21st Century
SOCIOLOGY

EDITORIAL BOARD

21st Century SOCIOLOGY
A Reference Handbook

Volume **1**

Edited by
Clifton D. Bryant
Virginia Polytechnic Institute, Blacksburg
Dennis L. Peck
The University of Alabama

A SAGE Reference Publication

SAGE Publications
Thousand Oaks ▪ London ▪ New Delhi

For information:

Sage Publications, Inc.
2455 Teller Road
Thousand Oaks, California 91320
E-mail: order@sagepub.com

Sage Publications Ltd.
1 Oliver's Yard
55 City Road
London EC1Y 1SP
United Kingdom

Sage Publications India Pvt. Ltd.
B-42, Panchsheel Enclave
Post Box 4109
New Delhi 110 017 India

Printed in the United States of America

Library of Congress Cataloging-in-Publication Data

21st century sociology: A reference handbook / coeditors in chief Clifton D. Bryant, Dennis L. Peck.
    p. cm.
Includes bibliographical references and index.
ISBN 1-4129-1608-9 or 978-1-4129-1608-0 (cloth : alk. paper)
  1. Sociology. I. Bryant, Clifton D., 1932- II. Peck, Dennis L.
HM585.H33 2007
301—dc22

                                2006018379

This book is printed on acid-free paper.

06 07 08 09 10   10 9 8 7 6 5 4 3 2 1

Publisher:	Rolf A. Janke
Developmental Editor:	Sara Tauber
Production Editor:	Melanie Birdsall
Copy Editor:	QuADS
Typesetter:	C&M Digitals (P) Ltd.
Proofreaders:	Cheryl Rivard and Joyce Li
Indexer:	Kathy Paparchontis
Cover Designer:	Michelle Kenny

CONTENTS

VOLUME ONE

Traditional and Core Areas

Volume Two

Specialty and Interdisciplinary Studies

PREFACE

Since its inception through the early decades of the twentieth century, the discipline of sociology was essentially monolithic in perspective, representing a rather narrow range of interests into social problems areas. Early sociologists were essentially generalists, and during the first 100 years of disciplinary activity, the literature of sociology expanded only incrementally. By mid-twentieth century, however, there was a sufficiently large body of sociological literature on which to draw and a much broader and energized sociological curiosity as to foster some degree of specialization.

With its new focus on theories of the middle range, sociological inquiry developed into a multifaceted perspective, representing a variety of specialty interests and an expanded literature in which a proliferation of knowledge is documented. Sociologists thus developed an expansive array of specialty knowledge that represents the variety of research and theoretical activity within the discipline. Now, in the twenty-first century, the success of the past century requires a comprehensive survey and assessment of the many specialty areas of sociology that is essential for organizing this vast information. The two-volume *21st Century Sociology: A Reference Handbook* accomplishes this organization with 106 essays that are authored by leading authorities from the United States, Canada, Australia, the United Kingdom, Germany, Scotland, Sweden, The Netherlands, France, Spain, Finland, and Singapore. Each chapter provides an up-to-date, comprehensive survey of one of these specialty areas. The *Handbook* also represents a thorough inquiry into the state of knowledge and scholarly thinking in each of these specialty areas by offering authoritative insightful essays of the various subfields in sociology, provide an assessment of contemporary knowledge, and end with brief projections of anticipated future theoretical development and research activity.

Several years ago, in response to the question "What is sociology?" a colleague responded, "Sociology is what sociologists do." As unusual a statement as this may appear to be, there is certainly an element of truth in it and perhaps even more than one might initially care to admit.

Indeed, for more than 100 years, sociological inquiry has covered a vast terrain of topics, theoretical perspectives, and methodologies that run the range of mainstream areas of interest, emerging new ideas, as well as topics considered to be peripheral to the discipline but nevertheless draw heavily on sociological literature for their framework. The work sociologists engage in is both pure and applied, and depending on time and space and shifts in the dominant orientation of the body politic, the substance of this work is more or less significant. Like all things, the discipline of sociology and its practitioners are subject to the changing needs of the society that we attempt to better understand. Sociologists have been from the beginning social activists and social policy analysts. These interests and foci continue in the present and will undoubtedly continue throughout the twenty-first century.

Increasingly, sociologists have engaged in exploring a wide range of topics, and this extensive activity is demonstrated through the large number of topical chapters presented in the *Handbook*. Thus, the model followed for this *Handbook* is one of inclusiveness in that a large number of topics are covered, but in so doing, the authors address each topic in a thorough, comprehensive manner. Although there is certain to be some modest theoretical and methodological overlap between some of the topics, each chapter is developed to reflect the unique historical development of the topic, offers a general overview of the current state of knowledge, and provides suggestions for how the area of inquiry is destined to develop as we move well into the twenty-first century. These topics are both interesting and informative in that the chapter content offers the reader insight into the rich legacy and development of the discipline of sociology while also providing the requisite reference information for advanced study and research into each substantive area. In this regard, there is a sufficient amount of information to support the rich sociological legacy of enabling public policy-oriented readers ample opportunity to learn while also providing important insights for those who enthusiastically embrace social activism as a part of the sociological enterprise.

We appreciate the fine professional effort by our colleagues in providing their insights and expertise for each of the areas covered. In this regard, one important feature of this *Handbook* is the international perspective that is brought to bear on the discipline. The American tradition of sociology is dependent on its rich European heritage, a fact that may, on occasion, be lost to a younger generation so influenced by the American empirical style and the dominant role American sociology has had throughout the twentieth century. Thus, as we presently experience yet another phase in globalization and social change, the international sociological perspective will direct the discipline's attention toward some of the same kinds of issues that begged the attention of sociologists at the turn of the twentieth century. Some of these issues are now so popular within the social sciences and the humanities that these are subject to interdisciplinary inquiry and understanding. We are pleased to offer many of these emerging areas of research in this *Handbook*.

The list is obviously not exhaustive, and other specialty areas, it can be argued, could be added to this impressive list of topics presented in this *Handbook*. Readers with a critical eye may specifically note the absence of entries on Black and Africana Studies, Women's Studies, and Latino Studies. It was our original intention to include entries on these topics. In the process of trying to identify and recruit suitable scholars to develop such entries, however, we were frequently informed by those in these fields that their areas of research and teaching were *not* specialties of sociology but rather were subdisciplines of their own that have developed a separate and distinctive orientation and literature. All drew on the literature of sociology along with the literature of various other disciplines, but they were autonomous and no longer within the purview of sociology. Indeed, we hold a special appreciation for those sociologists of the past who have been instrumental in contributing to the development of such areas. Thus, the articulation of specialty areas in this *Handbook* provides a nonexhaustive, albeit generous and appropriate, coverage of the discipline of sociology.

This *Handbook* represents a labor of love. But a work of this magnitude cannot be accomplished without the contributions of others; in this instance, many others. The most important individuals are those who contributed their insights and talents in developing the chapters. These are the authors/colleagues who first graciously accepted our invitation to develop a contribution for the *Handbook* and then reacted with a professional acumen to requests and suggestions that were made during the review process. The effort of so many dedicated individuals to portray their areas of expertise by thoroughly documenting this material for future generations of readers interested in the sociological perspective has been both stimulating and gratifying. The process has been stimulating because of the unique opportunity to learn of the rich heritage of the numerous subareas of study; it has been a gratifying experience to observe the effort of these international scholars to share their expertise and to do so despite the fact that each was busy with various other professional obligations. The opportunity to work with each of these individuals is indeed both a wonderful and humbling experience.

Our gratitude is expressed to the Associate Editors who served with distinction on the Editorial Board and took on various assignments during the preliminary organization of the project and throughout the development stage. Each contributed a great deal to the creation of the *Handbook*, beginning with suggestions for identifying authors with the requisite expertise to create the chapters and then in gracefully and diligently working with individual authors to bring each chapter to fruition. Our profound thank-you is extended to Drs. Rosalind A. Sydie of the University of Alberta, Harold R. Kerbo of California Polytechnic State University, J. David Knottnerus of Oklahoma State University, and Elaine Wethington of Cornell University.

In addition, the logistics for initiating and then managing a large project are made easy when the Managing Editor and the Assistant Editor are as competent as is Mrs. Patty M. Bryant and Mr. Steven J. Seiler. The ability of these two individuals to locate prospective authors and to demonstrate proficiency through their computer skills and in conducting various aspects of a long-term project such as this are acknowledged with our profound appreciation. Ms. Dianne Marshall of the Department of Sociology at Virginia Tech is to be thanked for her many secretarial contributions—typing, handling e-mail correspondence, duplicating manuscripts, and other clerical activities—to this project.

Finally, the foresight and encouragement of the Vice President and Publisher of Sage Publications, Mr. Rolf Janke, was instrumental in facilitating our efforts to create *21st Century Sociology: A Reference Handbook*. He was responsive to the initial overture to embark on this project and offered encouragement throughout the entire process. Sage development editors, Mrs. Sara Tauber and Mrs. Eileen Gallaher, provided the requisite encouragement and assistance at critical points in the process, while Mrs. Melanie Birdsall served well the need to establish a smooth production process involving so many contributors by adding her considerable expertise to this overall effort. We acknowledge the special contributions by each of these individuals with a deep appreciation.

Of course, there remains yet another element of major import, and that is the loving tolerance and support offered by our wives, Patty Bryant and Peggy Peck. Too often Patty and Peggy were called upon to forgive us for not being a functional part of the family during critical periods in the formulation and the process leading to what we hope will be a fitting tribute to a wonderful area of social inquiry. Know you each are much appreciated and loved.

—Clifton D. Bryant and Dennis L. Peck

ABOUT THE EDITORS

COEDITORS IN CHIEF

Clifton D. Bryant has been Professor in the Department of Sociology at Virginia Polytechnic Institute and State University (Virginia Tech) in Blacksburg, Virginia, since 1972. He was Department Head from 1972 to 1982. His specialty areas include the Sociology of Death and Dying, Deviant Behavior, Military Sociology, and the Sociology of Work and Occupations. Prior to coming to Virginia Tech, he enjoyed full-time faculty teaching appointments at Western Kentucky University (Department Head 1967–1972), Millsaps College (Department Head 1963–1967), and the University of Georgia (1960–1963). He was Visiting Professor at Mississippi State University (Summer, 1985) and at Pennsylvania State University (Summer, 1958). His research appointments include Visiting Scientist at the U.S. Army Institute for the Behavioral and Social Sciences (Summer, 1993), Visiting Research Scholar with the Mississippi Alcohol Safety Education Program (Mississippi State University; Summer, 1985), and Visiting Research Scholar with Training Technology Project operated by the Resource Development Office of Oak Ridge Associated Universities (Summer, 1987). His foreign teaching appointments include Visiting Fulbright Professor, Department and Graduate Institute of Sociology, National Taiwan University, Taipei, Taiwan, Republic of China (1987–1988), and Visiting Professor in the Department of Sociology/Anthropology, Xavier University, The Ateneo, Cagayan de Oro City, Mindanao, Philippines (1984–1985). He was a participant in the U.S. Department of Education's 1998 Fulbright-Hays Seminars Abroad Program in the People's Republic of China (Summer, 1998) and was also a participant in the U.S. Department of Education's 1993 Fulbright-Hays Seminars Abroad Program in Hungary (Summer, 1993). He served as President of the Southern Sociological Society (1978–1979) and as President of the Mid-South Sociological Association (1981–1982). He was the recipient of the Mid-South Sociological Association's Distinguished Career Award in 1991 and Distinguished Book Award in 2001 and also in 2004. He is also the recipient of the Southern Sociological Society's 2003 Distinguished Contributions to Teaching Award. Most recently, he was the recipient of the Virginia Tech 2003–2004 College of Liberal Arts and Human Sciences Excellence in Research and Creative Scholarship Award. He has been listed in the Who's Who in America since 1984 and in the Who's Who in the World since 1991. He is a member of Omicron Delta Kappa, Phi Kappa Phi, Phi Beta Delta, Alpha Kappa Delta, Pi Kappa Alpha, and Alpha Phi Omega. He was founder and chairman of the Editorial Board of *Sociological Symposium* (1968–1980). He was also the founder of *Deviant Behavior* and served as Editor in Chief of that journal from 1978 to 1991. He continues to serve as Chair of Editorial Policy Board for the journal. He was Editor of the *Southern Sociologist* (1970–1974). He was a member of the Editorial Board of Criminology (1978–1981), Associate Editor of *Sociological Forum* (1979–1980), Associate Editor of *Sociological Spectrum* (1981–1985), member of Board of Advisory Editors of *Sociological Inquiry* (1981–1985), and also Associate Editor of that journal (1997–2000). He was a member of the Board of Editors of *Society and Animals* (1997–1999) and was Associate Editor for a special issue of *Marriage and Family Relations* (Fall, 1982). His books include *The Handbook of Death and Dying* (two volumes), *The Encyclopedia of Criminology and Deviant Behavior* (four volumes), *Deviant Behavior: Readings in the Sociology of Norm Violations; The Rural Work Force: Nonagricultural Occupations in America, Sexual Deviancy and Social Proscription; Khaki-Collar Crime: Deviant Behavior in Military Context; Sexual Deviance in Sexual Context; Deviant Behavior: Occupational and Organizational Bases; The Social Dimensions of Work; Deviance and the Family; Social Problems Today; Dilemmas and Dimensions;* and *Introductory Sociology: Selected Readings for the College Scene.* He has published articles in a number of professional journals, including *Social Forces, Society, Sociological Inquiry, Sociology and Social Research, Rural Sociology, Sociological Forum, American Journal of Public Health, Journal of Sex Research, Journal of Veterinary Medical Education,*

Journal of Leisure Sciences, Sociological Spectrum, The Rural Sociologist, Psychological Reports, Free Inquiry in Creative Sociology, World Leisure and Recreation, Hort Technology, Anthrozoos, Applied Behavioral Science Review, Man and Environmental Systems, Southern Sociologist, and *Deviant Behavior.* He received his BA and MA degrees from the University of Mississippi, did advanced graduate work at the University of North Carolina (Chapel Hill), and received his PhD degree from Louisiana State University.

Dennis L. Peck is Professor of Sociology (1986) at The University of Alabama where he has been a member of the faculty since 1978. He is the Coeditor in Chief of *21st Century Sociology: A Reference Handbook,* served six years as Editor of *Sociological Inquiry,* he was Coeditor of volume 2 and Associate Editor of the four-volume *Encyclopedia of Criminology and Deviant Behavior* (2001), and was Associate Editor for the *Handbook of Death & Dying* (Sage, 2003). He has served and/or currently serves as a member of several editorial boards and in numerous professional association positions, including past president of the Mid-South Sociological Association and past president of the Alabama-Mississippi Sociological Association. His teaching and research interests are in the areas of demography, the sociology of law, and deviant behavior; he has authored and edited five books, edited two thematic journal issues, and published numerous articles and chapters in the areas of suicide, public health, psychiatric law, democracy, toxic waste disposal, life without parole, human sexuality, urban development programming, posttraumatic stress disorder, program evaluation, divorce, social policy, and civility. He served with the U.S. Air Force and the U.S. Public Health Service. While a member of the faculty at The University of Alabama, he had assignments with the Washington, D.C., Office of Evaluation Research at the Department of Housing and Urban Development, and he served as a policy analyst at the Department of Education. He was awarded the master's of science degree from the University of Wisconsin at Milwaukee and the PhD from Washington State University.

MANAGING EDITOR

Patty M. Bryant worked as an executive secretary for various corporations and agencies, including the law firm of Stennett and Stennett in Jackson, Mississippi, Orgill Brothers Hardware Corporation, Great Southern Box Corporation, Illinois Central Railroad, and the city of Blacksburg, Virginia. She has been involved in the editorial process of several journals, including *Sociological Symposium, Southern Sociologist,* and *Deviant Behavior,* for which she served as Assistant Editor and later Managing Editor. She has traveled extensively in Asia and lived both in the Philippines and Taiwan, where she worked with Clifton D. Bryant on conducting research on Asian culture. She was involved in the editorial process (with Clifton D. Bryant) on several books, including *Deviant Behavior: Readings in the Sociology of Norm Violation; Deviant Behavior: Occupational and Organizational Bases;* and *The Social Dimensions of Work.* Most recently, she served as Managing Editor of *The Encyclopedia of Criminology and Deviant Behavior* (four volumes; 2001), as Managing Editor of *The Handbook of Death and Dying* (two volumes; 2003), and most recently, Managing Editor of *21st Century Sociology: A Reference Handbook.* She graduated from Draughon's Business College in Jackson, Mississippi, and did undergraduate work at Western Kentucky University, majoring in sociology.

ASSOCIATE EDITORS

Harold R. Kerbo has been a Professor at Cal Poly since 1977 and is Chair of the Social Sciences Department. He has been promoting international education in the United States and abroad with study programs to Southeast Asia for Cal Poly students. He has also had extensive teaching and research experience in Asia and Europe since the early 1980s. In addition to other teaching experience in Tokyo, he was a Fulbright Professor during 1988/1989 at Hiroshima University as well as a Visiting Professor in the Law Faculty at Hiroshima Shudo University. During 1991, he was a Visiting Professor at the University of Duisburg, Germany, and returned to the Dusseldorf area during 1992 and 1993 as a Research Professor conducting research on employee relations in Japanese corporations located in Germany. In 1990, he received a Fulbright-Hays grant to study at Chulalongkorn University in Bangkok, Thailand, and for several months during 1994 to 1996 directed a research project on employee relations in American and Japanese corporations with operations in Thailand. During 1996, he was also a Visiting Professor in the MBA Program at the Prince of Songkla University in Thailand. During the winter term of 1999, he was a Visiting Professor at the University of Zurich, Switzerland, and was a Visiting Professor at the University of Wales, Great Britain, during the fall term of 1999. In 2002, he was a Distinguished Visiting Professor of Sociology at the University of Oklahoma and in 2003, a Distinguished Fulbright Chair in the Political Science Department at the University of Vienna. During 2006 to 2007, he was the recipient of an Abe Research Fellowship based in Japan. He will spend the year doing research on poverty reduction programs in Thailand, Vietnam, and Cambodia and spend part of the year in residence at the Center for Social Inequality at Tohoku University, Sendai, Japan. He has published several books and numerous articles on the subjects of social stratification, comparative societies, corporate structure, and modern Japan. He is the author of a basic sociology textbook *Sociology: Social Structure and Social Conflict* (1989). He is also the author of a textbook on social stratification, *Social Stratification and Inequality* (now in its 6th ed., translated into Spanish), and coauthor of *Who Rules Japan? The Inner-Circles of Economic and Political Power* (1995). He is creator and general editor of the *Comparative Societies Series,* which includes books on 11 countries. The first volume, *Modern Japan* (by Harold Kerbo and John McKinstry), was published in 1998. He has also coauthored the volumes *Modern Germany* (with Professor Hermann Strasser at the University of Duisburg, Germany) and *Modern Thailand* (with Robert Slagter), both of which were published in 2000. He is also a coauthor of the text *Social Problems* (now in its 9th ed., 2001). His latest book, *World Poverty: Global Inequalities and the Modern World System,* was published in 2005. His current research involves a comparative analysis of poverty reduction programs and their success in Southeast Asian countries.

J. David Knottnerus is Professor of Sociology at Oklahoma State University. His research interests are in the areas of social ritual, social theory, social psychology, group processes, social structure and inequality, and collective behavior/social movements. His recent books are *Structure, Culture and History: Recent Issues in Social Theory* (coedited with Sing C. Chew); *Literary Narratives on the Nineteenth and Early Twentieth-Century French Elite Educational System: Rituals and Total Institutions* (coauthored with Frederique Van de Poel-Knottnerus); *The Social Worlds of Male and Female Children in the Nineteenth-Century French Educational System: Youth, Rituals and Elites* (coauthored with Frederique Van de Poel-Knottnerus); and *Plantation Society and Race Relations: The Origins of Inequality* (coedited with Thomas J. Durant Jr.). Other recent publications (some of which are coauthored) include "The Theory of Structural Ritualization" (*Advances in Group Processes,* 1997); "Reproducing Social Structure in Task Groups: The Role of Structural Ritualization" (*Social Forces,* 2000); "Chinatown under Siege: Community Protest and Structural Ritualization Theory" (*Humboldt Journal of Social Relations,* 2006); and "Exposing Enron: Media Representations of Ritualized Deviance in Corporate Culture" (*Crime, Media, Culture: An International Journal,* 2006). He is currently working on projects relating to "structural ritualization theory," which focuses on the role symbolic rituals play in social life and the processes by which ritualization occurs and leads to the formation, reproduction, and transformation of social structure. At present, this work focuses on several topics, including deritualization, the enactment of ritualized practices in organizations and communities, structural reproduction, strategic ritualization and the role of power, rituals and the development of social inequality, collective ritual events and emotions, and applied research focusing on

risky behavior in youth. His goal is to conduct further research in these areas and expand the range of issues addressed by this theoretical/research orientation. He is presently preparing a book dealing with this perspective. He is a past president of the Mid-South Sociological Association and currently serves as a member of the Council for the Theory Section, American Sociological Association, and as a cosponsor and co-organizer of the annual meeting of the Sociological Imagination Group. He earned his PhD in sociology at Southern Illinois University at Carbondale.

Rosalind A. Sydie is Emeriti Professor of Sociology, and formerly Professor of Sociology (1989–2006), at the University of Alberta, Edmonton, Canada, where she served as Chair of the Department of Sociology (2000–2006). Her areas of interest include Social Theory, Gender and Feminist Studies, Art and Culture, and Comparative Historical Sociology. Among her numerous publications are two books, *Natural Women* (1987) and *Cultured Men: A Feminist Perspective on Sociological Theory* (1994), and the coauthored *Sociological Theory* (2001). She has published numerous journal articles and book chapters, including "Sex and the Sociological Fathers" (*Engendering the Social,* 2004, B. Marshall and A. Witz, eds.); "The Phallocentric Gaze: Leon Battista Alberta and Visual Art" (*Journal of Historical Sociology,* 1997); "Feminist Sociology" (*Advances in Sociological Knowledge,* 2004, N. Genov, ed.); and "Gendered Spaces of Domesticity" (*Design and the Social Sciences,* 2002, J. Frascara, ed.). Throughout her career she has been a frequent contributor of book reviews, conference papers, and creative session organizer for professional meetings; her professional standing is well recognized as witnessed by the many appointments and honors received throughout her career. In addition to her important role as an Associate Editor of *21st Century Sociology: A Reference Handbook* (2004–2006), she was Consulting Editor for the *Encyclopedia of Social Theory* (volumes 2–5; 2003); she served as Editor of the *Canadian Review of Sociology and Anthropology* (1994–1997), Associate Editor of *Sociological Inquiry* (1987–1993), Book Review Editor of the *Canadian Journal of Sociology* (1979–1980, 1990–1995), and English Language Editor of the *Canadian Review of Sociology and Anthropology* (1976–1979). She has been a periodic reviewer of manuscripts for several scholarly journals, book publishers, and funding agencies. In addition to many university-wide administrative positions, she is a past president of Western Association of Sociology and Anthropology. In light of her long career of distinguished service to her university and to the discipline, she is anticipating retirement along with the expanded opportunity to engage in some long-delayed research projects and to spending quality time with her grandchildren.

Elaine Wethington is Associate Professor of Human Development and of Sociology at Cornell University. She is a medical sociologist. She has an extensive background in survey research methods, epidemiology, and applied gerontology research and has directed numerous primary and secondary analyses projects since 1979. Her first research job was as data-collection manager for the "Social Supports of the Elderly" study. She is the author of papers on social support and adaptation to stressors, coping, life events, and life-turning points and has developed instruments to measure life events and chronic stressors, including the Structured Life Event Interview and the Daily Inventory of Stressful Experiences. Currently, she is the Coprincipal Investigator and Director of the Pilot Study core of the Cornell Institute for Translational Research on Aging, Co-investigator for a national longitudinal survey of mental disorders in the United States (the *National Comorbidity Survey 2*), and Coprincipal Investigator for *Work-Family Integration and the Diets of Multiethnic Adults* (funded by the National Cancer Institute). In the recent past, she directed *Pathways to Life Quality,* a Cornell University at Ithaca College longitudinal study of 1,000 older people. She was a network associate of the John D. and Catherine T. MacArthur Research Network on Successful Midlife Development. Her most recently published book is *Residential Choices and Experiences of Older Adults: Pathways to Life Quality* (2003, coedited with John Krout). Her papers have appeared in the *Journal of Health and Social Behavior, Journal of Marriage and Family, Annual Review of Sociology,* and *Advances in Life Course Research.* She received her PhD from the University of Michigan in 1987, specializing in the sociology of mental health and illness.

ASSISTANT EDITOR

Steven J. Seiler is a PhD student in the Department of Sociology at the University of Tennessee, Knoxville. He has taught courses in social justice and social change. His varied research interests include the political economy of social movements in the Global South, the impact of structural adjustment programs on Southeast Asia, and development and social change in Thailand. He is currently researching the socioeconomic and political consequences of structural adjustment programs in Thailand following the 1997 Asian economic crisis. In addition to his research in political economy, he has presented papers at professional conferences on labor relations in Thailand and critiques of social movement literature. Prior to pursuing a college education, he served four years active duty in the U.S. Navy. He earned a master's degree in sociology and a Graduate Certificate in International Research and Development from Virginia Technological and State University. He earned the undergraduate degree in sociology and political science from the University of Georgia.

About the Contributors

Barry D. Adam is University Professor of Sociology at the University of Windsor, Ontario, Canada. He is the author of *The Survival of Domination* and *The Rise of a Gay and Lesbian Movement,* and coauthor of *Experiencing HIV* and *The Global Emergence of Gay and Lesbian Politics.* He has also published articles on new social movement theory, on Nicaragua, on gay and lesbian issues, and on social aspects of AIDS.

Rebecca G. Adams is Professor of Sociology at the University of North Carolina at Greensboro. Her research has focused mainly on the sociology of adult and older adult friendship, including on friendship formation and community development among fans of a rock 'n' roll band, the Grateful Dead. Her publications on these topics include numerous articles and chapters in both the scholarly and popular press and several coauthored or coedited books, including *Deadhead Social Science* (2000, with Rob Sardiello); *Placing Friendship in Context* (1998, with Graham Allan); *Adult Friendship* (Sage, 1992, with Rosemary Blieszner); and *Older Adult Friendship: Structure and Process* (Sage, 1989, with Rosemary Blieszner). Her work has been discussed in most major newspapers in the United States and in many news, women's, teen, and special interest magazines as well as during interviews on more than 50 radio and television shows, including for BBC, NPR, NRS, HBO, MTV, and PBS. A past president of the Southern Sociological Society, a Fellow of the Gerontological Society of America, and a Charter Fellow of the Association for Gerontology in Higher Education, she is currently serving as Editor of *Personal Relationships* (official journal of the International Association for Relationship Research), as an Advisory Editor for George Ritzer's *Encyclopedia of Sociology,* and as a Member at Large of the Council of the American Sociological Association.

Benigno E. Aguirre is Professor of Sociology in the Department of Sociology and Criminal Justice at the University of Delaware, Newark. He is senior faculty member of the Disaster Research Center and a frequent contributor to the specialty areas of collective behavior,

disaster studies, and Latin American sociology. He is past president of the Research Committee on Disasters of the International Sociological Association. He earned his PhD from The Ohio State University in 1977.

Graham Allan is Professor of Sociology at Keele University, United Kingdom, and currently Visiting Professor in Family Studies at the University of British Columbia, Vancouver, Canada. His research has focused principally on the sociology of informal relationships, including friendships, family ties, and community sociology. He has published widely in these areas. His books include *Placing Friendship in Context* (1998, with Rebecca Adams); *The Sociology of the Family* (1999); *Families, Households and Society* (2001, with Graham Crow); *Social Relations and the Life Course* (2003, with Gill Jones); *Social Networks and Social Exclusion* (2004, with Chris Phillipson and David Morgan), and *The State of Affairs* (2004, with Jean Duncombe, Kaeren Harrison, and Dennis Marsden). His current project is concerned with stepfamily kinship. He is coauthoring a book on this topic with Sheila Hawker and Graham Crow, which is to be published in 2007. Recently, he has acted as an Associate Editor of *Personal Relationships* and as one of the Advisory Editors for George Ritzer's *Encyclopedia of Sociology.* He is also coeditor of the *Palgrave Studies in Family Sociology* book series.

Stephen J. Appold lectures in the Department of Sociology at the National University of Singapore and is a Visiting Researcher in the Kenan Institute of Private Enterprise at the University of North Carolina at Chapel Hill. His recent publications include "The Weakening Position of University Graduates in Singapore's Labor Market: Causes and Consequences" (*Population and Development Review*); "The Location Patterns of U.S. Industrial Research: Mimetic Isomorphism, and the Emergence of Geographic Charisma" (*Regional Studies*); and "Research Parks and the Location of Industrial Research Laboratories: An Analysis of the Effectiveness of a Policy Intervention" (*Research Policy*). With Jack Kasarda, he is investigating the interplay of air transport, urban development, and employment trends.

Ilkka Arminen is Professor in the Department of Sociology and Social Psychology, University of Tampere, Finland. He is one of the coauthors of *Alcoholics Anonymous as a Mutual-Help Movement: A Study in Eight Societies* (1996) and the author of *Therapeutic Interaction: A Study of Mutual Help in the Meetings of Alcoholics Anonymous* (1998) and *Institutional Interaction: Studies of Talk at Work* (2005). He has also published articles in a number of edited collections and journals, including *Acta Sociologica, Discourse & Society, Discourse Studies, Journal of Pragmatics, Personal and Ubiquitous Computing, Research on Language and Social Interaction, Text,* and the *Sociological Quarterly.*

Christopher R. Badcock, PhD, is Reader in Sociology at the London School of Economics, University of London, where he teaches courses on the social implications of evolution and genetics. He is the author of *Evolutionary Psychology: A Critical Introduction* (2000).

Kenneth D. Bailey is professor of sociology at the University of California, Los Angeles. He has served as Associate Editor of the *American Sociological Review* and was elected Secretary of the Society for the Study of Social Problems (SSSP); Vice President (North America) of Research Committee 33, Logic and Methodology, of the International Sociological Association (ISA); President of RC 51, Sociocybernetics, of the ISA; and also President of the International Society for the Systems Sciences (ISSS). He is the author of more than 115 articles, chapters, reviews, and books, primarily in the areas of methods and systems. His books include *Methods of Social Research* (4th ed., 1994); *Social Entropy Theory* (1990); *Sociology and the New Systems Theory* (1994); and *Typologies and Taxonomies* (Sage, 1994). His work has been translated into Bahasa Malaysian, Chinese, Italian, Korean, Slovak, Slovene, and other languages.

Carl L. Bankston III is Professor of Sociology and Codirector of the Asian Studies Program at Tulane University. He is author or editor of 14 books and over 85 journal articles and book chapters. His research and teaching interests include Asian and Asian American issues, international migration, race and ethnicity, and sociology of education.

Lori Baralt is a PhD student in Sociology at Michigan State University. Her current research interests include gender, social movements, and identity. She received her BA in women's studies and political science from the University of Florida.

Clemens Bartollas is Professor of Sociology at the University of Northern Iowa (UNI). He has taught at UNI for the past 24 years. He recently published the seventh edition of his *Juvenile Delinquency* text and is coauthor of *Juvenile Justice in America,* which has gone through four editions. His coauthored monograph, *Juvenile Victimization: The Institutional Paradox,* examined the degree of victimization that existed in a maximum-security juvenile training school in Ohio. He has published a number of journal articles related to juvenile offenders and the processes of institutionalization. In addition to his work with juveniles, he has written a number of publications on adult corrections, the criminal justice system, policing, and criminology. He received his PhD from The Ohio State University in 1973.

Loretta E. Bass is Associate Professor of Sociology at the University of Oklahoma. She focuses her research on children and stratification issues and completes research in West Africa, the United States, and France. She recently served as Guest Editor for an international edition of the *Sociological Studies of Children and Youth* (volume 10, 2005) and published a book, *Child Labor in Sub-Saharan Africa* (2004), which offers a window on the lives of Africa's child workers drawing on research and demographic data from 43 countries. Her research has appeared in *Population Research and Policy Review, Political Behavior, Anthropology of Work Review, International Journal of Sociology and Social Policy,* and *Journal of Reproductive Medicine.*

Amanda K. Baumle is Assistant Professor of Sociology at the University of Houston. She specializes in demography, social inequality, and the sociology of law. Her current research explores issues involving the demography of sexual orientation, labor demography, and gender inequality in the legal practice. Prior to obtaining her PhD in sociology at Texas A&M University, she earned a JD from the University of Texas and practiced labor and employment law.

Felix M. Berardo is Professor Emeritus in the Department of Sociology at the University of Florida. His long career interests embrace the areas of family sociology, social gerontology, the sociology of death and survivorship, and the sociology of risk. In addition to extensive publications in professional journals, he is the author, coauthor, or editor of more than a dozen major book-length works. He is former Editor of the *Journal of Marriage and Family* as well as a monograph series on *Current Perspectives in Family Research.* He is Deputy Editor of the *Journal of Family Issues.* He served as President of the Florida Council on Family Relations and as Associate Chair and Chair of the Department of Sociology at the University of Florida, Gainesville. He has been elected the President of the university's chapters of the National Honor Societies, Phi Beta Kappa, and Phi Kappa Phi. He was the recipient of the Arthur Peterson Award in Death Education and has been awarded Fellow status by the Gerontological Society of America and the National Council on Family Relations. His book *Emerging Conceptual Frameworks in Family Analysis* (with F. Ivan Nye) has been included among a select group of works considered "classics" in family sociology and recognized for its long-lasting impact on the field. In 2004, the National Council on Family Relations established the Felix M. Berardo Mentorship Award in honor of his outstanding contributions to student and faculty careers.

Fabrizio Bernardi is Associate Professor, Department of Sociology II (Social Structure), Universidad Nacional de Educación a Distancia, Madrid, Spain. From 1998 to 2001, he worked as an Assistant Professor of Sociology at the University of Bielfeld (Germany). Among his recent publications are "Public Policies and Low Fertility: Rationales for Public Intervention and a Diagnosis for the Spanish Case" (*Journal of European Social Policy,* 2005) and "Returns to Educational Performance at Entry into the Italian Labor Market" (*European Sociological Review,* 2003). His research interests focus on social inequality, the relationship between family and labor markets dynamics, as well as on quantitative methods for longitudinal analysis.

Bo Jason Bernhard is Assistant Professor in the Departments of Sociology and Hotel Management at the University of Nevada, Las Vegas, where he also serves as Director of Gambling Research at the university's International Gaming Institute. His work has focused on the impacts of gambling in society in a variety of national and international settings.

Lakshmi Kant Bharadwaj is Associate Professor of Sociology at the University of Wisconsin at Milwaukee, where he has been teaching sociological theory, environmental sociology, the sociology of religion, and social change. His research interests lie in exploring the role of social integration and personal efficacy in promoting personal well-being in different life domains, and the role of the family in both coping with social change and in mediating its impact upon the quality of life. His work has been published in various journals, including *Human Relations* and *Social Indicators Research.* His publications include an entry on human ecology and environmental analysis in the *Encyclopedia of Sociology* and a lead chapter on theories of demographic change in a collected work on Demographic and Structural Change. He is interested in the issues of peace, justice, and nonviolence and has served as the Director of the Peace Studies Program at the University of Wisconsin at Milwaukee. As a longtime member of the Milwaukee Association for Interfaith Relations, he has been actively involved in promoting interreligious understanding and dialogue among members of various faith communities. He was recently nominated by the governor of Wisconsin to serve a three-year term on the State Council for Affirmative Action. He earned his PhD from the University of Wisconsin at Madison.

Dwight B. Billings is Professor of Sociology at the University of Kentucky. He has written extensively on Appalachia and the American South. He is a past president of the Appalachian Studies Association and current editor of the *Journal of Appalachian Studies.* His most recent book is *The Road to Poverty: The Making of Wealth and Hardship in Appalachia* (coauthored with Kathleen Blee).

Bart Bonikowski is a doctoral student in sociology at Princeton University. He received his BA at Queen's University in Kingston, Ontario, and his MA in sociology at Duke University. His master's thesis, titled "Dancing to Darwin's Beat: A Dynamic Analysis of Cultural Niches in Blau Space," applied McPherson's ecological model of affiliation to changes in popular music consumption over two decades. His current research continues to explore the relationship between culture, inequality, and social networks.

Jac D. Bulk is Professor of Sociology at the University of Wisconsin at La Crosse. He has taught courses in Law and Society, Marriage and Family, Research Methods of the Social Sciences, Racial and Ethnic Minorities, Contemporary Issues in Racial and Ethnic Studies, and Hmong Americans. He has published journal articles on topics relating to legal studies and racial and ethnic studies, and he was honored with the first UW-System "Excellence in Ethnic Studies Award." He is currently engaged in a longitudinal study of the retention of three cohorts of minority students (2000–2003). He is also involved in a research project titled "Australian Aborigines and American Indians: A Comparative Study in Ethnic Preservation and Ties to Homelands." He has engaged in many university, community, and professional service activities. Most noteworthy has been his membership on the UW-System American Ethnic Studies Advisory Committee (1979–1987); Associate Editor to the *Wisconsin Sociologist* (1988–1991); member on the Race and Ethnicity Steering Committee (1980–1990); and conference organizer of the 25th Annual National Association for Ethnic Studies in 1997 held at the University of Wisconsin, La Crosse. He earned his undergraduate degree at Cornell University and his MS and PhD degrees at the University of Wisconsin, Madison.

Thomas J. Burns is Professor of Sociology at the University of Oklahoma. He does both quantitative and qualitative research on the interface between human social organization and the natural environment. In an ongoing project with a number of collaborators, he does statistical modeling of how macro-level social, demographic, political, and economic processes affect environmental outcomes including pollution, deforestation, and the ecological footprint. He also analyzes rhetorical practices surrounding environmental issues.

Tom R. Burns is Professor Emeritus at the Department of Sociology, University of Uppsala, Uppsala, Sweden. He is a Member of the EU Commission's Advisory Group on the Social Sciences and Humanities. Among his engagements, he has been a Jean Monnet Visiting Professor at the European University, Florence, Italy, 2002; Visiting Scholar, Stanford University, Spring, 2002, 2004, 2005; Gulbenkian Visiting Professor at the University Institute for Business and Social Studies (ISCTE), Lisbon, Portugal

(2002–2003); Visiting Fellow, Center for Interdisciplinary Research (ZIF), Bielefeld, Germany; Visiting Professor at the Wissenschaftszentrum, Berlin (1985); Clarence J. Robinson University Professor at George Mason University (1987–1990); Fellow at Swedish Collegium for Advanced Study in the Social Sciences (Spring, 1992; Autumn, 1998); and Fellow at the European University Institute (Spring, 1998). He has published more than 10 books and numerous articles in the areas of governance and politics, the sociology of technology and environment, the analysis of markets and market regulation, and studies of administration and management. He has also published extensively on social theory and methodology, with an emphasis on the new institutional theory, a social theory of games and human interaction, and dynamic systems theory.

Brian Castellani is Associate Professor of Sociology at Kent State University and Adjunct Professor of Psychiatry at Northeastern Ohio University's College of Medicine. He is the author of *Pathological Gambling: The Making of a Medical Problem* (2000). His research program sits at the intersection of medical sociology and complexity science. He is currently working on a monograph, *The Sociology of Complexity: A Guide to Modeling Complex Social Systems* (with Fred Hafferty), which presents readers an overview of the sociology of complexity, develops a theoretical framework for the study of social complexity called social complexity theory, and provides a step-by-step guide for modeling complex social systems called assemblage. He holds a master's degree in clinical psychology and a doctorate in medical sociology.

James William Coleman is Professor of Sociology at the California Polytechnic State University, San Luis Obispo. He is the author of numerous books and articles in the sociology of religion, criminology (especially white-collar crime), and social problems. They include *The New Buddhism: The Western Transformation of an Ancient Tradition* (2001) and the *Criminal Elite: Understanding White-Collar Crime* (2006). He earned his PhD from the University of California at Santa Barbara.

Richard A. Colignon is Professor and Chair of Sociology and Criminal Justice at St. Louis University in St. Louis, Missouri. His research centers on the social and political processes surrounding apparently rational procedures. His recent books include *Amakudari: The Hidden Fabric of Japan's Economy* (2003, with C. Usui) and *Power Plays: Critical Events in the Institutionalization of the Tennessee Valley Authority* (1997). His current interests include government-business relations around pensions and health care and cross-culture analysis of work design and managerial strategies.

Gerry R. Cox is a Professor of Sociology at the University of Wisconsin, La Crosse. He is the Director of the Center for Death Education & Bioethics. His teaching focuses on theory/theory construction, deviance, and criminology;

death and dying; social psychology; and minority peoples. He has been publishing materials since 1973 in sociology and teaching-oriented professional journals. He is a member of the International Work Group on Dying, Death, and Bereavement; the Midwest Sociological Society; the American Sociological Association; the International Sociological Association; Phi Kappa Phi; Great Plains Sociological Society; and the Association of Death Education and Counseling.

John DeLamater is Professor of Sociology at the University of Wisconsin. He has been conducting research and writing about sexuality for 25 years. His current research is focused on sexual expression in later life. Working with data from the AARP/Modern Maturity sexuality survey, he and his students have written two papers: (1) "Sexual Desire in Later Life" (*Journal of Sex Research, 42,* May 2005) and (2) "Sexual Behavior in Later Life" (under review). He is collaborating with Janet Hyde on a project employing data from the 2003–2004 Wisconsin Longitudinal Study on sexual expression. He is the current Editor of the *Journal of Sex Research.*

Norman K. Denzin is Distinguished Professor of Communications, College of Communications Scholar, and Research Professor of Communications, Sociology and Humanities, at the University of Illinois, Urbana–Champaign. He is the author, editor, or coeditor of numerous books, including *Performance Ethnography: Critical Pedagogy and the Politics of Culture; Screening Race: Hollywood and a Cinema of Racial Violence; Performing Ethnography;* and *9/11 in American Culture.* He is past editor of *The Sociological Quarterly,* coeditor of *The Handbook of Qualitative Research* (2nd ed.), coeditor of *Qualitative Inquiry,* editor of *Cultural Studies: Critical Methodologies,* and series editor of *Studies in Symbolic Interaction.* He earned his PhD in sociology from the University of Iowa in 1966.

Philippe R. DeVillé is Professor of Economics at the Université Catholique de Louvain (UCL). Committed to interdisciplinary work, his fields of interest in the past have been macroeconomics and employment issues, equity and education, and a systems approach to growth and development in a historical perspective. He was coauthor with Tom R. Burns and Thomas Baumgartner of *Man, Decisions, Society* (1985) and *the Shaping of Socio-economic Systems* (1986). He also coauthored with them a number of articles in the 1970s and 1980s. His recent work has been concerned with critical issues of market economies and the ethics of capitalism. He is currently working with Christian Arnsperger on two essays, "On the Ethics of Competition" and "Is *Homooeconomicus Neoclassicus* a Social Being?" He has been Visiting Professor at, among other universities, the University of Montréal, University of Québec in Montreal, the University of Sao Paolo (Brazil), and Quisqueya University (Haiti), and Fulbright Fellow at the Hoover Institution, Stanford University, Visiting Scholar at Stanford University and the University of Massachusetts, and Fellow at the Swedish Collegium for Advanced Study. He received his PhD in economics from Stanford University in 1973.

Frank Dobbin is Professor of Sociology at Harvard. His *Forging Industrial Policy* received the 1996 Max Weber Award. His *Economics Meets Sociology in Strategic Management* (2000, coedited with Joel Baum), investigates intellectual synergies between sociology and economics. His collection of classics *The New Economic Sociology: An Anthology* (2004) traces the roots of modern economic sociology and his collection of new studies *The Sociology of the Economy* (2004) showcases the range of the new economic sociology.

Peter Donnelly is currently Director of the Centre for Sport Policy Studies and a Professor in the Faculty of Physical Education and Health, at the University of Toronto. He taught at the University of Western Ontario from 1976 to 1979 and at McMaster University from 1980 to 1998. His research interests include sport politics and policy issues (including the area of children's rights in sport), sport subcultures, and mountaineering (history). His recent books include *Taking Sport Seriously: Social Issues in Canadian Sport* (1997; 2nd ed., 2000); *Inside Sports* (1999, with Jay Coakley); and the first Canadian edition of *Sports in Society: Issues and Controversies* (2004, with Jay Coakley). He is a former editor of the *Sociology of Sport Journal* (1990–1994), a past president of the North American Society for the Sociology of Sport (2001), and currently Editor of the *International Review for the Sociology of Sport* (2004–2006). He was born in Chester, England, studied physical education as an undergraduate, and taught in school for several years. In 1969 he moved to the United States where he completed undergraduate studies in New York City, and then received master's and PhD degrees in sport studies from the University of Massachusetts.

Andrea Doucet is Associate Professor of Sociology and Anthropology at Carleton University. She is the author of *Do Men Mother?* (2006) and has published book chapters and articles on feminist approaches to methodology and epistemology as well as on gender and domestic labor, mothering and fathering. Her work has appeared in journals such as *Signs, Sociology, The Sociological Review, Journal of Family Issues, Community Work & Family,* and *Women's Studies International.*

Timothy J. Dowd is Associate Professor of Sociology at Emory University. His research deals with the sociology of music, as well as with the sociologies of culture, media, and organizations. His publications include articles in *American Sociological Review, Social Forces, Annual Review of Sociology,* and *Administrative Science Quarterly.* He has also edited special issues for journals, including "Explorations in the Sociology of Music" (*Poetics,* 2002); "Music in Society: The Sociological

Agenda" (*Poetics,* 2004, with Richard A. Peterson); and "The Sociology of Music: Sounds, Songs, and Society" (*American Behavioral Scientist,* 2005).

John P. Drysdale is currently Professor Emeritus of Sociology at Concordia University, Montréal, Québec, Canada. He has held teaching appointments in the United States at the University of Southern Mississippi, Louisiana State University, the University of Kentucky, and the University of Iowa, and in Canada at Concordia University, Montréal. His main teaching fields are contemporary and classical sociological theory, the sociology of knowledge, political sociology, and the history of sociology. He has also held research and guest appointments at Harvard University's Center for European Studies, the Institut für Soziologie and the Max-Weber-Institut of the University of Munich, and Balliol College, Oxford University. His research interests include German, British, U.S., and Canadian social theory. He has published several articles and reviews on Max Weber's methodology, including "How Are Social-scientific Concepts Formed? A Reconstruction of Max Weber's Theory of Concept Formation" (*Sociological Theory,* 1996) and "Max Weber on Objectivity: Advocate or Critic?" (*Max Weber's "Objectivity" Revisited,* forthcoming, L. McFalls, ed.). He received his BA from Millsaps College and his MA and PhD degrees from Louisiana State University.

Riley E. Dunlap is Professor of Sociology at Oklahoma State University. He has served as President of the International Sociological Association's Research Committee on Environment and Society and as Chair of the American Sociological Association's Section on Environment and Technology, the Rural Sociological Society's Natural Resources Research Group, and the Society for the Study of Social Problems' Environmental Problems Division. Besides contributing to the theoretical development of environmental sociology, he conducts research on the nature and sources of public concern for environmental quality, including cross-national comparisons in such concern; the evolution of American environmentalism; and the efforts of the U.S. conservative movement to mount an antienvironmental "countermovement." He is senior editor of *American Environmentalism* (1992), *Handbook of Environmental Sociology* (2002), and *Sociological Theory and the Environment* (2002).

Thomas J. Fararo is Distinguished Service Professor Emeritus of Sociology at the University of Pittsburgh (Pittsburgh, Pennsylvania) where he teaches courses in sociological theory. His books deal with theoretical and mathematical sociology and include *Mathematical Sociology* (1973); *The Meaning of General Theoretical Sociology* (1989); *Social Action Systems* (2001); and *Generating Images of Stratification* (2003, with K. Kosaka). He is coeditor of *Rational Choice Theory: Advocacy and Critique* (1992, with J. Coleman); *The*

Problem of Solidarity: Theories and Models (1998, with P. Doreian); and *Purpose, Meaning and Action: Control Systems Theories in Sociology* (2006, with K. McClelland).

David Fasenfest is Associate Professor of Sociology and Urban Affairs and Senior Research Fellow at Wayne State University. His educational background is as an economist and sociologist, and his research focuses on regional and urban economic development, labor market analysis and work force development, and income inequality. His work has appeared in *Economic Development Quarterly, Urban Affairs Review, International Journal of Urban and Regional Review,* and *International Journal of Sociology.* In addition, he is the current Editor of *Community Economic Development: Policy Formation in the U.S. and U.K.* (1993) and *Critical Perspectives on Local Development Policy Evaluation* (2004). He is Editor of the journal *Critical Sociology* and is book series Editor of *Studies in Critical Social Science.*

Abbott L. Ferriss is Professor Emeritus retired from Emory University in 1982. He is a former president of the Southern Sociological Society, the founder and a past editor of *SINET: The Social Indicators Network News,* and a past editor of *PAA Affairs* and *The Sociologist.* He is the author of three books in the area of social indicators and has published numerous journal articles and reports on social indicators, child poverty, quality-of-life studies, and civility. He also coedited a thematic issue on civility for *Sociological Inquiry,* the international honor society journal of Alpha Kappa Delta. A member since 1942, in 2006 he was honored with the "Service Award" in honor of his contributions to the Southern Sociological Society.

Joanne Finkelstein is Dean of the Faculty of Arts and Education at Victoria University, Melbourne, Australia. Her sociological publications include *Dining Out, Fashion* and, most recently, *The Sociological Bent: Inside Metro Culture.*

Cornelia Butler Flora is the Charles F. Curtiss Distinguished Professor of Agriculture and Sociology at Iowa State University. She is also Director of the North Central Regional Center for Rural Development, covering the 12 Midwestern states. Her international development experience includes research, project evaluation, and project design primarily in Latin America and also in Africa and Asia.

Jan L. Flora is Professor of Sociology and Extension Community Sociologist at Iowa State University. He is also a Visiting Professor at the National Agrarian University–Molina in Peru. His current research analyzes the relationship of community social capital to economic, community, and sustainable development. His extension work focuses on involving Latino immigrants in the affairs of rural Iowa communities.

James H. Frey is Professor Emeritus of Sociology and retired Dean of the College of Liberal Arts at the University of Nevada, Las Vegas. He is author of *Survey Research by Telephone* (Sage, 1989) and *Sociology of Sport* (1996, with H. Nixon). He has published articles on gambling behavior and policy, survey research, sociology of work and leisure, and deviant behavior. He holds a master's degree in sociology from the University of Iowa (1968) and a PhD from Washington State University (1974).

R. Scott Frey is currently Professor of Sociology and Head of the Department of Sociology at the University of Tennessee, Knoxville. He has held appointments at Argonne National Laboratory, George Washington University, Kansas State University, the National Science Foundation, and the University of North Florida. He has contributed chapters to recent books on environmental issues and has published in numerous journals, including the *American Journal of Sociology* and the *American Sociological Review.* He received his PhD from Colorado State University in 1980.

Jan Marie Fritz is Professor of Health Policy and Planning in the School of Planning at the University of Cincinnati. She is also affiliated to the Department of Women's Studies and the Department of Sociology. She is the author of more than 80 publications, was a member of the International Sociological Association's (ISA) executive committee, and the ISA's representative to the United Nations. She is a past president of a national organization of clinical sociologists, the sociological practice section of the American Sociological Association, and the ISA's division on clinical sociology. She was a member of the U.S. Environmental Protection Agency's National Environmental Justice Advisory Council and currently is vice president of two divisions (RC 26 Clinical Sociology and RC 46 Sociotechnics—Sociological Practice) of the International Sociological Association. Over the past 20 years, she has mediated labor, special education, commercial, employment, and public policy disputes and served as a reviewer of programs for the Commission on the Accreditation of Applied and Clinical Sociology Programs and the Departmental Resources Group of the American Sociological Association.

Gilbert Geis is Professor Emeritus in the Department of Criminology, Law and Society, University of California, Irvine. He is a former president of the American Society of Criminology and recipient of its Edwin Sutherland Award for outstanding research. His recent books are *Criminal Justice and Moral Issues* (2006, with Robert F. Meier) and *White-Collar and Corporate Crime* (2006).

W. Richard Goe is Professor of Sociology at Kansas State University. He is presently completing a book that examines the effects of economic restructuring on the growth of nonmetropolitan cities and communities in the United

States at the end of the twentieth century. His research has been published in *Social Forces, Urban Affairs Review,* and *Work & Occupations and Rural Sociology,* among other journals.

Juan J. González is Tenure Professor of Sociology, Department of Sociology II (Social Structure), Universidad Nacional de Educación a Distancia, Madrid, Spain. He is Honorary Fellow at the Department of Sociology, University of Wisconsin at Madison (1992–1993) and Visiting Research Scholar at the Social Sciences Department, California Polytechnic University (2000–2001). His fields of teaching and research include Social Stratification, Political Sociology, and Rural Sociology. His publications include *Agricultura y Sociedad en el cambio de siglo* (Madrid, 2002) and *Tres décadas de cambio social en España* (Madrid, 2005).

Erich Goode is Professor Emeritus of Sociology at the State University of New York at Stony Brook and Senior Research Scientist in the Department of Criminology and Criminal Justice at the University of Maryland at College Park. He is the author of 10 books, mainly on drug use, deviant behavior, and paranormal beliefs; more than 40 articles that have been published in academic journals; and 20 invited book chapters and encyclopedia entries, as well as editor of five anthologies, the recipient of several teaching awards, and a winner of the Guggenheim fellowship. He has taught at a half dozen universities, which include—in addition to Stony Brook and Maryland—Columbia, New York University, The Hebrew University of Jerusalem, and the University of North Carolina at Chapel Hill. His textbooks include *Drugs in American Society* (6th ed., 2005) and *Deviant Behavior* (7th ed., 2005).

John Grady is Professor of Sociology at Wheaton College in Massachusetts and Senior Research Scholar at the Salt Institute for Documentary Studies in Portland, Maine. He has produced numerous documentary films, including *Mission Hill and the Miracle of Boston* (1979), *Water and the Dream of the Engineers* (1983), and *Love Stories: Women, Men and Romance* (1987). He has written extensively on visual research and communication. He was President of the International Visual Sociology Association (IVSA) from 1996 to 2000. He received his PhD from Brandeis University.

Frederic W. Hafferty is Professor of Behavioral Sciences at the University of Minnesota School of Medicine, Duluth. He is the author of *Into the Valley: Death and the Socialization of Medical Students* (1991) and *The Changing Medical Profession: An International Perspective* (1993, with John McKinlay). He is currently working on two books, the first (with Brian Castellani) on the sociology of complexity and a second on the hidden curriculum in medical education. He is past chair of the Medical Sociology Section of the American Sociological Association and is currently an associate editor of the *Journal of Health and Social Behavior* and a member of the Association of American Medical College's Council of Academic Societies. His current research focuses on the disappearance of altruism as a core medical value and the concurrent rise of "lifestyle medicine," the role of trust in the ideology of professionalism, social dimensions of medical effectiveness research, disability studies, and rural health issues. He received his undergraduate degree in social relations from Harvard University in 1969 and his PhD in medical sociology from Yale University in 1976.

Roberta Hamilton is Professor of Sociology at Queen's University, Canada. For the past 35 years, she has been engaged in scholarly work on feminist theories, historical sociology, Canadian political economy, and Québec society. Her most recent publications include *Setting the Agenda: Jean Royce and the Shaping of Queen's University* (2002), which won the Ontario History Prize (awarded triennially) for the best book in women's history, and *Gendering the Vertical Mosaic: Feminist Perspectives on Canadian Society* (2005).

Douglas Harper, Professor of Sociology at Duquesne University, was the last PhD student of Everett Hughes. Harper has completed ethnographies of railroad tramps (*Good Company: A Tramp Life*), a rural auto mechanic (*Working Knowledge: Skill and Community in a Small Shop*), and the industrialization of dairy farming (*Changing Works: Visions of a Lost Agriculture*). He has used photography as a part of his ethnographic studies, and also codirected a film, with Steven Papson, on the culture of a small sawmill in northern New York. He was the founding editor of *Visual Sociology* and has been active in the International Visual Sociology Association since its inception. His work has been translated into Italian, German, and French, and he has been a guest professor and lecturer at several universities in Europe. His current research, with Patrizia Faccioli, is a study of food and culture in northern Italy.

Michelle Hasday is now in her first year of a joint MA/PhD program in sociology at the University of Wisconsin at Madison, where she is a University Fellow. The main focus of her studies is the sociology of sexuality and gender. Her other current projects include a working paper, "Male Pornography Use and Orientations towards Sexual Relationships with Women," which will be ready for publication submission by fall of 2006. She is also beginning a new project examining the relationship between female self-objectification and power dynamics in intimate relationships. She received her BA in sociology from Brown University.

Jeff Hearn is Professor, Swedish School of Economics, Helsinki, Finland, and Linköping University, Sweden, and Professor of Sociology, University of Huddersfield, United Kingdom. He was previously Research Professor, University of Manchester, and has also worked at the

Universities of Bradford, Oslo, Tampere, and Åbo Akademi. His books include *'Sex' at 'Work'* (1987/1995); *The Sexuality of Organization* (1989); *Men in the Public Eye* (1992); *Men as Managers, Managers as Men* (1996); *Hard Work in the Academy* (1999); *Gender, Sexuality and Violence in Organizations* (2001); *Information Society and the Workplace* (2004); *Handbook of Studies on Men and Masculinities* (2005); *Men and Masculinities in Europe* (2006); and *European Perspectives on Men and Masculinities* (2006). He is Coeditor of the journal *Men and Masculinities.* He was Principal Contractor of the EU Research Network "The Social Problem of Men" and is currently researching "Men, Gender Relations and Transnational Organising, Organisations and Management."

Danielle Antoinette Hidalgo is currently a doctoral student in sociology at Tulane University, writing a dissertation on women in same-sex relationships in Thailand. She has published several journal articles and book chapters on sexuality and gender issues in Southeast Asia and the United States. She has completed an MSc in sociology at the London School of Economics.

Susan Hoecker-Drysdale is Professor Emerita of Sociology, Department of Sociology and Anthropology, Concordia University, Montréal, Québec; retired Visiting Professor, Sociology, the University of Iowa. She was a Visiting Fellow, School of Advanced Study, the University of London from 1997 to 1998. Her areas of teaching and research include classical social theory, feminist sociological theory, women in the history of sociology, gender, and Victorian sociology. She is a founding member of the British Martineau Society and the Harriet Martineau Sociological Society. Her publications include *Harriet Martineau: Studies of America, 1831–1868* (eight volumes; 2004, edited with introductions by Susan Hoecker-Drysdale); "Harriet Martineau: The Theory and Practice of Early Critical Social Research" (*Lost Sociologists Rediscovered: Jane Addams, Walter Benjamin, W. E. B. DuBois, Harriet Martineau, Pitirim A. Sorokin, Flora Tristan, George E. Vincent, and Beatrice Webb,* 2002, M. A. Romano, ed.); *Harriet Martineau: Theoretical and Methodological Perspectives* (2001, M. R. Hill and S. Hoecker-Drysdale, ed.); "Harriet Martineau" (*The Blackwell Companion to Major Classical Social Theorists,* 2000, Chap. 2, G. Ritzer, ed.); "Sociologists in the Vineyard: The Careers of Everett Cherrington Hughes and Helen MacGill Hughes" (*Creative Couples in the Sciences,* 1996, H. Pycior et al., ed.); "The Enigma of Harriet Martineau's Letters on Science" (*Women's Writings: The Elizabethan to Victorian Period,* 1995); *Harriet Martineau: First Woman Sociologist* (1992); and "Women Sociologists in Canada: The Careers of Helen MacGill Hughes, Aileen Dansken Ross, and Jean Robertson Burnet" (*Despite the Odds: Essays on Canadian Women and Science,* 1990, M. G. Ainley, ed.). She earned her PhD from Louisiana State University.

Carla B. Howery is the Deputy Executive Officer of the American Sociological Association (ASA). She serves as the Director of two of the ASA's six core programs: the Academic and Professional Affairs Program and the Sydney S. Spivack Program on Applied Social Research and Social Policy. During her 24 years at the ASA, she has worked on a number of issues, including the status of women in sociology, research on the profession, sociological practice, international sociology, graduate and undergraduate teaching, and membership concerns. Two recent major projects focused on minority opportunities through school transformation and integrating data analysis (in early undergraduate sociology courses). Raised in Wisconsin, she attended St. Olaf College, the University of Minnesota, and the University of Pennsylvania.

Valerie Jenness is Professor in the Department of Criminology, Law and Society and the Department of Sociology at the University of California, Irvine. She is the coeditor of one book, *Social Movements, Public Policy, and Democracy* (2005, with David Meyer and Helen Ingram), the author of three books—*Making Hate a Crime: From Social Movement to Law Enforcement Practice* (2001, with Ryken Grattet); *Hate Crimes: New Social Movements and the Politics of Violence* (1997, with Kendal Broad); and *Making It Work: The Prostitutes' Rights Movement in Perspective* (1993)—and articles published in the *American Sociological Review, Law & Society Review, Annual Review of Sociology, Gender & Society, Social Problems, American Behavioral Scientist, Sociological Perspectives, Journal of Criminal Law and Criminology, Law and Critique, Journal of Hate Studies,* and *Research in Social Movements, Conflicts and Change.* Her research has received awards from the Gustavus Myers Center for the Study of Bigotry and Human Rights in North America, the Society for the Study of Social Problems, the Pacific Sociological Association, and the University of California.

Gary F. Jensen is Professor of Sociology and Religious Studies and Joe B. Wyatt Distinguished University Professor at Vanderbilt University. He taught at the University of North Carolina, Chapel Hill, and the University of Arizona before moving to Vanderbilt as Department Chair in 1989. He has authored or coauthored, and edited or coedited 8 books and more than 75 articles or chapters primarily focusing on crime and delinquency. His most recent works include *Social Learning and the Explanation of Crime: A Guide for the New Century* (with Ronald Akers) and *The Path of the Devil: A Study of Early Modern Witch Hunts* (2006). He is working on the fourth edition of *Delinquency and Youth Crime* (with D. G. Rojek). He was initiated as a Fellow of the American Society of Criminology in 2001. He earned his PhD from the University of Washington in 1972.

Andrew K. Jorgenson is Assistant Professor of Sociology at Washington State University. His current research focuses on the social and environmental impacts of (1) foreign direct investment in different sectors and (2) the structure of international trade. His recent publications appeared in *Social Forces, Social Problems, Sociological Perspectives, International Journal of Comparative Sociology, Human Ecology Review, Humboldt Journal of Social Relations, Journal of World-Systems Research, Society in Transition,* and other scholarly journals and edited collections.

Linda Kalof is Professor of Sociology at Michigan State University. She has written articles on the cultural construction of femininity, edits the book series *A Cultural History of the Human Body,* and embraces both cultural studies and visual sociology in her research.

Michael S. Kimmel is Professor of Sociology at State University of New York at Stony Brook. His books include *Changing Men* (1987); *Men Confront Pornography* (1990); *Against the Tide: Profeminist Men in the United States, 1776–1990* (1992); *The Politics of Manhood* (1996); *Manhood: A Cultural History* (1996); *The Gendered Society* (2003, 2nd ed.); *Men's Lives* (2003, 6th ed.); *Handbook of Studies on Men and Masculinities* (2005); *The Gender of Desire* (2005); and *The History of Men* (2005). He is editor of *Men and Masculinities,* an interdisciplinary scholarly journal, a book series on *Men and Masculinity* at the University of California Press, and the Sage Series on *Men and Masculinities.* He is the spokesperson for the National Organization for Men Against Sexism (NOMAS) and lectures extensively on campuses in the United States and abroad.

Jerry Krause, Professor Emeritus Humboldt State University, fell in love with sociology in the early 1960s while an undergraduate sociology major at the University of California at Berkeley, where he was influenced by Herbert Blumer. In 1971, he assumed a professorship of sociology at Humboldt State University, where he remained until his retirement in 2005. He cofounded in 1991 and directed until 2005 the Center for Applied Social Analysis and Education (CASAE) at Humboldt State University and was instrumental in developing the Sociological Practice MA program. Working with Sociological Practice graduate students on a variety of CASAE projects, he pioneered the development of participatory research approaches to sociological practice. He earned a master's degree in sociology at San Jose State College in 1966 and a PhD in sociology from Louisiana State University in 1975.

Kelsy Kretschmer is a graduate student in sociology at the University of California, Irvine. She is interested in social movements and gender. Her current research focuses on dissident identity organizations and leadership in social movement organizations.

Nancy G. Kutner is Professor of Rehabilitation Medicine and Adjunct Professor of Sociology at Emory University, where she directs a U.S. Renal Data System Special Studies Center on Rehabilitation and Quality of Life funded by the National Institutes of Health (NIH). Her current projects focus on functional outcomes among persons with stroke and osteoarthritis, as well as chronic kidney disease. She has served on advisory committees for the Institute of Medicine, the Health Resources and Services Administration, and the Health Care Financing Administration (now the Centers for Medicare and Medicaid Services). In 2003, she was an invited speaker for the NIH Physical Disabilities through the Lifespan Conference held in Bethesda, Maryland.

Elise S. Lake is Associate Professor in the Department of Sociology and Anthropology at the University of Mississippi, where she teaches courses on the sociology of food, marriage and family, criminology, and deviance. Her research interests include the sociology of food, the sociology of literature, and teaching ethics.

Kenneth C. Land is the John Franklin Crowell Professor of Sociology and Demographic Studies at Duke University, Durham, North Carolina. His areas of research interest are in mathematical sociology/demography, statistical methods, demography, social indicators/quality-of-life measurement, and criminology. He is the coauthor or coeditor of five books and author or coauthor of more than 150 peer-reviewed journal articles and book chapters. He was the recipient in 1997 of the Paul F. Lazarsfeld Memorial Award of the Methodology Section and served in 2005 as Chair of the Mathematical Sociology Section of the American Sociological Association. He has been elected a Fellow of five professional societies, including the American Statistical Association.

Beryl Langer is a senior member of the program in Sociology and Anthropology at La Trobe University, Melbourne, Australia. Her current research on global children's culture is published in the *Journal of Consumer Culture, Thesis Eleven,* and *Childhood.* Her research interests include consumer culture, globalization, and Canadian literature.

Jack Levin, PhD, is the Irving and Betty Brudnick Professor of Sociology and Criminology at Northeastern University, where he directs its Brudnick Center on Conflict and Violence. He has authored or coauthored 28 books, including *Mass Murder: America's Growing Menace; Killer on Campus, Overkill: Mass Murder and Serial Killing Exposed; Hate Crimes Revisited; The Will to Kill: Making Sense of Senseless Murder; Why We Hate;* and *The Violence of Hate.* He was honored by the Massachusetts Council for Advancement and Support of Education as its "Professor of the Year." He has spoken to a wide variety of community, academic, and professional groups, including the White House Conference on Hate Crimes, the Department of Justice, the Department of Education, and the International Association of Chiefs of Police.

Zai Liang is Professor of Sociology at State University of New York at Albany. His current research projects include internal migration in China and international migration from China to the United States and Europe. He currently serves as Chair of the Asia and Asian America section of the American Sociological Association and Codirector of Urban China Research Network at the University at Albany. He received his PhD in sociology from the University of Chicago.

Linda Lobao is Professor of Rural Sociology, Sociology, and Geography at The Ohio State University. Her research focuses on spatial inequality, particularly the role of economic structure and the state in creating inequality across regions. She was President of the Rural Sociological Society from 2002 to 2003. Her publications include a book monograph, *Local and Inequality,* two coedited volumes, as well as articles in *Social Forces, Rural Sociology, Annual Review of Sociology,* and other journals.

David F. Luckenbill is Professor of Sociology at Northern Illinois University. His current research focuses on the violation and protection of intellectual property.

Brent K. Marshall is Associate Professor in the Department of Sociology, University of Central Florida. He has published articles in numerous sociology and interdisciplinary journals such as *Social Forces, Social Science Research, Sociological Spectrum,* and *Environment and Behavior.* His current research focus is on disasters, environmental risk, environmental justice, and ecosystem management. He is a member of the American Sociological Association's Gulf Coast Disaster Research Team.

Natasha S. Mauthner received her PhD from the University of Cambridge, where she conducted research on motherhood and postnatal depression. She took up a postdoctoral fellowship at Harvard University, where she continued with this work and subsequently published it in *The Darkest Days of My Life: Stories of Postpartum Depression* (Harvard University Press, 2002). She is currently Senior Lecturer in the Business School at the University of Aberdeen, where she writes book chapters and journal articles on gender, work, and family life, as well as on reflexivity, research practice, and the construction of knowledge. These include work on epistemological issues in archiving and reusing qualitative data, the politics of feminist research management, and epistemological and ontological issues in collaborative research.

Sabrina McCormick is jointly appointed in the Department of Sociology and the Environmental Science and Policy Program at Michigan State University. Her work has been published in a variety of journals and edited volumes, including *Sociology of Health and Illness, Sociological Forum, Social Science and Medicine,* and *Science, Technology, and Human Values,* among others. She received her PhD from Brown University in 2005.

Kathleen McKinney is the K. Patricia Cross Endowed Chair in the Scholarship of Teaching and Learning and Professor of Sociology at Illinois State University. She has published extensively in the areas of relationships, sexuality, sexual harassment, and college teaching. She is a past editor of Teaching Sociology and a Carnegie Scholar (2003–2004). She has received several teaching awards, including Illinois State University's Outstanding University Teacher, and the American Sociological Association's Hans O. Mauksch Award and Distinguished Contributions to Teaching Award. She earned her PhD from the University of Wisconsin at Madison.

Neil McLaughlin teaches sociological theory at McMaster University, in Hamilton, Ontario, Canada. He is interested in intellectuals, the sociology of knowledge, and creativity, as well as critical theories. He has published in such journals as the *Sociological Quarterly, Sociological Theory, Sociological Forum, Journal of the History of the Behaviorial Sciences,* and *Canadian Journal of Sociology and Dissent.* He is presently working on a study of Canadian professors as public intellectuals, the question of the global public intellectual, public sociology from a comparative perspective, and the academic/intellectual reputations of such thinkers as Orwell, Trilling, Chomsky, and Said.

Miller McPherson is Professor of Sociology at Duke University and Director of the Duke Center for the Study of Social Networks. He has developed an ecological evolutionary model of affiliation. Current projects include a test of that theory with nationally representative data from the Niches and Networks project, funded by the Human and Social Dynamics Initiative at the National Science Foundation. The project will create a representative sample of voluntary groups, and study their coevolution of group memberships and networks over time. He is the lead author of a paper in the June 2006 *American Sociological Review,* "Social Isolation in America: Changes in Core Discussion Networks over Two Decades."

David S. Meyer is Professor of Sociology, Political Science, and Planning, Policy, and Design at the University of California, Irvine, and a Faculty Fellow of the Center for the Study of Democracy. He is author, most recently, of *The Politics of Protest: Social Movements in America* (2007).

Michael Micklin is Chief of the Risk, Prevention, and Health Behavior (RPHB) IRG at the Center for Scientific Review (CSR), National Institutes of Health. He has authored or edited eight books, including the *Handbook of Population* (2005) and *Continuities in Sociological Human Ecology* (1998), both with D. L. Poston Jr. He contributed to this volume in his personal capacity. The views expressed are his own and do not necessarily represent those of the National Institutes of Health or the U.S. government.

Kirk Miller is on the sociology faculty at Northern Illinois University. He currently researches the behavior of law in a variety of arenas, including police traffic stops and intellectual property. He received his PhD from North Carolina State University.

Vincent Mosco is Canada Research Chair in Communication and Society, Queen's University, Canada. He is currently working on a project funded by the Canadian Social Sciences and Humanities Research Council that addresses labor and trade unions in the communications industries of Canada and the United States. He is the author of five books and editor or coeditor of eight books on the media, telecommunications, computers, and information technology. His most recent books are *The Digital Sublime: Myth, Power, and Cyberspace* (2004); *Continental Order? Integrating North America for Cybercapitalism* (2001, edited with D. Schiller); and *The Political Economy of Communication: Rethinking and Renewal* (Sage, 1996), translated into Chinese (two editions; Beijing and Taiwan), Spanish, and Korean. He is a member of the editorial boards of academic journals in the United States, United Kingdom, Turkey, Portugal, and Slovenia, and he has served as a contributor and a member of the editorial advisory board of the International Encyclopedia of Communication. He has written about electronic commerce for a new edition of the *Dictionary of American History*. He has held research positions in the U.S. government with the White House Office of Telecommunication Policy, the National Research Council, and the U.S. Congress Office of Technology Assessment, and in Canada with the Federal Department of Communication. He graduated from Georgetown University (Summa Cum Laude, Phi Beta Kappa) in 1970 and received his PhD in sociology from Harvard University in 1975.

Joel I. Nelson is a Professor of Sociology at the University of Minnesota. His publications focus on social and economic inequality. Current research interests consider the broad implications of the second industrial divide—particularly the connection between diversification in goods and services and widening disparities in earned income.

W. Lawrence Neuman is Professor of Sociology at University of Wisconsin at Whitewater. He recently published *Power, State and Society,* and his *Social Research Methods* is now in its sixth edition. At the University of Wisconsin at Whitewater, he is Director of the Pacific Asian Educational Resource Center and Coordinator of the Asian Studies Program. He earned his PhD in 1982 from the University of Wisconsin at Madison.

Gerd Nollmann has taught sociology at the Universities of Muenster and Duisburg-Essen where he is currently an Assistant Professor. He has worked as a publisher and marketing director for Bertelsmann and for Vandenhoeck & Ruprecht. In his scientific work, he focuses on the application of interpretive sociological theories to social research, as well as the analysis of social inequalities, and is the author/editor of 8 books and 15 articles in sociological journals. He received his PhD in sociology from the University of Muenster, Germany.

Sean Noonan is Associate Professor of Sociology at Harper College, near Chicago, Illinois.

Minjoo Oh is Assistant Professor in the Department of Sociology and Anthropology at the University of Mississippi. Her research concerns the intersection of eating practices and identity, in the context of globalization. Her other research interests include contemporary social theory, popular culture, and the sociology of food.

Erica Owens is Assistant Professor in the Division of Sociology and Anthropology at West Virginia University. Her article "Race, Sexual Attractiveness, and Internet Personals Advertisements" was published in Net.SeXXX (2004). Other empirical and theoretical articles on family processes and identity troubles have appeared or are accepted and pending in the journals *Family Relations, Symbolic Interaction,* and *Journal of Family Issues.* She is on the editorial boards of *Marriage and Family Review* and *Journal of Family Issues.* She is the current Vice President (2005–2006) of the Society for the Study of Symbolic Interaction. Her research interests include self-identity, coping, and romantic difficulty.

Michael Quinn Patton is an independent organizational development and program evaluation consultant, former President of the American Evaluation Association, and author of *Utilization-Focused Evaluation* (3d ed., Sage, 1997) and *Qualitative Research and Evaluation Methods* (3rd ed., Sage, 2002). He is recipient of both the Myrdal Award for Outstanding Contributions to Useful and Practical Evaluation Practice from the Evaluation Research Society and the Lazarsfeld Award for Lifelong Contributions to Evaluation Theory from the American Evaluation Association. The Society for Applied Sociology honored him with the 2001 Lester F. Ward Award for Outstanding Contributions to Applied Sociology. He earned his PhD in sociology from the University of Wisconsin.

Harry Perlstadt is a professor in the Department of Sociology, director of an interdisciplinary program in Bioethics, Humanities, and Society, and an affiliate faculty in the Institute for Public Policy and Social Research at Michigan State University. He earned his PhD in sociology at the University of Chicago, and Master of Public Health in health planning and administration from the University of Michigan. He specializes in medical sociology, health organizations and delivery systems, and evaluation research. Over the years he has conducted evaluation research for the W. K. Kellogg Foundation, Center for Substance Abuse Prevention (CSAP), Health Resource Services Administration (HRSA), National Institute for

Mental Health (NIMH), Centers for Disease Control (CDC), and World Health Organization (WHO). He has published on citizen participation in health care planning, attitudes and experiences of women lawyers, and several program evaluations. He has recently begun to focus on the human research protections process, developing a researcher's bill of rights and a framework for assessing risk in social research. He helped found and served as the first chair of the Commission on Applied and Clinical Sociology, which accredits undergraduate and graduate programs. He was chair of the American Sociological Association Section on Sociological Practice, and chaired the Science Board and Joint Policy Committees of the American Public Health Association. He also served on the Scientific Advisory Committee of the American Lung Association. He has served on the editorial boards of the *Journal of Applied Sociology, Journal of Health and Social Behavior,* and *The Nation's Health.* In 2000 he received the Alex Boros award for contributions and service from the Society for Applied Sociology.

Bernice A. Pescosolido is Chancellor's Professor of Sociology at Indiana University and Director of the Indiana Consortium for Mental Health Services Research. Her research agenda addresses how social networks connect individuals to their communities and to institutional structures, providing the "wires" through which society's energies (social interaction) and levels (contexts) influence people's attitudes and actions. In the early 1990s, she developed the network-episode model, which combined a social network, multilevel, and life course approach to understand how individuals come to recognize health problems, respond to their onset, and use health care services. She has also studied the role of social networks in suicide, in media influences, and in the underlying roots of stigma. She has published widely in sociology, social science, public health, and medical journals; served on the editorial board of a dozen national and international journals; and has been elected to a variety of leadership positions in professional associations, including Vice President of the American Sociological Association and Chair of the ASA Sections on Medical Sociology and Sociology of Mental Health.

Trevor Pinch is Professor of Sociology and Professor and Chair of Science and Technology Studies at Cornell University. He has published 14 books and numerous articles on aspects of the sociology of science and technology. His studies have included quantum physics, solar neutrinos, parapsychology, health economics, the bicycle, the car, and the electronic music synthesizer. His most recent books are *How Users Matter* (2003, edited with Nelly Oudshoorn) and *Analog Days: The Invention and Impact of the Moog Synthesizer* (2002, with Frank Trocco). *Analog Days* was the winner of the 2003 silver award for popular culture "Book of the Year" of *ForeWord* magazine. He has just completed a third volume in his popular series

of "Golem" books with Harry Collins, *Dr Golem: How to Think about Medicine.* He holds degrees in physics and sociology.

Dudley L. Poston Jr. is Professor of Sociology and the George T. and Gladys H. Abell Endowed Professor of Liberal Arts at Texas A&M University. He previously served on the faculties of Cornell University and the University of Texas. His research focuses on the demography of China and South Korea, the demography of homosexuality, and the social demography of gender. He is currently writing a book with Amanda K. Baumle and D'Lane R. Compton on the *Demography of Sexual Orientation.*

Antony J. Puddephatt is a PhD candidate in the Sociology Department at McMaster University in Hamilton, Ontario, Canada. His areas of interest include science and technology, sociological theory, and ethnographic research. He has published in journals such as *Symbolic Interaction, Sociological Focus,* and *Social Epistemology.* Most recently, he has revisited the theoretical contributions of George Herbert Mead to illustrate their implications for emerging developments in interpretive theory, as well as the sociology of knowledge, science, and technology.

Gordana Rabrenovic, PhD, is Associate Professor of Sociology and Education and Associate Director of the Brudnick Center on Violence and Conflict at Northeastern University. Her substantive specialties include community studies, urban education, and intergroup conflict and violence. She is author of the book *Community Builders: A Tale of Neighborhood Mobilization in Two Cities* (1996), coeditor of the book *Community Politics and Policy* (1999) and the *American Behavioral Scientist* special issue on *Hate Crimes and Ethnic Conflict* (2001), and coauthor of the book *Why We Hate* (2004).

Miguel Requena is full Professor of Sociology in the Department of Sociology II (Social Structure), Universidad Nacional de Educación a Distancia, Madrid, Spain. He is Visiting Professor in the Department of Spanish and Portuguese Languages and Cultures, Princeton University; and Senior Associate Member in St. Antony College, Oxford University (1994–1995). His fields of teaching and research include social stratification, demography and sociology of family, and sociology of age. His publications include *La emancipación de los jóvenes en España* (1996) and *Tres décadas de cambio social en España* (2005).

Dawn T. Robinson is Associate Professor of Sociology at the University of Georgia. She is Deputy Editor of *Social Psychology Quarterly* and Director of the Laboratory for the Study of Social Interaction (LaSSI) at the University of Georgia. She is currently Chair of the Sociology of Emotions section of the American Sociological Association. Her research focuses primarily on identity and emotion processes in face-to-face interaction and the relationship between network structures and social identities. She is currently conducting a series of National Science Foundation funded studies examining the relationship between identity, injustice, and emotion.

Paul M. Roman is Distinguished Research Professor of Sociology and Director of the Center for Research on Behavioral Health and Human Services Delivery, Institute for Behavioral Research, University of Georgia, Athens. Previously, he served on the faculty of Tulane University from 1969 to 1986. His research is focused on organizational and sociological aspects of drug and alcohol problems, with particular attention to the organization of treatment systems and to the workplace and the design of intervention efforts to deal with employees with substance abuse problems. He served on the Panel on Employer Policies and Working Families, National Academy of Sciences, and has had many years of service as member and chair of review groups and study sections at the National Institutes of Health. His current research is focused on the patterns of organizational structure associated with organizational innovation and change among substance abuse treatment providers, the impact of NIDA's Clinical Trials Network on adoption of innovations in treatment programs, and the organization and management of therapeutic communities. Other recent research has centered on referral patterns associated with different types of employee problems referred to employee assistance programs, national patterns of drinking and drug-related behaviors and attitudes among employed persons, and the structural and process characteristics of EAPs. Among his publications is a monograph, *Cost Effectiveness and Preventive Implications of Employee Assistance Programs* (1995, coauthored with Terry C. Blum) and *Drug Testing in the Workplace* (1994, coedited with Scott Macdonald). He received his PhD from Cornell University in 1968.

Eugene A. Rosa is currently the Edward R. Meyer Distinguished Professor of Natural Resources and Environmental Policy in the Thomas F. Foley Institute of Public Policy and Public Service, Professor of Sociology, Affiliated Professor of Environmental Science, Affiliated Professor of Fine Arts, and Faculty Associate in the Center for Integrated Biotechnology, all at Washington State University. He specializes in research on global environmental change and on risk, is currently a member of the Human Dimensions of Global Change Committee of the National Academy of Sciences, has published widely in both fields, including articles in *Science, Ambio, The American Sociological Review, Social Forces, Ecological Economics, Risk Analysis,* and others, and has published the award-winning book *Risk, Uncertainty, and Rational Action* (with Carlo Jaeger, Ortwin Renn, and Thomas Webler).

John Ryan, PhD, is Professor and Chair of the Department of Sociology at Virginia Tech, where he teaches the Sociology of Law and Sociology of Culture.

His research interests focus on the study of culture-producing organizations, copyright law, and the uses of symbolic culture. His recent work includes a study of the changing role of music producers in the digital environment and the effects of the Internet on musical taste.

Clinton R. Sanders is Professor in the Sociology Department at the University of Connecticut. He has served as President (2002–2003) and Vice President (1994–1995) of the Society for the Study of Symbolic Interaction. His work focuses on cultural production, deviant behavior, ethnographic research, and sociozoology. He is author of *Understanding Dogs: Living and Working with Canine Companions* (1999) and coauthor of *Regarding Animals* (1996, with Arnold Arluke), both of which received the Charles Horton Cooley Award given by the Society for the Study of Symbolic Interaction for the year's Most Outstanding Contribution to the Symbolic Interactionist Literature. He is coeditor of the series on "Animals, Culture, and Society," an associate editor of *Society and Animals,* and a member of the governing council of the American Sociological Association's section on "Animals and Society." In 2004, he was the recipient of the University of Connecticut Provost's Award for Research Excellence, and in 2006, he received the "Distinguished Scholarship Award" from the Animals and Society Section of the American Sociological Association.

Stephen K. Sanderson has now retired from full-time teaching and resides in Boulder, Colorado. He taught for 30 years at Indiana University of Pennsylvania. A specialist in sociological theory and comparative and historical sociology, he has authored or edited 10 books, as well as several dozen articles in professional journals, edited collections, handbooks, and social science encyclopedias. His most recent works are *Evolutionism and Its Critics: Deconstructing and Reconstructing an Evolutionary Interpretation of Human Society* (2006) and *Studying Societies and Cultures: Marvin Harris's Cultural Materialism and Its Legacy* (2006, coedited with Lawrence A. Kuznar). He is currently working on books on the concept of culture in sociology and anthropology and the sociology of Edward Westermarck. He received his PhD in sociology from the University of Nebraska at Lincoln in 1973.

Saskia Sassen is the Ralph Lewis Professor of Sociology at the University of Chicago and Centennial Visiting Professor at the London School of Economics. Her new book is *Territory, Authority, Rights: From Medieval to Global Assemblages* (2006). Just completed for UNESCO is a five-year project on sustainable human settlement involving a network of researchers and activists in over 30 countries; it is published as one of the volumes of the *Encyclopedia of Life Support Systems.* Her recent books are the coedited *Digital Formations: New Architectures for Global Order* (2005); *A Sociology of Globalization* (2006); and a third, fully updated edition of *Cities in a*

World Economy (Sage, 2006). *The Global City* was released in a new, fully updated edition in 2001. Her books have been translated into 16 languages. She serves on several editorial boards and is an advisor to several international bodies. She is a Member of the Council on Foreign Relations, a member of the National Academy of Sciences Panel on Cities, and Chair of the Information Technology and International Cooperation Committee of the Social Science Research Council (United States). Her comments have appeared in the *Guardian,* the *New York Times, Le Monde Diplomatique, Newsweek International,* the *International Herald Tribune,* and the *Financial Times,* among others.

Joseph A. Scimecca is Professor of Sociology at George Mason University, where he was previously Chair of the Department of Sociology and Anthropology and Director of the Institute for Conflict Analysis and Resolution. A former President of the Association of Humanist Sociology, he is the author of *Crisis at St. Johns: Strike and Revolution on the Catholic Campus; The Sociological Theory of C. Wright Mills; Society and Freedom: An Introduction to Humanist Sociology;* and *Education and Society;* coauthor of *Sociology: Analysis and Application* and *Classical Sociological Theory: Rediscovering the Promise of Sociology;* and coeditor of *Conflict Resolution: Cross-Cultural Perspectives.*

David R. Segal is Distinguished Scholar-Teacher, Director of the Center for Research on Military Organization, Professor of Sociology, and Affiliate Professor of Government and Politics and of Public Policy at the University of Maryland at College Park. He joined the Sociology Department at the University of Michigan in 1966. During the first years of the all-volunteer force, he directed the U.S. Army's sociological research program. He joined the Maryland faculty in 1976. He has received career achievement awards from the American Sociological Association, the American Psychological Association, and the District of Columbia Sociological Society, and has twice been awarded the U.S. Army Medal for Outstanding Civilian Service. His most recent publications include "Postmodernity and the Modern Military" (*Armed Forces & Society,* 2001, with Bradford Booth and Meyer Kestnbaum); "America's Military Population" (*Population Bulletin,* 2004, with Mady W. Segal); and "Bringing the Soldiers Back In: Implications of Inclusion of Military Personnel for Labor Market Research on Race, Class, and Gender" (*Race, Gender & Class,* 2005, with Bradford Booth). He earned his PhD from the University of Chicago.

Jane Sell is Professor of Sociology at Texas A&M University. Her research explores a range of issues related to group dynamics, including cooperation, the establishment and dissolution of inequality in groups, and the role of legitimacy in the establishment of group routine.

Constance L. Shehan is Professor and Chair of the Department of Sociology at the University of Florida, Gainesville. Her areas of expertise are gender, families, work/occupations, and aging. She has published widely in the areas of women's work and family life, work and well-being, and parent-child relations in later life. She is currently Editor of the *Journal of Family Issues.* She is also author of several books, including *Marriages and Families; Through the Eyes of the Child: Re-Visioning Children as Agents of Family Life;* and *Women at the University of Florida,* and coauthor of *Gendering the Body* (forthcoming 2007, with Sara Crawley and Lara Foley). She earned her PhD in sociology from Pennsylvania State University.

Linda G. Smith has worked for 30 years in the corrections field as a practitioner, researcher, and professor. She has taught at the University of South Florida, Georgia State University, and University of Maryland at College Park. She has conducted research and consulted in several states, including Pennsylvania, Maryland, Ohio, Minnesota, California, Indiana, Washington, Georgia, Delaware, Connecticut, and Florida, as well as for the U.S. Department of Justice, National Institute of Justice, and the U.S. Department of Education, Office of Correctional Education. She was also a federal court monitor overseeing a correctional institution in Florida and ran a large jail in Atlanta, Georgia. She has published in corrections/criminal justice journals and books and has written several technical reports for federal, state, and local governments. She is the 2003 recipient of the American Correctional Association Peter Lejins Research award for her contribution to the field. She received her PhD from the University of Florida.

Lynn Smith-Lovin is Robert L. Wilson Professor of Sociology in the Trinity College of Arts and Sciences at Duke University. She received the 2006 Cooley-Mead Award and the 2005 Lifetime Achievement Award in the Sociology of Emotions. Her research examines the relationships among social association, identity, action, and emotion. Her current projects involve an experimental study of justice, identity, and emotion as well as research with Miller McPherson on an ecological theory of identity (both funded by the National Science Foundation). Her recent publications include "Social Isolation in America" (*American Sociological Review,* June 2006) and "Gender Identity Recognition and Task Performance" (*Advances in Group Processes,* 2005). She has served as President of the Southern Sociological Society, Vice President of the American Sociological Association, and Chair of the ASA Sections on the Sociology of Emotion and on Social Psychology.

Robert A. Stebbins, FRSC, is Faculty Professor in the Department of Sociology at the University of Calgary. He has written over 150 articles and chapters and written or edited over 30 books, including *Between Work and Leisure* and *Volunteering* (2004); *Challenging Mountain Nature* (on mountain hobbies, 2005); *A Dictionary of Nonprofit Terms and Concepts* (2006, with D. H. Smith and M. Dover); and *Serious Leisure: A Perspective for Our Time* (2006). Stebbins was elected Fellow of the Academy of Leisure Sciences in 1996 and, in 1999, elected Fellow of the Royal Society of Canada. He received his PhD in 1964 from the University of Minnesota.

Ronald G. Stover is Professor of Sociology at South Dakota State University, where he has been employed since 1983. He was born and raised in Georgia. He taught at Clemson University before moving to South Dakota State University. He has published numerous chapters in books and articles in professional journals. In 1993, he published *Marriage, Family, and Intimate Relations* (with Christine A. Hope) and in 1999 published *Industrial Societies: An Evolutionary Perspective* (with Melodie L. Lichty and Penny W. Stover). He was twice voted Teacher of the Year by students at South Dakota State University. He earned the BA, MA, and PhD in sociology from the University of Georgia. He received his doctorate in 1975.

Hermann Strasser has taught sociology at the University of Oklahoma, Norman, and the University of Vienna, Austria. After his Assistant Professorship at the Institute for Advanced Studies, Vienna, he took over the Chair in sociology at the University of Duisburg-Essen, Germany, in 1978, where he is also the Director of the Academic Career Service Center. Moreover, he heads VERBAL, a private firm devoted to writing biographies for corporations and public personalities. In his scientific work, he focuses on the paradigmatic structure of sociological theories, as well as the analysis of social change and social inequality, and is the author/editor of more than 20 books and 100 articles in sociological journals. He received a PhD in economics from the University of Innsbruck, Austria, and a PhD in sociology from Fordham University, New York.

Robin Stryker is Professor of Sociology, Affiliated Professor of Law, and Scholar of the College (2004–2007) at the University of Minnesota. She is past Chair of the Sociology of Law Section and current Chair of the Theory Section of the American Sociological Association and past President of the Society for the Advancement of Socio-Economics. She has written extensively on the politics of social science in American regulatory law, including labor, employment, and antitrust law; on institutional politics and organizational and institutional change; on legal and political culture; on law and legitimacy; and on the comparative welfare state, politics, and gendered labor markets. Among her recent publications are "The Strength of a Weak Agency: Title VII of the Civil Rights Act and the Transformation of State Capacity at the Equal Employment Opportunity Commission, 1965–71" (*American Journal of Sociology, 110,* 2004, with Nicholas Pedriana); "A Sociological Approach to Law and the Economy" (2005, N. Smelser and R. Swedberg, ed., *Handbook of*

Economic Sociology, 2nd ed., with Lauren Edelman); "Mind the Gap: Law, Institutional Analysis and Socio-Economics" (*Socio-Economic Review, 1,* 2003); and "Disparate Impact and the Quota Debates: Law, Labor Market Sociology and Equal Employment Policies" (*Sociological Quarterly, 42,* 2001).

Richard Tewksbury is Professor of Justice Administration at the University of Louisville. He has worked for several correctional systems and studied and written extensively on issues of correctional programming, institutional culture and correctional education, and health issues. He is the 2006 recipient of the American Correctional Association Peter Lejins Research award. He holds a PhD in sociology from The Ohio State University.

Bryan S. Turner is Professor of Sociology in the Asia Research Institute, National University of Singapore. He is the research leader of the cluster on religion and globalization and is currently writing a three-volume study of the sociology of religion. He edited the *Cambridge Dictionary of Sociology* (2006). A book on human rights and vulnerability is to be published in 2006. He is a Research Associate of GEMAS (Centre National de la Recherche Scientifique, Paris), an honorary Professor of Deakin University, and an Adjunct Professor of Murdoch University, Australia. He recently edited *The Sage Handbook of Sociology* (2005, with Craig Calhoun and Chris Rojek). He is the founding editor of three journals: *Citizenship Studies, Body & Society* (with Mike Featherstone), and *Journal of Classical Sociology* (with John O'Neill). As Dean of the Faculty of Arts at Deakin University (1992–1998), he was the founder of the Deakin center for citizenship and human rights. His recent publications include *Classical Sociology* (1999) and *The New Medical Sociology* (2004). He coauthored *Society & Culture: Principles of Scarcity and Solidarity* (2001, with Chris Rojek) and *Generations, Culture and Society* (2002, with June Edmunds). He coedited the *Handbook of Citizenship Studies* (2002, with Engin Isin).

Jonathan H. Turner is Distinguished Professor of Sociology at the University of California, Riverside. He is the author of some 30 books as well as numerous journal articles and chapters in books. He is a general theorist who seeks to develop abstract models and propositions on the dynamics operating at all levels of social reality, from the neurology of the human brain as it affects emotions and interpersonal behavior to the dynamics of institutional, societal, and intersocietal phenomena. He has specific substantive interests in evolutionary sociology, the sociology of emotions, interpersonal behavior, stratification, history of social thought, and social institutions.

Chikako Usui is Associate Professor of Sociology at the University of Missouri at St. Louis. Her areas of research interests are comparative public policy, political economy of Japan, aging, and gender. Her recent publications include "Japan's Frozen Future: Why Are Women Withholding Their Investment in Work and Family?" (*Japanese Women: Lineage and Legacies,* Amy McCreedy Thernstrom, ed., 2005); "Continuity and Change in Paths to Political Office: Ex-bureaucrats and Chiiriyo in Japan" (*Asian Business & Management, 3,* 2004); "Women, Institutions, and Leadership in Japan" (*Asian Perspective, 27,* 2003); *Amakudari: The Hidden Fabric of Japan's Economy* (2003, coauthored with Richard A. Colignon); and "Japan's Aging Dilemma?" (*Asia Program Special Report, 107,* 2003).

Jean Van Delinder is Associate Professor of Sociology, with affiliated appointments in American studies and women's studies, at Oklahoma State University. Her research interests are culture, theory, and gender. Her recent publications include studies on the relationship between scientific management and dance. She serves on the editorial board of the *Society for Dance History Scholars* and edits their biannual newsletter. Her funded research includes grants to teach sociology of gender through service learning and collaborative studies with nutrition faculty on the relationship between culture and disease in Oklahoma Native American women. She earned her PhD in sociology from the University of Kansas.

Ruut Veenhoven studied sociology and teaches at Erasmus University of Rotterdam as a professor of social conditions for human happiness. His research is on subjective quality of life. His major publications are *Conditions of Happiness* (1984), *Happy Life-Expectancy* (1997), and *The Four Qualities of Life* (2000). He is Director of the World Database of Happiness and Editor of the *Journal of Happiness Studies.* He has also published on love, marriage, and parenthood.

Emilio C. Viano is Professor in the School of Public Affairs, American University, Washington, D.C. He is a specialist in the fields of victims of crime, terrorism, and human rights. He has published more than 30 books and 120 articles. He is frequently asked to lecture and consult in various countries of the world and also to be interviewed on international media like CNN, the BBC, Voice of America, and various radio and television stations and newspapers in the United States and abroad. He has been visiting professor at many universities worldwide, including the University of Paris. He has received many awards and prizes and was recently elected to the Board of Directors of the International Society of Criminology. He received his PhD from New York University and his LLM from Leicester University, United Kingdom.

Lee Garth Vigilant is Associate Professor of Sociology at Minnesota State University at Moorhead. He teaches in the areas of social theory, qualitative research methods, and urban social problems, while his research interests are in the sociology of health, healing, and illness. He is past recipient of the Donald J. White Teaching Excellence

Award for Sociology at Boston College (2000) and the TCU Senate Professor of the Year Award for Tufts University (2001). His recent publications have appeared in *Humanity and Society* (2004), *Deviant Behavior* (2005), and the *Handbook of Death and Dying* (2003). He is the coeditor of *Social Problems: Readings with Four Questions* (2006, with Joel Charon). He earned his PhD from Boston College in 2001.

Theodore C. Wagenaar is Professor of Sociology at Miami University, Ohio. He has served as Editor of *Teaching Sociology* and is a Carnegie National Scholar. He has served as a Program Analyst and an American Statistical Association Fellow at the National Center for Education Statistics. His publications address childhood socialization, the transition from youth to adulthood, teaching sociology, and other areas in education. Wagenaar also is a certified K–8 teacher.

Gary R. Webb is Associate Professor of Sociology at Oklahoma State University. He conducts research on the social aspects of disasters, including organizational and community preparedness for and response to large-scale crises. Currently, he is examining the governmental response to Hurricane Katrina. His publications have appeared in a variety of scholarly journals.

John Williamson is Professor of Sociology at Boston College. He is author or coauthor of 15 books and more than 120 journal articles or book chapters. He has written extensively on the comparative study of social welfare policies, particularly those dealing with the elderly. Some of his recent work has been based on the comparative historical method and some on quantitative cross-national analysis. His current research and writing efforts deal primarily with (1) quantitative studies of social, economic, and political determinants of cross-national differences in social policy and social justice issues such as income inequality, welfare state spending levels, physical quality of life, life expectancy, infant mortality, suicide rates, and homicide rates; (2) the comparative study of social security systems; and (3) the debate over generational equity and justice between generations in connection with Social Security policy in the United States.

Andrea E. Willson is Assistant Professor at the University of Western Ontario in London, Ontario, Canada, and was previously a postdoctoral fellow in the Carolina Population Center at the University of North Carolina. Her research is in the area of social inequality, health, and intergenerational relations over the life course. She is particularly interested in methodological issues related to the use of longitudinal data.

Frank Harold Wilson is Associate Professor in the Department of Sociology and Urban Studies Program at the University of Wisconsin at Milwaukee, where he teaches courses on sociological theory, urban sociology, and racial and ethnic relations. He has written widely in the areas of urban inequality, gentrification, poverty, and African American population. He is the author of *Race, Class, and the Postindustrial City: William Julius Wilson and the Promise of Sociology* (2004). He served as President of the Association of Black Sociologists and the Association of Social and Behavioral Scientists and as Senior Chair of the American Sociological Association, Committee for the Public Understanding of Sociology.

Allison K. Wisecup is currently a graduate student at Duke University. Her interests include gender, identity, emotion, and meaning. Her current projects include an examination of the effects of multiple-identity enactment for emotion production and research on gender differences in identity meanings. Her dissertation addresses the variation of identity and behavior meanings across sociodemographic space as a function of social distance. Her recent publications include "Gender Identity Recognition and Task Performance" (*Advances in Group Processes,* 2005, with Lynn Smith-Lovin and Miller McPherson).

William R. Wood is a PhD student at Boston College. His current interests are in juvenile justice and comparative criminology. He also studied at Union Theological Seminary in New York City where he received his master's degree in religious history. He has published articles in several areas of study, including the history of death and dying, the history of science and technology, and criminology. He expects to finish his degree in the fall of 2006.

Vera L. Zolberg is Professor in the Sociology Department of the New School for Social Research, New York City, where she has taught for over 20 years. Among her publications are *Outsider Art: Contesting Boundaries in Contemporary Culture* (1997, with J. M. Cherbo) and *Constructing a Sociology of the Arts* (1990; translated into Italian, Korean, Spanish, and Portuguese); she is coeditor of *After Bourdieu: Influence, Critique, Elaboration* (2004, with David Swartz). She was a founding member and then Chair of the Culture Section of the American Sociological Association and President of the Research Committee on the Sociology of the Arts of the International Sociological Association. Her research interests include contemporary and historical cultural policy and politics, art and culture, museums, African art, and collective memory. She has a BA from Hunter College, New York City; an MA in sociology and anthropology from Boston University; and a PhD in sociology from the University of Chicago.

PART I

THE DISCIPLINE OF SOCIOLOGY

1

THE SOCIOLOGICAL PERSPECTIVE

DENNIS L. PECK

The University of Alabama

CLIFTON D. BRYANT

Virginia Polytechnic Institute and State University

A commonly accepted definition of sociology as a special science is that it is the study of social aggregates and groups in their institutional organization, of institutions and their organization, and of the causes and consequences of changes in institutions and social organization. (Albert J. Reiss, Jr. 1968:1)

Within the contemporary context, sociologists are interested in human social interaction as people take one another into account as each behaves toward the other. Sociologists also take into analytical consideration the systemic units of interaction within social groups, social relations, and social organizations. As stated by Reiss (1968), the purview of sociology extends to

> Governments, corporations, and school systems to such territorial organizations as communities or to the schools, factories, and churches . . . that are components of communities. . . . are also concerned with social aggregates, or populations, in their institutional organization. (P. 1)

Sociology is, as Touraine (1990) suggests, an interpretation of social experience and is thus a part of the reality that the practitioners of the discipline attempt to observe and explain. To these areas we can add that sociology is a discipline that demystifies its subject matter, and it is, as Dennis H. Wrong (1990:21–22) notes, a debunker of popular beliefs, holds skeptical and critical views of the institutions that are studied (Smelser 1990), and challenges myth making (Best 2001).

The early history of sociology is a history of ideas developed in the European tradition, whereas the sociological approach of the last 150 years involved the development of concepts, methodology, and theories, especially in the United States (Goudsblom and Heilbron 2001). As American sociologists trained in the traditional theory and methods developed during the first eight decades of the twentieth century, we acknowledge our intellectual debt to the European founders. But beyond an earnest recognition of the classic work of the early founders, including Auguste Comte, Émile Durkheim, Alexis de Tocqueville, Frederic LePlay, Marcell Mauss, Max Weber, Karl Marx, and Harriet Martineau, most of whom were attracted to the European environment that included the liberalism, radicalism, and conservatism of the early to mid-nineteenth century (Nisbet 1966; Friedrichs 1970) and to what C. Wright Mills (1959) refers to as the *sociological imagination* that "enables us to grasp history and biography and the relations between the two within society" (p. 6), our approach to sociology is deeply embedded with and indebted to those individuals who established the Chicago, Harvard, Iowa, and Berkeley schools of thought. Similarly, as practitioners, our approach to the discipline of sociology is reflected in these distinctive American scholarly perspectives.

The American tradition of sociology has focused on social policy issues relating to social problems, the recognition of which grew out of the dynamic periods of social transformation wrought by the Industrial Revolution, the Progressive Era, world crises engendered by war, worldwide population shifts, increasing mechanization, and the effort of sociologists to create a specific niche for the discipline within a growing scientific community. This effort occurred first in North America and Western Europe and then, similar to cultural transitions of the past, within a global context. In every instance, the motives embedded within a science of society lie in the attempt to understand and offer proposals for solutions to whatever problems gain significant attention at a particular point in time.

In a most interesting work, Goudsblom and Heilbron (2001) pose that sociology represents a great diversity, or what some analysts may refer to as fragmentation, because the discipline grew as a part of the processes affecting societies and cultures worldwide throughout the nineteenth and twentieth centuries. Thus, as we move well into a new era and a new stage of academic development, it remains important that we recognize the sociological heritage as identified and discussed by these analysts. The five stages that sociology has experienced to date are (1) the predisciplinary stage prior to 1830, further identified as "protosociologies"; (2) the formation of the intellectual discipline, 1830–1890; (3) the formation of an academic discipline with diverging national traditions, 1890–1930; (4) the establishment of an international academic discipline, 1930–1970; and (5) a period of crisis, fragmentation, and attempts to develop a new synthesis, 1970–2000 (Goudsblom and Heilbron 2001:14574–80).

Consistent with the fifth stage, for almost four decades we have been witness to major changes in the substantive topics that undergo sociological inquiry both in the United States and, given the influence on the discipline by Canadian, European, and Scandinavian scholars, internationally. Among the areas more fully developed that might be identified as fragmentation are many of the most interesting sociological topics, including deviant behavior, the family, religion, gender, aging, health, the environment, science and technology, among so many seemingly unrelated topics. The unique conceptual paradigms of sociology serve as a template or pattern for seeing the social world in a special way. Every discipline and, indeed, every occupation employs templates or patterns to see and accomplish things in a unique fashion. Disciplines such as sociology rely on intellectual templates based on certain conceptual schemes or paradigms that have evolved through the development of a body of knowledge in those disciplines. Thus, the content of this two-volume reference reflects this rich legacy and current emphases within sociology. We have also asked the contributing authors to consider the prospects for sociological inquiry during the early decades of the twenty-first century, thus making the above-cited categories of the phases of development of the discipline of sociology most germane.

THE EARLY SOCIOLOGY

In its early era of the mid- to late nineteenth century, sociology was understood to represent anything relating to the study of social problems. Indeed, it was thought that the methods of the social sciences could be applied to social problems and used to develop solutions (Bernard and Bernard 1943). In focusing on such substance, O'Neill (1967:168–69) notes that periodicals of this early period had a sociological section in which news items relating to family matters, poverty, and labor often appeared. These early social scientists did not hold any special talents other than their training in theology. This situation was similar in the United States as well. It is not difficult, then, to imagine that, as Bramson (1961) notes, "For many American sociologists these problems evoked a moral response" (p. 75). Thus, the process of solving the problems of society was attempted by application of the conventional morality and the validation of Christian principles of piety rather than reform or progress.

Sociology was born as a result of a process, a process that directed a method of inquiry away from philosophy and toward positivism (MacIver 1934). Sociology was the result of a process caused by two major forces—namely, the Industrial Revolution and the French Revolution. The events, changes, and ideas that emerged from these two revolutions are found in the nineteenth-century thought pertaining to social order (Eisenstadt 1968). Following in the wake of the Age of Reason and the Renaissance, according to Nisbet (1966), this was a period of word formation:

> Perhaps the richest period of word formation in history . . . which were either invented during this period or were modified to their present meanings: industry, industrialist, democracy, class, middle class, ideology, intellectual, rationalism, humanitarian, atomistic, masses, commercialism, proletariat, collectivism, equalitarian, liberal, conservative, scientist, crisis . . . [among others]. (P. 23)

These were words that held great moral and partisan interest in the European economy and culture; such passions were identified with politics as well.

Identified with European conservatism, which became infused by and with science, the visionary perspective promoted by Auguste Comte during the 1830s in his six-volume *Positive Philosophy,* later translated from the French and condensed into two volumes by Harriet Martineau, was based on the medieval model of European society.

This model of family, community, authority, tradition, and the sacred became the core of scientific sociology that was to serve notice that a science of society was essential to provide for more than commonsense analysis and to reestablish social order (MacIver 1934). Although unsuccessful in his quest to secure a professorship, Auguste Comte was a positivist, mathematician, and promoter of the scientific identity of the engineering profession (Noble 1999). Comte argued that positivism and the still-to-be-identified area of "sociology" would serve as a means of supporting his intention to create a unique perspective of human relations and a system to reestablish the social order and organization of society. Reestablishment of this new social order was to proceed in accordance with the positivist stage of evolution with its ineluctable natural laws that could and would be established through engaging the scientific perspective. Along with the arts, the science of sociology, according to Comte, was to emerge as the queen of the sciences, the *scientia scientorum,* and would ultimately supplant biology and cosmology.

If the restoration of order in French society was a preoccupation for many early-nineteenth-century scholars, including Auguste Comte, it was also the case, as Bramson (1961) notes, that

> many of the key concepts of sociology illustrate this concern with the maintenance and conservation of order; ideas such as status, hierarchy ritual, integration, social function and social control are themselves a part of the history of the reaction to the ideals of the French Revolution. What conservative critics saw as resulting from these movements was not the progressive liberation of individuals, but increasing insecurity and alienation, the breakdown of traditional associations and group ties. (Pp. 13–14)

For social scientists of the early nineteenth century, many of the problems of the time were much more well defined than is the case in the contemporary experience.

Comte was fervently religious, and he believed those interested in science would constitute a "priesthood of positivism" that would ultimately lead to a new social order. According to Noble (1999),

> A theist in spite of himself, Comte declared that the existence of the Great Being "is deeply stamped on all its creations, in moral, in the arts and sciences, in industry," and he insisted, as had previous like-minded prophets since Erigena, that all such manifestations of divinity were equally vital means of mankind's regeneration . . . Comte was convinced that people like himself, science-minded engineering savants occupied with the study of the sciences of observation are the only men whose capacity and intellectual culture fulfill the necessary conditions. (P. 85)

The legacy of this enthusiastic perspective is that sociology has been at the heart of the positivists' contribution to the understanding of the human condition. It was also to serve in part as a basis for the reactions of conflict theorist

Karl Marx, especially as these writings referred to the religious *opiate of the masses* deemed by Comte as critical to the reorganization of society (Noble 1999:87). The discipline continues to present an array of perspectives that have served to stimulate much controversy within both society and the discipline (see Turner 2001).

Although the sociological legacy of Harriet Martineau is substantial, as outlined by Lengermann and Niebrugge-Brantley (1998), it was Martineau's effort to translate and condense Auguste Comte's six-volume magnum opus into a two-volume set of writings published in 1853 that allowed this important work to be available to the English-speaking world. Interestingly, Comte's English translation came after Martineau's sociological contributions, the richness of which was finally recognized by feminist researchers during the 1980s and 1990s. Martineau engaged in "participant observation" of the United States during the mid-1830s and subsequently published the two-volume *Society in America* (1836/1837), which is based on this excursion to the North American continent. Because of this experience, Martineau was able to lay the foundation for her treatise on research methodology in *How to Observe Morals and Manners* (1838).

THE FOUNDATION OF SOCIAL SCIENCE: STATISTICAL STUDIES

Perhaps it is ironic that the distinctive difference between the European theoretical sociology and the empirical sociology practiced in the United States was advanced by events in Europe. Indeed, the origin of empirical sociology is rooted in Europe. Statistical studies began in the 1660s, thereby preceding the birth of all of the social sciences by a couple of centuries. The early statistical gatherers and analysts were involved in "political arithmetic" or the gathering of data considered relevant to public policy matters of the state, and as noted by Reiss (1968), the gathering of such data may have been accelerated to meet the needs of the newly emerging insurance industry and other commercial activities of the time. But it was the early work of the moral statisticians interested in reestablishing social order in the emerging industrial societies that was to lay the quantitative foundation for the discipline, especially the early scientific work of the French sociologist Émile Durkheim (Whitt 2001:229–35).

The second stage in the early history of quantification may have been related to the development of probability theory, the rise of the insurance industry, other commercial activities, and political necessity (Lecuyer and Oberschall 1968; Reiss 1968). English political arithmeticians, including John Graunt and William Petty, were destined to be followed by the efforts of the moral statisticians who engaged in data gathering in Belgium and France. Indeed, as early as 1831, the Belgian Adolphe Quetelet and the Frenchman Andre Michel de Guerry de Champneuf, in building on the early efforts of the practitioners of the "political arithmetic" that first began in the 1660s, were engaging in the government-sponsored data-gathering activity pertaining to data on moral topics, including suicide, prostitution, and illegitimacy. Such activities would prove quite instrumental in the establishment of the empirical social sciences. Even many of the methodologies developed during this same era of the early nineteenth century, as well as awareness of important ecological methodological issues such as statistical interactions, the ecological fallacy, and spuriousness, were developed by early moral statisticians such as Andre-Michel de Guerry and Adolphe Quetelet. Later, the work of Henry Morselli, Enrico Ferri, and Alfred Maury during this same century were to serve well the needs of aspiring European sociologists and even later members of the Chicago School of Sociology (Whitt 2001:229–31).

THE RISE OF AMERICAN SOCIOLOGY

American sociology is one of the intellectual creations that has most deeply influenced our century. No other society (*the American*) has been more actively involved in understanding its own organizational change for the sake of knowledge itself. (Touraine 1990:252)

The birth of the social sciences in general and of sociology in particular is traced to the liberal democratic ideas generated by the British social philosophies of the seventeenth century—ideas that later were to be enhanced by the French Enlightenment of the eighteenth century and then transformed in the United States where these ideas served as the foundation for practical democratic society. The rise of American sociology can be traced to the early-nineteenth-century social science movement, a movement that by the mid-1800s became a new discipline that was widely introduced into college and university curricula. The movement also led to the establishment of a national social science association that was to later spawn various distinctive social sciences, including sociology, as well as social reform associations (Bernard and Bernard 1943:1–8).

Although the promotion of the social sciences in the United States began as early as 1865 with the establishment of the American Association for the Promotion of Social Sciences and then, in 1869, creation of the American Social Science Association with its association-sponsored publication the *Journal of Social Science,* prior to the 1880s there had been no organized and systematic scientific research in the United States. This was the case simply because, as Howard W. Odum ([1927] 1965:3–20) noted, there was no university per se in which research as a scientific pursuit could be conducted. It is within the context of the movement to organize such a university that sociology and many other social sciences were embraced as viable academic disciplines, thereby allowing systematic research to be conducted in a rigorous manner. This also was a period of great emphasis on pursuing

answers to new research questions through the evaluation of knowledge and the employment of methodological and statistical tools within an interdisciplinary context. Indeed, L. L. Bernard and Jessie Bernard (1943) posit that the vision of the founders of the American Social Science Association was "to establish a unified science of society which could and would see all human problems in their relationships and make an effort to solve these problems as unified wholes" (p. 601).

Thus, the social sciences in general and sociology in particular owe a great intellectual debt to the American intellects who studied at length with the masters of Europe. Included among these are notables such as William Graham Sumner, Lester Frank Ward, Albion Woodbury Small, Franklin Henry Giddings, John William Burgess, Herbert B. Adams, Thorstein Veblen, Frederick Jackson Turner, James Harvey Robinson, George Vincent, Charles Horton Cooley, Edward Alsworth Ross, George Howard, Frank W. Blackmar, Ulysses G. Weatherly, John R. Commons, and Richard T. Ely (see Odum 1951, [1927] 1965); each of whom were well versed in scholarly areas other than sociology, including history, theology, economics, political science, and statistics. With the decline of the social science movement and its national association, the general discipline that emerged from the remains of social science was in fact sociology (Bernard and Bernard 1943:835).

The development of an intellectual and academic American sociology, like sociology in any part of the world, was and continues to be dependent on the social and political conditions of the country. In the United States, a liberal political climate and, in the aftermath of the Civil War, the advent of a system of a mass public education system, American sociology flourished. Thus, in countries in which the structure of the system of higher education was open to free inquiry, research was supported by private foundations and government contributions (Wright 1895), and the university was organized albeit loosely, sociology, subject to the polemics of its status as an academic science, gained entry if not acceptance among university faculty. Where education was available to the elite rather than the masses, sociology was less apt to flourish (Reiss 1968).

Another important factor is that American sociology arose basically without roots other than the growing influence of the social science movement in the United States and the emphasis on the virtues of science that permeated the intellectual and social environs of this same period. As noted by Neil J. Smelser (1990:49–60), American sociology did not experience the yoke of either European feudalism or any peculiar intellectual history. Rather, sociology came into being within American higher education during the 1880s and only after several other disciplines, including psychology and economics, had been accepted within the academy. Attempts among adherents of these other disciplines led to the establishment of the scientific theme within the social sciences. Early sociologists embraced this same scientific theme.

A second factor that had a profound effect on the early adherents of the sociological perspective is the social reform theme of the 1890s. The legacy of these two themes—namely, scientific respectability and social reform—became the dual platforms on which the unique American sociological perspective was to be based.

Although there was a great, direct influence of European thought, research, and the philosophy of the British Social Science Association on sociology to focus on attempting to solve America's problems (Odum 1951:36–50), the rise of American sociology, at least during the first half of the twentieth century, was concomitant with the most dynamic period of technological, economic, and social reform changes ever recorded. In this context, Howard W. Odum (1951:52) views sociology as a product of the American social and cultural experience and places sociology's heritage to be as "American as American literature, American culture, and the freedoms of the new world democracy" (p. 3). American sociology is thus part European and part American. Indeed, American sociology was envisioned early on as a social science that could and would assist policymakers and concerned citizens in creating the "American Dream."

Consistent with this ideology, Odum (1951:59–60) identified three unique American developments, each of which influenced the direction of American sociology throughout the entire twentieth century. The first of these developments is the symbiotic relationship between the discipline and the American society and culture. The ideology that focused on the American Dream and its realization had a great influence.

The second development, according to Odum, is the emphasis on moral development and the motivation to establish ethics as a component of the educational curricula, American literature, and the social sciences, especially as these relate to ethical conduct, social justice, and public morality. Within sociology, this orientation is found in the application of sociological principles into economic and organizational behavior and the founding of the American Institute of Christian Sociology.

Finally, Odum (1951) notes, the American experience led to a research emphasis on social problems of a moral and economic nature. In an effort to better understand these social problems, sociologists organized the systematic study of issues such as waves of immigration, the working class, public disorder, neglect of children, violence toward women, intergroup conflict, urbanism, alcoholism, suicide, crime, mental illness, delinquency, and poverty (see also Fine 2006). This was the application side of sociology that held important social policy implication. However, there was also an early emphasis on a "general sociology" as opposed to a "special sociology" as was found at the more elite institutions of higher learning. Clearly, this difference foreshadowed the pure versus applied dichotomy that has generated so much discussion within the discipline (see Odum 1951:51–74).

Because of the important influence of the social science movement in the United States, there is some disagreement pertaining to who the founders and members of the first generation of American sociologists are (see Odum 1951, [1927] 1965). But publication of Lester Ward's book *Dynamic Sociology in 1883* does appear to mark the beginning of American sociology (Bramson 1961:84–85). On the other hand, there does not seem to be any disagreement as to the purpose of the American founders, and that was to establish a scientific theoretical base. Later, at the University of Chicago the goals were to establish a relationship between sociology and the classical problems of philosophy by focusing on process issues relating to elements of social control, such as conflict, competition, and accommodation (Kurtz 1986:95).

American sociology emerged concomitant with the challenges to legal philosophy and the discussion of questions relating to myriad questions that arose as the effects of industrialization were observed Calhoun (1919). Such questions have their focus on marriage, divorce, immigration, poverty, and health and how to employ the emerging scientific model to topical data that had been gathered by the nineteenth-century moral statisticians.

Leon Bramson (1961:47–48) observed that the most interesting aspect of American sociology in the first half of the twentieth century is that when affected by European theories of mass behavior and collective behavior, American sociologists, in their haste to establish a role for sociology in America, either transformed the meaning of the concepts to meet their needs or created new concepts to apply to the more liberal American social and political context. American sociologists, according to Bramson, also applied European theoretical concepts such as social pathology, social disorganization, and social control to the data referring to the American experience without regard for whatever special conditions should have been accounted for or even possible theoretical distortions; this issue is also discussed by Lester R. Kurtz (1986:60–83) in his evaluation of the Chicago School of Sociology.

Albert J. Reiss, Jr. (1968) notes that the first formal instruction of a sociology course in the United States was offered by William Graham Sumner, a professor of political and social science at Yale University, during 1876. The first, second, and third American Departments of Sociology were established at Brown University, the University of Chicago, and Columbia University, respectively (Kurtz 1986:93–97). Between 1889 and 1892, 18 American colleges and universities offered instruction in sociology, but in 1893, the University of Chicago was the first to develop a program that led to the granting of a Ph.D.

Despite the recognition of the emerging field of sociology as a distinctive area of inquiry, the focal point of a religious orientation and perhaps fervor expressed by social commentators in their discussions and analyses of the social issues that were to constitute the purview of sociology also engaged the attention of other early practitioners of the discipline. The social problems identified in the wake of expansion of the American West and the building of the railroads included issues relating to "the influx of immigrants, the rise of the factory system and the concentration of people in big cities. These comprised the now familiar catalogue of crime, delinquency, divorce, poverty, suicide, alcoholism, minority problems and slums" (Bramson 1961:75).

Alfred McClung Lee (1978:69) notes that ever since that time, sociologists have been attempting to divorce themselves from an ancestry that is historically rooted in the clergy, the police, utopian ideologues, social reformers, conservative apologists, journalistic muckrakers, radical thinkers, agitators, and civil libertarians.

Given the moral tone of much of the writing of many early American sociologists, it is noteworthy that in articulating the six "aims" of the *American Journal of Sociology* established at the University of Chicago in 1895, the scientific view of sociological concern so clearly defined several decades later by E. A. Ross (1936) was not so clear to many if not all of the moral philosophers of this earlier period. Witness the following comments offered by the founding editor of the *American Journal of Sociology,* Albion W. Small (1895):

> Sociology has a foremost place in the thought of modern men. Approve or deplore the fact at pleasure, we cannot escape it. . . . To many possible readers the most important question abut the conduct of the *Journal* will be with reference to its attitude toward "Christian Sociology." The answer is, in a word, towards Christian sociology sincerely deferential, toward "Christian sociologists" severely suspicious. (Pp. 1, 15)

These comments were of particular significance given that the *American Journal of Sociology* was not only the first journal of sociology created anywhere, but it was also, until 1936, the official journal of the American Sociological Society. Thus, the influence of both the Chicago School and the large number of contributions by its faculty and students to the *American Journal of Sociology* placed the work of the Chicago School at the forefront in shaping the early direction and substance of American, Canadian, and Polish sociology (Kurtz 1986:93–97). This was especially true in the subareas of urban and community studies, race and ethnic relations, crime and juvenile delinquency, deviance, communications and public opinion, and political sociology.

Leon Bramson (1961:73–95) identified three important phases in the rise of American sociology. The first period began in 1883 with the publication of Lester Ward's *Dynamic Sociology* to about 1915 or 1918 with the publication of Robert E. Park's essay on the city and/or the end of World War I, respectively. During this period, the founders began their earnest quest to establish the theoretical foundation as it related to the American experience focusing on "a liberal sociology of change and process, rather than one of conservation and equilibrium" (Bramson 1961:85).

This focus on change and process became even more evident during the second stage of American sociology,

identified as the period between the two world wars. This was a period of academic expansion, with major increases in faculty and students, but even more important, led by sociologists at the University of Chicago, this was a period of specialization and the beginning of differentiation within sociology as the quest to develop a viable methodology began in earnest. This also was a meaningful period during which sociologists worked to establish the scientific status of the discipline and to earn respectability and academic legitimization. It was also a period during which many of the conceptual problems of sociology first began to emerge as its practitioners developed an increasingly complex technical vocabulary, a vast array of classification schema, and other abstract systems categories of thought. Perhaps assuming the need to compensate for a past that included so many nonscientifically moral reformist-oriented representatives of the discipline, sociologists responded during this phase of development by creating complex theories that, for an extended period of time, were not only unintelligible to the layperson, but also the abstract nature of these grand theories exceeded the ability of social scientists to create methodologies appropriate to empirically test these theoretical models (Lee 1978). But despite this theoretical/methodological problem, this second stage of sociological development was also one in which much substance was created.

The history of sociology in America from prior to World War I to approximately the mid-1930s is, according to Kurtz (1986), a history of the school of thought promoted by the University of Chicago. If the second phase of American sociology is to be distinguished as a period dominated by the Chicago sociologists, it is also one that led Pitirim Sorokin to observe that American sociology was emerging as a distinctive brand:

> The bulk of the sociological works in America are marked by their quantitative and empirical character while the bulk of the sociological literature of Europe is still marked by an analytical elaboration of concepts and definitions; by a philosophical and epistemological polishing of words. (Cited in Bramson 1961:89)

The period is characterized by a marked increase in the development of new and expanding methodologies and measurement. These new techniques included a plethora of scales intended to measure the theoretical concepts developed previously.

As noted, Goudsblom and Heilbron (2001) identify five phases of development of the discipline that cover the period prior to 1830 to the very end of the twentieth century. But the third phase of the development of American sociology, identified by Bramson (1961) as covering the period from 1940 to 1960, is noteworthy because this was a period during which the development and adoption of theories of the "middle-range" advocated by Robert K. Merton led to even greater specialization and differentiation of the discipline. In turn, sociologists began to develop ever-expanding areas of inquiry. Robert K. Merton

([1957] 1968), who wrote in reaction to the abstractness of the previous dominant position of the functionalist school of sociology, stated that theories of the middle range are

> theories that lie between the minor but necessary working hypotheses that evolve in abundance during day-to-day research and the all-inclusive systematic efforts to develop a unified theory that will explain all the observed uniformities of social behavior, social organization and social change. (P. 39)

The all-inclusive efforts refer, of course, to the contributions of Talcott Parsons in *The Structure of Social Action,* originally published in 1937, and in 1951 with the appearance of *The Social System.*

The third phase of development can be characterized as the most enthusiastic period during which greater emphasis was placed on the application of sociological knowledge. As the field expanded, new outlets for sociological studies and knowledge were created, sociologists found employment in nonacademic settings such as government and business, and the new specialty areas of interest reflected the changes in American society, including a growing rise in membership in the middle class, the expansion of the suburbs, more leisure time, and the growth of bureaucracy. In lieu of the previous sociological interest in the reform of society and the more traditional social problems orientation of the discipline, the new sociology opted to leave such concerns to the social work profession and to special studies programs such as criminology. Thus, specialty areas emerged—areas such as the sociology of marriage and the family, and aging (later to be defined as gerontology), industrial sociology, public opinion, organizations, communications, and social psychiatry (later called mental health). From this point forward, the continued rise to respectability of sociology is attributed by analysts such as Robert Nisbet (1966) to the public recognition that societal problems are more integrative in nature than previously thought. This may also serve as a partial explanation for why the discipline is viewed by some as fragmented.

THE SUBSTANCE OF THE SOCIOLOGICAL PERSPECTIVE

The logic and ethos of science is the search for the truth, the objective truth. Thus, the most fundamental problem the social scientist confronts, according to Gunnar Myrdal (1969), is this:

> What is objectivity, and how can the student attain objectivity in trying to find out the facts and the causal relationships between facts? [That is,] How can a biased view be avoided? The challenge is to maintain an objectivity of that which the sociologist is a part. (P. 3)

Although the sociologies of the United States and Europe differ in perspective, both attempt to answer similar albeit distinguishable questions. In his discussion of "the two faces of sociology," Touraine (1990:240) states that these differences lie in the scholarly research response to two problems: (1) How does society exist? (2) How are culture and society historically created and transformed by work, by the specific way nature and its resources are put to use, and through systems of political, economic, and social organization? Because the intellectual legacy of American sociological thought has been shaped to a large extent by the historical experience of creating a nation in which the rights and the will of the American people have been dominant, American sociologists have long focused on "institution" as a central concept and the significance of efforts of reform movements within the American society to affect its social organization. Thus, the substance of American sociology has been on topics such as the family, social organization, community, the criminal justice system, and law and society among the numerous institutional-level areas of inquiry that are evaluated within the context of yet another American theoretical focus—namely, the emphasis on theories of the middle range. European sociologists, on the other hand, tend to focus on the second question while emphasizing the concept "revolution" in their analyses. Thus, even when similar topics such as social movements serve as the focus of inquiry, the American and European sociology responds from a different perspective (Touraine 1990). To understand the importance of this difference in perspective between the two sociologies, Alain Touraine (1990) poses the view that American sociology has a symbiotic relationship between culture and society, whereas European sociology integrates society and its history. Americans sociologists focus on society; the European sociology is focused on the rich history that serves as the backdrop for any attempt to understand social change.

Because the American experience is predicated on building a nation through the rule of law; the concepts of individualism, capitalism, and territorial conquest; and the attempt at integration of successive waves of immigrants to the North American continent, American sociology began its rise in prominence through an elitist intellectual process that dominated the academy during the early formative years of the discipline. Thus, it is perhaps ironic that an American sociology housed within the university setting would assume a critical teaching and research posture toward an elitist system of institutions that the early sociology assisted in creating. Within the context of certain kinds of social problems areas, such as ethnic studies, discrimination, and segregation, sociology and sociologists have been able to exert some influence. But in other important areas within which issues relating to elitist society may be involved, such as social class relations and economic and political power, the official and public perceptions of the efforts of American sociologists may not be as well received.

Many analysts of the past can be called on to render testimony in support of or apologize for the past efforts of sociologists to provide useful information, but none is perhaps more relevant than the following statement offered by George A. Lundberg (1947): "Good intentions are not a substitute for good techniques in either achieving physical or social goals" (p. 135). During the 1960s and 1970s, sociology, psychology, and other social science undergraduate job candidates customarily responded to interviewer queries with "I want to help people." Similar to those who attended graduate school after World War II, these individuals were influenced by the potential of sociology to make a difference. But good intentions aside, the real issue is, How do we go about assisting/helping people? Perhaps the more educated and sophisticated we become, the more difficult are the answers to social problems and social arrangements that are deemed inappropriate or at least in need of some form of rearrangement. That is, the more we believe we already know the answers, the less apt we are to recognize the importance of the sociological perspective. Within this context, sociology necessarily must adhere to and advocate the use of the methods of science in approaching any social problem, whether this is local or international in scope.

Sociology has utility beyond addressing social problems and contributing to the development of new social policy. Indeed, the sociological perspective is empowering. Those who use it are in a position to bring about certain behavior in others. It has been said that "behavior that can be understood can be predicted, and behavior that can be predicted can likely be controlled." It is not surprising that sociologists are often used to help select juries, develop effective advertising campaigns, plan political strategies for elections, and solve human relations problems in the workplace. As Peter Berger (1963) phrases it, "Sociological understanding can be recommended to social workers, but also to salesmen, nurses, evangelists and politicians—in fact to anyone whose goals involve the manipulation of men, for whatever purpose and with whatever moral justification" (p. 5). In some ways, it might be said that the sociological perspective puts one "in control."

The manipulation of others, even for commendable purposes, however, is not without critical reaction or detractors. Some years back, industrial sociologists who worked for, or consulted with, industrial corporations to aid them to better address problems in the workplace were sometimes cynically labeled as "cow sociologists" because "they helped management milk the workers." Knowledge is power that can be used for good or evil. The sociological perspective is utilitarian and empowering in that it can accomplish things for whatever purposes. Berger (1963) goes on to reflect the following:

> If the sociologist can be considered a Machiavellian figure, then his talents can be employed in both humanly nefarious and humanly liberating enterprises. If a somewhat colorful metaphor may be allowed here, one can think of the sociologist as a *condottiere* of social perception. Some *condottieri* fight for the oppressors of men, others for their liberators.

Especially if one looks around beyond the frontiers of America as well as within them, one can find enough grounds to believe that there is a place in today's world for the latter type of *condottiere*. (P. 170)

Responding to the question, "Can science save us?" George A. Lundberg (1947) states "yes," but he also equates the use of brain (the mind) as tantamount to employing science. Lundberg also posed the following: "Shall we place our faith in science or in something else?" (p. 142). Physical science is not capable of responding to human social issues. If sociologists have in a vain effort failed to fulfill the promise of the past, this does not indicate that they will not do so at some future time. Again, as Lundberg (1947) heeded long ago, "Science is at best a growth, not a sudden revelation. We also can use it imperfectly and in part while it is developing" (pp. 143–144).

And a few years later but prior to the turmoil that was to embroil the decades of the 1960s and 1970s, John Madge (1962) urged that a century after the death of the positivist Auguste Comte (now 150 years later) the structure of sociology remains incomplete. However, Madge recognized and demonstrates in *The Origins of Scientific Sociology* that sociology was slowly gaining in maturity and with this growth was on the verge of or within reach of achieving the status of a science. But it is also important to keep in focus the goals of science as articulated by Gunnar Myrdal (1969)—more specifically, "The goals of objectivity and effectiveness in research are honesty, clarity, and effectiveness" (p. 72). If the results of sociological research have been less than to the liking of policymakers and government and corporate leaders, then yet another of Myrdal's insights is especially germane. That is,

> Research is always and by logical necessity based on moral and political valuations, and the researcher should be obligated to account for them explicitly. When these valuations are brought out into the open any one who finds a particular piece of research to have been founded on what is considered wrong valuation can challenge it on that ground. (P. 74)

There are other reasons as well, reasons that complicate the delivery of the important message promoted by the discipline's practitioners, for as noted by Joel Best (2003:11), sociology "is a perspective built on relativism, built on the recognition that people understand the world differently." Indeed, many years earlier George C. Homans (1967) observed,

> If some of the social sciences seem to have made little progress, at least in the direction of generalizing and explanatory science, the reason lies neither in lack of intelligence on the part of the scientists nor in the newness of the subject as an academic discipline. It lies rather in what is out there in the world of nature. (P. 89)

Such statements lie at the heart of the epistemological debate that began in the 1920s (see Reiss 1968:10–11) and continues into the modern era. Despite the vastness of sociological inquiry, it is obvious that a strong orientation toward the scientific study of human behavior, social interaction, and organizations continues and that this scientific focus is predicated on the assumption that such study is possible because it is based on the examination of phenomena that are subject to the operation of universal laws, a point not lost in the minds of the discipline's founders. The counterpoint that the social sciences are cultural sciences and thereby fundamentally different from the physical sciences and also subject to different methodology and other evaluative criteria is representative of a long-standing European influence that also began in the 1920s.

Given the diversity and fluidity of the topics addressed and the levels of theories employed by sociologists, it is not surprising that many others do not agree. The counter-argument is based on the premise that given the circumstances behind the evolution of science and the support it received in the past and the more repressive attention it receives in the contemporary experience from powerful interest groups, objective social science and the establishment of universal laws that are based on such inquiry may not be possible (see Turner 2001).

Whether or not one argues that the study of human society is unique, it is still extraordinary given the vast array of extant theories used to express the human experience and capacity. Witness the statement of one contemporary analyst who, in an intriguing assessment of the contemporary American "wilding" experience, wrote,

Sociology arose as an inquiry into the dangers of modern individualism, which could potentially kill society itself. The prospect of the death of society gave birth to the question . . . what makes society possible and prevents it from disintegrating into a mass of sociopathic and self-interested isolates? This core question of sociology has become the vital issue of our times. (Charles Derber 2003:18)

Only in part is Derber referring to the American experience. His assessment also speaks to the experience of Western Europe. Much social change has taken place, and the efforts of sociologists to describe and explain this change and to draw upon these insights to develop predictive models has led to a diversity of theories. Indeed, over time, the scientific paradigm shifts more generally described by Thomas Kuhn ([1962] 1970) are obvious in our discipline (see Friedrichs 1970). There have been, there are at present, and there undoubtedly will be future paradigm shifts within this evolving and apparently expanding discipline of sociology, many of which will focus, as has been the case in the past, on the social change process. And for all the so-called objectivity of a scientific sociology advocated by analysts such as George A. Lundberg (1947), the development of which is so eloquently described by Leon Bramson (1961)), sociologists have been involved in social activism and social engineering, that first occurred during the embryonic years of the

discipline's development (Volkart 1968). Such activism occurred again during the 1960s and 1970s, in many social justice areas, and in occupational settings such as those of the criminal justice system.

At present, sociological inquiry represents a vast array of topics and offers many competing theoretical models while its practitioners attempt to make sense of a rapidly changing world. For all its middle-range theories and studies that reflect the efforts of those dedicated to cumulative knowledge, it is also important that we recognize that the building of a paradigm as well as challenges to an extant paradigm are not relegated to the gathering of information alone. Indeed, if sociology is to advantage itself in the twenty-first century, it may be imperative that a dominant paradigm begins to identify the kinds of community needs that it can usually serve, for as Joseph R. Gusfield (1990) so clearly notes, sociology has been at odds with and a critic of the classical economic and individualistic interpretations of American life. Thus, whatever issues sociology may need to address at this juncture, perhaps we are hampered only by the limits of the sociological imagination. Again, the following comment by Homans (1967) is noteworthy:

The difficulties of social science lie in explanation rather than discovery. . . . Our trouble has not been with making discoveries but with organizing them theoretically—showing how they follow under a variety of given conditions from a few general principles. (Pp. 79, 105)

The present diversity of the discipline welcomed by so many social critics also serves as a barrier to the creation of a dominant theoretical paradigm. Without this focus, sociology remains in the minds of many of the discipline's representatives a less-than-coherent discipline. Perhaps this is not different from the struggle of the 1960s as described by Gouldner (1970), a period that also was far less than organized and coherent and certainly far less civil in disagreement. It is important that sociologists take stock of their trade and question in earnest the utility of the work we do. As noted by Herbert L. Gans (1990),

By and large, we sociologists have been too distant from the society in which we operate and in which we are embedded, which funds us even if too poorly and which influences us surely more than we influence it. We are too busy trying to understand how that society functions . . . that we rarely think about our own functions—and dysfunctions. To some extent our failure to do so stems from a typical professional blindness, which results in our inability to distance ourselves sufficiently from ourselves and our routines to look systematically at what we are for and to whom. (Pp. 12–13)

Not all may agree, of course. Indeed, sociology in the United States and in Europe has been a critique of modern urban life with its emphasis on the individual, capitalism, and bureaucracy. In some instances, this critique of American society has been radical and reformist in its thrust (Gusfield 1990:31–46). And although American sociology had been shaped in part by psychology in establishing its methodology during the first two-thirds of the twentieth century, especially through a common social-psychological area (see, e.g., Reiss 1968), it can be safely stated that American sociology has been transformed during the latter decades of the twentieth century.

THE PASSION FOR SOCIOLOGY

Sociologists may be accused of engaging in an affair with their work. Witness the stirring comments of one colleague:

> I fell in love with sociology when I was twelve. . . . Sociology was my savior. It saved me from the vexing confusion caused by my once despising the mundaneness of everyday life and deeply loving and admiring my people. It stabilized me by articulating the dedication that I felt for social justice. (Shahidian 1999:303–04)

We share this passionate approach to social science based on the insightful development of theory and empirical research, an approach that has, in turn, led to a vast array of subject matter. Note the other 105 chapters represented in this two-volume *Handbook*. In light of these impressive contributions, the only aspect of this endeavor that may seem perplexing to some is that as we move further into the twenty-first century, there are those who continue to believe in and practice the scientific method; there also are those who argue that if the logic of science and the methods of scientific objectivity are to be carried to an extreme, sociology will lose or has already lost its humanistic perspective and, with this loss, the inclination toward active community involvement through social policy advocacy and practical intervention. As Peter L. Berger (1963) phrases it,

> At the same time it is quite true that some sociologists, especially in America, have become so preoccupied with methodological questions that they have ceased to be interested in society at all. As a result, they have found out nothing of significance about any aspect of social life, since in science as in love a concentration on technique is quite likely to lead to impotence. (P. 13)

This dichotomy certainly is a matter of considerable debate, but perhaps most advocates and active practitioners of the discipline would fall somewhere in between these two orientations (see, e.g., Reiss 1968:10–11). In this regard, we are also optimistic that the sociological imagination will continue to be an important part of the work of sociologists as they take into consideration "a quality of mind that will help them to use information and to develop reason in order to achieve lucid summations of what is going on in the world and of what may be happening within themselves" (Mills 1959:5).

THE FUTURE OF SOCIOLOGY IN THE 21ST CENTURY

More than 170 years ago, sociology began to emerge from its philosophical and biological roots to it current status as an important social science. Early sociologists achieved renown based on their interest in providing information useful to appraise social policy issues. However, in the contemporary instance, there are strong indicators that sociology has not achieved the eminent position envisioned by the founders. Note the less-than-enthusiastic assessment offered by Black (1999):

> The problems endemic to the discipline of sociology include the lack of a paradigm, disciplinary fragmentation, and the irreconcilability of science, ideology, and politics . . . and the lack of an occupational niche—[all these] place sociologists in the position of having constantly to defend the profession. (Pp. 261, 263)

Thus, as we move well into the twenty-first century, it is clear that sociology is engaged in yet another struggle to (re)identify itself. Perhaps such a struggle is to be expected of any science of human behavior. And nowhere is this situation more contentious than in the responses of representatives of the discipline to the question as to whether sociology is or is not yet considered an activity worthy of the label "scientific activity."

At the center of this struggle lies the heart of any discipline—namely, sociological theory. Among the eminent theorists reporting on the status of sociology in this *Handbook* are individuals who represent the very best of what the discipline has to offer. That the message is suggestive of a continuing debate within the discipline is both disheartening and encouraging. It is disheartening in that after a period of more than 175 years, representatives of the discipline should be able to exclaim with great pride the accomplishments of so much activity instead of debating their scientific worth. It is encouraging because the current debate over the theory and the substance of the work sociologists engage in can only lead to the exploration of new and challenging frontiers. But the substance of sociological inquiry also represents a matter of contention for many research- and practitioner-oriented representatives of the discipline. Some contemporary analysts who have observed the developments within the academy during the past several decades call for a critical reevaluation of that which sociologists identify as the substance of research and understanding. Sociology has given birth to and generated intense interest in many areas of study that are no longer identified with the discipline. Because the specific subareas developed by sociologists became well accepted as legitimate applied disciplines within the academy, independent, overlapping units within the academy have been created.

If the 1960s represent the *golden era* of sociology, it is also a period, as described by Turner and Sica (2006), that is "remembered as a time of violence, massive social change, and personal transformation" (p. 4). The period had a profound effect on an entire generation of students, many of whom were instrumental in creating the new sociological emphasis that today is criticized for its diversity, the lack of continuity, and a failure to develop a unified paradigm. Whatever reservations that may continue to exist as we progress well into the twenty-first century, these can be hailed as a challenge. Thus, at the same time that community involvement and applied research are increasingly being devalued in the academic world, there is a distinct pressure, according to Harris and Wise (1998), for sociologists to become increasingly involved in the community and society.

This call to establish a public sociology may well combine with the three types of knowledge identified by Burawoy (2005)—the professional, critical, and policy-specific databases. In each of these areas, the initiative would be consistent with enthusiastic proclamations of the past. George A. Lundberg's (1947) *Can Science Save Us?* serves as but one important example of those who promoted the application of social science insights to solve social problems. Of course, one major difference between the time when Lundberg wrote and now is that we are not rebounding from the tragedy of a world war. Indeed, it was during the post–World War II period and during the subsequent several decades that American sociology assumed its theoretical and empirical dominance (Odum 1951), especially in the area of deviant behavior (see Touraine 1990). Yet another important difference between then and now, as Harris and Wise (1998) suggest, is that sociologists need to be perceived as problem solvers rather than as social critics, and similar to the pleas of Marion Talbot (1896) at the end of the nineteenth century, much of the sociological may necessarily become interdisciplinary in nature. This perspective is supported as a portion of a more scholarly editorial philosophy articulated by Wharton (2006:1–2). Most noteworthy for our purpose are points three and four:

> (3) Be aware and reflective about the . . . broader contributions to scholarship, policy, and/or activism . . . ; (4) produce useful knowledge—not merely in the applied sense of solving problems, but knowledge that is useful as *basic* research that can help people better understand and transform the social world. (P. 1)

These same kinds of issues—social activism and public policy research—were recognized at the end of the nineteenth century as strengths of the new discipline.

Thus, there appears to be hopeful as well as worrisome aspects of sociology at the end of the twentieth century (Lewis 1999). But this kind of enthusiasm and concern appears to be periodic throughout the history of the discipline as sociologists attempt to both define and then redefine the parameters of what some argue is too extensive a range of topics to allow practitioners of the discipline to be

definitively identified (Best 2003). Witness the statement attributed to one of the coeditors of this *Handbook* who, in the early 1980s, wrote the following:

> Future prospects for sociology(ists) no doubt will depend upon our ability to identify and respond to community needs, to compete for funds available from nontraditional sources, to work in applied areas, and to establish creative problem-solving strategies. The challenge before us should generate a healthy response. (Peck 1982:319–20)

Since that time and in the wake of a declining influence of the social sciences, there has been a response as evidenced by the many new areas of inquiry, many interdisciplinary in nature, that currently curry attention from sociologists. Indeed, there does appear to be a fragmentation, but this so-called fragmentation is consistent with an assessment offered by Beck (1999), "Sociology today, as throughout its history, is not unified. . . . we have never been able to sustain . . . unanimity and consistency for very long. Thank goodness" (p. 121).

Perhaps we do not engage in "normal science," at least not in the sense that Thomas Kuhn ([1962] 1970) refers to it. That is, academic sociologists continue to function quite well even though they are outside the single frame of reference that usually serves as the paradigmatic foundation for the physical sciences. Normal science is rigid, but it is also burdened by uncertainty and inconsistency, as Friedrichs (1970) observes. In the case of sociology, this is found in the diversity of theoretical models and topical areas. Although some analysts lament the current state of the discipline, Jacobs (2004) recently observed that "some might view this diversity [of topics] as evidence of excessive fragmentation, (but) there are important theoretical connections" (p. v). Of course, the substance of manuscripts submitted for possible publication, the rubrics under which the research can be categorized, is quite different from the search for a common sociological paradigm. To wit, classic studies do exist, but none serve to forge a single paradigm. Thus, the future of the discipline will depend, as usual, on the contributions of those who may be relatively silent in the wake of less-than-acceptable "scholarship," as suggested by Lewis (1999), but who nonetheless commit themselves to excellence by producing significant contributions to theory and application (see, e.g., Rossi 1999) that should, in the long run, counter the myriad productions that are less significant. Concomitant with this effort will be an increased awareness of and involvement in the applied and an earnest effort to again be a viable force in the policy-related aspects of sociology and society. In other words, we believe there will be a reawakening of and involvement in those aspects of sociology that served the discipline well during its early years of development in the United States (see Ross 1936) even as the applied social work-oriented practitioners broke away to form their own professional association (Odum 1951; Rossi 1999). Indeed, there exists a need for answers to myriad policy-oriented questions as well as applied concerns at all governmental levels.

But in the end, sociologists may, as Beck (1999:123) suggests, go where they go, where they want to go. This may again mean that sociologists will abandon important areas of inquiry that they helped to establish, leaving the sociological legacy to others. Sociologists will also move to create other areas of inquiry while questioning past and present assumptions and knowledge claims in an ongoing quest to better understand social arrangements and to engage in, as Beck (1999) observes, "life, liberty, the pursuit of happiness, and the sociological imagination" (p. 124). To this we can add the quest to establish the meaning of social justice in a rapidly changing democratic society.

Thus, contrary to dubious predictions of an ominous obscure future, the content of this *Handbook* attests to a much more positive and grand future orientation within the discipline that will include much more than the rigorous efforts to clean up conceptual problems that sociologists are supposedly noted for. Moreover, the epistemological debates of the past will undoubtedly continue as Turner (2001) and Best (2003) suggest, but in so doing, the future of academic sociology will again be broadened. This expansion will again, we think, involve the applied aspects of the discipline and engagement of the public through active involvement of sociologists in the four traditional areas—namely, through a public sociology with an emphasis on further development of the profession and a critical civic activism with the intent to broadly influence social policy. Moreover, the increasing influence of European sociology in the global community will undoubtedly continue; this influence is not only important, it is most welcome. Given the above, it may well be that another call to arms will result. There has been a movement, albeit a small movement, among highly regarded intellectuals (the National Association of Scholars) to enhance the substance and quality of academic teaching and scholarly activity. This, too, is welcome in sociology.

The world that engages a scientist, as noted by Friedrichs (1970), is one that emerges from a scientific tradition, along with its special vocabulary and grammar and environment. Sociology's laboratory is the social world and on occasion its practitioners are criticized by those who argue the arcane nature of all that is considered scientific. If the normal science, as described by Thomas Kuhn ([1962] 1970) and Robert W. Friedrichs (1970), is to be realized within the discipline of sociology, then it may depend on efforts of young sociologists (see, e.g., Frickel and Gross 2005) who may capture the essence of such a paradigm in a general theory of scientific/intellectual movements. Such work may also serve to stimulate more thought as to the requisite initiatives essential for subsequently developing the kind of intellectual movement that will define once again, and actively promote, the substance of the sociological perspective.

If the emphasis of American sociology at the beginning of the twentieth century was unsophisticated, armchair science that "featured the study of general society and the 'system' of social theory, it reflected not only the almost universal philosophical approach but also the consistency of the best minds in interaction with European philosophy and American higher education" (Odum 1951:421–22). In the mid-twentieth century, sociology, similar to other social and physical sciences, struggled to determine whether the future of the discipline would continue to pursue a general systems theory of society or whether the discipline's practitioners would develop more theory and then relate these theories to research and the scientific method (Odum 1951:422). At this critical midpoint of the century past, and in recognition of the importance of the discipline, Odum (1951) wrote that there is

> the extraordinary need in the contemporary world for a social science to seek special knowledge of human society and welfare and meet the crises brought on by science and technology, so often out of perspective to human relations, and so to provide the basis for not only a social morale in an age of science but for societal survival as well. (P. 3)

At the end of the twentieth century, these comments rang clear, and as we move forward and well into the greater twenty-first-century experience, Odum's words seem no less germane today than in the past.

Toward establishing the prospects for the future of this great academic discipline, we hasten to add how critical it is and will be to again acknowledge the important work of the founding mothers and fathers of sociology. Thus, at the end of the twentieth century, the state of sociology may have been debatable, but during the initial decades of the twenty-first century, sociologists will undoubtedly take up the challenge to pursue answers to vexing social problems that are, as Fine (2006:14–15) states, embedded with complex, dynamic, interconnected social systems. Some of the solutions to be tendered in the near future may not serve well the needs of all citizens, but these should nonetheless address policy issues relating to social freedom, social justice, and social equality while recognizing that such policies determine the behavior of those actors whom sociologists are intent to study. Herein American sociologists may now have achieved the requisite disciplinary maturity to employ the kind of *sociological imagination* envisioned by C. Wright Mills (1959) half a century ago. Such a sociology would, in the tradition of Europe, encompass a biography and history within society, thereby allowing sociology to represent not only a scientific enterprise but also to serve as a sensitizing discipline that allows us to continue to view the world in a new and interpretive fashion.

Finally, in some peculiar ways, the vexing problems that capture our attention during the early portion of the twenty-first century parallel those of the early twentieth century; this is true at all levels of society and perhaps even more so within those sectors that heretofore were barricaded from a critical analyses. The actors may have changed but, in general, the public concerns regarding the kinds of behavior tolerated and considered to be appropriate tend to remain the same. And as the moral entrepreneurs of the twenty-first century push their agendas, the new prohibitionist movements continue to capture the attention of policymakers, which may of necessity be cause for some sociologists at least to revisit many of the same topics that held sway in the past. Thus, we will continue to use templates in our lives to understand the world, physical and social, in which we exist. The sociological templates derived from the many conceptual constructs available provide us with a unique and perceptive perspective. As sociology further develops, new conceptual constructs will be added and will contribute to its unique perspective, thereby enhancing our ability to better analyze and understand human social behavior.

2

THE HISTORY OF SOCIOLOGY

The European Perspective

GERD NOLLMANN

HERMANN STRASSER
University of Duisburg-Essen, Germany

George H. Mead (1936:116f.) taught us that each generation will write anew its history. Many histories of sociology have been written before, and the sociology of knowledge has made an interesting object of research out of them. However, today's history of sociology will set different priorities than those written 50 or 100 years ago, and it would be interesting to detect the reasons behind such changes. We want to present an overview of three aspects constituting much of sociology's dynamic development. The first aspect is the stepwise emancipation of sociology from philosophical thought. The second is the discovery that societal change and continuity are causally based on meaningful human behavior that needs to be understood and explained in social research. The final aspect is sociology's growing empirically validated knowledge. Finally, we will ask if there is a current tendency aiming at the reintegration of theories of human conduct and social research.

FROM THE ORIGINS TO THE FOUNDING FATHERS

The History of Ideas

The more people began to understand that society is not simply god-made, natural, or the traditional, unchangeable

way of life it always used to be, the more we see sociological thought emerge and develop. However, it is impossible to draw a clear historical line where sociology comes into the picture. Society has always been an object of curious interest of mostly philosophical thinkers such as Aristotle (1943), who considered the human being as *zoon politikon* that naturally tends to build up communities. Hence, his works discuss the essence and the tasks of the "good" state. Aristotle tries to determine institutionalized forms of power adequate to the human nature and, therefore, considered legitimate. For Aristotle, humans are unequal by nature. It is the main task of the state to help realize the good life of its citizens. Society is seen as something that is on the way to reaching a good, natural form. Empirically, Aristotle made clear that there is a wide variety of factual states and that societies he analyzed critically were at different stages of "goodness." But the point to be stressed here refers to the quite unquestioned assumption about the *nature* of society.

This assumption breaks down in modern social thought. It is quite common to see in Thomas Hobbes's (1588–1679) *Leviathan* (1904) the fundamental turning point. The reality of the British Commonwealth with its growing cities and spatial immensity, its ceaseless conflicts and problems, provide the empirical data from which Hobbes attempts to derive principles to solve a concrete social problem: the origin and persistence of social order.

Hobbes reverses Aristotle's assumption of the state of nature and conceives of it as one of war of all against all. This change fundamentally determines his social thinking. Since human desires are random and all men seek to realize them, individuals must necessarily strive for commanding means that secure the realization of these desires. Furthermore, since these means are limited, the control over means toward ends results in zero-sum games. Power becomes the facility for getting what one party wants by preventing another party from getting what it wants. If man is no longer considered a *zoon politikon* but rather relentlessly driven by passions, desires, and the will to survive, reason demands the overcoming of the state of nature. The Hobbesian state must be understood as a natural necessity. The social contract as the foremost goal of the state is not meant to protect man's freedom but to provide security to the people. In return for vesting the state with power monopoly and for being obeisant and loyal, the sovereign protects the subjects' right to live and to own property. The price for social security consists in restricting natural freedom.

Hobbes's man does not appear as capable of moral responsibility, but an atom whose movements in the social space must be regulated through socialization and social control. Social order is thus based on man's coercive subjection to the authority of a powerful state. Hobbes posited war as primeval and inherent in human nature and justified political absolutism in the name of peace and security.

As Hobbes's *Leviathan* shows quite clearly, the sociological quest for more knowledge about a society that evidently got involved in far-reaching social change and shocking revolutions and wars did not develop in a linear direction. Modern social thinkers were more or less stuck with the great philosophical tradition and combined their contemporary knowledge and experiences in often amazing ways with traditional certainties. The social thinkers who followed may also be characterized along the lines we want to highlight in our history of sociology: gathering more and more knowledge about events and amazing changes of their times while at the same time reconciling these changes with traditional assumptions.

We should look at these thinkers in a sociological way: Human beings are mostly conservative insofar as they do not easily give up expectations they have learned. Therefore, even those theorists we call visionary today have tried to grasp the salient change and adapted it to the traditional views of society they have learned from their teachers. This is, as we will show, why the history of sociology is characterized by many hybrid systems of thought that combine an increasingly radical sociological view with unquestioned traditional assumptions.

The trend, however, unequivocally pointed to giving more and more weight to man-made facts instead of discovering natural states, and looking for empirical proof of this shift. Even Hobbes's contemporary Spinoza (1632–1677; 1899) stressed the importance of social institutions for guaranteeing freedom. For him, the institutions of the state mirror the changing relations of social power. He rejected the proposition that the problem of social integration could be solved through a general value consensus or by subjecting people to an all-powerful state. Charles de Montesquieu (1689–1755; 1999) for the first time formulated social order as independent of such presuppositions as natural law or rationality. He did not deny the existence of a substratum of history like human nature. However, what can be deduced from human nature characterized by a drive for self-preservation, peace, reproduction, and sociability is merely the existence of human society, not its specific structure. The latter, and the social laws by which it is explained, can be derived only from the conditions of real human associations. Montesquieu did not believe that the structural principles of social order could be derived from abstract ideas. Rather, these principles were to be recognized through observation and analysis of "positive" facts—that is, social realities. To discover the structural laws of society, he focused *not* on moral principles (like Rousseau later) or some rational will of a powerful state (like Hobbes before) but on the variety and causality of existing *social facts.* In his examination of the relationship between types of political superstructure and their social foundations, Montesquieu argued that the problem of social integration was a different one in different societies. Analyzing different forms of state and society, he confined himself to stating that social conflicts spring from society. Contrary to Hobbes, he thought that they are less a human or natural than a *social* phenomenon. Conflict, war, and inequality of men are rather related to the essence of society, inseparable from collective life, and in need of being mitigated and moderated. Today, the pluralism attached to this concept appears particularly modern: Social order was not to be established on the basis of commonly accepted norms and values but by tolerating and legally channeling the various interests and rights.

Jean-Jacques Rousseau (1712–1778), like Hobbes, was interested in discovering the laws that governed human action in society. Unlike Hobbes, however, he arrived at the conception of the absolute sovereignty of the people by means of which the state should force the individual to be free. Whereas Montesquieu and Hobbes had been concerned with the integrative and disruptive effects of human action, the intellectual, social, and political changes the eighteenth century was undergoing generated the need for a new perspective. The focal point now shifts toward altering those forms of integration under the auspices of *progress.* This new frame of reference transcends the existing society and provides the potential view that man is the master of his own history. Man's will should now be translated into social reality. It was no longer important to determine the equilibrium of social powers by studying social laws. The imagined commitment of all members of society to a central cause, the *volonté générale,* now provided the criterion of relevancy and is, by definition, never wrong. The ideal of happiness replaces the ancient ideal of virtue.

Rousseau's conclusions and practical hopes are based on the assumption that man is a reasonable creature. Present evils could therefore be eliminated through emancipation of the individual by releasing him from the current form of society. The new society, or *contrat social,* should enable the individual to be absorbed into the common will, thus securing reconciliation among men as well as equality of all before an external power (Rousseau 1972). Man's "second nature" would thus be grounded in normative principles in accord with collective interests and social solidarity—the general will. When Rousseau submitted his prize essay, "The Origin of Inequality," he based his theory on the assumption that there is natural equality among men, thus replacing the Aristotelian premise of a natural rank order.

Because theoretically sovereignty is inalienable and indivisible, therefore for government to represent the general will would require, in practical terms, that the divergent opinions of individuals be brought to a common platform through permanent exchange of arguments and political conviction. Permanent discussion should guarantee that people become aware of their common interests, which are geared toward collective maintenance of the body social and toward general welfare. In contrast to Hobbes's compromise between liberty and security through subjection, Rousseau offers the alternative of radical emancipation through free submission to the general will. Rousseau envisions a society united by reason and founded on liberty. Finally, Rousseau states in the last chapter of the *Contrat Social* that a civic religion of sentiments of sociability could provide the primary integrative force to which everyone could commit himself.

Rousseau's fantastic ideas, to a large extent a reflection of his personal creed, stand in remarkable contrast to the tradition of sober empiricism in Great Britain where statisticians and world travelers initially developed the idea of a general theory of society on the basis of worldwide experiences of manifold cultures and diverse human societies. In the social sciences, the old empiricism had received important methodological impulses from Francis Bacon and later indirectly from Isaac Newton. Society was seen as a construct of nature. However, it was not until the middle of the eighteenth century that the first scientific system of this sort was presented by Adam Ferguson (1723–1816; 1773) in *An Essay on the History of Civil Society.* Ferguson showed perhaps even more than Adam Smith (1723–1790) that a science of society was an oppositional discipline against the *ancient regime* and developed new ideas of social order. Whereas Hobbes had committed men to common values and total institutions and Rousseau proposed the free choice of the general will, the Scottish moral philosophers now gave up the underlying assumption of a given human nature. They began to attribute to society the capacity to mold human nature, thus making man open for society. Man is now believed to be able to learn from his experience and subordinate his actions to rules and natural rights of others. The reason imputed

to the alter ego limits the claim to rational efficiency in ego's action. This limitation on utilitarian rationality has been achieved by introducing the postulate of the "natural identity of interests," thus evading successfully the Hobbesian problem of order. The new conception of the state of nature is materialized in a particular social structure with the *cooperatio omnium* as its basic principle. Under the guidance of reason and the subsequent recognition that human association is mutually gratifying, Hobbes's *bellum omnium contra omnes* turns into associative cooperation of all with all.

Among the Scottish philosophers, Adam Smith stressed the invisible hand that integrated the self-interested striving of individuals, while Ferguson and John Millar (1735–1801) stood at the beginning of a social conflict theory highlighting that social change resulted from conflicting interests. Smith pictured a society that, by means of a system of mechanisms, sets man's basic interests free and controls them at the same time. He did not see the Cartesian principle of reason as the great means of revelation to man. Rather, sensations and sentiments were taken as the empirical foundation of thinking. Therefore, in *The Theory of Moral Sentiments,* Smith (1971) analyzed such elements of interaction as passions, propensities, affections, and feelings, which make society last. Moral sentiments should be regarded as the immediate expressions of social life. According to Smith, man is endowed by God with moral sentiments that serve to bind men to each other. At the same time, his science of the social order is founded on the theory of reciprocity rather than conflict between the individual and the collective. In *The Wealth of Nations* (Smith 1963), he converted the concept of mutuality into the problem of exchange relations, fundamental to the economy of civil society.

It seems that the French Revolution (1789) destroyed this optimism of early social thinking about order. Auguste Comte (1798–1857), who gave the discipline its name, grew up in a counterrevolutionary environment and was continually disturbed by the disorder of his time (Lenzer 1998). Like his teacher, Henri de Saint-Simon (1760–1852), he saw the revolution as a turning point in the history of social affairs. Their message, like that of many other social thinkers of the nineteenth century, consisted mainly in the search for the new principles of the emerging industrial society (Strasser 1976). They also agreed that the actions of men were ill-directed, their system of thought disoriented, and their feelings lacked coherence and were without worthwhile objectives. Therefore, Comte's fight against the negative heritage of the revolution embraced all those individualistic ideas that had weakened the sources of morality and social solidarity. He felt strongly the need for an order of institutions that would be able to cope with the changes in society. For him, in its stringent legislation against French society as it existed at the time, the Revolution led to an intolerable centralization of government in the sense that the state absorbed social functions belonging properly to other institutions, thus accelerating the rate of moral disorganization. The essential problem was consequently neither a political nor an economic one but rather one of *societal* organization. Thus, in some pamphlets he called for the replacement of theology and war by science and industry and even drew "a plan of the scientific operations necessary for reorganizing society." All his life, he was devoted to the creation of an intellectual basis for a new social organization. Positive philosophy, he believed, could eventually deliver society from the peril of dissolution.

In this attempt, the law of the three stages is his key notion as it describes the evolutionary development of the individual and, finally, of all humanity. The theological stage supposes the phenomenon under consideration to be due to immediate volition, either in the object or in some supernatural being. It can be seen in the thinking of children and primitive societies with regard to the phenomena of nature. In the metaphysical stage, abstract force residing in the object and, yet existing independently of the object, that is nature, is substituted for volition. In this stage, men do not deify objects but they do reify and personify abstractions. They imagine that they are making deductions from eternal truths, when they are really neglecting in their reasoning what needs to be examined most. They imagine that freedom, equality, and sovereignty actually exist, whereas these are really human constructs with many meanings.

The final stage, the positive, is reached when the quest for certainty is abandoned, and men accept the scientific laws derived from experience as the highest form of knowledge within human grasp. Inherent or external volition and inherent force have disappeared from the minds of men. Therefore, the explanation of a phenomenon is meant to refer, by way of succession or resemblance, to some other phenomenon, resulting in the establishment of a relation between the given fact and some general fact. Comte's philosophy of science is inseparable from his philosophy of history and from the theory of progress. What the sociologist does is simply give an accurate account of the realization of the essential order of each society in history. Comte's sociology assumes a harmonious evolution as a progress of social order in which one stage is the inevitable result of the preceding one and itself the motor of the next stage.

Even though "sociology" had formally entered history by Comte's system, it is evident that in the nineteenth century, the new discipline was still far away from a completely successful emancipation from philosophy, especially from the speculations of the philosophy of history that dominated the coming Hegelian Age. The German alternative to the early French social criticism of the time formulated a conservative theory of society. Georg Friedrich A. Hegel (1770–1831) conceived of a Universal Consciousness or Spirit in place of God, existing before man and nature. Conceptual phenomena evolved and revealed themselves through world history. There was no eternal truth; rather, truth and thought were subject to constant progress and change. In the *Philosophy of Right*, Hegel (2005) attempts to explain the social forms of history based on human free will. The progression begins with the family as a property-holding unit, paving the way for civil society based on private interests and mutual needs. The Spirit finally culminates in the socioethical community of the state. In its monarchic stage, all contradictions of civil society are reconciled in the realm of thought. Hegel, like Marx after him, thought that mankind had reached maturity. The truth actually coincided with the given social and political order.

Karl Marx (1818–1883) rejected Hegel's separation of the act of thought from the human subject, which tended to reduce the individual to a predicate of the hypostatized thought. Nevertheless, Marx extracted the rational core of Hegelian dialectic. Marx put Hegel's theory, the pendant of truth, to a test. The truth, Hegel claimed, is pervasive so that every single element can be connected with the process of reason. If that cannot be accomplished, the truth of the whole is destroyed. Marx believed that he himself had found such an all-destructive element: the *proletariat*. According to him, the existence of the proletariat was marked by universal suffering and injustice that meant, to him, the negation of the reality of reason. An entire class gives proof that the truth has not been realized. In opposition to Hegel's society-oriented theory, Marx developed his individual-oriented theory of society. Marx implied that individual freedom presupposes a free society and that the true liberation of the individual requires the liberation of society. This emancipation required the abolition of the prevailing mode of labor that was rooted in the historical form of society. According to Marx, people's essence of existence is expressed by a definite mode of life, which coincides with their production, both with what they produce and with how they produce.

Marx and his collaborator, Frederick Engels (1820–1895), established three propositions on which they based their theoretical and empirical studies. First, in capitalist society, men work under material conditions independent of their will. Second, relations of production are fundamental in forming man's character, including his consciousness. Third, the materialistic nature of the prevailing social order, that is, the prevalent relationship between social being and social consciousness, is to be regarded as man's alienated condition. Marx's unending effort to fulfill the truth of the materialistic thesis in its negation, by leaving the domain of "necessity" and entering the domain of "freedom" in which men would begin consciously to determine their fate, can be seen as proof for the unity of his early writings with those of his maturity.

The Rise of Probabilism

So far, we have stressed the history of ideas from which sociology emancipated itself later on. However, the prehistory of modern sociology would remain incomplete without its second major heritage: the so-called probabilistic revolution. Probabilism thoroughly changed the way of explaining social phenomena. From a traditional viewpoint, something is either the cause of some effect or it is not. Such attribution of causes and effects is proposed by the structure of language, which often directs our attention to the assumed relation between *one* certain cause and *one* certain effect. As twentieth-century research on causal attribution shows, it can still be considered predominant in everyday behavior today, even though the beginnings of the probabilistic revolution date back to the eighteenth century.

The most important founding father of data collection and statistical reasoning on which later research could draw was Adolphe Quetelet (1796–1874), the Belgian multitalented astronomer who in his *social physics* gathered all kinds of information that might provide insight into societal regularities. Moral statistics rose with the industrialization, first of England, then of other European countries. The need arose to understand what kind of new social structure was developing and the forces governing it. After the success of the natural sciences, people started believing that not only natural and technical but also *social* affairs were governed by regularities and even laws (Kern 1982:37).

Quetelet was familiar with Laplace's "error curve," or, as it was called later, the normal distribution. He was fascinated by the fact that distributions of birth, death, crime rates, physical capacities, height, weight, and strength showed similar shapes. Furthermore, he analyzed bivariate relations between mortality, occupation, yearly seasons, divorces, age, gender, and suicide. He summarized his results in many tables and constructed a "l'homme type," a typical man with propensities to act in a certain way. By doing so, he hoped to answer questions such as which laws govern the development of man, how high the influence of nature is, and what consequences human conduct has on society. From his observations, Quetelet was skeptical about free will and its individual behavior because his statistics suggested that it was neutralized by large numbers and social conditions change only slowly and appear to be amazingly constant from one society to the next.

Looking back, one recognizes in Quetelet's ample statistical material the problem that has accompanied empirical social research until today: Regularities of the kind that were available at Quetelet's time may well indicate strong associations. However, they alone neither answer the decisive question what exactly accounts for social change nor tell us how we can shape such change. Causal hypotheses about social change must refer to actual regularities of *human conduct*. Despite great efforts and advances in attitude measurement, our knowledge about actual human behavior has remained a serious problem that is still—despite many attempts at synthesis—discussed as the irreconcilability of qualitative and quantitative research, of explaining and understanding (Quah and Sales 2000:11).

This is not to deny that Quetelet's enthusiasm managed to make some intuitively convincing hits. Also, it paved the way for statistical progress without which sociology could not work the way it does. In Germany, Wilhelm Lexis (1837–1914) and in France, Èmile Dormoy (1844–1871) found that statistical series showed greater dispersion than Quetelet's interest in population means had indicated and that it would be necessary to differentiate populations into more subgroups and variables such as age, ethnicity, occupation, and class. This movement finally led to breaking with Quetelet's approach—away from the *statistics of the average* to the *statistics of relationships* (Desrosières 1993). Further research led to a deeper interest into actual variation and laid the basis for the conception of correlation and regression as methods of dealing with two and eventually any number of variables of whatever kind (Stigler 1986).[1]

Weber, Durkheim, and Early American Sociology

Despite the successful expansion of administrative statistics, the problem of a balanced database necessary for explaining social change started to become manifest at the end of the nineteenth century. Quetelet directed the organization of Belgian official statistics, and they became a model for social statistics in other countries. So the European states and their statistical offices started producing more knowledge about contemporary societies. The conviction spread further that history is man-made. But the more that data were collected, the more often the question arose as to how one could interpret such data to achieve convincing solutions for public policy and social problems. A look at the discussion about the consequences of industrialization shows the urgency of this difficulty. Neither politicians nor scientists knew what kind of behavior would result from newly discovered regularities, especially the formation of new social classes.

It is not possible to go into the details of all early research problems, so we will focus on one of the key issues of early-twentieth-century research: the so-called social question and the state of workers' consciousness. How would workers in the long run react to the strains of industrialized work, low wages, and unemployment? Some speculated they would revolutionize society sooner or later. Others postulated that they would rather fall into apathy. Such questions were vital to the modern state, but science had no valid information about what behavior could be expected in such crucial situations.

Émile Durkheim (1858–1917) and Max Weber (1864–1920) were among the first who tried to solve this puzzle. Their main merit consisted, however, in ending the long-lasting struggle between the philosophy of society and the sociological study of society by calling for a thorough *empirical* study of human conduct and social structures without philosophical speculation or unproven assumptions. They set the stage for the rise of sociological theory and social research and may therefore be considered as the most important founding fathers of sociology. Almost all assumptions about the nature of society and man, the relation between consensus and conflict, good and bad, progress and history, were dropped and replaced by the empirical study of the variables of "social facts." Weber and Durkheim did not in the least postulate that efforts in theoretically founding sociology should be abandoned. The relation between theory and research was rather a matter of degree, not a question of all or nothing. But the theory of society became much more sober, guided as it is by methodological considerations and no longer by philosophical reflections. There is good reason to let the actual history of sociology start with Weber and Durkheim in addition to Georg Simmel (1858–1918), Ferdinand Toennies (1855–1936), Werner Sombart (1863–1941), Vilfredo Pareto (1848–1923), Norbert Elias (1897–1990), Herbert Spencer (1820–1903), Robert E. Park (1864–1944), Ernest W. Burgess (1886–1966), and George H. Mead (1863–1931), while most previous theorists may be regarded as more or less philosophical speculators who built on traditional assumptions that were not meant to be tested empirically.

Durkheim's contribution to the history of sociology appears at least twofold. On the one hand, he directed his attention to the moral elements of society. In his studies *The Division of Labor in Society* (Durkheim 1984) and *Suicide* (Durkheim 1952), Durkheim polemicizes against the utilitarian individualists and shows that the Comtean requisite of social order, the consensus of moral beliefs, requires new interpretation in the light of newly discovered social facts. Illustrative examples are the "higher" type of solidarity, "organic solidarity," as generated by the growing division of labor, the occupational corporations that could regulate interpersonal relations more effectively, even in a socialist society, and social cohesion, a low degree of which could lead to suicide. This normative paradigm was soon to become part of social theory through Talcott Parsons's structural functionalism.

On the other hand, in *The Rules of Sociological Method,* Durkheim (1938) left us with the seemingly clear instruction to explain the social by the social. Against much contemporary opposition, Durkheim insisted that social facts form a reality *sui generis,* not be reduced to individual or psychological qualities. Social institutions (e.g., marriage, court, market, church), norms, and social regularities (e.g., the growing division of labor in civilized countries, the shrinking of the traditional family, economic depressions) depend on their own laws to be discovered by sociology.

The best example Durkheim offered for this thesis is the development of suicide rates. At first sight, it seems that no other human action could be more individual than the decision to end one's life. However, Durkheim shows convincingly that suicide rates are amazingly constant in relation to social, religious, and professional groups, to winter and summer, to married or single people. Durkheim therefore distinguishes between different *types* of suicide: egoistic, altruistic, fatalistic, and anomic. The relative isolation of a human in society—if, for example, a young single sees all other boys walk with their girlfriends on a summer day—is a precondition for an egoistic suicide. In contrast, the altruistic suicide protects the community in which the person is strongly integrated: The military officer kills himself because he has done something dishonorable, which threatens his professional group. The term *anomie*—literally translated, *without law*—signifies a state of normlessness, irritation, confusion, and breakdown. Durkheim assumes that anomie will be found in times of increased social change when traditional values no longer have their binding authority and the new norms do not yet have enough power to guide human behavior. People will commit suicide more often in such a state of depression because they do not know what way their life is going. Durkheim's way of arguing with official statistics has made *Suicide* a paradigmatic study of sociological research and generalizing, probabilistic explanations on the basis of correlations.

Weber was also concerned with the problem of social order, but in a different way. As he did his dissertation and habilitation thesis in law, he started off with a completely different view on social life. The breakdown of social order is not his starting point but rather the simple observation that human conduct shows certain regularities that can be documented. If sociologists want to explain such regularities, they need a complex theory about human behavior that Weber (1949) developed gradually in his scattered methodological writings, later known as *The Methodology of the Social Sciences.* Weber's mature social theory, expounded in *Economy and Society* (Weber [1922] 1968) and *Some Categories of Sociology* (Weber 1981), calls for a combination of three elements:

1. "Objective" regularities ("devoid of meaning"), that is, all kinds of regularities, including unknown influences on human behavior as indicated in public statistics, for example, by *distributions* of income, education, resources, health

2. The meaning of human behavior, which is, as we know today, the subjectively believed reason for one's behavior and the way people usually attribute internally or externally behavior, especially as internally set goals ("I want to . . .") and values ("because it means so much to me") but also emotions and traditions ("we always did it that way")

3. The selection of a typical social relationship or *type of situation* the explanation refers to (in contrast to the unclear term *society,* which Weber refused to use); this element refers to questions such as, Which audience is listening? How many people are present? Is the situation formal or informal? What is the time horizon of the situation? What is the problem dealt with? Do people act on a consensual or on a conflictual basis?

Weber sees the fulfillment of all three requirements as crucial to achieve valid statements on consequences of human behavior. Even though all three elements may be closely connected in practical research, they need, however, separate efforts at empirical proof. In Weber's time, such data were not available. Weber wants us to have more concerns for local, microscopic ideas. For example, Marx neglected requirements 2 and 3 by focusing on objective regularities of surplus value distribution and exploitation and by simply maintaining that the typical motives of workers were "false." For Marx, it seemed that behavior in nineteenth-century society looked as if it could be understood from such distributions alone. The use of language unavoidably results, as Weber stresses, in statements about regularities of behavior *and* meaningful, that is, attributional, ideas. Even simple sentences imply far-reaching assumptions about behavior that are indeed difficult to prove empirically.

In his methodological writings, Weber liked to exemplify the *selective* function of causal statements by such everyday examples as the mother who attributes the causes of her own rude behavior against her child in a particular situation. Or to use a more contemporary example: We may say that in contrast to upper-class students, lower-class students do not believe as strongly in effort as upper-class students do. From Weber's view of causality, such a statement tells us that there is both an "objective" influence on behavior (class of father) and a selective meaning of behavior (small causal belief in one's effort). Furthermore, Weber wants the sociologist to locate the specific social relationship in which such a statement actually and typically occurs. Modern society is differentiated into many types of situations. Depending on where people show what kind of conduct, it will have different consequences. Weber was well aware that the rules that guide conduct vary considerably from one situation to the next. A science that was to elaborate on the consequences of meaningful behavior would have to pay attention to such situational differences, as our example demonstrates: Even lower-class students may agree to try harder *in the class-room* because effort attributions are highly institutionalized within school, while in the afternoon at home—the next type of situation—this attributional expectation may well lose its plausibility if the lower-class family and their peers do not impose equal pressure on more effort. The consequence of such different behavior in and outside the class may well be that lower-class students are not as successful in education because they cannot get rid of their social origin and unintentionally continue its structural disadvantages intergenerationally. In the end, their attitude and behavior at home are causally decisive for the outcome in their life course—despite all efforts on the parts of the teachers and the state. This is a consequence of unequal meaningful behavior that needs to be determined and possibly measured.

In Weber's time, such detailed research knowledge was, of course, not available. But his writings on meaningful behavior demand that we distinguish between objective ("devoid of meaning") and subjective ("meaningful") regularities both theoretically and empirically and combine

them because both regularities become causally effective in the end. Subjective understanding refers to typical situations in which people show differential expectations. In contrast, by elaborating objective causes, we may well detect forces (especially resource distributions, class positions, educational level) whose societal effects may overlap considerably, although they may be in explicit contrast to socially visible attributions. For example, people may think of themselves (and say this in surveys), more than ever before, as being self-determined, individualized decision makers of their life courses. And yet, as observers, we see that the influences of unequal origins, class positions, education degrees, access to institutions, and resource distributions (which can often hardly be changed by individual behavior) have not vanished. Therefore, sociological explanations must combine *seemingly* contradictory elements.

However, this paradox self-presentation of modern behavior is not new at all. Weber had a solution for the analysis of such a society by distinguishing between the *material* and the *idealist* aspect of human behavior. This distinction is indispensable because both dimensions have their own evolution in modern society. Material welfare has risen incredibly, and yet, at the same time, the causal ideas that people have with regard to their practical behavior have changed even more dramatically. More than ever before, people conceive of their behavior as self-determined and individualized so that "subjectively" the world will increasingly appear as ordered from inside instead of from outside, for example, by tradition, God, nature, or the collective fate of class. The elective affinity between religious ideas and capitalist materialism, discussed in *The Protestant Ethic and the Spirit of Capitalism* (Weber 2001), was just one example of the type of analysis Weber had in mind.

Today, many more examples *could* follow. "Understanding" therefore means doing research on the selective causal ideas that people show in their behavior. "Explaining" refers to the detection of the structural forces and distributions that "accompany" such behavior. Both views combined reflect the entire causal situation appropriately. This two-part model of an explanation will be convincing only if it is complemented by a statement on the meaning of behavior because it is the major source of social change in modern times. Therefore, Weber wants sociology to analyze human behavior by means of *both* an observer's and the participant's concept of causality.

Evidence for the argument that people have causal ideas about situations and behave accordingly has been usually taken from the tradition of attribution research established by Heider's (1958) analysis of everyday concepts of causality. It is amazing how little attention sociologists have given to Weber's (1949) obstinate discussion of causality. Weber insisted that human behavior can be explained causally just like explanations for natural phenomena. He therefore stressed that causality is not an objectively given feature of the external world but rather a practical tool of language that we use in our behavior. We *understand* both the historical and our contemporary world by attributing selectively certain causes and effects to it. The emphasis is on *selection* from a horizon of different possibilities that makes our views meaningful in a phenomenological sense.[2]

Weber did work on the empirical operationalization of such a scientific concept (Lazarsfeld and Oberschall 1962)—without much success, as demonstrated by his and his brother's early attempt at studying attitudes in the German *Verein für Socialpolitik* in 1908. Contemporary research had much information about conditions of workers' existence such as wages, work time and loads, nutrition, and living conditions in general. Little knowledge was available about their personality and the influence that industry had on their attitudes. The *Verein* decided to conduct a survey, which faced basic problems with respect to not only professional, reliable execution but also the question of what exactly one was to ask workers in order to obtain the expected knowledge about their actual behavior. However, the scientists administering the survey had virtually no idea about the mechanisms in which objective conditions are converted into subjective attitudes and in what way such attitudes shape structural opportunities. Therefore, no theory about the interview situation and an appropriate questionnaire design existed so that in 1911 the frustrated Weber concluded that the surveys had brought almost no reasonable results.

While Weber and Durkheim tried to master more or less successfully the requirements in a unified research program, representatives of early American sociology made clear that it would be difficult to keep the sociological research train on common rails. On the one hand, we find in Mead's theory of causality striking resemblances to Weber's insistence on the practical first-order character of causal statements. Like Weber, Mead (1936:114) argues that "everything in experience falls under the idea of causation." Human experience is ordered by a pragmatic construction of causes and effects:

> If in the past we find one event following another and this has been repeated, then we expect that it will happen again. That is all there is to the law of causality. It does not show that every cause must have a certain effect, every effect a cause; that there must be like causes for like effects; that there must be an adequate cause for every effect. We do not know this as a law of the universe. What we find is this fixed expectation— an expectation that comes so frequently, so unconsciously, that we are not aware of it. (P. 438)

This conception of causality is surprisingly radical. Mead does not even mention science in his definition of causality and stresses—like Weber—but the ordering power of practical everyday expectations. Nevertheless, Mead does not in the least intend to devalue scientific work on causes and effects. Mead is optimistic about the capacity of science to come up with causal knowledge, uniformities, and regularities and help society in directing

progress. Therefore, Mead's (1936:286) motto is, "The law is dead; long live the law!" With these views, Mead warranted later the microsociology approach that focused on qualitative regularities of human behavior (Blumer 1954; Strauss 1956; Goffman 1961). The study of social interaction, socialization, and group psychology was firmly established *within* sociology (Kalberg 2005:43).

On the other hand, early American sociologists stressed the necessity to study social change in the early twentieth century in macrosociological terms. Widespread immigration led to the establishment of demography within sociology—unlike in Germany, England, and France. Social change could not be studied solely by qualitative knowledge of human behavior; it required quantitative efforts. This exigency matched a quest for distinguishing sociology from the humanities and social work. The search for scientific procedures and laws became central (Oberschall 1972). Such scientific commitment promised further implications of research for social policy, for example, by alleviating tensions caused by massive population growth.

Concluding this section on the "prehistory" and the early constitution of modern sociology, we want to stress the enormous efforts undertaken until the beginning of the twentieth century. Not only had sociology had to emancipate itself from philosophical and speculative theories of society and the "great" history of ideas, it also had to elaborate its own concepts, which assumed that society is made up of meaningful human behavior and that, therefore, a methodological individualism would be appropriate. Finally, sociology needed to institutionalize itself in the academic community, thus establishing a link to the growing statistical knowledge about social affairs. These difficult tasks took a long time to accomplish but were solved by the time the founding fathers left the scientific scene in Europe and in America.

THE RISE OF SOCIOLOGICAL THEORY AND SOCIAL RESEARCH

The Sociological Research Program

If we want to explain the directions that the more recent history of sociology has taken, we need to look at two aspects: what sociologists had in mind and the structural opportunities under which the discipline developed. To be sure, the circumstances of scientific analysis changed dramatically in the course of the twentieth century. Sociologists managed to institutionalize the new discipline in the scientific community in the first half of the twentieth century. In the second half, the history of sociology is characterized by its expansion at the universities with many new chairs and emerging research fields, at least in Western societies. However, the institutionalization of sociology had unexpected side effects, the increasing specialization of scholars in particular. Social theory and social research developed along separate routes and not without conflicting relationships. In many countries, particularly in the United States, sociological theory was accused of promoting an undesirable regression to unscientific armchair research (Turner 1989:224). In contrast, in some European countries, particularly in France, Germany, and Great Britain, sociologists promoted theoretical efforts more than ever before.

We do not want to judge whose claims may be more or less justified in these continuing struggles. Rather, we take these conflicts within the discipline as a hint at the complexity of the sociological research program devised by its founding fathers. Weber's and Durkheim's legacies proved to be much more difficult to realize. Soon after Weber's premature death in 1920, a controversy started about what exactly his combination of explaining and understanding meant and in what way a theory of social action should be elaborated. Contenders to Weber's legacy were Alfred Schütz (1899–1959) and Talcott Parsons (1902–1979), both great admirers of Weber. They did develop, however, two completely different views of the master's intentions. Even though both Parsons and Schütz claimed that it was the perspective of the actor that should guide sociological research, Schütz disputed that Parsons's theory represented an analysis *adequate to meaning* (Schütz and Parsons 1977:57ff.). Weber's call for both *causal and meaningful adequacy* in sociological explanations was one thing, its concrete realization quite another.

This is one reason why sociology started splitting up in terms of its categories, intentions, and goals. Phenomenological sociology and its interpretive variants have stressed, against Parsons's structural functionalism, that sociological explanations must aim at meaningful adequacy and that it was necessary to understand the subjectively intended meaning of Ego's consciousness to explain social behavior and its outcomes. Some of the best discussions and exemplifications of this program can be found in Erving Goffman's (1959) studies of the *Presentation of Self in Everyday Life,* in Harold Garfinkel's (1967) *Studies in Ethnomethodology,* and finally, in many explications of the symbolic interactionist program originating in the social psychological writings of George H. Mead.

Another important discussion was drawn along the lines of conflict and consensus. Some of the key participants in this debate were Alvin W. Gouldner (1920–1981), Lewis A. Coser (1913–2003), and Ralf Dahrendorf (1929–), on the one hand, and Talcott Parsons (1902–1978) and Robert K. Merton (1910–2003), on the other hand. Especially in the 1960s, this debate polarized the sociological community with one side claiming a particular competence for the analysis of social change, whereas the other side was said to be obsessed by the question of social integration. Parsons never accepted the proposed challenge that his general theory of action had a conservative, static bias and was led by an oversocialized conception of man. He developed the basic postulates of his theory gradually from *The Structure of Social Action* (Parsons 1937) to *The Social System* (Parsons 1951), in which he elaborates two

familiar axioms of human action. First, following the utilitarians, Parsons assumes that in every situation, people aim at an optimum gratification of their needs. The second axiom relates individuals to situations assumed to be determined by culturally structured patterns or norms. Hence, the pursuit of aims is always based on culturally recommended action patterns. These patterns discipline action—the system of order thus supersedes men's interest. Norms, or better, the obligatory character of norms, function not only to avoid social war but also to overcome "double contingencies" generally. By recognizing that in society there are choices and uncertainties on my part and that of others, Parsons places the solution of the problem of these contingencies in the center of the interaction process. They are supposed to be overcome by internalized norms. In deciding the Hobbesian problem of order, Parsons refers to the common value system as *the* prerequisite for the constitution of social order.

The much-discussed relation between action and system is easy to express in Parsons's sense: Action *is* system, that is, social systems are formed by interrelated actions. Parsons gradually developed a conceptual scheme for the analysis of social systems. He maintains that a social system gets its system character from boundary maintenance and a tendency toward equilibrium. That is to say, members of some social entity are generally closer to one another than they are to nonmembers; there is more mutual understanding, and anticipated responses are more often validated in relations with insiders than with outsiders; there is a tendency with regard to insiders to repeat contact, to cooperate, and to continue relationships. On the other hand, social systems are also characterized by built-in mechanisms that tend to keep society unchanged over time or that tend to reestablish a lost equilibrium. From this point of view, social conflicts and societal change can only be conceived of as temporary deviations from stable structures. If any given social system is to persist or to undergo an orderly process of developmental change, the system must solve four functional problems: *a*daptation to the environment, goal *a*ttainment, *i*ntegration, and *l*atent pattern maintenance (AGIL). As they evolve, societies differentiate first along these AGIL lines and then into subsystems of each AGIL function (economic subsystem, etc.). However, the principle of differentiation is not sufficient. Segmentation and normative specification are also needed.

Even though Parsons's argument (actually taken from Weber) that empirical observation shows a certain stability of normative patterns is undoubtedly correct, his obsession with normatively stabilized social integration challenged his contemporaries to systematic criticism, and competing theories were developed that put more stress on social conflicts. In *The Functions of Social Conflict,* Coser (1956)—a student of Merton—presented a conflict-theoretical reanalysis of Simmel's *Conflict and the Web of Group Affiliations* and stressed that social conflicts are not necessarily in contrast to social order and have positive effects on societal development. Dahrendorf (1958) found his place in the social sciences of the twentieth century by delineating himself from Parsons. He points out that society is always characterized by two faces that unite static *and* dynamic components, integration *and* conflict. Nevertheless, both sides are by no means structures that are self-understood and closed, but "two equally valid aspects of every imaginable society" (p. 175). Hence, he focused on an extension of the structural-functional theory wherever its claim of universality hides the immanent capacity of explaining social change and conflict. Dahrendorf (1959) argued against the structural-functional primacy of integration that "the 'dynamically variable elements' which influence the construction of social structures do not necessarily originate outside the 'system' but may be generated by the structure itself" (p. 123).

The confrontation between structural functionalism, on the one hand, conflict theorists and phenomenological interactionists, and on the other hand, it also posed a challenge to Niklas Luhmann (1927–1999), whose devotion to systems theory relates him to Parsons, but only in a very limited sense. Luhmann argued that it does not make sense to develop competing theories for social integration and social conflict, interactionist and societal analysis. His claim is as high as Parsons's was: formulating a general theory of human conduct capable of treating every type of human conduct, be it consensual, be it conflictual. For Luhmann, there can be no doubt that research will inevitably lead to some alienation of meaningful first-order expressions because individual motives must be subsumed under more general categories to be part of sociological explanations. While many scientists continue to use Weber's problematic ideal types of human conduct, Luhmann (1990:53ff.) believes that the interpretation of action as a means-values-ends relation is a far too special view of human behavior to be able to constitute a *basic* tool. Undoubtedly the causal relation between means, values, and ends provides evidence to the observer, but it is not fundamental enough to reconstruct the broad ways in which meaning appears in the social world. Instead, Luhmann sees the attribution model of behavior as suitable for achieving meaningful *and* causal—that is, generalizable—adequacy in sociological research. This model summarizes conduct in four directions: internal versus external, stable versus variable interpretation. Internal attributions of behavior will appear as action based either on ability and/or effort. External attributions are interpreted as passive experience of the world, either as luck or fate. Hence, social action is not an ontologically, unquestioned given object of sociological research but a first-order interpretation based on the internal attribution of conduct. It is for this reason that Luhmann (1995:137ff.) places his level of analysis on social systems, or, to be more precise, on communication instead of social action.

From Luhmann's point of view, systems theory helps distinguish between the mental level, on the one hand, and the social level, on the other hand. This clear distinction reminds us that sociological explanations are—as Weber and Durkheim told us—based on the *social* rules that govern the attribution of meaning. Mental idiosyncrasies are of no interest to sociology. Therefore, the advantage of using systems theory appears as methodological—not only by providing a clear-cut distinction between the social and the mental level but also by breaking down, as Weber had intended by his notion of "social relations," the complex object of "society" into smaller units of observation, which Luhmann calls different kinds of social systems: face-to-face interactions, formal organizations, and functional subsystems of society. Such a theoretical use of the term *system* has nothing in common with Parsons's notion of "action as a system."

Nevertheless, Luhmann's solution of the problem of intersubjectivity must be understood in the context of the discussions between Parsons and Schütz. Luhmann takes Parsons's side against Schütz in this question and reinterprets phenomenologically the Parsonian distinction between the psychic and the social system. Both systems constitute two separate levels of meaning. Therefore, the distinction between psychic and social systems is not—as in Parsons's AGIL scheme—meant analytically but rather *empirically:* Luhmann (1995:12) assumes that there are psychic and social systems in the real world. Both consciousness and communication are based on meaning but each has its own logic and dynamic. Only communication—and not consciousness—forms the "intersubjective" level of the social on which sociological explanations must be found. This solution of the intersubjectivity problem makes the struggle between "subjective" and "objective" terminologies obsolete.

Luhmann's concept of understanding follows Schütz, who had objected to Weber's methodology that ideal-type understanding is not a privilege of the social scientist. Rather, in everyday life, actors apply interpretive schemes to grasp the meaning of what they do. Luhmann integrates this idea into his concept of communication and insists on practical first-order understanding as the object of sociology. Accordingly, communication consists of three combined elements: utterance, information, and understanding. The meaning of behavior is constituted by the *communicative* act of *understanding* that follows the *utterance* of *information* (Luhmann 1995:139ff.). Selective understanding constitutes meaningful social rules that help actors build up certainty about what to expect in the social world. Luhmann defines meaning phenomenologically as a means of selection. In other words, human behavior is meaningful as its motives are causal selections from a horizon.

Unfortunately, Luhmann's integration of systems theory and interpretive sociology has not been widely discussed in Anglo-Saxon sociology. Instead, Jeffrey Alexander's (1982) call for multidimensionality and Anthony Giddens's (1984) theory of structuration found more attention. Especially Giddens's approach generated some consensus on the relation between human behavior and social structures that are no longer considered as incompatible. Structures are now seen as both restricting and enabling conduct. The crucial question, however, that remained was what consequences this new consensus has for empirical research.

The Rise of Social Research

While theorists insisted on the meaningful behavior as the causal basis of social change, researchers did not wait for a consensus that might end theoretical controversies about the meaning of meaning. After World War II, Paul F. Lazarsfeld (1901–1976) became the founding father of modern social research. Together with Marie Jahoda (1907–2001) and Hans Zeisel (1905–1992), he conducted the famous study *The Unemployed of Marienthal* (Jahoda, Lazarsfeld, and Zeisel [1933] 2002). The task of Lazarsfeld's research group from the *Wirtschaftspsychologische Arbeitsstelle Wien* was to document the psychological effects of long-term unemployment. They used modern methods of data collection that allowed insights into the mechanisms between structural descriptions and subjective experiences that the affected persons themselves reported. The measurement of walking speed became famous as an indicator for individual coping. The group constructed types of attitudes, for example, the unbroken, the resigned, the apathetic, and the desperate. The answer to the by then much politically debated question about the social psychological consequences of unemployment was clearly the prevalence of apathy. Despite the qualitative and individual case study character, the group demonstrated that it is in principle possible to quantitatively measure complex social phenomena. In 1940, Lazarsfeld got a chair at Columbia University, New York City, where, in 1944, his *Forschungsstelle* became the *Bureau of Applied Social Research.*

Twentieth-century social research is well characterized by the development of Lazarsfeld's reader *Language of Social Research.* In the 1955 edition, Lazarsfeld and Rosenberg (1955:393) give an account of action (purchasing a good) that combines understanding and explaining, connecting the analysis of the "total make-up of the person" and "the total situation in which he finds himself." By the 1972 edition, empirical understanding of action largely disappeared together with qualitative research in favor of extensive multivariate analysis. Such quantitative methods as path analysis fulfilled a deep wish for sociological scientism—a stance that triumphed in the generation after World War II connected with names such as Otis D. Duncan (1984), William F. Ogburn and Meyer F. Nimkoff (1964), and Hubert M. Blalock (1982). A strong concern with methodology promised to cure sociology's inferiority complex on its way into academia and to provide equal strength in the competition of scientific disciplines.

In the quest for more quantitative, generalizing knowledge, researchers aimed at all major sectors of society (e.g., family, education, work, and health care). Funding agencies asked for more information about society to be able to modernize it, rebuild it, and make welfare state activities more efficient. Together with textbooks and research methods, American sociology's triumph of empiricism and scientific orientation were adapted widely. This is illustrated, among other things, by the establishment of various institutes for advanced studies in Europe after World War II (e.g., in Austria, Sweden, and The Netherlands).

One of the most important achievements is constituted by the development of class schemes. Class schemes uncover class *relations* instead of conceiving of them as a gradational difference of prestige. Therefore, Goldthorpe (1980:40) defines the class concept by typical market and work situations, including the proximity to occupational authority, the level of work autonomy, the way work is supervised, the opportunities for promotions, and job security. It has become common to confront the European Erikson/Goldthorpe/Portocarero, or EGP, scheme as "Weberian" with the American scheme of Wright's (1997:25) more "Marxist" scheme, which, too, is based on typical work relations but which focuses on the inherent relations of exploitation. Goldthorpe's scheme is widely used in comparative research.

Another major achievement of the twentieth-century social research was established by large-scale panel data and the implementation of longitudinal research designs. Longitudinal research aims at the collection of data over time, which is essential if one wants to measure social change (Mayer 2000). It may be based on repeated cross-sectional studies, prospective or retrospective data collection. Important examples of repeated cross-sectional surveys are the United Kingdom's General Household Survey and Family Expenditure Survey, and the European Union's Eurobarometer. Well-known prospective panel studies are the US Panel Study of Income Dynamics (PSID), the British Household Panel Study (BHPS), and the German Socio-Economic Panel (GSOEP). They are based on a random sample of respondents and repeated data collections at fixed intervals (up to a year). They all aim at grasping in more detail the nature of social change. The GSOEP is a prospective longitudinal survey that interviews a random sample of adults annually.

Cohort panels constitute a specific form of study taking into account generational replacement. It is assumed that a cohort experiences relatively similar life events. Researchers select an age group and administer a questionnaire to a sample to follow it over life courses with reinterviews usually every five years. Examples are the UK National Child Development Study and the German Life History Study (GLHS). The GLHS is a retrospective study of individual life courses that collects all information from birth on at one point. It consists of different birth cohorts for which information about education and employment history, parental status, marital and fertility history, and family and household composition are provided. In comparison to other panels (e.g., the American PSID), both the GSOEP and GLHS contain relatively little information about attitudes and other social psychological scales that might provide a deeper insight into the micro-dynamics and consequences of human behavior (Diewald 2001). This is also demonstrated by a more recent struggle in British Sociology where the National Child Development Study (NCDS) provided the basis for a debate on the more or less meritocratic character of contemporary labor markets (Bond and Saunders 1999; Breen and Goldthorpe 1999). This "race" between the causal weight of structural and individual factors did not have a definite result, which in turn stresses the need for more and deeper panel studies into the meaning of human behavior.

Interviews and surveys have become the major methodological instrument of data collection to measure both subjective attitudes and structural characteristics of classes and life courses. Whereas origins of surveying date back to the early nineteenth century, early political polls began to appear in the 1930s, and market research emerged only after World War II. Since then, survey and interview research has become dominant so that the majority of available data today stems from interview surveying. Such programs as the General Social Survey (GSS), European Social Survey Program (ESS), and the Eurobarometer today provide sociological research with interesting data about social change. Another example for recent international collaborative survey research is the International Social Justice Project (ISJP), which has explored popular beliefs and attitudes on social, economic, and political justice through two large-scale opinion surveys fielded in 13 countries in 1991 and 6 countries in 1996 (Kluegel, Mason, and Wegener 1995). The ISJP questionnaire combined structural and social psychological, attributional concepts—a research design that might prove to be an important tool for combining quantitative and qualitative aspects. It did show that beliefs about justice and inequality are much more individualistic in the United States than in other countries (see Kluegel and Smith 1986).

Survey and interview research has gone a long way—and not only in terms of internationalization, which makes it virtually impossible today to distinguish between European, American, and other sociologies in this field. It proceeded from merely collecting objective facts about the poor in the nineteenth century to surveying subjective phenomena and measuring specific human behavior and its contextuality in the past decades. The relation between attitudes that people will mention in surveys and their real behavior has continuously inspired research efforts (Ajzen and Fishbein 1980) and a more recent interest in the cognitive processes of the interview situation (Krebs and Schmidt 1993).

This is not to deny that case studies and "small N" qualitative research have played an important part in tracking social change, especially in areas of society with radical social change, dealing with public and private talk, all kinds of documents and texts, interviews of different style,

Internet communication, and visual data such as photographs, cartoons, videos, and advertisements (Silverman 2004). Important schools comprise conversation analysis, ethnography, ethnomethodology, and discourse analysis. Qualitative research in virtually all areas of society will also continue to be at the center of sociological efforts in the twenty-first-century sociology.

FROM SPECIALIZATION TO REUNIFICATION: PROSPECTS FOR THE 21ST CENTURY

In the twentieth century, sociologists have often been quite critical of their discipline because of its many rivaling schools and its seeming multiparadigmatic failure to focus on a unified approach to the study of society. One could argue, however, that it is not only the pronounced willingness of scholars to come into conflict over methodological and conceptual issues, it is also sociology's object of study—a highly differentiated society—which enforces methodological and theoretical pluralism.

Nevertheless, at the beginning of the twenty-first century, we find an extensive search for new goals and orientations as well as a lot of dissatisfaction with the development of social research. The deepest dissatisfaction seems to stem from the wide gap between our everyday and theoretical knowledge about human behavior and the available data. Despite ever-larger and differentiated data sets, research does not seem to have achieved convincing explanations that make the inequality and change of life courses sufficiently understandable, not to mention the lack of firm recommendations for political goals. The relation between understanding and explaining remains sketchy despite our certainty that it is only human behavior that can be the causal source of change and continuity.

Consequently, in recent years the nature of causal statements has (again) been critically discussed. *Sociological Methods & Research* even printed Abbott's (1998:174) overly pessimistic view that correlational analysis is a waste of time if you want to understand why social life happens the way it does. There is a wide dissatisfaction with the deficiency of research to make unequal human behavior more *intelligible,* as Goldthorpe (2000:178, 260) stresses in his quest for complementing statistics and hermeneutics. According to Goldthorpe, we do not exactly know how educational "decisions" are actually made and what kind of causal attributions people from different class backgrounds typically make. In fact, our methodology and data suffer from knowing a lot less about such situations on a general level than about the *results* of mobility processes, which are revealed by class schemes. As a consequence, research on meaningful behavior in such situations up to now is dominated by qualitative typologies gained from small N's. The results are interesting, but their underlying data sets lack a level of validity that would permit the test of specific hypotheses on social change between cohorts.

Nevertheless, looking back at the history of sociology, we see no reason to be overly pessimistic about sociology's scientific record. As we indicated at the beginning, sociology had to go a long way to free itself from philosophical theories of social life and society. Even today, philosophical, theoretical, and "armchair" conceptions of society remain rivals in public discourse. It is often difficult to find public sympathy for sociological research results, as the mass media favor simple answers to complex societal problems, and these do, however, inevitably involve multiple causal assessments. Often, political discussions assimilate sociological advice to their conflicting structures so that much of its actual value is lost when it is transferred to the public. Against this background, the sociological ideas about meaningful human behavior as the basis of societal change and continuity are difficult to defend—despite sociology's growing empirically validated knowledge.

Keeping these obstacles in mind, both the theoretical and empirical progress of sociology and some more-recent integration of theories of human conduct and social research are impressive. We believe that sociology will have to live with a continuous critical self-perception and public distrust against attempts at a sociological "enlightenment" of societal processes. Sociologists should present their research results with more self-confidence and insist on their high proficiency for a deeper understanding of modern societies and their problems. However, this goal will be achieved only by more integration of research and theoretical attempts at grasping the meaningful character of human behavior and its consequences. Theorists often forget that their efforts and controversies should actually contribute to or at least lay the basis for better empirical understanding and research designs. A more serious integration of theory and research could, as we believe, make sociology a leading discipline in the scientific community.

3

THE HISTORY OF SOCIOLOGY: THE NORTH AMERICAN PERSPECTIVE

JOHN P. DRYSDALE

SUSAN HOECKER-DRYSDALE

Concordia University, Canada

All histories are written from a particular perspective, time, and place, and are therefore partial and incomplete. To paraphrase Albion Small (1916:721–22), the history of sociology has less to do with facts and even ideas than it does with the context of those facts and the reasons for particular thoughts. As suggested by the recent volume *Diverse Histories of American Sociology* (Blasi 2005), the histories of North American sociology have been written from diverse perspectives and contexts, but always with the conviction that expanding the knowledge of its history would provide a greater and more sophisticated understanding of the discipline and its complexities (House 1936; Bottomore and Nisbet 1978; Bulmer 1984; Ross 1991).

THE VARIETIES OF HISTORIES OF SOCIOLOGY

Albion Small (1854–1926), one of the key founders of American sociology, produced several historical accounts of the discipline, including "Fifty Years of Sociology in the United States (1865–1915)" (1916) and *Origins of Sociology* (1924). Small (1924) maintained that sociology "came into existence as an organic part of this maturing of social science as a whole ... Sociology is a normal advance of human thought from less developed to more

developed dealings with human reality" (pp. 14–15). He recognized that the work of building sociology was done also by those outside of, or marginal within, academe who wished to explore the social world, to understand it, to answer questions, and to solve social problems. "Indeed," Small remarks, "there is the wherewithal for a brilliant Doctor's dissertation on the subject 'Sociology outside the Ranks of the Sociologists'" (p. 15). Small credited especially German sociology and philosophy as a watershed for the evolution or development of a social and historical self-consciousness in sociology, reflecting especially his own training and perspective. In addition, Small recognized how the history of sociology is shaped and influenced by factors of politics, nationality, and ethnicity (p. 19), and, we would add, race and gender. He asserted that an understanding of our discipline and its accumulated knowledge in whatever period requires an understanding of its history.

Nearly half a century later, Howard W. Odum (1951) began his history of American sociology reiterating and extending Small's point of view, reminding the reader of (1) the distinct history produced by each epoch, (2) the need for young sociologists to understand the history of sociology, (3) the dynamics of technological, economic, and social changes creating the context for the development of sociology, (4) North American sociology's roots in European as well as American culture, and (5) the expectations for sociology in the future. In his detailed and useful history, Odum takes an institutional approach to tell "the Story of Sociology in the United States through 1950."

Various approaches to the historical narrative of sociology have followed the early histories by Albion Small, including Harry Elmer Barnes's (1948) classic edited compendium, *An Introduction to the History of Sociology,* which views the topic through the sociologies of individuals who were pioneers (Comte, Spencer, Morgan, Sumner, Ward, Gumplowicz, German sociologists, non-German Europeans, English, and finally American). J. H. Abraham in *The Origins and Growth of Sociology* (1977) similarly looks at individual figures through a periodization from Plato and Ibn Khaldun to twentieth-century America and modern Europe. A voluminous and detailed account of the history of American sociology is L. L. Bernard and Jessie Bernard's ([1943] 1965) *Origins of American Sociology: The Social Science Movement in the United States,* which relates the rise of sociology to the social science movement, associationism, the impact of Comte and positivism, quantification, and sociology's emergence as a positive science.

Heinz Maus (1962) in *A Short History of Sociology* examines the history of sociology internationally from the nineteenth century to modern times. In analytical chapters, Maus considers how "American Sociology Faces Reality" and "American Sociological Theory and Teaching" in which he discusses the impact of the work of Park, Burgess, and Thomas and Znaniecki, as well as the influence of cultural anthropology on early American sociology. He notes that sociology in America has been significantly more influenced by social psychology than in other countries, that American social research has tended toward the quantitative and therefore away from history, but that the migration of European sociologists and social scientists to America in the 1930s and 1940s had a remarkable influence on the development of social theory and social research.

Jennifer Platt's (1996) *A History of Sociological Research Methods in America, 1920–1960,* is a comprehensive and well-contextualized analysis of research methods in American sociology in the twentieth century. Neil Smelser's (2003) "Sociology: Spanning Two Centuries" combines a historical view of sociology's development in the twentieth century with insightful projections about the movement of sociology in the new millennium.

Histories of the American Sociological Association (ASA) by Lawrence Rhoades (1981) and Katherine J. Rosich (2005) focus on the umbrella organization of American sociology. Other histories may be found that focus more specifically on subdisciplines, specific areas of study, academic departments, and professional organizations. *A Centennial Bibliography of the History of American Sociology* by Michael R. Hill, a comprehensive and well-developed research tool, was prepared for the 2005 Centennial Celebration of the ASA.

THE ORIGINS AND EARLY DEVELOPMENT OF NORTH AMERICAN SOCIOLOGY

The rise of sociology in the United States was not the result of a straightforward transplantation of European ideas to American soil. To be sure, early American sociologists drew upon the European legacy, but they did so selectively, in some cases critically, and adapted European ideas to American experience and conditions. In addition, some streams of thought, for example, pragmatism, appeared to arise from distinctive aspects of the nineteenth-century American context in the decades following the Civil War.

The European Legacy

In common with the other social sciences, sociology traces its modern intellectual lineage to the eighteenth-century Enlightenments of France, Germany, and Britain. It was in these contexts that both general and specific social sciences were first proposed and foundational ideas advanced. Of particular significance was the idea of distinguishing between state and society, including the assumption that state forms were malleable and contingent, subject to human design, whereas societies included both malleable and more or less permanent features resistant to human intervention or wholesale change.

Baron de Montesquieu pioneered a sociological approach to the classification and study of societies focusing on their social laws and institutional organization. Condorcet, his successor, extended the goal of the scientific study of society with a strong commitment to the idea of progress. In Germany, Immanuel Kant developed a synthetic view of knowledge showing the necessity of both rational and empirical aspects of any possible science. J. G. Herder developed the idea of societies as coterminous with cultures that could be understood as unified wholes based on common language and living patterns. In Scotland, Adam Smith pioneered the idea of making specific human institutions and processes, for instance, the division of labor, objects of new "moral sciences." Adam Ferguson and John Millar called specific attention to the significance of social rank or stratification as an object of study. In all of these cases, human societies, institutions, and practices were regarded as objects of systematic observation without recourse to theological speculation or nonnaturalistic modes of explanation. At the same time, the Enlightenment philosophers shared the view that increases in our knowledge and understanding of human societies and social processes could be expected to lead to the improvement of society and hence of human welfare. By the end of the eighteenth century, the way had been prepared for the establishment of social sciences as specific disciplines with defined frames of analysis and inquiry.

Taking their cue from Condorcet, both Henri de Saint-Simon and Auguste Comte worked out ideas for a new science of society to be called *sociology*. This new science was to comprise both rational and empirical methods in the study of both structural (*social statics*) and processual (*social dynamics*) aspects of society. Above all, this new science was to contribute to our knowledge of human social evolution and to the improvement of human societies by the application of sociological knowledge to social life. Comte set forth his detailed vision and program of sociology in his six-volume work *Cours de philosophie positive, 1830–1842*.

During the nineteenth century, the formative center of gravity of the new field of sociology shifted from France to England. First of all, the promulgation of Comte's ideas for sociology became the project of Harriet Martineau, the English political-economist and writer whose 1853 translation remains the standard version (Martineau 1853). Martineau, who in 1838 declined a publisher's invitation to preside over the establishment of a new journal of sociology, published over 70 volumes of essays and research over the next several decades on topical questions of the period, such as the effects of industrialization, occupational and social change, urbanization, work and work conditions, socialization, race relations, women's roles, to name but a few (Hill and Hoecker-Drysdale 2001; Hoecker-Drysdale 1992). Especially noteworthy were her empirical and critical macro-studies of American society based on extensive fieldwork, direct observation, and interviews conducted over a two-year period; her contributions to the public discourse concerning the abolition of slavery; and her analysis of the subjugation of women (Martineau 2004). Her *How to Observe Morals and Manners,* 1838, the first treatise on methodology in sociology, provides still valuable instruction for researchers (Martineau 1989).

The theoretical development of the social sciences was aided by John Stuart Mill, whose 1843 work, *A System of Logic,* outlined methodological ideas for the social sciences. Herbert Spencer wrote several influential books on sociology, including *Social Statics,* 1851, *The Study of Sociology,* 1873, and *The Principles of Sociology,* 1882. Spencer made extensive use of biological, especially organismic, analogies in his analysis of society ("society is an organism"), and is best known as a theorist of societal evolution paralleling the Darwinian model.

The Emergence of American Sociology: 1850–1890

Not unlike the situation in Britain and Europe, American sociology emerged out of a number of influences: the prevalence of, and interest in, political economy; concern with social problems, including poverty with increasing urbanization; workers' situations in nineteenth-century industrialization (Martineau, Florence Kelley, Edith Abbott); a strong interest in the methodologies of

social research (Martineau, Spencer, Comte, Durkheim, Charles Booth, Beatrice, and Sidney Webb); empirical investigations of families and workers (Booth, the Webbs, Jane Addams, Florence Kelley, and others); the increasing use of ecological and statistical analyses (Booth, Durkheim, Kelley, and Clara Collett); analyses of gender and class (Thorstein Veblen, Max Weber, the Webbs, C. P. Gilman, and Lester Ward) and race relations (Martineau, W. E. B. Du Bois, Annie Julia Cooper, Ida B. Wells-Barnett, Mary Church Tyrell, and Fannie Barrier Williams).

Generally, sociology's early figures practiced sociology as a response to the societal needs and problems, serious questions and issues about social change in urban industrial contexts, and the desire to know more about the social factors affecting people's lives. However, sociology was struggling for recognition as a positive science based on empirical observation, a progressive accumulation of facts, and provable theories. By the end of the second period in America, around 1920, sociology's history became regarded as anachronistic and unimportant, except, of course, for some, like Albion Small, who were committed to this aspect of sociology. New theories, concepts, and methodologies were seen to stand on their own, as abstract tools of timeless meaning. The various debates and tensions between theory and empiricism became pronounced by the mid-twentieth century in America. Today, however, in the early twenty-first century, though tensions remain, the history of sociology is acknowledged as essential to our understanding of sociology; to the critique of our research goals, tools, and findings; and to suggestions for new directions in our research.

The impetus for the rise of sociology in North America, first in the United States and later in Canada, was provided by a number of developments. First, a major influence among the North American founders of sociology, academic and nonacademic, was their philanthropic and humanistic, even moralistic, concerns. American Protestant ministers and/or offspring of ministers whose concern for the effects of the experiences of immigration, urbanization, industrialization, and accompanying dislocation, poverty, family disorganization, and crime combined an interest in exploring and understanding these developments with a desire to find solutions to society's problems. In the same way, women and black Americans were pursuing research to address social issues and problems of gender and race. "In short, like every other distinct thought-phenomenon, the American sociological movement was a child of its time" (Small 1916:724). Small points out that this quest to understand societal problems was prevalent as early as the mid-nineteenth century (pp. 723–24). The American Civil War and its Jim Crow aftermath created the realization that "work was ahead to bring American conditions into tolerable likeness to American ideals" (p. 725). Harriet Martineau had concluded in her antebellum studies of America that the contradictions between stated American values and the realities of race and gender discrimination and subjugation posed a grave danger to the social fabric of American society, and indeed to the survival of the young republic (Martineau 2004).

In their analysis of American sociology, Stephen Turner and Jonathan Turner (1990) emphasize the moral concerns, in large part fueled by abolitionist values and activities that fed into reform movements and professional organizations during and after the Civil War. Many reformers recognized that these provided more efficacious avenues for improvement in human affairs than political parties. The authors further point to the fact that this interesting relationship between sociologists and reformers became riddled with tensions between the establishment of sociology as a science, still regarded with trepidation by some, and the demands for social reform led by religious reformers, particularly (pp. 12–15).

As young women in the late nineteenth and early twentieth centuries began to attend universities in the United States and Canada, they applied their educations and training in empirical methods to pursue their philanthropic interests and social concerns about various groups and social problems in the community. The outstanding instance, rather parallel to the collaboration of Charles Booth and Beatrice and Sidney Webb in England, is Jane Addams and the Hull House women (Deegan 1988, 1991, 2002). A great deal of research along with fresh perspectives have revealed the critical roles in theory, empirical research, social policy, and applied sociology that women have played in the emergence of sociology since Harriet Martineau's generation (Deegan 1991; Lengermann and Niebrugge-Brantley 1998; Reinharz 1992, 1993); and indeed, in the Western world since the Enlightenment (McDonald 1993, 1994, 1998). For a look at North American women's narratives about their experiences as sociologists in the twentieth century, see works by Ann Goetting and Sarah Fenstermaker (1995), Barbara Laslett and Barrie Thorne (1997), and Deegan (1991).

The second factor in the emergence of North American sociology lay in the need to legitimate a new social science with its focus on society and collectivities that made claims not only to its own distinctive object of study but also to its place as a science among others following natural science paradigms, an objective perspective on social life using scientific methodologies, quantitative analyses, logical reasoning, and verifiable results (Smelser 2003). Tension between the model of sociology as a traditional scientific discipline and the model of sociology as a humanistic, interpretive field of study can be found in most decades and particularly in the interwar and post–World War II periods (Lundberg 1947; Lynd 1939). Certainly Lester Ward (1883) as well as Albion Small and George Vincent (1894) were interested in establishing sociology's scientific stature within the social sciences.

A third aspect of this endeavor has to do with the organizational foundations of this new field of study as an academic discipline, a recognizable and legitimate source of data for broader public use, and an acceptable, credible enterprise for the "study of mankind" (Stuart Chase). These foundations include not only the institutionalization of sociology in higher education but also recognition through the organization of professional associations and by governments, foundations, unions, business and industry, and society at large of the value of sociological research and of the profession. Sociology in the United States was born out of the concerns and interests of individuals trained in the related fields of history, economics, political science, psychology, and religion. Blasi (2004) shows that the early faculty in sociology often held doctorates in history (several at Johns Hopkins), philosophy (Dewey, Mead), and economics (E. A. Ross, Veblen). The earliest departments not surprisingly had at least one of the founding male academics associated with them: Yale—Sumner; Columbia—Giddings; Brown—Ward; Chicago—Small; and Wisconsin—E. A. Ross.

Fourth, it should be emphasized that in sociology's early period, many important sociologists were outside of academe so that while doing sociological theory and empirical research, they were generally not considered part of the founding generation nor what became the sociological establishment. Many of these were either trained in other disciplines, worked outside colleges and universities, and/or were women and minorities, particularly African Americans, who had specific perspectives on minority needs. The matter of trained membership in the profession becomes more complex when one considers the profound impact of European and other immigrant scholars in various time periods. In addition to research by academics, major projects took up pragmatic inquiries, as in the works of Ida B. Wells-Barnett on lynching (1892, 1900) and Ann J. Cooper on racism (1892) and *The Hull House Maps and Papers* in Chicago (1895). Survey research had begun in the American context with the Pittsburgh survey by Paul U. Kellogg, 1907–1909, and even earlier with the labor surveys of H. K. Oliver in the Massachusetts Bureau of Statistics of Labor in the 1870s that were successful in showing both the usefulness and the problems in survey research (Turner and Turner 1990:15, 32–33).

The Founding of Academic Sociology: 1890–1920

The early stages of American sociology can be best understood in terms of the major figures and the theoretical and methodological debates in North America at the time. Albion Small (1854–1926), Lester Frank Ward (1841–1913), William Graham Sumner (1840–1910), and Franklin H. Giddings (1855–1931), among the most influential of the male founders of sociology, were significantly influenced by the work and ideas of their European predecessors. Women founders in this generation, extending the tradition of Martineau, Besant, Butler, Tristan, and Webb (Lengermann and Niebrugge-Brantley 1998) and influenced by these predecessors, included Anna Garlin Spencer (1851–1932), Jane Addams (1860–1935), Charlotte Perkins Gilman (1860–1935), Florence Kelley (1859–1932), Edith Abbott (1876–1957), Sophonisba Breckinridge (1886–1948), Marion Talbot (1858–1947), Emily Greene Balch (1867–1961), Ida B. Wells-Barnett (1862–1931), and many others (Deegan 1991). Several of these women held faculty positions and most published in sociology journals and conducted sociological research within and outside of academe.

Sociology as a discipline entered academe in the form of courses, specific faculty interests, and ultimately departmental structures. Courses were offered in other disciplines, especially political economy and political science, that were sociological in content if not in title. The first sociology course was taught by William Graham Sumner at Yale in 1875. Albion Small, in 1890 at Colby College, announced that he had changed the focus of an important course to "moral science" and "sociological philosophy" that included "descriptive sociology," "statical sociology," and "dynamic sociology" (Coser 1978:292–93) and chaired the first Department of Sociology at Chicago in 1892.

From the beginning in North American sociology, there were differences in perspectives, predominantly between evolutionary naturalism that predicates immutable laws of evolution (Spencer, Sumner) and progressive evolutionism that suggested humans had evolved to a stage of emancipation and liberation from the imperatives of nature (Ward, Small) (Fine 1976; Smelser 2003:9–10). The conflicts in assumptions and approaches in sociology reflected differences in values and priorities for the study of society that had been embedded in the lives of the early sociological founders.

It was the struggle, then, between evolutionary, naturalism and social Darwinism against progressive evolutionism that dominated the intellectual and institutional development of sociology during its first two decades, as shown by William F. Fine (1976). The naturalistic or Darwinist evolution emphasized the inevitability of structures, classes, and natural processes that would shape the social world. Progressive evolutionism emphasized human distinctiveness, the creation of the sociocultural world, mastery over nature, humans' developing freedom, and pursuit of values. It challenged the evolutionist idea of inevitable transition according to natural laws and emphasized human agency, free will, and progress as consequences of human actions. Nevertheless, both perspectives identified the need, indeed necessity, for the scientific study of social life and for new knowledge to address specific developments and problems in society. Both sides were building the case for sociology. Turner and Turner (1990) comment on the blending of positivism, organicism, and individualism as American sociology moved forward to establish itself as a science:

What emerges in early American sociology, then, are programmatic commitments to (1) a science that seeks to develop abstract general theory and (2) a combination of individualism/mentalism that is reconciled in an uneasy alliance with evolutionism, organicism, and implicit functionalism. (P. 18)

One must recognize the additional fact of social reformism that was particularly dominant in America in the first two decades of the twentieth century.

During the last decade of the nineteenth century and the first decades of the twentieth century, a number of basic textbooks were published: Albion W. Small and George E. Vincent, *An Introduction to the Study of Society,* 1894; Lester Ward, *Outline of Sociology,* 1898; and Ernest Burgess and Robert Park, *An Introduction to the Science of Sociology,* 1921. Important studies produced in the United States included W. E. B. DuBois, *The Philadelphia Negro,* 1899; Thorstein Veblen, *The Theory of the Leisure Class,* 1899; Edward A. Ross, *Social Control,* 1901; Charles Horton Cooley, *Human Nature and Social Order,* 1902; William Graham Sumner, *Folkways,* 1906; Cooley, *Social Organization,* 1909; George Herbert Mead, "The Social Self," 1913; Ernest Burgess, *The Science of Sociology,* 1921; E. A. Ross, *Principles of Sociology,* 1901; W. I. Thomas, *The Unadjusted Girl,* 1923; Frederic Thrasher, *The Gang,* 1927; and Robert E. Park and E. W. Burgess, *The City,* 1925.

Studies by women that used the methodologies and analyses of sociology but were often done outside of academe included Ida B. Wells, *Southern Horror: Lynch Law in all its Phases,* 1892; Matilda Joslin Cage, *Women, Church and State,* 1893; Florence Kelley, *The Sweating System* and *Wage-Earning Children,* 1895; Charlotte Perkins Gilman, *Women and Economics,* 1898; Frances Kellor, *Experimental Sociology,* 1901; Emily Green Balch, *A Study of Conditions in City Life: With Special Reference to Boston,* 1903; C. P. Gilman, *Human Work,* 1904; Jane Addams, *The Subjective Need for Social Settlements,* 1892; *Democracy and Ethics,* 1902; "Trade Unions and Public Duty" and "Problems of Municipal Administrations," in the *American Journal of Sociology* and over 500 other publications; Edith Abbott, *Women in Industry,* 1910; and Olive Schreiner, *Women and Labour,* 1911.

The roles played by women sociologists during this period exemplified in many ways the tensions and differences in perspectives among the early founders of sociology. Women who were not Ph.D.s in sociology, such as Martineau, Beatrice Webb, Josephine Butler, Annie Besant, and Jane Addams, had been doing sociological research and theorizing in the nineteenth century in England, Europe, and North America. Their work was most often associated with social reform, philanthropy, social policy making, the abolition movement, and suffrage politics in large part because these educated and trained women identified community issues, social injustices, individual and group needs, and social trends that required study, exposure, and action.

As Mary Jo Deegan (1991:8) points out, there were a number of "firsts" for women sociologists in the nineteenth century. Rose R. Firestone received her doctorate in sociology from the University of Wooster (Ohio) in 1887; Mary Roberts Coolidge became an Assistant Professor in Sociology at Stanford University in 1894; Ida B. Wells-Barnett became the first black woman practicing sociologist (journalist) with her publications in the 1890s; Anna Julia Cooper (Ph.D., Sorbonne, 1925) wrote *A Voice of the South* in 1892; Marion Talbot became the first woman assistant professor sociologist at the University of Chicago in 1892.

Black American sociology made further inroads toward establishing its place within sociology with W. E. B. Du Bois's *The Philadelphia Negro,* 1896, a brilliant study using a variety of methodologies, and *The Souls of Black Folk,* 1903. Along with E. Franklin Frazier and later Oliver Cox, Du Bois not only produced groundbreaking analyses of blacks in America but also ensured that research on minorities would become a critical part of the sociological enterprise.

The Establishment of
Professional Organizations

Early organizational formations such as the American Social Science Association (1865–1885) founded by Franklin B. Sanborn brought together academics and nonacademics with scientific, historical, or philanthropic interests (Haskell 1977; Small 1916). In 1903, African American Jesse Lawson (1856–1927) formed the National Sociological Society (NSS), an organization of white and black men from the North and the South to address, among other things, the race problem (Hill 2005a:126–40). The organization collapsed a year later because of publicity problems, the splintering of potential members into several black organizations like the American Negro Academy, the reluctance of Du Bois and B. T. Washington to get involved in NSS, and the turn of the American Sociological Society (ASS) away from social reform and activism (Hill 2005a).

At the December 1905 Annual Meeting of the American Economics Association (AEA) at the Johns Hopkins University in Baltimore, C. W. A. Veditz of George Washington University called a meeting of the sociologists present, to be held on December 27, to determine whether a section of sociologists should be formed within the AEA or another existing association, or whether the group should form an entirely new sociological association. Sociologists were surveyed in advance to explore their general thoughts on the matter. The nearly 50 attendees included Albion Small, E. A. Ross, Lester F. Ward, Thomas Carver, William Davenport, Anna Garlin Spencer, and Franklin Giddings among others. In one day a subcommittee (Cooley, Veditz, Wilcox, Wells, and Lindsay) produced a constitution. All articles were passed unanimously after limited discussion, officers were nominated and elected, and the first Annual Meeting of the ASS's 115 members (women and men) was held on December 27–29, 1906, in Providence, RI. Of the charter members, 14 would serve as presidents of the ASS (Rhoades 1981:1–5). The first executive committee consisted of Lester F. Ward, president,

William G. Sumner, first vice president, Franklin H. Giddings, second vice president, and C. W. A. Veditz, secretary-treasurer, plus six elected council members. The *American Journal of Sociology,* the first professional sociology journal in America, founded in 1895 at the University of Chicago by Albion Small, became and served as the official journal of the ASS until the *American Sociological Review* was established in 1936.

The major and best-known figures in this founding generation were Albion Small, Lester Frank Ward, William Graham Sumner, and Franklin H. Giddings. Others such as George Vincent, E. A. Ross, Thomas Carver, and William Davenport were also active in the new discipline. The ASS became important in the promotion of the social sciences, the creation of the Social Science Research Council, the establishment of the *Encyclopedia of the Social Sciences,* the development of the American Council of Learned Societies, and the advancement of the social sciences in the curriculum of public schools. Other accomplishments included the journal *Social Science Abstracts,* the *Dictionary of American Biography,* a national social science fraternity—Alpha Pi Zeta, and the *American Yearbook* (Rhoades 1981:6–7). Membership in ASS increased from 115 in 1905 to 1,530 in 1930. As the society grew in size and complexity, controversy arose regarding structure, fragmentation, the annual meeting format, and publications (Rhoades 1981:11–17).

Albion Small trained for the clergy, studied in Germany for two years and at Johns Hopkins for a year, and served as professor and president of Colby College for three years before he went to Chicago. He was a key figure in the first two decades of the movement to establish sociology as a recognized social science because he took initiative in founding the necessary formal structures. He was appointed the first Head Professor of Sociology at the University of Chicago in 1892. He served as founding editor of the *American Journal of Sociology* for 30 years, and played a key role in the establishment of the ASS, of which he served as the fourth president in 1912–1913. Small was especially concerned that sociology study, understand, and compile its own history. He emphasized the importance for young sociologists to know the history of their discipline, an idea reiterated by ASA at its 2005 annual meetings when it recommended that every department establish a course on the history of sociology. Small's (1916) *Fifty Years of Sociology in the United States (1865–1915)* is an invaluable source of information on American sociology's earliest period. In many respects he reflects the creative tensions in early sociology to relate philosophy and sociology, science and value, historical and interpretive understanding of the social, and the application of specific knowledge to society's problems, issues, and conflicts.

Lester Frank Ward, president of the ASS in 1906 and 1907, published (at his own expense) the first major work in American sociology, *Dynamic Sociology,* in 1883. Ward, a man of working-class origins and a varied educational and work background, came to the discipline with an interest in the science of society, taking up an evolutionary theory of societal change that depended on the forces of matter, motion, and energy and moved in a progressive direction. Ward, in addressing the tension between the intellectual pursuit of understanding, on the one hand, and the application of sociological knowledge to improve society, on the other, saw sociology as a field with pure and applied divisions that studied both statics and dynamics, a Spencerian influence.

William Graham Sumner served as the second president of the ASS from 1908 to 1910. He had studied in Germany and England and spent most of his career teaching at Yale. In many respects Sumner can be seen as the pioneer of the anthropological tradition in sociology because of his compilation and theorizing about folkways and mores in societies. He was akin to Darwin and Spencer in defending the inevitability of social change and the imperatives of nature that worked in the social world as in the natural world. He disliked reformers and anyone who would pretend to social engineering. Sumner defended the status quo in such works as *What the Social Classes Owe Each Other,* 1883, and was convinced that social problems will take care of themselves through the elimination of people who perpetuate them. While both Ward and Sumner emphasized that human behavior was driven by biological and psychological drives as well as social motives, Ward emphasized the significance of the individual within a progressive collectivity. He believed that change, deliberate as well as natural, was dominant over a structured social order of inevitable social classes and group stratifications that Sumner emphasized.

Franklin H. Giddings, the fourth major founder, became the third president of the ASS, 1910–1912. Giddings worked as a journalist, had no graduate degrees, but received several honorary doctorates. Odum (1951) tells us that Giddings "was appointed to what is estimated the first full professorship of sociology in America in 1894" (p. 87) at Columbia. He was, above all, a teacher. "His influence upon sociology was measured in terms of his textbooks, his lectures and teachings, and the continued extension of his work by more than fifty PhD graduates who held top positions in college, university, publishing, and public affairs" (p. 87).

In the founding generation (1900–1920), many women began their careers with full intent to become professional sociologists and social scientists. Women such as Edith Abbott, Emily Balch, Sophonisba Breckinridge, Charlotte Gilman, Florence Kelley, and Annie Marion MacLean established connections with Jane Addams's Hull House where the theory and practice of Chicago sociology continued under her influence and collaboration (Deegan 1991:16). That women most often ended up in tangential departments (social work, statistics, anthropology, union work, labor departments, and community service) and often outside academe was a particular function of the male culture and personnel in sociology at the time.

Nonetheless, women contributed a great deal to sociological research, social policy, and social reform (Deegan 1988, 1991).

There were exceptions among the men of course. Albion Small offered Jane Addams (BA, Rockford Female Seminary, 1881) teaching positions in the Chicago sociology department, which she declined to work instead in the community through Hull House. Cooley, Ross, and Bogardus cited Addams's writings in their works, and Lester Ward was a defender of women's rights, talents, and contributions. George Herbert Mead was active in the suffrage movement (Deegan 1988:208–11). Jane Addams, representative of women who became committed to social causes and the movement to facilitate community change, led an active campaign for peace in the years before World War I, but suffered public ostracism and professional marginalization as a result. She was awarded the Nobel Peace Prize in 1931; Emily Greene Balch, a student of Giddings, also won the Nobel Peace Prize in 1946. Greene received support and encouragement from George E. Howard and W. E. B. Du Bois (Deegan 1991:55–62). Most important for our purposes here is the recognition and knowledge that women who experienced discrimination in educational environments nonetheless were present in every sense at the beginning and at every subsequent stage in the development of American sociology.

Securing the Place of Sociology as the Science of Society and the Study of Social Change and Crises: 1920–1940

In the period of transition from the post–World War I war decade to the realities of economic depression from 1929 onward, sociology expanded its repertoire of statistical analyses, use of survey methods, development of large research projects often at the impetus of government, and began to rise in visibility as the tools, methods, and approaches offered by this new social science became increasingly known and solicited. An historic project requested by President Hoover and headed by William F. Ogburn and Howard W. Odum resulted in the 1933 *Recent Social Trends,* which revealed the major trends in America in technology, the economy, population, the family, urbanization, education, and other areas. It was an exercise in demonstrating the potential of sociology to serve policy making as well as scientific goals. It was intended to provide background and context for reforms during the Depression and became a standard reference work for government and educators for some time to come.

New methodologies in sociology—participant observation, various types of interviews, questionnaires, use of government and private documents and archives—had been evolving since the nineteenth century. In their methodologically instructive *The Polish Peasant in Europe and America,* 1918, W. I. Thomas and Florian Znaniecki used a public call for immigrants' autobiographies as well as letters and diaries to explore the Polish experience in the early twentieth century. This project and W. I. Thomas's *The Unadjusted Girl,* 1923, were funded by philanthropists and social welfare leaders, Helen Culver and Ethel Surges Dummer (Platt 1996:143). The proliferation of empirical studies in sociology by 1920 brought with it the need for research funding, gleaned first from private individuals, then from foundations, and finally from government.

During this period the John D. Rockefeller Foundation, established by the man who founded the University of Chicago, was the largest single supporter of sociological research. The Laura Spelman Rockefeller Memorial Fund, 1918–1929, funded sociological research particularly at Chicago, Columbia, Harvard, North Carolina, and the Social Science Research Council (Platt 1996:144). The Institute for Social and Religious Research (ISRR) (originally the Committee on Social and Religious Surveys) at Chicago was supported originally by Rockefeller to conduct research and analyses of the church as an institution and on social and religious movements using the scientific approach (Turner and Turner 1990:39–84). The Institute sponsored the well-known Middletown studies in 1923 but later rejected Robert and Helen Lynd's book as long and too descriptive; Lynd left, published the books with Harcourt, and situated himself at Columbia. Rockefeller withdrew his support from ISRR in 1932, in spite of its support of research by Park and others, because the statistical rigor and absence of practical value of the research were not in line with the expectations of supporters and readers (p. 45). Rockefeller supported from 1927 to 1932 the Local Community Research Committee where Robert E. Park was a central figure and the Social Science Research Council (p. 51).

The Social Science Research Council, a federation of learned societies, was one of the first interdisciplinary research bodies with academics from economics, political science, sociology, and statistics involved in the encouragement of joint research and the development of a scientific methodology. The *Encyclopedia of the Social Sciences,* published in 1934, was also a cooperative project of all the social sciences. Symposia that explored the state of the social sciences resulted, in one instance, in *Recent Developments in the Social Sciences,* 1927, edited by E. C. Hayes. Social research in universities increasingly received monetary support from Rockefeller and others, particularly Howard Odum's Institute for Research in Social Science at North Carolina.

In the contexts of the Depression and World War II, sociologists were increasingly (1) funded to do massive reports on specific social problems or issues and (2) employed by various government agencies and departments: Works Progress Administration (1935–1943), the U.S. Department of Agriculture, Tennessee Valley Authority, the Natural Resources Committee, and other state and local agencies, as well as the Office of Strategic Services, the Office of Population Affairs, the Department of State, the Agricultural Experiment Stations at the

land-grant universities, the Bureau of the Census where Philip Hauser played a major role, and, from World War II on, the U.S. military departments (Platt 1996:150–53).

This period set the stage for the founding of other departments, graduate programs, journals, research institutes, and major empirical studies and their expansions in numbers during the 1920s. The figures show considerable growth. Not only had the general undergraduate population in the United States increased from 462,445 in 1920 to nearly a million by 1930 with a subsequent rise in interest in the social sciences, but also the number of undergraduate textbooks in sociology had increased from 10 before 1919 to 26 in the following decade. The number of graduate students trebled from 1920 to 1930; the number of graduate degrees increased threefold from 1918 to 1924; and the number of Ph.D. degrees awarded in 1930 was four times the 1920 figure (Hinkle and Hinkle 1954:18).

Sociology as an organized profession in the 1920s and 1930s was an almost exclusively white male enterprise. Nevertheless, institutions like Jane Addams's Hull House in Chicago became important centers for women to do research, publications, community service, and to develop a culture of women-centered sociological work. Interestingly, women were seen as strong in research, statistical work, and demography (Margaret Hagood, Alva Myrdal, Dorothy Swaine Thomas, and Irene Taeuber). The next generation of women sociologists being trained at Columbia in the 1930s and 1940s included Mirra Komarovsky, Gladys Meyer, Alice Rossi, and Grace Coyle, and at Chicago, Rose Hum Lee, Ethel Shanas, and Helena Znaniecki Lopata. Jessie Bernard, Helen McGill Hughes, Elizabeth Briant Lee, Carolyn Rose, and Alice Rossi were among the women who married men in sociology. The relationships "for better and for worse" often involved collaborative work as couples but frequently posed difficulties for the women's careers (Deegan 1991:18–20).

More quantitative research was accompanied by the expansion of descriptive sociology, that is, qualitative studies within communities beginning with Charles J. Galpin, *The Social Anatomy of a Rural Community,* 1915, which influenced Robert E. Park's work on the city (Park, Burgess, and McKenzie 1925); E. M. Thrasher, *The Gang,* 1927, 1936; Harvey Zorbaugh, *The Gold Coast and the Slum,* 1929; Nels Anderson, *The Hobo,* 1923; Ruth C. Cavan, *Suicide,* 1928; Louis Wirth, *The Ghetto,* 1928; Robert and Helen Lynd, *Middleton,* 1929; Franklin Frazier, *The Negro Family in America,* 1932; Paul Cressey, *The Taxi Dance Hall,* 1932; and many other such studies using multiple methodologies, surveys, interviews, participant observation, diaries, letters, and so on. The factors creating such realities and their actors were seen as multiple and multicausal, creating networks of social relations and communications of a very complex nature.

Increasingly, sociology was moving toward a broader range of subjects of research, often involving other disciplines and contexts, thereby expanding the relevance and visibility of sociology as a discipline. An example of this is the studies by Elton Mayo at the Hawthorne Western Electric Plant in Cicero, Illinois, from 1927 to 1932, as much a study in the sociology of work and industrial relations as in industrial psychology because it demonstrated that work group norms and the informal organization among workers determined productivity.

Professionalization, changes in funding patterns, economic effects of the Depression, and a continuing fragmentation of sociology into numerous associations, journals, subdisciplines, and changing departmental rankings generated conflicts between the oncoming generation of sociologists and the older generations (Turner and Turner 1990:57–65). An indicator of these developments was the decline in membership in the ASS to approximately 1,000 by 1940 (Rhoades 1981:74). Perhaps the most pragmatic division was the separation of rural sociologists from ASA to establish the Rural Sociological Society in 1935 and to establish their own journal, *Rural Sociology.* The impetus for this was, to a considerable degree, increased funding from government and to some extent from the Rockefeller foundation in southern colleges and universities for quantitative research in agricultural contexts (Turner and Turner 1990:51–53).

Added to this were the debates over methodology and scientism, leading to questions like *Knowledge for What? The Place of Social Science in American Culture,* the title of Robert Lynd's (1939) challenge to make sociological research both relevant and scientific. Turner and Turner (1990:39–84) draw our attention to the numerous disputes during the 1930s having to do with sociology's audiences, the efficacy of hypotheses in social research, the tensions between traditional scholarship and technical research and between science and reform, and quantitative versus qualitative methods (pp. 66–67). These debates may have been suppressed during wartime, but they perdured in sociology after the war (George Lundberg's [1947] *Can Science Save Us?*).

Major theoretical works were published during the 1930s. The most original domestic works were the posthumously published books of the social psychologist, George Herbert Mead, based at the University of Chicago (1934, 2001). Mead, a pragmatist, developed ideas of the processes of socialization and the development of the social self that formed the basis for what became known as "symbolic interactionism." Other major theoretical publications of the period included Talcott Parsons's *The Structure of Social Action,* 1937; Pitirim Sorokin's *Social and Cultural Dynamics,* 1937-1939; and Parsons's translation of Max Weber's *The Protestant Ethic and the Spirit of Capitalism,* 1939.

The Emergence of Canadian Sociology

Canadian and American sociology share not only the same continent but also, in some respects, a common history. There were, and perhaps still are, significant differences in the culture of sociology between the two countries, shaped particularly by historical, cultural, and linguistic traditions (see Nichols 2002). However, even given these differences, the histories of Canadian and American sociologies have been intertwined. Sociology in Canada, as in the United States, emerged in the context of the "social gospel" movement, social reform movements, immigration, urbanization, and industrialization. The imperatives of the social gospel movement resulted in the establishment of sociology courses in numerous denominational colleges and church-sponsored social research (Brym 1989:16).

The influence of the Chicago School on Canadian sociology was clear from the beginning of sociology when in 1922 McGill University hired Carl A. Dawson, a Canadian trained by Robert E. Park at Chicago. In 1925, the McGill Department of Sociology was established, new hires were inevitably from Chicago, and Rockefeller funding helped to build sociology at McGill (Brym 1989:17). Strong ties between Canadian and American sociology were thereby established and sustained through the following decades with a substantial traffic of scholars. It can be said that though Canadian research projects were limited in number compared to the United States, the projects and their subsequent books became classics and highly influential in sociology in both countries, the two earliest being Everett C. Hughes's (assisted by wife Helen Hughes) *French Canada in Transition,* 1943, a study of a small city in Québec (Hoecker-Drysdale 1996). Leonard Marsh's *Canadians In and Out of Work,* 1940, the first important analysis of social class in Canadian society. Hughes promoted Park's sociology and helped to accelerate the growth of sociology in Canada through his association with Father Georges-Henri Lévesque, who in 1932 founded l'Ecole des Sciences Sociales at Laval University, the center for early French Canadian sociology. Lévesque's successor, Jean-Charles Falardeau (Ph.D. Laval), another leader in French Canadian sociology, studied with Hughes at Chicago (Falardeau 1967). Léon Gérin (1863–1951), who produced many studies of Québec rural society, and Hughes were both influenced by Frédéric LePlay's family studies. Gérin studied the work of LePlay in Paris and Hughes absorbed the influence of LePlay from Park (Shore 1987:270).

Back in Chicago, Hughes began training Canadian as well as American sociologists, among them Jean Robertson Burnet and Aileen Dansken Ross. (Hoecker-Drysdale 1990:152–76). Although the singular influence of the Chicago School began to wane, the momentum of the traffic of sociologists between Canada and the United States has continued through the decades. Sociology in Canada is an amalgamation of French *sociologie,* the British tradition of political economy, and the American emphasis on social psychology, community studies, and new methodologies. The *éminence grise* of Canadian social science in its earliest decades was Harold Innis (1894–1952), a Chicago Ph.D. in political economy who spent his career at the University of Toronto and played an enormous role in advancing Canadian social science and in developing the privately funded Canadian Social Science Research Council in 1941, predecessor of the Canada Council, a government agency founded in 1957 (Acland and Buxton 1999).

THE "GOLDEN ERA" OF SOCIOLOGY IN THE UNITED STATES: FROM WORLD WAR II TO 1970

Following the dislocations of European sociologists caused by the rise of Nazism in Germany in the 1930s and the devastating consequences of World War II in Europe and the United Kingdom, the United States was positioned to take a preponderant role in the development of sociology in the postwar period. In fact, many of the pacesetting developments in both theory and research occurred in the United States during the years between the end of the war and 1970. This period was also marked by a great expansion on almost all fronts: academic development, professional organizations, journals, and scholarly publications, as well as the increasing role of governments in research funding (Lipset and Smelser 1961). While sociological research programs and methods proliferated in numerous directions, the trends in sociological theory showed a different pattern: at first consolidation around a single dominant paradigm, structural-functionalism, and then, by the 1960s, a substantial turning away from functionalism toward a variety of alternatives, including symbolic interactionism, exchange theory, phenomenology and ethnomethodology, conflict, and critical theory. With some justification Lawrence Rhoades (1981), in his *A History of the American Sociological Association,* designated the period from 1950 to 1970 the "golden era" of American sociology.

With the enrollment of returning American soldiers in large numbers in U.S. colleges and universities, sociology also began to expand rapidly as an academic subject. Although fluctuating, the number of undergraduate degrees awarded in sociology doubled between 1950 and 1965, and more than doubled again by the mid-1970s when they reached a peak of some 35,000 per year. The growth of graduate degrees awarded followed a similar pattern, rising from around 400 M.A.s per year in the 1950s to a high of more than 2,000 in the mid-1970s, and from around 150 Ph.D.s annually in the 1950s to a peak of more than 700 per year in the mid-1970s.

Theoretical Schools and Perspectives

The rise to preeminence of structural-functionalism both in the United States and abroad paralleled the period of postwar American dominance in world affairs. The most influential author of this school was Talcott Parsons of Harvard University, who in collaboration with colleagues in cultural anthropology and social psychology established the Department of Social Relations in 1946, an interdisciplinary

unit that subsumed and replaced the Department of Sociology. Along with various collaborators Parsons attempted to develop a comprehensive, abstract taxonomy of human society in such works as *Towards a General Theory of Action* (1951, edited with Edward Shils) and *The Social System* (1951). Using such concepts as *status, role, norm, value,* and *need,* he sought to develop an analytical language for the elemental properties of societies viewed as social systems, including their relations to personality and culture, also viewed as systems. His focus was on the structural aspects of societies and the *functional requisites* of social systems for their maintenance; hence, the name, structural-functionalism, later referred to more simply as *functionalism.*

Parsons, who was elected president of the ASA in 1949, was joined in promulgating functionalism by a number of his protégés and students. The most influential of these were Robert Merton, Kingsley Davis, Wilbert Moore, and Neil Smelser, all of whom also eventually served as presidents of the ASA. Merton, author of *Social Theory and Social Structure,* 1949, responding to critiques of the highly abstract level of Parsons's theorizing, became known as the advocate of "theories of the middle range." In attempting to clarify the relation between functions, consequences, and intentions, he distinguished between *manifest* and *latent* functions, according to the presence or absence of intention, and between *functions* and *dysfunctions,* according to whether the consequences were positive or negative for a designated social system. Latent functions were conceptually distinct from what Merton famously called the *unanticipated consequences of intentional (or purposive) action,* in that while such consequences are by definition latent, they may be either *functional* (positive) or *dysfunctional* (negative) for a given system. As the second most influential American functionalist, Merton contributed a number of conceptual analyses of several middle-range phenomena: anomie, social deviance, role, and reference group analysis.

In a 1945 article, "Some Principles of Stratification," published in the *American Sociological Review,* Kingsley Davis and Wilbert Moore articulated the so-called functional theory of social stratification. They argued that systems of stratification, for all their structured inequalities in the distribution of rewards (e.g., prestige, income), are universal because they are functionally necessary to provide motivations for people to seek to fill the positions a society most needs. The claim for the functional necessity of social stratification became identified as a signature position for functionalism and a point of contention in the eyes of later critics. While the claim of universality of stratification could be subjected to empirical test on the basis of the presence or absence of specific indicators of stratification, the claim of functional necessity was difficult if not impossible to prove or disprove, leading to the interpretation that functionalists provided justifications for the continuing existence of institutionalized forms of social and economic inequality, regardless of their "necessity."

Neil Smelser's affiliation with functionalism stemmed from his collaborative work with Parsons on *Economy and Society,* 1956, while he was still a graduate student at Harvard in the 1950s. He is properly considered a neo-functionalist on account of both a generational difference and a departure from the strict formulations of Parsonsian functionalism. In addition to economic sociology, the fields of social change and collective behavior have been the focus of his work. His focus on comparative methods, social change, and historical subject matter tended to set him apart from most of the other functionalists.

In his 1959 ASA presidential address, "The Myth of Functional Analysis as a Special Method in Sociology and Anthropology," Kingsley Davis proclaimed that functional analysis, rather than being simply one among several alternative "methods" of sociology, was tantamount to sociological explanation *tout court.* In the eyes of functionalists, this proclamation represented the moment of virtually complete ascendancy of functionalism as the preeminent, if not actually the only, paradigm of sociological theory and analysis. Yet by the late 1950s, functionalism had become the target of a number of influential critiques, including especially those by David Lockwood, Ralf Dahrendorf, and C. Wright Mills. The issues flagged by these critiques were, among others, charges of a functionalist bias toward value consensus as opposed to conflict, toward normative order instead of change, and toward abstract "grand theory" instead of empirically testable ideas. Lewis Coser's (1956) *The Functions of Social Conflict* attempted to bridge functionalism and the study of conflict.

The critiques of functionalism continued in the next decade. In his 1961 article in the *American Sociological Review,* "The Oversocialized Conception of Man," Dennis Wrong charged that functionalism's exaggeration of societal integration was based on a faulty conception of personality as being fully malleable to fit the needs of a social system. In 1962, Edward Tiryakian published *Sociologism and Existentialism,* in which he attempted to broaden awareness of the theoretical perspectives beyond the functionalist tradition. During the 1960s, functionalism was challenged not only by its critics, but also by rival perspectives that had been present but overshadowed by functionalism in the postwar period, especially *exchange theory* and *symbolic interactionism.* Exchange theory was developed by George Homans, a departmental colleague of Parsons at Harvard, as an attempt to explain the social behavior of the individual on the basis of principles drawn from Skinnerian psychology and elementary economics. According to Homans's views in his 1961 *Social Behavior: Its Elementary Forms,* neither the social group (as for Durkheim) nor the social structure (as for Parsons), but the individual, was the basic unit of analysis. The behavior of individuals is conceived as a set of exchanges that bring rewards and costs, the calculation of which is carried forward in the conduct of future behavior. Peter Blau, an Austrian émigré from the Nazi period, made a significant contribution to the study of bureaucracy with his 1955 *The Dynamics of Bureaucracy* before turning explicitly to exchange theory in his 1964 *Exchange and Power in Social Life.* While Blau, like Homans, relied on psychological propositions to explain individual orientations to exchange, he demonstrated a broader concern with social structure as both context and result of exchange processes. Through his analyses of processes of exchange based on individual decision making, Blau can also be regarded as a pioneer of *theories of rational choice.* Both Homans and Blau served terms as presidents of the ASA, Homans in 1964, and Blau in 1974.

The most prominent representative of *symbolic interactionism* in the tradition of Mead during this period was Herbert Blumer, who began as a student of Mead, and like Mead, spent half of his influential career in the sociology department of the University of Chicago. Known primarily as an interpreter of Mead's ideas, Blumer sought to distinguish more clearly between stimulus-response models of behavioral psychology and the symbolic or meaningful components of social interaction. In his 1969 *Symbolic Interaction: Perspective and Method,* Blumer argued the view that all stimuli are first interpreted by actors in terms of their meanings before the actor responds (acts). This means that sociological analysis must necessarily focus on the subjective aspects of behavior and take into account the standpoint of the actor. Social structures, when acknowledged at all by Blumer, were regarded mainly as constraints on action that nevertheless have to be interpreted by the actor. One of Blumer's students, Erving Goffman, continued the Meadean tradition by developing a variant called *dramaturgy.* In his 1959 *The Presentation of Self in Everyday Life,* Goffman refashioned the symbolic interactionist notion of role playing into what he referred to as *impression management,* as part of a set of theatrical metaphors. Goffman's 1961 *Encounters* and 1963 *Stigma,* influential works of the period, presented innovative ideas of self, identity, and interaction. The continuing influence of symbolic interactionism was indicated by the election to the presidency of the ASA of Blumer, in 1956, and his student, Goffman, in 1982.

The decade of the 1960s was a period of social and political turmoil in the United States and a time when received ideas in sociology were called into question in terms of their implications for public policy and social values. The most direct challenge to functionalism, widely portrayed as conservative and as morally indifferent to issues of poverty, racism, and the war in Vietnam, came from *conflict theories.* In spite of divergent views on certain questions, such as the necessity or universality of conflict, most conflict theorists claimed that conflict is endemic to most forms of group life and is often associated with power and coercion, phenomena neglected by functionalism. The type of conflict theory that came to the fore in the 1960s, however, reflected the view that much conflict and coercion was not only unnecessary but was actually oppressive and socially unjust with respect to issues of class, race, gender, and international relations (colonialism and imperialism).

C. Wright Mills of Columbia University had been first among American sociologists of this period to critique not only functionalism but the structures of class and power elites in American society. The critique of society was also put forward by neo-Marxist *critical theorists* of the Frankfurt School, several of whom had come to the United States in the 1930s as refugees from Nazi Germany, including Theodor Adorno, Max Horkheimer, Herbert Marcuse, Erich Fromm, and Leo Lowenthal. Their critique of advanced industrial societies attracted many of those who studied or entered sociology during the 1960s and who participated in the New Left, a broad and somewhat amorphous political and countercultural movement directed at first toward domestic issues of poverty and civil rights, and later became a significant anti-Vietnam War movement. Domestic neo-Marxist analyses were developed by Paul Baran and Paul Sweezy in their 1966 *Monopoly Capital.*

Among the significant alternatives to functionalism to receive attention in the 1960s were the developments in phenomenology. Having originated in European philosophy through the work and influence of Edmund Husserl, phenomenology was imported to the United States by the émigré sociologist Alfred Schutz. From his location in the New School for Social Research, he taught and influenced a number of sociologists who promulgated *social phenomenology.* Peter Berger, a student of Schutz and also an émigré, was perhaps the most prominent representative of this school during the 1960s, when he published his 1966 *The Social Construction of Reality,* coauthored with Thomas Luckmann, and subsequently, as he moved into the specific field of the sociology of religion. Also influenced by Schutz, Harold Garfinkel's contributions to social phenomenology, designated as *ethnomethodology,* are exemplified in his collection *Studies in Ethnomethodology,* 1967.

By the end of the 1960s, sociology had undergone a major transformation in its theoretical dimension. For most of the 1940s and 1950s, functionalism had been the predominant school, without significant challenge from competing perspectives. The dominance of functionalism had given the appearance of theoretical unity, if not scientific maturity, by the apparent lack of diversity in theoretical orientations. All this changed in the 1960s when functionalism was challenged not only by direct critiques but also by the rise of competing perspectives, especially symbolic interactionism, phenomenology, ethnomethodology, exchange, conflict, and critical theories. The substantial turn from the previously predominant functionalism led to a vigorous development of diverse perspectives in theory and research in later decades.

Sociological Research

Among the reasons for calling the postwar era "golden" was the flourishing of sociological research and the burgeoning of its funding.

Organization and Funding of Research

The primary sources of support in the immediate postwar period continued to be the major private foundations, especially Rockefeller, but over time also the Sage, Carnegie, and Ford foundations, among others. The choice of universities and scholars as recipients was highly selective, and Columbia and Harvard, along with Chicago, benefited especially from such funding in the first half of this period. The main development in the funding of research in this period, however, was, on the one hand, the enormous growth in the amount of available funding and, on the other hand, the increasingly predominant role of governments, especially the federal government, as the source of funding. Along with this change came others, such as the distribution of research funds to an ever broader array of universities, colleges, and institutes, and broader ranges of research topics, as well as new patterns of allocation processes, such as peer-review procedures.

The other major development occurred in the organization of research. While much sociological research continued to be done by individuals and sometimes by small collegial groups of collaborators, the postwar period witnessed the development of research institutes and centers usually affiliated with specific universities. Examples of research centers of national importance are the Bureau of Applied Social Research, founded during World War II by Paul Lazarsfeld of Columbia University; the Survey Research Center, founded in 1946, based at the University of Michigan; and the National Opinion Research Center, founded during World War II at Denver, but since 1947 based at the University of Chicago. Most of the largest centers, along with the Gallup Research Center and the Roper Center for Public Opinion Research, tended to focus mainly on survey research using nationwide sampling techniques. The same centers involved collaboration among various social science disciplines, including political science and economics, as well as sociology.

Major Studies

Among the most important and innovative of the large-scale studies that came out of this period were, first, Samuel Stouffer's four-volume *The American Soldier,* published in 1949, and second, Theodor Adorno's *The Authoritarian Personality,* published in 1950. Both of these works were conducted by teams of sociologists and other social scientists who contributed significantly to the research, both substantively and technically. The *American Soldier* research was mandated by the U.S. War Department to address problems of morale, cooperation, and combat effectiveness in the U.S. Army, along with questions of race relations and propaganda effects. Stouffer's team conducted extensive fieldwork and interviewing of American soldiers and employed sophisticated sampling and measurement techniques. Stouffer later served a term as president of the ASA in 1953. Adorno's *authoritarian personality* study, sponsored by the American Jewish Committee, developed the *f-scale* to tap prejudicial attitudes with the aim of understanding such problems as anti-Semitism and racial prejudice. The so-called authoritarian personality type exhibited tendencies of submissiveness to ingroup authority coupled with negative attitudes toward members of outgroups.

A third major study was Gunnar Myrdal's 1944 study, *An American Dilemma: The Negro Problem and Modern Democracy,* commissioned by the Carnegie Corporation to address persistent problems of racial discrimination. The "dilemma" referred to the juxtaposition of the societal ideals of egalitarianism versus practices of racial discrimination. On the grounds that most American social scientists were themselves prejudiced, at least in the sense of believing that racial prejudices were largely immutable, Carnegie chose the Swedish Myrdal, as an outsider, to lead the research. Indeed, one of the main conclusions of the research was that racial discrimination patterns were mutable, subject to change by intervention. Myrdal's findings were cited in the context and arguments leading to the U.S. Supreme Court's landmark 1954 decision in the *Brown v. Board of Education* decision overturning the legality of racially segregated public education.

Sometimes in collaboration with other social scientists sociologists published several important empirical or quantitative studies in the areas of communications research (propaganda, content analysis, and opinion polling), including studies by Robert Merton, Paul Lazarsfeld, Bernard Berelson, and Leo Lowenthal. Industrial sociology benefited from several studies by, among others, Elton Mayo, William F. Whyte, and W. E. Moore, an important theme of which was the importance of informal groups outside the formal organization of work that nevertheless had a significant impact on worker productivity. Some of this research was criticized by later sociologists (e.g., H. Sheppard and C. W. Mills) as displaying a managerial bias in its perspective. An important study that broke new ground in industrial sociology was *Union Democracy,* 1956, a study of the internal politics of a major trade union, led by S. M. Lipset, with the collaboration of Martin Trow and James Coleman, and supported by Columbia's Bureau of Applied Social Research. Lipset was ASA president in 1993. The study of work and occupations became an important subfield of industrial sociology during the 1950s.

Other fields that developed especially during this period were criminology and the study of deviant behavior, social psychology, and the study of small-group interaction, military and political sociology, as well as rural sociology and the study of social problems and race relations. Most of these fields also represented topics of courses typically offered in undergraduate programs. Occasionally, as with David Riesman's classic 1950 study, *The Lonely Crowd,* a sociological book also became a bestseller for the general public.

Scholarly and Professional Associations

The American Sociological Association, until 1959 called the American Sociological Society, the sole official national association of sociologists, grew sharply in membership during this period, rising from about 1,000 in 1940 to over 14,000 in 1970. This growth outpaced the increase in degrees awarded in sociology, reflecting a number of changes made in the policies and structures of the national association, as it became more open to members in terms of gender, race, and ethnicity, and to students as well as faculty in all types of educational institutions. After electing E. Franklin Frazier as the first black president in 1948, the ASA elected its first woman president, Dorothy Swain Thomas, in 1952, almost half a century after the founding of the association.

Regional and specialty associations also thrived during this period. The main regional associations had been established in the 1930s, including the Pacific, the Midwest, the Southern, and the Eastern. In the decades following World War II, a number of others were organized, including the Ohio Valley (later renamed the North Central), the Southwestern, and the Mid-South. Almost all the regional associations also formed their own journals, including some of the most important journals, such as *Social Forces* and the *Sociological Quarterly.* Literally dozens of specialty associations have formed, some of them born from discontent with the ASA. The most significant organization founded in this period has been the Society for the Study of Social Problems, founded in 1951. The latter developed with a concern with social policy that its members found lacking in the ASA's neglect of social issues during the 1950s and 1960s.

During the 1960s, the ASA experienced a number of internal conflicts that brought changes of lasting import. One of the salient internal schisms concerned the question of ASA policy toward U.S. involvement in the Vietnam War. In 1968, the membership voted not to take an official position on the war. The Sociology Liberation Movement was formed that year largely to give voice to strong antiwar sentiment. In the same year, the Caucus of Black Sociologists was formed, as was the Radical Caucus. Women sociologists formed the Caucus of Women Sociologists in 1969, later to become the Sociologists for Women in Society. Each of these movements and caucuses called for more openness, inclusiveness, and democratization in the ASA, reflecting broader concerns in the society at large for extended civil rights, gender equality, antipoverty, and antiwar policies. Many of these issues were to occupy the attention of the ASA and its members in subsequent decades as well.

SOCIOLOGY IN THE ERA OF GLOBALIZATION: FROM 1970 TO THE PRESENT

In the early 1970s, as the period of greatest student activism and social unrest crested, sociology was nearing the zenith of its most rapid growth in the United States as a discipline, profession, and academic subject. The peak for undergraduate degrees awarded was almost 36,000 in 1973, more than 2,200 master's degrees in 1974, and 734 doctorates in 1977, numbers not matched again in the twentieth century. ASA membership also peaked in 1972 at around 15,000 members in all categories (see American Sociological Association Web page).

Both Robert Friedrichs's *A Sociology of Sociology* and Alvin Gouldner's *The Coming Crisis of Western Sociology,* published in 1970, critiqued mainstream sociology as indifferent to societal issues. Jürgen Habermas's first book, *Toward a Rational Society,* was translated into English in the same year. Taken together, these critical works challenged sociology to reexamine its largely disengaged relation to the societies being observed and analyzed. Likewise, the ASA, when challenged internally on issues of gender and race, responded in the early 1970s by establishing standing committees on the status of women and on the status of racial and ethnic minorities in the profession.

Following the end of the Vietnam War in 1973, undergraduate student enrollments began to decline steeply, with degrees awarded falling by almost two thirds by 1985. ASA membership levels also began to decline, falling from a peak of about 15,000 in 1972 to about 11,000 in 1984, due mainly to declines in student memberships (thereafter membership levels rose gradually to reach almost 14,000 in 2005). Nevertheless, sociology as a discipline continued to grow into a more differentiated field of study, with the rise of new specialties. Gender joined race and class to form a strong core of variables examined by sociologists across most specialties. Long a majority at the undergraduate level, women formed majorities approaching and exceeding 70 percent from the 1980s onward. By 1980, women formed a majority of master's degree recipients, rising to about two thirds by century's end. In 1988, for the first time women comprised the majority of sociology doctorates, reaching about 60 percent by 2000. Men continued to occupy a disproportionately large share of leadership positions both in the academy and in the ASA. An indicator of gender lag in U.S. sociology is found in the fact that eight of the nine women ASA presidents from 1905 to 2006 have been elected since 1970.

U.S. Trends in Theory and Research

The theoretical perspectives developed in earlier periods continued to find followers in the most recent era.

Newer trends tended to spin off from already existing schools rather than arising as radically new innovations. Functionalism begat neofunctionalism; exchange theory continued in its earlier guise but also morphed into network analysis and rational choice theory; symbolic interactionism endured but so did its offshoot, dramaturgy and other variations; conflict theory partially gave way to critical theory; and finally, the study of race, class, and gender became more concerned than ever before with policy issues based on equality, redress, and reform.

Only a few of the major studies of this period can be mentioned. Few works of general theory attracted the interest of sociologists in this period. Jeffrey Alexander's ambitious *Theoretical Logic in Sociology,* 1982–1983, featured Parsons along with Marx, Weber, and Durkheim in a synthetic and neofunctionalist reading of the classic tradition. Neil Smelser's *Comparative Methods in the Social Sciences,* 1986, was among several of his more general works of this period; he served as ASA president in 1997. James Coleman's *Foundations of Social Theory,* 1990, attempted to develop a general statement of sociological theory, which nevertheless owed a great deal to the perspectives of exchange theory and rational choice. Coleman also authored important research in the sociology of education that contributed to public debate and policy changes in the area of racial desegregation of the public schools; he was ASA president in 1992.

The tradition of conflict sociology advanced with Randall Collins, *Conflict Sociology,* 1975; Harvey Braverman, *Labor and Monopoly Capital,* 1974; and Michael Burawoy, *Manufacturing Consent,* 1979. Work on various axes of inequality and diversity also tended to reflect emphases on conflict. Outstanding examples included Alice Rossi, ASA presidential address, "Gender and Parenthood," 1983; Patricia Hill-Collins, *Black Feminist Thought,* 1990; Nancy Fraser, *Unruly Practices,* 1989; and Erik Olin Wright, *Classes,* 1985, and *Interrogating Inequality,* 1994.

Microsociology, including social psychology, interaction, exchange, and network analysis, benefited from Richard Emerson's work in the 1970s; Harrison White, *Identity and Control,* 1992; and Linda Molm, *Coercive Power and Exchange,* 1997, in addition to the continuing work and influence of James Coleman and Peter Blau. Manuel Castells, *The Rise of the Network Society,* 1996, and Stephan Fuchs, *Against Essentialism,* 2001, are important synthetic works in the same tradition.

Although drawing on previous ideas, sociologists developed some newer directions and emphases in theory and research. Examples include theories of modernity, societal evolution, and globalization; theories of culture and emotions; the sociology of the body; and sociobiology. Studies of large-scale or macrosociological subjects came to the fore from the 1970s onward. Daniel Bell's *The*

Coming of Post-Industrial Society, 1973, attempted to assess current societal trends in a historical perspective. With his works on world systems theory, notably *The Modern World System,* 1974 onward. Immanuel Wallerstein has played a leading role in the development of macrohistorical sociology on a global scale. Reinhard Bendix, ASA president in 1970, noted for his earlier work in industrial, political, and historical sociology, contributed to comparative political sociology with his *Kings or People,* 1978. In the same area, Theda Skocpol published her *States and Social Revolutions,* 1979. Charles Tilly's major work in this field was his *Citizenship, Identity, and Social History,* 1995. Randall Collins attempted a global theory of intellectual change in his *The Sociology of Philosophies,* 1998. Sociologists also contributed to the conceptualization and study of globalization, as in the work of Roland Robertson, *Globalization: Social Theory and Global Culture,* 1992, and George Ritzer, *The McDonaldization of Society,* 1993.

Perhaps the greatest single growth area in sociological specialties in the past three decades has been the focus on gender (for several years, the ASA section on gender has had the largest number of members of all the sections). Among the major works in this area not already referred to above are Joan Acker, *Doing Comparable Worth: Gender, Class, and Pay Equity,* 1989; Margaret Anderson and Patricia Hill-Collins, *Race, Class, and Gender,* 1992; Jessie Bernard, *The Future of Marriage,* 1972; Janet Chafetz, *Gender Equity,* 1990; Nancy Chodorow, *Femininities, Masculinity, Sexualities,* 1994; Sandra Harding, *The Science Question in Sociology,* 1986; and Barbara Reskin and Irene Padavic, *Women and Men at Work,* 1994. Reskin was ASA president in 2002.

The study of race and racism has also been a vital area of sociological research and, as with the study of gender in this same period, has been connected to policy concerns. William Julius Wilson, president of the ASA in 1990, has made major contributions with his *The Declining Significance of Race,* 1978, and *The Bridge over the Racial Divide,* 1999. Joe R. Feagin, also a past president of the ASA, has authored several works on racism in American society, including his *Racist America,* 2001, and *The Continuing Significance of Racism: U.S. Colleges and Universities,* 2003.

At the same time, important developments occurred abroad and American sociologists became more aware of and receptive to sociological ideas and research in other countries. Outstanding examples of influential European works have been the republication in the 1970s and 1980s of Norbert Elias, *The Civilizing Process,* 1939; Michel Foucault's many works, including his *Discipline and Punish,* 1979; Pierre Bourdieu, *Distinctions,* 1984, including his idea of *cultural capital;* Anthony Giddens's work on *structuration,* as in his *The Constitution of Society,* 1984, and on modernity in *The Consequences of Modernity,* 1990; Jürgen Habermas, *The Theory of Communicative Action,* 1984–1987; Niklas Luhmann's work in systems theory,

including his *The Differentiation of Society,* 1982, and *Social Systems,* 1995; and Ulrich Beck, *The Risk Society,* 1992. These works are part of a growing international dialogue among sociologists. The writings of Giddens, Habermas, and Luhmann, for instance, address ideas of American provenance, for example, those of Mead and Parsons, while at the same time representing independent and innovative formulations of their own, which in turn have been addressed by their American readers. If the so-called golden era was one of American preeminence internationally, the period since 1970 has seen an internationalization of sociological discourse.

The Development of Sociology in Canada

The widespread development of sociology in Canada began in the 1960s. While sociology had been offered as an academic subject for several decades, the dominant tendency was for sociology to be offered in conjunction with another field such as political economy or cultural anthropology. The Canadian Association of Sociology and Anthropology was formed in 1965. Aside from its more recent development compared to the United States, Canadian sociology is marked by its linguistic duality; French-language sociology has its own institutions, journals, and associations, more or less paralleling those of the English language.

Sociology flourished at Québec's three major French-language universities from the 1960s onward. An important figure was Fernand Dumont, whose *Le Lieu de l'Homme,* 1968, and *Les ideologies,* 1974, contributed to cultural sociology. In the 1960s, Québec society underwent a so-called quiet revolution, a quite rapid transformation conventionally analyzed in terms of modernization, secularization, and liberalization. Québec sociology, which has seen itself at a significant intersection between French and Anglo-American intellectual traditions, has sought to address the peculiar nature of Québec society with its aspirations as a distinct *nation* in relation to Canadian society and the world at large. The sociology of culture and political sociology, perennially important in Québec, were further developed by Marcel Rioux in critical terms in his *Essai de sociologie critique,* 1978. Rioux also participated in the public discourse over the status of Québec with his *Québec in Question,* 1971. Widely recognized as the dean of Québec sociology, Guy Rocher, trained at Laval and Harvard and based at the University of Montréal, has made a major contribution to general sociology, beginning with his three-volume *Introduction à la sociologie générale,* 1969. His book *Talcott Parsons and American Sociology,* 1972, has been published in six languages.

English-language sociology in Canada drew upon British, European, and American sociological perspectives and personnel for the staffing of its fast-growing departments all across the country in the 1960s and 1970s before attempting the *Canadianization* of its curricula and research agendas. A senior sociologist of the period,

S. D. Clark of the University of Toronto, contributed to the discourse on the specificity of Canadian society with his *Canadian Society in Historical Perspective, 1976.* Beyond the exercise of national self-reflection, two especially strong areas of theory and research emerged in English-Canadian sociology: macroeconomic sociology and the study of gender issues. Both areas have been supported by a great deal of empirical and quantitative research as well as critical policy orientations.

The study of social stratification and power was greatly stimulated and influenced by John Porter, *The Vertical Mosaic: An Analysis of Social Class and Power in Canada,* 1965. Beginning in the 1970s, sociologists joined other social scientists in critical analyses of corporate capitalism. Major examples were Wallace Clement, *The Canadian Corporate Elite,* 1975, as well as his *Continental Corporate Power: Economic Linkages between Canada and the United States,* 1977; Robert Brym, edited collection *The Structure of the Canadian Capitalist Class,* 1985; and William K. Carroll, *Corporate Power and Canadian Capitalism,* 1986. The critical sociology of gender developed especially from the 1980s onward with major contributions from Margrit Eichler, *The Double Standard,* 1980; Bonnie Fox, *Hidden in the Household: Women's Domestic Labour under Capitalism,* 1980; Mariana Valverde, *Sex, Power and Pleasure,* 1985; Roberta Hamilton and Michele Barrett, *The Politics of Diversity: Feminism, Marxism, and Nationalism,* 1986; and Dorothy Smith, *The Everyday World as Problematic: A Feminist Sociology,* 1987.

One of the distinctive features of Canadian sociology has been its frequent interaction with research and perspectives of other national traditions. The boundaries of Canadian and U.S. sociology, in particular, have been permeable in both directions. Several Canadians have had careers in the United States, including Erving Goffman, Dennis Wrong, and Michèle Lamont. Several American sociologists have conducted important research in Canada, including Seymour Martin Lipset's *Agrarian Socialism,* 1950, and *Continental Divide,* 1990. Interaction between Canada and Europe has also been important in the development of Canadian sociology, exemplified by Marcel Fournier's work on Marcel Mauss; Fournier has also collaborated with Michèle Lamont on *Cultivating Difference,* 1992. Finally, Canadians also tend to be disproportionately active in international professional associations.

Challenges Facing Sociology Early in the 21st Century

The history of sociology has to be written anew by each generation. What Max Weber said about concepts applies at least as well to the writing of historical accounts. Weber famously claimed that concepts, once formed, are destined to become obsolete because the culture changes incessantly as does the intellectual culture of science and scholarship. Just as there can be no closed, permanent set of concepts, so can there be no fixed historical narrative

of sociology's past. As new insights, knowledge, and perspectives arise, they provide lenses for making new discoveries about the past, discoveries that in turn nourish reflection and innovation for oncoming generations. Of all the challenges facing sociology, we can highlight only three that are especially relevant to the writing of sociology's history.

Sociology as a Policy-Neutral Science versus Public and Critical Sociology

If there has been a single issue that has haunted sociology from the first generation until now, it is the status of sociology as an empirical science of social phenomena: Should sociology strive to be entirely value- and policy-neutral, or should it attempt to contribute to the reform and improvement of social life? The question itself spawns others: If sociology *should* attempt to be policy- and value-neutral, *can* it be neutral and nonpartisan, and if so, how? If, on the other hand, sociology should align itself with forces of social reform, how can sociologists know and decide which values and policies will lead to societal improvement? Or is the question of science versus reform wrongly put as an "either/or" alternative? Can ways be found to honor the ideals of both a resolutely empirical science and the humanitarian impulse to contribute to social justice and reform? How can sociology best contribute to the quest for the good society, while maintaining scientific credibility?

Although these questions have so far resisted resolution, an examination of the history of sociology can be instructive in various ways. For one thing, we learn about the rich variety of positions and arguments on behalf of scientific neutrality and reform commitments, and the nuanced as well as passionate positions taken by colleagues of the past. Historical knowledge can help the present generation to refine the questions and issues while sorting through possible paths toward resolution and consensus. Second, our historical account has shown that in the 1960s and 1970s, students flocked to sociology, and graduates entered the profession, particularly in a time of perceived social crisis with the expectation that sociology could address the opportunity for societal improvement. Third, an examination of recent ASA presidential addresses shows that leaders of the current generation share a commitment to sociology as both a science and as an instrument for the reform and betterment of society. Two in particular have highlighted the obligations of sociology toward society and the public: Joe Feagin's 2000 address, "Sociology and Social Justice: Agendas for the 21st Century," and Michael Burawoy's 2004 speech, "For Public Sociology." The question of science versus reform, a question that is older and broader than sociology itself, has not yet been resolved, but important steps have been taken to clarify the nettle of questions at stake and the opportunities to move toward workable resolutions.

Creating and Securing the Conditions of Dialogue

It is often observed that the present era is one of great fragmentation and diversity in sociology. Instead of a single paradigm, sociology has many; instead of a strong core of general sociological theory and research, we have many special sociologies, each with its own concepts, theories, and favored research methods. Lacking a strong core of theory, method, and knowledge, it has become increasingly difficult for sociologists to maintain a unified sense of the discipline as a whole. One of the great challenges facing sociology in the twenty-first century is to create and secure conditions of communication across lines that divide specialists from other specialists, and that separate sociologists from fruitful communication with social scientists in other disciplines, with sociologists and social scientists in other parts of the world, and with the potential constituencies and publics for sociological knowledge. There are a number of ways of addressing the need for greater dialogue and opportunities to learn from each other: greater use of professional associations, conferences, and technologies for wider communication across specialties and national boundaries; increased attention to developing synthetic theories of social phenomena in conjunction with other social sciences; and promoting awareness of the rich content of past sociological theory, research, and practice. An awareness of the history of sociology shows that neither unity nor fragmentation has prevailed for more than a generation. History also reveals the relative benefits and disadvantages of unity, and more importantly, measures of coping with the challenges posed in this generation by disunity, fragmentation, and diversity.

New Directions in the Writing
of the History of Sociology

The most recent period in North American sociology has witnessed several new developments in the writing of sociology's history. Turning from literal and descriptive accounts of previous sociology, Lewis Coser (1971), in his *Masters of Sociological Thought,* sought to emphasize the importance of examining earlier ideas in relation to their historical and social contexts. Irving Zeitlin (2001), the Canadian sociologist, in his *Ideology and the Development of Sociological Theory,* sought in addition to place the development of sociological theory into an overarching narrative in which the thought of Karl Marx was placed at the center as a "watershed." In a more comprehensive vein, Donald Levine (1995), in his *Visions of the Sociological Tradition,* analyzed the history of sociology in terms of national traditions and highlighted the need for dialogue to overcome disciplinary fragmentation.

Perhaps the greatest innovations of recent decades have stemmed from a thoroughgoing reexamination of the founding and early development of sociology. Both the ASA and the International Sociological Association have established vigorous sections and research committees on the history of sociology that foster exchange of ideas and research findings. The recent volume, *Diverse Histories of American Sociology,* 2005, edited by Anthony Blasi on behalf of the ASA section on the History of Sociology, exemplifies the broadening of the scope of contributions to the development of sociology. The most significant development of the recent past has been the rediscovery and acknowledgment of the role of women in the founding of sociology in the nineteenth and early twentieth centuries. Several U.S. and Canadian sociologists have participated in this work of rediscovery, including, among many others, Mary Jo Deegan (1988, 1991), Michael R. Hill (Martineau 1989), Susan Hoecker-Drysdale (1992), Shulamit Reinharz (1992), Lynn McDonald (1994), Patricia Lengermann and Jill Niebrugge-Brantley (1998), and Hill and Hoecker-Drysdale (2001).

An education that is concentrated only on the sociology of the present day and of a single country or society yields a seriously limited view of sociological knowledge. The obvious antidote is a sociological education that includes knowledge of the history of the discipline, the ideas, methods, and practices of the past and of other societies. Future work in the field of sociology has much to gain from greater awareness of its history.

4

SOCIOLOGICAL THEORY IN THE 21ST CENTURY

JONATHAN H. TURNER

University of California, Riverside

Theoretical sociology has differentiated into ever more schools of thought over the last 40 years, a trend that is facilitated by the lack of "grand theories" that seek to integrate more specialized theoretical programs. Differentiation is furthered by a lack of consensus over the very nature of theorizing in sociology, with the major fault lines of debate revolving around whether or not sociology can be a natural science. Without a commitment to a common epistemology or a core canon of early theoretical works, an increasing number of theoretical perspectives has emerged from a small early base of theories and philosophies—functionalism, conflict theory, utilitarianism, pragmatism, and phenomenology. And as theories continue to proliferate, the hope of ever reaching a consensus over the key properties of the social universe and the best epistemology for studying these properties has begun to fade. Moreover, there are now many highly specialized theories emerging out of research traditions that are only loosely affiliated with theories built from the ideas of the founding generation.

It is not a simple task, therefore, to survey theoretical sociology at the beginning of the current century. The best that can be done is to focus on the more general theoretical schemes that built on the early legacy provided by the founding generations of sociologists. These are the theories that dominate theoretical sociology.

THE RISE AND FALL OF FUNCTIONAL THEORY

Sociology's first theoretical approach was decidedly functional, examining social structures and processes for how they meet postulated needs and requisites necessary for societal survival. Both Auguste Comte (1896 [1830–1842]) and Herbert Spencer (1898 [1874–1896]) drew an organismic analogy calling attention to the systemic qualities of the social universe and to the functions of parts for maintenance of social systems. For Spencer, there were four basic problems that all systems, including organismic and societal, had to resolve: production, reproduction, regulation, and distribution. Later, Émile Durkheim ([1893] 1947) postulated only one master functional requisite: the need for sociocultural integration.

Functional theorizing might have died with Durkheim and the abandonment of Spencer's evolutionism were it not for anthropologists, particularly A. R. Radcliffe-Brown (1952) and Bronislaw Malinowski ([1944] 1964), who carried functionalism to the midpoint of the twentieth century. Since preliterate societies had no written history that could be used to explain the origins of cultural features of these societies, assessing the function of a particular cultural pattern for the survival of the society became another way to "explain" why a particular cultural pattern existed (Turner and Maryanski 1979). Radcliffe-Brown (1952) followed

45

Durkheim's lead and analyzed cultural patterns, such as kinship, for how they resolve integrative problems in pre-literate societies, whereas Malinowski adopted Spencer's more analytical strategy, emphasizing that social reality exists at different system levels (biological organism, social structure, and culture) and that each level of reality has certain functional requisites that must be met if that system level is to be viable in its environment.

It is this latter form of analytical functionalism that came to dominate sociological theory in the 1950s and the first half of the 1960s, primarily through the work of Talcott Parsons (1951) and colleagues (Parsons, Bales, and Shils 1953; Parsons and Smelser 1956). For Parsons, social reality consists of four action systems (behavioral organism, personality, social, and cultural), and each system must meet four fundamental requisites: (1) adaptation (taking in resources, converting them into usable commodities, and distributing them); (2) goal attainment (establishing goals and mobilizing resources to meet these goals); (3) integration (coordination and control among system parts); and (4) latency (reproducing system units and resolving tensions within them). Each action system was analyzed by Parsons in terms of how it meets these requisites; later, Parsons began to explore the input-output relations among the action systems. Near the end of analytical functionalism's brief dominance of sociological theorizing, particularly in the United States, Parsons (1966) posited a cybernetic hierarchy of control among the action systems, with those high in information (culture) providing guidance for those action systems lower in the hierarchy. Energy was seen as rising up the hierarchy from the behavioral organism through personality and social system to culture, while information from culture guided the organization of status roles in social systems, the motivated actions of the personality system, and the mobilization of energy in the organismic system. At the very end of Parsons's (1978) reign as the leading theorist in the world—indeed, not long before his death—he posited a view of the entire universe as four systems meeting the four functional requisites (a strategy that harkened back to Spencer's Synthetic Philosophy, where physics, biology, psychology, sociology, and ethics could be analyzed in terms of the same elementary principles of evolution).

Functionalism came under increasing attack from many quarters by the early 1960s. From philosophy, the idea that system parts should be analyzed in terms of their functions will produce illegitimate teleologies (outcomes cause the very events that lead to these outcomes) or tautologies (circular arguments in which parts meet needs and needs cause parts to emerge). On a more substantive level, the rise of conflict theories (or their resurrection) in the 1960s led critics to argue that functionalism produced a theory supporting the status quo because, in essence, it argued that existing structures must exist to meet needs for survival (Dahrendorf 1958)—a line of argument that biases inquiry against searches for alternative structures.

Functionalism did not completely die, however, because there are many scholars, especially in Europe (e.g., Münch 1987, 2001), who continue to use Parsonsian categories to perform functional analysis, while others retain the emphasis on systems without the same elaborate taxonomy revolving around multiple-system requisites (e.g., Luhmann 1982). In the United States, a brief neo-functionalist movement occurred in which theorists (e.g., Alexander 1985; Alexander and Colomy 1985) abandoned the notion of functional requisites and, instead, focused on the strong points of functionalism: the emphasis on structural differentiation and the integrative effects of culture. Neofunctionalism was not functional, for all its other merits, because what makes functionalism distinctive is the view that social structures and systems of cultural symbols exist because they meet fundamental needs or requisites for survival (Turner and Maryanski 1988).

Another effort to save what is important in functional theory revolves around viewing functional requisites as forces that generate selection pressures for social systems. For example, Jonathan Turner (1995) argues that human social systems are driven by forces—much like the forces such as gravity in physics and natural selection in biology—that push populations to organize in certain ways or suffer the disintegrative consequences. Many of these forces overlap with what hard-core functionalists have seen as survival requisites. Thus, for Turner, regulation, reproduction, distribution, production, and population drive the formation of macro-level institutional systems; differentiation and integrative forces drive meso-level formations of corporate units like organizations and categoric units such as social and ethnic classes (Turner and Boyns 2001); and another set of forces direct the flow of micro-level interpersonal behavior in encounters (Turner 2002). Such an approach is no longer functional because needs or requisites are not posited, but the approach still retains the appeal of functionalism: analysis of how the universal forces apply selection pressures on populations. Other theorists working from different theoretical traditions have also begun to pursue this selectionist line of theorizing (e.g., Runciman 1989; Sanderson 1995).

THE PERSISTENCE OF ECOLOGICAL THEORIZING

In the works of both Spencer and Durkheim can be found the essence of an ecological theory. Both argued that as populations grow, competition for resources increases, setting into motion selection pressures. Spencer's famous phrase "survival of the fittest" (uttered some nine years before Darwin's theory was presented) captures some of this view; those individuals and social structures revealing properties that allow them to secure resources in their environment will survive, while those that do not will be selected out. Durkheim took a more benign view of selection, arguing that if individuals and collective actors cannot secure resources in one resource niche, they will seek resources elsewhere, thus increasing the level of specialization (or social speciation) or differentiation in a society. Thus, from the very beginnings of sociological theorizing, social differentiation has been seen as an outcome of niche density and competition for resources.

The arguments of Spencer and Durkheim were downsized between the 1920s and 1940s by the Chicago School in the United States (e.g., Hoyt 1939; Park 1936). While the members of the department of sociology at Chicago pursued many diverse lines of research, one persistent theme was to view urban areas as a kind of ecosystem, with competition among diverse actors (individuals with varying incomes and ethnic backgrounds as well as varying business and governmental actors) for urban space. Their competition is institutionalized by real estate markets; fueled by these markets, the patterns of control of urban space, the movement of individuals and corporate actors in and out of urban space, and the overall distribution of actors across urban areas can be analyzed with ecological principles. Today, this tradition still operates under the label of urban or human ecology (e.g., Frisbie and Kasarda 1988); it has consistently proven a useful theoretical orientation in understanding processes of urbanization and differentiation within urban areas.

In the 1970s, a new type of ecological analysis, one that focused on the ecology of organizations (Hannan and Freeman 1977), emerged. All organizations can be viewed as existing in a niche, where they seek resources (customers, clients, students, memberships, or any other resource needed to sustain an organization). Once an organization sustains itself in a resource niche, other organizations enter this niche and, in so doing, increase the density of organizations. Thus, the number of organizations in a niche will initially increase, but eventually, niche density becomes so great that selection pressures lead to the "death" of those organizations unable to secure resources or, alternatively, to their migration to a new niche where they can sustain themselves. More than urban ecology, organizational ecology borrowed self-consciously from bioecology, transferring many concepts from ecological analysis in biology to sociology. And perhaps more than urban ecology, organizational ecology remains one of the dominant approaches to understanding the structure and distribution of organizational systems in societies (Carroll 1988).

As urban and organizational ecology flourished, one of the carriers of this tradition from the Chicago School, Amos Hawley (1986), began to move the ecological analysis from the meso level (urban areas and organizations) back to macro-level societal dynamics. In essence, Hawley completed a conceptual odyssey to Spencer's and Durkheim's macro-level ecological theorizing, adding new refinements. For Hawley, technology as it affects productivity, modes of transportation, communication systems, and markets will lower mobility costs (for moving people, information, and resources) across space; and as mobility costs decrease, differentiation among corporate units (organizations revealing a division of labor) increases. Differentiation is also influenced by the capacity of the state to control territories, manage capital investments in the economy, regulate markets, and encourage technological development. When centers of power can effectively accomplish these goals, mobility costs are lowered and sociocultural differentiation increases. With increased differentiation, new integrative problems inevitably arise, often posing threats to centers of power that, in turn, lower the capacity of the state to control territories and otherwise act in ways that make markets more dynamic, that increase productivity, that expand transportation, and that extend communication. Thus, the ebb and flow of differentiation in a society is mediated by the operation of centers of power as these centers raise or lower mobility costs. Thus, the legacy of Spencer and Durkheim is very much alive in modern macro-level ecological theorizing. Others (e.g., Turner 1994, 1995) have also followed Hawley's lead in carrying forward Spencer's and Durkheim's macro-level ecological theory.

THE CHALLENGE OF BIOSOCIAL THEORIZING

The persistence of Darwinian ideas in ecological theorizing has been supplemented in recent decades by another type of Darwinian theory: sociobiology and evolutionary psychology. Both of these approaches emphasize that humans are animals whose phenotypes (physiology as well as behavioral capacities and propensities) are influenced by their genotypes (genetic makeup) as this genotype has been honed by the forces of biological evolution (natural selection, gene flow, genetic drift, and mutation). This approach has been highly threatening to many sociologists because it is often interpreted as a new form of biological determinism that reduces understanding of culture and social structures to genetically driven behavioral propensities. Some of this skepticism was appropriate because early sociobiologists often made rather extreme statements (e.g., Wilson 1975). The basic argument of sociobiology is that behavioral propensities, culture, and social structure are, in essence, "survivor machines" that keep genes responsible for these propensities in the gene pool (Dawkins 1976). If particular behavioral proclivities and the sociocultural arrangements arising from these proclivities enable individuals to reproduce, they operate to maintain the genes of these individuals in the gene pool. Thus, behavioral strategies, social structures, and culture are survival machines, driven by "blind" natural selection to preserve those genes that enhance reproductive fitness (Williams 1966).

Evolutionary psychology (Cosmides 1989; Cosmides and Tooby 1989) adds to this line of argument the notion that there are "modules" in the brain that direct behaviors. These modules have been created by the forces of evolution as they have worked on the neurology of phenotypes (and the underlying genotype) to install behavioral propensities that enhance fitness. For evolutionary psychology, then, universal behaviors are driven by brain modules, as these have been honed by the forces of evolution (Savage and Kanazawa 2004).

These biosocial approaches represent a new way to address a topic that was often part of classical sociological theory: human instincts. Most early theorists had some vision of human instincts, but these views were often vague and disconnected to evolutionary biology. Bio-sociology offers a more sophisticated way to examine what is "natural" to humans as evolved apes, although the number of scholars pursuing this line of theorizing is comparatively small (but growing slowly). What this type of theorizing offers is a chance to reconnect sociology and biology in ways somewhat reminiscent of Comte's and Spencer's advocacy. (For sociological efforts to develop bio-sociology, see Horne 2004; Lopreato 2001; Lopreato and Crippen 1999; Machalek and Martin 2004; van den Berghe 1981.)

THE REVIVAL
OF STAGE MODELS OF EVOLUTION

Comte, Spencer, Marx, and, to a lesser extent, Durkheim all presented stage models that saw the history of human society as passing through discrete stages of development. These models were, in a sense, descriptive because they reviewed the features of societal types, from simple hunting and gathering through horticulture and variants of horticulture like herding and fishing to agriculture and on to industrialism (post-industrialism was added later as a stage by contemporary sociologists, as was a postmodern stage by other sociologists). Yet these descriptions of societal evolution were always seen as driven by some fundamental forces, converting descriptions of stages into theories about the forces driving movement from one stage to another. For Comte, Spencer, and Durkheim, the driving force was population growth as it unleashed the ecological dynamics summarized above. Moreover, Spencer in particular saw war as an evolutionary force because those societies that won wars were generally better organized (economically, politically, and culturally) than those that were conquered, with the result that winners of wars constantly ratcheted up the complexity of human societies through the evolutionary stages that Spencer described in great detail. For Marx, the driving force of history revolved around changes in technologies and modes of production as these worked to generate "contradictions" that led to class conflict. For two thirds of the twentieth century, stage model evolutionary theory remained recessive. But in the 1960s, it was revived not only by Parsons (1966) in his later works but more significantly by Gerhard Lenski (1966) in his analysis of stratification systems. And later, neo-Marxian approaches like world-systems theorizing (see below) often imply a stage of societal evolution (Sanderson 1999; Wallerstein 1974).

These more recent models of societal evolution avoid the problems of early models, such as seeing each stage of evolution as inevitable and as marching toward an end state personified by Western European countries. Instead, more generic forces such as environment, demographic features (population size, characteristics, and rate of growth), technologies (economic and military), dynamism of markets, levels of production of material goods and services, properties and dynamics of stratification systems, and nature of institutional systems are all seen as interacting in complex ways to drive the structure and culture of societies. Few theories would posit one master force as driving evolution; instead, sets of forces are highlighted in various theories.

Lenski (1966), often in collaboration with others (e.g., Nolan and Lenski 2004), emphasizes the effects of technology (knowledge as it is used to increase production), but these effects are influenced by other forces, particularly the biosocial environment, nature of cultural symbols (values and ideologies), population size and rate of growth, institutional systems (kinship, religion, education, and polity), and patterns of war. Larger populations in stable and resource-rich environments, revealing liberal ideologies encouraging technological innovation, and institutional systems that do not discourage innovations or divert resources away from the economy and that limit warfare will become more complex and able to adapt to their environments. Stephen K. Sanderson (1995) blends ideas from biosociology and Marxian analysis, stressing that natural selection still works on individuals (rather than on society as a whole), but like Lenski, he stresses that societies are driven by demographic, ecological, technological, economic, and political forces. And like all Marxists, Sanderson emphasizes the material conditions of life—production and distribution—as the base that drives the development of cultural ideologies, political systems, interactions with the ecosystem, and relations with other societies.

While all present-day evolutionary theories stress that it is possible for de-evolution to occur (as Spencer had also argued), they tend to see a direction to evolution toward greater complexity, higher rates of innovation, and increased interdependence among societies connected by global markets. And most theorists would argue implicitly that if human evolution were to be restarted, it would pass through the same evolutionary stages from hunting and gathering to post-industrialism. The virtue of theorizing on stages of evolution is the time perspective gained, with contemporary social formations seen as the outcome of a long evolutionary history driven by a few fundamental forces.

THE REVIVAL OF
CONFLICT THEORIZING

Both Karl Marx (Marx and Engels [1847] 1970) and Max Weber [1922] (1968) posited a conflict view of the social world. Each argued that inequalities generate tensions that, under specifiable conditions, increase the probability (for Marx, a certainty) that subordinates in the system of inequality will become mobilized to engage in conflict with superordinates in an effort to redistribute resources. Marx and Weber presented a similar list of conditions: High levels of inequality, large discontinuities between classes, and low rates of social mobility across classes all set the stage for the emergence of leaders who would articulate a revolutionary ideology. Each added refinements to this general model, but they both saw inequality as potentially unleashing forces that lead subordinates to pursue conflict.

Conflict theorizing remained prominent for most of the twentieth century in Europe, but in the United States, it was recessive until the 1960s. Partly emboldened by the European critique of functionalism and by the demise of McCarthyism in the United States as well as by protests against the Vietnam War, conflict theory supplanted functionalism as the dominant theoretical orientation by the 1970s, although today the conflict approach is so integrated into mainstream sociological theorizing that it no longer stands out as a distinctive approach. The essence of conflict theories is the recognition that social reality is organized around inequalities in the distribution of valued resources such as material wealth, power, and prestige and that these inequalities systematically generate tensions, which under specifiable conditions generate various forms of conflict between those who have and those who do not have these valued resources. At first, the conflict theory revival was used as a foil against the perceived conservative bias of functionalism, but over the decades as conflict theory prospered, it developed a number of distinctive variants.

Abstracted Marxism

The first variant of conflict theory sought to make the theory more abstract, drawing from Marx's analysis of class conflict and extending it to all social systems where inequalities of authority exist (Dahrendorf 1959). This approach took what was useful from Marx, modified the Marxian model with ideas from Weber and Georg Simmel, and generated an abstract theory of conflict in all social systems. In the several versions of this abstracted Marxism (Dahrendorf 1959; Turner 1975), the conditions generating awareness among subordinates of their interests in changing the system inequality are delineated, and these follow from Marx but add the important proviso that the more organized are subordinates, the less likely they are to engage in violent conflict (instead, they will negotiate and compromise). Indeed, in contrast to Marx, these approaches argue that incipient organization, emerging ideologies, and early leadership will lead to open and often violent conflict, whereas high levels of political organization, clearly articulated ideologies, and established leaders lead to negotiation and compromise, a line of theoretical argument that goes against Marx but takes into account Weber's [1922] (1968) and Simmel's [1907] (1990) critiques of Marx.

Analytical Marxism

Another variant of Marxism is what Erik Olin Wright (1997) has termed *analytical Marxism,* an approach that incorporates many of the key ideas of Marxian theory on the dynamics of capitalism while trying to explain with an expanded set of concepts the problems in Marx's approach, particularly (1) the failure of industrial societies to polarize, (2) the lack of revolutionary conflict in industrial societies, (3) the rise of the state as a source of employment (thus making problematic whether government workers are proletarians or state managers), (4) the expansion of the middle classes in industrial and post-industrial societies, (5) the contradictory class locations of individuals in industrial and post-industrial societies (as both workers and managers), (6) the multiple-class locations of many families (where one person is a manager or owner, while another is a wage worker), and (7) the blurring of class distinctions as some skilled blue-collar workers become high wage earners or even owners of highly profitable small businesses, while many white-collar workers become lower-wage proletarians in service industries.

These and other events that have gone against Marx's predictions have troubled present-day Marxists (for a review, see Burawoy and Wright 2001), and so they have set about revitalizing Marxian theory to explain contemporary conditions. In Wright's (1997) version of analytical Marxism, for example, a distinction between economic power (control of others and the ability to extract their economic surplus) and economic welfare (ratio of toil in work to leisure time), coupled with people's "lived experiences" and contradictory class location, dramatically changes the nature of exploitation and, hence, individuals' awareness of their interests and willingness to engage in collective organization. Moreover, the notion of "ownership" and "control" is broadened to include four basic types of assets: labor-power assets, capital assets (to invest in economic activity and extract surplus value), organizational assets (to manage and control others and thereby extract surplus), and skill or credential assets (to extract resources beyond the labor necessary to acquire skills and credentials). Depending on the nature and level of any of these assets for individuals and families, the rate of exploitation will vary, being highest among those who have only labor assets and lowest among those who have the other types of assets. Additionally, Wright has sought to account for the fact that the state employs a significant proportion of the workforce yet cannot be seen as part of the bourgeoisie. Here, Wright emphasizes a "state mode of production" made possible by the resources that come from taxes, tariffs, and fees; and from this mode of production comes conflicts between managers, who ally themselves with capitalists and political decision makers, on the one side, and government workers, who provide the actual services, on the other. These two classes of workers in government reveal conflicting class interests and, hence, increased potential for class conflict. In the end, Wright and other analytical Marxists work hard to retain the basic concern with emancipation of subordinates in Marx's thinking while adjusting Marxian concepts to fit the reality of post-industrial societies.

World-Systems Theory

This approach retains many ideas from Marx on the dynamics of capitalism but shifts the unit of analysis from nation-state to systems of societies and globalization (Chase-Dunn 2001). Immanuel Wallerstein (1974) codified this mode of analysis, building on earlier work by dependency theorists (e.g., Frank 1969), into a conceptualization of world systems. One type of global system is a world empire revolving around conquest and extraction of resources from the conquered, which are then spent on elite privilege, control, and further conquest. Such systems eventually face fiscal crises, leading to showdown wars with other expanding empires. Of more interest to world-systems theorists like Wallerstein is a world economy driven not only by war but also by the flow of capital and technology through world markets. Such world economies are composed of (1) "core states," which have power, capital, and technology; (b) "peripheral states," which have inexpensive labor, natural resources, and insufficient power to stop their conquest, colonization, and exploitation; and (c) "semiperipheral states," having some economic development and military power, which, over time, can allow them to become part of the core. Thus, for world-systems theorists, the core is seen to exploit the periphery, frequently aided by the semiperiphery, with analysis emphasizing the economic cycles of varying duration (Juglar, Kuznet, and Kondratief cycles) and the flow of resources from periphery to core. From such exploitation, conflict within and between societies can emerge. There are many variants of world-systems theory, which adopt the broad strokes of Wallerstein's approach but emphasize somewhat different dynamics. For example, Christopher Chase-Dunn (1998) introduces new variables, such as population growth, intensification of production and environmental degradation, and immigration and emigration processes, to world-system dynamics leading to conflict within and between nations (Chase-Dunn and Hall 1997). Thus, Marxian ideas have been given new life by the shift to globalization.

Abstracted Weberianism

Just as Marx's ideas have been abstracted and extended, so Weber's analysis of conflict has been converted to more general and abstract theories of conflict. Randall Collins (1975, 1986), for example, has blended Weber's analysis of domination with ideas from other theoretical traditions. Collins (1981) argues that macro-level social structures like organizations and stratification systems are built from micro-level interaction rituals that sustain class cultures, authority systems in organizations, and inequalities in resources. People carry varying levels of cultural capital, emotional energy, material wealth, prestige, and power; and they use these resources in face-to-face interaction, with those high in these resources generally able to dominate others and augment their shares of resources. True to his Weberian roots, Collins then analyzes the varying cultures of social classes, the power of the state, the ideologies used to legitimate state power, the economy, and even the geopolitics between nations in terms of the relative resources of actors. Those who receive deference because of their resources will have different cultures and orientations than those who must give deference; the nature of control in organizational systems will varying depending on the relative reliance on coercion, material resources, or symbolic resources; the scale of the state depends on a surplus of economic resources, the degree of consensus over symbols, and the ability to use resources to expand the administrative and coercive bases of power; and geopolitics will reflect the technological, productive, geographical, and military advantages of states. Thus, like Marx, Weber's ideas stand at the core of new forms of conflict theorizing.

Historical-Comparative Analysis

The ideas of Marx and Weber are often combined in historical-comparative analysis of conflict processes. These analyses tend to focus on several classes of historical events, particularly the rise of democracies, revolutionary conflict, and empire formation and collapse. All of these theories focus on the state and the mobilization of masses (and often factions of elites) for conflict against the state. There are two lines of argument in these theories. One lists the conditions that lead masses and elites to mobilize for conflict against the state, while the other specifies the forces weakening the state's power and its capacity to repress dissent and conflict (Li and Turner 1998). The first line of argument owes more inspiration to Marx, and to a lesser extent to Weber, while the second is more indebted to Weber than to Marx. Some adopt Marx's ideas and extend them to nonindustrial societies, as is the case with Jeffrey Paige's (1975) analysis of agrarian revolutions in which cultivators (agricultural workers) and noncultivators (owners of land and their allies in government) evidence a clear conflict of interest, with revolution most likely when cultivators can communicate, develop ideologies, and mobilize for collective action and when noncultivators do not enjoy large resource advantages over cultivators. Barrington Moore's (1966) analysis of the rise of democracy employs an argument very similar to that developed by abstracted Marxian theories, emphasizing that subordinates can effectively engage in conflict when they live in propinquity, communicate, avoid competition with each other, and perceive that they are being exploited by elites who no longer honor traditional forms of relations with subordinates (primarily because of the effects of markets in breaking down traditional patterns of social relations). Charles Tilly (1978, 1993) similarly develops a model of resource mobilization that draws from Marx and Weber, emphasizing that when subordinates have been kept out of the political arena, when segments of elites have similarly been disenfranchised, and when the state has been weakened (due to fiscal crises, inefficient tax collection, and poor administration), mobilization for conflict is likely. Theda Skocpol's (1979) analysis of revolution draws from Weber the effects of losing prestige in the world system, which comes with defeat in war, coupled with fiscal crises, which give subordinates opportunities to mobilize for conflict. Jack Goldstone (1991) introduces a demographic variable into these theories of revolutionary conflict, arguing that population growth will over the course of a century cause price inflation, displacement of peasants from the land, urban migrations, disaffection of some elites, and fiscal crises for the state. In turn, these lagged outcomes of population growth weaken the power of the state to repress mobilizations by peasants, migrations of restive peasants to urban areas, and disaffection of some elites. Finally, Randall Collins (1986) develops a Weber-inspired model of empire formation, arguing that expansion of empires increases when a society has a marchland advantage (natural barriers protecting its backside and flanks) and when, compared with its neighbors, it has a larger population, greater wealth, higher levels of productivity, more advanced technologies, and better-organized armies. But, as the empire expands, it will eventually lose its marchland and military advantages (as enemies copy its technology) while increasing its logistical loads to sustain the empire. Eventually, an empire will have a showdown war with another empire, causing it to collapse and implode back to its original home base. As is evident, then, Marx and Weber's theoretical legacy lives on in yet another theoretical venue, historical-comparative analysis of state and empire formation, revolutionary conflict, and war.

CRITICAL THEORIZING

From sociology's very beginnings, thinkers have often argued that sociology could be used to reconstruct society. Comte, for example, viewed positivism as a means for creating a better society, but his approach as well as that of his followers, such as Spencer and Durkheim, was not sufficiently critical of the condition of early industrial societies. Instead, it was Marx's critique of the evils of capitalism that pushed for a critical edge to theorizing, but as critical theorists in the early twentieth century sought to retain the emancipatory thrust of Marx's ideas, they had to take into account Weber's prediction that the state would increasingly dominate social relations through rational legal authority.

At the University of Frankfurt, early critical theorists like Max Horkheimer ([1947] 1972, [1947] 1974) and Theodor Adorno [1966] (1973) emphasized that critical theory must describe the social forces that work against human freedom and expose the ideological justifications of these forces. Theorists must confront each other, debating ideas, and from these debates "truth" will emerge, but this truth is not that of science but a practical knowledge that comes from human struggles against the forces of oppression. Others in the Frankfurt School, as it became known, took a more idealist turn. György Lukács [1922] (1968), for example, borrowed from Marx the idea of the "fetishism of commodities" and converted it into a notion of "reification" in which all objects, including people, become commodities to be marketed, whose worth is determined by their "exchange value," another concept taken from Marx and Adam Smith ([1776] 1976). Lukács saw this process of reification to be an evolutionary trend, coming to a similar conclusion as Weber's "steel cage" argument, but he proposed a way out: There are limits to how far human consciousness will tolerate reification, and so it is necessary to unlock this innate source of resistance to reification—a theoretical position that pushes critical theory into subjectivism.

Outside the Frankfurt School proper, critical theory also took a cultural turn. For example, in Italy, Antonio Gramsci [1928] (1971) returned to the early Marx, where the importance of ideology was emphasized in the critique of the Young Hegelians. For Gramsci, the power of the state is used to manipulate workers and others through the propagation of ideologies about civic culture that are seemingly inoffensive but that nonetheless become the dominant views of even those who are oppressed. Thus, workers come to believe in the appropriateness of markets, the commodification of objects and symbols, the buying and selling of labor as a commodity, the rule of law to enforce contracts unfavorable to workers, the encouragement of private charities (rather than structural reform) to eliminate suffering, the curriculum in schools, the state's definition of a "good citizen," and many other taken-for-granted beliefs of the oppressed population. Thus, the state controls a population not so much by a "steel cage" of repression and rational-legal domination as by a "soft" world of symbols that the oppressed accept as "natural and appropriate"—a more sophisticated version of Marx's arguments about "false consciousness." In France, Louis Althusser (1965) adopted a structuralist metaphor, seeing the individual as trapped in a "deeper" structural order dominated by the state, capitalist economic relations, and capitalist ideologies; and because people see this order as the way things must be, they do not perceive that they can escape from this structure. By failing to see the state and ideology as crude tools of power and by seeing self as subordinate to deep structures directing all social life, individuals come to believe that resistance to these oppressive structures is futile.

The tradition of the Frankfurt School has been carried forth by a number of scholars, the most notable being Jurgen Habermas (1981/1984), who begins by seeing science as one form of domination as the state propagates an ideology revolving around "technocratic consciousness." Habermas develops a broad evolutionary view of human history, incorporating theoretical elements from many contemporary theoretical traditions, but the basic argument is that the "lifeworld" (an idea borrowed from phenomenology) is being "colonized" by the state and economy; as this process proceeds, people's capacity for "communicative action" is reduced. For Habermas, communicative action is the process whereby meanings are formed, creating the lifeworld that is the principal means of integration for societies. As the lifeworld is colonized, the reproduction of the lifeworld is interrupted; and societal integration is maintained only by "delinguistified media" such as money and power. Habermas develops a larger philosophical scheme, but his arguments carry forth the legacy of the Frankfurt School.

Within the United States, the issues raised by the old and new Frankfurt School, and those outside Germany working with its legacy, have been less influential than the rise of a wide variety of more specific critical approaches. These critical approaches often borrow from Marx and philosophy, but they owe more inspiration to prominent social movements, particularly the civil rights and women's movements. These theories are generally philosophical, often anti-science, and critical of the social relations and ideologies that oppress specific subpopulations, such as members of ethnic minorities, women, and workers. Over the last two decades, this line of theorizing, if it can be called theory proper, has gained a strong foothold not only in sociology but also in many other disciplines such as English. Just how successful these ideologically loaded "theories" will be in the next decades is an open question, although they are now well established throughout academia and thus have a resource base that can sustain them. The result is that the debate of earlier generations of sociologists over the prospects for scientific theorizing has taken on a new polemical intensity, exceeding by far the comparatively muted debates among the founding generation of sociologists over the prospects for scientific sociology.

POSTMODERN THEORIZING

One of the most prominent new lines of theorizing in sociology is postmodernism, which, like critical theories, tends to be hostile to science (Lyotard 1979; Rorty 1979) and often takes a cultural turn from its Marxist origins. Economic postmodernism draws ideas not only from Marx but also from early theorists who were concerned about the "pathologies" of modernization, whereas cultural postmodernism emphasizes the increasing dominance of culture at the same time that symbols have become fragmented, commodified, and at times trivialized in ways that make individuals overly reflexive and unable to sustain a stable identity. Both economic and cultural postmodernists emphasize the dramatic transformations that come with global markets driven by capitalism; indeed, these transformations are so fundamental as to mark a new stage of human evolution: the postmodern.

Economic postmodernists stress particular dimensions of the transformation that come with globalization (Harvey 1989; Jameson 1984; Lash and Urry 1987). One point of emphasis is the effect of high volume, velocity, and global markets fueled by advertising. The result has been the commodification of objects, people, and, most important, cultural symbols that are ripped from their indigenous locations, commodified, and marketed across the globe. Marxist-oriented postmodernists, who often overlap with world-systems theorists, emphasize the rapid movement of capital over the world and its deconcentration from historical centers of capital. Advances in transportation and communication technology have also compressed time and space in ways that facilitate the flow not only of capital but also of goods, people, and symbols around the globe. Finally, economic postmodernists tend to emphasize the growing dominance of imaging technologies of reproduction over those for production.

Cultural postmodernists focus on the consequences of the transformations described by economic postmodernists (Baudrillard 1981/1994; Gergen 1991; Kellner 1995). The first significant consequence is the increasing dominance of culture and symbols over material structures. People increasingly live in a world of fragmented symbols, which has more impact on their identities and behaviors than material conditions. The increase in the power of culture is made possible by media technologies and markets that detach culture from local groups, local time, and local space and that send commodified cultural elements via media technologies or via markets around the global system. Indeed, humans live in a simulated world of symbolizations of symbols, viewed through the eyeglass of the media (Baudrillard 1981/1994). As a result of its detachment from its material base and free-floating signifiers, culture loses its capacity to provide stable meanings for individuals. As an outcome of this inability of culture to provide meanings and anchorage of individuals in local groups, self becomes more salient than group, leading to increased reflexivity about self in an endless loop of searching for meanings and for a true sense of self. Thus, at the very time that self is ascendant, it reveals less stability, coherence, and viability.

These themes in contemporary postmodern theory can all be found in the founding generations of sociologists. For example, Durkheim's concern over anomie and egoism; Marx's views on alienation; Simmel's analysis of the marginal and fractured self; Smith's, Comte's, Spencer's, and Durkheim's concerns about the differentiation and fragmentation of society; Weber's portrayal of rationalization and emphasis on efficiency over other types of action; Marx's and the later critical theorists' view of the power of ideology; and many other "pathologies" of modern societies that early theorists emphasized have all been recast in postmodern theory. In a very real sense, then, postmodern theorizing represents an extension of the concerns of early theorists about the effects of modernization on society and humans. Yet much postmodern theory consists of conjectures that have not been seriously tested, although many postmodernists, particularly the cultural postmodernists, would consider empirical tests in the mode of science to impose a "failed epistemology" on their modes of inquiry. Moreover, a great deal of postmodern theory overlaps with critical theorizing because few consider the "postmodern condition" to be a good thing; thus, postmodernism is heavily ideological in critiquing the contemporary world, often assuming implicitly that human nature has somehow been violated.

Like critical theorizing, postmodern theory is part of a much larger intellectual and cultural movement that extends across disciplines as diverse as architecture, social sciences, and the humanities. Within sociology, it has enjoyed a strong following for the last two decades, although there are signs that cultural postmodernists are losing ground, with the economic postmodernists moving more squarely into Marxian-inspired world-systems analysis.

INTERACTIONIST THEORIZING

Contemporary interactionist theorizing reveals a number of variants, each of which draws from a different theoretical tradition. Symbolic interactionism carries forth the pragmatist tradition synthesized by George Herbert Mead (1934); dramaturgical theory draws primarily from Durkheim's ([1912] 1947) analysis of rituals; interaction ritual theory also draws from Durkheim and dramaturgy while introducing elements from other modern theories; ethnomethodology represents the modern application of phenomenology (Husserl [1913] 1969; Schütz [1932] 1967), coupled with elements from other traditions; and there are several efforts to develop syntheses among all these strands of theorizing about face-to-face interaction.

Symbolic Interactionism

The ideas of Mead have been applied to a wide variety of topics, from roles (Turner 1968) and identity processes (McCall and Simmons 1978; Stryker 1980, 2001) through the sociology of emotions (Burke 1991; Heise 1979; Scheff 1988) to theories of collective behavior (Snow and Benford 1988; Turner and Killian 1987). The basic argument is that social reality is ultimately constructed from face-to-face interactions among individuals who communicate symbolically, develop definitions of situations, draw on cultural resources, play roles, and seek to verify self and identity (Blumer 1969). Identity theories are perhaps the most prominent theoretical wing of interactionist theory today (for recent statements by various theorists, see Burke 2006; Burke et al. 2003). Here, theorists view more global self-conceptions and situational role identities as a cybernetic control system, with individuals presenting gestures so as to get others to verify their self and identity. These theories also overlap with theories of emotions, since verification of self arouses positive emotions, whereas failure to verify self generates negative emotional arousal and leads to adjustments in behaviors or identities that bring identity, behavior, and responses of others into line. Some versions of symbolic interactionism extend these Gestalt dynamics not only to person but also to others, the identity of others, and the situation, with individuals seen as motivated to keep sentiments about these aspects of interaction consistent with each other (Heise 1979; Smith-Lovin and Heise 1988). As noted earlier, another set of symbolic interactionist theories incorporates Freudian dynamics to explain the activation of defense mechanisms when self and identity are not confirmed or when individuals fail to realize expectations or experience negative sanctions (Scheff 1988; J. Turner 2002). Role theory has also been influenced by symbolic interactionism, with each individual reading the gestures of others to determine the latter's role and with individuals also seeking to have others verify their roles and the self and identity presented in these roles (R. Turner 2001). Theories of collective behavior and social movements also adopt symbolic interactionists ideas, emphasizing the collective contagion and emotional arousal of crowd behaviors and the processes by which members of social movements frame situations in ways that direct collective actions (Snow and Benford 1988).

Dramaturgical Theories

Erving Goffman (1959, 1967) was the first to downsize Durkheim's ([1912] 1947) analysis of rituals and emotions as the basis of social solidarity in the most elemental social unit, the encounter, or episode of interaction. While Goffman was often seen as a symbolic interactionist, he was a Durkheimian who emphasized the importance of the cultural script, the dramatic presentations of self to an audience, and the strategic behaviors that individuals employ in presenting self on a stage in which props, sets, space and ecology, and interpersonal demography are employed to make a dramatic presentation and to realize strategic goals. In contrast to most symbolic interactionists, dramaturgy views self as purely situational and as something that individuals "put on" in presenting a "line" or in strategic acts of "impression management." Thus, in addition to the use of the front stage to manage a line, forms of talk, use of rituals, presentations of roles, and keying of frames (of what is to be included and excluded from the interaction) are all synchronized to present self in a particular light and to achieve strategic ends.

Interaction Ritual Theorizing

Randall Collins (2004) has extended Durkheim's and Goffman's analysis to a more general theory of ritual. For

Collins, the elements of what Goffman termed the "encounter" constitute a more inclusive ritual where individuals reveal a focus of attention, common mood, rhythmic synchronization of bodies and talk, symbolization of the positive emotional energy from rhythmic synchronization, and enhanced solidarity. When these elements of the ritual do not unfold, however, negative emotional energy is aroused, and solidarity becomes more problematic. Unlike most interactionists, Collins does not see self as a critical motivational force in these rituals. Moreover, he tries to develop a more general theory of meso and macro structures using interaction rituals as the "micro foundation" of all social structures (Collins 1981). More recent theories (Summer-Effler 2002, 2004a, 2004b) in this tradition have blended more symbolic interactionist elements into interaction ritual theory by expanding the analysis of emotions and introducing self and identity as key forces.

Ethnomethodology

Ethnomethodology emphasizes the methods or interpersonal techniques, especially in talk and conversation, that individuals employ to construct, maintain, or change their presumptions about what they share. This basic idea is adopted from phenomenology, a philosophical tradition (e.g., Husserl [1913] 1969) given a sociological character by Alfred Schütz ([1932] 1967). For Schütz, much interaction involves signaling to others not to question the presumption that parties to an interaction share a common view of reality. For ethnomethodologists, the gestures and signals that individuals exchange are "indexical" in that they have meaning only in particular contexts; and these signs are used to construct a sense of common meaning among individuals. Most ethnomethodological research examines finely coded transcripts of conversations to determine the ethno or folk methods that individuals employ to create or sustain a sense of reality. For example, turn-taking in conversations, gestures searching for a normal conversational form, ignoring gestures that may disconfirm reciprocity of perspectives, patterns of overlaps in conversations, allowing ambiguities in meanings to pass, or repairing in subsequent turns minor misunderstandings are all techniques that individuals employ to create and sustain the sense that they share a common intersubjective world (Garfinkel 1967; Sacks 1992; Schegloff 2001). The data presented by ethnomethodologists have been adopted by other theories, but unfortunately, the theoretical arguments of ethnomethodology appear to have taken a backseat to empirical analyses of conversations, often moving ethnomethodology into some version of linguistics.

Integrative Approaches

All of the above theoretical approaches involved some integration of both classic and contemporary theories. But some contemporary theorists have sought to develop more general and robust theories of interpersonal processes by integrating concepts and propositions from a variety of interactionist theories. Jonathan Turner (2002), for example, has blended elements from symbolic interactionism, dramaturgy, interaction ritual theory, the sociology of emotions, role theory, expectation states theory, and ethnomethodology into a view of encounters as driven fundamental forces: emotions, transactional needs, symbols, status, roles, demography, and ecology. Yet relatively few theories are as integrative as Turner's efforts; most microsociology tends to remain narrow in focus, producing a delimited set of generalizations and data sets designed to test these generalizations.

EXCHANGE THEORIZING

Exchange theory draws from both the behaviorist tradition of Edward Thorndike, Ivan Pavlov, John B. Watson (1913), and B. F. Skinner (1938) and the utilitarian tradition of the Scottish moralists. The basic argument is that individuals seek to gain profits in exchanges of resources with others, with profit being a function of the resources received, less the costs and investments spent in seeking these resources. All exchanges are also mediated by norms of fair exchange and justice, with the most prevalent norm of justice emphasizing equity or the distribution of rewards in proportion to relative costs and investments among actors. However, all exchange theories introduce the notion of power, in which one actor has the capacity to receive more rewards than others. Power is typically defined as the dependence of other actors on a powerful actor for valued resources, and the greater is the dependence of actors, the greater is the power of resource-holders over them.

Over the last four decades, exchange analysis has ventured into other areas of theorizing. Initially, exchange theory and network analysis were combined to understand the dynamics of networks in terms of the exchange dynamics that arise from power dependence (Cook and Rice 2001). The general finding is that power-advantaged actors use their advantage to exploit dependent actors by demanding additional resources. Under these conditions, dependent actors will seek other exchange partners, leave the exchange, learn to do without resources, or introduce new resources into the exchange that are highly valued by the previously advantaged actor (thus creating mutual dependence). Other findings emphasize that actors will develop commitments to exchanges, or engage in suboptimal exchanges, in return for certainty of exchange payoffs.

Another area where exchange theory has more recently penetrated is the sociology of emotions, in which power-dependence processes and network structures are analyzed in terms of the emotions that are aroused during the process of exchange (Lawler 2001). From theory and research, several generalizations emerge (Turner and Stets 2005). When payoffs are profitable and meted out in accordance with the norms of justice, positive emotions are aroused, whereas when payoffs are unprofitable, below expectations, and violate the norms of justice, negative emotions are aroused. If individuals are over-rewarded or their over-reward leads to unfair under-reward for others, they will experience guilt. Positive rewards in negotiated and reciprocal exchanges reveal a proximal bias in attributions (leading to feelings of pride), while negative rewards or under-rewards in such exchanges evidence a distal bias (arousing anger toward others, the situation, or group). High-power individuals are more likely to make self-attributions for success in profitable exchanges and external attributions for under-rewards than are low-power actors. The more profits are received in dense networks engaged in coordinated actions, the more likely are positive exchange outcomes to cause actors to make external attributions to the group, and the more they will become attached to the group. These and other generalizations document that exchange theories are becoming integrative, crossing over into other areas of theory and research in sociology.

STRUCTURALIST THEORY

All sociologists study social structures, but structuralist theorizing in sociology has special connotations. There are, in essence, two branches of structuralist theorizing, both of which derive considerable inspiration from Durkheimian sociology. One branch emphasizes material conditions as influencing the nature of social relations among individuals and collective actors. Marx, Georg Simmel, and especially the early Durkheim all agreed that structure is a set of connections among parts, with the goal of theorizing being to discover the cause of these connections and their dynamic properties. The other branch of structuralism seeks to discover the "deep structures" or "generative rules" guiding the formation of culture systems and social structural arrangements. What is observable empirically is seen as a surface manifestation of a deeper underlying system of generative rules and, in some theorists' minds (e.g., Lévi-Strauss [1958] 1963, 1979), rules directed by the neurology of the human brain.

The materialist version of structural analysis can be found in any theory that tries to explain the properties of social relations. One of the more prominent approaches in this tradition is network analysis, which views structures as nodes connected by relationships involving the flow of resources. In network theory, the form of the relationship is critical because different forms will reveal varying dynamic properties (for a review, see Turner 2002). The structuralism that also comes from Durkheim, via structural linguistics (de Saussure [1915] 1966; Jakobson 1962–1971) and structural anthropology, has inspired a revival of cultural sociology, even though some theories oftentimes see structure as being generated by the biology of the brain. But structuralism inspired a new concern with cultural codes and the practices that carry these codes to situations and that change or reinforce them. The

structuralism movement enjoyed a certain cache during the 1970s and 1980s, but by the turn into the twenty-first century, the interests of structuralists had been incorporated into the "cultural turn" of sociological theorizing. The more materialist versions of structural analysis continue, as they always have, in a wide variety of theoretical perspectives, although network analysis—the most formal of these materialist approaches—has become ever more concerned with computer algorithms for describing rather than explaining network structures.

THE CULTURAL TURN IN SOCIOLOGICAL THEORY

Over the last decades of the twentieth century, sociological theory has taken a cultural turn. There were, of course, classical antecedents to this turn, but all of them tended to see culture as a dependent variable, as something that is shaped by social structural arrangements. For Marx, culture is a "superstructure" driven by the material "substructure"; for Durkheim, the collective conscience is related to the nature, number, and relationships among system parts, although his work did inspire cultural structuralism; and for the modern functionalists, culture is conceptualized in highly analytical terms as a system composed of abstract elements such as value orientations. Only Weber ([1905] 1958) appeared to emphasize culture as a causal force, as illustrated by his analysis of the Protestant Ethnic and the rise of capitalism (although his analysis in terms of ideal types tended to reduce the culture of Protestantism and capitalism to a few analytical elements). As we saw, the critical theories of the Frankfurt School and others in this tradition like Gramsci often migrated to the analysis of ideologies, but again, culture was always connected to material and political interests. And during the 1960s, as Marxism and conflict sociology reemerged in the United States, culture was once again seen as an ideology reflecting the material interests of contending groups.

Jeffrey Alexander and Philip Smith (2001) have termed most sociological analyses of culture a "weak program" because culture is not explored as an autonomous system but, instead, as a dependent variable or superstructure to material conditions. They even criticize work that focuses explicitly on culture, including the Birmingham School's analysis of symbols in terms of Marxian structural categories, the efforts of Pierre Bourdieu (1977) to understand "habitus" and its connection to material conditions, and the works of poststructuralists like Michel Foucault (1972), whose "archeology" of knowledge ultimately uncovers the effects of power on culture. Similar cultural programs, such as Wuthnow's (1987) analysis of the moral order, are seen to emphasize the connection between the moral order and the material resource bases generated by wealth, leadership communication networks, political authority, and other structural properties. Likewise, Michèle

Lamont's (1999) analysis of culture as marking group boundaries is viewed as explaining culture by its attachment to stratification and economic systems.

In contrast to these "weak programs," Alexander and Smith (2001) propose a "strong program" where culture is treated initially as an autonomous sphere with deep textual analysis of its symbols in their specific context. Both the weak and strong programs emphasize cultural codes, discursive practices by which these codes are used, rituals directed at the code, and the objects denoted by codes, discourse, and rituals, but the strong program avoids connecting cultural analysis to material conditions, as least until the full exploration of the cultural codes has been completed. For example, Alexander's (2004) strong program of "cultural pragmatics" emphasizes that there are deep background "representations" that generate "scripts" and "texts" that actors decode and interpret; and these need to be analyzed before they are connected to individuals' actions in front of audiences. Although power and productive relations influence how actors extend culture to audiences through ritual performances, the elements of culture need to be analytically separated from their structural contexts, and their scripts and texts need to be thickly described. Only then can they be reattached to ritual, social structure, and audience to explain ritual practices and audience reactions. And as actors extend culture to audiences, they experience cathexis, which, in turn, influences the nature of the texts, discourse, and rituals.

Whatever the merits of these kinds of arguments, it is clear that cultural sociology has made an enormous comeback over the last decade of the twentieth century, and indeed, theorizing about culture is becoming as prominent in the first decade of this century as conceptualizations of material conditions were at the height of conflict theory in the 1960s and 1970s. Yet, for all the emphasis on thick description of texts, most analyses eventually become highly analytical, abstracting from these texts particular sets of codes that, in turn, are attached to material conditions.

PROBLEMS AND PROSPECTS FOR SOCIOLOGICAL THEORY IN THE 21ST CENTURY

The Decline of Grand Theory When It Is Most Needed

At the very time when sociological theory has differentiated into a variety of approaches, general and integrative theorizing has declined. All of the early theorists, especially Spencer, Marx, Weber, and Durkheim, were generalists who sought to explain a wide range of phenomena across long reaches of history. Functional theory in the modern era, particularly that practiced by Talcott Parsons and Niklas Luhmann, was also grand, but with the demise of these versions of grand theory, such theorizing fell out

of favor and has been replaced by narrower theories confined to one level of analysis and held in check by scope conditions. Relatively few theories today seek to explain all phenomena at the micro, meso, and macro levels. There are some exceptions, however. For example, Anthony Giddens's (1984) structuration theory is grand in the sense that it attempts to explain all levels of reality, although his scheme is more of a conceptual framework for describing a wide range of empirical cases. Jonathan Turner's (1995, 2002) efforts of theorizing approximate a grand approach because he consciously seeks to integrate existing theories at all levels of social reality. Randall Collins's (1975, 2004) interaction ritual theory is another approach that seeks to explain reality at the micro, meso, and macro levels. Still, most theorists shy away from this kind of integrative effort, at the very time that sociological theory is fragmenting into diverse and often hostile camps. In the future, it will be necessary for more integrative and, indeed, grand approaches to make a comeback if sociological theory is to reveal any coherence in the twenty-first century.

The Continuing Debate over Science

From the beginning, sociologists have debated the prospects for scientific sociology resembling that in the natural sciences. The founders were split, with Comte, Spencer, Simmel, and Durkheim pushing for scientific sociology, while Marx and Weber had doubts about the prospects for universal laws that could explain reality at all times and in all places. This split over the prospects for scientific sociology continued through the whole of the twentieth century and divides sociological theory (Turner and Turner 1990).

There are those who wish to perform rigorous analytical work but who view a sociology that apes the natural sciences as impossible; there are those who see the epistemology of the natural sciences as not only impossible but as a tool of repression; there are still others who see science as proposing grand narratives when the world does not reveal such an obdurate character; there are many who seek sociology as an art form or as a clinical field in which investigators use their intuiting to solve problems; and there are many who argue that sociology should be explicitly ideological, seeking to change the world. There is, then, a rather large collection of anti-scientists within sociology, especially sociological theory.

The end result is that scientific sociology is not accepted by many sociologists. Yet an enormous amount of theoretical growth and accumulation of knowledge has occurred over the last four decades, at the very time when many were having doubts about the appropriateness or possibility of a natural science of society. Thus, much of the new scientific understanding about the dynamics of the social world is ignored or viewed with hostility by those who have other agendas. Indeed, should sociology ever have its Einstein, only a few would take notice.

Chauvinism and Intolerance

Even among those who are committed to the epistemology of science, there is both chauvinism and intolerance. Some proclaim that certain processes occurring at a particular level of reality are the key properties and processes of the social universe, while being dismissive of those who think otherwise. And among those who do not believe that science is possible or even desirable, there is a smug condescension that is equally dismissive. For the former, theory becomes narrow and focused, building up barriers to other theoretical approaches, while for the latter group, theory becomes anything and everything—ideology, practice, philosophizing, textual analysis, moral crusading, critique, and virtually any activity. In being anything and everything, it becomes nothing in the sense of accumulating knowledge about the social world. Social theory, when not disciplined by the epistemology of science, becomes driven by intellectual fads and foibles, constantly changing with new social, cultural, and intellectual movements but never establishing a base of knowledge.

CONCLUSIONS

This summary cannot really do justice to the diversity of activity that occurs under the rubrics of "social" and, more narrowly, "sociological" theory. Humpty Dumpty has fallen off the wall, split into so many pieces that even grand theorists may never be able to put him back together again. In one sense, the proliferation of theories is a sign of vitality, especially among those narrow theories that seek to develop cumulative knowledge. But it is also an indicator of weakness because at some point, sociological theory will need to develop a more integrated set of principles and models about social reality. This effort is hindered by those who simply do not accept the epistemology of science. As a result, efforts to integrate theories will often be sidetracked by debate and acrimony as factions become intolerant of each other. As a consequence, at a time when enormous progress has been made in denoting the basic properties of the social universe, in developing abstract models and principles on the operative dynamics of these properties, and in assessing these theories with systematically collected data, it is not clear how many sociologists are listening. Fifty years ago, it seemed that sociology was ready to take its place at the table of science; today, this prospect seems more remote, despite the fact that sociology is far more sophisticated theoretically than five decades ago. Thus, as we move toward the end of the first decade of the twenty-first century, it is not clear just what the prospects for sociological theory will be. Will the scientists prevail? Will the anti-science factions win out? Or will the fight continue for another 100 years? Realistically speaking, this last prognosis is the most likely scenario.

PART II

INTERNATIONAL PERSPECTIVES

5

ASIAN SOCIOLOGY

CHIKAKO USUI

University of Missouri–St. Louis

Sociology in Japan and China, as in the West, arose out of dramatic economic and political change. Japan's Meiji Restoration and the end of China's dynastic rule marked periods of dramatic transformation. Sweeping changes took place in Japan with the Meiji Restoration, postwar occupation reforms, and rapid ascent to world economic superpower. Sociology in China was shaped by the end of dynastic rule, the Communist Revolution, the Cultural Revolution, the dramatic shift to a market economy, and diplomatic opening to the West. The importation of sociology from the West brought different traditions to each country, but sociology is now firmly institutionalized in these societies. New generations of sociologists take active roles in international communication and research collaboration, producing high-quality sociological works.

Differences in historical legacies, political and economic development, and contact with the West were responsible for distinctive paths of advancement in the two countries. Japanese sociology developed toward more abstract and formal German sociology, with academic production taking the form of individual scholars translating texts from the West for a domestic market. In contrast, Chinese sociology followed an American or British model, was applied in its orientation, and academic production

involved collaborative and empirical works with publication including an international audience. Japanese and Chinese sociology are distinguished by the degree of academic as opposed to applied and policy orientations and by the rate of diversification of substantive fields. In China, sociological research is more centrally planned and funded, including publications and establishing international links. In Japan, the discipline has grown and diversified, making it harder to capture its development as a whole.

INITIAL DEVELOPMENT OF SOCIOLOGY

1880s to Early 1940s: Japan

Japanese sociology emerged in the context of explosive efforts to modernize the country with the opening to the West following the Meiji Restoration in 1868. These efforts included selective importation of Western knowledge, technology, and institutions. Sociology blended ideas of traditional authority with modern, democratic principles of representative government. For example, Japanese law was modeled after German and French codes, and Japan's first constitution, written in 1889,

AUTHOR'S NOTE: The author is grateful to the following individuals for their helpful comments and information provided: Richard A. Colignon, Shujiro Yazawa, Yoshimichi Sato, and Noriko Iwai. The author also thanks Jian Sun and Chongyi Wei for their assistance in translation of Chinese sources.

rested on the principle of a divine emperor as an absolute ruler but with a parliament (the Diet). Significant institutional advances took place in education, initially with the establishment of the University of Tokyo (originally, Tokyo Imperial University) in 1877 and later in other public national universities where Western knowledge and technology were promoted.

Sociology was initially translated as *gun-gaku* (study of collectives) but changed to *shakai-gaku* (study of society) around 1885. In 1893, Masakazu Toyama (1848–1900) became the first Japanese sociology professor at the University of Tokyo and is generally considered the founder of Japanese sociology. In 1903, the University of Tokyo established the first sociology department. In the first decade of the twentieth century, sociological ideas mixed with academic and political interests and dynamics to create divisions between liberals and conservatives. Liberals looked to Herbert Spencer, J. S. Mill, and Jeremy Bentham on individual rights and freedoms in their push for an elected parliamentary assembly. Conservatives also relied on Spencer's work to justify the absolute power of the emperor in guiding modernization, needs for war (in the Sino-Japanese War of 1894), the Meiji Constitution (1889), and August Comte's sociology to justify Japan's existing social hierarchy (Kawamura 1994:5).

In contrast to the political involvement of sociology, there was also a movement toward a more academic style of sociology. Shotaro Yoneda (1893–1945), the first sociology professor at Kyoto University, introduced a formal sociology by promoting specialized areas (Kawamura 1994:55). He laid the groundwork for European (and later German) sociology in Japan by introducing social theories (of Gabriel Tarde, Émile Durkheim, George Simmel, Edmund Husserl, Hendrich Rickert, and Leopold von Wiese) during the first decade of the twentieth century. Yoneda was succeeded by his students Yasuma Takada, Junichiro Matsumoto, and Masamichi Shinmei, leading to the dominance of German sociology in Japan until World War II (Sasaki 2000:1477–78).

The reform movement for democratic rights and universal suffrage organized by workers, peasants, and intellectuals during the Taisho Democracy era of the 1920s further shaped the development of sociology. However, the rising militarization of Japan and government hostility toward liberal sociology redirected its development. The Great Depression of the 1930s and government oppression brought conservatives to prominence in academia, and sociology moved in a nationalistic direction. Conservative sociologists began criticizing socialism as an enemy of Japanese national polity, and liberal sociologists converted to conservative ideologies that supported the emperor system (Kawamura 1994:6). By the 1930s and 1940s, the focus of sociology shifted to "Japanism," an ideology built on the emperor system and the family system.

An empirical orientation had emerged in the 1920s, led by Teizo Toda, in family structures and rural sociology. Kunio Yanagita became the most influential twentieth-century scholar of folklore; he emphasized the development of indigenous theories of agricultural systems, kinship lineage, and common people (Kawamura 1994:69). In addition, the Japan Sociological Association was formed in 1924. However, prior to World War II, sociology remained a small venture; sociology departments existed at only a few public and private universities with a limited number of sociologists and sociological research projects.[1]

1890s to 1950s: China

Chinese sociology was similarly born out of the rapid transformation of society at the end of the nineteenth century. The Qing dynasty was imploding from rural poverty, lost wars, colonial incursions, and civil unrest. Sociology came out of the vacuum created from the declining support for the Confucian-based dynastic order. Chinese intellectuals had been questioning the adequacies of the old Confucian order and looked for a new foundation from which to steer China into the twentieth century. At that time, Beijing University (established as Metropolitan University in 1898 and renamed Peking University in 1911) was a central location for the development of Western ideas such as anarchism, monarchism, pragmatism, socialism, Marxism, democratic liberalism, and scientism (King 1978:39).

Yu Fu, the first president of Peking University, translated the work of Herbert Spencer into Chinese in 1897. St. John's University in Shanghai offered the first sociology course in 1914, and Peking and Tsin Hua Universities followed in 1915 and 1917, respectively. The first sociology department was created at Yanching University (merged with Peking University in 1922) (King 1978:38). Western scholars at private missionary colleges were instrumental in introducing and spreading sociology in the early twentieth century. American missionary colleges and organizations were leading importers of Western sociology to China in the 1920s and 1930s through direct teaching and training of Chinese sociologists with reformist, applied interests emphasizing theory, research, and methods (King 1978:41–42). In contrast to the Japanese style of a single established scholar translating a Western text and working with a group of students, Chinese sociology developed in a different direction by training young scholars in Western sociology and then engaging in collaborative research between domestic and foreign scholars and publication of community studies.

Sociology developed quickly in terms of infrastructure, professional body, and volumes of publication because of collaboration between Chinese and Western scholars. In addition, Chinese were oriented toward translation of their texts for an English-speaking audience (in contrast to Japanese who were oriented toward their domestic market). In the 1930s and 1940s, the sociological infrastructure began to develop. The Chinese Sociological Association was established in 1930. Universities rapidly created sociology departments, and courses as professional identity, and the legitimacy of sociology as an academic discipline firmly took root. By the end of 1930, 11 universities offered sociology curricula. By 1947, 19 universities had full-fledged sociology departments, and there were 143 academic sociologists and 1,500 students taking sociology as a college major (Whyte 2000). Chinese sociology (by Chinese and non-Chinese scholars) flourished with unique applied features combining social anthropology and social work, embarked on large-scale community studies, and produced fine ethnographies of Chinese villages (e.g., Li Ching-tan, Fei Xiao-tong), many of which were published abroad in English (Li et al. 2001:622; Whyte 2000:297–98).[2] Sociology was growing faster in China than anywhere else in the world outside North America and Europe (King 1978:39; Whyte 2000). Sociologists contributed to the development of the social policy of the Kuomintang government (1911–1948), even though some leading "leftist" Chinese sociologists caused irritation by their severe criticism of the government.

Sociology took root in China and matured rapidly with its own style through the use of domestic data as the content of sociology courses before 1949. Many of these studies were published abroad. However, after the Communist Revolution in 1949, Chinese sociology was reorganized. Marxism became the guardian of the communist political order and the sole legitimate national ideology, and Soviet-model reforms (which banned sociology) were implemented in higher education institutions. All social sciences were seen with suspicion, particularly sociology. Academic sociology denounced "bourgeois sociology" (Western sociology, in particular Comptean sociology imported from the United States) and accepted Marxist sociology (then called "new sociology"), but all types of sociology were banned in 1952. Ethnography continued to flourish because it was considered separate from sociology. Similarly, demography was established as an independent field in the 1970s. The new communist China rejected sociological contributions to social research and methods, and Mao's case study methods (proletariat in nature) became the rule. After a brief restoration movement in sociology in the mid-1950s, the discipline was finally silenced, along with political science and law, and it vanished in 1957 (for more details of this period, see Li et al. 2001).

1950s to 1970s:
Americanization of Sociology in Japan

Democratic occupation policies provided the context for the institutionalization of sociology at major public universities after World War II. Sweeping changes led by the Allied occupation reforms in the economy, land, and education as well as democratization accelerated the advancement of sociology. Sociology was integrated into the general university educational curriculum, and the Japan Sociological Society (JSS; 1924–present) joined the International Sociological Association in 1950. The central focus of sociology shifted to the study of American

sociology and its theoretical and empirical innovations (especially Talcott Parsons) (Lie 1996:63), in contrast to the conservative prewar stance of Japanese sociology, which drew heavily from the formal orientation of German sociology.

Sociology was dominated by those with prewar training, and their research focused on themes of modernization and democratization (Sasaki 2000:1478). The prewar emphasis on ethnographic research led to the development of two major specialized fields (substantive areas or subfields) that became most representative of Japanese sociology: rural sociology and industrial sociology. Rural sociology was established by Tadashi Fukutake (1917–1989), Eitaro Suzuki (1894–1966), and Kizaemon Ariga (1897–1979). Industrial sociology proliferated, with Kunio Odaka (1908–1993) at the University of Tokyo laying the foundation work (Nakao 1998:503). Other notable advances took place in mass communication through the work of Ikutaro Shimizu (1907–), sociology of culture by Rokuro Hidaka (1917–), and French sociology by Suketoshi Tanabe (1894–1962).

The 1950s brought large-scale time-trend national survey projects. The Social Stratification and Social Mobility (SSM) project by the Japanese Sociological Association in collaboration with the International Sociological Association began in 1952, and data collection has continued every 10 years to the present.[3] Also, in 1954 the Institute of Statistical Mathematics launched research on the Japanese character by conducting national surveys every 5 years and pioneering the use of identical questions over time to analyze changes in the social attitudes of the Japanese people. This survey became a model for the General Social Survey of the National Opinion Research Center at the University of Chicago (Sasaki 2000:1479). These two ongoing surveys have become the most well-known national social surveys in Japan.

1950s to 1978: Remission of Sociology in China

The development of sociology was suspended by the Chinese Communist Party, which perceived sociology incompatible with Marxism-Leninism and Maoism. Mao's grassroots investigation methods became the sole legitimate research methodology, and sociology was banned for nearly 25 years (1952/1957–1979). No sociology degree was given between 1952 and 1982. However, in the late 1950s, the United States, Japan, and Europe began sociological studies of China and developed elaborate methods to cope with difficulties of learning about China firsthand (Whyte 2000).

1970s to 1990s: Diversification of Sociology in Japan

Japanese sociology was marked by growth, diversification, and internationalization from the 1970s to 1990s. In the context of a booming economy, scholars' attention moved to issues of the consequences of rapid industrialization, such as inequality, social problems, and the environment.

Sociology became firmly institutionalized, as indicated by the growth in the number of sociologists, sociology programs, and publications. In the 1970s, some 300 sociologists were teaching, but by the 1980s, the number exceeded 1,000. Membership in the Japan Sociological Society increased from 870 in 1957 to 1,945 in 1985, 2,200 in 1990, and 3,034 in 1994. By the late 1980s, 33 out of Japan's 501 colleges/universities offered doctoral programs in sociology, with 700 graduate students (of which 490 were doctoral students). During 1977–1986, 41 Ph.D.s were awarded in sociology. The number of articles and books published in 1984–1988 exceeded 7,000 and 900, respectively (Sasaki 2000).

Continuing its orientation to American sociology, Japanese sociology experienced diversification of substantive areas, methodology, and theory, as exemplified by the proliferation of specialized sociological associations. New substantive areas that thrived during this period included organization, family, education, social psychology, social pathology, sport, labor, life course, law, and religion. Social surveys and empirical studies flourished in areas including family, rural/urban sociology, and popular culture (Lie 1996:65). Diversity of methodological approaches included subjective methodologies and phenomenological sociology, symbolic interactionism, and ethnomethodology (Sasaki 2000:1479). American influence became even stronger, and the new generation of sociologists increasingly turned to structuralist social theory. The theoretical focus shifted from macro to micro level and to multidimensional paradigms of Michel Foucault, Jürgen Habermas, Niklas Luhmann, Pierre Bourdieu, Anthony Giddens, and Alfred Schütz. Diversification of sociology (interests, theoretical orientation, and methodology) led to more specialized sociological associations (Yazawa 2000).

The orientation of Japanese sociology became more international through increasing participation in international conferences and associations. For example, the Japan Sociological Society organized the first conference of Asian sociologists (The Asia Congress of Sociology) in Tokyo in 1973, in collaboration with the International Sociological Association and U.N. Educational, Scientific and Cultural Organization (UNESCO) on themes of social development in Asia (Morioka and Yazawa 1993:1547). Japanese leadership continued in successive meetings in 1978, 1981, and 1984. Korea and China hosted the 1987 and 1991 conferences, respectively (Yazawa 2000).

Two issues remained. Access to the original survey data for secondary analysis was foreign despite the scores of statistical studies performed every year on an amazing array of topics by government agencies and private organizations (Matsui 1997; Tanioka and Iwai 2003). These raw data sets were not publicly shared. Research by individuals or teams in collecting and analyzing original data was

prized as scholarly work. In addition, with the adoption of Western sociology, empirical analyses were directed to fact-finding ventures, with little testing of theory. Efforts at theorizing from Japanese society remained limited.

1990s to the Present: Globalization of Sociology in Japan

Japanese sociology had become more international and continued to grow, diversify, and professionalize. In the late 1990s, Japan built an American-style graduate school system geared to global competitiveness. A new generation of Japanese sociologists undertook empirical research projects and expanded international research endeavors. For the first time, several universities opened national data archives to scholars for secondary analysis.

The late 1990s saw a clear shift in leadership and education reform by the central government. In this process, a new generation of sociologists has connected Japanese sociology more closely to American and European sociologists. Younger sociologists who were trained abroad with secondary data analyses sought the new direction in sociology. Others promoted the creation of a new environment, cultivating their own contacts and working with specialized sociological associations. (To name a few, such sociologists include Hiroshi Ishida, Noriko Iwai, Kenji Kosaka, Masamichi Sasaki, Yoshimichi Sato, Toshio Yamagishi, Shujiro Yazawa, and Kosaku Yoshino.)

The Japanese higher education system changed dramatically in the beginning of the twenty-first century, including more independent administration of national universities, a reduction in the number of national universities, and the institutionalization and reform of graduate schools. Reforms initiated by the Ministry of Education, Culture, Sports, Science and Technology (MEXT) focused on founding new and specialized graduate schools, a move toward an American-style education system that is appropriate for a postindustrial, mature economy. It gave each university more flexibility in university management and independence in creation of unique graduate programs. Competition among universities to survive the adverse market (due to the decline in the number of prospective students) has intensified. In restructuring higher education, MEXT has identified academic research as an integral part of knowledge production and global competitiveness.

Somewhat similar to the National Science Foundation (NSF) in the United States, MEXT has begun priority funding of creative research under the 21st Century Center of Excellence (COE) program. The program attempts to support the formation of centers of excellence in graduate training. Several initiatives in sociology have been selected and funded, including the Center for the Study of Social Stratification and Inequality at Tohoku University and Social Research for the Enhancement of Human Well-Being at Kwansei Gakuin University.[4]

The reform also made it easier to obtain graduate degrees in contrast to the previous system of doctorate training that consumed nearly half of one's career. Generally speaking, three years of course work (plus a dissertation) are required for a doctoral degree beyond a master's degree. Before the reform, doctoral candidates became teaching or research assistants first before completing their Ph.D. dissertations. These posts marked the beginning of one's lifelong tenured career at the university. They continued to work with the senior academic (master) and completed their dissertations at a later date, typically in middle age. This system was similar to the apprenticeship of European higher education systems such as the one in Germany. More recently, however, universities have restructured their Ph.D. programs that are similar to the American system and began awarding doctorate degrees in shorter duration and in larger numbers. Perhaps the most exciting and significant change in Japanese sociology was the development of a publicly accessible social science infrastructure. Prior to the 1990s, a widening gap of research infrastructures existed between Japanese and European/North American sociologies. Statistical studies performed by government agencies and private organizations focused on fact-finding rather than theory-testing in empirical analyses, and these rich data were not shared with academic researchers (Tanioka and Iwai 2003; Smith et al. 2005). This contrasted with accelerated infrastructure building abroad. In Europe, the movement led to the creation of several national data archives that provided an opportunity for international collaboration in the 1960s, and by 1976, Europe established the Council of European Social Science Data Archive (CESSDA). In the United States, the first data archive of public opinion polls opened at the Roper Center in 1946, and by 1962, the ICPSR (Inter-University Consortium for Political and Social Research) was established. The American General Social Survey (GSS) was created in 1972 with NSF funding.

In parallel fashion, the University of Tokyo created in 1996 the Information Center for Social Research on Japan (a unit within the Institute of Social Science) for specifically managing the Social Science Japan Data Archive (SSJDA 2005), which is funded by MEXT.[5] Shortly thereafter, with funding from MEXT, a team of sociologists launched the first nationwide General Social Survey (JGSS, parallel to the American GSS) to provide data on attitudes and behavior for secondary analyses by social scientists. The data for JGSS-2000 (Japanese version) was released by ICPSR in February 2004 (also scheduled for release in Cologne), and the English version of data files for JGSS-2000, -2001, and -2002 will become available soon (Iwai 2004). In 2005, MEXT funded the Educational and Social Survey Research Center (ESSRC) at Hyogo Kyoiku University, which is charged with the collection and dissemination of nationwide attitudinal surveys relating to educational issues. EERC is the first research center attached to a university in Japan.

Prior to the 1990s, Japanese sociology thrived in a large domestic market for translations of European and American sociological work (Lie 1996:60; Sasaki 2000:1482). General social theory dominated the most prestigious area of scholarship, involving the interpretation and reinterpretation of classical theories, introduction of contemporary theories, and theoretical syntheses. Mastery of classics was a mark of serious scholarship, and publication of books dominated the market. With a limited peer-review system, the quality of work in journal publications varied, and journal publication remained secondary to book publication. As a result, there were limited opportunities for the exchange of ideas, and intellectual stimulation among sociologists was not eagerly sought out[6] (Lie 1996:61; Sasaki 2000:1480–81).

The field of Japanese sociology grew to the second largest national sociology with a membership of over 3,000 and 30 specialization fields (Lie 1996; Sasaki 2000; Yazawa 2000). By 1997, 65 out of 586 colleges/universities offered a master's degree in sociology, and 47 offered a Ph.D. (Sasaki 2000:1481). (In the United States, there are nearly 120 Ph.D. programs in sociology.) The diversification of sociology in Japan since the mid-1960s paved the way for internationalization in the 1980s and 1990s. It was fueled by the development of social science infrastructure, increasing scope of activities in cross-national collaboration, and international and regional conferences. The diversity of membership and publication in subfields is indicative of the lack of a central or dominant theoretical or methodological orientation, or central figure or focus to Japanese sociology at present (Sasaki 2000; Yazawa 2000). In addition, sociologists with interpretive or phenomenological approaches, mathematical or formal sociology, and quantitative styles of research are more prominent today (Yazawa 2000). Cross-national research collaboration and participation in international conferences continue to grow, especially in the areas of comparative sociology, environmental sociology, culture, family, information and the mass media, mathematical sociology, rational choice, rural sociology, social psychology, and social stratification/social mobility.

The International Journal of Japanese Sociology (1992–), the official publication of the JSS in English, began annual publication. The articles represent diverse topics in more than 20 substantive sociological topics. Another significant change was the increase in the number of international conferences organized by Japanese sociologists. For example, Japan hosted the 30th World Congress of the International Institute of Sociology (IIS) in Kobe in 1991. Masamichi Sasaki served as the president of IIS from 1998 to 2002. The Japan Association for Mathematical Sociology (JAMS) established in 1986 has actively worked with foreign counterparts, developed original models, and positioned itself as a world leader of rational choice theory and social network analyses. JAMS and the Section on Mathematical Sociology of the American Sociological Association organized the first U.S.-Japan joint conferences in 2000 (led by Phillip Bonacich and Yoshimichi Sato), 2002, and 2005 (http://www.geocities.jp/rcusjapan/).

The Center of Excellence projects support large-scale data collection and are a significant departure from previous data collection practices in Japan. First, Japanese sociology has positioned itself to embrace a global model of social science research by building research infrastructures. Second, there is a clear generational shift in leadership. Third, Japanese sociology has moved beyond U.S.-centered sociology, building regional links in Asia and collaborating with European universities.

1979 to the Present: Robust Revival and Diversification of Chinese Sociology

After Deng Xiaoping's rise to power in 1977, China set a course of pragmatic changes toward economic reform. For the next two decades, the nation witnessed average annual growth rates of 9%. The revival of sociology took place in 1979, when Deng Xiaoping declared, "We have ignored the study of political science, law, sociology, and world politics for many years. Now we need to restart." This speech was followed by an appeal from Hu Qiaomu, president of the Chinese Academy of Social Sciences, to re-embark on sociological research. Since then, sociology has been identified as a key scientific field of study for its potential in helping the country move forward. Sociology as a profession has achieved a legitimate status, bent toward policy-relevant studies. Thus, it has received solid government priority and funding in research areas such as economic reform, social development, and social change.

The rehabilitation of sociology began with remarkable speed to the surprise of skeptics (Whyte 2000). It was led by a number of prominent pre-1949 Chinese sociologists such as Fei Xiao-tong. They were charged with reestablishing the discipline and training future sociologists. Their effort was aided by the recruitment of scholars from fields related to sociology such as philosophy. American and Japanese sociologists were invited to lecture. Chinese sociological associations were revived in 1979, and the first sociology department was created in Nankai University in 1981. Within a short time, sociology departments were created in leading universities, including Peking University, Zhongshan University, Renmin University, and Fudan University. As new sociologists were trained, more sociology departments were added throughout the country. The Institute of Sociology was established in the Chinese Academy of Social Sciences (CASS) in Peking in 1980, along with many provincial and city academies (Whyte 2000:300).

Sociology's reemergence took place in the context of education reform. In 1977, uniform national examinations were reinstated, and in 1984, over 1.6 million candidates took the test for 430,000 places in more than 900 colleges and universities (U.S. Library of Congress 2003). In 1985, China began to drastically reform the higher education system to meet modernization goals. More universities and colleges were created and allowed to choose their own teaching plans and curricula and to conduct joint research and international exchanges. Universities gained more freedom to allocate funds for their own goals. Student enrollment, the graduate assignment system, student financial assistantships, and the study-abroad system (for students and scholars) also were changed to reflect more closely the personnel needs of modernization.

Sending students and scholars abroad has been an important means of raising educational quality in modern China. A large number of students were sent to the Soviet Union until the late 1950s. Some 30,000 students were sent to 14 countries between 1978 and 1984, and the number of students coming to the United States quickly accelerated after diplomatic normalization between the two countries in 1979. During the 1980s, government control of higher education relaxed as China attempted to model the Yugoslavian and Romanian experiences of melding socialist and capitalist systems.

Government directives facilitated the development and diversity of sociology. China has had a centrally planned economy based on the Stalinist model since it became the People's Republic of China. It has implemented a series of five-year plans to guide its development (Aoi and Wakabayashi 1993). In these plans, the government articulated national objectives and policies. The sixth five-year plan (1980–1984) identified three major areas for sociological study: social theory and methods, rural and urban studies, and problems relating to population, labor, and family. In the seventh five-year plan (1985–1989), 12 sociological areas were articulated as priorities, including new areas such as rural families, social welfare and assistance, stratification, aging, and lifestyle.

In the 1980s, Chinese sociology focused on large-scale surveys and case studies with a strong bent toward applied sociology. "Small town" research by Fei (1984) was the most sustained and coordinated research (Xueguang and Xiaomei 1997). In addition, CASS carried out a 1983 survey of marriage and family with a 1994 follow-up survey and a survey of 100 counties in 1988. In Tianjin in 1988, the municipal government and sociologists at the Tianjian Academy of Social Sciences began a 10-year household survey leading to the investigation of life-course changes. In 1994, Ma, Wang, and Liu edited a volume containing 30 case studies of rural enterprises, examining market transactions in dense social relations. Research on lifestyle (gender, sexuality) also began as a new area of sociology.

The Tiananmen Massacre of 1989 led to criticisms of sociology (and other newly revived social sciences) by conservatives. It was once again denounced (because it teaches Western democratic ideas critical of the socialist regime). The central government exerted control over sociological publications and research projects. Except at Renmin University and Shanghai University, sociology departments were not allowed to enroll students (Aoki and Wakabayashi 1993). However, the discipline remained robust and intact as new stimuli came from different directions, including the end of the Cold War and the diplomatic normalization between China and the United States, which led to a surge in international research collaboration and exchange of scholars (Whyte 2000:301).

Chinese sociologists also began debating China's unique identity with the appeal for the discipline to become more Chinese. The debate centered on how to use Western ideas and concepts in the study of Chinese society as well as how to innovate theoretical and methodological techniques. By the 1990s, Chinese sociologists sought new approaches by distinguishing two major trajectories between capitalism and communism. This gave rise to a firmer sense of sociological community in which sociological knowledge is to be shared and marked the end of isolation of Chinese sociology from the rest of the world (Whyte 2000). Sociologists began to assume a stronger professional identity as sociologists. Sociology has come to be understood as a scientific discipline with its own methodology and objectivity to address China's unique problems (Merle 2004).

Greater specialization and professionalization of sociology has raised new questions about the applicability of Western sociology into research of China. In an effort to "indigenize," Chinese sociologists emphasize the importance of reflective sociology, which scrutinizes the past in understanding present-day China. A team of sociologists at Peking University launched an oral history project to examine social and economic transformation of peasant life over six distinct periods during the past 50 years across six villages in China (Merle 2004). The complex changes in the 1980s and 1990s opened up numerous new research agendas, with a new spurt of activity, publication, and abundant data focusing on the consequences of the Cultural Revolution and its radical policies, impact of the diplomatic opening, the nature of societal transitions, decollectivization of agriculture and peasant life, and comparison between Eastern Europe's market-oriented reform and that of China. The Institute of Sociology at CASS has hosted a number of conferences in recent years. For example, CASS hosted the 36th World Congress of IIS in Beijing in 2004, with the theme "Social Change in the Age of Globalization." More than 1,000 sociologists gathered for this major international symposium.

The relationship between government and social science research is still strong. Sociology institutes in the social science academies in China are well funded and function like government think tanks. Scholars enjoy prestige, and their research findings are published in journals and reports and are circulated widely. However, the government now encourages research institutes and researchers to obtain research grants on their own, from international agencies, private foundations, and nongovernmental organizations (Whyte 2000). The Chinese Sociological Society publishes its flagship journal, *Chinese Sociological Review.* Journal publication is still controlled by the government, though this has been relaxing.

CONCLUSION

Similarities in the Development of Sociology between Japan and China

As in the West, the emergence of sociology in Japan and China came at a time of momentous political transformation accompanied by economic transformation. During rapid economic development, sociology applied itself to the challenges of these two countries. Major themes of sociological inquiry involved problems of modernization and democratization for Japan and of economic reform and social change for China.

Both countries possess Confucian traditions of hierarchical organization and collective orientation as opposed to the more democratic and individualistic orientation of Western traditions. Yet out of this mismatch of political, economic, and cultural institutional contexts, sociology was imported from the West into Japan and China and took root in their soil of political, economic, and cultural transformation.

Initially neither country experienced sustained democratic political institutionalization that would nurture the free development of sociology. By the 1930s, Japan embarked on militarization and fascist orientation, and China never shook off the feudalism embarked on by communists in the early 1950s. The rise of militarism in Japan shaped the development of a conservative, nationalistic sociology in the 1930s and 1940s. The focus of sociology shifted to a type of "Japanism," an ideology built on the emperor system and the family system. At the same time, the development of sociology was held back by the Chinese Communist Party, which perceived sociology incompatible with Marxism-Leninism and Maoism.

By the latter part of the twentieth century, sociology in both countries benefited from government involvement in education and developed diversity of specialized areas in addressing issues of these political and economic changes. After World War II, educational reform led by the American occupation established sociology in Japan as part of the liberal arts educational curricula. Sociology was recognized as an independent field of social science and grew rapidly during the economic development of the 1950s and 1960s, heavily influenced by American sociology. In China, after the rise of Deng in the late 1970s, sociology took a sharp turn from a discipline that threatened the communist regime to one of indispensable knowledge for China's modernization.

Since the 1990s, sociology in Japan and China has become internationalized and more integrated in world sociology, albeit with two distinct trajectories. There has also been more collaboration among sociologists between the two countries in promoting sociology of East Asia, especially in the areas of social stratification, social mobility, and family changes. As the two major non-Western countries, Japan and China can contribute better understanding of the roles of cultural and historical forces to the

Euro-American-centered processes of societal organization and transformations.

Differences in the Development of Sociology between Japan and China

Differences in the development of sociology are associated with historical differences in the two countries. Sociology in Japan developed in the context of more or less democratic and capitalist institutions and dramatic economic transformation, whereas in China, sociology has grown in the context of developing economic and political institutions. Although both countries imported sociology from the West, Japan imported European (in particular German) sociology and developed an orientation toward a more abstract, formal, and theoretical sociology. Japanese sociology emphasized the interpretation of abstract, philosophical, and classical works. It took a conservative stance within a small number of universities in the context of the turbulent process of nation building as the only non-Western industrial and imperial power. Sociology in China began by importing British social anthropology and American sociology with emphases on applied and reformist orientation. A number of foreign sociologists came to China through missionary teaching and were involved in training Chinese sociologists in the early part of the twentieth century.

Japanese sociologists are in a unique position to study new issues of maturing political and economic institutions with a drastic decline in birth rates and unprecedented rate of population aging. Gender, popular culture, and ethnicity have become very important new areas of sociology. More recent sociological inquiry in China includes broad issues relating to the consequences of market reforms and social problems of dislocation, including the issues of inequality, a new middle class, democratization, civil society, migration, and unemployment. Chinese sociologists are in a unique position to study social change and societal transformation, including studies of the Cultural Revolution and its consequences, the transition to a market economy, the social consequences of a hybrid socialist and capitalist economy, and demographic issues of monumental proportions.

Japan developed a more domestically oriented sociology, whereas China's had a more international orientation. Japanese sociologists have taken the path of more homegrown sociology, gradually internationalizing its scope with further enrichment of quality in a number of specialized fields of sociology. Chinese importation of sociology led to a more empirical and policy-oriented discipline and international collaboration. As a result of a sudden surge in international interchanges between China and the United States, interests in China have more fully integrated to mainstream American sociology. This has led to tighter integration of Chinese sociologists in American sociology and raised global visibility of Chinese sociologists.

Japanese sociological work has developed a philosophical and humanities orientation, whereas Chinese sociology gained a legitimate status as a scientific field bent toward policy-relevant research. Infrastructure and dissemination of sociological research are more centralized and controlled in China. Research institutes function like government think tanks and receive solid government priority and funding in areas of economic reform, social development, and social change.

Future: Glocalization

East Asian sociology confronts the tension between the stubborn facts of empirical sociological enquiry and available theories from the West to help explain those facts. In Japan and China, sociology was introduced at the end of the nineteenth century and brought inspiration and tensions between Occidental culture and Confucian tradition. It posed the challenge of "indigenization." Development of sociological theories or concepts suited to a particular country has stood as a major challenge. As these countries have indigenized and localized sociology, fundamental questions have arisen about the applicability of Western social scientific concepts and relationships. Given that sociological problems for research emerge in any non-Western country, Western concepts do not necessarily have relevance in different domains of research. Khondker (2004) argued that globalization or "glocalization" should be seen as an interdependent process. The problem of simultaneous globalization of the local and the localization of globality (glocalization) can be expressed as the twin processes of macrolocalization and microglobalization. acrolocalization involves expanding the boundaries of locality as well as making some local ideas, practices, and institutions more global.

Both countries are well positioned to overcome cultural and linguistic barriers in building a better understanding of East Asia and offering insights to world sociology. The ascent of sociologies in East Asia provides opportunities for better articulation of the region's dynamic social transformation. It is always possible to be carried away with "methodological nationalism," a position that says each country or society should be examined in its own context through the devices of its own homegrown methodology. However, such a position would lead to intellectual closure of dialogue and understanding between societies. In the globalized world, such discourses have limited value. Yet it is important to take seriously the local context and variables and not to fall into the trap of blind application of Western ideas and concepts.

Lessons from East Asia include the demise of modernization theory and questioning of the assumptions of autonomous organizations in Anglo-American organizational sociology (Granovetter 1994). The rise of the Japanese economy in the 1960s and 1970s was a key element in the questioning of modernization theory. Here was an economy that did not follow the Anglo-American model of development but instead rode the logic of the "developmental state" to become the second largest economy in the world. The developmental state has provided a model of development adopted by several "Asian Tigers." Further, throughout the 1980s and 1990s, organizational sociologists increasingly recognized the theoretical importance and practical effectiveness of groups of organizations leading to the development of new approaches. Interest was sparked by the worldwide competitive successes of East Asian firms that rely extensively on network forms of organization (Gerlach 1992). The restructuring of the economies of China and the former Soviet republics and the failures of neoclassical economic theory to inspire policies to generate market economies also created interest in new approaches.

We may end with a set of globally valid concepts or concepts of limited application that help us examine processes of social transformation that are inextricably connected with global transformation. Thus, Japan and China need integration of theories with data, specification of causal mechanisms, and empirical verification to advance sociological knowledge. Such efforts will transcend sociologies of context-specific research to context-sensitive sociologies that have more general applicability. It is in this context that Robertson (1992) conceptualized globalization in the twentieth century as "the interpenetration of the universalization of particularization and the particularization of universalism" (p. 100).

6

SOCIOLOGY IN CANADA

NEIL MCLAUGHLIN

ANTONY J. PUDDEPHATT
McMaster University, Canada

Canadian sociology has a rich history, and the diverse fabric of the contemporary field has much to offer our discipline, our universities, and our intellectual life throughout North America and internationally. Established at McGill University in the 1920s and the University of Toronto in the early 1960s, sociology as a distinct academic discipline has since been institutionalized in universities throughout the country and is now a core element of Canadian liberal arts education and research-oriented social science (Brym and Fox 1989; Helmes-Hayes 2002; Hiller 1982; Shore 1987). We argue that sociology in Canada offers three major unique strengths to the discipline. First, as a result of its unique historical genesis, Canada's brand of sociology is remarkably diverse methodologically relative to other national traditions and is strong in historical, interpretive, and quantitative traditions. Second, Canada's position relative to the United States represents a complex "optimal marginality" that allows a place for critical analytic clarity due to its distance from the disciplinary core, which is largely centralized in the United States and Europe. Finally, as a result of the institutional context of Canadian sociology and its political culture, there is rich potential for public academic contributions in the discipline. These strengths will be discussed with regard to historical and contemporary contributions of Canadian sociology. We will proceed to explore some of the institutional and professional obstacles

Canadian sociology faces, and finally, we will provide thoughts on its likely future.

THREE RESEARCH TRADITIONS IN CANADIAN SOCIOLOGY

Perhaps more than any other brand of national sociology, the Canadian tradition is marked by a great deal of methodological diversity and an openness to competing but complementary approaches to research. It is true that sociology on the whole is characterized by diverse research methods, which are of course made up of competing paradigms of multivariate, historical/comparative, and interpretive sociology (Alford 1998). However, it is our contention that the Canadian model is probably more diverse than the European and American traditions in relative terms. European sociology is marked by a stronger emphasis on social theorizing and qualitative and historical methods. American sociology is dominated, in line with the flagship journals *American Journal of Sociology* (*AJS*) and *American Sociological Research* (*ASR*), by a quantitative approach. We argue that because of Canada's unique position and historical ties with respect to both British and American traditions, the Canadian tradition enjoys a more even methodological balance. We perceive this methodological diversity offered by Canada as a major

AUTHORS' NOTE: We would like to thank Dennis Peck, Robert Brym, and Kyle Siler for their careful reading of previous drafts and helpful editorial suggestions.

strength for the discipline and an example of the rich potential offered by multimethod approaches generally.

It is a major problem that sociologists have been divided by arbitrary distinctions created by methodological and theoretical orthodoxies. Most contemporary research consists of either qualitative ethnography linked to interpretive theory, quantitative statistical methods aligned with multivariate modes of theorizing, or archival data embedded in historical narratives. Contemporary efforts at "triangulation" improve on research done within one single paradigm of social inquiry, and discussion among different levels of inquiry improves the sociological imagination. The evidence for sociological theories is most compelling when these different methodological approaches are combined, and when the discipline allows a place for each type of research tradition. For a variety of geographic and historical factors, these three research logics of multivariate, interpretive, and historical-comparative have carved out relatively secure spaces in sociology in Canada.

Multivariate Research in Canada

The origins of Canadian quantitative sociology, as was the case in the British tradition we often draw on, lie with quantitative policy-oriented research dealing with poverty, social exclusion, and the welfare state. From the important early policy work of Leonard Marsh and, later, John Porter, sociologists in Canada have contributed an enormous amount to the research base for welfare state design and implementation as well as playing a pivotal role in the legitimation of state spending on social provisions (Helmes-Hayes 2002). Leonard Marsh's (1940) *Canadians In and Out of Work* represents the first book-length account of class analysis in Canada and its relation to the labor market, and his famous "Marsh Report" (1943) on social security provisions was a major step toward more egalitarian social policy based on solid empirical research (Helmes-Hayes and Wilcox-Magill 1993). Following in this tradition, John Porter's book *The Vertical Mosiac* (1965), in particular, is a classic study about nationality and ethnicity in the Canadian stratification system that has given rise to a rich tradition of quantitative research on elites. In dealing with Canadian government officials who were more concerned with the practicality of policy proposals than abstract theoretical arguments, many of the early Canadian sociologists developed skills at gathering and presenting quantitative data on policy-relevant issues. Numbers mattered in the emergence of sociology in Canada, and this tradition continues today with Canadian federal government-sponsored research on topics such as health care, poverty, immigration, and racism (e.g., Armstrong 2001; Armstrong and Armstrong 2003; Armstrong, Armstrong and Fegan 1998; Boyd 1979; Boyd et al. 1985; Boyd and Thomas 2001; Breton 1990; Breton and Reitz 2005; Fong 2003, 2004; Fong and Wilkes 2003; Li 1996, 1998, 2003; Reitz 1980, 1998; Sinclair 1985, 1988).

In the past 25 years or so, quantitative research in Canada has become more theoretically focused and has moved in more technical quantitative directions than was the case in its early Fabian-influenced origins. An English Canadian research tradition has emerged, for example, that has subjected the comparative U.S.-Canada research program of Seymour Martin Lipset to extended critique, revision, and expansion, based on a sophisticated set of statistical analyses (Baer 1990; Baer, Curtis, and Grabb 2001; Baer, Grabb, and Johnston 1990, 1993; Grabb, Baer, and Curtis 1999; Grabb and Curtis 1988, 2005; Grabb, Curtis, and Baer 2000, 2001; Ogmundson 1994). Recently, Andersen, Curtis, and Grabb (2006) have written a methodologically sophisticated critique of Putnam's arguments surrounding civic engagement based on a comparative and longitudinal statistical analysis of the United States, Canada, the United Kingdom, and the Netherlands. They show that the decline of civic engagement central to Putman's influential argument appears to be a uniquely American process and seems to be explainable not by television or a generational dynamics but by a decline of female civic participation in an American society that lacks collective social supports for child rearing. There is also extensive quantitative research done, for example, in Canada on voting behavior, the social origins of crime, social psychology, higher education, and work and occupations (Gartner 1991; Gartner and MacMillan 1995; Gartner and McCarthy 1991; Hagan 1989a, 1989b, 1991; Hagan and Foster 2001; Hagan and Leon 1977; Hagan, MacMillan, and Wheaton 1996; Hagan and McCarthy 1997; Hagan and Wheaton 1993; Nakhaie 1992, 1996, 2002). The methodological sophistication of Canada's best quantitative researchers rank with top international standards (Baer 2005).

Starting with the Marxist critique of Porter's student Wallace Clement in *The Canadian Corporate Elite* (1975), we have a vast scholarship produced in Canada that analyzes class dominance and the links between corporate class and major decision-making processes (Carroll 1986, 1992b, 2004; Clement 1975, 1977, 1986, 2001; Clement and Myles 1994; Fox and Ornstein 1986; Ornstein 1986, 1988, 1989). The combination of the sophisticated quantitative work of what is sometimes called the "York School" of Marxist elite studies and the influence of the social network approach of Barry Wellman at the University of Toronto has led to strong scholarly work on elites in Canada (Ogmundson 2002, 2005; Tindall and Wellman 2001; Wellman 1979, 1999). More recently, the dominance of *The Vertical Mosiac* as well as neo-Marxist and network paradigms have been challenged by quantitative scholars working from a feminist perspective, as well as by scholars raising questions about the centrality of race, for what are called "visible minorities" in Canada (Helmes-Hayes and Curtis 1998; Nakhaie 1997).

Ethnography in Canada

Canadian sociology is also characterized by a rich qualitative research tradition that is well known internationally. Formed initially at McGill University in Montreal, with close ties to the University of Chicago, qualitative symbolic interactionist research traditions have spread throughout Canadian sociology, leading to the development of a strong interpretive tradition in Canada. The sociology department at McGill was first founded by Carl Dawson in 1925, who was influenced in large part by the ecological tradition at Chicago, exemplified by the likes of Albion Small and Robert Park (Camara and Helmes-Hayes 2003).[1] These ties to Chicago brought over Everett Hughes, who had moved to Canada after marrying a Canadian woman from British Columbia (Helen Hughes) and conducted his landmark study *French Canada in Transition* while in Montreal, making use of ecological approaches to studying the city (Hughes 1943). Hughes pioneered ethnographic methods in Canada, and later taught the Canadian expatriate Erving Goffman while he was a foreign student at the University of Chicago. The ethnographic tradition continued at McGill, then McMaster, and now throughout Canadian sociology at a number of universities across the country.

The ethnographies produced by Canadians are rich and varied. Goffman (1959), of course, is the most famous of Canadian sociologists even though his links to his homeland were not strong after he left the University of Toronto as an undergraduate to pursue his Ph.D. in the United States. Orrin Klapp is also known as an important Canadian theorist of identity, and he also made use of qualitative cases to forward his conceptualization of public reputations in American society (Klapp 1962, 1964). Like Goffman, his ties to Canada are somewhat tenuous as much of Klapp's work was produced south of the border. Robert Stebbins is an example of the opposite kind of cross-border migration— an American who settled at the University of Calgary. Stebbins has studied deviance (Stebbins 1995), sporting culture (Stebbins 1987), and work and occupations (Stebbins 1984, 1990) and has developed the notion of "serious leisure" (Stebbins 2004) to help characterize devoted participation across both leisure and occupational spheres. Jack Haas and William Shaffir (1991) have explored the process of professionalization medical students undergo as a type of status passage into the world of medicine, and Shaffir has written extensively on religious orthodoxy (e.g., Shaffir 1974). Canadian scholars have written excellent ethnographic work on Afro-Canadians in Nova Scotia, gender and family, schooling, the dynamics of cities, and education (Albas and Albas 1984; Clairmont and Magill 1974; Eichler 1988, 2001, 2002; Fox 1993; Luxton 1980). Prus (1989a, 1989b) has studied sales and marketplace activity as it happens in process vis-à-vis concrete settings such as shopping malls and trade shows and has contributed to work on deviance in his work on professional hustlers and the hotel community (Prus and Irini 1980; Prus and Sharper 1977). Not satisfied, however, with simply describing various research sites, Prus (1996, 1997) has argued for fieldwork tactics that are combined with a conceptual framework of "generic social processes" by providing transcontextual theoretical comparison points for field observations.

Part of the strength of ethnography in Canadian sociology comes from an institutional legacy—many Canadian sociology departments remain as sociology and anthropology departments, even at departments that produce sociology Ph.D.s. Moreover, the professional body representing Canadian sociologists houses anthropologists as well and was called *The Canadian Sociology and Anthropology Association (CSAA)* for years, although this recently changed to *The Canadian Sociology Association (CSA)*. As a consequence of these factors, and because of our historical links to Great Britain, social anthropology plays a strong role in the intellectual life of Canadian sociology, providing the symbolic interactionist tradition with natural allies. In addition, the Fabian policy orientation of many Canadian sociologists and the focus on regional diversity in this highly decentralized federal state has often been combined with qualitative research approaches to produce rich research on fishing communities on the East Coast and logging on the West Coast as well as urban issues (Hannigan 1998; Marchak 1983, 1991, 1995; Marchak, Aycock, and Herbert 1999; Sinclair 1985, 1988).

The Historical Comparative Tradition in Canada

Finally, Canadian sociology has always been profoundly historical in its orientation. Canadian sociologists have long stressed the need to understand the deep historical roots of Canadian culture and life in our colonial past as well as our earlier reliance on natural resources such as fishing and fur trading. Furthermore, there has been a need to understand the complex relationships between our first nations, the French in Québec and the British in Upper Canada, in the forging of the nation, and our deeply ambivalent historical relationship with the United States. Historical sociology tends to be dominated by the great theorists produced in the United States, such as Barrington Moore, Immanuel Wallerstein, and Theda Skocpol, but Canadian sociologists have produced some excellent historical sociology in their own right.

Canadian historical sociologists have studied a variety of topics over the past 50 years, beginning with the influential work on social movements and regionalism by S. D. Clark (1948, 1959, 1976), who is often heralded as Canada's original historical sociologist. Harold Innis (1923, 1927, 1930, 1946), Clark's mentor and a groundbreaking economic historian and political economist, laid the foundation for a uniquely Canadian school of "staples" that stresses the importance of geography and the resource basis of Canada's original economy of fur, water, wood, and fish (Buxton and Acland 1999; Creighton 1957; Kroker 1984). More recently, Canadian historical sociologists have studied early state formation in Europe, comparative nationalisms, the origins of the welfare state in comparative perspective, slavery in the United States, labor history, work and class inequality, the transformations of Western welfare states, academic disciplines, political theory and the origins of the census in Canada, and religion (Budros 2004; Carroll 1986, 1989; Clark 1995; Curtis 2001; Hall 1986, 1988, 1994, 1996; McDonald 1993; Myles 1984; Ogmundson and Doyle 2002).

The dynamics of national and linguistic conflict and division in Canada between French and English, our origins and present condition as a country of immigrants, and the fact that our nation was, like the United States and Australia, founded on the realities of white settler colonialism has also created rich historical comparative research on these topics. Emerging from the tradition of writing on marginality and the hinterlands pioneered by S. D. Clark, there is also excellent historical sociology on regionalism in Canada (Brym and Fox 1989). Canada's geographic location adjacent to the United States, the economic and cultural domination exerted first by the British and French, and now the Americans, and the history of Québécois domination by English Canada has meant that there has always been an interest in various "dependency," "cultural imperialism," and "world systems" theories in Canada (Veltmeyer 1997). It probably helped, of course, that Immanuel Wallerstein taught at McGill University for a number of years. More recently, however, one can see these various issues analyzed in Canada from a historical-comparative perspective.

Obviously, Canada is not alone in having these three research paradigms inside the discipline of sociology. The argument is not that there is more or better multivariate, ethnographic, or historical-comparative research produced in Canada than in other countries. Canada is a relatively small national sociological community with approximately 800 full scholars teaching in the discipline (Curtis and Weir 2005). We have not produced enough of the broad historical-comparative research like Barrington Moore, and our ethnographic tradition is, after all, an American import from the University of Chicago. Nonetheless, if one takes the scale of the discipline into account and tries to come up with an empirically grounded estimation of what percentage of research in Canada is either multivariate, ethnographic, or historical-comparative, then the Canadian discipline would probably be closer to an equal proportion for each research logic than is the case, for example, in the United States, Britain, Germany, or France. This places Canadian sociologists alongside other small nations with diverse methodological traditions where quantitative research has not come to dominate the profession as it does in mainstream American sociology.

CANADIAN SOCIOLOGY AS OPTIMALLY MARGINAL

Anglo-Canadian sociology occupies a unique sociological and historical position relative to the United States that offers potential for unique insights. While Canadian sociologists have maintained close links with American sociology, they also retain a certain intellectual distance from the assumptions that dominate American culture and its sociology. As a result, Canadian sociology has been more open to various intellectual currents that are marginalized within the American tradition. Examples of this include the "standpoint feminism" of Dorothy Smith, radical Marxist sociology, and a greater attention to new developments in European social theory (Brym and Fox 1989; Carroll 1992a; Smith 1975, 1987, 1995, 1999). Canada enjoys a particular position of "optimal marginality," in that it is both close to the intellectual energy, cultural capital, and resources of America, yet maintains a certain distance from American political, cultural, and intellectual orthodoxy.

There is a long tradition in sociological analysis that emphasizes the creative potential that comes from strong links to core societal and institutional resources (Collins 1998; Gieryn and Hirsch 1983; Merton 1949; Wolfe 1998). Contrary to this view, an opposing tradition has argued that insights come not only from the core power centers of knowledge cultures but also and importantly from the margins of power and privilege. Strangers and nomads, from this perspective, can see society more clearly than those deeply embedded in existing power relations and social structures (Coser 1965, 1984; Galliher and Galliher 1995; Kauppi 1996; McLaughlin 1998; Seidman 1994). McLaughlin (2001) has argued that this long-standing debate is stale and irresolvable and that the concept of "optimal marginality" suggests that there may be some forms and combinations of social marginality that lead to insight and innovative ideas and others that do not. The case of Canadian sociology illustrates both possibilities.

An important contribution Canadian sociology can make to intellectual life is forwarding what Michael Burawoy called the "provincializing" of American sociology (Burawoy 2005a). What Burawoy means by this is that American sociologists, as scholars rooted in the dominant political and cultural power in the world at present, tend to inappropriately universalize the American experience. Articles in American sociological journals and textbooks tend to make broad references to the criminal justice system, higher education, the family, or race relations in general, when they are actually only presenting the American case. Scholars and individuals outside the United States tend, of course, to see through this obvious blindness to both the experiences of others and how the American sociological tradition must be understood as a particular form of intellectual work, shaped by a specific American history and set of institutional arrangements. At the same time, sociologists in the United States have pioneered a series of methodological approaches and research traditions that can help us better understand the world. The task is to take and modify the insights of the American sociological tradition, placing the literature on American society into a larger global context where fruitful comparisons can be made.

Canadian sociology is well positioned to contribute to this task of globalizing the sociological imagination. It is easy to dismiss the cultural arrogance implicit in the tendency of American scholars to read their own particular national experience as a universal sociological phenomenon. At the same time, there is no doubt that American sociology has produced a vibrant sociological tradition that is home to many of the most important figures in our discipline. Furthermore, the early founders of American sociology have drawn on the top European theorists as their paradigmatic exemplars. Sociology today is far more global than it was in the past, as the discipline has grown throughout the European community and in the global South. Sociologists in English Canada, with their links to both the American and the British sociological traditions, combined with Québec's links to sociology in France and Continental Europe, represent a sociological community that is literally in the global crossroads of two-way traffic between the discipline in the United States, Europe, and the world (Breton 1989; Leroux 2001).

There is an institutional angle to the optimal marginality of Canadian sociology, relating to the particularly flat structure of Canadian higher education (Davies and Guppy 1997). Canadian universities, when compared with American or European schools, are remarkably homogeneous across a range of institutions. That is to say, while there are elite universities in Canada, the differences between these institutions, less prominent research universities, and lower-tier teaching schools are comparatively small. The Canadian university system is flat in comparison with the divide between the private elite institutions like Harvard or Yale, elite public institutions, more mass public institutions, and the hundreds of public, local, and regional universities across the United States. Moreover, Canadian universities are essentially public, and thus the Canadian higher-education system does not have the scores of relatively elite liberal arts schools.

In Canada, a national market for universities does not exist as it does in the United States. Students generally go to university locally, or they go to the United States (Davies and Guppy 1997). This softens the brutal competitive edge that drives the American university system. Canadian universities are not dominated by an American-style "test" culture where competitive SATs (Scholastic Assessment Test) or GREs (Graduate Record Examinations) are central to the admissions process. The tuition is more or less the same low level at all English Canadian universities, and is even lower in Québec. In Ontario, for example, one can attend a massive and prestigious research-oriented university, a small teaching-oriented school, or a moderate-sized research institution all for essentially the same price. Canadian universities, moreover, do not have huge endowments and do not have a tradition of raising money from alumni. Nor are big business-oriented, high-profile sports programs a major part of the Canadian academic scene. Certainly, no Canadian universities have the long and rich elite traditions of Oxford, Cambridge, or the great French or German institutions of higher learning.

Some of this is changing, of course, as Canadian university administrators attempt to raise tuition in differential ways for professional programs, move toward a model of what has been termed "academic capitalism," and compete in a global context with major international universities (Slaughter and Leslie 1999). Nonetheless, this relatively flat structure and local culture creates a situation whereby the intellectual leadership of the elite institutions are not as influential or accepted lower down the institutional hierarchy (Polster 2001). The very idea of elite institutions of higher education runs against Canada's more egalitarian political milieu, although Canada's roots in the British Empire provides a background history of elitism that is still embedded in university practice and culture in various ways.

These points are documented in the comparative literature on education, but it needs to be emphasized how this particular structure of higher education shapes the dynamics of academic disciplines in distinct ways. The nonelitist structure of Canadian sociology seems to allow for more diversity and more of what might look like, to mainstream American sociologists, more innovative approaches. For example, the Canadian Sociological and Anthropology Association once gave its highest book award, the Porter Prize, to a book by David MacGregor on Hegel and Marx, recognizing the strength of the critical tradition in Canada (MacGregor 1984, 1992). And John O'Neill (1976), Arthur W. Frank (1995, 2004), and Barbara Marshall (1994) have done quality work on the sociology of the body and sexuality that would probably be further from the mainstream of the discipline in the United States than it is in Canada.

The relative unwillingness of different sociology programs in Canada to accept the intellectual leadership of more elite universities, especially the more American-oriented departments, undermines the intellectual control and power of mainstream sociology in Canada. This has advantages and disadvantages for the discipline. The school of Marxist sociology, the sociology of intellectuals and knowledge, and criminology and deviance are just three examples where alternative approaches have gained a stronger foothold in the disciplinary orthodoxy in Canada. In the following section, we discuss these examples of how Canadian sociology's marginality and flat institutional hierarchy have been "optimal" for the discipline, before outlining some of the challenges these historical and institutional realities create.

Marxism/Political Economy

Canada's marginal position has created a space for a very left-wing Marxist-oriented political economy tradition. While Marxist sociology is, of course, quite strong in the United States, Marxist studies of the Canadian political economy, as represented in the journal and network around *Studies in Political Economy,* are probably far closer to the center of mainstream Canadian sociology (Brym and Fox 1989). The most influential early Marxist scholarship in Canada emerged with Leonard Marsh's work, and as discussed above, a dialogue with the *Vertical Mosaic* tradition as young Canadians attempted to build on John Porter's (1965) "power elite" and policy-oriented analysis of social inequality in Canada (Clement 1975, 1977, 2001; Helmes-Hayes and Curtis 1998). Later, feminist scholars and sociologists, influenced by various critical theories of race, raised important questions about Porter's assumptions and analysis, and the debate has produced a positive and productive outcome for Canadian sociology. Analysis of the corporate networks central to Canadian politics and economic decision making, the historical origins of Canadian economic and cultural dependency, perspectives on the Canadian welfare state, and, more recently, socialist-feminist-inspired research have created a very strong critical tradition in Canadian sociology (Béland and Myles 2003; Eichler 2001; Ornstein 1986).

A central debate in Canadian sociology has revolved around the perspectives on Canadian society promoted and developed by Seymour Martin Lipset. Not strictly Marxist in its theoretical approach and political stance, James Curtis, Edward Grabb, and Douglas Baer are at the center of a materialist-oriented Canadian political economy tradition that questions Lipset's stress on values and history in shaping the U.S. and Canadian differences (Grabb, Curtis, and Baer 2000). The work of Grabb et al. (2000) combines historical-comparative analysis with a sophisticated use of survey data on volunteering, religion, and political opinions analyzed with advanced statistical methods. The argument has been that North America can be understood as four distinct regions: essentially the American Red and Blue states, alongside English Canada and Québec. The Curtis/Grabb/Baer tradition represents some of the best work Canadian political economy has to offer, despite various debates within the discipline regarding the ideological underpinnings (e.g., Carroll 2005).

There also exists an extensive feminist sociology in Canada that deals with gender dynamics within the family, critiques gender blinders, and adds a qualitative dimension to a Canadian political economy sometimes dominated by multivariate methods (Clement and Vosko 2003; Fox 1993). Clement and Myles's (1994) *Relations of Ruling* represents a sophisticated theoretical approach to combining class, race, and gender in critical comparative-historical research, a work that is clearly rooted in the Porter tradition but one that also extends beyond the original perspective in productive ways.

The influence of Canadian political economy has spread beyond the original networks of the founding generation of radical sociologists in Canada. There is a strong critical tradition in the analysis of health care politics in Canada, often linked to debates about the privatization of the national health care system (Armstrong 2001; Armstrong and Armstrong 2003; Armstrong, Armstrong, and Fegan 1998). There is extensive research in Canada on the sociology of aging and the politics of pensions, a tradition that is now far more empirical and less ideological than was the case in the 1970s and 1980s (Béland and Myles 2003; Marshall 1980; Myles 1984). Furthermore,

there is a growing social movement literature in Canada that combines the more traditional resource mobilization/political process/framing theories from American sociology with a critical edge and applied focus that has been forged in debates with the Canadian Marxist tradition (Carroll 1992b; Cormier 2004; Kowalchuk 2003a, 2003b; Staggenborg 1986, 1988, 1989, 1998, 2001; Tindall and Wellman 2001).

Sociology of Knowledge and Intellectuals

Canadian society has produced a unique sociology on the politics of knowledge and intellectuals. Modern society is no longer shaped centrally by industrial or even service production, but has become a knowledge society shaped by information and communication. Largely influenced by Luhmann's systems theory, Nico Stehr has pioneered an empirically based tradition that stresses the politics of knowledge and attempts to theorize the knowledge society (Stehr 1992, 1994). The dynamics of interdisciplinary knowledge production and use, science and technology governance, and the influence of the Internet are just some of the topics analyzed in this rich interdisciplinary Canadian sociology (Baber 1996; Wellman 1999).

Robert Brym has been at the center of a widely cited research tradition produced in Canada on intellectuals in both Russia and North America (Brym 1980, 1987, 1988, 2001; Nakhaie and Brym 1999). Intellectuals have also been central in this effort as Canadian sociologists draw on the work of Pierre Bourdieu and their own experiences in shaping the Quiet Revolution in a national/provincial context (Fournier 2001, 2002; Leroux 2001; Pinard and Hamilton 1984). Furthermore, Michele Lamont's research agenda on intellectual and cultural capital was originally conceived as research on the social sciences in Québec (Lamont 1987, 2000; McLaughlin 1998). Public intellectual Dennis Wrong (1998) is another Canadian who wrote extensively about the context of intellectuals and ideas in relation to social classes, institutions, power, and the state. The influence of Foucault in Canada, in particular, has resulted in studies of the historical origins of power dynamics rooted in knowledge production and state data gathering (Curtis 2001). Combining a historical-comparative sociological and a broad social theory orientation in the tradition of Irving Zietlin, Joseph Bryant (1996) has produced a broad-ranging and important study of the social origins of Greek philosophers that goes well beyond Alvin Gouldner's (1965) classic study of Plato.

Dorothy Smith has pioneered a critical sociology of knowledge tradition in Canada, arguing for a sociology for women and, more recently, a sociology for the people. Through the development of her socialist-feminist ethnomethodology, Smith has made Canadian sociology an important crossroad for a critical sociology of knowledge (Smith 1975, 1987, 1995, 1999). Today Smith's theories of institutional ethnography are widely influential in Canadian sociology, and she helped establish a critical perspective on knowledge now popular in Canadian social science.

There is a growing interest in science and technology in Canadian sociology. For example, Miall and Miall (2003) analyzed the social dynamics of geological science in their study of a research group working under the auspices of Exxon. Baber's (1996) work on science, Ungar's (1994, 1998, 2000) writings on global warming and the social construction of ignorance, and Woolgar and Pawluch's (1985) writings on "ontological gerrymandering" are also important parts of this Canadian-based sociology of knowledge, science, and technology.

In general, Canadian scholars have long focused on media, communications, and technology because of the influence of Harold Innis (1950) and Marshall McLuhan (1994). Harold Innis (1950) wrote extensively on the social dynamics of communication after moving away from his earlier focus on Canadian economic history. McLuhan's (1994) famous phrases "medium is the message" and the "global village" have become common terminology the world over. The body of scholarship produced means that Canadian scholars have been at the center of research on mass media, new information technology, and the Internet.

This critical focus on knowledge has expanded an already rich tradition of the history of sociology. The gender biases, in particular, have been critiqued by Canadian feminists, who critically look at the role of women in the founding of sociology; assumptions about gender in the classic canon of Marx, Weber, and Durkheim; and the broader epistemological issues essential to producing a sociology that is inclusive of women (Eichler 1988, 2001, 2002; McDonald 1993, 1994, 1998; Sydie 1987, 1994). There is also a poststructuralist body of literature that looks at the writings of Marx as forms of rhetoric, alongside work that critically examines the whole notion of canons, founders, and classics in the discipline (Baehr 2002; Kemple 1995). William Buxton's (1985) work, which has emphasized the nationalist ambitions and imperial blinders embedded in the sociological corpus of Talcott Parsons, is a good example.

An important early text in this area is Robert Brym and Bonnie Fox's (1989) *From Culture to Power,* a historical account of the political economy-oriented Canadian sociology as it emerged in critical dialogue with the Parsonian tradition. The critical history of demography in Canada is also well represented by Bruce Curtis's (2001) award-winning *The Politics of Population,* an analysis of the origins of Census research in British North America. The history of sociology holds a prominent position in Canada. Indeed, Canadians have been central to the rethinking of the history of sociology, often from a critical and feminist perspective (Eichler 2001, 2002).

Critical Criminology and Deviance

The relative marginality of social science in Canada, combined with a distinctive criminal justice system, has led to the development of a particularly strong and perhaps unique critical criminological tradition. With a smaller incarcerated population than in the United States, and thus far less employment opportunities in the applied sector of the field, criminology in Canada has a theoretical, critical, and grand historical orientation. Canada's historical links with Great Britain, moreover, have created a larger presence of the neo-Marxist, Birmingham School of cultural studies, and Foucault-styled analyses of criminology, as compared with the highly quantitative and policy-oriented tradition in the United States.

John Hagan has given the discipline in Canada an empirically focused and rigorous research program on the social origins of crime (Hagan 1989a, 1989b, 1991; Hagan and Foster 2001; Hagan and Leon 1977; Hagan, MacMillan, and Wheaton 1996; Hagan and Wheaton 1993), and he is not alone in producing first-rate mainstream criminology in Canada (Gartner 1991; Gartner and MacMillan 1995; Gartner and McCarthy 1991). Even when critical sociologists have criticized the work of Hagan and his students, the criminology literature represents a lively, interesting, and is far less rooted in the concrete demands of criminal justice practitioners as is the case in the United States. Furthermore, Canadian criminologists have strong links to empirical and theoretically driven multimethod research traditions found elsewhere (Ericson and Baranek 1982; Ericson, Baranek, and Chan 1987).

Perhaps the size of the Canadian criminal justice system and the low levels of national government funding for criminological research have left more opportunity for the development of deviance literature that is more theoretical and qualitative in nature. The ethnographic tradition has long been associated with the study of deviant groups, and the Canadian tradition has taken advantage of openings within the larger intellectual community to produce a successful research tradition. Robert Prus's (Prus and Irini 1980; Prus and Sharper 1977) landmark ethnographies of card and dice hustlers, and then hookers, cons, and the social organization of seedy hotel life, are widely recognized as Canadian classics in the interpretive tradition. Robert Stebbins (1995) has considered the relations of deviants to the larger community and their management of stigma and identity, which has inspired a generation of Canadian ethnographers on this same topic (e.g., Atkinson 2003). Daniel Wolf (1991) produced a classic ethnography of organized crime through covert participant observation among outlaw biker gangs. There is also a tradition of writing about youth and deviance in Canada, much of which challenges some of the Willis "resistance" orthodoxy (Davies 1995; Tanner 2001). Hagan and McCarthy's (1997) study of homelessness will likely remain influential for many years to come. Furthermore, Hagan's own study of American draft resisters in Canada perhaps exemplifies the point that certain forms of deviance can be discussed more openly in the broader political and intellectual climate in Canada (Hagan 2001).

Toward a Canadian Public Sociology

Canadian sociology is well positioned to contribute to the global discussion of what Michael Burawoy has called "public sociologies" (Burawoy 2004, 2005b). At issue is how sociologists can build on their core "professional" research, "policy"-oriented consulting, and "critical" sociology to take these ideas outside of the university to dialogue with laypersons through a "public sociology." This vision of a public sociology has given rise to an extensive debate, with some scholars arguing that this activist orientation threatens the professional standing of the discipline within the modern research university. Others suggest that Burawoy does not go far enough in challenging sexism, racism, and social inequality. A major task for the development of a global public sociology will be comparative research into how the specific institutional arrangements, cultures, and histories of countries such as South Africa, Brazil, Norway, Ireland, Denmark, and Sweden create different opportunities and challenges for bringing the sociological imagination into public debate and dialogue.

The Canadian case provides a particularly interesting and important example of public sociology. The Canadian parliamentary system and the relative social democratic consensus have created enormous opportunities for policy-oriented sociology in Canada. Beginning with the work of Leonard Marsh and John Porter, there is a long-standing Canadian tradition of policy-oriented research that assists in shaping government action on health care, immigration, poverty, social security, and multiculturalism (Brym and Myles 1989; Brym and Saint-Pierre 1997). As the global sociological community debates the intellectual and political issues at stake, the Canadian case will undoubtedly continue to provide a useful example.

Critical sociologists such as C. Wright Mills (1967), Alvin Gouldner (1970), and Canada's own Dorothy Smith (1975, 1987, 1995, 1999) have engaged in academic dialogues about the moral, political, ontological, and epistemological assumptions embedded in the professional activities and structures of the discipline. The strength of policy sociology in Canada has given rise to a particularly strong and vocal critical sociology. Dorothy Smith has long argued for a reform of the discipline from the standpoint of women. This has inspired a direct critique of mainstream American sociology and has fueled a strong agenda for Canadian policy-oriented scholars to get involved with direct interventions in the state. Critiques of mainstream sociological methods and theory are widespread in Canadian sociology departments.

Public sociology has always been strong in Canada, something that first emerged with the policy-oriented writings on social inequality of John Porter. This public sociology now includes issues relating to social movements, gender and sexuality, race, and, perhaps most prominently, health care. Perhaps representing more of the Gramscian "organic public intellectual" than the elite-oriented "traditional public intellectual" (Burawoy 2004), Canadian

sociologists like Wallace Clement (1975, 1977, 1986, 2001), William Carroll (1986, 1992a, 1992b, 2004), Patricia Marchak (1983, 1991, 1995, 1996), Gordon Laxer (1989, 1991), and Pat and Hugh Armstrong (Armstrong 2001; Armstrong and Armstrong 1978, 2003) have had a strong influence on Canadian intellectual life and debates about social policy.

THE FUTURE OF CANADIAN SOCIOLOGY

The portrait of a rich and lively Canadian sociology is only part of the picture. Canadian sociology faces many institutional and intellectual challenges that have been widely discussed in recent debates (Baer 2005; Brym 2003; Curtis and Weir 2005; Johnston 2005; McLaughlin 2005, 2006; Murphy 2005; Sydie 2005). Despite the many strengths discussed above, the discipline in Canada is challenged by at least five major problems: (1) a lack of resources rooted in the institutional flatness of the Canadian higher-education system, (2) our links to the British sociological tradition with its undeveloped disciplinary core and organizational permeability, (3) the sometimes excessive shrillness of a critical sociology that was forged in the 1960s without the foil of an established mainstream sociology, (4) the division between sociology in Québec and the rest of Canada, and (5) the relative weakness of professional sociology in English Canada.

The flatness of the Canadian education system is, from the perspective of the authors, a positive thing for Canadian society. It is true that the American combination of elite and public research universities, along with their unique system of liberal arts colleges, produces excellent research traditions, stable academic disciplines, and, for the lucky few, an excellent education. However, the system places an enormous financial drain on public funds and generates academics who are often more interested in research than in educating the new generation. This creates an enormous pressure on middle-class economic resources that permeate throughout the politics and culture of a society deeply divided by class and race. Canadian higher education provides far more modest resources for research, is less competitive and cut-throat, and, one could argue, does not drain the society of as much tax revenue and elite philanthropy.

As a consequence, however, Canadian universities, even the most elite and research oriented, do not have anywhere near the resources that are provided in the United States. Flowing from this context, Canadian sociology faces a highly competitive environment in higher education and often finds itself pushed in an applied direction toward health, criminology, welfare state policy, and vocational training, while being squeezed out, at the other end of the academic spectrum, by the new interdisciplinary subfields of cultural studies, communications, and critical/social theory. Canadian sociologists, for example, partly because of these resource issues, meet annually at an interdisciplinary scholarly meeting run by our federal government, not in an autonomous professional gathering as in the American Sociological Association. These factors often lead to the production of low-level policy research, excessively polemical ideology, specialized work in methods (either qualitative or quantitative), or studies on narrow topics that lack a larger theoretical vision. The possibilities for ambitious multimethod work become even more limited as publication pressures create disincentives for faculty to engage in book-length projects, tackle larger research projects, and attempt to combine complimentary methods.

Another challenge to the institutional health of Canadian sociology is rooted in our colonial relationship to the British Empire. Anglo-Canadian universities have always had a British flavor to them, something that can be seen in terms of faculty hiring, university governance, and culture. Steve Fuller (2000) describes England as "the major nation with probably the weakest institutional tradition in the field" (p. 508). A theoretically driven, empirical sociology came late to Great Britain, for a variety of reasons (Abrams 1968; Kumar 2001; Lepenies 1988). Furthermore, the dynamics of the publishing industry in the United Kingdom (Fuller 2000), the politically active intellectuals to the left of the Labour Party, and the relative weakness of an empirical research tradition have combined to produce a sociology that is dominated by a "Verso Press radicalism" that is polemical, politically engaged, and far less professionally oriented than what is produced in the United States. The English connection to Canadian sociology has been well documented by early commentators (Clark 1976) and contemporary historians of the discipline (Hiller 1982). Helmes-Hayes (2002) has argued that "from the early years of the century up until the thirties, scholars in traditional disciplines, many schooled in England, either ignored sociology entirely or worked actively (to) prevent its development" (p. 84). At the University of Toronto, in particular, Harold Innis and his protégé S. D. Clark were particularly hostile to American-style multivariate sociology (Helmes-Hayes 2002).

Canadian sociology is also challenged by the fact that the discipline was essentially founded in Canada during the social and political turmoil of the 1960s, and thus we brought cultural and political biases of the New and Old Left into scholarly discourse. American radical sociology in the 1960s transformed an institutionalized discipline, albeit one with liberal and conservative tendencies. The result for Canadian radical sociology in the 1960s, in contrast, was a weakly institutionalized discipline. Many Canadian sociology programs went much farther than American departments in institutionalizing student involvement in hiring and tenure processes. Simplistic critiques of liberalism dominate too much of Canadian

sociology, making for a discipline far less credible with our students and the public than it should be.

Sociology in Canada is also inhibited by the deep cultural division between the field in French-speaking Québec and the rest of Canada. Québécois sociology was deeply involved in the political turmoil of the late 1960s and 1970s, and they helped create an increasingly autonomous provincial culture and politics, separate from political dynamics in both English Canada and the United States. More linked to French and Continental intellectual traditions as well as the needs of provincial policymakers, there is remarkably little contact between French and English sociology in Canada. This resembles the reality of Canadian politics more broadly, with the French and the English connected only loosely by a weak national identity. It is difficult to imagine sociologists in Canada doing much to overcome the "two solitudes" of the national identity until the larger national polity is better able to bridge this ethnic and regional divide.

All these factors mean that professional sociology in English Canada is relatively underdeveloped. State policy interests in health care in particular and the priorities of the National Funding organization known as the Social Science and Humanities Research Council influence academic reward structures and hiring patterns significantly. Canadian sociology is shaped, to a remarkable degree, by the teaching demands of undergraduate education, the funding opportunities for applied research, and the fads promoted by university administrators. Theoretically oriented and empirically grounded research programs in sociology in Canada suffer from this institutional context, leaving a discipline far less vibrant, lively, and autonomous than it could be (Ogmundson 2002).

Despite these obstacles, not all is gloom. Recent events in Canadian sociology suggest a potentially bright future. A lively debate in the discipline indicates that there is the political will to resist pressures that would otherwise drown the Canadian sociological imagination in trendy efforts at interdisciplinarity. There is a new generation of excellent Canadian-trained sociologists active in the discipline today, alongside Canadians trained in the United States and Britain, and there is a healthy contingent of scholars who have moved to our nation to make it their new professional home. The recent debate about moving sociology away from excessive quantification and of the importance of public sociologies in the context of a new global vision brings some of Canadian sociology's particular strengths to the foreground. Canadian sociology's unique global position has generated a rich tradition of alternative perspectives, a vibrant multimethod sociological imagination, and a willingness to take sociology in new and innovative directions, suggesting real hope for the future.

7

European Sociology

Gerd Nollmann

Hermann Strasser

University of Duisburg-Essen, Germany

THE INSTITUTIONAL SHAPE OF EUROPEAN SOCIOLOGY

Several obstacles must be kept in mind when "European sociology" is on the agenda. First, European sociology encompasses quite diverse scientific activities so that we will have to deal selectively with it. By far the largest sub-units of European sociology are constituted by French-, English-, and German-speaking sociologists. Furthermore, the major scientific language is English. It has become good practice for many European sociologists to spend some time in the English-speaking community and publish in English. However, we must keep in mind that—even though most classical studies have been translated into different languages—current research diffuses selectively between the German, French, English, Italian, Spanish, Portuguese, Dutch, Belgian, Scandinavian, and Eastern European languages. Only rarely is it worthwhile for publishers to have foreign manuscripts translated into a language other than English. Although the competition for university chairs in Europe still works on a national level, it will not be rational for scientists to invest much time in studying French, Italian, Spanish, Dutch, German, Austrian, Polish, Scandinavian, and many more research results—let alone understanding the language. This kind of competition leads to a continuously high level of reputation of national professional journals that are often considered the most desirable place of publication in the quest for academic recognition. Quite similar to the slow rise of a European public, European sociology has only partially

developed a central focus of attention. The labor market of European sociology is only theoretically open. As long as this insulation continues, there will not be a unified European sociology (Nedelmann and Sztompka 1993:3).

This is not to deny that there is much exchange within European sociologies as well as many common research activities, often inspired by funds from the European Union. Also, there is a common institutional platform: The European Sociological Association (ESA), founded in 1990, is a professional association of sociologists and non-profit organizations related to sociology. With more than 700 individual and institutional members, its main goal is to facilitate sociological research and teaching as well as the communication between sociologists in Europe and to give sociology a voice in European matters. An ESA Conference is held every two years.

Historically, both commonalities and diversities of the national paths have developed. On the one hand, first chairs date back to the early twentieth century throughout Europe. After decades of growth, fascism and World War II brought about a setback to sociological research. The second half of the twentieth century is characterized by Western European sociology's amazing expansion at the universities with many new chairs, institutionalization of empirical social research heavily influenced by American standards, and emerging special research areas. However, this extremely successful institutionalization also led to an increasing specialization of scientists. In Europe, the crucial line of such specialization divides social theory from social research, each developing its own discourse and most unfortunately not sufficiently taking note of each other. By mid-1970, enthusiasm for both educational expansion and sociology started to cool down. Chairs were occupied and at the latest by mid-1980, a phase of continual shrinking was set in motion.

On the other hand, European history has led to some distinctive national developments. Stalinism defined sociology as a bourgeois pseudoscience to be replaced by Marxism-Leninism. The Cold War forced many Eastern European sociologists to follow Goffman's strategies, distinguishing between cautious front stages and authentic back stages. Despite long-lasting political suppression, Polish sociology produced many outstanding scholars with international reputation, that is, Florian Znaniecki, Ludwig Gumplowicz, Stanislaw Ossowski, Wlodzimierz Wesolowski, and Zygmunt Bauman, who were forced to emigrate from Poland or had left the country before communists came to power. The same applies to Hungarian sociology where many scholars risked their careers and lives in their struggle to correct the apologetic orthodox Marxist "two-class-one-stratum" model by their empirical research results.

In contrast, Sweden, Finland, Denmark, Norway, and Iceland have contributed to a specific "Scandinavian" sociology with some continuity by strongly believing in sociology as an empirical and value-free science. In these "Nordic" countries, social research in social problems and the American style of "positivistic" sociological creed were favored. Among their outstanding scholars, we find such names as Johan Galtung, Stein Rokkan, and Jon Elster.[1]

Looking at major achievements of European sociology, we shall look at major lines of research by showing that sociological research focuses on empirical knowledge about the continuity and change of human conduct in all areas of society and of its consequences for societal development. Goldthorpe (2000a:262) has called this the ideal of a "new sociological mainstream" involving both questions about theory, that is, the concepts and categories used to understand and explain human conduct and empirical tests.

To demonstrate sociology's journey through periods, national idiosyncrasies, and inventive concepts, in the following sections, we will present the European "founding fathers," the theoretical discussion of the concept of meaningful human behavior as the microbasis of sociological research, and the constitution and development of social research in stratification, class, and mobility. It should be clear that this distinction does not perfectly reflect the complete set of European sociology, although it should be helpful in delineating its distinctive character.[2]

THE EUROPEAN FOUNDING FATHERS

Émile Durkheim (1897, [1895] 1982), Georg Simmel (1908), Werner Sombart ([1913] 2001), Ferdinand Tönnies ([1887] 1957), Max Weber ([1905] 1930, [1904] 1949), and Vilfredo Pareto ([1916] 1980)—all born around 1860—are considered the European founding fathers of sociology as an academic discipline with specific methods and objects of research. Many other European scholars could be mentioned, such as the Germans Karl Marx (1859) and Norbert Elias ([1937] 1978/1982), the Austrians Karl Renner (1953) and Franz Borkenau (1973), the British Herbert Spencer (1898), the Polish Stanislaw Ossowski (1963), and the Russian Pitirim A. Sorokin (1937/1941). In the second half of the nineteenth and the first half of the twentieth century, this generation set standards of sociological imagination and developed systems of thought on which sociology keeps on relying up to the present. In contrast to Continental, particularly German and French sociologists of this first generation, British sociology has resisted the European theoretical tradition and was, at least until after World War II, overwhelmingly empirical.

Until today, Durkheim and Weber have remained most influential among the European founding fathers. Durkheim's (1897) *Suicide* has certainly become *the* sociological paradigm as it deals with a social phenomenon making the object understandable to the reader while using (at that time) elaborate statistical data and methods, thereby appearing scientific, empirically saturated, and professional. Even though it may seem that no other human action could be more individual than the decision to end one's life, suicides are not caused by individual, idiosyncratic reasons but correlate with the social integration of the individual.

Based on these rates, Durkheim determines three types of suicide completing his explanation by providing the corresponding motives: egoistic, altruistic, and anomic. Despite Durkheim's (1897:297) own prohibitions and his claim to explain the social by the social and nothing else, such a typology comes close to Weber's parallel call for "sociological rules" and the underlying understanding of motives of behavior. The relative isolation of man in society—if, for example, a young single seeing all other boys walk with their girlfriends on a summer day—is a precondition for an egoistic suicide. In contrast, the altruistic suicide protects the community in which the person is strongly integrated: The military officer kills himself because he has done something dishonorable that threatens his professional group. The term "anomie" is Durkheim's contribution to sociological theory and means, virtually translated, "without law." It signifies a state of normlessness, irritation, confusion, and breakdown. Durkheim assumes that anomie will be found in times of increased social change. Traditional values do not have their binding authority anymore, and the new norms do not yet have enough power to guide human behavior. People will commit suicide more often in such a state of depression because they do not know what way their life is going.

Durkheim's (1897) way of arguing with official statistics has made *Suicide* a paradigmatic study of sociological research and generalizing probabilistic explanations on the basis of correlations. Its combination of understandability and professionality has been quite charming to later sociologists, and *Suicide* is therefore read and taught with high frequency at the universities—probably much more than his *Rules of Sociological Method* (1895), which spells out this same conception in a more theoretical fashion.[3]

Weber was aware of and agreed with Durkheim's search for the so-called sociological rules that combine social regularities, that is, all kinds of probabilistic distributions, with motives of human conduct. He came to a quite similar conception of sociological explanations—but got there on a completely different route. The reason is biographical: Weber was trained as a lawyer, did his dissertation and habilitation thesis on legal issues, and became a sociologist only in his late years. He was quite "theoretical" in his discussions, even though for him it went without saying that such work must go hand in hand with empirical efforts. He started several projects of data collection and social research (Lazarsfeld and Oberschall 1962).

From his dispersed methodological writings, later sociologists quoted mostly the definition of sociology: It is meant to understand human behavior in order to explain its course and consequences. Applied to Durkheim's example, this means that the statistical form the number of suicides takes on must be made understandable by looking at the reasons humans themselves actually attribute to ending their lives. For Durkheim, the question of motives was settled by distinguishing several types of suicide that match the social regularities of suicides. Probably the question of motives was much more prominent for Weber because, as a lawyer, he was well aware that in everyday life, the reasons man's behavior is actually based on are much more complicated to determine as may seem at first sight. He knew that if we ask people about their motives, we will not necessarily receive valid answers because the actual reasons for conduct are often not clear to humans themselves. Nevertheless, Weber insisted on the significance of the named reasons and advised separate empirical efforts, that is, psychological experiments and surveys, in detecting their causal power.

Also, Weber's own empirical research efforts stress the weight of meaningful motives to explain social change. In his work on the *Protestant Ethic and the Rise of Capitalism* (Weber [1905] 1930), he develops his thesis that in order to explain social change, we must look at the altering selectivity of human behavior. The decisive change was to be found in Calvinism, which made people believe that one could not simply do good works or perform acts of faith to assure one's place in heaven. However, wealth was considered a sign a person was one of God's elected, providing encouragement to acquire wealth and be successful. The protestant ethic thus provided religious sanctions so that the social world was no longer experienced as externally natural and eternal but rather as an object of internal control of man—with far-reaching consequences. For Weber, it was clear that the rapid social change modern society has been undergoing can only be properly attributed to change in human behavior. This is why the study of motives was so central to him. He made clear that the greatest part of

everyday behavior simply follows traditional rules, and only a small part of it is calculated in rational terms. But it is this difference that accounts for the Western style of *disenchantment* of society.

Unfortunately, Weber (1968, 1981) was clear neither in his *Categories* nor in *Economy and Society* about the crucial role of understanding (*Verstehen*) in doing research on social change in modern society. But how could he have been? Weber did not even try to present perfect research results, let alone develop a theory of society. His *Protestant Ethic* was not more than an exemplary illustration with scanty empirical proof. Rather, his efforts were but a preliminary approach to a research program to be filled later on. As later discussion showed, it was far from clear what "understanding" actually means in social research and in what way valid data can be constructed on the course and consequences of meaningful human behavior.

THE MEANING OF MEANINGFUL BEHAVIOR

Whereas American sociology discussed the question of understanding only occasionally (Goldenweiser 1938; Tucker 1965) and preferred to analyze available data causally (Abbott 1998), the major representatives of European sociology have spent a lot of time discussing what Weber's concept of meaningful behavior means exactly and what the nature of explanations is really all about. One of the major historical crossroads between American and European sociology was the discussion between Schütz and Parsons. The differences are best demonstrated by their exchange of letters about how a theory of action should be developed. Schütz claimed that it was the perspective of the actor that should guide sociological research. He disputed that Parsons's theory was an analysis *adequate to meaning* (Schütz and Parsons 1977:57ff.)—an argument that Parsons, in turn, disputed. Schütz's phenomenological sociology and its later interpretive variants stressed, against structural functionalism, that sociological explanations must aim at *meaningful* adequacy. Schütz (1932) explained this idea on the basis of the phenomenological reorientation of philosophical thought. Edmund Husserl (1859–1938), founder of the European phenomenological movement, reformulated the classical epistemological relation between knowledge and the object of knowledge (Husserl 1931). He insisted that it is not a lonely subject that meets objects of knowledge in the world but that acts of consciousness always "intend," that is, encompass or, as it is said later, *constitute* their object. Therefore, it is not the allegedly problematic difference between subject and object but rather the *horizon* character of the world that needs to be analyzed. Speaking of the world as a horizon means replacing the old idea of the world as a sum of things by relating a "thing" to its environment from which it—by means of distinction—receives its identity. A chair remains a chair—no matter from what angle we look at it. Through our perception, we know that even the parts of the object we do not see immediately are still there. Perception simplifies the chaos of incoming stimuli into constant and variable units. It overemphasizes the stability of certain data while leaving out other perceptual aspects. Without such one-sided certainties, perception would not be possible.

Schütz applied this phenomenological revolution to the social world. By use of language, we generate stable characteristics in the form of typifying interpretive schemes shared by the inhabitants of lifeworlds. They select observations and rely on an unproblematic "stock of knowledge at hand" (Schütz 1967:7). It is sociology's task to focus on the typifications suitable in the lifeworld, establishing second-order constructions about first-order constructions. Such a sociology of knowledge shows, as Berger and Luckmann (1966) stress, how typifications become institutionalized.

From the unresolved controversy between Parsons and Schütz, European sociology was left behind with an abyss that has not proven fruitful. For several decades, it seemed that distinctions such as "action versus system," "micro versus macro," "conflict versus integration," "social definition versus social structure," and "explaining versus understanding" generated irreconcilable paradigms that must exist side by side. Looking back, one could argue that the exaggerated confrontation between those who insist on guarding the perspective of human conduct and those who allegedly did not was rather the result of a phase in European sociology in which it had lost sight of the research program that Weber had in mind when he stressed the importance of meaningful behavior for social change. It would not seem completely unfair to blame Parsons for this fatal misunderstanding: Parsons's theory was so challenging that many European sociologists saw their task as sufficiently fulfilled by confronting Parsons's analytical realism with the meaningful character of the social world (as Schütz did) or by criticizing his alleged neglect of material factors (Lockwood 1956). We do want to stress that this criticism has been necessary. However, it did not bring us closer to realize the research program of the founding fathers.

At least three European sociologists of the next generation have made substantial contributions to this debate that may be considered as real advances and shed some new light on the concept of the explanation of meaningful behavior. Anthony Giddens, in his typically British, anti-system thinking fashion, stresses *duality of structure.* In his *New Rules of Sociological Methods,* Giddens (1976) insists on the interpretive foundation of sociology and calls for a double hermeneutic: Understanding is not only an inevitable source of hypotheses about human behavior but also an element already inherent in the research object. Sociology needs to take into account that the social world is always preinterpreted. In this respect, Giddens criticizes "positively" the traditions of Schütz's phenomenology, ethnomethodology, and the Anglo-Saxon theory of action, which follows the late Wittgenstein.

At the same time, Giddens stresses that we would be mistaken if we looked at the social world only from the angle of its meaningful production. Rather, research must also keep in mind the material reproduction of social practice. In *The Constitution of Society,* Giddens (1984) summarizes his theory of structuration and provides a wide definition of social structures. These encompass not only rule structures, that is, meaningful expectations of humans' behavior, but also structures that limit human action, as illustrated by unequal distributions of resources. The term *structure,* as is well established in European sociology by now, therefore takes on a twofold meaning: It is seen as both enabling and restricting human conduct.[4]

Similar thoughts have been laid down by Niklas Luhmann and Pierre Bourdieu (Nassehi and Nollmann 2004). Luhmann's theory of social systems has become quite influential in European sociology. At first sight, his devotion to systems theory seems to connect him closely with Parsons. This connection is, however, justified only in a very limited sense. Actually, like Weber, Luhmann insists on meaning as sociology's basic concept. However, Luhmann (1990:53ff.) believes that the Weberian typology of action as a means-value-ends relation is a far too selective view of human behavior to be able to constitute *the* basic analytical tool. Instead, Luhmann favors the attribution model, which categorizes conduct in four directions: internal versus external, stable versus variable interpretation. Internal attributions of behavior will appear as "action" based either on ability and/or effort. External attributions are interpreted as (passive) experience of the world, either as luck or fate. Hence, "action" is not an ontologically given object of sociological research but a *practical* internal attribution of conduct. It is for this reason that Luhmann (1995:137ff.) assumes that human conduct is "systemic"; that is, the meaning of a behavioral event is constituted by the next event that selectively *understands* its predecessor. Luhmann's concept of understanding follows Schütz who had objected to Weber's methodology that ideal-type understanding is not a privilege of the social scientist. Luhmann insists on practical first-order understanding as the object of sociology. Accordingly, communication consists of three combined elements: utterance, information, and understanding. The meaning of behavior is constituted by the *communicative* act of *understanding* that follows the actor's *utterance* of *information* (Luhmann 1995:139ff.). Selective understanding constitutes meaningful social rules that help actors secure certainty about what to expect in the social world. Luhmann defines meaning phenomenologically as a means of selection from a horizon of other possibilities.

Luhmann makes three basic statements on the empirical distribution of practical first-order interpretations of behavior: First, in the course of societal evolution, there is a general trend toward more internal attributions. Organizations especially are based on the assumption that any kind of conduct can be interpreted as decisions so that people can be held responsible. Attributions to nature and

God do not disappear completely but require a specialized context to find support. According to Luhmann, however, it would be a mistake to assume that all actors can *really* shape the world according to their intentions in situations that are attributed internally. The internal attribution of meaning as responsible action is just one suitable way of interpreting the social world. Therefore, "freedom" does not mean that causal strains on human conduct are absent or that voluntarism has finally appeared in the social world. Rather, Luhmann sees modern appeals to freedom as a mere correlate of this general trend toward the practice of internal attribution. It is a reflex of societal structure, not the rise of human emancipation from external influences, that makes us describe ourselves as "free individuals." The recent discussion of *individualization* reflects just one more step in this direction.

Second, in modernity, interpretation of conduct depends on the context of media of exchange. For example, the appeal to "truth" leads to external attributions as "experience": In scientific discussions, we publicly discuss competing accounts of truth while we assume that the reason for rival concepts is not our dislike or hate of each other but rather our belief that the rival has not reached the externally given instance of truth. In contrast, conduct in the area of "power" accounts for interpretations as "action" for both ego and alter because political communication (and organizational behavior generally) aim at collectively binding decisions controlling citizens' behavior (Luhmann 1997:332ff.).

Third, as Luhmann (1973) shows in a study of the German civil service, attributional preferences and "styles" are distributed according to hierarchical positions in organizations. Civil servants were asked to determine the reasons for their own and their colleagues' promotions or the absence of promotions. More specifically, the interviewees had to locate the perceived causes of promotions according to Heider's (1958) attribution model. The general result of this study demonstrates that civil servants were more inclined to attribute promotions internally, the higher their position, success, upward mobility, satisfaction, and positive attitudes toward the organization. Those who reached higher levels prefer internal attributions of their professional careers as resulting from effort and ability. The lower the position, the more servants tended to interpret their life course as externally dominated by fortune, chance, and conduct of others they could not control.

Luhmann does not, as Parsons might have, take this result to be a proof of the view that in modern society "effort makes a difference." He preferred to refrain from normative statements of this kind and was content with interpreting his findings as supporting his theory, which predicts that attributional preferences are not randomly distributed in society but rather structured in a specific way. It is the elaboration of such "subjective" meaningful preferences that Weber wanted sociologists to pursue by combining social regularities with meaningful rules.

Pierre Bourdieu, in turn, developed his social theory against the background of French structuralism as represented by Ferdinand de Saussure (1857–1913) and Claude Lévi-Strauss (1908–). In *The Logic of Practice,* Bourdieu (1990) summarizes his views in a more theoretical fashion, whereas in *Distinction* (1984), he presents his major findings on the stratification of French society. Bourdieu identifies the structuralist tradition with the objectivist search for systems of rules. It aims at a complete and logically consistent model meant to analyze social phenomena. Individual and collective actors appear to be mere executors of social structures. The scientific observer is in a privileged position to have a more complete knowledge of social contexts than participants do. Bourdieu contrasts this viewpoint with the subjectivist tradition, which he sees represented by Jean-Paul Sartre's phenomenology, theories of rational choice (RC), game theory, and neoclassical economics. In these perspectives, the subjectively intended meaning actors attribute to their conduct is reconstructed. These attempts, according to Bourdieu, overemphasize the alleged decisions of the "lonely" consciousness.

Bourdieu sees the need to mediate between both traditions. He sees the main weakness of objectivist approaches in their tendency to project their own constructs into their object and to ignore the paradoxical statements, intentions, and motives found in practical behavior. The central category to synthesize these traditions is the *habitus.* It consists of schemes of perception and evaluation capable of generating practical behavior. They become internalized and form the self-evident preconditions of conformity and continuity of human conduct. They do not presuppose plans and reflexive decisions but enable humans to know automatically what should be considered reasonable and useful in practical terms. Like Weber, Bourdieu argues that human conduct is mostly nonreflexive and traditional. Such automatism is inevitable because practical behavior is under enormous pressure of time.

In *Distinction,* Bourdieu (1984) distinguishes between the space of social classes (high, middle, low) and the space of lifestyles with its corresponding types of "taste." The volume of capital, assembled in the course of life, determines the individual's position in these spaces. The habitus works as a mediator between objective societal distributions and subjective interpretive schemes and to some extent indicates the duality of structure as discussed by Giddens and Luhmann.

CRITICAL THEORY

So far, we have highlighted major European statements on the meaning of meaning in sociological research. This is not to say that European sociology offers much more relevant discussions. In the 1960s and 1970s, a widespread discussion took place, later known as *Positivismusstreit,* which was basically a controversy about Max Weber's call for a sociology devoid of value judgments. *Critical theory* played the major antipode in the *Positivismusstreit* and attacked assumptions of Gadamer's (1975) hermeneutic circle. Critical theory is usually associated with the Frankfurt School of Social Research and its leading figures Theodor Adorno (1903–1969;1972), Max Horkheimer (1895–1973), and Herbert Marcuse (1898–1979;1969). This tradition criticized instrumental reason as increasingly dominating the history of man. Their pessimism considers modern industrial society as a totalitarian form of domination. Instrumental reason not only sees the world but also sees other human beings in terms of efficient exploitation. Adorno's famous dictum that sociology should not simply reproduce the facts about society but rather take part in criticizing them constitutes the opposite of Weber's research program, which stressed that we actually know so little about the domain-specific regularities of human conduct.

The work of Jürgen Habermas (1929–)—the most well-known figure of the second generation of critical theory—draws on its heritage, but is more closely linked to the sociological mainstream. At the center of his theory of modernity is his twofold concept of society combining action and system theory. Two forms of integration correspond to these paradigms in social theory: social and system integration. Mechanisms of social integration refer to orientations of actors constituting societal order of values, norms, and communicative process. In contrast, market exchange and power as mechanisms of system integration transcend the orientations of actors and integrate nonintended contexts of action through functional networks. Whereas socially integrated interaction remains at least intuitively understandable for actors and can therefore be captured meaningfully, system-integrated contexts lie beyond the self-explication of actors and can only be explained from the point of view of the observer.

There are two concepts of society assigned to the mechanisms of integration, the concept of lifeworld and the concept of social system. From a practical point of view of actors, society is seen as a sociocultural lifeworld, whereas from the observer's point of view, it is regarded as a social system. By means of this conceptual duplex, Habermas describes all kinds of societies as systemically stabilized contexts of socially integrated groups.

For Habermas, lifeworld and system have been differentiated in the process of social evolution. In primitive societies, social and system integration are closely related, whereas in the course of societal development, the mechanisms of system integration become disconnected from social integration. With the transition to modernity, these two principles have become largely separated. In contemporary society, lifeworld and system exist in opposition to each other. The private and the public political and cultural spheres represent the institutional orders of the lifeworld. In these primarily socially integrated areas, the symbolic reproduction of society takes place (i.e., the tradition and innovation of cultural knowledge, social integration, and socialization). Therefore, symbolic reproduction represents

not just one but several functions that modern lifeworlds serve (Habermas [1992] 1996:77). The lifeworld consists of *culture, society,* and *personality.* With these three elements, modern lifeworlds develop the educational system, the law, and the family as institutions highly specialized to fill these functional specifications. According to Habermas, these lifeworld components remain connected to each other through the medium of language. Colloquial language imposes strict limits on the functional differentiation of the lifeworld so that its totality is not endangered.

With regard to the interpenetration of lifeworld discourses, Habermas ([1985] 1988:418) speaks of the capacity of intersubjective self-understanding of modern societies, keeping borders between the socially integrated areas open. All parts of the lifeworld refer to one comprehensive public, in which society develops reflexive knowledge of itself. Although the lifeworld is structured by communicative action, it does not, however, constitute the center of modern societies. Habermas sees rationality endangered because the communicative infrastructure of lifeworlds is threatened by both colonization and fragmentation.

Outside of the lifeworld, the capitalist economy and public administration are situated. These two functional subsystems of society use money and organizational power as their media of exchange. They specialize in the material reproduction of the lifeworld. Between the economy and private households, on the one hand, and the public administration and political-cultural public, on the other, exchange relations exist. Habermas conceptualizes economy and politics as open systems that maintain a systemic exchange with their social environments. From the point of view of the economy and the political system, the lifeworld is just a societal subsystem, whereas from the vantage of the lifeworld, the economic and administrative complex appears as rationalized contexts of action transcending the intuitive understanding of actors. As the media-based exchange relations between the lifeworld and system illustrate, the separation of system and social integration is, even in contemporary societies, far from complete. The economic and administrative complex remains connected to the lifeworld because the systemic media of money and organizational power are in need of an institutional anchorage in the lifeworld. Although communicative action, on the one hand, and capitalist economy and political administration, on the other, are asymmetrically related, the lifeworld remains, in contrast to the functional subsystems, the more comprehensive concept of social order. Only by anchoring legal institutions in the lifeworld can markets and the authority of the state persist. This is why the areas of system integration are constituted legally.

In *Between Facts and Norms: Contributions to a Discourse Theory of Law and Democracy,* Habermas ([1992] 1996) points to the significance the theory of communicative action attributes to the category of law. Modern law is connected both with the lifeworld and the functional subsystems, hence serving intermediary functions between social and system integration. Such lifeworld messages (i.e., public protest) must be translated into the language of law before they can be understood in economy and politics. Modern law works like a transformer that guarantees that normative messages circulate throughout society.

Habermas's theory of modernity has been criticized in many ways. One important line of criticism refers to the normative texture of the theory of communicative action. Rational potential of reflexivity is only imputed to the socially integrated lifeworld even though lifeworlds constitute only a part of modern societies. Also, the categorical distinction between functionally specialized subsystems (economy, administration, politics) and the specific parts of the lifeworld (education, law, family) is not as clear as it may seem at first glance. According to McCarthy (1986:209ff.), only a gradual distinction can be observed between these areas. Education, law, and family also suffer from unintended consequences of social action. At the same time, economy and public administration remain, just as the communicative structure of the lifeworld, dependent on the use of ordinary language. Even though Habermas has tried to combine the heritage of critical theory with some of the important results of interpretive sociology, it is not easy to see in what way such a critical theory will contribute to an empirical study of social change.

METHODOLOGICAL INDIVIDUALISM AND RATIONAL CHOICE

The opposite of this weakness can be seen in another important stream of European sociology represented by the tradition of RC. RC sociologists are united by the conviction that assumptions about human conduct must be tested in social research. Probably all RC theorists assume that actors' preferences (i.e., goals, wishes, motives) are conditions of their action. From the individual's point of view, such action contributes to the fulfillment of his goals. Many variants of RC are used in research. Therefore, it has become common to distinguish between wide and narrow versions and strong and weak versions. European sociology predominantly relies on wider and weaker versions of RC, denying the economic assumption that humans follow more or less exclusively egoistic goals. Humans are seen as guided by bounded rationality and not by completely linear probabilities. RC theorists assume that people will follow a behavior that they themselves consider to be useful to them. As this assumption is quite trivial, the discussion focuses on the question of how researchers can model such utility beliefs and the question of which designs are best to test RC empirically. One central problem concerns the way researchers should develop the so-called bridge hypotheses that are at the core of the much-discussed micro-macro link comprising the important expectations and evaluations of humans. European RC theorists seem to be methodologically open to various ways of data

generation on subjective preferences, be that case studies or surveys (Opp and Friedrichs 1996). More recently, the problem of measuring valid and reliable attitudes, for example, by the so-called factorial surveys, has been one focus of attention (Beck and Opp 2001).

Important areas of German RC research comprise the worldwide largest study in reasons and causes of divorces (Esser 2002), marriage and family (Brüderl and Diekmann 1994), political protest, especially the rise of the so-called Mondays' protests in the former German Democratic Republic (Opp 1998), ecological consciousness (Diekmann and Preisendörfer 1998), and the risky decision to help Jews in times of the Holocaust (Klingemann and Falter 1993). Probably the most well-known RC theorist in France, Raymond Boudon (1974) has widely analyzed the paradoxical and unintended effects of individual action, for example, with reference to the unexpected consequences of educational expansion or early purchases in a time of high inflation.

Besides these lines of social theorizing and empirical testing, European sociologists have stressed the significance of human conduct for social change. Michel Crozier has, together with Erhard Friedberg (1980), applied methodological individualism to organization theory without neglecting its systemic context. Alain Touraine (1969, 1983) has developed a theory of postindustrial society in which new social movements constitute the central force of action beyond the old class conflict. In Great Britain, John H. Goldthorpe (1997) has proposed a moderate version of RC for sociology. Furthermore, Peter Hedström and Richard Swedberg (1996, 1998) have shown in what way RC actually aims at the empirical realization of Weberian ideas.

EUROPEAN SOCIAL RESEARCH

Probabilism thoroughly changed the way of explaining social phenomena. From a traditional viewpoint, something is either the cause of some effect or it is not. Even for Durkheim, dependencies between variables seemed to be either complete or nonexistent, whereas Weber, as a lawyer, made us aware of the highly contingent and constructive character of statements that involve causality. Consequently, Weber not only devoted most of his methodological discussions to the problem of controlling valid causal statements but also explicitly demanded that sociological explanations consist of "chances," that is, more or less high probabilities that social regularities coincide with practical attributions of goals, means, values, and other assumed causes of one's behavior. Despite his clearly probabilistic approach, he himself—like most other founding fathers of sociology—did not have a thorough knowledge of statistics. At least, he was convinced that a close cooperation between sociology and statisticians was necessary. One of the early attempts at studying attitudes was made by the German *Verein für Sozialpolitik* in 1908 led by Max Weber and his brother Alfred. Their motivation exactly matched the situation described above. In the Germany of that time, research was conducted on social welfare and the labor question so that one knew a lot about conditions of existence: wages, work time and loads, nutrition, and living. Little knowledge was available about their personality and the influence that industry had on their attitudes. The *Verein* decided to conduct a survey on basic problems concerning the quality of work and the question what exactly one was to ask workers in order to obtain the required knowledge about their actual behavior. Such questions as "Is your work very exhausting? After how many hours of work do you get tired? Which goal do you hope to achieve in life? Which goals have you set earlier in your life?" led to disappointing results. The survey was not based on any idea about the mechanisms in which objective conditions are converted into subjective attitudes and in what way such attitudes—if at all—shape structural opportunities. In 1911, the frustrated Max Weber concluded that despite ample efforts, the surveys had brought almost no reliable and applicable results. The gap between theoretical reasoning and empirical research was deep and wide.[5]

Because of this scanty research situation, the early ideas of research questions on social structure and stratification were more theoretical than empirical. Not only did Weber see sociology's mission of explaining human behavior in understanding, he also criticized Marx's class theory in a fundamental way that became influential in later research. In *Economy and Society,* Weber extends Marx's simple dichotomy between those who control the means of production and those who do not by stressing the importance of education and social mobility, which showed that the working class was much more differentiated. His distinction between class, status, and party was meant to indicate that the distribution of power in society is more differentiated and that it is necessary to take into account the actual expectations of human conduct in the divergent social relationships.

Weber's classification of occupations inspired later research. Further discussion in stratification research has been sitting on the shoulders of the giants Marx and Weber. It has provided variations of the basic tension between these giants of social thought: the relation between interests and ideas, objective and subjective causal influences in the social world, the material and ideal aspects of human conduct. The heritage of Weber and Marx enables us to deduct all later research as offshoots of their core ideas. This is not to say that no progress was achieved in the meantime. But the basic positions of later research were fixed between the representatives who stress the material and structural aspects of social life and those who underline the "ideal," meaningful character of behavior because of its consequences for social change.

Furthermore, it deserves mentioning that early European reflections on social stratification presented good reasons why sociology should actually study social stratification—reasons that were often forgotten in later research. Simmel ([1897] 1983) in his essay "Roses: A Social Hypothesis" tells the completely fictitious story of a "terrible" form of inequality: All people have their own piece of land and can live from it. However, some of them grow roses. For a while, this difference is accepted like the natural distribution of beautiful and ugly. But slowly, the anger grows. Agitators say that all humans have a natural right to roses. With allusions to famous words of Rousseau, Nietzsche, and Marx, Simmel shows how even more envy is generated. A revolutionary party is created that sees itself in opposition to the owners of roses who try to legally assure their rose monopoly. However, in the name of justice, the revolutionary party manages to equalize rose property so that everybody—at least for a while—is happy. Unfortunately, new differences now become visible. Some roses are bigger and more beautiful than others. Again, anger grows about the unequal distribution of such differences and another revolutionary situation. This way, as in a fairy tale, the story will go on and on and on.

Simmel's sociological fairy tale makes clear what is really interesting about the study of social inequality: It is not only the change and continuity of the absolute distribution of goods but the change and continuity of people's *interpretations* of differences that have the most significant consequences in modern society. This position matches Weber's insistence on the *meaningful* character of modern human conduct, which needs to be studied in combination with "structural" distributions. Also, Simmel's ([1897] 1983) rose hypothesis stresses that more attempts at equality will lead to a higher consciousness of remaining inequalities. Humans are sensitive to differences. Inequality is a useful focus for political leaders aiming at popularity, but, as Simmel points out, revolutionary attempts at more equality will not be successful and do not necessarily lead directly to more happiness.

Simmel's early study took into account only two typical interpretations of differences: At first, people see the unequal distribution of roses as natural and traditional, that is, external to their own behavior. In the following stage, it is considered as unjust. There is an expression of an assumed common will that sees the distribution internally as unwanted and calls for a change ("We do not want this . . ."). Simmel implies that the latter attribution is on the rise in modern society substituting traditional understanding of stratification.

Another, more complex satirical story about the modern interpretation of inequality can be found in Michael Young's (1958) *The Rise of the Meritocracy,* which seriously challenges the common belief that *effort makes a difference* by taking it seriously and analyzing fictitiously to what consequences a real meritocracy would lead. Young confronts us with Great Britain in 2033 where intelligence and effort together make up merit constituting a complete justification of inequality. This code directs social selection and generates a perfect meritocracy. For Young, this is not the end but rather the beginning of his story in which he analyzes the resulting dynamics of equality and inequality. The most important means of professional careers are constituted by intelligence testing independent of social class of origin and money. Everybody has the right to get tested again after a while. All talent is thus concentrated in the upper class. The lower class consists of losers and fools. It degenerates into a stupid mass as it can no longer find such alternative interpretations of its inferiority as fate, bad luck, and the power of the upper class. There are compensatory programs so that a possible resistance against this meritocratic order will not even develop in the first place. But problematic inequalities do—despite the equalization of income—remain, and finally the alliance of young women and old socialist men leads to the new ideology of "cultivate variety" instead of "equal opportunity."

Obviously, these thoughts are still of eminent actuality, especially today. However, Simmel's and Young's satirical stories hardly inspired empirical research but their ideas retain salience today. It would be more than timely to find out how such interpretations of inequality are *really* distributed in contemporary societies and what consequences such beliefs might have for social change. However, neither European nor any other sociology made this task its most urgent one. Empirical research in meaningful behavior was later found to be more often in cognitive and social psychology against which European sociology remained quite reserved.

Major advancements of sociological research are attached to a researcher who originated from Vienna, Austria, and who later, after his emigration to the United States, became a founding father of survey research in American sociology: Paul F. Lazarsfeld (1901–1976). Together with Marie Jahoda (1907–2001) and Hans Zeisel (1905–1992), he conducted the famous study of *The Unemployed of Marienthal* (Jahoda, Lazarsfeld, and Zeisel 2002). Marienthal was a small industrial village founded to satisfy the labor needs of a textile company shut down in 1929/1930. Of the 478 families, 367 did not have work anymore so that the village was dominated by the consequences of unemployment. The task of Lazarsfeld's research group from the *Wirtschaftspsychologische Arbeitsstelle Wien* was to document thoroughly the social psychological effects of long-term unemployment. They used modern methods of data collection that allowed insights into the mechanisms between structural descriptions and subjective experiences reported by the affected persons themselves, that is, their attitude to their situation. The measurement of walking speed especially became famous as an indicator for individual coping. The group constructed such types of attitudes as the unbroken, the resigned, the apathetic, and the desperate. The answer to the by then politically much-debated question about the social psychological consequences of unemployment was clearly the prevalence of apathy. Despite the qualitative and individual case study character, the group demonstrated with great personal involvement that it is principally possible to

quantitatively measure complex social phenomena. In 1940, Lazarsfeld got a chair at Columbia University, New York, and in 1944, his *Forschungsstelle* became the *Bureau of Applied Social Research.*

After World War II, European sociology, like European societies, needed to recover, and in the period of reconstruction, the initial concentration was on the major sectors of society (family, education, work, health care) that were also critical political issues. Public funds were provided to produce more information about society in order to be able to modernize it, rebuild it, and make welfare state activities efficient. European sociology reeducated itself and imported American sociology's triumph of empiricism and request for scientific values. American textbooks and research methods were widely adapted.

European sociology very much followed the direction of its American counterpart after World War II, aiming at the generation of new data and the quantitative operationalization of research problems, slowly replacing philosophical and theological orientations in such countries as Austria, Germany, and Spain. One of the most important achievements of European sociology has certainly to do with the development of class schemes. *Occupational groups* offer access to the class structure of modern societies. Class schemes uncover class *relations* instead of conceiving of them as a gradational difference of prestige, as social strata have been mostly defined in the United States. Gradational and relational approaches to understanding social inequality must be seen through the historical lenses of the class concept, as it developed in European and American sociology over the last two centuries. Especially since Marx, class in the European sense is understood as a historical reality accompanied by an increasing consciousness of common interests to be realized *against* other classes. Classes in the American sense of strata represent a conglomeration of individuals differentiated according to such criteria as income, prestige, and education. These different definitions of class are related to different historical situations and experiences. European societies were characterized by fairly low mobility that took place primarily within specific class situations. In the United States, in contrast, capitalism was not preceded by feudalism but characterized by a rather weak labor movement and fairly extensive mobility rates. Whereas the European class view has traditionally focused on large groups, the American view has always referred to individuals and their social relationships. In other words, the European perspective has been one of conflicting interests of large groups, whereas the empirical reference in America has always been the belief that everyone is the master of his fate. Typical representatives of such class concepts on the European side are Marx and Weber and their epigones, whereas the American concept, actually founded by Alexis de Tocqueville in the 1830s, has been most strongly represented by Lloyd Warner; such functional theorists as Parsons, Kingsley Davis, and Wilbert Moore; and such prestige researchers as Donald Treiman and Robert W. Hodge.[6]

Goldthorpe (1980:40) defines the "European" class concept by typical situations of work in the labor market, including its proximity to occupational authority, the level of work autonomy, the way work is supervised, the opportunities for advancement, and job security. Goldthorpe (1980) developed his scheme in *Social Mobility and Class Structure in Modern Britain.* It later came to be known as the EGP (Erikson/Goldthorpe/Portocarero) or CASMIN scheme. The most important classes are farmers, petite bourgeoisie, workers, nonmanual routine, and the service class. Its fruitfulness has been validated several times (Evans and Mills 1998). Also, it has led to several controversies, for example, in the *class and gender debate* in Great Britain, in which feminist researchers criticized the scheme for ignoring the situation of women. In a more recent symposium, the foundations of class analysis have been criticized (Wright 2000, Sørensen 2000).[7]

The study of occupational classes has gradually developed into elaborate statistical ventures. Class research was also based on thoughts initially introduced by Dahrendorf (1959:153) with an *analytical* intention. He assumed that class theory can be divided into two elements: the theory of class formation and the theory of class action as a conflict theory. The charm of this *analytical* division consisted in the idea of class formation, which, till then largely neglected, now called for continuing studies. The scientist referred to the *classes in themselves,* but excluded the *classes for themselves* from his observation (Braverman 1974:26ff.). Discussions about class concepts up to the present time are based on Dahrendorf's distinction between class formation and class action. For example, Sørensen (2000) and Goldthorpe (2000a) distinguish between three main types of class concepts with hierarchically ordered levels of theoretical ambition, beginning with a concept that provides a purely nominal categorization of populations according to significant dimensions of stratification concerning life chances and conditions, attitudes, values, and patterns of action. The second level goes beyond this first concept by delineating class positions that may turn individuals into collectivities with recognizable cultural identities. The third, most ambitious, level aims at class action as it defines collectivities in terms of common interests and the motivation to engage in conflict with other classes. Both Sørensen and Goldthorpe look for a well-constructed theory that will inform the scientific observer *at all three levels* of theoretical ambition.

This is not to say that class-specific interpretations have not been explored in other ways as well. One important direction of research tried to link the class concept to typical images of society. Lockwood (1966) pointed to the fact that individuals

visualize the . . . structure of their society from the vantage points of their own particular milieus and their perception of the larger society will vary according to their experiences . . . in the smaller societies in which they live out their daily lives. (P. 249)

Consequently, he developed a typology of working-class views of society that corresponded to the fluctuations within their working situation.[8]

A more recent direction that connected European and American research in 10 countries tried to prove the action-relatedness of class by measuring class-specific *attitudes* (Erbslöh et al. 1988; Wright 1997). The results more or less mirror the hierarchical order of occupational groups. Unemployed workers show the highest, capitalists the lowest degrees of class-specific attitudes. Petite bourgeoisie, wage-dependent middle class, commercial and aggregated working class, and mechanical workers, in ascending order, occupied the slots between the extremes of attitudes expressed in responses to statements such as "In strikes, the management should not be allowed to hire other workers." But the study of social attitudes in stratification research never managed to attain the same amount of attention and data level as more "structural" research.

Another, more recent achievement of European research can be found in the German Life History Study (GLHS) and the German Socio-Economic Panel (GSOEP). They were both developed in the context of the research group on "Microanalytical Foundations of Social Policy," which started in 1979 and involved researchers from sociology, economics, and political science. The GSOEP is a prospective longitudinal survey in which a random sample of adults is interviewed annually. The GLHS represents a retrospective study of individual life courses consisting of different birth cohorts for which information about education and employment history, parental status, marital and fertility history, and family and household composition are provided. In comparison with other panels, for example, the American Panel Study of Income Dynamics, both studies contain relatively little information about attitudes and other social psychological scales that might provide a deeper insight into the microdynamics and consequences of human behavior (Diewald 2001).

This is also demonstrated by the National Child Development Study (NCDS) in Great Britain, which triggered a debate on the more or less meritocratic character of contemporary labor markets (Bond and Saunders 1999; Breen and Goldthorpe 1999). This "race" between the causal weight of structural and individual factors generated no definitive results, which, in turn, stresses the need for deeper panel studies into the meaning of human behavior and its consequences.

This deficiency may also be shown from the raging debate on individualization and the alleged *death of class* in European sociology (Beck 1992; Pakulski and Waters 1996; Marshall 1997; Grusky and Sørensen 1998). In this battle, the theorists of individualization argue that individuals no longer consider themselves as class members with a common fate and destination, while empirical studies still show a more or less unchanged effect of class membership on life courses and behavioral patterns. Despite the conflicting schools, more recently some scholars have stressed that these two points of view do not necessarily indicate irreconcilable assumptions but may simply refer to two different objects of sociological research and that more data would be needed about both "objective" regularities that indicate outcomes and antecedents of human action and "subjective" regularities of interpreted human behavior itself (Nollmann and Strasser 2002). This goes hand in hand with more recent calls for interdisciplinary data collection and the cooperation of large-scale data analyses and theories of human agency (Hedström and Swedberg 1996, 1998; Goldthorpe 2000a).

Concluding our section on social research, it seems necessary to stress that interviews and surveys have become the major methodological instrument of data collection for the measurement of both subjective attitudes and sociostructural data of classes and life courses. Whereas the origins of the survey date back to the early nineteenth century (Marsh 1982), early political polls began in the 1930s and market research emerged only after World War II. Since then, the survey and interview research have gained an overwhelming dominance so that the majority of available data today stems from this source (Kaase 1998). Programs such as the European Social Survey Program and the "Eurobarometer," which is based on the theory of value change (Inglehart 1977), today provide sociological research with relevant data on social change. Survey and interview research have gone a long way, and not only in terms of internationalization, which makes it virtually impossible today to distinguish between European, American, and other sociologies in this field. Also, it proceeded from merely collecting objective facts about the poor in the nineteenth century to surveying subjective phenomena and measuring specific human behavior in, for example, factorial surveys (Beck and Opp 2001). In this development, we see a kind of reunion of Goldthorpe's idea of a new sociological mainstream with some of the more recent developments in survey research, especially questionnaire designs that retrieve valid context-specific evaluations.

This is not to deny that case studies and "small N" qualitative research will play an important role in tracking down social change, especially in such highly innovative areas of society as the "new economy." Such research will also be necessary as a preparatory measure for developing hypotheses and setting the hermeneutic basis for generalizing quantitative data.

8

British Sociology

Bryan S. Turner

National University of Singapore

INTRODUCTION: THE ORIGINS OF VICTORIAN SOCIOLOGY

British sociology had its nineteenth-century origins in three streams of Victorian social thought. First, there was the liberalism of J. S. Mill, who made important contributions to the philosophy of the social sciences and to the analysis of democracy, in which he was much influenced by the study of American society by Alexis de Tocqueville. Second, the emergence of sociology was related to social reformism and town planning in such figures as Patrick Geddes and Charles Booth. Third, its major intellectual figure—Herbert Spencer—was part of a broader intellectual movement of social evolutionism associated with Charles Darwin. Spencer (1884) in *The Man versus the State* attempted to reconcile the liberalism of the British utilitarians with the evolutionary theories of Darwin. There were also early institutional developments at the London School of Economics (LSE) with the creation of the Martin White chair of sociology that went to the liberal philosopher Leonard T. Hobhouse, and the publication of the first series of *The Sociological Review*. Geddes and Branford founded the Sociological Society in London at the turn of the century (Mumford 1948). A small group of sociologists—L. T. Hobhouse, Victor Branford, and Morris Ginsberg—developed the subject in the 1930s. Robert McIver held a lectureship in sociology and philosophy at the University of Aberdeen before World War I. Karl Mannheim arrived in 1933 and became influential at the LSE. R. H. Tawney published his classic *Religion and the Rise of Capitalism* in 1926 before Ernst Troeltsch and Max Weber were translated into English.

Although these developments represented a promising start, British sociology has had an uncertain and weak institutional history. It has been highly dependent on continental social theory, and its great achievements after World War II were closely associated with a large influx of European (specifically Jewish) refugees who found refuge in British universities during and after the ascendancy of German fascism (Turner 1990). The peculiarity of British sociology is that while its professional development has been somewhat slow and uncertain, it has produced a rich, if heterogeneous, body of sociological scholarship. In short, the paradox of British, unlike American, sociology is that it has flourished in marginal, typically parochial, universities, and it has been carried out by people and institutions that have not been overtly connected to mainstream sociology departments. Although sociology has been well represented at the LSE, it has not flourished at Oxford or Cambridge. In contrast, it has enjoyed a distinguished history at provincial universities such as Leicester, Lancaster, Liverpool, Essex, Warwick, and Edinburgh. Leicester appears to have been especially significant, being the academic home of Rosemary Crompton, Eric Dunning, Norbert Elias, Anthony Giddens, John Goldthorpe, Ilya Neustadt, and others (Giddens and Mackenzie 1982). Another example is the success of the sociology of deviance and the York University Deviancy Symposium that attracted such figures as Stan Cohen, Mike Hepworth, Ian Taylor, Paul Walton, and Jock Young. Critical criminology (Taylor, Walton, and Young 1973) flourished in these provincial universities in opposition to the Cambridge criminology center that was largely funded by Home Office grants and whose intellectual orientation was the legacy of Sir Leonard Radzinowicz. The early development of the sociology of religion was closely associated with the University of Leeds, where Bryan Wilson, Roland Robertson, Robert Towler, and Tony Coxon had taught a traditional program, and where Wilson (1967) did his early research on the sociology of sects before leaving for All Souls College, Oxford. Perhaps the most influential social philosopher of the period—Alasdair MacIntyre—had also been a lecturer at Leeds before becoming a professor of sociology at the University of Essex. MacIntyre published *Secularization and Moral Change* (1967) and *Marxism and Christianity* (1968) before leaving for the United States to become the Richard Koret Professor of the History of Ideas at Brandeis University. MacIntyre's blend of philosophical reflection and critical social insight has remained a positive characteristic of British sociology and is currently illustrated by the philosophical and ethical reflections of the Polish-born Zygmunt Bauman, who is emeritus professor of sociology at the University of Leeds.

INDIVIDUALISM, SOCIOLOGY, AND EMPIRE

British sociology and British intellectuals must be considered within the context of the rise and fall of Britain as a capitalist nation and as an imperial power. Adam Smith, David Ricardo, and John Locke laid the foundations for the study of the market as both an efficient mechanism of exchange and the foundation of a free society. To establish political economy, Karl Marx had to struggle intellectually against this legacy—as did Émile Durkheim ([1893] 1960) in *The Division of Labor*. British social science has been strong in two major areas: economics and social anthropology. The first tradition reflects the strength and depth of British capitalism and the importance of individualism and liberalism as values. The second reflects the legacy of colonial administration, especially in Africa. British sociology does not have the international recognition accorded social anthropology, which can boast Mary Douglas, James Fraser, Ernest Gellner, Max Gluckmann, Sir Edmund Leach, Bronislaw Malinowski, and Peter Worsley. British social anthropology has been dominant in the elite universities, especially Oxford and Cambridge, partly because it enjoyed strong connections with imperial expansion. Perhaps the best illustration is the influence of Baldwin Spencer and F. J. Gillen's (1997) *The Northern Tribes of Central Australia* in 1899, which played an important role in Émile Durkheim's ([1912] 1954) *The Elementary Forms of the Religious Life.*

British social science has clearly produced or nurtured major sociological figures such as Percy Cohen, Ralph Dahrendorf, Anthony Giddens, David Glass, Stuart Hall, A. H. Halsey, Peter Laslett, John Rex, W. G. Runciman, Peter Townsend, Michael Young, and others—but the general social and cultural climate is hostile to intellectuals, and British intellectual life still suffers from the legacy of Thatcherism and its hostility to the "chattering classes." Despite much criticism of the theory and practice of Third Way politics, there has been a British civil society and public culture that has been shaped by sociologists, specifically in recent years by Giddens. However, in terms of sociology narrowly conceived, British sociologists have acted as a conduit between Continental European and North American intellectual fields. One can think of the ways in which French social theory—Louis Althusser, Pierre Bourdieu, Michel Foucault, and Nicos Poulantzas—has been received in Britain, often before academic recognition in France, and then exported to North America (Turner 1990). As a result, it is not clear that there is such a thing as *the* British tradition. The only exception from the past may have been the exceptional strength of class analysis in British sociology as illustrated in particular by Rosemary Crompton, John Goldthorpe, David Lockwood, Gordon Marshall, and Howard Newby.

In general terms, understanding the question of the intellectual in British life has been best answered by a group of intellectuals around the *New Left Review*—Perry Anderson, Juliet Mitchell, Tom Nairn, and Robin Blackburn—that provided an enduring diagnosis of British culture. We lack public intellectuals because we lack a vibrant public culture that is shaped by critical social philosophy or critical social theory. The underdevelopment of British social theory is a consequence historically of gradualism, a compromise culture, an aborted and premature revolution, evolutionary thought, and individualism. The Restoration was a compromise that put an end to civil war and set the scene for Locke's liberal theory of government, tolerance, and social contract. From the perspective of the *New Left Review* generation, the "origins of the present crisis" (Anderson 1964) rest on the social and political conditions that have produced a political social process of gradualism. The political trauma of the execution of the king and the civil war produced a political and legal settlement that institutionalized social conservatism. Marxist historians have argued that British history has subsequently been based on class compromise and cooperation. This traditionalism is illustrated by the breadth of the Anglican Church, which sought a national compromise as an alternative to sectarian warfare and the scope of the constitutional settlement that retained both the monarchy and the House of Commons.

The weakness of British sociology (and British social theory in general) is associated with the gradualness of the political transition to modern society and the hegemonic nature of possessive individualism. Whereas France had the Revolution, a passion for the concept of social solidarity and a revolutionary transition to modern society, Britain had a precocious revolution in the seventeenth century, beat off French republicanism in the early nineteenth century, and slid ineluctably into industrial capitalism by the middle of the nineteenth century. French

Catholicism was more congenial to sociology and public intellectuals than Protestant individualism. If sociology flourishes in response to social and political crisis, this may explain why the vitality of postwar British sociology owed so much to Jewish and other migrants, for example, Bauman, Elias, Gellner, Mannheim, Neustadt, and Sohn-Rethel.

POSTWAR DEVELOPMENTS

We can divide the achievements of twentieth-century sociology into three broad phases representing three different traditions. These are, first, the analysis of social class and citizenship that had its origins in social reformism before and after World War II. The main theme here was the tension between social class and welfare citizenship as illustrated in the sociology of T. H. Marshall. Second, the period of rapid university expansion in the 1960s and onward resulted in innovative intellectual fields, in which the "new universities" played an increasing role. The dominant theme was the rise of an affluent, consumer, postwar society. The late 1960s witnessed perhaps the most interesting period of British sociology—a period of extraordinary growth in university places to cope with the baby boomers, postwar reconstruction, and economic reorganization. Sociology was importantly connected with major international issues such as the Events of 1968, Campaign for Nuclear Disarmament (CND), and Anti-Apartheid. Third, the contemporary phase where there is relatively little intellectual coherence and sociology often finds itself as part of interdisciplinary studies (women's studies, leisure studies, cultural or sports studies). This phase has been somewhat dominated by cultural studies, resulting at its worst in "decorative sociology," namely, a sociology with little interest in historical and comparative research, little concern for macrosociological analyses of political institutions, and scant interest in ethical issues (Turner and Rojek 2001). The main exception is the ethical inquiries of Bauman in, for example, *Postmodern Ethics* (1993).

Throughout this period, the professional development of British sociology at the national level has been relatively weak. Unlike the social sciences in North America, British sociology has had a debilitated and uneven history of institutional development. The British Sociological Association has not had the controlling influence that has been enjoyed by the American Sociological Association, but in some respects that lack of professional regulation has permitted more experimentation and innovation. In substantive terms, the period from 1945 has been characterized by the decline of social class analysis and the growth of concern for postwar affluence as illustrated by research into consumer behavior, leisure activities, and sport. There has been a wave of publications in the 1990s illustrating this shift from the sociology of social class to the sociology of consumption (Featherstone 1991) and lifestyle (Shields 1992).

SOCIAL STRATIFICATION: CLASS, RACE, AND GENDER

Postwar British sociology, from Keynesian postwar reconstruction to the 1968 generation, was dominated by the exploration of the tensions between social class and welfare citizenship. T. H. Marshall's study analyzed the rise of citizenship rights in three stages: legal, political, and social. British sociology can be seen as the study of how and why universal social rights were frustrated by social stratification along three dimensions: class, race, and gender.

There is an argument to be made that John Maynard Keynes was perhaps the most influential sociologist of his period, and he clearly had a major impact both on postwar economic and social policy and on social theory (such as the nature of money and consumption). Perhaps the core British tradition was originally organized around the study of the promise and limitations of the welfare reform of capitalism and the tensions between social inequality and the egalitarian impulse of citizenship. However, this tradition was domestic in its interests, and comparative sociology was not a particular strength. T. H. Marshall's (1950) *Citizenship and Social Class and Other Essays* and Richard Titmuss's (1962) *Income Distribution and Social Change* were classical contributions to this approach. These sociological studies of citizenship were preceded by an early tradition of social history and historical sociology of inequality in the work, for example, of G. D. H. Cole and R. H. Tawney. At a somewhat later date, W. G. Runciman's (1966) *Relative Deprivation and Social Justice,* A. H. Halsey's (1957) *Social Class and Educational Opportunity,* and Ralph Dahrendorf's (1959) *Class and Class Conflict in an Industrial Society* made important contributions to the understanding of macroprocesses of inequality. The field of welfare policy, educational reform, and income redistribution came to be championed by a long list of distinguished British sociologists: David Glass, A. H. Halsey, Peter Laslett, Gordon Marshall, W. G. Runciman, Alan Scott, Peter Townsend, and John Westergaard.

British sociology was influenced by its connections to the Labour Party and social reformism. An important tradition of British empirical sociology examined the social and cultural circumstances of the working class in such classics as *Coal Is Our Life* (Dennis, Henriques, and Slaughter 1962). One consistent theme of postwar sociology, especially through the influence of Marxism, was the issue of the absence of a revolutionary working-class movement. Why was the British working class passive? This question produced a rich crop of sociological responses, including *Class and Class Conflict in an Industrial Society* (Dahrendorf 1959), *Consciousness and Action in the Western Working Class* (Mann 1973), and *Learning to Labour* (Willis 1977). *The Dominant Ideology Thesis* (Abercrombie, Hill, and Turner 1980) was critical of the idea that there was "a dominant ideology" in capitalist society and argued instead that the apparent complacency of the working class had to be explained by the material conditions of their lifeworld, not by liberal ideology. To understand their political acquiescence, we need to look not toward ideologies or forms of consciousness but to how the everyday needs of mere survival exert a dull compulsion over the lives of ordinary people. Everyday life does not require a coherent ideological legitimacy; it does not "require additional verification over and beyond its simple presence. It is simply *there,* as self-evident and compelling facticity" (Berger and Luckmann 1967:37).

This period was rich in important contributions that challenged the complacency of a society that had been told by Prime Minister Harold Macmillan that "you have never had it so good" and that the Conservative election success of October 1959 demonstrated a victory of the middle classes and a rejection of class conflict. This rich tradition of empirical work on class was associated with several major intellectual debates. These included the debate around Basil Bernstein's notions of restricted and elaborate codes of language and the impact of these codes in school settings (Bernstein 1971). There were important analyses of the nature of British politics and how to analyze them. In the famous confrontation between Ralph Miliband (1969) and Nicos Poulantzas (1969) in relation to the state and social class, Miliband defended the argument that there was a dominant class in British society rather than a cluster of separate elites, while Poulantzas dismissed Miliband's thesis by arguing that the state was an objective structure that could not be understood through empirical studies of the personal ties of ruling-class families (Urry and Wakeford 1973). Another important debate concerned the process of embourgeoisement and the incorporation of the working class. Perhaps the most influential study of this process was by John Goldthorpe et al. (1969) in *The Affluent Worker,* which demonstrated many changes in traditional working-class attitudes but rejected the view that the working class was joining the middle class. Workers in new industries no longer adhered to traditional working-class images of a divided and conflictual society.

The sociological analysis of social class was also important as a setting for the emergence of the sociology of citizenship that produced a long debate with the legacy of Marshall. His liberal theory of citizenship is one answer to the problem of individual rights and social inequality. Social rights expanded through three stages: the growth of legal rights in the seventeenth century produced habeas corpus, jury system, and rule of law; political rights in the nineteenth century resulted in the parliamentary system; and social rights in the twentieth century were associated with welfare state. Marshall argued that citizenship was a *status* position that compensated for or ameliorated the *class* inequalities that arise from a capitalist *market.* Marshall's view of the welfare state and citizenship can be regarded as the sociological dimension of social Keynesianism.

Michael Mann (1987) criticized Marshall's theory for its Anglo-centric and evolutionary qualities. Marshall's theory is an account of the liberal model of the institutionalization of class conflict. Mann identified several other viable forms in addition to Marshall's liberal model: reformist, authoritarian monarchist, fascist, and authoritarian socialist. Mann's alternative theory concentrates on the role of the ruling classes (dominant economic groups, military and political elites) and argues that social change is orchestrated by ruling classes and that radical change is probably only possible when the ruling classes are divided or fragmented. Sociology tends to exaggerate the impact of the Industrial Revolution, and at the same time neglects the impact of geopolitics and victory in world wars in explanations of social change. Despite these criticisms of Marshall, his study of citizenship remains influential in contemporary British sociology (Turner 1986, 1993; Turner and Hamilton 1994).

In the United States, sociology has been very closely associated with policy issues relating to race, ethnicity, and migration. Sociology was concerned with the stratification of ethnic groups in urban society. Class analysis and inequality were major sociological themes in postwar European sociology, where Marxist sociology was influential in the 1970s. But class as the key concept of sociology has declined. Class is more likely to be seen as simply one component of stratification alongside gender, ethnicity, and race. More important, the decline of Marxism has meant that sociologists have over the last 10 years at least had relatively little to say about poverty, income levels, or economics—namely, the "base" of society—and a great deal to say about the superstructure. The cultural has flourished while the social has been abandoned or merely subsumed under the notion of culture.

RACE AND RACE RELATIONS

Race and ethnicity were seen, as a consequence of postwar migration, to be a check on the enjoyment of citizenship. In the historical context of nineteenth-century liberalism and laissez-faire economics, there were almost no laws regulating refugees, and the official attitude was one of apathy and indifference. Postwar migration was largely economic and from the Commonwealth. The 1948 Nationality Act recognized the right of Commonwealth citizens to freely enter and work in Britain. The Act was overtly generous because it assumed an outflow, not influx, of Commonwealth citizens. By 1971 there were 300,000 Caribbean migrants who, for Conservative leaders like Enoch Powell, created a racial crisis. Powell's 1968 "river of blood" speech, however, found little active overt political support, apart from the 1971 Immigration Act that introduced work permits without a right of residency. The pragmatic reluctance of postwar British governments to become involved in colonial wars (after the Suez crisis) meant that overtly racist politics were unpopular. Harold Macmillan's African winds-of-change speech made Powellite visions of a white-dominated Commonwealth anachronistic. However, racism was an important feature of British life, and a considerable research effort went into understanding its social roots.

The study of race relations in Britain is closely associated with the career of John Rex. Born in South Africa, he held a number of professorial chairs in Great Britain. These included Professor of Social Theory and Institutions at the University of Durham (1964–1970), Chair of Sociology at the University at Warwick, Research Professor in Ethnic Relations at the University of Aston, Birmingham, and subsequently Professor of Ethnic Relations in the University of Warwick. As an influential interpreter of Max Weber's conflict sociology, he was critical of functionalism, because it could not develop an adequate theory of social action. Rex (1981) used Weber's sociology to understand race and ethnicity as features of the unequal distribution of power and resources in society. The result of this research was *Social Conflict: A Conceptual and Theoretical Analysis.* His work on the study of racial conflict was influential and wide ranging. With Robert Moore, he developed the concept of "housing classes" in his study of unequal access to mortgages, housing allocation, and ethnic divisions in Birmingham in *Race Community and Conflict: A Study of Sparkbrook* (Rex and Moore 1967). A number of influential publications on sociological theory and race followed: *Race Colonialism and the City* (1973b), *Race Relations in Sociological Theory* (1970), *Race and Ethnicity* (1986), and (with Sally Tomlinson) *Colonial Immigrants in a British City* (1979).

Although Rex was seen as a critical social theorist, a number of younger sociologists emerged as a second generation whose conceptual framework and interests were far removed from the British academic establishment. Stuart Hall was closely associated with the Birmingham Centre for Cultural Studies, and he drew on a range of social and cultural theories to explore the underclass of poor white and black youth in British cities. Hall and his colleagues examined various types of cultural resistance to the hegemonic culture such as punk subcultures (Hall and Jefferson 1976). Hall also, through a number of influential essays, became a public critic of the politics and policies of Margaret Thatcher and her Conservative governments (Hall and Jacques 1983). Another influential critic of British society was Paul Gilroy (1987) whose *There Ain't No Black in the Union Jack* accused British intellectuals and politicians of not taking race seriously. The question of racism and the sociology of race remain unresolved and bitter issues in British culture and were made even more contentious by the murder of Stephen Lawrence, the police investigations, the legal treatment of the offenders, and the subsequent Report of Sir William Macpherson in February 1999. Gilroy himself left Britain to take up a chair of sociology and African studies at Yale University in the United States. Hall and Gilroy can be regarded as contemporary representatives of a tradition of a black British intelligentsia that had its foundations in the work of radical writers such as C. L. R. James, who first came to London from Trinidad in 1932 (Worcester 1996).

GENDER

In the 1960s and 1970s, mainstream sociology, for example, the study of social class, had somewhat neglected feminist theory and gender. The debate about how to measure social class taking into account the class position of "unemployed" housewives is a classic example. Gender was thus examined in British sociology originally under the umbrella of the sociology of marriage and the family. Peter Wilmott and Michael Young (1960) undertook important studies of working-class family life in the east end of London, for example, in *Family and Class in a London Suburb,* to examine to what degree familial connections and working-class community were breaking down under the impact of urban development. British sociology has been significantly influenced by the work of Ann Oakley (1974). This tradition is now regarded as uninteresting, conservative, and out of date. In the 1970s and 1980s, feminist analysis and criticism assumed a more radical dimension. Through the influence of Michele Barratt (1992) and Juliet Mitchell (1966), feminist sociologists came to engage more productively with the legacies of Marxism and Michel Foucault, and also with a range of largely French feminists. Feminist thought eventually fragmented into materialist, socialist, and postmodern versions (Lovell 2000). There was also considerable conflict between gender studies, women's studies, lesbian studies, and gay studies. Feminism gave rise to a rich theoretical legacy perhaps best illustrated by the work of Judith Butler. These debates over gender, sex, and sexuality were heavily influenced by social constructionism through the general claim that anatomy is not destiny. The dominance of gender studies, lesbian studies, and Queer Theory has often meant, ironically, that the traditional sociology of the family and marriage has been somewhat neglected or even condemned as ideologically biased. Sociologists have explored gay and lesbian culture, especially within the framework of symbolic interactionism (Plummer 2000), and to some degree, an older tradition represented by the work of Laslett, Wilmott, and Young went into decay.

MODERN SOCIOLOGY

Cultural Studies

Stuart Hall was not only a tireless critic of Thatcherism and racism but played a major contribution through the Open University to establishing sociology and the study of race relations as a theoretically significant area, and sustained an important tradition of cultural studies from the Birmingham School. Cultural studies in Britain emerged partly out of academic debates in departments of English literature in terms of the established canon. *The Uses of Literacy* (Hoggart 1957) and *Culture and Society* (Williams 1958) were major contributions to the study not only of culture but also of British society. The theme of the first two texts was the loss of working-class community, the rise of consumer culture, and the dominance of middle-class individualism. Both authors lamented the erosion of the cooperative tradition of working-class autonomy and the transformation of the culture of northern cities like Leeds and Bradford by television and consumerism. Both Hoggart and Williams were grammar school boys who had risen from the working class to positions of influence in English literature and cultural studies. Williams's (1989) personal sense of alienation from Cambridge in *What I Came to Say* was a common experience of socially mobile academics.

Contemporary cultural studies in Britain has flourished and has to some extent overshadowed sociology departments. Whereas cultural studies has attracted large numbers of undergraduates and postgraduates to influential departments such as Goldsmiths College and Nottingham Trent University, sociology student numbers at university level have stagnated since the heyday of the 1960s. Cultural sociology has not developed significantly to compete with film studies and cultural studies. It is not clear yet, however, that there is anything that one can identify as a distinctive body of cultural theory as such, and cultural studies methodology is a relatively tame version of qualitative sociological methods. These weak theoretical foundations, inadequate methodologies, and limited political horizons have led to the accusation that the cultural turn is merely a "decorative sociology" (Rojek and Turner 2000).

Social Theory

Postwar British sociology was heavily dependent on continental social philosophy, much of which was inspired by the legacy of Marxism. This period was marked by the influence of Althusser and Poulantzas. There was a corresponding hostility to American sociology that was mistakenly seen to be represented by Talcott Parsons. The myth that Parsons's Marshall lectures at Cambridge University in 1953 delayed the development of academic sociology is difficult to erase, at least among Cambridge academics. The lectures, which eventually formed the first three chapters of *Economy and Society* (Parsons and Smelser 1956), were probably too ambitious at the time to gain support from either economists or sociologists. Whereas Parsons was either neglected or maligned, C. Wright Mills, and later Peter Berger and Thomas Luckmann (1967), were influential, and *The Social Construction of Reality* was employed as a critical weapon of political analysis.

An intellectually exciting sociology is not just the study of relevant contemporary problems; it has to make a more enduring contribution to the development of sociological theory or sociological methods. In the case of John Rex,

his publications on sociological theory included *Key Problems in Sociological Theory* (1961), *Discovering Sociology* (1973a), *Approaches to Sociology* (1974a), and *Sociology and the Demystification of the Modern World* (1974b). There is an important relationship between his empirical work on class and race and his employment of Max Weber's sociology to criticize the legacy of structural functionalism, especially the legacy of Parsons in *Key Problems in Sociological Theory* (1961)—one of the most influential theory books in the 1960s. The other influential theory book at the time was Percy Cohen's (1968) *Modern Social Theory.* However, Alan Dawe (1970), whose career at Leeds University was originally supported by Rex, was an influential teacher, and his article on "the two sociologies" played a significant role in shaping how younger sociologists saw the connection between political action and sociological theories of action.

The contribution of Anthony Giddens has been central for a number of decades. His early work involved the (re)interpretation of the classics, for example, in *Capitalism and Modern Social Theory* (1971), and he developed new ways of thinking about the traditional "agency and structure" debate in *The Constitution of Society* (1984). He was an early contributor to debates about postmodernism and globalization in his *The Consequences of Modernity* (1990). With the departure of John Major's Conservative government, Giddens played a role in shaping the emergence of New Labour in his *The Third Way* (1998). Giddens has had many critics, and his interest in social theory has not been associated with specific empirical research interests (Loyal 2003), but he has been an important spokesman for sociology in Britain. Giddens's eclecticism in social theory construction reflects the fact that British sociology has been distinctive at the university level in terms of its openness to foreign sociologists and to external intellectual trends. Much of British social theory can therefore be said to have been a reflection on Continental social philosophy. Giddens in a sense is no exception in that he has been influenced by European hermeneutics and more recently by the sociology of Ulrich Beck in the study of risk society (Beck 1992). Giddens's intellectual impact is partly a consequence of the role he has played with John Thompson and David Held in the development of Polity Press as a major publisher of modern social theory.

Sociology of the Body

Medical sociology has been an important subfield of British sociology, and *Inequalities in Health* (Townsend and Davidson 1982) was an influential indictment of health and health services in Britain and demonstrated many failures of the National Health Service. The notion of "medical sociology" was replaced by "sociology of health and illness," because it was assumed that medical sociology had become merely a servant of the medical profession. The journal *Sociology of Health and Illness* subsequently became one of the most creative journals in the field.

Out of this innovative sociology of health and illness, the sociology of the body emerged at the beginning of the 1980s (Turner 1984). Sociological studies were interested in the consequences of consumerism on the body, gender differences, body piercing, cosmetic surgery, sport, and aging (Featherstone, Hepworth, and Turner 1991). The journal *Body & Society* was founded in 1995. Once more the influence of continental social theory was particularly marked, especially in the work of Michel Foucault and Pierre Bourdieu. Another related development in British sociology was the study of the emotions, as illustrated by Jack Barbalet's (1998) *Emotion, Social Theory and Social Structure*. A new conceptual language emerged out of Bourdieu's pioneering work on practice, body, and social capital, namely, practice, embodiment, hexis, and habitus. Bourdieu's (1984) *Distinction* was a key text.

CONCLUSION: SOCIOLOGY AND THE AFFLUENT SOCIETY

In the period from 1945 to 1968, British sociology was primarily concerned with postwar reconstruction. This involved the study of the implementation of the Keynesian economic policies and the welfare state. This phase concluded with the first Thatcher administration of 1979–1983. British sociology then became, somewhat implicitly, the study of the rise of consumer society and the decline of the old collectivist values that lay behind the Labour Party and the welfare state. Thatcherism ushered in a new era of individualism, deregulation, and entrepreneurial values celebrating mobility and personal affluence. New Labour and Third Way politics have represented the attempt of the Labour Party to modernize itself and to adjust to the new consumerism. T. H. Marshall was the theorist of the first wave of British sociology and Anthony Giddens of the second.

Postwar British sociology spans the final collapse of the British Empire and the decline of Britain as a major world power. These conditions produced important generational differences and a specific consciousness that existed over and above specifically gender or class differences (Edmunds and Turner 2002). These postwar generations experienced the Cold War and came to maturity under conditions of increasing affluence, the decline of trade unionism, and the erosion of social class as the most important marker of identity. While these generations were always

threatened by disasters, they have been lived under conditions of (relative) peace. Military conscription, rationing of essential household items, and barrack room drill had come to an end. Internationally Aden, Suez, Kenya, and the Malaysian emergency were military episodes that marked the decline of British imperial power. The Suez crisis in 1956 demonstrated that Britain could no longer operate as a great power without American approval, and Britain subsequently withdrew from further significant colonial adventures (including Mrs. Thatcher's defense of British interests in the South Atlantic during the Falklands War in 1982). The pragmatism of Harold Macmillan, whose foreign policies allowed Britain to avoid the colonial confrontations that dominated France, Portugal, and Belgium in the postwar period, made the decline of Britain less painful than other European colonial powers. In short, British sociology has to be understood in terms of the rise and decline of the baby boomers. Their political activism was associated with CND and anti-apartheid movements, but their maturity was experience in the context of affluence, leisure, and the consumer boom.

There is, however, a new mood in British society in which the future looks insecure and the international role of Britain uncertain. The Iraq war and the London bombings in July 2005 confirmed that the sentiments announced by Macmillan—you have never had it so good—had come to an end. This mood of uncertainty explains the popularity of Ulrich Beck's (1992) *Risk Society,* and the negative aftermath of terrorist attacks in London will raise difficult questions about the failures of British race relations policy and multiculturalism especially with respect to its Muslim population. Britain has been relatively successful in providing its Muslim community with opportunities to achieve social inclusion (Ameli and Merali 2004), but it is unlikely that civil peace could be sustained in the face of determined, sustained terrorist attacks over a longer period. These social conflicts will make the sociological study of new wars and civil violence a more prominent feature of British sociology and political science (Hirst 2001).

The sociology of insecurity and terrorism will become the next areas of growth for sociological research and theory in Britain, but insecurity will also include biological risk and the globalization of new infectious diseases such as severe acute respiratory syndrome (SARS) and avian influenza. The question of the body and society will also include the management of cloning and genetic modifications. These are new conditions that demand public intellectuals and a relevant sociology for the twenty-first century.

PART III

THE SCIENTIFIC APPROACH TO THE STUDY OF SOCIETY

9

QUALITATIVE METHODOLOGY

NORMAN K. DENZIN

University of Illinois, Urbana–Champaign

Qualitative research is a field of inquiry in its own right. It cuts across disciplines, subfields, and subject matter.[1] A complex, interconnected family of terms, concepts, and assumptions surrounds the qualitative research orientation. These include the traditions associated with positivism, poststructuralism, and the many qualitative research perspectives or methods connected to cultural and interpretive studies.

In North America, qualitative research operates in a complex historical field that cross-cuts seven historical moments. These seven moments overlap and simultaneously operate in the present. They can be defined as the traditional (1900–1950), the modernist, or golden age (1950–1970), blurred genres (1970–1986), the crisis of representation (1986–1990) and postmodern, a period of experimental and new ethnographies (1990–1995), post-experimental inquiry (1995–2000), and the future, which is now (2000–). The future, the seventh moment, is concerned with moral discourse, with the development of a sacred texture. The seventh and eighth moments suggest that the social sciences and the humanities become sites for critical conversations about democracy, race, gender, class, nation, freedom, and community.

Successive waves of epistemological theorizing move across these moments. The traditional period is associated with the positivist, foundational paradigm. The modernist or golden age and blurred genres moments are connected to the appearance of postpositivist arguments. At the same time, a variety of new interpretive, qualitative perspectives were taken up, including hermeneutics, structuralism, semiotics, phenomenology, cultural studies, and feminism.[2] In the blurred genres phase, the humanities became

central resources for critical, interpretive theory and the qualitative research project broadly conceived. The researcher became a *bricoleur,* learning how to borrow from many different disciplines.

The blurred genres phase produced the next stage, the crisis of representation. Here, researchers struggled with how to locate themselves and their subjects in reflexive texts. A kind of methodological diaspora took place, a two-way exodus. Humanists migrated to the social sciences, searching for new social theory and new ways to study popular culture and its local, ethnographic contexts. Social scientists turned to the humanities, hoping to learn how to do complex structural and poststructural readings of social texts. The line between a text and a context blurred. In the postmodern, experimental moment, researchers continued to move away from foundational and quasi-foundational criteria. Alternative evaluative criteria were sought, those that were evocative, moral, critical, and based on local understandings.

North Americans are not the only scholars struggling to create postcolonial, nonessentialist, feminist, dialogic performance texts, texts informed by the rhetorical, narrative turn in the human disciplines (Delamont, Coffey, and Atkinson 2000). This international work troubles the traditional distinctions between science, the humanities, rhetoric, literature, facts, and fiction. As Atkinson and Hammersley (1994) observe, this discourse recognizes "the literary antecedents of the ethnographic text, and affirms the essential dialectic" underlying these aesthetic and humanistic moves (p. 255).

Moreover, this literature is reflexively situated in a multiple, historical, and national context. It is clear that

America's history with qualitative inquiry cannot be generalized to the rest of the world (Atkinson, Coffey, and Delamont 2001). Nor do all researchers embrace a politicized, cultural studies agenda that demands that interpretive texts advance issues surrounding social justice and racial equality.

Lopez (1998) observes that "there is a large-scale social movement of anti-colonialist discourse" (p. 226), and this movement is evident in the emergence of African American, Chicano, Native American, and Maori standpoint theories. These theories question the epistemologies of Western science that are used to validate knowledge about indigenous peoples. The Maori scholar Russell Bishop (1998) presents a participatory and participant perspective (Tillman 1998:221) that values an embodied and moral commitment to the research community one is working with. This research is characterized by the absence of a need to be in control (Bishop 1998:203; Heshusius 1994). Such a commitment reflects a desire to be connected to and a part of the moral community. The goal is compassionate understanding (Heshusius 1994).

These understandings are only beginning to enter the literatures on social problems and deviance. As they do, a blurring of the spaces between the hyphens that join researchers and those studied occurs. Definitions of sociological phenomena, including social problems and deviance, are thereby made problematic.

QUEERING THE INQUIRY

In the context of discussing the study of same-sex experience, Kong, Mahoney, and Plummer (2002) present compelling historical evidence to support the conclusion that "*the sensibilities of interviewing are altered with the changing social phenomena that constitute 'the interviewee'*" (p. 240, italics in original). Reviewing the interviewing of gays in North America and Europe over the past 100 years, they trace a movement from a "highly positivist mode of research through one where the boundaries become weaker, and on to a situation where interviewing has been partially deconstructed" (p. 240).

These authors distinguish three historical moments: (1) traditional, (2) modernizing, and (3) postmodern. Their analysis contrasts the three periods in terms of assumptions about interviewers, gays, lesbians, questions asked, approaches taken, wider cultural discourses, and politics. Interviewers are presumed to be objective and heterosexual in the traditional period, closeted in the modern period, and out in the postmodern moment. Same-sex experiences are approached clinically, in terms of pathologies in the traditional period, while they are normalized in the postmodern period, when discourses on disease give way to talk of liberation, politics, and postmodern ethics.

Kong et al. (2002:254) offer three conclusions relevant to the arguments presented in this chapter. Interviewing gays and lesbians today is very different from interviewing them at the end of the nineteenth century. With the arrival of postmodern understandings, new forms of interviewing and new kinds of findings are appearing. A form of reflexive, radical historicity should now be a part of all interpretive inquiry. Of equal importance, any form of inquiry, such as the interview, is itself a cultural form, in which questions and answers become self-validating.

READING HISTORY

Several conclusions can be drawn from this brief history, which is, like all histories, somewhat arbitrary. First, each of the earlier historical moments is still operating in the present, either as a legacy or as a set of practices that researchers continue to follow or argue against. The multiple, and fractured histories of qualitative research now make it possible for any given researcher to attach a project to a canonical text from any of the above-described historical moments. Multiple criteria of evaluation compete for attention in this field. Second, an embarrassment of choices now characterizes the field of qualitative research. There have never been so many paradigms, strategies of inquiry, or methods of analysis to draw upon and utilize. Third, we are in a moment of discovery and rediscovery, as new ways of looking, interpreting, arguing and writing are debated and discussed. Fourth, the qualitative research act can no longer be viewed from within a neutral or objective positivist perspective. Class, race, gender, and ethnicity shape the process of inquiry, making research a multicultural process.

QUALITATIVE RESEARCH AS A PROCESS

Any definition of qualitative research must work within this complex historical field. Qualitative research means different things in each of these moments. Nonetheless, an initial, generic definition can be offered.[3]

Qualitative research is multimethod in focus, involving an interpretive, naturalistic approach to its subject matter. This means that qualitative researchers study things in their natural settings, attempting to make sense of or interpret these things in terms of the meanings people bring to them. Qualitative research involves the studied use and collection of a variety of empirical materials—case study, personal experience, introspection, life story, interview, and observational, historical, interactional, and visual texts—that describe routine and problematic moments and meanings in an individual's life.

Three interconnected, generic activities define the qualitative research process. They go by a variety of different labels, including theory, method, and analysis, and ontology, epistemology, and methodology. Behind these last three terms stands the personal biography of the gendered researcher, who speaks from a particular class, racial, cultural, and ethnic community perspective. The gendered, multiculturally situated researcher approaches the world with a set of ideas, a framework (theory, ontology) that specifies a set of questions (epistemology), which are then examined (analysis, methodology) in specific ways. That is, empirical materials bearing on the question are collected and then analyzed and written about. Every researcher speaks from within a distinct interpretive community, which configures, in its special way, the multicultural, gendered components of the research act. This community has its own historical research traditions, which constitute a distinct point of view. This perspective leads the researcher to adopt particular views of the "other" who is studied. At the same time, the politics and the ethics of research must also be considered, for these concerns permeate every phase of the research process.

RESISTANCES TO QUALITATIVE STUDIES

The academic and disciplinary resistances to qualitative research illustrate the politics embedded in this field of discourse. The challenges to qualitative research are many. Qualitative researchers are called journalists, or soft scientists. Their work is termed unscientific, or only exploratory, or entirely personal and full of bias. It is called criticism and not theory, or it is interpreted politically as a disguised version of Marxism or humanism (see Huber 1995; also Denzin 1997:258–61 for a review).

These resistances reflect an uneasy awareness that the traditions of qualitative research commit one to a critique of the positivist or postpositivist project. But the positivist resistance to qualitative research goes beyond the "ever-present desire to maintain a distinction between hard science and soft scholarship" (Carey 1989:99). The positive sciences (e.g., physics, chemistry, economics, and psychology) are often seen as the crowning achievements of Western civilization, and in their practices it is assumed that "truth" can transcend opinion and personal bias (Carey 1989:99). Qualitative research is seen as an assault on this tradition, whose adherents often retreat into a "value-free objectivist science" (Carey 1989:104) model to defend their position. They seldom attempt to make explicit and critique the "moral and political commitments in their own contingent work" (Carey 1989:104).

Positivists further allege that the so-called new experimental qualitative researchers write fiction, not science, and they have no way of verifying their truth statements. Ethnographic poetry and fiction signal the death of empirical science, and there is little to be gained by attempting

to engage in moral criticism. These critics presume a stable, unchanging reality that can be studied with the empirical methods of objective social science. The province of qualitative research, accordingly, is the world of lived experience, for this is where individual belief and action intersect with culture. Under this model, there is no preoccupation with discourse and method as material interpretive practices that constitute representation and description. Thus is the textual, narrative turn rejected by the positivist orientation.

The opposition to positive science by the postpositivists and the poststructuralists is seen, then, as an attack on reason and truth. At the same time, the attack by positive science on qualitative research is regarded as an attempt to legislate one version of truth over another.

POLITICS AND REEMERGENT SCIENTISM

The scientifically based research (SBR) movement initiated by the National Research Council (NRC) has created a new and hostile political environment for qualitative research. Connected to the No Child Left Behind Act of 2001, SBR embodies a reemergent scientism (Maxwell 2004), a positivist, evidence-based epistemology. Researchers are encouraged to employ "rigorous, systematic, and objective methodology to obtain reliable and valid knowledge" (Ryan and Hood 2004:80). The preferred methodology has well-defined causal models using independent and dependent variables. Causal models are examined in the context of randomized controlled experiments that allow replication and generalization (Ryan and Hood 2004:81).

Under this framework, qualitative research becomes suspect. There are no well-defined variables or casual models. Observations and measurements are not based on random assignment to experimental groups. Hard evidence is not generated by these methods. At best, case study, interview, and ethnographic methods offer descriptive materials that can be tested with experimental methods. The epistemologies of critical race, queer, postcolonial, feminist, and postmodern theories are rendered useless, relegated at best to the category of scholarship, not science (Ryan and Hood 2004:81; St. Pierre 2004:132).

Critics of the evidence movement are united on the following points. "Bush Science" (Lather 2004:19), and its experimental, evidence-based methodologies, represents a radical masculine backlash to the proliferation of qualitative inquiry methods over the last two decades (Lather 2004). The movement endorses a narrow view of science (Maxwell 2004), celebrating a "neoclassical experimentalism that is a throwback to the Campbell-Stanley era and its dogmatic adherence to an exclusive reliance on quantitative methods" (Howe 2004:42). There is "nostalgia for a simple and ordered universe of science that never was"

(Popkewitz 2004:62). With its emphasis on only one form of scientific rigor, the NRC ignores the need and value of complex historical, contextual, and political criteria for evaluating inquiry (Bloch 2004).

Neoclassical experimentalists extol evidence-based "medical research as the model for educational research, particularly the random clinical trial" (Howe 2004:48). But the random clinical trial—dispensing a pill—is quite unlike "dispensing a curriculum" (Howe 2004:48), nor can the "effects" of the educational experiment be easily measured, unlike a "10-point reduction in diastolic blood pressure" (Howe 2004:48).

Qualitative researchers must learn to think outside the box of positivism and postpositivism as they critique the NRC and its methodological guidelines (Atkinson 2004). We must apply our critical imagination to the meaning of terms such as *randomized design, causal model, policy studies,* and *public science* (Cannella and Lincoln 2004; Weinstein 2004). Furthermore, we must resist conservative attempts to discredit qualitative inquiry by placing it back inside the box of positivism.

MIXED-METHODS EXPERIMENTALISM

Howe (2004) observes that the NRC finds a place for qualitative methods in mixed-methods experimental designs. In such designs, qualitative methods may be "employed either singly or in combination with quantitative methods, including the use of randomized experimental designs (p. 49). Mixed methods are direct descendants of classical experimentalism. They presume a methodological hierarchy, with quantitative methods at the top, relegating qualitative methods to "a largely auxiliary role in pursuit of the technocratic aim of accumulating knowledge of 'what works'" (pp. 53–54).

The mixed-methods movement takes qualitative methods out of their natural home, which is within the critical, interpretive framework (Howe 2004:54; but see Teddlie and Tashakkori 2003:15). It divides inquiry into dichotomous categories, exploration versus confirmation. Qualitative work is assigned to the first category, quantitative research to the second (Teddlie and Tashakkori 2003:15). Like the classic experimental model, it excludes stakeholders from dialogue and active participation in the research process. This weakens its democratic and dialogical dimensions and reduces the likelihood that the previously silenced voices will be heard (Howe 2004:56–57).

Howe (2004) cautions that it is not just the "'methodological fundamentalists' who have bought into [this] approach. A sizeable number of rather influential . . . educational researchers . . . have also signed on. This might be a compromise to the current political climate; it might be a backlash against the perceived excesses of postmodernism; it might be both. It is an ominous development, whatever the explanation" (p. 57).

THE PRAGMATIC CRITICISMS OF ANTIFOUNDATIONALISM

Seale et al. (2004:2) contest what they regard as the excesses of an antimethodological, "any thing goes," romantic postmodernism that is associated with this project. They assert that too often the approach valued produces "low quality qualitative research and research results that are quite stereotypical and close to common sense" (p. 2).

In contrast, Seale et al. (2004) propose a practice-based, pragmatic approach that places research practice at the center. Research involves an engagement "with a variety of things and people: research materials . . . social theories, philosophical debates, values, methods, tests . . . research participants" (p. 2). (Actually this approach is quite close to my own view of the *bricoleur* and bricolage.)

Seale et al.'s (2004) situated methodology rejects the antifoundational claim that there are only partial truths, that the dividing line between fact and fiction has broken down (p. 3). They believe that this dividing line has not collapsed, that we should not accept stories if they do not accord with the best available facts (p. 6). Oddly, these pragmatic procedural arguments reproduce a variant of the evidence-based model and its criticisms of poststructural, performative sensibilities.

I turn now to a brief discussion of the major differences between the qualitative and quantitative approaches to research.

QUALITATIVE VERSUS QUANTITATIVE RESEARCH

Qualitative implies an emphasis on processes and meanings that are not rigorously examined or measured (if measured at all) in terms of quantity, amount, intensity, or frequency. Qualitative researchers stress the socially constructed nature of reality, the intimate relationship between the researcher and what is studied, and the situational constraints that shape inquiry. Such researchers emphasize the value-laden nature of inquiry. They seek answers to questions that stress how social experience is created and given meaning. In contrast, quantitative studies emphasize the measurement and analysis of causal relationships between variables, not processes. Proponents claim that their work is done from within a value-free framework.

RESEARCH STYLES: DOING THE SAME THINGS DIFFERENTLY?

Of course, both qualitative and quantitative researchers "think they know something about society worth telling to others, and they use a variety of forms, media and means to communicate their ideas and findings" (Becker 1986:122). Qualitative research differs from quantitative research in five significant ways (Becker 1996). These points of difference turn on different ways of addressing the same set of issues.

1. Uses of Positivism and Postpositivism

First, both perspectives are shaped by the positivist and postpositivist traditions in the physical and social sciences. These two positive science traditions hold naive and critical realist positions concerning reality and its perception. In the positivist version, it is contended that there is a reality out there to be studied, captured, and understood, while the postpositivists argue that reality can never be fully apprehended, only approximated (Guba 1990:22). Postpositivism relies on multiple methods as a way of capturing as much of reality as possible. At the same time, emphasis is placed on the discovery and verification of theories. Traditional evaluation criteria such as internal and external validity are stressed, as is the use of qualitative procedures that lend themselves to structured (sometimes statistical) analysis.

Historically, qualitative research was defined within the positivist paradigm, where qualitative researchers attempted to do good positivist research with less rigorous methods and procedures. Some midcentury qualitative researchers (Becker et al. 1961) reported participant observation findings in terms of quasi-statistics. As recently as 1999, two leaders of the grounded theory approach to qualitative research attempted to modify the usual canons of good (positivistic) science to fit their own postpositivist conception of rigorous research (Strauss and Corbin 1999).

Flick (1998) usefully summarizes the differences between these two approaches to inquiry. He observes that the quantitative approach has been used for purposes of isolating "causes and effects . . . operationalizing theoretical relations . . . [and] measuring and . . . quantifying phenomena . . . allowing the generalization of finding" (p. 3). But today, doubt is cast on such projects:

> Rapid social change and the resulting diversification of life worlds are increasingly confronting social researchers with new social contexts and perspectives . . . traditional deductive methodologies . . . are failing . . . thus research is increasingly forced to make use of inductive strategies instead of starting from theories and testing them . . . knowledge and practice are studied as local knowledge and practice. (P. 2)

2. Acceptance of Postmodern Sensibilities

The use of quantitative, positivist methods and assumptions has been rejected by a new generation of qualitative researchers who are attached to poststructural, postmodern sensibilities. These researchers argue that positivist methods are but one way of telling a story about society or the social world. They may be no better or no worse than any other method; they just tell a different kind of story.

This tolerant view is not shared by everyone. Many members of the critical theory, constructivist, poststructural, and postmodern schools of thought reject positivist and postpositivist criteria when evaluating their own work. They see these criteria as irrelevant to their work and contend that it reproduces only a certain kind of science, a science that silences too many voices. These researchers seek alternative methods for evaluating their work, including verisimilitude, emotionality, personal responsibility, an ethic of caring, political praxis, multivoiced texts, and dialogues with subjects.

3. Capturing the Individual's Point of View

Both qualitative and quantitative researchers are concerned about the individual's point of view. However, qualitative investigators think they can get closer to the actor's perspective by detailed interviewing and observation. They argue that quantitative researchers are seldom able to capture the subject's perspective because they have to rely on more remote, inferential empirical materials.

4. Examining the Constraints of Everyday Life

Qualitative researchers are more likely to confront and come up against the constraints of the everyday social world. They see this world in action and embed their findings in it. Quantitative researchers abstract from this world and seldom study it directly. They seek a nomothetic or etic science based on probabilities derived from the study of large numbers of randomly selected cases. These kinds of statements stand above and outside the constraints of everyday life. Qualitative researchers, on the other hand, are committed to an emic, ideographic, case-based position, which directs their attention to the specifics of particular cases.

5. Securing Rich Descriptions

Qualitative researchers believe that rich descriptions of the social world are valuable, while quantitative researchers, with their etic, nomothetic commitments, are less concerned with such detail. They are deliberately unconcerned with such descriptions because such detail interrupts the process of developing generalizations.

These five points of difference described above (uses of positivism and postmodernism, acceptance of postmodern sensibilities, capturing the individual's point of view, examining the constraints of everyday life, securing thick descriptions) reflect commitments to different styles of research, different epistemologies, and different forms of representation. Each work tradition is governed by a different set of genres, each has its own classics, its own preferred forms of representation, interpretation, and textual evaluation. Qualitative researchers use ethnographic prose, historical narratives, first-person accounts, still photographs, life history, fictionalized facts, and biographical and autobiographical materials, among others.

Quantitative researchers use mathematical models, statistical tables, and graphs and usually write in an impersonal, third-person prose.

WORKING THE HYPHEN: THE "OTHER" AS RESEARCH SUBJECT

From its turn-of-the-century birth in modern, interpretive form, qualitative research has been haunted by a double-faced ghost. On the one hand, qualitative researchers have assumed that qualified, competent observers could with objectivity, clarity, and precision report on their own observations of the social world, including the experiences of others. Second, researchers have held to the belief in a real subject or real individual who is present in the world and able, in some form, to report on his or her experiences. So armed, the researchers could blend their own observations with self-reports provided by subjects through interviews, life story, personal experience, and case study documents.

These two beliefs have led qualitative researchers across disciplines to seek a method that would allow them to record their own observations accurately while also uncovering the meanings their subjects brought to their life experiences. This method would rely on the subjective verbal and written expressions of meaning given by the individuals studied, these expressions being windows to the inner life of the person. Since Dilthey ([1900] 1976), this search for a method has led to a perennial focus in the human disciplines on qualitative, interpretive methods.

Recently, as noted above, this position and its beliefs have come under assault. Poststructuralists and postmodernists have contributed to the understanding that there is no clear window into the inner life of an individual. Any gaze is always filtered through the lenses of language, gender, social class, race, and ethnicity. There are no objective observations, only observations socially situated in the worlds of the observer and the observed. Subjects, or individuals, are seldom able to give full explanations of their actions or intentions; all they can offer are accounts or stories about what they did and why. No single method can grasp the subtle variations in ongoing human experience. Consequently, qualitative researchers deploy a wide range of interconnected interpretive methods, always seeking better ways to make more understandable the worlds of experience that have been studied.

INTERPRETIVE PARADIGMS

All qualitative researchers are philosophers in that "universal sense in which all human beings . . . are guided by highly abstract principles" (Bateson 1972:320). These principles combine beliefs about *ontology* (What kind of being is the human being? What is the nature of reality?), *epistemology* (What is the relationship between the inquirer and the known?), and *methodology* (How do we

know the world or gain knowledge of it?) (see Guba and Lincoln 2000). These beliefs shape how the qualitative researcher sees the world and acts in it. The researcher is "bound within a net of epistemological and ontological premises which—regardless of ultimate truth or falsity—become partially self-validating" (Bateson 1972:314).

The net that contains the researcher's epistemological, ontological, and methodological premises may be termed a paradigm (Guba 1990:17) or interpretive framework, a "basic set of beliefs that guides action" (Guba 1990:17). All research is interpretive and guided by a set of beliefs and feelings about the world and how it should be understood and studied. These beliefs may be taken for granted, only assumed, while others are highly problematic and controversial. Each interpretive paradigm makes particular demands on the researcher, including the questions that are asked and the interpretations that are brought to them.

At the most general level, four major interpretive paradigms structure qualitative research: (1) positivist and postpositivist, (2) constructivist-interpretive, (3) critical (Marxist, emancipatory), and (4) feminist-poststructural. These four abstract paradigms become more complicated at the level of concrete specific interpretive communities. At this level, it is possible to identify not only the constructivist but also multiple versions of feminism (Afrocentric and poststructural),[4] as well as specific ethnic, Marxist, and cultural studies paradigms.

The positivist and postpositive paradigms work from within a realist and critical realist ontology and objective epistemologies and rely on experimental, quasi-experimental, survey, and rigorously defined qualitative methodologies. The constructivist paradigm assumes a relativist ontology (there are multiple realities), a subjectivist epistemology (knower and subject create understandings), and a naturalistic (in the natural world) set of methodological procedures. Findings are usually presented in terms of the criteria of grounded theory. Terms such as *credibility, transferability, dependability,* and *confirmability* replace the usual positivist criteria of internal and external validity, reliability, and objectivity.

FEMINIST, ETHNIC, MARXIST, CULTURAL STUDIES, AND QUEER THEORY MODELS

Critical theory is a materialist-realist ontology—that is, the real world makes a material difference in terms of race, class, and gender. Subjectivist epistemologies and naturalistic methodologies (usually ethnographies) are also employed. Empirical materials and theoretical arguments are evaluated in terms of their emancipatory implications. Criteria from gender and racial communities (e.g., African American) may be applied (emotionality and feeling, caring, personal accountability, dialogue).

Poststructural feminist theories emphasize problems with the social text, its logic, and its inability to ever fully represent the world of lived experience. Positivist and postpositivist criteria of evaluation are replaced by other terms, including the reflexive, multivoiced text that is grounded in the experiences of oppressed people.

The cultural studies and queer theory paradigms are multifocused, with many different strands drawing from Marxism, feminism, and the postmodern sensibility. There is a tension between humanistic cultural studies that stress lived experiences and a more structural cultural studies project that stresses the structural and material determinants (race, class, gender) of experience. The cultural studies and queer theory paradigms use methods strategically—that is, as resources for understanding and for producing resistances to local structures of domination. Such scholars may do close textual readings and discourse analysis of cultural texts, as well as local ethnographies, open-ended interviewing, and participant observation. The focus is on how race, class, and gender are produced and enacted in historically specific situations.

BRIDGING THE HISTORICAL MOMENTS: INTO THE PRESENT

Two theses have organized the discussion to this point. First, in its relationship to the field of sociological inquiry, the history of qualitative research is defined more by breaks and ruptures than by a clear, evolutionary, progressive movement from one stage to the next. These breaks and ruptures move in cycles and phases, so that which is passé today may be in vogue a decade from now. Just as the postmodern, for example, reacts to the modern, someday there may well be a neomodern phase that extols Malinowski and the Chicago School and finds the current poststructural, postmodern moment abhorrent.

The second assumption builds on the tensions that now define qualitative sociological inquiry. There is an elusive center to this contradictory, tension-riddled enterprise, which seems to be moving further and further away from grand narratives, and single, overarching ontological, epistemological, and methodological paradigms. This center lies in the humanistic commitment of the researcher to always study the world from the perspective of the interacting individual. From this simple commitment flow the liberal and radical politics of qualitative sociological research on social problems. Action, feminist, clinical, constructionist, ethnic, critical, and cultural studies researchers are all united on this point. They all share the belief that a politics of liberation must always begin with the perspective, desires, and dreams of those individuals and groups who have been oppressed by the larger ideological, economic, and political forces of a society or a historical moment.

This commitment defines an ever-present, but always shifting, center in the discourses of qualitative research. The center shifts and moves as new, previously oppressed, or silenced voices enter the discourse. Thus, for example,

feminists and ethnic researchers have articulated their own relationship to the postpositivist and critical paradigms. These new articulations then refocus and redefine previous ontologies, epistemologies, and methodologies, including positivism and postpositivism. These two theses suggest that only the broad outlines of the future can be predicted, as the field confronts and continues to define itself in the face of four fundamental issues.

The first and second issues are what we have called the crises of representation and legitimization. These two crises speak, respectively, to the other and its representations in our texts and to the authority we claim for our texts. Third, there is the continued emergence of a cacophony of voices speaking with varying agendas from specific gender, race, class, ethnic, and Third World perspectives.

Fourth, throughout its history, qualitative sociological research has been defined in terms of shifting scientific, moral, sacred, and religious discourses. Since the Enlightenment, science and religion have been separated, but only at the ideological level, for in practice religion and the sacred have constantly informed science and the scientific project. The divisions between these two systems of meaning are becoming more and more blurred. Critics increasingly see science from within a magical, shamanistic framework (Rosaldo 1989:219). Others are moving science away from its empiricist foundations and closer to a critical, interpretive project that stresses morals and moral standards of evaluation (Clough 1998:136–37).

Three understandings shape the present moment; these are,

- The qualitative sociological researcher is not an objective, authoritative, politically neutral observer standing outside and above the social world (Bruner 1993:1).
- The qualitative researcher is "historically positioned and locally situated [as] an all-too-human [observer] of the human condition" (Bruner 1993:1).
- Meaning is "radically plural, always open, and . . . there is politics in every account" (Bruner 1993:1).

The problems of representation and legitimation flow from these three understandings.

THE CRISIS OF REPRESENTATION

As indicated, this crisis asks the questions, "Who is the Other? Can we ever hope to speak authentically of the experience of the Other, or an Other? And if not, how do we create a social science that includes the Other?" The short answer to these questions is that we move to include the other in the larger research processes that have been developed. For some, this means participatory or collaborative research and evaluation efforts. These activities can occur in a variety of institutional sites, including clinical, educational, and social welfare settings.

For other researchers, it means a form of liberatory investigation wherein the others are trained to engage in their own social and historical interrogative efforts and are then assisted in devising answers to questions of historical and contemporary oppression that are rooted in the values and cultural artifacts that characterize their communities.

For still other social scientists, it means becoming coauthors in narrative adventures. And for still others, it means constructing what are called "experimental," or "messy," texts where multiple voices speak, often in conflict, and where the reader is left to sort out which experiences speak to his or her personal life. For still others, it means presenting to the inquiry and policy community a series of autohistories, personal narratives, lived experiences, poetic representations, and sometimes fictive and/or fictional texts that allow the other to speak for himself or herself. The inquirer or evaluator becomes merely the connection between the field text, the research text, and the consuming community in making certain that such voices are heard. Sometimes, increasingly, it is the "institutionalized other" who speaks, especially as the other gains access to the knowledge-producing corridors of power and achieves entry into the particular group of elites known as intellectuals and academics or faculty.

The point is that both the other and more mainstream social scientists recognize that there is no such thing as unadulterated truth, that speaking from a faculty, an institution of higher education, or a corporate perspective automatically means that one speaks from a privileged and powerful vantage point, and that this vantage point is one to which many do not have access, by dint of either social station or education.

Judith Stacey (1988) speaks of the difficulties involved in representing the experiences of the other about whom texts are written. Writing from a feminist perspective, she argues that a major contradiction exists in this project, despite the desire to engage in egalitarian research characterized by authenticity, reciprocity, and trust. This is so because actual differences of power, knowledge, and structural mobility still exist in the researcher-subject relationship. The subject is always at grave risk of manipulation and betrayal by the ethnographer (p. 23). In addition, there is the crucial fact that the final product is too often that of the researcher, no matter how much it has been modified or influenced by the subject. Thus, even when research is written from the perspective of the other, for example, women writing about women, the women doing the writing may "unwittingly preserve the dominant power relations that they explicitly aim to overcome" (Bruner 1993:23).

THE AUTHOR'S PLACE IN THE TEXT

The feminist solution clarifies the issue of the author's place in the text. This problem is directly connected to the problem of representation. It is often phrased in terms of a false dichotomy—that is, "the extent to which the personal self should have a place in the scientific scholarly text"

(Bruner 1993:2). This false division between the personal and the ethnographic self rests on the assumption that it is possible to write a text that does not bear the traces of its author. Of course, this is incorrect. All texts are personal statements.

The correct phrasing of this issue turns on the amount of the personal, subjective, poetic self that is in fact openly given in the text. Bruner (1993) phrases the problem this way: "The danger is putting the personal self so deeply back into the text that it completely dominates, so that the work becomes narcissistic and egotistical. No one advocates ethnographic self-indulgence" (p. 6). The goal is to openly return the author to the text in a way that does "not squeeze out the object of study" (p. 6).

There are many ways to openly return the author to the qualitative research text. Fictional narratives of the self may be written. Performance texts can be produced. Dramatic readings can be given. Field interviews can be transformed into poetic texts, and poetry, as well as short stories and plays, can be written. The author can engage in a dialogue with those studied. The author may write through a narrator, "directly as a character . . . or through multiple characters, or one character may speak in many voices, or the writer may come in and then go out of the [text]" (Bruner 1993:6).

THE CRISIS OF LEGITIMATION

It is clear that critical race theory, queer theory, and feminist arguments are moving farther and farther away from postpositivist models of validity and textual authority. This is the crisis of legitimization that follows the collapse of foundational epistemologies. This so-called crisis arose when anthropologists and other social scientists addressed the authority of the text. By the authority of the text, I refer to the claim any text makes to being accurate, true, and complete. That is, is a text faithful to the context and the individuals it is supposed to represent? Does the text have the right to assert that it is a report to the larger world that addresses not only the researcher's interests but also the interests of those who are studied?

This is not an illegitimate set of questions, and it affects all of us and the work that we do. And while many social scientists might enter the question from different angles, these twin crises are confronted by everyone.

COPING WITH THE PRESENT

A variety of new and old voices, critical theory, and feminist and ethnic scholars have also entered the present situation, offering solutions to the problems surrounding the crises of representation and legitimating. The move is toward pluralism, and many social scientists now recognize that no picture is ever complete, that what is needed is many perspectives, many voices, before we can achieve a deep understanding of social phenomena and before we can assert that a narrative is complete.

The modernist dream of a grand or master narrative is now a dead project. The postmodern era is defined, in part, by the belief that there is no single umbrella in the history of the world that might incorporate and represent fairly the dreams, aspirations, and experiences of all peoples.

CRITICAL THEORISTS, CRITICAL PEDAGOGY

The critical theorists from the Frankfurt to the Annales world systems and participatory action research schools continue to be a major presence in qualitative research, and they occupy a central place in social theory (Freire 1998; Kincheloe and McLaren 2000; Denzin 2003). The critique and concern of the critical theorists have been an effort to design a pedagogy of resistance within communities of differences. The pedagogy of resistance, of taking back "voice," of reclaiming narrative for one's own rather than adapting to the narratives of a dominant majority, was most explicitly laid out by Paolo Freire (1998) working with adults in Brazil. Critical pedagogy seeks to overturn oppression and to achieve social justice through empowerment of the marginalized, the poor, the nameless, and the voiceless. This program is nothing less than the radical restructuring of society toward the ends of reclaiming historic cultural legacies, social justice, the redistribution of power, and the achievement of truly democratic societies.

FEMINIST RESEARCHERS

Poststructural feminists urge the abandonment of any distinction between empirical science and social criticism. That is, they seek a morally informed social criticism that is not committed to the traditional concerns or criteria of empirical science. This traditional science, they argue, rests a considerable amount of its authority on the ability to make public what has traditionally been understood to be private (Clough 1998:137; Olesen 2000; Lather 2004). Feminists dispute this distinction. They urge a social criticism that takes back from science the traditional authority to inscribe and create subjects within the boundaries and frameworks of an objective social science. Feminist philosophers question the scientific method's most basic premises, namely, the idea that scientific objectivity is possible.

CRITICAL RACE AND QUEER THEORY SCHOLARS

There is yet another group of concerned scholars determining the course of qualitative social problems research: They are critical race (Ladson-Billings 2000) and queer theory scholars (Kong et al. 2002), who examine the question of whether history has deliberately silenced, or misrepresented, them and their cultures.

This new generation of scholars, many of them persons of color, challenge both historical and contemporary social scientists on the accuracy, veracity, and authenticity of the latter's work, contending that no picture can be considered final when the perspectives and narratives of so many are missing, distorted, or self-serving to dominant majority interests. The result of such challenges has been threefold: (1) the reconsideration of the Western canon; (2) the increase in the number of historical and scientific works that recognize and reconstruct the perspectives of those whose perspectives have been previously written out of the present; and (3) an emphasis on life stories and case studies, stories that tell about lives lived under the conditions of racism and sexism.

BACK TO THE FUTURE

The press for a civic social science remains (Agger 2000). We want a civic sociology—by which we mean not just fieldwork located in sociology but rather an extended, enriched, cultivated social science embracing all the disciplines. Such a project characterizes a whole new generation of qualitative researchers: educationists, sociologists, political scientists, clinical practitioners in psychology and medicine, nurses, communications and media specialists, cultural studies workers, and researchers in a score of other assorted disciplines.

The moral imperatives of such work cannot be ignored. Not only do we have several generations of social science that have solved serious human problems, but many times, such work only worsened the plight of those studied. Beyond morality is something equally important: The mandates for such work come from our own sense of the human community. A detached social science frequently serves only those with the means, the social designation, and the intellectual capital to remain detached. We face a choice, in the seventh and eighth moments, of declaring ourselves committed to detachment, or solidarity with the human community. We come to know each other and we come to exist meaningfully only in community. We have the opportunity to rejoin that community as its resident intellectuals and change agents.

And as we wait, we remember that our most powerful effects as storytellers come when we expose the cultural plots and the cultural practices that guide our writing hands. These practices and plots lead us to see coherence where there is none or to create meaning without an understanding of the broader structures that tell us to tell things in a particular way. Erasing the boundaries between self, other, and history, we seek to learn how to tell new stories, stories no longer contained within, or confined to, the tales of the past. And so we embark together on a new project, a project with its own as yet not fully understood cultural plots and cultural practices.

And what remains, throughout, will be the steady, but always changing, commitment of all qualitative social problems researchers. The commitment, that is, to study human experience and its problems from the ground up, from the point of interacting individuals who together and alone make and live histories that have been handed down to them from the ghosts of the past.

10

QUANTITATIVE METHODOLOGY

KENNETH D. BAILEY

University of California, Los Angeles

HISTORY OF SOCIOLOGICAL QUANTIFICATION

Quantitative reasoning is widely applied in the discipline of sociology and quantification aids sociologists in at least seven main research areas: quantitative modeling, measurement, sampling, computerization, data analysis, hypothesis testing, and data storage and retrieval. But sociologists differ widely in their views of the role of quantification in sociology. This has apparently always been true to some degree. While Durkheim was a proponent of quantification, Weber was less enthusiastic. However, while Weber advocated the nonquantitative method *Verstehen,* both Weber and Durkheim saw the importance of method as well as theory, as both authored books on method (Weber 1949; Durkheim [1938] 1964). Today, the situation is much different, as a wide gulf exits between theory and method in twenty-first-century sociology, with only a few authors such as Abell (1971, 2004) and Fararo (1989) simultaneously developing theory and quantitative methodology designed to test theoretical propositions.

The most vocal proponent of quantification in sociology may have been Lundberg (1939), who was known as the unabashed champion of strict operationalism. Operationalism, as originally defined in physics by Bridgman (1948), is the belief that "in general any concept is nothing more than a set of operations, *the concept is synonymous with the corresponding set of operations*" (Bridgman 1948:5–6). George Lundberg (1939, 1947) took the application of operationalism in sociology to an extreme. In Lundberg's view, one did not approach an already existing concept and then attempt to measure it. The correct

procedure in Lundberg's view is to use measurement as a way of defining concepts. Thus, if one is asked what is meant by the concept of authoritarianism, the correct answer would be that authoritarianism is what an authoritarianism scale measures.

When he encountered objections to his advocacy of the use of quantification in sociology, Lundberg (1939, 1947) replied that quantitative concepts are ubiquitous in sociology, and need not even be symbolized by numerals, but can be conveyed verbally as well. For example, words such as "many," "few," or "several" connote quantitative concepts. In Lundberg's view, quantification is embedded in verbal social research as well as in everyday thought and is not just an artificial construct that must be added to the research process by quantitative researchers.

After Lundberg (1939, 1947) and others such as Goode and Hatt (1952) and Lazarsfeld (1954) laid the foundation for quantitative sociology in the 1930s, 1940s, and 1950s, the field surged in the 1960s and 1970s. The 1960s saw increased visibility for quantitative sociology with the publication of books and articles such as Blalock's (1960) *Social Statistics,* Kemeny and Snell's (1962) *Mathematical Models in the Social Sciences;* White's (1963) *An Anatomy of Kinship;* Coleman's (1964) *Introduction to Mathematical Sociology, Foundations of Social Theory;* Duncan's (1966) "Path Analysis: Sociological Examples"; Land's (1968) "Principles of Path Analysis"; Blalock's (1969) *Theory Construction: From Verbal to Mathematical Formulations;* and White's (1970) *Chains of Opportunity.*

Quantitative methods became even more visible in the 1970s and 1980s with the publication of a host of mathematical and statistical works, including Abell's (1971)

Model Building in Sociology; Blalock's (1971) *Causal Models in the Social Sciences;* Fararo's (1973) *Mathematical Sociology;* Fararo's (1989) *Meaning of General Theoretical Sociology;* Bailey's (1974b) "Cluster Analysis"; and Blalock's (1982) *Conceptualization and Measurement in the Social Sciences.*

QUANTITATIVE DATA COLLECTION

Specific quantitative techniques make rigorous assumptions about the kind of data that is suitable for analysis with that technique. This requires careful attention to data collection. For data to meet the assumptions of a quantitative technique, the research process generally entails four distinct steps: hypothesis formulation, questionnaire construction, probability sampling, and data collection.

Hypothesis Formulation

A hypothesis is defined as a proposition designed to be tested in the research project. To achieve testability, all variables in the hypothesis must be clearly stated and must be capable of empirical measurement. Research hypotheses may be univariate, bivariate, or multivariate, and some may contain auxiliary information, such as information about control variables. The vast majority of hypotheses used by quantitative sociologists are bivariate. The classical sequence is to formulate the hypotheses first, before instrument construction, sample design, or data collection. Hypotheses may be inductively derived during prior research (Kemeny and Snell 1962) or may be deductively derived (Bailey 1973). Increasingly, however, quantitative sociologists are turning to the secondary analysis of existing data sets. In such a case, hypothesis formulation can be a somewhat ad hoc process of examining the available data in the data bank or data set and formulating a hypothesis that includes the existing available variables.

For example, Lee (2005) used an existing data set and so was constrained to formulate hypotheses using the available variables. He presented three hypotheses, one of which stated that democracy is not directly related to income inequality (Lee 2005:162). While many quantitative studies in contemporary sociology present lists of formal hypotheses (usually five or less), some studies either leave hypotheses implicit or do not present them at all. For example, Torche (2005) discusses the relationship between mobility and inequality but does not present any formal hypotheses (p. 124).

Questionnaire Construction

In the classical research sequence, the researcher designed a questionnaire that would collect the data necessary for hypotheses testing. Questionnaire construction, as a middle component of the research sequence, is subject to a number of constraints that are not always well recognized. First and foremost is the necessity for the questionnaire to faithfully measure the concepts in the hypotheses. But other constraints are also imposed after questionnaire construction, chiefly sampling constraints, data-collection constraints, and quantitative data-analysis constraints. The questionnaire constrains the sampling design. If the questionnaire is very short and easily administered, this facilitates the use of a complicated sample design.

However, if the questionnaire is complex, then sample size may need to be reduced. The construction of a large and complex questionnaire means that it is difficult and time-consuming to conduct a large number of interviews. It also means that money that could otherwise be spent on the sample design must now be used for interviewer training, interviewing, and codebook construction. In addition to such sampling and data-collection constraints, the chief constraint on instrument design is the type of quantitative technique to be used for data analysis.

That is, the questionnaire must be designed to collect data that meet the statistical assumptions of the quantitative techniques to be used. Questionnaires can quickly become long and complicated. Furthermore, there is a tendency to construct closed-ended questions with not more than seven answer categories. While such nominal or ordinal data are often used in regression analyses, they are marginally inappropriate for ordinary least squares (OLS) regression and other quantitative techniques that assume interval or ratio data. Clearly, one of the great advantages of conducting a secondary analysis of data that has already been collected is that it avoids dealing with the many constraints imposed on the construction of an original data-collection instrument.

Probability Sampling

Many extant quantitative techniques (particularly inductive statistics) can only be used on data collected with a rigorous and sufficiently large probability sample, generally a random sample of some sort. One of the questions most frequently asked of research consultants is, "What is the minimum sample size acceptable for my research project?" Based on the law of large numbers and other considerations, some researchers permit the use of samples as small as 30 cases (Monette, Sullivan, and DeJong 2005:141). There is clearly a trend in the sociological literature toward larger sample sizes, often achieved through the use of the secondary analysis of existing samples and the pooling of multiple samples.

Sociology had few if any research methods books of its own prior to the publication of the volume by Goode and Hatt (1952). Before 1952, sociological researchers relied primarily on psychology research books, such as Jahoda, Deutsch, and Cook (1951), which de-emphasized sampling by relegating it to the appendix. Psychology emphasized the experimental method, with a small number of research subjects (often 15 or less), and de-emphasized surveys. Furthermore, in the mid-twentieth century, it was common for both psychology and sociology to use a "captive audience" sample of students from the researcher's classes.

The chief research models for sociology before 1952 were psychology and (to a lesser degree) medicine. While psychology routinely used a small sample of subjects in experiments, samples in medical research were often quite small as well. If a researcher is conducting medical research, such as a study of pediatric obsessive compulsive disorder, it may be difficult to obtain more than 8 or 10 cases, as the onset of this syndrome is usually later in life. With psychology and medicine as its chief models before 1952, sample sizes in sociology tended to be small.

Over time, sample sizes in sociology have grown dramatically. The present emphasis is on national samples and multinational comparisons, as sociology moves away from the psychological model and toward the economic model. For example, Hollister (2004:669, table 1) did not collect her own data, but used secondary data with an N of 443, 399 to study hourly wages.

Data Collection

During the period 1950 to 1980 when social psychology was dominant in sociology, data collection was often a matter of using Likert scales of 5–7 categories (see Bailey 1994b) to collect data on concepts such as authoritarianism or alienation from a relatively small sample of persons.

Now that economics is becoming the dominant model (see Davis 2001), there are at least two salient ramifications of this trend. One is that an individual researcher is unlikely to possess the resources (even with a large grant) to collect data on 3,000 or more cases and so must often rely on secondary data, as did Joyner and Kao (2005). Another ramification is that researchers wishing to use these large economic data sets that are relatively prevalent must obviously use a different kind of data, and different quantitative techniques, than researchers did in an earlier era when psychology predominated. The psychological orientation resulted in data collection more conducive to analysis of variance, analysis of covariance, and factor analysis, in addition to multiple regression (OLS). Today things have changed, and the technique of choice for the large economic data sets is logistic regression.

MATHEMATICAL SOCIOLOGY

It is useful to divide the extant quantitative techniques in twenty-first-century sociology into inferential statistics (probability-based techniques with tests of significance) and mathematical models (techniques that lack significance tests and are often nonprobabilistic). Rudner (1966) makes a distinction between method and methodology. Although the two terms are often used interchangeably in

sociology and elsewhere, there is an important difference between them. According to Rudner, methods are techniques for gathering data, such as survey research, observation, experimentation, and so on. In contrast, methodologies are criteria for acceptance or rejection of hypotheses. This is a crucial distinction. Some mathematical models lack quantitative techniques for testing hypotheses, as these are not built into the model.

In contrast, inductive statistics, in conjunction with statistical sampling theory, provides a valuable means for sociologists not only to test hypotheses for a given sample but also to judge the efficacy of their inferences to larger populations. Tests of significance used in sociology take many forms, from gamma to chi-square to t-tests, and so on. Whatever the form or level of measurement, significance tests yielding probability, or "p," values provide not only a way to test hypotheses but also a common element for community with researchers in other disciplines that also use significance tests.

Mathematical sociology has traditionally used methods such as differential and integral calculus (Blalock 1969: 88–109). Differential equations are frequently used to construct dynamic models (e.g., Kemeny and Snell 1962; Blalock 1969). However, one of the problems with mathematical models in sociology (and a problem that is easily glossed over) is that they are sometimes very difficult to apply and test empirically. Kemeny and Snell (1962) state that mathematical models are used to deduce "consequences" from theory, and that these consequences "must be put to the test of experimental verification" (p. 3). Since experimental verification in the strictest sense is relatively rare in sociology, this seems to be an Achilles heel of mathematical sociology.

To verify the predictions by comparing them with the experimental data, Kemeny and Snell (1962) use the statistical test chi-square. That is, the mathematical model proves inadequate for hypothesis testing and must be augmented by a statistical test (p. 62). Kemeny and Snell (1962) then "improve" the model by stating that there may be some subjects to which the model does not apply and "adding the assumption that some 20 per cent of subjects are of this type" (p. 62). Unfortunately, such "model simplification," achieved by simply excluding a proportion of the population from the analysis, is rather common in quantitative sociology. Yamaguchi (1983) explains his failure to include women in the analysis by writing, "In this paper, I limit my analysis to non-black men to simplify the model" (p. 218).

The dilemma is real. If the sociological phenomenon is too complex, then the mathematical sociologist will not be able to solve all the inherent computational problems, even with a large computer. Fortunately, the future technological advances in computer hardware and software, along with the continued development of new mathematical techniques such as blockmodeling (Doreian, Batagelj, and Ferligoj 2005), ensure a bright future for mathematical sociology. While the challenges of social complexity are real, the rewards for those who can successfully model this complexity with mathematics are great. For additional commentary and references on mathematical sociology in the twenty-first century, see Edling (2002), Iverson (2004), Lewis-Beck, Bryman, and Liao (2004), Meeker and Leik (2000), and Raftery (2005).

STATISTICAL SOCIOLOGY

While statistical methods extant in sociology can all be classified as probability based, they can be divided into tests of significance (such as gamma) and methods used for explanation (often in terms of the amount of variance explained), prediction, or the establishment of causality. Among these techniques, the most commonly used are multiple correlation, multiple regression, logistic regression, as well as analysis of variance (the dominant method in psychology) or analysis of covariance. Other methods used less frequently by sociologists include cluster analysis, factor analysis, multiple discriminant analysis, canonical correlation, and smallest space analysis (Bailey 1973, 1974a), and latent class analysis (Uggen and Blackstone 2004).

Which statistical technique is appropriate for a given analysis can depend on a number of factors, one of which is the so-called level of measurement of the quantitative data involved. S. S. Stevens (1951) divided data into four distinct levels—nominal, ordinal, interval, and ratio. It is important to stress consistent measurement at all four levels, as lack of attention to consistent measurement across studies in sociology is problematic for the field.

Nominal

The reality is that nominal variables can be very important in both sociological theory and statistics, but unfortunately they have been badly neglected by sociologists and often are created and treated in a haphazard fashion. This is unfortunate because discussions of classification techniques are readily available to sociologists in the form of work on cluster analysis and various classification techniques for forming typologies and taxonomies (McKinney 1966; Bailey 1973, 1994a). Carefully constructed classification schemas can form the foundation for all "higher" levels of measurement. A sociological model lacking adequate nominal categories can be the proverbial house of cards, ready to collapse at any moment.

The nominal level of measurement deals with nonhierarchical categories. Many of the most theoretically important and frequently used sociological variables lie at this level of measurement, including religion, sex, political affiliation, region, and so on. Much of the statistical analyses at the nominal level consist of simple frequency, percentage, and rate analysis (Blalock 1979). However, the chi-square significance test can be used at the nominal level, as can a number of measures of association, such as Tschuprow's T, V, C, Tau, and Lambda (Blalock 1979:299–325). Sociologists often dislike nominal categorical variables because it is felt that they are merely descriptive variables that do not possess the explanatory and predictive power of continuous variables, such as interval and ratio variables. But more important, nominal (and also ordinal) categorical variables are disliked because they generally do not fit into the classical multiple regression (OLS) models that (until the recent dominance of logistic regression) have been widely used in sociology.

In univariate cases with a large number of categories, or especially in multivariate cases with a large number of variables, and with each containing a large number of categories, the analysis can quickly become very complex, so that one is dealing with dozens if not hundreds of categories. As Blalock (1979) notes, there is often a tendency for researchers to simplify the analysis by dichotomizing variables (p. 327). Unfortunately, such attenuation results in both loss of information and bias.

Another problem with categorical data is that the printed page is limited to two dimensions. Thus, if one has as few as five categorical variables, and wishes to construct a contingency table showing their interrelations, this requires a five-dimensional table, but only two dimensions are available. The customary way to deal with this, even in computer printouts, is to print 10 bivariate tables, often leading to an unmanageable level of complexity.

Ordinal

Nominal and ordinal variables share some similarities and problems. Measures of association such as Spearman's r_s and tests of significance such as the Wilcoxon test are also available for ordinal variables (Blalock 1979). As with nominal variables, ordinal variables cannot be added, subtracted, multiplied, or divided (one cannot add rank 1 to rank 2 to obtain rank 3).

The ordinal level shares with the nominal level the problem of the desire to simplify. Sociologists often wish to reduce the number of ordered categories to simplify the research project, but unfortunately they often conduct this simplification in an ad hoc manner, without any statistical or theoretical guidelines for reducing the number of categories. Again, this leads to problems of attenuation and bias, as noted for the nominal level.

Interval and Ratio

A sea change has occurred in sociology in the last 40 years, as shown later in the review of *American Sociological Review* (*ASR*). During the 1950s and 1960s, American sociologists relied primarily on percentage analysis, often using nominal and ordinal measurement. Later in the twentieth century, quantitative researchers stressed the use of interval and ratio variables to meet the assumptions of OLS multiple regression analysis. Now, as seen below, there has been a major shift back to the use of nominal and ordinal variables in logistic regression.

Interval variables are continuous, with "arbitrary" zero points, while ratio variables have absolute or "nonarbitrary" zero points. Theoretically, only ratio variables, and only those found in nonattenuated fashion with a wide range of continuous values, should be used in multiple regression models, either as independent or dependent variables. Although textbooks such as Blalock (1979) say that only interval measurement is needed, in my opinion ratio is preferred and should be used whenever possible (p. 382). In reality, continuous variables are routinely used in regression without testing to see whether they can be considered ratio or only interval.

Furthermore, while such continuous variables may theoretically or potentially have a wide range of values, they often are empirically attenuated, with extremely high and low values (or perhaps even midrange values) occurring infrequently or rarely. Also, attenuated variables that are essentially ordinal, and contain only five values or so, are often used in surveys (e.g., Likert scales). While these Likert variables do not meet the technical requirements of multiple regression, either as dependent or independent variables, they are often used in regression, not only as independent variables but also as dependent variables.

As noted earlier, sociologists have traditionally struggled to meet the requirements of OLS regression, especially when encountering so many nominal and ordinal variables in everyday theory and research. For example, Knoke and Hout (1974) described their dependent variable (party identification) by saying, "The set of final responses may be coded several ways, but we have selected a five-point scale with properties close to the interval scaling our analysis requires" (p. 702). While this dependent variable may indeed be "close" to interval, it remains severely attenuated, possessing only five "points" or values compared with the hundreds or even thousands of potential values in some interval variables. In addition to using attenuated ordinal scales in regression (even though they clearly do not meet the assumptions of regression), sociologists often use nominal variables in regression. These are often used as predictors (independent variables) through the technique of "dummy variable analysis" involving binary coding.

As shown later by my review of *ASR,* the most common statistical technique in contemporary sociology is multiple regression in some form, including OLS and logistic regression. However, many of the variables used in sociology are nominal or ordinal. Those that are interval or ratio are often recoded as ordinal variables during data collection. The result is that between the existence of "naturally occurring" nominal and ordinal variables and the (often unnecessary) attenuation of nominal, ordinal, interval, and ratio variables, the range of empirical variation is greatly attenuated.

A common example is when an income variable with potentially dozens or even hundreds of values is reduced to five or so income categories to make it more manageable during the survey research process (see Bailey 1994b).

While it is true that respondents are often reluctant to provide their exact income, other alternatives to severe category attenuation are available. These include the use of additional categories (up to 24) or even the application of techniques for dealing with missing data. In addition, some common dependent variables, when studied empirically, are found to have small empirical ranges, but the adequacy of correlation and regression is formally assessed in terms of the degree of variance explained. Considering the cumulative effect of variables that are empirically attenuated, added to those variables that are attenuated by sociologists during the course of research, it is not surprising that explained variance levels are often disappointing in sociology.

A generic multiple regression equation for two independent variables is shown in Equation 10.1.

$$Y = a + b_1 X_1 + b_2 X_2 \qquad [10.1]$$

The model in Equation 10.1 is quite robust and adaptable but should not be abused by using it with severely attenuated data. Although one cannot add additional dependent variables, additional independent variables are easily added. Also, the model can easily be made nonlinear by using multiplicative predictors such as $X_1 X_2$ or X^n.

Assume that the dependent variable (Y) is annual income, and the predictors are, respectively, age and educational level. One could conduct an OLS regression analysis for a large data set and experience a fairly small degree of attenuation if the data were collected properly and the variables were not attenuated through unnecessary categorization. But now assume that a second regression analysis is computed on Equation 10.1, but this time the dependent variable is whether the person attends college or not, coded 1 or 0, and the independent variables are sex (coded 1 for female and 0 for male) and age (coded 1 for 20 or younger and 0 for 21 or older). Running OLS regression on this will yield very little in terms of explained variance. The analysis can be converted to logistic regression by computing the odds ratio and taking the natural log (logit) to make it linear. The limitations of this model are that little variance exists to be explained and the predictors are inadequate.

IMPLICATIONS

While many of the logistic regressions one sees in the sociological literature have many more predictors, many of these are often dummy variables (ordinal or ratio), and the wisdom of running regression on such data remains debatable. What accounts for the tremendous popularity of logistic regression, when many times the degree of variance explained remains decidedly unimpressive (see the discussion below)? Perhaps logistic regression is now a fad, or perhaps users do not see an adequate alternative. Why do they not just present correlation matrices? Why is regression needed? Perhaps because typologies using nominal variables are said to provide description, correlation is said to provide explanation, and regression is said to provide prediction, with prediction considered to be the highest form of analysis (Blalock 1979).

The implications of the analysis to this point are clear: Sociologists have long struggled to deal with the analytical problems posed by the different levels of measurement, and they continue to do so. While the recent widespread adoption of logistic regression has surely changed the way that sociologists deal with nominal (and to a lesser extent ordinal) variables, for example, it is not clear that the fit between theory and method, or between empirical data and method, has been drastically improved. Changes are still needed, and some recommendations are presented below.

METHOD AND THEORY

As previously noted, method and theory have become sharply bifurcated within sociology over the past 40 years. While the *ASR* once published methods articles, now these articles are routinely segregated into journals, such as *Sociological Methodology, Sociological Methods and Research,* or the *Journal of Mathematical Sociology*. Thus, quantitative methods are not only separated from qualitative sociology (which has its own journals such as *Qualitative Sociology*) but also are separated from sociological theory (with its own American Sociological Association journal, *Sociological Theory*).

Kemeny and Snell (1962) state that one first inductively derives a theory through observation and empirical research and then uses quantitative models to deduce testable hypotheses from the theory. The procedure suggested by Kemeny and Snell (1962) is a sound one. The obvious problem with successfully using such an integrated theory/method research process in contemporary sociology is that the theory and quantitative methods knowledge segments are so segregated and widely divided that it is increasingly difficult for the individual researcher to have access to all of this separated literature. By segregating sociology into largely verbal theory (*Sociological Theory)* and quantitative sociology (the *Journal of Mathematical Sociology*), the process of developing theories and testing them is made more difficult than it should be.

In spite of the wide degree of artificial separation of theory and method in sociology, the quantitative area has changed in a manner that makes it more consistent with the needs of theory. To meet the goal of operationalizing sociological theory, the quantitative method area should minimally provide three main services:

1. Quantitative sociology must provide both diachronic (dynamic) models dealing with process and synchronic (cross-sectional) models dealing with structure. Until the last decade or so, statistical sociology provided mainly synchronic or cross-sectional models via OLS. Now many logistic regression models are longitudinal as in event history analysis (Allison 1984).

2. The second service that quantitative method (including both statistical sociology and mathematical sociology) must provide is to talk increasingly in terms of actors rather than primarily in terms of equations or variables. While theory talks in terms of action by individuals or groups (agency), quantitative method talks in terms of change in variables (mathematics) or relationships among sets of variables (regression). A good example of the use of actor-oriented dependent variables in logistic regression is provided by Harknett and McLanahan (2004) who predict whether the baby's mother will take a certain action or not (marry the baby's father within 30 days).

3. Quantitative sociology must do a better job of raising R^2s as variance explained in many regression analyses in sociology (whether OLS or logistic regression) remains unacceptably low. A lot of this may be due to attenuation of variables, both dependent and independent. As seen above, some of the attenuation is avoidable, and some unavoidable. Until recently, the dominant regression model was OLS regression, which did a poor job of incorporating nominal and ordinal variables. Logistic regression includes nominal variables aggressively, thus making it more compatible with theory that is replete with such nominal variables and providing a welcome means of bridging the theory-method gap. However, it is unclear that the incorporation of nominal variables (both dependent and independent) in logistic regression has raised the variance explained by any meaningful degree. It is important that we pay more attention to this problem and that we focus on R^2 values, not just on p values. That is, it is likely that there is actually more variance that can be explained empirically, but the techniques in use are not picking it all up. Perhaps sociology has lost sight of whether sociological models fit the data well, which is the primary point of prediction. To say it another way, if logistic regression is used in virtually every analysis in the *ASR,* it seems obvious that this method will fit the data better in some cases than in others. In the cases where it can be determined that the fit is not good, perhaps an alternative method of analysis should be considered.

HISTORICAL COMPARISONS

Perhaps most sociologists are at least vaguely aware of changes in quantitative techniques that have appeared in the sociological literature in the last 40 years, particularly the shift toward logistic regression. I decided that it would be helpful to illustrate these changes by conducting a review of the *ASR* over the last 40 years. While a full review of all issues was impossible due to time constraints, it seemed that a partial review would be illuminating. I compared the last full volume of the *ASR* that was available (2004) with the volumes 40 years before (1964), and 30 years before (1974), as shown in Table 10.1.

Table 10.1   Presence of Regression by Type (OLS or Logistic), *American Sociological Review,* 1964, 1974, 2004

Review, 1964, 1974, 2004

ASR Vol.	Q[a]	OLS[a]	LR[a]	Both[b]	NQ[c]	Total[d]
V. 29						
1964	28	2	0	0	12	40
	(70%)	(5%)	(0%)	(0%)	(30%)	(100%)
V. 39						
1974	51	25	0	0	8	59
	(86%)	(42%)	(0%)	(0%)	(14%)	(100%)
V. 69						
2004	35	3	25	4	2	37
	(95%)	(8%)	(68%)	(11%)	(5%)	(100%)

a. Q = number of articles with quantitative analysis (at least some numbers or percentages), OLS = number of articles with least squares regression only (not logistic), and LR = number of articles with logistic regression only.

b. Both = number of articles with both OLS and LR.

c. NQ = number of articles without any quantitative analysis (no numbers).

d. T = total number of articles. All percentages are percentages of this total, although some percentages reported in the text may use a different base.

Table 10.1 shows the presence or absence of quantitative analysis in every article of *ASR* in 1964 (Volume 29), 1974 (Volume 39), and 2004 (Volume 69). These volumes were not selected by scientific probability sampling but were arbitrarily chosen to reflect changes in quantitative methods. The first year (1964) shows the initial use of regression, 1974 shows the growth of OLS regression, and 2004 (the last full volume available) shows the dominance of regression, both the continuing presence of OLS and the predominance of logistic regression. Presidential addresses were omitted as they tended to be nonquantitative essays. I also omitted research notes, replies, and comments and included only the articles from the main research section of the journal.

The first row of Table 10.1 analyzes Volume 29 (1964) of *ASR*. It reveals that 70 percent of all articles (28 out of 40) were quantitative. The remaining 12 were verbal essays without any numbers. An article was counted as quantitative if it had raw scores or means. The predominant numerical method in 1964 was percentage analysis; however, there were two cases of regression analysis. These were OLS analyses with continuous dependent variables, although they were identified only as "regression analysis." There were no instances of logistic regression. Although regression was soon to dominate sociological statistics, this trend was not yet evident in 1964.

However, by 1974, the trend toward the use of regression was clearly visible. The proportion of the articles that were quantitative in 1974 was 86 percent, up from 70 percent a decade earlier. Although there were still no logistic

regression analyses in *ASR* in 1974 (regression with categorical dependent variables), fully 49 percent of all quantitative articles (and 42 percent of all articles in the entire volume) were OLS regressions showing clear evidence of its upcoming dominance in sociological analysis.

It should be noted that in 1974, many of the OLS regression analyses were presented in the form of "path analysis," with the "path coefficients" presented in path diagrams. While 70 percent of all *ASR* articles were quantitative in 1964 and 86 percent in 1974, by 2004 the proportion of quantitative *ASR* articles had climbed to a startling 95 percent, with logistic regression in some form accounting for the majority of these. Out of a total of 37 articles in Volume 69, only two were entirely verbal, lacking any numerical analysis at all.

Even more startling was the fact that in 2004, out of the 35 quantitative articles in *ASR*, 32, or 86 percent of all articles in the volume, and 91 percent of all quantitative articles were regressions. Still more surprising, of the 32 articles with regressions, only three had OLS regression only. The remaining 29 had logistic regression, with 25 of these containing logistic regression only, and with four more articles presenting both OLS and logistic regression in the same article. Four additional articles (not shown in Table 10.1) contained "hybrid" models, which used various combinations of OLS and logged dependent variables, or presented models said to be "equivalent to OLS," and so on. Of the three quantitative articles that contained no regression, one contained both analysis of variances and analysis of covariance, while the other two contained only percentage analysis.

When logistic regression occurs in 29 out of 35 (83 percent) of quantitative articles and 29 out of 37 total articles (78 percent), it obviously has an amazing degree of dominance for a single technique. In fact, in the last four issues of Volume 29 (Issues 3, 4, 5, and 6), 19 of the total of 20 articles contained logistic regression of some sort (the other article was entirely verbal, with no quantitative analysis of any kind). This means that fully 100 percent of the quantitative articles (and 95 percent of all articles) in the June through December issues of the 2004 *ASR* (Volume 69) contained at least one logistic regression analysis. This dominance prompts the rhetorical question of whether one can realistically hope to publish in *ASR* without conducting logistic regression. It appears possible, but the odds are against it. If one wishes to publish in *ASR* without logistic regression analysis, the article should include OLS regression.

What accounts for the fact that in 2004, 95 percent of all published *ASR* articles were quantitative, and of these, 83 percent contained at least one logistic regression analysis? Could it be that quantitative sociologists in general are taking over the field of sociology, and sociologists should expect a wave of mathematical sociology articles to be published in *ASR?* I did not see any publications in Volume 69 containing articles that I would classify as mathematical sociology. I did see two models in 1974 that I would classify as work in mathematical statistics (one stochastic model and one Poisson model), but none in 2004.

Comparing 1974 *ASR* articles with 2004 *ASR* articles, we see a sea change toward logistic regression. From the standpoint of quantitative methodology, I can certainly appreciate the heavy reliance that *ASR* currently has on logistic regression. While casual observers might say that "regression is regression" and that not much has changed in 30 years, in reality nothing could be farther from the truth. The 29 logistic regression analyses presented in Volume 69 of *ASR* differ from the 25 OLS regression analyses of Volume 39 in a number of important ways. The traditional OLS regression that was dominant in 1974 has the following features:

1. It uses a continuous (internal or ratio) dependent variable.

2. It uses predominantly continuous independent variables, perhaps with a few dummy variables.

3. It uses R^2 to evaluate explanatory adequacy in terms of the amount of variance explained.

4. It uses about 5 to 10 independent variables.

5. It usually reports values of R^2 (explained variance) in the range of .20 to .80, with most values being in the intermediate lower part of this range.

In contrast, the logistic regression that dominates twenty-first-century sociology has these features:

1. It uses categorical rather than continuous dependent variables (see Tubergen, Maas, and Flap 2004).

2. It often uses rather ad hoc procedures for categorizing dependent and independent variables, apparently without knowledge of proper typological procedures (Bailey 1994a) and without regard to the loss of information that such categorization entails, as pointed out by Blalock (1979). Some of these decisions about how categories should be constructed may be theory driven, but many appear to be arbitrary and ad hoc categorizations designed to meet the specifications of a computerized model.

3. It logs the dependent variable to "remove undesirable properties," generally to achieve linearity, and to convert an unlogged skewed distribution to a logged normal distribution, more in keeping with the requirements of regression analysis (see Messner, Baumer, and Rosenfeld 2004).

4. It uses more categorical or dummy variables as independent variables, on average, than does OLS regression.

5. It uses larger samples.

6. It uses more "pooled" data derived through combining different samples or past studies. This has the advantage of getting value from secondary data. While it is good to make use of data stored in data banks, in some cases this practice may raise the question of whether the data set is really the best one or is just used because it is available.

7. It uses more models (often three or more) that can be compared in a single article.

8. It uses more multilevel analysis.

9. It uses more "corrections" of various sorts to correct for inadequacies in the data.

10. It often does not report R^2 because it is generally recognized to have "undesirable properties" (see Bailey 2004), thereby providing no good way for evaluating the efficiency of the explication in terms of the amount of variance explained.

11. It generally reports statistically significant relationships with p values less than .05, and often less than .01, or even .001.

12. It presents more longitudinal analysis.

While the trends toward multilevel analysis, longitudinal analysis, and actor orientation are welcome, the plethora of categorical variables and the complexity of the presentations (often spilling over into online appendixes) are of concern. Also, while all computerized statistical programs are vulnerable to abuse, the probability that some of the "canned" logistic regression programs will be used incorrectly seems high due to their complexity. But the chief concern regarding the dominance of logistic regression is that while the recent logistic regressions appear more sophisticated than their traditional OLS counterparts, it is not clear that they have provided enhanced explanatory power in terms of variance explained. In fact, logistic regression in some cases may have lowered the explanatory efficacy of regression, at least when interpreted in terms of explained variance.

The binary coding of dependent and independent variables can obviously lead to extreme attenuation and loss of explanatory power, as noted by Blalock (1979). One of the most undesirable properties of R^2 for any dichotomous analysis is that the dichotomous dependent variable is so attenuated that little variance exists to be explained and so R^2 is necessarily low. If nothing else, the large number of cases when no R^2 of any sort is reported is certainly a matter of concern, as it makes it very difficult to compare the adequacy of OLS regressions with the adequacy of logistic regressions.

In lieu of R^2, users of logistic regression generally follow one of three strategies: (1) They do not report any sort of R^2 (Hollister 2004:670), relying solely on p values. The p values of logistic regression often are significant due (at least in part) to large sample size, such as Hollister's (2004:669, sample N of 443,399 in table 1). While large sample sizes may not guarantee significant p values, they make them easier to obtain than with the smaller sample sizes previously used in many traditional sociological studies; (2) they report a "pseudo R^2" (see Hagle 2004), such as those reported by McLeod and Kaiser (2004:646) for their table 3, ranging in value from .017 to .112 (the highest reported in the article is .245 in table 5, p. 648); or (3) they report some other R^2 term, such as the Nagelkerke R^2, as reported by Griffin (2004:551), in his table 4, with values of .065 and .079.

SUMMARY

In the middle of the twentieth century, sociology relied on careful percentage analysis as the backbone of its quantitative methodology, augmented by relatively rudimentary statistics, such as measures of central tendency, correlation coefficients, and tests of significance such as chi-square. Although sociologists were aware of multivariate statistics such as factor analysis and multiple discriminant analysis, the onerous computation that these methods required before computerization limited their use.

With the advent of mainframe computers in the 1960s and 1970s, sociologists could go to their university-computing center and run a variety of multivariate statistical analyses. Thus, by 1974, OLS regression became the dominant method. A major problem with OLS regression was that it could accommodate only a single interval-dependent variable, and the independent variables had to be intervally measured as well, except for "dummy" variables. Thus, many important theoretical variables, such as religion, race, gender, and so on, could not be properly accommodated in the dominant regression model.

But by 2004, all had changed. The sea change to logistic regression facilitated the use of multiple regression, as one no longer needed to limit the analysis to interval or ratio dependent variables. Also, the dependent variable could be logged. The advantages of logistic regression are great. These advantages include the facilitation of multi-level analysis (such as use of the individual and country levels) and the ease with which data can be pooled so that many surveys are used and sample sizes are large. Logistic regression makes good use of existing data sets and does a much better job of longitudinal analysis than OLS. Furthermore, the published logistic regressions are replete with categorical variables that were previously missing from OLS regression.

While the advantages of logistic regression are obvious, it may be debatable whether the dominance of this technique indicates that theory and method have merged in an ideal fashion in contemporary sociology. There are several reasons why. First, much sociological theory is not stated in terms of the binary-coded dichotomies favored in logistic regression. While the prediction of dichotomies is certainly theoretically significant in some cases, it would not seem to match the general significance of predicting the full range of values in an interval or ratio variable. That is, why limit the analysis to predicting 1 or 0, when it is possible to predict age from birth to death. Second, since sociological theory is generally not written in terms of logged

variables, it is difficult to interpret statistical analysis where the dependent variables are logged to normalize them.

In summary, the logistic regression analyses now dominating provide a number of benefits. These include, among others, advances in longitudinal analysis, in multi-level analysis, in the use of pooled data, in the presentation of more comparative models in each analysis, and in the presentation of more interaction analyses. But logistic regression sometimes appears to relinquish these gains by losing theoretical power when it is unable to provide impressive R^2 values. This is due in part to the excessive attenuation resulting from the widespread use of binary-coded dependent variables (often dichotomies).

PROSPECTS FOR THE 21ST CENTURY

The future for quantitative sociology will include the continued use of logistic regression. There also will be further developments in blockmodeling and also in longitudinal methods, including event history analysis. There will also be continued interest in multilevel techniques (Guo and Zhao 2000) as well as in agent-based or actor modeling (Macy and Willer 2002). There will also be increased interest in nonlinear analysis (Meeker and Leik 2000; Macy and Willer 2002). In addition, there will be continued advances in regression analysis in such areas as fixed effects regression, including Cox regression (Allison 2005) and spline regression (Marsh and Cormier 2001).

Davis (2001) writes, "In sum, I believe the seeming technical progress of logistic regression (and its cousins) is actually regressive" (p. 111). In another analysis of the logistic regression model, Davis writes,

> In short, despite the *trappings* of modeling, the analysts are not modeling or estimating anything; they are merely making glorified significance tests. Furthermore, these are usually merely wrong or deceptive significance tests because . . . they usually work with such large Ns that virtually anything is significant anyway. (P. 109)

Davis recommends a return to path analysis, in part because it is easier to measure the success or failure of path analysis (p. 110).

Sociologists rely on logistic regression because the variables used are conducive to this technique. Davis (2001) also notes the shift within sociology from using psychology as a model to the present reliance on economics. He writes that in the 1950s psychology was the "alpha animal," but now economics is a "Colossus" (p. 105). Quantitative researchers have long favored economic variables because they are easier to quantify. Furthermore, inequality research has benefited from the wide availability of economic coefficients such as the Gini (Lee 2005). Nevertheless, sociologists are now more likely to be citing *Econometrica* or *The World Bank Economic Review,* and the future influence of economics on sociology seems clear.

While the advantages of logistic regression are clear, there are other methods that deserve consideration as well. It is clear that sociologists will increasingly employ the methods of epidemiology, such as hazard and survival models and Cox regression (Allison 2005), and the methods and data sets of economics. But in addition, sociologists will undoubtedly continue to collect their own data sets while employing the OLS regression and path analysis models. They will also use relatively neglected techniques such as factor analysis, analysis of variance, analysis of covariance, multiple discriminate analysis, canonical correlation, and smallest space analysis.

11

COMPARATIVE HISTORICAL SOCIOLOGY

WILLIAM R. WOOD

JOHN WILLIAMSON
Boston College

A subfield of sociological works exists, often grouped together under the name "comparative historical sociology" (CHS). These are the works of a sociology that emerged in the late 1960s and early 1970s, partially in response to perceived shortcomings of functionalism and crude Marxism, and partially as a return to classical sociological questions regarding the apparent contradictions and problems of modernity itself. Although a "comparative" approach is used in virtually all branches of social scientific inquiry, within CHS it has largely followed the works of Karl Marx and Max Weber with regard to the comparison of macrounits of analysis—the state, social class, capitalism, and culture. Its themes and major practitioners are well known; examples include Wallerstein's (1974) study of the modern world-system, Moore's (1966) study of democracies and dictatorships, Skocpol's (1979) study of revolutions, and Mann's (1986, 1993) study of the origins of social power. Although these names are not exhaustive, they are representative of a sociology that relies explicitly on the past to explain and understand the origins, auspices, and arrangements of social structures, institutions, and processes.

On the other hand, there exists outside of the field of CHS a multitude of subdisciplinary pursuits, all of which evidence a degree of overlap with the topical and methodological concerns of comparative historical work. "Historical sociology" is quite similar to, and is even labeled interchangeably with, CHS. Social history in its various forms, particularly the *Annales* School work under Fernand Braudel, the "new history" of E. P. Thompson, the

new "new history" of Perry Anderson, along with various "history from below" projects, all likewise share CHS's interest in the formation and development of social class and nation-states. Feminist works such as Mies's (1986) *Patriarchy & Accumulation on a World Scale* also have taken a comparative historical approach to the study of gender and social class. Even the work of scholars such as Philippe Ariès (1981), whose *The Hour of Our Death* epitomizes the French emphasis on the history of *mentalités,* or "attitudes," is both comparative and historical insofar as it explicates differing social attitudes toward death and dying throughout Western history.

The issue, then, becomes where one should draw the line between CHS and other works demonstrating some degree of comparative sociohistorical investigation. In the case of CHS, this line was perhaps originally carved out between the grand theory of functionalism and the narrative singularity of historiography. As Stinchcombe (1978) has argued, "one does not apply theory to history; rather one uses history to develop theory" (p. 1) Thus, for Stinchcombe and many others in the field, CHS was, and remains, a fundamentally social-scientific endeavor, whose main purpose is not the narrative description of *wie es eigentlich gewesenist* ("the way things actually were") but rather the formulation of theoretical knowledge concerning historical processes and social structures. For many of its practitioners, CHS is not history, or even social history, per se, but rather represents the sociological analysis of history, particularly in relation to the rise of capitalism, social class, and the modern state.

This distinction between social science and history is not new. It is a tension that runs the gamut of sociological thinking, dating back to at least Comte's proposition of a "science of society," as well as to the succession of Enlightenment thinkers, who initiated the scientific study of economics, politics, and law. Marx and Durkheim both argued that their work was "scientific," although for Marx this "science" was intrinsically linked to the study of history. However, it was Weber who devoted the most serious consideration to the *methodenstreit* between the social and natural sciences—the question of whether sociology should be aligned nomothetically with the empirical sciences or idiographically with the traditions of hermeneutics and interpretation (Weber 1949).

More recently, within the last two decades, this tension between social science as either a nomothetic or an idiographic pursuit has become more pronounced. CHS has been criticized for its dependence on historical data, its proclivity for the use of small numbers of cases, and for its close association to qualitative research. This is also due, in part, to the rise of the so-called linguistic turn in the humanities and social sciences, which has affected not only CHS but also sociology in general in its claims to empirical knowledge and value-neutral methodologies. While much of the work in CHS still assumes Stinchcombe's proposition that history can be used to develop sociological theory, newer scholarship has questioned the limits of theoretical generalization within the field.

Arguably, it is not so difficult to trace the origins and seminal works within CHS. It is, however, decidedly more difficult to draw contemporary boundaries between this field of study and works within history, the humanities, culture studies, policy studies, international relations, and political science, which all appear to be moving with increasing ease between one another as disciplinary boundaries become more ambiguous. This chapter will look at the general contours of CHS: its origins, its major works, and its relationships to other fields of study. It will also look more closely at the debates regarding method, theory, and epistemology, giving special consideration to the longstanding tension between history and sociology.

ORIGINS

The foundations of CHS are present in its emergence as a distinct field within sociology in the 1960s and 1970s, as well as in the work of much of classical sociology that was itself vested in historical investigations of the rise of capitalism, the nation-state, and modernity. In this regard, CHS initially focused extensively, as it still does today, on the concepts of social class and the nation-state, where the influence of Marx and Weber are most present. Although a "comparative historical" approach can arguably be applied to a variety of phenomena, its emphasis on class and the state reflects basic concerns of Marx and Weber regarding the origins and role of social class, the rise of the modern state, bureaucracy, industrialization, and revolution. Despite their dissimilarities, these two thinkers both believed that history itself provided an important explanatory role in their respective analyses of social change. The peculiar aspects of social organization related to capitalism, industrialization, bureaucracy, and modern rationality could only be located and analyzed in the past histories of modes of production, "primary" accumulation, the division of labor, technology, religion, and government.

Durkheim is often left out of the discussion of CHS and "the classics." While Durkheim's work was, in some sense, no less dependent on history than Marx's or Weber's, for Durkheim history could not define the function of a particular social fact, nor could it provide a positivistic framework necessary for the analysis of social organization. Mathieu Deflem (2000) characterizes this as "the distinction between causal explanation and functional analysis," where "causal-historical research and functional-synchronic analysis were divorced and the latter was often the privileged perspective," particularly within midcentury American sociology.

The use of history for explaining and understanding social change and organization was also present in the work of other well-known late-nineteenth- and early-twentieth-century scholars. Sombart's ([1902] 1928) *Der moderne Kapitalismus* continued in the tradition of Marx's analysis of the history of capitalism. The early work of the *Annales* School under Bloch and Febvre in the 1930s, as well as its later direction under Fernand Braudel, has been influential within CHS and world-systems theory specifically. Polanyi's (1944) *The Great Transformation* analyzed the rise and apparent failure of the "market society." Hannah Arendt's (1951) *The Origins of Totalitarianism* compared the rise of Soviet communism and German fascism and their relationship to anti-Semitism. These works deserve mention because they mitigate the notion that the close relationship between history and sociology was "rediscovered" in the waning light of functionalism in the 1960s and 1970s. By the middle of the last century, American sociology had become the predominant locus of sociology itself; the work of Talcott Parsons and other functionalists came to dominate almost every major research university in the United States. Yet even within Parsonian functionalism, as well as in the work of other midcentury scholars such as Robert Merton, history per se was not ignored. Rather, with its emphasis on the search for a general theory of social organization, functionalism largely eschewed history as a viable means of sociological explanation.

Immanuel Wallerstein (2000) has called the era of functionalist dominance between 1945 and 1960 the "golden age" of sociology, the time when "its tasks seemed clear, its future guaranteed, and its intellectual leaders sure of themselves" (p. 25). Yet somewhat rapidly, sociology moved from the certainty and dominance of midcentury functionalism to the uncertainty of a discipline united in name only. One consequence of this sociological fracturing was a return to history, or, more specifically, a return to Marxist and other critical works that viewed social problems as immanently rooted in history itself—colonialism, capitalism, slavery, and war. Although Weber's work was also being reread, comparative historical works in the late 1960s and 1970s owed more to Marx than to Weber, influenced in part by new readings of Marx in Britain (E. P. Thompson, Perry Anderson, and Eric Hobsbawm) and France (Althusser and Braudel). While by no means homogeneous—for example, the disagreements between Thompson and Althusser—variations of Marxist analysis were by far the most prevalent within both "new history" as well as within the inception of the so-called second wave of historical sociology.

Although the works of Marxist historians were (and remain) influential within CHS, what separated "new history" and the *Annales* School from early CHS was the proposition that CHS could be empirical, and could generate generally applicable theory. This was evident in the use of comparative methodologies and particularly the development of the case studies approach. A principal concern of comparative historical sociologists was not so much the writing of history but rather the use of history for the development of empirically valid theories about large-scale social change: the transitions from feudalism to capitalism, agrarianism to industrialization, fiefdom to nation-state, and local culture to commodity culture.

However disparate in terms of individual works, the CHS that emerged from the late 1960s until the early 1980s was articulated largely as a "middle ground" between the grand theories of functionalism, teleological Marxism, and the perceived idiosyncratic tendencies of historiography. Tilly (1981) notes that such a "middle ground" was not an attempt to reconcile theory and history. On the contrary, it was a conglomeration of specialties that sought to "concentrate on human social relationships . . . deal with change over a substantial succession of particular times [and] . . . yield conclusions that are generalizable, at least in principle, beyond the particular cases observed" (p. 57). This approach is clear in the work of Wallerstein, Tilly, Skocpol, Stinchcombe and Moore, and others and remains a central position in comparative historical research today.

MAJOR THEMES AND WORKS

A majority of comparative historical works share important general features. Notably, CHS deals in macrosocial units of analysis. Charles Ragin (1987:8–9) makes a useful distinction between "observational units" and "explanatory units" of analysis within comparative work. This distinction is common throughout sociology, as Ragin (1987) notes:

For most noncomparative social scientists, the term [unit of analysis] presents no special problems. Their analysis and their explanations typically proceed at one level, the individual

or organizational level. This is rarely the case in comparative social science, where analysis often proceeds at one level (perhaps the individual level) . . . and the explanation is couched at another level (usually the macrosocial level). (P. 8)

Dependency theorists and neo-Marxists, for example, rejected the assumptions of early modernization and development theories by bringing attention to larger external factors involved in the purported "inability" of poorer nations to modernize. The sizable corpus of work on revolutions has documented the degree to which external and larger units of explanatory analyses are involved in the precipitation, as well as the successes or failures of revolutionary movements. Thus, early comparative historical work emerged out of a context in which an endogenetic model of social change was standard; a major focus of CHS has been to determine how and where larger social, economic, and political structures contribute to or determine historical processes and events.

Within CHS, the idea of an "explanatory unit of analysis" is not the same as the establishment of direct causality. Contrary to other comparative sociological approaches, for example, comparative cross-national analysis, CHS usually does not present or analyze casual determinacy through statistical methodologies. Even where quantitative analysis is sometimes used, the emphasis on outcomes is almost always on the identification of what Ragin (1987) calls "intersections of conditions," and it is usually assumed that any several combinations of conditions might produce an outcome.

One reason for the emphasis on "intersections of conditions" is that CHS focuses extensively on the identification and development of historical "cases." As they are used in comparative historical work, cases involve the identification of particular processes, institutions, or events as situated within a larger temporal setting. The development of cases thus requires extensive knowledge not only of the particular phenomenon being studied but also a broad understanding of the economic, social, and cultural milieu in which this phenomenon has occurred as well as its location within a temporal sequence of complex events and the identification of possible causal relationships.

The effort required in the development and identification of case studies explains, in part, why comparative historical work usually results in a small *n*. A second explanation for small *n* is that the macrosocial units of analysis that are of interest to comparative historical sociologists are often limited in number. Comparative historical works that use a small or single *n* are, therefore, more often qualitatively oriented, and rely on methodologies more suited to the development of rich and detailed description of individual cases, the identification of unforeseen or unanticipated phenomenon, and the proposal of general hypotheses that may be followed up through more detailed studies.

Another commonality within CHS is an interest in macrosocial changes over long periods of time, decades or even centuries. Fernand Braudel's work, in particular, remains influential for his notion of the *longue durée*. In CHS, world-systems theory remains most closely aligned with the study of the *longue durée*. Even where Braudel's work may be criticized for its Marxist structuralist approach, the overarching notion that the study of large social structures and processes requires a long durational setting is common throughout comparative historical work.

Finally, most comparative historical works draw from a variety of disciplines, not only history and sociology but also economics, political science, legal studies, geography, and more recently race, gender, and culture studies. This is often necessary both for the development of suitable comparative cases as well as for the analysis of macrosocial structures and processes, where different disciplines provide a contextual framework not readily apparent within sociology. Paige's (1997) *Coffee and Power,* for example, draws from various disciplines—economics, political science, gender studies, and culture studies—in comparing the histories of El Salvador, Nicaragua, and Costa Rica over the last century, and proposes that each case cannot be understood outside of the complex political, social, and cultural relationships each country has had in relation to this commodity.

Thus, even within these aforementioned similarities, any attempt at grouping the wide disparity of works within CHS requires an artificial thematic, theoretical, or methodological unity not borne out in the disparity of works in the field. Much debate exists regarding not only the merits of individual works but also in their respective classifications. For our purposes, Charles Tilly's classification of the various levels of comparison within the study of comparative history remains conceptually useful. Tilly (1984:60–61) categorizes comparative historical works into four categories: world-historical, world-systemic, macro-historical, and micro-historical. Of these, we will look at the first three, as they constitute an overwhelming amount of work within CHS.

WORLD-HISTORICAL APPROACHES

In the category of world-historical approaches, Tilly includes works from Toynbee and Braudel as exemplifying "schemes of human evolution, the rise and fall of empires, and of successive modes of production." Arguably, the work of Toynbee (1934), particularly his *A Study of History,* falls squarely into the category of "the rise and fall of empires," as does the work of those such as Oswald Spengler (1926) and Samuel Huntington (1997). For varying reasons, all of these scholars, except Braudel, have played fairly minor roles within CHS—Spengler and Toynbee, perhaps for their almost total lack of materialist analysis, and Huntington, who as Matlock (1999) has argued, "makes the same error Toynbee did in assuming that the many disparate elements that make up his 'civilizations' comprise a coherent, interdependent whole" (p. 432).

Marx and Weber

Marx's theoretical connection between the forces and relations of production as a means by which to understand and methodologically approach social organization and power remains central within sociology, and particularly germane to comparative historical analyses. Marx's work has also proved fruitful in CHS in the extension of his notion of the capitalist mode of production to larger geographical regions, such as in world-systems analysis, and in the comparative historical interest in revolutions. Finally, Marx remains central within CHS by way of influence of the Italian Marxist, Antonio Gramsci. Gramsci's concept of "hegemony," formulated in his analysis of the Italian working-class embrace of fascism, has been widely adopted, used, and critiqued in comparative historical work, particularly in Marxist work on the state.

In the case of Weber's influence on CHS, this is more difficult to trace to any single work or even particular theory, as his work was less organized than Marx's around a particular theme or organizing principle. The best known among Weber's ([1930] 2001) comparative works remains *The Protestant Ethic and the Spirit of Capitalism,* but this work has been less influential within CHS, and arguably sociology itself, than his other writings. In the case of CHS, Weber's work was also closely associated with that of Parsons's and structural functionalism. Outside of the more interpretive emphasis of Bendix and the pluralist approach of those such as Lipset, Weber was somewhat cast aside in favor of the reinvigoration of Marx that characterized much of CHS in the late 1960s and early 1970s.

By the later 1970s and 1980s, however, Weber's work was being widely read and used within CHS, including studies of nation-states and state policy, nationalism, and social movements. Contrary to Marx, for whom society was defined more or less as the forces and relations of production, Weber argued that class alone was not able to account for the variety of forms of social organization. "Status" and "party" were, in Weber's estimation, equally influential spheres of social life. This recognition alone has been most important for sociology, which now recognizes economics, politics, and culture as distinct and interrelated spheres of social organization and power.

Weber's influence on CHS, however, extends beyond his tripartite analysis of social organization. Weber's (1975:128) interpretive method (*Verstehen*) broadened the task of social analysis by proposing that sociology must elucidate not merely the causal sequence of events but also the meaning of social action. In Weber's estimation, people, institutions, and organizations act for a variety of reasons: class interest, obligation, honor, emotion, tradition, custom, or habit. Understanding the meaning of social action was therefore as important as the effects of such actions, insofar as they were both necessary components of causal explanation. As sociologists could rarely definitively know the actual motives of social actors, Weber stressed the need for "ideal types" of social action (e.g., instrumental rational action, value-oriented action, affective action, and traditional action) against which specific cases could be juxtaposed. Comparative analysis was useful and necessary for Weber both for understanding the differences between different cases as well as for refining ideal types.

At the same time, Weber argued that the nature of an "interpretive" science mitigated the possibility of causal attribution when juxtaposed against that of the natural sciences. As Giddens (1971) notes, "Weber stresses that causal adequacy always is in a matter of degrees of probability . . . [T]he uniformities that are found in human conduct are expressible only in terms of the probability that a particular act or circumstance will produce a given response from an actor" (p. 153). Here, Weber's work has seeped down thoroughly into CHS, which more often seeks "conjectural" explanations than "calculable" ones.

WORLD-SYSTEMS THEORY

Out of Tilly's four categories, "world-systems approaches" denotes the most cohesive corpus of work within CHS. While Wallerstein's (1974) *The Modern World-System* is generally regarded as the starting point of the world-systems approach, the last 30 years has seen the subsequent proliferation of works from many scholars. Wallerstein developed his concept of the "modern world-system" partially as a response to perceived deficiencies within modernization theory and partially in relation to Braudel's notion of the *longue durée* and the "world economy." In *The Modern World-System,* Wallerstein argued that contrary to the apparent "success" of capitalism in the West, and its apparent "failures" elsewhere, modern capitalism represented rather a single "world-system" based largely on the geographical division of labor between "core," "semiperipheral," and "peripheral" regions. For Wallerstein, there had been other "world-systems," largely articulated under a single political entity, but the modern world-system is unique in that it constitutes "a world-economy [that] has survived for 500 years and yet has not come to be transformed into a world-empire" (p. 348).

This uniqueness is explained through the historical rise of Western capitalism. According to Wallerstein (1974), "capitalism has been able to flourish precisely because the world-economy has had within its bounds not one but a multiplicity of political systems" (p. 348). Wallerstein's argument rests on the notion that within the modern world-system, capitalism relies on a particular geographical configuration of the division of labor but is at the same time not bound to any one geographical location. Arrighi (1997) notes,

> Central to this account [is] the conceptualization of the Eurocentric world-system as a capitalist world-economy. A world-system [is] defined as a spatio-temporal whole, whose spatial scope is coextensive with a division of labor among its constituent parts and whose temporal scope extends as long as the division of labor continually reproduces the "world" as a social whole. (Para. 5)

The division of labor under capitalism, while certainly present within early-modern Western European states, was for Wallerstein more pronounced as a division of labor and resources that began in the sixteenth century to define the respective core, semiperipheral and peripheral regions of Western Europe, Central Europe, Eastern Europe, and the Americas. Where Northwestern Europe was successful in amassing capital for purposes of industrial production, largely through war and colonization, it was also able to coerce or force semiperipheral and peripheral regions into the production of foodstuffs and cheap textiles, as well as the exportation of raw materials. While limited movement between these regions has occurred, most notably in the case of the United States as the now dominant "core" region, for Wallerstein the movement within regions is secondary to the arrangement of the system itself.

Wallerstein's analysis has been expanded on in a proliferation of works both critical and complementary to his theory of the modern world-system. One of the best known is Arrighi's (1994) *The Long Twentieth Century.* Arrighi follows Wallerstein's logic of a global world-system but emphasizes the ebb and flow of finance capital in what he calls "systemic cycles of accumulation." Arrighi identifies four major systemic cycles of accumulation, dating from the sixteenth-century Italian city-states (particularly Genoa), moving to Holland in the eighteenth century, Britain in the nineteenth century, and finally the United States in the twentieth century. For Arrighi, the study of the movement and growth of capitalism must take into account not only the division of labor or the periodic stability of production but also the periods of crises and instability by which capitalism is able to move expansively from one region to another. Profitability in trade and production, argues Arrighi, periodically reaches geospatial limits, at which point capital moves toward high finance, war, and eventual relocation into newer and larger spheres of trade and production.

Other world-systems scholars have argued that the world-system existed prior to the rise of European capitalism. Janet Abu-Lughod's (1989) *Before European Hegemony,* for example, suggests that the world-system as conceptualized by Wallerstein is actually a subset of a larger world economy that encompassed parts of China, Southeast Asia, Africa, and Europe from the twelfth to the fourteenth century. Andre Gunder Frank and Barry Gills (1993) have also argued that Wallerstein's world-system is itself part of a larger world-system, but unlike Abu-Lughod, they see this world-system dating back not to the eleventh or twelfth century but 5,000 years. For Frank and Gills, the conceptualization of a larger and more truly global world-system represents more than an attempt to "reorient" Wallerstien's unit of analysis on an even larger scale. It also questions major assumptions within world-systems theory, and indeed much of classical sociology itself, regarding (1) the analysis of capital accumulation as a peculiarly European phenomenon; (2) the notion that "core," "semiperiphery," and "periphery" are relatively new or exist only within the European development of capitalism; and (3) whether or not cycles of expansion and contraction within European capitalism are in fact only part of an interrelated world-system "that extend[s] back many centuries before 1942" (pp. 3–4).

MACRO-HISTORICAL APPROACHES

In Tilly's categorization of differing levels of comparative analysis, macro-historical approaches fall in between world-systems approaches and micro-historical approaches. Tilly (1984) argues that "at this level, such large processes as proletarianization, urbanization, capital accumulation, statemaking, and bureaucratization lend themselves to effective analysis" (pp. 63–64). In describing different units of analysis, Tilly is also making an argument that the "macro-historical" approach deals with the largest units of analysis from which empirically verifiable arguments can be derived from comparative case studies. Although this point remains contentious, it is the case that the large majority of work in CHS focuses on the processes taking "states, regional modes of production, associations, firms, manors, armies, and a wide variety of [other] categories" as their units of analysis (p. 63).

Nation-States

Virtually all historical comparative works engage various aspects of nation-states in the study of different forms of government, social class, revolutions, militarism, social welfare, civic society, social citizenship, and cultural studies. States are used both as descriptive and explanatory units of analysis. Over the last half-century, the most well-known approaches to the study of the state are structural-functionalist theories, including pluralism and early modernization theory; elitism, Marxism, and class-centered theories; the state-centered approach, and institutionalism or new institutionalism.

Pluralist and Modernization Theories of the State

Pluralist theories of the state such as those put forth by Parsons (1966, 1969, 1971) and Smelser (1968) have tended to view the liberal democratic state and particularly the United States as a neutral mechanism for the "equilibration" of competing actors and groups. Social class has on occasion been identified as an important or central interest group, but pluralist approaches have more frequently emphasized the ability of the free market and representative democracy to mitigate the concentration of power. A variation of pluralist theory known as "elite

pluralism" or "polyarchy" concedes that elites maintain a disproportional amount of power and influence within liberal democracies but views competition among different elite groups as prohibitive of the creation of a single ruling class.

Pluralist theory has been largely confined to analyses of modern Western states. Its functionalist correlate for the study of nonindustrial Western nations is found in early modernization theory (also called development theory). Here, nation-states are assumed to develop in a similar unilinear fashion, and modernization theorists have argued that a "dichotomy" exists between traditional and modern states. The question for modernization and development theorists such as Rostow (1960), Almond and Powell (1966), and Eisenstadt (1966) was thus how to "encourage" policies of industrialization and democratization similar to those that had occurred in the West.

Marxist and Class-Centered Theories of the State

Marxist theories of the state became quite popular by the 1960s in both Europe and North America. The well-known "Miliband-Poulantzas," often referred to as the "instrumentalist-structuralist" debate, seen as crucial at that time, was between Marxists who viewed the state as more of a direct or subjective extension of class interests (e.g., as an "instrument for the domination of society"; Miliband 1969:22) and those who viewed the state as a distinct set of structures and practices through which the logic of capitalism was naturalized and reproduced. While the instrumentalist position was quite popular, structuralist theory has fared better within sociological analyses of the state, particularly in its ability to analyze the state less as the subjective extension of the elite than as an objective relation of economic, political, and social structures or "state apparatuses." Structural Marxists, for example, have investigated (1) the manner in which capitalism was reproduced in "institutional form[s] of political power" (Offe and Ronge 1975:139), (2) the use of social welfare to stabilize class conflict (Gough 1979), and (3) the successes and failures of states to mediate fiscal crises (O'Conner 1973) and legitimization crises (Habermas 1973; Offe 1973). The work of Offe, in particular, recognized important contradictions between state institutions, as well as circumstances where states acted against the interests of elites.

Where structural Marxism has fared better is within works that are more historically oriented. The structural Marxism of Althusser and the anthropological structuralism of Lévi-Strauss, on the other hand, have largely fallen out of favor for their tendency toward transhistorical or functionalist analysis of deeply rooted social structures that were seen as totalizing or teleological by other Marxists (e.g., Anderson 1974; Thompson 1963).

Perry Anderson's (1974) *Lineages of the Absolutist State,* along with the work of Moore (1966), represented a decidedly different class-centered approach to the study of states, suggesting that history was far more important in understanding the development of modern states than most structural Marxists had allowed for. These two works were central in the development of the "comparative historical" method. Both Moore's and Anderson's work cast significant doubt on the idea that states followed anything like a normative or unilinear progression of development. Anderson argued that contrary to the idea that an emerging bourgeoisie had merely supplanted the landed feudal aristocracies of Europe, absolutist monarchies had rather helped to foster the bourgeoisie. For Anderson, however, this did not occur at the same level throughout Eastern and Western Europe, and particularly in England. A large part of Anderson's analysis was therefore directed toward explaining the "lineages" of absolutist states from relatively similar feudal relations to decidedly different modern economic and political paths.

Barrington Moore's (1966) *Social Origins of Dictatorship and Democracy* set the stage for a generation of comparative historical work on nation-states. His general thesis is often summed up as "no bourgeoisie, no democracy." In each case study, Moore argued that the relative strength of the bourgeoisie was decisive in the formation and outcome of different revolutions or revolutionary movements. Moore then linked these different revolutionary typologies to the development of differing forms of modern governments—democracy, fascist dictatorship, or communist dictatorship.

For Moore, however, the presence or absence of a strong bourgeoisie was important *within* a sequence or ordering of specific historical events. In this sense, Moore's was one of the first comparative historical works that analyzed cases both structurally and temporally. As Mahoney (2003) notes, "Since the publication of *Social Origins,* nearly all comparative historical scholars have come to theorize about the ways in which the temporal ordering of events and processes can have a significant impact on outcomes" (p. 152). More generally, Moore's work suggested that class conflict itself was not given to any one specific historical trajectory or outcome.

State-Centered Theory

By the late 1970s and early 1980s, comparative historical sociologists were questioning the usefulness of Marxist analyses. If there had existed any thematic or theoretical unity in the field under its earlier Marxist cohesion, the 1980s (1) witnessed not only the demise of any such cohesion but the beginnings of a proliferation of different approaches to the study of states that rejected earlier assumed groupings of capitalism and the state as cohesive or binomial components of "society-centered" approaches, (2) questioned the limitations of class conflict and the division of labor as an analytical approach to the study of modern states, and (3) analyzed the "agency" and efficacy of states, elites, and institutions.

The single biggest shift in the historical comparative study of states was the development of the state-centered approach of Evans, Giddens, Mann, Reuschemeyer, Skocpol, and Tilly in the early 1980s. Although varied in their respective emphasis on different aspects of state formation and activity, this approach was a redress of what Skocpol called "society-centered" functionalist, pluralist, and Marxist approaches to the study of the state that, as Skocpol (1985) argued, tended to view states as "inherently shaped by classes or class struggles [that] function to preserve and expand modes of production" (pp. 4–5).

State-centered theorists drew heavily from Max Weber's work on bureaucracy and political sociology. Contrary to Marx, Weber had developed a comprehensive and systematic theory of the state, one that agreed with Marx's analysis of class divisions but rejected Marx's primacy of class itself as determinate or even central in the formation or logic of modern states. Weber ([1919] 1958) argued rather that "sociologically the state cannot be defined in terms of its ends . . . Ultimately, one can define the modern state sociologically only in terms of the specific *means* peculiar to it, as to every political association, namely, the use of force" (pp. 77–78). The primary goal of the state was, in Weber's analysis, sustained sovereignty over a particular territory through the monopoly of the legitimate use of physical force.

Using Weber's work, proponents of the state-centered approach thus argued that states themselves should be considered as "weighty actors" able to "affect political and social processes through their policies and patterned relationships with social groups" (Skocpol 1985:1). Jessop (2001) summarizes nicely the major assumptions and research foci of the state-centered approach:

> (1) The geo-political position of different modern states within the international system of nation-states . . . (2) the dynamic of military organization and the impact of warfare in the overall development of the state; (3) the distinctive administrative powers of the modern state . . . (4) the state's role as a distinctive factor in shaping institutions, group formation, interest articulation, political capacities, ideas, and demands beyond the state . . . (5) the distinctive pathologies of government and the political system—such as bureaucratism, political corruption, government overload, or state failure; and (6) the distinctive interests and capacities of "state managers" (career officials, elected politicians, etc.) as opposed to other social forces. (P. 153)

The state-centered approach opened up or expanded on several avenues of comparative historical research, including the study of economic policy (Evans 1985; Reuschemeyer and Evans 1985), revolutions (Farhi 1990; Goodwin 1997; Skocpol 1979; Wickham-Crowley 1991, 1992), and militarism and war (Giddens 1987; Mann 1988; Tilly 1985).

Institutionalism

Popular throughout the 1980s, state-centered theory largely merged with or moved toward what is called historical institutionalism. In the late 1980s and early 1990s, two new institutional approaches, rational choice theory and historical institutionalism, emerged as interdisciplinary pursuits within political science, organizational studies, economics, and sociology. Within CHS, historical institutionalism is closely aligned with the state-centered approach insofar as it recognizes the state as a potential locus of action. However, historical institutionalists such as Hacker, Immergut, Pierson, Skocpol, Steinmo, Thelen, and others have moved away somewhat from the notion of the state as actor, toward the investigation of how institutions themselves are both agents and objects within larger networks of structurally limited possibilities. A central focus of historical institutionalism is the emphasis on historically contingent institutional "paths" or "path dependency."

Pierson (2000) describes path dependency as "increasing returns" where "the costs of switching from one alternative to another will in certain social contexts increase markedly over time" (p. 251). Path dependency thus seeks to explain the "initial conditions" or "critical junctures" that precipitate specific institutional paths, recognizing that small events or actions can lead to large outcomes. Historical institutionalists also recognize that while paths may become more stable or determined through positive feedback, outcomes are not predetermined. Emphasis is placed on the "timing" or "sequence" of events in an attempt to explain institutional movement or development.

Historical institutionalism also argues that questions of power and legitimacy are almost inexorably linked to institutional processes. Comparative historical sociologists and political scientists have used this approach extensively when explaining why similar institutional structures and choices vary widely between states in the case of social welfare (King 1992; Orloff 1993; Pierson 1994; Skocpol 1992), social health care policies (Immergut 1992), taxation (Steinmo 1993), and labor movements and democratization (Collier and Collier 1991; Mahoney 2002).

Social Class and Labor

A key theme in the comparative study of social class has been the historical formation of modern classes. Researchers interested in "transition periods" in Europe and the United States have developed different theories about the movement from feudalism to capitalism and from agrarianism to industrialism. Hobsbawm (1965) argued that a "general crisis" within seventeenth-century Europe had been central to the development of European capitalism. Brenner (1977) proposed that levels of peasant organization and revolt could explain the emergence of variant forms of capitalism in Europe, particularly the early development and force of industrialism in England. The work of Moore and Anderson (discussed above) was also central in transitional literature. E. P. Thompson's (1963) *The Making of the English Working Class* was a redress to structural Marxism (specifically Althusser), and this work continues to be influential for his thesis that class is not merely a

structural category but rather "an active process, which owes as much to agency as to conditioning" (p. 9).

Comparative historical sociologists such as Tilly have argued that the nineteenth century represented a substantial shift in the formation of social class. Tilly's (1975, 1978) work emphasizes the change in later-nineteenth-century Europe from collective "reaction" to more deliberative or purposive collective action such as labor organization strikes. As Eder (2003) notes, "What changes in 1848, the year chosen by Tilly as a convenient time marker, are the claims and the action repertoire. Claims become more proactive; new rights are claimed, rather than old rights defended" (p. 279).

The comparative study of organized labor in Western twentieth-century states has looked at general patterns of labor strength and organization between states, as well as produced several notable comparative works on specific labor movements and unions (see Haydu 1988; Taylor 1989; Tolliday and Zeitlin 1985). Voss's (1993) work on the Knights of Labor rejects the "American exceptionalism" explanation for the conservatism of American labor movements and concludes that the fall of the Knights of Labor shifted the direction of American labor unions toward a decidedly different and more conservative course. Stepan-Norris and Zeitlin's (2002) *Left Out: Reds and America's Industrial Unions* argues that the post-World War II decline of unions can be traced to the anticommunist purging that effectively crippled many unions. Kimeldorf's (1988) *Reds or Rackets* explored how longshoremen's unions on the East and West Coasts of the United States developed, respectively, toward conservative and radical political affiliation.

Comparative studies of class have also looked at the changing structures of labor itself in the West, particularly in the later part of the twentieth century. The world of Mills's "white-collar" managers and the division between the managerial and working classes has given way to a complex arrangement of labor sectors and relationships. Myles and Turegun (1994) argue,

> By the 1970s virtually all class theorists—Marxist and Weberian—had converged on the centrality of two broad strata for understanding the class structure of advanced capitalist societies: the growing army of mid-level corporate officials engaged in the "day-to-day" administration of the modern firm . . . and the professional and technical "knowledge" workers who have become virtually synonymous with postindustrialism. (Pp. 112–13)

Moreover, as Myles and Turegun note, the rise of the latter group has been categorized alternatively as "the service class" (Goldthorpe 1982), as part of "new petite bourgeoisie" (Poulantzas 1975), or as "knowledge workers" (Wright 1978).

The division of bourgeoisie/proletariat or owner/worker has thus become more complex with the rise of managerial and "middle" classes, and comparative historical sociologists have sought explanations for differences or varieties of class formation—largely in comparative studies of states. Katzenstein (1984, 1985) has identified differences between liberal (e.g., the United States and Britain), statist (e.g., France), and corporatist (e.g., Germany, Austria, and smaller European states) systems of capitalism as crucial for the development of class and the relationship between labor and capital. Others such as Zysman (1983) and Arrighi (1994) have emphasized the central role of financial systems and finance capital in the structuring of industry, labor markets, and social class.

The comparative historical study of class and labor in other regions besides Europe and the United States is still limited but has increased somewhat more recently, partially in relation to the rise of global commodity chains and the rapid change in labor relations under structural adjustment policies and flexible accumulation. Bonacich et al. (1994), Candland and Sil (2001), and Silver (2003) have all looked at global production schemes or changes in global labor trends and relations. Studies of labor relations in Latin America include Collier and Collier's (1991) case studies of eight Latin American countries and the relationship between labor movements and political developments in the twentieth century; Bergquist's (1986) *Labor in Latin America,* which looks at the experiences of workers in the export-oriented economies of Argentina, Columbia, Chile, and Venezuela; Huber and Stafford's (1995) *Agrarian Structure and Political Power;* and Murillo's (2001) *Labor Unions, Partisan Coalitions, and Market Reforms in Latin America.* Studies of labor in Asia include Frenkel's (1993) edited volume *Organized Labor in the Asia-Pacific Region: A Comparative Study of Trade Unionism in Nine Countries;* Gills and Piper's (2002) edited volume *Women and Work in Globalising Asia;* and Hutchison and Brown's (2001) *Organizing Labour in Globalizing Asia.* Comparative historical work on Africa is perhaps not surprisingly the most underrepresented within the field, the work of Michael Burawoy (1972, 1981) being the notable exception.

Revolutions

In many respects, because the study of revolutions and states in CHS are so closely tied to one another, the movement of research and theory about revolutions parallels research on the state itself. Midcentury American thought on revolutions tended to follow a functionalist analysis, using variants of early modernization theory to explain revolutions as disequilibria between traditional and modern forms of social organization. However, as Goldstone notes (2003:58–59), large *n* studies attempting to link "the strains of transition" to revolutions have been only partially successful at best. The most notable finding that came out of these studies, argues Goldstone (2003), was the realization that "different countries were different in important ways, and that revolutions themselves were different in how they unfolded, their levels of violence, and which elites and groups were involved" (p. 59).

The assumption of unilinear development from premodern to modern society is not unique to functionalist analysis of revolutions, however. In the case of historical materialist accounts of revolution, as Comninel (2003) notes, "The classic formulation of this transformation has been as 'bourgeois revolution'—a historically progressive class of capitalist bourgeois taking political power from an outmoded landed class of feudal aristocrats" (p. 86). Moore's (1966) work, however, cast significant doubt on both orthodox Marxist and functionalist depictions of any unilinear progression from premodern to modern states, and the role that revolutions play in this transformation. While Moore argued that class conflict, and particularly the strength of peasant movements, was central to the potential for and shape of revolutions in his case studies (Russia, France, Germany, Japan, the United States, Great Britain, and India), his analysis also showed that varying forms of class conflict led to very different types of revolutions and subsequently to different types of modern states. Tilly's (1978) work *From Mobilization to Revolutions* also centered on class conflict as central to revolutionary movements, although for Tilly, revolutionary conditions did not emerge from class exploitation alone. Rather, revolutions were a form of "collective action" that required specific political opportunities, access to resources, and an organizational structure capable of attracting support and mounting a sustained challenge.

Skocpol's (1979) *States and Social Revolutions* challenged what she has called in various places "society-centered" analysis of states and revolutions. In this seminal work, Skocpol argued that the success of revolutions in France, Russia, and China were as much or more the result of external forces—markets and militarism—than of internal political instability. Moreover, Skocpol argued that in each case, successful revolutions depended on other structural factors as well, namely, competition or conflict between rulers and elites, and the organizational ability of revolutionaries.

More recently, Skocpol's work, and social-structural theory in general, has become less popular in light of research on the numerous revolutions and revolutionary movements that have occurred within the last half-century. If anything, the differences between revolutions in Eastern Europe and the former Soviet Union, Iran, the Philippines, Central America, and Asia have made comparative historical scholars cautious toward theorizing too broadly about the causes of revolutions. Yet the current lack of any single dominant theoretical approach to the study of revolutions has been greeted by a deluge rather than a dearth of work in the area. As Goldstone (2003) notes,

The elements of revolutionary process [have been] expanded to include international pressures, fiscal strain, intraelite conflict, a wide range of popular protest and mobilization, underlying population on resources, and coordination between opposition elites and popular protest to produce revolutionary situations, as well as the pivotal role of revolutionary ideologies in guiding outcomes. (P. 69)

Social Movements

Social movements have been of keen interest to comparative historical sociologists not only for determining the conditions under which such movements may emerge but also in understanding why they succeed or fail in their respective aims. By "aims," the study of collective action recognizes that very often such action constitutes more than mob violence or disorganized reaction to external political, social, and cultural pressures. Prior to the American civil rights movement and subsequent social movements, much of the thinking on the topic was centered around functionalist and behavioralist theories in North America and Marxist theory within Europe. The civil rights movement, along with the antiapartheid movement, environmental movements, and other social movements, were clear indications, however, for sociologists that collective action could not be adequately explained as spontaneous reaction to the short-term breakdown of social norms (functionalism), or merely as response to material inequalities or oppression.

More recent approaches include resource mobilization and political process theories. These approaches argue that social inequality is endemic throughout social relations, and that collective actions and social movements cannot be explained solely by inequality (e.g., "relative deprivation") or oppression itself. Rather, resource mobilization and political processes theories argue that social movements are created and engendered by "opportunity structures" and access to resources otherwise unavailable to potential collective actors. "New" social movement theory has argued that modern social movements differ from earlier forms of collective action in that the contested terrain encompasses not only class conflict and material inequality but the symbolic production of meaning and identity (Canel 1997; Cohen 1985; Melucci 1980, 1985).

METHODOLOGICAL AND EPISTEMOLOGICAL CONSIDERATIONS

Within the last two decades or so, there has been significant debate regarding the role of method and theory in comparative historical analysis. These debates encompass not only particular critiques of various works and theories but more generally the historical comparative claim to theoretical knowledge, the reliability of causal explanation in comparative historical work, and the purported division in comparative historical work between sociology and history. Moreover, these debates can be linked to the "linguistic turn" that has occurred throughout the social sciences and humanities, particularly in relation to the various postmodernist and poststructuralist critiques of epistemology and knowledge/power relations.

In the case of methodology and subsequent claims to theory generation, Jeffery Paige (1999:782) has characterized the polarities of this debate in CHS as one of "advancing general theories of society," on the one hand, and "explaining historical conjectures," on the other. This division is a revival of the *methodenstreit* confronted by Max Weber, focusing on the question of whether to situate sociology nomothetically, which is within the realm of empirical sciences, or idiographically, within the realm of hermeneutics and interpretation.

Although CHS takes history as its "field of study," its earlier practitioners generally sought to situate the field on the *other* side of the *methodenstreit*. Calhoun (1998) notes that

> rather than emphasizing sociology's substantive need for history—the need for social theory to be intrinsically historical—Skocpol and Tilly among others argued that historical sociology should be accepted because it was or could be comparably rigorous to other forms of empirical sociology. (P. 850)

Part of this "rigor" lay in the notion that CHS could speak *scientifically* about history, not only by distinguishing causal sequences of events but also by generating broader theories about society itself through the study of history.

With a few exceptions, this view of CHS was the predominant view through the mid-1970s. By the late 1970s and early 1980s, however, the nomothetic/idiographic assumption was being questioned both within CHS as well as within sociology itself. Philip Abrams's (1982) *Historical Sociology* was one of the first serious critiques of this assumption, where Abrams argued that "in terms of their fundamental preoccupations, history and sociology are and always have been the same thing" (p. x). While the notion that there are *no* differences between history and sociology was and remains perhaps not as widely held as critics of this position decry, comparative historical analysis in the last two decades has undoubtedly seen a growing divide along the lines of "historical conjecture" and "general theory."

Sociologists such as Goldthorpe (1991), Burawoy (1989), Kiser and Hechter (1991), and others have moved to counter the growing "historicism" within sociology, something that Goldthorpe (1991) has called "mistaken and—dangerously—misleading" (p. 225). Instead, Goldthorpe argues,

> History may serve as a "residual category" for sociology, marking the point at which sociologists, in invoking "history," thereby curb their impulse to generalize or, in other words, to explain sociologically, and accept the role of the specific and of the contingent as framing—that is, as providing both the setting and the limit—of their own analyses. (P. 212)

Here the debate becomes as much epistemological as methodological. The question becomes "What counts as legitimate knowledge within comparative historical analysis?" This is a difficult question and one that has plagued not only CHS but also sociology and the social sciences in general. Currently, nothing like the cohesion of functionalism in sociology or the dominance of Marxism exists within CHS. Some like Kiser and Hechter see the concomitance of sociology and history as a dangerous vacuum. Others see this as the movement away from a confining and limiting sociology.

Much of the current work in CHS arguably falls somewhere in the middle. Some, such as Mahoney and Rueschemeyer's (2003) edited work *Comparative Historical Analysis in the Social Sciences,* seek to show that historical comparative work can be empirically rigorous and that the field has been successful not only in individual projects but also in the accumulation of knowledge in the field itself. Paige (1999:785), on the other hand, has argued that many "second-generation" comparative historical sociologists have developed "neither case-specific conjectural explanation, nor universal theory, but rather historically conditional theory," which Paige defines as the practice of "examining anomalies in theoretical frameworks presented by particular time-place conjunctures." Yet these historically conditional theories resemble less a gradated continuum than myriad trajectories of method and approach to theory.

Moreover, it is not only CHS that has changed but the discipline of history as well. Thus, within comparative historical analysis, the question of the relationship of history to sociology is hardly settled. The turn toward history within sociology itself, the overlap between sociological and historical work, the emergence of differing methodological strategies, and the growing interdisciplinary nature of the field have created a decidedly complex and contentious blurring of the boundaries of the field. If anything, it is questions of method and epistemology that appear most daunting for the future of comparative historical studies.

THE FUTURE OF COMPARATIVE HISTORICAL SOCIOLOGY

At this point, conclusions are difficult. Part of this stems from the possibility that the field itself has become unwieldy. This would not be surprising except for the fact that so few historical comparative courses are taught when compared to other sociological subfields. Outside of a

dozen or so "classic" works in the field, lists of readings for "comparative historical" courses vary widely, as does the inclusion or exclusion of methods, and works in the history of the field itself.

The literature in the field has in fact become subsets of literatures that have largely moved toward specialization, as well as being connected with other disciplines and fields of study. For some, the emergence of subspecializations runs the risk of "turning [students] into skilled technicians" competent in specific methodologies but "crippling" their ability "to think like social scientists" (Wallerstein 2000:33). For others, the overlap with other disciplines and fields of study is seen as a corruption of or regression away from the goal of empirical research and the construction of general theory (Burawoy 1989; Goldthorpe 1991; Kiser and Hechter 1991). For yet others, the movement of comparative historical analyses into other areas such as feminist and culture studies is indicative of the "domestication" of the field itself, where CHS has lost its once "critical edge" to other disciplines and fields (Calhoun 1996).

In many ways, CHS is today less diverse or "transdisciplinary" than merely divided along differing thematic, methodological, theoretical, and epistemological positions. There seems to be much hope in "trans- or "postdisciplinary" approaches. There is also decidedly less actual work that can be pointed to as examples of what such work should look like, particularly in several major sociological journals that for the last decade or so have played host to a series of various attacks on and defenses of what CHS is or is not.

However, it is not at all clear that these growing divisions are as dangerous as many claim, or that CHS as a meaningful rubric has not outlived its usefulness. Its initial growth in the United States and Europe was as much a social as an academic movement, a type of collective identification against the perceived shortcomings of sociology and its inability to address problems of social injustice, exploitation, and war. As this collective identity has faded, so too has the notion that comparative historical work must be grounded in these larger theoretical concerns. In this sense, a truly transdisciplinary approach must begin not with greater emphasis on interdisciplinary research but with the more reflexive question of whether or not the field has outgrown its conceptual boundaries. It must confront the fact that today the landscape of the field resembles a contested and contentious division of comparative historical "sociologies."

PART IV

THE FABRIC OF SOCIAL LIFE

12

THE SOCIOLOGY OF CULTURE

LAKSHMI KANT BHARADWAJ

The University of Wisconsin–Milwaukee

The word *culture* is derived from the Latin *cultura* (from the root *colere:* to cultivate, to dwell, to take care, to tend and preserve), which shows its affinity to "agriculture" and also to religious worship. Throughout most of history, culture has been virtually synonymous with religion. Prior to modern times, culture was not one arena of life but was a whole way of life inextricably bound up with religion. Weber has traced the roots of Western capitalism to the ascetic impulse of Calvinism and the idea of work as a calling. As capitalism came into its own, the religious impulse got detached from the work ethic, and religious asceticism gave way to the reign of unbridled hedonism. With the phrase "the disenchantment of the world," Weber tried to capture the radical changes that attended the rise of Western capitalism. By the time of Henry Ford, work itself had become religion, and now for the "modern, cosmopolitan man, culture has replaced both religion and work as a means of self-fulfillment or as a justification—an aesthetic justification—of life" (Bell 1976:156). With the separation of the church and state and the secularization of culture, religion lost its public character and became instead a matter of personal belief and the private affair of each individual. Modernity thus marked a radical break with the past. It is precisely at the point when culture became detached from religion that both religion and culture became the subject matter for social scientific study. In short, culture has become a theoretical problem for the West only because it has already become socially problematic (Milner 1994:4).

Culture has been the master concept of anthropology since its very inception. But within the last hundred years, the sociological study of culture has also come into its own. A basic problem has been the lack of a common definition of "culture." A half-century ago, Kroeber and Kluckhohn ([1952] 1963:149) enumerated almost 300 definitions of culture in their critical review of this most significant concept in cultural anthropology. Radcliffe-Brown (1957) went farther and denied the very possibility of a science of culture, insisting that "you can study culture only as a characteristic of a social system. Therefore, if you are going to have a science, it must be a science of social systems" (p. 106). After noting the bewildering variety of definitions, and Radcliffe-Brown's (1957) lament that "the word culture has undergone a number of degradations which have rendered it unfortunate as a scientific term," Leslie White ([1954] 1968) settled for a nominalistic definition: "*Culture,* like *bug, is a word* that we may use to label a class of phenomena—things and events—in the external world. We may apply this label as we please; its use is determined by ourselves, not by the external world" (pp. 15–16). As against Kroeber and Kluckhohn's conception of culture as "intangible abstractions," White ([1954] 1968) insisted on drawing a distinction between the *conception* of culture and what it stands for: "Culture as the name of a class of things and events in the external world" that are objective and observable, and "the conception of culture [that is] in the mind of the culturologist. Let us not mistake the one for the other" (p. 20). Anthropologists, however, have continued to be exercised by questions such as the following:

> Is culture real or just an abstraction from reality? If real, then what is the nature of this reality, and where does this reality have its locus? If an abstraction, then how can we speak of it as influencing the behavior of individuals? (Kaplan [1965] 1968:20)

130

The long-standing opposition between Culture and Nature in the West was played out in the split between two divergent methodological approaches for studying socio-cultural phenomena. While sociologists have continued to be of one mind that the discipline ought to be "scientific," the question of methodology has divided the practitioners into two camps. On the one side were those such as Auguste Comte who treated man himself as a natural object and believed that the natural scientific method alone was appropriate for the study of social reality. On the other side were sociologists, such as Wilhelm Dilthey (1976) and Max Weber ([1904] 1949), who argued that the subject matter of sociological investigations is not nature but man himself—with his plans and projects, motives and intentions, culture and institutions—and therefore a method other than that of the natural sciences was needed to study and apprehend social reality. The sociological study of culture owes much to the great methodological contribution made by Dilthey through his contrast between the empirical-observational methods of the natural sciences (*Naturwissenschaften*) and the hermeneutic method of understanding of the cultural sciences (*Geisteswissenschaften*). As such, those who took the latter course claimed that "understanding" should be the central category of sociological analysis. They argued, in short, that sociology should be an interpretive science rather than a science in the manner of the natural sciences. Weber's method of subjective understanding (*Verstehen*) and the symbolic interactionists' and the ethnomethodologists' "definition of the situation" focus attention on the crucial importance of understanding meaning structures and the meanings the actors attach to their own actions. The basic problem with this approach has been that having found it well nigh impossible for one reason or another to understand what people do in terms of the meaning they themselves attach to their action or the way they define their own situation, the sociologist has been forced to "impute" a meaning to their action in terms of his or her own model of "rationally" acting subjects or homunculi. This has led to strenuous attempts to vouch for the validity of this operation (see, e.g., Schutz [1953] 1963:342–43).

One of the reasons for the relative neglect of the study of culture by sociologists is the generally accepted division of labor between sociologists and anthropologists, whereby the former have focused their attention on society and the social, and the latter have carved out culture and cultural practices as their special field of interest. Durkheim's ([1895] 1938) insistence that all social facts must be explained by other social facts also kept sociologists focused on the social to the neglect of the individual and cultural. Thus, in trying to explain suicide as a social fact, Durkheim's emphasis fell on explaining differences in suicide rates by other social factors while neglecting the part played by individual meanings, motives, and intentions in explaining why, under the same social conditions, certain individuals end up committing suicide while others do not. Since culture is above all symbolic, the positivist strain in sociology that abjured any concern with consciousness and meaning also militated against the study of culture. And functionalists such as Talcott Parsons (1951) looked at culture primarily as a source of norms and values that regulated society and kept it together and helped it adapt to the challenges and contingencies of the environment. Their focus on consensus and equilibrium made the functionalists neglect sociocultural contradictions and conflicts that mark the other face of society.

Finally, and no less important, the study of culture also got a short shrift from Marxist sociologists who were wedded to Marx's base/superstructure dichotomy that relegated all things cultural and subjective to the superstructural aspects of society. Whereas his study of religion and charisma had led Max Weber to emphasize the role of ideas and the individual in history, Marx subordinated both to the primary role played by productive forces and production relations within each historical period. As a dialectical materialist, Marx borrowed the dialectical method from Hegel but claimed that Hegel was wrong in giving primacy to the Spirit over matter. As Marx put it, Hegel was as a result standing on his head, and it was he (Marx) who put him back on his feet. Objective factors determine subjective ones, for, as Marx ([1904] 1959) declares in the oft-quoted passage from his *A Contribution to the Critique of Political Economy,* "It is not the consciousness of men that determines their existence, but, on the contrary, their social existence determines their consciousness" (p. 43). Marx thus asserts the primacy of the objective, material factors over ideas, consciousness, culture, and institutions, which are all treated by him as part of the superstructure. Culture here is reduced to economic factors and is again denied an independent role in Marxian theory. Much controversy still surrounds the exact nature of the relationship between the base and the superstructure: Does the base "determine" the superstructure, or is the superstructure a mere reflection of the base? In either case, does the superstructure react back on the base at all? The overall result has been that in Marxian theory, cultural factors have seldom been given their due or treated as central variables in their own right but have been included among other variables to round out or further specify the relationships being examined.

THE CLASSICAL HERITAGE

Western sociology was born with the recognition that Christianity no longer provided the basis for an ordered social existence. Given his conviction that "ideas rule the world or throw it into chaos," Auguste Comte, the father of sociology, wanted the discipline to come up with the new first principles (scientific laws) of social order by applying the method of the natural sciences to the study of society. Realizing that a society is essentially held together by religion, both Comte and Durkheim put forward this new discipline of sociology as the new "religion of humanity."

Although Durkheim was deeply troubled by the destructive consequences of modernity, he was much more sanguine than Weber about the future of modern society. Durkheim ([1915] 1965) saw religion as an indispensable integrative force, but, like Comte, was convinced that the old religion will not do, that the future society needed a new "scientific" religion. He therefore set about to establish the synonymy of God and society, with God being nothing but society transfigured and expressed as a symbol. He harbored the conviction that once men had become sociologically sophisticated, they would transfer their allegiance from God to society and would hold society itself in awe and reverence.

Contra Marx, Weber recognized the autonomy and efficacy of religious ideas and the role of charismatic individuals in history. But capitalism, he said, had come into its own with the death of the religious impulse that had brought it into being and fueled its growth. And a secularized modernity for Weber spelled the death of true charisma, the very principle of creativity and rejuvenation that strikes roots and thrives in the religious soil of a traditional society. Weber saw the unending, universal process of rationalization as ultimately destructive both of society and the individual. The future of capitalism appeared to him bleak indeed—an "iron cage" in which the individual had been reduced to a mere cog in the bureaucratic machine. But while Weber had earlier placed great emphasis on the role of ideas in history, the reality of the First World War made him recognize the crucial role played by material factors in the success of ideas:

> Not ideas, but material and ideal interests directly govern man's conduct. Yet very frequently the "world images" which have been created by "ideas" have, like switchmen, determined the tracks along which action has been pushed by the dynamic of interests. (Weber 1958:280)

Durkheim ([1915] 1965) had rightly understood that the real characteristic of religious phenomena lay in the division of the whole universe into the sacred and the profane. Religion was to him a unified system of beliefs and practices, wherein religious beliefs expressed the nature of sacred things. He defined the sacred as those things that are set apart and held in awe and reverence. He argued that since these beliefs and practices are unanimously shared by group members, they must be of social origin. And in keeping with his insistence on the autonomy and specificity of religious symbols, he went on to affirm the utmost importance of keeping the profane distinct and distant from the sacred, "Unless the profane [were] to lose its specific characteristics and become sacred after a fashion and to a certain degree itself." And, given the "aptitude of society for setting itself up as a god or for creating gods," Durkheim ([1915] 1965) notes that right at the beginning of the French Revolution, secular things, "things purely laical by nature were transformed by public opinion into sacred things: these were the Fatherland, Liberty, Reason" (pp. 244–45). Durkheim

([1915] 1965) thought that the reason why such ideas and ideals are not able to create the same ardor in us is not because they are profane symbols that have become, as he put it, "sacred after a fashion and to a certain degree," but "because we are passing through a stage of transition and moral mediocrity" (p. 475). Weber had talked about modernization in terms of the separation of value spheres and the irreversible march of rationalization. But while Weber was full of apprehension about the future, Durkheim ([1915] 1965) was certain that "this state of incertitude and confused agitation cannot last for ever," for "there are no gospels which are immortal, but neither is there any reason for believing that humanity is incapable of *inventing* [italics added] new ones" (p. 475). In all this, sociology was to play a pivotal role as the new science of society.

THE STRUCTURALIST TURN IN THE STUDY OF CULTURE

The structuralist turn in the study of culture owes much to the work of Claude Lévi-Strauss (1966). Drawing on the insights of Durkheim's later work regarding the moral and symbolic ordering of society and de Saussure's (1960) semiotic linguistics, Lévi-Strauss treats society like a language that has an "underlying grammar"—the "grammar of mythology which has its foundation in the universal nature of the human mind itself" (Walsh 1998:287). Myths represent collective problem-solving strategies, and one can decipher their meaning by "looking beyond their manifest content to the structures of symbolic opposition and sequence that organize these various narratives" (Norris 1991:37). The structuralist aim is to go beneath the surface differences among cultures to lay bare their common but deep underlying patterns that constitute their structure. As Tudor (1999) points out,

> At its simplest, this [method] involves taking diverse myths, breaking them into their constituent units . . . and trying to show how their combinations and permutations, their inversions and transformations, can be understood [following de Saussure] in terms of fundamental binary oppositions such as those between Life and Death, Nature and Culture, Raw and Cooked. [In this account] both the social and the individual recede in the background [and] it is difficult to say anything about the social role of cultural forms except at the most general level. (P. 69)

And since rules and symbols are viewed as arbitrary by the structuralists, meaning in culture as in language becomes a matter of difference, with the cultural system now seen as having "the potential to realize an infinite range of realities" (Jenks 2005:196).

Jacques Derrida (1974), on the other hand, denies that language ever settles into a stable order of meaning. His methodology of deconstruction is "avowedly 'post-structuralist'" because it rejects the structuralist view of "the text as a bearer of stable . . . meanings and the critic as a faithful seeker after truth in the text" and denies that "the idea of structure [is] in any sense given or [is] objectively there in a text" (Norris 1991:3). Paul de Man (1979), on the other hand, has drawn attention to the dilemma faced by the interpreter engaged in deconstruction. As Norris points out, de Man shows that Derrida's "reading must open up an endless series of further deconstructions, each latching on to those rhetorical aspects that can never be expunged in its own performance." And the only way to get out of this "dizzying regress," then, is to exercise "a figural will power beyond reach of deconstruction" (p. 106).

As a Marxist, Althusser (1971) gives structuralism a materialistic turn. Going beyond a simple base/superstructure model, he attempts to show how through its dominant culture, the capitalist state and its ideological apparatus mold and channel individual consciousness and effort in the service of the system (Walsh 1998:287–88). It is then left to Gramsci (1971) to reaffirm the role of consciousness, culture, and human agency in explaining how capitalism maintains its status quo through its hegemonic culture. As a result,

> Revolution can begin only by the proletariat challenging the dominant cultural apparatus to form a consciousness of its own in relation to its conditions within the capitalist system . . . Culture is [therefore] an arena of critique and struggle for Gramsci and not just a structural, collective and unconscious determinant of subjectivity. (Walsh 1998:288–89)

THE SEMIOTIC TURN IN MARXIST THEORIZING

Twentieth-century attempts to salvage Marxism have not only turned Marx on his head, they have driven his ideas toward sheer irrelevancy. In trying to save what was essentially Marxist in Marx, these efforts have only succeeded in paving the way for destroying the whole edifice of Marxian theory. Declaring that "Marx is being turned on his head," Albert Bergesen (1993) coined the term *Semiotic Marxism* to not only highlight the fateful reversal of the Marxist base/superstructure logic but to document how the logic of the cultural and ideological superstructure itself has now come to constitute the logic of the whole social formation. Bergesen's own description of the four stages in this semiotic transformation of Marxism may be summarized as follows:

1. In the first stage, Gramsci inverts the base/superstructure logic by transforming class rule into rule by the consent of the governed. Class relations now are no longer derived from the ownership of the means of production but from the control of the state apparatus. As a result, the functions of the hegemonic state "become coterminous with the cultural functions of civil society—legitimizing,

socializing, in maintaining moral order," and the class struggle itself becomes an ideological struggle for the control "over the structure of consciousness [as] the prerequisite for control over the structure of production" (Bergesen 1993:2–3).

2. In Althusser's (see Althusser and Balibar 1970) theory of the "Ideological State Apparatus," the ideological and the political merge and go on to absorb the logic of the economic in Stage 2. Bergesen uncovers a basic similarity between the logic of the ideological state apparatus (ISA) and de Saussure's logic of language, whereby the "structural logic of language becomes the Althusserian logic of ideology" so that "to produce a 'worker, a boss' is to reproduce the social relations of production which now implicitly suggests the economic sphere is reproduced by the ISA, that is by the superstructure." Bergesen (1993) goes on to show that "this logic of semiotic systems is implicitly applied [by Althusser] to social formations, and social class relations are now treated as relations between semiotic signs" (p. 5).

3. In the third stage, the now fused ideological/political superstructure is merged with the economic base in the work of Nicos Poulantzas (1973, 1974, 1978), and all three spheres are said to codetermine each other. As a result, "the tri-partite division of society into economic, political, and ideological spheres, is now reduced to three interdependent branches of the [capitalist] state apparatus: the Ideological State Apparatus, the Repressive State Apparatus, and now the Economic State Apparatus" (Bergesen 1993:6).

4. In the last stage, the "final unhinging of the sociological logic of Marxism" is accomplished by Laclau and Mouffe (Laclau 1988; Laclau and Mouffe 1985; Mouffe 1979, 1988) by renaming the Marxian social formation as the "discursive formation," thus "reflecting the now explicit semiotic assumption that the substance of collective existence is 'discourse,' not social relations." The Marxian base/superstructure logic is then "not only inverted (by Gramsci, Althusser, and Poulantzas) but now completely dissolved as all economic, political, and ideological elements float in the weightless void that is the discursive formation." With all social relations dissolved into discursive relations, the post-Saussurian logic of signs formally becomes the new Marxian logic of classes (Bergesen 1993:8).

Bergesen (1993) interprets these developments as heralding the "complete triumph of the semiotic over the material" and the disappearance of all causation. The result is a "purely semiotic Marxism, where there is no difference between what one thinks of reality and reality itself." What this Semiotic Marxism completely disregards, though, is that in real life "we are no longer dealing with just signifiers and symbols, but with classes, groups, parties, organizations and institutions" (p. 10).

THE CULTURAL TURN IN SOCIOLOGY

The problematic of a sociological study of culture derives from the very crisis of the social sciences, occasioned by the mounting critique and a failure of nerve regarding the Western "enlightenment project"—which promised peace, prosperity, progress, and the perfectibility of the individual—as well as the failure of Auguste Comte's positivistic sociology to provide adequate explanations, much less uncover the "scientific" laws of society and social living. As a result, the "epistemological, disciplinary, political, and even moral foundations of the social sciences are [now] very much at issue" (Bonnell and Hunt 1999:1). This critical state of affairs has brought about a marked shift in emphasis from the social to the cultural in the social sciences and has resulted in a "cultural turn," which has taken us back to the interpretive/hermeneutical tradition of a Wilhelm Dilthey, Max Weber, or Alfred Schultz.

The history and the future direction of the cultural turn in the social sciences have been addressed in a series of essays included in the volume titled *Beyond the Cultural Turn: New Directions in the Study of Society and Culture* (Bonnell and Hunt 1999), a central text in the new and emerging fields of cultural sociology and cultural history. The book was to be a part of a series of related publications that defined the concept of culture "in the broadest sense to encompass the study of mentalities, ideology, symbols and rituals, and high and popular culture" (Bonnell and Hunt 1999:ix). The cultural turn thus marked the ascendance of "culture" to a preeminent position, both as a central focus of academic interest and as an explanatory variable in its own right. Briefly, the intention behind the cultural turn, as expressed by Bonnell and Hunt (1999:1–27), was as follows:

1. To insist that culture was not just an appendage of the social structure or merely a reflection of more basic socioeconomic processes (such as industrialization or modernization) but that it made an independent contribution of its own to the sociohistorical process, and as a result, the "social" lost some of its privileged explanatory potential

2. To recognize that the natural scientific approach was inadequate, even inapplicable to the study of culture and society and therefore to abandon the quest for positivistic explanations and objective laws in favor of interpretive understanding and the hermeneutic search for meaning; culture should be viewed as linguistic and representational.

3. To acknowledge the bankruptcy of all metanarratives or master paradigms and to insist that there is no exclusive methodology or preferred paradigms for studying cultural phenomena

4. To acknowledge the dissolution of disciplinary boundaries and recognize that the study of culture would have to draw from diverse disciplines and be truly interdisciplinary in nature

5. To recognize that under present realities, the scope of such studies would have to range from the local to the global

Bonnell and Hunt (1999:8) divide the historical period leading to the cultural turn broadly into three periods:

1. *The 1950s and 1960s:* The 1950s were marked by the "semiotic revolution" ushered in by the structuralism of Claude Lévi-Strauss, "which traced all meaning to the functioning of signs or symbols" and insisted that "culture itself could be analyzed much like a language, and all behavior got its meaning from often unconscious or implicit structural codes embedded in it." The turbulent 1960s, however, ended up placing both agency and history back again at the center of the intellectual agenda.

2. *The 1970s:* Hayden White's (1973) argument that all historical texts are basically constructed by the author as a "poetic act" and Clifford Geertz's (1973) conception of culture as text to be studied by the semiotic approach are singled out by Bonnell and Hunt as having had a radical impact on both theory and method in the social sciences. Roland Barthes, Pierre Bordieu, Jacques Derrida, Marshall Sahlins, Raymond Williams, and Michel Foucault are mentioned as the other theorists who made a deep impact during the 1970s on how culture was to be approached and studied.

3. *The 1980s and 1990s:* The postmodernists and the poststructuralists, who dominated the field during this period, reduced all scientific explanations to "simply an exercise in collective fictionalization or mythmaking," and undermined any remaining faith in objectivity and objective truth.

Geertz's (1973) work has inspired an outpouring of interest in ethnographic field work after the cultural turn. His injunction that the anthropologist should "strain to read" culture as an "ensemble of texts" "over the shoulders of those to whom they properly belong" (p. 452), however, points to the serious methodological and epistemological dilemmas created by the cultural turn itself:

If analysis of culture, as Geertz insisted, depended on the interpretation of meaning rather than a scientific discovery of social explanations, then what served as the standard for judging interpretations? If culture or language permeated meaning, then how could any individual or social agency be identified? . . . Could "culture" be regarded as a causal variable and did it operate independently of other factors, including the social or institutional? [In short,] the cultural turn threatened to efface all references to social context or causes and offered no particular standard of judgment to replace the seemingly more rigorous and systematic approaches that had predominated during the 1960s and 1970s. (Bonnell and Hunt 1999:9)

However, it appears that the sociologists who have been influenced by the cultural turn have been unwilling "to accept the obliteration of the social implied by the most radical forms of culturalism or postculturalism" (Bonnell and Hunt 1999:11).

But this is hardly the end of the story, for as Dirks (1996) emphasizes, "the debate continues [with] textuality . . . seen less as a metaphor inviting a new range of critical interpretive practices than an invitation to nihilism and relativism. . . . If historical reality is a text, then it can neither be important nor real" (p. 33). In a section titled the "Perils of the Text," Ian Davies records that

> the temptation, always, even in pre-Marxian days, was to find salvation in the text. But what text? . . . Much of the debate was around the status of "text" in the analysis, its relation to the context of both production and consumption, and to the analysis of audience. (Davies 1995:120, 122)

And by focusing "on anthropological texts as literary creations, fictions which present themselves as facts but which have no priority to that claim over other potential orderings of the world" (Linstead 1993:108), postmodern ethnography presents the frightening prospect that "we may be developing a semiotic ethnography [where] there are no texts, no audiences. There is only an instance of the process of making and circulating meanings and pleasures" (Fiske 1988:250, quoted in Davies 1995:123). The postmodernist and poststructuralist critique has thus been so thoroughgoing that it is highly unlikely that social sciences will again find a secure foothold. Bonnell and Hunt (1999) have summed up the predicament as follows:

> The cultural turn and a more general postmodern critique of knowledge have contributed, perhaps decisively, to the enfeebling of paradigms for social scientific research. . . . The failure of Marxism has signaled a more general failure of all paradigms. Are the social sciences becoming a branch of a more general interpretive, even literary activity—just another cultural study with claims only for individual authorial virtuosity rather than for a more generally valid shared knowledge? (P. 4)

Among sociologists engaged in the study of culture, the work of Jeffrey Alexander invites close attention. His call for a *cultural sociology,* which he defines as the study of cultural structures, is framed within the context of "the linguistic turn in philosophy, the rediscovery of hermeneutics, the structuralist revolution in the human sciences, the symbolic revolution in anthropology, and the cultural turn in American historiography" (Alexander 2003:6). The distinction between the analytical (or heuristic) autonomy of culture and its concrete (or empirical) autonomy is maintained in this approach. So is the distinction between reality and appearance, for cultural sociology is given the task of bringing "the unconscious cultural structures that regulate society into the light of the mind." Cultural sociology thus attempts to bring the social unconscious for view to "reveal to men

and women the myths that think them *so that they can make new myths in turn* [italics added]" (Alexander 2003:4).

Between tradition and modernity, the choice for Alexander is clear. He places himself squarely on the side of the latter and invokes the social constructivist notion of "man, the myth-maker" to underwrite the task assigned modern men of making new myths. That is a worthy goal indeed but leaves as many questions unanswered: What myths? Whose myths? Would any do? Any how, in keeping with the self-defined vocation of sociologists as the new "myth-makers" (see Greer 1969), Alexander's (2003) own work is rooted in "pragmatic, broadly normative interests" (p. 6), admittedly to serve the interests of a capitalist democracy and to defend modernity against those conservative "friends of culture [who] have betrayed a nostalgia for the organicism and solidity of traditional life" (p. 9). A similar commitment, we are told, leads him to bracket the reality claims of other intellectual groups as well as to relativize the reality claims of intellectual-cum-political authority (p. 7).

To establish continuity between the past and the present, Alexander (2003) wants to establish how the new discipline of cultural sociology can help bridge the gap left open between religion and social structure in the work of Weber and Durkheim. He pursues this goal in a series of essays on topics such as cultural trauma and collective identity, a cultural sociology of evil, the discourse of American civil society, and Watergate as a democratic ritual. He tries to accomplish his goal by extending Durkheim's ideas on primitive religion to demonstrate how "the love of the sacred, the fear of pollution, and the need for purification have continued to mark modern as much as traditional life" (pp. 7–8). And, contra Weber, he points out how "faith was relevant [not] only to the creation of modernity, [but also] to the project of its ongoing institutionalization," and "how practical meanings continue to be structured by the search for salvation," with "fantasies and myths [continuing to] inspire giant efforts at practical transformation" (p. 8). These "giant efforts at practical transformation" and the unceasing global attempt to remake the world and to recast it in the modern Western image have historically been part and parcel of the self-defined telos and destiny of the modern man.

What mattered to Durkheim, as a classical functionalist, was the integrative function performed by the various beliefs and practices, regardless of the truth of their content. On this reckoning, though, any beliefs and any practices would do, for, as he put it, "The only thing necessary for a society to be coherent is that its members have their eyes fixed on the same goal, concur in the same faith" (see Farganis 2004:84). Since religious forces for him were human forces, he was quick to note how modern society has come up with its supporting myths, symbols, rituals, and rites. And it did not take long for later sociologists, such as Robert Bellah (1970), to declare "civic religion" as the functional equivalent of traditional religious beliefs:

> On this view, the Constitution, the Bill of Rights, and our democratic institutions affirming human rights represent the

fundamental moral consensus of society. The national anthem, the flag, and the national holidays are contemporary symbols and common rituals of unity in the presence of diversity and differentiation. (Farganis 2004:58)

By the 1980s, however, Bellah noted that this consensus seemed to have all but evaporated as aggressive individualism took off on its own in the age of greed, greatly weakening the sense of community and the civic society and creating a critical "crisis of meaning." As Seidman points out, "in the aftermath of the enfeeblement of the American civil religion and the failure of the new religions to move beyond sectarianism," Robert Bellah turned "cynical toward his earlier argument that national civil religions might function as socially cohering symbolic configurations" (Bellah 1975; Bellah et al. 1985; Seidman 1990:222). Recognizing the contingent character of intention and interpretation, Alexander and Smith (1993) attempt to bypass the problem of consensus by focusing instead on commonly shared cultural codes that allow people to "speak a language."

It is the essence of a symbol, which is not merely a sign, that behind the representation there always stands the represented. But for Robert Wuthnow (1987), it is the form that determines content. Since what is of importance to him is the relationship between symbols, and not what the symbols themselves represent, he would not hesitate to disregard the content of these symbols as long as they do their job of maintaining moral boundaries (see Rose 1999:221–22). The alleged continuity between tradition and modernity, between the past and the present, posited by Alexander is based also on the same conviction that whatever serves or could serve the function of religion is religion. Expressing her strong opposition to the functionalizing of all concepts and ideas by social scientists and disparaging the widespread tendency to regard communism, for instance, as a "new religion"—"notwithstanding its avowed atheism, because it fulfills . . . the same function traditional religion fulfilled and still fulfills in the free world"—Hannah Arendt ([1954] 1968) declares that

> their concern is only with functions, and whatever fulfills the same function can, according to this view, be called the same. It is as though I had the right to call the heel of my shoe a hammer because I, like most women, use it to drive nails into the wall. (P. 102)

Furthermore, she points to the bankruptcy of such an argument, for

> if it is only a question of function and how a thing works, the adherents of "false religion" can make as good a case for using theirs as I can for using my heel, which doesn't work so badly either. (P. 102)

Her stricture about all these so-called functional equivalents is well taken. She is also convinced that the break between the past and the present, between tradition and modernity, is final and not subject to debate and that none of the modern revolutionary attempts, or sustained efforts to substitute the thread of historical continuity for tradition, have been successful in bridging this gap (p. 19). Gallagher (1979) and other modernization theorists also support this notion by holding that modernity and its basic tenets (pragmatism, relativism, high mobility, etc.) are "diametrically opposed to the basic tenets and world views of all traditional societies, no matter how much the latter may differ among themselves" (p. 10).

As against sociologists who posit a radical, dichotomous break between the present and the past, Alexander (2003) rejects the contention that "only in simple, religiously ordered, undemocratic, or old-fashioned societies do myths, and narratives and codes play a fundamental role." Still asserting that there is "continuity between the religion of early societies and the cultural life of later more complex ones," he makes a series of continuity assumptions between the postmodern and modern, and between modern and traditional societies (pp. 5–9). As "the tradition of the new," modernity for others, however, implies a clear break with the past. As Daniel Bell (1976) has pointed out, "The old concept of culture is based on continuity, the modern on variety; the old values tradition, the contemporary ideal is syncretism" (p. 100).

Modern thinkers seek in vain to find a principle of continuity and coherence that would provide meaning to life and its pursuits in a fragmented culture that has lost its traditional legitimacy. Sewell (1999:52) would like to view culture in terms of a dialectic between system and practice, a move he believes would help counter the attempt to treat culture as a coherent, self-enclosed system. But unwilling to give up on all sense of coherence, he prefers to opt for a thin coherence that is "as much the product of power and struggles for power as it is of semiotic logic" (p. 57). Such an approach, of course, makes sense within the context of modern and modernizing societies in which coherence is always problematic and a difficult, unstable, even rare achievement. Alexander (2003) comes up with another major difference between the past and the present: "In our postmodern world, factual statements and fictional narratives are densely interwoven. The binaries of symbolic codes and true/false statements are implanted one on the other" (p. 5). In fact, the very distinction between truth and fiction is obliterated in the modern/postmodern world when simulations are consciously used to mask, subvert, and replace the real (see Baudrillard [1981] 1994).

In her take on the cultural turn, Sonya Rose (1999) has provided an insightful critique of Jeffrey Alexander's ideas pertaining to continuities in the vocabularies of moral discourse. In addition to questioning the assumed continuity between the past and the present, she also deals with the question of the presumed autonomy of culture. Rose points out that while Jeffrey Alexander and Phillip Smith (1993), for example, argue that the continuity in the "discourse of civic society" is ensured by the "underlying consensus as to the key symbolic patterns of American civil society," they fail to indicate how the underlying consensus was created in the first place: "The idea that this structure is historically durable because it enjoyed such widespread consensus is neither directly demonstrated empirically nor explained theoretically" (Rose 1999:225). Rose (1999) also draws attention to the circular nature of their argument regarding durability or continuity:

> Their formulation, while appealing because it seems to suggest that particular cultural forms endure because they are deep, in the end relies on circular reasoning. If a cultural form or practice endures, it is deep. It is deep because it is part of common sense and it is pervasive. It is part of common sense and pervasive because it is structured in a particular way. But if all cultural forms are structured by antinomies, why are some durable and others not? (P. 226)

These concerns prompt her to reject "a formal analysis that theorizes cultural processes as fully autonomous from patterned social relations and practices, a theoretical position that . . . places cultural forms outside of history" (Rose 1999:233–34).

The most pertinent question these concerns raise is related directly to the study of culture. While Alexander (2003) believes that understanding cultures demands the understanding of "the true power and persistence of violence, domination, exclusion, and degradation," he is also convinced that "we can separate knowledge from power and not become only a servant to it" because cultural sociology tells us that "reflection and criticism are imbedded in myths that human beings cannot be entirely reflective and critical about" (pp. 7, 9). Rose (1999), on the other hand, raises the related but most basic question of "how . . . a particular discourse becomes dominant—and how are meanings fixed, however temporarily? How is it possible for discourses to produce systematic effects?" (p. 230). She endorses Laclau and Mouffe's (1985) argument that at the back of a discourse lay the attempt "to dominate the field of discursivity, to arrest the flow of difference, to construct a center" (p. 112). These considerations lead her to conclude that

> moral discourses specify a single standard of virtue, while denigrating or marginalizing alternative practices. . . . Morality, in other words, is elaborated in a struggle over symbolic power, which is ultimately the power to define social categories and groups and to establish as legitimate a particular vision of the social world. (Rose 1999:230)

There is therefore a persistent danger that "knowledge" in the service of "pragmatic" interests may merely be "power in disguise: the power to impose one's beliefs and, ultimately, one's values on others who do not share them and are thereby both marginalized and dominated by this imposition of a particular view of the world" (Martin 1992:418, quoted in Schwartz 2000:111). To paraphrase Dirks (1996), one should say that cultural analysis is not just a game; it has real stakes and real effects (p. 36).

THE PRACTICE TURN IN THE STUDY OF CULTURE

The term *practice* has come to acquire a privileged position in the discourse on culture. Briefly stated, two central ideas undergird practice theory: (1) "that the forms of human activity depend on the practices in which people participate" and (2) that not individuals, but "practices are the source and carrier of meaning, language, and normativity," which opens them up "to determination by the social factors that affect practices, for example, power and politics" (Schatzki et al. 2001:11–12). In his introduction to *The Practice Turn in Contemporary Theory,* Theodore Schatzki specifies the threefold thrust of practice theory as the attempt to "free activity from the determining grasp of objectified social structures and systems, to question individual actions and their status as the building block of social phenomena, and to transcend the rigid action-structure oppositions" (Schatzki, Cetina, and von Savigny 2001:1).

While "action" has been recognized as a central category, and even a basic unit of analysis by most sociologists, the problem of understanding "action" has proved intractable from the beginning. Sociologists have tried to handle the problem by attempting (a) to substitute "imputed meanings" for the subjective meanings of the actor, and to judge his/her actions against the model of a "rational actor" (Weber); (b) to use the rational "means-ends" schema to understand action, thereby reducing action to work or labor (Parsons); (c) to use the sociologist's own rational puppets (or homunculi) to interpret action (Schutz); (d) to understand action in terms of taken-for-granted activities, thereby reducing action to routine practices (the ethnomethodologists); and, finally, (e) to bracket the actor's intentions, meanings, hopes, fears, and so on and replace action with conditioned responses or with automatic, unconscious routine behaviors/practices (behaviorists; the practice theorists).

In her contribution to the volume on the practice turn in contemporary theory, Ann Swidler (2001) tries to figure out what it is that anchors cultural practices. The focus of attention in practice theory is on the "unconscious," "automatic," and "un-thought" practices embedded in taken-for-granted routines. As a result,

> Practice theory moves the level of sociological attention "down" from conscious ideas and values to the physical and the habitual. But this move is complemented by a move "up," from ideas located in individual consciousness to the impersonal arena of "discourse." (Swidler 2001:75)

Swidler (2001) notes Stephen Turner's (1994) serious concern about the notion of practices being silent and hidden but rejects his focus on "habit" as too individualistic. She also finds the individualistic imagery underlying Bourdieu's (1977) concept of "habitus" and Sewell's (1992) concept of "cultural schemas" as less appealing. She finally comes to the conclusion that "it is the practice itself that anchors, and in some sense reproduces, the constitutive rule it embodies" (pp. 82–83). However, this focus on culture as practices in interaction, which she says is quite in line with "Lévi-Strauss's notion that animals are good to think with" (Swidler 2001:75), reduces human action to behavior and the human actor to an automaton or an unthinking animal. Contra Parsons or Weber, she insists that culture is not the result of "some abstract stuff in people's heads":

> Rather, cultural practices *are* action, action organized according to some more or less visible logic, which the analyst need only describe . . . [I]f one studies "practices," whether linguistic or not, one is already studying behavior and the problem of the causal connection between one form of behavior and another is at least staved off, if not resolved. (Swidler 2001:76)

In addition to conflating action and behavior, Swidler (2001) also admits that even after bracketing the individual actor and his actions and disregarding the content of what he or she says or has to say, the practice theorist still cannot entirely escape the subjectivist demand for interpretation. He or she still needs to figure out and make "implicit claims about what the symbols mean to individual actors or group of actors." The only saving grace, then, seems to be that at least the "discourses and practices are concretely observable in a way that meanings, ideas, and values never really were" (p. 76). However, such an exercise may very well conceal the personal and cultural biases of the researcher who now assumes a superior authorial position with regard to his or her subjects. Another problem relates to the fact that the "structure/practice contrast recognizes only one kind of structure—synchronic connections among signs—to the exclusion of structures (and thus ways of making meaning) that are lodged in the processual execution of practice" (Biernacki 1999:74). To make matters worse, a further problem for research and interpretation is raised by the fact that "the same belief can support varied practices [and] the same practice [can] be supported by different beliefs" (Biernacki 1999:75). And if culture is viewed as a symbolic "tool kit" that individuals use for choosing effective strategies of action to cope with the world (Swidler 1986), then it would be pertinent to ask, What determines their differential access to this tool kit? Does its effective use by one group negatively affect its use by other groups? And would the academic users of this kit be as eager to see their own practices historicized? Historians, for one, we are told, "have bridled at the historicization of their own ground" (McDonald 1996:12; see also Dirks 1996:40–41).

THE GLOBAL TURN IN THE STUDY OF CULTURE

The study of culture took a global turn in the early 1980s when the term *cultural globalization* replaced the term *cultural imperialism* that had gained special currency during the 1970s (Elteren 2003:170–71). As a result, the new metanarrative of globalism came to replace the earlier imperial and colonial metanarratives (Filmer 1998:242). At the same time that the worldwide commodification of the postmodernist cultures of consumption threatens to absorb the cultural into the economic, globalization also furthers a culture of performance and expressive individualism at home that "fits into a more general shift of emphasis from narrative to performance as the primary source of meaning and gratification in contemporary Western culture. [As a result,] McWorld threatens local democracy and, more generally, civil society" (Elteren 2003:180).

In addition to the critical problem of the very survival of local traditional cultures, Gayatri Chakravorty-Spivak's ([1985] 1988) "Can the Subaltern Speak?" identifies representation as the central problematic of global culture. An Eurocentric discourse on the "Other" raises serious concerns of its own, and what is true of the discourse on history is equally true of the discourse on culture:

> Insofar as the academic discourse of history . . . is concerned, "Europe" remains the sovereign theoretical subject of all histories, including the ones we call "Indian," "Chinese," "Kenyan," and so on. There is a peculiar way in which all these other histories tend to become variations on a master narrative that could be called "the history of Europe." In this sense, "Indian" history itself is in a position of subalternity: one can only articulate subaltern subject positions in the name of this history. (Chakrabarty 1992:1, quoted in Davies 1995:98)

Davies (1995) adds that

> One reason for all this is that historians, by and large, write for other historians and that the dominant historical institutions, associations, and research resources are in the West. Thus history from below, even though it uncovers a layer of experience that was formerly absent in historical research, creates an appropriation of its subject-matter that makes "representation" essentially tokenish. . . . In the end, the issue of representation is related directly to the question of who is being represented by who to whom, and under what auspices." (Pp. 98, 105)

Rather than effecting a separation of knowledge and power, this last sentence again places knowledge cultures squarely within an all-encompassing logic of power (see Foucault 1980).

Commenting on E. P. Thompson's (1963) focus on conflict and difference and his attempt to rescue the marginalized and the bypassed from "the enormous condescension of posterity," Davies feels, "It was, perhaps, more of an appropriation of these people to another cause (Thompson's own) than to fully reveal them as they were." "Was 'history from below,'" Davies (1995) goes on to ask, just "another form of 'Orientalism,' to use Said's ([1978] 1995) language, a grasping for the 'people' to validate one's own culture?" (p. 96). Dirks (1996) points out that "the operations of difference . . . seem always to produce hierarchical relations between 'us' and 'them' (however these categories are constructed) and never exist outside of representation itself" (p. 30).

Modernity and postmodernity have already passed a death sentence on traditional societies and cultures, the wholesale destruction of aboriginal (and all other) spiritual traditions having been a key element of the process of colonization (Kulchyski 1997:622). The fragmentation and destruction of the cultural coherence of traditional societies is well documented in Feierman's (1999) study of the brutal colonial suppression of public healing practices in Africa. To underwrite the inevitability involved in the disappearance of traditional societies and to explain why the world has come to consist of "culturally homogeneous pools" called nation-states, Ernest Gellner invokes the "sociological necessity" of the industrial world having "room only for a limited number of nation states" (Gellner 1979, cited in Gallagher 1979:58). The argument is especially specious when "under conditions of postmodern discourse, sociological theory itself as a discourse on the social necessarily loses all viability" (Camic and Gross 1998:467).

METHODOLOGICAL APPROACHES TO THE SOCIOLOGICAL STUDY OF CULTURE

The major turns during the past several decades have given rise to a diversity of methodological approaches to the study of culture. With its crisis of representation and rejection of metanarratives, the emphasis on self-reflexivity, and the focus on multiple voices in a polysemic world, postmodern ethnography has itself played a leading role in the fragmentation of the field.

In keeping with our emphasis on the developments since the cultural turn of the 1980s, the following discussion is limited to more recent methodological approaches in the field. Vaillancourt (1986), however, provides a good reference for those interested in exploring the various research strategies employed by the Marxists that have general application. These include the qualitative, subjective strategies used by philosophical Marxists; strategies that draw on the resources of dialectical and historical materialism; the strategies employed by the structuralists, with or without Althusser; and, finally, the research done by the materialists. A good introduction to the rational choice theory approach is provided by Coleman and Fararo (1992). Hall and Neitz (1993) identify institutional structures, cultural history, production and distribution of culture, audience effects, and meaning and social action as the major frames around which theoretical and methodological work on culture has been focused. Wuthnow and Witten (1988), on the other hand, identify public moral discourse, science, organizational culture, and ideology as

the main substantive areas that will have an important bearing on the future course of cultural analysis.

The cultural turn in particular has aroused a great deal of interest in the study of cultural beliefs and practices. Mohr (1998) reviews a wide range of techniques and methods, including semantic differential, survey, content analysis, symbolic interactionism, and participant observation, that have been used by the researchers. He also identifies research studies that explore the role of culture in the prediction of status attainment, the study of organizations and their environment, the study of social movements, and the processes of identity formation. A central concern in the study of culture has been the measurement of the underlying structures of meaning attached to symbols and various cultural productions. While a large number of studies have been ethnographic or qualitative in nature, quantitatively oriented scholars have also been turning their attention to researching meaning to deal with the increased interest in bridging the divide between culture and social structure. In an overview of some of the quantitative research being done in this area, Mohr (1998) has focused on studies that have used a structural approach to interpret institutional meanings or have relied on advanced statistical techniques (such as multidimensional scaling and clustering, network analysis, correspondence analysis, Galois lattices, and hierarchical classification models) to facilitate the understanding of complex meaning structures. Tilly's (1997) study of the parliamentarization of British politics is identified as one of the several others that have employed structural methods for measuring meanings. Mohr singles out Karen Cerulo's (1988, 1995) treatment of national anthems (and national flags) as cultural meaning systems to exemplifying the central principles of this type of comparative structural analysis. Mohr also draws attention to Griswold's (1987, 1993) attempt to formulate rigorous empirical approaches that try to bridge the gap between the understanding of meaning contained in literary and other texts and the study of social structure.

Clifford Geertz's work has provided the model for the ethnographic study of discourse and practice "either through micro observation of largely mute and unnoticed practices [or] through 'thick description' of the publicly observable symbolic and ritual practices" (see Swidler 2001:76). Lewandowski (2001), however, is uncertain whether Geertz's reading is "deep" or is merely perspectival/local. Roseberry (1982) has criticized Geertz's approach for its lack of concern with the material and the historical context of cultural performances such as the Balinese cockfights, but by focusing only on the material dimension, Roseberry unfortunately ends up subordinating culture to history (discussed in Dirks 1996:25–28). Sewell (1997) on his own has tried to add a diachronic dimension to Geertz's approach. Since cultures for Lewandowski "are not so much deep texts or manuscripts as contexts in which the social critic and social practices are embedded in various ways," he is very concerned that "Geertz's method of text reading is in his own characterization one way—we only hear from him"

(Lewandowski 2001:12–13). Geertz's (1983) exclusive focus on publicly available symbols and practices rules out any direct concern with the "native's" point of view and raises questions about the validity of his own interpretations. All such attempts to interpret the cultural/religious meanings and practices of "others" through "asymmetrical translations and transcreations of non-Western texts . . . by reframing and re-encoding [indigenous] signs precisely within a Euro-centered imaging of the world" raise disturbing questions regarding "how or what does one compare if categories in the typology of belief, crucial to understanding one side of the symbolic system being juxtaposed, are decisively absent in or irrelevant to the other tradition or system" (Bilimoria 2003:346).

Paula Saukko (2003) has recently taken a fresh look at both the classical and the new methodological approaches to the study of culture. Given the fact that the phenomenological/hermeneutical approach to understanding other people's lived experience is contradicted by the poststructuralist critique of "discourses" that mediate the world of multiple realities and that "cultural studies can no longer know the whole truth, or even claim to approach it" (Clifford 1986:25), Saukko (2003) gives up the old criterion of validity as "truthfulness" and settles instead for the notion of multiple validities to identify "good" or valid research (pp. 11–35). And taking into account Grossberg's (1998) criticism of "cultural-turn" methodologies for neglecting to address material and economic developments and the increased sensitivity to the voice of marginal groups (women, minorities, non-Western people), Saukko recommends combining Marcus's (1998) "multisited ethnography" with Appadurai's (1997) notion of "scapes" as the best strategy for dealing with the contemporary realities of a globalized culture that has breached the boundaries between experience, culture, and reality—or "lived experience," "texts," or "discourses"—and the social/ global context (Saukko 2003:176–96). At the same time, Appadurai's concept of "flows" ("of people, media-images, things, money, etc.") helps her to study social issues and events from different locations and perspectives by combining the two dimensions of multiple locales ("sites") and the different spheres of life (financescape, mediascape, ethnoscape, etc.). To come to grips with the problem of representation, she then counts on Hannah Arendt's (1958) notion of the agonal nature of public/political discourse rather than the Habermasian (1992) notion of rational public discourse to provide the theoretical underpinnings of her multisited/ multiscaped qualitative strategy

that carefully listens to the specificity of individual perspectives both in terms of content ("take" or opinion) and their form (the way in which they relate to the world . . .) while aiming to bring them into conversation with one another . . . not for the sake of difference, but in order to bring . . . into dialogue different research and social points of view. (Saukko 2003:192)

The shift in attention from grand theory to more empirical but qualitatively oriented studies in sociology since the 1980s continues to further the trend toward embracing ethnographical fieldwork as the preferred approach for studying culture. There is also a greater appreciation of the historical or the time dimension and a consequent interest in specifying the diachronic character of cultural change, especially among social historians (see Sewell 1997). In addition to continuing the traditional emphasis on comparative and cross-cultural research, the twenty-first century is likely to witness a concerted drive to further expand disciplinary boundaries and to draw freely from theories and methods being developed in a wide range of disciplines ranging from the social sciences to humanities and literary studies.

FUTURE DIRECTIONS IN THE SOCIOLOGICAL STUDY OF CULTURE

Displacing the nineteenth-century concept of "race" as a way of differentiating people, "culture" proved to be "one of the most useful intellectual tools of the twentieth century," even as the cultural field became "a critical domain of intellectual and of social struggle" (Kulchyski 1997:605). By the late 1980s, culture had already emerged as a "major growth industry" (Wuthnow and Witten 1988:49). The vast intellectual outpouring of interest in the study of culture, especially since the cultural turn of the 1980s, now directs our attention to where it is headed in the twenty-first century.

The cultural studies approach of the Birmingham Centre was one of the first on the scene. Although Marxist in orientation, it moved away from a rigid base/structure dichotomy to focus on its Gramscian concern with conflict over discourses that reflect different power positions. Following Williams' (1981) injunction that culture is always implicated in relationships of dominance and submission, this approach viewed culture as the site where language and the meaning of words and symbols are always in contention. While the central thrust of cultural studies has been the study of popular culture, its focus on the political and race-class-ethnicity-based dynamics of culture (see Hall 1992) made these discourses politically salient, and cultural studies "soon mushroomed to cover diverse interests involving women's studies, gay and lesbian studies, multicultural studies, etc." (Bonnell and Hunt 1999:11).

Reflecting on the wrong turn Marxist and sociological scholarship had taken at the end of the twentieth century, Bergesen (1993) noted with obvious distress that

the theoretical corpus of Marxism has fled the intellectual terrain of social structure (class relations in material production) to be re-invented in the sphere of culture/ideology as the discursive formation with class relations re-theorized as signed subject relations governed by the linguistic logic of symbolic difference [and] that [the earlier] faith in social structure—Marxian, Durkheimian, Weberian—now seems shattered. (P. 11)

He pins his hope on

another surge of paradigmatic theory about the structure of human existence—not theory of the ideas or discourse about structured human life—not semiotics/hermeneutics/meaning analysis/discourse analysis (although for the realm of ideas that is fine)—but theory about the global web of relations that entrap and ensnarl human existence, is hopefully on the horizon. (P. 11)

To bridge the gap between cultural and structural analysis, Anne Kane (1991) has drawn a useful distinction between the analytical and the concrete forms of cultural autonomy. To accomplish this task, Kane (1991) asks that the cultural analyst "must demonstrate that the culture structure he or she has found at the analytic level is the one which the social group truly shares and acts on in the specific historical situation being studied" (p. 55). Apart from the empirical problem of finding a concrete culture structure that a group actually shares *in common* and acts jointly on, the proposal raises again the old problem faced by Alfred Schutz ([1954] 1963:342–45), namely, that of relating the first-order constructs of the culture structure by the group members to the analyst's second-order constructs, however constructed, of the culture structure at the analytical level. She is right though in criticizing Robert Wuthnow (1987) for "giving up 'the problem of meaning' in cultural analysis in order to cure its illness of subjectivity," Ann Swidler (1986) for her culture as a "tool kit" vision that "denies both the logic of cultural systems and the role of a coherent belief system in concrete social action," and Archer (1988) for neglecting meaning and for making culture fully dependent on the social system (Kane 1991:67). Ann Swidler's practice approach does not obviate the need for interpretation and the imputation of meanings by the analyst either. The structuralist and linguistic/semiotic approaches, as Allan (1998) points out, also neglect agency and affect-meaning by making human action and interaction dependent on the structural dynamics of the sign system; postmodernism, on the other hand, not only celebrates the death of the subject but also effects a decisive break between the sign and reality (pp. 8, 10).

Coming from the other direction, Eisenstadt (1989) had expressed his serious reservations about the growing disjunction between the study of culture and the study of social structure and had noted with great concern the increasing marginalization of some of the central areas of sociology of culture (sociology of knowledge, religion, and the arts). He claimed,

The conceptualization of culture, social structure, and personality as "real" ontological entities, the mutually exclusive deterministic approaches, the neglect of the analysis of rules, norms, or of the emergent systemic qualities of social

structure—pointed to the inability of most analyses to address themselves to the central questions of sociological analysis which were . . . opened during this period, particularly the relations between the different constituents of social order, of the ways in which culture is constitutive, as an inherent component of social order and structure (even if it does not constitute it), and, conversely, the degree to which social structure is constitutive of culture. . . . Accordingly, all of these developments were also unable to resolve the classical problem of the order-maintaining as opposed to the order-transforming functions of culture, as well as the related problem of the degree to which social structure determines culture or vice-versa—i.e., the extent of mutual determination of culture, social structure, and social behavior. (P. 9)

Alexander (1990) has rightly emphasized the critical importance of understanding both subjective meanings and structural constraints in the study of culture, but his attempt to distance himself from the traditional *sociology of culture* approach, which has been concerned with "the significant effects of cultural meanings," and to nurture instead the new field of *cultural sociology,* focused on "interpreting" collective meanings, reflects a long-standing rift between the positivist and interpretive approaches within the field of sociology (p. 26). By the late 1980s, however, a major rift had appeared within cultural sociology, between

those who have thought of culture as an implicit or subjective facet of social life [and] those who portray culture in terms of specific kinds of discourse, texts, or other symbolic products. Moreover, competition has arisen between those who regard cultural sociology as more legitimately concerned with the social contexts in which culture is produced and those who wish to focus attention more clearly on the content of these products themselves. It is, in fact, this intellectual competition among contending orientations that promises to animate innovative work in cultural sociology in the immediate future. (Wuthnow and Witten 1988:65)

Somers has used the concept of "knowledge cultures" to document how a metanarrative, such as that of citizenship theory, strives to take on "the role of an epistemological gatekeeper—by defining not only the range of rational argument and worthwhile questions but also the rules of procedure by which those questions can rationally be answered" (Somers 1999:145). The current fixation on "difference" will ensure that cultural analysis, of whatever hue, will continue to focus on the perceived threat or promise of "the other" (Brantlinger 1990:163). However, as the twenty-first century rolls on, all universalizing master narratives will increasingly be called into question as previously submerged voices become assertive and clamor to be heard. And whatever may be the merits of Samuel Huntington's (1996) forebodings about an imminent clash of civilizations, the proper understanding of the knowledge/power nexus (see Foucault 1980) and of the most pressing political and moral struggles being waged around the world acquires a new urgency.

A quarter-century ago, an exhaustive overview of the different approaches to culture had led Peterson (1979:160) to conclude that none of the perspectives he had considered had come up with a convincing paradigm to relate culture and society. The sociological task for the study of culture in the twenty-first century remains the same it has been all along: of how to reconnect culture and social structure and to explore the way they affect one another and human relationships and the human condition, both locally and on the global landscape. In addition to the long-standing ideal/material, macro/micro, structural/conjunctural, quantitative/qualitative divisions, this task will continue to divide those who wish to hold on to the positivist generalizing/empirical mission of the conventional sociology of culture from those who feel called on to pursue in one form or another the new and emerging interpretive/textual approaches of cultural sociology. Unwilling to let go of the first for the second, most sociologists would perhaps find it congenial to carve out a position between the two extremes.

13

THE SOCIOLOGY OF SOCIALIZATION

LEE GARTH VIGILANT

Minnesota State University, Moorhead

JOHN WILLIAMSON

Boston College

Socialization is the most interdisciplinary subfield in the social sciences because of the rich history of arguments across disciplinary lines, discourses between psychology and sociology, sociology and anthropology, and between the social and natural sciences (Clausen 1968; Goslin 1969; Watson 1924). The idea that environmental forces are responsible for human behavior was in direct opposition to the view that instinctual and hereditary factors were largely in charge. This debate came to prominence in the mid-1800s beginning with Darwin's natural selection and adaptation discoveries ([1872] 1966) and has continued over the last century with varying degrees of intensity.

By 1900, the *nature* (*hereditary*) versus *nurture* (*environment*) argument concerning whether biological and instinctual forces were overriding social and environmental ones in determining human behavior was at its most intense. Moreover, the emerging discipline and social movement of eugenics in the Americas, which was a natural extension of the idea that hereditary forces were more important than social ones in human development, did much to demarcate the two approaches (see Stepan 1991). In fact, it was the father of eugenics himself, Francis Galton, who noted in the introduction of his book that hereditary factors were overriding all other social factors, and that it was possible to improve the race by the "careful selection" of traits that were more desirable than others (Galton [1869] 1972, quoted in Stepan 1991). Eugenists

and hereditarians were utterly convinced that no amount of intellectual training, moral development, or resocialization would ever have an intervening impact over the predetermining genetic ones. "No degenerate or feebleminded stock," said Karl Pearson, Francis Galton Professor at University College, London University, "will ever be converted into healthy and sound stock by the accumulated effects of education, good laws, and sanitary surroundings. We have placed our money on environment when heredity wins by a canter" (quoted in Stepan 1991:28).

Debates between social scientists who were aligned with the *interactionist approach* and evolutionary biologists and other "social" scientists who were in the *hereditarian camp* (Thomas 1999) were passionate and raging (see Bernard 1924; Lombroso 1911; Watson 1924). In fact, each discipline within the social sciences brought its own insights on how individuals develop a sense of self and how they internalized the norms and values of society apart from hereditary influences.

For anthropology, socialization was "seen as enculturation or intergenerational transmission," for psychology it was "the acquisition of impulse control," and lastly, for sociology, socialization was conceptualized as "role training or training for social participation" (LeVine 1969:505). These disciplines brought unique theories to the problem of the individual's personal and social development along the life course while emphasizing dissimilar pathologies to explain failed socializations. Anthropology's main contribution was to conceptualize the child as tabula rasa repository of cultural values. Children came into the world with clean slates, and society wrote the cultural script onto their blank pages; they were, at least initially, passive receptors of cultural values, norms, and mores. Moreover, anthropology was one of the first social sciences to challenge the received view of biological determinism that posited genetic or instinctual causes for human actions and social pathologies (see Bernard 1924; Lombroso 1911; Wilson 1975; Wilson and Herrnstein 1985). Its emphasis on cultural transmissions between parent and child and between culture and the individual were the basis of its understanding of socialization (see Mead 1930).

In psychology, socialization analysis centered on the development of the personality system in individuals, and here, the psychoanalytic theories of Sigmund Freud (1923, 1946) had pervasive influence. One of the central ideas of Freudian psychoanalytic theory of socialization is that inborn instinctual drives are controlling our behaviors, influencing our choices, and affecting our interpersonal interactions. However, these instinctual drives often come into conflict with rules, mores, and norms imposed on us initially by our parents, then our culture, and other socializing agents. The individual, and his or her personality system, is in a constant struggle to balance the inborn instinctual drives for *eros,* defined by Freud as the insatiable desire for, and pursuit of, pleasure, with the demands of society for discipline, order, and moral stability, which are naturally anathema to the pleasure principle. The child quickly learns to restrain his or her demands for pleasure in acquiescing to society's norms and mores. As such, Freud reasoned that the personality system that adults have is the sum of socialization and is composed of three parts: the *id,* which is the most primordial; the *ego,* which develops after the id; and lastly, the *superego,* which embodies values that come from the outside world values that have a delimiting impact on the id (Freud 1923).

In the psychoanalytic theory of socialization, although the id and the superego were clearly irreconcilable by themselves, they did share an important character according to Freud: The past was having an overriding influence on each psychical agency. Influencing the id were biological drives that were genetic and hereditary, while the superego was reflecting the norms, mores, and values of society *inherited* from previous generations (Freud 1949). Interestingly, Freud's psychoanalytic approach saw parents, teachers, and others as having a profound influence on the personality system through socialization. These socializing agents acted on the personality system through the superego, by promulgating society's norms to especially impressionable minds. They act to control the id, because an unrestrained id pursuing eros unhindered by normative constraints was ultimately pathological. Likewise, and in contrast, a person who was overly obsessed with the superego's normative impositions on the psychical system would become socially stifled. The ego is the mitigating influence between these opposite agencies. The ego is the harmonizing agent that prevents extremes in the personality system from either the instinctual pursuit of pleasure or the crippling compliance to normative constraints. While sociologists appreciated the emphasis on the superego, namely, society's imposition of values and moral codes, and the role of socializing agents in assuaging the unconscious biological drive for eros, ultimately Freud's socialization paradigm was in stark opposition to sociological theories on the development of the self because of its emphasis on how instinctual forces influence behavior.

Another important contribution from psychology was the cognitive development theory of Jean Piaget (1950, 1954; see also Piaget and Inhelder 1969), especially his ideas on human reasoning. Piaget's insights on the analytical maturity of children were an important contribution to the nature versus nurture debate in the sciences because, like Freud, he sought an effective integration of biology and sociality in explaining human reasoning. For Piaget, there was no real nature versus nurture debate with regard to analytical proficiency because both factors had prevailing influence at different periods in a child's life. For instance, hereditary factors played a role in the maturation of the child's nervous system, which in turn affected reasoning. According to Thomas (1999:33), "Piaget initially accounted for children's progress through the four stages by the internal maturation of their nervous system as governed by their genetic endowment." Thus, like Freud, Piaget conflated ideas from both camps in developing his stage theory of cognitive development.

The first stage of analytical development in Piaget's theory was the *sensorimotor stage,* from birth to age 2. In this stage, the infant's senses mediate understanding of her or his surroundings by what she or he can feel, touch, taste, see, and hear. The infant does not posses the capacity to reason as such, but can only manipulate objects via the senses. The second stage is the *preoperational stage,* from ages 2–7. The child begins to manipulate rudimentary speech patterns and symbols to solve problems, even though she or he may not be fully cognizant of their meanings. The third stage is the *concrete-operational stage,* from ages 7–12. With this stage comes the ability to think logically and analyze *concrete* examples that are easily imagined. The final stage is the *formal operational stage,* from the age of 12. This stage is where the child can undertake abstract or philosophical reasoning. Egocentric appeals to the senses no longer dominates the child as in the preoperational stage, nor does she or he mostly rely on what others say or feel about an issue, as in the concrete reasoning stage. The child now has the ability to raise and answer critical questions that require abstract thought.

Freud and Piaget's psychological theories on socialization contained strains of biological determinism because of their emphasis on instinctual drives and/or maturation in shaping human personality (see Thomas 1999). As such, their theories are still oppositional paradigms to the somewhat "oversocialized" (Wrong 1961) view of human development in sociology, the next social science paradigm on socialization.

Sociology's contribution to the socialization debate begins in earnest in the late 1800s with an emphasis on the self and social role acquisition, the former relating to how individuals come to a sense of self by internalizing the impressions of othersand the latter referring to how individuals come to participate in society by assuming role obligations. Although sociology shared with Freudian psychoanalysis emphasizes on the superego's influence with respect to the developing self, it differed, according to LeVine (1969), by "stressing positive social prescriptions rather than proscriptions or prohibitions, and in seeing no necessary conflict between conformity and individual satisfaction" (p. 507). In sociology's conception of socialization, there was no struggle between the individual's desires and those of the social order. Rather, sociology saw society as having an overriding influence on the development of the self—as opposed to instinctive biological drives—by imparting norms and values onto the developing child, and these moral "social facts" (Durkheim [1895] 1964) were enabling and empowering, as opposed to constraining.

In emphasizing the *interactional* over the *instinctual,* sociology departed from the claim that hereditary factors were influencing social behavior by stating unequivocally that the individual's mind and self were indivisible from the social order, and in fact, that the individual was a reflection of society (Mead 1934). Indeed, it was C. H. Cooley's ([1902] 1964) analogy of the "looking glass" that became the key symbol of the lifelong development of his "social self" ideal. Cooley believed that the self developed through social interactions, namely, by interpreting and internalizing the reactions and judgments of others. Our self-concept was the looking glass that reflected our thoughts about the impressions of others through the ability to see ourselves from their point of view. His looking glass concept had three parts. We first consider how we appear to others. Then, we weigh their reactions and estimations of our appearance to them. Lastly, we internalize their reactions and evaluations, and in so doing, develop our own emotions and judgments about their estimation, which in turn shapes our self-concept. The self is a mere reflection of a multitude of social interactions over the life course, and this is why it is a mirror reflecting our interconnectedness.

A contemporary and close friend of C. H. Cooley, George Herbert Mead's (1934) contribution to socialization theory has been the most enduring of the early sociologists who undertook this debate. Mead began his analysis by stating unequivocally that the self is a social creation: "The self, as that which can be an object to itself, is essentially a social structure and it arises in social experience" (p. 140). In Mead's socialization theory, the self, which is a product of society and social interaction, has two parts to its existence, the "I" and the "me." In children, the "I" is the most primordial aspect of the self, initially unaffected by socialization. It is self-centered, egocentric, and undersocialized; it is the self as *subject.* It is only through socialization that a more complete sense of the self emerges, the

"me." This part of the self internalizes and assumes the "attitudes of others"; it is the self as *object* (p. 175).

George Herbert Mead (1934) saw play as an essential part of the development of the self in children. Through play, children are able to "take the role of the other" by trying out various tasks (pp. 364–365). These role-taking recreations are essential for the development of the self in children and proceed along a continuum beginning with the *imitation stage,* birth to age 3, where children impersonate the gestures and responses of others without fully understanding what those gestures mean. Then, the *play stage,* from ages 3 to 6, where children play at role taking by acting out occupational or status roles they have observed in adults. Finally, there is the *game stage,* age 7 and beyond, where children can now take on multiple roles while participating in highly organized activities such as sports. Taking on the role of "significant others" and the expectations of "generalized others," which Mead (p. 154) defined as the "organized community or group which gives to the individual his unity of self," is essentially how the child comes to see himself or herself as connected to the social world. The child learns to modify his or her behavior to comply with the values, norms, and expectations of the "general" community, and this is an essential part of the socialization process in children.

THE STRUCTURE OF SOCIALIZATION

Sociology's approach to the study of socialization emphasizes social learning throughout the life course, from birth to death; socialization is not limited to the young, but rather, it occurs in varying degrees at all points in the life course of the individual (see Marshall and Mueller 2003; Mortimer and Simmons 1978). Moreover, social learning theory (see Bandura 1977) has been the dominant paradigm in sociological analysis on socializing processes, positing that individuals learn both approving and deviant behaviors through social interactions (see Bandura 1969; Sutherland, Cressey, and Luckenbill 1992). However, the indelible contribution that sociology makes to understanding human socialization is its analysis of how structural forces affect the quality and form of socialization. According to Inkeles (1969), ecological, economic, political, and moral structures are continually affecting the socialization people receive. Ecological factors such as population dynamics and density, for instance, will affect proximally the type of interactions people have. Likewise, economic factors, such as a person's income and assets, which largely determine an individual's access to goods and services, have a crucial impact on socialization, especially when they impose limits on a child's education and access to cultural capital (see Bourdieu and Passeron 1977; Keister and Moller 2000; Kozol 1991; Shapiro 2004). Political structures affect socialization throughout the life course from state policies and laws that harm poor and improvised families to nation-state repression that curtail free and open discourse (see Edin and Lein 1997). Finally, values or preferences concerning both prescribed and proscribed behaviors influence both social interactions and personal choices (see Crittenden 1990; Windermiller, Lambert, and Turiel 1980). Structural factors affect the socialization individuals receive, and as such, sociology pays keen attention to how the aforementioned variables affect an individual's socialization into social class, race, and gender.

THE AGENTS OF SOCIALIZATION

Besides illuminating the impact of structural variables on socializing processes, sociology noted the existence of agents of socialization, namely, people and institutions that function as conduits of social facts. These agents influence our attitudes, preferences, and worldviews by imparting values and norms, which, once internalized, affect our preferences and our behaviors. While the list of potential agents of socialization is exhaustive, sociologists have focused on the family and community, schools, peer groups, religion, media, the arena of competitive sports, and the workplace as the main sources of socialization. Each of these institutions transmits particular values that buttress—or sometimes oppose—the values of other attending socialization agencies. For instance, the values propagated by religious agents of socialization, are, usually, the values that families in their congregation try to promulgate to their children in primary socialization—values that affect parenting styles and parent-child relations (see Pearce and Axinn 1998; Wilcox 1998).

On Primary Socialization: The Family and Community, Schools, and Peer Network

Primary socialization incorporates the foremost socializing agents that children encounter: family and community, schools, and peer networks. Our family gives us our sense of self and social location, and this has an enduring impact as we move through the life course. The family transmits norms and values to us that shape our preferences (Denzin 1977; Elkin and Handel 1984; Handel 1988). The family socializes us into our social class, gender, and racial and ethnic identities (Anderson 1990; Lorber 1993; MacLeod 1995; Ontai-Grzebik and Raffaelli 2004). Families impart religious or nonreligious worldviews that, at least initially, orient our ethical, political, and ideological leanings (Acock and Bengtson 1978; Hunsberger and Brown 1984; Martin, White, and Perlman 2003). Moreover, families, and parents in particular, play a crucial role in facilitating the moral socialization of children by providing them a forum for moral "role taking," that is, the ability of children to take the moral standpoints and perspective of parents through communication and reciprocal exchanges on morality (Kohlberg 1969).

Although the sociological research on family socialization is overwhelming, recent studies all point to the importance of family life in influencing adolescents'

involvement in deviant groups and delinquent behaviors (Whitbeck 1999), in illicit drug use (Donohew et al. 1999; Oetting and Donnermeyer 1998; Oetting, Donnermeyer, and Deffenbacher 1998), alcohol consumption (Barnes Farrell, and Cairns 1986), and sexual activity (Ramirez-Valles, Zimmerman, and Juarez 2002). Consequently, the socialization children receive from their parents is an important predictor of future deviant behaviors. Family abuse, for instance, has been shown to be a strong predictor of adolescent delinquency, including deviant peer affiliation for both boys and girls, for drug abuse and risky sexual activity (Whitbeck 1999). Children model the behavior of parents, thus the primary socialization they encounter influences their choices in adolescence and beyond. One researcher, using the social learning theory of socialization that underscores the importance of "anticipatory socialization" and the modeling hypothesis, where a person might prepare in the present to assume an anticipated future role (Bandura 1977), has shown that the best predictor of future alcohol abuse is parental behavior: Parents who are heavy drinkers are more likely than non-heavy-drinking parents to have children who become heavy drinkers (Barnes et al. 1986).

Community life is also an important socialization agent for children and adults. Neighborhood life can play an important role in buttressing—or negating—the socialization children receive at home. Several studies on poor inner-city neighborhoods have shown that community socialization often filters into the home and vice versa (Anderson 1976; Brooks-Gunn, Duncan, and Aber 1997; Clark 1965; MacLeod 1995; Rainwater 1970; William and Kornblum 1990; Wilson 1987, 1996). Elijah Anderson's (1990) research on the neighborhood life and family structure of inner-city residents describes two types of families that coexist in extreme poverty: "decent families" and "street families." The former, although poor and struggling to make ends meet, have accepted mainstream social values of hard work and self-reliance, while taking an interest in their children's education and moral development. The values they impart at home are anathema to the realities of the street, and these families do their best to insulate children from the surrounding pathologies of crime and deviance. On the other hand, the "street families" have abandoned the mainstream American values of hard work and self-reliance, and, what's more, are actively propagating the "code of the streets" in their socialization patterns, a code that values interpersonal respect and the use of violence to ensure its prolongation.

Schools and Socialization into Social Class

Schools perform an essential work in the socialization of children by first transmitting the culture's values. In fact, Émile Durkheim (1973) proposed a protracted role for educators in socializing children into morality. Moral socialization was the first work of every school. Durkheim thought it was the duty of schools to instruct their pupils into society's values and norms, a task that he thought too overwhelming for the family unity (Durkheim 1973). Schools also impart the knowledge and intellectual skills necessary to assume adult roles, while performing essential functions in social integration, career gatekeeping, and social placement for society, and these are manifest functions (see Collins 1977, 1979; Hallinan 1994; Kilgore 1991).

Durkheim notwithstanding, the most crucial socialization role that schools perform today is in preparing students for economic and social class reproduction. The charge that schools are socializing children in such a way to assure class reproduction is a contested and hotly debated issue among social scientists. The debate is, however, less about whether schools *do* socialize children in such a way to produce class reproduction and more about *how* they go about accomplishing this function.

The strongest proponents of the socialization into class reproduction thesis are Samuel Bowles and Herbert Gintis (Bowles 1977; Bowles and Gintis 1976, 2002). Their work on social reproduction has influenced a host of other similar studies (Cookson and Persell 1985; Kozol 1991; Willis 1976). Bowles and Gintis (1976) advance a thesis known as the "structural correspondence" principle, which argues that there are structural similarities between the way schools and workplaces are organized, and this corresponding likeness is designed to socialize students into the demands of a modern capitalist workforce.

Bowles and Gintis (1976; Bowles 1977) also believe that public schools in working-class and poor communities are much more highly regimented, emphasizing control, rules, and discipline and order over independence, while schools in middle-class suburbs flex less direct control and supervision over students' curriculum and their interpersonal interactions emphasizing problem solving and critical thinking. Middle-class public school students are in training, Bowles and Gintis (1976) reason, to be managers, supervisors, and professionals, that is, to assume the same social class position as their parents. Working-class and poor public school students, however, receive a pedagogy that prepares them to take orders and to be biddable employees.

Other theorists on educational socialization, like Pierre Bourdieu (1974, 1977) and Basil Bernstein (1965, 1977), stress the importance of socialization into cultural and linguistic capital. According to Bourdieu (1974, 1977), children in middle- to upper-class families receive a primary socialization that stresses the attainment of gainful cultural competencies that are designed to give advantages especially in the world of careers. These cultural competencies, which include things such as linguistic skills and familiarity with the aesthetics, tastes, and preferences of the power elite, are desired by wealthy and middle-class parents. Basil Bernstein (1965, 1977) notes that parents in the middle and upper classes orient their children toward a linguistic code that is *elaborated,* where their vocabulary and syntax patterns reflect a wide range of possible linguistic tools. On the other hand, children from working-class

and poor backgrounds have a linguistic code that is *restricted,* limited to a predictable linguistic range. Naturally, schools in middle- and upper-class communities orient themselves to the achievement of linguistic and cultural capital, and in so doing, impose a system of implicit disadvantage to children coming from poor communities and less privileged backgrounds. Moreover, Cookson and Persell's (1985) research on the educational socialization that elite boarding schools transmit is especially instructive of the role of cultural capital in this process. These schools emphasize a classical curriculum with a plethora of elective courses on the arts, languages, and music. They provide students with opportunities to travel and study abroad and stress the value of competition and *esprit de corps* through sports and intramural activities. Cookson and Persell (1985) argue that elite boarding schools are preparing students to assume the reins of power in society, and they are using the acquisition of cultural capital as the primary instrument to achieve this goal. Of course, the analogous argument follows for those students who come from working-class and poor backgrounds. The education they receive is socializing them for social reproduction (see Kozol 1991; MacLeod 1995).

Peer Group and Cohort Socialization

The last agent of primary socialization is peer groups. Peer groups are an important socialization agent throughout the life course because we often see others in our generational cohort as comparative metrics of our own social standing (see Heinz and Marshall 2003). Our contemporaries are an index of our social location, and we look to them for guidance on everything from consumer tastes, to political and ideological orientations, to socialization into old age. Elkin and Handel (1984) note that each peer group will have several common features, among them, these: (1) similar age cohort or social position; (2) members with different levels of power and influence within the peer group; and (3) social concerns that are unique to its members or cohort. Peer groups are especially important for adolescents, and several studies document the importance of this socializing agent.

The research of Ogbu (1978, 1983), Fordham and Ogbu (1986), Fordham (1988), and recently McWhorter (2001) suggest that Afro-American teens face tremendous downward pressure toward academic mediocrity because many of their peers link academic success to desires to "be white." Fordham and Ogbu (1986) find that many Afro-American children deliberately underperform in school, settling for Ds and Cs instead of Bs and As, to avoid being labeled and stigmatized by their peers. Patricia and Peter Adler (1998), in their study of peer socialization among elementary students, found that peer groups exercise power by "techniques of inclusion and exclusion." With regard to exclusion techniques, Adler and Adler (1998) found that adolescent peer groups exercise power and influence through *out-group subjugation,* by bullying and harassing outsiders; by *in-group subjugation,* or picking and niggling lower-ranked members of the clique; by *compliance,* or not openly challenging the harassing behaviors of more powerful group members; by *stigmatization,* where the group subjects a member to stigmatizing labels and derisive comments; and finally, *expulsion,* or getting kicked out of the group. Peer influences are important because as adolescents move along the life course, the other agents of primary socialization flex a diminishing level of influence over their attitudes and preferences; and much evidence suggests that peer influences, especially around attitudes of drug use, begin to have an overriding influence over those of parents as children mature (Downs 1987; Kaplan, Martin, and Robbins 1984; McBroom 1994). Notwithstanding this evidence, there is a vigorous debate concerning the power of peer influence over adolescent socialization into both deviant and conforming behaviors.

Control theorists see deviance and delinquency as resulting from a weakening of the bonds of attachment and commitment to primary groups, namely, family, community, and school. Deviance is the outcome of weakened social control on the part of parents and teachers, which then leads to weakening self-control on the part of the individual, and this is due to peer influences. Baron and Tindall (1993), in their research on delinquent attitudes common among juvenile gang members, find support for control theory that emphasizes strong social bonds as the correlates of conforming behavior and weak social bonds as leading to deviant outcomes (see Gottfredson and Hirschi 1990; Hirschi 1969). Peer influences should not have a more influential impact than other primary socializing influences if individuals are highly attached and committed to their family, community, and school. Indeed, in a recent essay on the limitations of peer socialization, Hartup (1999) points to several factors that make the relative influence of peer socialization hard to gauge, partly because of a lacuna in research. Among Hartup's (1999) constraining influences are (1) the nebulous social characteristics of children who are doing the socializing versus the children being socialized; (2) the conditions (coercion, reward, etc.) that make behavior change possible might be different for groups of children; and (3) the constraining influences of cognitive and affective maturity that limit children's influence over each other. While the question regarding which primary socialization agent is most powerful in determining adolescences' deviant outcomes is open for debate, the research is clear on the point that the influence of peer groups increases over time, while the influence of parents generally decreases.

Religious Socialization

Sociology has always placed an emphasis on the importance of religious institutions in social life. Émile Durkheim ([1915] 1965), in *The Elementary Forms of the Religious Life,* defined religion as a set of beliefs and practices on sanctified things that provide a basis for the development of moral communities. Durkheim saw religion as an "eminently social" creation that strengthened collective solidarity by bringing together individuals who share similar moral worldviews (pp. 21–22). Westerhoff (1973) writes that religious socialization "is a process, consisting of lifelong formal and informal mechanisms, through which persons sustain and transmit faith, worldview, value system and way of life" (p. 121). Religious institutions contribute to socialization by helping individuals sustain and transmit values, worldviews, rituals, and other aspects of sacred culture. Current research links levels of religious socialization to everything from voting patterns to educational outcomes (Jelen and Chandler 1996; Regnerus 2000).

Much of the early work on religious socialization focused on why religious socialization fails, that is, why many adults abandon the faiths of their youth by either becoming apostates, agnostics, and/or nonchurched individuals (Hadaway and Roof 1979; Hunsberger 1980, 1983; Martin et al. 2003; Roof and Hoge 1980). Most researchers in this field recognize the importance of three socializing agents as playing a significant role in religious socialization: parents, churches, and peer groups. These agents, particularly parents, socialize children into religion by *channeling* them to institutions and experiences that will strengthen the ethical values and religious worldviews taught at home. This explanation is known as the *channeling hypothesis* (Himmelfarb 1980; Martin et al. 2003). Churches, synagogues, mosques, and other religious institutions can have an *indirect* impact on the socialization of children if parents view them largely as normative "reference groups" (Merton 1968). Yet the intensity of religious socialization in childhood has a *direct* effect on the apostasy rate of adults (Hunsberger and Brown 1984). For instance, in a study of the intensity of religious socialization among a sample of 878 college students, Hunsberger and Brown found that the home environment, particularly the influence of mothers, had the strongest influence on later levels of religiosity. Hunsberger and Brown (1984) note that the stronger the religious socialization in adolescence, the more likely individuals are to remain in their faith, and the less likely they are to become apostates. Finally, a bourgeoning area of religious socialization research focuses on the role of religious socialization in influencing people's attitudes on a variety of political and "family values" issues, from abortion to premarital sexual relations (Hammond, Shibley, and Solow 1994; Hayes 1995; Jelen and Chandler 1996; Wilcox and Jelen 1990).

SOCIALIZATION INTO GENDER, RACE, AND THE LIFE COURSE

Gender socialization is the mechanism by which individuals acquire the expected roles associated with their respective sex (see Weitzman 1979). Gender role socialization begins with the internalization of norms and—most significant—expected behaviors that society ascribes to males and to females. The earliest "socialization" perspective on the rise of gender identities in children was Sigmund Freud, who saw the emergence of gender as entangled in psychosexual development, namely, the Oedipus complex for boys and the Electra complex for girls (see Freud 1923). Girls come to first define themselves as girls by *the lack of* a penis, while boys come to define themselves principally through *the possession of* a penis. The problem of lack, that is, "I lack a penis," becomes the seminal experience of girls, who now must come to terms with their "penis envy." Boys, on the other hand, are privileged for not suffering from the problem of lack, while girls must contend with this potential neurosis. Gender, as both a social and personal concept for the child, is first linked to the recognition of *difference,* a dispensation with innumerable recompense for males, and anatomical determinism for girls.

Rejecting Freud's theory of lack, Nancy Chodorow (1978) proposed a psychoanalytic and sociologic model of gender emergence that was less constrained by anatomical determinism, or "penis envy." Chodorow saw a child's gender identity as emerging through the process of breaking away from the mother to form a unique identity. But the real strength of Chodorow's (1978) theory on the reproduction of mothering is its emphasis on *social* learning of both gender and mothering. According to Chodorow, the process of severing the bond between mother and child, which was necessary for the emergence of a unique identity in the child, was invariably more violent for boys than it was for girls because boys saw themselves as more separate and distinct from their mothers than girls did. A girl's socialization into gender and femininity is a more fluid process because of her identification with, and closeness to, the mother. Masculine identity, on the other hand, requires a complete break—or loss—to achieve a culturally sanctioned socialization into manhood. If women experience a sense of *lack* in Freud's understanding of the emergence of gender, then the problem for boys, in Chodorow's socialization paradigm on gender, is one of loss and disconnection from the mother: It is *masculinity* that is troubled and lacking.

Parental Influence on Gender Socialization

Notwithstanding the aforementioned psychoanalytic theories on gender, the existing research in the areas of gender socialization suggests that gender is socially constructed, and that parents have an overriding influence beginning with how they interact with their sons versus their daughters (Goldberg and Lewis 1969; Hoffman 1977). Socialization into gender begins at home, with children modeling the behaviors of their parents. Moreover, marriage itself is a primary tool that socializes children into gender role expectations (Ex and Janssens 1998; Risman 1998). Socialization into gender roles often

takes subtle forms in the home such as the division of household work. Peters's (1994) research among 448 high school students found that traditional gender role behaviors were most evident in the division of household chores, where boys did most of the yard work and girls typically attended to the inside of the home. Peters (1994) also found that girls were much more likely to have an earlier curfew than their brothers were.

The Influence of Language on Gender Socialization

One of the most potent methods of socializing individuals into gender is through language. A recent study suggests (Gelman, Taylor, and Nguyen 2004) that one of the ways children learn gender differences is by "implicit essentialist language" that privileges one sex (male) over another (female). According to Gelman et al. (2004),

> Children may infer from their parents' implicit essentialist language that their parents endorse gender-stereotyped responses, and adopt these beliefs. Although children are active learners and parents are unlikely to shape children's beliefs directly, mothers' linguistic input does seem to convey subtle messages about gender from which children may construct their own essentialist beliefs. (P. 111)

Language as a tool of gender socialization can work in three ways, according to Henley (1989): (1) Language might be used in explicit and pejorative ways to subjugate women; (2) language might be used in implicit ways that result in the exclusion of women, as in the use of masculine pronouns; and lastly, (3) language might be used to proliferate gender stereotypes (as cited in Gelman et al. 2004). Children internalize these implicit and subtle verbal cues that support, whether consciously or not, the gendered hierarchy that privilege the masculine over the feminine. Moreover, children's storybooks and fairly tales are replete with the use of sexist violence and imagery of female subordination: "*Peter, Peter, pumpkin eater, had a wife, but couldn't keep her. He kept her in a pumpkin shell, and there he kept her very well*" (Davies 1991; Purcell and Stewart 1990; Weitzman et al. 1972).

The Influence of the Mass Media on Gender Socialization

The mass media is a crucial secondary agent of gender socialization that supports gender role stereotypes and stratification. Television, movies, video games, music, magazines, advertisements, the Internet, books, and other secondary media sources of socialization are especially important to adolescents as their parents' influence begin to diminish and as the influence of peers takes precedence (Arnett 1995; Kelly and Donohew 1999; Van Evra 1998). Research abounds on the gender role stereotypes and violence against women that are perpetuated in the mass media, a result of what some feminist scholars have referred to as the "feminist backlash" (Faludi 1991). No other time in history has witnessed such a perfect convergence, proliferation, and intensification of consistent gender role stereotypes in all forms of mass-mediated imagery, from Internet manga and hentai marketed to adolescents and young adults (Powell-Dahlquist and Vigilant 2004), to beer commercials, popular music, movies, and videos (Cooper 1985). What's more, these media sites portray a relatively consistent and overwhelmingly stereotypical ideal of girls and women according to the most recent studies (Deitz 1998; Furnham and Bitar 1993; Glascock 2001; Kolbe and Langefeld 1993; Signorielli 1989). Deitz's (1998) content analysis on the portrayal of violence and gender role sets in video games found that the stereotypical depiction of women as sexual objects was common, and that 21 percent of the video games analyzed had violence directed at women.

While the media are powerful agents of socialization, most sociologists still conceptualize their influence as a secondary one (Kelly and Donohew 1999). The media largely strengthen the values, norms, and worldviews that come out of primary socialization. The media might encourage both prosocial and antisocial behaviors in their portrayals, but the data on whether there is a unidirectional link between violence and/or sexism in the media and actual behaviors are still contested (see Van Evra 1998).

Racial Socialization

Over the last 20 years, research has intensified in the area of *racial socialization,* one of the newest areas of socialization analysis in the social sciences (Brega and Coleman 1999; Constantine and Blackmon 2002; Hughes 2003; Hughes and Johnson 2001; Miller and MacIntosh 1999; M. F. Peters 1985; Scott 2003; Stevenson, Reed, and Bodison 1996; Thompson, Anderson, and Bakeman 2000). Racial socialization is the mechanism by which parents transmit values that increase ethnic pride and strengthen self-concept in hopes that this will insulate children from the effects of racism or ethnic prejudice. Racial socialization typically involves conversations between parent and child about the social meaning of race, and admonitions about the difficulties they might face because of their race or ethnicity. It may also include the sharing of race-related experiences such as a parent's experiences with discrimination. Some researchers even suggest that racial socialization is a requisite tool for successful coping during discriminatory experiences (see Fischer and Shaw 1999; Miller and MacIntosh 1999; Ward 2000).

An adolescent's level of racial socialization is typically measured by an instrument called the Scale of Racial Socialization for Adolescents (SORS-A), while a teen's level is measured by the Teenager Experience of Racial Socialization Scale (TERS), both developed by Howard Stevenson (1994). One study on the prevalence of racial socialization among Afro-Americans found that 79 percent

of respondents had conversations with their parents that fit the racial socialization definition (Sanders-Thompson 1994), while another reported 73 percent (Biafora et al. 1993). Other studies find that minority children who experience racial socialization for the likelihood of future racial or ethnic discrimination, and who receive counteracting messages about racial and ethnic pride, have higher levels of self-esteem and social competence (Constantine and Blackmon 2002). Moreover, a different study finds an association between high-achieving Afro-American students and higher levels of racial socialization (Sanders 1997; see also McKay et al. 2003). The study of racial socialization seems to be an increasingly important and bourgeoning area of analysis for understanding both the effect of racial socialization on coping with perceived or real discriminatory actions and prejudicial experiences, and their affect on adolescents' well-being.

Life-Course Socialization

The life-course theory of socialization represents one of the most extensive subfields of socialization research, and as such, deserves separate space to do justice to the depth and breadth of its concerns (see Marshall and Mueller 2003; Mortimer and Simmons 1978, for two comprehensive reviews). The most frequently cited researcher in the life-course perspective is Glen Elder (1974, 1975, 1994, 1998), who has done more than any other life-course theorist to advance this perspective. The very notion of the life course, however, infers developmental stages, biological, psychological, and social, that individuals experience as they mature from infancy to death (Cain 1964; Erikson 1959; Riley 1979). The life-course theory of socialization divides the life cycle into several important stages beginning with childhood, then adolescence (13–17), young adulthood (18–29), middle age (30–65), and old age (65 and beyond). Entrance into each of these stages requires learning new sets of norms and expectations. Exiting these stages may also involve their own *rites of passage* and *status passage* (Cain 1964; Glaser and Strauss 1971), as, for instance, acquiring the driver's license and registering with selective service may signify passage from adolescence into young adulthood. Each stage in the life course involves adopting new roles and learning new role expectations. At times, entrance into a new role along the life course might involve radical resocialization, or completely altering the norms and expectations of a previous stage, as, for instance, going from independent living to an assisted-living facility or nursing home in old age.

Finally, life-course theorists have highlighted a peculiar similarity between the resocialization into total institutions (Goffman 1961) such as prisons and mental hospitals, which begins with a degradation ceremony (Garfinkel 1956), and the resocialization that growing old requires. Irving Rosow (1974) notes that growing old poses a special problem for adult socialization because it involves the *forced* socialization into an undesirable position, whereas normal status passages involves the entrance into a valued position. According to Rosow (1974), the reasons why socialization into old age is difficult include (1) the devalued status that aging represents, (2) the ambiguity of norms around the old-age "role," (3) role discontinuity, (4) loss of previous status, and (5) resistance to current role socialization (p. 118). The strength of the life-course perspective is its emphasis on the importance of socialization throughout the life cycle of the individual.

ORGANIZATIONAL SOCIALIZATION: FROM TOTAL TO GREEDY INSTITUTIONS

Work is the primary arena for adult socialization, and professional organizations have been the focus of much socialization research (Mortimer and Simmons 1978). Naturally, the socialization that takes place in organizations will reflect the type of structure that exists. For instance, Goffman's (1961) description of the "total institution," where every aspect of an individual's life is controlled by an authoritarian body, depicts an organization that is expressly concerned with the resocialization of individuals such as prisoners and military enlistees. Others, like Lewis Coser's (1974) "greedy institutions," may encourage the professional socialization of members into the organization's values, while requiring unrealistic allegiance and undivided fidelity. Studies point to the role of professional socialization in, for instance, learning how to lie as a requisite for "successful" assimilation into some greedy institutions (Schein 2004), and in preparing for an anticipated future occupation, for example, the anticipatory socialization into careers such as social work (Barretti 2004a, 2004b). Studies on the anticipatory occupational socialization among nursing students find a dichotomy between classroom education on the one hand and service learning on the other, where students apply their knowledge firsthand, thus achieving both academic and professional socialization at the same time (Melia 1984).

A considerable body of work in recent years has focused on the role of gender in institutional socialization, especially on the socialization of women into traditional male-dominated fields (Carlson, Thomas, and Anson 2004; Gomez-Mejia 1983; Okamoto and England 1999; Worden 1993). Research has also focused on how the demands of greedy institutions affect family life (Perlow 1997). Finally, occupational socialization theory has been dominated by four explanatory models over the last 25 years, each seeking to explicate how socialization takes place in bureaucratic organizations: socialization tactics theory, uncertainty reduction theory, social cognitive theory, and sense-making theory (see Saks and Ashforth 1997 for a comprehensive discussion of each of these occupational socialization models).

Military Socialization

As a subfield of occupational analysis, military socialization has received considerable sociological attention. Most studies tend to treat the military as both a total and a greedy institution because of the control the uniformed armed forces exercise over their enlistees, and for the demands they make for unwavering commitment and loyalty to their values (see Segal 1986). The military's *raison d'être* is to resocialize individuals to meet rigors of war, and basic training is the most pronounced and shocking method of resocializing young soldiers into the values of military service (Bourne 1967). Moreover, the drill sergeant plays a crucial role in this resocialization process (see Katz 1990). Faris (1975) notes that drill instructors are key to resocialization because of their use of degradation ceremonies to break and remake individuals and for their efforts at maintaining group solidarity. Bourne's (1967) study on the psychosocial character of basic training found four distinct periods of resocialization during the course of basic training beginning with the following: (1) the initial shock of being removed from one's normal social environment and being segregated from the mundane world; (2) the stripping away of any semblance of one's unique individuation; (3) the period of acquiring new skills and identities that are reinforced by the institution; and finally, (4) a period of personal transformation marked by a sense of accomplishment where individuals are fully socialized into their new identities as "soldiers."

Other studies focus on hypermasculinity as the principal quality of military basic training (Karner 1998; Levy 2000). Several studies point to the armed forces as propagating the warrior ideal through an ethos of the masculine mystique, an image criticized as bogus and inflammatory, and specifically designed to capture the imaginations of young men who are searching for their own masculine self-identities (Arkin and Dobrofsky 1978; Shatan 1977).

Finally, there is a body of research on the military's role in the political socialization of soldiers (see Bachman et al. 2000; Franke 2000; Goertzel and Hengst 1971; Stevens, Rosa, and Gardner 1994). One study on political socialization among enlistees between the years 1976 and 1997 found that military enlistees were more likely to support greater military expenditures and a protracted role of the military in world affairs than their nonenlistee cohort (Bachman et al. 2000).

SUMMATION: PROSPECTS FOR FUTURE DEVELOPMENT IN SOCIALIZATION THEORY

Social interaction has seen tremendous changes due to the development of the Internet. The rise in virtual communities on the World Wide Web has posed several challenges for society. Without question, the Internet is both enabling—and radically altering—traditional social interactions. Yet studies on the Internet and socialization processes remain relatively underdeveloped. The Internet empowers self- and anticipatory socialization because of how readily available and easily accessible information has become, and these Net-based socialization modes demand enquiry.

The new age of virtual connection and instantaneous access is also indelibly changing personal orientation, if we are to believe the social psychiatrist Robert J. Lifton (1993). The cybernetic age is one that demands, according to Lifton (1993), a *protean personality* that is fluid and nebulous just like the contours of late-modern society. This *proteanism* has multiple personas that adapt easily to the ever-shifting social landscape of a late-modern world that is, itself, amorphous. In a sense, Lifton's ideas are not at all new. Sociology is the science of the industrial age; its first concern was to understand the changes wrought by the shift from a *Gemeinschaften* to a *Gesellschaften* social order (Toennies [1887] 1988), from a *quantitative* to a *qualitative individualism* (Simmel 1950). Social changes affect culture and the socialization that individuals receive. Lifton's theory on the development of a postmodern proteanism is not out of step with sociological observations from the last great social change, the Industrial Revolution. Sociology can make an important contribution by studying the "new" protean socialization throughout the life course.

The role of children as an important socializing agent for other children, and increasingly for parents, is a phenomenon that deserves greater attention (see J. F. Peters 1985). How are parents socializing children to meet the demands of a late-modern culture and society that is marked by cultural, political, economic, and moral globalization? Moreover, how are children assisting the socialization of their parents into this milieu? The old assumption of a unidirectional socialization becomes increasingly farcical in late modernity where, because of technological interventions, parents *seem* to be exercising less direct control over their children's interactions. Sociology needs more exploration on how communication technologies are influencing the socialization of children and adolescents, as well as how their own *self-socialization* is taking place through the use of these media (see Arnett 1995). Finally, there is a need for cross-cultural and longitudinal studies on how the new technologies are changing socialization throughout the life course. Is there a McDonaldization (Ritzer 1993, 1998) effect on socialization processes because of the changes imposed by technocultural forces? How is globalization affecting the socialization of individuals throughout the life course? Without question, these are important areas of future analysis for the sociology of socialization.

14

SOCIAL PSYCHOLOGY

J. DAVID KNOTTNERUS

Oklahoma State University

While social psychology has played a vital role in sociology during the twentieth century, the nature of this role has changed through the years. Earlier in the century, social psychology was viewed by many as a separate body of research distinct from other, more accepted parts of sociology. Today, however, this field occupies a much more central role in the discipline, increasingly interconnected with other areas of sociological research. In this chapter, the nature and history of social psychology will be addressed, with special attention to key developments in this area, especially in recent decades.

An event critical to the formalization of the field of social psychology in sociology was the founding of the journal *Social Psychology Quarterly* (first titled *Sociometry*) in 1937 by the American Sociological Association (ASA). Furthermore, social psychology forms a major section within the ASA. Among its activities are the publication of a newsletter and the awarding each year of the Cooley-Mead Award, which is given in recognition of those individuals who have made outstanding contributions to theory and research in social psychology. Work in this area also appears in many mainstream journals in sociology and in more specialized volumes, especially the research annual *Advances in Group Processes,* which has been published for over two decades.

Reflecting the advances that have taken place in this area, several decades ago the ASA commissioned the publication of a volume that would serve as a sourcebook and textbook for the field of social psychology. Under the editorship of Morris Rosenberg and Ralph H. Turner, a number of scholars contributed to *Social Psychology: Sociological Perspectives* (1981), reporting on major research and theory in the mid-twentieth century. An updated and expanded examination, *Sociological Perspectives on Social Psychology,* was subsequently produced by Cook, Fine, and House (1995). Other sources that summarize major research and theoretical developments include the *Handbook of Social Psychology,* edited by John Delamater (2003), and the *Handbook of Social Psychology,* Volumes 1 & 2, edited by Daniel T. Gilbert, Susan T. Fiske, and Gardner Lindzey (1998).

In terms of substantive interests and orientations, both sociologists and psychologists populate this field of study and have defined its basic character. This situation has resulted in what some analysts refer to as "sociological social psychology" and "psychological social psychology." In the past years, these differing perspectives have been portrayed as being in marked competition (House 1977); however, today one finds a greater degree of overlap between them. While differences still exist, the relationship between the two perspectives is not marked by a pronounced sense of conflict. As noted by Cook et al. (1995) and Delamater (2003), social psychology is truly interdisciplinary. According to Cook et al. (1995),

Social psychology represents an interdiscipline lodged between the disciplines of psychology, which examines inner lives and selves, and sociology, which examines the relationships between collectivities and organizations. Social psychologists argue that it is essential to examine how self and system interpenetrate. (P. xii)

HISTORY OF SOCIAL PSYCHOLOGY

Interest in social psychological issues has a historical legacy. Indeed, writers such as Aristotle, Hegel, Rousseau, and Hobbes raised many questions about why social behavior takes the forms that it does, and their work provides a foundation for the growth of social psychology. During the nineteenth century, theoretical and philosophical thought focused on social issues clearly foreshadowed the development of the science of social psychology. Analysts such as Auguste Comte put forth specific explanations for how social reality influences people, while others including Gabriel Tarde focused on the role imitation plays in conformity in social life.

The first two textbooks on social psychology were written in 1908, each reflecting the intellectual background of its authors. E. A. Ross (1908), a sociologist, focused on the place of imitation in social life and the group mind that had been discussed by Gustave Le Bon and Gabriel Tarde. William McDougall (1908), a psychologist, emphasized instinctive, internal motivations for social behavior. Shortly thereafter, other theoretical orientations began to influence the growth of psychology and social psychology. Behaviorism as developed by John B. Watson influenced social psychology through its emphasis on environmental determinants of learning and behavior and the use of experimental methods. Psychoanalytic theory, developed by Sigmund Freud, stressed other dimensions of social behavior, including the importance of socialization and the role of nonrational factors such as emotions.

Social psychology began to assume greater definition with the publication of Floyd Allport's (1924) social psychology text, which stressed experimental methods, the development of theory, and the importance of social influence. Shortly afterward, in 1934, George Herbert Mead's writings established the foundation for what would later become a major approach toward social psychology, namely, symbolic interaction. Two years later, Muzafer Sherif (1936) published *The Psychology of Social Norms,* a very different type of work, which investigated social interaction and conformity to social norms by employing a laboratory experiment. In the same decade, Kurt Lewin (1943) advocated a deductive approach for the development of general theories that could be tested through experiments. World War II followed and provided impetus to the growth of the field. For instance, Hovland, Janis, and Kelley (1953) initiated a series of persuasion studies focused on attitude change, particularly with regard to developing effective propaganda programs. Research on attitude change continued after the war and became a major area of study that continues to the present day.

Over the next several decades, social psychology blossomed. Samuel Stouffer and colleagues (1949) and Merton and Rossi (1950), for example, introduced the concept *relative deprivation,* using it to explain the differences in World War II soldiers' feelings of satisfaction and dissatisfaction between themselves and others. Other important sociological approaches emerging during this period include reference group theory and role theory (Rosenberg and Turner 1981).

At the same time, Solomon Asch's (1956) research on conformity and Stanley Milgram's (1965, 1974) studies of obedience to authority generated numerous follow-up studies and further strengthened a long-standing concern with social influence and norm formation in social psychology (see Blass 2000). Other research, such as the simulation study of prisoners and guards conducted by Zimbardo and Haney (Haney, Banks, and Zimbardo 1973; Zimbardo, Maslach, and Haney 2000), also demonstrated how a social situation could profoundly affect actors. Leon Festinger's (1957) cognitive consistency theory focused on the effects of social situations and the ways in which cognitive inconsistency motivates people to restore consistency. For at least the next 15 years, research on this perspective proliferated, addressing issues ranging from consumer behavior and conversion of beliefs among prisoners of war to the ways in which cult members reconcile disconfirmation of group beliefs (Harmon-Jones and Mills 1999).

By the 1960s, social exchange theory began to emerge. Based on the premise that social behavior is best understood as an exchange of valued resources, social exchange theory represents one of the major research programs in sociological social psychology. Other approaches also began to develop in the last several decades of the past century. In particular, the 1960s witnessed the emergence of attribution theory (Heider 1958; Jones and Davis 1965; Kelley 1967), a perspective that focuses on social inferences. This approach represented a major departure from the behaviorist paradigm, a paradigm that had been dominate in psychology and contributed to a growing interest in the ways in which people perceive and process social information. This important breakthrough ultimately resulted in the cognitive or social cognition approach. Although psychologists have dominated this perspective, sociologists have also shown interest in recent years (Fiske and Taylor 1991; Howard 1995).

During the second half of the twentieth century, symbolic interactionism flourished, albeit its development has taken a variety of paths. Other perspectives related to symbolic interactionism have also emerged over the last four or five decades, each of which focus on different aspects of daily life. These include the work of Erving Goffman, ethnomethodology, and conversation analysis. Finally, another contemporary theoretical program that has come to play a major role in social psychology is expectation states theory (EST), a theory that focuses on the decisions made by social actors and group dynamics.

Many different research issues and agendas currently exist, of which some issues play a dominant role in the developing intellectual landscape of the field. In the following sections, several of the more recent perspectives that contribute to the growth of social psychology will be discussed.

SYMBOLIC INTERACTION

Symbolic interaction is a perspective that emphasizes the crucial role meaning, symbolization, communication, and action play in social relations (Reynolds and Herman-Kinney 2003). As Manis and Meltzer (1978; see also Reynolds 2003) point out, the major antecedents of symbolic interaction are (1) evolutionism, (2) German idealism, (3) Scottish moralism, (4) pragmatism, and (5) functional psychology. Approaches such as American pragmatism, developed by William James, John Dewey, and Charles Peirce, played an especially important role in shaping symbolic interaction due to pragmatism's emphasis on activity, the importance of the meaning for action, and the dynamic nature of reality. George Herbert Mead, Herbert Blumer, William Issac Thomas, Everett Hughes, and Robert E. Lee Park were influenced by such intellectual sources as they, in turn, directed attention to a number of issues dealing with roles, the social self, socialization, and interaction throughout the first half of the twentieth century.

The philosopher and psychologist George Herbert Mead established many of the basic principles of symbolic interaction. Presented in a series of lectures, his ideas were later edited and published by his former students, the most important book being *Mind, Self, and Society* (Mead 1934). Mead's perspective emphasized how human survival depends on communication involving symbols that are held in common. These symbols develop through social interaction; mind, self, and society each emerge out of this social process.

Mead discussed how the self emerges through a social process in which an actor views "oneself reflexively by adopting the standpoint of others to attach meanings to self" (Stryker 2001:215). Two key parts of the self are identified: "the 'me,' or organized attitudes of others with reference to the person, and the 'I,' or the person's responses to these attitudes of others" (p. 216). An internal conversation between the "I" and the "me" (in which the "I" represents creativity and the "me" stands for the social or organized social meanings) is the basis for behavior. Mead also discerns how the self emerges through a developmental process involving stages that are integrally shaped by social interaction and the developing language skills of the child through play and games. At first, the child learns to take the role of specific individuals or others. At a more advanced stage, the child learns to respond to the multiple behaviors and expectations of others (e.g., being able to play an organized team sport). In demonstrating how the self and society influence each other, Mead created one of the first developmental models of socialization in the social sciences.

Herbert Blumer, a student of Mead, had a great influence on the growth of this perspective. By creating "symbolic interactionism" in the 1930s, Blumer (1969) presented many of the key ideas of this approach in *Symbolic Interactionism*. Blumer (1969) outlined what many believe are the fundamental assumptions of symbolic interaction:

> The first premise is that human beings act toward things on the basis of the meanings those things have for them . . . The second premise is that the meaning of such things is derived from, or arises out of, the social interaction that one has with one's fellows. The third premise is that these meanings are handled in, and modified through, an interpretative process used by the person dealing with the things he [or she] counters. (P. 2)

Blumer argued that Mead provided the foundation for a social psychology that stood in marked contrast to much of the sociological research that he associated with deterministic arguments, quantitative methods, and natural science. Blumer's work inspired a version of symbolic interaction that some view as abandoning the dictates of science and inadequately attending to the role of social organization in society (see Maines 1977; Prendergast and Knottnerus 1993; Reynolds 1993; Stryker 2001).

Blumer's arguments were focused on methodological issues and an approach that stood in contrast to conventional sociological theory and research. He was a spokesperson for the use of qualitative/naturalistic methods involving ethnographies and field studies. Indeed, Blumer advocated an inductive approach in which the researcher strives to come in contact with the empirical social world and learn as much as possible about how actors define social reality through a method of inquiry he proposed as "exploration" and "inspection." To carry out this qualitative research, Blumer argued for the use of "sensitizing concepts" rather than "definitive concepts," which provide a clear definition of characteristics that identifies an instance of a class of objects. Sensitizing concepts suggest directions of inquiry while providing researchers with a general sense of guidance.

During the twentieth century, the contributions of Manford Kuhn and McPartland (1954) provided an alternative to Blumer's approach. Arguing for the development of theoretical generalizations grounded in symbolic interactionist thought and the testing of these concepts through more standardized conventional research strategies, Kuhn and McPartland argued that once social structure is formed, it then influences and constricts social behavior:

> To implement that insight, he brought elements of role theory and reference group theory into his framework, adopting the former's conceptions of social structure as composed of networks of positions in structured relations among people and of role expectations as associated with these positions. (Stryker and Vryan 2003:17)

From the perspective of Kuhn and McPartland (1954), the self is more enduring and determinate in nature. While acknowledging that the dynamics of the self and role-taking exhibit a creative dimension, their discussion of the core self emphasizes how stable meanings associated with the self create stability and predictability in social behavior. Among the more famous research tools is the Twenty Statements Test, a measure of people's attitudes about self. In asking respondents to respond to the question "Who am I?" Kuhn argued for the need to provide precise measurements of concepts that seek to explain and predict social interaction. Through research such as this aimed at testing interactionist theory, Kuhn sought to develop a cumulative body of knowledge.

THEORIES OF EVERYDAY LIFE

The first approach involves the work of Erving Goffman, who is considered to be one of the most creative theorists of interaction processes. Goffman (1983) referred to the interaction order. His goal was to promote the study of face-to-face interaction as a substantive, legitimate area of investigation. His work centered on mapping and categorizing the many different occasions and forms of social interaction that occur in a host of settings, including public and more personal situations (Goffman 1971). In *The Presentation of Self in Everyday Life,* Goffman (1959) emphasized that any instance of interaction can be analyzed as a theatrical performance. Building on the ideas of Kenneth Burke, Goffman's dramaturgical approach demonstrates that people as performers play rehearsed lines and roles that create impressions for others. Various ideas include *front* and *back* regions of everyday interaction and *impression management,* which are concerned with the way actors influence and control the impressions of self that others form (see Brisett and Edgley 1990).

Goffman's contributions include a focus on mental illness that led him to analyze the ways in which people are stigmatized and how stigma is managed (Goffman 1963). Goffman's (1961) investigation of a mental institution in *Asylums* led to the idea of a total institution or a place where individuals who are cut off from the wider society lead a formally administered round of life and his analysis of how people respond to and adjust to conditions in such institutions. Elsewhere, he demonstrated how face-to-face interaction is shaped by rituals (Goffman 1967), and magazine advertisements are based on implicit assumptions about gender (Goffman 1976). Last, in *Frame Analysis,* Goffman (1974) focuses on the way situations are defined, the organizational principles underlying these definitions, and their consequences.

Ethnomethodology has also exercised considerable influence in social psychology. Garfinkel (1967) defines ethnomethodology as the study of ethnomethods or members' methods. The focus is on how people exhibit a social competence in their normal, everyday lives. That is, this approach is concerned with the ways in which people make sense of their social world. Strategies used to obtain data for analysis range from in-depth interviews and videotaping to "breaching experiments," a method involving disruptions of people's taken-for-granted, everyday activities. An example

of the topics explored by ethnomethodologists would be "accounting," which involves actors' verbal accounts or announcements to explain their actions and the meaning they derive (Sudnow 1967; Maynard and Clayman 1991).

Finally, conversation analysis focuses on one specific dimension of everyday interaction, namely, verbal utterances. This approach was influenced by both Garfinkel's ethnomethodology and the work of Goffman. Pioneered by Harvey Sacks and Emmanuel Schegloff, this tradition has grown into an interdisciplinary endeavor that provides detailed analyses of conversation (Schegloff 1991; Sacks 1992a, 1992b). Conversation analysis assumes that utterances depend on context, especially the sequential placement or organization of talk. In examining naturally occurring talk, this research tradition directs much of its efforts to the investigation of the organization of sequences or the nature or forms of serial conversation, turn taking in speaking, and repair, the ways in which actors deal with conversational and interactional problems (Maynard and Perakyla 2003). Conversational analysis has contributed to expanding studies dealing with language, interaction, and structure (e.g., Whalen and Zimmerman 1987; Zimmerman and Boden 1991; Maynard 2003).

SOCIAL EXCHANGE THEORY

One of the most active theoretical research programs in social psychology is represented by social exchange theory. Originating in behavioral psychology, this perspective focuses on the contingent exchange of resources among persons who seek to adjust their level of reward. Sociological contributions to this approach are noteworthy, oftentimes involving theory-driven research whose goal is the accumulation of scientific knowledge. Of special note is the work of George Homans (1958, 1961, 1974), who presented the first principles of exchange theory. In reacting to the work on functionalist theory by Talcott Parsons (1951), Homans (1964) argued for "bringing men back in." Homans (1961, 1974) suggested that sociology should shift its focus from large-scale social systems to elementary social behavior and interaction. Homans argued that social interaction could be analyzed using five basic behavioral propositions, principles that are derived in part from the contributions of B. F. Skinner (1976).

Other important contributions to exchange theory include that of Peter Blau (1964), who drew on economic theory and utilitarianism to present a microexchange theory. This theory emphasizes how relationships can influence the development of larger groups and institutions. By focusing on the emergence of larger social arrangements from associations between social actors, Blau sought to emphasize the linkages between the microlevel and macrolevel social structures (Knottnerus and Guan 1997).

During the 1970s, the development of research and theory on exchange processes was enhanced through the contributions of Richard Emerson (1972a, 1972b). Emerson's theoretical discussion of power-dependence relations was focused on power and social exchange. Emerson demonstrated how power is relational and how social networks emerge from individuals engaging in social exchange. Guided by this conceptual framework, Emerson (1976, 1981) and other analysts such as Stolte and Emerson (1977) and Cook (1977) have shown that position in an exchange structure affects exchange rates. In this area, Jonathan Turner (1986) argued that the most important contribution of power-dependence theory is its demonstration that network structure has independent effects on power and exchange processes. Among Emerson's other contributions is his discussion of how exchange relations tend toward structural balance or an equivalence of dependence and four principles of structural change, each of which denotes the ways in which exchange networks achieve a balanced state (Emerson 1962).

David Willer and his colleagues (cited in Willer and Anderson 1981) spearheaded the development of elementary relations theory—an approach that argues that three types of social relations are predominant in social life, namely, exchange relations, conflict relations, and coercive relations. Most of the research conducted in this program focuses on exchange structures, uses an experimental format like power-dependence research, and places a special emphasis on structural conditions such as exclusion (Markovsky, Willer, and Patton 1988; Willer 1999). In a different vein, Linda Molm (1997) expanded exchange theory by examining alternative sources of power, especially punishment power. Additionally, Molm (1997) has delineated exchanges that possess different kinds of properties.

Other dimensions of social exchange theory have addressed the role of uncertainty and risk and commitment formation (Cook and Emerson 1978; Kollock 1994; Molm, Takahashi, and Peterson 2000), while Lawler and Yoon (1996) sought to deal with emotions and solidarity in a relational cohesion theory demonstrating how social exchange can create positive emotions and strengthen social ties. It should also be noted that exchange theory continues to contribute to our understanding of the emergence and transformation of social structure, as reflected in Whitmeyer and Cook's (2002) assessment of this topic and Simpson and Willer's (2002) application of elementary relations theory to the structural dynamics operating in ancient Rome.

EXPECTATION STATES THEORY

One of the most important traditions of social psychological research focused on group dynamics is EST. Dedicated to deductive theorizing and cumulativity, EST employs experimental procedures to progressively develop an array of formulations intended to explain a wide range of group processes involving the development of social inequality and social structure. Joseph Berger along with Bernard P. Cohen and Morris Zelditch pioneered the growth of EST.

Status characteristics theory is the oldest and perhaps the most developed branch of EST. It provides an explanation for the repeated finding that status differences such as race, gender, occupational rank, or ability determine the distribution of power, prestige, and influence in problem-solving task groups (Berger et al. 1977; Berger, Rosenholtz, and Zelditch 1980; Berger and Zelditch 1985; Webster and Foschi 1988; Wagner and Berger 1993). In focusing on "state-organizing processes," the theory begins with the observation that individuals differentiated by socially valued characteristics such as sex, race, age, or occupational rank receive differential attention, authority, or respect in a task situation irrespective of whether the characteristic is relevant to the group task. Status characteristics theory argues that social characteristics serve as cues from which people develop expectations about their own and others' task abilities. Once formed, these expectation states shape the power and prestige order of the group. A set of formally defined principles—salience assumption, burden of proof assumption, sequencing assumption, aggregation assumption, and the basic expectation assumption—provide the explanatory basis on which various predictions have been made about social interaction. Among the issues examined is how actors process multiple status characteristics. Years of research in this branch of EST have generated a great deal of knowledge about how status stereotypes create and perpetuate inequalities in social interaction.

EST also posits that one's expectations for rewards are interdependent with performance expectations. Unequally distributed rewards among group members, therefore, create a status hierarchy (Berger et al. 1985). Moreover, verbal and nonverbal cues such as initiating conversation, making suggestions, and making eye contact can influence performance group expectations and inequalities (Ridgeway 1987; Fisek, Berger, and Norman 1991).

Other issues currently under investigation include how status expectations created in one setting influence the status structures that develop in subsequent situations (Freese 1974; Markovsky, Smith, and Berger 1984). Status construction theory (Ridgeway 1991, 2001; Ridgeway and Balkwell 1997) addresses the question of how status beliefs are formed in society by combining EST principles with structural perspectives such as Peter Blau's (1977) macrostructural theory. Double-standards theory (Foschi 1989, 2000) focuses on how different standards may be used to create performance expectations for actors in different status groups. Additional research has also examined how legitimacy develops in group interaction and increases compliance with the group status order (Ridgeway and Berger 1986; Berger et al. 1998). Finally, recent work has begun to provide an explanation for how second-order expectations—beliefs about others' expectations—influence actors and the inequalities that emerge in groups (Webster and Whitmeyer 1999).

OTHER RESEARCH AND
THEORETICAL APPROACHES

Numerous research problems are being examined by social psychologists today. One such line of inquiry is social identity and the ways in which it may affect social behavior. Among the more sophisticated theoretical formulations and research programs, four warrant mentioning (Owens 2003). Role-identity theory (McCall and Simmons 1966) focuses on the role that actors construct for themselves when occupying specific positions and the ways in which individuals deal with multiple-role identities. Identity theory (Stryker 1980) emphasizes the interconnections between individuals and social structures and networks of social relations in which particular attention is given to how the self involves a hierarchical ranking of identities and an actor's role commitment.

Identity control theory (Burke 1991; Burke and Stets 1999; Stets and Burke 2002) provides a cybernetic control model of identity focused on the internal dynamics of the self and how negative emotions conceivably result from whatever discrepancies exist between a person's perception of self-relevant meanings in a situation and identity standard meanings. Affect control theory (Heise 1977, 1979, 2002; Smith-Lovin and Heise 1988; MacKinnon 1994) is a highly researched identity-based perspective that offers a cybernetic feedback and control model while emphasizing how deflections between fundamental and transient feelings created in interaction situations influence peoples' emotions and social relations.

Social psychologists have also given attention to the role of emotions in social behavior, interaction, and society (Stets 2003). Peggy Thoits (1990), among others, defined the essential components of emotions, while Kemper (1987) and Turner (2002) developed taxonomies of primary and secondary emotions. Kemper (1991) emphasizes how emotions are grounded in structural conditions involving power and status. Others focus on how culture contributes to the development of emotions. For instance, Hochschild (1983) argues that feeling rules define the emotions we should have in different situations, and people manage their emotions to fit these cultural standards (Gordon 1990). Other approaches focus on the roles that social interaction and self-processes play in generating emotions. Identity control theory (Burke 1991), as previously noted, argues that a lack of fit between how actors see themselves in a social setting and their identity standards results in negative emotions. So, too, affect control theory (Heise 1979) emphasizes how the confirmation or disconfirmation of people's identities in situations influences how we feel.

Interest in the role of emotions continues to expand in other ways in social psychology. For example, relational cohesion theory (Lawler and Yoon 1996; Lawler and Thye 1999) argues that group cohesiveness is determined by the frequency of exchange agreements and the positive emotions they generate. Other analysts have directed attention to the status processes that shape emotions (Ridgeway and Johnson 1990) and the ways in which group sentiment structures may influence performance expectations (Shelly 2001). Finally, Scheff (1990, 1994, 1997; Retzinger and Scheff 2000) argues that emotions play a crucial role in shaping social relations. Emotions such as shame are expressions of social bonds, which under certain conditions lead to undesirable outcomes, including conflict and violence.

Another research issue of increasing interest over the last several decades concerns the life course and socialization. In this area, Mortimer and Simmons (1978) and Brim and Wheeler (1966) demonstrate how adult socialization differs from childhood socialization. Other analysts, including Elder (1985, 1998; Elder and Caspi 1988), show how transitions and trajectories occur over historical periods and positions in social structure. The life-course paradigm focuses on the social dynamics operating at different life stages and demonstrates how social structure affects individuals at different points of their lives. Research in this area continues to expand, addressing issues relating to how the childhood period involves children engaging in an "interpretative reproduction" of culture (Corsaro and Eder 1990; Corsaro 1997).

Another area of research focuses on social dilemmas or the pervasive social situation where a conflict exists between group incentives and individual short-term incentives (Sell, forthcoming). The discussion surrounding social dilemmas has been strongly influenced by Mancur Olson's (1965) and Garret Hardin's (1968) treatment of the topic. Subsequent cross-disciplinary research based on rational choice assumptions and game theory concentrates on various strategies and factors influencing the solution of dilemmas (Messick and Brewer 1983; Ostrom, Gardner, and Walker 1994; Yamagishi 1995; Wilson and Sell 1997; Sell and Wilson 1999; Sell et al. 2002).

Last, topics surrounding legitimation are of increasing interest. In this area, Walker, Rogers, and Zelditch (2002), Zelditch and Walker (1984), and Zelditch et al. (1983) have investigated issues involving how the legitimacy of acts, persons, and positions influences compliance with authority. And EST has shown how status beliefs linked to status characteristics provide legitimation for status hierarchies (Ridgeway and Berger 1986; Ridgeway, Johnson, and Diekema 1994; Berger et al. 1998).

All this research is contributing to a growing body of knowledge concerning social interaction, identity, and the relationships between actors and social systems.

OTHER AREAS OF INTEREST

Social psychology represents a diverse field of inquiry. While it is not possible to discuss all the topics addressed by social psychologists, such as social justice, social movements/collective behavior, stratification/mobility, and cross-cultural concerns, the present discussion is intended to highlight key traditions of thought and to identify major sources.

Many of the research topics addressed by social psychologists hold relevance among applied researchers and for public policy issues. Research on the social psychology of work has addressed topics such as the benefits of work for men and women (Sorensen and Mortimer 1988) and has demonstrated the importance of the organization of the work environment for psychological functioning and work orientations (Kohn and Schooler 1983). Other research has examined the significance of social psychological influences on health, such as the role of chronic stress in causing illness (Mirowsky and Ross 1989).

Social psychological scholarship has also contributed to our understanding of crime and deviance. Control theory (Hirschi 1969) and labeling/societal reaction perspectives (Becker 1963) demonstrate the crucial role that social interaction, relationships, and participation in group activities play in both creating and mitigating deviant behavior. Groundbreaking studies such as Goffman's (1961) investigation of total institutions help us understand how social milieus such as prisons lead to various psychosocial outcomes that oftentimes are contrary to the stated goals of such institutions.

As a final example, a body of applied research in EST focuses on status intervention strategies to lessen inequalities among status groups. This work has been especially concerned with developing techniques for reducing the pernicious effects of negative-status stereotypes such as race, gender, or nationality among schoolchildren (Cohen and Roper 1972; Cohen 1993; Cohen and Lotan 1997).

The dynamic aspects of social psychology are further demonstrated through new research and theory development. For instance, current work in the area of structural ritualization theory (Knottnerus 1997, 2002; Knottnerus and Van de Poel-Knottnerus 1999; Sell et al. 2000) focuses on the role ritual plays in social interaction and the ways in which ritual can create, reproduce, or transform social structure. This perspective, which is committed to cumulativity, discusses how social action and structure develop and may be maintained even when actors are not rewarded for their behavior and it may not benefit a group. A number of issues are currently being investigated by this approach, including the reproduction of ritualized social practices in groups embedded in a larger social milieu, the spread of legitimation, the development of ritualized activities in organizations, the strategic use of rituals, and the impact disruptions of ritualized behaviors have on social practices and groups.

Because symbolic interaction is characterized by a variety of theoretical perspectives, assumptions, and methods, it seems likely that this perspective will expand in the years ahead and that work in this area will continue to exhibit a vital and influential role in social psychology. This is evident in the impact of this tradition's ideas and findings on a number of areas, including the study of institutions such as the family, science, medicine, education, and religion and phenomena such as deviance, collective behavior/social movements, gender, emotions, socialization, and race/ethnic relations. Symbolic interactionism's influence is also evident in various approaches that have broadened in theoretical scope to address interaction processes and other issues such as identity or emotions. Stryker's (1980) analysis of structure and identity, Heise's affect control theory (1977), and Burke's identity control theory (1991) attest to this continuing influence.

More broadly, symbolic interactionism has contributed to a central insight involving the general principle of social construction or the power of individuals to shape their social setting. Through social interaction and interpretations, people construct, maintain, and change their social world. Symbolic interactionism emphasizes how people create a shared reality that is experienced as subjectively meaningful and objectively real (see also Berger and Luckmann 1966). This insight should continue to inform theory and research in the years ahead.

PROSPECTS FOR THE 21ST CENTURY

Prospects for the development of social psychology in the twenty-first century are quite promising. Research and theorizing should continue at a rapid pace. Moreover, there is no apparent reason to think that the gradual reduction in competition between sociological and psychological approaches to social psychology will reverse itself. While differences will continue to exist, and a certain degree of disciplinary rivalry will most likely characterize this area, there will continue to be some overlap and dialogue between the two approaches.

All indications are that the specific traditions of theory and research discussed in this chapter will continue to develop in the next decade or two. And certain areas will quite likely receive especially increased attention. Research into legitimation is one such area that should expand as researchers explore the various social mechanisms contributing to the legitimacy of group arrangements and authority structures (e.g., Johansson and Sell 2004; Johnson 2004). Theorizing and research about the role emotions play in social action, relationships, and society as a whole should also increase. Some of this work, such as the development of relational cohesion theory, will be integrative in nature, involving linkages with research addressing other components of social behavior and societal processes.

Moreover, the continued growth of the discipline will undoubtedly represent some of its greatest challenges. As research continues to expand, social psychology may face the possibility of a widening gulf between these various theoretical and research programs. Knowledge production within the social sciences rests on the assumption that the best ideas arise from a vigorous competition between alternative perspectives and bodies of evidence. When carried to extremes, however, especially in areas of inquiry marked by vigorous growth of diverse approaches, such tendencies can lead to unproductive consequences. Thus, it will be crucial that in the future, social psychologists recognize the value of cooperative research and theoretical development (Knottnerus 2005). Cooperative efforts broaden explanations of social processes while generating new insights and lessening the possibility of fragmentation and limited communication.

Such cooperation may involve multimethod research embracing different methodologies, such as laboratory experiments, historical studies, and ethnographic research, to test and exemplify theoretical formulations. On a conceptual level, the development of a common vocabulary and framework, for example, the idea of institutional rules (Lovaglia et al. 2005), could serve to frame and coordinate different perspectives addressing the same issue, such as the social dynamics operating in different kinds of groups. Cooperation could also involve different theoretical approaches creating direct linkages and either the integration of ideas or the building of conceptual bridges to deal with issues relating to status, power, exchange, emotions, legitimacy, or rituals in social behavior. Finally, the proposed integrative endeavors could focus on how social processes operate across different structural levels (from the most micro to the most macro), to explain how groups nested within larger groups can by influenced by the latter and smaller groups may affect the wider social environment.

PART V

SOCIAL AGGREGATIONS

15

THE SOCIOLOGY OF SOCIAL STRUCTURE

Fabrizio Bernardi

Juan J. González

Miguel Requena
Universidad Nacional de Educación a Distancia, Madrid, Spain

In the most general sense, the notion of "structure" refers to a set of relations between elements that has some measure of coherence and stability. It is, then, a concept with a heavy load of abstraction, a concept that we could, in principle, apply to any parcel of reality where we perceive a certain order. The way it is commonly used in the social sciences, it simply designates the deepest, most recurrent aspects of social reality, its framework or underlying form. In this sense, it is often used to distinguish the fundamental elements of society from the secondary ones, the essential aspects from the superfluous ones, the stable ones from the contingent ones (Boudon 1968). The idea of social structure refers, in this general case, to the idea of an ordered or organized arrangement of elements (Smelser 1992). On other occasions, the structure of a social aggregate is equivalent to the distribution of its elements in given positions. Sometimes the structure of a social entity is simply identified with its form or shape.

As the previous paragraph suggests, the meaning of the term *social structure* is not free from ambiguity. Adapting a famous joke of Raymond Aron's (1971) on the heterogeneity of the approaches of sociology, we could say that the only thing that the sociologists who deal with social structure share is that they all acknowledge how hard it is to define social structure. But the reference to Aron's joke may be more than just an analogy. Due to the importance of the concept of social structure in sociology, its definitions end up reflecting the plurality and heterogeneity of

approaches that characterize the discipline. As the late Robert Merton aptly said (1976:32), the evolving notion of social structure is not only polyphyletic—because it has more that one ancestral line of sociological thought—but also polymorphous—because these lines differ partly in substance and partly in method.

Where does this semantic ambiguity that envelopes the term *social structure* come from? The Latin source of the word *structure* is *struere,* which means "to build." And the most general notion of this term does, in fact, refer to the framework of elements and materials that constitute and support a building (López and Scott 2000). Another relevant and more recent (nineteenth century) historical source of meaning for the term *structure* comes from the anatomy of living beings, where the term designates the relation of the parts to the organic whole. In his classic work on structuralism, Jean Piaget (1970) went far beyond the constructive and organic analogies to specify three important characteristics that define the idea of structure in a great variety of scientific fields and disciplines. Every structure is, first, a *totality* whose properties cannot be reduced to those of its constituent elements. Second, it is a *system* with its own laws or mechanisms for functioning. And third, it is a *self-regulated entity* that to some degree maintains itself or preserves itself throughout time. These characteristics that Piaget pointed out have, in one way or another, impregnated the meaning of the concept structure in the social sciences and, more specifically, the use of the term *social structure* in sociology. As we will see, however, this Piagetian minimum common denominator has not been enough to produce a paradigmatic consensus on the concept of social structure. In addition, the contributions from neighboring disciplines have not always facilitated the task of achieving this paradigmatic consensus. The use of the idea of social structure in social anthropology, where it moves at very different levels of abstraction (Radcliffe-Brown 1940; Nadel 1957; Lévi-Strauss [1949] 1968) and is oriented toward very diverse empirical referents (e.g., Murdock 1949), is a good illustration of this.

In this chapter, we have three principal objectives. First, we will present two main visions of social structure that correspond to two important currents of structural sociological thought: on one hand the institutional or cultural vision and on the other the relational or positional vision. Both visions try to determine which element of society is the most *structural* one, in the sense of the element that conditions others the most, by answering the following question: What is social structure and what does it consist of? These visions of social structure, although they share some generic traits, can be distinguished because they give analytic priority to certain aspects of the social structures as opposed to others. Deep down, the difference between these visions reflects the discussion about the relationship between the sphere of culture and the sphere of social relations, a discussion that repeats itself throughout the development of sociological theory. Nevertheless, we will discuss some efforts at a theoretical synthesis of the two visions that have arisen. Afterwards, in the rest of the chapter, we wi'l try to organize the debate on the notion of social structure by presenting two key aspects that are clearly interdependent from the analytic point of view but that should be treated separately for the sake of explanatory clarity. The first aspect refers to the definition of the different levels of social structure and the analysis of the relations that hold among them. Here, the relevant question is, How many levels of social structure is it possible to identify and what is their configuration as a whole? (Prendergast and Knottnerus 1994). The second matter has to do with the margins of freedom and creativity left by social structure to individual action, and how individual action tends to modify or reproduce the structure (Sewell 1992; Kontopoulos 1993). The question, in this case, is, What relationship is there between social structure and individual action?[1] We will end the chapter with a summary of the main ideas presented.

VISIONS OF SOCIAL STRUCTURE

The different approaches to the term *social structure* make it quite clear that there is no basic paradigmatic consensus. To illustrate these relevant differences, we are going to examine two different visions of social structure—the institutional and the relational visions—that, without exhausting the inventory of existing approaches, point to the two main currents in structural sociological thought and, more generally, in sociological theory.

Institutional or Cultural Vision

In the first place, we will consider the *institutional* or *cultural* vision of social structure. From this point of view, the basic elements of social structure are the norms, beliefs, and values that regulate social action. A complete, influential sociological tradition understands social structure to be an *institutional* structure—namely, a set of *cultural* and *normative* models that define actors' expectations about behavior. The structural sociology that favors the ideational contexts of action—for example, norms, beliefs, values—has clear antecedents in the currents of thought that defend some kind of cultural determinism of human behavior. But the idea that the social structure consists of institutions, understood to be cultural phenomena and collective representations that regulate social action, is present above all in the functionalist theorization of the 1940s and 1950s. The clearest and most systematic expression of the relevance of cultural models for understanding the basic structure of social relations can be found in the work of Talcott Parsons. In fact, Parsons (1951) imagined a *social system* made up of differentiated roles that maintained structured (systemic) relations among themselves. Each role is defined in the value system shared by the individuals who form the society, so that the society is ruled by cultural norms that are transmitted from one generation to the next by a process of socialization. Individuals internalize these roles in their infancy: They learn to behave and to relate to others according to these shared cultural models. What we wish to highlight is that the social institutions—namely, the shared norms that reflect the fundamental values of society—constitute the skeleton of the social system (Parsons 1951). As Hamilton (1983) observes, in Parsons's theorization, social structures coincide with the systems of expectations—normative orientations—that regulate the relations between the actors, with the objective of satisfying the society's functional needs. In this approach, society's material structure itself derives from its cultural structure. This means that we can apprehend the basic structure of social relations (from kinship to stratification) from the contents of the culture that the members of the society share.

After a hiatus of almost 20 years, these visions of social structure have reappeared with renewed energy in the current of thought known as neo-institutionalism (Brinton and Nee 1998). The most recent position of the neo-institutionalists, particularly in economics, political science, and the sociology of organizations, is much less ambitious and deterministic than the version of Parsons and his more orthodox followers. In other words, there is no attempt to provide a general explanation of how society functions, nor is the idea that the cultural/value sphere constitutes the ultimate essence of social structure held.

In fact, the neo-institutionalists in economy and political science "limit" themselves to acknowledging the importance of institutions as shared norms and cultural representations that regulate individual action. Institutions function as "game rules" and procedures that give a sense of stability and order to interactions and reduce the insecurity of market transactions. On the other hand, neo-institutionalism in the field of the sociology of organizations has introduced the concept of institutional isomorphism to describe how the emergence of similar structures among previously different organizations is the result of the diffusion of organizational languages and cultures (DiMaggio 1994).

Relational and Distributive Vision

Second, we have the *relational* perspective. From this point of view, the elements that make up social structure are, basically, social relations, and the analysis of social structure focuses on the tissue of social relations that connects individuals, groups, organizations, communities, and societies. With reference to the antecedents of this perspective, we must mention, first of all, the Marxist tradition, which interprets social structure as a system of relations between class positions, with the basic relations being the relations of exploitation of the dominated classes by the dominant classes; these relations are defined by the modes of production of a given society in a particular historical period (Marx [1859] 1936). Authors such as Simmel ([1908] 1950), for whom society exists insofar as individuals enter into association or reciprocal action, should not be forgotten as pioneers of this vision of social structure.

For the sociology of social structure, however, this relational perspective has its nearest origins in British social anthropology. English anthropologist Radcliffe-Brown (1940:2), for example, saw human beings "connected by a complex network of social relations" and used the term *social structure* "to denote this network of actually existing relations." Social structure thus includes both all person-to-person social relations and the differentiation of individuals and of classes by their social role. Of course, contemporary applications of this approach go well beyond the anthropological study of small groups and communities. And, in all probability, the main development in this vein nowadays is modern network analysis, with a really broad range of studies, from personal relationships to kinship, from organizations to markets, from cities to world economy. Modern network (or structural) analysis aims to study "the ordered arrangements of relations that are contingent upon exchange among members of social systems" and claims that social structures "can be represented as *networks*—as sets of *nodes* (or social systems members) and sets of *ties* depicting their interconnections" (Wellman and Berkowitz 1988:3, 4). Network theorists try to map social structures, studying regular and enduring patterns of relation in the organization of social systems and analyzing how these patterns affect the behavior of individual members (see, e.g., Granovetter 2005, for an analysis of the impact of social networks on economics outcomes).

An important variation on this second vision of social structure is the *distributive* or *positional* perspective. From the distributive point of view, social structure is an ordered or hierarchical set of positions. For example, according to Blau (1976b, 1977a, 1977b, 1980, 1994), social structure is defined quantitatively in terms of the distributions of the members of a population in different social positions. In Blau's own words (1976b), social structure refers "to population distributions among social positions along various lines—positions that affect people's role relations and social interaction" (p. 221). A set of parameters—or criteria of social distinction, such as age, sex, race, and socioeconomic status—defines a social structure, which is composed of social positions and social relations. Under these assumptions, Blau's theory essentially deals with two things: (1) establishing the structural conditions of a specific society—namely, defining the quantitative properties of its social structure (e.g., the number of individuals who occupy the different social positions and the size of the different groups and social strata) and (2) analyzing how a society's structural conditions, understood in quantitative terms, affect the models of social interaction or of association (e.g., marriage or friendship) among those who occupy its different social positions. Furthermore, Blau's theory of social structure is not only distributive but also macrostructural and multidimensional. One of the objectives of the social structure theory of Blau (1977b) is to explain certain forms of social inequality. In a similar vein, Lin (2001:33), in his recent work on social capital, defines a social structure as consisting of "(1) a set of social units (*positions*) that possess differential amounts of one or more types of valued resources and that (2) are hierarchically related relative to *authority* (control and access to resources), (3) share certain *rules* and procedures in the use of the resources, and (4) are entrusted to *occupants* (*agents*) who *act on* these rules and procedures."[2]

Some Attempts at Synthesis

A persistent problem in the debate between the cultural vision and the relational vision is that it often leads to a dual representation of the social structure and to a split image of society. In some classic authors, such as Durkheim ([1893] 1964) and Weber ([1921] 1968), and in other contemporary ones, such as Dahrendorf (1972), Giddens (1984), Sewell (1992), and Bourdieu (1989), we can find a broad conception of social structure that attempts to include both the ideational and the relational aspects. Dahrendorf (1972:163) uses the expression "the two faces of social structure" to refer to this idea. According to Dahrendorf (1972:157ff.), the categories of integration and values, on one hand, and the categories of authority and interests, on the other, correspond to these two faces of social structure.

Giddens (1984) presents a very elaborate development of a dual theory of structure that encompasses both the relational and the ideational aspects of social reality. According to Giddens, social structure represents a kind of grammar that orients social action. While the action constitutes an activity that is situated in space and in time, the structure has only a virtual existence that becomes explicit in the actors' models of action. Another fundamental distinction in Giddens's theorization is made between structure and social system. As has already been mentioned, the notion of structure denotes basic, deep principles: Structure consists of "rules and resources" that the actors employ to manage in situations of social action and interaction (Giddens 1984). However, when he uses the term *social system,* Giddens refers to the concrete relations between actors and collectivities. A social system can, then, be considered to be the manifestation and updating of a particular social structure. The application of rules and resources by the actors involves the production and recursive reproduction of the social structure and, consequently, of the social system. The structure does not consist of the models of social practices that make up the social system but of the principles that give models to the practices. Thus, the two key ideas of Giddens's structuration theory can be as follows: (1) Structure, understood to be the set of rules and resources belonging to a specific social system, limits and makes possible the action of individual actors; and (2) action, insofar as it consists of carrying out and updating the structure, contributes to reaffirming it and transmuting it and, consequently, to reproducing and transforming the social system.

Giddens's theorization has been the object of numerous criticisms, some radical and others more favorable. Among these last ones, Sewell's (1992) stands out: He upholds a revision and broadening of Giddens's theory and focuses on two aspects: the nature of moral rules in the structure of legitimization and the immaterial character of resources. Sewell (1992) criticizes Giddens's concept of rules and advocates substituting it with the "schema" to include "not only formally established prescriptions but also the schema, metaphors, and presuppositions that are assumed by these prescriptions, which are informal and not always conscious" (p. 8). These are procedures that can be generalized to the most diverse contexts of interaction, known or new, and that are applied on several levels of depth, from the deepest levels described by Lévi-Strauss to the most superficial ones, such as protocol norms. The schemata are, therefore, not distinguished by their field of application, as Giddens's distinction between semantic rules in the field of communication and moral rules in the field of sanctions suggests, but by their level of depth.

Sewell's notion of "schema" comes close to Bourdieu's (1989) notion of *habitus,* a system of "durable and moveable" dispositions that generate sensible practices and perceptions capable of giving meaning to the practices that are generated in this way. The dispositions that form the *habitus* operate as mental schemata that routinely orient individuals' actions and offer a practical knowledge of the meaning of what has to be done and of how it should be done. The crucial point is that the mental schemata operate like a filter that puts the options available to the actor in order, without the actor having to actively worry about them (López and Scott 2000:103). Bourdieu (1989) defines the *habitus* as a "structuring structure," since the logical categories with which the social world is perceived are, in turn, a product of the division of social classes. This is the same as saying that the dispositions of the *habitus* depend on the position that the actor occupies in the society's system of differential positions.

Other attempts at synthesis present a kind of contextual vision of social structure that is much broader than the institutional and relational visions but also much more diffuse and indeterminate. From this other point of view, social structures are, simply, the context in which social action happens and develops. According to another exponent of this current, Rytina (1992), social structure

> is a general term for any collective social circumstance that is inalterable and given for the individual. Social structure thus provides a context or environment for action. The size of organizations, distribution of activities in space, shared language, and the distribution of wealth might all be regarded as social structural circumstances that set limits on feasible activities for individuals. (P. 1970)

Clearly, with this broad contextual perspective of social structure, we have moved far from the bounded field of norms, or of social relations and positions, to situate ourselves in the diffuse world of all those factors that—inso-far as they are, in some measure, structured—can influence social action.

In summary, the two broad visions of social structure share some generic traits that are implicit in the very idea of structure, but at the same time they present crucial differences. As for the similarities, we will mention three common features. First, the elements of the structure are organized or ordered in some way; in other words, they maintain patterned or nonrandom relations—and, precisely because of this, we can say that they form a structure. Second, these relations among the elements of social structures are constituted by regular or recurring behaviors that are repeated and that give the structures a certain permanence in time and space. And third, these regularities that constitute the social structures condition, in several ways, many social choices and behaviors. As for the differences, it is obvious that these visions of social structure differ, above all, in the specifications they make about which is the fundamental dimension of social structure: normative contexts of action or social positions and relations. This disagreement has, in addition, crucial sociological implications because the analytic key to the explanations of social action depends on which structural aspects or dimensions are judged to be most relevant. In other words, the relevant dimensions of the social structure—norms or relations and positions—are not only *structured* in the sense that they are ordered, regular, persistent sets, but they are also *structuring* in the sense that they offer opportunities and establish constraints for social action.

THE PROBLEM OF THE LEVELS OF SOCIAL STRUCTURE

Another problem that any approach to social structure must resolve, no matter which aspect or dimension receives priority, is the question of choosing the units or elements that make up the social structures on which the analysis will focus. The obvious candidates for becoming units of analysis are those social entities that are susceptible to establishing relations, occupying positions, or constituting contexts that are relevant for action. But it is difficult to make an exhaustive list of all the social entities that can operate as units of analysis for social structures. Why is it so hard to make a complete list? The difficulty arises because opting for one entity or another depends, on one hand, on the kind of range that the phenomenon we want to investigate has; it is, thus, an eminently empirical problem that can have many solutions. On the other hand, it depends on the theoretical and methodological orientation chosen, which will favor some structural units over others in explaining the phenomena studied. Furthermore, several inventories of elements are also possible, depending on the degree of abstraction at which we wish to move.

Prendergast and Knottnerus (1994) identify six levels of social structure: interpersonal relations, networks among individuals, relations in organizations, relations among organizations, societal stratification, and the world system. Other classifications are, logically, feasible. But, keeping in mind that the identification of levels reflects growing ranges of complexity, one possibility for classifying these different levels is to resort to a triple scheme that distinguishes, moving from simple to complex, three main social levels: micro, meso, and macro. The crucial factor that allows us to clarify on which level of social structure we should be moving is not only the range of the phenomenon we wish to study but also—and this is equally fundamental—the theoretical and methodological assumptions that we adopt in our explanations of social action.

If we consider that the relevant structural units are individuals and their relations, then we will be getting involved in some form of microsociology of social structure (Homans 1976; Collins 1981; Coleman 1990). As Homans (1987) clearly stated, those who practice this sort of individualist sociology "are most interested in how individuals create social structures" (p. 73). If, for whatever reasons, our interest is focused on intermediate entities such as groups, networks of relations, communities, and organizations, which we consider to be causal agents or independent variables in the social structures analyzed, then we will be practicing some kind of mesosociology. The

sociology of organizations (Perrow 1986) fits into this formulation. Finally, if what attracts our attention are social entities or aggregates that are very complex—either because of the number of elements they contain or because of their high relational density—and if we judge that these complex social structures are the explanatory instances of our dependent variables, then we will situate ourselves in the area of macrosociology. Excellent examples of structural macrosociology can be found in Blau's theories of social structure, in which he explains the phenomena of inequality and heterogeneity (1977a, 1977b) and formulates a set of axioms on the models of social association and interaction drawn from the quantitative characteristics of social structure (Blau 1994).

Sociological literature has resorted, also, to different metaphors to explore the relations among the different levels of the structure (López and Scott 2000). We will present three here. The first one represents the levels of the social structure as being fitted one within the other, such as Chinese boxes. The second one resorts to a geological image and distinguishes between one level that is the base of the structure and the others that are on top of the structure and are conditioned by it. A third metaphor divides social structure into system and subsystem levels.

A Chinese box-type of metaphor is used by Prendergast and Knottnerus (1994) to explain the relation among the different levels of social structure. Both authors understand social structure as systems of social relations that manifest themselves with different levels of complexity and that maintain among themselves nested ties. Blau (1981) has expressed this idea very clearly: "social structures are nesting series with successive levels of more and more encompassing structures" (p. 12). In this perspective, the most complex systems of social relations include the simplest ones, although each level has its own properties and characteristics. Besides, the logic of each level of social structure is not determined by the higher or lower levels of the structure. The notion of social structure that can be deduced from Simmel's ([1908] 1950, [1908] 1955) theorization offers an example of the Chinese box metaphor. Simmel analyzes how the quantitative determination of the group influences the form of its structure. The simplest groups are those made up of only one, two, or three elements. The movement from one of these groups to the next bigger one occurs through the presence of a single added element. Nevertheless, the presence of this added element deeply modifies the structure of group relations. The movement from the dyad to the triad opens up the possibility of new forms of relations that were impossible in a relationship between just two elements. These forms are the "impartial mediator," the *tertius gaudens* (the third who rejoices), and the *divide et impera* (divide and rule). What matters here is that the three types of social configuration—the single element, the dyad, and the triad—can be considered to be forms of elemental relations that are within one another and that, nevertheless, are qualitatively different among themselves. In general, we feel it is important to underline that this kind of conception of social structure remains essentially neutral with respect to the matter of which is the ultimate, basic element of social structure that conditions the rest.

The base and superstructure model identifies two main levels of social structure and suggests that there is a causal relationship between them (López and Scott 2000). One level, the base or infrastructure, conditions or determines the other, the superstructure. In some versions, this model translates into a strong determinism, according to which the superstructure is nothing more than a simple product or epiphenomenon of the base. In others, some degree of autonomy is acknowledged and the analysis focuses on demonstrating the limits of this autonomy.

The clearest formulation of the base and superstructure model can be found in the theory of Marx. According to this author, the basic structure of a society coincides with the mode of production that characterizes it. Marx distinguishes between the material basis of the social relations of production and the superstructures formed by the political and legal apparatuses and the collective representations (values, norms, ideologies) that are associated with them. In addition, the superstructure reflects the nature of the mode of production and does not have a logic of its own. As for the political superstructure, the institutions of the State and their ways of functioning are designed according to the needs of the productive structure, to guarantee its maintenance by different means of coercion; something similar happens with the ideological superstructure, built to serve the interests of the bourgeoisie by persuading the proletariat of the goodness of the system. In the "Preface" to his *A Contribution to the Critique of Political Economy,* Marx ([1859] 1936) described his approach as follows:

> In the social production of their existence, men inevitably enter into definite relations, which are independent of their will, namely relations of production appropriate to a given stage in the development of their material forces of production. The totality of these relations of production constitutes the economic structure of society, the real foundation, on which arise a legal and political superstructure and to which correspond definite forms of social consciousness. The mode of production of material life conditions the general process of social, political and intellectual life. It is not the consciousness of men that determines their existence, but their social existence that determines consciousness. (Pp. 517–18)

The vision of social structure as something that is formed of systems and subsystems tends to be associated with the theory of Parsons and the school of systems theory that his work has inspired. The idea that is behind Parsons's (1951) AGIL scheme is that to survive, every social system has to fulfill four functional prerequisites: (1) adaptation to the environment (A), (2) the ability to achieve goals (G), (3) integration (I), and (4) latency or maintenance of a latent pattern (L). In the case of the social system as a whole, the following functional subsystems correspond to

each function prerequisite: the economy (A), politics (G), the legal system and the community (I), and, finally, the family, school, and cultural institutions (L). Each of these subsystems can, in turn, be divided into four other subsystems (Collins 1988). The political system, for example, is subdivided into the subsystems of administration (A), executive (G), legislation (I), and Constitution (L). These subsystems can, in turn, be subdivided into other subsystems that fulfill the four functional prerequisites.

What it is important to underline is that in this vision of social structure as opposed to the model of base and superstructure, there is no hierarchical relationship that separates the subsystems into lower and higher levels. A subsystem of action is an analytic aspect that can be abstracted from the total processes of action but does not, in any concrete sense, exist independent of them. On the other hand, the subsystems fit into one another laterally to form the logical and coherent unit of a system of action.

THE PROBLEM OF STRUCTURE AND ACTION

Once the main visions of social structure and the problem of its different levels have been presented, the second part of the debate on this important sociological notion that we will deal with in this chapter refers to the relation between the structural elements and the action of individual actors. Our question here is, To what extent does the structure condition and determine the action of individuals? Or, taking the opposite perspective, To what extent can the structure be considered nothing more than the product of the action of individuals? To present the different responses to these questions, one can distinguish, following Kontopoulos (1993), three main perspectives: the strategy of reduction (or strong individualism), of systemic transcendence (or holism), and of construction (or methodological individualism).[3]

The strategy of reduction in the physical and natural sciences is based on the idea that the structures are nothing more than the parts that make them up and that the highest levels of organization of phenomena are totally determined and explained by the lowest levels of organization. In the case of sociology, the lowest levels of organization from which the higher levels derive are individuals. In other words, the individual actors are the atoms, and structure takes its form and existence from their aggregation. As examples of the strategy of reduction, one can consider Homans's behaviorist sociology and Collins's microtheory of the chain of interaction rituals.

According to Homans (1967), any structure is created and maintained throughout time by the action and interaction of individuals. Thus, to explain a social phenomenon, it is necessary to reduce it to psychological propositions about human conduct and, in particular, to the actors' optimizing intentions. It is important to note that the behaviorist paradigm does not conceive the social structure to be an entity that is separate and autonomous of individual action. In one of his latest works, Homans (1987) claims,

> When I speak of social structures I shall mean any features of groups that persist for any period of time, though the period may not be long. I shall not attempt, nor shall I need to attempt, any more sophisticated definition. (P. 72)

On the other hand, he acknowledges that individual action is subject to the influence of and to certain restrictions from the actions of other individuals, but he rejects the idea that institutions, organizations, and other structural factors, such as the social stratification system, are anything other than the result of interaction among individuals. In his own words, "The characteristics of groups and societies are the resultants, no doubt the complicated resultants but still the resultants, of the interaction between individuals over time—and they are no more than that" (Homans 1974:12).

Along the same lines, in an article from the early 1980s, Collins (1981) proposed a microfounding of sociology based on a theory of the chains of ritual interactions. According to this theory, all social phenomena, including social structure, are nothing more than microrepetitions of certain behaviors in the real world. In strict terms, according to Collins's proposal, things such as the "State," the "economy," or a "social class" do not exist.[4] All that exist are collections of individuals who act in specific types of microsituations.

The strategy of systemic transcendence or collectivism is characterized by a strong determinism of the micro parts by the macrosystem interpreted to be an autonomous entity, on the highest level, superimposed on the systemic parts of the lower level in a kind of hierarchical control. In the case of sociology, the approaches that share this epistemic strategy imply a relation between structure and action that opposes the strategy of the theorizations studied up to this point. In other words, the structure is what fundamentally conditions and determines action. In this view, the existence of a deep structure, whether material, cultural, or of another kind, is assumed. This deep structure generates the observable forms of social action and, therefore, is independent of them, so that it can be studied "objectively." Individuals' actions turn out to be nothing more than a reflection of the logics and properties of the structural elements of the system. Examples of these collectivist or holistic kinds of views can be found in the theoretical traditions with functionalist orientations and in some structuralist variants of Marxism.

The clearest origin for this approach can be found in Durkheim's definition of the sociological method and social facts. To found a new social science subjected to the method applied in the natural sciences, Durkheim granted "social facts" a reality independent of individual impulses, whose erratic appearance was disturbing in comparison with the "astonishing regularity" of social phenomena. One basic assumption of Durkheim's sociology is that social facts are be considered and treated as *things* that are external to, and coercive of, the actor. He thus defined social facts as ways of acting, thinking, and feeling that are external to individuals and have coercive power over them. This exteriority is due to the fact that individuals are born into an already constituted society and they are no more than a minimum element in the totality of social relations. The coercive characteristic derives from the mechanisms of social sanction and punishment that are instituted to preserve the network of moral obligations that society is and from the resistance that these mechanisms pose to reform. Individual action is, to a great extent, determined by social causes that cannot be explained by means of individual psychology but only by their relation with other social facts (Durkheim [1895] 1938). According to this approach, complex processes such as the progressive "division of social work" can be described leaving out any reference to the attitudes and preferences of those who participate in them and can be explained by other processes that are also objective, such as the increase in population density, the improvement of communication, or competition for scarce resources.

At the "materialist extreme" of structural approaches, we can also find reasonings according to which individual action is, to a great extent, determined by the structural position occupied. The Marxist terms *class consciousness* and *class action* referred, originally, to thoughts and behaviors derived from the individual's position in the system of production. The social classes' ways of political thinking and acting rest on and are shaped by economic interests. At any rate, it is true that clearly holistic positions have been more frequent among Marxist sociologists than in Marx himself. However, some more recent readings of Marx—particularly the current called analytic Marxism (Roemer 1986)—question an overly deterministic interpretation of his thought and put greater emphasis on the actors' capacity for choice.

Finally, the strategy of construction represents an intermediate position between the two extremes that we have presented in the preceding paragraphs. In recent decades, this approach has been acquiring greater relevance in sociology, perhaps due to its remarkable capacity for orienting empirical research and interpreting the results that it produces. In this approach, the relation between structure and action is bidirectional. On one hand, the restrictions and opportunities of the structural context in which the actor finds himself capacitate and constrain his action. In other words, the structure limits and conditions action. Nevertheless, individuals do not cease to have a margin of freedom in their actions. On the other hand, the aggregation and combination of individual actions can result in emerging, unforeseen, or undesired effects of change in the social structure. In other words, the structure itself is the product of the complex aggregation of individual actions (Boudon 1981). This view demonstrates that individualism and collectivism are not logically incompatible, necessarily opposed positions.

The basic propositions of methodological individualism can be summarized as follows. In the first place, there is a structure of constraints and opportunities associated with the different positions in a given social context. In the second place, the unit of analysis is the individual actor and his intentional actions. The individual actor chooses his course of action intentionally, from among the available options and according to his preferences. Intentional action is understood to be a purposeful action—namely, an action directed toward achieving an objective. The influence of the structure is manifest both in what the actor can do (i.e., his available options) and in what he wants to do as his preferences have been formed in a specific social context. Third, individual actions can produce effects on the structure of constraints and opportunities that are undesired or unexpected by the individuals. These propositions cover and connect different levels of analysis. As Coleman (1990) has observed, the first proposition (how the structure condition individual action) implies a movement from the macrolevel of structure to the microlevel of the actor, while the third (how individual actions can result in a change of the social structure) implies an inverse movement from the microlevel to the macrolevel.

One key aspect of this explanatory model is the actions of individuals. What does it mean when we say that the individual actions depend on the structure of the actors' situation? To answer this question, it is necessary, according to Boudon, to *comprehend* why an individual in a specific situation chooses a particular course of action. Following Weber, comprehending a social action implies, for Boudon (1986), getting enough information to analyze the motivations that inspire the action. An observer *comprehends* the action of the subject observed when he can conclude that in an identical situation, he would have acted in the same way. In general terms, this operation of comprehension implies that the sociologist adopts a particular model of the individual actor. To this end, Boudon and the majority of the sociologists who share the epistemic strategy of construction have used a model of an actor with a rationality limited by the character of the situation in which he finds himself (Simon 1982; Gambetta 1987; Elster 1989). With respect to the economists' classic model of the rational actor,[5] this model observes that there are limits in access to all the relevant information for making a decision. Second, it acknowledges that in certain situations that share a strategic dimension, it is impossible to univocally establish which behavior is the rational one. In situations of this kind, individuals resort to representations that are more or less solidly founded as norms, traditions, or imitations of others to make a decision.

To summarize, the causal explanation of a social phenomenon requires the description of the structural context in which the actors find themselves, a comprehension of the actions in this context, and the reconstruction of the aggregation process of these actions. Boudon (1986) defines this explanatory model as the "Weberian paradigm of action." For the purposes of this chapter, it is important to underline that on the epistemological level, this model attempts to conjugate the explanation of the structure with the phenomenological comprehension of the actor's action. On the analytic level, it seems to offer a flexible, useful framework for investigating the interdependence of structure and action.

CONCLUDING REMARKS

In this chapter, we have discussed some basic aspects of the sociology of social structure around three questions: (1) What is the ultimate nature of social structure? Or in other words, is it fundamentally collective representations such as norms and values, or relations among actors who occupy social positions? (2) How many levels of structure are there and how do they combine with one another? And finally, (3) what is the relation between structure and the action of an individual actor?

As we have seen, the sociology of social structure is not an intellectually unified field because it lacks a unitary conception of social structure. When sociologists use the term *social structure,* they usually refer to a set of social entities—the elements or constitutive units—that are ordered, organized, or hierarchized in some way and that maintain patterned, nonrandom relations among themselves with a certain permanence in time and space. But beyond this perfunctory commonality in the use of the term, there is no clear agreement about what the fundamental dimension of social structure is.

In this chapter, we have presented the two broad visions of social structure that have been most influential in sociological thought. On one hand, we considered the *institutional* or *cultural* vision of social structure, for which the basic elements are the norms, beliefs, and values that regulate social action. From this point of view, social structure is an *institutional* structure—namely, a set of *cultural* and *normative* models that define the actors' expectations about their behavior. We have also explained how this cultural vision of social structure has developed theoretically in structural functionalism and in the work of its most outstanding representative, Talcott Parsons, and, more recently, in neo-institutionalism. On the other hand, we distinguished the *relational* vision, for which the elements that make up the social structure are, basically, social relations. From this point of view, the analysis of the social structure focuses on the tissue of social relations that connects individuals, groups, organizations, communities, and societies. Modern network analysis exemplifies this second vision very well. A relevant variant of this second vision is the distributive or positional perspective. The representatives of this current of structural thought, among whom we highlighted Peter Blau, consider the social structure to be, above all, an ordered or hierarchical distribution of positions that share certain attributes and that affect people's social relations and interactions.

To the extent that the foundations of both visions—cultural and relational—imply a split image of social reality, several attempts at synthesis have been made to try to overcome this double representation of social structure. Here we have examined some recent theorizations (those of Giddens, Sewell, and Bourdieu) that try to integrate the basic assumptions of both visions in a single analytic framework, considering the normative and relational dimensions of social action jointly. Another attempt to avoid this dual representation of social structure is the definition of social structure in very broad and diffuse terms as the contexts in which social action develops—namely, the varied social circumstances that, being inalterable and given for the individual, provide the surroundings for his social action. From this last point of view, the precise conceptualization of social structure depends, in each case, on the type of social action theory that it defends and on the causal factors to which the proposed explanations point.

In addition to identifying the fundamental dimensions of the social structure, structural sociology faces the matter of choosing the units or elements that make up the social structures. Many classifications are possible, but we advocate a schema that discriminates three broad levels of complexity—micro, meso, and macro. However, deciding on which level of social structure to move depends not only on the phenomenon that we wish to study but also on the theoretical and methodological assumptions of our explanations of social action. Another interesting matter in relation to the levels of social structure is the matter of the images or metaphors that represent the relation among the different levels of the structure. We have presented three metaphors here. The first one represents the levels of social structure fitting into one another as if they were Chinese boxes. The second one resorts to a geological image and distinguishes between one level that is the base of the structure and the others that rest on top of the structure.

A third metaphor divides the social structure into levels of a system and subsystems.

With reference to the relation between structure and action, we have presented two main epistemological and methodological strategies that are opposed: individualism and holism. While the first consists of reducing the structural phenomena to the individual behaviors that form them, moving from the microlevel to the macrolevel, the second one considers individual behaviors as a reflection of the logic of the social structures and moves from the macrolevel to the microlevel. We have also seen that the approach called methodological individualism offers a possibility of overcoming the opposition between individualism and holism. According to this approach, the restrictions and opportunities defined by the structural context in which the actor finds himself condition his action. Nevertheless, individuals do not cease having margins of freedom to choose their courses of action. Besides, the aggregation and combination of individual actions can produce emergent, unforeseen, or undesired effects of change in the social structure. It is important to highlight the idea that the restrictions and opportunities that condition the actor's action can be of a relational nature, as well as cultural or ideational. In other words, they can be determined both by the actor's position in a specific system of social relations and by the cultural, normative, and value orientations that prevail in this system.

Given the current state of our discipline, it is hard to envisage the future development of a fully unified sociology of social structure. As always, theoretical and methodological preferences will determine the results of research on this topic. But the analysis of social structures will keep on being a fruitful field as long as it is able to solve the persistent problems of specifying the pertinent levels of social reality, define the relevant social entities that compose social structures, and disentangle the mutual relationship between social structures and individual action.

16

THE SOCIOLOGY OF GROUP DYNAMICS

JANE SELL

Texas A&M University

The study of groups and their structure has variously been termed *group dynamics, small groups,* and *group processes.* The sociological and the psychological interests in groups coincided in the early development of sociology and psychology and still coincide. The close relationship between the psychological and sociological investigations of groups is one of the important characteristics of this area of study. In fact, this interdisciplinarity, which existed at the beginning of its development, has continued, is still one of its most distinctive characteristics, and has further developed to include economics and political science.

Groups, their organizations, and their processes were important foci of many of the early sociologists. In an influential book, *Small Groups,* edited by A. P. Paul Hare, Edgar F. Borgatta, and Robert F. Bales (1965), the editors pay allegiance to the early theorists Émile Durkheim, Georg Simmel, Charles B. Cooley, and George H. Mead. In particular, the editors emphasize Durkheim's generic interest in group organization and his theoretical ideas of division of labor, which can be translated easily into role differentiation and stratification within groups. Both Cooley and Mead are important ancestors for the specific framework of symbolic interaction and frequently addressed the central importance of groups, especially small groups. Cooley, for example, developed and elaborated the idea of primary groups. Mead's (1934) theoretical conceptualizations in *Mind, Self, and Society* were important for developing concepts central to the development of group dynamics. Such concepts involved the centrality of groups and the importance of role-taking. Within these discussions, Mead used the example of a ball game

in which the attitudes of a set of individuals are involved in a cooperative response in which the different roles involve each other. In so far as a man takes the attitude of one individual in the group, he must take it in its relationship to the action of the other members of the groups; and if he is fully to adjust himself, he would have to take the attitudes of all involved in the process. (P. 163)

Simmel ([1907] 1971) wrote about many of the concepts and perspectives that have preoccupied group theorists for the 100 years since he detailed them. His discussions of conflict and exchange framed issues in the form of dynamic. For example, he argued that exchange was pervasive in human life:

Most relationships among men can be considered under the category of exchange. Exchange is the purest and most concentrated form of all human interactions in which serious interests are at stake. Many actions which at first glance appear to consist of mere unilateral process in fact involve reciprocal effects. The speaker before an audience, the teacher before a class, the journalists writing to his public—each appears to be the sole source of influence in such situations, whereas each of them is really acting in response to demands and directions that emanate from apparently passive, ineffectual groups. (P. 43)

What are group processes or group dynamics? What makes this line of investigation unique and distinct from other investigations? First, as indicated by the discussions of early theorists, the group is the unit of analysis (or in later work, one important unit of analysis). Second, in part because of the area's early alliance with psychology, it has traditionally accepted and developed laboratory studies, although experimental research has not been exclusively employed.

While it is impossible to be exhaustive, I summarize and discuss areas that seem to define the area by virtue of their continued attention by researchers. In particular, I focus on status, cooperation and competition, exchange, justice, and legitimation. I provide an assessment of trajectories of research and suggest particular questions or approaches that appear particularly promising.

STATUS AND STATUS EFFECTS

Status is one of the most important concepts in the discipline of sociology. In fact, much of sociology can be conceptualized as questioning what constitutes status and the effect of status. Status is usually defined as a position in a social network. Importantly, these statuses involve status beliefs, beliefs about the social worth of the individuals who occupy these statuses, such as the belief that a person who occupies one position is "better than" a person who occupies another position (see Sewell 1992).

Early studies in status tended to examine leadership. While these studies sometimes examined individual "styles" of leadership, most studies focused on general types of leadership approaches. A well-known study by Kurt Lewin, Ronald Lippitt, and Ralph White (1939) involved an experimental investigation of three different kinds of leadership: autocratic, democratic, and laissez-faire. The groups consisted of 10- and 11-year-old boys in after-school groups, and all the leaders were adults. On the basis of their experiment, the researchers found evidence that the democratic group resulted in more "we-ness" and group goals and less scapegoating compared with the autocratic group. Interestingly, autocratic groups spent more of their time working than did the democratic groups, who in turn spent more time working than did the laissez-faire groups. However, when the autocratic leader left the room, the boys stopped working, while the boys in the other groups continued working.

Bales (1950) and researchers at Harvard developed different kinds of analyses to map behaviors within the group. Interaction process analysis (IPA), described in 1950, was then an innovative technique and still shapes many group investigations. In its original form, it consisted of 12 categorizations of behavior. These categorizations separated out behaviors into positive and negative social emotional behavior and neutral task behaviors. So, for example, asking for opinions, disagreeing, and giving suggestions were coded, depending on their specific context. In particular, Bales and his colleagues were interested in the kind of interaction that occurred and how the particular behaviors of one group member conditioned the behaviors of another. These studies provided important evidence that status was *relative* to the group (Borgatta and Bales 1953), a central insight for group dynamics. This insight was critical for most of social psychology because it was the beginning of the powerful idea that while people might possess the same characteristics from one setting to another, these characteristics did not have the same salience in different settings. Such an idea took many years to develop but took root in new thinking about characteristics such as sex (or gender) and ethnicity.

Many sociologists have suggested that status significance is acquired through resources. In an analysis of one process through which nominal characteristics, such as race and sex categories, might acquire status-value and status beliefs, Cecilia Ridgeway (1991) developed and then tested aspects of status construction theory (Ridgeway and Erickson 2000; Ridgeway et al. 1998). This theory posits one mechanism through which a characteristic previously not status-valued might acquire such value. According to the theory, members differ in the level of material resources they possess—they differ on an unordered nominal characteristic, and resources are correlated with the "state" or category of the characteristic (Ridgeway 1991, 1997).

Status has been examined from a number of different perspectives. One of the most developed research programs, in many ways a direct descendant from Bales's research in group processes, is expectation states theory. The theory has several subsets. One portion of the theory, status characteristics theory, is concerned with how status characteristics generate and then sustain inequalities of power and prestige within groups. (Summary statements of the theory involved in this process can be found in Berger, Conner, and Fisek 1974; Berger, Wagner, and Zelditch 1992; Berger et al. 1977; Correll and Ridgeway 2003; Humphreys and Berger 1981.)

There are two types of status characteristics that have different properties. Specific status characteristics are those associated with a specific ability, such as the ability to score soccer goals or the ability to do accounting. These characteristics consist of two or more "states" that correspond to an expectation or assessment of how the individual will perform in the completion of a task. A diffuse status characteristic is a characteristic that also possesses at least two states of differential evaluation. However, associated with each state, not only are there associated specific performance expectations, but there are also associated general performance expectations "without limit as to scope" (Webster and Foschi 1988).

If individuals are within a task group and all are motivated to succeed on that task, status characteristics that differentiate among the group members are activated in the first step of a status organizing process, the burden-of-proof process. Unless some other characteristic or event intervenes, the status characteristics organize interactions such that those who are higher in social status receive higher amounts of power and prestige than those lower in status. The burden of proof rests on a demonstration that the status should NOT be used. The process proceeds in several steps; importantly, while the process might be conscious, it can be unconscious as well.

Much of the recent expectation states theory in general and status characteristics theory in particular has been explicated and elaborated through graph-theoretic models (see, e.g., Berger et al. 1977, 1998; Webster and Hysom 1998). These models serve to depict how different characteristics within the group and outside the group structure expectations and subsequent behavior.

Because of the burden-of-proof process, status can serve to organize the interactions within a group and help legitimate power use (or the lack of power use). The acceptable use of power can make a group function relatively smoothly and can generate an acceptance of inequality. Additionally, however, power use can generate negative sentiment and interrupt the process through which power use translates to status (see Lovaglia and Houser 1996; Lovaglia et al. 2005; Walker et al. 2000; Willer, Troyer, and Lovaglia 2001).

Dissolving status hierarchies involves more than just a reversal of the burden-of-proof process. Once a status hierarchy is created at an initial point in time, the deference granted at time one serves to reinforce subsequent power differentials. Because of this, initial differences become more and more entrenched. Consequently, it seems that interventions must either occur early in the group interaction or serve to severely contradict the expectations generated by other characteristics. Most researchers who have investigated this have considered how the addition of certain kinds of characteristics can serve to "dampen" or even eliminate the effects. Some research has investigated decreasing the effects of diffuse status through adding performance information (or specific status characteristics) that contradicts the evaluation associated with the diffuse status characteristics. Such investigations include those of Pugh and Wahrman (1983) and Wagner, Ford, and Ford (1986) for sex and Freese and Cohen (1973) for age. One important caveat to this research (and an implication from the graph theory) is that characteristics that equate actors do not contribute to the formation of expectations and to the subsequent observable power and prestige (Martin and Sell 1985; Webster 1977). Consequently, if both actors have equally high (or low) specific status characteristics and they are differentiated by a diffuse status characteristic, only the diffuse status characteristic organizes their interaction.

Another approach was suggested by Fisek in 1991 and then expanded and tested by Goar and Sell (2005). This approach emphasizes how changing the nature of the task might change the inequalities generated in the group: specifically, if the group task involves different abilities that are inconsistent with each other, group participation tends to equalize.

A long-term research and application program associated with expectation states theories was initiated and developed by Elizabeth Cohen and her colleagues (see Cohen 1982, 1993; Cohen and Roper 1972). These studies developed intervention strategies to reduce the participation differences between minority and majority children.

Additionally, the strategies were applied to other kinds of labeling, including reading ability (Tammivaara 1982).

The investigation of inequality within groups and how it relates to status remains an important area within the group dynamics area. Early studies stressed descriptions of groups, while later studies investigated possible ways in which status hierarchies might be modified or disrupted. One of the most exciting and promising areas of investigations is that of studies that examine different groups, how these groups are nested, and how status differences translated from one group to others. For example, Lovaglia et al. (1998) developed a formulation that assesses how status differences created in a group translate to individual-level performances on standardized tests.

LEGITIMATION

Closely related to the issues of status are issues of legitimation. Legitimation is the process through which a principle or set of rules is adhered to, deferred to, or supported even in the absence of obvious incentives to do so. These principles may or may not be written, and they can refer to persons, positions, and acts. This process is often taken for granted in the establishment and maintenance of social structure.

Max Weber, although not often discussed in terms of small-groups analysis, was important for initial conceptualizations of power (and subsequently exchange) and types of authority. He conceptualized three types of authority: charismatic, traditional, and legal rational (Weber [1924] 1978). Traditional authority is based on time-honored traditions, and charismatic authority is legitimated based on personal qualities of the leader. Legal rational authority, a characteristic of the modern bureaucracy, stresses universal rules, calculability, and efficiency.

Early studies on leadership (mentioned above) can be considered part of legitimation studies (see Burke 2003). In the context of leadership, an important study by Evan and Zelditch (1961) specifically tested some aspects of Weber's formulation and was one of the first experimental studies that created a bureaucracy in the laboratory. They investigated authorization as a source of legitimation and tried to separate the *legal* and *rational* components of Weber's theory of bureaucratic authority, finding that the source of legitimation was more important than the competency of the authority when it came to eliciting compliance.

Dornbusch and Scott (1975) elaborated a theory of authority, based on Weberian concepts of power, authority, and legitimacy. Different dimensions defined authority. One dimension refers to the norms that underlie the power relationship. Dornbusch and Scott (1975) refer to this dimension as either validity, collective support for a normative order, or propriety, individual belief in the fairness of norms. A second dimension refers to the sources of legitimacy. The power *structure* becomes legitimated through authorization, endorsement, or both. The third dimension of authority refers to its formal or informal character.

Expanding, modifying, and further developing these formulations, Bell, Walker, and Willer (2000), Zelditch and Walker (1984), Walker, Rogers, and Zelditch (2002), and Zelditch (2001) argued that theories concerned with the emergence of legitimacy must deal not only with types (validity and propriety) and sources (authorization and endorsement) but also with multiple objects such as acts, persons, and positions. For example, Thomas, Walker, and Zelditch (1986) found that collective approval can override personal approval.

Read (1974) created leaders with different sources of support: election, appointment by expert external authority; appointment by nonexpert external authority; and usurpation by a self-appointed leader. The study pointed out an important aspect of legitimation: What is given or the "status quo" is usually not questioned until something unusual occurs that calls into question the existing arrangements. Read concludes, "The leader selection process may establish a relationship between group members and the agent of selection which remains unexpressed until the leader places unusual demands upon group members" (p. 202). Subjects chose to retain the elected leader more than they did the expert appointed leader even though the expert leader had more task influence. This suggests a complex relationship between source of authority and influence, even in small informal groups.

Questioning the status quo was also a focus for research on revolutionary coalitions. Such coalitions were called revolutionary because they existed to "overthrow" some given arrangement within the group or organization (Lawler 1975; Webster and Smith 1978). Research in this area also suggested that endorsement was a particularly powerful source of authority. When the leader was responsible for a payment scheme that vastly underpaid some members, the disadvantaged were likely to revolt against the leader (Lawler and Thompson 1978). And in further demonstration of the importance of endorsement, Sell and Martin (1983) and Martin and Sell (1986) found that such a revolution could occur even if a legitimate authority had specifically prohibited the act.

In face-to-face group situations, it is often the case that influence and legitimacy are intertwined. (For a discussion of these concepts and how they are similar and different, see Lovaglia et al. 2005.) Berger et al. (1998) consider specifically the emergence and consequences of the legitimation (and delegitimation) of power and prestige orders. They describe legitimation as a social process that mediates the relationship between social actors and social structures. It is also a multilevel process. "Referential belief structures" or commonly held socially validated beliefs exist on a cultural level and can then be imported into a local setting, such as a task setting. The theory of reward expectations connects to this process by describing the relationship between performance and reward expectations that are based on the valued status characteristics. Rewards are then allocated to valued status positions in line with referential belief structures.

Another theory that addresses how legitimation can be transported from one arena to another is the theory of structural ritualization (Knottnerus 1997). The theory details how ritualized social practices can be reproduced, even in the absence of incentives and even when their reproduction may not be beneficial to the group (see Knottnerus 1997; Knottnerus and Van de Poel-Knottnerus 1999; Sell et al. 2000). Such a theory helps explain paradoxical behaviors, such as how those subjected to coercive practices eventually come to adopt and then support these same practices.

Legitimation concerns began with studies of individuals, specifically leaders, and their support from other group members. A particularly critical development within this area is the recognition and then elaboration of how different groups and organization can be "nested" and consequently how legitimation in one area can be imported into other areas. A particularly promising area for further investigation is how the sources and origins of legitimation can determine the stability of a group or organization, the potential development and dissolution of routines (see Johansson and Sell 2004), and the sudden development of crisis. In this regard, however, there must be further investigation of time. Even though the term *group dynamics* refers to change and time, strangely, "most research on groups neglects the role of time" (Arrow et al. 2005).

Much of what legitimation addresses relates to ideas of justice and fairness. Historically, the areas seem to have developed somewhat independently, with legitimation issues more often studied and applied in more "macrosociological" contexts, while justice and equity was more often studied in dyads or microsociological contexts. Recently, however, the two areas seem to be integrating.

JUSTICE

Within psychology there is a large literature related to issues of interpersonal justice. This literature aims to answer how individuals might make assessments of justice regarding their own and others' benefits (see, e.g., Adams 1965; Homans 1974; Walster, Walster, and Berscheid 1978). As Hegtvedt and Markovsky (1995) point out, sociological contributions to justice theorizing and research sought to extend justice decisions beyond the individual. Only by going beyond the individual can we begin to see the dynamics involved in the relative infrequence of revolution, for example (see Moore 1978).

One of the most important steps in this sociological focus was the status-value theory of distributive justice (Berger et al. 1972, 1985). The importance of a referential structure was developed and highlighted in these formulations. Such a structure is the general belief about how the social characteristics of generalized others correspond to social rewards. This structure is important for the judgment of actors about their local or immediate situation. So, for example, when professors assess whether their immediate situation is fair, the referential structure of "professor" is activated, and then a comparison between "what should be" and "what is" occurs. When there is congruence, the situation is evaluated as just.

Jasso (1980, 1988, 2001) developed a series of theoretical arguments and resulting models that use the insight of the referential structure. Her mathematical models allow estimates of the degree of felt injustice, and she argues that they can be extended to a wide variety of group-level phenomena, including such disparate acts as robbery and playing games of chance.

Markovsky (1985) developed a multilevel justice theory that highlighted the importance of the type of comparison, and the empirical results from differing comparisons. Specifically, he demonstrated that increased group identification could change actors' targets of comparison and therefore assessment of justice from interpersonal to group.

As mentioned, many of the sociological concerns with justice seem linked with legitimation and the question of authority. Hegtvedt and Johnson (2000) and Hegtvedt and Clay-Warner (2004) make the connection explicit. In particular, the literature makes it clear that different norms can be more or less valued or supported, depending on the way in which the norms were developed. Much of this idea relates to the referential comparison and the strength of different types of authority.

EXCHANGE

As Simmel ([1907] 1971) noted,

> Exchange is not merely the addition of the two processes of giving and receiving. It is, rather, something new. Exchange constitutes a third process, something that emerges when each of those two processes is simultaneously the cause and the effect of the other. (P. 57)

Group dynamic investigations of exchange emerged in the 1950s in both sociology and psychology. Homans (1950, 1958, 1961) adapted behavioral or operant learning tenets to describe behavior among individuals and, in doing so, gave homage to Simmel and his insight into human behavior. He presented human exchanges as involving rewards and costs and said that people responded to these in ways in which benefits outweighed costs. Blau's (1964) work on interactions in bureaucracies indicated that people compete for scarce resources and trade different social commodities (such as advice).

In psychology, Thibaut and Kelley (1959) developed their theory of social power, which involved the idea that the amount of power one individual or group possesses is determined, in part, by the alternatives present. Thus

individuals gauged whether to engage in exchanges on the basis of the value of the exchange itself and whether alternatives were available.

Emerson's (1962, 1964, 1972) formulation of power dependence theory in social relations took these previous conceptualizations and developed an overarching theory. It specified a relational aspect to power that placed the exchange relation as central. Power was inversely related to dependence: For a given exchange relation, the more powerful an individual or group, the less dependent it was on the relation. Furthermore, Emerson's theory posited a continual balancing mechanism in exchange relations. If people had power, they used it because it gave them an advantage. But if power was used, it was (incrementally) lost. This shift of power leads to continual balancing. In tests and extensions of the theory, Cook and Emerson (1978) demonstrated that power was a function of relative dependence. Empirical tests of the formulation supported this balancing notion (see, e.g., Cook et al. 1983), but other developments in the area questioned it (Willer 1987).

Further distinctions in different kinds of exchange emerged in work that followed. Specifically, Molm distinguished two types of exchange that had different properties. Negotiated exchange involves bargaining and negotiation and then agreement on the terms of the exchange. In contrast, reciprocal exchange does not involve negotiation but instead consists of individual acts performed for an other or others without knowledge about a future reciprocation. (For these distinctions, see Molm 1990, 1997a.) Given equivalent costs and benefits, reciprocal exchanges generate more trust and affect than do negotiated exchanges (Molm, Takahashi, and Peterson 2000). Part of the reason for this is that, at least under some conditions, risk generates trust (see also Kollock 1994).

Molm (1994, 1997a, 1997b) investigated coercive power in these nonnegotiated exchanges as well. Coercive power (in the sense of punishing others) is seen by participants as intentional and most likely to be used when an actor has little reward power. This is probably the case because coercion is risky and can decrease the possibilities of future beneficial exchanges. (We can see such coercive power use in examples of terrorism.) So, even though punishment can be an effective strategy if it is consistently and contingently applied, actors use it relatively infrequently.

While there are differences between negotiated and reciprocal exchanges, there are similarities as well. One important similarity rests with the negative emotion that can be generated with power use. For example, the conflict spiral, a theory about bargaining processes, documents that unequal power, even without punishment, can produce negative emotion (Lawler 1986; Lawler, Ford, and Blegen 1988).

Much of the research on negotiated exchange has countered part of Emerson's power dependence theory claims. While most of this research has supported the statement that "to have power is to use it," not all research has supported the second part of this, "to use it is to lose it." Much of the research within this area has focused on the idea of alternatives to valued resources and so considered exchange networks. Relative power of positions in simple networks can be analyzed by calculating the alternatives to a given position. Suppose there is a network in which there are three actors, Alphonse, Brunheilde, and Constantine (or A, B, and C). If Brunheilde can exchange with either Alphonse or Constantine, but Alphonse and Constantine can only exchange with Brunheilde, then B has alternatives while the others do not. As a result, in negotiations, B can demand much, and A and C can demand very little. This type of network has been termed strong power (Cook et al. 1983; Markovsky, Willer, and Patton 1988).

This network approach to negotiated exchange has flourished and other important exchange relations have been explored. One of the most important is weak power. Weak power yields exchange results intermediate between equal power and strong power (Markovsky et al. 1993; Willer 1999).

There have been a number of attempts to find methods of predicting power in networks that vary in structure and size. There is the graph-theoretic approach (Lovaglia et al. 1995), a game-theory approach (Bienenstock and Bonacich 1993), and an expected-value model (Friedkin 1992), among others. However, as discussed in Lucas et al. (2001), a general solution for a range of networks that vary in complexity is not yet clear.

As mentioned earlier, recent work within exchange perspectives has begun to consider how emotion is implicated in the exchange process. The affect theory of social exchange, for example (see, in particular, Lawler 2001; Lawler and Yoon 1993, 1996, 1998), maintains that while social exchange has an instrumental and individual function, the exchange itself involves a group product that fosters emotional, affective processes. While rational choice formulations had examined how commitment in exchange networks was fostered by uncertainty reduction, Lawler, Thye, and Yoon (2000) demonstrated that affect, in and of itself, also generated commitment. They also present the argument that such affect is particularly strong in productive exchanges. These exchanges occur in settings in which group members have equal power, coordination issues exist and must be solved, and the interdependence of group members is necessary for the production of the outcome.

While the study of exchange has always been important to group dynamics, the addition of emotion and notions of risk, trust, and uncertainty has transformed early investigations of simple cost and benefit. The transformations have expanded both the depth and scope of exchange formulations. For example, depth has been transformed by analysis of actors' strategies in the face of contingencies, and scope has been transformed by analysis of the network configurations under which exchange occurs. In this regard, the effects of economics in terms of game theory, anthropology in terms of studies of gift exchange, and psychology in terms of risk have been particularly influential.

COOPERATION AND COMPETITION

Very early studies in cooperation drew attention to the incentive structures that "steer" actors toward cooperating with others or competing with others (see Coser 1956, 1967; Thibaut and Kelley 1959). In a study meant to reflect on why people might "panic" in settings, Mintz (1951) provided people with incentives if they withdrew their playing pieces successfully. However, only one person could withdraw at a time. When incentives or costs for not withdrawing were high, cooperation decreased and consequently success decreased. These findings illustrated that early ideas of mob or panic "mentality" were not appropriate social psychological models of group behavior. In fact, actors respond to perceived immediate individual incentives that might result in long-term negative results both for themselves and for the group. In other words, panic situations could be analyzed in terms of incentive dilemmas.

Social dilemmas are one of the most studied phenomena within the area of cooperation and competition. A social dilemma is any setting in which there is a conflict between individual short-term incentives and overall group incentives (see Dawes 1980). Common examples of social dilemmas include the creation of collective movements, such as civil rights movements, and the maintenance of resources, such as fisheries or fragile ecosystems. Such settings are very different from market settings, in which individuals pay a price (money, time, etc.) to obtain a private good. Social dilemmas can only be solved through group effort, yet individuals cannot be excluded from the benefits, even if they have not contributed. For example, even if an individual does nothing to preserve a fragile ecosystem, he or she benefits by it. This feature of social dilemmas creates the "free-riding problem," the temptation for individuals to reap benefits but not contribute. Of course, if every individual reacts to the immediate incentives and free rides, the public good or resource is not provided. Social dilemmas are pervasive and appear in all levels of interaction.

Two statements often used to frame the issues surrounding social dilemmas are Mancur Olson's (1965) book *The Logic of Collective Action* and Garret Hardin's (1968) article "The Tragedy of the Commons." Olson's book is about public goods, while Hardin's article addresses common property resources. Because both types of problems have an incentive structure that pits individual against group interest, they are considered social dilemmas; however, there are social psychological differences between the public good problem, which involves "giving up" individual resources for the group good, and the resource good problem of establishing individual restraint from using the resource (see Brewer and Kramer 1986; Sell and Son 1997; Sell et al. 2002; Son and Sell 1995). There are many further categorizations of social dilemmas. An important distinction is between a two-person (or -actor) dilemma and multiperson dilemmas, termed *N-person dilemmas*. Other distinctions relate to the timing and structure of the incentives and to the relationship between cooperation (and the reverse of cooperation, defection) and group gains.

Because social dilemmas are so pervasive, most of the social sciences have investigated them. As a result, there is an especially rich cross-disciplinary literature. Particularly important has been game theory. Game theorists have concentrated on formal solutions that invoke the mathematics involved in expected utility arguments. One very important formulation for advancing the possibility of "rational" cooperation is the folk theorem. The folk theorem posits a whole range of history-contingent strategies that allow for cooperation if, at some point, it is the case that an actor's cost of contributing exceeds the cost of contribution and the discount rate is sufficiently large for contributing to remain an individually rational strategy. This means that social dilemmas can be solved rationally, without resorting to explanations such as altruism. However, while the folk theorem does suggest many possibilities for purely rational cooperation, it does not rule out many possibilities.

In line with this, there are a number of conditional cooperation strategies (for a discussion, see Yamagishi 1995) that have been investigated. One of the simplest and most investigated strategies is the tit-for-tat strategy (see Axelrod 1984). This strategy suggested a "nice response" of initial cooperation and thereafter cooperating when a partner cooperates and not cooperating when the partner does not.

Many solutions to social dilemmas involve changing the basic structure of the dilemma and thereby affecting incentives (see Messick and Brewer 1983; Samuelson and Messick 1995). Such solutions include factors such as punishment mechanisms for not cooperating (one class of which includes "trigger strategies") and incentives for cooperating (see Ostrom, Walker, and Gardner 1992; Sato 1987; Sell and Wilson 1999; Yamagishi 1988).

Other solutions to social dilemmas have focused on "social" factors—namely, factors affected by group interaction. After much research, it is apparent that communication among group members facilitates cooperation (Sally 1995). The reasons include the creation of commitments (Kerr and Kaufman-Gilleland 1994; Orbell, van de Kragt, and Dawes 1988) and the development of in-group identity (Brewer and Kramer 1986). However, simply sending signals of intention, or "cheap talk," is not enough to increase cooperation (Wilson and Sell 1997).

Two other very powerful social factors are social identity and trust. Social identity is the sense of "we-ness" that accompanies shared significant social categories that indicate some extent of common fate. Trust is a more diffuse property, which may or may not relate to social identity but does entail a sense of predictability of others' actions. If an actor trusts others to cooperate, and so acts on that basis, the original incentives of the social dilemma can be transformed and the dilemma solved (see Brann and Foddy 1987; Kollock 1998; Scharlemann et al. 2001; Yamagishi 1995). Some cross-cultural research indicates that there are indeed initial differences in levels of trust and cooperation,

a difference we might expect based on cultural differences in social identity (see Hwang 1987; Kopelman, Weber, and Messick 2002; Sell et al. 2002; Yamagishi 1988, 1995).

Studies of cooperation and competition continue to be a primary focus in group dynamics. This area, perhaps more than any other, promises further interdisciplinary work because it already possesses an interdisciplinary base, which includes many different disciplines. Early studies emphasized incentive structures, and because of this, much of the literature is characterized by a rational choice perspective. Such a perspective does not inhibit analysis of trust and social identity but demands that it be placed within the incentive structure. It is this combination of "rational choice" along with the more traditional social psychological emphasis on "not so rational" choice that provides an intriguing combination for further innovative theory.

NEW DIRECTIONS AND NEW INNOVATIONS

The study of group dynamics or group processes has been an important part of sociology since its inception. It was closely allied with psychology and, perhaps because of this, never abandoned the methodological acceptance of laboratory experiments. Later developments, especially in the areas of legitimation and cooperation, included contributions from political science and economics. Studies of coalition formation in political science and collusion in economics, for example, were important in the development of principles in cooperation.

Because of its interdisciplinary approach, for the most part, group dynamics research has not fallen into an insular pattern in which reference is made only to sociological developments. In fact, recent research reaches across not just to the social sciences but to the biological sciences as well (see, e.g., McCabe et al. 2001; Robinson, Rogalin, and Smith-Lovin 2004). Such interdisciplinary and cross-disciplinary research will almost certainly guarantee greater theoretical development and more attention to application. If the area is to remain vibrant, researchers cannot be reticent about attempting new methodologies that might be less well known and accepted. Such techniques might include physiological measurements and techniques, simulations, and explorations of virtual reality experiments.

A common vocabulary and framework also helps to frame different approaches to a similar problem. Lovaglia et al. (2005) and Sell et al. (2004) argue that one common vocabulary that might unite research across different areas in group dynamics is that of institutional rules. Institutional rules are formal or informal rules that specify who can engage in certain acts and under what conditions this can occur (see Crawford and Ostrom 1995 for a general discussion of institutional rules). Institutions might be an important framework for integration because they enable comparisons among very different groups. So, as an example, we can speak of the boundary rules of groups: who is and who is not in the group. These rules specify the permeability of the group. Can people easily come and go from the group, or are there membership rules that prevent entrance and exit? As another example, position rules define who gets to act and when he or she gets to act. Such position rules might specify leaders and a hierarchical form of group governance or the complete opposite, a total equalitarian governance.

The institutional framework allows comparison and also highlights the structural dimension of group dynamics. It can enable comparisons of the structure and dynamics of groups of schoolchildren, groups of circus entertainers, groups of world leaders, and groups of workers and CEOs in a bureaucracy. These rules could also help strengthen the development and analysis of nested groups. There is an important theoretical push in group dynamics to consider how smaller groups might be nested within larger groups and *at the same time* how larger groups are affected by smaller groups (see Lawler, Ridgeway, and Markovsky 1993). Institutional language can also aid this theoretical endeavor because it enables assessment of how rules compare within and across levels. The idea of nested groups is especially important for the development and elaboration of group dynamics because it points out that the study of "small groups" is really not necessarily about small. Groups can have a powerful impact on "big" structures. Indeed, the topics of status, exchange, legitimation, justice, and cooperation reach out to and into all domains of society.

17

THE SOCIOLOGY OF ORGANIZATION

RICHARD A. COLIGNON

St. Louis University, St. Louis, Missouri

The literature on the sociology of organizations is vast and represents a refracted history of the study of bureaucracy. The object of study is variously labeled bureaucracy, complex organizations, and formal organizations, but the concept of organization and the notion of organizing principles subsume all these labels. Thus, according to Blau and Meyer (1987), "the concept of bureaucracy, then, applies to organizing principles that are intended to achieve control and coordination of work in large organizations" (p. 3). This vast literature will be reviewed by dividing the field into approaches distinguished by their organizing principles and discussed more or less in the chronological order of their emergence. This provides the reader with a context and addresses these organizing principles in readily digestible portions. However, the chronology does not imply that the field developed in a linear fashion, nor does the division into major approaches suggest that all scholarship fits neatly into distinct approaches. The discussion of each approach is followed by a critique, and the review concludes with speculation on the future of the sociology of organizations in the twenty-first century.

The study of organizations varies within sociology, between academic disciplines, and across the globe, limiting in-depth communication. Studies of political parties by political scientists, private-sector firms by economists, and employees by industrial psychologists and sociologists within the United States and abroad may claim to predate the sociology of organizations. However, according to Scott (2003:9), there are three defining features of the sociology of organizations: (1) Examination is empirical, not normative; (2) organization is considered *sui generis*, not the aggregate of its members; and (3) an effort is made to generalize the analysis beyond analysis of the specific form of organization studied. These criteria became institutionalized after the 1960s and will be used to explore its refracted development.

EARLY WRITING

The Pyramids at Giza, the Roman conquests, and the spread of Christianity were accomplished through organizations and illustrate how the issues of organization stretch back in time. These large-scale organizational efforts represented attempts to grapple with the ambitions and stubborn facts of their day. The stability of societies was at stake, and their survival attracted powerful intellectual contemplation. As James March (1965) comments, "There is scarcely a major philosopher, historian, or biographer who has overlooked the management and perversities of organization. The church, the army, and the state had to be managed" (p. xi). After all, religions passed into obscurity, armies were defeated, and states fell. Impressive as an intellectual fascination and operational challenge, the term *bureaucracy* appears rather late in Western history.

The concept of bureaucracy appeared in the eighteenth century as a semantic partitioning of society and a new element in the stratification of society. The French term *bureau,* understood as *table,* took on the additional meaning of where officials worked. Bureaucracy represented a new group of rulers and a new method of government in contrast to monarchy, aristocracy, and democracy. The concept of bureaucracy began to refer to power over the population. By the nineteenth century, the theme of bureaucracy as a threat to democracy developed into ideas that democracy was the fundamental corrective to the routine, inflexibility, and power that came to characterize bureaucracy.

John Stuart Mill (1861) provided an interpretation of bureaucracy and democracy by comparing different types of governments and raising the question of the locus of decision making and power. Gaetano Mosca ([1895] 1939) continued the theme of bureaucracy acquiring power relative to other forms of governance, classifying all governments as either feudal or bureaucratic. Bureaucracy was not an element of society but represented society. Robert Michels ([1911] 1962) reversed the logic of nineteenth-century thought by arguing that democracy was inconceivable without bureaucracy. He also viewed bureaucracy as a particular example of a more all-embracing category of social organization, and he investigated the generic features of this modern structure (Albrow 1970:36). In addition, Michels ([1911] 1962) reasoned that if salaried officials were a necessary part of bureaucracy, oligopoly was the result, in his notion of the "iron law of oligarchy" or the tendency of organizational leadership to maintain itself. Yet a systemic treatment of the concept of bureaucracy was left to Max Weber.

Weber's renowned work on bureaucracy is spread across his theoretical, comparative, and historical analyses but may be briefly sketched in the following themes. Similar to Michels, Weber built his analysis of bureaucracy on the generic concept of *verband,* a group whose task it was to maintain the organization, including a leader and staff and a distinctive set of rules. *Verband* was broader than bureaucracy and included such differing notions as the state, political parties, commercial enterprise, and the church. Bureaucracy simply meant an "administrative body of appointed officials" whose work and influence could be seen in all kinds of organizations (Albrow 1970:42).

Using bureaucracy as a generic administrative body, Weber developed the theme of the affinity between Western rationalization and the rationality of bureaucracy and its inevitable importance. Precision, continuity, discipline, and reliability made bureaucracy the most satisfactory form of organization, both for authority holders and for other interests (Weber 1958, 1968, 1981). Weber's theoretical and empirical writings identify and develop key elements of government and profit-making organizations in Western society (Swedberg 2003). On the inherent tendency of bureaucracy to accumulate power, Weber advocated representative government as both a critical context and a training ground for leaders who could counterbalance the increasing power of bureaucracy.

Although his theory of organizations is much broader, Weber developed the ideal type of rational-legal bureaucracy as a methodological tool for his empirical work. Weber believed that rational bureaucracy was a major element in the rationalization of the modern world. Based on his position that legitimacy was fundamental to all systems of authority, Weber set out 5 related beliefs of legal authority, devised 8 propositions about the structuring of rational-legal authority, and then formulated 10 characteristics of the ideal-type bureaucracy. These include observing only professional duties, a clear hierarchy of authority, specification of functions of the office, appointment on the basis of contract, personnel selection on the basis of examination, graded salary positions, official's post as sole occupation, a career structure where promotion is based on seniority or merit, no appropriation of position or resources, and the organization being subject to unified control and discipline (Albrow 1970:44–45). This ideal type was then used to identify the degree of bureaucratization and its explanation in historical and comparative work.

Weber's theory of domination is based on a special type of power, authority, and the belief of the ruler to have the right to rule and the ruled to have an obligation to obey. This nexus of beliefs in the legitimacy of the administrative apparatus becomes fundamental for more specific discussions of rational-legal bureaucracy and the issues of domination, depersonalization, and exploitation. For Weber, bureaucratic power was both the cause and the consequence of the rise of capitalism and democracy in the West. Bureaucracy was the outcome of economic, political, and cultural features of the West, necessary for the development of democracy, and a tool of power affecting the rationalization of society and domination of its people. This broad intellectual canvas provided a rich legacy for the study of organizations.

ORGANIZATIONAL SOCIOLOGY IN THE UNITED STATES

The sociology of organizations began in the 1940s with Robert Merton's translation of a small portion of Weber's work. Indicatively, Weber's work that is typically cited in organizational sociology is "Bureaucracy" in Gerth and Mills's (1946:196–244) *From Max Weber,* representing a small excerpt from Weber's (1968:956–1002) *Economy and Society.* This pagination illustrates how Weber's work on organizations was narrowly and selectively imported into the American academic scene. At that time, Merton was promoting the application of his "empirical functionalism" to "theories of the middle range" that circumscribed an emerging definition of organizations by focusing on elements of ideal-type bureaucratic structure as a self-perpetuating, legally recognized entity with goals and clearly defined and defended boundaries (Scott 2003).

However, this dating of the origin of organizational sociology overlooks sources of the key conceptions of organizations provided by Chester Barnard (1938), Philip Selznick (1943, 1948, 1949), and Herbert Simon (1957). Barnard's work was the first comprehensive theory of an organization as a unit of analysis as a "cooperative system"

(Perrow 1986:53). He develops a behavioral theory of organizations that includes coordination and decision making, rather than the legalistically and formally based theories. Influenced by a biological system heuristic and the Human Relations School, Barnard's theory emphasizes the social aspects of organizations conceived as social systems seeking stability and equilibrium of its internal and external relationships. The organization was a cooperative system, with interdependent elements (workers/ management, organization/environment) that must be consciously structured to address the maintenance needs of the organization and to obtain resources from the environment and use them in order to induce contributions from organizational members (Barnard 1938:73). Although in different forms, these themes are repeated in subsequent approaches to the sociology of organizations.

Selznick pioneered a structural functional theory of organizations, establishing the (old) institutional approach. Merging Weber's rational-legal elements of bureaucracy with Barnard's social elements of a cooperative system, Selznick stresses how formal structure never completely succeeds in conquering the social elements of organizational behavior. Therefore, Selznick emphasizes the importance of normative controls of values and norms that are both internalized by actors and enforced by others in social situations. Out of the dynamic interaction of human features and structural elements, Selznick developed a goal-oriented theory of adaptation for organizational survival. The adaptive interaction of human action and formal organizational structure is shown to produce unanticipated consequences, establishing the "exposé'" tradition associated with the institutional school.

At about the same time, an important interdisciplinary development was under way at Carnegie Institute of Technology (Carnegie Mellon University), where Herbert Simon had gathered political scientists, economists, engineers, and psychologists to focus on a decision-making theory of administration. Simon combined rational aspects with social factors in his view of organizations as decision-making entities. He proposed a "boundedly rational" theory of decision making, based on the limitations and biases of individual decision making, in reaction to economic assumptions of rational maximizing models. People are intentionally rational but have structural and cognitive limits on their information. This leads to the notion that the search for alternative choices, rather than free, represents increasing costs, so that decision-makers settled for "satisfactory" rather than continuing to search for optimum solutions. Bounded rationality and satisfactory solutions lead to incremental decision making and the use of rules, standard operating procedures, routines, and habitual patterns of behavior (Pfeffer 1982:6–7). As in Barnard, organizational equilibrium represented a balance between the contributions of members and their organizational rewards. Later, the decision-making scholars recognized that organizational policies were the outcome of multiple and competing objectives of organizational participants and people who controlled the organization represented a coalition of interests that affected the organizational structures and processes (Cyert and March 1963). Later approaches adopt this view that human problem-solving processes determine the basic features of organizational structures and functions.

By the 1960s, the master features of organizational sociology were becoming institutionalized through the publication of textbooks, handbooks, and a new journal, *Administrative Science Quarterly,* emphasizing the interdisciplinary character of the study of organizations. The new field of study underwent a conceptual transformation: The central features of organizational structural elements turned into dependent variables, rather than independent variables, whose variation became the focus of explanation (Scott 1975:2). Within this causal transformation, the field shifted back and forth between various approaches, with some emphasizing the causal import of a purposive organization involving goals, decision making, and strategies, while others emphasized a more passive organization shaped by its environment (Hall and Tolbert 2005).

DEVELOPING APPROACHES

Prior to 1980, several approaches emerged in the sociological study of organizations. They questioned the presumed tight linkage between actions and outcomes and instead postulated a looser relationship between the organization form, its members, and its environment. The approaches identify economic and social factors that disrupt tight interrelationships, causing problems of organizational performance. To manage these problems, each approach is distinguished by the adaptive mechanisms offered that change organizational structure, strategies, and practices that are designed to improve organizational performance. These approaches include strategic contingency, resource dependency, and neo-institutional and transaction cost analysis. The population ecology approach represents an exception to this pattern by assuming that individual organizations cannot change or change too slowly, so where problems of organization-environment interdependency occur, some organizations must fail.

The *strategic contingency* approach was popularized in the late 1960s and became prominent as a loose framework for synthesizing the principal notions of organizations as open systems with objectivist empirical research. The organization represents a configuration of strategies, structures, and processes, and the structural features that best fit the demands of environmental and internal contingencies are by definition the most efficient. Similar to economic models, the contingency approach emphasizes efficiency, but like sociology models, it contends that the structure of the organization depends on various environmental and strategy contingencies (Donaldson 1996). Environmental contingencies include firm size and the complexity, predictability, and interdependence of technological and market changes.

Strategy and environmental factors are the contingencies affecting organizational structure, and efficiency is found in the fit or alignment of the environment and strategies with organizational structures. Strategies are considered part of the normative culture of the organization, with a presumption of an efficiency-seeking orientation among managers. The notion of fit between the organization and its environment resides somewhere in management perception, interpretation, and action. Managers are constantly surveying their environments, interpreting "strategic contingencies" that affect corporate performance (Child 1972). Having perceived such contingencies, they would, for example, create new programs or specialized departments or adjust administrative rules or structures to adapt to these contingencies.

The contingency approach moved the sociology of organizations away from notions of a tight relation between the organization and the environment and that there was one best way to organize toward the notion that the better way to organize depended on the particular environmental contingencies confronting the organization. However, critics question the tautological character of organization-environmental fit and the capacity of managers to perceive and change organizational structure (Pfeffer and Salancik 1978). Also unspecified are the internal dynamics that affect managerial strategies and the notion that the perception of environment contingencies may be social and political constructions rather than objective facts (Pfeffer 1982).

The *resource dependence* approach emerged in the late 1970s, in part as a reaction to the structural contingency approach. The environment was now the "task environment," including customers, suppliers, competitors, creditors, and regulators (Dill 1958), with increasing emphasis on the structures and processes of organizational operations sensitive to resource flows, such as information, raw materials, markets, and credit. Resource requirements forced exchanges with other organizations, not for efficiency but for survival, and the scarcity and importance of a resource supplied by another organization determined the degree of power/dependence between the two organizations. These resource requirements entangle the organization in patterns of power-dependence relationships. Similar to the contingency approach, the emphasis on economic or technological resources implicitly orients the framework toward private firms.

Managers are responsible for gaining favorable exchanges and avoiding debilitating dependencies. They seek discretion to maintain their own power and to permit subsequent adaptations to new environmental dependencies. The distribution of power within the organization is seen as an outcome of environmental dependencies. Thus, decision making is a function of the internal power structure, which interprets and defines the most critical dependencies and the choices of strategies to address them. The actors' position in the internal power structure depends on their ability to control and solve dependencies (Pfeffer and Salancik 1978) through their positions within the firm, their specialized knowledge, or their links to the outside world (Fligstein 1987). Management mediates the relationship between the environment and the organization by adapting the organizational structure, negotiating favorable terms of exchange, and using a range of strategies from stockpiling supplies to joint ventures and mergers. Organizations are seen as loosely connected to the environment, so managers are capable of "enacting the environment" by defining environmental dependencies and the practical options to address them. The sheer capacity to enact an environment implies that the resource dependency model is most appropriate for large, powerful, and dominating organizations.

The resource dependency model focuses greater attention on internal organizational decision making and the efforts of managers to strategically adapt to the environment. However, the larger pattern of asymmetrical relations in which the focal organization is enmeshed is left largely unexplored.

The *neo-institutional* approach began with the work of Meyer and Rowan (1977). Building on the earlier institutional school of Selznick, this approach represents a reaction to economic contingency and resource dependency models that postulate that organizational structure is the result of technical and economic contingencies in the environment. Instead, this approach presumes that many sectors and even parts of organizations are free of these technical and economic constraints and that organizational structure is more the result of efforts to fulfill normative expectations in the environment. The emphasis is on how organizational decision making is shaped, mediated, and channeled by normative institutional arrangements (DiMaggio 1991), where these arrangements take the form of routines, operating procedures, and standard ways of perceiving the environment and agreed-on value priorities. Broadly shared patterns of beliefs and habitual practices mitigate problems of uncertainty, leading to emphasis on the role of ideas and belief systems in supporting and structuring organizations. Thus, organizations involve established procedures and rule-bound and standardized behaviors, and researchers attend to the process of infusing such procedures and behaviors into the organization as regularized and stable features (Jepperson 1991).

Isomorphic mechanisms infuse the organizations' structures with normative expectations of reference group organizations or the generalized expectations of the environment. Organizational structures become similar as organizations interact and formal or informal rules emerge to govern these interactions. Once institutionalized, or taken for granted, these rules exert powerful normative effects on subsequent organizational interactions, and changes in organizational structure result more from issues of legitimacy than from rational adaptation or efficiency. DiMaggio and Powell (1983) contend that the primary institutionalizing mechanism is imitation, which also works through coercive and regulatory mechanisms of the state and professions that disseminate and elaborate sets of beliefs and rules about appropriate organizational structure and practices. Their point is that modern organizations cannot be adequately understood in terms of efficiency and adaptations to technical and economic contingencies because of the often contradictory demands of maintaining organizational effectiveness and legitimacy. One solution to this dilemma is for organizations to "decouple" their formal structure from their everyday operations. They adopt formal structures that are legitimate, while informal everyday activities pursue effective operations, independent of the formal structure.

The institutional approach is more applicable to public sector organizations because of its greater sensitivity to issues of normative expectations and legitimacy. The approach is criticized as tautological in the sense that outcome is the evidence for the cause and there is a lack of specification of what practices, procedures, and behaviors are institutionalized and which ones are freer to vary (Hall and Tolbert 2005). Also, the emphasis on normative features deflects attention from issues of interests, power, and conflict (Perrow 1986) and the technical and economic challenges to the organization.

The *population ecology* (or *natural selection*) approach began with the works of Hannan and Freeman (1977) and Aldrich and Pfeffer (1976) and presumes a tight relationship between the organizational form and the environment by stressing the impact of the environment on organizational survival. In contrast with approaches that explain organizational change through adaptation of individual organizations, population ecology scholars emphasize selection processes such as competition embedded in the environmental or ecological conditions of a population of organizations. This approach operates at the level of groups or populations of organizations that carry out similar activities, compete with each other, and are dependent on similar resources within the same ecological niche. They examine the birth or death rates of types or forms of organizations to identify the survival rates of a particular form. Organizational form changes not as a result of adaptation of existing organizations but through the replacement of one form of organization with another (Hannan and Carroll 1995:23). There is no commonly accepted definition of organizational form, but rather, it represents a "heuristic" generally based on the interests of the researcher (Romanelli 1991:81–84).

The research objective is to explain the variation in form, the longevity of that form, and its birth rates and death rates (Hannan and Carroll 1995). Three evolutionary processes are viewed as the mechanisms linking the environment with the survival of the organizational form or activity. Variation in forms and activities of organizations may occur in a "planned or unplanned" manner. Some organizational forms or activities are selected over alternatives as a result of better fit in a given environment or "niche" (Aldrich and Pfeffer 1976). Researchers explain this selection based on characteristics of the niche representing a distinct combination of resources and density of organizations as a kind of organizational ecology. Narrow niches have been shown to support specialized forms of organizations, while broader niches support a more generalized form of organizations. Finally, the selected forms or activities are retained through some type of reproduction process, and reproduced forms generate variations that begin a new cycle of selection and retention.

The emphasis on ecological niche adds to the present knowledge of specific industries, and their longer time frame of analysis provides a historical perspective absent in other approaches (Hall and Tolbert 2005). However, the source of the initial variation or mutation is not specified. The notion of "fit" between organizational forms and environment resources is left unspecified, representing a tautology similar to that of the contingency approach. The logic of this approach suggests that large, powerful public and private organizations and government sponsorship of certain environments neutralize the selection process by enacting their environments, thus limiting the applicability of the approach. Finally, focusing on the selection effects of competing organizations directs attention away from more symbiotic and cooperative interorganizational arrangements (Scott 2003).

The *transaction cost* approach is the economic approach best known to sociologists and has become an important foil for their arguments. Oliver Williamson (1975, 1981) has promoted an approach focused on the creation and changes in governance structure to explain organizational efficiencies. Organizational governance structures are arrangements for establishing and safeguarding economic exchanges of the firm. The approach postulates two broad governance structures of economic exchanges: markets and organizations. Markets represent immediate exchanges, but when exchanges involve future transactions, the market becomes less useful for securing satisfactory exchanges. Organizations appear as an alternative to markets as a governance structure for exchanges, and the structure of the organization varies by the types of exchanges to be governed.

This approach attends to the efficiency of autonomous firms and the cost of exchanges of goods and services within the organization and between the organization and the market. It assumes that actors are boundedly rational, based on the limits of information, and opportunistic in that they will lie, cheat, and steal. The issue is that not all eventualities can be anticipated in contracts and that actors may deceive. One solution is to bring transactions inside the organization to control opportunism through authority relations. Then, firms respond to issues of bounded rationality by subdividing operational problems, making simpler decision guidelines, channeling information, and creating standard operating procedures. Bounded rationality and opportunism present transaction cost problems for the firm when contracting outside the organization, where tasks are difficult to specify and monitor. Transaction costs include searching for information on quantity, quality, and price; negotiating and monitoring agreements; and providing incentives for cooperation and resolving disputes. Organizations may respond by writing contingent contracts and creating auditing and controlling systems to safeguard the efficiency of exchanges. Opportunism is aggravated when firms have few exchange partners representing transaction disadvantages such as monopoly prices. The emphasis on transaction costs shifts analysis toward the governance structures as the organizational form created and adjusted to search, create, and monitor exchanges. Thus, the form of the organization is a function of the transaction costs to which it needs to adapt.

Transaction cost scholars' attention to "small numbers bargaining" provides a notion of the greater leverage of large, powerful firms in their interorganizational relations. Also, since the theory can be applied to both interfirm and intrafirm exchanges, it provides a fertile link between the nature of markets and intra-organizational relations (Swedberg 2003). However, the fact that an organizational form (governance structure) reduces transaction costs does not explain its creation. All organizations that exist are not, by this fact, efficient. In addition, the arguments about efficiency ignore power and goal ambiguity, and therefore the analysis of decision making is simplistic. Finally, the approach neglects the extent to which search, creation, and monitoring of economic behaviors are embedded in social relations (Granovetter 1985).

CHANGING CONTEXT FOR ORGANIZATIONAL SOCIOLOGY

Since the 1980s, organizational sociologists have recognized the theoretical importance and practical effectiveness of groups of organizations, leading to the development of new approaches. Recognition was sparked by the worldwide competitive successes of East Asian firms that rely on network forms of organization (Hamilton and Biggart 1988) and the limits of economic theory in restructuring the economies of the former Soviet republics (Stark 1996). Also, changes in technology, labor markets, and laws governing rules of competition and cooperation in the United States contributed to a rethinking of organizational processes (DiMaggio 2003). The global movement and management of money also led to conceptual questions about coordinated activities among groups of organizations (Davis and McAdam 2000). Furthermore, sociologists began to use economic theories as a foil for their arguments because of the overwhelming dominance of economists in discussions of corporate and industrial policy and their theoretical vulnerability from simplistic assumptions about organizations (Biggart 2002).

Sociologists used the concept of a network of organizations as a way of analyzing the cooperative interconnections among groups of firms. This shift in attention to interactions among organizations in level of analysis from the single firm to a collection or network of firms represents a substantial theoretical shift. Furthermore, the recognition of how collective meaning among network firms makes a difference provided a new sense of organizational culture and took the form of attention to "organizational fields." In addition, the success of East Asian economies and a careful historical analysis of Western development led to new questions of how the state shaped organizational environments. These responses reconnect the organizational sociology literature with a Weberian framework for studying organizations by moving from the internal and external interactions of autonomous organizations to how groups of organizations fit within the social organization of society.

Network approaches represent a synthesis of strategic contingency recognition of the complexity and uncertainty of the environment with a resource dependency framework of relations among suppliers, customers, competitors, and regulators. Some network approaches move to groups of organizations as the unit of analysis and reorient the framework to confront economic theories of efficiency. These approaches deal with the types and patterns of relationships and the causes and consequences of those types and patterns. Networks represent "any collection of organizations that pursue repeated, enduring exchange relations with one another and lack a legitimate interorganizational authority to arbitrate and resolve disputes that may arise during the exchange" (Podolny and Page 1998:58–59).

The causes of network formation are technical and environmental complexity, speed of market change, bounded rationality of decision making, need for efficient and reliable information, and defense against a hostile environment. Networks foster access to resources (Powell and Smith-Doerr 1994), mutual interests and defense (Gerlach 1992), legitimacy or public approval (Galaskiewicz 1985), and better and quicker response to external demands (Uzzi 1996). The interdependence of products, services, and flexible resources and the specialization of member firms provide the conditions and adjustment mechanisms for networks of organizations. Additional factors facilitating the formation of networks include geographical proximity of customers and suppliers (Saxenian 1996) and products whose value is not easily measured and whose members have an orientation to innovation (Powell 1990). Network analyses on groups of private firms tend to look at outcomes of efficiency and product quality, while analyses in the nonprofit sector typically look at outcomes of status, legitimacy, integration, and coordination.

At the level of networks, structural patterns include the centrality and structural equivalence of firms in the network (Nohria and Eccles 1992). The interactions among the organizations in a group representing the pattern and form of the network are adaptive mechanisms of networks. However, there is less agreement on the nature or type of relations that constitutes the network that represents these adjustments. Some authors emphasize the normative context and affective elements of network relationships, including reputation, identity, trust, loyalty, mutuality of orientation, friendship, and altruism. Others focus on the behavioral issues. For example, networks of organizations represent multiple owners that manage a specific subset of resources, leading to increasing decision-making participation, greater specialized niche seeking, customized production, forms of "relational contacting" (Dore 1984), and organizational learning (Saxenian 1996). Boundaries between the organization and the network are often vague, and familial traditions and societal obligations provide social norms that substitute for formal controls. Identities, norms, and actions define an informal boundary between organizations in the network.

Network analysis points to areas of the network that may be buffered from dependencies on other organizations, density of relations in different parts of the network, and stratification of the organizations within the network. Yet criticisms include the lack of clear specification of the social mechanisms of adjustment to changing contingencies of the network. There is also neglect of the role of interests that would provide a mechanism of change (DiMaggio 1988), and it is not clear whether managers' perceptions and intervention or emergent properties of network relations affect network configurations. Finally, there is a bias toward viewing networks as positive, and the constraints and dysfunctions of network membership are underexamined.

The *field* approach developed, in part, in reaction to the network approach's exclusive focus on the interactions of firms and its relative neglect of the roles of normative beliefs, politics, and the strategies of member organizations. This approach attempts to synthesize organizational goals and strategies with the articulation of the environment. DiMaggio and Powell (1983) define the field as "those organizations that, in the aggregate, constitute a recognized area of institutional life: key suppliers, resource and product consumers, regulatory agencies, and other organizations that produce similar services and products" (p. 148). Invoking Weberian concerns for rationalization and the bureaucratization of organizational behavior, these authors contend that firms within a field are defined through their objective practices and the perceptions of managers as to the reference group for their firm. Different authors posit isomorphic mechanisms of imitation, coercion, and regulation or conflict and struggle as the adaptive mechanisms of organizations within the field.

The field is formed as the interdependence among organizations, competition for resources, and monitoring of the behavior of other organizations become increasingly intense, elaborating a strategic vision and tactical maneuvering on the part of managers to the point where the practices of the organization take on the characteristics of a game with goals, rules, and players. The very ground is in motion, and the goal of each organization is to stabilize its relationships and institutionalize its existence (Emery and Trist 1965; Warren 1967). This field dynamic represents a melding of the destiny of the organization with that of the field members, in which the organization's goals cannot be defined independently of the fate of the field (Martin 2003).

DiMaggio and Powell (1983:148) contend that the field develops its structural elaboration through the emergence of interorganizational relations of domination and coalitions among groups of organizations that are involved in mutual enterprise. The patterning of the field is the result of both direct and indirect relationships. Even hostile firms that do not share direct linkages may be drawn closer together because they share suppliers, distributors, competitors, and regulators. In addition, DiMaggio and Powell provide agents of alignment among groups of organizations by identifying the state and professions as the social mechanisms facilitating the homogenization of forms, practices, and perceptions of the organizational field.

Fligstein (1996, 2001) further develops the notion of field by emphasizing conflict and struggle among firms as the adaptive mechanisms of the field and elaborates its political and cultural components. He highlights the organizations' motivation to produce a system of domination and the elimination of competition. This system of domination and competition is supported by a local culture rendering a cognitive map of the role position of the organization in the field. The cognitive maps define social relationships and help managers interpret the organization's location in the field and status expectations in a set of social relationships; and these interpretations are reached through political processes. The field is stratified between dominant firms, which benefit the most from current arrangements, and subordinate firms, which benefit less. Dominant firms seek a set of collective understandings that allow for accommodation in the field and legitimation of those understandings by the state. Once in place, the interaction in the field becomes "games," where dominant firms use the accepted institutional rules to reproduce their power.

The field approach provides a corrective to the normative and structural deterministic notion of the organizational environment by linking the analysis to the struggles that produce those structures and cultures (Swartz 1997:119). However, some contend that the field itself is not directly measurable and its existence can be proved only by its effects (Martin 2003:8–9). Furthermore, some suggest that seeing life as antagonistic games ignores the myriad interactions that are not strategic but altruistic, civil, and "downright pleasant" (Martin 2003:33) and may limit application of this approach to certain competitive sectors. Also, the transformation of the field relations and adaptation mechanisms of the field are underdeveloped.

The *organization and state* approach is reminiscent of Weber's work because it highlights the distinctive power of large corporations in the context of the development of capitalism and the state. This approach raises both historical and functional questions, including how large industrial organizations emerged in Western countries (Dobbin

1994; Perrow 2002) and how private corporations, markets, and industries produce stable arrangements for economic exchanges (Colignon and Usui 2003). Scholars examine how states shape the environment of organizations, affecting their emergence and decline, form, and effectiveness, and how large organizations, in turn, affect the patterns of interactions and the subsequent policy directions of the state. Some work includes organizational goals, strategies, choices by managers, and how they are linked to alliances and antagonisms involving state and societal interests (Colignon 1997).

The organization-state approach takes up key elements of Weber's work by linking powerful organizations to the interactions of markets and the state, material and ideal interests, and how large organizations dominate state policy patterns. Historical studies focus on the emergence of large, dominating organizations that reflect and define the corporate and government policy directions of their countries. Researchers identify critical historical moments and potential policy alternatives that not only define practical policy possibilities involving the passage of laws, wars, and legislation but may also involve the less formal interventions of state actors. Some studies identify those actors promoting and resisting different alternatives, their capacities, alliances, and good fortune (Colignon 1997; Roy 1998).

Another strand of the organization-state approach asserts that states and societal actors negotiate property rights, governance structures, and rules of exchange that function to define the market environment for organizational operations. Property rights are rules defining ownership and control over the means of production, such as partnership forms, patents, and credentials. Governance structures are rules and regulations defining relations of competition and cooperation among firms and how firms should be organized, such as corporate hierarchies and industrial associations (Campbell and Lindberg 1990). Fligstein (2001:34–35) adds rules of exchange that define who can transact with whom and the conditions under which transactions are carried out, such as setting standards of weights, enforcement of contracts, and setting health and safety standards. These features direct attention to an interface between government agencies and the economy contested by organizations, industrial associations, government, labor, and consumers that varies across sectors, country, and time providing a framework for comparative analysis of the political struggles among institutions, organizations, and interests and the historical conflicts.

Although this approach resonates within developed countries, it is not clear how it fits with developing countries, where legal and administrative instruments are not as well developed. Furthermore, there is an underdevelopment of the specific mechanisms of change and the importance of changing state structures to the deinstitutionalization of old organizational forms and the institutionalization of new forms (Guillen 2003).

CONCLUSION: THE FRACTURING OF ORGANIZATIONAL SOCIOLOGY IN THE 21ST CENTURY?

The information explosion at the end of the twentieth century generated new organizational forms that are flatter, networked, nimble, and global (Castells 1996). These new organizations created enormous wealth, while mergers, acquisitions, restructuring, and bankruptcies have transformed the nature of decision making and employment. At the same time, government organizations played important roles in the development of these new organizational forms and the deinstitutionalization of older forms of organization. The passage of laws, allocation of resources, changing regulatory frameworks, and provision of failure protection (bankruptcy protection and assuming medical and pension obligation) changed organizational environments and advanced the interests of some organizations. While these changes are taking place in industrialized countries, the gap between technologically rich and poor countries has widened with little attention. In the face of these changes, what does organizational sociology have to offer for the twenty-first century?

This chapter sketched different approaches to the sociology of organizations implying a few theoretical and empirical programs for the twenty-first century. Theoretically, there is the need to examine the broad landscape of organizational theory as well as to attend to the more rigorous and nuanced application of the different approaches. Some approaches are more applicable to public or private organizations by emphasizing normative expectations or, alternatively, the technical and market contingencies of the environment. The performance of some organizations is determined by normative attitudes and expectations, while for others it is the result of technology and markets. Furthermore, some approaches are more applicable to large, dominant, monopolistic organizations, whereas other approaches are better suited to smaller, weaker, competitive, or "trivial" organizations (Perrow 1986). Some approaches view organizations and environments as so tightly linked that failure is imminent, while other approaches assume the linkage is so loose as to remove organizational failure as an outcome. Both distinctions, public versus private and dominant versus trivial, suggest a decoupling of the study of different types of organizations from the pursuit of a general theory of organizations. Ironically, both distinctions are evident in Weber's historical and comparative work (Swedberg 2003).

All too often organizational theory is overdrawn and analytic subtlety is lost. There is a tendency to present differences between approaches in oppositional terms, such as legitimacy versus markets or dominant versus subordinate organizations, but these differences are more complex. For example, public and private firms face constraints of both markets and legitimacy. Multiple approaches may be relevant in explaining markets for the funding of public organizations and issues of legitimacy for the forms and practices of private organizations. Similarly, the mechanisms of adjustment for dominant and subordinate organizations may be not only qualitatively different but also a matter of degree. Small organizations may gain flexibility in ways similar to large organizations but are restricted to their local environments. The theoretical effort should be to unravel the ways in which the contingencies of markets and legitimacy are intertwined for both public and private and dominant and subordinate organizations.

The defining features of organizational sociology may limit the capacity of sociologists to address issues of organization in the twenty-first century. The master features of organizational sociology that were institutionalized after the 1960s may hobble the abilities of sociologists engaged in explaining social developments surrounding new organizational forms and environments in the twenty-first century. As organizational sociologists institutionalized these defining features, they reduced their analyses to the impact of the environment on the organization and failed to locate the organization in the broader role structure of industry and society. Empirical examination of distinct types of organizations, public and private, dominant and subordinate, fell within the drive for a universal theory that would fit all organizations.

The approaches of organizational networks, fields, and state-organization relations circumvent this problem by substituting a view of organizations as a relational process inseparable from their interactional context (Weick 1995), rather than *sui generis* structures, and moving up levels of analysis to incorporate the location of the organization in its group, industry, or society. This allows them to incorporate issues of interests and power and examine the consequences of organizational actions. These approaches combine normative and instrumental elements reminiscent of Weber's work. Their general applicability and flexibility regarding goals, environments, interdependencies, and mechanisms of change provide the possibility for a more unified theoretical development. Yet even these new approaches suggest that variation in industry and societal location may create and enforce substantially varied environments that require comparative analyses.

All the approaches reviewed in this chapter may benefit from comparative analysis across social situations and between different theories. Many of these theories have developed in specific sectors or national contexts. For example, the concept of "opportunism" is central to both transaction costs analysis and resource dependency, but its meaning varies by social situation, which has rarely been addressed. In addition, empirical work tends to concentrate on variables identified with a particular theoretical approach. Research does not so much test the applicability

of different approaches as illustrate the application of a particular approach. Consequently, it is difficult to assess the viability of pursuing a general theory for the sociology of organizations. For example, neo-institutional and ecological approaches, which minimize interests and strategy, would be well served by comparative hypothesis testing across sectors with variables from other approaches, including decision making, transaction costs, structural contingency, and resource dependency, which share the key assumption that strategic adaptation matters in organizational performance.

The examination of the relationship between people and organizations is another area of neglect that followed from the institutionalization of organizational sociology in the 1960s. Empirical work on decision making and employment experience was neglected as the approaches to organizational sociology increasingly focused on the correspondence between organizational structures, strategies, and the environment. Favored approaches in organizational sociology pay minimal attention to the changing internal dynamics, such as agency, voice, power, and resistance practices. These approaches describe relations between environmental changes and organizational forms by relying on near-tautological explanations instead of examining the social mechanisms of human interaction that mediate the effects of the environmental changes and changing forms of organization. The neo-institutional perspective would benefit from a deeper and more fine-grained analysis of decision making and work activities to specify the processes of institutionalization and the conditions under which institutionalization takes place (Tolbert and Zucker 1996).

The future of organizational sociology depends on practical application of key assumptions and more rigorous comparative and longitudinal examinations of key concepts and relationships to better address the organizational forms and environments of the twenty-first century. Otherwise, it stands to relinquish its academic birthright to scholars from disciplines that are less encumbered by these assumptions. For at least 30 years, organizational sociologists (trained in sociology departments) have been taking positions in business schools to provide them with analytic rigor in the study of organizations. This has created a situation where scholars with an institutional location outside of sociology contribute considerably to the development of the sociology of organizations. A review of the top organizational books over the last several decades and a casual examination of the editorial boards of journals and handbooks of organizational studies reveal the extent of the interdisciplinary nature of the field of organizational sociology.

18

INDUSTRIAL SOCIOLOGY

RONALD G. STOVER

South Dakota State University

Trying to define and then describe industrial sociology is a challenge because there is no general agreement among sociologists about the definition of industrial sociology or even the content of the subdiscipline (Miller 1984). This disagreement has produced alternative labels for the subdiscipline from "sociology of work" to "work and occupations" to "organizational sociology." Furthermore, there is no sense of identity among social scientists conducting industrial sociology investigations. While important industrial sociological research is being conducted, it is spread among many different disciplines, including sociology, economics, and business. Here, industrial sociology will be defined as the study of work and work organizations, careers and adjustments by workers, and the relations of workers and work organizations to the community and society (Miller 1984; Stover, Lichty, and Stover 1999).

THE HISTORY

Investigations of topics that would eventually be labeled industrial sociology began in the early part of the twentieth century. In-depth studies of occupations such as prostitutes, teachers, salespeople, physicians, waitresses, and ministers were conducted in the 1920s at the University of Chicago (Taylor 1968). However, the subdiscipline of industrial sociology is generally considered to have begun with the famous Western Electric research program conducted at the Hawthorne Works in Chicago (Whyte 1968). These studies, conducted during much of the Great Depression, were designed to understand the factors involved in worker productivity (Simpson 1989). When the studies ended, the researchers claimed to have determined that the social environment—the work group of the worker and the way workers were treated by management—had a powerful effect on worker performance (Roethlisberger and Dickson 1939). Although disagreement now exists about whether their results actually support their claims (Carey 1967; Franke and Kaul 1978; Jones 1992), there is little doubt that their conclusions captured the imagination of social scientists interested in worker productivity and culminated in substantial research projects dealing with work, workers, and the workplace.

That research activity eventually became known as industrial sociology and represented, for a time, one of the most vibrant sociology subdisciplines (Miller 1984). (For examples of the research being conducted during this time, see Chinoy 1955; Walker 1950; Walker and Guest 1952; Walker, Guest, and Turner 1956.) Guest provides an example of the importance of this research when he describes the results of one of his projects. In 1948, he and his team launched a two-phase project on a community whose U.S. Steel plant was to be shut down. The first phase was to be a study of the plant and the community before the shutdown and the second was to be a study of the community after the shutdown. After the first phase was completed, the results were published in the book *Steeltown*. A year later, he contacted the head of public relations for U.S. Steel and asked why the mill had not yet closed. The director was surprised that Guest had not heard what had happened. Apparently, the head of engineering for U.S. Steel had read the report, realized the importance of the skill in the mill's workforce, and convinced top management to upgrade the mill to keep it in operation. The director concluded by saying, "You won't have a ghost town to study, but I'm sure that if you went back for a visit the Chamber of Commerce would parade you down Main Street as heroes. Everyone knows the story" (Guest 1987:8).

THE SPLINTERING

During the 1960s, industrial sociology began to splinter. As sociologists recognized the potential value of the information available from a study of the workplace, they carved out specialty areas of study. Some began to study industrial organizations instead of the workers within those organizations; others focused on nonindustrial organizations (e.g., government, education, and welfare organizations); still others focused on the characteristics of the labor force (e.g., the unequal distribution of wages among various occupations). At the same time, others chose to leave sociology and to affiliate with business schools. Miller (1984) argues that industrial sociology research began to spread outside of sociology when business schools abandoned their "trade school" image in the late 1950s and created new sociology-based courses with labels such as Business and Society, Personnel and Organizational Behavior, Management and Labor Relations, and Dynamics of the Labor Force. Through the appointment of sociologists to academic positions in business schools, sociological expertise was transferred to other disciplines (Miller 1984). This splintering is at least partially responsible for the current status of industrial sociology as a very important but underappreciated subdiscipline within sociology.

MILESTONE INVESTIGATIONS

Social scientists have investigated and described numerous exceptionally important industrial sociology topics. Among the more important are those pertaining to changes in society due to industrialization and to changes in the design and operation of industrial organizations.

Societal Changes

Convergence versus Divergence

Perhaps the most important of the topics that industrial sociologists have investigated pertain to the consequences of the industrial process. What happens to a society as it industrializes? Two opposing theories have been described. The *divergence theory of industrialization* suggests that although the industrialization process changes the production system of a society, the culture of a society is so strong and durable that the industrialization process has minimal, if any, effect on it. In contrast, the *convergence theory of*

industrialization argues that the industrialization process is so strong it substantially transforms any society that is industrializing. Substantial research supports the convergence theory (Form 1976; Form and Rae 1988; Inkeles 1960; Inkeles and Rossi 1961). For a time, it appeared that Japanese workers might be exceptional and provide support for the divergence theory. However, formal investigations support the conclusion that Japan is not an exceptional case (Cole 1971; Marsh 1984; Marsh and Mannari 1976; Naoi and Schooler 1985).

Deindustrialization of America and the Development of a Service Economy

The concept *deindustrialization* means the loss of industrial capacity and, implicitly, the loss of goods-producing jobs. The phrase *deindustrialization of America* refers to both the loss of industrial capacity and to the economic and social consequences of that loss for the United States. The development of the service economy is the counterpart to that trend. Service-producing jobs have arisen to take the place of goods-producing jobs.

The change started in the 1960s when the United States lost the virtual monopoly it had maintained on many markets since World War II; in fact, the United States was forced out of several markets (Bluestone and Harrison 1982; Harrison and Bluestone 1988). Corporations responded in several ways. As Harrison and Bluestone (1988) state, "They abandoned core businesses, invested offshore, shifted capital into overtly speculative ventures, subcontracted work to low-wage contractors here and abroad, demanded wage concessions from their employees, and substituted part-time and other forms of contingent labor for full-time workers" (p. xxvii). Bluestone and Harrison (1982) suggest that somewhere between 32 and 38 million jobs were lost during the 1970s alone as the direct result of private disinvestment in American businesses (p. 9).

The consequences of this deindustrialization are substantial. First, the ability of a country to continue to develop economically depends on having a strong and growing manufacturing base. Many industries (e.g., trucking and railroads) are highly dependent on goods production because they move parts to the assembly plants and then move the finished products to the distributors.

Second, the nature and character of the jobs available to workers change. The United States has developed a service economy. The combination of the loss of a substantial number of goods-producing jobs with the creation of a huge service sector has produced a substantial shift in the nature of the jobs available in the U.S. economy. Good jobs with good pay, good fringe benefits, job security, and guaranteed civil rights are being destroyed or moved overseas and are being replaced by bad jobs with poor pay, few fringe benefits, no job security, and little protection of civil rights.

In 1970, the proportion of workers in the goods-producing sector of the economy was about 44 percent; by

2003, it had dropped to about 27 percent. While the number of jobs in the goods-producing sector increased slightly from about 35 million in 1970 to 37 million in 2003, the number of service-producing jobs increased from about 44 million to slightly more than 100 million (*Statistical Abstract of the United States* 1997, table 649; 2004–2005, table 601).

The change in the characteristics of the available jobs is also clearly evident. Thurow (1987) demonstrates that in the 1963 through 1973 time frame, almost half of newly created jobs were well-paying jobs, whereas only about 20 percent were poor-paying jobs. Yet only six years later, the proportions had reversed; over 40 percent were poor-paying jobs, whereas only 10 percent were well-paying jobs (Thurow 1987). Average hourly and average weekly earnings peaked in the early 1970s; both have declined substantially since then (U.S. Bureau of Labor Statistics 2005a, table B-16; *Economic Report of the President* 1994:320).

The Decline of U.S. Private Sector Unionization

The 1930s and early 1940s were periods of solid growth for organized labor in the United States. The three decades following World War II were years of relative stability for unions. However, since the mid-1970s, private sector unionization has experienced a precipitous decline (Clawson and Clawson 1999). Whereas at its peak in the 1950s, almost one in three eligible workers were union members, today the number is slightly more than 12 percent and still declining (U.S. Bureau of Labor Statistics 2005b). Nationwide, total membership is down from the historic high of about 21 million in 1979 to about 16 million today (Chang and Sorrentino 1991:48; U.S. Bureau of Labor Statistics 2005b, table 1).

Two contradictory trends complicate the discussion of the decline of membership in the American labor union movement. One trend applies to private sector union membership and the second pertains to public sector union membership (essentially, governmental employment). While the unionization rate for private workers has dropped from almost 40 percent in 1960 to about 8 percent in 2005, the unionization rate for public employees shows the exact opposite trend; it has risen from about 10 percent in 1960 to close to 36 percent in 2005 (Stover, Lichty, and Stover 1999:238; U.S. Bureau of Labor Statistics 2005b:1).

The reasons given for the decline include the abandonment by management of the tacit agreement it had with unions to maintain the standard of living of current union members in exchange for the abandonment of (or at the least a diminution of) aggressive union-organizing activities, the actual attempts by management to hamper union activities among the workers in an organization, the shift by many companies of their operations to nonunion geographic areas such as the South and West, the failure of unions to successfully organize work in nonunion areas such as the South and West, the failure of unions to successfully organize traditionally nonunion work such

as women-dominated occupations and service work (Kimeldorf and Stephan-Norris 1992), the choice of increasing numbers of workers to eschew unions (Farber and Krueger 1993), and changes in the legal climate making it more difficult to be protected from retaliation for union activities (Freeman and Medoff 1984; Geoghegan 1991; Weiler 1993). Structural changes in the economy—(a) the development of a service economy, (b) the shift within the manufacturing part of the economy from "traditional" to "high-tech," and (c) the increasing importance of the export component part of the economy—have also been noted as reasons for the decline in private sector unionization (Troy 1990).

Trends in Unionization Outside the United States

But what about unions in other industrialized countries? The discussion is complicated because countries vary in their approach to organized labor. For some countries, generalizations are difficult because little is known about their policy toward organized labor. For example, the status of unions in the former Eastern Bloc nations—the former United Soviet Socialist Republics (USSR) and its East European allies—is hard to describe because those unions have been free of political control for such a short period of time that it is unclear how they will be treated. For other countries, commenting on the status of unions is a useless endeavor because organized labor has little or no legal standing. Unions in some developing countries (such as the Philippines) are either outlawed or have had their activities severely curtailed by the laws of the country (McGinnis 1979). Unionization in Japan deserves special consideration because of its variety. Many unions are company unions and are controlled to a great extent by company management (Berggren 1992; Ginsbourger 1981). Others are either industrywide unions or members of nationwide coalitions that are sometimes able to achieve worker demands (Kerbo 2006). Finally, German unions must be distinguished from unions in other industrialized countries because of their special relationship to management. Germany's labor-management relationship is qualitatively different from that of other industrial countries because of its *Mitbestimmung* labor-management system—a legally mandated formal arrangement between workers and management requiring cooperation between workers and management. (For details, see the section below titled "Germany's *Mitbestimmung* Labor Policy" and also Kerbo 2006:538–543.)

Accepting these caveats, several overall trends in unionization rates among various countries since World War II can be described (Chang and Sorrentino 1991; Kassalow 1984; Stover, Lichty, and Stover 1999:255). First, the proportion of the labor force unionized in most of these countries has remained remarkably stable over the last two to three decades. There have been fluctuations—some minor declines and some minor increases—but overall there is a great deal of stability. Second, France and the

Netherlands, like the United States, have experienced substantial declines in unionization rates since World War II. Third, two countries—Sweden and Denmark—have experienced substantial increases. In both the countries, virtually the entire labor force is unionized.

Four differences have been noted concerning differences in the approach taken by Western European nations to organized labor and that taken by the United States (Kassalow 1984; Thurow 1992). First, there seems to be a much greater acceptance of unionization as a societal institution in European countries. While unions in the United States are the subject of considerable ambivalence, if not outright hostility, unionization in Europe is accepted as a matter of course. Second, while the United States is experiencing growth in industries that were previously heavily unionized, much of that growth is not covered by union contracts. That type of growth of nonunion employment in an industry covered by union contracts typically would not occur in Europe; the workers in a new mill or new mine would be covered automatically under the terms of a previously existing, industrywide contract.

Third, management responses to the adverse economic conditions of the 1970s and 1980s were radically different. Members of many unions in the United States had to accept severe declines in their quality of life either through pay cuts or fringe-benefit givebacks. Other unions faced attacks on their existence as companies developed tactics to convince workers to decertify their unions. Such attacks tend not to be the case in Europe. Although some union members in Europe have had to accept concessions, these concessions generally do not threaten the standard of living of the workers, and they do not represent an assault on the existence of the unions. Fourth, while workers in both high-tech and service industries—both high-growth areas in mature industrial societies—will be covered by existing contracts in Europe, they will not be covered by such contracts in the United States.

Organizational Changes

Challenges to Frederick Taylor's Scientific Management

With his success in popularizing his scientific management theory in the late nineteenth and early twentieth centuries, Frederick Taylor (1911) saw many of his ideas about how to run organizations eventually dominate management practices (Braverman 1974; Hill 1981; Kanter 1977). As Hill (1981) notes, "Taylorism . . . established the basic philosophy of work organization which has dominated the administration of work through to the present day" (p. 27). However, there have been numerous industrial sociology investigations into the consequences of his management philosophy for workers, and calling into question the validity of his insistence that the best way to manage an industrial organization is to have managers conceptualize and plan work and to have workers carefully controlled and carefully

instructed on exactly how to do the work. Berggren (1992) argues that the consequences of Taylorism—such as alienation, massive job dissatisfaction, worker absenteeism and turnover, deskilling, and worker powerlessness—were so negative there was a virtual revolt against it during the 1970s in the Western industrial world (p. 232). (For discussions about concerns with the limitations and negative consequences of Taylorism, see Blauner 1964; Braverman 1974; Chinoy 1955; Gersuny 1981; Goldman and Van Houten 1981; Gottfried 1998; Harvey 1975; Roy 1952, 1954, 1958; Walker and Guest 1952; Weil 1962.)

Sociologists have described three especially striking international challenges to the basic principles of Taylorism: (1) Germany's *Mitbestimmung* labor policy, (2) Spain's Mondragon industrial complex, and (3) sweden's automotive assembly system.

Germany's Mitbestimmung *Labor Policy*

Industrial and political leaders of West Germany planning to rebuild the economy of the country after the devastation of World War II decided not only to rebuild the physical plant of industry but also to restructure labor-management relations as well. They embarked on a policy of *Mitbestimmung* (roughly translated, *Mitbestimmung* means codetermination) to ensure that the interests of workers would be given serious consideration in industrial organizational planning (Frege 2003; Furstenberg 1977; Kerbo 2006; Putman 1977). Workers have extensive rights and representation in all but the smallest companies through workers' corporate board representatives and worker councils elected by employees of the company. Kerbo (2006) notes,

> Workers must be given extensive information about all matters affecting them and the whole company; works councils must be consulted on any changes in policies affecting work time arrangements, overtime, work breaks, vacation times, plant wage policy systems, the introduction of new technologies and any other alterations in the work environment, as well as the hiring, transfer, reclassification, or firing of workers. (P. 540)

Furthermore, under German law, workers are assumed to have rights, legal protection, and authority equal to that of stockholders. The supervisory board of large German corporations (roughly equivalent to an American board of directors) must include representation for workers equal to that of stockholders; the supervisory board must be made up of 10 employee representatives and 10 stockholder representatives (see Diamant 1977; Rowley 1977 for critiques of *Mitbestimmung*).

Spain's Mondragon Industrial Complex

After World War II, a Catholic priest began a radical experiment in industrial development in the Spanish town of Mondragon. The radical nature of the experiment stems from the way the work organizations are owned and managed. The workers own and control the organizations. Only workers own the organization in which they are employed, and all workers own a share of the organization in which they work. Workers, acting through worker councils in each of the product or service organizations, establish the policies of the company and hire management to carry out the policies; managers are thus the subordinates of the workers. Managers do not make policy, and they have little say in the policies that are created. They must carry out policy; managers who fail to carry out worker directives can be fired (Johnson and Whyte 1977; Whyte and Whyte 1991).

The Mondragon experiment has recorded substantial organizational success. Of the 103 worker cooperatives (and supporting organizations) created between 1956 and 1986, only 3 failed (Whyte and Whyte 1991:3). The number of cooperatives now exceeds 160 industrial and service organizations, and the complex as a whole is recognized as one of the most successful industrial complexes in Europe (see Mondragon 2003, 2005). There has also been success in terms of creating jobs. Employment grew from 23 workers in 1956, to 25,322 in 1992, and to 68,200 in 2003 (Mondragon 2003, 2005; Whyte and Whyte 1991:3).

For a different perspective on the success of the Mondragon experiment—one that focuses much more on the political aspects and implications of the Mondragon experiment—see Kasmir (1996). Writing the results of her ethnographic study from a working-class perspective, Kasmir argues that workers in cooperatives face the same strains as do those not in cooperatives—shift work, assembly line work, routinization of tasks, and demands for ever-increasing productivity. Furthermore, she insists that the cooperatives have political implications. For example, they divide the working class—those in cooperatives from those not in cooperatives—in terms of trying to achieve working-class goals.

Sweden's Automotive Assembly System

In the 1960s, Swedish auto companies faced a labor crisis consisting of very high rates of turnover (which approached 100 percent per year), high rates of both short-term and long-term absenteeism, and the inability to recruit new workers. Searching for an answer to their labor crisis, the Swedish automobile industry leaders discovered the results of studies by sociologists working in industry—especially those studying workers on the assembly line. Based on the results of the studies, those leaders began to completely revamp their production processes (Berggen 1992; Freyssenet 1998).

Volvo was a leader in the changes as it experimented with a series of different assembly systems. All the systems with which they experimented had two distinct features. First, they represented efforts to eliminate the traditional assembly system by having teams assemble major components—for example, an engine or a transmission. Second, they replaced the traditional shop floor hierarchy with work groups responsible for shop floor assembly decisions. The role of the foremen was changed to that of coordinating and planning the activities of the work groups and of providing the logistical and informational support for the activities of the groups. Volvo's Kalmar plant—the first plant designed with the new assumptions—opened in 1974. At that time, it was the world's first auto assembly plant without mechanically driven assembly lines. Speaking of the importance of the Kalmar plant, Berggren (1992) suggests that it was important in several ways; it demonstrated that there were feasible alternatives to the traditional rigid assembly line, that a small factory could produce efficiently because it was more productive than a Volvo plant five times as large, and that a small plant could produce high-quality products because in one of the years of its operation its cars had the highest standards in the history of Volvo (p. 129).

In 1993, Volvo closed Uddevalla—a three-year-old plant designed with their new automotive production principles. Some argued that the failure of the plant cast doubt on the potential success of Volvo's principles, whereas others argued the closure could be explained by other factors (for the debate, see Adler and Cole 1993; Berggren 1994).

A Critique of the Japanese
Lean Automotive Production Model

In 1982, Japanese automobile transplants first appeared in the United States with the opening of the Honda plant in Marysville, Ohio (Graham 1995:6). The success of the Japanese automobile industry relative to that of the U.S. automobile industry spurred industrial sociology research into the nature of organizational and management practices of the Japanese. That research agrees that Japanese management practices are as authoritarian as they are under scientific management (Berggren 1992; Graham 1993, 1995). In fact, management—especially in the guise of the foremen—seems to have even greater authority and decision-making power than ever. There are strict and precise management controls concerning (a) the distribution of power—workers have virtually no decision-making authority at all, (b) the way a worker works, (c) the way a worker dresses (he or she will wear company uniforms), and (d) the way the worker thinks (under the "Kaizan" system of continuous improvement, a worker who does not constantly think of new ways of improving productivity is assumed to have the "wrong" attitude and will be sanctioned or even fired) (Berggren 1992).

The Quality Revolution

The Quality Revolution refers to the increasing emphasis by consumers for quality goods and services; it is a label for a revolution of rising expectations in terms of quality. Numerous investigations, including those by industrial sociologists, documented how this revolution affected the operations, success, and sometimes failure of U.S. organizations (Dobyns and Crawford-Mason 1991; Kanter 1989; Main 1994; Thurow 1992; Womack, Jones, and Roos 1990). Japanese companies provided the stimulus for this revolution when, after World War II, they emphasized quality in production. Womack, Jones, and Roos (1990), based on their multiyear study of the automobile industry, stated,

> Today, Toyota assembly plants have practically no rework areas and perform almost no rework. . . . American buyers report that Toyota's vehicles have among the lowest number of defects of any in the world, comparable to the very best of the German luxury car producers, who devote many hours of assembly-plant effort to rectification. (Pp. 57–58)

American companies were forced to change their operations, adapt to the new production standards, or go out of business.

Workplace Democracy

As U.S. industrial organizations struggled with the challenges of the Quality Revolution and with the negative consequences of Taylor's Scientific Management, many analysts concluded that the power and authority that were once restricted to management should be redistributed throughout the organization (Blumberg 1968; Fantasia, Clawson, and Graham 1988; Grenier 1988; Guest 1957, 1987; Hodson 1996; Hodson et al. 1993; Kanter 1995; Knights and Collinson 1985; Kornbluh, 1984; Parker 1985; Parker and Slaughter 1988; Peters 1987; Ramsay 1977; Safizadeh 1991; Sorge 1976; Thomas 1985; Turner 1991). Efforts to redistribute this power have various labels—Workplace Democracy, Worker Participation, Participative Management. These efforts range from moderate "fine-tuning" of the traditional worker-management relationships to radical revisions of them. This range can be categorized into four major groupings: (1) humanization of work, (2) labor-management quality-of-work-life (QWL) committees, (3) worker-owned companies, and (4) worker-owned/worker-managed companies (Zwerdling 1978a).

Humanization of work experiments are explicit attempts to improve productivity by improving the workers' QWL. Their underlying assumption is that by improving the QWL, the worker will feel better about work, and if the worker feels better about work, he or she will be a more productive worker.

Labor-management QWL committees experiments represent a more radical step in that they involve significant changes in the power relationships between labor and management because the worker has meaningful power over his or her working conditions. The basic assumption of these experiments is that improving the QWL is a worthy goal in and of itself and that one of the best ways to improve the worker's QWL is to give him or her real power.

Worker-owned company experiments are those in which workers actually own but do not manage the company. The workers own all or part of the company; that ownership may involve a coequal share of the company or may involve unequal ownership. Worker-owned company experiments are particularly important for labor-management relations for two reasons. First, they change the workers' attitudes toward the company because the company belongs to them, and they know their economic future is tied to that of the company. Second, with ownership, workers can have a meaningful say in both the policy and the production decisions that affect their lives. In other words, such experiments have the potential of bringing democracy to the workplace.

Worker-owned/worker-managed companies are obviously the most radical of the workplace democracy experiments and are, therefore, the most infrequently tried. Zwerdling (1978a) suggests that a "true" worker-owned/worker-managed company has the following characteristics. First, it is owned and operated by the people who work in it: Only the workers have control. Second, there is no stock, since stock implies that control is turned over to someone else. If capital is needed, the company uses debt financing. Third, all profits, in excess of operating expenses and investments in productivity enhancement, are divided equally among all workers. Fourth, it is run democratically. All workers regardless of skill and experience make decisions on how the business is run. Each worker has one and only one vote. Fifth, although workers can loan money to the company, their loan will be treated like any other loan and will not entitle them to any special privileges because those special privileges would conflict with the democratic principles on which the organization is based. The Mondragon system discussed earlier is an example of such an organization (for American examples, see Pencavel 2001; Perry 1978; Zwerdling 1978b).

NEEDED INVESTIGATIONS

There are several industrial sociological topics that deserve thorough investigations. Among them are a sociology-based explanation for the British Industrial Revolution, a sociological understanding of the great depressions, and an exploration of the impacts of globalization.

A Sociology-Based Explanation for the British Industrial Revolution

Given the profound consequences of industrialization for the organization not only of work but also of society itself, it is surprising that relatively little sociological effort has been invested in explaining why the first Industrial Revolution—the one that occurred in Great Britain approximately in 1750 to 1850—occurred (for two such sociological explanations, see Brown 1966; Campbell

1987). To date, the best explanation is an ecological one (Charlton 1986; Wilkinson 1973). In an important study dealing explicitly with ecological analysis and cultural evolution, Wilkinson (1973) argues that the underlying explanation for the Industrial Revolution can be found in ecological factors. He states,

> The ecological roots of the English industrial revolution are not difficult to find. The initial stimulus to change came directly from resource shortages and other ecological effects of an economic system expanding to meet the needs of a population growing within a limited area. (P. 112)

He illustrates the process by describing how the timber shortage caused by the cutting down of the forests of England resulted in the shift to coal as the country's principal energy source. That shift, in turn, led to the invention of Newcomen's atmospheric engine (which was eventually modified by James Watt into a steam engine) because of the need to pump water out of the flooded coal mines. In effect, he argues that Great Britain's Industrial Revolution was a series of necessary adaptations resulting from the degradation of an environment whose carrying capacity had been exceeded.

Although there is convincing evidence that environmental changes played an important role in the British Industrial Revolution, single-factor explanations for such an historical event should be considered suspect. The driving force in Wilkinson's theory is population increase. Yet for the century preceding the Industrial Revolution, the population of England was relatively stable (Deane 1965:11; Wilkinson 1973:71). Why, starting at about 1750, did the population of England dramatically increase? It is reasonable to assume that social factors played a part.

A Sociological Understanding of the Great Depressions

Industrial societies endure depressions—severe economic downturns characterized by drastic declines in production and extremely high levels of unemployment. There have been three economic depressions so far. While there is widespread acknowledgement of the Great Depression of the 1930s, there is little acknowledgement of the two prior depressions endured by industrial societies. The United States was not industrialized enough to be severely affected by the first depression—the one that devastated England from roughly 1820 to the mid-1840s (Gordon 1978). However, the industrial boom that the United States experienced after the American Civil War resulted in an industrial nation susceptible to economic fluctuations, and it was hard-hit by the second depression. For almost 20 years, starting in 1873, the economies of the United States and other industrialized nations endured what economic analysts at that time called the "Great Depression" (Gordon 1978; for a good summary of that depression, see Parshall 1992). In the United States, that depression

resulted in such a massive concentration of business power that an alarmed federal government was forced to intervene as "trust busters" during the first two decades of the twentieth century. The Great Depression of the 1930s changed the United States in even more fundamental ways than had the second depression. In response to the collapse of the American economy, the National Industrial Recovery Act was passed to give the federal government extraordinary powers to intervene in the economy. The federal government was also forced to provide massive support to the U.S. economy (Watkins 1993). That support continues today: the housing industry is supported by legislation that allows homeowners to claim as tax deductions interest paid on home mortgages, the agricultural industry is supported by a multi-billion-dollar farm subsidy program, and numerous businesses are protected from international competition by high import tariff and import quotas. Given the enormous social organization consequences of depressions, it is curious that industrial sociologists have not devoted more time and effort to describe the depressions and their consequences and understand why they occur.

Understanding the Implications of Globalization

Markets were once primarily restricted to small geographic areas because of the limitations of transportation systems. As transportation systems developed, markets became regional and then national. Today, neither consumer nor labor markets are national. Consumers have access to products and services from a world market. And those customers are increasingly taking advantage of that world market. They demand quality products and services, and they use that world market in their search for those products and services. Consumers now have access to a world economy. Furthermore, labor markets are becoming international because companies can now "source" their production worldwide (Friedman 2005). That is, they can shift their jobs to whatever location they decide is best for their company, irrespective of the effects of these shifts for the workers, communities, and countries they leave.

The potential consequences of changes in both these markets for the status of industrial organizations and their workers are profound. As Kanter (1995) notes, "Globalization is surely one of the most powerful and pervasive influences on nations, businesses, workplaces, communities, and lives at the end of the twentieth century" (p. 11). There is currently great concern and divergence of opinion about globalization. There are those who focus on the potential of globalization for all societies, not just industrial ones (Friedman 2005). There are others who describe the tremendous costs of globalization. The opposition to the North American Free Trade Agreement and the often violent protests whenever the World Trade Organization meets illustrate their concern (see also Gern 1995; Kamala 1998; Lewis 2002; Michalowski and Kramer 1987 for other expressions of concern). Investigations into globalization have documented benefits (Firebaugh and Goesling 2004) and costs (Horn 1993; Sass 2000; Storm and Rao 2004). Further investigations by industrial sociologists into the implications of globalization seem warranted (for examples of such investigations, see Ciccantell and Bunker 2004; Howes 1993; Johnson 1991, 2002; Kanter 1991, 1995; Kanter and Corn 1994; Kappel 1995; Perrucci 1994; Reich 1991; Ross and Trachte 1990; Sallaz 2004; Wolf 2005).

THE FUTURE OF INDUSTRIAL SOCIETIES

The social sciences have documented numerous instances of societal collapse (Catton 1993; Diamond 2005; Tainter 1988). Investigators are intrigued by the survival potential of industrial societies. What are the possibilities?

Every production system negatively affects the environment in some way. The degree and permanence of that environmental degradation, however, varies tremendously. In some cases, it is very limited and short term, whereas in others it is extensive and long term. As societies become larger and more complex, their environmental degradation becomes more pervasive and more permanent.

The degradation is a threat to both individuals and society. In the 1960s, the USSR dumped huge quantities of highly radioactive waste into Lake Karachay. The lake is now so radioactive that anyone standing on its shore for an hour or two will receive a lethal dose of radiation (Lenssen 1992:53). In the early 1980s, the town of Times Beach, Missouri, suffered severe, widespread chemical contamination. Rather than attempt the very costly procedure of rectifying the environmental damage, the U.S. Environmental Protection Agency bought out the residents and declared the town off-limits for humans (Boraiko 1985).

The threat of environmental degradation also extends to the actual survival of society itself. There are numerous instances of societies that have overexploited their resources and degraded their environment to such an extent that the society collapsed. Three of the most well-known examples are Easter Island, the Classic Maya, and the Anasazi of the U.S. Desert Southwest (Catton 1993; Diamond 2005, chap. 4; Pennsylvania State University and WQED 1993; Thorne 1989). (For other examples of societal collapse, see Chedd 1980; Diamond 2005; Tainter 1988.)

What, then, can be said about the future of industrial society? After all, industrial societies are among the largest and most complex of all societies and create some of the most pervasive and permanent environmental degradation. Predictions of the future of industrial society differ greatly. This range of alternatives can be collapsed into three major categories: pessimistic, moderate, and optimistic.

Pessimists point out that industrial societies are complex, resource-consuming, and environmentally degrading societies. The dismal history of other such societies suggests that industrial societies have a limited life span. Societal complexity, high rates of resource consumption, and extensive environmental degradation all seem incompatible with societal longevity. Few, if any, complex societies have survived for even a thousand years. Some analysts (Daily, Ehrlich, and Ehrlich 1994; Pimentel et al. 1994) claim that the world community has already exceeded the world's carrying capacity and the resultant environment degradation will inevitably lead to the collapse of society. An early investigation into the consequences of human population growth was conducted by researchers at the Massachusetts Institute of Technology (Meadows et al. 1974). They conducted a series of computer simulations focusing on "the five basic factors that determine, and, therefore, ultimately limit, growth on this planet—population, agricultural production, natural resources, industrial production, and pollution" (Meadows et al. 1974:xi). In the course of their investigation, they systematically varied the value of each of the crucial factors. Despite changing the assumptions, the end result was almost always the same. The system continued to grow beyond what could be sustained and collapsed within a hundred years. Their computer models indicated that there was only one possible set of conditions that would stabilize the system and that was to simultaneously control population and industrial output. In other words, industrial societies had to be radically redesigned. Two decades later, the team updated their original study (Meadows et al. 1992). They discovered that their original time frame was wrong. Their analyses suggested that without substantial change—not just minor "fine-tuning"—industrial society would collapse in as little as 20 years. Pessimists, then, argue that industrial societies as they currently operate cannot survive, and that without substantial change, industrial society as we know it will collapse. In fact, some argue that the negative impacts of such societies are so severe that they should not survive (Lewis 2002).

Proponents of moderate scenarios share with the pessimists the common theme that industrial society is sustainable indefinitely only if changes are made in its basic operating assumptions (Dobkowski and Wallimann 2002). Whether they argue for developing a "steady-state economy" (Daly 1973; Postel and Flavin 1991), or for the importance of building a "sustainable society" (Brown 1981), or for the value that "small is beautiful" (Schumacher 1973), they insist that industrial societies can survive long term only if the premises on which they are based are substantially changed. And the core change centers on the concept of sustainability. In a sustainable society, renewable resources are used at a rate that ensures the indefinite survival of the resource, while the use of nonrenewable resources is de-emphasized or even abandoned. In sum, proponents of moderate scenarios are optimistic about the future of industrial societies. They argue that moderate, not radical, changes in the operation of industrial societies will allow industrial societies to survive.

Optimists insist that despite all the problems facing industrial societies, the future is not bleak but is instead filled with possibilities. They suggest that not only are industrial societies not threatened by the problems that have been documented but also that the problems may ultimately disappear as pressing human concerns (Budiansky 1994; Simon 1981). The optimists focus their attention on what they believe to be a misplaced emphasis on the problems of overpopulation and resource limits. They argue that even if the pessimists are right about resource limits, technological innovations will overcome any problems created by the limits. They note, for example, that as copper has become more expensive, fiber-optic cable has been used in its place (Simon 1981). According to the optimists, then, the future of industrial society is bright. The creativity and innovation of people in industrial societies and the productivity of industrial production systems will yield increased wealth and a better quality of life for all. Population growth will cease to be a problem, and resources will become more abundant and less expensive (Simon 1981).

SUMMARY

There is little reason to believe that the subdiscipline of industrial sociology will ever attain its former prominence. However, given the importance of work in industrial societies, there is little doubt that there will continue to be theoretically and practically important investigations into industrial sociology topics.

19

THE SOCIOLOGY OF VOLUNTARY ASSOCIATIONS

BART BONIKOWSKI

Princeton University

MILLER MCPHERSON

Duke University

Voluntary associations, understood as "formally organized named groups, most of whose members—whether persons or organizations—are not financially recompensed for their participation" (Knoke 1986:2), have been both hailed as the building blocks of American democracy and disparaged as instruments of social exclusion that reproduce racial and ethnic conflict. Similarly, individuals' membership in voluntary associations has been found to have important benefits for their economic, emotional, and mental well-being but also to reaffirm their negative social stereotypes. Regardless of which characteristics of voluntary associations one chooses to emphasize, one thing is certain: The United States has long been and continues to be a "nation of joiners" (Tocqueville [1835] 2000). The voluntary associations that operate in the United States serve a myriad of purposes, many of which supplement functions offered by the state and the private sector. These associations cover the full gamut of human activity, from economic cooperation to emotional support, from professional development to philanthropy, and from religion to recreation.

Given the prevalence of associations in the United States and the fact that they lend themselves well to the study of social interaction, it is not surprising that sociologists have been interested in voluntarism since the earliest days of their discipline. The body of research motivated by this interest spans nearly 10 decades and includes thousands of articles and books from such diverse subfields as the sociology of religion and demography. Our brief review will outline a history of this rich field of inquiry, delineate its major intellectual currents, summarize its most important empirical findings, and offer some new directions for future research.

HISTORY OF VOLUNTARY ASSOCIATION RESEARCH

Alexis de Tocqueville occupies a central position in the origin story of voluntary association research. His rich observations of nineteenth-century American life (Tocqueville [1835] 2000) helped shape an emerging liberal paradigm in political theory, which treated voluntary associations as the building blocks of civil society—the intermediary between the family, political institutions, and the market. Previously, classical political theorists, from Aristotle to Hobbes and Hegel, had viewed civil society as the commonwealth of elites protected by the state, which shared in "the virtuous tasks of ruling and being ruled" (Edwards 2004:6). In contrast, the liberal democratic framework developed by Madison, Tocqueville, and other Enlightenment thinkers defined civil society as the aggregate of voluntary associations whose primary role was the protection of local interests from the intrusion of government authority. In addition to "curbing the power of centralized institutions, protecting pluralism and nurturing constructive social norms" (Edwards 2004:7), voluntary associations enabled the mobilization of resources toward common goals, increased social cohesion within communities, and supported political debate. This liberal understanding of civil society became fundamental to the pluralistic school of thought in American political theory.

The civil society approach championed by pluralist theorists dominated voluntary association research in the first decades of the twentieth century. However, beginning in the 1920s, its hegemony became increasingly challenged by a newly emergent discipline of sociology. The highly theoretical and abstract arguments that characterized the civil society literature gradually gave way to grounded empirical research pioneered by the Chicago School of urban sociology. Its members systematically studied community life from an ecological perspective, treating neighborhoods as systems of interrelated institutions and practices. The importance of voluntary associations in community life was captured in such sociological classics as Thomas and Znaniecki's (1927) *The Polish Peasant in Europe and America,* Lynd and Lynd's (1929) *Middletown,* and Whyte's (1943) *Street Corner Society.*

While the first wave of the Chicago School was still in its heyday, a number of sociologists began advocating a more generalizable approach to sociological research, one based on quantitative analysis of survey data. While their methodological perspective made considerable inroads into American sociology during the interwar years, it experienced a veritable explosion after World War II. Generous government funding facilitated the collection of unprecedented volumes of survey data on virtually every topic of interest to social scientists, shifting the methodological balance decisively in favor of large-sample quantitative research. This survey revolution produced much of the foundational research in social stratification, sociology of education, demography, and many other core subfields of sociology. Its impact on the study of voluntary associations was no less groundbreaking.

The availability of nationally representative survey data allowed scholars of volunteerism to explore two fundamental questions: Who joins voluntary organizations, and what are the consequences of their membership? To answer the former question, researchers correlated countless sociodemographic variables with voluntary association membership. Race, gender, income, education, geographic location, religious preference, and many other individual-level characteristics were shown to significantly affect the likelihood of affiliation. Some studies introduced more nuanced understandings of the dependent variable by distinguishing between various types of voluntary associations. The most recent additions to this research tradition

have reproduced the older participation models in a comparative context, usually at the international level.

Research on the consequences of voluntary association membership has been similarly affected by the proliferation of survey data: Researchers have correlated membership with such diverse outcomes as mental health, life satisfaction, social mobility, and political participation. Since the typical level of analysis in these studies has been the individual, survey research on the consequences of voluntary participation can be seen as a counterpart to the civil society perspective, which has theorized the effects of participation on the political system as a whole.

A handful of researchers have recently begun using survey data to study the dynamic processes that shape the life cycles of voluntary associations. Treating associations themselves as the units of analysis, they have examined the effects of administrative structures, political and economic conditions, and interorganizational competition on the associations' size, composition, and stability. Institutional studies have focused on the first two factors, arguing that associations must be nimble enough to adjust to a continually changing social environment. Structural-ecological studies have built on structuralist theory, social-evolutionary logic, and social network analysis to emphasize the third *explanans*—interorganizational competition—as the fundamental mechanism that drives associational change.

Both the institutional and structural-ecological approaches have two important characteristics that set them apart from the majority of previous research: (1) They strive to develop a general theory of voluntary associations, and (2) they view voluntary associations as collective phenomena rather than mere aggregates of individual behaviors. To examine these properties, researchers have developed new methods for measuring system-level variables, such as organizational size and density, with traditional survey data.

In addition to the growth of structural approaches, the 1990s were characterized by a powerful revival of the civil society tradition in political science, sociology, and international relations. This neo-Tocquevillian phase reached its height in the early 2000s, with the publication of Putnam's (2000) enormously popular treatise on the decline of American volunteerism, which combined traditional pluralist arguments with social capital theory. Although Putnam's work has been widely critiqued, it continues to define much of the contemporary discourse on volunteerism.

TYPOLOGIES OF VOLUNTARY ASSOCIATIONS

Researchers of voluntary associations have developed a number of classificatory schemes based on the defining features of associations, such as the associations' size, internal structure, level of outside control, social function, source of support, geographic location, and membership characteristics (Smith and Freedman 1972). Since all these criteria have proved useful for the study of various aspects of voluntarism, none of them can be viewed as definitive.

Perhaps due to its simplicity and flexibility, the most enduring and widely employed typology is Gordon and Babchuk's (1959) distinction between expressive and instrumental associations. The primary function of expressive organizations is the facilitation of interaction between members. Hence, participation in such organizations is an end in itself. In contrast, the primary manifest function of instrumental associations is the exertion of influence over specific social conditions. Thus, participation in these organizations is a means to particular extraorganizational ends. Since many associations do not fit neatly into either of these two categories, Gordon and Babchuk (1959) combined them to form a third association type: Instrumental-expressive associations place equal priority on both these dimensions.

Many typologies developed over the past three decades have built on Gordon and Babchuk's original scheme. For instance, DeVall and Harry (1975) distinguish between utilitarian, normative, and normative-utilitarian associations; Palisi and Korn (1989) employ the categories of total voluntary, instrumental, and expressive associations, while Wilson and Janoski (1995) classify voluntary action as self-oriented or community oriented.

The other common approach to classifying associations focuses on their substantive sphere of activity. For example, McPherson and Smith-Lovin (1982) distinguish organizations related to economic activities from those related to community or domestic affairs, while Knoke (1986) lists 14 "functionally specialized" types: "labor unions, churches and sects, social movement organizations, political parties, professional societies, business and trade associations, fraternal and sororal organizations, recreational clubs, civic service associations, philanthropies, social welfare councils, communes, cooperatives, and neighborhood" (p. 2). This approach closely resembles industry classifications used by economists and policymakers. In fact, Knoke's (1986) categories overlap with Salamon's (2002) typology of the nonprofit sector, which includes the following fields of activity: culture, education, health, social services, environment, development, civic and advocacy, philanthropy, international, religious, business and professional, unions, and others.

None of the above classificatory approaches provide a perfect representation of the functioning of actual voluntary associations; each one reduces these complex social phenomena to simplistic and often overlapping ideal types. Nevertheless, these typologies provide convenient and useful conceptual tools for examining various properties of a myriad of diverse organizations. Hence, each typology must be evaluated in light of specific research questions and appropriate empirical evidence. For instance, Richmond (2003) divides voluntary associations into local and cosmopolitan, regardless of their function or purpose.

This is an entirely reasonable decision in the context of his study, which examines the relationship between association membership and geographical mobility.

MEMBERSHIP STUDIES

In response to the widespread availability of individual-level data and dedicated survey analysis techniques, researchers have produced hundreds of studies correlating voluntary association membership with sociodemographic variables. Since a complete bibliography of this body of research would occupy far more space than is available in this volume (see Pugliese 1986), we will limit our overview to the most significant determinants of participation. In each section, we will outline the conclusions reached by previous literature reviews and supplement them with more recent findings.

Age and the Life Course

In their 1972 review of voluntary association research, Constance Smith and Anne Freedman conclude that voluntary participation declines with age due to a variety of psychological and structural factors. In a subsequent review, David Smith (1975) concurs but adds that the pattern is actually curvilinear, with the youngest and oldest persons participating less than those in their middle age. The decline in participation in the latter stages of the life course is more "pronounced for instrumental (e.g., occupation-related) [associations] than for expressive ones" (Smith 1975:253). Similarly, Janoski and Wilson (1995) find that as people age their interests shift from "self-oriented" to "community-oriented" associations.

Reviewing the literature on volunteering, Wilson (2000) acknowledges the curvilinear age pattern but notes that participation is actually higher in adolescence than in young adulthood and that its overall decline in old age is accompanied by an increase in the hours of commitment among those already volunteering. In addition, young people participate predominantly in associations related to "self- and career-oriented activism," and middle-age people prefer "more community-oriented work," while older volunteers "turn away from youth-related, political and ethnic groups and toward service organizations, recreational clubs and agencies to help the elderly" (Wilson 2000:227). Other evidence suggests that between 1974 and 1994, age became a less important determinant of the types of voluntary associations people joined (Monti et al. 2003).

In contrast to the above findings, Hendricks and Cutler (2001) demonstrate that the curvilinear pattern of membership disappears once cohort composition is taken into consideration. They argue that after controlling for compositional factors, the rate of volunteerism peaks in late middle age and remains stable thereafter, regardless of whether unions and religious organizations are included in the analysis. This conclusion is consistent with Cutler's (1976) study, which finds no independent drop in participation after the age of 44.

All the above studies agree on one fact: People volunteer substantially in middle age. To help explain this phenomenon, some researchers have turned to the life-course perspective. Using event-history analysis, Rotolo (2000) demonstrates that changes in participation rates are a result of important role transitions that occur at particular points in the life cycle. For instance, marriage and child-rearing increase rates of participation. Furthermore, Rotolo distinguishes between rates of joining and leaving associations, arguing that transition out of work and marriage, which occurs in old age, results both in fewer new memberships and in fewer terminations of existing memberships. Other explanations for the curvilinear effect of age on voluntarism have emphasized changes in people's attitudes, human capital, and psychological needs.

Gender

Studies conducted in the early 1970s found that men participated in more voluntary associations than did women (Smith and Freedman 1972; Smith 1975) but that this difference narrowed when the level of commitment was taken into account (Smith 1975). By the mid-1980s, most of the difference in overall participation rates had disappeared (Knoke 1986; Monti et al. 2003), and by the 1990s, women were volunteering more than men (Wilson 2000). Although some explanations for the high overall participation rate among women rely on essentialist cultural arguments (Wilson 2000), the long-term shift in the effect of gender on volunteering suggests that structural factors, such as the entry of women into the labor force, play a more important role (Gustafson, Booth, and Johnson 1979; Knoke 1986).

Despite the equalization of overall participation rates between men and women, important differences persist in the type and quality of their respective memberships. Analyses of the sex composition of voluntary associations reveal striking patterns of segregation, which are exacerbated by the tendency of women to participate in smaller associations (McPherson and Smith-Lovin 1982, 1986). This pattern does not seem to diminish over time (Popielarz 1999). Furthermore, women's groups are far more homogeneous with respect to age, education, and occupational status than are men's groups (Popielarz 1999).

Gender also functions as a mediating variable for other determinants of volunteering. For instance, while work instability has a general negative effect on rates of voluntary participation, this effect is more pronounced for women than for men (Rotolo and Wilson 2003). Unstable work histories decrease women's participation in all associations other than unions and farm organizations, while for men, they only decrease membership in job-related associations. Gender also shapes the effects of life-course transitions on joining and leaving voluntary associations, with marriage disproportionately increasing the likelihood of women leaving job-related organizations (Rotolo 2000:1152).

Race

According to Smith (1975), research from the 1970s demonstrates that blacks exhibit lower rates of participation in voluntary associations than do whites, though this difference disappears once socioeconomic status (SES) is taken into consideration (Smith 1975). In contrast, Smith and Freedman (1972) report higher overall rates of participation among blacks, regardless of SES, especially in expressive organizations (Smith and Freedman 1972; cf. London 1975). More recently, researchers have found that once SES is controlled for, blacks consistently volunteer more than whites (Wilson 2000; Stoll 2001).

The relatively high rates of volunteering among African Americans are often attributed to ostensibly higher levels of cohesion in black communities, driven by strong racial identification and shared perceptions of social injustice (Knoke 1986; Ellison and London 1992). This argument is supported by evidence that black volunteers show a strong preference for organizations that serve the needs of the African American community (Wilson 2000). However, research on blacks' general attitudes toward altruism and volunteering is inconclusive, calling into question affective explanations of racial differences in participation rates (Wilson 2000).

Studies of the role of social context on volunteering have demonstrated a tendency toward higher participation in ethnically homogeneous neighborhoods (Rotolo 2000; Stoll 2001). Since African Americans continue to experience acute residential segregation, this finding partly explains the relatively high propensity for voluntarism among members of this group.

Like gender, race is also a strong predictor of the internal composition of voluntary associations. Researchers have consistently found that most associations in the United States are racially homogeneous (Christerson and Emerson 2003; Dougherty 2003); for instance, Dougherty (2003) reports that only 8 percent of Christian organizations are racially diverse. The homogeneity of voluntary associations may be a result of the sociodemographic properties of social networks through which members are recruited (Popielarz and McPherson 1995). Because social ties tend to be homophilous, meaning that individuals interact most often with people similar to themselves, the social groups that form at the intersections of these ties tend to be composed of similar members. Structural-ecological theory suggests that new members who are dissimilar from current members are unlikely to remain in the group for a lengthy period of time, while those who are similar have a higher probability of retaining their memberships. A recent study of racially and ethnically heterogeneous religious organizations (Christerson and Emerson 2003) supports this argument, demonstrating that ethnic and racial minority members incur higher social costs of membership than do majority members.

Socioeconomic Status and Labor Market Variables

Most SES indicators are found to positively affect rates of voluntary participation. This is particularly true for occupational status and education (Smith 1975). Some researchers have also observed that specific job characteristics and not just occupational status have an effect on participation. For instance, individuals with a high degree of control over their jobs tend to volunteer more hours and do so for a wider range of organizations. Although education has been consistently found to positively influence rates of voluntary participation, its effect varies by organization type. For example, the effect is consistent for political groups but not for informal community associations or emergency service organizations (Wilson 2000).

The evidence for the effect of income on volunteering is mixed. Some studies find that wages are negatively associated with volunteering; others suggest that higher overall income increases the propensity to volunteer, while others argue that higher wages increase voluntary activity but higher levels of wealth decrease it. Furthermore, income may be linked to the type of associations joined, with higher-income individuals volunteering more for health- and education-related associations but not for religious and informal ones.

Childhood Socialization

A number of studies point to the importance of socialization in promoting voluntary association membership. Researchers have found strong evidence for the positive effect of parents' participation in voluntary associations on the participation of their offspring, net of SES factors (Smith 1975). Similarly, volunteering during high school years has been found to positively affect the propensity to join voluntary associations later in life (Wilson 2000). It is unclear whether values and attitudes play a mediating role in the transmission of voluntaristic behavior or whether the phenomenon is a result of structural factors, such as social networks and social roles.

Social Context

Although social context has been an underemphasized correlate of voluntary participation, a few studies in the 1970s did examine the role of social networks, work environments, and neighborhood characteristics on volunteering (Smith 1975). They demonstrated that coworkers, family members, and other personal contacts, especially those of high status, have an important impact on voluntarism. A positive effect was also found for SES-homogeneous neighborhoods, longer residential tenure in

a community, and communities with less than 50,000 inhabitants (Smith 1975).

Attention to social networks and structural explanations increased significantly in the 1980s and 1990s, giving rise to new traditions of voluntary association research, many of which treat organizations as units of analysis. Social networks have been found to play a crucial role in disseminating information, mobilizing resources, and creating opportunity structures for voluntary participation. Similarly, demographic characteristics of communities have been shown to affect the composition of voluntary associations. For instance, McPherson (1982) demonstrates that the number and size of associations found in a community, as well as the density of interorganizational and interpersonal links, is strongly affected by the size of the community's population (McPherson 1982). Rotolo (2000) argues that neighborhood heterogeneity has a negative effect on participation since it lowers the probability of homophilous social ties through which association memberships are transmitted. This effect is particularly strong for racially heterogeneous neighborhoods. Stoll (2001) finds that neighborhood poverty also decreases the number of memberships present. Finally, Richmond (2003) demonstrates that geographic mobility differentially affects individuals' propensity to join local and cosmopolitan associations.

Cross-National Differences

As outlined above, the growing interest in organization-level analyses has led many researchers to shift their attention from simple correlation studies to more theoretically sophisticated analyses that examine the impact of contextual factors on voluntary association membership. Despite this considerable progress, traditional survey studies of participation still constitute a considerable portion of the field. This is in no small part due to the growing volume of cross-national research conducted by James Curtis and his associates. Initially inspired by Lipset's (1989) theory of cultural differences between Canada and the United States and later by Putnam's (2000) thesis on the contemporary decline of social capital, these researchers have devoted the past decade and a half to comparing the overall membership rates of industrialized nations using data from the World Values Survey.

In contrast to Lipset's (1989) thesis, their findings demonstrate that, with the exception of religious organizations, Americans are no more likely to join voluntary associations than are Canadians (Curtis et al. 1989; Grabb and Curtis 1992). Similar results are found when the participation in the United States is compared with that of other countries, such as Australia, the Netherlands, Norway, Sweden, and Northern Ireland (Curtis, Grabb, and Baer 1992). According to Curtis, Baer, and Grabb (2001), high national rates of participation are correlated with "multidenominational Christian or predominantly Protestant religious compositions" (p. 783), longer traditions of democratic governance, social or liberal democratic systems, and high levels of economic development. Finally, in response to Putnam (2000), Baer, Curtis, and Grabb (2001) argue that the overall levels of participation have not declined in 12 of the 13 countries examined, including the United States and Canada (but see McPherson, Smith-Lovin, and Brashears 2006).

Correlation studies of the determinants of membership have made many contributions to our descriptive understanding of voluntary associations. However, with some important exceptions (e.g., Knoke 1981; Rotolo 2000), most of them have failed to formulate systematic theoretical explanations for the links between sociodemographic variables and volunteering. As prime examples of abstracted empiricism (Mills 1959), these studies place far more emphasis on the presentation of raw empirical findings than on uncovering the mechanisms that shape voluntary associations.

The few studies that have made educated guesses about the causes of the observed correlations have typically relied on individualistic conceptions of social action, emphasizing the role of attitudes, norms, affects, and cost-benefit calculations in decision-making processes. This framework is questionable because its conclusions are based on loose assumptions that are not grounded in systematic empirical research. Even Wilson (2000), who is generally sympathetic to motive-based explanations, concludes in his review of the literature that "overall, the relation between values and volunteering is weak and inconsistent" (p. 219). Since few researchers of voluntary associations have access to data on people's motivations, individualistic explanations of voluntary participation seem to be granted validity solely because they echo commonsensical understandings of human behavior.

In contrast, recent research on organizational dynamics has demonstrated that patterns of voluntary participation can be better explained using structural arguments that treat associations themselves as units of analysis. Since these arguments are based on measurable properties of social systems rather than imputed motives of individuals, they offer a more reliable and general explanatory framework for the study of voluntary associations. Where appropriate, in the preceding section, we have used explanations generated by this research tradition to supplement the findings of conventional correlation studies.

CONSEQUENCES OF MEMBERSHIP

Research on the consequences of voluntary association membership mirrors the study of participation, since it too is based on the correlation of membership with various individual-level variables. Although this tradition has also been facilitated by the proliferation of survey data and analysis techniques, its scope is considerably smaller than that of participation research. The two areas that have gained the most attention in studies of outcomes are

political mobilization and psychological well-being. Others include demographic variables, geographical mobility, physical health, and socioeconomic status. Overwhelmingly, these studies demonstrate that membership in voluntary associations results in numerous material, emotional, and political benefits for individuals. This reinforces the need for continued examination of the unequal distribution of memberships across social groups. In the following sections, we outline some of the important findings for each of the categories of outcomes.

Political Mobilization

One of the most frequently studied outcomes of voluntary participation is individual political action, particularly voting behavior. There is a high level of consensus among researchers about the positive effect of membership on political participation, although explanations of this phenomenon vary. Knoke (1986) concludes that "associations act as mobilizing mechanisms in democratic societies, transforming nonpolitical organizational involvements into political participation" (p. 8) by broadening individuals' interests, expanding their social networks, exposing them to social interaction and leadership, and creating channels for effecting political change (see also Olsen 1982). Other possible reasons for this correlation include sharing of information, development of organizational skills (Schulman 1978), fostering of generalized trust, political socialization (Wilson 2000), and the creation of a sense of community (Cassel 1999). Some studies have found that the level of mobilization is positively influenced by members' commitment to their organizations, while others find no such effect (Knoke 1986).

Psychological Well-Being

The effects of membership in voluntary associations on various psychological outcomes have also attracted considerable research attention. Most studies have found that membership has positive effects on various mental health variables (Wilson 2000), including self-validation, self-confidence, and life satisfaction. Membership has also been found to lower the risk of depression (Rietschlin 1998) and protect the elderly from "hazards of retirement, physical decline and inactivity" (Fischer and Schaffer 1993:9). There is some evidence that the subjective benefits of membership vary by geographical location, SES, age, and marital status (Cutler 1981; Palisi 1985), as well as by type of organization and the salience of participation for the individual (Hougland 1982).

A few studies have examined the negative outcomes of voluntarism. Christerson and Emerson (2003) find that minorities bear relatively high personal costs of membership in ethnically diverse religious organizations, while Erickson and Nosanchuk (1998) argue that membership increases the likelihood of individuals holding negative ethnic and racial stereotypes. Whether this is a selection effect or causal effect is unclear—for instance, Betz and Judkins (1975) have argued that voluntary associations are more likely to reinforce members' prior attitudes than to alter them or cause the development of new ones.

ORGANIZATIONAL DYNAMICS

Since most of the participation studies described above rely on cross-sectional data, they rarely pay serious attention to the inherently dynamic processes that affect the composition of voluntary associations. By failing to formulate convincing theoretical accounts of the formation, persistence, and dissolution of associations, these studies tend to make simplistic assumptions about their subject matter, akin to Rose's (1956) textbook truism, "a voluntary association develops when a small group of people, finding they have a certain interest (or purpose) in common, agree to meet and to act together in order to try to satisfy that interest or achieve that purpose" (p. 305). Such nonexplanations of the origins of voluntary associations are variants of what Mayhew (1980) once described as the central tenet of individualistic sociology: "people do things because they want to" (p. 354).

The investigation of organizational dynamics treats associations themselves as the primary objects of analysis. Scholars in this tradition seek to explain the rise, growth, transformation, and decline of voluntary associations using such explanatory factors as organizational structure, environmental conditions, and ecological competition (Knoke 1986). Although the methods used in this research program range from ethnography to computer simulation, they all share a commitment to examining voluntary associations from a diachronic perspective.

As in most sociological subfields, the methodological approaches used to study organizational dynamics reflect researchers' epistemological convictions, with some committed to the formulation of complex, particularistic explanations and others to the development of cumulative, parsimonious general theory. The former category includes many of the historical analyses and case studies of voluntary associations, while the latter consists predominantly of statistical treatments of survey data obtained through random-sampling techniques.

Historical Studies

In contrast to case studies of particular organizations, analyses of organizational dynamics that employ historical methods examine changes in overall patterns of voluntary association activity in particular time periods and geographical locations. Although their findings may generate theoretical insights, they are rarely directly generalizable to other spatiotemporal settings.

Two paradigmatic examples of this genre are Brown's (1973) study of colonial New England and Eisenstadt's (1972) analyses of the Yishuv (Jewish Palestine) and the

nascent state of Israel. Brown (1973) is concerned with explaining the historical roots of secular voluntary associations in post-Revolutionary Massachusetts. Although religious associations had existed in the region since the time of European settlement, their secular counterparts did not gain popularity until the latter half of the eighteenth century. The activities of the secular associations were initially confined to the Boston area, but at the turn of the century, they gradually expanded to other urban centers. Yet even after this period, most associations continued to draw their membership from local populations, operating largely through face-to-face interaction. Brown attributes the rise and expansion of secular associations to three primary causes: the emergence of a new republican ideal of citizenship after the American Revolution, individuals' recognition of emotional rewards stemming from membership, and the increasing density of New England communities. Thus, his explanation relies on a historically conditioned combination of cultural, psychological, and structural factors.

Eisenstadt's (1972) study seeks to explain the transformation of voluntary associations during the political transition from Jewish Palestine (the Yishuv) to the nascent state of Israel. He argues that associations in the Yishuv consisted primarily of primary groups closely related to social movements and political parties, which performed vital community services and were strongly committed to the dominant Zionist value orientation of the community. After the transition, purely social groups multiplied; associations that performed civic duties became less prevalent, giving way to purely philanthropic organizations, and the political functions of voluntary associations became confined to special interest groups that exerted direct pressure on the government. The value system of the new organizations separated social activities from political participation, placed little emphasis on civic duties, and did not encourage political change. Furthermore, the status structure shifted from one that rewarded political and intellectual involvement to one that valued economic and occupational success.

Eisenstadt attributes the changes in the voluntary system to the reconfiguration of power relations in the new Israeli state. The creation of a complex government and military bureaucracy led to "an immense increase in the political power available for allocation and distribution" (Eisenstadt 1972:6). This shifted many functions away from the voluntary sector, changed status evaluation criteria, and increased the social distance between elite and nonelite social groups. As a result, associations became increasingly stratified and specialized, moving away from the pursuit of communal well-being and toward the production of social advancement for individuals and groups.

In Eisenstadt's (1972) study, a crucial factor in the transformation of the voluntary sector was the tension between individuals' status positions and aspirations, both of which were altered by the new political system. In general, each voluntary association "developed its activities in the direction and social sphere in which its members felt that their status-aspirations and references were not affirmed" (p. 11). Thus, for instance, highest-status individuals did not join many organizations, while those in relatively high economic positions mainly joined cultural and social groups.

The findings from both the above studies contribute to our understanding of the organizational dynamics of voluntary associations in specific historical contexts. They suggest that associations develop at the complex intersection of cultural values, demographic and political changes, status group struggles, and individual motivations. As such, this form of research is quite useful for the construction of more general theories of voluntary association dynamics. However, due to its particularistic focus, it is less well suited for the rigorous testing of existing theoretical models.

Institutional Analyses

A number of researchers have stressed the internal structure of associations and their embeddedness in the broader social environment as factors that influence associational lifestyles. This tradition treats the shifting objectives of particular associations, and their ability to fulfill these objectives, as functions of the configurations of decision-making responsibilities within the associations and of the constraints and enablements imposed on them by external institutions. Hence, an association's survival is dependent on its ability to fulfill its objectives, provide sufficient incentives to retain its members, and adapt to a changing political and economic environment.

One way of addressing these questions is to conduct detailed case studies of the development of specific associations. This is the approach taken by Watson (1982), who analyzes a Canadian health advocacy association in an attempt to explain its gradually declining membership and efficacy. He argues that the association's hierarchical administrative structure precluded it from adapting to a changing environment of health-care provision. As shifts in government policy and advances in scientific knowledge made the association's goals increasingly outdated, a number of members advocated a transition to a federative administrative structure with independently managed local chapters. However, those in leadership positions used their control of the association's communication channels and policy-making capabilities to strongly resist the proposed changes. The resulting internal conflict debilitated the association and prevented it from making the changes necessary for its continued operation in a shifting context.

Mead (2000) also analyzes the decline of a specific voluntary association, in this case, an elite Argentinean women's organization focused on delivering assistance to poor women and children. The study is both historical and comparative since it examines the association's transformation during a 40-year period from 1880 to 1920 and generates explanations based on a comparison of the Argentinean social context with that of France and the United States. Mead cites three reasons for the initial success of the organization: the support of the federal government, Catholic values, and an anti-immigration rhetoric that resonated with the public. Conversely, the Beneficent Society's ultimate decline was a result of its failure to cooperate with newly emerging women's organizations, as well as the professionalization of male-dominated medical care in Argentina, which restricted the association's ability to continue its role as a primary provider of health services to the poor.

The above case studies point to similar determinants of associational well-being. First, internal cohesion is essential for the association's ability to carry out its objectives and to adapt to a changing environment. An excessively rigid administrative structure and high membership heterogeneity can negatively affect this ability by exacerbating conflict between competing interest groups within the association. Second, the actions of external institutions can hinder the association's efficacy by withdrawing financial or political support, exerting pressure over the association's actions, or drastically altering the policy landscape in which the association functions. Both these explanations rest on the underlying assumption that associations must adapt to a changing context by continually adjusting their objectives and administrative structures.

Case studies of voluntary associations tend to focus almost exclusively on advocacy groups, ignoring less instrumental associations (Gordon and Babchuk 1959), such as churches, fraternal organizations, sport clubs, and youth groups. Since instrumental groups tend to formulate more explicit goals, which often focus on the social environment external to the association, it seems reasonable to evaluate their well-being on the basis of their ability to satisfy these goals. However, this is more difficult for expressive organizations, whose goals are often more implicit. Furthermore, it is entirely possible for an association, whether instrumental or expressive, to thrive without fulfilling its overt objectives. Members may continue to participate in the group for reasons that differ from its initial purpose. Consequently, efficacy is a tenuous measure of associational success.

To deal with the above problem, a number of researchers have used a simpler and more reliable indicator of associational well-being: the rate and strength of membership. Since membership levels are relatively easy to measure, they are well suited for survey research, which enables the estimation of trends across a wide population of voluntary associations. This is the strategy used by Knoke (1981) in his study of the effect of associations' political structure on the strength of membership commitment.

Structural Ecology

One approach to the study of organizational dynamics was initiated by McPherson's (1983) article on the ecology of affiliation. Drawing heavily on the evolutionary logic in bioecology, McPherson argues for a general theory of voluntary association that does not rely on assumptions about individual or group motivations. Building on the work of human ecologists, he instead seeks to capture the system-level processes that shape the behavior of voluntary associations. This inherently relational and dynamic approach views associations as interdependent entities that compete with one another for members. The characteristics of the ecological system have important implications for the growth, persistence, transformation, and decline of individual associations.

The structural-ecological model of voluntary affiliation rests on a few simple assumptions about the nature of the social world. First, social entities are primarily transmitted through social networks; that is, people acquire their behaviors and attitudes from those with whom they interact. Second, social ties are homophilous. Since individuals occupying similar social positions are more likely to interact with one another, entities transmitted through networks tend to be clustered in particular regions of social space. Third, individuals have finite resources, including time and energy. Since each social entity, such as a voluntary association or a cultural preference, consumes a portion of those resources, there is a limit to the number of entities with which each individual can affiliate. Hence, social entities must continually compete with one another for individuals' resources.

McPherson argues that the behavior of voluntary associations is analogous to that of biological species in natural ecosystems. The transmission of memberships across homophilous social ties, which occurs within an inherently competitive ecological system, causes associations to cluster into finite social niches. As memberships are gained and lost at the niche edges, niches gradually shift their position in social space. This process is a direct result of niche competition—members are lost in areas of high competition, characterized by high niche overlap, and gained in areas of low competition, characterized by low niche overlap, causing the niche center to move away from the former and toward the latter.

The same mechanism causes associations to become more or less diverse. An association surrounded by areas of low competition, namely, an association whose niche does not overlap with the niches of other associations, will gain members in all directions of social space, thus becoming more generalist. Conversely, an association surrounded by regions of high competition will lose members in all directions of social space, thus becoming more specialized. In these cases, the standard deviation of the association's membership will change, while its mean, which defines its position in social space, will remain constant.

In addition to its theoretical interest, McPherson's model has a practical advantage for sociologists of voluntary associations: It allows them to explore the effect of social networks on organizational dynamics with conventional survey data. Traditional approaches to network analysis depend on specialized data sets that completely describe the relationships between the nodes of specific networks. Data of this sort are in short supply, restricting the types of research questions that can be addressed using network logic. In contrast, structural ecology incorporates network mechanisms into its model of social space, making it possible to analyze the behavior of voluntary associations using standard sociodemographic variables.

CIVIL SOCIETY

One of the overarching questions that have occupied political theorists since times of antiquity is what constitutes the "good society." The philosophical and pragmatic challenge presented by this question has been taken up by some of the greatest minds in human intellectual history, including Plato, Aristotle, Hobbes, Locke, Montesquieu, Hegel, Tocqueville, and Marx. In its modern incarnation, the debate over the best way to organize the political structure of society has increasingly emphasized the notion of civil society, understood as "a sphere of social interaction between economy and state, composed above all of the intimate sphere (especially the family), the sphere of associations (especially voluntary associations), social movements, and forms of public communication" (Cohen and Arato 1992:ix).

Philosophers of the early Enlightenment, such as Hobbes and Rousseau, argued that associations were a necessary evil—they were important for democratic rule but had to be closely regulated by the state. In contrast, liberal democrats such as Tocqueville, Locke, and Mill, as well as their pluralist successors, claimed that democratic systems depended on the existence of independent and unregulated associations. They argued that associations maximized the capacities of individuals, kept government power in check, and socialized the polity (Smith and Freedman 1972). Contemporary pluralists expanded this list of functions to include the role of voluntary associations in distributing power in society, leading to satisfaction with the democratic process, providing mechanisms for change, increasing social cohesion, giving people a sense of efficacy and identification, and enabling individual advancement (Smith and Freedman 1972).

Over the past few decades, pluralist thought rooted in Tocquevillian liberal democratic theory has come under severe criticism. Mills and Marcuse argued that pluralism is a mere façade for elite rule, Barber claimed that it necessarily leads to the development of bureaucratic oligarchies, Pinard and Gusfield questioned its ability to prevent totalitarian rule, and Lowi critiqued it for leading to pathological interest group politics (Smith and Freedman 1972). Others have charged that pluralism relegates political action to the private sphere, thereby "deflect[ing] from political participation or activism on the part of citizens" (Cohen and Arato 1992:18).

Although the basic tenets of pluralist theory, with its focus on voluntary associations, have been successfully challenged by many of its critics, its idealistic spirit remains dominant in contemporary political theories as diverse as communitarianism and neoconservative antistatism. This spirit is particularly palpable in Robert Putnam's (1995, 2000) work on social capital and community, which has contributed to a powerful revival of the civil society debate among scholars of voluntary associations (see Edwards and Foley 1998; Ladd 1999; Paxton 1999; Rotolo 1999; Shapiro 2000/2001; Edwards and Foley 2001; Etzioni 2001; Wilson 2001).

Putnam (1995, 2000) argues that social capital rooted in voluntary association membership has been declining steadily in America as a result of generational changes in social values. As baby boomers have allegedly abandoned the voluntaristic ethic of the Great Depression and World War II generations, they have contributed to the rapid deterioration of associationalism in the United States, which, in turn, has depleted overall stocks of social capital among its citizens. After demonstrating myriad correlations between social capital and various social and economic outcomes, Putnam concludes that the ostensible decline in the former may have devastating consequences for American society. He goes on to recommend a number of measures for addressing this dire situation.

Aside from its interpretive conclusions, *Bowling Alone* (Putnam 2000) makes a number of empirical claims that have inspired a wealth of subsequent empirical research. The two most crucial of these are that (1) voluntary association memberships in America have declined systematically over the past few decades and (2) social capital embedded in voluntary associations is an inherently beneficial social phenomenon.

The first claim has led a number of scholars to examine trends in membership rates in American voluntary associations and compare them with those in other countries. Rotolo's (1999) analysis challenges Putnam's conclusions by demonstrating that while overall voluntary association participation decreased briefly after 1974, it increased substantially in the early 1980s (but see McPherson et al. 2006). Similarly, Baer et al. (2001) find that between the early 1980s and 1990s, voluntary association activity in the United States, as well as in Canada, Germany, and the Netherlands, has been increasing steadily. Monti et al. (2003) concur, stating that between 1974 and 1994, "Americans have managed the tension between their private lives and broader public duties better and more creatively than we could have imagined" (p. 143). Finally, Warde et al. (2003) corroborate these findings in the British context, arguing that the volume of social capital in Great Britain has not declined in the past decades.

The second empirical claim made in *Bowling Alone* is that voluntary association membership (cum social capital) is an inherently beneficial social phenomenon. This suggestion has inspired a number of studies that present evidence for the insidious aspects of voluntarism. One of the most influential of these is Kaufman's (2002) *For the Common Good? American Civic Life and the Golden Age of Fraternity*. Kaufman does not challenge the argument that participation in voluntary associations has declined in the twentieth century. However, unlike Putnam, he sees this decline not as a sign of the unraveling of American democracy but as a mark of a progression toward a more open and inclusive society. At the core of this normative evaluation lies Kaufman's belief that American associationalism has always been a tool of social exclusion, whose legacies include

> a long-standing tradition of racial prejudice and interethnic hostility; a pernicious political system dominated by special-interest groups; an ominous love for guns, accompanied by a menacing fear of government; a weak and subservient labor movement; and a half-hearted tradition of public social service provision, capped by the repeated failure to pass even the most rudimentary universal health insurance legislation. (P. 10)

Kaufman's findings provide a significant challenge to Putnam's view of civic participation. This challenge is bolstered by past studies, which have demonstrated the tendency of voluntary associations to be internally homogeneous along various sociodemographic dimensions (McPherson, Smith-Lovin, and Cook 2001) and hence to reproduce structural inequalities in American society (McPherson and Smith-Lovin 1982; Popielarz 1999; Christerson and Emerson 2003; Dougherty 2003). These findings demonstrate the need for a more cautious normative interpretation of empirical data on voluntary participation.

One lesson we may be wise to draw from the civil society debate is that complex social phenomena are often morally ambiguous. Since normative arguments that lament social change and warn of impending social crises often reduce this ambiguity to simple predictive and prescriptive judgments, they should be viewed with a degree of skepticism. Associations can play positive roles, such as when they champion the political claims of marginalized groups or provide material and emotional support for the disadvantaged, as well as profoundly negative ones, such as when they contribute to gender, racial, and economic segregation and perpetuate stereotypical conceptions of social others.

THE FUTURE OF VOLUNTARY ASSOCIATION RESEARCH

Each of the approaches discussed has contributed important elements to our understanding of voluntary associations. The civil society literature was the first to alert scholars to the vital role played by volunteerism in American democracy. Tocqueville's insightful work, along with that of other prominent political theorists of the Enlightenment, helped reshape the perennial discussion about the nature of the "good society," shifting its emphasis from the state's control of the polity to the protection of communities from abuses of state power. As a result, voluntary associations became revered in public discourse as symbols of American entrepreneurship, compassionate individualism, and traditional community life. This perspective continues to characterize civil society research today, as is evidenced by the discussion surrounding Putnam's work.

The tone of the civil society debate has been predominantly normative, as is the case for most work in political theory. Considering the central problem of this research tradition—the achievement of the good society—such a normative outlook is legitimate and understandable. However, the fundamental questions that have concerned most sociologists of voluntary associations, beginning with the Chicago School, were of a different nature. Rather than trying to place volunteerism in the context of idealized political systems, sociologists have sought to understand the functioning of voluntary associations—who joins them, at what rate, and why it matters. The result has been an accumulation of a vast volume of information about the determinants and consequences of membership.

An important limitation of sociological research on voluntary associations has stemmed from its inability to develop coherent theoretical explanations of its subject matter. This shortcoming has led a number of researchers to turn their attention to what we have termed *organizational dynamics*. However, their efforts have been substantially constrained by the inadequacy of available data. With a few exceptions, most sociological surveys of voluntarism have been cross-sectional and individualistic. As such, they have failed to capture the dynamic relationships between members, organizations, and the broader social context.

The challenge for future research is to overcome the limitations presented by traditional survey data. Nationally representative longitudinal or panel data that track the creation and dissolution of both individual memberships and entire associations are essential for shedding theoretical light on the empirical observations gathered by correlation studies. Such data would allow researchers to disentangle the causal relationships between membership changes, social networks, organizational dynamics, and large-scale historical developments. They would also enable the investigation of general trends, such as the alleged national decline in voluntary association memberships (Putnam 2000). Furthermore, researchers could map the distribution of memberships by social characteristics over time to disaggregate general trends and test theories about underlying causal mechanisms.

In the past, the complex data sets necessary for such research were beyond the reach of sociologists. However, due to advances in survey research methodology and data collection technology, as well as to the growing theoretical sophistication of the field, funding agencies are becoming increasingly willing to support these new lines of inquiry. These changes have the capacity to significantly alter the way sociologists study voluntarism, just as was the case with the survey revolution of the 1950s.

Voluntary association research is entering an exciting stage of development. Combining new theoretical frameworks, such as structural ecology and life-course analysis, with sophisticated multilevel dynamic data promises to significantly improve our understanding of the creation, transformation, and dissolution of voluntary associations. If researchers capitalize on this potential, the field will progress far beyond the correlation paradigm that has defined it over the past few decades. As evidenced by existing studies that incorporate voluntary association research and social network analysis (e.g., Mark 1998; McPherson et al. 2006), the progress is well under way.

20

THE SOCIOLOGY OF SOCIAL NETWORKS

BERNICE A. PESCOSOLIDO

Indiana University

Social networks have come to take on prominence in sociology, other academic disciplines, many policy areas, and even in the public discourse in recent years. "Networking," "six degrees of separation," "social support," and "social capital" have been adopted in the business world, among poets and playwrights, and among friends. Yet the diffusion of the underlying terms and concepts from a social network perspective has produced both acceptance and confusion in academic and community circles. Simply stated, a social network is a "structure of relationships linking social actors" (Marsden 2000:2727) or "the set of actors and the ties among them" (Wasserman and Faust 1994). Relationships or ties are the basic building blocks of human experience, mapping the connections that individuals have to one another (Pescosolido 1991). As network theorists claim, the structure of these relationships among actors has important consequences for individuals and for whole systems (Knoke 1990).

Some sociologists see social networks as the essence of social structure (Burt 1980); others see social structure governing these networks (Blau 1974); still others see networks as the mechanism that connects micro and macro levels of social life (Coleman 1990; Pescosolido 1992). To many, the power of network explanations lies in changing the focus of social structure from static categories such as age, gender, and race to the actual nature of the social contacts that individuals have and their impact on life chances (White 1992; Wilson 1987, 1996). In any case, there is a clear link between networks and sociology's central concerns with social structures and social interaction.

THE ROOTS OF A SOCIAL NETWORK PERSPECTIVE IN SOCIOLOGY

Despite the many varieties of "sociology" in contemporary theory, the role of social interactions may be the single commonality (Pescosolido 1992). Social relationships have always been at the heart of sociological understandings of the world. Many sociologists trace the introduction of the structural approach to social interactions to Georg Simmel (1955) in *Conflict and the Web of Group Affiliations* (Pescosolido and Rubin 2000; White, Boorman, and Brieger 1976). In this work, Simmel (1955) began with the classic statement, "Society arises from the individual and the individual arises out of association" (p. 163). Like the founding sociologist, social interaction was the currency that set Simmel's work apart from other social sciences and philosophies. In Durkheim's (1951) *Suicide,* for example, two types of social interaction (integration and regulation) were seen as combining to create four distinct types of social structures (anomic, fatalistic, altruistic, and egoistic), which shaped the behavior of individuals who lived within them. To map these social structures, Durkheim referred to different kinds of "societies," social groups or institutions such as the family, polity, or religions. While consistent with a network approach, Durkheim's approach was more implicit than explicit on social ties (Pescosolido 1994).

Simmel suggested that it was the nature of *ties* themselves rather than the social group per se that lay at the center of many human behaviors. In his attempt to

AUTHOR'S NOTE: I thank Brea Perry, Stanley Wasserman, and Ann McCranie for their comments on an earlier draft of this chapter.

understand the transition from agrarian to industrial society, Simmel discussed two ideal configurations of social networks, commonly referred to as the "premodern" form of concentric social circles and the "modern" form of the intersection of social circles. For each, Simmel described and considered their effect on individuals, including the way personality and belief structures are formed. Briefly, social networks in premodern society were encapsulating and comforting but often intolerant of outsiders (Blau 1993; Giddens 1990). They provided a sense of security and solidarity, which minimized psychological "tensions" for the majority of individuals. Yet such a structure, as Simmel noted, limited freedom, individuality, and diversity. These networks were, as Suchman (1964) was later to call them, "parochial."

Modern society brought "cosmopolitan" networks characterized by intersecting circles. The transition to modern society allowed individuals to increasingly participate in a greater number of networks with more numerous, but fewer multistranded, ties (Blau 1977). Individuals craft unique personalities that stand at the intersection of all the social networks they have inherited and built (Burt 1976). Individuals are more unique and tolerant.[1] But with greater choices possible, individuals deal with greater uncertainty and less support (Giddens 1990; Maryanski and Turner 1992).

Sociological research continued to develop, making heavy use of Durkheim and referring less often to Simmel's network perspective. However, in the 1930s, J. L. Moreno (1934), a psychiatrist and a prolific writer, published *Who Shall Survive? Foundations of Sociometry, Group Psychotherapy, and Sociodrama*. This work marked the major reemergence of the social network metaphor into sociology and, equally important, across the social sciences and into social policy. Working within the context of a girls' school of the time, Moreno and his colleagues developed sociometric techniques that mapped the relationships among individuals (e.g., Jennings 1943; Moreno and Jennings 1938). The goal was not only scientific but pragmatic, with Moreno (1934) using network data to develop "interpersonal therapy," discussing its use with national leaders, including then president Franklin D. Roosevelt.

Moreno laid out a dictionary of network terms, many still used in the same way today (see the next section). More important, the sociogram, a visual technique that graphed the ties between social actors, became the main analytical tool of sociometry. For the first time, these pictures of social relationships made clear the structure of friendships, leadership, and classrooms (Jennings 1943; Northway 1940). Each individual was represented by a circle with lines showing connections and arrowheads indicating whether the tie was sent or received (see Figure 20.1).

As the number of cases increased, and the technique was applied to housing units and communities as well as individuals, the sociograms became increasingly difficult

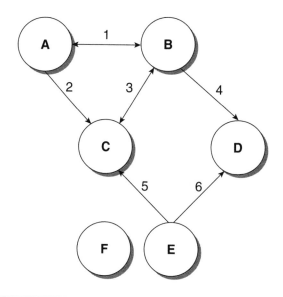

Figure 20.1   Representation of Network Ties in a Sociogram

to read and understand (e.g., see Barnland and Harlund 1963). This was complicated by attempts to introduce other factors, such as sociodemographics or tie intensity, into the graphs. While sociograms continued to appear, these limits saw the graphic approach fall into disuse, and with it, much of the intellectual force that the network approach had brought to sociology. The introduction of graph theory in the 1940s led to the development of mathematical techniques to deal with large networks (Harary, Norman, and Cartwright 1965) and forced Moreno to the sidelines. While Freeman (2004) refers to this period through the 1960s as the "Dark Ages," balance theory formalized the study of network influences and dramatically influenced theory and data collection in social psychology (e.g., Newcomb 1961).

The next important break came in the 1970s, when Harrison White and colleagues developed new principles to rethink the analysis of network data. Using matrix algebra and clustering techniques, block modeling (White et al. 1976), the essential insight of their approach, rested on five basic ideas.[2]

But the development of the Harvard School represented more than an answer to an analytical problem. It began a resurgence of theoretical interest in sociology that was limited to neither the kinds of data nor the analytical techniques developed by White and his colleagues. For example, both Granovetter's (1982) strength-of-weak-ties concept and Fischer's (1982) documentation that urban alienation was thwarted because people live their lives in small worlds, had roots in this environment. Such a review is not meant to imply that other important work across the social sciences was lacking or should be dismissed. In England, Bott's (1957) work on social networks in the family was seminal; in psychology, Milgram (1967) traced chains of connection in "small worlds"; in medical sociology, Kadushin's (1966) "friends and supporters of psychotherapy," Suchman's (1965) "parochial versus cosmopolitan" network distinction, and Rogers's (1971) similar distinction between "localites" and "cosmopolities" became the mainstays of theoretical development and research agendas.

Nonetheless, the developments at Harvard under Harrison White revived interest in social networks, stemming from the realization that the magnitude of social structural problems could now be matched with adequate theoretical and analytical tools. Carrington, Scott, and Wasserman (2005) saw another recent but unexplained spike in network research and interest beginning in the 1990s. This resurgence captured not only the social sciences but also epidemiology, administrative science and management, physics, communications, and politics. Barabasi (2003) contends that the increased emphasis on networks reflects a broad-based realization that research, traditionally (and successfully) searching for "pieces" of social and physical life, could not consider these pieces in isolation. This recognition, he argues, comes in the wake of the emergence of the Internet with its focus on networks (see also Wasserman 2003; Wellman and Gulia 1999). Paralleling these efforts is the development of a wide range of network analytical techniques catalogued in *Network Analysis* (Wasserman and Faust 1994) and recent additions in *Models and Methods in Social Network Analysis* (Carrington et al. 2005).

MAIN CONTRIBUTIONS: PRINCIPLES UNDERLYING THE SOCIAL NETWORK PERSPECTIVE

There is no single network "theory"; in fact, Knoke (1990) sees this as unlikely and even inappropriate. The network approach is considered by most, who use it as more of a perspective or frame that can be used to develop specific theories. Yet sociologists share, across studies, basic principles that often underlie much research using a network frame and guide the development of specific investigations and analyses.[3]

1. Social actors, whether individuals, organizations, or nations, shape their everyday lives through consultation, information and resource sharing, suggestion, support, and nagging from others (White et al. 1976). Network interactions influence beliefs and attitudes as well as behavior, action, and outcomes.

2. Individuals are neither puppets of the social structure nor purely rational, calculating individuals. Individuals are "sociosyncratic," both acting and reacting to the social networks in their environment (Elder 1998a, 1998b; Pescosolido 1992). They are, however, always seen as interdependent rather than independent (Wasserman and Faust 1994). Some theorists (e.g., Coleman 1990) see

networks in the purposive action, rational actor tradition, but this represents only one view that can be subsumed within a network perspective (Pescosolido 1992).

3. Important but often daunting and abstract influences such as "society," "institution," "culture," the "community," and the "system" can be understood by looking to the set of social interactions that occur within them (Tilly 1984). Networks set a context within groups, formal organizations, and institutions for those who work in or are served by them, which, in turn, affects what people do, how they feel, and what happens to them (Wright 1997).

4. Three characteristics of social networks are distinct—structure, content, and function. *Structure* targets the architectural aspect of network ties (e.g., size, density, or types of relationships). *Content* taps what flows across the network ties. They are "channels for transfers of material or non-material resources" (Wasserman and Faust 1994). That is, attitudes and opinions, as well as more tangible experiences and collective memory, are held within networks (Emirbayer and Goodwin 1994; Erikson 1996; Stryker 1980). Finally, networks serve a variety of *functions,* including emotional support, instrumental aid, appraisal, and monitoring (Pearlin and Aneshensel 1986).

5. Network influence requires the consideration of interactions among these three aspects. Structural elements (e.g., size) of a network may tap the amount of potential influence that can be exerted by the network (i.e., the "push"). However, only the content of the network can provide an indication of the direction of that influence (i.e., the "trajectory"). For example, large networks can influence individuals on the Upper West Side of Manhattan to seek out medical professionals (Kadushin 1966) while keeping individuals in Puerto Rico out of the medical system (Pescosolido, Wright, et al. 1998). The intersection of the structure and content of social networks together calibrates whether and how much individuals will be pushed toward or away from doctors and alternative healers or even rely only on family for assistance (Freidson 1970; Pescosolido 1991).

6. Networks may be in sync or in conflict with one another. Different contexts can circumscribe different sets of networks (Simmel 1955). Family, peer, and official school-based networks, for example, may reinforce messages or clash in priorities for teenagers. The level of discordance in the "culture" of networks and the *interface* of social circles may be critical to understanding the behavior of social actors (Pescosolido, Wright, and Sullivan 1995). They may also be different from the perspective of interacting parties in ways that provide insight into social action and outcomes (Pescosolido and Wright 2002).

7. Social interactions can be positive or negative, helpful or harmful. They can integrate individuals into a community and, just as powerfully, place stringent isolating regulations on behavior. The little research that has

explored negative ties in people's lives has found them to have powerful effects (Berkman 1986; Pagel, Erdly, and Becker 1987). Portes (1998), Rumbaut (1977), and Waldinger (1995) all document how tight social interactions within ethnic groups lead to restricted job opportunities for those inside and outside of the ethnic networks.

8. "More" is not necessarily better with regard to social ties. As Durkheim (1951) pointed out, too much oversight (regulation) or support (integration) can be stifling and repressive (Pescosolido 1994). Further, "strong" ties are not necessarily optimal because "weak" ties often act as a bridge to different information and resources (Granovetter 1982), and holes in network structures (Burt 1980) provide opportunities that can be exploited. The focus on social support, and now social capital, may have obfuscated the focus on the "dark" aspects of social networks (see below).

9. Networks across all levels are dynamic, not static, structures and processes.[4] The ability to form and maintain social ties may be just as important as their state at one point in time. There may be changes in the structure of networks or changes in membership. In fact, early work on this topic suggests that turnover rates may hover around 50%, while the structure (e.g., size) tends to remain stable (Perry 2005a). As Moody, McFarland, and Bender-deMoll (2005) note, "An apparently static network pattern *emerges* through a set of temporal interactions" (p. 1209). Further, the underlying reasons for changing networks may mark important insights into the influence of networks (Perry 2005a; Pescosolido and Wright 2004; Suitor, Wellman, and Morgan 1996; Wellman, Wong, Tindall, and Nazer 1996). This focus represents some of the newest work in sociology and some of the greatest theoretical, methodological, and analytical challenges (Bearman, Moody, and Stovel 2004; Snijders 1998). In fact, Carrington et al. (2005) refer to the analysis of social networks over time as the "Holy Grail" of network research. New analytical methods and visualization approaches are becoming available to see how social networks look and trace how they change (Bearman et al. 2004; Freeman 2004).

10. A network perspective allows for, and even calls for, multimethod approaches. Jinnett, Coulter, and Koegel (2002) conclude that quantitative research is powerful in documenting the effects of social networks but only when accompanied by qualitative research that describes why they operate and look the way they do. There is no standard way to chart network relationships—they may be derived from a list on a survey where individuals are asked to name people they trust, admire, or dislike or with whom they share information. Alternatively, the information may come from observing the behavior of individuals (e.g., who they talk to in their work group; Homans 1951, 1961). Network information can be collected through archival sources such as citation records (Hargens 2000) or by documenting the behavior of organizations or countries (e.g., trade agreements; Alderson and Beckfield 2004). Even

simulated data can be and have been used to examine network processes (Cederman 2005; Eguiluz et al. 2005; Moss and Edmonds 2005).[5] In sum, deciding which kinds of social networks are of interest, how to elicit the ties, and how to track their dynamics remain critical issues (Berkman 1986; House, Robbins, and Metzner 1982; Leik and Chalkey 1996; O'Reilly 1998; Suitor et al. 1996; Wellman et al. 1996).

11. Sociodemographic characteristics are potential factors shaping the boundaries of social networks but provide, at best, poor measures of social interaction (Collins 1988; Morgan, Patrick, and Charlton 1984; White et al. 1976). Originally, networks were circumscribed by the place where people lived and their customs (Fischer 1982; Pescosolido and Rubin 2000; Simmel 1955; Wellman 1982). But a process of "disembedding" (Giddens 1990) from local places has been replaced by a "re-embedding" at the global level. While we may continue to see gross differences in, for example, the number of network ties by these "actor attributes" (Monge and Contractor 2003) or "composition variables" (Wasserman and Faust 1994), these static characteristics only indirectly tap the real underlying social forces at work—the content, structure, and function of social interactions.

Used in combination with social network factors, these characteristics offer two possibilities. First, complicated issues—for example, that men tend to report more networks but that women's networks are more intimate (Campbell and Rosenfeld 1985; Moore 1992)—can now be more readily examined with analytical techniques (Carrington et al. 2005; Freeman 2004; Koehly and Pattison 2005). Second, networks may operate differently for different groups. That is, considered as potential interactive factors, rather than simply shaping ones, attribute variables may provide insights into how social network processes create different pathways of beliefs and behaviors for social actors.

12. Individuals form ties under contextual constraints and interact given social psychological and neurological capacities. Thus, social networks exist in a multilevel environment. Some of these levels (e.g., organizations) may also be conceptualized in network terms. For example, an individual's network ties within the religious sphere exist within geographic areas that themselves have a structure of religious network types and a more general social capital profile (e.g., areas where the religion is dominant or in a minority; Pescosolido 1990). Such a view leads to additional research questions about whether network structures operate in the same way in different contexts (Pescosolido 1994). Similarly, other factors (e.g., laws) may set structural conditions on relationships (e.g., within organizational or business organization fields).

Further, individuals' social networks are not divorced from the body and the physical/mental capacities that individuals bring to them (Leventhal, Leventhal, and Contrada 1997; Orlinsky and Howard 1987; Rosenfield and Wenzel 1997). As Fremont and Bird (2000) report, when social interactions are the source of social stress, the impact appears to be more devastating in magnitude (see also Perry 2005b). Social psychological characteristics (e.g., self-reliance) may also influence the effect of network ties. Biological challenges may lie at the heart of dramatic changes in individuals' social network systems both for those affected directly and for caregivers (Dozier 1993; Dozier, Cue, and Barnett 1994; Lysaker et al. 1994; Rosenfield and Wenzel 1997; Suitor and Pillemer 2002). It has long been known that children with physiological or neurological deficits have difficulties in establishing social relationships (Perry 2005b). Sociologists know that these early social relationships affect adult educational outcomes (Entwisle, Alexander, and Olson 2005).

Networks may also affect biology. In trying to understand why social networks matter—for example, in cardiac health—researchers have linked constellations of social networks to biological processes (e.g., plasma fibrinogen levels; Helminen et al. 1997). Furthermore, social support has been shown to influence the phenotypic expression of genetic predispositions (Caspi et al. 2002).

NETWORK BASICS

Even with some agreement on network foundations, a myriad of concepts and approaches confront the network approach with the necessity of clarifying terms (see also Monge and Contractor 2003). The most frequently referenced terms are briefly described below. This is neither an exhaustive nor a technical lexicon of network terminology; rather, the goal is to provide an orientation to network language and its basic variants.

• *Node, social atom, actor:* These terms refer to the central "units" that have networks. Social actors often refer to individuals; however, actors may also be families (Padgett and Ansell 1993), organizations (Galaskiewicz 1985), nations (Alderson and Beckfield 2004; Snyder and Kick 1979), or any other entity that can form or maintain formal (e.g., legal, economic) or informal (friendship, gossip) relationships (Figure 20.1: A, B, D through F represented as circles are "actors").

• *Ties, links, relationships, edges:* The network connections between and among actors are referred to as ties. Ties can be directed (sent or received) or not directed (joint organizational memberships). In Figure 20.1, a tie is sent from B to D (out-degree); D receives a tie from E (in-degree). A and B send and receive ties to each other. Double-headed arrows indicate "mutual," "bidirectional," "symmetrical," or "reciprocal" ties. They may map the existence of a relationship or have an intensity (ties in Figure 20.1 are lines 1 through 6). The two-actor connectors are dyads; three-actor connections are triads.

• *Subgroups:* When the focus is on some subset of actors and their linkages, the search is for subgroups.

• *Sociogram:* This is a picture of the relationships among members in a social network (Figure 20.1).

• *Sociomatrix/adjacency matrix:* Network ties can also be recorded and depicted as a set of numbers in a square table that consists of rows (recording ties sent) and columns (ties received) (see Figure 20.2).

• *Type of tie:* Networks can depict or illustrate different kinds of relationships called "types." For example, Padgett and Ansell's (1993) study of a Florentine family included both marriage and business ties.

• *Sociometric star:* In a social network, an actor(s) receiving a relatively high degree or number of ties is considered to be a "star." In Figure 20.1, C is a sociometric star with four in-degrees, more than any other actor.

• *Isolate:* An ego or node receiving no ties is an isolate (F in Figure 20.1, Actor 6 in Figure 20.2).

• *Network path:* Paths are determined by tracing ties to determine the number of degrees of separation between two actors. If two actors are directly connected, the value of the path is 1 (Figure 20.1, the path between A and B). The path value between E and A is 3 since E can be connected to A by tracing the path from E to C, C to B, and B to A.

• *Size:* In a network, the number of social actors constitutes the network size (in Figure 20.1, $n = 6$; in Figure 20.2, $N = 100$). In ego-based networks (see the next section), size refers to the number of ties listed for each social actor (e.g., How many confidants do you have?).

• *Density:* The "tightness" or "connectedness" of ties among actors in a network is calculated by the proportion of ties existing in a network divided by the possible number of ties that could be sent and received. Density

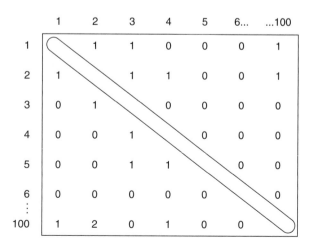

Figure 20.2 Representation of Network Ties with a Sociomatrix

answers the question of how well all the members of a network are connected to one another (Figure 20.2: 30 possible ties, 9 ties sent, yielding a density of 9/30 or 0.33).

- *Content/function:* Both describe the meaning or nature of the tie.
  - ○ *Strength:* This is a measure of intensity or potency of a tie. It may indicate frequency (e.g., how many trading agreements countries share), closeness (How close do you feel to X?), or another relevant quality that offers a value to the tie or defines a name generator (How many close business associates do you have in this firm?).
  - ○ *Multiplexity:* When ties are based on more than one relationship, entail more than one type of social activity or social role, or serve more than one purpose, they are thought to be multiplex, "many stranded," or "multipurpose" (Barnes 1972). Multiplex ties tend to be more durable and deeper than those based on only one connection (Holschuh and Segal 2002; Morin and Seidman 1986; Tolsdorf 1976).
  - ○ *Instrumental support:* Ties that offer practical resources or assistance are said to deliver instrumental support.
  - ○ *Emotional support:* Ties that provide love, caring, and nurturing offer emotional support (Thoits 1995).
  - ○ *Appraisal:* This targets network assistance in evaluating a problem or a source of aid (Pearlin and Aneshensel 1986).
  - ○ *Monitoring:* When network ties watch, discipline, or regulate the behavior of other social actors, the monitoring function is fulfilled (Pearlin and Aneshensel 1986).

- *Latent versus activated ties:* Latent ties represent the number, structure, or resources of those ties on which actors expect to rely on a regular basis (Knoke 1990; Who can you rely on generally?). Activated ties represent a list of those persons, organizations, and so on that actors actually contacted in the face of a specific problem or task (e.g., Who did you consult?).

- *Network "holes"/network "bridges":* Holes refers to places in a network structure where social actors are unconnected (Burt 1992, 2001). These holes afford opportunities to build bridges where social actors can connect different subgroups or cliques, bringing new information to each (Granovetter 1982).

- *Binary/valued data:* These terms differentiate between the reporting of whether a tie exists or not and reporting ties where there is some sort of assessment (How close are you to X? Rate from 1 to 4).

- *Diffusion:* This type of network analysis focuses on the flow of information through a network—for example, why some social actors adopt a new idea and others do not (Deffuant, Huet, and Amblard 2005; Valente 2005).

FOUR TRADITIONS OR APPROACHES

Part of the complexity of understanding the contributions and future directions of social network research in sociology lies in the different ways in which the idea of network ties has been incorporated in research. The approaches have also been characterized by differences in theoretical starting points, data requirements, and methods of data collection. In this sense, they are not strictly different traditions but nonetheless represent different strands of research. They continue to use different terms and draw only sporadically from one another (Thoits 1995).

The first two represent quantitative traditions. The *complete or full* network approach attempts to describe and analyze whole network system. The *local or ego-centered approach* targets the ties surrounding particular individual actors. The *social support* perspective is more general and theory oriented, often using network imagery but tending to focus on the overall state of an individual's social relationships and summary measures of networks. The *social capital* perspective is the most recent, focusing on the "good" things that flow along network ties (i.e., trust, solidarity), which are complementary to the more economically focused human capital (e.g., education; Lin 2000).

As Wasserman and Faust (1994) note, the first question to ask and the one most relevant to distinguish many of these traditions is "What is your population?"

The Whole, Complete, or Full Network Approach

This tradition, in many ways, represents the "purest" approach. Here, all network ties among members of a population are considered. This allows for a mapping of the overall social network structure. And the most advanced techniques have been developed to determine and describe that structure. Full networks have been described in hospitals (Barley 1986), elite or ruling families (Padgett and Ansell 1993), laboratory groups and other scientific collaboration (Breiger 1976; Powell et al. 2005), business structures (Galaskiewicz et al. 1985), world trading partners and global economic systems (Alderson and Beckfield 2004; Snyder and Kick 1979), policy-making systems (Laumann and Knoke 1987; Laumann and Pappi 1976), and schools (Bearman et al. 2004).

In keeping with Wasserman and Faust's (1994) questions, this approach requires that the universe of network members can, in fact, be delineated. That is, it must first be possible to list all the members of the social structure in question and to elicit, in some way, the ties or bonds that exist among them. To make the analysis effective, data must be collected from all members of the population. While assumptions can be made to fill in missing data (e.g., assume that ties are reciprocal), this solution becomes more questionable as the response rate decreases even to levels considered acceptable for nonresponse in surveys. Furthermore, unlike regression techniques, there are no well-established and tested options to deal with missing data. These requirements for defining the population and having nearly 100% response or completion rates make this approach unfeasible for many questions.

However, problems that can be matched to these stringent data requirements have at their disposal a rich range of possibilities for analysis. This analysis of complete network data begins with the construction of the sociomatrix or adjacency matrix of the type depicted in Figure 20.2, which lays out all ties. The data can be summarized across rows and columns in a number of ways, and individuals can be clustered together to examine clique structures or blocks. For example, in the block model approach (White et al. 1976), the assumption of structural equivalence is used to bring together columns of data that share *both* a similarity of ties and an absence of ties. As an illustration, in Figure 20.3, Panel A, an original matrix of zeros and ones for 100 actors has been clustered into four blocks of structurally equivalent social actors. Essentially, in this reordered matrix, the rows and columns have simply been reassigned from their original position in Figure 20.2 into blocks that reflect groupings (e.g., within the first block, the social actors with original IDs 1, 10, 11, 14, 77, and 81 have been grouped together based on the similarity of ties). Within each block of this new matrix, called the density matrix, the percentage or proportion of ones (indicating the presence of ties of the number possible) has been computed. So, for example, among the social actors in Block 1, 60% of the possible ties that can exist do exist. This indicates that this block may, in fact, be a clique or subgroup. However, only 10% of the ties that can exist between Block 1 and Block 3 have actually been recorded, indicating that those actors in Block 1 *do not* tend to be connected to those in Block 3.

The interpretation of the block structure begins with a conversion of the block proportions into ones and zeros. In the most stringent analysis, the cutting point between ties and no ties is a pure zero block (no ties). However, as can be seen in this more typical result, there are no such blocks (though Blocks 3 and 4 come close). The conversion from a density matrix to an image matrix, in most cases, requires a decision about an acceptable cutting point, which is often facilitated by having a good knowledge of the data collection setting. In the absence of that information (and often when the site is familiar), the conversion depends on the analyst's decision. Here, one choice might be to use a cutting point of 0.4 or above. A more stringent choice might be 0.6 or above. Figure 20.3, Panel B, uses the less stringent 0.4 criteria to represent the image matrix. There is no statistic that can determine either the proper number of blocks or the density cutting point, making the decision making relatively arbitrary.

To this point, then, actors were partitioned into structurally equivalent sets with the density of ties computed, and the structure of relationships was mapped into a set of images indicating whether subgroups exist and how they related to other blocks. To get a better sense of the

Panel A

	1 1 10 11 14 77 81	2	3	4
1 10 11 14 77 81	.60	.40	.10	.06
2	.80	.90	.14	.21
3	.65	.87	.11	.67
4	.18	.51	.01	.48

Panel B

	1	2	3	4
1	1	1	0	0
2	1	1	0	0
3	1	1	0	1
4	0	1	0	1

Panel C

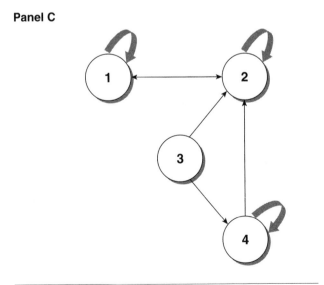

Figure 20.3 Hypothetical Density, Image, and Socio-Matrix from a Block Model Analysis of a Complete Network

structure of relationships, a sociogram can be constructed using the blocks, not actors, as nodes in the diagram (Figure 20.3, Panel C). The actors in Blocks 1, 2, and 4 appear to form subgroups because they send and receive ties to each other. Note, however, that the individuals in Block 4 are similar only in the patterns of their ties to other actors but do not in themselves form a subgroup. This also suggests that this group may be of lower prestige since they send ties to all other groups but do not receive ties in return (i.e., asymmetry). Furthermore, only the actors in Blocks 1 and 2 have a mutual relationship.

In sum, the complete network tradition is concerned with the structural properties of networks at a global or whole level (Doreian, Batagelj, and Ferligoj 2005). The primary issue in taking this approach is the identification of the boundaries of the network, which requires answering the question "Who are the relevant actors?" (Marsden 2005; Wasserman and Faust 1994).

The Local or Ego-Centered Approach

If the first approach is the purest, then this approach is the most typical. While data requirements may be less strict, there are more limits to what can be done analytically. Here, the focus is on a set of social actors who are defined as a sample. The effort centers on gathering information about the network from the standpoint of the social actors situated within it (Marsden 2005). Since it is impossible to include, for example, all individuals in a large community, each social actor is asked about his or her own ties. In Figure 20.4, each social actor (A, B, C through E of a small to very large *N*) was selected under some purposive sampling plan, whether a random sample, deliberate sample, or convenience sample. Here, each selected social actor (A through E) is typically asked to list other social actors in response to a name generator. This list may record all the individuals with whom a respondent is friends, loans money to, receives money from, and so on. The first case (Ego A) names three alters, Ego D names seven, and Ego B lists only one. In some cases, the individuals who are named may also be contacted using a snowball sampling technique (see Figure 20.4, Egos A or E). The original respondents may be called egos or focal respondents (FRs), while those they name, who are followed up, may be called alters or network respondents (NRs) (Figure 20.4).

The NRs may be asked about the networks that the original FR has, perhaps for

corroboration or theoretical purposes (Pescosolido and Wright 2002). In this case, the dashed line indicates that Alter A1 does, in fact, have a relationship with the FR or ego, as does Alter A2. However, Alter 3 indicates no such tie to FR A. Finally, the alters may also be asked about their *own* ties. In caregiver research, it is a typical strategy to ask "Who cares for the caregivers?" Here, as indicated by the dotted lines, Ego E reports two network ties (Alters E2 and E1). They, in turn, have reported their ties. E1 mentions two actors, including the original person (Ego E). However, Alter E2 mentions five supporters but does not include Ego E among them. Such relationships have theoretical implications for both the stability and the durability of each ego's network support system as well as for the ability of each caregiver to experience "burnout" (e.g., Suitor and Pillemer 2002).

While more limited network mapping can be done compared with complete network data, factors such as the size

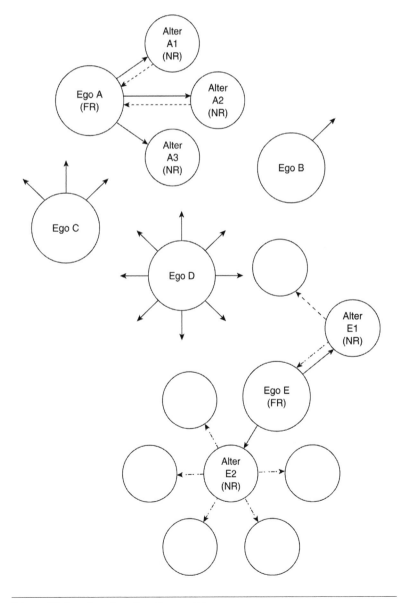

Figure 20.4   Local or Ego-Centered Structures

(as a count of mentions), density (by asking the FRs to indicate whether each NR they mention as a tie knows each other tie), or reciprocity (by asking the FRs if they also provide friendship, assistance, etc., or by asking the NRs in a first-stage snowball) can be constructed and used to test theoretical ideas about the influence of social networks. Attribute information can be collected on each tie (e.g., gender, age, ethnicity, attitudes), which can be used to examine, for example, the influence of network homogeneity on structural and context issues. Even the interaction of network size and content, noted earlier (Principle 5), can be operationalized, though recent methodological concerns surround the appropriate construction of such interactions (Allison 1978; Long 1997; for substantive examples of different approaches, see Pescosolido, Brooks-Gardner, and Lubell 1998; Pescosolido, Wright, et al. 1998).

The Social Support Approach

This tradition, unlike the two described above, comes primarily from a social psychological, rather than a structural, perspective. As Thoits (1995) notes, social support is the most frequently studied psychosocial resource and has been documented to be a powerful influence, for example, in occurrence of and recovery from life problems. While social support is seen similarly as resources available from family, friends, organizations, and other actors, researchers here tend to use a summary social integration strategy, looking less to network structures (Barrera 1986). Emanating from a concern with actors' responses to stressful situations, social support is considered a social reserve that may either prevent or buffer adverse events that occur in people's lives (Pearlin and Aneshensel 1986).

Social networks represent one component of social support (House, Landis, and Umberson 1988), in contrast to the structural perspective that tends to see social support, conversely, as a possible type of tie, a resource that flows over ties, or content that may or may not occur (Faber and Wasserman 2002; Wellman 1981). However, the social support tradition does not ignore structure altogether, noting that indicators of structural support (i.e., the organization of an individual's ties in terms of size, density, multiplexity) are important (Barrera 1986). Yet the focus in this approach is on the sustaining qualities of social relationships (Haines, Beggs, and Hurlbert 2002). Researchers tend to ask study respondents whether they have/had enough support in everyday life issues or critical events. Questions may target either perceived social support (i.e., the belief that love, caring, and assistance are potentially available from others; latent networks in the structural tradition) or received support (i.e., the actual use of others for caring, assistance, appraisal [Thoits 1995], activated networks in the structural tradition). In fact, social support research has documented that perceived support is more important than actual support received (House 1981; Turner and Marino 1994). Even more surprising, Cohen

and Wills (1985) suggest that the simplest and most potent indicator is whether individuals report that they have a single intimate tie in which they can confide.

The Social Capital Tradition

According to Monge and Contractor (2003), the ideas underlying the investigation of social capital were introduced in the 1980s to refer to resources that accrue to social actors from individuals to nations as a result of networks (Bourdieu and Wacquant 1992; Coleman 1990; Lin 2000)—that is, because individuals participate in social groups, there are benefits to be had. Individuals invest in and use the resources embedded in social networks because they expect returns of some sort (Lin 2000). Resources are not equally available to all individuals but are differentially distributed across groups in society (Lin 2000). Thus, social capital in the form of trust, social norms of reciprocity, cooperation, and participation resides in relationships, not individuals, and therefore shares roots with many aspects of classical sociology and other network traditions (Paxton 2002; Portes 1998).

Although some contend that the social capital approach brings no novel ideas to network perspective, offering only a "more appealing conceptual garb" (Portes 1998; see also Etzioni 2001; Wilson 2001), three unique aspects of this approach are notable. First, more than the other traditions, social capital research has been popularized to describe the state of civil society (e.g., Putnam's [1995] concept of "bowling alone") or differing geographical areas (e.g., neighborhoods, Rahn 2004) and to relate to large public policy issues. For example, Wilson (2001) suggests that social networks constitute social capital to the extent that they contribute to civic engagement. As such, these resources can be measured at multiple levels (the individual, the neighborhood, the nation), a measurement task difficult under the other traditions. Social capital data have been collected in a variety of ways, from the number of positive networks or connections that individuals have to overall geographical characteristics (e.g., migration rates, voting rates). Second, social capital focuses attention on the positive qualities (though not necessarily consequences) of social ties, downplaying the potential "dark side" of networks. As Edwards and Foley (2001:230) note, social capital comes in three "flavors"—good, better, and best. From a social network perspective, this aspect is perhaps the most troubling. Like the social support tradition, this emphasis on positive contents limits the theoretical import of ties. Third, the social capital approach has broadened the appeal of a network perspective to those in other social science disciplines outside sociology. By providing sociability that is parallel to "human capital" and "fiscal capital," the introduction of social capital reinforced the sociological thesis that social interaction can have powerful effects on actors.

These unique contributions produce other curious corollaries. Because of its affiliation with other forms of "capital," the social capital tradition has been more likely to adopt a rational choice foundation. Social capital theorists often talk about the costs and benefits of establishing ties, as well as how and why actors deliberately construct or maintain ties in the service of creating opportunities and resources. This discussion of "investment strategies" or "fungibility," "opportunity costs" or "resources to pursue interests" (Baker 1990), does not question the self-interested and antisocial nature of individuals, a debate in sociology still not settled by those who see an inherent sociability. By basing the perspective in the notion of purposive action (Lin 1999), the roles of "habitus" and emotions are underplayed, if not absent, in the rational choice perspective that undergirds most social capital research (Pescosolido 1992).

THE FUTURE OF SOCIAL NETWORKS: CHALLENGES AND OPPORTUNITIES

The network perspective poses many challenges to routine ways of doing sociological research. Two seem to be most pressing. The first entails questions about social networks themselves, their dynamics, and how the network approach might be integrated into the life-course approach. Such questions include the following: To what extent do ties persist? Why do some persist more than others? How do changes affect actors' networks and intersect with larger changes in society? How are network dynamics intertwined with change in other life arenas? (Pescosolido and Wright 2002; Suitor et al. 1996). The second topic addresses the interplay of social and biological forces. The biological and social network interaction across the life course represents some of the most recent considerations that have been posited (Elder 1998b; Giele 2002; Klovdahl, Graviss, and Musser 2002; Shonkoff and Phillips 2000). Relevant questions include the following: How are social networks shaped by and shape lives through psychological and biological processes? Can we understand what happens in social life by reference to the limits that social networks, genetics, personality, and biology set for one another?

Patterns, Pathways, and Trajectories of Networks and Their Influence

The life-course perspective views lives as organized socially across both biological and historical time (Elder 1998b; see also Werner 2002). The social network perspective suggests that what links the lives of individuals to the time and place in which they live are their connections to others (Kahn and Antonucci 1980). However, these interactions can exist at many levels—individuals interacting with other individuals, individuals interacting within large social groups or organizations, and individuals interacting in larger climates or contexts that may differentially affect outcomes. Simultaneously embracing the dynamics and multiple levels of the life course—that is, understanding social networks as attached to time and place—reveals a complex interplay of forces to be examined. If social networks mark the social interdependence that continuously shapes and redirects lives, then exploring how they play a role in pathways, trajectories, and transitions becomes critical (Elder 1985; Moen, Robison, and Dempster-McClain 1995; Pavalko 1997; Werner 2002).

The Multidisciplinary Evolution and Prominence of Social Networks

From its beginning, the network approach has been embraced by a variety of social science disciplines, particularly anthropology (e.g., Barnes 1954; Bott 1957; Mitchell 1969). The network approach has come to be a major force in the areas of health and medicine (Levy and Pescosolido 2002); communications research (Monge and Contractor 2003); mathematics, physics, and other sciences (Barabasi 2003; Watts 2003); and political science (Fowler and Smirnov 2005; Huckfeldt and Sprague 1987; Rahn 2004). Yet these areas remain unconnected. Taking seriously the life-course perspective's principle of "linked lives" (Elder and Pellerin 1998; Werner 2002), the network perspective offers a way to synthesize disciplinary insights.

While network theory may reject focusing on individuals alone, mental events, cognitive maps, or technological determinism (White 1992), identity, cognition, technology, and biology may be intertwined in complex ways. Agenda-setting reports on health and medicine, for example, have embraced this possibility. In an Institute of Medicine report, *From Neurons to Neighborhoods* (Shonkoff and Phillips 2000), social network relationships are viewed as the "fundamental mediators of human adaptations" and the "active ingredients of environmental influence." Yet the response of sociology in leading the theoretical agenda has been slow. If we see, as Castells (2000) suggests, that social structure is made up of networks in interactions that are constantly on the move, similar to self-generating process images in molecular biology, sociologists' familiarity with conceptualizing multilevel, dynamic processes becomes essential to understanding social life.

21

WORK AND OCCUPATIONS

DOUGLAS HARPER

Duquesne University

The study of work has been part of sociology since its beginning. Karl Marx described how capitalist relations of production transformed work from the creative matter of subsistence to the alienated activity of mass production manufacture. Max Weber also studied work: the emergence of capitalism via the culture of Calvinism, and, later, the dehumanization of work in bureaucracies. Émile Durkheim approached work as part of the study of the division of labor. In prior societies (which he referred to as having mechanical solidarity), work was an expression of one's sameness to others; in the modern societies (which Durkheim referred to as having organic solidarity), specialization led to evermore differentiated divisions of labor and job specialization. The study of work (as an extension of identity) locates most naturally in societies that are organically organized, while occupations belong to societies characterized by mechanical solidarity.

While work (and, by implication, occupations) compelled these and other sociologists' writing in the first decades of our discipline, almost no sociologist studied the cultural definition of work; none entered the factory, farm, or firm to understand how work was defined and managed by those who work. The closest thing to an ethnography of work was Frederick Engels's ([1845] 1973) *The Condition of the Working Class in England,* written when the author was 24 years old.

Engels describes how machines have simplified work and changed its social character:

> The human labour, involved in both spinning and weaving, consists chiefly in piercing broken threads, as the machine does all the rest. This work requires no muscular strength, but only flexibility of finger. Men are, therefore, not only not needed for it, but actually, by reason of the greater muscular development of the hand, less fit for it than women and children, and are, therefore naturally superceded by them. Hence, the more the use of the arms, the expenditure of strength can be transferred to steam or water power, the fewer men need be employed; and as women and children work more cheaply, and in these branches better than men, they take their places. (P. 179)

From this passage, it is clear that these revolutionary changes altered working-class family life as work replaced work previously based on skill and strength with the repetitive movement of the assembly line.

For the child workers, the conditions in the factory were horrific. Engels described narcotics use among children. The repetitive work produced physical deformity. Children were punished for minor infractions and suffered work-related injury, stunted growth and imagination, as well as the decline of home life. The culture of early industrialized work was a kids' world of full-fledged exploitation.

One of the strongest themes in the book concerns the impact of industrial life on family culture: Roles were reversed as women were forced into the workforce. These themes would be returned to 100 years hence.

This book was based on field research in the working-class slums and factories of industrial England. What is not generally remembered is that Engels, the privileged son of a factory owner, was guided into the dark neighborhoods and oppressive factories by his working-class Irish girlfriend, Mary Burns. All fieldworkers need an entry to the field!

WORK AND OCCUPATIONS
IN AMERICAN SOCIOLOGY

The study of work and occupations began during the 1920s at the University of Chicago, as an aspect of the Chicago School of sociology. University of Chicago sociologists, under the tutelage and theoretical guidance of W. I. Thomas and Robert Park, applied an ecological orientation to the study of urban institutions, including work and occupations. One of first graduate students to focus on work was Everett Hughes, who earned his Ph.D. in 1927 for a study of the Chicago Real Estate Board. Hughes was especially interested in the contested steps in the process of how occupations claimed the designation of "profession." These themes would reemerge as the subfield developed, especially during the 1950s.

A competing, yet largely mutually exclusive trend in the study of work and occupations during the formative era was "industrial sociology," that is, a sociology applied to the problems of management. Frederick Winslow Taylor (1911), the chief intellectual figure in what was also referred to as the "human relations school of industrial management," argued that "scientific management" would locate the control of work squarely in the hands of management, thus displacing the oppositional cultures that emerge in all work settings. One of the most famous applications of Taylor's theories is found in Elton Mayo's (1945) "Hawthorne Experiments," in which workers were experimented on to measure the conditions under which their work became more efficient. These fascinating experiments, which would be unlikely to pass Institutional Review in today's world, showed that workers' productivity improved under several imposed changes. It is now commonly accepted that the improvements in production were the result of the selected workers becoming a mini-culture of their own. Industrial sociology has developed as an aspect of applied sociology rather than as the sociology of work and occupations per se.

The sociological study of work and occupations, outside of the research done in the service of management, is attributed to Everett Hughes. In 1952, Hughes became editor of the *American Journal of Sociology* and devoted his first issue to the study of work. Hughes ([1952] 1971) wrote in the editorial Foreword to that issue,

> Why give a large part of an issue of this Journal over to such whimseys [sic] as the special culture of the few professional boxers who fly up like moths from the morass of the slums and drop back again in a little while and as the disappearing breed of small custom-furriers; to such oddities as janitors and schoolteachers? (P. 299)

By way of answer, Hughes cited the "double burden" of sociologists to analyze the processes of human behavior free of time and place, while also becoming "ethnologist of his own time and place" (p. 299). Finding variety and contrast in case studies would allow sociologists to study similar sociological processes from the vantage points of occupations.

The study of work and occupations had begun to adopt the case studies approach. Prior to Hughes's work in the 1950s (as researcher, graduate professor, chair of the Department of Sociology at the University of Chicago, and editor of important sociology journals), Stone (1946) studied the social construction of status and leadership in an aircraft fighter squadron; William Foote Whyte (1949) studied the social structure of the occupational worlds of the restaurant; and Oswald Hall (1948) had analyzed the subjective dimensions of medical doctors' careers. Themes found in this research, including understanding the coordinated lines of work that constitute the social structure of a work environment, and study of the career as defined inwardly as well as by the calendar, became important themes in the study of work and occupations. Similarly, these studies showed the usefulness of examining what Hughes (1970) called "the humble and the proud," that is, the cultures of the most highly trained professionals and the most mundane of service jobs.

The ethnographically oriented studies of work and occupations during the 1950s were dominated by Hughes and his students, while the macro, functionalist orientation otherwise dominant in American sociology was represented in Caplow's (1954) influential text on the sociology of work, republished several times, and translated. Several texts subsequently followed Caplow's example.

Among Hughes's insights was an interpretation of Taylor's understanding that in all work settings there was an ongoing struggle over who would control the productive output. For Taylor, this amounted to a problem for management. Hughes ([1952] 1971) saw it as a generic sociological principle:

> Restriction of production . . . is generally defined [as] . . . the willful refusal by workers in industry to do as much work as their employer believes they can and ought to do. The latter, having hired a man's [woman's] time, expects some large power over its disposition. It is assumed by the employer that his will—enlightened, informed, and reasonable—should determine how hard a man should work. (P. 301)

Sociologists have continued to identify these patterns in virtually all work settings. Two examples are Donald Roy's (1952) study of "goldbricking" (the hidden cultural processes through which workers organized their activities to restrict production in the machine shop) and Burawoy's (1984) study of worker resistance in the assembly line world.

Becker (1952) was the first to study the occupational culture of artistic workers, which introduced the importance of worker interaction with their publics. The jazz musicians Becker studied, for example, had conflictual relationships with their audiences. Their decisions about what to play, how to play the songs, and even how to occupy the stage reflected how musicians collectively managed their relationships with audiences they largely disdained. Sanders (1974) examined the folk singers' performance strategies from this perspective, and Stebbins (1969) updated Becker's argument to the then contemporary jazz scene. Becker's (1982) tour de force, Art Worlds, continued to define art as a negotiated process between audience and producer.

The early sociology of work and occupations also included several studies of work as coordinated activity. Robert Wilson (1954) applied Whyte's perspective on teamwork in the restaurant to the operating room; and Fred Davis (1959) offered the first of many studies of the client and provider in a fleeting relationship, here between the cabbie and his fare.

Finally, sociologists of the early era began to study work, or occupational socialization, a theme that has had an important role to this day. The seminal study was by Becker et al. (1961), a participant observation study of the informal aspects of medical school education. The study of the formation of a professional identity noted, for example, how the "precynical" attitudes of the young student were invariably replaced with the "cynical" (socialized for failure) attitudes of the doctor. Becker and Geer's (1958) excerpt from that study went further, labeling this the "fate of idealism" in medical school. In the 1980s, Haas and Shaffir (1982, 1984) restudied the ideological conversion of medical training in a Canadian medical school with specific reference to Becker and Hughes's pioneering study.

By the 1950s, the study of work and occupations had gained a strong foothold in American sociology. These close-up case studies (ethnographies in the modern parlance, though not called that at the time) served as an alternative to American sociology dominated by survey research and a methodological concern with scientific rigor, what Gouldner and others referred to as "positivist grand theory." It was largely through the study of work and occupations that fieldwork, during these decades of methodological and theoretical hegemony, remained viable as a method.

The 1960s and 1970s saw the application of previously introduced themes to new subject areas. The most significant was work socialization, but now focused across the full range of occupations and sociological themes. For example, Blanch Geer and Howard Becker studied occupational socialization in a five-year research project, "Educational Experiences for Non-College Youth," which led to Geer's (1972) edited volume on trade work socialization. Sociologists studied how violence and abusive socialization integrated workers into dangerous work roles in the coal mine (Fitzpatrick 1980; Vaught and Smith 1980) and how hip seminaries socialized ministers to the political correctness of the day (Kleinman 1984). Others studied military socialization and the normalization of deviance (Bryant 1974a) and the process through which workers internalized values and norms in the skilled trades (Riemer 1977). The challenge of these studies remains in the development of truly comparative analyses of similar social processes in different settings.

During the 1960s, the study of work and occupations became more critical and phenomenological. For example, Egon Bittner's (1967) ethnomethodological study of peacekeeping on skid row described the "practical accomplishment of police work"; Jerry Jacobs's (1969) study of a social welfare agency applied Weber's understanding of rationalization to the crushing irrationalities of bureaucratic life. Critical studies of industrial work, recalling Marxian themes of alienation and control, were developed in Eli Chinoy's (1964) study of assembly line workers. Zucher's study of Hughes's (1959, 1960, 1965) several papers on the relationship between occupations and professions captured the interest of scholars studying law, medicine, funeral directors, and others.

The study of people involved in so-called deviant occupations, such as strippers and prostitutes, became common during the 1970s (e.g., Heyl 1977), and others studied how deviant activity such as theft or drug use was integrated into nondeviant work roles. For example, Ditton (1977) showed how delivery workers in the United Kingdom learned to cheat customers. Bryant (1974b) detailed the routines of deviant use of drugs and alcohol in the military. I (Harper 1982) studied how railroad tramps cycled through identities that cast them as homeless alcoholics, masters of the complex railroad migration, and fruit harvesters in the Pacific Northwest. Haberstein's (1962) study of funeral directors showed how an occupation can be both professional and deviant.

Hochschild's (1979) study of the emotion work of airline stewardesses was the seminal study of emotion work. Subsequent studies of emotions on the job focused on how workers managed boredom, fear, anger, and love as part of the cultural mastery of work. One of the most compelling is Haas's (1977) study of techniques for mastering fear as part of the emotional socialization of high steelworkers.

Several scholars who subsequently became major contributors to the subfield first published in the 1970s. These included John Van Maanen (1973, 1976), who contributed several important books and papers on police socialization and occupational phenomenology, and Robert Faulkner (1973a, 1973b), who described the contingencies of the career of musicians in a low-prestige orchestra. Robert Bogdan (1972) studied the interactive milieu of face-to-face sales; Jack Haas and William Shaffir (1982, 1984) returned to the subject of the professional socialization of medical doctors; and Gary Fine (1985) studied trade school students learning to cook for a social class above their own.

During the 1980s, sociologists began to study the impact of increasing gender equality in the workforce. Many studies showed the problematical aspects of female socialization into previously male occupational worlds. For example, Vaught and Smith (1980) examined women's experience of degrading initiation rituals in an underground coal mine, Lembright and Riemer (1982) studied the socialization of women truckers via the apprenticeship system, and Jurik (1988) was but one of several sociologists to study the socialization of female corrections officers. Many of these studies documented the pervasive effect of male occupational cultures that remained resistant to gender integration of previously male work worlds.

I identified, in the past 15 years (1990–2005), 93 article- or chapter-length studies of work and occupations. This compares to 65 during the 1980s, 52 during the 1970s, 20 during the 1960s, 18 during the 1950s, and a handful before that time. In fact, for the past four decades there has been, curiously, about the same number of published studies, between 50 and 60 per decade. The subject matter of the recent scholarship has reflected earlier preoccupations (the professions, with 24 studies during the 1990s and 10 in the past five years, have outnumbered all other job classifications), but the specifics of these studies have changed. Garot's (2004) ethnomethodological study of bureaucratic emotions may be at one extreme; Groce and Cooper's (1990) study of women in rock and roll bands, a study of gender and artistic division of labor, at the other. An important direction, represented by Macias's (2003) study of the role of informal networks among Mexican-American professionals, combines the study of ethnicity with job culture. Several studies of professions are located outside the United States, notably Lewis's (1997) study of female judges in Korea and Alvesson's (1998) study of gender dynamics in a Swedish advertising firm.[1]

Studies of the working class (nine) were internationally and topically eclectic, including studies of the phenomenology of Icelandic fishing (Thorlindsson 1994), the work ethic of Mexican brewery workers (Firestone et al. 2005), and Dant's (2004) visual study of the garage mechanic. What were largely absent were studies on previous themes of worker resistance on the assembly line, arguably because most assembly lines had migrated to areas of the world where few sociologists plied their trade.

All seven studies of deviant work focused on prostitution, exotic dancing, or stripping for a living (this does not include the study of deviant activities in nondeviant occupations, such as Dabney and Hollinger's [1999] study of illicit prescription use among pharmacists). Indeed, one can draw many conclusions from this one-dimensional focus, but likely the most reasonable is that the area is dominated by a handful of scholars who publish on different aspects of their primary research interests.

Finally, there were two significant additions to the canon. The most important were several studies that explored work in the caring professions, including Isaksen's (2002) study of body and disgust among female caregivers, Murray's several studies of family care work (notably Murray 2000), and Perakyla's (1991) study of what she calls "hope work" by caregivers for the terminally ill. These and several similar studies have given the studies of work and occupations a place in the "caring service work" studies that are increasingly relevant.

The other new addition to the canon has been the study of welfare reform work, the experience of unemployment, and the shift of work from the workplace to the family. These studies have demonstrated the relevance for sociologies of work that abandon the old settings of an economy that is rapidly changing.

WORK CULTURES AND SOCIAL STRUCTURES

Blue Collar Work

We now approach the sociology of work and occupations from the vantage point of job type. We define blue-collar workers as workers who make things, typically using their hands, tools, and machines. Through history these workers would have included skilled castes such as blacksmiths, who had special status and privilege in their communities because their skill was so esoteric and important.

We are interested in how craft work evolved to factory work, and what happened to the culture of work in the meantime. This historical frame of reference necessarily addresses the matter of skill. The craft workers, whether making a wooden wagon wheel (which is very hard to make) in the fourteenth century or fabricating a repair by welding steel in the twentieth century, share a grounding in human mastery that involves both the body and the mind.

On the matter of work culture, we can imagine, largely through historical novels and some fine arts records, the culture of the shop. Here, skilled craftspeople form raw materials into objects that are used by their local communities. The shop of guild members makes everything from stained glass windows and iron latches for a 100-year job building a local cathedral to the beer the workers drink. In the guild, one attains membership by being born into a guild member's family. The first stages of training are marked by the formal status as apprentice, followed by the middle stages as journeyman, and after long years of development, one becomes a master. Thus, the skill one develops in a guild or similar shop circumstance is melded into one's aging. As one gets older, the body deteriorates, but lack of strength and dexterity is balanced against increasing knowledge and ability to apply it.

The skill of modern blue-collar workers is found in the trades such as the high steelworkers studied by Applebaum (1981). In these occupations, self-esteem comes from shared mastery of dangerous work, where small mistakes lead to death. The cultures of unions and union shops, barely studied by sociologists, have declined with the precipitous drop in unionized work in the United States, where most of this sociology is written. Thus, the cultures of skilled workers have declined as work has transformed.

Thus, we turn briefly to the transformation of work via industrialization and its impact on work cultures. The story is a common sociological theme. A craftsman works on a single work process and applies a complex combination of hand, body, and intuitive knowledge to an ever-evolving set of tasks. The things a craftsperson makes are all slightly different, and thus they embody the mind and body of the worker. Industrialization included elements such as knowledge of metallurgy sufficient to make machines that could withstand the rigor of massive pounding and snapping and engineering skill that led to machines of previously unimagined complexity. But separating the skill in manufacturing out of the manufacturing process itself meant that the actual human actions involved in manufacture would be repetitive and endless actions connected to the unvarying rhythms of the machine, typically as manifested on the assembly line. The computer I type on was made on an assembly line. The automobile I drive home was, as well. The food I eat, whether fast food, fresh, or packaged, was at least partially processed and assembled on assembly lines.

Humans, however, do not adapt well to unvarying actions that have no intrinsic meaning. Karl Marx described the dehumanization of the industrial process as alienation/separation of the worker from the product, from other workers, and from what Marx called the worker's "species being," that is, the qualities that make a human a human.

Sociologists have entered the workplace as participants (meaning, they take the jobs and report on their experiences) and hence became observers. Others have reported on jobs they had in industrial settings prior to becoming professional sociologists. For example, Donald Roy worked in a machine shop in 1944–1945 in which one was paid "piecemeal" for what one accomplished. Roy discovered that counter to what one would expect, workers did not work as fast as they could to increase their salaries, for if they did, the time-motion experts would adjust the rate of their pay downward. Their hourly pay would not increase with greater effort; working harder would only produce harder work. So the workers found ways to restrict their production and to hide this from management. This, indeed, was work culture: workers, often implicitly, creating networks of culture in which the shared interests of workers prevailed against management (Roy 1952, 1953).

Several sociologists studied how shop settings, background cultures, and forms of work influenced the cultures of alienated, industrial work. Molstad (1986), who studied and worked in a brewery, hypothesized that workers chose boring tasks in the factory over work in which they might have greater responsibility, but less control. Molstad theorized that the uncertainty posed by more interesting work was the dominant factor. In other words, the workers Molstad studied (and worked with) preferred to be alienated rather than challenged.

Degraded work, however, does not necessarily lead to alienation, as shown by Bryant and Perkins's (1982) study of poultry butchers:

> Workers must snatch live birds from cages unloaded from tractor trailer trucks and hang them, upside down, on shackles attached to moving conveyor lines. The hanging job may involve 30–40 pound turkeys. The hangers are subjected to wing battering by the dirty, squawking birds who infrequently urinate and/or defecate on the workers handling them. As the flopping, noisy birds move down the line, they undergo an electric shock intended to relax all muscles for a thorough bleeding after the throat is cut. This step also results in additional execratory discharges from the birds. All five senses of the workers are assaulted. One hanger who was interviewed revealed that, on weekends, he took six to eight showers trying to rid himself of the stench. (P. 203)

Yet the authors noted that "poultry processing employees managed to accommodate themselves; they were pretty satisfied and sustained morale through widespread network of social interaction both on and off the job" (p. 200). They liked chicken work. They bought the results of their work in chicken sales and feasted on the product of their hard work. Why? The workers were from a regional culture in which options were limited. They were uneducated and unexposed to opportunities elsewhere. The wages in the poultry-processing factory were above average. But, most tellingly, the workers found ways to connect on and off the job to form a culture, a collective that gave their lives meaning. One worker, ill with cancer, lovingly told of how her coworkers arranged a bake sale that produced several hundreds of dollars for her (and some great cake!). The hard and unpleasant work of the poultry factory was part of a culture in which a lot of life was rather hard and unpleasant, but a life in which people stood together.

The boredom of assembly line work, that is, the challenge to make one's mind minimally engaged, that is, sufficient to the task, but otherwise available to daydreams, fantasies, and sabotage, is a central theme of working-class life. Perhaps the best article on this subject was written by Roy (1959–1960), where he describes how a stupendously monotonous job with a small coterie of "old-timers" is endured and even enjoyed. "Banana time" has come to stand for the phenomenon in which factory workers create routines of mirth and playfulness to make the time go by. But these rituals, as Roy learned, are fragile. A misstated joke, in Roy's case, wrecked havoc on his ephemeral work culture.

Many sociologists find that the circumstances of a job work against the formation of a job culture. For example, Susan Mulcahy and Robert Faulkner (1977) studied how the physical organization of machines in a shop eliminated the possibility of collective work experience, and thus work culture. Many sociologists and philosophers have addressed the matter of work alienation in the abstract, but few have studied it in the concrete. Those who have discover that in the most unlikely circumstances, workers find richness and meaning in human connection. The sad fact remains unchallenged: Alienated industrial work, begun in England in the 1830s, continues. Our factories are now largely in countries far from our shores (and thus purview), and the workers are likely to be women and children as well as adult men. The work, however, is dehumanizing because of it its organization.

The Professions

The study of work and occupations has long focused on the professions. Much of what we say draws heavily on Hughes's several essays on professions and occupations. But Hughes ([1952] 1971) pointed out that the topic of professionalization was of interest to the founding figures of sociology: Comte observed that the "same engineer had kept the waterworks of Paris going before, during and after the Revolution" (p. 365). For Herbert Spencer, the professions all "elaborated, extended or elevated life . . . part of the development of society" (p. 365). And Durkheim noted the propensity of professional groups to generate social rules and to become "impermeable to attempts of outsiders to control them." Durkheim also imagined that occupational groups would provide the basis for social solidarity in an increasingly individualized world.

The earliest professional was a person who took religious vows. By the late seventeenth century, the meaning had become secularized and had come to indicate a special degree of qualification necessary for a category of occupation. Hughes' defined it as "the occupation which one professes to be skilled in and to follow . . . A vocation in which professed knowledge is used in the affairs of others" (Hughes [1952] 1971: 375).

The modern professions developed during the early eras of capitalism in Europe, but they were distinctive in societies increasingly dominated by the logic and spirit of the market. Hughes summed this up by comparing the familiar theme of a capitalist world, caveat emptor ("let the buyer beware"), with that of the professional, credat emptor ("let the taker believe in us").

Hughes took a special interest in the license and mandate of the professions. The occupations claimed license to act and justified actions with mandates for special status, autonomy, and privilege. The license to touch, cut into, or dispose of bodies was granted to the medical and funeral professions. The license to instill ideas and values into the minds of children were assumed by the educational professionals. Religious professionals claim the license to judge our sins and to arrange for their forgiveness, and accounting professionals assume the license to learn and manipulate our finances. Hughes pointed out, however, that with the license to cross these boundaries comes the mandate not to use the knowledge gained by privileged access to further ones' own interests, be they prurient or legitimate. The doctor is not supposed to be ghoulish or sexually aroused by his or her work. The priest is not supposed to become titillated on hearing the sins of others. Educators are not supposed to preach their private orthodoxy (a theme that, incidentally, traces to Max Weber). Of course, professionals and professions are rift with conflict over precisely the forgotten or ignored mandates and misused license.

In exchange for providing these services, professional occupations expect to be self-regulated. They previously defined the schooling necessary to prepare for the profession and determine what tests and examinations will certify the successful aspirant. They also fight for, and usually win, the right to judge and punish themselves. For example, only a university awards or terminates tenure. In some professions, the autonomy has eroded: For example, individuals have won the right to pit one set of professionals—lawyers—against another—medical doctors—in malpractice suits. The state has initiated the process of accreditation, which has radically diminished the independence of professions.

In essence, the concepts of license and mandate indicate that the professional asks to be trusted to act in the good faith of his or her client. This trust is effected within the reality—perceived more fully by the professional than the client—that not all problems are solvable; only some diseases may be cured and one side loses every law case.

Professional knowledge is assumed to have such depth that it can be mastered by only the brightest and the most dedicated. The knowledge is also distinctive due to its intellectual abstraction: Professionals think objectively about matters that are generally in the realm of the sacred, passionate, or personal spheres of life. This translates to many as irreverence or, ironically, as greater-than-life and creates a distance that sets the professional apart.

Of course, there are those within the professions who deal with the individual and thus use the most concrete forms of professional knowledge (the lawyer who tries cases) and others in the profession who develop professional knowledge itself (those who study law for their entire career, teach in law schools, and write philosophically and analytically about the law). As professions become more powerful, their mandate also expands: Doctors not only become more skilled and knowledgeable about treating disease, but they are called on to define the nature of health, and, by extension, the nature of the good, or most desired life. Politicians are largely recruited from lawyers, who in that role assume the responsibility to organize society legally.

The independence of thought connected to professional life was once reflected in the social independence of the professional. The archetypical professional was contracted individually for services rendered. Hughes reminds us that the original professor of the European university earned the right to teach by gaining the doctoral degree and used the university as a forum and form of validation: His fees were earned directly from students. Indeed, due to the anti-Semitism of the German university system in the late nineteenth and early twentieth centuries, Georg Simmel, one of the most important first-generation sociologists, never attained a university position in his home city of Berlin, yet his lectures (his identity was as a "free-floating intellectual") were highly popular and his earnings were lucrative.

The professional ideal type is barely recognizable in modern society. Most professions and professionals have become socially, economically, and politically powerful and are viewed as primarily serving their own interests. The term *professional* has a attained a folk definition that indicates those who earn a living doing only one activity, such as the professional athlete, who are extravagantly paid, and who seldom demonstrate any meaningful social altruism. Even the expectation of service among professions such as the clergy and teachers and professors has eroded by scandals in the church and political maneuvering among the teaching professions. The ease with which people leave the professions, such as university teaching for more lucrative occupations, confirms the decline of professional calling in modern life and the blurring between the professions and the business world.

Finally, we continue to interpret the category of profession as socially constructed rather than as a description of intrinsic qualities of special occupations. Hughes ([1952] 1971) notes that occupational social mobility was described as early as 1933 in the United Kingdom and in 1939 in America. Professionalization as a process involves extending the educational preparation required for the profession and often the creation of special degrees to certify professional standing, establishing professional societies and licensing boards, establishing a research tradition within the profession that defines its special characteristics, and organizing politically to gain legal power.

Hughes also recognized that the category of "semiprofessional" indicated those occupations that had made a successful claim to full professional status, rather than an indication of the occupation's intrinsic quality. Lively's (2001) study of the professionalization of paralegals demonstrates the continuing vitality of this line of thought.

The sociological study of professions includes relationship with clients. Behind the scenes of professional routine, sociologists see the client/professional relationship as negotiated and constructed, often emerging from norms that seem inconsistent with the service ethic that is argued to characterize professional ideology. Sander's (1994) study of how veterinarians deal with what they term "annoying customers" is one example of studies that document this phenomenon.

Professionalization and Bureaucratization

The single most powerful force affecting professionalization is bureaucratization. As noted, the professional originally was an autonomous provider of services. As these services became more available, it became necessary to regularize fees and to spread the paying of fees in such arrangements as insurance arrangements or state funding.

Bureaucratization has been an inevitable consequence because it provides the most efficient means to organize the increasingly complex process through which professional services are allocated and funded. Further, bureaucracies, such as townships, purchase professional services (such as from engineers) that are often embedded in other bureaucracies. Simply managing the interactions of complex bureaucracies becomes the specialty of yet another branch of a profession of law and civil administration. The spreading of costs through medical insurance allowed doctors to vastly increase their fees (most are startled to realize that before World War II medical doctors and professors made equivalent salaries), but it has robbed the medical doctors of their autonomy. Doctors are often employees of bureaucracies as varied as hospitals and health maintenance organizations (Hoff 1999); while they are still well rewarded financially, their work has been routinized and can be as controlled as are the tasks of an assembly line worker (though they are not). The relationship between the client and the professional is eroded in the bureaucratized professional environment: Both parties see each other as dehumanized agents rather than as individuals.

The study of the self and the professional identity has been expressed as role closeness, neutrality, or distance in a study of classroom teachers (Khleif 1985). The matter of the professional in organizations has been examined critically in studies of proletarianization or the routinization of professional work and gender inequality within professions such as law (Podmore and Spencer 1982).

Finally, however, the matter of professional culture remains enigmatic. Lines between professions and other occupations are increasingly blurred. Society's appreciation of professional distinctiveness is vastly diminished, even as the economic inequality that follows the professional fault line increases. The tendency of sociologists to "study down" the social ladder and ability of professions to avoid the gaze of inquiry makes case studies of professional worlds rare. The blurring between the world of commerce and the previous professions also influences this matter. Jackall's (1988) study of corporate culture (to be distinguished by the spate of books by apologists of the corporate world) is a rare exception.

Service Occupations

We are well used to the idea that our society has moved from a productive economy to a service economy. This means, at the most simple level, that in the late twentieth century, the suddenly prosperous working class (at least in the case of unionized work, such as the steel industry of the American Northeast) priced itself out of existence in a global economy, and as their jobs moved to countries with less well-paid labor forces, the economy has restructured partly around the delivery of services. Professions, of course, deliver services, but we are speaking of service jobs as the doing of tasks or the servicing of people's needs at the other end of the economic and social spectrum. We might speak of the service occupations as "degraded professions" in that they do not require esoteric knowledge or long periods of training; they do not assume that the practitioners internalize a sense of license or mandate.

It is in the beginning of the twenty-first century that service jobs that depend on telephone service have migrated to the cheaper labor of the less-developed world. The work cultures of the corporate "campuses" of India, where much of our phone-based service work is now performed, have received attention in the popular press but not yet sustained sociological study.

Still, the world of service occupations close to home is sociologically varied and rich for study. At one end of the sociological spectrum are jobs in child care and elder care (Applegate 1993) and other examples of caregiving that are not strictly in the medical profession. In the United States, these are often poorl paying and carry an ambiguous social status. These workers are expected to be motivated by professional ethics but carry few if any of the rewards. The jobs of family domestics and au pair girls— family servants by another name—have special characteristics that have gained sociological attention. They are "paid in smiles" (Murray 2000) and often they compete with natural mothers for the love of their children (Murray 1998). The focus on the sociology of emotions in the cultural study of work has led to several studies of the emotional labor, and often the emotional rewards, of these semiprofessional service jobs.

However, the primary focus on the service world concentrates on the exploitation of service workers in highly rationalized work environments. This is the core of the McDonalized world: human robots delivering poor-quality products or automatic services to customers who pass by in a blur. These jobs, which do not involve selling, but rather servicing customers, are automated out of existence as grocery and other stores find ways to have customers do the work that was previously performed by this sector of the service economy.

However, the matter of selling, that is, making a pitch and trying to snag a buyer, has been much studied, going back to the beginning of the specialty. Sales involve manipulating the client's view of her or his needs, and the most successful sales personnel do exactly that. Of course, the more expensive the product, the heavier the game and the bigger the bet. But the matter of interactive manipulation is the same, no matter the level.

Finally, there are a small number of studies of the "craft" of service work, especially in the semiskilled occupations. Lawson's (1999) study of barbering shows the skill and interactive context in which it is played out. Bell's (1976) study of bartending is one of a few studies of the aesthetic character of a service occupation. The one study of the small-shop mechanic (Harper 1987) uses photographs in interviews that probe the meaning of a bricoleur's work: his skill, tools, materials, and social life that emerged from his work. The project was the first to integrate visual sociology methods to the cultural study of work.

We conclude this section with Everett Hughes:

Persons and organizations have problems; they want things done for them—for their bodies and souls, for their social and financial relations, for their cars, houses, bridges, sewage systems; they want things done to the people they consider their competitors or their enemies . . . it is in the course of interaction with one another and with the professionals that the problems of people are given definition. (Hughes 1994:72)

Seen this way, the professions and their related poor cousins, the service occupations, remain essential to the cultural study of work.

The Future of Work and Occupations

What are the most important trends in the study of work and occupations? How should the subdiscipline develop? Looking at about 400 studies published in the past 50 years, I note the persistence of the case study method. Recent years have brought new research in gendered work, work and welfare policy, and work at home. What was once a branch of American sociology has seen increasing contributions from sociologists abroad, especially from the United Kingdom and France, where Hughes and Becker remain figures of importance. The setting of the case studies was once the factory or the boardroom; now it is increasingly the global system.

This being said, there is vastly unrealized potential in the sociology of work and occupations. Sociologists have focused increasingly on the professions, with 34 of 93 article-length publications in the past 15 years, leaving the remaining two-thirds of the canon to address issues relating to proletarian work, welfare reform work, theory, service work, semiprofessional work, and deviant work. Within the professions, sociologists disproportionately study the medical field, which partly reflects the specialist journals in specialized medical areas (nursing, physiotherapy) that have encouraged the development of occupational ethnography. Many professions are glaringly missing (or nearly) from sociological scrutiny: the political world (at all levels), professional sports, the legal world (lawyers, judges, and others), the clergy, and university work cultures. The question of access is undoubtedly responsible for some of this missing research, but since sociologists successfully find their way into medical work settings, this cannot be the whole problem.

The cultures of the corporate world have also largely escaped sociological study. Robert Jackall's (1988) study of the culture of the corporate world, penetrating and highly critical, is the single thick description of arguably the most influential form of work in the modern world. The corporate world produces its own canon of ideological and self-congratulatory books about what they describe as "corporate culture," and the corporate world aggressively protects itself from sociological scrutiny. Jackall got access to his research sites almost by accident, and it is likely true that the firms he studied never really understood what he was doing there. The corporate world continues to suffer crises of legitimacy due to "Enron"-type scandals and will likely remain wary of ethnographic investigation.

Studies of working-class labor have moved from the factory to fishing boats, meatpacking plants, and, significantly, the world of day labor. While the broadening of topics is welcome, the final work on assembly line work has certainly not been written. The study of work in the factories of the Third World is indeed a gaping hole in the literature.

This brings me to my final point. The sociology of work and occupations has begun to embrace the globalized work worlds. Two studies deserve special mention. One is Collins's (2003) study of the global apparel industry. Collins shows how contemporary manufacture of thread, cloth, and clothes evolved from the paternalistic mill towns of the American Southeast, first to factories in Mexico that were tied to specific manufacturing firms and, most recently, to the "just-in-time" manufacturing strategies of firms like Liz Clairborne. Collins calls her work a "multi-sited" work ethnography and, indeed, applies her sociological lens to the corporate boardrooms of Liz Clairborne (admittedly, more could be done in that setting), to the Mexican factories, and to the international middlemen who increasingly shift orders from one factory to another; from Thailand to Hong Kong; from China to India, depending on the fraction-of-a-cent difference on an estimate. Collins has successfully married the microanalysis of work ethnography (and, in the case of Mexican workers, the ethnography of home and work in combination) with the largest patterns of industrial structure.

The globalization of work is but an aspect of the separation of work from its immediate context. The teaching profession clings to the idea that their presence in the classroom is an important aspect of their work; increasingly sophisticated computer systems create distanced learning processes in which the teacher is disembodied and otherwise separated from the objects of their labor.

The second project that examines micro and macro aspects of globalized work (though not as thoroughly) is Brandt's (2002) study of the "trail of the tomato." Brandt has long worked as a sociologist, as well as an activist, and was able, like Collins, to do meaningful fieldwork among the migrant Mexican tomato harvesters. Her book weaves the family and work stories of these workers into a global context, which places their work systems into the work worlds of single-mother cashiers in the Canadian supermarkets where the tomatoes are eventually sold. The sinew holding these stories together is a worldwide system of food production characterized by high transportation costs, genetic engineering, and environmental irrationalities. Like Collins, Brandt reveals systems in which specific work cultures unfold.

The future study of work and occupations will depend on a continuing supply of sociologists trained in the intensive field methods tradition. Luckily there remain important graduate centers where field methods and ethnography balance the dominant methodological paradigms. Certainly, one can easily see that many of the most important questions in sociology have been approached by the subdiscipline, while, at the same time, it is clear that much remains to be done.

PART VI

SOCIAL DISTINCTIONS AND DIVERSITY

22

Social Stratification

Harold R. Kerbo

California Polytechnic State University, San Luis Obispo

Since the earliest-known writings on the nature of human societies, there has been recognition that social stratification is a central part of all human organization (Lenski 1966). In his *Politics,* in 350 BCE, Aristotle wrote of the natural ranking of free people and slaves. More recently, during the Age of Enlightenment, philosophers such as Locke, Rousseau, and Montesquieu wrote of the feudal system of social stratification and its inequities (Zeitlin 1968; Strasser 1976). By the mid-1800s, the classic sociological theorists such as Marx, Durkheim, and Weber began more systematic analyses of system of social stratification using concepts that remain with us to this day.

From the root word *strata,* we can recognize that social stratification refers to a ranking of people or groups of people within a society. But the term was defined by the earliest sociologists as something more than the almost universal inequalities that exist in all but the least complex of societies. *Social stratification* refers to a system with rather predictable rules behind the ranking of individuals and groups, which theories of social stratification are meant to uncover and understand. The existence of a system of social stratification also implies some form of legitimation of the ranking of people and the unequal distribution of valued goods, services, and prestige. Without belief systems justifying the inequality and unequal ranking, it is unlikely that a stratification system would remain stable over time. Beyond agreement on a definition of social stratification, however, the classic sociological theorists agreed on little else. From this classic period of sociology, we have, in fact, a triple legacy of social stratification theories from the works of Karl Marx, Émile Durkheim, and Max Weber.

More than anyone, it was Karl Marx who attempted a more or less comprehensive theory of social stratification. Along with Engels, in 1848, Marx began one of the world's most famous political writings on the subject, *The Communist Manifesto* (Marx and Engels 1964), by writing,

> The history of all hitherto existing society is the history of class struggles. Free man and slave, patrician and plebeian, lord and serf, guild-master and journeyman, in a word, oppressor and oppressed, stood in constant opposition to one another, carried on an uninterrupted, now hidden, now open fight, a fight that each time ended, either in a revolutionary reconstitution of society at large, or in the common ruin of the contending classes. (P. 5)

But when Marx was finally about to undertake a more detailed and systematic discussion of class at the end of the third volume of *Capital,* he died (see Dahrendorf 1959:8). Although Marx referred to several different classes or class segments throughout history, he clearly saw the ownership of property as the basis of class divisions. In preindustrial agricultural societies, the primary division was between the landowners, or landed aristocracy, and those who owned no land, peasants and serfs. In capitalist industrial societies, the primary division was between the owners of industrial capital and the working class, or proletariat. It was this exclusively economic definition of class—that is, owners versus nonowners—that allowed Marx to conclude that the elimination of private property in any future communist nation would eliminate extensive inequality and even social stratification itself.

In strict contrast to a Marxian theory of social stratification are functional theories of social stratification. In tracing the development of functional theory, most historians of social thought draw a direct line from Saint-Simon and Auguste Comte, through Durkheim, to modern functional theorists such as Talcott Parsons (see Gouldner 1970; Giddens 1973; Strasser 1976). More than anyone else, though, it was Durkheim who established this general perspective, though interestingly he had little to say about social stratification specifically. This is somewhat understandable when considering that Durkheim's holistic perspective focused on how parts and processes within societies work for the good of the whole. Divisions between people within societies were given little recognition.

Durkheim, however, did make brief mention of inequalities within societies. He saw two types, what he called *external inequality* and *internal inequality*. As he described them in *The Division of Labor,* external inequalities are those imposed on the individual by the social circumstances of birth, in other words, ascribed status. It was in mechanical solidarity, or preindustrial societies, that these external inequalities predominated. In industrial society, on the other hand, there was a need for internal inequality: "All external inequalities compromise organic solidarity" (Durkheim 1964:371)—that is, threaten social order and the proper functioning of the division of labor in industrial societies. Internal inequalities were seen as inequalities based on individual talent, or achieved status. For the proper functioning of the industrial system, Durkheim implied that the people with the proper talents must be allowed to move into positions for which their talents are best suited.

What Durkheim anticipated was a meritocracy based on equality of opportunity. Inequality would be there, but he believed an inequality based on merit was needed. And although Durkheim's ideas paralleled somewhat those of many modern functionalists, given his overriding concern with solidarity and moral integration in society, his stress was different. The dominance of internal over external inequality, he believed, was most important for the maintenance of social solidarity. If external inequalities were forced on individuals, "constraint alone, more or less violent and more or less direct, binds them to their functions; in consequence, only an imperfect and troubled solidarity is possible" (see Lukes 1973:175). Thus, in contrast to Davis and Moore (1945), Durkheim was more concerned with moral integration and cooperation than he was with the efficient staffing of "important" positions in industrial society.

Soon after Marx's death, sociologist Max Weber took issue with Marx's unidimensional view of social stratification in writings often referred to as a debate with Marx's ghost. Weber recognized that humans have always been divided by not only economic ownership but also occupational skills, status, and organizational power or *class, status,* and *power/party* (see Gerth and Mills 1946:181–94). In a sense, Weber recognized two forms of economic divisions under the term *class*—divisions based on ownership as well as divisions based on occupational skills (or one's

relation to the marketplace). Weber then recognized that people could be divided over honor, status, or prestige with respect to a strongly held value system (particularly one based on religion) and political or organizational power. It was this power/party dimension that Weber believed would be increasingly important in modern industrial societies, especially because of the necessity of political and corporate bureaucracies and organizations (such as labor unions), which challenge those in higher ranks in these bureaucracies.

Max Weber's multidimensional view of social stratification became the most accepted perspective among twentieth-century sociologists. Among other things, Weber's more complex view of social stratification allow sociologists to explain the rapidly growing middle class, as more occupations emerged between the owners of capital and the unskilled working class. Equally important, Weber's multidimensional view of social stratification could explain why social stratification and inequality did not go away in twentieth-century societies that called themselves communist. As Weber predicted, when one dimension of social stratification is minimized, such as private ownership of property, another dimension would come to be more important. In communist societies, this was the dimension of power and control over state bureaucracies.

A HISTORY OF SOCIAL STRATIFICATION IN AMERICAN VERSUS EUROPEAN SOCIOLOGY

Although today most American sociologists consider social stratification as one of the most important areas of study, this has not always been the case. In fact, the importance of this subject in understanding societies and human behavior has been widely recognized by American sociologists only in the past 50 years. The contrast to European social thought is clear. Sociology as a separate discipline of study in the United States dates back only to the early 1900s. But in the works of the founders of American sociology (e.g., William Graham Sumner, Albion Small, and Edward Ross), we find a rather classless view of American society (Gordon 1963; Page 1969; Pease, Form, and Huber 1970). The relative neglect of social stratification is not surprising, however. Unlike in European societies, the old rigid class and estate inequalities were less in evidence. The value system stressed equality of opportunity for all, and at least an appearance of opportunity and democracy was in greater evidence. Not until the Great Depression of the 1930s was this classless image seriously reexamined, and then only by a few American social scientists. Even then, many years passed before the study of social stratification was able to make a significant break with American classless mythology.

The first detailed American study in social stratification appeared in 1929 with Robert and Helen Lynd's (1929) *Middletown,* followed later by *Middletown in Transition*

(1937). This first work was to establish a long tradition of stratification studies of small community life in the United States. But the general conflict perspective of this study was only much later a part of this tradition. The Lynds' focus was on power and economic inequalities, and the overpowering image of equality of opportunity in American society was exposed as a myth (see Gordon 1963:66). With the end of the Great Depression, their view of American society was placed on the shelf and all but forgotten for three decades.

Of the social stratification research stimulated by the Great Depression, Lloyd Warner's work (in the 1930s and 1940s) had the most significant impact, at least for the next 20 to 30 years. Like the Lynds' research, Warner's many-volume *Yankee City* study was centered on social stratification in small communities (Warner and Lunt 1941, 1942; Warner and Srole 1949). Using various methods of study, from survey research to detailed participant observation, these works sought to examine the extent of inequality and social mobility, as well as the meaning of social stratification for the people involved. But the Warner School differed from the Lynd tradition in three ways. Most important, the Warner School came to define social stratification in terms of status (Weber's second dimension of social stratification). As Warner and Lunt (1941) wrote, "By class is meant two or more orders of people who are believed to be, and are accordingly ranked by the members of the community, in superior and inferior positions" (p. 82). With such a view, inequalities of economics and power were easily ignored, and the dynamics of conflict related to these stratification dimensions were dismissed. Second, the Warner School failed to examine the actual extent of equality of opportunity critically. In the face of contrary experience highlighted by the Depression, this research tradition continued to stress a reality of social mobility for all who had the talent and ambition to succeed, a finding now disputed in a reanalysis of *Yankee City* (Thernstrom 1964). We find in the Warner School, therefore, an emphasis on social stratification as functional and necessary for complex societies like our own. The conflict, the structured and hereditary nature of inequalities, the harsh conditions for workers, and the extensive poverty all too often found in the expansion of American capitalism were all but ignored.

Despite its neglect of class and class conflict, a tradition of stratification theory and research was at least begun. The Warner School stimulated many students, and there was soon a wide variety of research on subjects such as differing class values and lifestyles, occupational prestige, and the degree and causes of social mobility (Pease et al. 1970). One review of the early stratification literature found at least 333 research articles and books on the subject published between 1945 and 1953 (Pfautz 1953). By 1954, the first American textbook on the subject was published (Cuber and Kenkel 1954).

The break with functional theory came first with Floyd Hunter's (1953) study of community power, then most dramatically with C. Wright Mills's (1956) description of a power elite on the national level. Before Watergate, Vietnam, and America's discovery of poverty and discrimination in the 1960s, these works were ahead of their time. There were soon new neo-Marxist theories, more empirical research on elite power and conflict, and a greater recognition of the long history of conflict theories of social stratification from the European traditions.

SOCIAL STRATIFICATION THEORY TODAY

Toward the end of the twentieth century, many theorists began combining the insights of Marx and Weber for more realistic explanations of social stratification. For example, rather than accepting Marx's view of the state as simply an institution run by and for the capitalist class to control others, the concept of state autonomy emerged as a means of understanding how political elites are able to control or regulate modern economic systems to prevent the meltdown of capitalism predicted by Marx (see, e.g., Skocpol 1979; Skocpol and Amenta 1985).

Class Categories and the Meaning of Class

Other theorists began combining dimensions of stratification from Marx and Weber for more sophisticated conceptions of class categories. The most impressive of these attempts has been Erik O. Wright's empirical work (Wright 1978a, 1978b, 1997; Wright et al. 1982; Wright and Martin 1987). By following Marx's idea that class must be defined in relation to the productive system in the society (i.e., by one's relation to the means of production), rather than simply occupational status levels, as functionalists suggest, Wright has developed a four-class model. With this four-class model, Wright is able to show the usefulness of both the Marxian and the Weberian views of class.

Defining class in relation to the productive system, we have what Wright calls capitalists, managers, workers, and the petty bourgeoisie. Capitalists own the means of production (factories and banks), purchase the labor of others, and control the labor of others. Managers merely control the labor of others for capitalists and sell their labor to capitalists (such as managers of corporations). Workers, of course, have only their labor to sell to capitalists, while the petty bourgeoisie own some small means of production but employ very few or no workers.

Most previous empirical research in social stratification has been done from the functional perspective. Class positions, or, more accurately, occupational status positions, are viewed by functionalists as skill and status rankings on a continuum from lowest to highest. Pay, status, and education levels are all assumed to roughly follow this continuum. In other words, functionalists do not consider class divisions, but rather rankings, as on a ladder. However, these previous functional studies have many problems. For one, research shows no simple relation between these occupational grades and income. Another problem is that education level does not predict income very well (see Jencks et al. 1972 on these problems).

Research by Wright (1978b, 1997) has produced some interesting findings using these new class categories. With national samples of people in the labor force, Wright's research found class position (the four categories described earlier) to be about as good in explaining differences in income between people as are occupational status and education level. It is also interesting that capitalists have higher incomes, even controlling for or eliminating the effects on income from education level, occupational skill, age, and job tenure. In other words, being a capitalist, and especially a big capitalist, irrespective of other factors such as education and occupational skill, brings more income (see also Aldrich and Weiss 1981).

There are other interesting findings using Wright's class categories. For example, education does not on the average help workers attain a higher income, but more education does bring more income for the managerial class. And, examining people within class categories, there is not much difference between males and females, blacks and whites on income. The male-female and black-white overall income differences (males and whites have higher incomes) are due primarily to class position. That is, females and blacks have lower average incomes because they are proportionately more often than white males to be in the working class, as defined by Wright.

Another recent conceptualization of class has been made by Pierre Bourdieu, a French sociologist who came to be respected in the United States in the 1990s. From a French structuralist tradition, Bourdieu (1993) focused on how meanings people have of the world are shaped or limited by objective structures in the society. In social stratification, Bourdieu argued that economic class positions shape the worldviews of members of distinct class positions. Thus, these class subcultures result in class differences in tastes, lifestyles, and even preferences of values (Bourdieu 1984, 1996). Through differing class subcultures, people of different classes tend to draw lines around their class "in-group" and the "out-group" of people in other class positions. Thus, people in higher-class positions come to define those of lower-class positions as different and perhaps not as capable of fitting into higher positions in the class system. One can say that from this perspective, "people compete about culture and they compete with it" (Jenkins 1992:128). While there are questions about the extent to which these class subcultures are as important in the American mass culture context, this perspective has contributed to our understanding of how social mobility might be restricted or enhanced by how people in higher-class positions (such as teachers with lower-class children) evaluate others in terms of their knowledge of higher culture (DiMaggio 1982; DiMaggio and Mohr 1985).

Despite the wide acceptance of these new conceptualizations of class, there are still retractors who favor older, more functionalist views of continuous hierarchies rather than classes at all. Years ago, Dennis Wrong (1959, 1964) outlined what he called realist versus nominalist definitions of class. As Kingston's (2000) recent attempt at revival shows, the realist places emphasis on clear class boundaries in people identifying themselves as members of a particular class and interacting most with others in the same class; in other words, forming distinct social groupings based on class divisions. There is evidence that Americans are less likely to think about common economic class interests and are more likely to associate with others on the basis of nonclass lifestyle or subcultural preferences rather than within their own economic class (Kingston 2000). For the nominalist, however, most important are the common characteristics that groups of people may have that influence their life chances and share of valued rewards in the society, such as education level, occupational position, or bureaucratic power position. People are then placed in class categories in terms of these common characteristics whether or not they are aware of these characteristics and associate with others in the same class.

Related to this realist view of class are recent questions about the extent to which economic class conflicts are important enough to influence voting behavior. There is evidence that voting in national elections is now more likely based on moral or value issues rather than economic class issues (LeDuc, Niemi, and Norris 1996; Evans 1999; Clark and Lipset 2001). However, this decline in class voting is occurring to a great extent in the United States only, and the United States is most unique in lower-class *nonvoting*. In other words, something in the United States has led to the neglect of issues important to the less affluent (Kerbo and Gonzalez 2003). The majority of sociologists who continue to argue that class divisions remain powerful argue that when the interests of the less affluent are being ignored in the political system, this in itself suggests an element of class conflict.

SOCIAL MOBILITY AND STATUS ATTAINMENT

During the second half of the twentieth century, there has been more research in the area of social mobility and status attainment in the United States than any other area in social stratification (Kerbo 2006a, chap. 12). *Social mobility* refers to the extent of movement up and down the stratification, while the subject of *status attainment* refers to the process and factors leading individuals to movement up or down with respect to their parents' position. The most detailed studies of social mobility in the United States following the functionalist occupational categories were conducted by Blau and Duncan (1967), and then 11 years later by Featherman and Hauser (1978). Since the 1973 data, there has been no research as comprehensive from a functionalist perspective, though we have smaller studies providing updated information. Blau and Duncan's (1967) mobility data were collected with the help of the U.S. Bureau of the Census in 1962, with detailed information on the family backgrounds, educational experience, and occupational history of over 20,000 males in the labor force. Blau and Duncan's study *The American Occupational Structure* is considered the landmark study of social mobility in the United States. The Featherman and Hauser study (1978) *Opportunity and Change* is designed as a replication of this landmark study, with a similar sample of over 30,000 employed males in 1973. Hout (1988) updated this research with new data from 1972 to 1985.

The basic conclusions of this research are that intergenerational mobility has been rather extensive in the United States, at least between the 1950s and 1980s. Furthermore, there has been more upward mobility than downward mobility, primarily because of changes in the American occupational structure. That is, with more jobs being created in the middle and upper-middle occupational categories compared with lower occupational positions in this time period, there has been more upward mobility due to occupational changes. However, most people move only short distances in the occupational structure, and those toward the bottom have substantially lower rates of upward mobility than those born toward the middle.

Unfortunately, large-scale social mobility studies of the Blau and Duncan or Featherman and Hauser type have not been done since the 1970s. But smaller studies indicate that changes in the American occupational structure due to corporate restructuring and changes in the global economy have led to much less upward social mobility. Even during the 1972 to 1985 time period, Hout (1988) found that the overall rate of social mobility was slowing for the first time in the years we have data on the subject. He also found that while there was still more upward than downward social mobility, upward social mobility had slowed. When we move from indicators of intergenerational occupational mobility to the intergenerational changes in income attainment, all indicators suggest less upward mobility and significant increases in downward mobility. For example, data on income attainment between 1980 and 1995 in Europe and the United States show that the income of the middle class, or incomes of 25 percent above and below median income, has shrunk by 4 percent in the United States, the highest shrinkage of all industrial nations (Pressman 2001). In almost half of the European Union countries, in contrast, there was in fact an increase in the percentage of the income of middle class. In another study of income mobility employing a sample of over 6,000 American families, Hertz (2004) found considerable drops in upward social mobility and increases in the inheritance of low income over the generations. Other research has found the rate of income mobility to drop between 1979 and 1998. In this time period, almost 70 percent of sons remained in the same 20th percentile income position as their fathers. At

the top 20 percent income group, however, most sons had attained more income than their fathers, indicating only significant upward mobility for those born toward the top (Perrucci and Wysong 2003). And finally, other research shows that the position of the United States has dropped below that of Canada and several European countries with respect to income mobility in recent decades (Solon 1992).

As noted, one of the limitations of previous research on social mobility has been exclusive focus on occupational status. In addition, this earlier research was primarily limited to social mobility patterns for sons compared with their fathers. Wright, with research using class categories developed from both Marx and Weber, has overcome these limitations. In particular, the capitalist ownership category and the authority category have been completely missed in previous studies of social mobility. Using a large data set from the United States, Canada, Norway, and Sweden, Wright found that the capitalist property boundary is the least permeable, while the authority boundary is the most permeable in all four countries (Western and Wright 1994; Wright 1997:169–201). In other words, there is more intergenerational mobility into higher positions of authority than mobility into the category of capitalist property ownership. This is especially so for the United States (and to some extent Canada), which in many ways is the most capitalist of all the industrial societies, has more inequality based on the ownership of property, and has more power in the hands of capitalists and the corporate class than other industrial nations (Wright 1997:186–90).

In this research, they also investigated the expertise category, which we can generally call a category of professionals and technical experts. The likelihood of moving into this expertise category was mixed in the four countries, but generally between the capitalist property category and authority category in permeability. Thus, given the importance of wealth in the United States, and given that there are different chances of mobility into the capitalist (or owner) class than into a higher occupational position (occupational skill level and expertise category) and authority positions, it is here that we find the old studies of social mobility focused only on occupational status. In an interesting addition to this research, Wright also examined cross-friendship patterns in these four countries with respect to these class categories (Wright and Cho 1992; Wright 1997:203–22). As expected, fewer people from outside the capitalist property boundary had friendship ties to people in this capitalist class category compared with friendship ties across the other class categories. In other words, it is harder to break into the capitalist class and even more difficult to form friendship ties with people in this class if the person is not already in it.

Another issue of comparative mobility rates can now be addressed that was impossible to address before the Erikson and Goldthorpe (1992) study and Wright's (1997) class categories research on comparative rates of social mobility for women. If the family unit of women is considered (thus the position of the husband entered into the measure), what is most significant "is the evidence of how little women's experience of class mobility differs from that of men" (Erikson and Goldthorpe 1992:275). On the other hand, when the occupations of women are considered, there is more social mobility compared with men, but much of it is downward to manual employment. Women tend to experience more limited prospects of moving into top positions in the society, even when born into families at or close to the top of the occupational structure.

Wright (1997) has found some differences in the social mobility patterns for women across countries. For example, higher-authority positions are slightly less difficult for women to attain in the United States compared with Europe (Wright 1997:192). Recent research in the United States on women engineers has also suggested that the "glass-ceiling" effect for American women may be becoming less of a problem for younger women (Morgan 1998).

Finally, another issue of comparative mobility rates can be made clear with the studies of Erikson and Goldthorpe (1992) and Wright (1997). The United States has the reputation of being the land of opportunity among many people in the world. These studies, however, indicate that the United States is only about average with respect to its rate of circulation mobility, or equality of opportunity in general. In fact, none of the advanced capitalist societies are radically different with respect to their overall rates of circulation mobility. But in some places in the stratification system, especially toward the bottom, the chances of moving up are below average in the United States.

RECENT TRENDS IN SOCIAL STRATIFICATION AND STRATIFICATION RESEARCH

In terms of the specific subjects researched in the second half of the twentieth century, a content analysis of the five leading sociology journals in the United States showed that more than half of the published research in the general area of social stratification focused on some aspect of social mobility (Kerbo 1981, 2006a, chap. 12). In the last couple of decades of the twentieth century to the present, there is a shift toward more research on race, ethnic, and gender inequalities. But there remains a kind of ambivalent relationship between the field of social stratification and these areas of research. Are theory and research on race, ethnic, and gender inequalities to be considered subareas of social stratification, or are they to be considered subareas of sociology in their own right? The trend seems to be toward the latter as more and more of the research and theory seem less connected to broader theories of social stratification. There are, however, other recent trends in research and theory on social stratification in recent decades.

Historical and Comparative Research

Within sociology more generally, there has been a clear trend toward more historical and comparative research, especially in American sociology. As many have observed, since the early days of American sociology there was less interest in research that compared different societies on the same issue, or even research focused on historical trends within the United States. The research methodologies and interests of the classic European sociologists seemed to fade quickly as the young discipline was transported to the United States (Gouldner 1970). Perhaps globalization has had its impact on American sociologists, but new research methods requiring fewer cases and allowing for time series analysis no doubt helped bring about this new research trend.

Despite the value of more historical and comparative research, most of this research has been quantitative and less sensitive to the qualitative differences that exist across societies thereby making indicators and measures of key variables misleading. For example, when comparing rates of social mobility across a sample from modern industrial societies, the issue is whether social mobility up and down a standard ranking of occupations is equally important in all societies. It is known that there is a strong correlation between how people in different countries rank occupations in terms of status (Treiman 1977). But there are certainly other dimensions to status or economic ranking that differ cross-culturally. In Japan, being an electrician or a manager for Toyota or Sony brings much more status and long-term rewards than holding similar positions in small companies (Kerbo and McKinstry 1995). There has recently been more qualitative historical-comparative research that can counter these problems in the quantitative historical-comparative research, which will likely expand in coming years.

Modern World-Systems Theory and Research

Over the last couple of decades, it has become clear that one of the most important new theories related to social stratification comes under the general title of the modern world-systems theory. It is now evident that no clear understanding of social stratification in the United States or any other country can be achieved without reference to the affects of the modern world system. The growing income inequality in the United States, the growing class conflict in Europe over changes in class relations and rewards, the Asian economic crisis beginning in 1997 (earlier for Japan), to name just a few topics, must be considered in relation to changes in the modern world system. We must also include major world events, such as colonialism, World War I, World War II, and the Cold War, along with all the events and conditions these world-shaping events caused, as related to changes in the modern world system.

In brief, from the works of Wallerstein (1974, 1977, 1980, 1989, 1999), Frank (1969, 1975, 1978, 1998),

Bornschier (1995), Chase-Dunn (1989), and Chirot (1986), modern world-systems theory considers nations to be ranked in ways similar to the international system of social stratification. From about 1500 AD, when the new modern world system began, nations have been in competition with each other for dominance over other nations, especially with respect to economic domination. Core nations are the richer nations on top of the modern world system, with semiperiphery and periphery nations in lower ranks in this system, much like middle class, working class, and the poor in an internal stratification system. Throughout this period of core nation competition and conflict, aspects of a country's political economy, including its system of social stratification, have had negative or positive affects on the country's ability to maintain or improve its ranking in the world of nations. Conversely, this modern world system has had effects on domestic political economies and systems of social stratification in both rich and poor countries.

THE GREAT U-TURN

Another new topic of comparative-historical research in social stratification shows the importance of the modern world system in understanding domestic trends in social stratification. Earlier research had established that as nations become more economically developed, there was a clear long-term trend toward reduced income inequality (Jackman 1975; Harrison and Bluestone 1988). New research, however, has shown a clear trend toward increasing inequality in the most advanced and richest nations in the world, especially in the United States (Alderson and Nielsen 2002). Other research has recently shown that government policies can strongly affect the level of income inequality and poverty in advanced industrial nations. The questions become, Why is income inequality increasing in several advanced industrial nations (most extensively in the United States), and why have not more governments attempted to reduce income inequality and poverty?

Modern world-systems theory suggests two related explanations (Kerbo 2006a, 2006b). First, the greater ability of corporations to move across the world more freely has brought many workers in advanced industrial nations in more direct competition with low-wage labor in less affluent countries. Where the working class has less political influence in rich nations, these workers have their standards of living eroded. Second, in advanced industrial societies where workers have less protection, corporations from these countries are in a stronger position to compete successfully for greater profits in the global economy. While the incomes, benefits, and job security of workers in countries with stronger traditions of working-class political action are more protected in the short term, a history of core competition in the modern world system suggests that the competitive position of their corporations in the global economy may be eroded, and thus their standards of living

may be reduced in the future. But this outcome is far from certain because, as German unions and many German executives argue, more job security and employee influence within the company will give German and other European corporations a long-term advantage in global competition (Thelen 1991; Turner 1991; Kerbo and Strasser 2000).

RESEARCH ON POVERTY

One of the biggest contrasts between sociological research in the 1960s and 1970s compared with the present has been a lack of research on domestic poverty in recent years. The reason is rather obvious; the Great Society Programs of the 1960s generated more interest and funding for research on American poverty in these years. There is evidence of new interest and research on American poverty, however, with several recent books with 1960s-style titles and tables of contents recently published (e.g., Danziger and Haveman 2001; Iceland 2003; Rank 2004). Ironically, with this new interest in American poverty, under the American administration of the early 2000s, there has been less research support and even less data, as shown in the 2004 Annual Census Bureau report, which combined the previously separate census reports on income and poverty into one report that left out much of the information about poverty that has been provided for many years (U.S. Bureau of the Census 2004).

The reemergence of interest in American poverty is likely related to the continued growth of inequality in the United States as well as the fact that poverty was reduced only slightly and temporarily with the longest economic boom in American history between 1991 and 2001. New data also show that the poor are poorer in the United States than in previous years as measured by how many are below 50 percent of the poverty line, and the percentage of poor people in families with a full-time worker has been increasing steadily in the last two decades (Kerbo 2006a, chap. 9).

The new interest in comparative research in social stratification has also been evident in research on poverty in rich nations. Not surprisingly, comparative research has shown less government action to reduce poverty in the United Sates than other rich nations, with U.S. government programs reducing American poverty by about 28 percent of what it otherwise would be compared with reductions of 50 to 80 percent in the original 15 European Union nations (Smeeding 1997; Mishel, Bernstein, and Schmitt 1999:377; Smeeding, Rainwater, and Burtless 2001).

There is something of a surprise in this area of research, however. Previous comparative studies of poverty in rich nations had to use spotty data on absolute poverty rates compared with relative poverty rates. Absolute poverty rates are measured using a poverty line that estimates the actual costs of basic necessities. Relative poverty rates are set at 50 percent of median income in each nation. With the United States having the highest rates of income inequality, the finding of higher rates of relative poverty in the United States is hardly surprising. Now, although, the new Purchasing Power Parity (PPP) measures of income across nations has provided a new tool. The measures for PPP are set at what U.S. dollars would buy and then adjustments are made for real currency when comparing incomes across nations. The current U.S. poverty line is set at about $11 per day using PPP. Thus, we now have figures for many more countries on a poverty line also set for $11 per day in these other countries. The surprise is that about 13 percent of the American population lives below $11 per day (about the figure below the poverty line estimated by the U.S. Census Bureau), while the figures from Great Britain is 15.7 percent and Australia is 17.6 percent (Smeeding et al. 2001). Absolute poverty rates for other rich countries range from 9 to 4 percent of the population.

There has also been increased interest in global inequality and poverty in recent years, no doubt stimulated by figures showing that world inequality has been at unprecedented levels in recent decades (Kerbo 2006a, chap. 17, 2006b), and growing protest since the 1999 World Trade Organization protests in Seattle. New PPP measures have provided new perspectives on world poverty, especially with findings that about 1.3 billion people live on less than $1 per day and almost half the world's population lives on less than $2 per day (World Bank 2000).

The belief among antiglobalization protestors has been partly supported by research from the modern world-systems perspective. One of the most important research questions has been whether poor countries have *more or less* long-term economic growth when they become extensively tied to multinational corporations from rich nations. While there is certainly variability among periphery nations, especially in Asia, several early studies indicated that many periphery nations do have less long-term economic growth when overly dominated by outside multinational corporations (Chase-Dunn 1975, 1989; Bornschier, Chase-Dunn, and Rubinson 1978; Snyder and Kick 1979; Stokes and Jaffee 1982; Nolan 1983; Bornschier and Chase-Dunn 1985). Poor nations that receive extensive multinational corporate investments, of course, tend to have some economic growth in the short term. But the longer-term prospects for growth (over five years or more) are in many cases actually harmed by the kinds of outside aid and investment these nations have received. This research has also indicated that outside corporate investment increases income inequality within poorer nations. As noted above, the historical pattern for rich nations until recently has been one of reduced income inequality as economic development proceeds (Jackman 1975; Hewitt 1977; Stack 1978a, 1978b; Weede 1980). In the case of poor nations, however, the rich tend to get richer while the poor are either poorer or no better off (Chase-Dunn 1975; Rubinson 1976; Bornschier et al. 1978; Stack 1978b; Bornschier and Ballmer-Cao 1979).

After the first wave of research on the effects of multinational corporate investments in poor countries, however, more recent research has shown less consistent and even contradictory results. Some research using larger and more recent data sets of poor nations has found that extensive multinational corporate investment now tends to produce more positive economic growth in the long term, while another using recalculations of older data also finds outside investment results in more long-term economic growth (Firebaugh 1992, 1996; de Soysa and Oneal 1999). Other research has shown that outside corporate investment in poor nations does not lead to less economic development when the types of goods imported or exported to and from the poor nations are considered, or if the outside corporate investment is accounted for by several rich nations rather than just one or two (Bollen and Appold 1993; Kentor 2001; Kentor and Boswell 2003). When many multinational corporations have smaller amounts of investment within a poor country, they are less able to dominate the economy and political system and, in fact, must compete among themselves giving workers in poor countries some advantage. Still other studies have questioned the negative effects of multinational investments in poor nations, such as increases in income inequality and a lower standard of living among the poor masses of people. These studies suggest a more complex relationship between multinational corporate investment and income inequality with evidence that the poor in many of these nations do have improved lives because of multinational investment (Alderson and Nielsen 1999; Firebaugh and Beck 1994). Some authors of original research showing that multinational corporate investment harms poorer nations have conducted research using data from the 1990s to conclude that their original research was correct but that the negative effects on poor countries tend to be less today (e.g., Herkenrath and Bornschier 2003). The current conclusion is that the effects of location in the modern world system are more complex than originally thought, and the global economy itself is changing. The conflicting research results on the impact of outside corporate investment on poorer countries is also due to rapid economic growth in Asian nations with extensive outside investments compared with countries in Latin America and Africa (Kerbo 2006b).

GLOBALIZATION AND THE FUTURE OF DOMESTIC SYSTEMS OF SOCIAL STRATIFICATION

One has to be cautious about overstating the impact of globalization on domestic systems of social stratification around the world, but we must recognize that the impact is certainly increasing for both rich and poor nations. Furthermore, new comparative analyses of political economy, or social stratification more generally, show that a nation's competitive position in the modern world system is affected by the nature of its system of social stratification.

Table 22.1   Competing Forms of Capitalism

	Corporate-Dominated Capitalism (Neoliberal)	Cooperative Capitalism (Corporatist)	State Development Capitalism (Asian Development Model)
Countries	United States, Canada, United Kingdom	Western European Union countries	Japan and developing countries in East and Southeast Asia
Characteristics	Small state, little government regulation, weak unions, low labor costs	Large welfare state, state regulation of the economy, economic planning, strong unions	Strong state intervention, extensive regulation/planning, weak unions
Outcomes	Cheap production costs, high inequality, low benefits to workers, less job security, low unemployment, high poverty, low taxes	High production costs, low inequality, high worker benefits, high job security, high unemployment, low poverty, high taxes	Medium production costs, low inequality, medium worker benefits, medium job security, low unemployment, low poverty, low taxes

SOURCE: Kerbo (2006b, chap. 3, 2006a, chap. 14). Also see Esping-Anderson (1990), Goodin et al. (1999), and Kerbo and McKinstry (1995).

Esping-Anderson (1990) and Goodin et al. (1999) have specified two distinct models of capitalism and shown their differing outcomes for people in differing class positions within a nation. To their two models of capitalism, which are found mostly in Europe and North America, we can add a third Asian model as indicated below (Kerbo and McKinstry 1995; Kerbo 2006b). There are differing outcomes for people in different class positions in each of these three models of capitalism as summarized in Table 22.1. As noted earlier, much future research on class systems and the modern world system, such as the great U-turn, will be devoted to whether or not one of these three models will become the dominant one as global competition proceeds throughout the twenty-first century.

Less-developed nations in the modern world system today are divided between those forced into the neoliberal model of capitalism by rich nations and the International Monetary Fund (especially in Latin America and the Philippines), those with development states (primarily in East and Southeast Asia), and those that can best be described as "predator states," that is, states captured by particular subgroups in the society and used primarily for the enrichment of that subgroup only (most often in Africa, but also in some other countries such as Burma) (see Kerbo 2006b). The questions for these countries will be which form of capitalism will be able to sustain economic development in the twenty-first century, and which form of capitalism will be able to promote more equally spread economic development that reduces poverty. Current trends point to the Asian development model as being most sustainable and able to reduce world poverty, though Japan's long stagnation since 1990 and the Asian economic crisis of 1997 suggest that the answers are far from certain.

23

THE SOCIOLOGY OF RACIAL AND ETHNIC RELATIONS

FRANK HAROLD WILSON

University of Wisconsin–Milwaukee

Racial and ethnic relations are salient dimensions of social distinction and diversity. Although institutional changes, the civil rights movement, and federal policies have diminished the traditional problems of discrimination and segregation across racial and ethnic groups, the "color line" remains as a complex system of cultural and institutional patterns, inequality markers, and social constructions of reality. At the beginning of the twenty-first century, the traditional Black-White color line, which defined the most salient boundaries of social distance in American race relations, is complicated and augmented by the increasing growth of recent immigrants from Latin America and Asia and the emergence of a new color line that has additional layers of cultural and color stratification and distinction.

Sociologists usually view racial and ethnic groups as deriving from social interactions and social definitions in which physical and cultural characteristics are distinguished and used as identifiers or markers in relationships. While a racial group is defined as a social group that persons inside or outside the group have decided is important to single out as inferior or superior on the basis of physical characteristics, an ethnic group is typically defined as a social group distinguished or set apart on the basis of cultural and nationality characteristics such as language, religion, and history. Sociologists and other social scientists such as anthropologists, psychologists, and historians have discredited any scientific basis of race or racial classification and have emphasized the interrelationships between culture and social structure in shaping different group and individual life chances and behaviors. Social definitions of racial group are to be distinguished from "natural," biogenetic, and popular conceptions that define race in terms of biological traits, such as skin color, hair texture, and other physical characteristics, and generalize from these surface manifestations deeper underlying differences between groups in intelligence, temperament, physical aggression, and sexuality.

The study of racial and ethnic relations in sociology has been an important concern throughout the twentieth century and shows signs of continuing in significance in the twenty-first century. Not only have academic concerns among sociologists contributed to the focusing and refocusing of problems and controversies of race relations. Simultaneously, larger historical, social, cultural, economic, and political factors have interacted to redefine what is meant by race and ethnicity and the social factors explaining this phenomenon. As such, the concept of race relations has been to an important degree an interdisciplinary one, which has implications for knowledge. This essay will examine the following concerns: (1) the classical theoretical perspectives of race and ethnic relations, (2) the post–civil rights sociological controversies concerning the changing significance of race and ethnicity, (3) the current state of knowledge on racial and ethnic inequality, (4) how sociology has brought its understanding of race relations to the public, and (5) the prospects for future research in racial and ethnic relations.

CLASSICAL THEORETICAL PERSPECTIVES OF RACE AND ETHNIC RELATIONS

Among the earliest generations of sociologists, the interests in racial and ethnic relations were initially influenced by cultural discourses focused on explaining the "race problem" or "Negro problem" that preceded the development of a scientific sociology (McKee 1993:95). From the end of the Civil War to the turn of the century, the race problem in the United States centered on explaining the lower status and morality of Blacks in the South who had come out of slavery and Reconstruction and remained largely subordinated and impoverished. Early sociologists drew from social Darwinism and biogenetic assumptions of human society to argue a natural inequality of the races (Lyman 1972). In defining different human populations as races, it was fallaciously assumed that these races (1) represented natural and separate divisions within the human species based on visible physical differences and (2) were biologically distinctive and homogeneous populations that were unambiguous, clearly demarcated, and uninfluenced by migration. The social construction of race was both a classification and ideological system that rationalized European attitudes and actions toward conquered and enslaved groups such as Indians and Africans and justified the inequalities in status, power, and privilege between dominant and subordinate groups.

Accompanying the development of a scientific sociology, classical sociologists refocused the discourse by emphasizing the historical and sociological contexts of race relations based on cultural contacts and group competition. Robert Park's (1930) initial conception of race relations as a "cycle," set within the contexts of an urban and secular society, hypothesized that global and cross-national movements of populations produced contacts between racially different groups on a frontier that were followed by processes of competition, conflict, accommodation, and assimilation. During the stages of competition and conflict, struggles between racial groups for resources resulted in prejudice, antagonisms, race consciousness, and the eventual development of a social order with dominant and subordinate groups. The antagonistic cooperation and "bridge building" in accommodation would eventually be followed by assimilation processes "by which people of diverse racial origins and different cultural heritages occupy a common territory, achieve a cultural solidarity sufficient at least to sustain a natural existence" (p. 281). According to Park ([1939] 1950), the concept of race relations came to refer to all relationships which are capable of producing race conflict and race consciousness and which determine the relative status of groups in the community. The term *race relations* eventually came to refer to the social processes and social structures arising from the contacts and interaction of people with varied social characteristics.

Park's framing of a race relations cycle identified important concepts such as racial frontiers, racial conflict, subordinate and dominant groups, racial antagonisms, assimilation, and prejudice. The inevitability of assimilation was relatively untested in the race relations scholarship until generations later. His conceptualization of the processes in the cycle contained in its logic assumptions of a greater significance of "racial differences" in its earlier stages and a "declining significance of race" in the latter stages.

The expectations of assimilation in race relations were challenged in part by caste and class perspectives. During the 1930s, social anthropologists such as William Lloyd Warner, John Dollard, and Allison Davis popularized a conceptual scheme for analyzing race relations in the southern region of the United States, which viewed Black-White relations as organized by a color caste system that shaped economic and political relations as well as family and kinship structures (Warner 1936; Dollard 1937; Davis, Gardner, and Gardner 1941). In caste and class perspectives, American race relations were viewed as an intractable system of formal and informal racial control and subordination that were characterized by different black and white caste systems with separate class systems in each caste. Within each of the two castes, social classes existed in which social status was based on income, education, and family background and reflected in distinctive life styles. Caste and class comprised a sociocultural system that functioned to distribute power and privilege unevenly and punished individuals who questioned the system by word or actions.

Although the institutional, organizational, and quality-of-life conditions were unequal between the races, the caste and class system functioned as a stable social order to provide economic, political, cultural, psychological, and emotional advantages to both Blacks and Whites. Unlike assimilation conceptions, the contacts between different groups were not competitive nor would these lead to racial conflict.

The refocusing of race relations into race and ethnic relations accompanied the entry of the concept of minority. Although minority had been used by some classical sociologists such as Robert Park and Louis Wirth, it was not central in defining or analyzing race relations. During the 1930s, the pairing of racial and ethnic groups grew out of sociological textbooks such as Donald Young's *American Minority Peoples* (1932). Young objected to the earlier literature that had created the impression that "Negro-white relations are one thing, while Jewish-Gentile, Oriental-white, and other race relations are vastly different from each other" and emphasized that "the problems and principles of race relations are remarkably similar, regardless of what groups are involved; and that only by an integrated study of all minority groups can a real understanding and sociological analysis of the involved social phenomena be achieved" (Young 1932:xii–xiii). The concept of minority was introduced to apply to groups distinguished by biological, language, and alien cultural traits. The conceptual category of minority in these textbooks suggested the theoretical similarities of racial, religious, and nationality groups. Although race was beginning to be broadened into racial and ethnic relations, this discourse did not represent the consensus or conventional wisdom in sociology.

The concept of minority was inspired by the experiences of Eastern European ethnic groups that made up parts of the growing immigration to the United States through 1924. In Eastern Europe, minority had been used to refer to suppressed racial and national groups that were accorded equal rights, and these rights were protected by proportional representation. Among early generations of sociologists, nationalities were defined as racial groups that had attained social consciousness, race pride, and moral independence. Louis Wirth's (1928) reference to the ghetto as "one historical form dealing with a dissenting minority in a large population" (pp. 4–5) was based on the experiences of European Jews. In the United States, the concept was initially applied to areas of first settlement of immigrants (ethnic ghettos), areas of ethnic groups new to the city, and the racially segregated communities of Black Americans in northern cities.

During the post–World War II years, the sociology of race relations was enlarged by the growing presence of liberal practitioners in human relations who were committed to the possibilities of social intervention in race relations. Drawing from the pragmatic, interventionist, and social reform experiences of New Deal programs and the social planning values, many sociologists came to view the earlier conceptions of an objective study of race relations detached from political intervention as limiting. These sociologists did not view race relations as intractable, slow to change, or singularly affected by the relationships between majority and minority groups. Instead, they came to view race relations as a social problem that might be influenced by applied sociological research and the increased introduction of sociological knowledge on race relations into public policy. Following the lead of the Carnegie Corporation, important foundations such as the Marshall Field Foundation, the Phelps Stokes Fund, and the Rockefeller Foundation became involved in funding scholarships and educational projects that emphasized the reduction of prejudice through education, reducing hostilities between racial groups, and identifying strategies for controlling discrimination.

By the 1940s and 1950s, sociologists paid increasing attention to the conceptual and analytical distinction between prejudice and discrimination, which had not been earlier articulated. While prejudice referred to the negative and faulty attitudes associated with groups, discrimination referred to the patterned behaviors and actions that differentiate and subordinate groups. In Park's earlier concepts, there was no clear distinction between prejudice and discrimination. Instead, the path to assimilation grew out of racial groups that had acquired group consciousness, race pride, and solidarity through racial conflict.

An American Dilemma (Myrdal 1944) represents the most comprehensive and influential statement of race relations during the post–World War II years. While refocusing race relations from "race and cultural contacts" and minority groups to the Negro problem, race prejudice was identified as "the whole complex of valuations and beliefs which are behind discriminatory behavior on the part of White Americans" (p. 52). The significance of race in American culture and social structure was highlighted as a moral contradiction between theory and practice in the hearts, minds, and consciences of White Americans that was reflected in the conflict between universal values of the American Creed—the doctrine embodied in the Constitution and Bill of Rights, high Christian precepts, and the Golden Rule—and the particular discriminatory practices in race relations that resulted from regional doctrines, local customs, conformity pressures, and individual prejudices (Myrdal 1944).

Myrdal also identified a "vicious cycle" where each of the major social institutions through discriminatory practices contributed to the discrimination and exclusion of Black Americans in other institutions and organized life. Conversely, once social change in race relations was initiated with social reforms in discrimination laws and practices and the reeducation of prejudiced beliefs and attitudes, the cumulative effects led to a "virtuous cycle," which began to reverse historic discrimination and improve the quality of life. By emphasizing cumulative causation, the continuities rather than discontinuities between prejudice, discrimination, and the social status of racial minority groups were underscored. Over time, its ideas of optimism, progress, and integration resonated with federally initiated executive orders, legislative reforms, and Supreme Court interpretations such as *Brown v. Board of Education* (1954).

The post–World War II focus on prejudice and discrimination was further reflected in leading theoretical arguments. Robert Merton's (1949) essay "Discrimination and the American Creed" offered a logical set of combinations of prejudice and discrimination that had empirical referents and identified both continuities and discontinuities. In his conceptual and analytical distinction of the unprejudiced nondiscriminator ("all weather liberal"), the "unprejudiced discriminator," "fair weather liberal," the "prejudiced nondiscriminator," "timid bigot," and "prejudiced discriminator" ("active bigot"), he emphasized more complexities between prejudice and discrimination. Merton emphasized that individual discrimination did not lead directly to prejudice and vice versa. In his discussion, most persons conformed to norms, laws, and institutionalized practices even when that behavior came into conflict with their own attitudes (Merton 1949). Consequently, effecting social change in discrimination did not require that attitudes be changed first. Sociological proposals for reform in race relations were usually premised on affecting discriminatory behaviors because racial attitudes were slower and more resilient to change. *The More Perfect*

Union (MacIver 1948) redefined the problem of controlling discrimination as a necessary strategy in developing larger objectives of national unity. Discrimination and segregation not only contradicted American moral values but also contradicted economic efficiency values in terms of high costs, duplication, and wastes. As a strategy, the nation's struggle against discrimination was centered on increasing opportunity in institutional areas of the economy, politics, and education and also identified the importance of innovation by the leadership of corporations, churches, and trade unions.

The focus of classical theorizing on race relations during the first half of the twentieth century was largely influenced by the color line or the relationships between White and Black Americans. Although the examination of immigrant and ethnic groups had always been an important focus in sociology, this topic was not initially conceptualized as race relations.

Distinctions between racial and ethnic groups were usually made clear. Black Americans, in terms of historical, social, and cultural conditions, were usually viewed as a unique case.

During the latter half of the twentieth century, the "liberal expectancy" paradigm of increasing integration and assimilation, based on the experiences of immigrant and ethnic groups in the North, came to represent the dominant line of interpretation among sociologists for analyzing racial and ethnic relations. Accordingly, optimism and progress are expected to characterize race relations over the long run as the historic inequalities of race are diminished. Not only are most European ethnic groups viewed as substantially assimilated, but the middle classes of racial minority groups are analyzed as becoming increasingly integrated and assimilated. In Milton Gordon's (1964) paradigm, the experiences of different ethnic groups might be analyzed by stages of cultural, structural, identificational, civic, marital, attitude-receptional, and behavioral-receptional assimilation.

By contrast, the "conservative expectancy" or "caste and class" paradigm, based on the color line experiences between Blacks and Whites in the rural South, has been reflected to a lesser degree in leading sociological interpretations of race relations with the exception of the National Advisory Commission on Civil Disorders observation that "America is moving toward two nations, one black, one white, separate and unequal" (National Advisory Commission on Civil Disorders 1968) and Andrew Hacker's (1992) *Two Nations*. The conservative expectancy views the objective social facts bearing on race relations as more intractable and slower to change than the theories and perceptions that are more influenced by public policy controversies and cultural beliefs. It predicts important continuities of the southern rural color line race relations in the contemporary cities and metropolitan areas of the North.

During recent years, many sociologists in analyzing racial and ethnic relations have continued to view the experiences of Black Americans in terms of the history of slavery and continuing institutional discrimination as unique and qualitatively different from immigrant and minority groups.

POST–CIVIL RIGHTS SOCIOLOGICAL CONTROVERSIES IN RACIAL AND ETHNIC RELATIONS

Since the late 1960s, one important theoretical development has been to shift the object of analysis toward issues of social inequality and mobility that have brought racial and ethnic relations into a closer convergence with paradigms of social stratification. Theorizing and research in stratification have usually been more national (or societal) in scope and less directly concerned with many of the urban and community relationships such as race and cultural contacts, assimilation, and segregation that characterized classical discussions. The increasing concern with social class, and race-class intersections, has been influenced by stratification interests. Another development informing post–civil rights theorizing has been the emergence of power conflict perspectives that have questioned the adequacy of assimilation (social order) theories. Instead of identifying the primacy of assimilation processes across racial and ethnic groups, these have emphasized the salience of institutional and organizational processes in structuring racial inequality. Power conflict discourses reintroduced Oliver Cromwell Cox's criticisms of classical assimilation and caste perspectives and the crucial intersection between capitalism and race relations (Cox 1948). Accompanying the growth of industrial capitalism, employers make use of ideologies of racism to segregate, divide, exploit, and control Black and White workers. Ideologies of racial superiority/inferiority, antagonism, and hatred function to hinder contact and constrain strong labor organizations between racial groups (pp. 485–88). Power conflict perspectives such as Van den Berghe's (1967) have noted that the development of racism and economic exploitation within modernizing industrial societies functioned to justify the contradictions between principles of freedom and equality and practices of slave labor and colonialism. Carmichael and Hamilton (1967) introduced the concept of institutional racism to identify the complex intersection between institutional actions, cultural beliefs, and policies that contribute to the subordination of Blacks.

Power conflict perspectives, such as internal colonialism, distinguish between minorities who are "conquered peoples" (colonized minorities) and those who are not (immigrant minorities). While colonized minorities are characterized by histories of conquest, forced and restricted movement, unfree and slave labor, and systematically harsh treatment with respect to group culture and social organization, immigrant minorities are characterized by histories of voluntary movement, free labor, and less intense group cultural and social organization conflicts. The concept is useful in distinguishing Native, African, Mexican, and Puerto Rican Americans (colonized minorities) from European, Asian, and other Latin Americans (immigrant minorities) (Blauner 1972). The concept of "racial formation" recognizes the role of the government in creating racial and ethnic definitions and institutionalizing discrimination (Omi and Winant 1986). Contemporaneously, the government has continued to socially define race and institutionalize discrimination through weakened enforcement of civil rights, voter dilution, and disenfranchisement in minority districts, "driving while black" practices among law enforcement officials, and the enactment of sentencing legislation that disproportionately targets the users of crack cocaine as distinct from users of pure cocaine.

The post–civil rights sociological theories are based on different perspectives of the changing nature of racial and ethnic stratification in the United States, the role of the economy and public policy, and the macrosociological and microsociological variables identified. With respect to the principal object of analysis, these derive from different sociological prisms of what has occurred and is likely to occur in the future. These models may be defined as follows: (1) the "declining significance of race" model, (2) the "continuing significance of race" model, and (3) the "increasing significance of ethnicity" model.

The "declining significance of race" model argues that as a consequence of a growing post–civil rights economy, the increasing integration of minorities in the corporate and governmental sectors of the economy, public policies of nondiscrimination, and more favorable attitudes among White Americans toward principles of equality and affirmative action, the effects of racial discrimination and segregation on the lives of racial and ethnic minorities are decreasing in significance. While civil rights policies have decreased the significance of historic discrimination, economics and class factors more than race factors are hypothesized as accounting for current racial and ethnic inequalities. William Julius Wilson's contemporary classics *The Declining Significance of Race* (1978), *The Truly Disadvantaged* (1987), and *When Work Disappears* (1996) have best exemplified these arguments. In disaggregating the effects of changing race relations across class lines, Wilson has hypothesized different outcomes for the new black middle class, who has become increasingly integrated, and the black underclass, who has experienced increasing social dislocation and joblessness.

In this paradigm, macroeconomic change factors, such as corporate growth, central-city plant closings, the decline of high wage, unionized manufacturing employment, the growth of low-wage service employment, and spatial mismatches between suburban employers and prospective central-city employees, are more primary in structuring opportunity rather than direct discrimination. Simultaneously, the differences across racial and ethnic groups in their acquisition of microlevel human capital characteristics such as increased education, training, and employment and social capital characteristics such as social

networks, organizational experiences, and work behaviors are relevant to their status in the racial and ethnic hierarchy. The most impoverished minority groups who remain behind are characterized by economic dislocations, "concentration effects," and "social isolation." "Declining significance of race" models interpret indirect discrimination in labor markets and housing and statistical discrimination as more important in inequality than direct discrimination. Historic discrimination, the "legacy of slavery," and the effects of past discrimination are acknowledged, while continuing discrimination is understated.

The "continuing significance of race" model argues that despite a growing economy, nondiscrimination and affirmative action policies, and increasingly favorable attitudes toward equality, recent post–civil rights trends in economic inequality have been accompanied by the persistence of racial and ethnic inequality in the lives of people of color. Drawing from "caste and class" and power conflict perspectives of racial stratification, these emphasize continuing segregation, institutional discrimination, and labor market segmentation (Hacker 1992; Oliver and Shapiro 1995; Omi and Winant 1986). These underscore that contemporary practices of institutional discrimination in the economy, politics, housing, education, and other areas of organized life continue to invidiously differentiate and lessen the life chances of racial minorities. Simultaneously, these emphasize that majority group White American attitudes and beliefs are ambivalent about the implementation of existing programs to bring about equality, view inequality as more individually rather than structurally caused, and commonly hold on to ethnic and racial stereotypes.

The increased visibility of a "new ethnicity" among third and fourth generations of ethnic groups, which were expected to become assimilated, was a cause for some sociologists to argue a resurgence of ethnicity, the limitations of assimilation, and the "end of the melting pot" (Glazer and Moynihan 1970; Greeley 1974). Not only had full assimilation not occurred for most ethnic groups, but its likelihood of occurring in the near future was questioned. In the "salad bowl," a more pluralistic interpretation of the transition to assimilation emerged that recognized ethnic groups becoming increasingly acculturated and structurally assimilated to the dominant society while retaining dimensions of ethnic group culture, identity, institutions, and organizations. The ethnic paradigm emphasized the immigrant analogy in accounting for the differences between ethnic and racial minorities, the primacy of the ethnic in racial and ethnic relations (or ethnic studies), and the salience of cultural factors in ethnic group adaptation and assimilation. Racial groups such as American Indians, African Americans, and Asian Americans were subsumed under broadened concepts of ethnic group. Race was included as an additional ethnic factor alongside language, religion, and nationality or redefined as an outcome of culture and self-definition. These discourses assumed that the histories of people defined as racial minorities were essentially similar to the experiences of European ethnic groups who experienced significant economic integration and assimilation in American society.

THE CURRENT STATE OF KNOWLEDGE ON RACIAL AND ETHNIC RELATIONS

Sociological research provides a basis for validating the competing theoretical perspectives while highlighting the distinction between empirical generalizations and social facts in contrast to the public policy discourses and cultural beliefs that may often confound what is known. Empirical sociological research knowledge may be distinguished by different approaches. While macrosociological research is focused on the "big questions" of how structural and institutional processes continue to be relevant to racial and ethnic inequality, microsociological research is focused on making sense of the cognitive, affective, and predisposition to action dimensions of racial attitudes, social distance, and ethnic identification.

Macrosociological Research

During the post–civil rights years, race has continued to structure the life chances of different groups. Despite important civil rights reforms such as *Brown v. Board of Education* (1954), the Civil Rights Acts of 1964, the Civil Rights Act of 1965, the Fair Housing Act 1968, and affirmative action, race continues to socially structure U.S. metropolitan areas, housing, education, the workforce, and other social institutions and organizations. Racial segregation remains as a social structure, practice, and symbol of racial and ethnic inequality. Patterns of segregation and desegregation experienced by racial and ethnic groups symbolize the status of these different groups in the social hierarchy and their access to the opportunities and resources connected to the American Dream.

Sociologists use the "segregation index" (or index of dissimilarity) to measure the degree of segregation, ranging from 0 for full integration and 100 for complete segregation. Values above 60 reflect high levels of segregation. During the twentieth century, the urbanization of Black Americans has been accompanied by high levels of racial segregation indicative of restricted socioeconomic opportunity and housing discrimination. Historic trends that accompanied the "Great Migration" through the post–World War II migration indicate progressively higher levels of segregation experienced by Blacks in cities between 1900 and 1970 (Taeuber and Taeuber 1965; Lieberson 1980; Massey and Denton 1993; Massey 2001). Since 1970, relatively small but steady decreases in Black segregation have occurred in the metropolitan areas with the largest Black populations. In 2000, the average Black-White segregation index in U.S. metropolitan areas was

65, and in the Northeast and Midwest it was 74 (Iceland, Weinberg, and Steinmetz 2002). Southern and western metropolitan areas, which initially had lower segregation levels, experienced relatively larger decreases.

Massey and Denton have conceptualized Black segregation as a multidimensional construct based on five dimensions of spatial variability—evenness, isolation, clustering, concentration, and clustering. Based on their criteria of index scores of at least 60 on four of the five dimensions, twenty metropolitan areas were identified as "hypersegregated" that contained roughly 11 million Black Americans (1990) and constituted 36 percent of the entire U.S. Black population. These levels of segregation approach the degree of Black-White segregation in South Africa under apartheid.

Hispanic segregation in metropolitan areas increased amidst relatively moderate levels of segregation (average scores ranging from 46 to 55 between 1970 and 1990). Hispanics who identify themselves as Black or racially mixed on the census have indices higher than 60, while those who identify as White have an index in the low to moderate range (Denton and Massey 1989:803). The greatest increases in Hispanic segregation were associated with metropolitan areas that experienced large Hispanic migration and population growth. Metropolitan areas with smaller Hispanic population growth experienced slower segregation growth.

Simultaneously, Asian segregation in metropolitan areas has been relatively lower than both Black and Hispanic levels (averaging 36 to 44 between 1970 and 1990). The growth of Asian segregation has accompanied the most rapid Asian migration and population growth (Massey 2001:407–409).

Historic patterns of European ethnic group segregation have usually been much lower than patterns of Black and Hispanic segregation and trends indicate more integration. Comparisons of segregation trends between Blacks and South/Central/Eastern European ethnic groups between 1890 and 1930 indicate that despite higher initial levels of isolation than Blacks, European ethnic groups experienced substantially more integration (Lieberson 1980).

During the post–civil rights years, the persistence of high levels of residential segregation was associated with high levels of racial segregation in schools. Although decreases in segregation accompanied judicially enforced desegregation between 1968 and 1980, during the 1980s and 1990s increasing segregation accompanied the government inaction and deregulation of mechanisms to desegregate schools. Levels of schooling segregation have been higher in the Northeast and Midwest than in the South and West (Orfield 2001). Racial minorities who attend segregated urban schools are less likely to take college preparatory courses and to attend college than those in more integrated and suburban schools. Teacher assignment practices are likely to reinforce inequality by assigning the least proficient teachers to the least desirable schools, which are often in minority neighborhoods. Yet even in more integrated schools, minorities experience disadvantages in terms of tracking and lower expectations by teachers.

During the post–civil rights years, continued improvements were made in completing high school across racial groups, which reflected in a narrowing of the racial gap. Although actual and percentage levels of college graduation increased for all groups during the 1990s, there has been a growing racial gap in the college graduation rate between Whites and Blacks and between non-Hispanic Whites and Hispanics (Blank 2001:25–26). Asian American college graduation has been substantially higher and increasing more rapidly than other groups (Kerbo 2006). Accompanying the growth of informational technology, there is a growing "digital divide" reflected in computer access and use across racial groups. While public access to computers through schools and libraries are almost universal, Black and Hispanic children are much less likely than White children to own or use computers at home.

Continuing racial segregation and discrimination has also affected the accumulation of wealth, earned incomes, and employment chances across racial groups. Oliver and Shapiro (1995) indicate that racial differences in wealth, which reflect inequality that is passed on intergenerationally, and current asset ownership are more extreme than income differences. Wealth differences reflect differences in home ownership, which are not merely the result of income differences but rather a product of the historical legacy of residential segregation, Federal Housing Authority (FHA) and Veterans Administration (VA) policies, and redlining. Blacks at similar income levels as Whites are rejected for home loans 60 percent more, Blacks pay more in mortgage interest rates than White families, and the valuing of homes and equity is color coded by segregation (Oliver and Shapiro 1995).

During the late 1960s through the early 1970s, the increasing returns to education received by highly educated Blacks recently entering the labor force translated into a convergence of income with similarly educated Whites (Featherman and Hauser 1976). The near parity of wages earned by Black college-educated graduates reversed during the 1980s and eventually came full circle in 1994 (Smith 2001:63). From 1972 to 1995, the overall ratio of Black/White household income remained between 57 and 60 percent and improved to 66.3 percent between 1995 and 2000 (Kerbo 2006, table 11–1).

Segregation in labor markets, which are associated with different formal and informal social networks, is reflected in higher chances of unemployment and joblessness among racial minorities. Unemployment rates for both Blacks and Hispanics have remained roughly twice the White unemployment rate, and recent trends indicate that among college-educated graduates, the Black rate increased to 2.5 times the White rate (Wilson, Tienda, and Wu 1995). Joblessness among racial minorities may be partly enabled by selective recruitment strategies such as the referrals of employees, avoiding placing ads in city and ethnic newspapers, and passing over applicants from the public schools, welfare programs, and state employment service programs (Wilson 1996).

High levels of Black segregation in U.S. metropolitan areas are not empirically explained by the class differences between Black and White Americans. When disaggregated by income or occupation, Blacks of higher status are as equally segregated from Whites of higher status as the Black poor are segregated from the White poor (Farley 1977). The high levels of segregation are also not accounted for by Blacks' preferences to live in predominantly Black neighborhoods since most Blacks "express support for the ideal of integration." High levels of segregation are explained by a complex of institutional discrimination practices that exist despite the Civil Rights Act of 1968. Housing audit studies, which measure the differences in treatment of potential Black and White homeowners and renters, indicate that Blacks are shown substantially fewer properties and are more likely to experience steering practices (Yinger 1998).

Sociologists have challenged the prediction of the resurgence of ethnicity. Stephen Steinberg argues that "cultural pluralism principles symbolic of resurgent ethnicity have been on the ascendancy precisely at a time when ethnic differences have been on the wane" (Steinberg 1989:254). Particularly important in explaining the status differences between ethnic groups is the intersection between social structure (class) and culture. Ethnic groups that were in the economically advanced sectors in their countries of origin had distinct historic advantages and chances of mobility over ethnic groups that were in more economically backward sectors (agriculture) (Steinberg 1989). Relatedly, Gans (1979) emphasizes that recent generations of ethnic groups express their identities through ethnic symbols that capture an identification with the old country, ethnic holidays, rites of passage, and political issues in contrast to earlier generations, who experienced ethnic identities through dense interactions within ethnic group institutions, organizations, and cultures in ethnic ghettos. In contrast to the more substantive ethnicity that was associated with the working classes, symbolic ethnicity is most likely to occur among those who have left the immigrant ghettos—the middle classes.

Microsociological Research

According to "liberal expectancy" hypotheses, racial prejudices and antagonisms are predicted to decease as a function of individuals increased social and economic integration into the society. Trend studies of racial attitudes in public opinion studies have documented a predominant trend toward positive change in the goals of integration and equal opportunity among White Americans (Schuman et al. 1997; Bobo 2001). With respect to endorsing principles of racial equality and integration, there has been a steady and dramatic movement supporting the more public and impersonal areas of jobs, employment, and schools. By contrast, more private and personal areas of racial equality, such as housing and racially mixed marriages, while experiencing change are characterized by more resistance and lag. Despite dramatic improvements in attitudes favorable to principles of integration and equality, racial attitudes in public opinion studies indicate a difficulty in translating these into concrete support for social policies that enable integration and equal treatment. The racial differences in the conceptions of integration indicate that most White Americans prefer to live in overwhelming White neighborhoods with a small number of Blacks, and Blacks prefer integrated neighborhoods with substantial numbers of Blacks (Bobo 2001:273).

Public opinion studies emphasize that both Blacks and Whites support compensatory programs that aim to equip minorities to be more effective competitors or that engage in special outreach and recruitment efforts. Policies that call for the more explicit racial preferences are unpopular and are resisted by both groups. Blacks and Whites support affirmative action-type policies, when these are aimed at improving training, competitive resources, and preferences for minorities in hiring and promotion. While a majority of Whites support the more compensatory types of policies, fewer support preferential policies.

Important disagreements concerning the prevalence of current discrimination exist between racial groups in opinion surveys. Where a majority of Blacks, Hispanics, and Asians perceive a prevalence of discrimination and see it as more institutional in character, a majority of Whites are more likely to view discrimination as a historical legacy of the past or as isolate discrimination that is declining in significance. White Americans' perceptions and beliefs concerning racial economic inequality that emphasize individualistic explanations (Blacks "should try harder," "should get ahead without special favors," and "fall behind because they lack motivation") are higher than structural explanations ("Blacks don't have the same chance for education" and "discrimination") (Kluegal and Smith 1986; Kluegal 1990). Contemporary racial attitudes have replaced the traditional anti-Black prejudice (or overt racism) during the post–civil rights years. While traditional racism was explicit in emphasizing innate biological differences between the races and the importance of maintaining racial segregation, contemporary racism is based more on cultural and political values. Objections to policies such as busing, affirmative action, and race-targeted programs among White Americans have more to do with broad American values, such as fairness, justice, individualism, and traditional conservatism, than with racism and prejudice (Kluegal and Smith 1986; Kluegal 1990; Schuman et al. 1997). This indirection in racial attitudes has been termed *symbolic racism* and *laissez-faire racism.*

While objective social indicators point to continuing structural sources of inequality, discrimination, and segregation, these are not necessarily reflected in the subjective indicators of racial attitudes. Recent macroeconomic changes and changing intergroup relations are often in contradiction with the dominant cultural beliefs.

BRINGING SOCIOLOGY INTO THE PUBLIC'S UNDERSTANDING OF RACE AND ETHNICITY

Sociology's involvement in discussions of race and ethnic relations has grown primarily from scientific concerns and secondarily from practical concerns. As an emerging social science, sociology's entry into discussions of race relations grew out of a need to place the question of race into its larger historic, cultural, and social structural contexts. By emphasizing the importance of the social environment and socialization in the social construction of race, sociologists challenged earlier dominant American cultural beliefs in the general public. Sociologists increasingly identified the variability of behaviors across and within racial groups and connected these with factors such as migration, demographic structure, social organization, class and status, and culture. Sociologists identified the roles of life chances and opportunity. Sociologists and other social scientists increasingly questioned and discredited the "natural" and innate explanations of intelligence, athletic performance, and social inequality.

Practical concerns driving interests in race and ethnic relations have grown out of "race problems" that demanded the understanding that sociological knowledge and research might play in social reform, social planning, and public policy. In addressing these, sociologists have conducted special studies and collaborated with public, private, and nonprofit agencies in formulating objectives and plans. Sociologists have acted as interpreters of contemporary social problems and social trends while often being consulted as experts.

Sociologists and other social scientists have a continuing track record of collaborating with public, private, and nonprofit agencies in formulating objectives and plans in areas such as desegregation. Research and expert testimony by the social psychologist Kenneth Clark, dealing with the adverse consequences of segregation on the self-concept of black children, represented a portion of the evidence used by the NAACP in the litigation of *Brown v. Board of Education* (1954). Sociologists predicted a gradual and uneven acceptance of school desegregation that would occur first in the Appalachians, Upper South, and Middle South and later in the Black Belt areas. The acceptance of desegregation was hypothesized as being correlated inversely with the percentage of Blacks in the population and the degree of prejudice in communities (Pettigrew and Back 1967:700). Sociologists, such as Reynolds Farley, have provided demographic research on current and projected metropolitan segregation patterns to enable civil rights organizations and courts to develop desegregation and busing programs.

Sociologists have brought sociological concepts, hypotheses, and empirical generalizations into the public understanding of changing race relations. During the post–civil rights years, the goals of controlling discrimination in institutional areas, such as the schools, the workplace, and the military, became the conventional wisdom that was both reflected and challenged in influential research and public policy. In response to the Civil Rights Act of 1964, James Coleman was commissioned by the Department of Health, Education, and Welfare to direct a survey focused on explaining the lack of equal educational opportunities for individuals by reason of race, color, religion, or national origin in public educational institutions in the United States. The chief findings in the report validated the then conventional wisdom of desegregation indicating that (1) most children attended schools with students of the same race, (2) schools attended by Whites had advantages in physical resources over those attended by Blacks, and (3) an academic achievement gap among Black children grew larger with each passing year. Simultaneously, the Coleman report challenged conventional beliefs concerning desegregation with other findings that emphasized that the effects of family background were greater than the quality-of-school effects in academic achievement, and the next important factors related to academic achievement were the social composition of the school and the student's sense of control of his environment (Coleman 1966). Although providing evidence to support policies of racial integration, subsequent research by Coleman emphasized the limitations of public schools in furthering desegregation and equality (Coleman, Kelly, and Moore 1975). Consequently, the concept of equality of opportunity in national discussions became increasingly distinguished by "equality of access" and "equality of outcomes."

The military has experienced significantly more racial integration than other civilian institutions with respect to minority access, promotions, and leadership. Sociologists studying race relations in the military have identified the army's organizational goals of accomplishing missions, maintaining an absolute commitment to nondiscrimination, promoting uncompromising standards of performance, and articulating opportunity channels as relevant to integration (Moskos and Butler 1996).

In response to the increasing racial polarization around issues of race relations during the post–civil rights years, William Julius Wilson in *The Truly Disadvantaged* (1987) and *When Work Disappears* (1996) introduces two sets of public policy approaches relevant to changing race relations: (1) universal policies and (2) race-specific policies. Universal policies emphasize broader policies, such as macroeconomic growth, higher wages, quality public education, health care, and child care, that benefit groups across the racial and class divide. Race-specific policies emphasize programs, such as civil rights and affirmative action, which have experienced greater ambivalence and resistance among the White American majority.

In a recent Supreme Court case on affirmative action, *Grutter v. Bollinger* (2003), the American Sociological Association, the Law and Society Association, the Society for the Study of Social Problems, the Association of Black Sociologists, and Sociologists for Women in Society filed a friend of the court brief in support of the respondents (University of Michigan) arguing that universities have a compelling interest in considering the life experience of growing up Black, Latino, or Native American in making admissions decisions and that race may be considered in university admissions when it is narrowly tailored and considered as one among many life experiences of individual applicants.

Sociologists have also been important critics in sociological controversies of race relations that have relevance for public policy. Following the publication of Daniel Patrick Moynihan's (1965) *The Negro Family: The Case for National Action,* sociologists were among its strongest critics (Rainwater 1967). While the report was designed to rally support for increased manpower programs in the Department of Labor that would benefit the most disadvantaged, the descriptions and analyses of social problems had implications that were easily misinterpreted and misused by public officials. As such, these had the potential of derailing equality and opportunity policies and programs. Richard Herrnstein and Charles Murray's (1994) *The Bell Curve* resurrected long-discredited arguments of intelligence as IQ and "substantially heritable" to explain social inequality and rationalize practices such as the removal by adoption of at-risk youth, choice programs such as vouchers and tax credits within the public schools, and reallocating some federal funds focused from the disadvantaged to programs for the gifted. Critics emphasized that the research evidence confused statistical conditions of correlation with causation, did not systematically account for rival explanations, introduced cultural superstitions about race as scientific facts, reduced intelligence to a single measure, and classified intelligence as a group phenomenon (Fraser 1995; Jacoby and Glauberman 1995; Willie 1995; Wilson 1995). Sociologists usually interpret social inequality as the product of historical and contemporary social, economic, political, and educational circumstances rather than as the consequence of biological inheritance.

Despite traditional American cultural beliefs and superstitions, a majority of social scientists and natural scientists at the beginning of the twenty-first century are coming to recognize race as a social construction rather than as a scientific fact. The American Anthropological Association in its "Statement on Race" emphasized that "Evidence from the analysis of genetics (e.g., DNA) indicates that most physical variation, about 94 percent, lies within so-called racial groups, and conventional geographic "racial" groupings differ from one another in only about 6 percent of their genes. This means there is greater variation within racial groups than between them (American Anthropological Association 1998:1). Related research from the Human Genome Project has underscored that the genes accounting for skin complexion, hair texture, and eye color account for less than 4 percent of the human genes.

The recognition of race as a social construction has been accompanied by proposals to eliminate racial categories for the purposes of collecting public data. By continuing the collection of official racial statistics, some argue that there is the social reproduction of racist thinking and the probable perpetuation of racial discrimination. By contrast, the American Sociological Association has argued that the measurement of differential experiences, treatment, and outcomes across racial categories is necessary to track disparities and to inform policy making to achieve greater social justice, and this has greater merit than discontinuing the concept of race altogether or not measuring the social consequences of race (American Sociological Association 2002:1–2).

THE PROSPECTS OF RACIAL AND ETHNIC RELATIONS IN SOCIOLOGY DURING THE 21ST CENTURY

At the beginning of the twenty-first century, the older conception of race as a biological scientific fact in sociology has been replaced by a newer conception that race and ethnicity are social constructions of reality. The social definition of race has developed from the convergence of scientific facts and political actions. In their continuing attempt to explain human variation, sociologists, other social scientists, and natural scientists have accumulated a body of scientific facts that emphasize that (1) there is a unity and common inheritance among all humanity, (2) greater variation exists within racial groups than between racial groups, and (3) there are no biologically distinctive and homogeneous racial groups. Although there is a consensus concerning the social definition of race, there is much less agreement concerning what are the most salient factors explaining racial and ethnic inequality in the United States and the possibilities of economic growth, public policy, and social action in changing these conditions. Underlying the political action components are values, ideologies, and cultural beliefs that are often in tension with scientific facts. Public policy and cultural discourses remain important in the sociological analysis of race and ethnicity but may also contribute to the reproduction of cultural beliefs, superstitions, myths, misinformation, and stereotypes.

There are many signs that racial and ethnic relations will continue to constitute an important sociological area of interest. Not only will theoretical, research, and teaching concerns inside academic sociology drive these interests but so will public policy controversies and struggles for social justice outside of sociology. Societies, such as the United States, South Africa, and Brazil, that dominated cross-national discussions of race relations in the twentieth century will continue to be important social laboratories. Advanced industrial societies such as Great Britain, France, and Germany, which are experiencing the tensions of economic reorganization, immigration, and ethnic conflicts, will increasingly inform the theorizing on assimilation, economic integration, and segregation. Within other Caribbean, Central American, and South American societies are possible clues concerning the emerging forms of "Latinization" in social consciousness and solidarity

that are coming to compete with and supplant the older Black-White color line in the United States.

Globalization trends, which are increasingly integrated into economic, political, educational, and legal institutions in much broader national and cross-national contexts, have the possibilities of connecting racial and ethnic relations into larger struggles of human rights. Simultaneously, globalization in terms of communications has regressive possibilities of socially reproducing and exporting stereotypes, beliefs, and symbols of racial subordination.

The recent demographic growth of ethnic and racial minority groups such as Hispanic, African, Asian, and Native Americans has led to some projections that the United States may become a nation primarily made up of racial and ethnic minorities before the middle of the twenty-first century. In some states such as California and New York and in several major cities, the possible future of an increasingly diverse multiethnic America has already occurred.

How this multiracial demographic growth translates into increasingly differentiated systems of stratification and intense intergroup patterns of competition and conflict, as opposed to multiracial political coalitions and organized struggles for social justice against racism, is an important question that has implications for reexamining the processes of assimilation and racial and ethnic stratification, and broadening the empirical research and sociological theories in the area. Simultaneously, it is not certain whether new forms of color and status consciousness, including multiple-race identification and categories, will replace the dominant Black-White classification or merely augment it in the near future.

The disconnect between what is believed and practiced by people in public and private encounters will continue to demand understanding and explanation by sociologists studying public opinion. Greater optimism concerning principles of integration and equality, as opposed to support for policies enabling desegregation and affirmative action, are associated with both moral ideals and economic uncertainties. The traditional support for segregation has been increasingly replaced by stronger principles of freedom of choice and individualism. As the United States continues to experience the social dislocations of globalization, economic reorganization, and multiethnic population growth in the twenty-first century, sociologists will be asked to identify to what degree a more universal, democratic, and social rights model of American society is emerging as opposed to a more local, fragmented, and contentious model in which race is a wedge issue.

The racial divide that increasingly intersects with growing trends of social class and income inequality and acts as a wedge on democracy will represent a most challenging problem for sociological theory, research, policy, and social justice. Sociologists will continue to address many of these questions through traditional academic research and simultaneously be challenged to play an increased role in consciousness raising and public policy.

24

THE SOCIOLOGY OF GENDER

ROSALIND A. SYDIE

The University of Alberta, Canada

The use of the concept of gender to explain the social differences between males and females is a fairly recent focus in sociology. This is not to say that differences between the two have been ignored by sociologists but that those differences were understood as immutable biological facts and that the social was, in the last instance, powerless to change. The presumed "natural" binary of sex was taken for granted by nineteenth-century and most twentieth-century theorists, for whom men were the primary focus of sociological interest, with women making an appearance usually in discussions of marriage and the family.[1]

The relative invisibility of women in the sociological enterprise, as in all Western intellectual traditions, was challenged with the advent of second-wave feminism in the 1960s. The challenge was not confined to the academy. Betty Friedan's (1963) popular best-seller, *The Feminist Mystique,* and Kate Millet's (1970) *Sexual Politics* critiqued the oppressive nature of male/female relationships, and the numerous consciousness-raising groups as well as feminist groups that emerged from various left and civil rights organizations also mounted trenchant critiques. Central to the critiques was the conviction that the "personal is political," that feminist scholarship must be allied to feminist activism. In the academy, the marginality of women to the "intellectual, cultural, and political world" (Smith 1987:1) was contested, and vital interdisciplinary exchanges began the process of putting the natural binary under the microscope (Hess and Ferree 1987).

SEX ROLES

In the early years, research focused on *sex roles* rather than *gender.* Sex as well as class and race were "traditional" variables used in social science research, with the assumption that sex, as a biological given, simply meant checking a box for male or female on government or social science survey forms. Using the concept of sex roles was a way of introducing social and cultural factors into the research. The assumption was that socialization into appropriate male/female roles, although resting on a "natural" biological foundation, allowed, in theory at least, some possibility of social change in the unequal relationships between men and women. But the influential work of Talcott Parsons indicated that there were limitations to the use of role theory. Parsons and Bales (1955) linked sex roles to differences in social functions, with males normatively adopting instrumental functions and females expressive functions. These functional *social* roles were, however, tied to the dictates of a biological binary, and any profound variation in the roles and functions, such as women having careers, was understood to be dysfunctional to the stability of the social system (Parsons [1942] 1954).

Sex-role research was fruitful, however, in producing several empirically based studies on male/female differences (Maccoby and Jacklin 1975), which tended to show that there were no significant differences and that "*women and men are psychologically very similar,* as groups" (Connell 2002:42). Later research refined the concept of sex roles as defining "*situated identities*—assumed and relinquished as the situation demands—rather than *master* identities, such as sex category, that cut across situations" (West and Zimmermann 1987:128). It was also pointed out that roles are prescriptive expectations that vary culturally and historically and are not enacted passively; rather, both men and women actively and reflexively shape their sex roles (Connell 1987; Stacy and Thorne 1985). Consequently, the "functional ideas embedded in the concepts of 'sex role' and 'socialization'" were shown to be "inadequate" because people often "do not become what they are expected to be" (Hess and Ferree 1987:14). More significant, critics pointed out that the concept of sex roles could not explain why men were nearly always the more valued members of any social group. In addition, the concept was theoretically problematic because sociologists did not refer to "race roles" or "class roles" (Eichler 1980; Hess and Ferree 1987).

Critiquing the concept of sex roles did not, however, eliminate the problem of the foundational assumption of immutable biological differences, which made the issue of significant change in male/female relationships problematic. In attempting to navigate the nature/nurture binary, Stoller's (1968) distinction between "sex" as the biological evidence from chromosomes, hormones, and external genitalia and "gender" as the social, psychological, and cultural manifestations was influential. The distinction was initially used in psychoanalytic work on sex and gender "anomalies," such as hermaphrodites and transsexuals (see Money and Ehrhardt 1972). For feminists, the distinction was a useful way of acknowledging the significance of sex and at the same time freeing them to concentrate on the social elaborations of gender differences. As Dorothy Smith (2002) points out, the distinction was a "political move" because "we had to believe that change was possible, that the repressions to which women were subjected were not the simple effect of biology" (p. ix). For example, Rubin (1975) suggested that the existence of two sexes gave rise to the social organization of gender in kinship systems, which are the "observable and empirical forms of sex/gender systems" (p. 169). Rubin's analysis retained the assumption of two sexes as foundational, whereas Delphy (1984) maintained that gender precedes sex and that choosing the "bodily type" to explain the hierarchical division of men and women is an arbitrary choice that does not make sense either logically or historically. Biology itself does not necessarily "give birth to gender," and to assume that it does means that the "existence of genders—of different social positions for men and women—is thus taken as a given and not requiring explanation" (p. 25). It became apparent that the ubiquity of the two-sex model needed to be dismantled if gender was to, as Delphy (p. 24) put it, to "take wing" theoretically.

Before looking at how gender "took wing," two points need to be made about the following discussion. First, the initial investigations into gender were largely undertaken by feminist researchers. Some male researchers did initiate research on male roles and masculinity, but these discussions were often marginal to the central feminist debates theorizing gender (Brod 1987; David and Brannon 1976; Farrell 1975; Kimmel and Messner 1989; Pleck 1981). The focus of most research, as the subsequent discussion will illustrate, was mainly on the position of women and their experiences, to the extent that it often seemed that men did not "have" gender, that the universal male subject of Western theory remained intact. The second point has to do with the sex/gender distinction, which will loom large in our discussion. As Donna Haraway (1991:127) discovered, when asked to contribute the sex/gender entry to a feminist keywords text, this is a distinction that other languages and other non-English-speaking feminists do not make. The concept of sex/gender remains a problem for cross-cultural feminist debates, exemplified most recently in the responses to Felski's (1997) article "The Doxa of Difference" and Hawkesworth's (1997) article "Confounding Gender" and the responses to Hawkesworth's article. To the extent that the following concentrates largely on the work of English-speaking feminists, the somewhat contested epistemological status of the sex/gender distinction should be kept in mind.

THEORIZING GENDER

By the late 1970s, gender was the central concept for feminist research, although the issue of "sex" in relation to gender remained contentious. For example, sociobiology maintained that women's reproductive biological destiny invariably results in social, sexual, political, and economic double standards that favor males (Barash 1977; Dawkins 1976; Wilson 1975). The sociobiological position was not uncontested, but sex became the "Achilles' heel of 1970s feminism" despite its being relegated to the "domain of biology and medicine" (Fausto-Sterling 2005:1493). In general, gender was used to "supplant sex" but "not to replace it" (Nicholson 1994:80).

In the initial forays into gender research, Marx and Freud were the two theorists whose work provided a basis for critique. Marxist analysis, with its focus on oppression and exploitation, seemed to promise an appropriate revolutionary perspective for change. Both Marx and Engels agreed that the first form of class subordination was the subordination of women to men, and for this reason, Engels (1935) maintained that "in any given society the degree of women's emancipation is the natural measure of the general emancipation" (p. 39). Critiquing Freud's work was seen as a necessity because it provided the psychological theory that supported the idea of universal patriarchy and offered an explanation for women's compliance with these arrangements. At the same time, Freud's assumption of pre-Oedipal bisexuality and a common libido offered the possibility of reconceptualizing the development of sexual difference.

Some of the first approaches concentrated on "documenting gender difference" and understanding "how gender difference is constructed" (Marshall 2000:26). In this context, unpacking the historical and social nature and impact of patriarchy was a central issue. Max Weber ([1925] 1978) had defined patriarchy as the power of "men against women and children; of able-bodied as against those of lesser capability; of the adult against the child; of the old against the young" (p. 359). Following Weber, *patriarchy* was used as a general term denoting the near-universal male domination of women, having its basis in the family and household. Gerda Lerner (1986) pointed out that the foundation for family patriarchy was the control of women's "sexual and reproductive capacity," which occurred "*prior* to the formation of private property and class society" (p. 8). Women's subordination preceded the formation of class societies, so class "is not a separate construct from gender; rather, class is expressed in generic terms" (p. 213).

Although Lerner was at pains to point out that patriarchy was tied to the appropriation of women's sexual and reproductive capacities, it was class issues filtered through Marx that initially took theoretical precedence in Anglophone sociology. Many feminists pursued the issue of patriarchy through vigorous debates over the connection between patriarchy and capitalism (Barrett 1980; Eisenstein 1979; Firestone 1970; Mitchell 1973; Sargent 1981; Walby 1990). What quickly became clear was that it was not possible to analytically separate the two, that *capitalist patriarchy* formed a unitary system. The debates produced important work on social class (Acker 1973; Giddens 1973; Kuhn and Wolpe 1978; Sargent 1981); the nature of women's labor, especially domestic labor (Fox 1980; Luxton 1980; Oakley 1974; Seccombe 1974); and the variable role of the State in the perpetuation of gendered power relations (Balbus 1982; Coontz and Henderson 1986; Coward 1983; Eisenstein 1979; Elshtain 1982; Lowe and Hubbard 1983). In the last context, a considerable amount of work focused on the ways in which gender, class, and race have played out in civic entitlements, especially with respect to welfare benefits (Fraser 1989; Gordon 1994; Marshall 1994; Pateman 1988; Pringle and Watson 1992).

The focus on capitalist patriarchy, however, tended to leave traditional Marxist analyses of productive relations intact and simply added a "separate conception of the relations of gender hierarchy" (Young 1981:49). For example, the domestic labor debates of the 1970s pointed to the usefulness of domestic labor to capital but "became trapped in trying to assess whether housework produced surplus value or was just unproductive labor" (Thistle 2000:286). Furthermore, the dualisms of work/home, public/private appeared not as "mutually dependent but as separate and opposed. It is accordingly, virtually impossible to bring them together within a logically coherent and consistent account of social life" (Yeatman 1986:160). In general, the debates did not displace in practice or in theory what Connell (2002:142) calls the *patriarchal dividend*.[2] The dividend refers to the very real advantages that men, as a group, derive from the unequal gender order. These advantages operate at all levels, from the local to the global, whatever the cultural, racial, or social differences. Connell concludes that most men have an interest in "sustaining—and, where necessary, defending—the current gender order" (p. 143).

The concern with class and stratification was also critiqued as ignoring race, ethnicity, and sexuality. The assumption seemed to be that the visibility of gender oppression required the invisibility of race, ethnicity, sexual orientation, and even class (Mohanty 1992:75). Many women of color, as well as gays and lesbians, correctly identified the way in which earlier discussions had privileged the position and interests of white, Western, heterosexual women, similar to the way in which "man" had been shorthand for white, Western, heterosexual males in post-Enlightenment sociological discourse (Barrett 1980; Collins 1990; hooks 1981; Rattansi 1995).

At the beginning of the United Nations Decade of Women, 1976, the idea of a "global sisterhood" suffering the same gender oppression came under fire, and it was pointed out that many white, privileged Western women were implicated in the patriarchal dividend enjoyed by their male counterparts (Bhavnani 2001). Critics pointed out that gender is constructed in and through differences of "race and class and vice versa" (Lovell 1996:310) and that race is "integral to white women's gender identities" (Glenn 1992:35).

But recognizing "race" often resulted in black women, Third World women, and native women becoming the trendy "Other." Ann duCille (1994) asked, "Why have we—black women—become the subjected subjects of much contemporary investigation, the peasants under the glass of intellectual inquiry in the 1990s?" (p. 592). Gayatri Spivak (1988) also critiqued the privileging of "whiteness" as the natural, normal condition that produced the colonial object on the assumption that race is something that belongs to others. A particularly important observation was that many white, Western, academic feminists were complicit in the "othering" process in using "native" informants to "build their academic careers, while the knowledgeable 'objects of study' receive nothing in return" (Mihesuah 2000:1250).[3]

The focus on race was particularly significant to U.S. sociology given its history of race relations. Patricia Hill Collins (1990) conceptualizes the black experience in the United States, in its critical difference from the experiences of "whites," as embodying an "outsider-within" perspective. She illustrates how African American women have their own take on their oppression and that they are "neither passive victims of nor willing accomplices in their own oppression" (p. xii). Collins points to the significance of everyday practices as the basis for understanding the intersection of race and gender that produces a "Black *women's* standpoint," not a "Black *woman's* standpoint," emphasizing the "collective values in Afrocentric communities" (p. 40, fn. 5).

In Collins's work and that of others, the key point is that there are multiple and interlocking layers of oppression and domination (see also B. Smith 1983; D. Smith 1987). The "matrix of domination" points to power relations tied to an individual's location on the interrelated structures of gender, race, class, and sexuality (Collins 1990). A significant part of the matrix was a "heterosexual norm" that produced taken-for-granted assumptions about sex, sexual identity, sexual desire, and sexual practice (Blackwood 1994). Sex and the biological binary, always an undercurrent in any of the debates discussed above, took on greater significance as feminists examined how people "have" and "do" gender and how or if, when considering human reproduction, biological essentialism can be avoided.

HETEROSEXUAL NORMALITY AND BIOLOGICAL/SOCIAL REPRODUCTION

Feminists recognized that Freud's theories provided psychological support to biological assumptions of "natural" sex differences that, in turn, supported the structural subordination of women under patriarchy (Coward 1983; Mitchell 1975). Jacqueline Rose (1986) suggested that Freud's work gave an "account of patriarchal culture as a trans-historical and cross-cultural force" that "conforms to the feminist demand for a theory which can explain women's subordination across specific cultures and different historical moments" (p. 90). As Jean Walton (2001) points out, psychoanalysis has always excluded race. The reworking of Freud by Lacan and the comments of other theorists such as Foucault and Derrida provided, and continue to provide, significant contributions to these debates (Braidotti 1991; Butler 1990, 1993; Butler and Scott 1992; Diprose 1994; Irigaray 1974; Kristeva 1986; Rose 1986). A key issue addressed was the presumed inevitability of a tie between biological reproduction and social mothering, which, in turn, was tied to the assumption of heterosexual normality. Chrys Ingram (1994) maintains that the idea that "institutionalized heterosexuality constitutes the standard for legitimate and prescriptive sociosexual arrangements" is one of the "major premises" of sociology in general and of some "feminist sociology" (p. 204). And Rosalind Petchesky (1980) pointed out "women's reproductive situation is never the result of biology alone, but of biology mediated by social and cultural organization" (p. 667).

The significance of reproduction, reproductive choice, motherhood, and mothering was the focus of what has been called maternal feminist debates. Nancy Chodorow's (1978) work was important to these debates. She suggested that while there are historical and cross-cultural variations in family and kinship structures, it is generally the case that women mother. This "mother-monopolized childrearing produces women who are able to *and will want to mother* in their turn" in contrast to men "who have a separate sense of self and who lack the capacity or the desire to nurture others" (Sydie 1987:151). Chodorow's (1978)

object-relations psychoanalytic analysis focuses on the primary, pre-Oedipal identification of both male and female children with the mother and the different ways in which separation occurs for each child. While the son's identification with the father follows the process described by Freud, that of the daughter is different. Chodorow maintains that the daughter, who shares her sex with her mother, does not completely reject the mother, and in her "personal identification with her mother" she learns "what it is to be womanlike" (pp. 175–76). It is not biological sex as such but the "early social object-relationships" located mainly in the unconscious that determine the development of sexed identities and, in the case of women, produce mothers (p. 54).

Masculinity is thus more difficult to achieve and is largely predicted on distinguishing self from the feminine. Dorothy Dinnerstein (1977), whose work parallels Chodorow's in many respects, suggested that both sexes have a terror of "sinking back wholly into the helplessness of infancy" so that for "Mother-raised humans, male authority is bound to look like a reasonable refuge from female authority" (pp. 161, 175). According to Dinnerstien, Freud was unable to account for the near-universal fear and hatred of women, but she maintains that this stance is the logical result of mother-monopolized child rearing, producing the male need to control women and women's more or less willing submission. Both Chodorow and Dinnerstein suggest that the solution is to change the nature of parenting to include both men and women.

The accounts by Chodorow and Dinnerstein were criticized on several counts, not the least of which were the implicit Western nuclear family model they assumed and the lack of clarity as to how men might be incorporated into parenting and what happens if this does occur, for the child's primary identification (Hirsch 1981; Lorber 1981; Spelman 1988). In such a situation, would the identification be bisexual, and if so, what are the consequences? (O'Brien 1981; Sayers 1982). Interestingly, Freud did posit an original bisexuality and common libido in the pre-Oedipal child that the castration fear resolves and that "normally" produces heterosexual gender identities (see Irigaray 1974). In general, it is this assumption of the normality of heterosexuality in these accounts that is a problem. MacKinnon (1982) summarized the heterosexual norm's effects on women as follows: "Sexuality is to feminism what work is to marxism: that which is most one's own, yet most taken away" (p. 515).

Adrienne Rich's (1980) "Compulsory Heterosexuality and Lesbian Existence" was an influential intervention into the sexuality and maternal feminist debates. Rich claimed that heterosexuality, like motherhood, needed to be "recognized and studied as a *political institution*" (p. 637). She points out that the structures that maintain heterosexuality and the ideology that claims its normality ensures the compliance of most women in their own subordination. Rich asks "*why in fact women would ever redirect that search*"

(p. 637) if women are the primary love object. Her answer is that they are forced to do so because women's identification with women could make them "indifferent" to men, introducing the possibility that "men could be allowed sexual and emotional—therefore economic—access to women *only* on women's terms" (p. 643). Consequently, heterosexuality is something that has to be "imposed, managed, organized, propagandized, and maintained by force," and lesbian existence and the lesbian continuum of "women-identified experience" throughout women's lives has to be denied.

Many of the critiques on the hegemony of heterosexuality looked at its manifestations in and on the body, and about the body as a "*text* of culture" and a "*practical, direct* locus of social control" (Bordo 1989:13).[4] The body as "text" was indebted to Foucault's concept of bio-power and body aesthetics. Other critiques concentrated on the Western conception of the organically discrete, natural, two-sex human body as a social construction (Laqueur 1990; O'Neill 1985; Schiebinger 1993). Donna Haraway (1991) went further in her claim that the naturalized body was a fiction, that bodies must be understood as "biotechnical-biomedical" bodies in a "semiotic system" that produces the "cyborg" as "our ontology" (pp. 150, 211). While not necessarily producing cyborgs, biotechnological and biomedical interventions in reproduction, such as in vitro fertilization, surrogacy, sex selection, and cloning, have been critiqued as not necessarily producing positive outcomes for women's health and their social, political, and economic welfare (Overall 1989; Sawicki 1999; Shildrick and Price 1998).

BODIES, SEX, AND GENDER

Michel Foucault's (1976) conceptualization of the body as the site for the exercise of power through "disciplines of the body and the regulation of populations" and his understanding of power as productive as well as prohibitive and punitive provided an initial entry into the conceptualization of the body as the effect of discourse. In addition, Foucault's demonstration that sexuality has been a "central preoccupation" of modern society that required the confession of a "true" sex identity—male or female, certainly not hermaphrodite—was suggestive. For Foucault, sex was the "naturalised product of a moral code which, through techniques of discipline, surveillance, self-knowledge, and confession organizes social control by stimulation rather than repression" (Foucault 1980:57). But as several feminists pointed out, Foucault's observation that power is all-pervasive and constituted in the practices of the subjected prompts the question, How is resistance possible? (Diamond and Quinby 1988; Fraser 1989; Ramazanoglu 1993; Sawicki 1991). Further, the relations of power/knowledge charted by Foucault may change, but they seem to do so by reaffirming "women's marginal status" (Ricci 1987:24), and there appears to be "no moral high ground where the individual can exercise agency outside of the social codes which constitute desire asymmetrically" (Diprose 1994:24). Foucault himself was not particularly concerned with the gender of dominated subjects of a power/knowledge regime and did not take account of the "relations between masculinist authority" and, therefore, the gendered "language, discourse and reason" (Diamond and Quinby 1988:xv).

Judith Butler (1990), however, found Foucault's notion of the constructed subject useful. She pointed out that this does not preclude the possibility of the subject's agency; on the contrary, the construction is the "necessary scene of agency" (p. 147). If subjects are discursive productions and identities unstable fictions, then this allows feminists to "contest the rigid codes of hierarchical binarisms." The binaries anyway produce "failures"—the assertive female, the effeminate male, the lipstick lesbian, and so on (p. 145). Gender is not simply constructed; it is performed and performed in relation to the sexual obverse—that is, heterosexual and homosexual bodies and practices are interdependent, produced by the regulative norms of compulsory heterosexuality. Furthermore, gender must be continually reproduced; there is no "original." Nor does anything, performatively, go. In *Bodies That Matter,* Butler (1993) points out that the construction and performance of gendered bodies does not mean that some constructions are not necessary constructions. For example, Evelyn Fox Keller (1989) suggests that it is the "vital process that issues in the production of new life" that has compelled "people of all kinds throughout history, and across culture, to distinguish some bodies from others" (p. 316). We may play with, perform, and deconstruct sex and gender, but how can we develop "strategies for eliminating (not only resisting) certain kinds of gendered and sexual subordination and violence, precisely those that are not easily subject to resignification" (Brown 2003:368)? And it is reproduction, and its extension mothering, that seems especially resistant to resignification.

The deconstruction of sex *and* gender and their manifestations in bodies was important in the development of queer theory and for the increasing focus on the "trans"—transgender, transsexual, intersexuality, bisexuality, and various other "transgressions" of sex and gender dimorphisms (Findlay 1995). More specifically, Eva Sedgwick (1990), in her *Epistemology of the Closet,* claimed that to understand "virtually any aspect of modern Western culture," it is necessary to "incorporate a critical analysis of modern homo/heterosexual definition" (p. 1).

Queer theory seeks to challenge the "master categories" of heterosexuality and homosexuality as "marking the truth of sexual selves," by understanding them as "categories of knowledge, a language that frames what we know as bodies, desires, sexualities, identities: . . . a normative language that erects moral boundaries and political hierarchies" (Seidman 1994:174). Queer theory also points to the poverty of sexuality studies in mainstream sociology, which has used labeling theory and/or a deviance perspective to study gay, lesbian, and alternative "subcultures" (Namaste 1994:227), although Epstein (1994:193) claims that the "involvement of sociologists in the study of sexuality" was a significant subset of mainstream sociology, stemming initially from Kinsey's work, which has diminished only in recent years.

There has been a veritable explosion of research under the general rubric of queer theory, although much of the work also falls under the general rubric of cultural studies rather than sociology (for a general review of the academic history and current status of queer theory, see Marcus 2005). Steven Seidman (1994) states that although queer theory challenges the "regime of sexuality itself" and "aspires to transform homosexual theory into general social theory or one standpoint from which to analyze whole societies," to date, "queer theory and sociology have barely acknowledged one another" (p. 174).

A critical issue for queer theorists remains the underlying question of how biology figures in these social constructions. Seeing identities as "multiple, unstable, and regulatory" as well as "pragmatic" and relating this to "concerns of situational advantage, political gain, and conceptual utility" may be a laudable standpoint for the contested social and cultural arena of sex/sexuality/gender studies (Seidman 1994:173). Meanwhile biology, especially evolutionary biology, continues to retain a binary take on physical bodies based on the assumption of natural chromosomal, hormonal, and genital binary difference (Haraway 1991).

Ignoring biology and concentrating on social construction seems to be a misguided position for feminists given the focus of some recent medical research. For example, medicine has searched for gay genes and for differences in brain structures between men and women as well as homosexuals and heterosexuals, and in biology, the studied attempts to deny the existence of "homosexuality" as well as the general "plethora of sex diversity" in the nonhuman animal world persists (Hird 2004). Anne Fausto-Sterling (2005) points out that although contemporary biomedical research seems to deal with sex "in the 1970s feminist meaning of the word, sex sometimes strays into arenas that traditional feminists claim for gender" (p. 1497). Fausto-Sterling concludes with a "call to arms" for feminists to recognize that "culture is a partner in producing body systems commonly referred to as biology" (p. 1516).

Attention to the treatment of the body of the intersexed is one of the ways in which the culture/body relation has been examined in recent years (Heyes 2003; Hird 2000, 2003, 2004; Kessler 1990). According to Hird (2003), the intersexed, defined as "infants born with genitals that are neither clearly 'female' nor 'male,'" (p. 1067) are estimated to comprise up to 2 percent of births. These infants present a "profound challenge to those cultures dependent on a two-gender system," and intersexed infants are "routinely surgically and hormonally gender reassigned" (p. 1068). The reassignment occurs despite some compelling evidence that for many of these infants, the process is traumatic and often less than successful in producing a stable gender identity in later years (see Hird 2004:135 on the John/Joan case). A critical point in the definition of and treatment of the intersexed is made by Wilchins, who asks, "Why are [intersex] people forced to produce a binary sexed identity? . . . What kinds of categories of analysis would emerge if nontransgendered anthropological bodies were forced to explicate themselves in terms of intersexuality, rather than the other way around?" (quoted in Hird 2003:1068).

Feminist attention to medical treatments of sex identity is more than warranted given the fact that although medicine "requires a biological definition of the intersexual's 'sex,' the surgeons, endocrinologists and psychiatrists themselves clearly employ a *social* definition" (Hird 2004:136). Kessler (1998) calls medicine's surgical interventions a "failure of the imagination" in not recognizing that "each of their management decisions is a moment when a specific instance of biological 'sex' is transformed into a culturally constructed gender" (p. 32). Furthermore, the insistence on choosing one of two "sexes" is ironic given the fact that the majority of human cells are intersexed, chromosomes have no sex, and there are many species that do not require sex for reproduction. In sum, although the corporeal body in its external fleshy manifestation is important, "beneath the surface of our skin exists an entire world of networks of bacteria, microbes, molecules, and inorganic life," and they take "little account of 'sexual difference'" and indeed exist and reproduce without any recourse to what we think of as reproduction" (Hird 2004:142). In addition, the insistence on "identity" as the manifestation of a sovereign "human" subject is compromised by the fact that the Human Genome Diversity Project has shown that humans share the vast majority of their genes with animals, especially with primates. The Genome Project "far from fixing 'proper' human identity . . . has shown it to be impure and fluid from the start," illustrating "profound interconnections and shared genetic identity, with everyone drawing on a common gene pool" (Shildrick 2004:162, 160).

This more recent feminist focus on science, especially biological science, in attempting to sort out sex, sexuality, and gender returns to but confounds the old nature/nurture problem that the sex/gender and biology/social distinctions were to address. The distinctions were initially a fruitful way for feminism to mount important critiques of social-cultural gender inequity, but they were always unstable. Understanding the complexity of our animality is a part of the recognition that dichotomies, in any context, are poor science and poor sociology.

GENDER AND FUTURE RESEARCH: WHAT MIGHT BE DONE

As the discussion above illustrates, the concept of gender has proven to be ambiguous, complex, and contradictory, and this is unlikely to change in the near future. In the midst of the debates, Chafetz's (1999) point is worth remembering: "All theory pertaining to gender is not feminist, although all feminist theory centers much or all of its attention on gender" (p. 4). There is still a need to unpack the "taken-for-granted assumptions about gender that pervade sociological research, and social life generally" (Ferree, Lorber, and Hess 1999:xii). For example, Stephanie Knaak (2004) points out that when the "standard 'gender = male/female' variable" is used in research "as the main proxy for gender," this superficial assumption threatens the "overall quality of our research" (p. 312).

There are some directions that might be fruitfully explored in the future, although they by no means exhaust all possibilities; others may have quite different ideas of how to go on in the sociological enterprise. One suggestion is to "bring men back in." Jeff Hearn (2004) suggests that it is

> time to go back from *masculinity* to *men,* to examine the hegemony of men and about men. The hegemony of men seeks to address the double complexity that men are both a *social category formed by the gender system* and *dominant collective and individual agents of social practices.* (P. 59)

Hearn points out that "men" are "*formed in* men's hegemony . . . and *form* that hegemony" and that the individual as well as the collective hegemony of men is reproduced and contested in all societies "both as a social category and in men's practices" (p. 61). Tania Modleski (1991), however, registers a caution with respect to scholars who, under the guise of feminist sympathies, appropriate "feminist analysis" to "negate the critiques and undermine the goals of feminism—in effect delivering us back to a prefeminist world" (p. 3).

The second direction to explore in greater depth is the way in which control by bio-power is deployed on a global scale as bio-political power. Rather than the disciplined subject "whose behaviour expresses internalized social norms," control, according to Clough (2003), "aims at a never-ending modulation of moods, capacities, affects, potentialities, assembled in genetic codes, identification numbers, ratings profiles and preference listings; that is to say, bodies of data and information (including the human body as information and data" (p. 360). If sex and gender are deployed as "natural" binaries in national and global statistical reports about "distributed chances of life and death, health and morbidity, fertility and infertility, happiness and unhappiness, freedom and imprisonment"

(p. 361), the use of such information for any emancipatory practices is limited. For this reason, a return to macrolevel stratification theory on the order of Lenski's application of POET—"population, organization, ecology and technology"—as suggested by Huber (2004:259), could be useful.

Gender theorists still contend with "two powerful, mutually canceling truths in feminism: on the one hand, there is no stable sex or gender and on the other, women too often find themselves unable to escape their gender and the sexual norms governing it" (Brown 2003:366). These two conceptions must also contend with the frequent reports of the "death of feminism," most particularly from a variety of conservative, often religiously inspired, traditionalists—both male and female (Hawkesworth 2004). The view from the antifeminist or nonfeminist women must not be simplistically dismissed as "false consciousness"; what is needed is to "know how they think as they do, how and in what terms and with what conflicts they experience their femininity" (Scott 1997:701).

Finally, sociologists as gender theorists need to contend with the tendency of the discipline to marginalize or co-opt gender issues, especially when these issues are linked to systems of inequality in the politics of everyday life (Young 1994). This returns us to the initial starting point of feminist appropriation of gender—the recognition that the concept is a political, economic, and social marker of inequality, whatever its theoretical stability. As Nancy Fraser and Nancy A. Naples (2003) contend, some of the debates in recent feminist theory that tended to see inequities as problems of culture left us "defenseless against free-market fundamentalism" and helped to "consolidate a tragic historic disjunction between theory and practice" (p. 1117). This is particularly troubling given the "acceleration of globalization" and the transformation of "circumstances of justice" by undermining the sovereignty of states. The struggle over governance as "representation" must therefore be added to the "(economic) dimension of redistribution and the (cultural) dimension of recognition."

The above suggestions are but a few that emerge from feminist struggles with the concept of gender. The issues, like all the issues and debates outlined above, are not confined to the disciplinary boundaries of sociology however they may be construed. But if sociology is to have any relevance in the twenty-first century, then gender, as a critical focus of sociological analysis, is important, especially if sociology is to be true to its origins as an engaged political and ethical scientific practice.

25

THE SOCIOLOGY OF SEXUALITY

JOHN DELAMATER

MICHELLE HASDAY
University of Wisconsin–Madison

THEORIES OF SEXUALITY

Many disciplines contribute to an understanding of human sexuality. While disciplines in the humanities address the range of behaviors, thoughts, and feelings associated with human sexuality, it is the sciences that seek to create and evaluate overarching explanatory theories.

Assessing the development of sexual theory, Irvine (2003) claims that sociology "has an impressive history of denaturalizing sex and theorizing its social origins in a body of scholarship dating from the early twentieth-century Chicago School" (p. 430), which viewed non-institutional forms of sexual expression as the result of a breakdown in informal controls such as family and neighborhood. Anthropologist Gayle Rubin notes that "the work of establishing a social science approach to sex . . . and challenging the privileged role of psychiatry in the study of human sexuality was mostly accomplished by sociologists" (as cited in Irvine 2003:430).

Based on the fundamental assumption that human behavior is socially learned, sociological theories of sexuality do not deny the existence of forces inherent in individuals. Rather, they assert that the specific thoughts and behaviors exhibited by individuals are a product of social rather than biological forces. This position is taken by Kimmel and Fracher, who state, "That we are sexual is determined by a biological imperative toward reproduction, but how we are sexual—where, when, how often, with whom, and why—has to do with cultural learning, with meanings transmitted in a cultural setting" (as cited in Longmore 1998:44).

Two sociological frameworks have substantially influenced the study of human sexuality, symbolic interactionism and scripting theory. Both perspectives fall within the broad paradigm of social constructionism (Berger and Luckmann 1966), the premise of which is that there is no objective reality; rather, reality is socially constructed. Such social construction rests on language, which enables humans to form shared meanings of experienced phenomena. These meanings in turn shape subsequent experience and behavior.

Symbolic Interactionism

Symbolic interaction theory is based on the writing and teaching of George Herbert Mead. For symbolic interactionists, objects acquire meaning, thus becoming symbols, through communication. The self is seen as not only subject but also object, and like other objects, it too becomes imbued with meaning through interaction. Importantly, the self is seen not only as an object to others but also to oneself. That is, people have the ability to take on the role of others and thus see the self as others see it—objectified. This view of self as other contributes to behavioral decision making, because people act in ways intended to foster certain perceptions of themselves on the part of others.

Within symbolic interactionism, there are two schools of thought with distinct methods of inquiry. Situational symbolic interactionists "focus on how individuals define situations and thereby construct the realities in which they live" (Longmore 1998:46). Accordingly, they study face-to-face interactions using predominately qualitative methods like ethnography, in-depth interview, and participant observation to uncover the individual and interactional construction of situations. Structural symbolic interactionists, on the other hand, focus on the ways in which location in the social structure influences the self and the self's construction of reality and thus tend to use quantitative methods like statistical survey analysis to examine the relationships between individuals and their location within the large institutions that comprise social structure. In studying sexuality, both analyze the way in which people construct their sexual realities, from which follow their sexual beliefs and practices.

For structuralists, major social institutions thought to influence sexuality are religion, family, economy, law, and medicine. Each institution is associated with a sexual ideology or discourse (Foucault 1998). Most religions in the United States promulgate the Judeo-Christian ideology, which emphasizes marital relationships as the appropriate context for sexual intimacy. Religious leaders use this discourse in public statements and official documents; the clergy base their interactions with parishioners on it. Economic institutions promote capitalism; income requires employment, and households (families) require income. Thus, the economy has profound effects on patterns of sexuality, especially marriage and childbearing (Teachman, Tedrow, and Crowder 2000). The family has traditionally been a strong institution, supported by both religion and the legal system and associated with a discourse that emphasizes family functions of support and child rearing, norms of fidelity, and the incest taboo. Medicine has become increasingly important in the conceptualization and control of sexuality, a trend referred to as the *medicalization of sexuality* (Tiefer 2004). The medical discourse defines certain aspects of sexual functioning in terms of health and illness and prescribes treatment for problems of sexual functioning. The influence of this discourse has increased dramatically with the widespread marketing of drugs to improve sexual functioning. Finally, there is law, which defines certain sexual practices as illegal and creates social controls that are used to enforce the law. Ultimately, the legal system reflects the interests of dominant groups in the society.

Scripting Theory

The premise of scripting theory is that sexual behavior "is the result of elaborate prior learning that teaches us an etiquette of sexual behavior" (Hyde and DeLamater 2006:40). During the 1970s, Simon and Gagnon explained that "without the proper elements of a script that defines the situation, names the actors, and plots the behavior, little is likely to happen" (as cited in Longmore 1998:51). Socially learned sexual scripts tell people who to have sex with (e.g., what the race, gender, and age of an appropriate sexual partner should be), when and where it is appropriate to have sex, and what acts are appropriate once sexual behavior is initiated.

Sexual scripts are not rigid or absolute. Accordingly, scripting is theorized on three levels: cultural, interpersonal, and intrapsychic. Cultural sexual scripts are defined as "the instructions for sexual and other conduct that are embedded in the cultural narratives that are provided as guides or instructions for all conduct" (Laumann et al. 1994:6). However, these cultural scripts are interpreted on both interpersonal and intrapsychic levels, which accounts for both the range of sexual behaviors and the sense of individual expression inherent in sexual encounters. Laumann et al. (1994) defined interpersonal scripts as "the structured patterns of interaction in which individuals as actors engage in everyday interpersonal conduct," and intrapsychic scripts as "the plans and fantasies by which individuals guide and reflect on their past, current, or future conduct" (p. 6). Thus, the intrapsychic dimension of scripting allows individuals to derive personal meaning from cultural scripts, while the interpersonal dimension opens the door for situational symbolic interactionism, where reality is defined by interaction.

Sociologists studying sexuality also make use of two additional frameworks. These are the social exchange framework, which is based upon economic as well as sociological principles, and sexual strategies theory, which falls under the umbrella of evolutionary psychology.

Social Exchange Theory

The social exchange framework, developed in the 1960s, focuses on the exchange of resources between people and has been used extensively in the study of relationships. All social exchange theories share a number of basic principles centered on the concepts of rewards, costs, and reciprocity (Sprecher 1998). Specifically, social exchange models share three basic assumptions: "(a) Social behavior is a series of exchanges; (b) individuals attempt to maximize their rewards and minimize their costs; and (c) when individuals receive rewards from others, they feel obligated to reciprocate" (p. 32). These principles are applied to the exchange of sexual resources for other resources that can be sexual or nonsexual, such as intimacy, commitment, social position, or money. People are portrayed as entering, staying in, and leaving sexual relationships based on the reward-cost balance experienced. The interpersonal exchange model of sexual satisfaction (Byers 2005) focuses on the exchange of specifically sexual resources and consequences for sexual satisfaction; other theories look at relationship satisfaction more generally. As a group, these theories have been applied to understanding and predicting sexual behaviors, including partner selection, premarital sex, relationship longevity or dissolution, and extradyadic sexual relationships.

Sexual Strategies Theory

Much contemporary social research into human sexuality is based on sexual strategies theory (Buss 1998), which falls within the evolutionary psychology paradigm. The premise of evolutionary psychology is that sexual selection in the early stages of human evolution resulted in the proliferation of certain traits in men and women that continue to be present today. One example would be that men are sexually jealous because in the ancestral environment it was more likely that women would bear the children of jealous mates than of nonjealous mates and thus more likely that the trait of male jealousy would be perpetuated in their (male) offspring.

Sexual strategies theory places desire at the foundation of human sexuality. Its arguments are based on the premise that not only do men and women have different problems to overcome to ensure mating success but also that they have to negotiate differing problems in short-term versus long-term mating. Accordingly, the theory looks at what qualities will be desired by men and women when pursuing short-term versus long-term mates, as well as when and why each sex might desire one type of mate over the other. Predictions based on this theory have included sex differences in the desire for sexual variety and sexual jealously, and what contexts will trigger sexual conflict between men and women (Buss 1998). Sexual strategies theory's compatibility with sociological theories is based on its emphasis on the importance of context in determining how sexual desire will manifest in mating decisions. Thus, while sexual strategies theory suggests that there are some universals in what men and women look for in mates, it leaves a great deal of room for how social context influences everything from when and why they pursue particular strategies to how their desires might be shaped by social position.

THE HISTORY OF SEX RESEARCH

The history of empirical sociological research on sexuality can be traced to Kinsey, Pomeroy, and Martin's (1948, 1953) landmark volumes, based on interview data from thousands of men and women. Although Kinsey et al. did not use representative sampling techniques, they did attempt to produce a heterogeneous sample by interviewing members of diverse groups. The first qualitative study of sexual expression to achieve wide recognition was Humphreys's (1970) *Tearoom Trade*, an observational study of men who have sex in public restrooms. The first survey of representative samples of 18- to 23-year-olds was reported by DeLamater and MacCorquodale (1979); and the first survey of a representative sample of the U.S. population, ages 18–59, was reported in 1994 (Laumann et al. 1994).

Between 1995 and 2005, several surveys of representative samples of subpopulations have been carried out and the results analyzed, most notably the Add Health survey of teens. Ethnographic and interview studies have been conducted on a wide variety of noninstitutional forms of sexuality. Research combining quantitative and qualitative research, such as Laumann et al.'s (2004) study of four neighborhoods within the city of Chicago, are beginning to appear and are especially valuable for the breadth of material they provide.

SEXUAL EXPRESSION

There is a great variety of ways in which humans derive sexual satisfaction. One continuum for sexual expression is the involvement of other persons, ranging from asexuality through autoerotic sexuality, partnered sexuality, and finally multipartnered sexuality at the other extreme.

Asexuality

Asexuality refers to having no sexual attraction to a person of either sex (Bogaert 2004). In a national sample of 18,000 British residents, about 1 percent reported no sexual attraction. The National Health and Social Life Survey (NHSLS) (Laumann et al. 1994) involved interviews with 3,432 Americans ages 18–59; 4 percent of male and 11 percent of female respondents reported having no sexual partner and engaging in little autoerotic activity in the preceding 12 months. In both studies, those who reported little or no sexual activity were more likely to be single (including divorced, widowed), older, and less educated. It is likely that some/many of these persons do not experience sexual desire or attraction to others.

Autoeroticism

Sexual self-stimulation can be produced by masturbation or by fantasy. In the NHSLS (Laumann et al. 1994), 62 percent of men and 42 percent of women reported masturbating in the past year; 27 percent of men and 8 percent of women reported masturbating at least once a week. Masturbation is not a substitute for partnered activity; people who report more frequent masturbation report more frequent partnered sex. A survey of older adults found that 35 percent of men and 20 percent of women ages 60–69 reported masturbation; among both, the principal correlate was frequency of sexual desire (DeLamater and Moorman, forthcoming).

Sexual fantasy refers to sexual thoughts or images that alter a person's emotions or physiological state. Most men and women, including gays and lesbians, report having sexual fantasies; men are more likely to fantasize about sexual activity, whereas women fantasize about playing a role in sexual interaction (Leitenberg and Henning 1995). Sexual fantasy may enhance one's sense of attractiveness, provide opportunities for rehearsing sexual scripts, increase sexual arousal, and facilitate orgasm.

Dyadic Relationships

Casual Relationships

Two kinds of casual relationships are common: casual dating relationships and casual sexual relationships. Casual dating commonly begins in adolescence. The precursor to dating is generally mixed-gender group friendships that form in preadolescence. These are followed developmentally by group dating, then by dyadic (or couple) dating, and finally by cohabitation and/or marriage. As teens move from mixed-gender friendship to group dating to couple dating, their levels of intimacy, commitment, emotional maturity, and sexual experience tend to increase (Connolly et al. 2004; Gallmeier, Knox, and Zusman 2002). Friendship networks often play important and varied roles in the dating process (Harper et al. 2004; Kuttler and La Greca 2004). In general, adolescent dating does not lead to long-term committed relationships but rather allows adolescents to develop and practice intimacy and communication skills for later relationships.

There is evidence that the context of teen sexual behavior shifted in the 1990s to relationships as opposed to casual sexual contexts (Risman and Schwartz 2002). Most adult sexual behavior occurs in the context of marriage (Hyde and DeLamater 2006). Thus, casual sex is most commonly the province of young adults ages 19–25. There is good reason to believe that practices such as "hooking up" have now become normative in college settings. Young adults, however, do not seem entirely comfortable with these practices. Lambert, Kahn, and Apple (2003) report that college women and men were less comfortable with many casual sexual behaviors than they thought their same-sex friends were, and that women and men both believed that members of the opposite sex were more comfortable with such behaviors than they really were. Lambert et al. conclude that "it is likely that most students believe others engage in these hooking-up behaviors primarily because they enjoy doing so, while they see themselves engaging in these behaviors primarily due to peer pressure" (p. 132). In their article on sexual compliance (which is agreeing to have sex with someone when it is not genuinely desired), Impett and Peplau (2003) offer another explanation for why women may engage in casual sex, namely, "to increase the probability of a long-term commitment from their sexual partners" (p. 97).

Committed Relationships

Many adolescents and adults form close or intimate relationships with others, relationships characterized by affective, cognitive, and physical closeness. Intimacy often grows out of self-disclosure by each person, creating a sense of a unique relationship. Many people believe that it is appropriate for two people who are committed to each other or "in love" to engage in sexual intimacy. Beliefs about the appropriateness of sexual activity with particular kinds of persons reflect social norms that are embedded in the groups one belongs to and enforced by friends and family. The norms in most societies include homogamy in sexual relationships, that is, that the partner be of similar age, race/ethnicity, religion, and social status. A common pattern among adolescents and adults in some societies is serial monogamy, in which people engage in a series of intimate relationships, often being faithful while in a relationship. For some people, this is a stage in development as the person moves from more casual relationships to a committed, long-term or lifelong relationship. According to the NHSLS, among married persons, ages 20–29, in the United States, 40 percent of the men and 28 percent of the women had two or more sexual partners prior to marriage (Laumann et al. 1994).

Cohabitation refers to an unmarried (heterosexual) couple living together (whether or not they share only one residence). These relationships represent commitment, because the couple is making a public declaration of their sexual relationship. In some developed countries, cohabitation is an alternative to marriage. In the United States, in 2000, 5 percent of all households were composed of unmarried partners; 90 percent of these involved a heterosexual couple, 5 percent involved two men, and 5 percent involved two women (U.S. Bureau of the Census 2005). One-third of heterosexual cohabiting relationships last less than one year. Sixty percent lead to marriage; these marriages are more likely to end in divorce than marriages not preceded by cohabitation (Smith 2003).

Marriage refers to a relationship between two people based on a religious or legal compact. The compact confers recognition and certain rights on partners in an intimate sexual relationship. For centuries, most societies have had established procedures for and recognized marriages involving one man and one woman. Some societies now provide for and recognize marital relationships involving two men or two women, including Belgium, Canada, the Netherlands, and Spain. In the United States, a few states allow such marriages as of 2006. At least 90 percent of the men and women in almost every country in the world marry (United Nations 2000), with men generally marrying at older ages than women. Marriage is the social relationship within which sexual expression has the most (in some countries the only) legitimacy. The frequency of and specific practices that make up sexual expression reflect social norms. In the United States, the frequency of vaginal intercourse within marriage ranges from twice a week among couples ages 18–29 to twice a month among couples ages 60–69 (Smith 2003). It is likely that a similar decline occurs in most societies. The frequency of sexual intercourse in a long-term relationship reflects both biological (changes associated with aging, illness) and social (habituation to partner, quality of the relationship) factors. There is wide variation in frequency, with some young couples who never engage in intercourse and some older couples who engage in it several times per week. Other forms of sexual expression also occur in marriage, including oral-genital sexuality, anal intercourse, and bondage and discipline. Couples also report the use of sex toys and erotic materials.

Extramarital sexual activity is reported by 25 percent of married men and 15 percent of married women (Laumann et al. 1994). Typically, the spouse is unaware of such activity. Many men and women will engage in this activity only once while they are married, although others engage in it throughout their marriages. The incidence varies by ethnicity; 27 percent of blacks report extramarital sexual activity compared with 14 percent of whites (Smith 2003). Hispanics report the same incidence as whites (Laumann et al. 1994). Several reasons have been suggested for extramarital relationships, including perceived inequity (Sprecher 1998), dissatisfaction with marital sexual relationships, dissatisfaction with or conflict within the marriage, and placing greater emphasis on personal growth and pleasure than fidelity (Lawson 1988). Recent research has broadened the study of "cheating" by looking at couples who are cohabiting or in a committed relationship and inquiring about involvement with a third person. One study of such extradyadic relations, with a sample of 349 persons ages 17–70 (48 percent married), found that 28 percent of men and 29 percent of women had cheated on a current partner (Hicks and Leitenberg 2001).

Nondyadic Sexual Relationships

Polyamory is emotional and sexual involvement with more than one person at a time, with the informed consent of all parties. Relationships can be centered around a primary relationship between two people (one or both of whom have secondary relationships), they can be hinged (where one person has equal relationships with two or more other persons but the others do not have relationships with each other), or they can be group relationships (where three or more people are all involved with one another equally). Additionally, they can be open, which means that relationship partners are free to take on additional lovers, or closed, which means members are restricted to established relationships. Sometimes two of the people in a polyamorous arrangement are legally married. Polyamorous people may live with none, one, or more than one of their relationship partners. The main distinguishing features are more than one sexual partner (distinguishing it from monogamy), an emotional connection to all partners (distinguishing it from swinging and other casual sexual arrangements), and complete honesty with all partners (distinguishing it from cheating). Polyamory is also characterized by nonpossessiveness, acceptance of varied sexual practices and identities, and high levels of gender equality. These characteristics distinguish it from the more traditional and historically rooted practice of polygamy (Wikipedia 2005). For many practitioners, polyamory is

not simply a type of relationship but a philosophical way of life. This is especially true of people in open polyamorous relationships (Ramey 1975).

Although there are no precise estimates of incidence, there are some indications that polyamory may be practiced by a sizeable minority. According to a survey by Blumstein and Schwartz (1983), 15 percent of married couples and 28 percent of cohabiting (heterosexual) couples had "an understanding that allows non-monogamy under some circumstances" (p. 585). Of course, it is not known which of these "understandings" are truly polyamorous, as opposed to an allowance for occasional one-night stands, for example. There has been very little scholarly attention given to polyamory. While the instability of the monogamous nuclear family has been widely discussed, cohabitation and not polyamory has emerged as a common relationship alternative. Additionally, polyamory has not leveraged the same degree of political visibility as homosexuality. Those studies that have been performed were conducted in the 1980s (e.g., Rubin and Adams 1986). Thus, we have no accurate sense of how many people practice polyamory currently, how their practices are conducted and perceived, or whether there are significant differences in couple stability, happiness, and other characteristics of sexual relationships or personal development.

SEXUALITY THROUGH THE LIFE COURSE

In this section, we will outline the process of sexual development that occurs across a person's life. This process is a biopsychosocial one, influenced by biological maturation/ aging, progression through socially defined stages, and by the person's relationships with others.

Childhood (Birth–7 Years)

The capacity for sexual response is present from birth. Male infants have erections, and vaginal lubrication has been found in female infants in the 24 hours after birth (Masters, Johnson, and Kolodny 1982). Infants have been observed fondling their genitals; the rhythmic manipulation associated with adult masturbation appears at ages 2½ to 3 (Martinson 1994). In the United States, children between the ages of 3 and 7 show a marked increase in sexuality. They form a conception of marriage or long-term relationships and of adult roles. They learn that there are genital differences between males and females (Goldman and Goldman 1982) and may show interest in the genitals of others. Children may engage in heterosexual play, for example, "playing doctor." Although there is little impact of childhood sex play on sexual adjustment at ages 17 and 18 (Okami, Olmstead, and Abramson 1997), in response to such play, parents may teach children not to touch the bodies of others, or their own genitals, and may restrict conversation about sex. This leads many children to rely on their peers for sexual information.

The quality of relationships with parents is very important to the child's capacity for sexual and emotional relationships later in life. Early childhood is also the period during which each child forms a gender identity, a sense of maleness or femaleness, and begins to be socialized according to the gender-role norms of the society (Bussey and Bandura 1999). Such gender identities eventually become vital components of adolescent and adult sexuality.

Preadolescence (8–12 Years)

In many societies, children at this age have a homosocial organization, that is, the social division of males and females into separate groups (Thorne 1993). One result is that sexual exploration and learning at this stage is likely to involve persons of the same sex. In some societies, this separation continues throughout life. During this period, more children gain experience with masturbation. About 40 percent of the women and 38 percent of the men in a sample of U.S. college students recall masturbating before puberty (Bancroft, Herbenik, and Reynolds 2003). U.S. adolescents report that their first experience of sexual attraction occurred at ages 10–12 (Rosario et al. 1996), with the first experience of sexual fantasies occurring several months to one year later. Group dating and heterosexual parties may emerge at the end of this period.

Adolescence (13–19 Years)

The biological changes associated with puberty lead to a surge of sexual interest. These changes begin as early as age 10 and as late as age 14, and include increases in levels of sex hormones, which may produce sexual attractions and fantasies. In the United States, many males begin masturbating between ages 13 and 15; the onset is more gradual among women (Bancroft et al. 2003). Bodily changes during puberty include physical growth, growth in genitals and girls' breasts, and development of facial and pubic hair, and they signal to the youth and to others that she or he is becoming sexually mature.

Several psychosocial developmental tasks face adolescents. One is developing a stable identity. Gender identity is a very important aspect of identity; in later adolescence, the young person may emerge with a stable, self-confident sense of manhood or womanhood, or alternatively may be in conflict about gender roles. A sexual identity also emerges—a sense that one is bisexual, heterosexual, or homosexual—and a sense of one's attractiveness to others. An important influence is the cultural norms regarding gender roles and sexual identities. Another task in adolescence is learning how to manage physical and emotional intimacy in relationships with others (Collins and Sroufe 1999). In the United States, youth ages 10–15 most frequently name the mass media, including movies, TV,

magazines, and music, as their source of information about sex and intimacy. Smaller percentages name parents, peers, sexuality education programs, and professionals as sources (Kaiser Family Foundation 1997). Youth learn different relationship and sexual scripts depending on which are most influential.

While biological changes, especially increases in testosterone, create the possibility of adult sexual interactions, social factors interact with them, either facilitating or inhibiting sexual expression (Udry 1988). Permissive attitudes regarding sexual behavior are associated with increased masturbation and the onset of partnered sexual activity, whereas restrictive attitudes and participation in religious institutions are associated with lower levels of sexual activity.

Toward the middle and the end of adolescence in the United States, more young people engage in heterosexual intercourse. Women are engaging in sexual intercourse for the first time at younger ages compared with young women 35 years ago (Trussel and Vaughn 1991). In the United States, patterns of premarital intercourse vary by ethnic group. African Americans have intercourse for the first time, on average, at 15.7 years, whites at 16.6 years, Hispanics at 17 years, and Asian American men at 18.1 years. Among blacks and Hispanics, men begin having intercourse at younger ages than women (Upchurch et al. 1998). These variations reflect differences in family structure, church attendance, and socioeconomic opportunities in the larger society (Day 1992). It is likely that similar differences are characteristic of other developed, multiracial societies.

Changing rates of premarital intercourse are associated with two long-term trends in Western societies. First, the age of menarche has been falling steadily since the beginning of the twentieth century. The average age is 12.5 years for African Americans and 12.7 years for whites (Hofferth 1990). Second, the age of first marriage has been rising. In the United States, in 1960, first marriages occurred at (median) age 20.3 for women and 22.8 for men; in 2003, it was 25.3 years for women and 27.1 years for men (U.S. Bureau of the Census 2004). The effect is a substantial lengthening of the time between biological readiness and marriage; that gap is typically 12–15 years today. Thus, many more young adults are having sex before they get married than in the 1960s. In the United States, many sexually active teenage persons do not use contraception, which led to a corresponding rise in pregnancy rates among single adolescents from 1970 to 1991. However, from 1991 to 1999, the rate of teen pregnancy declined by 25 percent.

This recent decline in teenage pregnancy rates reflects increased attention to the importance of pregnancy prevention, increased access to birth control, and increased economic opportunities for teenagers (Ventura et al. 2001). However, there may be other factors in this decline as well. Examining teen sexual behavior trends more closely, Risman and Schwartz (2002) emphasize the steadily decreasing percentages of sexually active teens throughout the 1990s, as documented by reliable and well-sampled studies. They hypothesize that as cultural norms for female sexuality have changed to allow and even expect premarital sexual activity, patterns of teen sexual behavior have shifted—first sexual intercourse now happens most often within the context of nonmarital relationships. Given evidence that women are more responsible regarding risks of disease and pregnancy (Risman and Schwartz 2002), girls' greater control of sexual intercourse would certainly help account for trends of decreasing teen pregnancy.

In the United States, 10 percent of adolescent males report having sexual experiences with someone of the same gender, compared with 6 percent of adolescent females (Bancroft et al. 2003). These adolescents usually report that their first experience was with another adolescent. In some cases, the person has only one or a few such experiences and the behavior is discontinued.

Adulthood

Our discussion of forms of sexual expression identified several sexual lifestyle options that are available to adults. One task in this life stage is learning to communicate effectively with partners in intimate relationships. A second task is developing the ability to make informed decisions about reproduction and prevention of sexually transmitted infections.

A significant challenge facing adults, particularly those who have chosen to enter long-term dyadic relationships, is the changes most will eventually experience. These changes may result from developing greater understanding of self or partner, changes in the nature and content of communication, accidents or illnesses that alter one's sexual responsiveness, or major stressors associated with family or career roles. Again, we see the combined effects of biological, psychological, and social influences on sexuality.

The dissolution of a long-term relationship is a major life stage transition, and persons who experience it, especially women, face complex problems of adjustment. These problems may include reduced income, lower standard of living, the demands of single parenthood, and reduced availability of social support (Amato 2001). These problems may increase the motivation to reestablish a relationship, though at the same time making it difficult to do so.

Persons who lose their partner through divorce or death have the option of new sexual relationships. In the United States, most divorced women, but fewer widows, develop an active sexual life; 28 percent of divorced women and 81 percent of the widowed report being sexually abstinent in the preceding year (Smith 2003). By gender, 46 percent of divorced and widowed men and 58 percent of divorced and widowed women reported engaging in sexual intercourse a few times or not at all in the preceding year (Laumann

et al. 1994). There is a higher probability of being sexually active postmaritally for those who are under 35 and have no children at home (Stack and Gundlach 1992). Men and women with low incomes report relatively higher rates of partner acquisition after dissolution of a cohabiting or marital relationship (Wade and DeLamater 2002).

Sexuality and Aging

Biology, a major influence in childhood and adolescence, again becomes a significant influence on sexuality at midlife (ages 50–60). In women, menopause is associated with a decline in the production of estrogen, beginning between the ages of 40 and 60. The decline in estrogen causes the vaginal walls to become thin and inelastic, and the vagina itself to shrink in width and length. By five years after menopause, the amount of vaginal lubrication often decreases noticeably. These changes make penile insertion more difficult and vaginal intercourse uncomfortable or even painful. There are a number of ways to deal with these changes, including estrogen replacement therapy, supplemental testosterone, and use of a sterile lubricant.

As men age, they experience andropause (Lamberts, van den Beld, and van der Lely 1997), a gradual decline in the production of testosterone; this may begin as early as age 40. Erections occur more slowly. The refractory period, the period following orgasm during which the man cannot be sexually aroused, lengthens. These changes may be experienced as a problem; on the other hand, they may be experienced as giving the man greater control over orgasm.

In addition to such biological changes, an important influence on sexuality is the attitudes held by others and derived from the culture, particularly those attitudes that define specific behaviors as acceptable or unacceptable. This is especially evident with regard to older persons. In the United States, there is a negative attitude toward sexual expression among the elderly. It seems inappropriate for two 75-year-old people to engage in sexual intimacy, and especially to masturbate. These attitudes are quite obvious in residential-care facilities where rules prohibit or staff members frown upon sexual activity among the residents. These attitudes affect the way the elderly are treated and the attitudes of the elderly themselves and may, in fact, be a more important reason why many elderly are not sexually active than the biological changes they experience. In the United States, analysis of survey data from a representative sample of more than 1,300 persons ages 45 and older found that negative attitudes toward sex for older persons was associated with reduced sexual desire (DeLamater and Sill 2005). Another major influence on sexual behavior is the presence of a healthy partner. As persons age, they may lose the partner through death; in some cultures, including the United States, women in heterosexual relationships are much more likely to experience this than men.

THE EFFECTS OF SOCIAL GROUP MEMBERSHIP ON SEXUALITY

Sexuality varies as a function of individual experience and is influenced by cultural norms. However, it is also influenced by membership in certain social categories. In the United States, sexual behavior and attitudes vary systematically by gender, social class, ethnicity, and religion.

Gender

Throughout this chapter, we have noted research that has documented the variations in sexual expression by gender in the United States. Women are more likely to report little or no sexual activity in the preceding year. Fewer women than men report masturbating in the past year or the past month. Women are less approving of and less likely to report sexual activity with casual partners. Men in some racial/ethnic groups report engaging in intercourse for the first time at younger ages than women. Following the loss of a partner, especially to death, women are less likely to resume sexual activity. Several explanations for these differences have been offered. One emphasizes the role of cultural factors, particularly differing norms for male and female sexual behavior, often referred to as the double standard. Some cultural groups are more accepting of sexual behavior and sexual exploration by men than by women. There may be several reasons, including the fact that women carry pregnancies and give birth, and that society (men) wants to control women's sexuality to ensure paternity of any children. Another explanation relies on the concept of sexual scripts. The traditional sexual script specifies the male as the initiator of sexual activity and the female as the object of male advances; thus, males engage in more sexual activity. Additionally, women tend to place more importance on the interpersonal as opposed to sexual aspect of relationships, which has been offered as an explanation for research showing women to be less permissive regarding premarital and extramarital sex but more tolerant of homosexuality than men (Treas 2002).

Recent trends, however, suggest that traditional norms of female sexuality are changing. People of both sexes, especially those who are younger and more educated, are becoming more accepting of premarital sex for women (Treas 2002). A review of 30 studies found that the double standard still exists but is influenced by situational and interpersonal factors, and that it differs across ethnic and cultural groups (Crawford and Popp 2003). According to Risman and Schwartz (2002), American college women find premarital sex equally acceptable for men and women in the context of relationships and equally unacceptable for both sexes outside of relationships.

Social Class

Using education as the measure of class, research in the United States reports differences in sexuality by class (Laumann et al. 1994). Education is positively related to both frequency of masturbation and frequency of orgasm from masturbation, among both men and women. Education is also positively associated with whether persons engage in active and receptive oral sex; men and women with advanced degrees are much more likely to have engaged in both than men and women who did not finish high school. There is a weaker relationship between education and participation in anal intercourse. Thus, greater education is associated with greater variety of sexual practices. It is also associated with greater acceptance of varieties of sexual behavior in others, although the gap between those with less education and those with more has declined between 1972 and 1998, due to a decline in disapproval for minority sexual practices among the less educated (Treas 2002).

Race/Ethnicity

In the United States, as in many other societies, race/ethnicity is associated with social class. Members of racial and ethnic minority groups disproportionately are found among the poorer and less-educated members of society. Variations in sexual behavior across these groups are the result of differing cultural heritages, as well as differences in current economic and social conditions. Thus, it is difficult to clearly attribute the source of observed differences.

African Americans

Black men and women are much less likely to report masturbation in the past year compared with members of other groups. They are also less likely to report having engaged in active oral sex. These may reflect differences in religious traditions. Black men and women are twice as likely as whites to remain single at ages 30–34. This reflects, in part, the gender ratio among African Americans; there are only 84 men for every 100 women. It also reflects the obstacles that black men encounter in seeking and keeping employment that provides enough income to support a family. Finally, blacks are twice as likely as whites to report two sexual partners in the preceding year, which may reflect the larger percent who are single.

Interesting data on differences in sexual expression by race/ethnicity are reported from the Chicago Health and Social Life Survey (CHSLS) (Laumann et al. 2004). Using a combination of sample surveys, key informant interviews, and ethnographic data, a nuanced analysis is provided of four neighborhoods. Southtown is an African American neighborhood with high unemployment; one-fifth of the households are below the poverty line; the churches are the social center of the community. Residents have relatively nonpermissive attitudes toward homosexuality and abortion but are relatively accepting of premarital sex, cohabitation, and divorce. There is a high incidence of multipartnering; almost half report two or more sexual partners in the last year and 40 percent of the men report having two partners concurrently.

Latinos

In the United States, Latino is used to refer to persons from several cultural backgrounds, including Cuban Americans, Mexican Americans, and Puerto Ricans. Despite many differences, these groups have a distinct cultural heritage, heavily influenced by the Roman Catholic religious tradition. Latino culture is relatively conservative sexually. The CHSLS provides an analysis of the (primarily Mexican American) Westside neighborhood in Chicago in which residents were found to have very strict attitudes about sexuality, and there was strong social disapproval of premarital sex and homosexuality. Few (14 percent) residents had had more than one partner in the past year; and more than half had never had a one-night stand (Laumann et al. 2004). Also, in traditional Latin American cultures, rigidly defined gender roles are emphasized in childhood socialization (Raffaelli and Ontai 2004).

Asian Americans

This category includes several different cultural groups, such as Chinese Americans and Japanese Americans, and newcomers such as Vietnamese Americans. In general, Asian cultures have had repressive attitudes toward sexuality. Core Asian values include collectivism, placing priority on family over individual, conformity to norms, and emotional control. As a result, Asian Americans are sexually conservative. They have the lowest incidence of multiple sexual partners and of same-gender sexual experience.

Religion

Religious affiliation and religiosity are correlated with sexual practices and attitudes. Research findings have shown that the primary influence on maintenance of female virginity is religious and moral values (Marsiglio, Scanzoni, and Broad 2000; Rostosky et al. 2004). Using General Social Survey data from 1972 to 1998, Treas (2002) found that more frequent attendance at religious services predicts the likelihood of condemning homosexual behaviors. There have been few studies examining the relationship between religiosity and sexual practices other than intercourse, the interactions between religiosity and romantic involvement in sexual behavior, and the effects of religiosity on racial minorities and men (Rostosky et al. 2004).

MEDIA AND SEXUALITY

The potential for media to affect socialization is well supported by many theoretical frameworks. Social learning theory is premised on the idea that people learn appropriate behavior based on whether behavior is rewarded or punished and recognizes the importance of observational learning. Scripting theory implies that "young people can easily learn scripts through watching television that establish when it is appropriate to have sex with someone or what outcomes one can expect from sexual encounters" (Farrar et al. 2003:9). Media influence people via cultivation, whereby people come to believe that media depictions are accurate representations of culture (Gerbner, Gross, and Morgan 2002), and agenda setting, the ability of media to shape what people see as important based on what they choose to depict and how they depict it.

Influences of media as a source of information have been documented. In a study by the Kaiser Family Foundation (1997), youth ages 10–15 most frequently named mass media as an information source about sexuality. Farrar et al. (2003) claim that "in the realm of sexual socialization, television is thought to contribute to young people's knowledge about sexual relationships, their judgments about social norms regarding sexual activity, and their attitudes about sexual behavior, among other influences" (p. 7). This statement has been supported by multiple studies (Farrar et al. 2003). Interest in what young people may be learning from the media is the motivation for content analysis, which is used to form a clearer picture of what messages are actually being presented by the mass media. Broad analyses of content are particularly important in realms like media where "influences on social beliefs, attitudes, and behaviors generally [occur] through a gradual and cumulative process that develops with repeated exposure over time to common and consistent messages" (p. 9).

Television

Analyses of sexual content in television are quite remarkable for the similarity in findings across different researchers and different genres. All television content analyses identify trends of increasing numbers of sexual behaviors and references (while references continue to be more common than behavior), increasing explicitness in sexual behaviors and references, and very few references to sexual risk or responsibility.

In 2000, Nielsen Media Research confirmed that prime time (8–11 p.m.) attracts the largest audience of any time of day. Seventeen of the 20 shows most frequently viewed by adolescents in 2000 were broadcast during prime-time hours (Farrar et al. 2003). The Parents Television Council (2000) found a 300 percent increase in the number and explicitness of sexual portrayals during prime time between 1989 and 1999. Farrar et al. (2003) found statistically significant increases in both percentage of programs including sexual behavior, and the average number of scenes per hour containing sexual behavior between 1997 and 2001. They also found that only 9 percent of shows with sexual content incorporated any messages of risk or responsibility. Twelve percent of all instances of sexual intercourse during prime time happen between characters who have just met—a risky sexual practice. Other studies have confirmed the significant lack of messages regarding the more dangerous aspects of sex like unwanted pregnancy and sexually transmitted diseases (Hyde and DeLamater 2006).

Analyses of television content outside prime-time hours have included studies of soap operas, cable movie networks, and music videos. Again, the messages are consistent. Greenberg and Busselle (1996) found that the most frequent sexual activity depicted in soap operas was sex between unmarried people, that soap operas contained an average of 6.6 sexual interludes per episode (in 1994), and that sexual safety was mentioned infrequently. Fisher et al. (2004) found that cable movie networks have the highest proportion of programs with sexual content, and that the most frequent portrayals are unmarried heterosexual intercourse. They also found that cable movie network programs often contained intercourse coupled with alcohol and drug use. Summarizing two decades of research on sex in music videos, Andsager and Roe (2003) found that sexual innuendo was very common (though explicit sex was not), that women were presented in revealing clothing or positions of implied nudity five to seven times more frequently than men, that women tended to be portrayed as subordinate sexual objects in traditionally female roles, and that even when women were portrayed as powerful and independent (which was rare), they were still generally highly sexualized.

Other Research

Many of the same trends seen in television have been found in analyses of other media. Greenberg and Busselle (1996) found that R-rated movies contain an average of 17.5 depictions of sexual behavior per hour, and that these depictions are significantly more explicit than sex during prime time. Analyses performed by Soley and Kurzbard (1986) and Reichert (2002) show trends of increasing proportions of advertisements with sexual content, increasing nudity and partial nudity in this sexual content (especially for women), and increasing explicitness in depictions of sexual behavior in advertisements across multiple mediums. Magazines are also responsible for a great deal of exposure to sexual content. One central theme of women's magazines is appearance, as it relates to the acquisition of sexual partners (Hyde and DeLamater 2006). A study of two globally top-selling women's magazines found that sex is the primary content (McCleneghan 2003). A closer look at *Cosmopolitan* showed that sex is portrayed as the source of female power in relationships as well as the workplace (Machin and Thornborrow 2003). And in one of the few sociological studies addressing effects, Thomsen, Weber, and Brown (2002) found correlations between adolescent females' reading of women's magazines and their practice of certain pathological dieting techniques. In the

recent decades, comparable men's lifestyle magazines have emerged, garnering a readership rivaling that of their female counterparts (Jackson et al. 1999). Analyses of men's lifestyle magazines have showed an overall trend of depicting a narrow male sexuality oriented toward sexual variety (Taylor 2005).

The Internet

The role of media in sexuality is not limited to purveyor of messages about sexuality. While "Personals" sections in newspapers have long been a means for people to actively use media to find relationship and sexual partners, the emergence of the Internet has truly normalized media use in the search for sex and love. As Internet use becomes more and more integrated into people's daily lives, one would expect its use to find partners to continue increasing as well. Social scientists have generated a number of hypotheses about the potential effects of Internet dating services. Like Tyler (2004), who refers to the use of personal advertisements and dating services as "the rational pursuit of the self as an entrepreneurial project" (p. 86), some are critical of this new phenomenon. However, others are excited about the possibilities of Internet use in dating by helping people with compatible (and sometimes atypical) interests, lifestyles, relationship desires, and sexual practices find one another. There has also been hope that online matching would encourage "deeper" interpersonal connections based on ideas, feelings, and other fundamental aspects of individual character by mitigating the role of appearance, although the realization of this hope must be questioned with the proliferation of pictures on dating sites.

While dating relationships are one forum for sexuality that has been affected by computers, sex outside the confines of a relationship (i.e., casual sex) has also been significantly affected. Internet chat rooms and message boards have provided a new (and immediate) way for those interested in casual sex to locate one another. The Internet has also created the practice of cybersex. These uses of the Internet in facilitating sexual communication and interaction, however, are more controversial than dating services. In a sample of 10- to 17-year-old Internet users, Finkelhor et al. (2000) found that about 20 percent had been sexually solicited over the Internet in the past year. The Internet has also been shown to be one way people establish and maintain extramarital sexual relationships (Hyde and DeLamater 2006).

Pornography

A discussion of the role of media in sexuality cannot responsibly omit the highly charged and controversial topic of pornography. The majority of research that has been done on the effects of pornography use is experimental as opposed to survey based, probably owing both to the suitability of experiments for exploring causality and the lack of reliable and representative data on pornography use. Thus, sociological inquiry has focused on the content of pornographic material. With the recent proliferation of Internet and computer use, sociologists are examining the role of changing media technologies in patterns of pornography access and use. The Internet is important because it offers the greatest (and often least expensive) access to pornography.

Acknowledging the increase of widely available pornographic media over the decades, Barron and Kimmel (2000) conducted an analysis comparing the content of magazine, video, and Internet (specifically Internet newsgroup, or Usenet) pornography, finding a highly significant and large increase in violent content on the Usenet compared with magazines and videos. They found that more than a quarter of Usenet scenes contained coercive or nonconsensual sex (compared to less than 5 percent for both magazines and videos). In Usenet scenes, men were disproportionately the perpetrators of violence and women the victims. Although this pattern was also seen in videos (though not magazines), unlike both videos and magazines, where the vast majority of violence occurred in the context of consensual relationships, the violence on the Usenet was primarily nonconsensual or coercive.

Focusing on the content of rape-themed Internet pornography, Gossett and Byrne (2002) found the most common theme to be graphic depictions of pain inflicted by anonymous men on exposed, powerless, and usually innocent women. This contrasts with other forms of media, they claim, where both the "rape myth" (where women enjoy being raped) and the depiction of promiscuous women who "deserve" what they get are common. Additionally, they explore the medium itself, positing that the interactive features of many rape sites (which offer a choice of the race of the woman to be raped and the location of the rape act, among others) add a sense of control for the user that has not been present in other mediums. Finally, Gossett and Byrne (2002) discuss how the unprecedented access to such sites, as well as the prevalent practice of violent sites providing links to other violent sites, makes the relatively small proportion of violent pornography to nonviolent pornography on the Internet potentially meaningless.

The ease of access to pornographic materials that the Internet has made possible is provocative. Barak et al. (1999) found that the *only* correlate to men's use of sexually explicit Internet sites was their past experience with sexually explicit media, so ease of access may be encouraging greater use, both in terms of frequency and numbers of users. Furthermore, Mitchell, Finkelhor, and Wolak (2003) found that 25 percent of youth ages 10–17 had experienced unwanted exposure to pornography online. Although they identified risk factors associated with unwanted exposure, a full 45 percent of those exposed had no risk factors.

THE FUTURE

In predicting the future, we hope to see a continuation of several recent trends. First, the need exists for more research involving quantitative and qualitative methods. This combination holds the promise of illuminating the broad picture with generalizable results while capturing the detailed experience of the phenomenon being studied. Second, a greater proportion of the published research relying on representative instead of convenience, volunteer samples will enhance the quality of the findings. In particular, researchers should abandon their reliance on samples of college students. Technological developments and the availability of census and other geographical data make it possible to locate concentrations of people by age, race, ethnicity, social class, and sexual orientation. Third, we hope a greater integration of theory and research will develop. This may require the development of more midrange theories focusing on specific phenomena, such as sexual desire or sexual orientation and testing propositions drawn from such theories. Finally, the need exists to further develop and test biopsychosocial theoretical models of human sexual expression (Lindau et al. 2003).

As for new directions, there is some indication that advances in genetics, which allow the incorporation of genetic alleles as explanatory variables in otherwise traditionally sociological models, may encourage some researchers to pursue biosocial research methods. Additionally, we hope to see advances in methodologies for studying the effects of the Internet on sexuality.

There is, however, cause for concern about the future of such research. Since 2001, opposition to sex research has increased, as evidenced by the targeting of four federally funded projects in 2002 and the "hit list" compiled by the Traditional Values Coalition (DeLamater 2005). It is possible that an increasing hostility will lead to fewer resources for research on human sexuality. Given that several pressing social problems involve sexual expression and that sexual health is the right of every person (WAS 2005), this would be a step backward.

PART VII

SOCIAL INSTITUTIONS

26

The Sociology of Love, Courtship, and Dating

Erica Owens

West Virginia University

The question of "What is love?" has piqued curiosity and engendered frustration for much of history. The exasperated answer that you "just know" when you are in love is reflected in the body of sociological literature on the phenomenon. Sociologists do not seem to agree on a uniform definition, although there are several competing but complementary typologies that attempt to pin down those emotional and behavioral states that add up to romantic "love."

Love scholarship can be roughly divided into two philosophical camps: (1) that which argues love must have certain components to be genuine, for instance, to differentiate it from mere liking or lust, and (2) that which suggests that love is a publicly informed but privately experienced state that is whatever the person "in love" believes it to be. Research on romantic love attachments often addresses the behaviors used in dating or, more infrequently, courtship; however, not all research on dating and courtship specifically addresses love. In this chapter, I will treat the three topics as separate. This is a conceit; clarity may be improved by separating the threads of romantic entanglement, but in research, as in life, the division is nowhere near as neatly accomplished.

It should also be mentioned here that the experience of love as understood in modern Western society has not been shared by all cultures in all times. In ancient Greece, true love between equals was seen as possible only between two men; although men married for purposes of procreation, a close emotional bond with a woman was seen as undesirable (Hendrick and Hendrick 1992). Romantic love as featured in novels and film began in the twelfth century. At this time, love came to be understood as an intense and passionate relationship that made the lover somehow a better person and was thus a worthy pursuit, albeit one with elaborate rules and rituals that required time and resources (Singer 1984). The ability to participate was associated with aristocrats or members of the "court," and it is this circumstance that gives us the term *courtship.*

Still, the expectation that one would love one's spouse was many years in coming. According to Stone (1980), changes in economic production and labor markets, together with public health measures, helped to encourage young persons to marry for love. Families had less sway over the choices of young people as production moved away from the family and into the factory, and as life expectancy increased, so did the emotional investment a spouse was willing to make in his or her partner. In some cultures where partners are still chosen by a young person's family, love is still not seen as a requisite for marriage. In this view, romantic love is a poor basis for forming a lasting union—and this normative stance is evident in research on spousal choice and sentiment. In one study (Levine et al. 1995), researchers asked participants in 10 countries whether they would marry a person who had the traits that they hoped for in a spouse, but whom they did not love. In the United States, fewer than 5 percent of people said that they would make such a match, while in nations such as Pakistan and Japan, young people were much more likely to consider such a union (50.4 and 35.7 percent, respectively). In nations where familism takes precedence over individual goals and desires, love and marriage are not always experienced together. Should love develop between the two, so much the better—but if not, the marriage is based on a solidly practical foundation designed to maintain familial and community stability.

WHAT IS AND IS (PERHAPS) NOT LOVE

With such an elusive topic, it is perhaps not surprising that many scholars who study love resort to metaphors to try to explain what love is. The rich and varied collection of metaphors include love as a "story" that we tell ourselves and one another (Sternberg 1998), expressions of love as policy statements that set forth the terms and expectations of the relationship (Van de Vate 1981), love as intensely focused and sustained attention in another person (see Brown 1987; Rowntree 1989), and love as emotion via decision (Hatfield and Rapson 1987).

Many scholars differentiate between the "falling in love" state of early romantic attachment and the more companionate state of being in a love relationship after the original flush has worn off (see Hendrick and Hendrick 1992). The intensity of early love is impossible for most couples to maintain. As the relationship progresses, partners come to have a warmer and closer feeling of intimacy, termed *companionate love,* rather than the all-encompassing passion experienced when the relationship was new (Berscheid and Walster 1978).

Dorothy Tennov's (1979) work on "limerence" is perhaps the most systematic exploration of the difference between falling in love and being in a committed love relationship. According to Tennov, limerence is a transient state that involves preoccupation with the "limerent object" (i.e., the person one is falling for) together with idealization, mood swings, and physiological arousal. Limerence may be positive, that is, mutual, or negative/unrequited. Much of limerence occurs in the mind of the one experiencing the emotion. Most people will become limerent at some point in their lives. The experience is generally not permanent—a limerent state lasts an average of around two years—but may occur more than once in a lifetime. What some people experience as a loss of passion, to Tennov, is the waning of the limerent state.

LOVE TYPOLOGIES AND THEORIES

Other research suggests that love is what the lover defines it to be. Lee's (1973) famous typology of "love styles" identifies six basic types of love experience; not all of the styles of love fit widespread cultural definitions of how romantic love develops and progresses. The primary styles of *eros, ludus,* and *storge* and the secondary styles of *mania, pragma,* and *agape* reflect different beliefs regarding love and loving behavior as well as personal preferences and comfort levels. The style that most closely resembles ideals of romantic love is termed *eros.* Lovers who have the eros style tend to value sexual and sensual contact with the beloved, to have a well-formed image of the beloved or a "type" that they tend to be drawn to, to become sexual fairly quickly in a relationship, to define the experience as "love" quite quickly, and to feel that the experience of the relationship is of great importance and scope. By contrast, lovers with styles of *ludus, storge, mania, pragma,* and *agape* do not fit the stereotypical mold of romantic love presented in novels and film, although manic lovers fit negative stereotypes of obsessed love. Ludus-style lovers are most interested in the conquest possible when chasing a potential partner. Love, to the ludus lover, is a game of strategy. These lovers are more likely to be pursuing multiple partners and to attempt to limit emotional displays with a partner or potential partner in an effort to maintain an advantage in the dyad. Sexual contact may be more likely to have an aspect of accomplishment and play in these pairings. Storge-style lovers, by contrast, focus on comfort and emotional closeness in a relationship. A relationship between partners with storge style of loving is generally not very physical and passion is not of paramount importance. To outsiders who equate the intense and exquisite experience of limerence as love, storge lovers can seem more like close friends. This is not altogether incorrect, as deep friendship is the basis of this form of love. Lovers who tend toward the pragma style are practical and stress what the potential partner brings to the bargaining table. These lovers are seeking to make the best deal for future life circumstances as possible. Manic love, on the other hand, is not reasoned. This form of love is love for love's sake; manic lovers value love to the point of obsession and experience an emotional roller coaster of jealousy, insecurity, and elation. The manic lover does not allow the relationship to develop over time but instead attempts to force the partner to make a declaration of love and intention. If ludic lovers enjoy the experience and have fun with love, manic lovers, for all that they yearn for love, generally feel miserable while in a relationship. The final style in Lee's typology, agape, is very rare in romantic love. This form of love is selfless and based on an almost spiritual desire for the other's good. Generally, this type of love is considered an ideal.

Sternberg (1998) also suggests an individual and subjective approach to the experience of love. Sternberg's work shows how lovers story their experiences; the resulting catalogue of love "stories" shows how individuals draw on shared understandings of what love is to fashion coherent and yet individual accounts of the love experience. Some love stories identified by Sternberg include love as science, love as journey, love as art, and love as war.

Most couples who profess a permanent bond (whether in a marriage or other commitment ceremony) describe their partnership as strong and explain that they have great love for their partner. But, over time, evaluations shift. Some couples lose the intense feeling of love and closeness, while other couples experience what can be termed *global adoration,* which seems to increase marital satisfaction and stability (Neff and Karney 2005:480).

The closeness experienced by partners determines the form of love experienced according to Sternberg (1986). Sternberg's well-known triangle theory of love suggests that love is a triangle with three points, each formed by a component of love: intimacy (i.e., emotional investment and closeness), passion (excitement and arousal, both emotional and physical), and commitment (a decision to maintain the relationship over time). A love relationship may be stronger in one or two areas and thus have a different character than would another relationship that features a different combination of attributes. For instance, infatuated love features great passion but lacks both intimacy and commitment, fatuous love includes passion and commitment without intimacy, and consummate love completes the triangle with all three components present.

COURTSHIP

Love and courtship are associated in Reiss's (1960, 1980) wheel theory of love. Unlike Sternberg's triangle theory, wheel theory assumes a standard progression of romantic relationships that encourages love to develop during the courtship process. These stages are sequential, each successful completion leading to the next step in the courtship process. First, couples experience *rapport,* or a feeling of ease with one another. Often, this is the result of shared attitudes and backgrounds, which encourages homogamy (or the tendency of people to marry others who are similar to themselves in background and experience). When a couple has rapport, communication is easier and the next stage of *self-revelation* is facilitated. In this stage, each partner exposes "who I am" to the other; within the norms of their social class and culture, partners will reveal information about themselves to the other, which helps to build closeness. As partners learn more and more about one another and begin to feel closer, the sentiment of *mutual dependency* grows. In this stage, each partner begins to rely on the other and feel as part of an interdependent unit. If this stage is fully experienced, and the relationship continued, the partners will take on unique significance for one another. One doesn't merely have "a girlfriend" who could be easily replaced by another female of similar background and attractiveness. This person brings unique benefits not easily found with others and thus *this* person has special status. If the couple completes the final stage of *intimacy need fulfillment,* by each partner deciding that the relationship fits his or her needs for closeness and disclosure, the relationship will likely result in an official partnering.

Another metaphor for partner choice during courtship is a "filter." Alan Kerckhoff and K. E. Davis (1962) posited a filter theory of partner choice based on couples successfully passing through a series of filters, including social characteristics, similarity of values, and need complementarity.

At each stage, potential partners who are not acceptable are excluded from further consideration. Murstein (1970) refined this theory with his stimulus-value-role (SVR) model of partner selection. In brief, partners progress from the stimulus stage, where social similarity and physical attractiveness first catch one's attention, through the stage of value where partners compare attitudes and beliefs on a variety of issues to check for fit and compatibility, and finally to role, to see if the potential partner fits with the idealized expectations that each has for a potential mate. Interestingly, Murstein notes that while physical attraction is very important for the initiation of a partnership, people generally choose partners whose attractiveness is similar to their own rather than seeking to find the most physically impressive partner possible.

Generally, courtship differs from dating in that it is more structured and subject to cultural norms. Courtship, unlike the looser dating, is acknowledged as codified behavior designed to lead to a permanent partnership or marriage (Cere 2001). Some researchers who detail courtship norms and patterns suggest that the erosion of courting behavior in Western societies in the twentieth century, while not solely determinant, corresponds to a lack of preparation for marriage and the attendant rise in rates of divorce (see Kass and Kass 1999).

Theories of Courtship

Courtship as a field of inquiry in modern sociology has been called "virtually moribund" (Glenn, cited in Cere 2001). Few academics in family sociology now study the more traditional pathways that young adults take to marriage. According to Cere (2001), studies of courtship are now found within three general schools of inquiry: sociobiology, exchange theory, and close-relationship theory (p. 55).

Willard Waller (1937) was one of the first sociologists to note that the marriage contract was based on a bargain that was becoming less and less explicit. In Waller's view, couples placed greater stress on love as a basis for marriage because of the lack of understanding of agreed-on and culturally sanctioned bases for marriage.

Courtship, then, stopped being a proving ground for potential partners to check one another for fitness as mate. Beth Bailey (1988) detailed the evolution of courtship from a private enactment of cultural expectation to a more public and also more sexually intimate "dating" brought about by market courtship. Courting moved from the home environment of family, church, and culture to the paid arena of dating sites such as restaurants, movies, and clubs. Courtship, beginning to morph into dating, became something to be purchased rather than something to be performed.

Gary Becker (1974) suggested the now well-known exchange theory model of courtship. In brief, people marry when the perceived benefits of a given pair bond outweigh the perceived costs of the bond. Each party is aware of what preferences or characteristics they require, and what resources, or attributes they have to offer another are part of the deal they wish to strike. From this perspective, courtship is akin to a long interview in which each party attempts to broker the best deal possible given the resources they may possess. However, this theory is criticized for its inability to account for the great persuasive and compelling nature of "love" and the desire to form a permanent bond with a partner who, to an outsider, might seem like a very poor choice. Exchange theory requires that each party be a rational actor with sufficient insight into their own and their partner's motivations and qualities to be able to evaluate and strike the desired bargain.

Sociobiological theories of courtship focus on partners' selection of a mate who will provide maximum reproductive success. Stated broadly, men seek out women who show physical signs of fertility (i.e., youth, attractiveness, and the appearance of health), while women are more likely to seek a partner who is able and willing to support a family (see Buss 1988; Tooke and Camire 1991; Benz, Anderson, and Miller 1995).

Courtship also has a retrospective character. Couples spending time together generally define their activity as dating; after the pair has become engaged or has married, the period of dating becomes the courtship that led to the decision to permanently partner. Courtship as experienced and referenced, then, is increasingly the province of memory and redefinition and is produced and reproduced in family storytelling occasions. Ponzetti (2005) identifies courtship tales as a major theme in family storytelling and explains that the courtship story serves as a ready explanation of how the pair decided to marry, thus chronicling the beginning of a family unit. By cofashioning the tale of courtship, spouses can fashion a partnership history that may help them to transcend present difficulties.

DATING

While the term *courtship* generally refers to mate selection leading to long-term partnership, *dating* has a much more casual connotation. Dating behavior as studied by sociologists runs the gamut from the very casual "hanging out" that isn't "really dating" (Owens 2005) to spending time with one or more potential partners, to having fun without any expectation of permanence. Dating can be difficult to distinguish from friendship at times, especially among young adults and teens who spend unstructured time hanging out with one another but who do not necessarily seek to define their relationships and who may deny that they have been on a "date." In some instances, young adults form committed sexual and emotional relationships that are durable, although they do not necessarily have an expectation of permanence while reporting that they have "never dated" or "never been on a date" (Owens 2005).

The difference in goals present in dating and courtship gives a "two-tiered system of heterosexual interaction" to

modern romance (Cate and Lloyd 1992:24). In fact, the goal and seriousness of the relationship is often the basis for marking whether the couple is "dating" or "courting," with dating evolving into courtship when the couple becomes both serious and sexually exclusive. Homogamy is present among dating, cohabiting, and married couples and forms an aspect of partner selection at all levels of commitment, but there does seem to be a "winnowing process" whereby the requirements and expectations of a partner become more and more stringent as the relationship moves from mere dating to a more permanent partnership (Blackwell and Lichter 2004:719).

Studies of the early stages of partner choice in dating tend to focus on initial attraction (Buss et al. 2001) and the techniques that people use to draw partners to them (see Clark, Shaver, and Abrahams 1999). Frequently, this literature deals with the ideal or goal relationship that a partner holds going into a potential relationship. Studies of the early stages of a dating relationship, therefore, often gauge the predating expectations or desires of partners. An example would be Yancey's (2002) study of who interracially dates; factors such as religious background, political stance, residential region, and educational background influence whether a person will date outside their own racial or ethnic background.

Relationship Troubles

Dating troubles are also a popular avenue for inquiry. Dating involves a plethora of potential difficulties, including dishonesty, infidelity, emotional turmoil, miscommunication, and struggles over power and dominance. Deception, therefore, is part of the mating dance. Both men and women understand that a potential partner will likely hide or minimize negative attributes and highlight other characteristics that would make him or her more attractive in the dating arena. In heterosexual pairings, deception follows gendered norms of what is and is not attractive in a potential spouse. As previously noted, men place a higher premium on youth when considering potential partners, while women are more likely to stress ability to support a family. Interestingly, each sex understands that the other is trying to appeal to these norms. Men acknowledge that women are going to be deceptive about intentions to maintain a youthful and attractive appearance, while women and men agree that men are more likely to be deceptive about financial prospects for the future (Benz et al. 1995).

Couples deceive one another not only to attract a partner who might otherwise not be interested but also to hide "competing relationships" or "outside-relationship activities," and to gloss over the "state of the relationship," including decreasing of contact (Tolhuizen 1991, cited in Cate and Lloyd 1992:87). Whether a partner chooses to stay or leave after discovering deception is influenced by communication patterns and the person's style of attachment (Jang, Smith, and Levine 2002).

Deception is not the only serious complication that couples face. More direct forms of aggression in relationships also exist. Intimate partner violence began receiving widespread attention in the 1980s. Although earlier studies may have made brief mention of violence in intimate relationships, it was not until the 1980s that explicit acknowledgement was offered that sexual assault and other forms of violence occurred in courtship and dating (Cate and Lloyd 1992). This oversight is surprising, as physical violence occurs in as many as 40 percent of dating couples (Simons, Lin, and Gordon 1998). Both male and female partners report experiencing common couple violence such as pushing or slapping, but men are more likely than women to engage in serious violence against a partner (Johnson and Ferraro 2000). Lifetime chances of being the victim of intimate partner violence are also skewed by gender. About a quarter of women but fewer than 10 percent of men will be physically assaulted by an intimate partner (see Tjaden and Thoennes 1998).

RECENT TRENDS IN SCHOLARSHIP ON ROMANTIC PAIRINGS

Much of the sociological literature on romantic pairings prior to 1970 focused on homogamy, propinquity, and complementarity of roles among young heterosexual couples. In more recent decades, researchers have included homosexual couples in studies of love, dating, and partnering (for a notable example, see Vaughan 1986). Moreover, studies of dating and courtship now include older daters, who may or may not have children from previous unions or who may be grieving the loss of a spouse due to divorce or widowhood (see Huyck 2001; Dickson, Hughes, and Walker 2005). Among adults in later life, dating relationships follow traditional gender norms (McElhany 1992) and provide a great deal of personal satisfaction and emotional closeness whether or not the relationship leads to marriage (Bulcroft and O'Conner 1986). Still, seniors who date experience some drawbacks unique to their life circumstances. Older women in the dating market feel vulnerable to being taken advantage of financially and practically in what Dickson et al. (2005) term the "nurse and purse phenomenon" (p. 78).

Work in this field evolves as people find new and innovative ways to relate to one another sexually and romantically. At present, two subfields are emerging as very important to the study of romantic pairings: work on love relationships that involve distance, such as cyber-romance or "living apart together" (LAT) relationships (Levin 2004), and on the liminal and open-ended pairings usually, but not exclusively, experienced by young adults and which have been termed *friends-with-benefits* relationships (Hughes, Morrison, and Asada 2005).

The more well-known of the two areas of inquiry is an exploration of what in the past was combined into the notion of "long-distance relationships." These relationships

have exploded with the advent of the Internet; it is now possible to meet partners, disclose personal information in real time through messaging, and even be physically intimate virtually. Online relationship research is a burgeoning field that includes work on Internet personals as a way to meet potential partners (see Groom and Pennebaker 2005), online chat as a gateway to potential real-world infidelity (Mileham 2003), online intimacy as a form of sexual exchange (Waskul 2002), and e-mail messaging (Hovick, Meyers, and Timmerman 2003) as a means of relationship maintenance.

The LAT relationship is a "historically new family form" that developed due to changing norms and societal circumstances over the past 30 years (Levin 2004). Partners in LAT relationships view themselves as a committed couple and their social network shares this image, but the partners maintain separate residences—sometimes hours away from one another—due to work or familial obligations or even personal preference. These relationships are distinguished from commuter marriages or relationships in that the pair does not share a primary home part-time, with one partner also renting an apartment during work or school.

A very recent trend in relationship research involves the friends-with-benefits relationship (FWBR) that involves sexual intimacy but not necessarily an explicitly emotional romantic connection as "romance" is traditionally understood. These pairings may or may not involve expectations by partners that the relationship will evolve into something more emotionally intimate (Hughes et al. 2005). These relationships combine the benefits of a friendship with that of a sexual relationship, but without the responsibility and time constraints present in more traditional romantic relationships.

FUTURE DIRECTIONS FOR THE 21ST CENTURY

Research on love, courtship, and dating will continue to evolve as new modes of pairing up and maintaining emotional closeness become more accessible. It is likely that electronic modes of relating will receive more attention from scholars. Not only has the Internet reduced much of the stigma of placing the "personals ad," but early stages of courting and relating can now be conducted with little—or no—in-person contact. Obviously, such circumstances come with attendant complications: How does one establish rapport and trust without the many cues in-person contact allows? What are the effects of distanced relating on disclosure and truth telling? Do these pairings become sexual more quickly because of a heightened sense of intimacy and "knowingness"? Extrarelationship pairings via electronic media will also continue to garner increased attention, as the definition of what "counts" as cheating moves further from a physical-contact model to a more flexible conceptualization of contact that takes attention, time, and focus from the primary relationship.

Studies of relational power and earnings will also factor strongly in family scholarship in the coming decades. Women have always worked, as family scholars who detail the historical family unit of production have noted. However, if current trends continue, women will be the majority of college graduates and may begin to catch up to men in their professional accomplishments and dollar earnings. This transition, if it occurs, will not be a simple one as it will challenge long-held notions of gender and place within a heterosexual pair bond.

Taking into account both electronic modes of relating and economic pressures felt by couples, we can also expect to see more scholarship on distance relationships and commuting. Established couples may choose to live apart due to career or educational necessity. Electronic communications and other forms of technology (e.g., cellular telephones that can be used to call one another or to send photos or text messages) may be used to maintain emotional closeness despite geographic distance.

27

MARRIAGE AND DIVORCE IN THE UNITED STATES

DENNIS L. PECK

The University of Alabama

The perpetuity of marriage is enforced by law as a protection for children, for whose education and support society as such makes no other provision than the frequently aborted attempt to compel an efficient guardianship of the parent by penal enactments. (Andrews 1975:12)

The Romans bemoaned their high divorce rates, which they contrasted with an earlier era of family stability. The European settlers in America began lamenting the decline of the family and the disobedience of women and children almost as soon as they stepped off the boats. (Coontz 2005:1)

No trend in American life since World War II has received more attention or caused more concern than the rising rate of divorce. (Cherlin 1992:20)

As an often-cited U.S. government report indicates, "Current concerns about the condition of the American family, as well as discussion about 'family values' indicate a need for timely information about factors contributing to major shifts in family structure" (Norton and Miller 1992:iii). With the emphasis on marriage, divorce, and remarriage, the government is looking closely at well-known sociological facts pertaining to changes in the family, sex and gender roles, and issues relating to human sexuality. As noted by Cherlin (1992), "Although the family undoubtedly has a future, its present form differs from its past form in important aspects, at least in part because of recent changes in patterns of cohabiting, marrying, divorcing, and remarrying" (p. 2).

Although marriage may in fact be a weakened institution (Cherlin 1992) and there is a global concern that a marriage crisis exists (Coontz 2005:2–3), social attitudes do not necessarily reflect a consistent view of these phenomena. Early alarmists who viewed the family as a weakened institution and thus as a focus of sociological analysis, including William F. Ogburn (1927) and Ogburn and Nimkoff (1955), raised significant questions about marriage and divorce. Family issues raised by these sociologists were based on the recognition that by the 1920s, the economic, protective, recreation, and religious functions of the family had changed. Thus, functions such as protection, education, economics, religious training, and recreation have been transferred to other entities (Newman 1950; Zellner 2001:38–39). Indeed, the economic unit functions of the family had been replaced by the factory, the restaurant, and the store, while the protective functions had been assumed by the courts, the school, and health departments (Ogburn 1927:7).

William Fielding Ogburn (1927) wrote that marriage is an important social institution because it is related to happiness. Ogburn also may have been the first analyst to recognize the important difference in the lower death rate among married males compared with single men. He recognized that divorce is of special concern to society because, as he notes (p. 7), divorce usually occurs with the idea that another family will be formed through remarriage.

PUBLIC PRONOUNCEMENTS
AND VITAL SOCIAL STATISTICS

The registration of vital events has a long history in the United States that began in 1632, when the Grand Assembly of Virginia required ministers from throughout the commonwealth to register all burials, christenings, and marriages. In 1639, the Massachusetts Bay Colony passed a law requiring government officials to record all births, deaths, and marriages. Other colonies, such as the Plymouth Colony in 1646 and the Connecticut Court of Elections in 1644 and 1650, were soon to follow by ordering town clerks or registrars to record similar birth, marriage, and death data. But it was not until 1842 that a standard registration procedure and form was formulated in Massachusetts, where responsibility for gathering such information was placed on the Secretary of the Commonwealth (Jacobson 1959:7–8).

Although the collection of vital information did not become an important function of the official state census gathering until the mid-1850s, vital statistics such as births, deaths, marriage, and divorce were well-recognized pronouncements of public significance. Perhaps for this reason alone, the ideology pertaining to marriage and divorce, particularly in the United States, has long been encumbered by social, religious, and political interpretations. Further legislation was interrupted by the Civil War, but in 1889, an issue of the *Political Science Quarterly* lent credence to the fact that issues relating to marriage and divorce were receiving significant exposure. Dike (1889) noted the following:

> Twenty years ago President Woolsey's *Divorce and Divorce Legislation* contained in a dozen scanty pages about all the existing statistics regarding both this country and Europe. Since then, the collections of their statistics by four or five more states (in a meager way, excepting the excellent work in Massachusetts begun by Mr. Wright, the Commissioner of Labor in 1879 and contained since under provision of statute); [and] the few additions by the National Divorce Reform League. (P. 592)

Lobbying for more efficient registration legislation led to important advances at the federal level by the early twentieth century with the creation in 1902 of the Bureau of the Census and, in 1903, a Congressional resolution calling for a cooperative effort between the states and the newly established Bureau to establish a uniform system of birth and death registration for the entire country. At the time, only 15 states and the District of Columbia had established a central filing system; by 1919, all states had legislation that required such registration even if strict enforcement did not occur (Jacobson 1959). Despite these advances in statistical gathering procedures, as late as the mid-twentieth century only three-fourths of the states had a provision for recording marriages and about one-half for divorces (Newman 1950).

In 1877, the first official database on marriage and divorce was created, and the initial analysis of the data therein was conducted by Walter F. Willcox (1891, 1893, 1897). Since that time a great public discussion has taken place as many analysts use the vital statistics data to question aspects of what was to become a complex social matrix involving the structure and function of the family institution.

In the 1950s, it was suggested that divorce was more characteristic of the lower socioeconomic classes and that the highly publicized divorces of high-profile middle- to upper-class people gave an unwarranted view of the true extent of divorce in the United States (Monahan 1955). By the late 1980s, however, the claim was made that two-thirds of all first marriages would end in divorce (Martin and Bumpass 1989). Following this claim, White (1990), arguing that divorce is a macro-level problem, wrote that "A shift in the lifetime divorce probability from 10% to well over 50% cannot be explained at the micro level" (p. 904).

Such a view of and debate over marriage and divorce issues continues in the contemporary experience, prompted in part by the findings reported and commentary attributed to analysts such as Martin and Bumpass (1989), Riley 1991, and Cherlin (1992). Andrew J. Cherlin wrote (1992:7) that "During the 1980s the divorce rate declined slightly but remained high enough that about half of marriages, at current rates, would end in divorce." Cherlin (1992) also observed that divorce "rates in the 1980s, although stable, still imply that about half of all the marriages begun in the mid-1970s will end in divorce or separation" (p. 30). Such information is also cited in the most learned of reference publications, as noted by Norton and Miller (1992) and Kurz (2001:3811), for example, who, drawing upon Cherlin (1992), among others, state, "The USA has one of the highest divorce rates—50 percent of all marriages now end in divorce." Because of the respectable position these analysts hold, other analysts make good use of the information to further perpetuate the myth of a 50 percent divorce rate. For example, Ruggles (1997), in citing Cherlin's work, stated, "Only about 5% of marriages contracted in 1867 were expected to end in divorce, but over one-half of marriages contracted in 1967 are expected to end in divorce" (p. 455). And of course, publications that champion women's issues cannot neglect the divorce problem, as noted in Deborah Perry's discussion on the economy: "with more than half of marriages ending in divorce, many stay-at-home women may not be entitled to the Social Security benefits of their former spouses" (Malveaux and Perry 2003:109).

Because of its seemingly authentic quality, the popular perception of the 50 percent divorce rate has held sway during the final decades of the twentieth century, and the myth continues to thrive into the early part of the twenty-first century. Despite its mythological quality, the inferred high rate of divorce places the institution of marriage and the divorce event among a critical core of social issues that challenge our sensibilities. Indeed, it is the case that ever since the publication of the first public report of the marriage and divorce data occurred approximately 100 years ago, myths of a more glorious past surrounding marriage and the family institution have been in evidence (Calhoun 1917, 1919; Coontz 1992, 2000, 2005). But careful consideration of the data indicates that the 50 percent divorce rate myth is not supported by the social facts.

The use of official government documents serves as the basis for a discussion of the incidence and rate of marriage and divorce and for exposing the myth of the United States' 50 percent divorce rate. In the following sections, such data are brought to bear on the historical and contemporary U.S. marriage and divorce experience. These official data indicate that the prevailing myth of a decline in the traditional family arrangement and the continued exponential growth in the U.S. divorce rate represent a social construct that is unsupported by fact.

In the following sections, some of the issues relating to the study of marriage and divorce are addressed. But these topics, as Newman (1950) long ago noted, cannot be addressed in isolation because the study of marriage and divorce is related to vast changes in a complex social order that require inquiry into the cultural, social, political, and economic aspects of the family, including changes in the structure and function of family. If this assessment was true more than a half-century ago, the message is perhaps even more appropriate in the early part of the twenty-first century.

THE HISTORY OF MARRIAGE AND DIVORCE

If civilization is to be founded on family life, then marriage also is essential. The family in its current form emerged during the sixteenth and seventeenth centuries, when the conjugal family developed concomitant with the soon-to-be-discovered concept "childhood." At that point in time and over the next two centuries, the primary task of the family was to train and nurture children; family life became increasingly oriented toward children. Thus, the modern family developed the concept "home" with its characteristics to include privacy, isolation, and the domestic life (O'Neill 1967:4–6). The history of the marriage institution and the cross-cultural complexity of divorce became well chronicled in an early-twentieth-century three-volume treatise titled *A History of Matrimonial Institutions*. Written by George Elliott Howard and published in 1904, this grand, scholarly series addressed the vast accumulated knowledge of marriage and divorce within a global context. Published during a period when many interesting questions were being raised about the family institution (see, e.g., Shively's ([1853, 1889] 1975) edited work *Love, Marriage, and Divorce, and the Sovereignty of the Individual: A Discussion between Henry James, Horace Greeley, and Stephen Pearl Andrews*), a previously unpublished work by

Stephen Pearl Andrews (1975, edited by Shively) titled *Love Marriage, and the Condition of Women,* and the references found in the cross-cultural and regional comparative analyses of Willcox (1893), such resources established the import that subsequent research would offer policymakers of the future.

Walter Willcox's demographic work was the first influential empirical assessment of marriage and divorce and helped to establish the foundation for future population analyses. But the first scholarly American study of the family appears to have been published in 1887 by Charles F. Thwing ([1913] 1887), a minister and later university president, whose analysis of divorce led to the belief that excessive individualism and modern secularism were the root causes of the divorce problem (as cited in O'Neill 1967:170–71). Thirty years later, Arthur W. Calhoun's three-volume set *Social History of the American Family* (1917–1919) was to serve social analysts and policymakers well. In the latter instance, the important sociological inquiry into the family institution helped to establish a university-level curriculum for the developing discipline of sociology.

A more limited but no less important inquiry into the history of American divorce is offered by Blake (1962), whose work builds upon the issue of "migratory divorce" raised by Cavers (1937) a generation earlier. Blake's questions about the conservative New York State's position on divorce led him to further explore the issue on a national basis, especially as it led to Nevada's liberal divorce laws. Willcox (1893:90), on the other hand, recognized long before Nevada's developing reputation that states like Rhode Island offered more liberal opportunities, including divorce, to the residents of New York State.

Marriage

Rapid expansion of the American frontier emerging from pioneering, development of industrialism and urbanization, and the increasing quality of life in the northern portions of the United States held important consequences for the evolution of the American family. This included an increased emphasis on marriage, early marriage for both males and females, and high birth rates to ensure large families (Calhoun 1918:11–25). The cultural need of these early Americans is reflected in the following statement. Marriage, according to Lowie (1933), is human mating that receives moral appraisal

> according to the norms distinctive of each society. Marriage denotes those unequivocally sanctioned unions which persist beyond sensual satisfaction and thus come to underlie family life. It is therefore not coextensive with sex life, which embraces matings of inferior status in the social scheme of values. (P. 146)

A single standard definition of marriage is difficult to formulate, as noted by Coontz (1992, 2000, 2005), because of the richness of the cross-cultural anthropological research literature (see, for example, Lowie 1933). However, marriage is a form of cooperation between the sexes that is intended to ensure perpetuation of the race and ultimate survival (Hankins 1931).

Despite the conceptual problems that exist, marriage and divorce are two family-related issues that have for more than 125 years received a great deal of discussion, analysis, and intense scrutiny. Arthur W. Calhoun (1917) described the American family institution as resulting from three evolutionary phases: "the complex of medieval tradition . . . on the basis of ancient civilization . . . ; the economic transition from medieval landlordism to modern capitalism; and the influence of environment in an unfolding continent" (p. 13). Later, this author, in the third in a series of volumes on the history of the American family, indicated that systematic study of the family began in earnest about the same time as the introduction of early inventions (i.e., telephone, incandescent lamp, trolley car, and typewriter) into the American culture, each of which was to have dramatic effects on communications and transportation (Calhoun 1919:7–10). Similarly, Ogburn and Nimkoff (1955:iii) note that changes in the American family and family living from the early 1800s are affected by what they describe as three clusters of inventions and discoveries, namely, steam and steel, contraceptives, and the myriad scientific discoveries that have had an effect upon religious beliefs. Almost 90 years after the publication of Calhoun's family treatise, one can safely state that the American family institution continues to be influenced by a fluid social environment even if the economic forces that thrive differ dramatically from those of the past.

Official records of marriage behavior generated and maintained by states can be traced to the act of 1842, wherein the state of Massachusetts began to collect marriage statistics, including information on age, sex, and place of birth (Monahan 1951). According to Willcox (1893) and Jacobson (1959), information pertaining to marital status first became available in state censuses such as those of Michigan in 1854 and New York in 1855. Twenty years later, several other states also began recording similar census data. But the national effort to collect and analyze data was to occur at the national level several decades later, when Willcox (1891, 1893, 1897) applied newly learned methods to several areas of interest to population analysts. Interestingly, Willcox (1893) notes the following: "Only in five states, Vermont, Massachusetts, Rhode Island, Connecticut and Ohio, and in the District of Columbia, can the number of marriages be obtained with approximate completeness for each of the twenty years [1867–1886]" (p. 73).

Divorce

Divorce has long been of interest to sociologists, and the topic has even been cast in importance alongside other social problems. Witness the effort of one eugenics-oriented author, D. George Fournad (1929), who wrote in the *Journal of Educational Sociology,*

> The unfortunate fact . . . remains that the homes of millions of farmers, miners, laboring men, and especially bootblacks are actually cursed by six or more poorly brought up, if not perfectly neglected children, for no other reason than the lack of eugenics or the need of birth-control information. Small wonder that crime, insanity, suicide, homicide, divorce, and physical or mental degeneration are steadily on the increase. (P. 179)

But other analysts project a more optimistic view, noting that American divorce has a long and venerable history in that Puritan settlers introduced it in the American Colonies during the 1600s (Howard 1909:767). Howard demonstrates that the granting of divorce had for four centuries undergone liberalization. Indeed, long before divorce became a matter of considerable debate during the twentieth century, the meaning of what a liberal granting of divorce would mean for society served as a matter of considerable discussion among moralists, theologians, and policymakers. In essence, then, the resulting institution of American divorce was vital, and growing, long before late-twentieth-century Americans carried it to its current state (Riley 1991:3).

Some early social analysts of divorce and its increase offer their lamentation while describing the demise of the traditional family. But the frequency of divorce alone was not the object of concern. Rather, in the early part of the twentieth century, divorce was viewed as "an evil which seriously threatens the social order, which menaces our deepest thought, our ripest wisdom, our most persistent courage and endeavor" (Howard 1909:767). This is the same lamentation Riley (1991) indicates first developed during the Victorian era of the late 1800s, a period that has been identified by some contemporary alarmists as the model for family life. But as Coontz (2005:2–3) argues, each generation of the past 100 years seems to be dissatisfied with the present arrangement, thinking that the marriage relationships of previous generations of parents and grandparents were much more satisfactory.

Despite differences in orientation toward divorce between the northern and southern regions of the United States, even the religious influences that led to these regional differences were not sufficient to prevent divorce from being recognized as a social safety valve that ensures the continuity of marriage (O'Neill 1967:6–10). From this perspective, divorce is not an indicator of a family system in disaster but represents an essential feature of the Victorian patriarchal and industrial families. Nevertheless, for the postindustrial/postmodernist family, there continue to be echoes of concern about the appropriate role of the husband and wife and their children.

Some contemporary social critics characterize a high incidence of divorce as somehow placing the institution of marriage at risk while decrying the liberal legislation that supports this behavior as undermining traditional family stability. However, neglected is the notion that the decline of the patriarchal family is consistent with the trend toward political democracy that conditioned American children and young adults during the eighteenth and nineteenth centuries (Calhoun 1918:53). The data reported later in this chapter tend to support this representation. But such lamentations and the image of an ideal, traditional marriage that is always somewhere in the past are not a recent phenomenon, nor have they become so since the passage of the No-Fault Divorce Act legislation. Indeed it has a much longer legacy. Witness the opinion crafted by Justice Thornton in *Martin v. Robson,* 1872:

> The maxims and authorities and adjudications of the past have faded away. The foundations hitherto deemed so essential for the preservation of the nuptial contract, and the maintenance of the marriage relation, are crumbling. The unity of husband and wife has been severed . . . she no longer clings to and depends upon man. (as cited in Vernier 1935:3)

Moreover, Howard (1904:1–160) documents that during the colonial period, it was established that there would exist a free and tolerant divorce policy, and throughout the century following the founding of the United States, divorce legislation was liberalized even further. And during the mid-nineteenth century, social analysts such as Stephen Pearl Andrews (1975:12–13) recognized that despite the need to provide for and succor children, divorce might be a necessary option to maintaining a relationship between two individuals who never loved one another or who may have ceased to love.

As the legal dissolution of marriage, divorce is a cultural problem-solving technique (Honigmann 1953), and it is a normal remedy for those who are in less-than-fortunate family situations (Blake 1962:iii). John J. Honigmann (1953:38) recognized that divorce is a standardized social response that people employ to change their interpersonal relationships, and, as indicated by Hankin (1931:177), divorce is designed to relieve hardships placed upon and experienced by individuals because of customary marriage rules. And like marriage, divorce also

> is a product of social evolution, therefore it is normal and to be accepted . . . inasmuch as certain functions of the parent have passed to the state we must begin to reconcile ourselves to the idea of state care of children to the virtual exclusion of home influence. (Calhoun 1919:10)

According to Calhoun (1919:7–10), the National Divorce Reform League, which began in the early 1880s, and in 1897 became the National League for the Protection of the Family, developed its focus on "existing evils relating to marriage and divorce" (p. 8). Although the extent of the poverty and divorce were unknown at the time, some analysts thought of poverty and divorce as important components of the emerging sociological studies of the family. In Volume III of the three-volume treatise *Social History of the American Family,* Calhoun documents this emerging

relationship through the writings of analysts of the late nineteenth century who were looking into the "divorce question" and the "problems of marriage and divorce." Many questions were raised, including those relating to polygamy, charity, and children as well as education, economics, politics, and religion—each of these issues and related questions was raised within the context of the lack of information pertaining to the 1880s' American family.

THE SOCIAL MYTH SURROUNDING DIVORCE

> A false idea once implanted is hard to dislodge, and the difficulty of dislodging it is proportional to the ignorance of those holding the idea. (George Cantor's law of the conservation of ignorance)

The mythology surrounding the American divorce rate is supported by individuals who develop what Sears et al. (1988:98) refer to as the "illusory correlation." Thus, two factors, the "high divorce rate" and the perceived "breakdown of the family" as a viable social institution, are believed to be highly correlated. Both factors may be contrary to commonly shared set of values, but repeated exposure to such illusory correlation stimuli is consistent with Canter's law of the conservation of ignorance: Myth eventually assumes the character of a social fact. Within this context, the news media and responsible citizens establish a portion of the public agenda that is based on an inappropriate social reality of the U.S. divorce problem. Dissemination of information in which the work of scholars is either misinterpreted or misrepresented serves to perpetuate social myths (see, for instance, Norton and Miller 1992:1; Kurz 2001).

The lack of public information is also important. In quoting a number of prominent analysts of divorce, Hurley (2005) noted the following:

> Part of the uncertainty about the most recent trends (in marriage and divorce) derives from the fact that no detailed annual figures have been available since 1996, when the National Center for Health Statistics stopped collecting detailed data from states on the age, income, education and race of people who divorce. (P. D57)

Perhaps because of the more recent paucity of information, some analysts of the past contributed information that continues to receive notoriety (see, for example, Martin and Bumpass 1989; Cherlin 1992). Despite the fact that Cherlin did not have access to actual data to support his contention, he predicted that approximately one-half of the marriages contracted during the 1970s would end in divorce. Further misunderstanding emerges. In assessing the rise of divorce and separation in the United States during the period from 1880 to 1990, for example, Ruggles (1997), citing Cherlin's work, stated, "Only about 5% of marriages contracted in 1867 ended in divorce, but over one-half of marriages contracted in 1967 are expected to end in divorce" (p. 455).

DIVORCE RATES AND RATIOS

Factual knowledge of the American marriage and divorce situation was first investigated by Walter F. Willcox (1891, 1893, 1897), a pioneer demographer who served as a statistician for the U.S. War Department, an academic scholar and university administrator, and a statistical adviser to nations (Notestein 1968). During the late 1880s, Willcox's interest in the divorce question led him to prepare a dissertation on the legal philosophy of this topic. But when he traveled to Berlin, Germany, to study empirical methods, Willcox was so taken by what he learned that he soon applied these new techniques to the U.S. marriage and divorce census data and later to other issues that emerged in this enlightened era and environment. Special topical areas that Willcox helped to develop include demography studies relating to birth, death, migration, and population composition, as well as the methodological problems affecting the gathering and analyses of census and vital statistics data. The following offers a brief discussion of this important foundation.

The persistency of the myth surrounding the U.S. divorce problem may be attributed in part to the large number of marriages and divorces recorded annually. Thus, it is important to understand the method used for determining the divorce rate, which is equal to the number of divorces occurring in a population during a specific year divided by the number of marriages, number of married males, or number of married females in the population. Thus, the crude divorce rate formula is

$$Divorce\ rate = D \times K/P,$$

where D is the number of divorces occurring in one year, P is the population at risk to divorce, and K is a constant, 1,000. This resultant ratio when multiplied by 1,000 provides a crude rate because, as Saunders (1988:41) notes, the entire population of marriages of all ages is represented in the denominator and the number of divorces of all ages is included in the numerator.

The general divorce rate records the behavior of a population actually exposed to the risk of divorce. This refined rate is the number of divorces in a given year per 1,000 females of age 15 and above or, in some jurisdictions, age 18 and above. The formula for this refined divorce rate is

$$Divorce\ rate = D \times K/P_f\ (15+),$$

where D is the number of divorces occurring in a population in a given year, $P_f(15+)$ is the number of females ages 15 and above in the population, and K is a constant, 1,000. Thus, the rate represents the number of divorces per 1,000

women over age 15, a measure that compares the number of divorces with the total number of women eligible for divorce (adult married women) and hence is a more valid indicator of the propensity for divorce (Lamanna and Riedmann 1991:546).

As noted by Nock and Kingston (1990:245), the divorce ratio divides the number of divorced persons by the number of married people per the constant 1,000. Thus, in a population of 1,000 people in which 20 divorced people live, the divorce ratio is

$$Divorce\ ratio = \frac{20\ (divorced\ people)}{980\ (married\ people)}$$
$$20/980\ .0204081 \times 1,000$$

Divorce ratio = 20.4081

The crude rate of divorce, based on 10 divorces in the same population, would be

$$Divorce\ rate = \frac{10}{1,000} \times 1,000$$
$$= .01 \times 1,000$$

Divorce rate = 10.0

In the following, official data are reported to establish an historical documentation to demonstrate the fallacy of the 50 percent divorce rate. The marriage and divorce data reported in the tables show the incidence, the rates, and, when available, the ratios in separate columns.

THE MARRIAGE AND DIVORCE DATA

William L. O'Neill observes that divorce was rare during the eighteenth century, and, according to Jacobson (1959) and Furstenberg (1990:382), during the 1800s formal divorce was difficult to obtain; thus dissolution of some marriages resulting from desertion were undercounted. But as shown in Table 27.1, during the next century, marriage and divorce were considered important enough to warrant official documentation, an accounting that began under the stewardship of Carroll D. Wright, then Commissioner of Labor (Dike 1889:592).

The first assessment of the American marriage and divorce question was addressed by Walter F. Willcox (1891, 1893, 1897). Portions of the data shown in the tables reported in this section are from these initial reports. These data beg the question as to why the myth of the 50 percent divorce rate prevails. One possible explanation may lie in the salience of attitude toward divorce reported by Peck (1993). Since the passage of the No-Fault Divorce Act in 1972, divorce, a fairly common event during the final decades of the twentieth century, emerged as a subject of considerable debate with important social policy implications. First, divorce is considered problematic when the union dissolution affects children. This is especially true when the quality of family life in terms of social, economic, and health-related factors for women and children, affected by diminished financial resources, is at risk (Furstenberg 1990). Divorce thus remains a salient issue, especially in terms of the conservative public attitude toward so-called traditional family values.

Evaluation of marriage and divorce in the United States is possible based on data from 1867 to the early twenty-first century. Included in these data are those published in the first statistical study conducted in the United States and the national vital statistics gathered throughout the course of the twentieth and early twenty-first centuries.

Marriage and divorce data for 1887 to 1906 first became available in 1908, and sociologists quickly acknowledged the information as representing a "great report" (Howard 1909:766). The data shown in Table 27.1 are from this first effort to offer an overall view of marriage and divorce in the United States. The researchers avoided reporting data in Part 1, actually reported in 1909, due to general underreporting/nonreporting jurisdictions. Indeed, Calhoun's (1919:199) assessment of these initial numbers indicates that few jurisdictions outside New England did anything more than supply some numbers. But it is noteworthy that the period from 1896 to 1905, according to Calhoun (1919), was "distinctly prone to marriage" (p. 199) and divorce, which Howard (1909:776) argued was frequent in the two most enlightened and democratic nations in the world, namely, the United States and Switzerland.

Clifford Kirkpatrick (1968) argues that divorce is an imperfect index of marital and social disorganization. The reason is straightforward: There can be disorganization in the family without divorce. This is one oft-cited reason why the divorce laws have liberalized in Western societies from the early to mid-twentieth century (Kurz 2001). Moreover, when the modern family became the dominant form during the nineteenth century, divorce became much more common (O'Neill 1967). Then, during the Progressive Era from approximately 1880 to 1919, a more liberal interpretation of marriage and divorce arose among the urban, industrial middle class. Indeed, O'Neill (1967:viii) found that as the Victorian family was to represent the ideal throughout the nineteenth century, divorce was to become the first in a series of adjustments that emerged from the clash between ideas surrounding the patriarchal family and the new sexual ethic arising in turn from the new urban, industrial society.

Despite the suggested inaccuracy of the data and ofttimes inconsistent method in recording and reporting procedures through which these data were gathered, at least some data are available. During the 40-year period from 1867 to 1906, a total of 1,274,341 divorces were reported in the then states, the District of Columbia, and the Indian Territory (U.S. Bureau of the Census 1908). As shown in Table 27.1, there is a steady increase in the number of divorces from 1867 on and in the number of marriages from 1887 to 1906. One would anticipate such a trend, given the growth of the general population during this same period. Yet this did not seem so logical to those analysts who defined divorce in problematic terms. Note the not-uncommon statement of the early twentieth century attributed to William Fielding Ogburn (1927),

> In 1924, there was one divorce granted to about every 7 marriages performed indicates that divorce is very common. Moreover, the chances of a marriage entered in 1924 being broken by divorce may perhaps be nearer to 1 to 5 or 6 than 1 to 7. There were in 1924 about 15 to 16 times as many divorces as there were in 1870, and yet the population is only about 3 times as large. (P. 7)

A similar, albeit misguided, statement is even later attributed to Newman

Table 27.1 Incidence of Marriages and Divorces: 1867 to 1906

Year	No. of Marriages	No. of Divorces	Year	No. of Marriages	No. of Divorces
1867	—	9,937	1887	483,069	27,919
1868	—	10,150	1888	504,530	28,669
1869	—	10,939	1889	531,457	31,735
1870	—	10,962	1890	562,412	35,540
1872	—	12,390	1892	577,870	36,579
1873	—	13,156	1893	578,673	37,468
1874	—	13,989	1894	566,161	37,568
1875	—	14,212	1895	598,855	40,387
1876	—	14,800	1896	613,873	42,937
1877	—	15,687	1897	622,350	44,699
1878	—	16,089	1898	625,655	47,849
1879	—	17,083	1899	650,610	51,437
1880	—	19,663	1900	685,284	55,751
1881	—	20,762	1901	716,621	60,984
1882	—	22,112	1902	746,733	61,480
1883	—	23,198	1903	786,132	64,925
1884	—	22,994	1904	781,145	66,199
1885	—	23,472	1905	804,787	67,976
1886	—	25,535	1906	853,290	72,062

SOURCE: U.S. Bureau of the Census (1909:7, 12).

NOTE: Prior to the 1909 report, many states lacked compulsory requirements for the recording of marriages. Thus, the number of marriages was first gathered for the 1909 report, at which time two states—namely, New York and South Carolina—did not have marriage license requirements. However, in the 1908 publication, which is actually Part II of this important report, it is written that for the 1867 to 1906 period a total of 1,274,341 divorces were recorded, of which 845,652 were granted to the wife (table 7, p. 203).

Table 27.2   Number of Marriages and Divorces, 1887 to 1932

Year	No. of Marriages	No. of Divorces	Granted to Husband	Granted to Wife — Number	Granted to Wife — Percentage	No. of Divorces per 1,000 Marriages
1887	483,069	27,919	9,729	18,190	65.2	
1888	504,530	28,669	10,022	18,647	65.0	—
1889	531,457	31,735	11,126	20,609	64.9	—
1890	542,537	33,461	11,625	21,836	65.3	—
1891	562,412	35,540	12,478	23,062	64.9	62
1892	577,870	36,579	12,577	24,002	65.6	63
1893	578,673	37,468	12,590	24,878	66.4	63
1894	566,161	37,568	12,551	25,017	66.6	65
1895	598,855	40,378	13,456	26,931	66.7	66
1896	613,873	42,937	14,448	28,489	66.4	67
1897	622,350	44,699	14,765	29,934	67.0	70
1898	625,655	47,849	15,988	31,861	66.6	72
1899	650,610	51,437	16,925	34,512	67.1	76
1900	685,284	55,751	18,620	37,131	66.6	79
1901	716,621	60,984	20,008	40,976	67.2	91
1902	746,733	61,480	20,056	41,424	67.4	85
1903	786,132	64,925	21,321	43,604	67.2	82
1904	781,145	66,199	22,189	44,010	66.5	83
1905	804,787	67,976	22,220	45,756	67.3	85
1906	853,290	72,062	23,455	48,607	67.5	84
1907	936,936	76,571				84
1908	857,461	76,852				
1909	897,354	79,671				
1910	948,166	83,045				
1911	955,287	89,219				
1912	1,904,602	94,318				
1913	1,021,398	91,307				
1914	1,025,092	100,584				
1915	1,007,595	104,298				
1916	1,040,684	112,036	33,809	74,893	68.9	108
1917	1,144,200	121,564				
1918	1,000,109	116,254				
1919	1,150,186	141,527				
1920	1,274,476	170,505				
1921	1,163,863	159,580				
1922	1,134,151	148,815	47,359	100,416	68.0	131
1923	1,229,784	165,096	52,999	111,480	67.8	134
1924	1,184,574	170,952	52,984	115,328	68.5	144
1925	1,188,334	175,449	52,147	121,333	69.9	148
1926	1,202574	180,853	52,834	126,563	70.5	150
1927	1,201,053	192,037	54,637	134,048	71.0	160
1928	1,182,497	195.939	55,065	137,277	71.4	166
1929	1,232,559	201,468	57,148	142,187	71.3	163
1930	1,126,856	191,591	52,554	137,309	72.3	170
1931	1,060,914	183,664	49,591	132,612	72.8	173
1932	981,903	160,338	42,335	117,375	73.5	163

SOURCES: U.S. Bureau of Statistics 1911:No. 33, table 45, p. 76; 1930:No. 52, table 98, p. 91; U.S. Bureau of the Census 1931:table 3, p. 5, table 13, p. 20; U.S. Bureau of the Census 1941: *Statistical Abstract of the United States, 1940,* table 96, p. 97; U.S. Bureau of the Census 1940:*Statistical Abstract of the United States, 1939,* table 94, p. 96.

(1950:89), who looked at the numeric increases instead of the rates of marriage and divorce.

In Table 27.2, the divorce "granted to whom"—husband or wife category—for most of the period from 1887 to 1932 is shown. Although not available for all years, the percentage column for "granted to wife" represents a statistic that is noteworthy. Without exception, for each year two-thirds or more of divorces granted are to the wife. The first data for calculating ratios noting the number of divorces per 1,000 marriages also are shown. With a few exceptions, notably the years 1913, 1918, 1921, and 1922, the number of divorces increases throughout the period from 1887 to 1929. For the period from 1930 to 1932, however, the data show a moderate downward trend toward fewer divorces. With the exception of 1928 and the period from 1930 to 1932, the same observation can be made for marriages in that the trend in the marriage rate is downward.

Perhaps the most important aspect of these rich data is the fact that they were to serve well the needs of an admiring and ever-growing community of scientists, and these analysts began to raise important theoretical and methodological cause-and-effect questions. Prominent among these early sociologists was George Elliott Howard (1909), whose interest in the complexities of sex, marriage, and the family and especially the role education might play in solving social problems led him to focus on the officially recorded cause of divorce. Other less obvious reasons for establishing the importance of causal factors of what became known as a "divorce movement" included the excessive use of liquor and the platform advocated by the Temperance Movement.

The most frequently cited legal ground, as noted by Hankins (1931) and shown in Tables 27.3a, b, and c, represents the legally recognized grounds for divorce—namely, adultery, cruelty, desertion, drunkenness, and neglect to provide. Each was common during the period from 1887 to 1891 and for some time thereafter, lending support to the contention by Flexner and Fitzpatrick ([1908] 1996), who, in 1908, wrote, "Women were only granted divorces in instances of 'adultery, desertion, non-support, and

extreme cruelty.'" Other grounds for divorce, although less frequently cited, included bigamy, coercion, conviction of a crime, impotence, insanity, incompatibility, misconduct, fraudulent representation, vagrancy, infection with venereal disease (Hankins 1931). But what is perhaps most interesting is that even though the legal reasons for divorce currently cited may be less offensive by virtue of the descriptor employed, the general reasons for dissolving marriages cited in the past continue in the present.

The numbers and causes of divorces granted to a husband and wife for the five-year periods for 1887 to 1906 (Table 27.3a) and for 1906 to 1932 (Tables 27.3b and c) are shown. As noted in Table 27.2, throughout the period 1887 to 1906 a total of 1,274,341 divorces were granted. Of this total, 428,687 divorces were granted to the husband; to the wife the number is almost double, at 845,652, and serves as testimony that the women's movements of the nineteenth and twentieth centuries worked to gain recognition from the courts to allow the initiation of divorce on behalf of women. As one can ascertain from these data, in the United States this right was granted to women in the nineteenth century (Anderson and Wolchik (2001). The causal factors identified within a legal context seem to hold at least up to the mid-twentieth century, for which period Harmsworth and Minnis (1955:316) reported that the legal functional categories, such as extreme cruelty, desertion, adultery, and nonsupport, represent overt manifestations of the factors leading to divorce but these did not necessarily represent the *causes* of divorce.

Table 27.3a   Number and Causes of Divorce[a], Granted to Husband and Wife, by Quinquennial Periods, 1887 to 1906

Causes	1887–1891		1892–1896		1897–1901		1902–1906	
	Number	Percentage	Number	Percentage	Number	Percentage	Number	Percentage
Granted to husband								
Adultery	17,139	31.2	19,956	30.4	24,269	28.1	29,526	27.0
Cruelty	4,047	7.4	6,069	9.2	9,385	10.9	13,678	12.5
Desertion	27,150	49.4	31,805	48.5	43,186	50.0	54,142	49.6
Drunkenness	592	1.1	765	1.2	986	1.1	1,093	1.0
Neglect to provide	—	—	2	[b]	1	[b]	3	[b]
Combinations of preceding causes	2,654	4.8	3,190	4.9	3,681	4.3	4,805	4.4
All other causes[b]	3,398	6.2	3,836	5.8	4,798	5.6	5,994	5.5
Granted to wife								
Adultery	10,880	10.6	13,714	10.6	16,915	9.7	21,360	9.6
Cruelty	25,200	24.6		26.7	48,797	28.0	64,541	28.9
Desertion	35,666	34.8	43,153	33.4	58,382	33.5	74,018	33.1
Drunkenness	5,397	5.3	6,913	5.3	8,828	5.1	11,942	5.3
Neglect to provide	4,605	4.5	6,857	5.3	10,423	6.0	12,779	5.7
Combinations of preceding causes	13,770	13.5	15,757	12.2	19,979	11.5	25,013	11.2
All other causes[c]	6,826	6.7	8,414	6.5	11,090	6.4	13,748	6.2

SOURCES: U.S. Bureau of the Census 1908:table 2, p. 4; table 7, p. 203; U.S. Bureau of Statistics 1911:table 46, p. 77.

a. All causes of divorce (1867–1906): Husband (428,689), Wife (845, 652).

b. Less than one-tenth of 1 percent.

c. Other causes include crime against nature, impotency, conviction of a felony and imprisonment in a penitentiary, and pregnancy prior to marriage, as well as unknown factors.

Table 27.3b   Number and Causes of Divorce, Granted to Husband and Wife, 1906 to 1926

Causes	1906		1916		1922		1924		1926	
	Number	Percentage	Number	Percentage	Number	Percentage	Number	Percentage	Number	Percentage
Granted to Husband										
Adultery	6,378	27.2	6,850	20.3	8,333	17.6	8,263	15.6	7,799	14.8
Cruelty	3,128	13.3	5,895	17.4	11,818	25.0	14,251	26.9	14,968	28.3
Desertion	11,512	49.1	16,908	50.0	20,979	44.3	24,059	45.4	24,059	45.5
Drunkenness	228	1.0	271	0.8	120	0.3	190	0.4	185	0.4
Neglect to provide	—	—	—	—	—	—	—	—	—	—
Combinations of preceding causes	996	4.2	1,440	4.3	2,182	4.6	1,761	3.3	1,538	2.9
All other causes	1,213	5.2	2,445	7.2	3,927	8.3	4,462	8.4	4,285	8.1
Granted to Wife										
Adultery	4,643	9.6	5,636	7.5	7,720	7.7	8,669	7.5	8,911	7.0
Cruelty	14,368	29.6	24,857	33.2	39,212	39.0	48,278	41.9	54,087	42.7
Desertion	15,895	32.7	23,082	30.8	27,528	27.4	31,323	27.2	32,944	26.0
Drunkenness	2,568	5.3	3,381	4.5	1,416	1.4	2,027	1.8	2,589	2.0
Neglect to provide	2,782	5.7	5,146	6.9	6,212	6.2	6,232	5.4	7,092	5.6
Combinations of preceding causes	5,396	11.1	7,892	10.5	10,667	10.6	9,884	8.6	9,938	7.9
All other causes	2,955	6.1	4,809	6.5	7,661	7.6	8,915	7.7	11,002	8.7

SOURCES: *Marriage and Divorce, 1924* (U.S. Bureau of the Census 1926:tables 12 and 13, pp. 22–23); *Marriage and Divorce, 1928* (U.S. Bureau of the Census 1930:tables 16 and 17, p. 23); *Marriage and Divorce, 1929* (U.S. Bureau of the Census 1931:table 16, p. 23); *Marriage and Divorce, 1932* (U.S. Bureau of the Census 1934:tables 4 and 7, pp. 4–6).

Table 27.3c   Number and Causes of Divorce, Granted to Husband and Wife, 1928 to 1932

Causes	1928		1929		1930		1931		1932	
	Number	Percentage	Number	Percentage	Number	Percentage	Number	Percentage	Number	Percentage
Granted to Husband										
Adultery	7,309	13.3	7,265	12.7					4,210	9.8
Cruelty	17,350	31.5	18,514	32.4					15,174	35.8
Desertion	24,177	43.9	24,660	43.2					17,884	42.2
Drunkenness	241	0.4	236	<0.1					143	0.3
Neglect to provide	—	—	—	—	—	—	—	—	—	—
Combinations of preceding causes	1,576	2.9	1,857	3.2					1,687	4.1
All other causes	4,412	8.0	4,616	8.1					3,237	6.9
Granted to Wife										
Adultery	8,908	6.5	9,245	6.5					7,395	6.3
Cruelty	60,648	44.2	62,770	44.1					53,072	45.2
Desertion	33,819	24.6	34,401	24.2					26,721	22.8
Drunkenness	3,098	2.3	3,353	2.4					2,035	1.7
Neglect to provide	7,883	5.7	7,741	5.4					6,620	5.6
Combinations of preceding causes	10,553	7.7	11,778	8.3					11,026	9.5
All other causes	12,368	9.0	12,899	9.1					10,505	8.4

SOURCES: *Marriage and Divorce, 1924* (U.S. Bureau of the Census 1926:tables 12 and 13, pp. 22–23); *Marriage and Divorce, 1928* (U.S. Bureau of the Census 1930:tables 16 and 17, p. 23); *Marriage and Divorce, 1929* (U.S. Bureau of the Census 1931:table 16, p. 23); *Marriage and Divorce, 1932* (U.S. Bureau of the Census 1934:tables 4 and 7, pp. 4–6).

Table 27.4a   Percentage Distribution of Divorces for Each Specified Cause, by Party to Whom Granted: 1887 to 1929 and 1930 to 1932

Cause and Party to Whom Granted	1887 to 1906	1916	1922	1923	1924	1925	1926	1927	1928	1929
All Causes (100 Percent)										
To husband	33.4	31.1	32.0	32.2	31.5	30.1	29.5	29.0	28.6	28.7
To wife	66.6	68.9	68.0	67.8	68.5	69.9	70.5	71.0	71.4	71.3
Adultery										
To husband	59.1	54.9	51.9	49.4	48.8	49.0	46.7	45.9	45.1	44.0
To wife	40.9	45.1	48.1	50.6	51.2	51.0	53.3	54.1	54.9	56.0
Cruelty										
To husband	16.1	19.2	23.2	23.3	22.8	21.7	21.7	21.4	22.2	22.8
To wife	83.9	80.8	76.8	76.7	77.2	78.3	78.3	78.6	77.8	77.2
Desertion										
To husband	42.5	42.3	43.2	43.8	43.4	43.3	42.2	41.6	41.7	41.8
To wife	57.5	57.7	56.8	56.2	56.6	56.7	57.8	58.4	58.3	58.2
Drunkenness										
To husband	9.4	7.4	7.8	10.8	8.6	7.4	6.7	7.1	7.2	6.6
To wife	90.6	92.6	92.2	89.2	91.4	92.6	93.3	92.9	92.8	93.4
Neglect to Provide										
To husband	—	—	—	—	—	—	—	—	—	—
To wife	100.0	100.0	100.0	100.0	100.0	100.0	100.0	100.0	100.0	100.0
Combinations of Causes										
To husband	16.1	15.4	17.0	14.9	15.1	13.7	13.4	15.9	13.0	13.6
To wife	83.9	84.6	83.0	85.1	84.9	86.3	86.6	84.1	87.0	86.4
All Other Causes										
To husband	31.0	33.3	33.9	37.6	33.4	26.9	28.0	27.7	26.3	26.4
To wife	69.0	66.7	66.1	62.4	66.6	73.1	72.0	72.3	73.7	73.6

SOURCES: *Marriage and Divorce 1929: Statistics of Marriages, Divorces, and Annulments of Marriage,* Eighth Annual Report, 1931 (U.S. Bureau of the Census 1931:table 18, p. 25).

Despite such issues, the position assumed by Howard (1904:Vol. 3, pp. 1–160) appears to be supported by the data reported in Tables 27.3a, b, and c and Tables 27.4a and b: Throughout the eighteenth and nineteenth centuries, divorce legislation became more liberalized, reflecting a social need caused by migratory expansion and social changes in attitudes toward the marital bond. Competing definitions of need and justifiable causes also are reflected in the diversity of state legislation, which led to liberal legislation and thereby an increased number of legally acceptable causes for divorce. By 1891, for example, Washington State's code included 11 causes, of which at least one cause codified a previous more abstract cause.

To this point the data raise interesting issues as to whether the traditional family some contemporary critics argue existed in the past did in fact really exist. Based on these five-year-period data, images of the traditional family may have been just that—images but not necessarily a reality of positive marital bliss. Some interesting findings reported in Tables 27.3a, b, and c include "adultery" and "desertion." Although the data for divorces granted to the wife based on allegations of adultery and desertion are most extensive, the divorce data for these same categories

granted to the husband also are noteworthy. Other categories include cruelty, a combination of causes granted to the wife. Such historical times hardly seem idyllic. Perhaps it can also be suggested that the reasons cited for divorce have not changed since 1887, albeit the contemporary law allows categories such as irretrievable breakdown of the marriage, incompatibility, or irreconcilable differences to serve as the more general reasons for filing for divorce, reasons allowed even if the divorce being sought is not mutually agreeable (Kurz 2001:3811). But other causes include crimes against nature, impotency, conviction of a felony and imprisonment, pregnancy prior to marriage, and unknown factors.

As with the information reported in Tables 27.3a, b, and c, the data in Tables 27.4a and b show the proportion of divorce by cause granted to husband and to wife. These data are broken down into proportions for the periods 1887 to 1927 and 1930 to 1932. Again, the "adultery" cause for divorce granted to husband is noteworthy as is the steady decreasing trend for this specific category. Of course the opposite effect for the "adultery" cause is noted for the "granted to wife" category. Focusing on the "desertion" cause category, the percentages are markedly consistent

Table 27.4b   Percentage Distribution of Divorces for Each Specified Cause, by Party to Whom Granted, 1887 to 1927 and 1930 to 1932

Cause and Party to Whom Granted	1930	1931	1932
All Causes (100 Percent)			
To husband	27.7	27.2	26.5
To wife	72.3	72.8	73.5
Adultery			
To husband			36.3
To wife			63.7
Cruelty			
To husband			22.2
To wife			77.8
Desertion			
To husband			40.1
To wife			59.0
Drunkenness			
To husband			6.6
To wife			93.4
Neglect to Provide			
To husband			—
To wife			100.0
Combinations of Causes			
To husband			13.3
To wife			86.7
All Other Causes			
To husband			23.6
To wife			76.4

SOURCE: *Marriage and Divorce, 1932* (U.S. Bureau of the Census 1934:table 4, p. 4).

Table 27.5   Numbers and Rates of First Marriage and Divorce: Three-Year Averages, 1921 to 1989

Three-Year Period	First Marriage		Divorce	
	Thousands	Rate	Thousands	Rate
1921 to 1923	990	99	158	10
1924 to 1926	992	95	177	11
1927 to 1929	1,025	94	201	12
1930 to 1932	919	81	183	10
1933 to 1935	1,081	92	196	11
1936 to 1938	1,183	98	243	13
1939 to 1941	1,312	106	269	14
1942 to 1944	1,247	108	360	17
1945 to 1947	1,540	143	526	24
1948 to 1950	1,326	134	397	17
1951 to 1953	1,190	122	388	16
1954 to 1956	1,182	120	397	15
1957 to 1959	1,128	112	381	15
1960 to 1962	1,205	112	407	16
1963 to 1965	1,311	109	452	17
1966 to 1968	1,440	107	535	20
1969 to 1971	1,649	109	702	26
1972 to 1974	1,662	103	907	32
1975 to 1977	1,508	85	1,070	37
1978 to 1980	1,580	83	1,167	40
1981 to 1983	1,632	84	1,191	39
1984 to 1986	1,595	80	1,179	38
1987 to 1989	1,564	76	1,165	37

SOURCE: Adapted from U.S. Bureau of the Census (1992).

throughout the entire periods from 1887 to 1927 and from 1930 to 1932 for both the husband and the wife.

Finally, the incompleteness of the data for the early 1930s is attributed to the fact that Congress mandated that the Marriage and Divorce study in progress since the early part of the century cease after publication of the 1932 study phase. By 1959, analysts such as Jacobson (1959) emphatically stated that marriage and divorce statistics represent the least developed branch of American vital statistics even though national data on divorce were available for many years before such information was available for births and deaths (p. 9).

Table 27.5 shows the 1921 to 1989 three-year average data for marriage and divorce. The three-year average rates increase from 1921 to 1923 up to the 1978 to 1980 period, and then a modest decline throughout the decade of the 1980s is documented. More important perhaps is that these data are from the oft-cited U.S. government report referred to above. It is important to recognize the historical rise and fall in the rate of first marriages. When placed within an historical context to include the relative prosperity of the 1920s, the Depression years, World War II, the tranquil years of the 1950s, and then the more activist years of the 1960s and 1970s, these data provide interesting

information pertaining to the sexual behavior of the American people.

Frank F. Furstenberg Jr. (1990) suggests that "Americans have always had a higher propensity to divorce than do Europeans and people of North Atlantic Countries," a contention that receives empirical support from sources such as the Statistical Office of the European Communities report covering the 1960 to 1988 period. Although the United States is shown to have the highest divorces per 1,000 married women, the same reports indicate that the United States also had the highest marriages per 1,000 persons for this period.

The incidence, rate, and ratio of marriages reported for the United Status during the period from 1887 to 2004 are reported in Table 27.6. Although the data on the number of marriages are incomplete for the entire period, they are both interesting and suggestive. Ranging from a low of 7.9 for the year 1932 (the heart of the Depression period) and then 7.6 for 2003 and 2004 to a high of 16.4 in 1946 (the end of World War II), the marriage rate had been declining or at a steady state since the peak period from 1980 to 1982. The rates recorded for 2002 through 2004 are the lowest since 1932, at which time the 7.9 rate was the lowest ever recorded for the United States. Trendwise, the highest marriage rate for the entire 118-year period was during 1940 to 1950 or just prior to and immediately after World War II.

Table 27.6 Incidence, Rate, and Ratio of Marriages:
United States, 1887 to 2004

(Continued)

Year	Number of Marriages	Rate per 1,000 Total Population	Rate per 1,000 Women 15 Years and Older	Year	Number of Marriages	Rate per 1,000 Total Population	Rate per 1,000 Women 15 Years and Older
2004	2,223,000	7.6	—	1939	1,403,633	10.7	—
2003	2,224,000	7.6	—	1938	1330,780	10.2	—
2002	2,254,000	7.9	—	1937	1,426,000	11.0	—
2001	2,345,000	8.2	—	1936	1,369,000	10.7	—
2000	2,329,000	8.2	—	1935	1,327,000	10.4	—
1999	2,251,000	8.3	—	1934	1,302,000	10.3	—
1998	2,258,000	8.3	—	1933	1,098,000	8.7	—
1997	2,384,000	8.9	—	1932	981,903	7.9	28.3
1996	2,344,000	8.8	—	1931	1,060,914	8.6	30.8
1995	2,336,000	8.9	—	1930	1,126,856	9.2	—
1994	2,362,000	9.1	—	1929	1,232,559	10.1	—
1993	2,334,000	9.0	—	1928	1,182,497	9.9	—
1992	2,362,000	9.3	—	1927	1,201,497	10.2	—
1991	2,371,000	9.4	—	1926	1,202,574	10.3	—
1990	2,443,000	9.8	24.1	1925	1,188,334	10.4	—
1989	2,404,000	9.7	23.9	1924	1,184,574	10.5	—
1988	2,395,926	9.8	24.0	1923	1,229,784	11.0	—
1987	2,403,378	9.9	24.3	1922	1,134,151	10.3	—
1986	2,407,099	10.0	24.5	1921	1,163,863	10.8	—
1985	2,412,625	10.1	24.9	1920	1,274,476	12.0	—
1984	2,477,192	10.5	25.8	1919	1,150,186	11.0	—
1983	2,445,604	10.5	25.7	1918	1,000,109	9.7	—
1982	2,456,278	10.6	26.1	1917	1,144,200	11.2	
1981	2,422,145	10.6	26.1	1916	1,075,775	10.7	
1980	2,390,252	10.6	26.1	1915	1,007,595	10.1	—
1979	2,331,337	10.4	25.8	1914	1,025,092	10.5	
1978	2,282,272	10.3	25.7	1913	1,021,398	10.6	—
1977	2,178,367	9.9	25.0	1912	1,004,602	10.6	
1976	2,154,807	9.9	25.2	1911	955,287	10.2	
1975	2,152,662	10.0	25.6	1910	948,166	10.3	
1974	2,229,667	10.5	27.1	1909	897,354	9.9	
1973	2,284,108	10.8	28.2	1908	857,461	9.6	
1972	2,282,154	10.9	28.8	1907	936,936	10.7	
1971	2,190,481	10.6	28.2	1906	853,079	10.5	
1970	2,163,000	10.6	28.4	1905	804,016	10.0	
1969	2,145,000	10.6	28.9	1904	780,856	9.9	
1968	2,069,000	10.4	28.3	1903	785,926	10.1	—
1967	1,927,000	9.7	26.9	1902	746,364	9.8	
1966	1,857,000	9.5	26.4	1901	716,287	9.6	
1965	1,800,000	9.3	26.0	1900	685,101	9.3	
1964	1,725,000	9.0	25.3	1899	650,585	9.0	
1963	1,654,000	8.8	24.7	1898	625,253	8.8	—
1962	1,577,000	8.5	23.9	1897	622,112	8.9	
1961	1,548,000	8.5	24.0	1896	613,719	9.0	
1960	1,523,000	8.5	24.0	1895	598,633	8.9	
1959	1,494,000	8.5	23.8	1894	565,798	8.6	
1958	1,451,000	8.4	23.5	1893	578,457	9.0	—
1957	1,518,000	8.9	24.9	1892	577,335	9.1	
1956	1,585,000	9.5	26.4	1891	562,004	9.2	
1955	1,531,000	9.3	25.8	1890	542,307	9.0	
1954	1,490,000	9.2	25.4	1889	530,937	9.1	—
1953	1,546,000	9.8	26.7	1888	504,373	8.8	
1952	1,539,318	9.9	26.8	1887	482,680	8.7	—
1951	1,594,694	10.4	28.1				
1950	1,667,231	11.1	29.8				
1949	1,579,798	10.6	28.5				
1948	1,811,155	12.4	33.0				
1947	1,991,878	13.9	36.8				
1946	2,291,045	16.4	42.8				
1945	1,612,992	12.2	30.5				
1944	1,452,394	10.9	27.8				
1943	1,577,050	11.7	30.6				
1942	1,772,132	13.2	34.8				
1941	1,695,999	12.7	33.7				
1940	1,595,879	12.1	32.3				

SOURCES: U.S. Bureau of the Census 1931:table 3, p. 5, National Center for Health Statistics (1978), U.S. Bureau of the Census (2004:tables 70 and 113, pp. 60 and 88. *Statistical Abstract of the United States, 1940.* 1941:table 96, p. 97. *Statistical Abstract of the United States, 1947* table 101, p. 90. The data for 1940–1988 are from the *Monthly Vital Statistics Report* Vol. 40, No. 4(S), August 26, 1991. The data for 1989–1992 are from *Monthly Vital Statistics Report* Vol. 38, No. 10 (April 4), 1990; Vol. 40, No. 13 (September 30), 1992; and Vol. 41, No. 13 (September 28), 1993. U.S. Bureau of the Census *Statistical Abstract of the United States: 1999:*table 156, p. 110. National Vital Statistics Reports Vol. 53, June 28, 2005 and Vol. 54, No. 7, December 22, 2005, No. 21. Data for the years 1920 to 1929 are from U.S. Bureau of the Census (1975).

Table 27.7 Incidence and Rate of Divorces and Annulments: United States, 1887 to 2004

(Continued)

Year	Divorces and Annulments	Rate per 1,000 Total Population	Rate per 1,000 Women 15 Years and Older	Year	Divorces and Annulments	Rate per 1,000 Total Population	Rate per 1,000 Women 15 Years and Older
2004	—	3.7	—	1938	244,000	1.9	8.4
2003	—	3.8	—	1937	250,000	1.9	8.7
2002	—	3.9	—	1936	236,000	1.8	8.3
2001	—	3.9	—	1935	218,000	1.7	7.8
2000	—	4.1	—	1934	204,000	1.6	7.5
1999	1,640,000	4.1	—	1933	165,000	1.3	6.1
1998	1,135,000	4.2	—	1932	164,241	1.3	6.1
1997	1,163,000	4.3	—	1931	188,003	1.5	7.1
1996	1,150,000	4.3	19.5	1930	195,961	1.6	7.5
1995	1,169,000	4.4	19.8	1929	205,876	1.7	8.0
1994	1,191,000	4.6	20.5	1928	200,176	1.7	7.8
1993	1,187,000	4.6	20.5	1927	196,292	1.6	7.8
1992	1,215,000	4.8	21.2	1926ª	184,688	1.6	7.5
1991	1,187,000	4.7	20.9	1925	175,449	1.5	7.2
1990	1,182,000	4.7	20.9	1924	170,952	1.5	7.2
1989	1,163,000	4.8	20.4	1923	165,096	1.5	7.1
1988	1,183,000	4.7	20.7	1922	149,815	1.4	6.6
1987	1,166,000	4.8	20.8	1921	159,580	1.5	7.2
1986	1,178,000	4.9	21.2	1920	170,505	1.6	8.0
1985	1,190,000	5.0	21.7	1919	141,527	1.3	—
1984	1,169,000	5.0	21.5	1918	116,254	1.1	—
1983	1,158,000	4.9	21.3	1917	121,564	1.2	
1982	1,170,000	5.0	21.7	1916	112,036	1.1	—
1981	1,213,000	5.3	22.6	1915	104,298	1.0	
1980	1,189,000	5.2	22.6	1914	100,584	1.0	
1979	1,181,000	5.3	22.8	1913	91,307	0.9	—
1978	1,130,000	5.1	21.9	1912	94,318	1.0	
1977	1,091,000	5.0	21.1	1911	89,219	1.0	
1976	1,083,000	5.0	21.1	1910	83,045	0.9	4.7
1975	1,036,000	4.8	20.3	1909	79,671	0.9	
1974	977,000	4.6	19.3	1908	76,852	0.9	
1973ᵇ	915,000	4.3	18.2	1907	76,571	0.9	—
1972	845,000	4.0	17.0	1906	72,062	0.9	
1971	773,000	3.7	15.8	1905	67,976	0.8	
1970	708,000	3.5	14.9	1904	66,199	0.8	—
1969	639,000	3.2	13.4	1903	64,925	0.8	
1968	584,000	2.9	12.5	1902	61,480	0.8	—
1967	523,000	2.6	11.2	1901	60,984	0.8	4.0
1966	499,000	2.5	10.9	1900	55,751	0.7	—
1965	479,000	2.5	10.6	1899	51,437	0.7	
1964	450,000	2.4	10.0	1898	47,849	0.7	
1963	428,000	2.3	9.6	1897	44,699	0.6	
1962	413,000	2.2	9.4	1896	42,937	0.6	—
1961	414,000	2.3	9.6	1895	40,387	0.6	
1960	393,000	2.2	9.2	1894	37,568	0.6	
1959	395,000	2.2	9.3	1893	37,468	0.6	—
1958	368,000	2.1	8.9	1892	36,579	0.6	
1957	381,000	2.2	9.2	1891	35,540	0.6	
1956	382,000	2.3	9.4	1890	33,461	0.5	—
1955	377,000	2.3	9.3	1889	31,735	0.5	
1954	379,000	2.4	9.5	1888	28,669	0.5	
1953	390,000	2.5	9.9	1887	27,919	0.5	
1952	392,000	2.5	10.1	1880 and 1870		0.4 and 0.3, respectively	—
1951	381,000	2.5	9.9				
1950	385,000	2.6	10.3				
1949	397,000	2.7	10.6				
1948	408,000	2.8	11.2				
1947	483,000	3.4	13.6				
1946	610,000	4.3	17.9				
1945	485,000	3.5	14.4				
1944	400,000	2.9	12.0				
1943	359,000	2.6	11.0				
1942	321,000	2.4	10.1				
1941	293,000	2.2	9.4				
1940	264,000	2.0	8.8				
1939	251,000	1.9	8.5				

SOURCES: National Center for Health Statistics (1978), U.S. Bureau of the Census (1975), U.S. Bureau of the Census (2001, 2004, tables 70 and 113). *Statistical Abstract of the United States, 1940.* 1941. No 62, table 96, p. 97. The data for 1940–1988 are from the *Monthly Vital Statistics Report* Vol. 39, No. 12, May 21, 1991. The data for 1989–1992 are from the *Monthly Vital Statistics Report* Vol. 39, No. 9, January 3, 1990; Vol. 40, No. 2, June 12, 1991; Vol. 40, No. 13, September 30, 1992; and Vol. 41, No. 13, September 28, 1993. U.S. Bureau of the Census, *Statistical Abstract of the United States: 1999:*table 155, p. 110. National Vital Statistics Reports: "Births, Marriages, Divorces, and Deaths" Vol. 53, No. 21, table A, updated October 18, 2005 and Vol. 54, No. 7, table A, December 22, 2005.

a. Statistics for annulments were collected for the first time in 1926.

b. No-Fault Divorce Act, California. No-Fault Divorce Act takes effect in the State of California.

Finally, the ratios are important as well. Because of their refinement (but missing for the final decade of the twentieth century and the early twenty-first century), the ratios that are reported in this table may be more representative of the state of marriage.

Calvin L. Beale (1950) recognized the important role separation held as a factor in divorce, especially from the year 1940 onward, a period that includes the years prior to, during, and in the aftermath of World War II. Aside from couple separation as a major factor, as shown in Table 27.6, an upward trend in the divorce rate can be observed for the period from 1961 to 1981. Since 1981, however, the divorce rate declined, ranging between 5.2 and 4.0. The persistent myth of an increasing U.S. divorce problem may be attributed in part to a focus on the *number* of marriages and divorces recorded annually, rather than the divorce rate.

In Table 27.7, the rate of divorce and annulments for the United States during 1887 to 2004 are presented. Most noteworthy is the declining divorce rate since the year 1981, at which time a high of 5.3 per 1,000 population was recorded. The estimates for the years 2003 and 2004, 3.7 and 3.8, respectively, are the lowest since 1972, one year prior to the passage of the California No-Fault Divorce Act legislation.

Use of the ratio for the years from 1920 to 1996 offers a more balanced representation of divorce in the United States. The highest divorce ratio recorded officially is for the year 1979 (22.8). Early ratios offered by the federal government were the number of divorces divided by marriages for a given year; such data are not useful and tend to offer some modest if ill-informed support to the mythical oft-cited 50 percent divorce rate. The empirical facts differ from the myth. Indeed, the data show that after peaking to a high in 1979 (5.3 and 22.8, respectively), the U.S. divorce rate has decreased beginning in 1982 (5.0 and 21.7).

DISCUSSION

The reaction to divorce data represents an emotional response to social change, and this reaction may be especially noteworthy when the effect of divorce influences the delivery of social services. One example is the national concern that a large number of children from single-parent families are denied the requisite financial support to allow them the opportunity to prepare for the future. This concern has generated policies to make parents, especially males, more financially accountable for the well-being of their children (Anderson and Wolchik 2001). But the traditional view that men were responsible for women throughout their entire life changed with the passage of the no-fault divorce legislation. Women are now expected to provide their own support through employment to be supplemented by child support and an equal distribution of property (Kurz 2001:3811).

Second, as noted by Sears et al. (1988:134–135), the social milieu affects salience. More than a generation of conservative thinking and a changed economy affect social values. The divorce and marriage rates also may be affected by the economic conditions of the late 1980s and early 1990s that prompted people to consider the financial effects of divorce. The reasons for this kind of decision, such as "for the sake of the children," "the cost of making two housing payments," and "to keep intact an estate," are similar to those reported after research carried out by Cuber and Harroff (1966) in a classic study of the attitudes held by upper-middle-class Americans toward maintaining an unhappy marriage. Another salient factor is the emotional desire to bond to one individual and the strong public attitude toward AIDS. Such external constraints, according to Sears et al. (1988:136), are likely to be salient factors that continue to target divorce as a social issue of import. In addition, the experience of growing up in a single-parent home, according to Dickinson and Leming (1990), is the cause of people viewing marriage differently compared with the past.

However, any discussion of the nature and origin of civil laws in debates over divorce remain relatively unexplored. If introduced into such discussions, evaluation of divorce law usually is confined to family law or the no-fault divorce statutes of the 1970s, especially the California Act of 1973. Thus, the argument as to whether the no-fault divorce laws are the cause or an effect of the U.S. divorce rate continues unabated. What is known is that the statutes currently referred to as "no-fault divorce" eliminate the requirement of providing proof in a court of law, as was required under common law, that one of the marital partners had engaged in adultery or some other act unacceptable to the marital relationship. No-fault divorce statutes eliminate the need to enumerate anything derogative as a sufficient ground for divorce. In other words, the no-fault divorce legislation eliminates the requirement to provide potentially damaging evidence by providing for the dissolution of a marriage based on the finding that the relationship is no longer compatible or viable (www.law.cornell.edu—retrieved January 23, 2003). Other acceptable reasons that lie outside the incriminating criteria used under the common law now include irreconcilable differences and incompatibility.

MARRIAGE AND DIVORCE IN THE 21ST CENTURY

In the sixteenth century, reformists viewed divorce as the medicine for the disease of marriage, while in 1919 Calhoun observed that the American people demonstrate a remarkable inclination toward marriage, a statement that was supported by the census of 1890 and the census Special Reports *Marriage and Divorce 1867–1906* (U.S. Bureau of the Census 1908, 1909). In 1933, Robert H. Lowie wrote, "It may be safely predicted . . . that the future of marriage will be shaped not merely by utilitarianism but largely on the basis of pregnant ideologies

(p. 154). And in 1931, Hankin observed, "Divorce, a symptom of the liberalizing tendencies of modern culture, seems likely to increase as long as underlying conditions continue their present trends" (p. 184). Such statements hold a general appeal—the ideas are not spatially bound or time bound—so that it may be safe to predict that a similar statement offers to forecast the initial decades of the twenty-first century. Witness the early returns. During the first three years of this century, the marriage rate averaged 8.1 per 1,000 population, while the yearly divorce rate averaged 4.0 per 1,000 population. These figures also characterize the final two decades of the twentieth century in that the marriage and divorce rates were lower than in previous years and both these rates declined throughout the final years of the past millennium. Indeed, the rate of divorce in the United States is at its lowest level since 1971, and this downward trend will probably continue or at least remain steady if only because of yet another trend observed by Norton and Miller (1992). These analysts documented the decline in the percentage of ever-married males and females between 1975 and 1990, thereby providing the evidence essential to understanding more recent marriage and divorce patterns in the United States.

Although some modest efforts to counter the myth of the 50 percent divorce rate do occur (see Hurley 2005), this misconception continues because it is reinforced by the news media, clerics, government officials, and even portions of the academic community. The data simply do not support this public misperception. A doubling of the divorce rate was a trend that occurred between 1940 and 1972. The divorce rate increased to 5.3 per 1,000 by 1981, and the decline in the annual rate has occurred since that time, representing an important trend that suggests a return to what may be identified as the normalcy divorce rate. Still, resistance to this fact and the perpetuation of the myth that a 50 percent divorce rate is undermining the family institution will probably continue because of other unrelated salient social issues. As Carter's law of the conservation of ignorance suggests, a false idea, once implanted, is difficult to dislodge from the human psyche.

Changing social mores throughout the nineteenth and twentieth centuries and changes in the divorce laws removed the legal constrictions and social taboos pertaining to divorce, in turn providing important new perspectives on divorce (Cherlin 1992). Thus, any explanation of marriage and divorce that is inclusive of an historical perspective is to be valued. Within this context, the historical data and a sociohistorical assessment of these data serve to address two sociological issues: (1) Was historical family life as good as some analysts would have us believe? and (2) Is the present family bond as bad as the common wisdom suggests? In focusing on the marriage and divorce topic in this manner, insights that are essential to challenging a longstanding myth pertaining to the solidarity of the traditional family and the most misleading social myth pertaining to the 50 percent divorce rate can be explored.

The importance of economic factors and marital stability was not recognized until the 1940s (Goode 1951), when employment status, occupation, deviant behavior, and public assistance variables were first taken into consideration. Given the important changes in the role of women during the past one-half century, and the call among some reformers to again relegate women to the domestic role, findings such as those reported by Schoen et al. (2002) serve to enhance our current views of marriage and divorce. Past perceptions that dual careers pose a threat to the family and that a persistently high divorce rate will eventually undermine the very foundations of the family institution do not hold up to long-term scrutiny, and it is this kind of analysis of marriage and divorce that must be undertaken within the context of historical change (Scott 2001). Note, for example, that the wife's employment status, according to Schoen et al. (2002), may be influenced by their labor force participation to end an unhappy marriage, but the wife's employment status does not appear to affect happy couples. As these analysts note, "There is an interaction involving wife's employment and marital happiness with marital disruption . . . [but] wife's employment is not associated with increased risk of disruption when both partners are happy in their marriage" (p. 569).

Thus, it can be suggested that if the cyclical prediction offered by William Strauss and Neil Howe in *The Fourth Turning* (1997) has merit, then we can anticipate a continued movement toward an American bonding experience throughout the early decades of the twenty-first century, including interpersonal relationships that emphasize the importance of the family. Thus, the marriage rate should remain stable or increase while the divorce rate will also remain stable or decline. If the past does indeed provide a lesson, this fourth turning crisis may thus reunite society by providing the requisite common purpose to reenergize and regenerate society. One possible result is that families are again strengthened, major public order questions are resolved, and a new order is established (Strauss and Howe 1997:256).

The assessment of the contemporary family system in general and of divorce in particular can emerge from a minority point of view to become a part of the new perspective of what the family represents and how this emerging definition fits into the social structure. As noted by O'Neill (1967), and consistent with the historical context emphasis advocated by Cherlin (1992), the period from 1880 to about 1919 was and continues to be important for understanding why the American rate of divorce increased and for identifying the change in the public attitude toward divorce. Thus, it would be erroneous to argue that divorce was, currently is, and will in the future serve as a sign of decadence that is corrupting the family institution.

Thus, as the American society strives to enter into a new cycle or era in which everything seems to be as it should be, Furstenberg's (1990:381) view that the rate of divorce during the 1980s reflects the state of role conflict and ambiguity within the marriage system can be used to explain the marriage system of the past 25 years. Referring to what he identifies as a voluntaristic form of marriage in the United States, Furstenberg argues that divorce has become an intrinsic part of the family system. Although it may take up to several decades of the twenty-first century to resolve most if not all of the issues that constitute the current "cultural wars," the outcome of these wars will determine the overall status of the cohesiveness and social bonding elements of the American society, of which the family system remains the most important. In the past, the most important social issues were related to fairness and justice for women; at the end of the twentieth century (Galston 1996) and as we move well into the twenty-first century, the public and moral issues seem to be related to our commitment toward children, which, as noted by Calhoun (1919), also was the case at the end of the nineteenth century. Perhaps the themes Stephanie Coontz has established are most appropriate for the twenty-first century when exploring family issues involving "the way we never where" and "the way we really are" in books with these titles. Certainly, the move toward legal sanctions for civil marriages among gay and lesbian couples and the questions and problems attendant on such unions or pairings really do not differ significantly from those that we are accustomed to.

Although sociologists have long employed divorce data (see, e.g., Ogburn and Nimkoff 1955) and permanent separation data (Beale 1950) as indicators of instability, the limitations of such census data are severe, as Ruggles (1997) noted. Despite the call by then Chief Statistician of the Marriage and Divorce Analysis Branch of the National Office of Vital Statistics Samuel C. Newman (1950) for better vital statistics, and the declaration by White (1990) that bigger and better data sets were available during the 1980s, currently less information is available on marriage and divorce. In turn, we have less rather than more insights into the complex issues surrounding marriage and divorce (Ruggles 1997). But data-gathering problems and methodological issues certainly are not new, and such problems continue. During the 1800s, formal divorce was difficult to obtain, and, for this reason, dissolution of some marriages resulting from desertion were undercounted (Furstenberg 1990:382). Even so, the published historical data were more comprehensive than those available during the final decades of the twentieth century.

Changes in recording practices occurred during the last two-thirds of the twentieth century, and in 1996, the collection of detailed marriage and divorce data was suspended by the federal government because of limitations in the information collected by and from certain states as well as budgetary considerations. Although the total numbers and rates of marriages and divorces at the national and state levels are available in the *National Vital Statistics Reports,* the paucity of data available for public and scholarly consumption will undoubtedly continue well into the twenty-first century. Moreover, the total picture will remain less well defined than in the past because of an increasing number and rate of informal marriages formed by cohabitation that will go unrecorded.

28

FAMILY SOCIOLOGY IN THE 21ST CENTURY

FELIX M. BERARDO

CONSTANCE L. SHEHAN
University of Florida, Gainesville

The beginning of a distinctive family sociology had its roots in centuries of accumulated writings on the subject. As Christensen (1964) noted in his attempt to frame that early history, "There has developed a vast literature on the family, running all the way from superstition-based folklore, to imaginative fiction, to poetic outpourings, to philosophical speculations, to popularized magazine articles and advice columns, and finally to reports of scientific investigations" (p. 3). It was generally recognized that family phenomena have widespread ramifications with respect to personal happiness and social stability. Indeed, the "wide range of commentary, analysis, and political action, over a period of twenty-five hundred years, suggests that throughout history we have been at least implicitly aware of the importance of family patterns as a central element in human societies" (Goode 2005:16).

We, of course, make no attempt here to cover this varied and expansive range of literature. Instead, we restrict our focus to North American family sociology, beginning with Christensen's overview of family studies, which he saw as historically sequencing through four partially overlapping stages: *preresearch* (prior to the middle of the nineteenth century), *social Darwinism* (last half of the nineteenth century), *emerging science* (first half of the twentieth century), and *systematic theory building* (1950 up to 1964, when his work was published as the first *Handbook of Marriage and the Family*).

Christensen gave little attention to the preresearch era, characterizing it as primarily emotional, speculative, infused with mythology, and highly superstitious in content. There was little in the way of generalizations (which were often contradictory) that could be identified as resulting from the rigorous application of scientific methodologies. It should be noted, however, that many influential philosophers, political scientists, and historians, as well as the early feminists of this period, offered important writings on the family. Thus, to dismiss all writings about families that appeared before the mid-twentieth century as lacking in value is unwarranted.

The social Darwinian period saw the emergence of a body of empirical literature (mostly anthropological) that viewed the family through broad historical, institutional, and comparative perspectives. Starting with evidence regarding biological evolution, an analogy regarding social evolution emerged. Its proponents concentrated on establishing phases of evolutionary development of family forms. However,

> the methods of data collection were poor, resting upon historical and anecdotal records of doubtful validity built up from reports of travelers and missionaries with minimal training in ethnography. Methods of analysis were descriptive and impressionistic, producing few firm propositions that could be left unchallenged. (Hill 1962:425)

During the latter half of the nineteenth century and the early part of the twentieth century, a focus on a variety of urban family problems and on a social reform agenda also developed. A number of prominent women sociologists worked at this time.

> The Industrial Revolution had brought on or intensified such conditions as poverty, child labor, women's restlessness accompanying emancipation [sic], prostitution, illegitimacy,

and divorce. The relationship of these to the family was quickly seen, and the result was a small amount of research, but considerably more agitation, directed toward social reform. (Christensen 1964:8)

The social Darwinian evolutionary emphases of this period faded and were eventually replaced by an emerging science with a self-avowed value-free orientation and a more rigorous methodological stance. Social survey techniques, statistics, and systematic testing of hypotheses were now increasingly used in family research. Moreover, in Christensen's (1964) view,

the most pronounced characteristic of twentieth-century family study is its emphasis upon the internal relationship of family members . . . Interest in studying the family broadly, as a social institution, has materially shifted to an interest in studying it more narrowly and internally as an association. This is the social-psychological approach . . . It has been expressed through expanding research, teaching, and counseling on such social phenomena as dating, mate selection, marriage adjustment, parent-child relationships, and personality formation within the family context. (Pp. 8–9)

Others have characterized this as a shift from the macroscopic to microscopic approach to family studies. During this transition, there was a gradual decline in the resistance to research on sensitive family issues and a greater public acceptance of such inquiries.

Finally, a period of systematic theory building began and continued throughout the latter half of the twentieth century. There were now "serious attempts to pull together and assess the various researches of the past, and to first delineate and synthesize the several schools of thought or theoretical frames of reference which have been used in family study" (Christensen 1964:9–10). Interestingly, this period also saw a revival of cross-cultural and comparative family studies. However, unlike those of the past, these were "more scientific and more suitable to sound theory building than were their earlier counterparts" (p. 10).

Among Christensen's conclusions was an observation of a growing concern over theory building in family sociology and the delineation of several distinct theoretical approaches. At the time, five of these were deemed sufficiently promising to be included in the first version of the *Handbook of Marriage and the Family* (1964): the institutional, the structural functional, the interactional, the situational, and the developmental. In subsequent years, these and other alternative conceptual frameworks or orientations seen as useful for family research were elaborated (e.g., Nye and Berardo 1966).

FAMILY SOCIOLOGY AND FAMILY HISTORY

Scientific disciplines, of course, do not develop in isolation from other fields. Indeed, their expansion and sophistication are often assisted by reciprocal contributions from other areas of inquiry. Such is the case with respect to various knowledge interchanges between family sociology and the multidisciplinary field of family history, whose scholars have challenged long-held generalizations about historical developments of family forms and practices (Coontz 2000). For example, the work of social historians has led to a questioning of earlier sociological paradigms that posited a uniform process of family formation. Their research revealed the fallacies underlying "unilineal" assertions regarding the impact of industrialization and modernization on family types and changing family relationships.

The most important contributions made by family historians to other social science disciplines deal with the themes of diversity, uneven change, and human agency (Baca Zinn and Eitzen 2002:34–38). Cross-disciplinary interchanges have stimulated a large and growing body of work on family diversity. "Historians have discovered so much diversity that any discussion of 'the Western family' must be qualified. Instead of a prevailing type of family at any one time, several types were present from the beginning" (Baca Zinn and Eitzen 2002:34). Especially noticeable has been a greater focus on racial and ethnic categories and their implications for familial roles and processes, especially those of women, which has shed light on adaptations necessitated by changing economic or political constraints and opportunities (Coontz 2000:285).

Social historians of the family have challenged the view that there is one family form or process that is superior to others. Instead, they have offered more inclusive definitions of families to encompass the various dimensions of family diversity, spurred by a growing recognition that "there are many different types of families, with many different needs, and many different ways of meeting those needs. Family diversity is a way of characterizing the variability within and among families" (Demo, Allen, and Fine 2000:1–2). This position has pretty much been incorporated into contemporary sociological perspectives, though it has not quelled the ongoing political debate over the priority of certain family structures and "family values" over others (Benokraitis 2000). Nevertheless, the current sociological position argues for recognition and acceptance of family diversity. In fact, family diversity has emerged as a prominent subspecialty within family sociology. Today it covers a wide range of topics, illustrated by the *Handbook of Family Diversity* (Demo et al. 2000), which focuses on structural and processual forms of diverse families, along with variations of family well-being, and gives particular attention to a wide spectrum of issues related to the social stratifications of race, social class, sexual orientation, and age. It also examines the application of diversity to such areas as clinical practice, family life education, and family policy. Scholarship in this area has prompted a reexamination of the definition and meaning of the term *family* itself to take into account an expanding range of family configurations. These efforts have also contributed to the ongoing paradigm shifts in family sociology.

PARADIGM SHIFTS IN FAMILY SOCIOLOGY

The history of all sciences reveals periodic paradigmatic shifts triggered by new theoretical and empirical developments in a particular discipline. Over the past several decades, family sociology has experienced such shifts in its major orientations. Prior to the 1950s, the field was characterized by a variety of theoretical frameworks, including the interactional, family-life-cycle, and family problems approaches, along with an early institutional-functional approach derived mostly from anthropology. However, by the mid-1950s, Parsonian functionalism had become the dominant perspective in family sociology:

> For Parsons, the family's remaining functions involve primarily expressive roles, whereas outside of the home modern societies require that impersonal, instrumental roles prevail. He generalized these social roles linking female roles with expressive roles and male roles with instrumental roles, claiming that this division of labor is more stable, complementary, and efficient. Hence a heterosexual, nuclear family with clearly defined breadwinner-homemaker roles is the most functional family form in modern societies. (Mann et al. 1997:318)

In subsequent decades this viewpoint was increasingly challenged by

> new scholarship depicting the diverse experiences of women and men from different classes, races, and ethnicities spawned in part by the Civil Rights Movement, the rise of the New Left, and the modern Women's movement. These new voices called into question many of the underlying assumptions of the structural functionalist viewpoint on families and highlighted the conflict, inequality, and diversity in family experiences. (Mann et al. 1997:371)

While the structural functional approach has by no means disappeared, the diversity of family studies that emerged from this new emphasis led to a rise in theoretical pluralism in family sociology and an interest in assessing its changing paradigmatic status.

Mann and colleagues (1997) attempted to assess paradigmatic transformations in family sociology from the 1960s through the 1990s by examining the major theoretical perspectives employed in multiedition textbooks designed for advanced-level courses: functionalism, exchange theory, symbolic interactionism, developmental theory, conflict theory, and feminist theory. They found evidence of a slow but definite integration of more critical theoretical frameworks into subsequent editions of family textbooks to counter the more traditional approaches to, for example, family-related social class issues. However, they also discovered that macrolevel functional theory and microlevel life-cycle theory had continued as the prevailing frameworks during this period, with two notable exceptions—the treatment of African American families and gender issues. Over time, these areas received wider coverage by the textbook authors, who increasingly drew on a growing critical and more conflict-oriented literature. Regarding African American families, they noted that

> in most cases, the integration of this new literature was associated with a shift toward more critical theoretical analyses by textbook authors. Indeed, the findings on this topic are especially notable, because this is the first time we have seen the clash between competing paradigms result in a transformation of the perspectives of many authors. (P. 334)

A similar development was noticeable with respect to gender issues. Textbooks began to incorporate theories of gender oppression, along with critical analyses of traditional gender roles. At the end of the 30-year period examined by Mann and colleagues (1997), other areas of study in family sociology, such as domestic violence, had begun to show small, incremental movements toward employing more critical theoretical approaches. In the most recent textbooks, for instance, life-course analysis has replaced life-cycle analysis because it is better suited to revealing the diversity of family experiences. Mann and her coauthors concluded that textbooks "included more critical literature that shifted their foci from convergence to diversity, from differentiation to stratification, and from consensus to conflict" (p. 340). These and other findings "suggest that the degree to which social movements become institutionalized may be a significant factor determining paradigm shifts in academic textbooks" (p. 340).

The paradigmatic shifts in family sociology, involving, among other things, modern ideas about diversity and social context, are increasingly noted in the most recent textbooks. Among these, *Diversity in Families* (Baca Zinn and Eitzen 2002:24) is illustrative. These authors adopted a structural diversity framework that has as its major premise that "families are divided along structural lines that shape and form their dynamics" (p. 24) and incorporates several thematic guidelines:

> Family forms are socially constructed and historically changing; family diversity is produced by the very structures that organize society as a whole; the social locations in which families are embedded are not the product of a single power system but are shaped by intersecting hierarchies; family diversity is constructed through social structure and human agency; and understanding family diversity requires the use of wide-ranging intellectual traditions. (Pp. 24–25)

Each of these is spelled out in greater detail in their textbook with a focus on multiple family forms. In their view, the key to understanding family diversity is the structural distribution of social opportunities. For example,

> the uneven distribution of work, wages, and other family requirements produce[s] multiple family realities. . . . At any particular time, a society will contain a range of family types that vary with social class, race, region, and other structural conditions. (Baca Zinn and Eitzen 2002:24)

These structural conditions result in differential opportunities for individuals within families as well as for families as social units.

FAMILY SOCIOLOGY AND FEMINIST SCHOLARSHIP

A number of social movements and various demographic shifts have played a role in the development of family sociology since the middle of the twentieth century. Perhaps one of the clearest examples of how social movements can influence paradigmatic developments can be seen in the women's movement and the impact of its associated feminist literature on family sociology.

As we noted earlier, much of the sociological literature from the 1950s and early 1960s portrayed contemporary marriage as an arrangement of love between equals, using terms such as "companionate marriage," "egalitarian marriage," and "symmetrical family." Theories of the time argued that men's "instrumental" roles and women's "expressive" roles were functional in advanced industrial societies (Parsons and Bales 1955). Feminists have argued, however, that the "reduction of gender divisions to a language of roles obscures realities of power and conflict and provides, at best, a shallow understanding of complex dynamics of gender" (Lopata and Thorne 1978). Feminist scholars began to call attention to the conflicted and unequal aspects of family relationships, using the concept of patriarchy to highlight the family as the locus of domination by gender and age (Osmond and Thorne 1993).

One of the earliest and most influential feminist voices in family sociology was Jesse Bernard (1972), whose book *The Future of Marriage* questioned the viability of an institution that subordinated women. Another scholar whose work foreshadowed later feminist emphases in family studies was Safilios-Rothschild (1969). Her insights about the effects of interviewing only one person to provide information about a marriage or family called attention to what would later be referred to as "standpoint" in feminist work.

Feminist scholars also attempted to demystify the ideology of the monolithic family, arguing that it reinforced the economic exploitation of all women. In the 1980s, feminist research shifted from an emphasis on patterns of domination and constraint to women's resistance and negotiation of the structures that dominated them. Attention to the intersecting influences of gender, race, and class on individuals' lives within and outside families gained increasing momentum (Stacey 1990).

Thorne and Yalom (1992) identified five themes that are central to a feminist rethinking of the family. First, feminists have challenged the ideology of the monolithic family (i.e., the nuclear family with the breadwinner husband and full-time wife and mother as the only legitimate family form). Second, feminists have focused on underlying and encompassing structures of gender, generation, sexuality, and race and class rather than on the family as the unit of analysis. Third, feminists have given voice to experiences within families that run counter to the idea of the family as a loving refuge, highlighting men's dominance and women's subordination within and outside of families, varying experiences of motherhood, and the presence of inequitably distributed work, conflict, and violence. Fourth, feminists have raised questions about family boundaries, challenging traditional dichotomies between private and public and between family and society. Finally, feminists seek a realistic and complex understanding of families as part of a larger program of social change. Other periodic assessments of the state of family sociology have documented the increasing influence of feminism (Ferree 1990; Fox and Murry 2000; Thompson and Walker 1995).

CONCEPTUAL FRAMEWORKS AND FAMILY THEORY

For some time, family sociology was criticized for slow and uneven progress in formulating theory (Settles 2000). However, the large and rapidly growing body of research in this area eventually led several scholars to shift their attention to evaluation and classification systems and better codification and synthesis of results. Consequently, the 1950s and subsequent decades increasingly saw formal delineations of several distinct conceptual frameworks or theoretical approaches, which, it was hoped, would enhance generalizations and theory building. Conceptual frameworks have been defined in various ways. For some scholars, they merely represent a group of concepts employed principally as a taxonomy. These involve the specification of

> a small number of definitions which delineate the few aspects of reality with which sociology deals. These definitions, broadly speaking, tell the sociologist what is important for him [sic] to pay attention to when he views a human relationship, a group, or society. (Zetterberg 1963:7–10)

Others have employed broader definitions of such frameworks (Klein and Jurich 1993).

Among the early attempts to specify the role of conceptual frameworks was that offered by Hill and Hansen (1960), who saw their identification as crucial to the inventory and codification of family research and to the development and accumulation of propositions in family sociology. They were successful in identifying several frameworks. Five of these—the institutional, structural-functional, interactional, situational, and developmental approaches—were deemed sufficiently developed by Christensen to be included in the initial *Handbook of Marriage and the Family* (1964). At about the same time, Nye and Berardo (1966) published *Emerging Conceptual Frameworks in Family Analysis*. Reflecting the multidisciplinary aspect of family studies, its contributors were able to specify 11 approaches. In addition to covering the 5 just noted, they detailed the anthropological, psychoanalytical, social psychological, economic, legal, and Western Christian. In the ensuing years, other scholars adapted or refined some of these and other emerging frameworks (Nye and Berardo 1966; Sprey 1990; White and Klein 2002; Winton 1995).

The next edition of the *Handbook of Marriage and the Family* (Sussman and Steinmetz 1987) took notice of the growing emphasis on systematic theory building and cited a dozen conceptual frameworks: symbolic interaction, situational, structural-functional, institutional, household economic, learning-maturational, developmental, psychoanalytical, systems, exchange, conflict, and phenomenological (Thomas and Wilcox 1987:87). The evolution and current status of these often competing approaches were given some attention in this work. It was noted that the earlier analytical confusion arising out of the multidisciplinary study of the family represented by these frameworks (due to differences in underlying assumptions, concepts, value orientations, and focus) had begun to diminish. Several approaches (e.g., those most closely tied to household economics and psychology) were dropped, while those with the greatest relevance to sociology remained, resulting in less competitiveness among the disciplines represented.

Thomas and Wilcox (1987) also noticed a more careful attempt among family scholars to define family theory and an emerging consensus as to the central place of propositions in its development (p. 87). The distinction between conceptual frameworks and family theory, as well as the relationship between the two, has been and continues to be somewhat ambiguous. The ongoing debate as to whether family sociology should stress conceptual frameworks or propositional theories has not been resolved. Some scholars take the position that conceptual frameworks are theory, while others vehemently deny such a claim, seeing them merely as summarizing devices. Still others view conceptual frameworks as a necessary step in theory formulation (Klein and Jurich 1993:37–39).

Apart from this as yet unresolved ambiguity, however, formal theory construction in the family field has been an ongoing activity since at least the 1970s, when a two-volume treatise titled *Contemporary Theories about the Family* (Burr 1979) was published. The process of theory building in family sociology has often involved the application of "mainstream sociological theoretical thinking to family theory," which "has generated some notable accomplishments" (Thomas and Wilcox 1987:93). Thomas and Wilcox (1987) concluded their review of the history of family theory building on an optimistic note:

> Building increment on increment of one research project after another in any area of the family field . . . [is] necessary foundation work that will eventually succeed in creating theory capable of explaining the phenomena under investigation. Better theory will increase the power of explanation,

predictions, and control. These will all result in a payoff in the practical realm of helping families solve problems. (P. 93)

The more recent progress in theory construction, as well as in methods, in family sociology has been tracked and evaluated through extensive scholarly overviews, including two editions of the *Sourcebook of Family Theories and Methods*. The first of these appeared in 1993, and it was reissued a decade later. Among the shifts noted in the first *Sourcebook* was a movement away from family theories guided by a positivistic philosophy of science context, which basically saw theory driven by the accumulation of empirical observations, to one of postpositivism, which saw theory as *preceding* such observation and which takes the position that there are no facts without theories and that all theories are socially constructed (Boss et al. 1993:5).

Other emerging developments in the field, which cannot be detailed here, include the four-volume *International Encyclopedia of Marriage and Family* (Ponzetti 2003). Specific chapters on extant theories dealing with the family appear under a range of content headings, which include the following: dialectical, developmental, human ecology, life course, phenomenology, relationship, role, social exchange, structural-functional, and symbolic interaction. The growth of alternative perspectives or models in recent decades has necessitated in part some "metatheoretical stocktaking" to avoid polarization among adherents of competing frameworks and also to bring a degree of clarification to the field.

SUBSTANTIVE TRENDS IN FAMILY STUDIES

Along with the trend toward greater theory construction, there has been a parallel process of stocktaking, reflected, for example, in the several decade reviews that have appeared over the last 40 years and that have tracked changing trends in substantive topics in family research. Although there have been earlier periodic evaluations of family research trends, the series of decade reviews published in the *Journal of Marriage and the Family* are perhaps most indicative of the directions of contemporary scholarship in this field.

To determine trends in the topics or issues that have received attention from family scholars over the past 50 years, we examined the four decade reviews published in the *Journal of Marriage and the Family* (1970, 1980, 1990, and 2000) and special issues released by the *Journal of Family Issues* since its inception in 1980. Content analysis revealed that the predominant topics appear to have followed changes in family patterns and social movements (see Berardo and Shehan 1984). In the 1970s, for instance, research on adolescent childbearing, domestic violence, and divorce and remarriage proliferated. None of these topics had been the focus of a decade review article in

1970 but were treated as primary in the 1980 review. The epidemic of teen pregnancy was highlighted in research conducted throughout the 1970s. The 1980 decade review continued to reflect this emphasis with articles on premarital sexuality and adolescent childbearing. This focus is also seen in the 1990 review but was discontinued in the following decade, paralleling the decline in teen pregnancies.

Research on "sex roles" noticeably increased in the 1970s, coinciding with the emergence of the second wave of feminism, and was a topic in the 1980 decade review. This emphasis was continued in the next decade, reflecting the growing interest in gender. However, the language used to refer to this area changed from "sex roles" to "gender," denoting the shift away from the characteristics of individuals to the structural dimension of social life. Not all research examining gender in families took a feminist perspective. The emergence of a strong feminist cadre of researchers during the late 1970s and 1980s was reflected in the 1990 review, which examined feminist perspectives in family research. As a result, attention on gender issues and feminist approaches to research was integrated throughout many of the subsequent articles on other substantive topics (e.g., violence).

Over the 1980s, research on the causes and consequences of divorce intensified, reflecting the dramatic rise in rates of marital dissolution, which began in the mid-1960s. In the 1970 decade review, there was no special attention given to this topic, but the following decades saw substantial space devoted to issues of divorce, desertion, and remarriage, including the impact on children. The latter emphasis most likely reflected the initiation of longitudinal studies of children of divorce. As the rates began to stabilize, the coverage of divorce and remarriage declined somewhat.

A similar pattern involving research pertaining to the intersection of employment and families can be identified. It wasn't until the 1990 decade review that articles on parental employment appeared. Not coincidentally, this followed a dramatic increase in the employment of mothers of young children. In the 2000 decade review, this focus expanded to include a renewed interest in the division of household labor. The broader economic circumstances of families and households began to receive extensive attention in the 1980s, and this trend has continued to the present. As noted earlier, the growth in research on family diversity is also observable.

Special issues published in the *Journal of Family Issues* since 1980 reveal similar trends. During the 1980s, a number of these focused on parenting, including the transition to parenthood, the impact of parenthood on psychological well-being, and childlessness. Other frequent topics included divorce, remarriage, and widowhood. Throughout the 1990s, parent-child relationships continued to receive concentrated attention. As reflected in our analysis of the *Journal of Marriage and the Family* decade reviews, employment, economic issues, and household labor also emerged as central concerns in papers published in the *Journal of Family Issues* during the same time period. Most recently, greater attention has been given to aging families and elder care, no doubt reflecting our aging population.

IDEOLOGICAL INFLUENCES ON FAMILY SOCIOLOGY

Over the course of its evolution, family sociology has felt the influence of various and often opposing ideologies reflected in the works and activities of its researchers, theorists, and practitioners. This perhaps became most apparent in the long-standing debate over the connection between social change and the alleged decline of the family. Vincent (1966) long ago noted that "since the earliest writing available, changes occurring in the institution of the family have been used and interpreted to support either an optimistic or a pessimistic premise concerning social change, and the pessimists have consistently outnumbered the optimists" (p. 31). Popenoe (1993), for example, describes several such changes that, in his view, signal family disorganization and decay. These changes include the decrease in traditional nuclear households, a historical decline in fertility, a continuously high divorce rate, changing family structures through divorce and remarriage, the rise in dual-worker families, expanding equalitarianism, and the spread of cohabitation among the unmarried.

Others have challenged such assertions, emphasizing instead the family's remarkable resiliency and ability to adapt to environmental flux by reorganizing its structures and relationships.

> The fact is that the family, like other institutions, is in a perpetual state of evolution rather than dissolution. It interfaces with those institutions in a panorama of complex transactions . . . Its ability to mediate, translate, and incorporate social change in the process of socializing its members is one of its major strengths. (Berardo 1987:427)

Similar observations about the adaptability of the family have been made by others (Berardo and Shehan 2004). The controversy and associated rhetoric over the presumed decline of the family are important insofar as which group—the pessimists or the optimists—gains influence in defining what is and what is not a family problem and the impact such views have politically on the development of family policy.

The ideological positions regarding this and other family matters sometimes get articulated in the major textbooks in the discipline. For example, one analysis of family textbooks that was published between 1994 and 1996 argued that most were poor to mediocre in terms of a balanced treatment of controversial issues, coverage of crucial topics, and scholarship or interpretation of evidence. "Misrepresentations of the literature, misstatements of facts, faulty reasoning, and misinterpretations of evidence abound in books" (Glenn 1997:204). Glenn, a well-known family sociologist, was highly critical of what he perceived to be strong liberal or radical ideological biases in these books, especially with regard to the institutional aspects of marriage. In Glenn's view, textbooks typically presented only negative images of marriage, with comparatively little attention given to its beneficial consequences. They also offered an overly adult-centered orientation, with a de-emphasis on child-related topics (for example, juvenile delinquency and violence, child abuse and neglect, and the effects of parental separation or divorce) and a failure to sufficiently stress the impact of family life on children.

Other equally respected scholars have strongly rejected these conclusions and charge, in part, that Glenn and his colleagues at the Council on Families are actively promoting a politically conservative agenda. We simply note here that these opposing viewpoints, and their associated charges and countercharges, continue to be expressed (Coleman and Ganong 2003). The so-called "family wars," sometimes involving ad hominem attacks, remain part of the twenty-first-century sociological landscape.

CONTINUING CONTROVERSIES

The authors of the latest *Sourcebook of Family Theory and Research* (Bengtson et al. 2005) note several controversies in the field that have generated "firestorms of debate" among family scholars and that must be dealt with in the future. They

> reflect differences in definitions, assumptions, and labels in studying families (and) conflict concerning the moral ends toward which theory should be directed. . . . Each issue reflects divisions of opinion concerning theory and epistemology—how we define families, the questions we ask, the knowledge we have about families, and the methods we use to gain such knowledge . . . Epistemological issues frame the ways we approach and define families. Definitions, assumptions, labels, and moral stances have powerful implications. They can be picked up by the mass media and misconstrued. (P. 614)

Among these issues, several were identified as having the potential to polarize family sociology: (1) the divergent epistemological perspectives of *positivism, postmodernism,* and *modernism;* (2) issues concerning gender *heteronormativity* and so-called queer theory; (3) the application of existing sociological theories to families, precluding the need for development of specialized family theories; (4) challenges to historical or traditional conceptualizations of the family; and (5) controversy over the *individualization* of family research and the resulting need for scholars to examine structural factors and influence from multiple levels in studying families.

FAMILY SOCIOLOGY: THE FUTURE

We now shift our sights forward and speculate about the directions in which family sociology seems to be heading with respect to its research and theoretical agendas. Prognostications about the future, like most if not all scientific forecasting, must of necessity be framed in terms of degrees of probability, especially with respect to the fluid events covered by the social sciences.

The questions addressed by family scholars are influenced by a number of factors, such as serendipity, personal interest, the number and diversity of family professionals, social movements, the impact of key scholars and their germinal works, interactions between researchers and practitioners, the willingness of the public to participate in research, and values (Berardo and Shehan 1984). Moreover, the influence of the broader sociohistorical context on family scholarship also plays a role.

Hence, long-range forecasting about the future development of the family as well as family sociology must be approached cautiously and stated with somewhat less certainty than might be desired. Nevertheless, if present trends continue, especially if they are evident on a worldwide basis, then certain predictions are feasible. It is within the context of these short-range trends that forecasts are most likely to attain a reasonable degree of accuracy rather than being uninformed conjecture (Nye and Berardo 1973:423–24).

Analysis of Global Trends

There are several trends apparent around the globe that have and will continue to capture the attention of family scholars. Among these are

> the spread of contraceptive knowledge and accessibility, rising rates of cohabitation, the movement toward more open mate-selection systems, a delayed age at first marriage, reductions in family size, the continued flow of women into the paid labor force and their expanded role as economic providers for their families, the increasing number of dual-earner families, rising divorce rates, and a growing surplus of elderly women as a result of extended life expectancy. (Berardo and Shehan 2004:257)

One research focus that will continue throughout the coming decades will be the changing roles of women, which are redefining family relationships. While this and other trends, such as the aging of populations, are occurring at very different points in time across societies, and at different accelerations, their evolution helps frame the research agenda of twenty-first-century family sociology worldwide.

In this context, Giddens (2005) notes a "global revolution" in progress with respect to changes affecting our personal and emotional spheres in terms of "how we think of ourselves and how we form ties and connection with others. It is a revolution advancing unevenly in different regions and cultures, with many resistances" (p. 26). It is manifested in intense discussions of issues surrounding sexual equality, the regulation of sexuality, and the future of the family, often reflecting the struggle between tradition and modernity (p. 27). As a result of numerous social changes, most family life, he contends,

> has been transformed by the rise of the couple and coupledom . . . In the traditional family, the married couple was only one part, and often not the main part, of the family system. Ties with children and other relatives tended to be equally or even more important in the day to day conduct of social life. The couple came to be at the centre of family life as the economic role of the family dwindled and love, or love plus sexual attraction, became the basis for forming marriage ties. A couple once constituted has its own exclusive history, its own biography. It is a unit based upon emotional communication or intimacy . . . "Coupling" and "uncoupling" provide a more accurate description of the arena of personal life now than do marriage and the family . . . Marriage is no longer the chief defining basis of coupledom. (P. 29)

Shifts in attitudes toward marriage, divorce, sexual orientation and behavior, reproduction, and out-of-wedlock births have all been part of this process. What is emerging is what Giddens (2005) labels a "democracy of emotions" as the principal context of all relationships, including marriage. Such relationships are based on equalitarianism, respect, and communication, as well as the "processes of active trust—opening oneself up to the other. Self-disclosure is the basic condition of intimacy" (p. 30). Finally, he sees emotional communication and intimacy replacing past ties in three areas that bind together our personal lives—in sexual and love relations, parent-child relations, and friendship.

If Giddens is correct regarding such a worldwide trend, then what it portends for the future dynamics of marriage and family relationships will of necessity become an area to be analyzed by theorists and researchers in the discipline. This does not mean, of course, that the family will cease to exist. Indeed, "in most of the world, the traditional family may be shaken, but the institution will probably enjoy a longer life than any nation now in existence" (Goode 2005:14). Sociological study of families and intimate relationships will continue to be a prominent feature of the intellectual landscape for decades to come.

29

THE SOCIOLOGY OF RELIGION

JAMES WILLIAM COLEMAN

California Polytechnic State University, San Luis Obispo

The task of building a scientific understanding of religion is a central part of the sociological enterprise. Indeed, in one sense the origins of the sociology can be attributed to the efforts of nineteenth-century Europeans to come to grips with the crisis of faith that shook Western society during the revolutionary upheavals of its industrial transformation. Most of the great European intellectuals of this era sought to formulate some sort of rational scientific paradigm to replace the religious foundations of Western culture, and such founding sociologists as Comte, Marx, and Durkheim were no exceptions.

Since the early sociologists were trying to break free from the hegemonic religious paradigm that had long dominated European thought, it is not surprising that they were fascinated with the phenomena of religion itself. As they became increasingly aware of the fecund diversity of religious life around the world, a number of basic questions arose that still lie at the heart of the quest for a sociological understanding of religion. Why are religious beliefs and practices so universal? Why do they take such diverse forms? How do social forces help shape those beliefs and practices? What role does religion, in turn, play in social, economic, and political life?

WHAT IS RELIGION?

The first step in understanding religion is obviously to decide what it is, but as is so often the case, defining this basic concept is a far more difficult business than it appears at first glance. A good place to start is with Émile Durkheim. According to this classic sociologist, religion is a "unified system of beliefs and practices relative to sacred things, that is to say things set apart and forbidden—beliefs and practices which unite into one single moral community called a Church, all those who adhere to them" (Dukheim [1915] 1965:62). Although this definition clearly requires some surgery to remove its Eurocentrism, it shows remarkable insight into the fundamental sociological characteristics of religion. The most obvious change that needs to be made is to remove the word "church," because that normally refers only to Christian religions. There are, however, some more fundamental problems especially with Durkheim's inclusion of the concept of the sacred in his definition. While "sacred things" play a major role in most religions, they are certainly not the sine qua non of religious life. In the Buddhist view, for example, there is nothing "set apart and forbidden" about meditation, ethical behavior, the cultivation of wisdom, or the other central tenets of their beliefs and practices. On the other hand, however, it doesn't seem justified to call any system of beliefs and practices a religion. The Christian theologian Paul Tillich's (1967) contention that religion involves issues of "ultimate concern" is far more broadly applicable (see Kurtz 1995:8–9).

For sociological purposes, at least, we can then say that religion involves three key elements: beliefs, practices, and a social group. Although religious beliefs are not always as systematically organized as Durkheim seemed to believe, those beliefs deal in some way or other with the questions of ultimate concern the believers face. The realm of religious practice is too vast to enumerate here, because it involves everything from rituals and ceremonies to dietary and behavioral standards and various spiritual disciplines, but it is clearly a central part of religious life. Finally, religion is a social phenomenon that involves groups of people. The solitary philosopher does not become a religious figure until one shares his or her ideas with a group of people.

SOCIOLOGICAL THEORIES OF RELIGION

Sociology starts with the rather eccentric figure of August Comte (1798–1857). Like many young intellectuals of his time, Comte believed that religion was an archaic holdover from the past. Comte held that in the course of history, theological thinking gave way to metaphysical thinking, which in turn gave way to scientific thinking or what he called "positive philosophy." Science, then, was the replacement for religion. When applied to the systematic study of society, it could be used to construct a rational social order guided by the sociologists that would eliminate the ancient problems that plagued humanity. Ironically, this determined opponent of religion suffered a mental breakdown toward the end of his life and refused to read anything but a medieval devotional text known as *The Imitation of Christ.*

Marx

Marx (1818–1883) was of course far more influential than Comte, and he was the first of the sociological giants to address the issue of religion. Although he shared the idea with many nineteenth-century thinkers that religious faith was an unscientific holdover from earlier times, his economic determinism and revolutionary commitment gave his views a particular slant. Religion in his perspective was merely part of the ideological superstructure erected on and shaped by the underlying economic realities and had no kind of independence of its own. Nonetheless, religion does play an important and clearly negative social role. For Marx (1844), religion was a profound form of social alienation because

> the worker is related to the product of his labor as to an alien object. . . . The more the worker expends himself in work the more powerful becomes the world of objects which he creates in face of himself, the poorer he becomes in his inner life, and the less he belongs to himself. It's just the same as in religion. The more of himself man attributes to God the less he has left in himself. (P. 122)

Religion in capitalist society provides a comforting illusion that obscures the realities of class conflict and class interest and, thus, is a profound example of false consciousness. By consoling the frustrated and oppressed, it helps prevent collective action to change the real source of their problems. Thus, religion was, in Marx's famous phrase, "the opiate of the masses."

Others in the Marxist tradition have taken a more nuanced position on religion, including his benefactor Fredrich Engels. Engels recognized that religion in some circumstances actually supported the struggle of the oppressed, as he felt was the case with early Christianity (Marx and Engels 1957). Most contemporary Marxists follow Engels's position holding a general skepticism and suspicion of religious institutions, but recognizing that some religious developments, such as liberation theology in Latin American Catholicism, can be a progressive force.

Durkheim and the Functionalists

While religion was of only a passing concern to Marx, it was central to the foundational French sociologist Émile Durkheim (1858–1917). In his major work on the sociology of religion, *The Elementary Forms of Religious Life,* Durkheim ([1915] 1965) studied the religious life of the Australian aborigines on the questionable assumption that it was more primitive and simple than in the European nations and thus reflected religion in its most basic forms. Durkheim was particularly fascinated with the totemistic aspects of aboriginal religion. He concluded that the totems, objects or animals held in special awe by a particular clan, actually had little to do with the supernatural but were in fact symbols of the social group. He went on to argue that if the totem "is at once the symbol of the god and of the society, is that not because the god and the society are only one?" (Durkheim [1915] 1965:236). Thus, even in European society, Durkheim saw the worship of God to be nothing more than the worship of society. Society is the transcendent reality that religion symbolizes, and it not only has its own needs but even takes on a kind of anthropomorphic form in some of his writings. Society personifies itself in the form of totems or Gods to be revered and worshiped because it needs to reaffirm its legitimacy and worth to its members. And just as the Gods symbolize society, the soul is the symbol of the social element within the individual that lives on long after the people themselves.

Although the almost metaphysical elements in Durkheim's thought were not particularly influential, his idea that religion functioned to meet basic social needs became a sociological truism. Over the years, functionalist theory grew more complex and sophisticated and is now one of the most widely used theoretical paradigms in the sociology of religion. Of particular importance was the contribution of Robert Merton (1957), who introduced the concept of the dysfunction. In his view, social institutions not only perform functions for society, but they also have dysfunctional consequences. Over the years, functionalists have developed a long list of the functions and dysfunctions of religion. Following O'Dea (1966:4–18), we can divide the human needs that religion meets into two categories—expressive and adaptive. Religion helps meet our expressive emotional needs by providing a supernatural context in which the hard realities of human life—powerlessness, uncertainty, injustice, and the inevitability of death—can be given meaning and purpose. Religion provides support and consolation, and its cult and ceremonies can encourage a sense of security and identity with something larger than the self. According to the functionalists, religion's most important adaptive function is the way it sacralizes and reinforces the norms and values on which social order depends. Common rituals and common beliefs also help bind people together into a common community. In a different context, however, each function can become a dysfunction. By comforting and consoling people, religion may also discourage action for the needed social change. By making norms and values sacred, it not only strengthens them, but it may make them much harder to change when the times require it.

Weber and the Historical-Comparative Approach

Like Durkheim, Max Weber (1864–1920) devoted a great deal of his enormous intellectual energy to the study of religion. Ever the rationalist, however, he was disinclined toward Durkheim's kind of philosophical speculation or Marx's political partisanship. If there is one underlying objective of Weber's richly detailed historical and comparative examination of religion, it was to understand the relationship between religion and economic life. Where Marx saw a simple economic determinism, Weber saw a complex reciprocal interaction. In his most famous work, *The Protestant Ethic and the Spirit of Capitalism,* Weber (1930) argued the revolutionary thesis that Puritanism was one key factor in the Industrial Revolution. It was not, as Weber's argument is sometimes misconstrued, just that Puritanism encouraged hard work (a strong work ethnic is certainly found in many non-European cultures). But also that Puritanism saw economic success as a sign of divine favor while demanding extreme rational self-control and a frugal lifestyle—conditions ideally suited to encourage the capital accumulation needed for the process of industrialization. Weber subsequently expanded his studies by examining the obstacles to economic rationalization posed by the religious and cultural traditions in other parts of the world, especially in China (1951) and India (1958).

Weber (1952, 1963) saw the influence of socioeconomic forces on religion in terms of what he called elective affinities. Weber felt that people in social groups with different lifestyles had an affinity for different kinds of religious beliefs. Those affinities may be based on the characteristics of entire societies, such as the tendency for foragers to believe in nature spirits or the appeal to monotheism for pastoralists. Or they may affect smaller-status groups, such as merchants who are attracted to rational calculating religions, or privileged elites with their proclivity for elaborate ritual and ceremony. However, Weber saw these relationships only as affinities, not as fixed and deterministic. Historical forces such as a foreign conquest can induce persons from a particular status group to adopt a religion for which they do not have a natural affinity.

The Sacred Canopy

One of the most popular of the more recent sociological theories of religion is built around Peter Berger's (1969) metaphor of the "sacred canopy." Drawing on the phenomenological and interactionist traditions, Berger holds human society to be an enterprise of world-building. It is, in other words, an effort to create a meaningful reality in which to live. This is a dialectical process that has three underlying movements. The first is "externalization," which "is the ongoing outpouring of human beings into the world, both in the physical and the mental activities of man" (Berger 1969:4). Next comes the process of "objectivation," which gives the products of this activity a reality and power that is independent of those who created it. Finally, individuals take this socially constructed reality into their own inner life in the process of "internalization." Through this process society creates a *nomos*—a meaningful order that is imposed on the universe. The most important aspect of this socially established nomos is that it is "a shield against terror" protecting us from the "danger of meaninglessness" (Berger 1969:22).

Religion plays a key role in this process because it is the human enterprise by which a sacred cosmos is established. It is, in turn, the awesome mysterious power of the sacred that confronts the specter of chaos and the inevitability of death. According to Berger (1969), the "power of religions depends, in the last resort, upon the credibility of the banners it puts in the hands of men as they stand before death, or more accurately, as they walk inevitably, toward it" (p. 51).

The Religious Marketplace

Despite the powerful way Berger's theory links the existential and the social dimension of religion, the idea that religion provides a single scared canopy over today's pluralistic societies has it limitations. A number of current scholars are now using a different theoretical paradigm— rational choice theory—to construct a model that explicitly recognizes the reality of religious diversity (Stark and Bainbridge 1985; Finke and Stark 1992; Warner 1993; Iannaccone 1994). The basic idea is that the kind of consumer decision making analyzed by economic theory also applies to religious behavior. This approach looks at the public as consumers of religious who are out to satisfy their needs by obtaining the best "product." Religious organizations are entrepreneurial establishments competing in a religious marketplace ruled by the laws of supply and demand.

Although religious "merchandise" is considered in just the same way as any other product, there is one important difference. The costs and benefits the consumers must weigh are often supernatural (such as the promise of an afterlife) and therefore cannot be empirically proven. This leaves the religious organization free to make almost any kind of claims it wishes, but it also creates the problem that the consumers are often uncertain about whether or not they will actually receive the benefits it promises.

Thus, demanding groups that require high commitment often have the most attractive product, because they create greater feelings of certainty among consumers that they will actually receive the promised rewards. Another important point stressed by these theorists is that greater religious pluralism will encourage greater religiosity among the public, because it stimulates competition among different religious groups to improve their "product" in order to protect and expand their market share. Societies with a state religion, on the other hand, will tend to have less religious vitality because the established religion will be less responsive to the needs of the public (Finke and Stark 1992).

The metaphor of the marketplace is a useful tool for sociological analysis, but it can also be seriously misleading because there are also some fundamental ways in which religion is unlike an economic commodity. One of the most obvious is that the majority of people stay in the religion into which they were born and do not change even if another religion in the "marketplace" offers more benefits and less costs. Moreover, "religious products" are not really subject to market exchange, because they have no direct monetary value. A church cannot put its product on sale if the customers don't come. Finally, as in other aspects of human life, rational choice theory fails to recognize the deep emotional forces involved in religious life that are often quite impervious to the beckonings of reason.

THE SOCIAL PSYCHOLOGY OF RELIGION

This examination of the theory of religion would not be complete without mentioning one other great nineteenth-century thinker, Sigmund Freud (1856–1939). His thinking contains many similarities to the more sociological-oriented theorists who have grappled with the problem of religion. Like Berger, for example, Freud saw religion as an attempt to deal with the fundamental problem of human existence. For Berger, that problem was the need for meaning, whereas for Freud, it was our inability to obtain the things we want and need. Religion in Freud's (1957) words "is born of the need to make tolerable the helplessness of man" (p. 54). Religion helps create a world in which we feel less threatened and more at home. But like so many other social scientists of this time, Freud felt that while religion may be comforting, it is a comforting illusion. Thus, religion is a kind of infantile wish fulfillment. In the face of our helplessness and defenselessness, we crave the solace and support we received from our parents when we were children, so we project a father figure into the heavens and call it God. While more recent psychological thinkers do not necessarily share Freud's metaphysical position, the idea that the patriarchal God of Western monotheism is a father figure and that the female Goddesses in other traditions are symbolic representations of the mother is widespread.

The Religious Experience

Because these sociological and psychological theorists focus on the roles religion plays and the needs it meets, they often lose sight of the experiential foundations of religious life. But no matter how skeptical one may be about their meaning, there is no doubt that many people have religious or mystical experiences. Indeed, most of the world's major religions trace their origins to such events. The experience Moses had when Yahweh gave him the Ten Commandments, Mohammad's experience as the Angel Gabriel revealed Allah's words in the *Koran,* and Siddhartha Gautama's great enlightenment experience under the Bodhi tree are just a few examples of religious experiences that have literally changed the course of human history. But how, then, is the social scientist to understand such events? Freud, Durkheim, and Marx along with many of the other founders of the sociology of religion would dismiss such experiences as hallucinations, but that hardly seems to do such momentous events justice. Believers in the various faiths founded on such visions would say their accounts of what happened are literally true, but that of course leaves the problem that the "truths" revealed in one religious tradition often contradict the "truths" of another. The inescapable fact is that fact experiences that lie completely beyond the bounds of the ordinary must be still expressed in terms of the cultural expectations, assumptions, and language of the individuals who try to report them.

In his classic study *The Idea of the Holy,* Rudolf Otto (1923) argues that religious experiences involve what he calls *mysterium tremendum et fascinosum.* That is, the experience of the holy is one of a terrifying power, fascinating yet absolutely unapproachable and wholly other. Ironically, most mystics in the Asian tradition and many Westerners as well describe such peak experiences in just the opposite way—a complete dissolution of the bounds of the normal self that produces an absolute unity with the entire universe (see Anonymous 1978; Kapleau 1989).

Of course, all religious experiences are not so overwhelming and profound. Like other experiences, they come in all ranges of intensities and in countless different forms. The feeling of holiness and tranquility one feels when entering a beautiful church or the sense of wonder and joy when seeing a mountain sunset are milder forms of religious experience, as are the states produced by effective rituals that invoke a sense of reverence and awe in the participant.

There is often a considerable difference in the importance placed on religious experience even among religious groups with relatively similar backgrounds. Among Protestant Christians, for example, the Pentacostalists give great importance to the direct emotional experience of the spirit of God, whereas the Puritans reject such emotionalism in favor of Bible studies and ethical discipline.

Religion and Identity

In societies with a single dominant faith, religious affiliation often becomes a taken-for-granted assumption and does not necessarily play a significant role in personal identity. The more religiously divided a society is, however, the more central the religion is likely to become in defining who one is. In pluralistic countries such as the United States, religious affiliation commonly provides a sense of belonging amid the anonymous institutions of mass society.

Religious identity is often mixed with ethnic identity—to be an Arab in many parts of the world is to be a Muslim, just as Serbs are identified with Orthodoxy, Croatians with Catholicism, and Thais with Buddhism. This combination can be an explosive one in areas with high levels of ethnic conflict. Religious differences aggravate ethnic conflict by providing emotionally charged symbols, systems of meaning that compete for cultural dominance, and a certain tendency to see one's own group as having a monopoly on the truth.

Religion can play another role in personal identity by reinforcing a definition of oneself as a particular kind of person. Those with high levels of religious involvement and commitment often define themselves as more moral, more spiritual, or more wise than other people. Many religious groups hold that their faith is the one true faith, and even that fellow believers are an elite group that will receive heavenly rewards in the afterlife, whereas all others will suffer horrible torments. So the members of such groups tend to see themselves as part of a special elite of the "saved." Although such beliefs can obviously reinforce self-esteem, they can also foster fear and anxiety if one fails to live up to the expectations of the religious group or begins to doubt the truth of its doctrines. They can also encourage a sense of hostility or even violence toward nonbelievers.

Religion may also have a critical role in sustaining identity change. In most societies, religiously rooted rites of passage publicly declare and reinforce changes in social status and the new identity that goes with them, for example, coming of age or marriage ceremonies. Religious groups may play a critical role in helping individuals make other radical changes in their lives as well. Religious organizations have often succeeded in helping drug abusers and compulsive gamblers where other programs have failed, because they offer an attractive new identity and a strong community to support it. A religious conversion or recommitment often follows various kinds of personal crises for much the same reasons.

Conversion and Commitment

Although there is a considerable amount of sociological research about "religious conversion," the concept is in some ways an unfortunate one for it seems to imply an all-or-nothing dichotomy. One is a member of one religion and then "converts" to a different one. In many cases, however, a "conversion" is more like a renewal or return to existing religious beliefs. Moreover, despite the exclusivity of many Western religions, there is no particular reason to assume that people must leave their old religion before joining a new one. A substantial percentage of the population of Japan would, for example, identify themselves as both Shintoists and Buddhists.

Most of the sociological research on conversion and commitment focuses on one of two types of religions—fundamentalist Christians and members of what are called the new religious movements. The most striking finding of the research on conservative Christian faiths is that most of their "converts" actually came from the same kind of conservative Christian background. Richardson and Stewart's (1978) study of the Jesus Movement in the 1960s and 1970s found that most of their converts were "hippies" who were returning to their original fundamentalist roots. Bibby and Brinkerhoff's (1974) study of fundamentalist churches in a large metropolitan area in the United States also found that most converts were already religious insiders from evangelical backgrounds. Unlike the popular image of religious conversion, Zetterberg (1952) found that only 16 percent of converts to the Christian Church he studied experienced a sudden change in lifestyle. For most of his subjects, religious "conversion" was more like a "sudden role identification" in which they identified themselves more clearly in religious terms.

The media attention in the 1960s and 1970s to religious cults that appeared to be brainwashing young converts stimulated considerable sociological attention on this subject. To avoid the stigma attached to the term *cult*, however, sociologists now more often use the term *new religious movements* (NRMs) (see Roberts 2004:187–197). But somewhat confusingly, the term does not apply to any new religion only but to groups outside the religious mainstream that have an intense encapsulating community and often a strong charismatic leader. The most well-known study of conversion to NRMs is John Lofland's work on the Unification Church of Reverend Sun Myung Moon. Lofland (1966) found that conversion to the Unification Church followed a series of stages. First, the potential convert was "picked up" by members of the group, then he or she was showered with attention and "hooked." In the next stage, they are "encapsulated"—isolated from contacts with those outside the group—and the final result is "commitment" to the group. Lofland's model has been criticized for giving potential converts too passive a role in the process, something he himself later recognized (Snow and Phillips 1980; Lofland and Skonovd 1981).

Like other researchers, Lofland (1966) concluded that people with high levels of emotional tension and dislocations are more prone to religious conversions. Conversion or a renewed religious commitment is, then, one possible response to intractable personal problems. Thomas O'Dea (1966) argued that religious conversion was also part of a "quest for community." Migrants, marginalized people seen as deviants by mainstream society, and others suffering from anomie and social disorganization are therefore prime candidates for a transforming religious commitment.

Sociologists, however, often neglect the obvious point that in addition to the desire to deal with pressing personal difficulties and to be part of a supportive community, people also make religious conversions for religious reasons. That is, they seek some kind of spiritual growth or religious experience. The members of the Western Buddhist groups that Coleman (2001) surveyed ranked the desire for spiritual growth as a more important reason for getting involved in Buddhism than a desire to deal with personal problems or to be with other members of those groups. More tellingly, the average respondent reported that they began to meditate about four years before they joined a Buddhist group—obviously, not something we would expect of someone whose primary goal was to find a supportive social community.

RELIGIOUS MOVEMENTS

There is probably no other sphere of human life in which more effort is made to maintain unchanging traditions than in religion. Yet religious life everywhere is in a constant state of dynamic change. Even in the most stable eras, religious beliefs and practices are undergoing continual change from generation to generation, and new religious movements often spring up unexpectedly to challenge orthodox views.

Weber traced the origins of most religious movements to charismatic leaders, who are often the bearers of radical new religious ideas. The charismatic leader, according to Weber (1947), has "a certain quality of . . . individual personality by virtue of which he is set apart from ordinary men and treated as endowed with supernatural, superhuman, or at least specifically exceptional powers or qualities" (pp. 358–59). The qualities and insights of the charismatic leader are creative, out of the ordinary, and spontaneous, and as such she or he is a major source of social change and innovation. When the charismatic leader issues a call, people follow, and things change. Thus, charismatic leaders are often seen as a threat to established religion, which may respond with various repressive measures.

In its early days, the charismatic religious movement draws its legitimacy and inspiration from its leader. But once the charismatic leader dies, the movement is thrown into crisis. If the movement is to survive, it must undergo a process Weber termed the "routinization of charisma." The special inspiration and magical quality of the leader must be incorporated into the routine institutionalized structures of society. In literate societies, the words and actions of the leader are written down and become revered holy books. The followers who gathered around the leader are typically subsumed into a formalized religious institution with the charismatic figure's inner circle as its leaders. Rules, rituals, and specialized roles are developed to keep the leader's message and the religious movement going.

This process of institutionalization is essential if the movement is to survive, but ironically, it can also sap its religious vitality and even subvert the intentions of the founder. As religious institutions become more powerful and more bureaucratic, the goals of the leaders are often displaced from spiritual objectives to the maintenance and enhancement of their own positions. Rituals and practices that were once vital and alive become stale, and the enthusiasm of the original converts is replaced by the complacency of those born into the faith. As this trend continues, the religion often generates revival movements that seek to shake things up and return to the original message of its charismatic founder.

The success of a new religious movement depends on both the qualities and skill of the charismatic leader and its sociological context. The religious message of the successful movement must have a stronger affinity to the needs and aspirations of particular status groups than competing religions. Political power is often critical to the expansion of the religion, as when conquering Islamic warriors propagated their faith across North Africa and the Middle East, or when the Christian faith of the European colonialists was spread throughout the vast empires they subjugated.

RELIGION AND SOCIAL STRUCTURE

The most widely used typology of religious organization is probably Weber's church-sect dichotomy. This useful, if somewhat Eurocentric, typology has been the subject of repeated elaborations and refinements over the years. Niebuhr (1957) added a third category, the denomination, between the first two, and some add a fourth (the cult), while still others have created subcategories within each broad type (Troeltsch 1931; Yinger 1970; Stark and Bainbridge 1985). Unfortunately, as the categories proliferated and their contents were elaborated in different ways by different sociologists, the classificatory scheme has become increasingly unwieldy.

The basic idea behind Weber's original classification is, however, still a valuable one especially when conceptualized as a continuum rather than a series of ideal types. At one end is the "church" or, less Eurocentrically, the "established religion." It is broad and universal and its members are usually born into the faith. It is well accommodated to the established order and, indeed, often receives official state support. At the other end is the sect, which is small and exclusive. Membership in the sect is by choice, and it demands a high degree of commitment and involvement. The roots of sectarianism are usually in some kind of protest movement, and in contrast to the established religion, there is an ongoing tension between the sect and the social order. As time goes by, however, both extreme types of religious organization tend to move more toward the middle. As the original members of the sect are succeeded by later generations, it tends to accommodate itself with the dominant social order, while established religions eventually split or see their hegemony eroded by new religious competition. European Christianity, for example, started as a sect, grew into an established religion, and then fragmented into multiple denominations.

Sectarian movements are most popular among the poor and disprivileged, groups that are naturally in a greater state of tension with the established order. But there are significant class differences even within established religions. In general, lower social strata have an affinity for emotional and expressive religion, while the middle and upper middle classes prefer more self-controlled rationalistic practice, and the upper class shows an attraction to elegant ceremony. In traditional Japan, for example, devotional Pure Land Buddhism was most popular among the peasants, and the disciplined Zen sect among the samurai, while the ritualistic Shigon held special appeal to the royalty.

Religion commonly plays another important role in the stratification system by legitimizing social inequality. One classic example concerning class inequality is the Hindu belief that someone who diligently carries out the obligations of their caste will be reborn into a higher caste in the future. Religion often plays a similar role in perpetuating gender inequality. First, many religious doctrines explicitly relegate women to subordinate positions. The *Koran,* for example, instructs women but not men to obey their spouse, dress modestly, and limit themselves to a single marital partner. Second, religious organizations often themselves discriminate against women as a matter of official policy. In Christianity, for example, the Roman Catholic, Eastern Orthodox, and many Protestant churches categorically exclude women from the clergy. Many religions, especially in the Western tradition, also encourage or even require discrimination based on sexual orientation. However, because organized religion has often sided with the privileged and the powerful, it does not mean that it always does, and there are also numerous examples of religious movements that sought to overturn or reform an unjust social order.

The relationship between religion and politics is therefore a complex one. In some cases, religious groups are an oppositional force challenging the established order, although some form of accommodation or active support is far more common. But even in the latter case, the relationship between religion and government takes many forms. At one extreme we have the theocracy, such as contemporary Iran, in which religious elites dominate state organization. At the other extreme are the totalitarian states that rigidly control religious practice, as occurred in most of the Communist countries, or that use religion as a tool of government policy, as was the case with State Shinto in Meiji Japan. Religion offers a way to legitimize ruling elites in much the same way as it does for the overall stratification system as, for example, in the European belief in the divine right of kings. Equally important, it can provide a palate of powerful symbols that can be used to justify specific government actions. In the contemporary conflicts in the Middle East, for example, one side justifies its actions in terms of an Islam Jihad, whereas the other does the same in terms of what Bellah (1970) termed America's "civil religion" (the belief that God supports America and that it has a moral duty to spread freedom and democracy around the world).

RELIGION IN AN AGE OF GLOBALIZATION

Like all social institutions, religion has undergone a sweeping transformation as a result of the Industrial Revolution and the global changes it has wrought. Many of the early founders of the sociology of religion saw this religious change in relatively simplistic terms as a process of secularization in which old religious ideas and institutions were being replaced by new rational-scientific ones. Over the years, the advocates of this secularization thesis moderated their claims holding merely that the influence of religion on society and social life has declined as a result of this process of modernization (Roberts 2004:305–28). More recently, a number of scholars have challenged this thesis holding that people are as religious as they ever were and that the process of secularization has ground to a halt (e.g., Stark and Bainbridge 1985). Such claims touched off a powerful counterattack, and this remains one of the most hotly debated issues in the sociology of religion (Bruce 1996).

Much of the differences between the contestants rest on conflicting definitions of secularization, and, polemics aside, several points seem clear. First, although the trend is more marked in the core than the periphery, societies in all parts of the world are becoming more secular if by that we mean mythical and magical thought is being replaced by rational-scientific thought in many (but certainly not all) areas of social life. The world, in Max Weber's term, is being "disenchanted."

Second, there has been a sharp decline in the political and social hegemony of organized religion in European societies as they have undergone the process of modernization. This trend is, however, much less pronounced or nonexistent in other parts of the world. In societies where hegemonic monotheism never took root, religion played a much weaker political role from the start. The Animistic religions do not have much in the way of distinct religious institutions, and Asian societies have always tended more toward totalitarianism than theocracy. For example, the Chinese government under Mao Tse-tung began a harsh repression of organized religious activities *before* any significant process of modernization had taken place, and since then has slowly been loosening its grip as industrialization has proceeded. In recent years, religion has also become an organizing principle for various movements reacting against the contradictions and dislocations caused by the process of modernization and the global spread of consumer capitalism. The Islamic fundamentalist movement is a political/religious response both to the relegation of the Islamic cultures to a peripheral position in the world system with the foreign domination that that implies and to the spread of Western consumer values. Interestingly, Islamic fundamentalism was stimulated to a significant degree by the success of another political/religion movement, Zionism, in taking control of formerly Islam territories. And the growing militancy of Islamic fundamentalism, in turn, stimulated a counterreaction in India sometimes known as Hindu fundamentalism. Even the United States, with its hegemonic position in the world system, has seen the growth of its own political/religious movements. The rise of the religious right in America was, however, obviously not the result of foreign domination, but a response to changes in traditional family institutions and sexual mores that resulted from the growth of consumer capitalism.

Third, although individual religiosity is difficult to measure, there seems little reason to believe that people are any less interested than they ever were in the matters of "ultimate concern" that are the foundation of most religions. Of course, social crises can stimulate a change or intensification of religion interests. The rise of Sufism after the Mongolian conquest of the Middle East is one example, as was the rapid growth of new religions known as the "rush hour of the Gods," which occurred in Japan following its devastating defeat in World War II. Nonetheless, no matter what form of social organization we adopt and what our historical circumstances are, the existential dilemmas that give rise to the religious impulse remain a fundamental part of the human condition.

THE FUTURE OF THE SOCIOLOGY OF RELIGION

Whatever the excesses of its early days, the sociology of religion played a vital role in establishing the independence of the social sciences from the religious worldview that dominated European thought. By making religion an object of scientific investigation like any other social phenomena, it broke through a deep cultural barrier to the understanding of the social world. Today, this critical freedom is often taken for granted, but it ranks as one of the major successes of the sociological enterprise.

As the twenty-first century unfolds, the challenges before the sociology of religion are quite different ones. The roots of the global political economy go back at least as far as the fifteenth century, but only with relatively recent advances in communications and transportation are we seeing the emergence of a truly global community. As the peoples of the world are bound ever more inextricably together, the protective social distance between the hegemonic claims of different religious groups have evaporated and smoldering conflicts burst into flame. The critical task of the sociology of religion in this new era is to free itself from its remaining bonds of Eurocentrism and to provide a balanced vantage point from which to begin unraveling the twisted knots of religious claims and conflicts. It is relatively easy for sociologists to laud the contribution that different religions have made to the common weal. It is a far greater challenge to point out the ways in which they foster violence, bigotry, and intolerance without fanning the flames of sectarian conflict. The sociology of religion is, nonetheless, in a unique position to provide the kind of cool rational voice needed to help foster a just pluralistic foundation for the emerging world community. But the success of this enterprise depends on sociology's ability to live up to its own illusive ideals of objectivity and impartiality.

30

POLITICAL SOCIOLOGY

W. LAWRENCE NEUMAN

University of Wisconsin, Whitewater

*P*olitical sociology is the study of power and the intersection of society and politics. Power is a pervasive, fundamental dimension of social relations and institutions, while politics refers to institutionalized processes by which social groups (i.e., classes, genders, and races) acquire, extend, apply, maintain, and struggle over power. The field's relevance extends beyond explaining political behavior to generating broad understandings of power, and it is more a perspective that cuts across many diverse topics than a fixed content area. It is a dynamic field that has periodically reinvented itself. Orum (1996) remarked, "Political sociology in the past fifteen years or so has come to look vastly different from a generation ago" (p. 142), and others (Nash 2000) see a "new" political sociology emerging. Other areas of sociology borrow from political sociology forging links across diverse subfields (Dobratz, Buzzell, and Waldner 2003).

Political sociology is interdisciplinary—where political science and sociology intersect. Like other interdisciplinary fields (e.g., social psychology, historical sociology, political philosophy), the boundary line shifts and is permeable, allowing for interchange and creativity (see Hicks 1995). Political scientists and political sociologists may study the same phenomena (e.g., voting processes, public policy development, and protest) but tend to concentrate on different issues, ask, different questions, and apply distinct analytic perspectives. Thus, political sociologists and political scientists both study elections, but the political scientist asks, Who won and by how much? Who voted for which candidate? How did a political party mobilize its supporters? By contrast, a political sociologist asks, How does voting compare to other means of gaining power? Does an election outcome influence life chances for various social sectors? Can elections alter the distribution of power among the major classes/groups/sectors of a society?

Political scientists focus the operation of political institutions (empirical political science) or consider ideal forms of governing (normative political science). They might examine the committee structure of legislative body, study how alternative voting rules affect election outcomes, or consider what makes a law "just" or "fair" relative to a set of political principles. Political scientists concentrate on the "front stage" of the "game of politics" in government at local, national, or international levels and map out their operations (e.g., voting in elections, passing new laws, administering policy). They focus on government's internal structure (e.g., unified or divided, centralized or decentralized, tall or flat hierarchy) and mechanics (e.g., who gets elected, what laws are passed, which agency budget grew).

By contrast, political sociologists see government as one of the multiple sites of concentrated power—simultaneously a site of power and an apparatus over which groups contest for control. They examine how social institutions/groups/forces interface with the political sphere of governing and struggles for power. They see "the political" permeating society—evident as sexual politics, cultural politics, racial politics, religious politics, educational politics, or environmental politics. Political sociologists synthesize ideas, issues, and research techniques with traditional sociological concerns by focusing on power relations wherever they appear. While a few areas of political sociology are applied (e.g., voting outcomes, policy contests), most effort is directed at developing a critical understanding of fundamental power dynamics.

305

HISTORICAL DEVELOPMENT
OF THE FIELD

Political sociology emerged out of late-nineteenth-century German and Italian social and political thought. Its founders include Karl Marx (1818–1883), Vilfredo Pareto (1848–1923), Gaetano Mosca (1858–1941), Max Weber (1864–1920), Robert Michels (1876–1936), and Antonio Gramsci (1891–1937). They tried to explain how capitalist industrialization displaced feudal institutions/relations and sparked clashes among peasants, merchants, workers, and owners, and how the nation-state altered the consolidation of elite power and sparked demands for democratic citizen participation.

After World War II, political sociology's center shifted from Western Europe to the United States, and the "classic era" of contemporary political sociology began. With the defeat of fascism, the onset of the Cold War, and the demise of colonialism, Americans saw themselves as the undisputed world leader of industrial capitalism with democratic politics and economic freedom. Strong domestic economic growth and social stability fostered a mood of optimism and self-assurance. One central question became, Why do some societies become democratic while others become totalitarian (e.g., the fascist regimes of Germany, Japan, Italy, and Spain or the communist regimes of Soviet Union, Cuba, China, and North Korea)? As Janowitz (1968) summarized, "Political sociology has come to be linked to the analysis of the economic, social, and psychological preconditions for political democracy" (p. 306). Political sociologists applied modernization theory to outline the societal conditions that reinforced or threatened democracy (Almond and Verba 1963; Apter 1965; Bendix 1964; Deutsch 1966; Huntington 1968; Lipset 1959b, 1963; Moore 1966). To them, liberal democracy emerged from advancing industrial capitalism, an expanding secular and educated middle class, and a defeat of traditional ruling elites. Democratic government required "modern" social-political institutions and values that favored popular participation, rule of law, and tolerance for dissent.

A second concern was to analyze the social bases of voting. This grew from a belief that formal democratic processes facilitated a peaceful resolution of conflicts among contenting groups. Two paradigmatic works of the 1960s, Lipset's *Political Man* and Campbell et al.'s *The American Voter,* emphasized societal consensus and an absence of irreparable social divisions or polarizing ideologies. Both argued that Americans were only modestly interested in politics and voted to advance the interests of their social group. After Lenski (1966) outlined a theory of multidimensional stratification, the impact of status inconsistency on political behavior occupied attention (Rush 1967; Segal 1969; Segal and Knoke 1968), but the issue proved to be a dead end. Expanding social programs of the era were seen as responsive democratic governments addressing the changing demography and evolving social needs of an industrial society (Cutright 1963, 1965; Wilensky 1975; Wilensky and Lebeaux 1958).

A third issue was to identify supporters of right-wing or left-wing political extremism and to discover why others were tolerant and defended civil liberties (Bell 1964; Rush 1967; Stouffer 1955). The intolerant were a mass of uneducated, low-income, marginal people who did not embrace establishment norms. Kornhauser (1959) warned, "The main danger to political order and civil liberty is the domination of elites by masses" (p. 228). Lane (1962) found that while few people were intensively involved in politics, most embraced basic democratic values. By implication, a well-educated middle class of professional white-collar workers, business owners, and upper-level managers were the bastion of a stable democratic society.

Political sociologists also examined Michels's "iron law of oligarchy," that is, large-scale bureaucratic organizations that spread in modern industrial society and produced antidemocratic tendencies. This contradicted the idea that modern industrial societies were becoming more democratic. Lipset, Trow, and Coleman (1956) examined blue-collar workers in a large bureaucratic union setting and discovered that they operated on democratic principles, contradicting both the iron law of oligarchy and distrust of "marginal" blue-collar workers. Yet the union was atypical; it had well-educated, high-skill workers who strongly held professional norms and had an intense sense of community. Thus, the findings reinforced the thesis that middle-class values sustained democratic politics.

In this period, political sociology shared structural functionalist assumptions about a societal value consensus. Bell (1960) argued that rising living standards, an expanding middle class, and increased education levels would weaken ideological thinking and strengthen democratic values. At the same time, studies found few Americans informed or involved in politics, and most people lacked consistent, stable political views (Berelson, Lazarfeld, and McPhee 1954; Campbell et al. 1960; Converse 1964). The apparent contradiction between widespread apathy and participatory democracy was reconciled by arguing that people were uninvolved because they were satisfied. This reinforced the idea that slow evolution was preferable to rapid, disruptive social change that might generate social strains or disturb the equilibrium of a smooth-functioning social system (Smelser 1963).

A few classic-era mavericks rejected mainstream views and questioned the prevailing democratic image (Domhoff 1967; Hunter 1953; Mills 1956; Williams 1964), and found an American "power structure" of elites with great power. Others (Edelman 1964; Gusfield 1963) emphasized symbols in politics and saw political actors using emotional appeals or manipulating symbols to distract people and advance their own political goals. Still others (Downs 1957; Olson 1965) applied economic models, now called rational choice theory, to politics. At its zenith in the mid-1960s. classic era political sociology had become a well-established field with sophisticated theory, critical questions, and an established body of knowledge (see Bendix 1968; Bendix and Lipset 1957; Janowitz 1968; Lipset 1959a; see also Hall 1981).

Political sociology sharply changed direction in the 1970s because it had failed to anticipate and could not explain a dramatic turn in political events. Theoretical breakthroughs transformed the field just as graduate programs expanded, producing a flood of new scholars without a commitment to previous concerns. Attention shifted to protest movements. In the classic era, protest was understood as irrational outbursts by isolated malcontents. New research contradicted such a view. It found that most protesters were socially integrated with a deep commitment to democratic ideals but wrestling power from entrenched elites (Gamson 1968; Lipsky 1968; Orum 1966; Piven and Cloward 1971, 1977; Ransford 1968). Others showed how parts of the American government were engaged in antidemocratic actions against its citizens who questioned political elites (Wolfe 1973). More than conformity to American values, democracy advanced when a range of social groups competed and fought (Paige 1975; Skocpol 1979; Tilly 1975; Wolf 1969). All nations were not inevitably progressing toward industrialism and democracy. Instead of spreading democracy, First World governments and corporations worked with local dictators to suppress grassroots pro-democracy worker and peasant movements (Baran and Sweezy 1966; Frank 1967; Petras 1969; Wallerstein 1976; Zeitlin 1967).

Many questioned the prevailing classic-era assumptions and asked whether America has a ruling class. At the same time, Europeans debated the larger capitalism-state relationship and how capitalism shaped state forms and actions (Miliband 1969; Poulantzas 1973). Others (e.g., Korpi 1978) saw social welfare programs as hard-won concessions only granted by rulers facing demands by politically mobilized and militant workers. Historically oriented studies said that early popular democratic impulses in America were squashed (Goodwin 1976), large corporations controlled Progressive Era business regulation (Kolko 1963; Weinstein 1968), and corporate elites dominated U.S. foreign policy (Shoup and Minter 1977). Meanwhile, classic-era thinkers continued to blame the social unrest of the 1960s era on "excessive democracy" (Crozier, Huntington, and Watanuki 1975).

Dispersion and Fragmentation

By the 1980s, unrest had faded and politics shifted rightward in much of the Western world (Kourvetaris and Dobratz 1982, 1983). Simultaneously, funding for social science research declined, graduate programs shrank, and student interest waned. New academic fields (i.e., environmental studies, urban studies, race and ethnic studies, cultural studies, women's studies) grew and borrowed heavily from political sociology. By the end of the twentieth century, Orum (1996) observed, "There no longer is any kind of coherent paradigm that guides the work of political sociology in America" (p. 132). This is not a negative assessment. As Hicks, Janoski, and Schwartz (2005) observed, "the field's great diversity of theoretical arguments is a sign of health, stimulating vigorous debate and self examination" (p. 30).

CURRENT THEORETICAL APPROACHES AND CONTENT AREAS

Political sociologists apply several theories to substantive issues. While each theory claims to be comprehensive, they were developed to address specific issues and rarely directly compete. They also operate at different levels of analysis, and what one treats as a major issue, another may view as peripheral (Alford and Friedland 1985).

Theoretical Approaches

The approaches were developed and gained adherents in different eras. Pluralism was dominant in the classic era but waned by the 1970s. It sees politics primarily as a contest among competing interest groups, and the emphasis is on the first (most overt, visible) dimension of power (Lukes 1974). Pluralism shares the assumption of societal consensus with structural functionalism and treats the state as a neutral apparatus that balances competing popular demands that people expressed through elections and public opinion. Although much stronger in political science, a few sociologists (see Burstein 1981, 1998; Burstein and Linton 2002) embrace pluralist theory.

A managerial (Alford and Friedland 1985) or the state-centered approach (Amenta 1998; Clemens 1993; Evans, Rueschemeyer, and Skocpol 1985; Finegold and Skocpol 1995; Orloff and Skocpol 1984; Skocpol 1985; Skocpol and Amenta 1985) grew from organizational and classic elite theory (e.g., Michels, Mosca, and Pareto). In it, nation-states are "conceived as organizations claiming control over territories and people" with "goals that are not simply reflective of the demands of interests of social groups, classes, or society" (Skocpol 1985:9). It explains state actions by looking at constraints from organizational structure, semiautonomous state managers, and interests that arise from the state as a unique, power-concentrating organization, including the state's role in an international system of nation-states.

A third major approach, class analysis, gained dominance from the mid-1970s to the early 1990s. Two versions were outlined in the structuralist-instrumentalist debate of the 1970s (see Barrow 1993): an Anglo-American power structure model (called instrumentalist by detractors) (see Domhoff 1970, 1974, 1978, 1980, 1983, 1990; Miliband 1969, 1977, 1982) and French structuralism (represented by Louis Althusser, Roland Barthes, Michel Foucault, and Claude Lévi-Strauss). The power structure model posited a ruling class of capitalists and a powerful "inner circle" (Useem 1984) who are class-conscious political actors. Common socialization, internal cohesion, class awareness, and collective action by mobilized class actors created a class that directly rules. By contrast, structuralist theory (Block 1981, 1987; Clark and Dear 1984; Jessop 1982, 1990; O'Connor 1973, 1984; Poulantazas 1973, 1974, 1978; Wright 1978) saw little need for active, direct rule by capitalist class actors. This is because a functional relationship (i.e., the state's structural position in capitalism) requires the state to satisfy system needs for capital accumulation and political legitimation. Thus, the structure of capitalism, not class members actively using the state as an instrument, assures capitalist dominance. A key mechanism is structural dependency (see Swank 1992) in which the state's reliance on a capitalist economy for revenue forces conformity to capitalist system requirements. Structuralists explained stagflation (high inflation with slow growth) and welfare state growth of the 1970s with the concept "fiscal crisis of the state" (Block 1981; O'Connor 1973). The crisis arose from a contradiction between the requirement to advance capital accumulation and to provide political legitimation (i.e., being responsive to the popular demands and providing tax-absorbing social programs). As taxes rose to satisfy legitimation demands, they slowed capital accumulation and economic growth, creating serious fiscal problems.

Another class analysis model moved beyond the structural-instrumentalist impasse to emphasize class struggles and relative autonomy. State-relative autonomy means that while the state cannot contradict core capitalist economic principles, state actions are not strictly predetermined. State managers have maneuvering room, but the mobilization and struggles among classes, subgroups within classes, and nonclass groupings can shape state actions in specific historical contexts (Gilbert and Howe 1991; Hooks 1990a; Zeitlin, Neuman, and Ratcliff 1976). The degree of autonomy expands or contracts based on domestic and external factors. Thus, attention shifted from issues of capitalist class cohesion, the class background of state managers, and economic functionalism toward explaining political conflicts and class alliances in specific historical conditions.

Other sociological theories (rational choice, constructionism, and new institutionalism) influence political sociology. Rational choice is strongly embraced by political scientists and used by some political sociologists (e.g., Brustein 1996; Hechter and Kanazawa 1997; Kiser and Hechter 1991; Marwell and Oliver 1993). Social constructionism adds a cultural dimension and is used at the micro and macro levels (Eliasoph 1998; Gamson 1992; Neuman 1998; Steinmetz 1999). Lastly, "new" institutionalism (Amenta and Zylan 1991; Campbell 2004; Clemens and Cook 1999; Immergut 1998) emphasizes how institutional arrangements shape political context while incorporating rational choice and organizational and cultural factors.

Content Areas

The substantive issues of contemporary political sociology fall into six major areas: (1) State, citizenship and civil society, (2) social cleavages and politics, (3) protest movements and revolutions, (4) surveillance and control, (5) state-economy relations, and (6) the welfare state.

1. *State, Citizenship, and Civil Society.* The modern nation state emerged from the demise of feudalism and was coincident with the rise of industrial capitalism. Political sociologists examine this process to understand state structures and processes of state transformation. Postmodernization theories of change emphasize the significance of warfare and state consolidation of control over territory and people, especially in seventeenth- to nineteenth-century Europe (Brubaker 1992, 1996; Ertman 1997; Mann 1988, 1993; Rueschemeyer, Stephens, and Stephens 1992; Tilly 1990). In addition to the importance of geopolitical conflict, resource extraction, and power consolidation, these developments helped form a civil society with a public sphere (Calhoun 1992; Ferree et al. 2002; Somers 1993). They also contributed to expanding citizenship (Janoski 1990; Korpi 1989; Mann 1987; Orloff 1993; Roche 1992; Tilly 1996), including franchise expansion (Ramirez, Soysal, and Shanahan 1997). Citizenship studies are a distinct subfield focusing on social inclusion and are tied to the welfare state (see below).

2. *Social Cleavages and Politics.* Since the classic era, political sociologists examined how social cleavages get expressed politically, and class was the most salient cleavage with the "democratic class struggle thesis" (Alford 1963; Hout, Brooks, and Manza 1995; Korpi 1983; Lipset 1960). They retain an interest in social class but also examine other social cleavages (Brooks 2000; Brooks and Manza 1997a, 1997b; Manza and Brooks 1997, 1998, 1999; Manza, Hout, and Brooks 1995). They argue that class remains important but has changed form and is not alone in affecting voting. Thus, increased female labor force participation generated a new gender effect on voting, new religious cleavages appeared, professionals and managers differ in voting, and racial differences are salient. Several political scientists (Dalton, Flanagan, and Beck 1984; Inglehart 1997; Inglehart and Baker 2000) and some sociologists (Hecther 2004) argue that social class is no longer relevant, and it has been replaced by cultural divisions (e.g., religion, nonmaterialist values such as environment or health) and status differences (e.g., gender, race, ethnic group).

The debate over class versus cultural cleavage effects on voting appears at an impasse. New inquiry has moved in several directions. One considers nonvoters (Piven and Cloward 2000; Teixeria 1992); another reconceptualizes class and other social cleavages (Hall 1997; Lee and Turner 1996; Wright 1997); and a third examines the effect of class on nonelectoral forms of political mobilization (McNall, Levine, and Fantasia 1991).

3. *Protest Movements and Revolutions.* The study of collective behavior changed as studies on movements merged with political sociology. By the 1970s, collective protest was understood to be a political phenomenon, and the resource mobilization approach explained movements in terms of their ability to acquire and use key resources (Gamson 1975; Jenkins and Perrow 1977; McCarthy and Zald 1977; Piven and Cloward 1977; Tilly 1978; Zald and Berger 1978; see also Jenkins 1983; Minkoff 1999). An

offshoot of resource mobilization theory, the "political process model" (McAdam 1982), placed movements firmly within political sociology. It looked beyond internal movement organization to include micromobilization processes, follower identity transformation, and the broader political environment (Klandermans 1984; Klandermans and Oegema 1987; McAdam 1989; Morris 1981, 1993; Opp and Gern 1993; Snow, Zurcher, and Ekland-Olson 1980; Whittier 1997). Others conceptualized environmental conditions as "political opportunity structures" (Almeida 2003; Amenta and Zylan 1991; Gamson 1996; Jenkins, Jacobs, and Agnone 2003; Kitschelt 1986; Meyer and Minkoff 2004; Meyer and Staggenborg 1996; Soule and Olzak 2004). The political opportunity model was expanded to account for waves or cycles of protest over time (Koopmans 1993; Minkoff 1997; Tarrow 1994) and to more closely tie the study of movements to historical processes (Roy 1984). A symbolic-cognitive dimension was added with cognitive liberation (Morris 1992) and movement frames (Ferree 2003; Gamson and Modigliani 1989; Snow et al. 1986; see also Benford and Snow 2000). Later research synthesized movement frames, political opportunities, and organizational forms (Clemens 1993; Diani 1996; Snow and Benford 1992). Some studies examined "new social movements"—that is, movements focused more on cultural issues or identity affirmation than traditional political protest (Buechler 1995; Laraña, Johnston, and Gusfield 1994; Pichardo 1997). The significance of media attention (Gamson and Wolfseld 1993; McCarthy, McPhail, and Smith 1996; Myers and Caniglia 2004, Mueller 1997; Oliver and Maney 2000; Oliver and Myers 1999), police responses to protests (della Porta and Reiter 1998; Earl, Soule, and McCarthy 2003; Wisler and Giugni 1999), and "spillover" from one movement to another (Dixon and Roscigno 2003; Isaac and Christiansen 2002) highlighted movements' dynamic-interactive politics. Some examined protests' impact on electoral or policy outcomes (Andrews 1997, 2001; McAdam and Su 2002), while others explored the mobilization of specific societal sectors, including corporations (Akard 1992). Movement concepts were applied to the business community that mobilized to exert political power through political action committees (Boies 1989; Burris 1987, 1991, 1992; Clawson and Clawson 1987; Clawson and Neustadtl 1989; Clawson, Neustadtl, and Bearden 1986; Clawson, Neustadt, and Weller 1998; Clawson and Su 1990; Mizruchi and Koenig 1986). A few researchers studied major societal transformations or revolutions (Goldstone 1991; Goldstone, Gurr, and Moshiri 1991; Lachmann 2003; Rasler 1996).

4. *Surveillance and Control.* Building on Foucault's (1986) concept of governmentality, Giddens's work (1987) on surveillance, and Althusser's concept (1978) of the ideological state apparatus, political sociologists examine surveillance and social control to understand how state authority penetrates into and regulates many spheres of social life, including activities to count, monitor, and regulate its population (Alonso and Starr 1987; Anderson and Fienberg 1999; Becker and Wetzell 2005; Kertzer and Arel 2002; Scott 1998; Skerry 2000; Torpey 2000). Traditionally, criminal justice was treated as an apolitical, technical-administrative field, but political sociologists see the legal system and the criminalization of behaviors as mechanisms of domination and tactics deployed in power struggles. They consider targeting certain social sectors for criminalization, historical and international patterns of imprisonment, felon disenfranchisement, and political-ideological agendas that shape crime policy (Beckett 1994; Behrens, Uggen, and Manza 2003; Garland 2001; Jacobs and Helms 1996; Jacobs and Kleban 2003; Kent and Jacobs 2004; Savelsberg 1992, 1994; Savelsberg, Cleveland, and King 2004; Sutton 2000, 2004; Uggen and Manza 2002). The tension between politicized legal-criminal issues and technical-scientific processes is itself an issue (see Stryker 1989, 1990, 1994).

5. *State-Economy Relations.* The state's relationship to the class of investors/capital owners and market operations has been an ongoing political sociological concern. Studies examined how political-institutional arrangements (e.g., laws and taxes, property ownership, investment and regulatory policy) and business political activism shaped corporate capitalism's expansion (see Campbell 1993; Campbell and Lindberg 1990; Dobbin 1992, 1994; Dobbin and Dowd 2000; Fligstein 1996; Prechel 1990, 1997; Prechel and Boies 1998; Roy 1997). This included noting how institutional arrangements, including their idea systems, shape economic outcomes (Campbell 2004; Campbell and Pedersen 2001). Others examined how de facto industrial policy and business regulation in specific areas, including military-industrial expansion, altered economic affairs and politics (Grant 1995; Grant and Wallace 1994; Hooks 1990b, 1991, 1994; Prechel 1990, 2000). Related studies (Calavita, Pontell, and Tillman 1997; Glasberg and Skidmore 1997) looked at corporate welfare as an alternative to industrial policy in the United States and, specifically, at the U.S. savings and loan bailout. After the dissolution of communist regimes' command economies, neoliberal ideology and state-economy arrangements diffused in a post-Cold War environment, and political sociologists shifted to discussing "varieties of capitalism." They examined alternative structural state-economy arrangements among the advanced capitalist nation-states that form integrated configurations (Campbell 2004; Fligstein and Sweet 2002; Hall and Soskice 2001; Kitschelt et al. 1999). Alternative arrangements and state policies developed historically and reinforced specific patterns of corporate capitalism with implications for economic expansion, interstate relations, and domestic labor relations and business practices.

6. *The Welfare State.* Measured as total social spending, the percentage of the population covered, or range of different programs, the welfare state expanded in all advanced

capitalist democracies. This became a major area of comparative research and the focus of competing theoretical explanations. In the 1980s, researchers (Hicks and Swank 1983; Isaac and Kelly 1981; Jenkins and Brents 1989; see also Fording 1997) explored Piven and Cloward's (1971, 1977) thesis that social unrest stimulated welfare spending. By the 1980s, a power resource model gained broad acceptance. It says that conflicts among opposing social classes in specific social-historical settings explain the timing, size, and form of welfare states. The largest, most comprehensive, and proegalitarian welfare states appear in nations that have a strong and politicized labor movement organized into social democratic or labor parties that regularly win national elections (Hicks and Kenworthy 1998; Huber, Ragin, and Stephens 1993; Huber and Stephens 2001; Korpi 1978, 1989; Quadagno 1984, 1988).

After Esping-Andersen's (1990) pathbreaking work, the notion of multiple welfare state regimes spread and has been elaborated on (Castles and Mitchell 1992, 1993; Ferrara 1996; Jones 1993) and extended to identify alternative pathways of welfare state expansion (Hicks 1999). Despite initial assumptions, poverty reduction has not been a major outcome of the welfare state (Korpi and Palme 1998; Moller et al. 2003). During the 1990s, studies documented how the specific structure and operation of a welfare state reinforced particular gender relations, household patterns, and intrafamily labor allocations (Gornick and Jacobs 1998; Huber and Stephens 2000; Korpi 2000; Orloff 1993, 1996), and in the United States, built on past programs (Skocpol 1992) and reinforced racial inequalities (Lieberman 1998; Manza. 2000; Quadagno 1990, 1992, 1994; Soule and Zylan 1997). The major welfare state regimes (liberal-market, Christian democratic, social democratic) were found to have different effects. Thus, over time, attention moved from welfare state expansion, to alternative welfare state forms, to ways welfare state operations affected a range of social and economic relations. More recently, what had appeared to be an inevitable expansion of the welfare state since World War II stalled in most countries during the 1990s. Debates over causes of stagnation have focused on neoliberal ideological dominance, domestic political outcomes or institutions, and the economic effect of globalization (Iversen 2001; Iversen and Cusack 2000; King and Wood 1999; Korpi 2003; Pierson 2001; Stephens, Huber, and Ray 1999; Swank 2002).

FUTURE DIRECTIONS

As political sociology advances into the twenty-first century, four lines of inquiry are posed for further development: (1) legitimacy and identity, (2) governmentality, (3) politics beyond the nation-state, and (4) a synthesis of new institutionalism, rational choice, and constructionism.

Political sociologists examined legitimacy since the nineteenth century, but issues of social identity and culture are increasingly a concern. Racial-ethnic, sexuality, lifestyle, religious, and other value-based cultural identity affirmations are potential sources of political division that can be triggered under certain conditions. The ways such identities evolve, get expressed, and overlap take place within political structures and involve power/dominance relations. Nation-states and other political structures try to regulate and prevent conflicts among the identities to uphold their legitimacy. This suggests reviving or adjusting Gramsci's notion of hegemony.

Repressive social control and state surveillance continue to interest political sociologists. Their attention has shifted to more subtle forms of domination and coercion, such as that captured by Bourdieu's concept of symbolic violence or Foucault's of governmentality. There is also a shift from treating the state apparatus as the sole site of concentrated power and domination to examining how power gets accumulated and exercised throughout numerous social institutions and relationships. In addition to examining the state's policing, taxing, and other powers, interest is turning to how coercion and power are embedded in the relations of a workplace, courtroom, classroom, shopping mall, hospital, television programming, religious community, and so forth. This moves attention to the symbolic-cultural-idea realm. It includes how collective memories, communication messages, and institutional arrangements impose social-ideational dominance and constrain free and autonomous public sphere for open participation and discourse, an idea elaborated by Habermas.

Few political sociologists expect the nation-state to disappear in the twenty-first century, but they expect changes and greater salience for nonstate politics. New global political structures are arising from accelerating cross-national border flows of information, investments, culture, and people in governments and nongovernment institutions (e.g., corporations, NGOs, social movements). New local multicultural or hybrid forms are emerging both in cities and small-scale units as well as in global institutions larger than the nation-state (see Boli and Thomas 1997; Meyer et al. 1997; Soysal 1994).

Political sociology emerged as a distinct field only since 1950 with its theories built on three core ideas: democratic participation and civic sphere for citizens, domination by elites in state and nonstate bureaucracies, and owner power in capitalist social-economic formations. These mid-twentieth-century concerns correspond to the pluralist, managerial, and class paradigms cogently outlined by Alford and Friedland (1985). As we begin the twenty-first century, political sociology is focusing on institutions and trying to incorporate more sophisticated and cross-discipline modeling as well as integrate emotive-cognitive-symbolic dimensions of social-cultural life.

31

THE SOCIOLOGY OF EDUCATION

THEODORE C. WAGENAAR

Miami University, Ohio

Education deals with the most fundamental human need: how to influence children to become competent adults. In this regard, "the sociology of education is perhaps one of the broadest fields within sociology itself," as Saha observes (1997a:1). He notes that one reason for such broadness is that almost everyone engages in some form of education. Another factor may be that both schools of education and departments of sociology lay claim to the field, often leading to turf issues. The school of education locus may also focus the field more on problem solving than on systematic sociological analysis. The field is also very popular; it is one of the largest special interest sections in sociology professional associations in the United States, the United Kingdom, and Australia. No major study in virtually all fields of sociology fails to include the level of education as either a cause or an effect.

Sociology of education is relevant because it examines the kind of issues people care about. Reducing the dropout rate in high school and college is an important measure of academic success. Understanding how classroom social structures can make disadvantaged children feel socially competent and connected will help mitigate the experiences of being disadvantaged. Teasing out the effects of various pedagogical strategies on boys and girls may help create better learning environments for both. Clarifying the impact of education on the values graduates hold helps clarify the values in a society. Diagramming the social matrix in middle school may help develop strategies for reducing early drug and alcohol use.

Sociology of education has had a split identity, as reflected in its name change. Until the 1960s, it was commonly called educational sociology and tended to focus less on theory and large-scale research and more on within-school behaviors. Willard Waller's (1932) study of teaching is one classic example of a brilliant analysis of the school as a locus where competing interest groups, which include teachers, students, administration, and community, negotiate for influence. The administrative structure of schools drew much attention in the first half of the twentieth century. The shift in nomenclature signaled a shift from a less empirically rigorous and less theoretically grounded field that often dealt with how to improve teaching to a field steeped in theory and empiricism.

Today, sociology of education lies at the heart of sociology. Societies across time have invested considerable resources in socializing their young to become productive citizens. The two institutions most responsible for this role transition are the family and education, the informal and the formal players. Historically, it has been difficult to alter family socialization patterns, and most societies fiercely protect the autonomy of the family. But where do we turn when concerns arise about how to teach children well? The answer is often *the schools*.

Many societies at various points in their histories have used the educational institution to guide the socialization of their future citizens. The notion of a melting pot figured prominently in education in the United States at the turn of the twentieth century as American society attempted to respond to the social forces of immigration, industrialization, and urbanization. Capitalism took root, and education was needed to socialize future workers and teach them skills and to credential them. Schools have been used to promote values, norms, and beliefs thought salient for a particular society, ones that societal leaders often worried were incompletely taught at home. The current focus on intelligent design versus evolution, and with sex education, for example, demonstrates the close relationship between the family and educational systems as these relate to the socialization process. Sociology of education also lies at the heart of sociology because of education's prominent role in status attainment, something that families also aspire to teach and transmit to their young.

Sociology of education is multidisciplinary, for many of the same reasons. Social psychologists study how individuals negotiate the schooling process and provide insight on how meaning and interpretation affect the values, attitudes, and aspirations of students. Economists examine the return on schooling investment for both individuals and societies. Corporate leaders have shown increasing interest in public education because its quality affects the competence of future workers. Corporate-sponsored education efforts rival those in the public sector. Political scientists examine power struggles and how educational decisions emanate from these struggles, providing sociological insight into educational decision making.

Anthropologists have traditionally examined the role of education and schooling across cultures to illustrate how schools reflect cultural values. More recently, anthropologists have contributed important insights by providing ethnographic accounts of school life at the elementary, secondary, and higher-education levels and of how college students respond to and attempt to redefine the culture of their schools. Historians have shown how the organization, focus, and outcomes of education have varied across time and space, providing sociological insights into the connections between societies and their education systems. All these contributions are relevant to sociologists studying education because they differentiate and analyze the social structural forces in education. Therefore, to borrow from Comte, it may be accurate to say that sociology of education is the queen of the social scientific approaches to education.

HISTORY

Lawrence J. Saha (1997b) notes that the earliest definition of sociology of education, then called educational sociology, goes back to a 1913 encyclopedia definition: "one of four special approaches utilized in that scientific study of education which founds its philosophy or inclusive theory upon detailed observation and analysis" (p. 106). Bidwell and Friedkin (1988) note that the sociology of education is "the analysis of educational activities—their form and content, their embeddedness in broader social structures, and their outcomes for individuals and collectivities" (p. 449). In reality, sociologists *have* examined just about everything involving education, ranging from macrolevel analyses of how educational systems reflect culture to microlevel analyses of classroom and playground behavior. But what distinguishes the sociological view from other approaches is its sustained attention to relevant structural and contextual dimensions, as well as its emphasis on

sociological theory and research. Hansen (1967) highlighted this role for sociology when he urged that the term *educational sociology* be reserved for what he called "normative" analyses of education, a form of analysis that suggests what schools ought to do. Sociology of education, he continued, should be reserved for sociological theory and research. He was writing at a time when the field was undergoing a transition from educational practice oriented to more systematically sociological.

With the exception of Durkheim, early sociologists generally ignored issues relating to education. But Banks (1971) details the rise of sociology of education in the United Kingdom; almost 200 universities were offering courses in the field by 1927. Interest in the area then began to decline. In fact, throughout the 1940s, educational sociology was marginalized (Saha 1997b). Most sociologists attached little significance to education as a field of study, and most educators thought sociology to be too far removed from the day-to-day operations of schools to be useful to educational practitioners. Even the number of courses in the field dropped by 1940 in the United Kingdom because it was taught outside the departments of sociology, a testament to its low status in the discipline.

By the 1970s, however, there was a growing interest in Marxist and radical theories. This interest is noteworthy given that the journal *Educational Sociology,* founded in 1927, bridged the gap between the normative and descriptive orientations of educational sociology and the scientific analysis of education of what later was to become sociology of education. In 1963, the American Sociological Association (ASA) assumed responsibility for the journal, titling it *Sociology of Education.* Lawrence Saha (1997b) notes that "the ambivalence about the sociology of education prevailed elsewhere in the English-speaking world," but "by the mid-1980s, the sociology of education was one of the most popular and productive areas within sociology" (p. 108).

Several factors contributed to this renewed interest. One was the new focus that caused researchers to emphasize qualitative techniques in their analyses of classroom interaction and language, and the curriculum (Riehl 2001). Another was the nascent empirical study of status attainment and the central role of education in that process. Critical theory gave another tool that provided greater prominence for a field of inquiry that emphasized the notion that the ideology of dominant groups is employed in schools to oppress the less powerful groups.

Another analytical approach was based on the view of education as an institution that reinforces and reflects cultural rules. Examples include studies of citizenship as well as the rise in enrollment of women.

THEORETICAL ORIENTATIONS

The sociology of education first emerged in Western Europe. Most scholars agree that sociology of education was birthed in the work of Durkheim, particularly his *Education and Sociology* ([1922] 1956). The early theorists in sociology of education, primarily Durkheim, Marx, and Weber, focused on issues relating to social control, concentrating their efforts on establishing how educational systems produced competent citizens, reinforced dominant ideologies, and provided status markers for individuals.

Lawrence Saha (1997a) notes that Durkheim ([1922] 1956) was both a sociologist and a "pedagogist," a combination that provided him with keen insights into the crucial role of education in societies. Countless scholars after Durkheim were to benefit from his insights into the relationships between societies and their educational structures. Of course, Durkheim is best known for his stance and thoughts pertaining to moral education and how well such education is correlated with the norms and values of society. Durkheim believed that education was central to the continuation of a society; thus, his writings centered on social order, the factors that gave rise to social order, and the social consequences when that order breaks down. Durkheim was particularly concerned with the role of education in creating future citizens. He also examined the connections between education and social institutions such as religion. In this area, Durkheim promoted a functionalist view, and his analyses of the roles of the family and education for socialization have informed countless research and theoretical articles.

In light of the interest in Marxist theories of education in the United States and the United Kingdom, it is interesting to note that Marx actually paid little attention to education in his analyses of the capitalist class other than to note its role in perpetuating unequal class systems. It is also noteworthy that Marx's views included aspects of functionalism (Saha and Zubrzycki 1997) in that he believed that economic institutions dominated and that education served an important socialization function in capitalist societies. Schools inculcate appropriate values to those students of the working class who would later be in the employ of the ruling class. Later Marxists and neo-Marxists contemplated what an educational system could look like if it did not simply serve the needs of the ruling class.

Although Weber did not specifically address education in his vast writings, his work on bureaucracy and rationalization does pertain to education. School systems in the United States rapidly became more bureaucratized in the first half of the twentieth century, and Weber's writings about bureaucracy and the salience of rationalization played a central role in analyzing how school systems were organized. Many sociologists have examined the implications of the bureaucratic structure of schools, such as Corwin's (1970) study of the organizational impact on teacher militancy. Weber added to Marx's class analysis as the basis of society by using power and status. Education played an important role in generating power and status but also fueled conflict with those who had less. Weber's notion of *Verstehen* encouraged sociologists to look at the

subjective meanings people experience, including that which emerges from membership in organizations; this orientation has yielded many sociological studies on the inner lives of schools and teachers (e.g., Metz 2000). Lawrence J. Saha and J. Zubrzycki (1997:17) conclude that "Weber has been relatively neglected by sociologists of education" because "he never developed a unified theory of society" (p. 17). This assertion may be somewhat overstated given all the studies employing Weber's ideas on bureaucracy and rationalization and his differentiation of class, status, and power. Certainly, education is a factor for each of these variables.

Jonathan H. Turner and Douglas E. Mitchell (1997) observe that "the emphasis in the sociology of education on applied problems has tended to blunt theoretical development at the micro and meso levels" (p. 21). These analysts outline what they consider to be the major paradigm contributions to sociology of education. First, the functionalist paradigm examines the social role of education, particularly in modernizing societies. Examples include the credentialing function that schools perform and the role of education in status attainment and mobility (Brown 2001).

Second, the utilitarian paradigm assesses the costs actors are willing to incur in pursuit of desired resources, which assumes a rational view of humanity. This paradigm appears most prominently in human capital and cost-benefit analyses and in the prominence of education for accruing human capital. More contemporary applications involve the assessment of the process in which policymakers and other interested parties engage in deciding on such issues as parental choice and school vouchers.

Third, the conflict paradigm has a rich history in sociology of education. The Marxist wing centers on the role of ideology in reinforcing unequal social structural relations among various economic classes. These relations are institutionally reinforced by education, the economy, and the polity and to a lesser extent by religion and the family. Some Marxist-oriented thinkers take a more radical view, stressing either the role of the hidden curriculum (e.g., Bowles and Gintis 1976) or the role of the formal curriculum (e.g., Giroux 1981) in maintaining and reinforcing the capitalist system. Other analysts, such as Anyon (1983), provide the empirical support for theoretical arguments by demonstrating how schools approach students who are from variant social classes in terms of how they teach, what is taught, and how students are evaluated. Conflict theorists examine the manner in which cultural ideologies perpetuate the class system within the context of the school system. In so doing, they highlight the role of status groups in this process. Perhaps the best-known sociologist who works in this area is Randall Collins (1979). Collins depicts how schools and educational systems construct and reinforce cultural differences, particularly through the process of credentialing on the basis of status definition and maintenance.

The interactionist paradigm takes a micro approach by examining the role of education in defining roles and the self. Symbolic interactionists assess how teachers and students define their conceptions of self and social position, how the roles they play contribute to these definitions, and the consequences of both the definitions and the roles for school functions. They are particularly concerned with the sources and consequences of teacher expectations and labeling, as seen in the famous study by Rosenthal and Jacobsen (1982). Erving Goffman's (1972) dramaturgical perspective is useful for examining how teachers and students engage in self-presentation and saving face. Other interactionists, such as Bernstein (1977), use linguistic analysis to show how restricted or elaborated linguistic codes are used in schools to reinforce class differences among students.

Finally, interactionist phenomenology examines the social reality as defined by teachers within the context of the educational institution. Students who do not conform to this teacher-defined model are shunted into less desirable tracks. Other social psychologists examine student attitudes and values, the impact of teacher attributions on student behavior, the role conflict experienced by teachers, the salience of reference groups, peer culture, and the sociometry of classrooms and schools (Bank and Biddle 1997).

Hallinan (2000c) outlines several problems with relying on general sociological theory to analyze education and schools. One such problem is that sociological theories fail to specifically address the unique situation of schools. Second, as a result, such approaches offer little for understanding the uniqueness of the educational institution as well as its many internal variations. Finally, she notes that using subdisciplinary approaches, such as stratification and social psychology, leads to similar problems.

MAJOR ISSUES

The analyses of schools and the school experience fail to match the progress made in other areas during the latter half of the twentieth century. Maureen Hallinan (2000c) posits three reasons for the greater success in other areas. First, models such as the general linear model were developed in other fields during the 1960s, which were then widely used to study schooling processes. Second, many well-crafted and statistically representative data sets were created using schools, teachers, and students. These data sets were mostly developed under federal auspices and yielded many longitudinal studies that helped spawn school outcomes research. Third, sociologists studying education saw the potential impact of their research on educational practice and policy, ranging from the local to the federal level.

Many approaches are employed to organize the major issues examined by sociologists of education. In this chapter, I draw on two of the most comprehensive works in this area, by Hallinan (2000a) and Saha (1997b). The use of both macro and micro approaches is one issue.

Macrolevel-oriented sociologists use quantitative methodologies to study the impact of social structure and cultural ideologies on, for example, the status attainment process. Such analysts view individuals as constrained by the social structural arrangements of which they are a part, demonstrating the differential consequences for individuals.

The relationship between education and development represents one such topic of interest. The goal is to encapsulate the relationship between education and social progress. Macrolevel sociologists also are interested in the impact of school on the workforce, and in doing so, they map the societal developments that influence how educational systems vary across time and space. These methods are used to establish the relationship between expanded educational opportunity and other aspects of society through examining the process by which national policies emerge and how these polices are implemented at the local level.

Microlevel sociologists use both quantitative and qualitative methodologies to study subjective interpretations, suggesting that individuals are less constrained by social structural arrangements than macrolevel sociologists argue. The gap between these two approaches has not been successfully bridged. Microlevel sociologists examine the role of schools as a socialization agent and provide detailed accounts of the differential experiences of students, controlling for social class. They portray the means by which schools come to reflect the normative orientation of culture, how this process affects the manner in which students are able to internalize the values and norms of the general society, and how students negotiate their surroundings. They examine how teachers assume their roles while still attending college, the process of becoming a teacher, and the trajectory of teachers' lives as professionals. Robert Dreeben (2005) examines the professional status of teaching and concludes that teacher competency—the use of research-based as well as practical knowledge—may represent the missing link for professionalizing teaching. Regrettably, the teaching profession and the actual work engaged in by teachers receive little attention.

Critical pedagogy and postmodernism play important roles in the discipline of sociology, and this is no less true throughout the last third of the twentieth century; their impact on education is evident. Critical pedagogy encourages resistance to the external definition of individual roles and life experiences and promotes the role of education in a democratic culture to free students from dominant ideologies. Postmodernism rejects the notion of an underlying reality and hence defines the resistance attempts of critical pedagogy as meaningless. Postmodernists view education as potentially contributing to more democratic theory and practice, although little impact of this perspective on educational policy is evident.

Inequality is perhaps the most substantive issue in the sociology of education. Educational systems function to reproduce social systems that are grounded in inequalities, but these same institutions are also widely thought to help reduce inequalities. Gender and race play prominent roles in these processes. Pamela B. Walters (2000) notes that educational expansion in the United States has occurred in response to demands for equity, but in reality it is largely a strategy to enhance attainment for disadvantaged groups while simultaneously maintaining the advantages held by higher-class people. She also found that school reform does not reduce educational inequalities. A related issue is the role education plays in maintaining, enhancing, or reducing cultural pluralism. Research centers on the educational experiences of minorities and the manner in which that experience is defined by the dominant cultural ideologies. On the more micro level, Hallinan (2000b) concludes that researchers need to address differential learning opportunities because they perpetuate inequalities. She notes that "researchers have focused on ways in which the organization of students for instruction, the content of the curriculum, student access to the curriculum, and informal social processes within a school limit access to learning" (Hallinan 2000c:7).

The effects of schooling are often examined from a sociological perspective. For example, private schools affect social capital more than is the case for public schools. Caroline H. Persell (2000) asserts that differential values and control mechanisms in public and private schools tend to offer different student experiences. She posits that it is the influence of higher-class parents that carries the most impact in private schools. In this body of literature, sociologists pay particular attention to the experiences of students who are traditionally less rewarded by educational systems. For example, Hallinan (2000b) links the literature on sociology of race and ethnicity with that on sociology of education to conclude that schools affect students differentially by race and ethnicity. Other sociologists depict how the status attainment process differs among minorities and whites and also how it differs within a specific minority group. Much of this work has led sociologists to employ the race and ethnicity variable as a causal variable, although Hallinan (2000b) concludes that race and ethnicity have a minimal impact on what sociologists think about the schooling process.

At the micro level, sociologists examine how students and teachers cope with schooling. Alienation occurs for both. For example, Wagenaar (1987) outlines the individual and structural causes of dropping out of school and posits policy changes to address the structural dimensions. Sociologists also contribute to our understanding of teachers and teaching. They have discussed why the field is so feminized in the United States, particularly at the lower levels, and why students select teaching as a career. They have considered the implications of the 50 percent dropout rate among young teachers within their first five years of teaching. The socialization process of teachers is also examined. For example, an effective mentoring system can substantially reduce the dropout rate among teachers by reducing the isolation of new professionals and creating a more collective responsibility for teaching and learning.

Professional collaboration is one hallmark of a profession, raising questions once again about the professional stature of teaching. Bidwell (2005) argues that sociologists should focus more on the academic and social lives of students as well as on how teachers function in the classroom, and relate these to both the organization and the curriculum structure of schools. But he also makes a more general proposal by observing that schools and classrooms represent social systems, and he highlights how reforms imposed by sources outside the school system are tempered by the power structure and the day-to-day activities of teachers and students.

At the organizational level, sociologists have examined the causes and consequences of specific structural arrangements, including for consideration factors such as leadership style, teacher interaction style, and teacher efficacy (Gamoran, Secada, and Marrett 2000). They clarify how organizational resources such as material, human, and social resources affect teaching practices, which in turn affect learning. They conclude that professional development is central to effecting change and that professional development needs to be "sustained, coherent, collaborative, and reflective" (Gamoran et al. 2000:52). Following sociological research that showed that smaller high schools help generate higher achievement, the Gates Foundation supported the reorganization of large high schools into smaller units in many cities throughout the United States. The degree to which school personnel work well together and hold high expectations for students also affects achievement. In this same area, Hedges and Schneider (2005) note how the organizational structure of schools and the microsociology of schools and classrooms affect the student learning process.

Schools are known to operate as loosely coupled organizations, in which the connections between the hierarchical structure and the actual teaching activities that occur are weak and rely on the professional knowledge of practitioners (Weick 1976). As a result, schools historically have not tightly controlled the curriculum and teaching methods due to the professional stature of teachers. This loose coupling has implications for staff compliance with the bureaucratic rules as well as staff accountability. It also raises questions about the disparity between teacher professionalism and autonomy and a bureaucratic emphasis on organizational performance. Ingersoll (2005), among others, tempers this view, however, by noting that classrooms are not as free from administrative and political influence as the model would suggest. This, then, may represent the crux of the problem: the tension between the control ideology of bureaucratic structures and the autonomous professional ideology of the "true" professions.

In the classroom, sociologists have examined how the sociometric choices of students affect both their academic and their social standing (McFarland 2005). Although social network theory remains relatively underused, the types of subunit social structures teachers employ in the classroom are known to affect the educational experience. Elizabeth Cohen and Rachel Lotan (1997) employed expectation state theory to develop specific strategies that teachers can use with students, but without placing them in tracks, to provide an equitable way for teachers to teach when the classrooms has students of unequal status or experience. In this area, sociologists have long provided insight into how the gender and race of both teachers and students affects both the learning experience and social relations. Yet the specific mechanisms at work when schools as structures and teachers and students as individuals intersect remain to be articulated clearly.

Sociologists have also examined the long-term outcomes of schooling. Private school attendance has different student outcomes than does public school attendance. Participating in high school extracurricular activities is linked to civic engagement as adults. Girls who attend single-sex schools generally have higher subsequent levels of achievement. Schooling facilitates the transition to work, but this effect differs by society. Alan Kerckhoff (2001) notes that three factors affect the transition from school to work in different societies: (1) how much inequality exists in the educational system, (2) how much standardization exists in the educational system, and (3) the nature of educational credentials in a system. Globalization no doubt has affected the impact of education on the transition to work. Vocational education may help students secure work and does not necessarily inhibit attendance at college, particularly in more contest-based societies such as the United States. The impact of education on employment is greater in Germany and Japan than in the United States. One possible reason could be the tighter connections between school personnel and employers in countries such as Japan and Germany (Rosenbaum and Jones 2000). Comparative analyses of school effects are rare, but they can help refine the intervening mechanisms at work and how they vary by culture.

Education influences altruistic behaviors, such as volunteering. People with more education are more connected socially. They tend to marry and have children later. Their schooling experiences greatly influence the available pool of marriage candidates. Those with more education tend to have better physical and emotional health. Sociologists examine the impact of attending higher education and how these effects differ according to the type of school attended. They study how the effects of attaining higher education vary by society and why. We have encountered some good international comparisons but have yet to fully understand the differential causal processes at work in different societies. One can learn much about promoting higher-education attendance from research in other societies. There are status advantages gained by attending elite colleges, and these benefits vary by race and social class.

Other sociologists have examined the connections between the home, the school, and the community, and they have articulated the role of each in accruing social capital (e.g., Epstein and Sanders 2000). Different patterns of home-school cooperation have different outcomes. Participation by family members has a strong effect on students' performance, particularly when the school involves family members in its planning efforts. Epstein and Sanders (2000) found that teachers recognize how important parental involvement is, but teachers are lacking in a confidence as to how to effectively encourage parents to become involved.

Sociologists have examined the impact of school and residence neighborhoods on school functioning. Others have examined outlier schools that were predicted to have lower achievement but defied that prediction. Charter schools represent the current nexus of community involvement in education. They are alternative schools with a particular mission, such as strengthening achievement among low-performing minority students. Publicly funded charter schools are largely free from the regulations governing public schools. The dramatic rise in charter schools reflects community involvement through the creation of new schools that are not inhibited by traditional credentialing methods. Although little research has been conducted on charter schools, it is known that in Ohio, at least, many charter schools perform poorly on state assessment indicators. The charter school movement also intersects with the political climate—many parents disaffected with public schools have used the political system to create alternatives that more accurately teach their beliefs.

One of the most recent issues in the educational arena holding political and scientific connotations is "intelligent design" versus evolution. The religious and ideological issues involved gain the limelight, prompting both proponents and opponents to become involved politically by joining school boards. This and other conflicts highlight the intense political foundation of American education.

THE FUTURE

Societies continue to imbue their educational systems with extraordinary expectations for solving social problems. This rich legacy bodes well for the future of the sociology of education. Sociologists will continue to study and contribute to this popular area. Given that the field continues to progress both theoretically and methodologically, in the future, social interest groups also will become more vocal about what they desire from the educational system. Such events will undoubtedly make it difficult to compose a compelling unified rationale for educational policy, and public interest groups may also deflect the perceived need for and impact of pure research. Still, sociologists may and perhaps should have much to say about future policy and practice implementation processes.

Recent years have seen more national-level education policies. For example, in the United Kingdom, national efforts to assess and categorize institutions of higher education were used for funding decisions, with substantial political fallout. In the United States, the No Child Left Behind Act of 2002 exerted a substantial federal force in a nation that prides itself on local autonomy, especially in educational decision making. The act requires states to develop measures of academic progress in reading and mathematics, institutes minimum teacher credentials, and requires narrowing of the performance gap between students of various ethnic and ability groups. Specific strategies are required to assist students in low-performing schools. For example, after several years of school underperformance, school systems must provide tutoring outside the school and allow students to transfer to better schools. Accountability testing in science will soon be added to help reverse a rank of 16th of 21 countries in science and 19th in mathematics for the United States. Yet the United States leads most other countries in scientific accomplishments, so sociologists could help explain the disparity.

Sociologists have shown considerable interest in the No Child Left Behind Act. A special add-on series of presentations, sponsored by the Sociology of Education section of the ASA, has become a fixture at the annual meetings of the ASA. In the future, sociologists will examine how the act came into existence, how it is related to political ideologies, how the evaluation measurement of the act will affect school curricula and operations, how individual states respond and what factors determine these responses, how the teaching profession may be negatively affected by the further eroding of teachers' involvement in the decision-making process, the manifest and latent functions of the current test-taking mentality, and the consequences of such a national program among states and local districts accustomed to local autonomy. The act and other political developments once again highlight the intersections between education and the family and economic, political, and religious institutions.

Accountability and its effects represent a related theme. Accountability demands intersect closely with how schools affect students and bring issues of social control to the forefront. Sociologists will investigate who does the defining of success and the criteria by which such success is measured. Business definitions of success have factored into educational governance since the early twentieth century, and some argue that such definitions now permeate education. Accountability discussions often confuse school inputs, throughputs, and outputs—that is, what types of students and resources are admitted into school, what processes occur while at school, and what students gain after completing their schooling. We know little about the validity and reliability of recent accountability programs. Sociologists have made some progress in assessing the value added by schools, but more insight into how school characteristics connect with high scores on assessment tests is needed.

Moreover, little is known as to whether accountability demands have a linear connection with changes in student achievement. Accountability demands will undoubtedly continue to rise. These demands are intended to establish a firm base for bringing every student up to some minimal set of standards, document achievement, and compensate for such shortcomings as students may experience at home. The corporate school model also gives rise to accountability demands, including the expectation that neither financial nor educational losses should occur as schools respond to accountability demands.

In the United States, a shift to the religious right and issues relating to the demand for accountability have led to a sharp rise in the number of charter schools. In the future, sociologists will document how the daily lives of teachers and students change in response to these demands. Sociologists have yet to tease out the functional and dysfunctional and the manifest and latent consequences of the accountability movement. But anecdotal evidence suggests that teachers are teaching for, and students are studying for, the mandated tests. Areas not tested, such as art and social studies, have withered. This test-centric focus may alter teacher creativity and may have substantial effects on the decision to either enter or leave the profession.

Australia, Western European countries, the United Kingdom, and the United States have each experienced a substantial inflow of immigrants in recent decades. In the United States, about one in five persons under the age of 18 is either an immigrant or a child of immigrants. This demographic movement has an effect on educational systems in ways that "question the relevance and efficacy of longstanding administrative, curriculum, instruction, and evaluation practices" (Luke 1997:50). Sociologists help to dissect the impact of immigration and to test alternative structural arrangements for meeting the needs of immigrant populations. Carol L. Schmid (2001) notes that external and intrinsic factors affect the uneven absorption and educational achievement of immigrants. External factors include economic opportunities, racial and ethnic status, and group reception. Intrinsic factors, on the other hand, include human and social capital, family structure, community organization, and cultural and linguistic patterns. Politically, arguments have arisen over whether local schools should be fiscally and otherwise accountable for the performance of recent immigrants. In Australian higher education, substantial increases in the numbers of foreign students have led to charges of inferior education being offered at some schools. In the United States, sociologists have much to say about the merits of bilingual education. They will continue to examine demographic issues at a macro level, advise policymakers on national policy, determine how shifts in student characteristics affect student outcomes, and examine the consequences for the dominant cultures. Sociologists will assist in clarifying the role of education in promoting democracy and citizenship, thereby leading to yet another debate on the role of education in promoting values.

Gender, race and ethnicity, and social class will continue to play a dominant role in sociological research because these remain important social variables. Recent research shows, for example, that in the United States, male students at all levels of education are falling behind females on many educational indicators (Tyre 2006). In this area, sociologists will examine the roles of culture, institutions, the media, parents, schools, and teachers in this shift. Bidwell (2005) argues that researchers understand little on how national and global change affects the classroom experience. This too represents an important area for future research. More research similar to that conducted by Riegle-Crumb (2005) is needed to confirm the findings that mathematics and science performance among girls and boys in various countries is affected by their opportunities to participate in the home, the labor force, and the government. Of special interest is the finding that the gender gap performance is lower in countries where women hold high governmental positions. Also well known is the fact that race and ethnic differences persist in many countries in spite of efforts to reduce them. Although many sociologists have noted that class, race, and gender need to be analyzed conjointly, the frequency of such research is still low. In the future, sociologists will continue to shed light on the macro and micro social forces that may mitigate these inequalities.

Although their presence is currently meager at best (Suter 2001), sociologists will become involved in the analysis of alternative pedagogical strategies. Sociologists are uniquely qualified to identify the social and cultural dimensions of learning and how these pedagogical strategies promote learning. At both the secondary and the higher-education levels, the numbers of students participating in distance education are rising rapidly. Distance learning may alter the social structure of classrooms and may affect student performance. Student-centered pedagogies alter the authority and position of teachers. Schools have long been used as an example of cultural lag, where one part of a society moves more slowly than the other parts. That lag may decline with the rise of technology. Sociologists will examine how technology and the ready access of information help redefine learning and the role of teachers. We currently know very little about the sustained short-term and long-term learning consequences of greater exposure to technology, and we have been unsuccessful in bridging the digital divide (Natriello 2001). Riehl (2001) argues that sociologists studying pedagogical strategies need to link with work in cognitive psychology and other disciplines that view learning as situated and sociocultural.

Homeschooling is on the rise, but few sociologists have examined the nature and kinds of parents who homeschool their children and with what effects (Wagenaar 1997). Preliminary research shows that homeschooled children perform well in college, but a selection factor may be operating. Some school districts allow homeschooled children to participate in extracurricular activities and even some academic activities. These differences in the homeschool experience should provide an ideal laboratory for assessing the effects of formal schooling.

In the United States, high schools and colleges place increasing emphasis on community engagement and service learning as pedagogical strategies. The literature demonstrating the effects of such engagement is somewhat scanty, but in the future, sociologists will isolate more clearly the consequences of such engagement. The rise in school-community partnerships will also provide ample opportunity for further research activity. In yet another area, sociologists will focus some attention on classroom-teaching behaviors to enhance our understanding at the micro level.

During the past 30 years, we have been witness to a greater involvement in policy planning and reform efforts as suggested and encouraged by sociologists. The increase in qualitative research in the sociology of education enhances the sociological influence on educational policy and practice. The involvement should continue as sociologists become more interested in applied issues and as decision makers on education become more aware of the benefits to be derived from sociology in their decision-making procedures. The political consequences of this involvement can also be expected to increase, particularly at the local levels. There is anecdotal evidence that in the United States, individuals with strong political and educational ideologies are increasingly running for office and winning school board seats. At the national level, Shain and Ozga (2001) lament the impact of strong national policy statements in England stating that sociological research in education must be both relevant and useful for policymakers, adding that those who wish to study the broader social complexities of education outside application may not provide a useful service at this time.

Sociologists will continue to make major contributions to our understanding of the many social forces at work in the educational institution. They will do so at the micro level, the macro level, and the levels in between. Societies can ill afford to overlook sociologists' contributions to identifying relevant causal factors, using research to tease out the connections among such factors, and providing policy advice relevant to solving educational problems.

32

ECONOMIC SOCIOLOGY

FRANK DOBBIN

Harvard University

Karl Marx, Max Weber, and Émile Durkheim sought to understand modernity by comparing precapitalist societies with capitalism. Marx explored the transition from feudalism to capitalism; Weber the capitalist impulse that arose with Protestantism; and Durkheim the rise of capitalism's division of labor. As capitalism was in its infancy, none were certain that modern industrial capitalism would take widely different forms, although Weber described a number of different forms—booty, political, imperialist, colonial, adventure, and fiscal capitalism (Weber 1978:164–67; see also Swedberg 1998:47). I review the growing field of economic sociology and, within it, studies that follow on the work of Marx, Weber, and Durkheim to explain the substantial variation found in economic behavior even in modern settings. While the classic studies of economic sociology sought to understand how emerging capitalism would be different from the system of feudalism, economic sociologists increasingly came to see that modern capitalism could take many different forms and sought to explain those forms by looking at different social processes. Economic sociologists have been looking at how power relations, institutions and social conventions, and social networks and roles interact at the societal level to create different sorts of economic systems; how these forces shape change within economic systems; and how they shape individual behavior.

Economic sociology has undergone a revival since the early 1980s. Sociologists have always studied aspects of economic behavior, but in the middle decades of the twentieth century, the social sciences adhered to the Parsonsian division of the world into, roughly, economy, society, polity, and culture. Each area was the province of one discipline. Sociologists generally stuck to society and left economic behavior and institutions to economists. This divide began to crumble from both sides by the early 1980s; sociologists were again explaining economic behavior, and economists began to explain social behavior generally and not merely economic behavior.

Sociologists returned to the study of economic behavior because they were dissatisfied with the models economists were developing, finding that because they neglected social factors economists were unable to predict people's economic decisions. And sociologists found economists' models of limited use in that they did not predict the broad differences in economic behavior across nations. Sociologists saw economic behavior as just one more example of social behavior, shaped by the same forces as other sorts of social behavior, particularly power struggles, conventions, and social milieu. Economic behavior, they reasoned, isn't shaped by rational choice narrowly construed because what people view as rational is shaped by societal conventions, power, and networks. Because what it means to be rational depends on what society you are standing in, people are not able to simply behave rationally even when they seek to do so.

In this chapter, I review the theoretical foundations and recent insights of three broad schools in economic sociology that have flourished since the early 1980s: power, institutional, and network approaches. Then I turn to a survey of studies that illustrate the utility of these approaches.

HOW POWER, INSTITUTIONS, AND NETWORKS SHAPE ECONOMIC BEHAVIOR

Most economic sociologists proceed inductively, looking at how economic behavior varies over time or across countries and tracing that variation to something about social context. This is quite different from the approach of most neoclassical economists, who proceed deductively from the premise that individual self-interest explains economic behavior. Studies of investment among early Protestants, management of new enterprises in China's market-oriented sector, and business strategy among Argentine wine producers have produced myriad insights about the forces that shape economic behavior. But sociologists have usually found that one of three different social processes is at the heart of the matter, and these processes have been spelled out in power, institutional, and network theories.

Power

Power relations shape economic behavior, both directly, as when a powerful firm dictates to a weak supplier, and indirectly, as when a powerful industry group shapes regulation to its own advantage. The structural theory of power is the direct inheritor of Marx's ideas, even if not all of its practitioners would call themselves Marxists. They include Neil Fligstein (1990), Bill Roy (1997), Beth Mintz and Michael Schwartz (1985), Mark Mizruchi (1992), Michael Useem (1996), and Charles Perrow (1992, 2002). Their concern is most often with how powerful groups succeed in promoting management practices and public policies that are *in their interest* as being *in the common interest.* Marx described the capitalist state as a tool of the capitalist class, which justified its existence under the guise of political liberalism. His idea was that modern states serve one group while claiming to embody principles that benefit everyone. Structural theorists of power explore how power plays a role in determining the state policies, corporate strategies, and individual behaviors that we take to be transparently rational. When a particular group succeeds in promoting its favorite public policy or business strategy—in making that approach the new convention—that group can reinforce its own power or wealth without having to exercise constant coercion.

Institutions

Social institutions shape economic action by constraining options (regulatory institutions) and by establishing behavioral scripts (conventions). Weber (1978) argued that social conventions must be understood in terms of their subjective meaning to individuals because we behave in ways that are meaningful to us—that we understand (see Swedberg 1998). Sociological institutionalists understand economic behavior to be regular and predictable not because it follows universal economic laws but because it follows meaningful institutionalized scripts (Meyer and Rowan 1977; DiMaggio and Powell 1983; Powell and DiMaggio 1991; Scott 1995). The meaning underlying modern behavior patterns is highly rationalized but, institutionalists argue, that doesn't make it any less meaningful than, say, behavior acknowledged to be spiritual in orientation. Meaning is not the antithesis of rationality. Economic customs carry meaning, and economic customs (and their meanings) often spread as rational fads. In the 1980s, management consultants offered downsizing (workforce reduction) as a solution to the problem of stagnant profits, and suddenly firms were doing it whether they needed to or not (Budros 1997). Downsizings are conventions, but since the time of Weber, institutionalists have also pointed to the ways in which wider social institutions—religious, educational, labor market—influence economic activity by regulating it and by defining social means and goals. For institutionalists, regulatory institutions are just another form of social convention, and they are held in place like management conventions by belief in their efficacy. They spread across provinces and nation-states because their proponents frame them as efficient.

Social Networks

It is a sort of modern truism that peer groups and role models provide concrete illustrations of how one should act in a given situation and enforce sanctions for misbehavior. Network theory builds on Simmel's and Durkheim's ideas about how the individual's position in a social milieu shapes both his behavior and his underlying identity. For Durkheim, social networks shape the actions of individuals not only negatively, by undermining antisocial behavior, but also positively, by establishing accepted behavior patterns. Mark Granovetter (1985) spells out the implications of the network approach in an article challenging transaction-cost economists' understanding of price gouging, in which gouging occurs when a supplier finds that he is the sole seller of a needed good. Granovetter argues that the norm against price gouging is enforced informally by members of an industry network; a seller who price gouges in times of scarcity will find that buyers turn elsewhere in times of plenty. Interpersonal networks thus enforce norms by sanctioning members who do not follow them. Development theorists find that societies with strong social networks have an advantage in development, in part because they can effectively carry out both positive and negative sanctioning.

As will be evident in the survey that follows, sociologists studying power, institutions, and networks are increasingly bringing their insights together to explain economic behavior. Economic sociology is thus moving from being a multiparadigmatic subfield to being a subfield with one broad way of understanding economic behavior encompassing three paradigmatic viewpoints. Economic practices—behavior patterns such as pricing strategies and firm structures—emerge in networks of actors, via the institutionalization of scripts for how to behave in order to achieve particular ends. Powerful actors try to shape the scripts that are constructed and the rules of the game that become institutionalized in public policy. Many recent studies in the field synthesize ideas about institutions, power, and networks as we will see below.

POWER: ON THE SHOULDERS OF MARX

While Marx's prophesy that communism would triumph over capitalism died with the breakup of the Soviet Union, his method and core insights are very much alive in economic sociology. His main insight was that it is not merely abstract ideas that drive economic history but production processes and social relations. Like neoclassical economists, Marx argued that self-interest shapes economic behavior. But for Marx, self-interest leads people to try to shape the world to their advantage rather than to merely achieve the best price in every transaction. Economic sociologists focusing on labor-management relations, such as Burawoy (1979) and Biernacki (1995), often build on Marx's (1894) final work and magnum opus *Das Kapital.* But Marx's early writings on the transition from feudalism to capitalism have been more widely influential, including *The German Ideology* (1974), *The Eighteenth Brumaire of Louis Napoleon Bonaparte* ([1852] 1963), *The Communist Manifesto* (Marx and Engels [1872] 1972), and the wide-ranging notes for *Das Kapital, The Grundrisse* (1971).

In *The German Ideology,* Marx (1974) explores how changes in the system of production alter the relative power of the aristocracy and bourgeoisie. Under feudalism, a nascent class of craftspeople and manufacturers grew by actively selling their wares and building their production capacity. They challenged the traditional political rights and privileges of feudal lords, encouraging policies that favored industry, such as free labor and free elections. As they gained resources, they gained the capacity to shape the political and economic realm to their own advantage. Marx argued that the modern state imposed capitalist rules of economic behavior on a society in which the vast majority were not capitalists, under the rhetoric of political liberalism rather than under that of capitalist domination. Recent power theorists have taken from this the idea that modern states impose a particular set of rules, regulations, and institutions shaping economic life. Modern power theorists point to the role of conflict and power in creating these ground rules and in forming conventional business practices.

Power and Change in the Corporate Form in America

The major changes in corporate form and strategy were pushed by successive groups (textile mill owners, Wall Street financiers, finance-trained executives, and institutional investors, respectively) that won power struggles with other groups. Each group institutionalized a new model of how to run a business that would soon become taken for granted. What is striking about the studies charting these changes is that they show that new business strategies spread under the rhetoric of efficiency but that each new model was merely one of several options that would likely have been about equally efficient. New policies clearly promoted the interests of their backers, but they did not so clearly improve on the status quo or best alternatives in the competition.

Charles Perrow (2002) traces the early rise of huge textile mills and gigantic railroads in America not to their greater efficiency (as compared with smaller enterprises) but to the fact that the Constitution gave state officials little power to regulate industry. The American state, designed as the antithesis of tyrannical European states, had meager administrative capacities and was deliberately opened to influence by the very groups it might have sought to control. This invited the powerful to reshape property rights—the laws that govern trade and corporate form—to their own taste. The American business elite changed property rights to the advantage of big corporations early in the nineteenth century. These legal advantages encouraged firms to use capital-intensive rather than labor-intensive methods, to build huge firms—even when labor-intensive methods would have been equally profitable.

If early capitalists shaped business strategy by shaping public policy, financiers pushed industry toward oligopoly in many industries at the dawn of the twentieth century. William Roy (1997), in *Socializing Capital: The Rise of the Large Industrial Corporation in America,* argues that the initial enforcement of antitrust in 1897 had an unanticipated effect on the balance of power between small and large firms. While antitrust was designed to prevent the concentration of economic power, by preventing collusion among firms, it gave big firms an advantage over small ones. Under antitrust, a group of small firms could not set prices together, but if they merged, the resulting large firm could set a single price. Roy argues that the advantage big firms had over small firms was not one of scale economies (Chandler 1977), for the merger wave at the dawn of the twentieth century swept across industries that could not benefit from scale economies as well as those that could. Instead, under antitrust, large firms demanded that smaller competitors sell out or face certain death in price wars. The ensuing mergers had less to do with manufacturing efficiency than with the fact that antitrust law put an end to the refuge of small firms, the cartel. Timothy Dowd and Frank Dobbin found that antitrust similarly stimulated a merger wave in railroading (Dobbin and Dowd 2000). When the Supreme Court enforced antitrust law in 1897, financiers, who typically held stock in many different railroads, decried price wars that would destroy the value of the small firms whose stock they held and heralded amicable mergers that would sustain the value of all the railroads they held. J. P. Morgan led financiers in threatening to withhold future financing from firms that engaged in price wars.

The next huge shift in corporate strategy was diversification. What drove diversification? Neil Fligstein's (1990) *The Transformation of Corporate Control* traces competition between three different management factions for the leadership of American corporations: production, marketing, and finance managers. Fligstein shows instead that a power play by finance managers was at the heart of the matter. After the Celer-Kefauver amendments to antitrust in 1950, which made it more difficult for firms to expand into related businesses, finance experts sketched a new theory of the firm in which large firms should act like investors with diversified portfolios. Finance managers succeeded largely by force of argument—by convincing boards and investors that the diversified conglomerate was the way of the future and that they, finance managers, were uniquely qualified to pursue this model of growth. This group came to hold most CEO positions.

In the 1980s, the diversified conglomerate next gave way to the core-competence/shareholder value firm, and this of course challenged the efficiency arguments underlying portfolio theory. By 1990, big firms were buying others in the same industry to take advantage of their own core competence—of their core managerial abilities. As Davis, Diekmann, and Tinsley (1994) and Fligstein and Markowitz (1993) have argued, this new model arose because institutional investors and securities analysts found the diversified conglomerate difficult to place a value on and assigned higher values to single-industry firms. Firms had begun compensating executives based on stock performance, and this gave executives an incentive to cater to investors and analysts. The result was that the typical firm became less diversified. In this change, the power of key groups outside of the firm brought about a reversal in corporate strategy.

Marx (1974), Perrow (2002), Roy (1997), Fligstein and Markowitz (1993), and Davis et al. (1994) show that power shapes economic behavior by shaping prescriptions for how firms should behave. Powerful industries often shape their own regulations (Useem 1984), and it is often power struggles among management factions that determine what is defined as rational firm behavior. With each change, a powerful group managed to propose a new business strategy that gave it particular advantages in the economy with the argument that the new strategy would be good for the economy as a whole—that it would be efficient.

INSTITUTIONS: ON THE SHOULDERS OF WEBER

Weber's work inspired many studies of how social institutions, customs, and conventions determine economic behavior. In *The Protestant Ethic* (2002), in his various studies of the world religions ([1916] 1951, [1917] 1952, [1916] 1958, 1963), and in his opus on capitalism, *Economy and Society*

(1978), Weber tried to understand the actual customs of different societies, the thinking behind those customs, and the forces that lead to changes in customs. For Weber, it is the beliefs underlying customs that sustain them. Thus, he argued for the importance of understanding the meaning of an action to the actor. Rationality is not in the eye of the beholder, but in the mind of the actor. Weber argued for a broad view of the causes of economic behavior, arguing that economic behavior is influenced by social institutions in different realms—law and the state, the religious system, and the class system (Swedberg 1998).

National Economic Institutions

Weber traces modern ("rational") capitalist customs to the rise of a particular brand of early Protestantism. Weber saw in Protestantism a religious ideology that was compatible with capitalism and wondered why Protestantism, alone among the world religions, developed such an ideology. Early Calvinism taught predestination, or the idea that one's destiny in the afterlife was fixed at birth. While one could not earn a place in heaven, God gave everyone an earthly calling, and for the anxious, working hard and achieving success in business might at least signal divine approval. Calvin's God also demanded self-denial and asceticism. The idea of God's calling led Protestants to devote themselves to their work, and the idea of asceticism led them to save. Some argue that Catholicism promoted the same kinds of behavior (e.g., Novak 1993), and others argue that Protestantism's main effect was to promote bureaucratization of the state (Gorski 1993), but what is novel about Weber is not so much this particular argument as his vision of how economy and society were intertwined.

A decade after writing *The Protestant Ethic,* Weber began work on three thick volumes on the world religions and economies, *The Religion of China* ([1916] 1951), *The Religion of India* ([1916] 1958), and *Ancient Judaism* ([1917] 1952). In comparing the world's religions, Weber found that all were oriented to salvation but that they espoused very different ideas about how to achieve salvation (Swedberg 1998:138). In Protestantism, salvation was signaled (if not earned) through piety, asceticism, and devotion to one's calling. In Chinese Confucianism and Indian Hinduism alike, salvation was achieved by accepting one's given station and withdrawing from the world in prayer. These religious ethics fostered traditionalism and complacency rather than activism and entrepreneurialism. Ancient Judaism discouraged rational capitalism by favoring the life of religious scholarship over that of entrepreneurialism. What Weber demonstrated in these comparative studies, and what he argued in *Economy and Society,* was that economic customs were related to wider social institutions—the law and the state, religion, class—and that to understand economic conventions one must understand their links to these other institutions.

Richard Whitley's National Business Systems approach does for the varieties of contemporary capitalism what

Max Weber did for the world religions, sketching the logic underlying each form of capitalism to grasp the meaning of conventions for actors and linking economic conventions to the wider institutional milieu. Whitley (1992a, 1992b) finds that different national ideas about efficiency, as institutionalized in national business systems, correspond with different prescriptions for economic behavior. National economic and political institutions offer particular understandings of the relationships between state and industry, buyer and supplier, finance and industry. Institutions arise for reasons of history and happenstance, but over time ancillary customs and conventions emerge that hold them in place. Whitley (1992a) first set his sights on East Asian business systems. In Japan, the large corporation, or *kaisha,* dominates; the bank-dominated business group, the descendent of the prewar *zaibatsu,* brings together large diverse firms; and the state actively promotes exports and plans industry expansion. In Korea, the family-controlled conglomerate, or *chaebol,* dominates; symbiotic relationships among conglomerate members characterize interfirm relations; and the state actively promotes the rise and expansion of huge and stable empires. In Taiwan and Hong Kong, smaller Chinese family businesses dominate; interfirm relations are relatively unstructured, with a few medium-sized family business groups (*jituanqiye*); and the state leaves firms largely to their own devices. These different systems influence all kinds of economic behavior. For instance, they influence market entry in new export sectors, with new firms sponsored by business groups in Japan; new firms sponsored by families that own small businesses in Taiwan and Hong Kong; and new firms subsidized by the central state under the auspices of existing *chaebol* in Korea. What is rational under one system—starting up a company with family backing—would be folly in another. Whitley argues that the Asian Miracle is built on at least three different systems (see Johnson 1982; Cumings 1987; Westney 1987) and in subsequent studies has found just as much diversity in European business systems (Whitley 1992b; Whitley and Kristensen 1996).

Weber shows that across different societies, early religious institutions shaped economic practices. In *Forging Industrial Policy: The United States, Britain, and France in the Railway Age,* I show that across different societies, early political institutions shaped government industrial strategies and industry itself (Dobbin 1994). Modern industrial strategies were based on the logic of state–private sector relations. In the United States, the polity was organized around self-governing communities with a federal state in the role of umpire. Americans applied the same principles to railroading, and so the federal government became referee in a free market of self-governing enterprises. In France, the polity was organized through a strong central state designed to dominate intermediate groups that could threaten its sovereignty—theirs was a form of democracy antithetical to the American form. The French applied the principle of central coordination to railroading,

with the state becoming the ultimate planner and ruler of the system of private railroads. Britain's polity produced yet a third form of democracy, based on the idea of affording maximum autonomy to the citizen. When the British considered the railroads, they could not imagine that the state would regulate markets as the American state did or plan routes as the French state did. The British state left railroaders to their own devices, and to protect them from other railroads, they created cartels that would quell cut-throat competition. In each country, the structure of the polity shaped emergent regulatory institutions that would persist for a century or more. The economy thus came to reflect the polity, with the federal state as market umpire in the United States, the central government as the guardian and planner of key industries in France, and a state committed to maximizing individual initiative in Britain.

Agency and Economic Institutions

Many neo-Weberian institutional analyses neglect interest and agency in the formation of institutions, and that is certainly true of the studies reviewed above (Swedberg 2001). Others emphasize that the agency of individuals shapes, or is shaped by, economic institutions. Carruthers (1996) shows how early British stockholders used trading to further their political aims.

Gary Hamilton and Nicole Biggart argue that in the years after World War II, political leaders in Japan, South Korea, and Taiwan chose industrial strategies that built on traditional authority systems—but they emphasize that these leaders did *choose,* and could have chosen, other alternatives (Hamilton and Biggart 1988; Orrù, Biggart, and Hamilton 1991). Postwar politicians pursued strategies of legitimation that built on certain aspects of traditional authority structures. Postwar state-industry relations arose by design, but history provided the alternatives from which designers chose. Japan has powerful intermarket industry groups under a state that helps them plan and coordinate. After the American occupying regime dissolved the prewar *zaibatsu,* politicians built directly on the Tokugawa and Meiji authority system, in which the *shogun* or emperor was "above politics" and provided a weak center surrounded by strong but loyal independent powers (Hamilton and Biggart 1988:S81). The postwar Taiwanese and South Korean states built on two different legitimating aspects of the Confucian political system. When Korea was embroiled in a civil war, the state directed industrial growth and presidential cronies became leaders of huge empires. The Rhee and Park regimes drew on the imagery of the strong, centralized Confucian state, with weak intermediate groups. The result was large family-dominated business groups beholden to the state. In Taiwan, Chaing Kai-shek modeled the state on the late imperial Confucian state's principle of fair treatment of the population. The postwar Taiwanese state allowed private parties to pursue their own projects. The resulting system mirrored late imperial China, with small family-run firms that had direct contacts with suppliers and buyers. In each case, politicians who were determined to build new economic institutions that would have some legitimacy in terms of tradition deliberately employed aspects of traditional authority structures that suited their own goals. Old political institutions shaped new economic institutions, but only through the agency of calculating politicians.

In another approach to unpacking agency, Mauro Guillén's (2001) *The Limits of Convergence* explores the very different firm and industry strategies found in the emerging economies of Argentina, South Korea, and Spain. Guillén finds politicians, entrepreneurs, and managers relishing and building on their industrial idiosyncrasies to distinguish themselves and to develop unique market niches. Across industries—wine making, banking, automobiles—broad public policy strategies have advantaged different sorts of industry structures and owners. South Korea's ardently nationalistic and centralized growth policies have favored huge integrated business groups over multinationals and smaller firms. Spain's pragmatic and flexible approach to regulation has resulted in a large presence of multinationals, a wide range of smaller domestic firms, and huge domestic firms in traditionally oligopolistic sectors. Argentina's populist policy orientation has discouraged foreign multinational penetration in some sectors but has promoted business groups that can provide stability and the economic basis for wider competition. Once established, a particular system becomes self-reinforcing as individuals develop economic strategies that build up its strengths.

Edgar Kiser and Joachim Schneider (1995) take a very different tack on agency that builds on rational choice theory. Weber argued that the early Prussian state was particularly efficient in collecting taxes because it was so bureaucratic. Kiser and Schneider show that the Prussian state was an efficient tax collector even before it became bureaucratic, and they use agency theory to show that it was efficient because it diverged from the bureaucratic ideal in ways that were particularly effective given the situation. Agency theory suggests that rulers seek to maximize tax revenues, their agents (tax collectors) seek to maximize their own take from taxes collected, and tax payers seek to minimize payments. Prussia developed a system that aligned interests to maximize the take of the ruler by, for instance, establishing long-term conditional contracts for tax farming that could minimize the cost of rent collection. Kiser and Schneider are part of a small group of economic sociologists who apply rational choice principles from agency theory.

Bruce Carruthers's (1996) analysis of early British stock trading exemplifies a related tradition in historical economic sociology, of showing that politics, and not narrow self-interest alone, drive economic behavior. Weber had argued that political institutions often shape economic behavior. Carruthers (1996) finds that stock trades were driven by politics as well as by price. *City of Capital: Politics and Markets in the English Financial Revolution* questions a central tenet of price theory in economics, namely, that sellers choose the buyer offering the highest price. There were strong political battle lines in place in the early 1700s, and large companies exercised significant influence over political decision making. Who controlled the East India Trading Company was of some importance, and major stockholders were aware of this. In consequence, Carruthers finds that stockholders with clear political leanings were significantly more likely to sell to members of their own political party even though this typically meant that they were constraining competition for the shares they had to sell. Politics shaped economic behavior even in the first instantiation of the modern stock market.

Change in National Economic Institutions

The institutional studies reviewed up to this point echo two of Weber's points: Economic institutions follow logics that are meaningful to the participants who enact them, and economic institutions are shaped by surrounding institutions, particularly political institutions.

In *Economic Ideology and Japanese Industrial Policy* (1997) and in *Japan's Economic Dilemma* (2001), Bai Gao asks how Japan's unique industrial strategy emerged and then evolved after 1930. Japan pursued strategic planning of the economy, the restraint of competition through the governance of markets, and the suppression of short-term profit orientation in favor of long-term orientation. The approach was influenced by economic thought from Europe: Marx's ideas about the downside of unbridled competition, Schumpeter's ideas about innovation, and Keynes's ideas about state management of economic cycles. Japanese policymakers and capitalists who favored economic stability and industry self-governance (as opposed to cut-throat competition) used these ideas to formulate Japan's unique industrial policy stance. In *Japan's Economic Dilemma*, Gao (2001) traces the consequences of this system in the 1990s. Industry self-governance had worked well when the economy was booming, but in an economic downturn firms were free to engage in cut-throat competition and to make ill-conceived investments to counter declining profits. If *Economic Ideology* supports the Weberian notion that ideas can shape economic institutions, *Japan's Economic Dilemma* supports the Weberian notion that institutions become resistant to change. Japan found it hard to change its industrial policy midstream, even when the old policy had clearly gone awry.

Whereas Gao highlights continuity in the Japanese industrial order, John Campbell, Rogers Hollingsworth, and Leon Lindberg's (1991) *Governance of the American Economy* shows the diversity of industry governance structures found in the United States and develops a Weberian approach to explaining change in governance. In studies of eight industries, contributors identify a series of different industry configurations—markets, mergers, monitoring systems, obligational networks, promotional networks, and associations. Historical change in industry governance begins with an external shock that leads different groups to vie to define a new structure. Power is key at critical moments of change. Campbell et al. challenge the prevailing view from transaction cost economics (Williamson 1985), which suggests that firms change governance forms when it is efficient to do so. Poor profitability may stimulate a search for new governance mechanisms, but many other kinds of shocks can stimulate change as well, and power rather than efficiency typically shapes the new equilibrium. The theory that Campbell and colleagues (1991) articulate is, then, in keeping with the theories of corporate strategy reviewed above in the section on power.

National Management Institutions

Reinhard Bendix's (1956) sweeping *Work and Authority in Industry: Ideologies of Management in the Course of Industrialization* traces the roots of management practice and ideology in four settings that differed on two dimensions: early versus mature industry and independent versus state-subordinated management. His two-by-two table included early English industry (independent management), early Tsarist Russian industry (state-subordinated management), mature American industry (independent management), and mature East German industry (state-subordinated management).

Successful management practices emerged where industry was autonomous, not where it was merely mature. It was in the two settings where management was autonomous, mature America and early Britain, rather than in the two where management was mature, America and East Germany, that managers developed ideologies that co-opted workers by suggesting to them that they too could benefit from social mobility, as current managers had. In Tsarist Russia and Communist East Germany, where managers were not autonomous, they did not succeed in countering the idea that managers' positions were undeserved and that management was a function of state oppression. In all four settings, the legacy of old ideas about class relations, and the reality of present class-state relations, shaped management patterns. For instance, in early England, the aristocracy's power vis-à-vis the state and their antipathy toward industry meant that the state left capitalist enterprises alone. In Tsarist Russia, by contrast, the state fostered early entrepreneurial activities and held early capitalists in its grasp, just as it held agricultural aristocrats in its grasp. In the wake of the collapse of Communism, an important punch line is that where the state subordinates entrepreneurs and industry to rule workers directly, the chances for the development of a successful managerial ideology are weak. Like Weber, Bendix was interested in the articulation between ideas and economic practices. He found that broadly similar economic practices could attain legitimacy in one setting, but not in another, largely on the basis of how well the attendant ideology of management meshed with the prevailing view of social relations.

Wolfgang Streeck's (1992) recent comparative studies of industrial relations systems build on Weber's insight that economic conventions are embedded in a broad set of societal institutions. *Social Institutions and Economic Performance* compares industrial relations systems across countries and links those systems to success in the global economy. For Streeck, history has produced different sorts of institutional configurations—labor markets, public employment policies, educational institutions—in each country, and these institutional configurations shape the industrial relations system. These industrial relations systems have different advantages. Nations with strong institutions (Germany and Japan) can make choices about how industry and training will be configured, and those choices can give them a comparative advantage over more marketized nations (Britain and the United States) where decisions are left to individuals. Germany's strong labor unions and rich educational system have allowed it to choose to make high value-added products that require skilled employees. Britain and the United States simply do not have the institutional capacity to make the same decision. The German and Japanese cases suggest that competitiveness in the modern economy depends on social institutions that permit countries to pursue collective goals through their industrial relations systems, educational systems, and corporations.

Geert Hofstede (1980) has taken the Weberian task of characterizing the work orientation of individuals to its logical conclusion, developing a scheme for understanding values in 40 different countries. His study is based on a survey of employees of a single multinational corporation with offices around the world. In describing authority relations and work values across countries, he identifies four dimensions: power distance (acceptable degree of supervisory control), uncertainty avoidance (degree to which people avoid the unknown to manage stress), individualism (importance of the individual vs. the group), and masculinity (relative importance of earning and achievement vs. cooperation and atmosphere). Hofstede correlates cultural types with societal institutions, arguing that the psyche is shaped by those institutions. One implication is that rational action takes very different forms across contexts, depending on whether close supervision is seen as improper, whether uncertainty elicits stress, whether individuals are valued over and above the group, and whether achievement is valued over cooperation. Hofstede thus fleshes out dimensions of the work ethic that Weber describes in *The Protestant Ethic*, and like Weber, he identifies societal institutions as the ultimate cause of differences.

Since the postwar Japanese Miracle caught the attention of economic sociologists, many have sought to bring Weber's comparisons of East and West up to date, to understand the characteristics of Japanese society and workplace that produced unparalleled growth rates after World War II. William Ouchi (1981) brought the case of Japanese management practices to a wide audience, showing that the same practices that worked well in Japan could have positive effects on American firms. But Ronald Dore's (1973) *British Factory–Japanese Factory* pioneered factory comparisons in the two hemispheres, showing dramatic differences between Britain's market-oriented management system and Japan's welfare corporatism. In Britain, Dore found high labor mobility between firms, wages set by the external market, weak employee loyalty, paltry fringe benefits, and poor integration of unions. In Japan, he found low external labor mobility but an elaborate internal labor market with extensive training, wages set under the internal career system, high employee loyalty, elaborate fringe benefits, and enterprise unions that play an integral role in the workplace. Dore rejected the idea that culture explains these differences, tracing them instead to the timing of industrialization and to the conditions under which industrialization occurred. Japan's industrial form was forged in the postwar period, with the most advanced management thinking available at the time—ideas about worker involvement and long-term incentives to orient employee goals to firm goals. Britain's factory conditions were forged in a much earlier era, before modern ideas about employee motivation were developed and before the idea that union-management collaboration could be effective was popular. Dore's (2000) recent work suggests that countries have converged little.

Weber suggested that the spirit of capitalism was fueled by Calvinism. One lesson of Dore's work is that work ethic is also shaped by concrete workplace conventions. James Lincoln and Arne Kalleberg's (1985) study of some 8,000 workers in the United States and Japan suggests that work practices are important. While corporatist practices are more common in Japan, they increase worker commitment in both countries. The Japanese wage system presumes the absence of an external labor market—wages are shaped by tenure in the firm's career system. In the United States, the wage system presumes competition across firms, and thus wages reflect job characteristics, position in the hierarchy, and union representation in the United States (Lincoln and Kalleberg 1990). The received wisdom about differences between Japan and the United States was that they were cultural—that both worker commitment and employer commitment (to the worker) were part of a broader cultural system. Lincoln and Kalleberg's (1985) findings show that work practices themselves shape commitment.

The Diffusion of Management Institutions

While Weber was most interested in how customs differ among societies, recent works in economic sociology have focused on the factors that facilitate diffusion across organizations or across societies (Meyer and Rowan 1977; Powell and DiMaggio 1991). Mauro Guillén's (1994) *Models of Management: Work, Authority, and Organization in a Comparative Perspective* charts the spread of three important management paradigms among

the United States, Britain, West Germany, and Spain. Guillén stands on Bendix's and Weber's shoulders, exploring the social structural and ideological factors that influence the spread of three management paradigms: scientific management, the human relations school, and structural analysis. Religion plays an interesting role. In Spain, the Catholic Church supported the human relations school for its humane treatment of workers. In Germany, Protestants supported the scientific management movements for its emphasis of individualism and self-reliance. New practices do not diffuse universally; rather, they diffuse where existing social institutions are compatible with them and where systems have the capacity to effect change. This finding supports Weber's notion that societal institutions reinforce one another when they share an "elective affinity."

Marie-Laure Djelic's (1998) *Exporting the American Model: The Postwar Transformation of European Business* explores why France and Germany succeeded in importing American-style capitalism after World War II and why Italy failed. What mattered most was the character of institutions, both international institutions and national political institutions. France and Germany adopted the corporate structure (rather than independent ownership), the multidivisional form (rather than the simple unitary form), and enforced price competition (rather than cartels). Support from international institutions, in the form of the Marshall Plan, from the local political system, and from the business community mattered. In the case of Italy, industry resistance to change, the emphasis of Marshall Plan administrators on infrastructure over industry, and the disarticulation of the recovery plan worked against the American model.

Weberian studies of economic institutions share a focus on the meanings of social conventions to actors and on the articulation of different social institutions. Economic conventions are only replicated to the extent that those who enact them understand them; so understanding is key to the persistence of conventions. Economic conventions are forged, and enacted, in social networks, and it is to networks I now turn.

NETWORKS AND ROLES: ON THE SHOULDERS OF DURKHEIM

Economic behavior is fundamentally role-oriented in the view of most economic sociologists. Émile Durkheim explored how social networks and social roles varied across different societies, and much of the new work in economic sociology builds on his insights. Durkheim tried to understand the emergence of industrial capitalism through the concrete social networks that gave rise to an increasing division of labor. For Durkheim, social networks gave individuals the roles and scripts they followed in economic life. Interpersonal networks varied dramatically among the societies that Durkheim studied, from the totemic, tribal societies of the South Pacific to the complex industrial societies of early-twentieth-century Europe. The division of labor, where the tasks of sustaining life were divided up, was what set modern societies apart. Durkheim's (1933) *The Division of Labor in Society,* explores how social attachment was restructured with industrialization, as individuals developed primary attachments to their occupational or professional groups rather than simply to their local communities. In Durkheim's view, economic behavior was shaped by social role, and in modern societies role identity was formed increasingly by occupation. People identify with those in their occupations, behaving according to occupational scripts and norms. One implication is that executives, physicians, accountants, and janitors follow economic customs rather than making rational calculations about how to behave in every situation they face. Occupational conventions may be based on rational ideas, but day-to-day behavior is guided by tradition rather than by active rational choice.

Changes in Networks and Roles

Durkheim's (1933) central question in *The Division of Labor* was in a sense a question about change, because he was interested in the simple early social structures of mechanical solidarity that were replaced by the complex social structures of organic solidarity. Since Durkheim's time, sociologists have focused on particular roles and network positions. Viviana Zelizer (1987) explores how particular roles change, showing that a network of social reformers altered the role of children under capitalism, redefining rationalized roles and changing behavior. With the rise of paid labor under early industrial capitalism, the labor of children was bought and sold just like the labor of adults. In realms ranging from factory production to life insurance to foster care to litigation, children were treated as laborers. Life insurance for children was designed to replace children's income. Foster parents favored older boys because of their earning potential. The courts awarded the parents of children killed in accidents remuneration based on the child's lost wages. A network of social reformers sought to protect children from the industrial labor market, describing childhood as a sacred category and defining children's value to parents as primarily emotional rather than economic. Their successes could be counted in institutional changes. Most forms of child labor were outlawed. Life insurance for children was transformed to provide parents with compensation for their grief over the loss of a child. Adoptive parents came to favor baby girls, who were inferior workers but superior objects of emotional attachment. The courts awarded grieving parents compensation for their emotional loss. Between 1870 and 1930, new norms about the role of children in capitalism were institutionalized. Employers themselves came to argue that children's time was better spent in schooling that would prepare them for the workforce. A social movement thus brought about a new rationalization of childhood centered on education rather than on labor.

Like Kiser and Schneider, Julia Adams (1996) is interested in the problem of agency and revenue collection among early European states. She argues alongside Durkheim that identity often causes individuals to conform to economic norms. But identity, in this case as honorable members of the Dutch colonial empire, was not always enough. The early Dutch East India trading network brought substantial revenues back to Holland. With the growth of Britain's parallel East India trading network, Dutch agents found an alternative trading route and many of them became free agents, acting for their own enrichment rather than for the good of their principal, the empire. The weak incentives to stick with the Dutch network were to blame. The British Empire reduced incentives to leave their network, and its agents were less likely to defect. The structure of the social network and its efficacy at binding individuals to society were key to predicting whether agents would stand by their principals.

Networks and Economic Development

Network position also shapes the roles that different nations play in the international order. Marx recognized this, and so especially did Lenin ([1916] 1971) in his work on imperialism. Immanuel Wallerstein's (1976, 1980) sweeping historical studies of the evolution of the world system suggest that late developers will follow a different pattern than early developers in part because their profits will be drawn toward early developing countries rather than remaining at home. Core countries, in Wallerstein's model, will buy raw materials and agricultural goods from peripheral countries at low prices. Power, in terms of core countries' capacity to make war and control technology, keeps peripheral countries in subordinate positions. Wallerstein's studies built directly on the work of Paul Baran, who similarly contended that differences in a country's location in the global trade network would shape the pattern of development and that power was the key factor that permitted developed nations to extract value from underdeveloped nations (Baran 1957; Baran and Sweezy 1966).

Cardoso and Faletto's (1979) *Dependency and Development in Latin America* took on the problem of the economic dependency of underdeveloped nations on developed nations. (Cardoso is best known for holding Brazil's presidency from 1994 to 2002.) Baran (1957) had argued that development would be stalled in underdeveloped nations by the fact that developed nations extract value from them—by the fact that they pay little for farm products, wood, oil, and minerals. Cardoso and Faletto (1979) refine the idea, arguing that class characteristics of developing countries shape their relations of dependency with core countries and thus shape industry. Cardoso and Faletto describe different patterns of local class incorporation in the international economy that correspond to typical phases in the evolution of dependency. At first, commercial groups are involved in the transfer of raw materials. Later, the urban middle classes and the industrial bourgeoisie play roles, as countries begin to trade in manufactured goods. When a country starts to substitute local products for imports, a wider range of social groups becomes involved in manufacturing. At each stage, the collaboration of local elites helps shape the kind of relationship a dependent country will have with the core, with export platform manufacturing requiring a very different pattern of cross-national class relations than, say, mining and lumbering. Here, international cross-class networks shape the pattern of development.

Whereas Cardoso and Faletto (1979) find that the international network shapes how export industries will be structured in developing countries, Gary Gereffi's (1983) systematic analysis of a single industry in 14 countries shows a similar pattern based on the strength of multinationals. Gereffi shows that powerful multinationals producing steroids suppress the development of domestically owned competitors in all these settings—multinational power trumps all kinds of domestic configurations. It is their market power and their willingness to bend the rules, rather than their efficiency, that keep multinationals in charge of this industry. Gereffi and colleagues (Gereffi and Korzeniewicz 1994) have refocused comparative studies of development, turning away from the dependent nation to the production network, or the "commodity chain." They trace goods from the extraction of raw materials to the consumer. As transnational corporations made the production process truly global in many industries, commodity chains became increasingly complex, wending through many countries. Case studies of different industries reveal that transnational corporations make use of unregulated extractive industries in one location, low wages in another, and advanced manufacturing techniques in a third. They practice the concept of comparative advantage, shopping for the best wages, environmental regulations, and so on, for each stage in the production process.

Peter Evans has focused on how networks of bureaucrats, multinationals, and local capitalists can foster development. Conventional wisdom suggests that laissez-faire state policies produce growth. In two books, one principally on Brazil (*Dependent Development* 1979) and one comparing Brazil with Korea and India (*Embedded Autonomy* 1995), Evans amends this wisdom. First, he finds that in virtually all successful cases of development, the state takes an active role in the promotion of industry. Comparisons across industries in Brazil make this clear. Second, he suggests that states need to be *autonomous* to develop successful growth strategies. Weberian norms of rationality make states effective managers of the economy. Where capitalists hold state bureaucrats in their pockets, dynamic growth rarely ensues. Third, in successful cases of development, states need to be embedded in societal networks in order to gain information on industry and to be able to influence industry. A comparison of the information technology industries in Brazil, Korea, and India provides evidence. For successful development, bureaucratic rules must contain the power of societal groups over the state, but the state must play an active role in development, and to do so effectively, state elites must be involved in networks of entrepreneurs and financiers.

Roles and Institutions in the Transition to Capitalism

The transition to capitalism has provided a sort of natural laboratory for analyzing rapid shifts in economic practices in Eastern Europe, in the former Soviet Union, and in China. In the short run, the plans for transition via "shock therapy" sketched by economist Jeffrey Sachs (1989) appeared to have failed, and this brought greater interest in sociological analyses of the transition. Followers of "shock therapy" believed that by destroying socialist economic forms, such as collective ownership, they would unleash the power of markets. Sociological analyses suggest that no one particular system fills the void—not American-style neoliberalism, but certainly not Japanese-style state-industry collaboration either. As Weber would predict, institutions do not change so easily. As Durkheim would suggest, social roles and social networks often explain which systems do change.

Iván Szelényi (1983) documented the emergence of proto-capitalist enterprises even before socialism fell, abruptly, in Eastern Europe in 1989. In *The Intellectuals on the Road to Class Power,* Konrád and Szelényi (1979) showed that intellectuals were becoming the ruling class under modern socialism. Yet by the late 1980s, Szelényi et al. (1988) found that a new bourgeois elite was rising in Hungary, contrary to all expectations. It was a farming elite, producing agricultural goods for sale in private markets. Szelényi found that the participants were typically from families that had been entrepreneurial even before the advent of communism in Hungary. Some 40 years later, the entrepreneurial inclination survived in these families, and some developed active and quite successful businesses targeting unmet demand for agricultural goods in private, unregulated markets. Szelényi argues that the continuity in family roles explains this. In Hungary, those whose families were on the path to embourgeoisement in 1944 put their ambitions on hold but revived those ambitions as a private, secondary economy emerged that allowed them to behave as entrepreneurs. The role in the old network proved to be the defining characteristic of the role in the new.

David Stark's laboratory is Eastern Europe after the fall of communism, and there he finds that societies with strong social networks that encourage political participation have the greatest potential for growth (Stark 1992a, 1992b; Stark and Bruszt 1998). Stark's study of post-1989 privatization strategies challenges the idea of "cookbook capitalism"—the idea that one can use a single recipe to create identical capitalist systems everywhere. Countries pursuing the recipe for privatization built very different systems, based on pre-1989 institutions and assumptions

(1992). States chose either corporations or individuals to acquire stock in state-owned firms, and they distributed stock either to those who could buy it or to those who, they deemed, had a right to it. Czechoslovakia and Poland chose citizens to acquire stock, the former selling it in a voucher auction and the latter distributing it through citizen grants. East Germany and Hungary both chose corporations to acquire stock, the former selling it and the latter reorganizing enterprises that would own themselves. The form of public ownership of corporations under communism, and the structure of elite networks, account for these differences. Some transitions are more successful than others. Stark and Bruszt's (1998) *Postsocialist Pathways* shows that the structure of social ties matters more than the extent to which nations have approximated the neoliberal model of the market. Consistency in the property rights regime is a precondition to success, and consistency is a consequence of a society's network structure. Where there is a "deliberative association" of producers that generates a market that is open and participatory, policy continuity and growth ensue. The Czech Republic's consistent policies are one result, and they contrast starkly with Hungary's policy vacillations.

Victor Nee (1989, 1991, 1992, 1996) studies the ways in which policy institutions have shaped the interests of elites in the Chinese transition to capitalism and the implications for the transition. The implicit story is that economic practices and structures persist because they produce a sort of equilibrium of interests, but that change in policy can alter interests and economic patterns. When public policy encouraged entrepreneurialism, government officials were the first out of the gate because they had the requisite knowledge and access to resources (Nee 1991). Yet when state cadres used privileges of position to build enterprises, they created a crisis of legitimacy in party socialism that further hastened the move toward capitalism (Nee 1996). Here a change in the incentives created by public policy brought about a new set of economic behaviors that fed back into the political system. Policy incentives can also shape the forms of enterprise that emerge under capitalism. In "Organizational Dynamics of Market Transition," Nee (1992) shows that China's transformation did not spawn a single enterprise form, because public policy continued to support hybrid forms such as cooperatives and enterprises owned by local governments. These forms were not inherently uncompetitive when they came head-to-head with private enterprises organized on the Western model. Their competitiveness depended on whether public policy encouraged efficiency in the particular form. Nee's rich analyses point to the importance of long-standing social networks for the transition to capitalism.

Douglas Guthrie's (1999) *Dragon in a Three-Piece Suit: The Emergence of Capitalism in China* charts changes in Chinese management practices during the 1990s, as a growing number of enterprises adopted Western management conventions. It is not those that need reform that move toward the Western conventions of bureaucratic wage and promotion systems, market pricing, diversification into the profitable service sector, and adoption of company law as a governance form. Two things matter. Networks matter, and specifically links to Western ideas, through the training of managers or through joint contracts with Western firms. And enterprises that had received significant public subsidies in the past change quickly after being cut off from public funding. Guthrie thus finds that institutional theory, with its emphasis on crises catalyzing change and its emphasis on the spread of new strategies through networks, better explains new corporate strategies in China than does efficiency theory.

CONCLUSION

Since its renaissance began in the late 1970s, the field of economic sociology has explored how three mechanisms produce economic behavior patterns in modern societies. First, in studying power, Marx (1974) had found that the emerging bourgeoisie under late feudalism used their newfound economic resources to move public policy in their direction, so that policy favored capitalist activities. The modern state professes neutrality in matters economic, Marx contended, but in fact it pursues policies that favor particular groups in the name of the collective good. By analogy, William Roy (1997) shows that the legal rules that made the corporation the most profitable governance structure were backed by a particular group of capitalists, who succeeded in convincing society at large that limited liability and kindred legal forms were good not only for the owners of corporations but also for the society.

Second, existing economic institutions and customs shape the new institutions and customs that emerge. This happens in part because existing institutions provide models of how the world should be organized and resources for organizing new fields of activity in the way that old fields were organized. Historical studies find dramatic shifts in economic behavior and institutions over time, but they also find that countries build on past experience. Hamilton and Biggart (1988) trace the modern industrial strategies of Japan, South Korea, and Taiwan not to postwar innovations in industrial policy but to the strategic use of traditional forms of state–private sector relations.

Third, networks are the conduits through which new economic customs diffuse as role prescriptions and through which power is exercised. Social networks take very different forms, and concrete networks determine what is possible in economic life and what is not. For Gao (2001), the close ties between state officials and corporations in Japan, and the resulting absence of formal controls over corporate activity, played a role in the economic collapse of the 1990s. Networks also define social roles for their members, and many studies have shown that individuals follow social norms promoted by networks unthinkingly in economic life rather than making rational calculations at every crossroad.

Economic sociologists have not challenged the idea that people seek profits or the idea that economic institutions have become more efficient over time. As a group, they have challenged the idea that profit-seeking translates transparently and straightforwardly into behavioral prescriptions. If the society you live in influences how you seek profits, then understanding how it does so is the job of economic sociology. Economic sociologists may emphasize one process or another when they are trying to explain economic behavior, but increasingly they find all three of these processes at work (Fligstein 2001).

In the twenty-first century, economic sociologists will increase their attention to how growing international exchange is shaping domestic economic behavior patterns and institutions. Their empirical focus will be on how new economic practices travel from one place to another. Their theoretical focus will be on how these three mechanisms interact to generate economic practices and institutions. Whereas economic theorists have often concerned themselves with where the economy is going—with what changes will emerge—economic sociologists have been concerned with how the economy gets there—with how change comes about. For economic sociologists, understanding how changes occur is the key to understanding which changes occur.

33

MEDICAL SOCIOLOGY

FREDERIC W. HAFFERTY

University of Minnesota, Duluth

BRIAN CASTELLANI

Kent State University

With a formal institutional history that dates back more than 50 years, the academic discipline of medical/health sociology is both rich and varied. As one of the largest subfields in sociology, it has explored a long list of health care issues, including the physician-patient relationship, illness behavior, stress and coping, the social distribution of health, medical professionalism, health care policy, and public health. It also has drawn on and made excellent use of a wide range of sociological theories, including structural functionalism, symbolic interactionism, feminism, and postmodernism. Finally, it has intersected with a variety of other social sciences, including medical anthropology, health psychology, and epidemiology, to produce an important literature that has helped to improve the practice of medicine and the health and well-being of people worldwide.

In light of this richness and diversity, we seek first to identify resources that will enable readers to have a deeper appreciation for the field of medical/health sociology. Second, we highlight ways of thinking about medicine and health care from a sociological perspective, which, in turn, may enhance our understanding and possibly assist in managing what has become society's most complex social institution.

This chapter is organized into three sections. First, we briefly explore medical sociology's historical roots. Second, we address the issue of what makes medical sociology sociological. That is, we assess how sociology contributes to our understanding of health and illness and how medical sociology contributes to the general sociological discourse. Third, we examine medical sociology in terms of the major sociological theories it draws upon to study health care issues.

Throughout this chapter (and per above), we will use the terms "medical sociology," "health sociology," and "sociology of health and illness" interchangeably or in some combination (e.g., medical/health sociology). Over the years, there has been considerable debate about what to label academic sociology's foray into the world of medicine, health, and illness. Herein, it is important only to note the debate.

HISTORICAL ROOTS

Medical sociology can trace its intellectual lineage to the late 1800s. In the waning decades of the nineteenth century, two nascent disciplines, sociology and allopathic medicine, began to cross paths in small but significant ways. For allopathic medicine, this time period witnessed the beginnings of medicine's ongoing attempts to consolidate its professional powers and social legitimacy. Meanwhile, *sociology* (the term being first coined by Auguste Comte in 1838) was beginning to emerge as a distinct discipline. In the United States, for example, Herbert Spencer's *The Principles of Sociology* (three volumes, 1876–1896) was a seminal publication, along with the establishment of the first American sociology course ("Elements of Sociology" at the University of Kansas, Lawrence, in 1890), and the founding of the first department of sociology (at the University of Chicago in 1892 by Albion Small—who three years later also would launch the first sociology journal, *American Journal of Sociology* [*AJS*], in 1895).

Examples of work from this time period that formally link "medicine" and "sociology" include two articles by Charles McIntire (1915, 1991) ("The Importance of the Study of Medical Sociology"—first published in 1894 and reprinted in *Sociological Practice*—and "The Expanse of Sociologic Medicine") along with two key books, the first by Elizabeth Blackwell (1902) (*Essays in Medical Sociology*) and the second by James P. Warbasse (1909) (*Medical Sociology: A Series of Observations Touching Upon the Sociology of Health and the Relations of Medicine*). The second McIntire article is of particular interest because of where it appeared—in the *Journal of Sociologic Medicine,* which was published not by a sociology association but by the *American Academy of Medicine.* This journal, with its distinctive sociological title and medical "residence," existed for a scant four years (1915–1919) before both the parent and the journal disappeared from view. The American Public Health Association hosted a similar sociologic offspring—its "Section of Sociology"—for a slightly longer period of time (1909–1921), but with a similar demise (Bloom 2002). It would take another quarter century before the next medical sociology journal (*Journal of Health and Human Behavior*—see below) appeared.

The initial timing and brief duration of these links between medicine and sociology reflected a much broader transformation taking place within allopathic medicine and between medicine and society, as both rushed to affirm the "scientific side" of medicine (Starr 1982; Stevens 1971). As medicine grew in clinical effectiveness and organizational complexity, however, the social-psychological and behavioral sides of medicine began to atrophy—with instruction, research, and principles relegated to "second-order" medical fields such as psychiatry and public health. While scattered "sociology of medicine" articles would continue to appear (albeit infrequently) in medical journals between 1920 and 1950 (Lawrence J. Henderson's [1935] "Physician and patient as a social system" being a notable example), the few that did surface would have a far greater impact on sociology than on medicine (one famous "benefactor" of the Henderson article, for example, was Talcott Parsons). In 1960, E. Gartly Jaco published what would become the first substantive disciplinary journal in medical sociology, the *Journal of Health & Human Behavior* (*JHHB*). In the spring of 1967, the American Sociological Association (ASA) took *JHHB* under its organizational wing where it was renamed the *Journal of Health and Social Behavior* (*JHSB*). Eliot Freidson was the first editor. This same year also marked the first issue of *Social Science & Medicine* (*SS&M*), with its distinctively

international and multidisciplinary social science focus. By the early 1970s, the medical sociology section of the *British Sociological Association* had established its own organizational footprint, and in 1979 published its own "medical sociology" journal (*Sociology of Health & Illness*). Like *SS&M,* it too would have an international and multidisciplinary focus (Jobling 1979).

During the 1950s and 1960s, the field of medical sociology underwent an explosive period of growth—before peaking in the early 1970s (Bloom 2002; Day 1981). During these two decades, the field enjoyed considerable academic excitement and success, including what today might be considered a lavish amount of grant support, both from private foundations and the federal government. At its peak in the early 1970s, for example, the National Institute of Mental Health subcommittee for social science training was awarding 1,500 graduate student stipends per year—80 percent of which went to sociology departments. The number of stipends was well in excess of what was needed to support medical sociology graduate students— and thus the entire field of sociology benefited from this philanthropic and federal largess (Bloom 2002). Even the founding of the medical sociology section itself and the ASA's decision to adopt the *JHSB* were underwritten by outside funding.

Membership in the new ASA section (established in 1959) was mercurial. In less than a year, the medical sociology section grew to 561 members. By 1964, membership had soared to nearly 900 (which, not incidentally, is close to the section's membership today). In less than a half dozen years, the field went from publishing introductions to the field (Anderson 1952; Hall 1951) to summative reviews (one notable example is Eliot Freidson's [1961] "The Sociology of Medicine: A Trend Report and Bibliography," published as a special issue in *Current Sociology*).

By the mid-1970s, however, there were signs of trouble (Bloom 2002; Day 1981). Established funding streams had dried up and were not replaced by alternative resources. Section membership had plateaued and coverage of medical/health issues in flagship sociology journals, such as the *AJS* and the *American Sociological Review,* became more infrequent. Meanwhile, colleges and universities were undergoing their own upheavals. Faced with considerable financial pressures, schools looked to trim programs, and sociology was high on a number of lists. As one small but indicative example, Yale University's Department of Sociology, which housed the first medical sociology program in the United States, decided in the 1990s to eliminate that program.

The 1980s and 1990s were a difficult time for allopathic medicine as well. The rise of managed care, the commodification of medical services, and the discovery of medicine by Wall Street and corporate America during the "go-go" years between 1985 and 1997 had earth-shattering implications for the future of medicine as an autonomous profession.

The 1970s through early 1990s also were a time of vigorous debates within academic sociology about the fate and future of allopathic medicine as a profession (Hafferty and Light 1995; Hafferty and Wolinsky 1991). Beginning with Eliot Freidson's (1970a, 1970b) transformative *Profession of Medicine* and *Professional Dominance,* a number of distinguished medical sociologists in the United States (Mark Field, David Frankford, Marie Haug, Eliot Krause, Donald Light, John McKinlay, Fredric Wolinsky) and elsewhere (David Coburn, Julio Frenk, Rudolf Klein, Magali Larson, Gerald Larkin, Elianne Riska, Evan Willis) began to debate the changing fortunes of organized medicine's status as a profession (Hafferty and McKinlay 1993). Once again medicine and sociology crossed paths. It is worth noting, however, that by the time organized medicine began to mount a campaign to reestablish its professional status and stature, sociologists had moved on to other debates (Castellani and Hafferty 2006).

Issues of Identity and Identification

From its very conception as an academic entity, medical sociology has been plagued by issues of identity (self) and of identification (others). On the one hand, the study of medical and health issues offered sociology great challenges and opportunities (Fox 1985). On the other hand, these same opportunities had the potential to strip sociology of its unique perspective (Bloom 1986). One hallmark of this tension is the now 50-year-old debate about whether the *ASA*'s section should be named "medical sociology" or whether it should sport some other marquee such as "health sociology" or the "sociology of health and illness." Many of these tensions are reflected in Robert Straus's (1957) famous distinction between a *sociology of* and a *sociology in* medicine. The problem is one of placement and perspective. The former (*of*) reflects situations where sociologists maintain their disciplinary base (an academic sociology department for example) and train their sociological lens on fields of inquiry (such as medicine) for the purpose of answering sociological questions. The latter (*in*) connotes a state of affairs where sociologists work, for example, in a medical setting and employ sociological concepts and perspectives to solve problems that are defined as such by medicine. *Sociology of* medicine thus became considered (by academically based sociologists) as more in keeping with the sociological tradition, with the presumption being that those operating from a *sociology in* medicine ran the risk of being co-opted or at least corrupted by the medical perspective. More recently, there have been efforts to "retire" this distinction by insisting that sociology has passed through its *of/in* phase and has graduated into a *sociology with* medicine (Levine 1987). This is wishful thinking. Organized medicine remains one of the most powerful social institutions in modern times—forces of deprofessionalization notwithstanding. Furthermore, medicine has little incentive (then or now) to welcome sociology to its table unless it feels that sociology can help solve issues or problems—*as defined by medicine* (and not sociology). Under such circumstances (and expectations), any working relationship between sociology and medicine involves considerable potential for sociology to undergo disciplinary co-opt. Sociologists who work in medical settings must be particularly sensitive to these issues. Often they function betwixt and between, receiving little respect from physicians or from their academically based peers who consider their "wayward" colleges to be too "applied." Whatever the particulars, organized medicine retains considerable institutional power and social legitimacy within today's society. Medicine has been able to establish its knowledge, skills, and culture as the everyday, taken-for-granted order of things, and this is what makes the medical perspective so potentially corrupting.

Medical Sociology and Medical Education

The move to introduce medical sociology into the medical school and nursing curriculum played an important role in the discipline's evolution as an institutional entity. The first beachhead came in 1959, when Robert Straus founded the first Department of Behavioral Science at the University of Kentucky. Straus also helped to found, in 1970, the discipline's first professional association (Association for the Behavioral Sciences and Medical Education). For Straus, "behavioral science" (note the singular form) reflected the intersection of medical sociology, medical anthropology, and medical psychology—and therefore represented a unique and transcending social science discipline. The field quickly established a presence within a number (but not all) of medical schools during the 1960s and 1970s, particularly in those 40+ community medical schools that were being founded during the 1970s and 1980s. Nonetheless, the field's fundamental identity within the basic science and clinical arms of the medical school was—and would remain—marginal and suspect.

As departments and programs of behavioral science(s) began to grow in number and size, once supportive allies such as psychiatry and community medicine began to mount counteroffensives to reestablish control over domains of medical knowledge and instruction that once had been their exclusive jurisdiction. Today, there are only three formally labeled "Departments of Behavioral Science(s)" in the United States: the University of Kentucky College of Medicine, the University of Minnesota Medical School–Duluth Campus, and Northeastern Ohio Universities College of Medicine (NEOUCOM).

Another indicator that points to the rather persistent marginal status for the behavioral sciences (including medical sociology) within medicine and medical education is reflected across the numerous national committees, commissions, and reports (dating back to the 1920s) that have emphasized the necessary role of the social sciences in medical education (Christakis 1995)—yet with little change over these decades in actual institutional and instructional practices by medical schools. Bloom (1986) famously likened this ongoing state of affairs to "reform without change." Straus's sociology *of* and *in* medicine also raises the question of whether there are two (or more) medical sociologies. One way to answer this question is to ask whether the medical sociology taught/presented to medical and/or other health science students, for example, is the same medical sociology presented to undergraduate and graduate medical sociology majors. Although we do not pretend to answer the question here, there is a sufficiently large body of relevant material to at least raise the question and suggest that there are, indeed, differences. Books by Thomas (2003) and Taylor and Field (2003), along with articles written for medical journals depicting sociology (Bilkey 1996; Chard, Lilford, and Gardiner 1999; Chard, Lilford, and Court 1997; Chaska 1977; Petersdorf and Feinstein 1981; Ruderman 1981) are a good place to begin any such inquiry.

Finally, we note that for some sociologists and sociology programs, the label *applied* is something to be courted, not condemned. There is a vigorous movement within organized medical sociology (and sociology in general) to make sociology training more explicitly "applied" and or "clinical" in focus—with the goal to make students more "job ready" or employable postgraduation (Dolch 1990; Gabelko and McBride 1991; Haney, Zahn, and Howard 1983; Hoppe and Barr 1990; Sengstock 2001).

Medical Sociology as Sociology: Or, What Makes Medical Sociology Sociological?

Any new or emergent subfield must draw on its parent discipline for theoretical, conceptual, and methodological sustenance. Thus, when Talcott Parsons (1951) began to craft his now famous Chapter 10 of *The Social System* ("Social Structure and Dynamic Process: The Case of Modern Medical Practice"), he drew on core aspects of sociological theory (e.g., the sociology of deviance, role theory, etc.) to reframe issues of health and sickness from a functionalist perspective. Similarly, Eliot Freidson (1970a, 1970b) drew on the sociology of knowledge and the framing of social order as the product of ongoing human production (Berger and Luckman, 1966) to help shape his analytical approach to medical work, language, and knowledge. As a final example, two of the most famous early studies of medical education, Robert Merton, Leo Reeder, and Patricia Kendall's (1957) *The Student Physician* and Howard Becker et al.'s (1961) *Boys in White* were less studies of medical education per se than they were efforts to test competing theories of social action, including adult socialization. The Merton camp advocated a structural functionalist perspective and the Becker camp a symbolic interactionist perspective. In short, the core issue was sociological theory, not occupational training, and therefore both studies were a *sociology of* rather than a *sociology in*. Medical education was "simply" the backdrop or battlefield (Hafferty 2000).

It seems reasonably self-evident that "medical sociology" must involve the application of sociological knowledge and concepts to issues of health and illness. It is distinct in its approach because it considers the import that social and structural factors have on the disease and illness processes as well as on the organization and delivery of health care. This includes factors such as culture (e.g., values, beliefs, normative expectations), organizational processes (e.g., the bureaucracy of hospitals), politics (e.g., health care policy, political ideology), economics (e.g., capitalism, the stock market, the costs of health care), and microlevel processes such as socialization, identity formation, and group process.

All of this conceptual blocking notwithstanding, what we have remains too limiting a definition. It is not enough that someone labeled a "sociologist" employs sociological concepts to answer questions if the questions themselves are defined/framed in a nonsociological manner. Asking sociologists to help solve the "problem of patient compliance" proposes that the sociologist take on a medical definition of the situation (where any deviation from "doctor's orders" is considered the responsibility and fault of the patient). Lost in the shuffle of who gets to define the topics and terms is the fact that physicians and patients interact within a highly complex system involving medicine and society, along with broader social issues such as the role of experts in society or the social management of risk.

There is another question here as well. Where and how does medical sociology contribute to the greater sociological enterprise? More specifically, where do we find evidence that medical sociologists/sociology directly contributes to the advancement of sociological theory or methods? The question is not rhetorical. Much of Anselm Strauss's early work on grounded theory (Glaser and Strauss 1967) came via research on the topics of death and dying (Glaser and Strauss 1965, 1968; Strauss and Glaser 1970). On the other hand, while it is clear that Erving Goffman's (1986) work on stigma has been widely employed within medical/health sociology, and while it is equally clear that the concept has great applicability to the sociology of chronic illness and the sociology of disability/disability studies, it is less clear how studies in these areas have contributed to the conceptual development of stigma as a sociological concept and therefore as a tool that can be applied by social scientists studying issues other than medicine.

Finally, we have a third question related to the multiple medical sociology question raised above. It is not always self-evident how the work of medical sociology differs from that of medical anthropology, medical economics, health policy, medical epidemiology, and public health. As such, is medical sociology itself a unique and singular perspective? Asked in a more sociological manner, Can we disentangle "medical sociology" from the broader social context in which it functions? To answer this question, we will briefly explore differences between U.S. and British medical sociology.

THE CASE OF BRITISH MEDICAL SOCIOLOGY

In addition to the possibility that medical (nursing, health science, etc.) students receive a different medical sociology than what is taught to sociology graduate students, there appears to be considerable (and important) differences between British and American medical sociology. We begin by noting that the parent disciplines (British and American sociology) themselves harbor key differences (Abbott 2000). British sociology is more theoretically inclined, more accepting of qualitative research strategies, and more critical of "abstract empiricism" (not only with respect to data analysis but also with respect to the very definition of data itself). There also are differences in theoretical constructs. British sociology, for example, has a strong tradition focusing on the "sociology of the body" (e.g., "constructing the body" or "gender, sexuality, and the body") (Shilling 2004; Turner 1992, 1996)—something much less visible in U.S. sociology. There also are differences in the use of analytic concepts—the British use of social class and the American use of socioeconomic status being one example (Halsey 2004; Reid 1979; Stacey and Homans 1978). Finally, we can point to significant differences between the U.S. and British health care systems. The American system is more capitalistic and "market oriented," while the British have a national health system organized and controlled by the state. Indeed, there are those who believe that while the British have a coherent and organized health care "system," the American arrangement of competing capital interest is, at best, a "nonsystem system."

All these differences are reflected in the focus and tone of British versus American medical/health sociology. Comparisons between White (2002) and U.S. textbooks such as Conrad (2005) and/or Weitz (2003) show differences in content and context. Chapter titles in White (e.g., "Foucault and the Sociology of Medical Knowledge," "Postmodernity, Epidemiology and Neo-Liberalism," and "Materialist Approaches to the Sociology of Health") have no parallel in Conrad or Weitz.

We continue to see these same differences in the medical/health sociology taught to British medical versus American medical students. One major difference is the use of medical/health sociology textbooks. Not only is there a market for such textbooks within British medical (and/or other health science) education, but the volumes themselves are formally identified as health and/or medical sociology text (Scambler 2003; Taylor and Field 2003; Thomas 2003). There are no such textbooks in the United States. Furthermore, in the rare instance when textbooks are used in the United States, the operative label used is "behavioral science" (Sahler and Carr 2003). Even here, most "behavioral science" textbooks sold in the United States are "board review" (Fadem 2001) or biostatistics (Gravetter and Wallnau 2003) books.

Similar differences can be found with other types of medical curriculum materials (Cook 2004; Iphofen and Poland 1997; Kitto 2004; Turner 1990). The article by Cook (2004), for example, describes course materials for health professional students built around "the concepts of differentiation, commodification, and rationalization (associated with the work of Émile Durkheim, Karl Marx, and Max Weber, respectively)," with these materials providing "a useful conceptual 'launching pad' for understanding key changes to medicine and doctor-patient relationships since pre-modern times" (p. 87). Similarly, the article by Kitto (2004) describes a new "health, knowledge, and society" curriculum for medicine, nursing, and health sciences students built around "aspects of C. Wright Mills' sociological imagination to teach 1st year medical students the importance of analysing the social aspects of health and illness in medical practice" (p. 74). Course materials with titles or rationales such as these simply do not exist within U.S. medical education. In the United States, behavioral sciences faculty are urged by students (via course evaluations) and administration (also driven by student evaluations) to be "relevant," "applied," "practical," "case based," and/or "patient centered"—all antonyms for the dreaded terms "theory" or "theoretical" (which are interpreted by U.S. medical students as having little to no applicability to issues of patient care). Moreover, even if we were to sweep away the stigmatizing presence of theoretical materials, the fact remains that medical students (along with many basic science faculty) consider the entire field of behavioral/social science to be "soft" and "subjective" when compared with the remaining basic sciences (pathology, pharmacology, molecular and cell biology, etc.) and clinical coursework. Within U.S. medical education circles, data demonstrating that U.S. medical students learn better when course materials are "patient oriented" rather than "theoretically oriented" (Leigh and Reiser 1986) have great face validity.

Theoretical Passages through Medical Sociology

As William Cockerham (2001) explains in his essay "Medical Sociology and Sociological Theory," because medical sociology is an applied field of study, there is a tendency to think that it lacks a theoretical rationale for the various topics it studies. Such conclusions are false. As we explained above, the general aim of medical sociology (whether the sociologist be Talcott Parsons or a newly hired junior faculty person or research associate) is to apply sociological theory and concepts to the topics of health and health care. This is true of both the sociology *of* and *in* medicine (Bloom 2002; Gerhardt 1989).

Obviously, an important part of what medical sociologists "know"—independent of what they study—is sociological theory. As each cohort of medical sociologists is trained, they learn not only the older canon of sociological theory—what has gone on before them—but also the latest theoretical advances. One hallmark of any academic discipline is how each new cohort of scientists goes about applying this "new-found" theoretical knowledge to what they seek to examine and understand. This, in turn, advances the field. A survey of the medical sociology literature suggests just this process to be the case (Gerhardt 1989).

While such an unfolding of the field certainly represents *advancement,* this progression, for medical sociology, has not been linear, nor has it been entirely cumulative. There also is much debate within medical sociology about the validity of applying various sociological theories to the fields of medicine and health care—one such example being the case of postmodernism (Cockerham 2001). Moreover, there are a variety of rifts in the field over the epistemological assumptions behind many of these theories. These rifts concern, for example, the validity of deductive reasoning and the linear model of statistics, the reliability of qualitative methodology and scientific representation, the appropriateness of various sociological units of analysis—micro, meso, macro—and the authority of medical and sociological knowledge (Annandale 1998; Levine 1995; Link 2003; Williams 2001). Finally, it appears that while different theories are useful in some areas, are less appropriate in others. Postmodernism, for example, is a useful way to critique the power of medical knowledge. It is, however, not much help in studying social stress or the social distribution of health and illness.

Despite the complexity and nuances of these differences—yet in many ways because of them—medical sociology is a theoretically rich and diverse field of study. Our purpose in this section is to provide a quick overview of this richness by surveying some of the more important sociological theories that have been employed by medical sociologists over the past 50 years. While no strict chronology is implied in our review, it is historically accurate to label the first four theoretical orientations as "classical" sociological theory, while the remaining three are more recent in both origin and application within the field.

The first major theoretical passage through medical sociology is structural functionalism. Grounded in the work of Talcott Parsons (1951), this theory takes a systems view of health and illness, focusing on the functional role that social institutions such as medicine play in maintaining the well-being of society. Despite the controversy that ensued during the 1960s and 1970s regarding the legitimacy of this perspective, it retains considerable influence and relevance (Williams 2005). Not only did the presence of Parsons (as probably the most famous sociologist of his time) and the utility of structural functionalism help to establish the study of health and illness as a worthy sociological endeavor, this lineague and apparent applicability also helped to develop several of the field's most important areas of research: the patient-physician relationship, the

sick role (which later became known as illness behavior), the medicalization of deviance, and medical professionalism

The second major theoretical passage is symbolic interactionism. Unlike structural functionalism, this perspective focuses more on the "microlevel" social processes of health and health care and the important role that patients and health care providers play in the creation, development, and transformation of the larger health care systems of which they are a part. Through the work of Anselm Strauss, Erving Goffman, Howard Becker, Norman Denzin, and Kathy Charmaz (to name a few), this perspective has examined such important topics as how medical schools socialize physicians, how patients learn the role of being chronically or mentally ill, how physicians and nurses use the tools of medicine and the medical model to impose on patients the normative expectations of society, how patients and their families manage the emotional labor of "illness," and how patients and health care providers negotiate the "politics" of daily medical encounters (Charmaz and Paterniti 1999; Gerhardt 1989). Like structural functionalism, symbolic interaction theory predates the origins of modern-day medical sociology. For example, and as noted above, the two most famous studies of medical student socialization, the Merton and Becker studies, built their respective investigations around this theoretical divide.

The third major theoretical passage is conflict theory. Building on the work of Karl Marx and Max Weber and represented by more contemporary conflict theorists such as Randall Collins (Collins and Makowsky 2004), this perspective demonstrates how a society's health and health care system is the result of a complex network of conflicting and competing aims and interests based on differences in income, gender, ethnicity, occupation, education, political affiliation, and so on (Navarro 2002). Conflict theory has been an important addition to the field of medical sociology because it has provided a much-needed theoretical framework for the *sociology of medicine,* which has enabled medical sociologists to study such important topics as the social distribution of health and illness, inequalities in the health care delivery system, the politics of health care policy, the economics of health insurance, and the failures of medicine to meet the health care needs of society (Gerhardt 1989; Henderson et al. 1997; Navarro 2002).

The fourth major theoretical perspective is feminism (Annandale 2003; Bury 1995; Clarke and Olesen 1999; Harkess 2000). Drawing on a variety of theories within sociology, including symbolic interaction and conflict theory, this perspective is concerned with the role that patriarchy, sexism, and gender play in the health and well-being of women. This perspective has examined important issues such as the medicalization of the female body, the quality of health care women receive, and the role that patriarchy has played in the construction of medical knowledge.

The fifth major theoretical framework is poststructuralism. Based on the work of the French philosopher and historian Michel Foucault, this perspective examines how people use the discourses of medicine, psychiatry, and science to care for and control themselves and others (Petersen and Bunton 1997). Like Parsons before him, Foucault (1980, 1987, 1988) examined many of the key topics in medical sociology, such as the history of madness, the medicalization of deviance, the birth of the modern medical clinic, and the various ways in which health care providers and everyday people use medical knowledge—think of, for example, the self-help literature, medical diets, and plastic surgery—to master and control the body.

The sixth major theoretical passage is postmodernism. Building on the work of Lyotard, Baudrillard, and Derrida (Best and Kellner 1991, 2001; Fox 1994), this perspective makes two radical assertions. First, it asserts that medicine and biomedical science are nothing more than discourses; powerful textual strategies that use a variety of binaries to control such important issues as (a) who is a medical expert (physicians versus traditional healers), (b) what constitutes valid medical knowledge (biology versus sociology), and (c) what sits outside "normal" ideas about health and health care (allopathic medicine versus alternative medicine). Second, it asserts that the dominating discourses of medicine and biomedical science need to be deconstructed and re-created to form new ways of thinking about health and health care, ways that are better able to address the postindustrial, globally interdependent, culturally fragmented, and nonlinear world in which we now live.

While postmodernism has provided an effective critique of modern medicine, critics point out that its wholesale dismissal of medicine and science as little more than normative ways of thinking oftentimes appears to "throw the baby out with the bathwater." While modern medicine and biomedical science are hierarchically ordered and still decidedly patriarchal, it hardly seems reasonable to issue a blanket dismissal of biomedicine as little more than dominating textual strategies, given its role in improving the health of populations throughout the world. It is for this reason that postmodernism has had a limited presence, impact, and utility in medical sociology.

The seventh major theoretical passage is multiculturalism (Lupton 2003; White 2002). Drawing on the theoretical perspectives of symbolic interactionism, conflict, feminism, poststructuralism, and postmodernism, this perspective has three major foci. The first is to examine the negative impact that racism, sexism, homophobia, ethnocentrism, and cultural intolerance have on the health and well-being of people. The second is to examine the ways in which culture affects the practice of medicine and biomedical science. The third examines the ways in which culture affects the health behaviors of different populations and, in turn, their use of contemporary Western health care (Lupton 2003; White 2002).

TWO SUBSTANTIVE THEORIES

Two important substantive theories have played a major role in medical sociology: (1) stress and coping (Cockerham 2004; Mirowsky and Ross 2003) and (2) professionalism (Hafferty and Light 1995; Hafferty and McKinlay 1993). Stress and coping is situated at the intersection of sociological traditions such as symbolic interactionism, conflict theory, and the sociology of work. The sociological study on stress and coping itself has two foci: (1) the role that certain social factors (e.g., chronic poverty, lifestyle, health behaviors, occupation, gender, etc.) play in the creation and exacerbation of stress and conversely, (2) the role that other social factors (e.g., marital status, strength of kinship networks, financial stability) play in assuaging stress.

The sociological study of professions has a longer and more storied history. While the sociological study of professions and occupations date back to the turn of the century (Carr-Saunders and Wilson 1928), modern-day discussions of medical professionalism are linked to Parsons and his conception of medical dominance and autonomy as necessary/functional for the well-being of both patients and society. Since Parsons, medical sociology has been engaged in an extended (and critical) examination of American medicine's claim to be a profession and the extent to which medicine has been able to maintain and live up to this claim. More specifically, medical sociology has examined the impact that medicine's professional status has on the lives of physicians and patients, as well as also on the entire issue of how work is organized relative to free market and bureaucratic organizational forms (Freidson 2001). According to the sociological analysis of medicine as a profession, medicine has gone through four major transformations: professional reform and rise (1890s–1930s), professional dominance (1940s–1960s), deprofessionalization (1970s–1990s), and organized medicine's efforts to reclaim and redefine its professional status (1990s–present) (Castellani and Hafferty 2006). As an aside, both traditional and modern-day medical sociology have strong disciplinary ties to the sociological study of profession. For example, the germination of medical sociology at Columbia, including *The Student Physician* study, arose out of a seminar organized by Robert Merton and William J. Goode on professions ("University Seminar on the Professions in Modern Society").

EMERGING THEMES

We see two emergent lines of sociological investigation as we move to examine the future of medical sociology—each related to the other. The first is globalization. It is clear that the world in which we live is going through major transformation. This is particularly true of health and health care. We now live in a world where the spread of disease is global and where the poor health of one country affects the well-being of others. Global financial markets and economic competition are challenging the ability of business and governments to provide affordable health care. As such, we can expect that as globalization increases, so will its importance as a major theme in medical sociology (Bury 2005). There are an increasing number of studies examining issues of health and illness in countries other than the United States or Britain—far more than can be listed here. Resources such as Mechanic and Rochefort's (1996) "Comparative Medical Systems" and Cockerham's (2004) *The Blackwell Companion to Medical Sociology* (with its 17 chapters on the United States, Canada, Mexico, Brazil, the United Kingdom, France, Germany, Sweden, Russia, Poland, the Czech Republic, South Africa, the Arab world, Israel, Australia, Japan, and the People's Republic of China) provide an excellent beginning.

The second and related theme is "complexity science." As argued by a growing list of scholars, and due to key factors such as the information revolution and globalization, anj emerging theme within twentieth-first-century science is complexity (Capra 1996, 2002). One example is the study of complex health networks (Freeman 2004; Scott 2000). While this perspective has been an important part of medical sociology since the 1970s, primarily in terms of explaining the role that social support and kinship networks play in promoting health and well-being, the latest advances in the study of complex networks (e.g., small worlds, scale-free networks) are providing new insights into the processes by which diseases spread and the ways that health care providers can improve the health and well-being of large populations (Watts 2004).

As these two new themes suggest, the theoretical framework of medical sociology continues to change to meet the new and contextually grounded needs of health care providers and patients. Medical sociology is—and remains—a theoretically rich area of study.

CONCLUSION

Medical sociology is a rich and diverse field that has, in its short history, gone through an appreciable amount of institutional and intellectual development. Some of these changes have been good, as in the case of the continuing application of sociological theory to the field. Others, such as the continued institutional difficulties medical sociology has had in finding a home in both sociology and medical education, continue to plague the field, both in terms of its legitimacy and the impact of its ideas. Despite these struggles, medical sociology remains an important part of the sociological family and the field of health care. This is particularly evident given the increasing relevance that health and health care issues have—along with a "sociological understanding" of these issues—to the global world in which we now live. Following a tradition that emphasizes theoretical relevance, the current generation of medical sociologists are once again embracing the latest theoretical advancements in sociology (e.g., network analysis, complexity science, globalization) and advancing them to help us better understand (as a global society) the evolving patterns of social relationship we call health and health care.

34

THE SOCIOLOGY OF LAW

ROBIN STRYKER

University of Minnesota

Sociology's canonical classical theorists, Karl Marx, Max Weber, and Émile Durkheim, confronted dramatic societal transformations. Studying law was a central task for Durkheim and Weber, as they sought to understand, explain, and predict the interrelated changes in technology, economy, polity, and culture constituting the rise of democratic capitalism (Sutton 2001; Stryker 2003). At the dawn of the twenty-first century, sociologists again confront profound and interrelated macrotechnological, institutional, and cultural transformations. These are reshaping everything from the nature of work, employment, and economic careers; to political institutions, policies, and culture; to religious and family life. Again, law is an important object of sociological inquiry. As did the classical theorists, contemporary sociological researchers of law provide windows into possible, alternative, or likely futures for national and global political economies and cultural life (Dezalay and Garth 1996, 2002; Stone 2004).

This chapter reviews sociological treatments of what law is and how it works, how law is produced and what law in turn produces, and how law relates to other aspects of social life. Understanding how law works requires not only considering legal rules or doctrine but also—and especially—legal actors or action and legal structures or institutions.

The first section provides entrée by discussing classical theories of law and social change that continue to shape the field. The second section addresses the question: What is law? Sociologists with different answers to this question likewise ask different questions and have different ideas about how law works in society. The third through fifth sections review legal sociologists' key contributions to answering basic questions that motivate sociology as a

scholarly field: (1) Who does what, how, and why? (2) Who gets what, how, and why? Studies of law's legitimacy, of legal culture and consciousness, and of legal mobilization and obedience to law respond especially to the first question. Studies of how legal rules/schemas, resources, and institutions reinforce or undercut economic and social inequalities respond especially to the second. Studies of how legal norms shape and are reshaped by social norms and of the causes, mechanisms, and consequences of legal change respond to both.

THE CLASSICS

Classical sociological perspectives on law are identified primarily with Karl Marx, Max Weber, and Émile Durkheim. Excellent in-depth reviews of their perspectives are available in Sutton (2001) and Trevino (1996), who also cover Sir Henry Maine's evolutionary theories and Cesare Beccaria's classical criminology. Remembered today primarily for proposing that modernization involved moving from legal rights and duties based on status deriving from family relations to legal rights and duties based on contract or bargains between individuals, Maine is an important precursor to Durkheim and Weber. With its intense criticism of the European penal institutions of the eighteenth century, Beccaria's *On Crime and Punishment* prefigures Durkheim's preoccupation with punishment theory and practice and links to contemporary treatises on penology (Foucault 1979; Garland 1990).

Durkheim's [1893] (1933) ideas on law, crime, and punishment are an important part of *The Division of Labor in Society,* his doctoral dissertation promoting sociology as a new professional field. In *The Division of Labor,* Durkheim provided an evolutionary theory of economic modernization that found its key indicators in the changing nature of law. A rudimentary division of labor was associated with *mechanical solidarity,* a type of moral bond based on similarity. A more advanced division of labor was associated with *organic solidarity,* a type of social bond based on difference. Durkheim classified law according to whether legal sanctions were penal/retributive, emphasizing punishment, or restitutive, emphasizing compensation for harm. These two kinds of sanctions became observable indicators for mechanical and organic solidarity. In lieu of Maine's idea of transition from status to contract or Marx's idea of class conflict as the motor force of economic transformation, Durkheim thought that the signpost of societal development was an increasing division of labor. This would be accompanied by a rising preponderance of organic solidarity. Thus, for Durkheim, the path of societal transformation was evidenced by an increasing preponderance of restitutive law over repressive law.

Durkheim's sociological classification of law served as an indicator for presumed normative *effects* of the increasing division of labor. But these effects—organic solidarity—also had a function (or secondary feedbacks) that reinforced and promoted the division of labor itself, by increasing social regulation and social integration (Durkheim [1893] 1933). Similarly, Durkheim distinguished "negative" from "positive" restitutive law and assumed that the two types indicated different stages in the transition from mechanical to organic solidarity (Sutton 2001). Negative restitutive law protected actors from particular interferences or harms and was exemplified by property and tort law. Positive restitutive law facilitated economic and social ties or improved disputing actors' circumstances and was exemplified by family law, administrative law, contract law, commercial law, and constitutional law.

Durkheim's laudable goal of formulating empirically testable hypotheses is marred by difficulties in operationalization, most notably his unwarranted assumptions about equivalent rates of translation of uncodified repressive and restitutive *customs* into codified and thus measurable repressive and restitutive *laws*. Substantial empirical research since Durkheim's time shows that his presumption of little restitutive law in societies lacking substantial division of labor is false. However, his argument that the division of labor in its *normal* as opposed to *pathological* forms produced solidarity rather than alienation and class oppression was an important attempt to refute Marx's theory of economic and social development.

Marx, like Durkheim, viewed law predominantly as a dependent variable rather than as an independent variable in social change. Indeed, Marx's historical-materialist philosophy of history relegated law to superstructure—an expression or reflection of changing economic modes of production. For Marx, changing modes of production—from, for example, the ancient slave societies of Greece and Rome, to feudalism, to capitalism, to socialism and communism—result from class conflict. Each mode of production entails its own characteristic means of production, for example, land in feudalism and capital in capitalism. Each production mode likewise entails its own characteristic class structure and conflicts between owners and nonowners of private property in its means of production, for example, between nobles and serfs in feudalism and between proletariat and bourgeoisie in capitalism. In the grand sweep of Marx's historical materialism, law primarily references economic categories of property, class, and labor as it codifies preexisting production relations in economy and society.

In historical materialism's general tenets, law is like the state, political, and cultural ideologies and religion in reflecting or following changing class relations of exploitation without being a force in producing them (Sutton 2001). This is an oversimplified, deeply flawed account. But Marx's journalistic writings and his empirically oriented writings on capitalism reveal a more nuanced treatment. For example, his analysis of the nineteenth-century Factory Acts in England presents law as being an object and outcome of class struggle rather than simply reinforcing bourgeois domination. In *Capital,* Marx suggests that the Factory Acts, restricting the work day's length, resulted from persistent working-class mobilization (Edelman and Stryker 2005).

Similarly, a young Marx wrote essays about law pertaining to theft of wood while the Rhine Assembly was debating a proposed law against gathering wood in Rhenish forests. Marx criticized the proposed law for what he assumed would be its effects—state legal mobilization in defense of expanding unequivocal private property interests of forest owners and against peasants' customary "use-rights . . . [to] dead timber" from the forests that had accompanied the prior mixed regime of private and common-use property (Trevino 1996:100). For Marx, the proposed law was unjustly vague in failing to distinguish between gathering wood that had dried and fallen on its own—subject to the common-use custom—versus gathering wood the peasants felled themselves—arguably an assault against forest owners' property rights. Illustrative of a talented scholar and activist's multiple strands of thought, Marx the journalist fought the proposed law on theft of wood, hoping his critique could make a difference. Marx the historical materialist would have predicted precisely such legal shenanigans and contradictions as those outlined by Marx the journalist.

Of all classical sociologists, Weber provided the most foundation for more contemporary sociology of law (Swedberg 2002; Edelman and Stryker 2005). Weber wrote on state legitimacy stemming from a belief in legality based on state action adhering to formal-rational rules (Hyde 1983; Tyler 1990; Stryker 1994). His detailed historical, comparative research included studies of law and the rise of capitalism, in which he consistently emphasized law's centrality for transforming and legitimating economic organization and activity (Ewing 1987; Stryker 2003).

According to Weber ([1921] 1978), for political stability, raw power must be converted to legitimated authority. Tradition served as the dominant source of legitimating political order in premodern societies, and charisma could serve as a source of legitimacy for rulers in societies undergoing institutional transition. But where charismatic leaders derive authority from their unique personal characteristics and traditional leaders derive authority from behavior in accord with what was done in the past, the legitimacy of modern democratic-bureaucratic states rests on belief in legality. Democratic leaders take office pursuant to legal rules and derive their authority from being bound by legal rules. Bureaucratic officials derive authority from impartial application of formal rules in accord with expertise derived from educational training and credentials. Authority adheres to the office—and to officials as incumbents of offices—rather than to persons.

Weber's systematization of his life's work, in *Economy & Society* [1921] (1978), emphasized interconnections among economic, political, legal, and religious action and institutions. According to Weber, rationalization of law was "a corollary to the rise of capitalism, the democratic-bureaucratic nation state and the advance of science and technology" and resulted from continuous power struggles, including those between state and church and among diverse status groups (Stryker 2003:338). In turn, legal rationalization promoted and reinforced rationalization of structure and action in other arenas of social life, including especially the economy.

Scholars continue to debate the meaning and adequacy of many aspects of Weber's arguments for the conjoint rise of formal-legal rationality and of capitalism (see, e.g., Trubek 1972; Ewing 1987; Trevino 1996; Swedberg 2002). Still, some key features of the argument seem clear and unassailable. Trevino (1996) suggests important reasons that Weber presumed the rise of formal-legal rationality facilitated capitalist economic behavior and institutions.

First, stable rules providing legal rights and guarantees to parties to exchange operate to increase predictability and certainty in contracting. Guaranteeing that contracts will be enforced according to known rules increases the likelihood that promises will be kept. All this encourages people to make contracts and to engage in other types of business activity on which market exchange depends. This increases the probability of developing market exchange, which, in turn, provides more opportunities for contract and business law to grow, diffuse, and adapt to new economic circumstances. Weber understood that markets and economic exchange could exist without legal enforcement of contracts. But without such enforcement, emergence of a full-blown capitalist economic system would be unlikely.

Second, formal legal rationalization promoted rational capitalism by making available new tools, especially the legal ideas of agency, negotiability, and the legal person. For Weber, all three of these ideas probably were necessary conditions for the development of economic action and institutions with a high degree of calculability, predictability, and systematization (Stryker 2003). Without the idea of agency—allowing one person (the agent) to represent another (the principal) with that other's consent—and without negotiable instruments—legal documents such as checks, bank notes, and bills of exchange that represent in writing an unconditional promise to pay—commercial transactions would be much harder and more risky, though not impossible.

In addition, the idea of the juristic or legal person makes expectation, liability, and responsibility, instead of magic, prophecy, or privilege, the core focus of contracts (Trevino 1996). This facilitates and regulates exchange relations, as does knowing where each officer and member of a business organization stands with relation to each other and to other firms. Such knowledge would be impossible without the idea of the business organization as a legal person—a legitimate economic actor and party to a contract with legal standing to ensure that the contract be enforced.

Third, the idea of legal personhood makes business organizations bearers of universal rights and duties entitled to formal equal treatment under law. The idea of the juristic person connects "rule of law" and "belief in legality in the polity [to] the construction and reproduction of capitalist ideologies, actors and institutions" (Stryker 2003:339).

In sum, Weber believed sensibly that legal tools such as agency, negotiable instruments, and the legal person were necessary preconditions but not in themselves sufficient for "a full blown formal and purposive rationalization of economic life" (Stryker 2003:239). Full-blown capitalism emerged from the confluence of many factors, including prior economic and legal preconditions and diverse political and religious factors. Where legal innovation functioned as a *necessary* condition for institutionalization, diffusion, and growth of capitalist forms of economic organization, Weber also suggested that the "ethic" of Protestantism was a sufficient albeit *not* a necessary condition for the rise of a capitalist "ethos" (Stryker 2003).

Notwithstanding empirical errors in Weber's work, including in his treatment of non-Western law, Weber's scholarship provides a starting point for much contemporary sociological inquiry into law, social order, and social change. This is appropriate because Weber demonstrates convincingly that law helps constitute and mobilize economic, political, and cultural actors, norms, values, interests, and power. Law also is a source of political-economic and cultural meaning. Revisiting Weber naturally leads to discussing contemporary ideas and findings from the sociology of law.

WHAT IS LAW AND HOW DOES IT WORK?

There may seem to be almost as many concepts of law as there are sociolegal scholars. But the concepts fall under a small number of broad categories that include law as social control, law as rule or institutionalized doctrine, law as resource, and law as legality. Whereas some concepts emphasize "law on the books," others highlight "law in action." Whereas some are especially conducive to thinking about legal actors, action, and interaction, others are especially useful for thinking about legal institutions or fields. All concepts embody ideas about how human agency relates to social structure, capturing sociology of law's dual focus on social action and social organization and institutions.

Inspired by Durkheim, scholars studying crime, law, and punishment tend to define law by its societal function as an institutionalized system of social control (e.g., Davis 1962; Spitzer 1975; Black 1976). For example, Davis (1962) stated that "law is defined as a formal means of social control that involves the use of rules that are interpreted, and are enforceable by the courts of a political community" (quoted in McIntyre 1994:10). Black (1976) defined law as "governmental social control . . . in other words, [law is] the normative life of a state and its citizens, such as legislation, litigation and adjudication" (p. 2).

The social control concept of law invites research on punishment theory and practice and on how law relates to social custom, morality, and power (e.g., Foucault 1979; Lanza-Kaduce et al. 1979; Garland 1990; Savelsberg 1992, 2002). Similarly, this concept promotes investigating how criminal and civil sanctions operate as external constraint or as behavioral standards that people internalize through socialization. It also spurs research on how formal and informal control mechanisms interrelate and on how legal actors and organizations such as police, prisons, courts, and regulatory agencies operate (e.g., Black 1989; Grasmick and Bursick 1990; Tyler 1990; Yeager 1990; Ayres and Braithwaite 1992).

Introductory sociology texts introduce the idea of law as a particular *type* of norm when discussing the broader concept of norms as patterned rules or expectations for behavior (Farley 1998:67). Thus, law as social control brings front and center questions about the relationship between legal and social norms while also distinguishing between law proper—rules enacted and enforced by formal state institutions—and other social norms or rules for behavior. Such other norms include customs and also formal rules enacted by nonstate institutions, including the due process grievance procedures that American firms adopted in response to post–World War II legislation and judicial rulings governing the workplace and social welfare provision (Bohannan 1965; Lempert and Sanders 1986; Sutton et al. 1994; Dobbin and Sutton 1998).

Because norms are rules, accounts of law as social control resemble doctrinal legal scholars' conceptualization of law as rules. But where traditional legal scholars typically think about rules expressed in written, institutionalized doctrine—"black-letter law," legal codes, and court opinions—sociologists of law typically are less interested in such law "on the books" than in what law and society scholars call "law in action" (see Cotterrell 1995;

Friedman 1995; Trevino 1996). Law-in-action research examines how law is socially produced and what are its social consequences. Calls to study law in action accompanied the mid-1960s founding of the Law & Society Association and produced rich, variegated insights and findings. A key contribution has been to highlight gaps between what law on the books says—or appears to say—and how legal actors and institutions, including prosecutors, courts, prisons, and regulatory agencies, operate in practice (Lempert and Sanders 1986; Black 1989; Friedman 1995; Stryker 2003).

Some sociologists of law question the utility of the concept of law as rules, promoting instead a concept of law as legality. In their influential *The Common Place of Law*, Patricia Ewick and Susan Silbey (1998) invoke legality to

> refer to the meanings, sources of authority and cultural practices that are commonly recognized as legal regardless of who employs them or for what ends. In this rendering, people may invoke and enact legality in ways neither approved nor acknowledged by the [formal] law . . . Rather than something outside of everyday social relations, legality is a feature of social interaction that exists in those moments when people invoke legal concepts and terminology associating law with other social phenomena. (Pp. 22, 32)

The idea of law as legality grew out of—and has further promoted—much current research on legal consciousness, exploring how law is experienced, understood, and enacted by people in their interactions with formal-legal authorities and in their everyday lives (Sarat 1990; Ewick and Silbey 1998, 2003; Boyle 2002; Hoffman 2003; Hull 2003; Marshall 2003; Saguy 2003; Nielson 2004). Law as legality also is associated with substantial research on legal mobilization as a strategy for promoting change in law and the state, as well as in broader economic, social, and cultural concepts and practices (Fuller, Edelman, and Matusik 2000; Kostiner 2003; Stryker 2003; Edelman and Stryker 2005). To the extent that scholars of legality consider that they *supplement* rather than *replace* prior sociological focus on formal-legal actors' organization and behavior, including interpretation and application of formal legal rules, law as legality begins to merge with a rule-resource concept of law (Stryker 2003; Edelman and Stryker 2005). Both rule-resource and law as legality concepts anticipate that formal-legal institutions and action will be constructed and their consequences for society played out through *political* and *cultural* processes. As well, they both point toward investigating how symbols, ideologies, and enactments of legality spill over and change across boundaries of formal-legal institutions and other fields of social life (Stryker 2003; Edelman and Stryker 2005).

Stryker (2003) proposed merging the idea of law as rule with the idea of law as resource to provide a concept of law that, like the idea of law as legality, emphasizes the agency-structure duality of all social life. The rule-resource concept is broadly institutionalist and thus a good fit with the growing popularity of institutional perspectives among sociologists more generally (see Edelman and Suchman 1997; Steinberg 2003; Pedriana and Stryker 2004). Stryker (2003) suggests that the rule-resource concept especially helps show how law shapes and is shaped by inequality and how legal and social change are interrelated (see also Stryker 1994; Dezalay and Garth 1996, 2002; Fligstein and Stone Sweet 2002; Edelman and Stryker 2005).

The rule-resource concept suggests that law contains rules, operating as resources for actors in and outside legal institutions. Key terms—rules and resources—are defined broadly so that rules encompass any "generalized procedures applied to the enactment/reproduction of social life" (Giddens 1984:2). Both doctrinal rules emphasized by lawyers and the orienting schema emphasized by scholars of legality receive empirical attention. Similarly, sociologists of law must attend both to state law and to the nonstate but lawlike formalized procedures that increasingly pervade the workplace. As do ideas of law as legality, the rule-resource concept points to examining boundaries between formal law and other institutional spheres, including the economy, polity, school, and family.

Both human attributes and nonhuman objects and tangible and intangible objects are positive resources toward meeting actors' goals or interests to the extent that they can be used to attain, enhance, or maintain those goals. When actors use law strategically to get what they want—whether money, power, social status, or self-esteem—legal rules operate as cultural resources that are mobilized instrumentally. When legal rules provide interpretive scripts to help actors define and understand and/or evaluate themselves, others, and their situations, they are resources operating—often unselfconsciously—in constitutive or normative fashion. Thus, law shapes social action and institutions through *cognitive or constitutive, normative, and instrumental* social mechanisms (Stryker 2003; Edelman and Stryker 2005). Because all institutions, and not just formal-legal ones, embody both rules for behavior and resource arrays, the rule-resource concept also invites inquiry into how legal resource arrays shape and are shaped by resources provided in other institutional fields, including the economy and polity. Studies of law and inequality focus on this question and the prior one of for whom, and how, legal rules provide resources.

LAW AND SOCIAL ACTION

One major category of research on law and social action focuses on why most people in most places most of the time obey the law and what causes variation in law violation (see, e.g., Grasmick and Bursick 1990; Tyler 1990). Studies of law's legitimacy are part of this first category, while bridging to a second category of focus on legal culture, consciousness, and mobilization. A third category focuses on how and why laws are enacted and how cognitive, normative, and instrumental mechanisms come

together to produce the political and institutional processes through which laws on the books are interpreted and enforced in action (Stryker 2000b, 2003; Edelman and Stryker 2005).

One explanation for obedience to law emphasizes deterrence, while another highlights legitimacy. Though often treated as competing, the two perspectives may well provide complementary accounts, each of which provides insight but neither of which is sufficient. Deterrence theory posits that crime and refraining from crime are products of rational choice.

> Given the opportunity to commit a criminal act, the person presumably weighs the costs and rewards of doing so in comparison to other behavioral options. The more the person presumes that "legal sanctions [will be] certain, swift and/or severe, the greater is the perceived cost of crime and thus the possibility of deterrence." (Williams and Hawkins 1986:547)

With expected costs held constant, as the expected rewards from crime go up, the deterrent effect of legal sanctions should diminish. Opportunity is a scope condition for this model; if there is no opportunity for criminal behavior, we cannot test whether or not deterrence works. When a person has the opportunity to commit a crime but refrains from doing so because he or she fears sanctions, including fine, imprisonment, or execution, deterrence is operating.

Deterrence scholarship distinguishes between general and specific deterrence (Williams and Hawkins 1986). General deterrence occurs when people refrain from crime due to perceived threat or fear of sanctions. Specific deterrence pertains to the subset of persons who have experienced legal sanctions. If such persons avoid further crime because they fear they will be punished, this constitutes specific deterrence (Williams and Hawkins 1986).

Early empirical research on deterrence varied the likelihood and severity of punishment (for reviews, see Zimring and Hawkins 1973; Blumstein, Cohen, and Nagin 1978; Gibbs 1986). Implicitly or explicitly, researchers presumed that variation in respondents' *perceptions* of the likelihood, swiftness, or severity of sanctions tracked variation in whether and how sanctions were applied (Grasmick and Bursick 1990). Consistent with Williams and Hawkins's (1986) admonition to theorize "the perceptual processes implied by the [rational choice deterrence] model" and directly measure the impact of "perceptual variables" (pp. 548, 549) more recent research has examined the impact of variation in *perceptions* of the likelihood and severity of sanctions.

Where cross-sectional perceptual studies consistently found that perceived certainty had a negative impact on self-reported criminal behavior, only one study found a significant negative effect of perceived severity on self-reported crime (Jensen, Erickson, and Gibbs 1978; Paternoster et al. 1982; Williams and Hawkins 1986). Most cross-sectional studies suffer from a "temporal order problem."

Since perceptions [were] measured after law violations [had] taken place, . . . the analysis . . . may indicate that individuals who were actively involved in crime in the past have lower perceptions of certainty and severity in the present precisely because they have escaped being caught and punished for their crimes. (Williams and Hawkins 1986:551)

Correcting the temporal order problem, panel research examined whether or not perceptions of certainty and severity remained stable over time and whether or not such perceptions at Time 1 had independent effects on self-reported crime at Time 2. Panel studies showed that perceptions of legal sanctions were unstable over time and their impact was smaller than that previously suggested by cross-sectional studies (Saltzman et al. 1982; Paternoster et al. 1983). But many of these studies were conducted on samples of juveniles, whose experiences and perceptions were not yet fully formed, leaving open the possibility that stability of perception may be greater among adults. Later panel studies on adults showed adult risk perception too may be unstable over time, and researchers have not agreed on the appropriate lag time for measuring perceptions relative to criminal behavior (Piliavin et al. 1986; Williams and Hawkins 1986).

One well-thought-out study asked a random sample of adults in face-to-face interviews about their intentions to cheat on their taxes, engage in petty theft, and drive drunk (Grasmick and Bursick 1990). Perceived certainty of legal sanctions was measured by items tapping the respondent's perception that she would be caught if she engaged in the behavior. Similarly, severity of legal sanctions was measured along a scale tapping the respondent's assessment of how big a problem would be created if she were caught and the courts had decided on the punishment. Using logistic regression to predict whether the respondent *intended* to commit the crime in the future, given her perceptions of certainty and severity today, controlling for gender, age, education, prior offending, and also controlling for the perceived potential for "extralegal" sanctions of shame and embarrassment, perceived threat of legal sanctions had substantial, statistically significant negative effects on intent to commit all three offenses (Grasmick and Bursick 1990).

Much research has examined whether or not execution deters homicide more so than does long-term incarceration. After an influential econometric analysis suggested that the death penalty had substantial deterrent effects, that study received searching criticism as part of a broader inquiry into the impact of legal sanctions on crime rates published by the *National Academy of Sciences* (Erlich 1975; Klein, Forst, and Filatov 1978). In their recent literature review, Radelet and Borg (2000) reported that "the vast majority of deterrence studies have failed to support the hypothesis that the death penalty is a more effective deterrent to criminal homicides than long term imprisonment" (p. 45). For a time, general deterrence was the most-invoked rationale for the death penalty, but this argument

waned as both criminologists and law enforcers became convinced by the research that if the death penalty were to be supported, it must be for reasons other than deterrence (Radelet and Borg 2000).

Piliavin et al.'s (1986) longitudinal study is one of the few measuring the reward as well as the cost side of deterrence logic. The authors specified, estimated, and tested a structural equation model of deterrence on data collected from three populations of respondents at high risk for formal sanctions. They found that self-reported crime rose as the perceived reward expected from committing the crime increased. However, Piliavin et al. failed to find deterrent effects of varying perceived costs. Neither perceived risk of legal nor extralegal sanctions was associated with rates of self-reported crime.

A major controversy concerns how extralegal sanctions are related to formal-legal sanctions and whether or not the former produce deterrence. Much research on the impact of extralegal sanctions presumed a Durkheimian mechanism of internalized social control or a Meadian self and identity mechanism responsive to the attitudes and behaviors of significant others (Williams and Hawkins 1986). Grasmick and Bursick (1990) reconceptualized internalized norms as conscience and argued that offending against one's conscience creates the cost of shame. Similarly, they recast significant others' attitudes in terms of costs—embarrassment—that likewise should decrease the utility of crime. They found that expecting shame had a greater effect on intent to cheat on taxes than did expecting legal sanctions. The impact of shame on intent to drive drunk or engage in petty theft was similar to that of legal punishment, while expecting embarrassment did not significantly affect intent to engage in any of the three behaviors.

Williams and Hawkins (1986) point out that to the extent formal-legal crime control occurs, deterrence is only one of the possible mechanisms. Incapacitation and habituation are two mechanisms independent of both perception and deterrence through which law can have its effects. Perceptual mechanisms outside of deterrence include "enculturation (conform[ity] out of respect for authority), moral condemnation (self-defined dislike of an act) [and] normative validation (seeing others punished reinforces the view that an act is wrong)" (p. 562). Perceptual factors that are part of deterrence include stigma from arrest, attachment costs, and commitment costs. The first and third—loss of self- and social esteem and respect and loss of friends, respectively—tap processes similar to what Grasmick and Bursick (1990) conceive of as shame and embarrassment. The second—the cost of arrest for realizing future goals—is similar to how Grasmick and Bursick (1990) operationalize and examine the direct impact of formal law enforcement.

Adding a final layer of complexity to scholarship on obedience is the idea of law's legitimacy and how this may work independent of or in tandem with deterrence. Theories about the role of legitimacy stem from Weber's seminal treatment discussed earlier. Though the concept of legitimacy has detractors (Hyde 1983), it

> has been considered essential for understanding how legal and social order are maintained. Current approaches contain three themes: legitimacy as cognitive orientation to binding [legal] rules . . . legitimacy as attitudinal approval of those rules; and legitimacy as behavioral consent to those rules. (Stryker 2001a:870)

The behavioral consent tradition typically emphasizes instrumental, interest-based sources of legitimacy beyond the specific cost-benefit analyses of sanctions considered by deterrence researchers (for a review, see Stryker 1994). However, most sociologists of law emphasize cognitive or normative definitions and sources of legitimacy. They suggest that legitimacy is of great social import to the extent that it motivates individuals to obey law even when law's application works against their self-interest (Hyde 1983; Tyler 1990; Stryker 1994). Tyler and his colleagues have conducted the most sustained, influential line of research on the sources and consequences of law's legitimacy for obedience (Tyler, Casper, and Fisher 1989; Tyler 1990, 1994; Lind, Kulick, and Ambrose 1993).

Suggesting that legitimacy has a normative basis, Tyler (1990) argues that its best definition is perceived internalized obligation to obey the law. A secondary definition is attitudinal support of legal authorities or institutions. Deterrence requires enforcement of legal controls and thus is costly to states, but legitimacy produces voluntary compliance. Legitimacy is distinct from personal morality. The latter involves following one's personal sense of right or wrong, independent of formal law, and is akin to Williams and Hawkins's (1986) idea of moral condemnation (Tyler 1990).

Using a representative sample of Chicago adults and focusing on six behaviors including parking violations, littering, petty theft, making noise and disturbing neighbors, speeding on the highway, and drunk driving, Tyler (1990) conducted both cross-sectional and panel analyses. When the dependent variable was legal compliance during the period between Times 1 and 2 of the survey, legitimacy measured at Time 1 (by a scale constructed based on items reflecting internalized obligation to obey) significantly and substantially increased compliance at Time 2, controlling for demographics and diverse attitudinal factors. Among attitudinal controls were variables tapping perceived likelihood of getting caught, that is, deterrence. When assessed independently in a multiple regression including other legitimacy measures, support for police had a weak but statistically significant effect on compliance. Support for courts was statistically insignificant.

In contrast to strong effects found for legitimacy, Tyler's (1990) analyses provided only weak evidence for deterrence. When he examined a possible interaction effect between legitimacy and deterrence, Tyler found that his respondents were "almost equally likely to comply with the law because they view it as legitimate whether they think the likelihood of their being caught is high or low" (p. 63).

Because legitimacy's import proved substantial, Tyler (1990) investigated empirically the sources of variation in law's legitimacy among Chicagoans. Stryker (2001a) summarizes her results as follows:

> Tyler (1990) found that a "process perspective" on procedural justice was a more powerful predictor of law's legitimacy than was an "outcome perspective." The outcome perspective presumes that people assess the fairness of procedures based on the degree to which they feel they can control the *content* of the decision. The process perspective presumes that people focus on more formal criteria like neutrality, impartiality or lack of bias. To some extent, Tyler's (1990) findings echo Weber's assumptions about how rational legal authority is legitimated, since in Tyler's data, people who perceived they had been treated neutrally, impartially, honestly, politely and with respect exhibited enhanced support for police and courts, but the effect of process control was greater than that of decision control. An important caveat is that neither perceived process control nor outcome control was directly related to the measure of legitimacy with the most impact on compliance to law: *perceived obligation to obey.* (P. 8702)

Exploring outcomes ranging from individuals' attitudinal support for judges and courts to corporations' behavioral acceptance of nonbinding arbitration decisions in federal contract and tort disputes, sociologists of law continue to examine how variation in law's legitimacy relates to variation in perceived procedural justice and to variation in subjective and objective desirability of outcomes achieved (Tyler et al. 1989; Lind et al. 1993). Finally, in a separate line of work grounded in experimental results showing that, over time, collective recognition of a binding rule produces the internalization of that rule by many members of the collective, Stryker (1989, 1994, 2000b) examined the relationship between the legal system's incorporation of scientific modes of reasoning and evidence and law's legitimacy. Whereas Weber failed to distinguish clearly between formal-legal and scientific rationalization, later scholars did so. This made it possible for Stryker (1994, 2000b) to theorize the cognitive, normative, and instrumental mechanisms linking legitimacy of litigation processes and results to the expanding role for cause-effect reasoning, scientific experts, and evidence within litigation. Because Stryker (1994, 2000b) focuses especially on how compliance and failure to comply are part of a broader set of processes producing both legal stability and legal change through legal and political mobilization and conflict, her work segues between the topic of obedience to law and the second major category of research on law and social action, that of legal consciousness and mobilization.

Lawrence Friedman (1989) distinguished between legal culture and popular legal culture. The former refers to ideas, ideals, beliefs, values, norms, attitudes, and behavioral predispositions about and toward law held and practiced by those working within formal-legal institutions. For example, the concept of precedent is an important part of American legal culture and of all common- or case-law-oriented legal culture. Without understanding what precedent is and how it works, no lawyer can practice nor can any judge adjudicate disputes by interpreting and applying prior adjudicative law (Shapiro and Stone Sweet 2002). Popular legal culture refers to ideas, ideals, beliefs, values, norms, and behavioral predispositions about and toward law held and practiced by laypeople. The study of popular legal culture, now relabeled legal consciousness, is a current growth enterprise among sociologists of law, who, like their counterparts in other sociological subfields, experienced a cultural turn. Legal consciousness is intimately related to legal mobilization, since "how people envision law affects whether and how people mobilize legal tools at their disposal" (Edelman and Stryker 2005:530, citing Fuller et al. 2000).

Substantial scholarship exists investigating the extent, patterns, and outcomes of mobilization of specific types of law, including labor, employment, and civil rights law (Bumiller 1987; Burstein 1991; Forbath 1991; McCammon and Kane 1997; McCammon 2001). For example, McCammon (2001) analyzed time series data for the period 1948–1978 and found that the filing of unfair labor practice charges by workers increased as union representation elections increased. Examining the post–World War II period, McCammon and Kane (1997) found that the likelihood of court rulings for workers increased as the number of unfair labor charges filed against employers increased. However, this effect became smaller when employer associations also were mobilized.

With respect to legal consciousness more generally, Merry (1985, 1986) observed persons using lower civil and criminal courts to deal with everyday business, family and neighborhood and romantic problems. She found that working-class Americans understood legal rights to be about "control [of] . . . one's property . . . and rights not to be insulted, harassed or hit by neighbors or family members without sufficient reason" (Merry 1985:67). As they gained experience with the courts,

> The meaning of rights shift[ed] . . . Rights bec[a]me resources, not guarantees. They bec[a]me opportunities for action . . . the ideology of formal justice exercises some control . . . but it is not passively received. Definitions of legal rights in social relationships are constructed by litigants and court officials as they deal with day to day problems in court. (Merry 1986:266)

Sarat (1990) investigated the "legal consciousness of the welfare poor" (p. 343) through participant observation at local welfare offices. He concluded that "the welfare poor understand that law and legal services are deeply implicated in the welfare system and are highly politicized.

As a result, they are both uncertain and afraid when they seek legal assistance" (p. 374). Nonetheless, they also hope. While some try to mobilize the technical legal rules of the welfare bureaucracy to fight the bureaucracy, others "try to use law and lawyers to get the welfare bureaucracy to live up to its own raison d'etre" (p. 374). Still others mobilize needs-oriented discourses, appealing to shared humanity of welfare recipients and professionals.

A common theme of research by Sarat (1990), Merry (1985, 1986), and others (e.g., Yngvesson 1988; Conley and O'Barr 1990) is that lay legal understandings are plural, representing both opportunity and constraint. There is built-in pessimism in foundational work on legal consciousness, because plural discourses mobilized by welfare recipients "reaffirm law's dominance even as they are used to challenge the decisions of particular legal officials" (Sarat 1990:374). Law's dominance itself is a key part of sustaining elite power and of the ideological and institutional maintenance of an inegalitarian democratic capitalism (Stryker 2003; Edelman and Stryker 2005). Ewick and Silbey's (1998) book culminated much work on legal consciousness, paving the way for early-twenty-first-century studies on street harassment, sexual harassment, and gay marriage (Hull 2003; Marshall 2003; Saguy 2003; Nielson 2004).

Based on in-depth, face-to-face interviews with more than 100 persons in four New Jersey counties, Ewick and Silbey (1998) suggest that three types of everyday legal consciousness interact to produce law as legality, blurring boundaries between strictly legal and broader social ideas and institutions. Labeling these "before the law," "with the law," and "against the law," the authors show how all three can be identified along four dimensions: normativity, constraint, capacity, and time and space. Respondents exhibiting "before the law" consciousness viewed law as a

> formally ordered, rational, hierarchical system of known rules and procedures . . . relatively fixed and impervious to individual action . . . a realm removed from ordinary affairs by its objectivity [and to which] they turn . . . only when they can imagine their personal problems as having general import . . . Law is understood to be a serious and hallowed space. (Ewick and Silbey 1998:47)

This is similar to law's own partially mythical, partially apt depiction of itself. Even when frustrated at their powerlessness, people exhibiting before the law consciousness defer to legal system claims of autonomy and legitimacy based on formally neutral procedures.

People expressing "with the law" consciousness emphasize law's value as a strategic resource to meet individual rather than collective goals:

> Law is described and "played" as a game, a bounded arena in which pre-existing rules can be deployed and new rules invented to serve the widest possible range of interests and values. It is an arena of competitive tactical maneuvering where the pursuit of self interest is expected and the skillful

and resourceful can make strategic gains. (Ewick and Silbey 1998:48)

When exhibiting "against the law" legal consciousness, people show their

> sense of being caught within the law or being up against the law, its schemas and resources overriding their own capacity either to maintain its distance from their everyday lives or to play by its rules . . . [They] described their attempts at "making do" using what the situation momentarily and unpredictably makes available—materially and discursively—. . . to forge moments of respite from the power of law. (Ewick and Silbey 1998:48)

Here, there is acute appreciation of the power and costs of law and there is momentary, individual-level resistance to evade those costs. Resistance is recounted with pride and a sense of justice. But it is not the sort of resistance that ordinarily leads to collective action to use the law to change the law.

On the one hand, Ewick and Silbey (1998) argue that both the plurality of legal consciousness and the contradictions among the types of consciousness reinforce the overall structure and potency of legality. Recognized violations of "before the law" consciousness may be explained by invoking a "with the law" consciousness, and people readily switch between the two to negotiate everyday life. That the very same people exhibit multiple, contradictory forms of legal consciousness is an important finding. The authors suggest this as a key reason for the durability and power of legal institutions (Ewick and Silbey 1998:230–33).

On the other hand, and in spite of their previous argument, the authors also suggest that sharing stories of resistance with others may bridge between personal resistance and collective action. They argue that "the recognition of these contradictions (i.e., that law is both a transcendent realm of rule bound authority and yet available to resourceful skilled players) is . . . at the heart of resistance" (Ewick and Silbey 1998:233). Avoiding the inconsistent empirical predictions implied by the authors requires future theory and research to address *conditions under which* contradictions among types of legal consciousness reinforce the structures of legality, *conditions under which* contradictions promote individual resistance, and *conditions under which* individual resistance becomes collective resistance. Ewick and Silbey (2003) have begun tackling these issues. However, more must be done to integrate studies of legal consciousness with those of collective action and legal and social change.

A final set of studies on law and social action focus on the politics of legislation and law enforcement (Stryker 2000a). Because politics in the broad sense involves individuals, groups, and organizations mobilizing tangible and intangible resources to influence authoritative decision making in accord with their understandings, interests, and values and also includes how attempts to influence authoritative decision makers are shaped by "rules of the game,"

it includes both institutional and cultural processes (Stryker 2003). It likewise includes both *overt* resource mobilization, countermobilization, and power and the *covert* power that creates nonissues and tends to limit overt power struggles to those taking place well within unchallenged foundational assumptions of democratic capitalism (Stryker 2003; cf. Edelman and Stryker 2005).

Stryker (2000a, 2003) and Edelman and Stryker (2005) review literature on the politics of diverse regulatory and social welfare legislation, interpretation, and enforcement. They may be consulted for more references and details about perspectives used to explain and predict the origins and enforcement of legislative law. Some explanatory perspectives emphasize the costs and benefits of diverse types of legislation to competing economic interests and also the resources available for mobilization by such interest groups. Other perspectives emphasize the political institutions that shape policymakers' and politicians' interests and through which both they and societal groups and organizations must work (cf. Stigler 1971; Wilson, 1980 with Moe 1987; Vogel 1996).

Traditionally, economic and political science variants on these approaches were appropriate for modeling comparative statics but not for understanding dynamics. Meanwhile, the class and historical-institutional perspectives devised by sociologists are less oriented to formal modeling but more focused on understanding and explaining dynamics of law and policy evolution (Stryker 2000a). An increasing amount of empirical research suggests that although theoretical accounts emphasizing politicians' interests and political institutions ordinarily are treated as competing, both perspectives offer partial insight and must somehow be integrated to understand the origins and evolution of legislative law (Stryker 2000a). Politics internal to the enforcement agency combine with conditions in the agency's external environment to shape regulatory legislation and enforcement (Stryker 1989). Technical experts play an important role in regulatory dynamics. Economic analysis is relied on heavily to promote deregulation and procompetitive regulatory reform but is also mobilized to promote more stringent regulation (cf. Yeager 1990; Rose-Ackerman 1992; Vogel 1996 with Stryker 1989).

Sociologists of law have shown

> how regulatory enforcement and cycles of regulation and deregulation evolve over time in response both to structural constraints of a capitalist economy and to active struggles over regulation by classes and class segments . . . many aspects of U.S. regulatory processes make it likely that laws passed against powerful economic actors will be limited in impact or will have unintended effects that exacerbate the problems that initially caused the regulation. (Stryker 2000a:1102)

For example, Yeager (1990) suggests that because the capitalist state depends on taxes from private capital accumulation, it tends to resolve conflict over negative externalities of production, such as pollution, conservatively to protect economic growth. Melnick (1983) shows how the highly structured, narrow, reactive, and adversarial legal processes through which U.S. pollution control takes place have led courts to simultaneously extend the scope of Environmental Protection Agency (EPA) programs while reducing EPA resources to achieve those goals. Yeager (1990) demonstrates that EPA sanctioning decisions, though rational given economic, political, and legal constraints on the agency, reproduce private sector inequality by favoring large corporations that have financial and technical resources.

Skewed financial and technical resources are but one reason that advocates of tough enforcement of laws regulating business are likely to lose out to resource-rich segments of the business community. Another reason emphasized by both Yeager (1990) and Edelman (1992) is the tendency of courts and regulatory agencies policing powerful economic actors to emphasize procedures over substance—a tendency that Edelman (1992) argues is prevalent especially when statutory law is ambiguous. Enforcement processes themselves may increase rather than decrease legal ambiguity (Kelly 2003). Meanwhile, as understandings about costs, benefits, and appropriate trade-offs are negotiated in regulatory arenas, shared cognitive and normative orientations often develop between regulators and regulated parties, leading to ongoing regulatory cultures that sometimes, but not always, amount to the "capture" of government regulators by the interests they are supposed to regulate (Meidinger 1987; Yeager 1990; Ayres and Braithwaite 1992; but see Sabatier 1975; Pedriana and Stryker 1997, 2004).

Part of a larger community of new institutionalist scholars of law and organizations (e.g., Sutton et al. 1994; Dobbin and Sutton 1998; Kelly 2003), Edelman (1992) and her colleagues (Edelman, Uggen, and Erlanger 1999) developed a "managerialist" perspective on civil rights and employment law enforcement. In this perspective, ambiguous statutes, such as Title VII of the Civil Rights Act of 1964, which failed to define discrimination, are interpreted in the first instance by managerial elites who must decide what the law means as they take steps to comply. Managers and human resource professionals engage in a normative process of "organizational mediation" of law in ways consistent with what they already regard as good business practice (Edelman 1992:1531). They absorb the new antidiscrimination requirements mandated by Title VII (and Executive Order 11246, mandating affirmative action for government contractors) into a managerial logic that already assumes that a "legalized" workplace, emphasizing formalized rules and due process grievance procedures, enhances smooth business operation and productivity (Edelman 1992; Sutton et al. 1994). In accord with this logic, managers create formal structures, including affirmative action offices and policies, providing "visible symbols of compliance" both to government regulators and to employees (Edelman 1992:1531).

Presuming that these symbols rarely convert to substantive impact, Edelman et al. (1999) suggest further that as symbolic compliance strategies diffuse broadly, courts will adopt ideas of compliance institutionalized in the economy without inquiring deeply into whether or not these compliance strategies are effective. Formal law itself will become an outcome of, or endogenous to, economic practice in ways that undercut tough enforcement and lessen the law's impact. Because Title VII was enacted in large part to increase the economic equality of African Americans and whites (Pedriana and Stryker 1997), any lessened impact of it or other antidiscrimination legislation due to judges' formal-legal validation of managers' constructions of compliance will leave racial and other inequalities intact. The next section further examines law and inequality.

LAW AND INEQUALITY

Liberal legal philosophy holds that Western legal systems are neutral, impartial as between the parties and autonomous from the rest of society, such that law is indifferent to economic, political, and social inequalities among litigants. "On the books," all have formal equality before judges, courts, and the law (Lempert and Sanders 1986; Friedman 1995, 2005; Trevino 1996). But sociologists of law have shown that economic and social inequalities often produce legal inequalities (Galanter 1974:81); Pedriana and Stryker 2004; Edelman and Stryker 2005). Because dominant classes and social groups have interests in perpetuating their dominance, and because wealth, status, and economic and social power provide myriad resource advantages for influencing legislation, many legal systems purposely enact economic and social stratification systems into law. Examples include historical restrictions on voting based on property and gender prior to the onset of adult universal suffrage in Western Europe and the United States, laws perpetuating second-class citizenship for African Americans in the post-Reconstruction American South, the racial and property laws of South Africa under Apartheid, and laws that continue to perpetuate women's economic and social subordination in North Africa and South Asia (Frederickson 1981; McIntyre 1994; Agarwal 1995; Charrad 2001).

Even legal systems that are formally egalitarian on the books often operate in inegalitarian ways in practice, perpetuating social inequality. For example, much research is devoted to detailing class, race, and gender biases of the American criminal justice system (Liska and Tausig 1979; Frohman 1997; Sampson and Lauritsen 1997; Baldus et al. 1998; Cole 1999; Feld 1999). Most sociologists of law agree that even where democracy, the rule of law, and formal equal access to the legal system exist, law tends to reproduce economic and social inequalities, and there are limits to how, and how much, legal rules can be mobilized as positive resources for economically and socially subordinate groups (Lempert and Sanders 1986; Trevino 1996; Stryker 2003). Previously discussed environmental law research by Yeager (1990) offers an important case in point. Similarly, Stryker (1989) shows how internal conflict within the National Labor Relations Board (NLRB) coupled with political backlash from a unified capitalist class led Congress to dismantle the NLRB's economic unit, reducing the agency's enforcement capacity on behalf of American labor. Galanter's (1974) seminal essay "Why the Haves Come Out Ahead" points to some key reasons why inequality reduction through litigation is limited.

Galanter (1974) distinguished between "one shot players who have only occasional recourse to the courts . . . and repeat players who are engaged in many similar litigations over time" (p. 97). Accused criminals and spouses who file for divorce ordinarily are one-shot players; prosecutors, insurance companies, and major corporations ordinarily are repeat players. Galanter (1974) suggests that the two kinds of players usually have different goals in going to court and find it strategic to "play the litigation game" differently. A one-shot player is concerned with the outcome of her or his particular case—parents fighting over child custody care only about their child's placement, not the general rules in child custody cases. Repeat players, such as large corporations engaged in tort litigation, pick and choose strategically among cases, allocating more resources where more is at stake in legal precedent and financial interest and choosing to settle cases likely to produce legal rulings unfavorable to them. In civil cases, a one-shot player may gain certain monetary compensation by settling. In criminal cases, he or she may settle to avoid maximum penalties such as death or lifetime incarceration.

Additional resources for repeat players include prior familiarity with the particular legal actors and processes adjudicating their cases. Repeat players also find it rational to invest in developing expertise, including ready access to specialist attorneys and other experts. Thus, when any given litigation begins, repeat players already know a great deal about the relevant legal precedents, increasing their capacity to pursue strategically cases likely to produce maximally favorable legal rules. The upshot is that, other things equal, being a repeat player gives the actor mobilizing the courts more litigation-relevant resources. The body of legal precedents produced by litigation between one-shot and repeat players is likely to be skewed systematically in favor of the repeat players (Galanter 1974).

Because lawyers are a type of repeat player (Galanter 1974), access to lawyers gives litigating parties an advantage. Since big companies who are repeat players have enduring relationships with in-house counsel and may routinely retain the same corporate law firms specializing in litigation, this amplifies their advantage. When a one-shot player gains access to a specialized lawyer, this may help balance the scales. But since the highest-prestige, highest-paying jobs in law involve representing high-status, wealthy, and powerful clients (Heinz and Laumann 1983), many skilled lawyers choose to represent "haves." Because retaining lawyers ordinarily is expensive, have-nots may find themselves without lawyers or with lesser-quality legal counsel, though reforms that increase, rather than continue to decrease, availability of legal services to the poor would help the disadvantaged (Galanter 1974; Lempert and Sanders 1986). Increasing the pro bono work done by major law firms also would help. Overloaded criminal and civil court dockets may work in the opposite direction, with financially well-off civil defendants able to use delay to their advantage, and harried public defenders in the criminal justice system lacking time to familiarize themselves with pertinent details of their clients' cases (Galanter 1974).

In American culture, lawyers who work on a contingency basis, receiving as payment a portion of the monetary compensation awarded to plaintiffs in civil cases on the condition that plaintiffs win the case, often are denigrated as "ambulance chasers" especially if they are personal injury lawyers. But contingency fees also increase access of the disadvantaged to attorneys and courts, assuming that prospective counsel deems disadvantaged clients to have strong cases given extant legal precedents. Similarly, public interest law firms "playing for rules" can provide those who ordinarily would be one-shot players with some of the advantages of repeat players (Galanter 1974; Chesler, Sanders, and Kalmuss 1988). In the 1960s, public interest law firms and lawyers devoted themselves almost exclusively to liberal causes. By the mid-1970s, legal organizations devoted to conservative causes entered the scene. Since then, both types have multiplied, sustaining debate around the concept of public interest legal practice (Southworth 2005).

As a testimony to Galanter's influence, in 1999, the *Law & Society Review* published a commemorative issue on his 1974 essay, documenting the continued relevance of his ideas (Grossman, Macauley, and Kritzer 1999). But as Lempert (1999) noted, Galanter's (1974) concern was with a particular type of have-not defined by action in legal institutions. Many sociologists focus instead on the divide between those who are economically, politically, and socially disadvantaged versus those who are not (Lempert 1999; Stryker 2003; Pedriana and Stryker 2004). The two types of haves and have-nots may coincide empirically. But distinguishing them analytically allows us to ask about the impact of reforms that provide to the poor, homeless, minority religious, ethnic and racial groups, women, and workers some of the advantages typical for repeat players (Harris 1999; Stryker 2003; Pedriana and Stryker 2004).

Some scholars are very pessimistic about mobilizing the legal system to mitigate class, race, gender, and other inequalities, but others are more optimistic (cf. Rosenberg 1991 with Chesler et al. 1988). Research by Edelman and colleagues (Edelman 1992; Edelman et al. 1999), reviewed in the previous section, is consistent with Galanter's (1974) observation that equality-producing laws on the books tend not to decrease inequality in practice. But reviews of econometric studies that try to estimate directly the impact of civil rights and antidiscrimination law on workplace inequalities find positive effects of such laws on the economic status of African Americans and white women relative to white males *in some periods* and *under some conditions* (Donahue and Heckman 1991; Reskin 1998; Stryker 2001b; Harper and Reskin 2005). Donahue and Heckman's (1991) exemplary evaluation and critique of extant empirical evidence on the impact of U.S. equal employment law seeks to isolate legal effects, taking into account diverse other factors shaping black-white employment outcomes. They conclude that in conjunction with federal antidiscrimination efforts in voting rights and education, federal equal employment law improved the economic status of African Americans between 1965 and 1975.

Early studies of affirmative action programs suggested that inequality reduction was greatest when companies monitored and rewarded managers for affirmative action performance, just as they did for performance on other business goals such as profitability (see Stryker 2001b). Harper and Reskin's (2005) recent review article emphasized that

> the intensity of employers' AA [affirmative action] efforts has varied with the politics of AA . . . and the impact of AA in employment among federal contractors depends almost entirely on the OFCCP's [Office of Federal Contract Compliance Program] enforcement. (Pp. 367–68)

It is easy to confound the specific impact of affirmative action with the impact of antidiscrimination law more generally and "with increasing human capital among minorities and women" (Harper and Reskin 2005:368). But, as in other legal arenas, it is clear that law's distributional impact on society is shaped profoundly by the politics of court and agency enforcement (Stryker 2000a).

Starting in the mid-1970s, adjudicative rules interpreting American antidiscrimination law began to lose their teeth (Stryker 2001b; Harper and Reskin 2005). Providing historical periodization of Title VII's administrative and judicial enforcement, Pedriana and Stryker (2004) investigate how early interpretations of Title VII may have helped produce the inequality reduction documented by Donahue and Heckman (1991). When it came into being, Title VII was considered a weak law with a weak enforcement agency, the Equal Employment Opportunity Commission (EEOC). From 1965 to 1971, civil rights advocacy organizations in interaction with the EEOC turned weakness into strength. They accomplished this in large part by winning an uphill litigation battle culminating in the Supreme Court's 1971 endorsement of the disparate impact method of proving employment discrimination. This method is based on showing that business practices have a disproportionate negative *impact* on members of minority groups rather than on showing that employers acted with discriminatory *motive* or *intent*. Empirical research has shown that interpretations of legislative law focusing on effects rather than intent tend to maximize the positive impact of legislative laws designed to benefit the disadvantaged (Lempert

and Sanders 1986; Chesler et al. 1988; Pedriana and Stryker 2004).

Pedriana and Stryker (2004) highlight how state legal capacity to promote equality reduction is a moving target, expanding and contracting over time. Aggressive and effective implementation of legislative law designed to benefit the disadvantaged is most likely to happen when there is sustained social movement pressure from below on government law enforcers. Movement pressure enhances the likelihood that enforcement agencies and courts will give such legislation an effects-based rather than intent-based interpretation. This in turn maximizes law's capacity for inequality reduction (Pedriana and Stryker 2004). Sabatier (1975) shows that regulatory agencies that lack sustained social constituencies to push for tough enforcement may create them proactively, thus increasing social communication, technical capacity, and monitoring.

Juxtaposing studies by Sabatier (1975), Pedriana and Stryker (2004), and Chesler et al. (1988) with those of Edelman (1992), Edelman et al. (1999), Stryker (1989), and Burstein (1991) highlights the import of strategies providing the economically and socially disadvantaged with resources normally available to repeat players. Edelman (1992) emphasizes that making individual discrimination victims responsible for bringing enforcement action is a recipe for weakness. However, when advocacy organizations such as the National Association for the Advancement of Colored People (NAACP) Legal Defense Fund took on civil rights and employment litigation at their own expense, providing specialized legal and technical expertise to many clients and coordinating litigation to play for favorable legal rules in key precedent-shaping cases, they increased the egalitarian impact of laws designed to benefit the disadvantaged (Chesler et al. 1988; Pedriana and Stryker 2004).

Equal employment laws provide ways for individual plaintiffs to overcome financial and expertise disadvantages by pooling resources for litigation. For example, the federal government can enter a lawsuit as a party on behalf of alleged individual victims. Class actions are a form of collective action involving the consolidation of many similar individual claims into a single lawsuit played for large stakes in terms of monetary awards and legal precedent (Galanter 1974; Burstein 1991; Stryker 2001b). Examining the impact of legal mobilization on the *final outcomes* of Title VII and other equal employment litigation cases from 1963 (when the Equal Pay Act, mandating that men and women be paid equally for the same work, was adopted) until 1985, Burstein (1991) found a statistically significant and substantial positive effect on plaintiff-employees' chances of winning a discrimination lawsuit when government was a party in the case. He also found class actions to be significantly and positively associated with plaintiff victory. Class actions were the most common form of collective action, with government as a party a distant second, and federal and nonfederal organizations writing amicus briefs an even more distant third. Of course, not all case wins create long-term equality producing legal precedents. Rogers (1990) and Albiston (1999:860) point to the "paradox of losing by winning."

In sum, capitalist democracies, committed to *formal equality,* generally provide unequal effective access to law, influence over law, and treatment by law between economic and social haves and have-nots. Formal equality usually exacerbates rather than mitigates substantive economic and social inequality. Conditions maximizing law's equality-producing impact on society are legislative law that is substantively skewed to provide benefits to the disadvantaged *coupled with* effects-based rather than intent-based legal interpretation and enforcement and also with government enforcement and class actions. The latter, whether brought by government or private plaintiffs, are collective avenues of legal mobilization for collective ends. Sustained social movement pressure from below facilitates effects-based interpretation of legislative law designed to benefit the disadvantaged. Considering law and social movements connects the topics of law and inequality and law and social change.

LAW AND SOCIAL CHANGE

Though sociologists of law agree that legal doctrine and institutions are not autonomous from society, Shapiro and Stone Sweet (2002) provide an especially lucid social science discussion of how precedent functions in "law in action" to create doctrinal path dependencies contributing to evolutionary change in "law on the books." Pedriana and Stryker (1997, 2004) also address the issues of path dependency and policy feedback in legal doctrine and institutions.

Pedriana and Stryker (1997) show how societal and government actors mobilized legal language and the central value of equality already embodied in U.S. antidiscrimination law to redefine the legal concept of equal employment opportunity. The redefined equal opportunity concept included remedial affirmative action aimed at producing equality results. Based on their analyses of equal opportunity symbolic framing, Pedriana and Stryker (1997) suggest that cultural resource construction is a key mechanism through which legal feedbacks more generally occur. As affirmative action policies diffused through American business, these and other legislative law-inspired innovations transformed the American workplace (Edelman 1992; Sutton et al. 1994; Dobbin and Sutton 1998; Edelman et al. 1999; Stryker 2001b).

Recently, Edelman and Stryker (2005) proposed an explicit "political-institutional" theory of the mutually endogenous character of change in law and the economy. Grounded in a broad review of extant scholarly ideas and findings, they suggested that both *overt* legal and political resource mobilization and countermobilization by economic actors and more *covert* diffusion and modification of cultural meanings and norms across the boundaries of legal and economic-organizational fields create a reciprocal

shaping process. In chicken and egg fashion, legal change creates social change creates legal change, and there is a mutually constitutive relationship between law and society.

For example, Dobbin and Dowd (2000) show how a U.S. Supreme Court ruling that unexpectedly upheld key portions of the Interstate Commerce and Sherman Acts set off a politics of mobilization and countermobilization around alternative principles of business competition. Because the Court made collusion among competitors illegal without mandating an alternative, the Court undermined cartels without providing a business replacement. In the competition over alternatives, the greater structural resources of finance capitalists allowed them to prevail, so finance capitalists had a subsequent disproportionate impact on later American business development. Casting law as independent variable to society's role as dependent variable, Dobbin and Dowd (2000) usefully but artificially start their time clock with a particular Supreme Court decision. But political resource mobilization and countermobilization by both economic actors and political figures within extant political and legal institutions also created the Interstate Commerce and Sherman Acts, without which the Court decision discussed by Dobbin and Dowd (2000) could not have occurred. Fligstein and Stone Sweet (2002) explicitly posit and examine empirically the joint construction of European Union (EU) law and EU market integration. Using a combination of quantitative research and qualitative, historical analyses, they find that "contests between the European Court of Justice and national legal regimes affected trade patterns, which in turn spurred more litigation. More litigation both further expanded cross-border trade and promoted EC-level legislation and lobbying, which then increased trade still further" (Edelman and Stryker 2005:539).

With respect to the mutually endogenous relationship between legal change and more general cultural change, Albiston (2005) analyzed interview data from American employees who negotiated workplace leaves pursuant to the 1993 Family and Medical Leave Act. She found that "although the law constructs leave taking as legitimate, implicit [institutionalized] norms about work, gender and disability may construct very different interpretations of the same behavior" (p. 13). Thus, "competing systems of meaning shape workplace rights mobilization . . . and negotiations over FMLA rights can both reinforce and transform deeply entrenched understandings of work, gender and disability" (p. 13). Similarly, Holtzman (2003) found a mutually endogenous relationship between more general *cultural* concepts of good parenting and the *legal* concepts of good parenting pervading child custody litigation between biological and nonbiological parents. Stryker (2003, 2006) reviews substantial literature on how law shaped the "exceptionalism" of the American labor movement in comparative perspective. She shows how change in U.S. legal doctrine and institutions and change in ideologies, behavior, and institutional forms of the U.S. labor movement were mutually endogenous through political-institutional processes involving cognitive, normative, and instrumental social mechanisms.

Clearly, much of the research described in previous sections of this chapter pertains to law and social change as well as to the topics under which it was described. Studies of regulatory origins likewise are studies of legal change. Many studies of law enforcement, including especially those focusing on dynamics, are at least implicitly—and sometimes explicitly—about mutually endogenous legal and social change. Studies examining law's distributional and redistributional effects on economy, polity, and society likewise speak to issues of law and social change, as do many studies of legal consciousness and mobilization. As highlighted in the previous section, social movements combining legal mobilization and broader political mobilization are a key mediating factor among law on the books, law in action, and social change. Not only are social movements important for understanding the mobilization and impact of law, law also is important for understanding the nature and course of social movements (McCann 1998; Pedriana 2006).

Asking "how and to what degree can [social movements] work through . . . legal traditions to advance their cause," McCann (1998:82) notes that "movements from the start are embedded within a (more or less) legally constituted environment rather than outside the law." Broad political movements of marginalized groups can be promoted by highlighting legal rights, as activists mobilize legal norms to name, claim, blame, and recruit new activists (McCann 1998). Thus, law is a central part of the opportunity structure for social movements (Pedriana 2006). High-profile court cases offer excellent opportunities for media publicity, popular mobilization, and broader cultural framing to accompany litigation. Thus, as McCann (1998) notes, movements can produce desired social changes even when they do not win lawsuits. Conversely, when movement opponents mobilize law, this may undermine the efficacy of the movement (see also Forbath 1991; McCammon and Kane 1997).

In sum, and consistent with research reviewed in the section on law and inequality, exactly how much and in what ways law matters for social movements and for legal and social change depends on "a variety of extralegal factors" as well as on formal-legal action and institutions (McCann 1998:85). Litigation is most effective in producing social change when it is combined with broader political activities (Sabatier 1975; McCann 1998; Pedriana and Stryker 2004). Kostiner (2003) points out that social change has multiple definitions. These include specific, measurable results, the creation of mass movements, and the transformation of thoughts. Kostiner (2003) reframes debates on law and progressive social change around the empirical question of how activists conceive of this relationship. She finds three general operating schemas: law as a way to acquire concrete resources, law as empowerment, and a vision of social change as transformation of thought—in which law plays a role, but one that is marginal.

CONCLUSION

Especially with its focus on law, legitimacy, politics, culture, the economy, and social change, contemporary sociology of law circles back to the classical sociological theorists, building on their insights and correcting their mistakes. At the dawn of the twenty-first century, American sociologists of law also are becoming increasingly drawn to global and comparative perspectives and topics on the interrelationships among diverse types of legal and social change. Drawing on world polity perspectives, legal sociologists have focused on changing human rights law and its impact (Boyle 2002; Dezalay and Garth 2002). Drawing on political and institutional perspectives, they have compared the evolution of race laws in France and Britain (Bleich 2003), examined how French feminist activists and legal actors responded to American sexual harassment law (Saguy 20003), and explored variation in evolution of family law and gender relations in North Africa (Charrad 2001). Research on "cause lawyers" likewise has gone global (Sarat and Scheingold 2001). Other research on the changing legal profession mobilizes Bourdieu's perspective on power struggles among actors drawing on diverse types of social and cultural capital to illuminate the construction of international business arbitration as a legal field (Dezalay and Garth 1996). Still other research shows the conjoint growth and asymmetric power relations in global political fields between actors and institutions oriented to economic liberalism and those oriented to human rights (Dezalay and Garth 2002). Constructing the EU as a multilevel legal-institutional system likewise is a subject of growing interest, as is cross-national research on regulatory law and politics and comparative and historical research on international and national law and the economy (Stryker 2000a; Carruthers, Babb, and Halliday 2001; Fligstein and Stone Sweet 2002; Stone 2004; Stryker 2006).

The upswing in comparative and global foci among sociologists of law should continue for the foreseeable future. Similarly, studies of legal consciousness and legal mobilization, legitimacy and the rule of law, and political and institutional perspectives on interlinked legal and social ideas, actors, institutions, order, and change are likely to continue. In sum, sociology of law in the twenty-first century remains grounded in questions of societal transformation that motivated sociological theorists of the nineteenth and early twentieth centuries. However, given the cumulative number of theoretically rich, empirical studies of law that now exist, future legal sociologists attempting grand theory of the scope of a Marx, Durkheim, or Weber will be far more informed empirically than were the classical sociological theorists of law and society.

35

MILITARY SOCIOLOGY

DAVID R. SEGAL

University of Maryland, College Park

THE FOUNDATIONS

As sociology evolved as a discipline in the nineteenth and twentieth centuries, it was strongly influenced by the ideological and humanistic concerns of the day. Military organization and war as a social process were given little attention. However, the institutional presence of the military was acknowledged. Herbert Spencer (1908), an early social Darwinist, saw social organization evolving from primitive military forms to advanced industrial societies. In contrast, Karl Marx and his followers saw military forces as necessary for the imperialism that capitalist industrial societies would have to pursue as they exhausted domestic raw materials and markets. More frequently, the military provided the organizational context within which theorists who were concerned with grand narratives addressed general substantive concerns. For example, Max Weber (1968), in his economic sociology, acknowledged the role of the military as the agent of the state for the legitimate monopolization of organized violence and drew heavily on the Prussian Army as the prototype for his general model of bureaucratic organization, and Émile Durkheim (1951) viewed participation in the military as one of the social conditions affecting the rate of suicide in his study of social integration. It is still the case that sociologists whose primary interest is not the military institution use the military as a site for research on a range of more general social phenomena (e.g., Bryant 1979).

Spencer's expectations have not been realized in the modern world. Most major industrial societies are also military powers, and neo-Marxist scholars point to the role of the military in international capitalist expansion. In many nations, such as Switzerland and Israel, the military plays a major integrative role in society. In developing nations, the military has repeatedly played a significant role in modernization, although there is little consensus on the reasons for this. Even in modern nations, where the military frequently plays a less central role, it is likely to affect the lives of a large proportion of the population through its impact on economic, political, familial, and educational institutions. In the early twenty-first century, one cannot read a newspaper in any major city in the world without being struck by the impact of the military. In contrast, if one's reading were confined to sociology journals, one might not know that the military existed.

EARLY 20TH CENTURY

Boene's (2000) analysis of the growth of military sociology in the United States reflects its slow start. Of his catalog of publications in the field, only about 5 percent were published before 1942. He attributed the slow growth of the field largely to ideological liberalism, a meliorist orientation to social problems within the discipline, and war weariness after World War I. This was not to say that war and the military were disregarded by social science generally. Many of the early contributions were by psychologists and political scientists, and while this ultimately produced an interdisciplinary orientation in "military sociology" that

AUTHOR'S NOTE: The preparation of this chapter was supported in part by the Army Research Institute under Contract W74V8H-05-K-0007. The interpretations presented here are solely those of the author.

353

has continued, it also emphasized less sociological objects and units of analysis. Psychologists, particularly during World War I, focused on individual abilities and behavior and sought to make contributions through the development of aptitude testing for the military (Yerkes 1921) and the understanding of effectiveness (Munson 1921). Since then, military forces have been drawing on the contributions of psychologists, particularly in the areas of psychometrics and training.

Political scientists, for their part, sought to understand war as part of the process of international relations, reflected, for example, in Charles Merriam's project on the causes of war, conducted at the University of Chicago with support from the Social Science Research Council. This project ultimately led to Quincy Wright's (1942) seminal study of war. Little attention was paid to the military as a social institution, an organization, an occupation, or a profession.

WORLD WAR II

The World War II period was a turning point both for the sociological study of the military and for sociology generally. The United States mobilized large numbers of academic sociologists, and other social scientists, in a variety of research and analysis roles in support of the war effort. Thus, the field of military sociology was initially dominated by Americans. Because the problems studied, like most important social issues, were not contained within the boundaries of a single discipline, these sociologists established a pattern of interdisciplinary collaboration, particularly with social psychologists. Because the army was the largest service, military sociology emerged primarily as the sociology of ground combat forces. And because the research was aimed explicitly at helping to manage the army and the war, it emerged primarily as an applied field—one oriented toward organizational and small-group processes rather than toward national or transnational concerns. As a policy science, it was concerned with army policies regarding soldiers and small units, rather than national policies regarding the army, and because of the nature and size of the mobilization, it focused primarily on the enlisted ranks rather than the officer corps.

Many of the sociologists who were mobilized in nonresearch roles in World War II recorded their experiences and observations in the sociological literature, for example, George C. Homans's (1946) observations of social relations on a small warship, which ultimately contributed to his formulation of exchange theory, and Tamotsu Shibutani's (1978) study of demoralization in a company of Japanese American soldiers. Reuben Hill (1949) conducted a landmark study of the stress that military service imposes on families, a topic that has come dramatically to the fore in the twenty-first century. The field of military sociology was greatly enriched by the contributions of sociologists who did not specialize in the military but had

recorded their wartime observations. Indeed, in 1946, the major sociological journal of the day, *American Journal of Sociology,* published a special issue titled "Human Behavior in Military Society." This issue included Arnold Rose's (1946) study of military social structure, Alfred Lindesmith's (1946) observations of the effects of their status in service on the self-esteem of teachers, and August Hollingshead's (1946) article on adjustment to army life and to subsequent civilian life. Sociologists from other specialties continued to use the military as a venue for research and theorizing in the post–World War II years and to enrich the field by doing so. This trend has continued into the twenty-first century.

World War II also saw the War Department drawing on the knowledge of manpower economists to help manage the personnel assets of the nation in support of the war (e.g., Ginzberg et al. 1959). This disciplinary perspective has become increasingly important within the U.S. Department of Defense (DoD) in the decades since World War II.

The major substantive sociological knowledge base of the field in the World War II period, as well as major conceptual and methodological advances in the discipline of sociology, came from the reporting of the results of experiments and surveys conducted by the Information and Education Division of the War Department. This program demonstrated the permeability of the boundary between social research and personnel management. The four volumes of *Studies in Social Psychology in World War II,* including the two-volume *American Soldier* studies authored by Samuel A. Stouffer and his colleagues (Stouffer, Lumsdaine et al. 1949; Stouffer, Suchman et al. 1949), covered a range of topics including cohesion, leadership, primary groups, morale, race relations (the army was still racially segregated), communication, and persuasion, which helped establish the research agenda of sociology and social psychology for years to come. The methodological contributions of this team to survey research, data analysis, and experimental design changed the face of quantitative sociology. Indeed, 35 years after the publication of *The American Soldier,* the major journal in sociological social psychology, *Social Psychology Quarterly,* published a retrospective review of the impact of this work (Clausen 1984a, 1984b; Lumsdaine 1984; Smith 1984; Williams 1984). As a result of these studies, the American military continued to use survey research as a personnel management tool after World War II, much as it had adopted selection and classification tests from psychology after World War I.

Other World War II studies, such as the work of Edward Shils and Morris Janowitz (1948) on the social dynamics of German army units based on interrogation of prisoners of war—a research strategy not permitted under current U.S. federal regulations regarding research on human subjects, demonstrated the permeability of the boundary between social research and military intelligence. A larger example of this was the U.S. Strategic Bombing Survey, a presidential commission established in 1944 to evaluate the effects of bombing civilian targets in Germany and the Pacific through the analysis of observations, documents, interrogations, and interviews. Hundreds of military and civilian personnel were involved under the direction of a board that included the economist John Kenneth Galbraith and the psychologist Rensis Likert. The reports generated by this survey argued for the ascendancy of air power in post–World War II conflicts and helped justify the establishment of the Air Force as a separate service.

In general, the topics that were studied during World War II have retained central positions in the current research agenda of military sociology, even as that agenda has been broadened by changes in military organization, civil-military relations, the nature of military conflict, and other global trends.

THE COLD WAR

After the war, sociologists who had participated in the war effort returned to their colleges and universities or, in a few cases, their more applied pursuits and, with few exceptions, turned their research efforts to other social institutions and processes. Although publications reflecting wartime experiences continued to appear, there was little new research, despite a minor increase during the Korean War. However, after World War II, the American military became a significant continuing institutional peacetime presence for the first time in American history (Burk 2001). After earlier military conflicts, starting with the Revolutionary War, America had demobilized its forces. In contrast, after World War II, because of the new bipolar tensions in the international community reflecting the Cold War, America maintained a large force under arms (Segal and Segal 2004:4–5).

During the Korean War, the focus on group processes that had started in World War II continued. Roger Little (1969) conducted research reaffirming the importance of interpersonal processes for motivation and support in combat, and the Special Operations Research Office of Johns Hopkins University studied race relations in the newly integrated U.S. Army (Bogart 1969). Both the army and the air force became principal sponsors of extramural research on small-group processes, in part as a consequence of the army's research on leadership and cohesion in World War II and the Korean War and also influenced by the apparent success of the Chinese People's Liberation Army in using principles of group dynamics in support of troop indoctrination and the building of military morale (Lifton 1963) as well as demoralizing American prisoners of war through "brainwashing." This research was never well integrated into the field of military sociology, although it has continued to have influence in military psychology.

In the mid-twentieth century, there were occasional attempts by scholars to describe the structural relationships between military forces and their host societies in the modern world. C. Wight Mills's (1956) *The Power Elite* and Harold D. Lasswell's (1941) developmental model of "the garrison state" were among the most important of these. However, it was not until the 1960s that military sociology emerged as a viable academic field. At the turn of the decade, Samuel P. Huntington (1957), a political scientist at Harvard University, and Morris Janowitz (1960), a sociologist at the University of Michigan, published books on the nature of the military profession and its relationship to the state (in Huntington's case) and to society (in Janowitz's case). The professionalism theme came to dominate the research agenda of this field, and sociologists in several nations began to address the issues raised by Huntington and Janowitz in their own nations. At the University of Maryland, Charles Coates and Roland Pellegrin (1965) published the first (and still the only) textbook on military sociology. This concern with the relationships among the military, the state, and society added civil-military relations to the sociological agenda and shifted the focus of military sociology from the conscripts and enlisted personnel who held center stage in the World War II research to the officer corps and the nature of the military profession.

The 1960s saw the growth of an organizational infrastructure in military sociology with the establishment of the Inter-University Seminar on Armed Forces & Society (IUS), a small group of American scholars from several universities with interests in military sociology who met periodically to discuss their research, initially at the University of Michigan and then at the University of Chicago. The IUS has grown to an international and interdisciplinary group of more than 600 scholars; it meets every two years but still maintains the atmosphere of an invisible college rather than a professional association. At the international level, the Research Committee on Armed Forces & Society of the International Sociological Association was formed and began to bring military sociologists from a number of nations together every four years at the World Congresses of Sociology. This research committee has evolved into the Research Committee on Armed Forces & Conflict Resolution. More recently, scholars concerned with military sociology in Europe have formed the European Research Group on Military and Society.

Another reflection of the internationalization of the field was its incorporation of social scientists who were concerned with development processes in former colonized territories. One of the dimensions of this concern was the role of the military in the development process (e.g., Janowitz 1964). While much of the concern in this area was focused on authoritarian military rule in these areas, a special interest among American scholars was the ongoing war of national liberation in French Indo-China, the subsequent Americanization of the Vietnam War, and the eventual implications of that war for American military organization and military manpower policy.

THE VIETNAM WAR

Presidents Kennedy and Johnson, for the first time in American military history, elected not to use the military's reserve components to mobilize for the Vietnam War but to depend on selective conscription of the large baby-boom generation to man the force. The social unrest in America during the 1960s was largely directed at the inequities of this conscription process, which placed the burden of waging the war disproportionately on the shoulders of the poor. Research on the internal dynamics of the armed forces during Vietnam was focused largely on themes that had characterized military sociology during World War II and the Korean War: group dynamics of leadership and cohesion (e.g., Savage and Gabriel 1976) and race relations (e.g., Moskos 1973). Added to these were drug use (e.g., Helmer 1974) and the shortcomings, inequities, and failures of the system of military conscription then in place (e.g., Curry 1985). A more long-term consequence was concern about the reentry of war veterans into society and the way the nation treated its military veterans (e.g., Scott 2004).

Before the Vietnam War was over, debates had begun in America, and among military sociologists, on ending conscription and manning America's military force with volunteers. The debate on conscription brought labor economics into a central position in the social scientific analysis of the military, as the nation discussed whether labor market dynamics could be substituted for conscription as a means of raising America's Cold War military (e.g., Friedman 1967). The issue of military conscription was widely debated in the early 1970s, and the 1972 defense appropriation provided funds for the establishment of an all-volunteer military force (Segal 1989:34–38). In January 1973, the U.S. DoD announced the end of peacetime conscription for the first time since World War II.

This would not be the first all-volunteer military force that America had. Voluntarism had been the rule, rather than the exception, through American history, and conscription had never been a popular alternative. However, it would be the first time America maintained a large standing force on a voluntary basis. Earlier in our history, we had ended conscription and demobilized in interwar periods. Given the bipolar tensions between East and West at the end of World War II and the advent of military aviation and nuclear technology, which deprived nations of the luxuries of time and distance from the battlefield when war broke out, we had never demobilized after World War II and starting in 1973, sought to maintain a standing Cold War force on a voluntary basis. Our national leadership decided that it had also been an error not to mobilize the reserve components for the Vietnam War. The failure to use these citizen-soldiers disrupted a historical linkage between the American military and the American people, and steps were taken to reconfigure the force so that we would not go to war again without the reserves. The appropriate role of the reserves in the total force has emerged as an important concern in military policy and military sociology.

The decision to end conscription in 1973 had a number of major impacts on military sociology. First, the American military recognized that while previously there had been volunteer military forces in the United States, they had always been demobilized interwar cadre forces. The nation had never attempted to maintain a large standing force on a volunteer basis. A large volunteer force was a challenging social experiment. The services showed a new willingness to draw on, and support, behavioral science research in support of organizational effectiveness to make this experiment a success. While the behavioral science programs of the Naval Personnel Research and Development Center, the Air Force Human Resources Laboratory, and the Army Research Institute for the Behavioral and Social Sciences (Zeidner and Drucker 1983) were dominated by psychology, they all had sociological components. Thus, military sociology grew in terms of both in-house research and extramural funded research, both in universities and in the research and development industry. Indeed, the post–Vietnam War volunteer military has undergone a major evaluation by social scientists at least once a decade (e.g., Bowman, Little, and Sicilia 1986).

Second, the substantive focus of the field was broadened. During the Vietnam War and the post-Vietnam years, there was increasing recognition that social trends in America were having an impact on the military. The armed forces had been racially integrated during the Korean War, but both America and her armed forces had been punctuated by racial tensions during the Vietnam War and postwar periods. Drug use had increased greatly among the American youth population, and this was reflected in the young people coming into the military. Women were entering the American labor force in increasing numbers, and the military had to confront the issue of gender integration. The manifestations of these trends in the military all became part of the subject matter of military sociology.

Third, the growth and broadening of the field led to significant increases in research and writing at a time when the major sociological journals, perhaps because of the ideological opposition to the Vietnam War that existed within the discipline, were unwilling to publish articles on war and the military. This, coupled with the increasing fragmentation of publication outlets in sociology, led to the establishment of two specialized journals, *Armed Forces & Society,* which was published by the IUS, and *Journal of Political and Military Sociology.* Both are now in their fourth decade of publication.

Fourth, military sociology began to reconceptualize the nature of military service and its relationship to society. One facet of this reconceptualization was to question the uniqueness of the military institution as the state's agent for the legitimate management of violence and to explore the isomorphism between military service and other forms of employment (Biderman 1967). In particular, Moskos

(1977) suggested that with the replacement of conscription by a volunteer force recruited by labor market dynamics, military service was being transformed from a value-based vocation to an economically based job. Moskos's formulation, which was referred to as the institutional and occupational models, had implications for understanding both the individual soldier and the military organization (D. R. Segal 1986), turned the focus of military sociology from the officer corps to enlisted personnel once again, and came to dominate the research agenda of military sociology as increasing numbers of nations abandoned conscription in favor of volunteer forces (Haltiner 1999) and scholars in other nations applied Moskos's models to their nations (Moskos and Wood 1988).

Many of the dimensions of change specified in Moskos's formulation, as well as derivatives of the formulation, came to dominate the agenda of military sociology in the last quarter of the twentieth century and into the twenty-first century. For example, one derivative of the hypothesized convergence between military service and civilian occupations was the potential for military unionization, and this became an active area of research in the 1970s (e.g., Taylor, Arango, and Lockwood 1977). Closer to the specifics of Moskos's model, the formulation suggested that the basis for legitimacy of the military institution was shifting from normative values of service to the dynamics of the market economy and that therefore recruitment appeals would shift from character qualities such as duty, honor, and country to compensation. This change was assumed by the military recruiting structure, and only recently has it been acknowledged that even in the absence of appeals to character in recruiting advertising, patriotic values have been as important, or more important, in the recruiting process as economic considerations (Woodruff, Kelty, and Segal 2006).

The formulation also assumed that military personnel would become less committed to the general military role of soldier and more to their specific occupational specialty and that their reference groups would be people who shared their occupations outside the military rather than other soldiers in different occupations. Research has shown that the former expectation is correct, and military personnel in the late twentieth century defined their appropriate duties in terms of specific military occupations (D. R. Segal 1995). However, in terms of general reference groups, military personnel were more likely to root their identities in their familial roles (Woodruff 2003) or religious affiliations (Trainor 2004) than in their military roles or in an external occupational community.

Moskos's formulation suggested that women would increasingly be integrated into the military on an equal basis, and indeed, while full equality has not been achieved, major changes have taken place in the numbers and roles of women in military service both in the United States and in other nations (M. W. Segal 1995). This dimension is just one reflection of increasing concerns with diversity, including continuing concerns with racial

equality (Moskos and Butler 1996) and emergent concerns with sexual orientation integration (Scott and Stanley 1994). Moskos's formulation also posited a change in the nature of the relationship between the military and the families of its personnel, from a posture of inclusion to one of exclusion. In fact, the modern military is an increasingly married force that competes for commitment with the families of its personnel (M. W. Segal 1986), has faced demands from those families (Stanley, Segal, and Laughton 1990), and has attempted to accommodate to them in recognition of the effect they have on commitment, retention, and performance (Bourg and Segal 1999).

Perhaps most dramatically, Moskos's formulation posited that the missions of the occupational model would focus less on the waging of conventional interstate wars and more on the constabulary or peacekeeping types of operations that Janowitz had hypothesized to be the focus of military professionals in the post–World War II world (e.g., Moskos 1976). Indeed, while the major powers largely avoided involvement in United Nations peace operations during the Cold War, the United States did get involved on a continuing basis in peace operations conducted under other auspices (Segal and Segal 1993).

THE CURRENT STATE OF KNOWLEDGE

The nature of military organization and the relationship between the armed forces and society began to change markedly in the 1980s. Some of the changes that have been observed reflect the military increasingly adopting management strategies from civilian corporate enterprise. When the Cold War ended in Europe, military budgets in many nations were diminished and the size of military forces was reduced significantly (Segal and Babin 2000). At the same time, military missions were redefined from the waging of large-scale wars to contingency operations such as peacekeeping and humanitarian assistance. Downsizing, a strategy used in the corporate world to deal with economic downturns, was adopted by the military, and as was the case in the corporate world, military downsizing produced problems both for victims and for survivors of the process (Wong and McNally 1994). These processes took place overseas as well (Hamilton et al. 2001).

As forces were downsized, some military bases grew as a result of realignment of functions, and their growth had positive effects on the economies of the surrounding communities (e.g., Hicks and Raney 2003). However, a larger number of military bases were closed down, and civilian communities that hosted those bases experienced the same kinds of economic challenges that are confronted when industrial plants close down. Thus, the relationship between military bases and their host civilian communities became a focus of sociological research. We learned that communities that have a major military presence have less racial segregation in housing and less racial inequality in employment than other communities, supporting the assertion by most host communities that military bases were an economic asset. However, we also learned that gender discrimination in employment, in terms of higher unemployment, lower wages, and lower returns to human capital for women, was higher in communities with a major military presence (Booth et al. 2000).

While forces were being downsized, the number of contingency operations expanded markedly, and the survivors of downsizing—both individuals and military units—found that they were asked to do more work with fewer available resources, in terms of both taking on new missions (e.g., Segal et al. 1999) and deploying for old missions more frequently. Both processes have potential implications for morale and for retention (Reed and Segal 2000).

One way of accomplishing an increasing number of operations was to have those jobs most clearly requiring military competence and military status performed by military personnel but taking other jobs that had previously been performed by military personnel and having them done by civilian employees of the services. The U.S. DoD, for example, employs roughly 700,000 civilians, making up about 20 percent of the DoD workforce. An additional 20,000 military positions were scheduled to be transferred to civilian employment in 2004 to 2005, with more civilianization conversions in 2006 and beyond.

Another adjustment involved adopting yet another corporate strategy: outsourcing. Rather than having government employees perform tasks that had previously been done by military personnel, the military services increased the degree to which they contracted out support and, in some cases, core functions. The use of civilian contractors to support the U.S. military is not a new process. Civilian contractors have been used to support military operations since before the Civil War. However, the period starting with the end of the Cold War in Europe represents a unique phase in this relationship, during which civilian contractors are being used to offset a downsizing of the active military force when the number of missions and frequency of deployments is increasing. The sociological implications of having large numbers of civilian contractor personnel, who are not subject to military discipline and are not combatants under the terms of the laws of war, colocated with military personnel in a combat zone are in the very early stages of exploration (e.g., Kelty 2005).

One strategy to deal with increased numbers of missions and deployments with a reduced active military force that was not drawn from the civilian corporate world was a change in the use of reserve forces. As noted above, the reserves had not been mobilized in the Vietnam War, and despite the fact that in the post-Vietnam years the active and reserve components have been conceptualized as a "total force," the image of the reserves has been that of a force in reserve, to be used only in the case of an emergency. For the National Guard, which serves as an agent of state government unless federalized, the state missions were regarded as paramount.

With the downsizing of the active force, by the end of the 1980s, almost as much of the army's combat force was in the National Guard as in the active army. When the United States went to war in the Arabian Peninsula in 1990 after Iraq invaded Kuwait and threatened Saudi Arabia, the total force was called up. At the maximum strength of Operation Desert Storm, more than 73,000 Army Reserve and National Guard personnel were in the combat theater, accounting for about a quarter of all army personnel there. However, the reserve units that were deployed were largely transportation, medical, military police, and other support units. Three National Guard combat brigades that were intended to bring active-duty combat divisions to full strength were activated but not judged combat ready and were not deployed. In the wake of the Gulf War, programs were put in place to improve the deployability of the National Guard.

In the mid-1990s, the army experimented for the first time with overseas deployment of reserve component personnel for contingency operations, initially serving as the majority of the American contribution to the Multinational Force and Observers in the Sinai Desert in support of the Camp David Accords between Israel and Egypt (Phelps and Farr 1996). The success of that experiment led to expanded use of the reserves for contingency operations, generally in relatively small numbers, for six-month deployments. America's invasion of Iraq in 2002, however, changed the role of the reserves from participants in contingency operations to participants in continuous operations, called up in larger numbers than at any time since World War II (between 40 and 50 percent of the personnel in Iraq in 2005 have been from the reserve components) and for longer periods of time—sometimes a year or more. This has had implications not only for the reserve component personnel but also for their families and their civilian employers. And it has required that the research agenda of military sociology, which had focused on the active force, be expanded to include the reserves as well.

Many of the topics of current research extend long-term research traditions. Despite the increasing international disfavor with military conscription and the belief that the less universal conscripted service is, the more inequitable it is likely to be, discussions in the United States about whether the Global War on Terrorism can be sustained without a return to conscription and in both Western and Eastern Europe about the future of conscription (Malesic 2003) have kept this a focus of current research. The nature of the military profession likewise remains an active research area, and where early Cold War conceptualizations of the profession were limited to the active-duty officer corps, the era of more highly educated, technically competent, and career-oriented volunteer forces has raised questions of whether enlisted personnel and noncommissioned officers, both active and reserve, should be included in the profession, whether the specialization of armed forces requires that we regard each branch as an autonomous profession, and the ways in which changes in the military profession reflect broader changes in the sociology of professions (Abbott 2002).

The processes of group dynamics that became focal points of research have continued to be active areas. The study of leadership has largely been left to social psychologists, who to a large extent have abandoned contingency and transactional approaches in favor of transformational models of leadership, based on charisma-like qualities (Bass 1998). Major changes have taken place in the conceptualization of cohesion in military units, focusing in part on the fact that the social cohesion based on homogeneity that was identified in World War II research as being important for the military has been used repeatedly as an argument against diversity in military forces without being shown to have a positive impact on performance (Segal and Kestnbaum 2002), while task cohesion, based on contributions to common goals, does not require homogeneity.

While many of the topics of military sociology remain unchanged, the sociological perspectives brought to bear on them reflect changes in the discipline. Thus, in the 1990s, questions that had been raised during the days of conscription by Janowitz and Huntington about relations between the military, the state, and society, and reflected in the early years of the volunteer force in attitude research by Bachman, Blair, and Segal (1977), were recast in terms of the trend toward culture studies in the social sciences, and questions were raised on whether the culture of the military was divergent from the culture of its host society (e.g., Feaver and Kohn 2001). Research showed that the American military does have a distinct culture, as would any profession studied, but that it is consistent with the culture of the broader society that it defends. This research topic achieved sufficient visibility in the late twentieth century so that like the topics of organizational change and military professionalism in the 1960s and 1970s, it has become a focus of European military sociology in the twenty-first century.

Another focus of late-twentieth-century sociology was postmodern theory, and the language of postmodernism increasingly appeared in analyses of soldiers (e.g., Battistelli 1997) and military organization (e.g., Moskos 2000). Moskos's formulation has been particularly influential. Like his earlier conceptualization of the transition from an institutional to an occupational model, he postulated a shift from modern to postmodern military organization along a number of empirical dimensions, some of which mirrored the components of his earlier formulation, such as gender roles and the relationship between the family and the military. Others referred to more strategic and macro-organizational dimensions, such as changes in major mission and force structure, whereas the I/O model had focused on more micro-organizational dimensions such as recruitment appeals and role commitment. Like the I/O model, the postmodern model has been applied in a range of national settings (Moskos, Williams, and Segal 2000). The major finding has been that while Western industrial nations vary in their degree of modernity, there is no truly postmodern military. Indeed, a major critique of the postmodern military formulation pointed out that the template used to study it was rooted in positivistic science, which postmodernism would reject, and that a truly postmodern military would be no military at all (Booth, Kestnbaum, and Segal 2001).

One of the dimensions of Moskos's postmodern model was the sexual orientation integration of the military, a process that has taken place in most European nations and to which a considerable amount of social science literature has been devoted. Two other trends in sociological research on diversity in the military are notable. The first is that other nations began to pay greater attention to gender integration in their armed forces (e.g., Dandeker and Segal 1996). The second was that increased attention has been paid to the intersections of race, class, and gender rather than focusing on disadvantaged statuses one at a time (Booth and Segal 2005). Important examples, which reflect an important emerging historical perspective in military sociology as well as the concept of intersectionality, are Moore's (1996, 2003) studies of African American and Japanese American women who served in the U.S. military in World War II.

Another contemporary perspective that has been applied to traditional problems in military sociology is that of the life course. While much research was done in the last quarter of the twentieth century on the postservice status of veterans compared with their peers who did not serve, it was primarily done from a status attainment or bridging environment perspective. In the main, it suggested that men who served in World War II or the Korean War benefited from their service relative to their peers who did not serve, that this benefit did not extend into the Vietnam War and current volunteer force periods, that minority men benefited more than white men, and that among women veterans, minority women benefited more than white women (Segal 2005). More recently, the life-course perspective has been used to clarify the dynamics by which military service, and particularly service in wartime and in combat, affects the postservice life trajectories of veterans (e.g., Sampson and Laub 1996).

The changes that have taken place in the missions of the twenty-first century and the technological and political contexts within which those changes have taken place have broadened the scope of military sociology. Changes in communication technology have altered the relationship between armies deployed at war and the society they defend and between deployed soldiers and their families back home. World War II was seen on the home front through the eyes of war correspondents, whose copy passed through the hands of military censors before it appeared in the next day's newspapers and in newsreels the following week. Headlines from the Vietnam War appeared on television the same day, with film on the evening news. The Gulf War was covered in part by CNN reporters in Baghdad reporting on the arrival of American bombs and rockets. And Operation Iraqi Freedom has been covered in part by reporters from the print and broadcast media embedded in military units and using modern communications media to file their stories in real time. These changes have altered the relationships between the military, the media, the state, and society.

At the level of the individual soldier, communications technologies for contact for families back home have progressed from mail, through telephones and faxes, to widespread use of the Internet (Ender and Segal 1998). These technologies alter the relationships within military families when soldiers are deployed and raise issues of information security to new levels.

The nature of the missions on which these soldiers are deployed has also expanded the scope of military sociology. The field as it grew during World War II focused on conventional military forces, allied with similarly organized forces and facing similarly organized adversaries. The Vietnam War sensitized military forces, and military sociology, to the differences associated with unconventional war, which reduced the relevance of large conventional military formations and emphasized the political dimensions of warfare, although the Gulf War closed the twentieth century with a conventional war.

The late twentieth century saw major nations like the United States moving into the arena of peace operations. They had largely been excluded by Cold War peacekeeping doctrines that emphasized impartiality, since the major nations were likely to be interested parties in any area of the world in which conflict occurred. Thus, during the second half of the twentieth century, peacekeeping had largely become the domain of "middle powers," such as Canada, the Netherlands, the Nordic nations, and smaller nations such as Fiji.

In the late twentieth and early twenty-first centuries, with the Cold War over in Europe, peacekeeping norms changed, with more deviations occurring from impartiality, minimum use of force, and host nation consent. Major powers became increasingly involved in peace operations, not only becoming less martial and more constabulary in their orientations but also challenging the primacy of the middle powers in the peacekeeping arena. At the same time, nations with more pacific security policies, such as Japan and Germany, which had been limited by their post–World War II constitutions with regard to their military forces and to out-of-area military operations, were encouraged under new international norms of burden sharing to become involved in multinational peace operations, becoming more martial in their orientations (Segal and Kurashina, forthcoming). And the operations, in turn, became increasingly concerned with nonstate actors such as insurgencies and terrorism rather than conventional military operations. All of these changes have been incorporated into the field of military sociology.

While military sociology is still a small subfield of the discipline, in the last half century, and particularly since the end of the Cold War in Europe, it has grown significantly in substance, in size, and in impact both within the discipline and more broadly in society. It is increasingly common to find military sociologists quoted in news stories about armed forces and military operations in both print and broadcast media. Interest in the applied aspects of the field has grown in other nations—most dramatically in the nations of Eastern and Central Europe, as they have dealt with issues of potentially ending military conscription, adopting democratic models of civilian control of the military, modernizing and professionalizing their forces, and addressing issues of gender integration and military families. Indeed, the center of gravity of military sociology seems to be shifting from North America to Europe. There has been a moderate growth of academic interest in military sociology, with a slowly growing number of colleges and universities offering courses in the field, accompanied by a growing concern with the national and transnational implications and consequences of the nature of the military institution and its relationship to the state and to citizenship (e.g., Kestbaum 2002). And there has been increased sociological attention paid to air and naval forces. The field has retained a strong interdisciplinary orientation, with sociologists who study armed forces and society seeing their professional community consisting as much of other social scientists who study the military institution (economists, psychologists, political scientists, historians) as of sociologists who study other social institutions.

PART VIII

SOCIETAL PROBLEMS AND DISAFFECTIONS

36

SOCIAL PROBLEMS

HAROLD R. KERBO

JAMES WILLIAM COLEMAN

California Polytechnic State University, San Luis Obispo

The study of social problems in the United States is no doubt one of the most difficult to summarize and analyze within sociology. In contrast to family sociology, criminology, social stratification, the sociology of sport, and so on, the study of social problems is always shifting in terms of what is included or excluded as the focus of study. But there is also the matter of shifting perspectives and theories within all the core issues within the field of social problems, such as racial discrimination, crime and delinquency, and sexual deviance, to name only a few of what have been among the core issues in the study of social problems in America.

In what follows, we will briefly consider how social problems have been studied in early American history and then consider how social problems have been defined in sociology textbooks and look at the trends in these textbooks over the years. In the second half of this chapter, we will examine more critically how the particular pattern of American values have influenced our definitions of social problems, along with the impact of wealth and power on these definitions. With this examination of wealth and power, we will consider the impact of social movements on what comes to be defined as social problems. A complete understanding of the impact of social movements, however, also requires brief consideration of the causes of social movements. Finally, we will consider how solutions to social problems are also shaped by power, wealth, and American value orientations.

A BRIEF HISTORY OF THE STUDY OF SOCIAL PROBLEMS IN THE UNITED STATES

The first book in the United States with the title *Social Problems* was mostly likely that by Henry George, first published in 1883 (George 1939). But sociologists such as George Herbert Mead were already discussing the nature of social problems and the need for social reform in the late 1800s (see Mead 1899; Schwendinger and Schwendinger 1974:452–56). As industrialization took off dramatically in the final two decades of the nineteenth century, so did many conditions that came to be defined as social problems, such as urban poverty, unemployment, and crime. As the great historian Hofstader (1955) noted, it was soon after this that the United States entered one of its reoccurring cycles of reform movements (also see Garraty 1978). It was also a time when sociology was emerging as a major discipline of academic study in the United States (Gouldner 1970; Schwendinger and Schwendinger 1974). The timing of these two events is no doubt a reason why the study of social problems became one of the major subareas in American sociology. But it was also the unique set of utilitarian and individualistic values in the United States that affected the development of American sociology. A crusading spirit accompanied the emergence of American sociology, with many of the early American sociologists coming from Christian clergy backgrounds to a new secular orientation toward understanding the problems of the newly industrialized nation (Gouldner 1970).

It was also a liberal critique of the American society rooted in the early discipline of U.S. sociology, different from that found in European sociology. From the mid-nineteenth century, European sociology had developed with the full range of perspectives, from radical critiques of basic institutions provided by Marx to conservative support of the status quo from the likes of Herbert Spencer. American sociology through the first half of the twentieth century, in contrast, "came to dwell on those concrete institutional areas and social problems" (Gouldner 1970:93) accepted by the dominate society from a perspective of how to make them work better rather than suggesting basic change. "Indeed, nothing like Marxian sociology was even recognized by American sociology until well after World War II" (McLellan 1973). There were, of course, Marxian perspectives among European immigrants and the early labor movement in the United States, but little of this found its way into academic halls. It is telling that Talcott Parsons's major book, designed to introduce Americans to European sociology in the early 1930s, had not one mention of Marx or Marxian theory (Parsons 1937). To this day, social problems are not considered a major sub-area in European sociology or offered as a course in many European universities. The exception to this was sociology in the old Soviet Union, where the Soviet government found the social problem orientation of functional sociology a useful perspective for "fine-tuning" the Soviet society without criticism of the basic Soviet institutions (Gouldner 1970:447–52).

WHAT IS A SOCIAL PROBLEM? TEXTBOOK DEFINITIONS

Standard "textbook" definitions of social problems are generally grouped into three categories, with the second two categories most often used by sociologists themselves. As we will consider in the following, however, there are many more underlying assumptions about the nature of society and humans that shape what sociologists as well as the general public come to define as social problems.

The public generally sees a social problem as any condition that is harmful to society; but the matter is not so simple, for the meanings of such everyday terms as *harm* and *society* are far from clear. Social conditions that some people see as a problem harm some segments of society but are beneficial to others. Take trade policy as an example. Shareholders and others affiliated with multinational corporate manufacturers typically argue that any kind of trade restriction is a problem because government regulation interferes with the free enterprise system and drives up costs to consumers. On the other hand, domestic workers and manufacturers argue that the government's failure to exclude products produced in low-cost nations is a social problem because it costs jobs and hurts domestic

business. As we will discuss in more detail later, one person's social problem, in other words, is often another person's solution. In fact, most people and organizations define something as a social problem only if it harms (or seems to harm) their own interests.

Sociologists have tried to take a less biased approach with mixed results. Most of the early sociological works on social problems held that a *social problem exists when there is a sizable difference between the ideals of a society and its actual achievements.* From this perspective, social problems are created by the failure to close the gap between the way people want things to be and the way things really are. Thus, racial discrimination is a social problem because although we believe that everyone should receive fair and equal treatment, some groups are still denied equal access to education, employment, and housing. Before this definition can be applied, however, someone must first examine the ideals and values of society and then decide whether these goals are being achieved. From this perspective, sociologists and other experts thus decide what is or is not a problem because they believe they are the ones with the skills necessary for measuring the desires and achievements of society (see Merton and Nisbet 1971).

Critics of this approach point out that no contemporary society has a single, unified set of values and ideals. When using this definition, sociologists must therefore decide which standards they will use for judging whether or not a certain condition is a social problem. Critics charge that those ideals and values used as standards are selected on the basis of the researcher's personal opinions and prejudices, not objective analysis.

The "social constructivists," who have become the dominant school in social problems research, take a different position, holding that *a social problem exists when a significant number of people believe that a certain condition is in fact a problem.* Here, the public (not a sociologist) decides what is or is not a social problem. The sociologist's job is to determine which problems affect a substantial number of people. Thus, in this view, pollution did not become a social problem until environmental activists and news reports attracted the public's attention to conditions that had actually existed for some time (see Blumer 1971; Spector and Kitsuse 1973).

The advantage of this definition is that it does not require a value judgment by sociologists who try to decide what is and is not a social problem: Such decisions are made by "the public." However, a shortcoming of this approach is that the public is often uninformed or misguided and does not clearly understand its problems. If thousands of people were being poisoned by radiation leaking from a nuclear power plant but didn't know it, wouldn't that still be a social problem? A potentially more serious shortcoming of this approach is its hidden political bias. Obviously, in a mass society it is not simply the seriousness of the problem that wins it public attention but the way the corporate media present it. Furthermore, relatively powerless groups with little money or political organization are not able to get their problems recognized as social problems in the way that dominant groups can. Sociologists using the constructivist approach in the study of social problems creation have generally been very sensitive to the role power plays in this process, but researchers focusing more narrowly on individual social problems have often unreflectively accepted the definitions of problematic conditions provided by funding agencies or popular opinion (Galliher and McCartney 1973; Useem 1976a, 1976b; Kerbo 1981, 2006a:254–59).

But even these conflicting views of how social problems are to be defined miss important underlying assumptions that influence what people come to define as a social problem. These underlying assumptions account for how social problems are differently conceived across societies, through history, and across lines such as race, class, and religion within societies at one particular time. And it must be recognized that sociologists have also been influenced by these underlying and often hidden assumptions about humans and societies.

THE FIELD TODAY: TRENDS IN "SOCIAL PROBLEMS" TEXTBOOKS

The question of which problems are serious enough to warrant sociological attention has been a difficult and controversial one over the years. We will consider this issue from another perspective in the following. But for now, we can note that the pressure of social movements is one of four interwoven factors that determined which problems draw the most sociological attention. The public's perception of its problems is a second important factor that, of course, is strongly influenced by the media of mass communication. Space does not permit an exploration of all the factors that influence the media's decisions to turn its attention on one problem and not another, but certainly the corporate interests of the media conglomerates and the various political and financial pressures to which they are exposed are of prime importance (see, for example, Domhoff 2006, on the "policy formation process"). But in addition to the media, the public's perception of social problems is also shaped by the actual experiences of everyday people. So a third factor is the social crises that have a wrenching impact on the public from time to time, as well as the ongoing contradictions of industrial capitalism. In January of 2001, for example, terrorism was not mentioned as a major problem in the Gallup Poll, but by the start of 2002, it was the number one problem identified by the respondents. With the start of the Iraq war the following year, warfare and international tension replaced terrorism on the list of national concerns. In 2001, less than 0.5 percent of the poll respondents mentioned warfare and international tensions as the nation's most serious problem, but by 2003, 35 percent did so (Gallup 2004). A final factor involves the sociologists who are selecting the problems for consideration.

Since most practicing sociologists hold some kind of academic position, they function as semi-independent intellectuals in the arena of social problems creation. As such, they have considerably more independence (although less visibility and influence) than scientists and advocates working for the corporations or other special interest groups. But as noted in the foregoing, they are, nonetheless, still constrained by the need to obtain financial support for their research and the political climate of their universities. The paradigmatic shift that has occurred in sociology in the last 50 years as it moved away from the functionalist perspective to a more critical conflict orientation has certainly been an important influence both in the problems that are given attention and in the ways in which they are analyzed.

Since the focus of ociological research itself is determined as much by the priorities of the funding agencies as by the sociologists who carry it out, one of the best guides to the changes in sociological concerns is the content of the social problems textbooks. A comparison of contemporary texts with those from the earlier decades of the postwar era shows that although organizational styles and definitions vary, there is a significant group of problems that have maintained consistent sociological attention. If any social problems can be said to occupy the center of sociological concern, they are the ones related to crime and deviance. Certain types of crime and deviance were given more coverage in one era than another, but all the major texts have an extensive coverage of this topic. Other constants are the problems of the family, ethnic relations, population, and poverty or economic inequality. A second group of problems appears in some texts but not in others without any clear chronological pattern of increasing or decreasing attention. Surprisingly, given their importance in public opinion polls, economic problems other than poverty are not consistently covered. Other problems in this category include those of urbanization, sexuality, and education.

Finally, a third group of problems has shown an increase or decrease in sociological interest over the years. The first edition of the best-selling text by Horton and Leslie (1955) had chapters on two problems that are not seen in later texts: "Religious Problems and Conflicts" and "Civil Liberties and Subversion" (the focus of the latter being primarily on the dangers of communism). New social movements during this period also brought new problems to the foreground. By the time Joseph Julian's text replaced Horton and Leslie as the top seller in the 1970s, several new problems had joined the core of sociological interest. In response to the rise of the environmental movement, Julian's (1973) first edition contained a chapter on environmental problems—something that became a mainstay of social problems texts either on its own or with a presentation of population growth as a social problem. The feminist movement succeeded in adding another critical topic—gender inequity—to the mainstream texts. The extremely influential text, edited by Robert K. Merton and Robert Nisbet (1976), first added a chapter on gender in its fourth edition, and Julian (1977) added a similar chapter the following year. More recently, there has been growing attention to the problems faced by gays and lesbians, even though this topic has generally not been treated in an independent chapter of its own. Although chapters on the problems of aging are not quite as common, they also started showing up around the 1970s.

The main focus of most of these texts, like that of American sociology itself, has been on domestic issues, but there have been some important changes there as well. As the memories of World War II began to fade, there was some decline in interest in events beyond America's borders. Horton and Leslie originally had two chapters with an international focus, "Population" and "Warfare and International Organization," as did the Merton and Nisbet text in its early editions. In 1976, however, Merton and Nisbet replaced their chapter on "Warfare and Disarmament" with a chapter on "Violence," which focused on criminal behavior, and Julian never had a chapter on warfare. However, as the process of globalization won increasing public attention in the 1990s, this trend was slowly reversed. Not only did many of the texts begin including more comparative material, but some added a chapter on global inequality as Coleman and Cressey (1993) did in their fifth edition.

Three overall trends are therefore evident in the sociological study of social problems in North America. As just indicated, one trend has been toward greater inclusivity. First African Americans, then other ethnic minorities, then women, and finally gays and lesbians have slowly won inclusion in what was originally an exclusively white male vision of the world. A second trend has been the slow expansion of sociological horizons to recognize the importance of environmental concerns as well as to take a more global perspective.

A third trend, not as easily recognizable from our previous analysis, has been an underlying paradigmatic shift. To the extent that they used any explicit theoretical approach, the earlier texts were based on functionalist assumptions. Following Horton and Leslie (1955:27–32), they tended to argue that there were three theoretical approaches to social problems: social disorganization, personal deviance, and value conflict. The value-conflict approach should not, however, be confused with contemporary conflict theory inspired by Marxian thought. Its basic assumptions were clearly functionalist: Society needed value consensus, and "value conflict" was therefore a cause of social conflict (Fuller and Myers 1941). As sociology slowly adopted a more critical perspective, a few books with an exclusively conflict orientation were published, and for most of the other textbooks, this tripartite approach was recast. The social disorganization approach was expanded and renamed to include all functionalist theory. The personal deviance approach expanded to become the interactionist approach, which had less of a functionalist cast and included other social psychological phenomena in addition to deviance. Finally, the issue of value conflict was subsumed under the much broader and more critical umbrella of a conflict approach (for example, see Coleman and Cressey 1980).

Of the new trends that seem to be developing for the twenty-first century, an increasing globalization perspective is most important. There is now greater recognition that for the United States, globalization is creating new social problems or making old ones such as poverty and unemployment worse. The movement of U.S. factories overseas and outsourcing of all kinds of work have helped reduce wages for the bottom half of the American labor force (see Kerbo 2006b:chaps. 2 and 3). In addition to this, the antiglobalization movements of recent years, as well as research on the negative impact of globalization for developing countries (Kerbo 2006b:chap. 4), have brought greater attention to the subjects of world poverty, environmental pollution, and global migration for most books on social problems. With global inequality expected to continue increasing for many years into the twenty-first century, the trend will likely become more pronounced.

PARADIGM ASSUMPTIONS AND DEFINING SOCIAL PROBLEMS

In his classic work *The Sociological Imagination,* C. Wright Mills (1959) argued we should distinguish between "'the personal troubles of milieu' and 'the public issues of social structure'" (p. 8). For him, of course, it was "the public issues of social structure" that should be the focus of sociology when defining the nature of a social problem. Mills offered this example:

> In these terms, consider unemployment. When, in a city of 100,000, only one man is unemployed, that is his personal trouble, and for its relief we properly look to the character of the man . . . But when in a nation of 50 million employees, 15 million men are unemployed, that is an issue . . . Both the correct statement of the problem and the range of possible solutions require us to consider the economic and political institutions of the society, and not merely the personal situation and character of a scatter of individuals. (P. 9)

Mills, obviously, offers a definition of social problems that focuses on the breakdown of basic social institutions that must take care of individuals and assure the survival of the society and its social institutions. His plea for a focus on social institutions seems straightforward and obvious; but he made such a plea because of the particular aspects of American culture that create a bias against this focus.

It has long been recognized that power (generally defined) and values interact to determine what comes to be seen as social problems. Those with wealth and influence in government and/or the mass media in modern societies are the ones most able to shape what the society comes to view as a social problem. But there are many forms of influence held by those below the top ranks in the society, making the study of social problems overlap with the study of social movements. Several years ago, for example, one of the basic American social problems textbooks employed the title *Social Problems as Social Movements* (Mauss 1975). As we will consider in the following, however, assuming that social movements help define social problems is also problematic because of the complex set of forces that make the emergence of social movements possible. But in addition to this, the recognition that social movements help define social problems continues to neglect the question of cultural assumptions and values that make one country, in one historical epic, view conditions differently for people in other times and places, as well as neglect the ability of those with wealth and power to shape the perspective on the causes and solutions to social problems once they have been defined as such.

Sociological analyses of sociology itself, a form of "deconstructionism" popular among professional sociologists during the 1960s and 1970s, long before the current fad in humanities, has shown that "paradigm assumptions" or "metatheoretical assumptions" shape all sociological theories at least to some degree (Gouldner 1970; Strasser 1976; Ritzer 2005). And while all scientific disciplines are influenced by these political, religious, or cultural assumptions (Kuhn 1970), these assumptions shape some fields within the social sciences to a greater extent than others. Theories and research on politically sensitive subjects such as crime and poverty, along with most subjects within the general area of social problems, are most influenced by these paradigm assumptions (Galliher and McCartney 1973; Useem 1976a, 1976b; Kerbo 1981).

To understand theories and research on social problems in the American society, it is first important to examine some of the general American values that shape views on these subjects. Various international opinion polls show the following: Americans have the highest scores on (1) individualism (Hofstede 1991), (2) beliefs in the existence of equality of opportunity, (3) beliefs that government cannot and should not reduce inequality or poverty (Ladd and Bowman 1998), and (4) beliefs that high levels of poverty and inequality are acceptable (Verba et al. 1987; Ladd and Bowman 1998). For the study of social problems in general, this has meant that American values suggest that individuals themselves are responsible for their problems rather than some aspect of the society or basic institutions. In contrast to the early appeals of C. Wright Mills noted in the foregoing, content analyses of articles on social problems published in American sociology journals through the second half of the twentieth century confirm that the focus tends to be on the characteristics of individuals rather than problems of society (Galliher and McCartney 1973; Useem 1976a, 1976b; Kerbo 1981, 2006a:254–59).

This research also shows that it is not simply the views of sociologists themselves that set the trend toward blaming the characteristics of individuals for social problems as much as the assumptions of funding agencies; most social science research is funded by government agencies and private foundations that are more interested in controlling social problems rather than changing aspects of the society that are often at the root of social problems (Kerbo 1981). Interviews with social scientists indicate that they are most often conducting research on questions that they know will get funding rather than on what they think are the most important sociological questions or subjects in which they are most interested (Useem 1976a, 1976b). What this research suggests is that while the rich and powerful may not always define what is seen as a social problem, they do have extensive influence over what we think are the causes and solutions to social problems. They help set the research agendas, what gets research attention, and what gets talked about in government circles and the mass media through this influence on the social sciences through research funding (see Domhoff 2006:77–132).

This is not to say, however, that the assumptions and interests of the less affluent and politically powerless do not shape what we come to define as social problems. For example, an abundance of research has shown that the civil rights movements of the 1960s, and especially the violent demonstrations and riots of that period, shaped the American society's definition of poverty as a social problem (Piven and Cloward 1971, 1977). Indeed, several studies have shown strong correlations between urban riots of the 1960s and the expansion of welfare benefits to the poor (Betz 1974; Kelly and Snyder 1980; Isaac and Kelly 1981).

The tie between social movements and what comes to be defined as social problems is especially critical in the United States. Compared with the rest of the industrialized world, of course, a much smaller percentage of Americans tend to vote during national elections. But an even bigger contrast to other industrialized nations is the class makeup of those who do vote in the United States: Toward the upper-income levels, some 70–80 percent of Americans who are eligible to vote do so, compared with 30 percent or less for people with a below-average income. This is not the case with other industrial societies, where the voter turnout is about the same at every income level (Piven and Cloward 1988, 2000; Kerbo and Gonzalez 2003). This is to say, therefore, that when the less affluent and less politically powerful in the United States have influenced definitions of social problems, it has been comparatively more often done in the streets than through the political process.

THE CAUSES OF SOCIAL MOVEMENTS AND THEIR IMPACT ON DEFINITIONS OF SOCIAL PROBLEMS

Recognizing that social movements are important in identifying what a society comes to view as a social problem forces us to ask how social movements themselves emerge. It is not our intent to review all the literature on the causes of social movements, but a brief summary of this literature is essential when considering how social problems have been defined in the United States.

For many years the study of social movements was dominated by theories based on some form of "deprivation" argument. In other words, social movements were seen to emerge and attract widespread membership because participants felt a sense of anger or outrage at their condition. Recognizing that long-standing deprivations do not always or even often spark widespread social movement activity (such as decades or centuries of discrimination and exploitation of a minority group by the majority), most deprivation theories of social movements attempted to explain how some type of change leads to a redefinition of the situation. The most popular of this type of theory has been called "relative deprivation theory" or "J-curve theory" (Davies 1962, 1969; Gurr 1970). During the early 1800s, Tocqueville (1955) recognized that, ironically, social movements and revolutions tend to emerge when conditions are actually improving. More recent refinements of "relative deprivation theory" distinguish between what is called "value expectations" and "value capabilities." When value capabilities are low (such as high levels of poverty) and have been so for a long period of time, people come to accept their situation or assume improvements are unlikely or impossible. People in deprived situations are often, even likely, to be persuaded that they themselves are responsible for their condition and thus have no one else to blame (Piven and Cloward 1971; Gans 1972). This is to say that low-value capabilities are usually associated with low-value expectations over long periods of time. Thus, to understand the emergence of social movements, relative deprivation theories suggest the need to understand how value capabilities and value expectations move apart.

Obviously, the gap between the two can develop because value capabilities worsen (such as a big jump in unemployment of the working class), thus creating a gap between previous expectations and newly lowered capabilities. Faced with a sudden crisis, people seldom assume their situation is hopeless or that they deserve their worsening situation. However, as Tocqueville (1955) was first to recognize, social movements and revolutions actually seem to occur when long-standing conditions of deprivation are actually improving. Refinement of relative deprivation–type theories has come to suggest that improving conditions quickly raise levels of expectation, but improving conditions seldom occur without fluctuation, meaning that a sudden downturn in improving conditions creates the gap between value capabilities and value expectations. It is anger or fear that improvements finally achieved will be short lived that motivate more and more people to join a social movement.

While research has shown that some form of "relative deprivation" seems to have preceded many social movements, others have noted that this is not always the case— nor is anger or a sense of deprivation in and of itself usually sufficient to make a social movement. In recent years, what is generally referred to as "resource mobilization theory" has become much more popular among sociologists attempting to explain the development and spread of social

movements (for original development of the perspective, see McCarthy and Zald 1977). In its basics, resource mobilization theory is a form of conflict theory focused on the balance of power between authorities (or the more powerful in a society) and those with possible grievances. Reduced power of authorities, increased power among those with a grievance, or both can lead to a strong social movement.

The concept of "resources" in resource mobilization theory refers to any value or condition that can be used to the advantage of a group. Obviously important are such things as money, publicity, arms, and the ability to interact with and organize larger numbers of people for the cause. In one of the first studies using resource mobilization theory, for example, Paige (1975) was able to show that certain kinds of crops and certain types of agricultural organization (such as wet rice agriculture with absentee landowners) are more likely associated with peasant revolts and revolutions because of the ability peasants have to interact freely, share common grievances, and be organized to oppose landowners. Likewise, the loss of legitimacy and the ability to punish opponents or hide information are conditions that reduce the power and resources of authorities. Ted Gurr (1970) has produced a long list of possible resources that includes things such as terrain (ability to hide or ability of authorities to uncover rebels), food supplies, and outside allies that can influence the power and size of social movements.

Perhaps more than any other social movement in recent American history, the new resource mobilization theory of social movements led to a reanalysis of the civil rights movement. Because of this extensive reanalysis of the causes of the civil rights movement, it is worth considering in more detail here how a particular social problem, racism and discrimination, came to be widely defined as a social problem in the second half of the twentieth century.

Civil Rights Movement

Considering the importance of the civil rights movement in the United States for defining racism, discrimination, and poverty as social problems, it is useful to consider how this social movement emerged and to consider the value of the social movement theories described in the foregoing.

Relative deprivation theory has some success in explaining why the more violent stage of the civil rights movement emerged in the mid-1960s. Sociologists using this perspective argue that the more violent stage of the civil rights movement was in response to a white "backlash" that resulted in some setbacks to the earlier achievements of the civil rights movement from the 1950s (Davies 1969). However, relative deprivation theory has difficulty in explaining why the civil rights movement suddenly appeared in the early 1950s, while so many other attempted social movements by black Americans failed in earlier American history. In recent years, research has shown resource mobilization theory to be a powerful tool in understanding why the civil rights movement became widespread and powerful when and where it did so (McAdam 1982).

In summary, the civil rights movement benefited from several changes that occurred in the American society after World War II. Among the most important changes was agricultural mechanization, which moved a majority of black Americans from rural areas and agricultural jobs into large cities all over the United States. Larger concentrations of black Americans in urban areas provided the ability to reach and organize far greater numbers of social movement participants than before. A key to organizational ability was also found in the huge churches dominated by black Americans in large cities in the southern United States. These black churches made possible organization within the denomination and across churches all over the South. At the same time, these large black churches provided support for social movement participants and their families when they were jailed or injured in social movement activities.

Among other new resources in the 1950s were more mass-media exposure to actions against black Americans and social movement activities that had remained relatively hidden in small cities and rural areas throughout the South in previous generations. But related to this was political change, as the Democratic Party lost its previously solid majority in the South. To counter this loss, the Democratic Party decided to "go for" new urban concentrations of potential black votes in the late 1950s. It was politicalization of black grievances in the presidential election of 1960 that gave black social movement activists more resources of many kinds and John F. Kennedy the presidency in one of the closest elections when newly organized black voters gave him overwhelming support.

Movements of Affluence

The foregoing analysis of social movements and their causes as instrumental in defining what comes to be seen as a social problem, however, should not be seen as reinforcing the common assumption that social movements are primarily by and for the poor and oppressed. We must recognize the distinction between what has been called "movements of crisis" and "movements of affluence" (Kerbo 1982). Most movements of crisis are made up of people who face critical problems such as poverty, discrimination, or some other deprivation. Most movements of affluence, on the other hand, involve people who are relatively comfortable, if not affluent, and have the luxury of devoting their attention and energy on "moral issues." Current social movements in the United States that are usually pushed by people on the political right (such as the anti-abortion movement) as well as the political left (such as the environmental movement and antiglobalization) must be included among these movements of affluence,

which focus on moral issues or issues that are not of immediate harm to individual social movement participants.

SOLUTIONS TO SOCIAL PROBLEMS

We can conclude with an examination of what are considered "solutions" to social problems. While the possible solutions to social problems are seldom recognized, they are equally, if not more, shaped by power and influence in a society. Over the last four decades in the United States, the extent and seriousness of many, if not most, social problems have remained relatively unchanged. For example, while violent crime and property crime have dropped in recent years, violent crime especially remains at high levels compared with other industrial nations. Drug use has gone up and down within only a narrow range. Teenage pregnancy has dropped only slightly. Poverty rates have ranged between 11 and 15 percent of the American population in the last 40 years, among the highest in the industrialized world. These continuing high levels of social problems in the United States might suggest that relatively little has been learned about the subject in the last half century of sociological research. The reality, however, is quite different. Even more complex than definitions of social problems is finding solutions that do not adversely affect groups with more political and/or economic power or impinge on important values of the dominant group in the society. Consideration of possible solutions to poverty and inequality will be useful in demonstrating the point.

In most of the original European Union countries, poverty rates are substantially below the American rates. Using the purchasing power parity (PPP) method of estimating currency values, and using the poverty line established by the U.S. Census Bureau (roughly $11 per day per person), during the late 1990s (the most recent years we have data for several European countries) the U.S. poverty rate was over 13 percent, compared with about 7 percent in Germany and the Netherlands and around 4 percent in Scandinavian countries (Smeeding, Rainwater, and Burtless 2001:51). But while the American poverty rates are comparatively high, unemployment at around 4 to 5 percent in the same time period was low compared to over 10 percent unemployment in most original EU countries. There are two interacting explanations for this: First, in contrast to the United States, European labor unions are strong enough to force government action to keep poverty low even at the expense of higher unemployment rates (Esping-Anderson 1990; Thelen 1991; Goodin et al. 1999; Kerbo and Gonzalez 2003). Second, opinion polls indicate that Europeans are more concerned than are Americans about high inequality and poverty among their citizens and believe that governments have the responsibility to reduce poverty and inequality (Verba et al. 1987; Ladd and Bowman 1998). These two explanations are also behind

Table 36.1	Comparative Impact of Welfare and Unemployment Benefits on Reducing Poverty[a]		
Country	*Poverty (Prewelfare Payments) (%)*	*Poverty (After Welfare Payments) (%)*	*Percentage Reduction*
Sweden	34.1	6.7	−80.4
Denmark	26.9	7.5	−72.1
England	29.2	14.6	−50.0
Belgium	28.4	5.5	−80.6
Germany	22.0	7.6	−65.5
The Netherlands	22.8	6.7	−70.6
France	21.6	7.5	−65.3
Italy	18.4	6.5	−64.7
Spain	28.2	10.4	−63.1
United States	26.7	19.1	−28.5

SOURCE: Constructed from data presented by Smeeding (1997), Mishel, Bernstein, and Schmitt (1999:377), and Nieuwbeerta (2001).

a. Poverty measured by income below 50 percent of median income in the nation. Data are available from 1989 to 1994.

the figures we see in Table 36.1. Without government action, poverty rates in Europe would be about the same or even higher than in the United States. But government interventions in Europe reduce poverty rates by 50 to 80 percent, compared with only a 28 percent reduction in the United States. Not surprisingly, the EU country with the weakest unions today and values closest to the United States, the United Kingdom, has the lowest rate of reducing poverty through government action in Europe and, using the PPP $11 per day poverty line, a poverty rate of 15.7 percent compared with 13.6 percent in the same time period in the United States (Smeeding et al. 2001:51).

The contrast between Germany and the United States is most clear. The influence of the American corporate elite, in the context of American values stressing individualism, has led the American public to generally accept the argument that the government should not be allowed to raise taxes, increase unemployment benefits, or raise minimum-wage laws to reduce poverty. Rather, the argument is that corporations and the rich should be left alone as much as possible to generate wealth that will then expand job opportunities that will reduce poverty among Americans. (For a broader discussion of this German vs. American contrast, see Kerbo and Strasser 2000, Kerbo 2006b:chap. 3.) In Germany, by contrast, the power of labor unions and labor laws already instituted with labor union pressure will not allow such government inaction as a presumed solution to the problem of poverty.

Another example can be briefly considered. Several studies indicate that high employment rates are instrumental in producing crime (Blau and Blau 1982; Williams 1984), which at least in part helps explain the lower crime rates in the United States from the early 1990s to the present. Thus, a guaranteed job after release from prison would significantly reduce the rate of recidivism. But since the 1930s, American politicians have not been willing to create employment through government programs in times of high unemployment or guarantee jobs to felons released from prison. The American corporate elite have been successful in blocking such government job guarantees or jobs created by government, even though it is clear this would be one viable solution to high rates of crime.

There are many other examples: Decriminalizing drugs would likely help reduce both property crime and drug addiction as it has in some European countries, and more sex education and freer access to condoms would help reduce teenage pregnancy rates, which are far higher in the United States than in Europe. But as with definitions of what is or is not a social problem, power and influence in combination with particular societal value orientations that can be exploited by those with power are also involved with what come to be viewed as accepted solutions to social problems.

37

THE SOCIOLOGY OF DEVIANCE

GARY F. JENSEN

Vanderbilt University

*D*eviance is the concept chosen by sociologists to encompass a variety of forms of human conduct that have been defined or reacted to by members of a social system as wrong, bad, immoral, illegal, or worthy of condemnation or punishment, and the *sociology of deviance* is the study of the social forces and processes involved in the formulation of such evaluative standards, violations of those standards, and reactions to such violations. The specific subject matter typically includes the study of behaviors defined as illegal (crime and delinquency) and forms of conduct that are disapproved or stigmatized by a sizeable proportion of members of a society such as suicide, mental illness, some forms of sexuality, and certain forms of alcohol and drug use. Although the concept has become a derogatory public term, sociologists originally adopted the concept as a more objective and neutral conceptual category than those in use by the public.

The discipline of criminology, defined as the study of law making, law breaking, and reactions to law breaking, and the sociology of deviance both encompass illegal conduct, but the sociology of deviance is unique in its concern for themes and principles that are supposed to apply to a variety of violations of shared standards. Indeed, the most significant scholarship in the early evolution of the sociology of deviance was Émile Durkheim's ([1897] 1951) study *Suicide*. Although suicide has been treated as a crime in some societies at some times, it is not encompassed in contemporary categories of criminal conduct, and it is not studied by criminologists. However, suicide and suicidal behavior remain of interest in the sociology of deviance. Moreover, because it is not limited to behaviors defined by criminal statutes, the sociology of deviance encourages

consideration of the possible relationships among different forms of deviance. For example, Durkheim hypothesized that homicide and suicide acted like two different "streams" of deviance with nations that had high suicide rates having low homicide rates. Similarly, when questions are asked about the relationships between such behaviors as criminal violence and noncriminal forms of deviance such as mental illness and alcohol use, a search for answers bridges the study of "deviance" and the study of "crime." In short, the sociology of deviance encompasses the study of relationships among criminal and noncriminal violations of shared evaluative standards (norms) as well as the search for general principles or themes that apply to deviance in general.

BASIC THEMES AND THEORIES

The most basic themes in the sociology of deviance include the observations that (1) the specific forms or instances of conduct that fall in such categories vary over time and among societies (cultural and temporal relativity), (2) there is greater social consensus on the impropriety of some forms of behavior than others (variable normative consensus), (3) some members and groups within the system have more influence on definitions and reactions to specific forms of deviance than others (power and moral enterprise), and (4) involvement in forms of disapproved conduct are not randomly distributed but are shaped by variable socialization, social learning, social control mechanisms, and other social influences and constraints. Every textbook on the sociology of deviance incorporates and builds on some version of these basic themes.

In addition to core themes, there is a general consensus on categories of distinct sociological theories of deviance. Three categories of theories concerned with "causes" of criminal and noncriminal forms of deviance that seek to explain measurable, observable variations in deviant conduct have dominated sociological discourse: (1) social disorganization, (2) cultural conflict-differential association, and (3) structural-cultural strain. Each of these three types of theories has distinct characteristics and each focuses on different features of society, groups, and categories of people in the attempt to explain real behavioral differences. In addition to these causal theories, at least two major types of perspectives have been critical of the focus on "causes" and the emphasis on measurable variations in conduct: (4) social constructionism and (5) radical and feminist theories.

When the concept of social disorganization was introduced, it was considered to be the underlying condition that explained the convergence of a variety of forms of deviant conduct in identifiable ecological territories. It was applied to the explanation of crime, delinquency, and other social problems by sociologists at the University of Chicago in the early 1900s. Rapid growth and change were viewed as "disorganizing" or "disintegrative" forces contributing to a breakdown in the teaching and learning of "social rules" (Thomas and Znaniecki 1927). Edwin Sutherland (1934) invoked the concept of social disorganization to explain increases in crime that accompanied the transformation of preliterate and peasant societies where "influences surrounding a person were steady, uniform, harmonious and consistent" to modern Western civilization, which he believed was characterized by inconsistency, conflict, and "un-organization" (p. 64). Although criminal and delinquent conduct were central to the development of the theory, Robert E. L. Faris (1948) extended the concept of social disorganization to explain "social pathologies," including crime, suicide, mental illness, mob violence, and suicide.

By 1939, Sutherland (1939) had modified his theory and proposed an explanation that emphasized (1) conflicting definitions of appropriate and inappropriate conduct as key to the distribution of crime among social settings and (2) differential association with people communicating conflicting definitions explained variations in criminality. Sutherland's systematic elaboration of a theory of both crime and criminality in a set of nine fundamental propositions earned him honors as the most influential theoretical criminologist of the twentieth century. Applied to delinquency, the central proposition of differential association was simply that "a person becomes delinquent because of an excess of definitions favorable to violation of law over definitions unfavorable to violation of law (Sutherland 1947:76). Although his propositions dealt with criminal and delinquent conduct, the theory emphasized normal mechanisms of symbolic interaction that applied to all forms of behavior (deviant and nondeviant). By the late 1930s, the notion that certain areas of cities were criminogenic because they were disorganized had been replaced by the notion that such areas were differentially organized. High-rate areas had different traditions or competing and conflicting subcultural traditions. With his work on *Culture, Conflict and Crime* in 1938, the criminologist Thorsten Sellin played a major role in reinforcing the shift away from social disorganization and toward conflicting subcultural norms in the explanation of crime.

A distinct theoretical tradition emphasizing a specific type of disorganization was elaborated by Robert K. Merton in 1938. Merton expanded on Durkheim's argument that economic crises and fluctuations could drive people to suicide because rules regulating behavior become unstable, and ambitions get out of step with reality. Applying a similar logic, Merton argued that high rates of deviance are generated in anomic social systems where there is a strong emphasis on economic success coupled with inequality in opportunity to realize success legitimately. The pursuit of success by illegal "innovative" means is viewed as one adaptation to this form of disorganization. Illegal innovation in pursuit of commonly shared success goals is viewed as a common lower-class response to frustrated ambitions, but Merton argued that there are other ways to adapt as well. Some people might adapt to strain by giving up the pursuit of success goals and retreating through the use of drugs, suicide, or mental illness. Still others might rebel and attempt to change the system. The logic of Merton's theory with its emphasis on widely shared goals coupled with unequal opportunity is the basis for designating it as a "strain" theory. Other theorists have followed the same logic introducing other forms of discrepancy between goals and means as a source of frustrated ambitions.

In one form or another, these basic theories have endured and are reflected in contemporary theories that assume real variations in measurable forms of conduct to be explained by measurable features of the social world. Modern "social control" and "self-control" theories (e.g., Hirschi 1969; Gottfredson and Hirschi 1990) share features with social disorganization theory in that they emphasize the absence of social and personal constraints as the crucial variables in the explanation of criminal and noncriminal deviance. Such theories focus on all forms of force and fraud and view noncriminal forms of rule breaking as early indicators of the absence of control. Modern social learning theory elaborates on Sutherland's work (see Akers 1977, 1998; Akers and Jensen 2003, forthcoming), differentiating a variety of distinct learning mechanisms that have separable consequences for deviance. The mechanisms apply to both nondeviant behavior as well as to crime and delinquency and other forms of deviance. Finally, modern versions of Merton's theory emphasize concepts such as "institutional anomie" (Messner and Rosenfeld 1997) and "general strain" (Agnew 1992), and both institutional anomie and general strain theorists attempt to specify different types of deviant responses to frustrating circumstances. New ideas have been introduced, but the basic explanatory frameworks provided by these three traditions have endured for more than six decades.

CONSTRUCTIONIST, RADICAL, AND FEMINIST CRITIQUES

As noted above, these "causal" theories assume that there are real, observable variations in conduct that violate discernible shared norms that can be explained by measurable features of society, groups, and/or people. However, a popular perspective on deviance for the last 30–40 years focuses on the construction and application of deviant labels and their consequences for those so labeled. This perspective has been called "labeling theory," "constructionist theory," and "interactionist theory." Although there is no one authoritative definition of the perspective, the basic characteristics are widely understood by sociologists. A very simple definition of social constructionism in the study of deviance is expressed in Rubington and Weinberg's (2005) statement that social constructionists take deviance as "subjectively problematic" as opposed to "objectively given" (pp. 1–2). Goode (1994) proposes that "to the constructionist, definitions have no absolute, objective validity" and that "*reality depends on perspective, and perspective is to a degree arbitrary*" (pp. 32–33). Warren and Karner (2005) propose that "the logic of qualitative inquiry" is social constructionist and specify the two basic assumptions of that logic as embrace of the view that "the analysis of society is made from some standpoint or perspective that informs the analysis" and that "social constructionists use qualitative methods to try to understand the meanings that people bring to social worlds they inhabit and construct" (p. 4).

The typical approach to delineating the features of the constructionist perspective is to contrast it with an opposing, "traditional," and "quantitative" alternative referred to under terms such as *absolutism, realism, naturalism,* or *positivism.* When taken to the extreme, the alleged positivist takes for granted that the problems or problem people studied are really "out there" and that people fall in such judgmental categories because they have violated widely accepted societal norms. Because these problems and problem people are assumed to be real, positivists ask what other measurable characteristics of people or their social world determined that reality. Although researchers adopting such methodological approaches may not see themselves as "positivists," the quantitative search for "causes" and correlates of deviant behavior based on survey or agency data at the micro, meso, or macro level are generally defined by constructionists as the central feature of that epistemology.

The constructionist critique shares many features in common with another critique that emerged first in challenges by "radical criminologists" and later in challenges by advocates of "feminist" perspectives. Both British and American criminologists (see Taylor, Walton, and Young 1973, 1975; Platt 1975; Quinney 1975; Chambliss and Mankoff 1976) mounted radical challenges to traditional criminological theories and methods and located the source of societal problems in the capitalist political and economic systems. Crime among the disadvantaged was an outcome of their economic marginality. With little or nothing to lose, few promising alternatives, and continual pressures to prove one's worth through material possessions, criminality becomes a relatively rational and attractive choice. Radical critics also believed that the focus of criminology on street crimes and the crimes of the powerless detracted from attending to more fundamental criminogenic problems in society such as inequality and racism. Like the constructionist, they challenged the value of data presumed to measure real behavioral differences and questioned the results of research using quantitative methodologies. A basic argument was that criminological research has served the interests of ruling classes to the disadvantage of other groups, and that the data and methods used were biased as well.

Feminist critiques have extended that argument and criticize the focus of research on males as well as the natural science methodologies dominating the sociological study of deviance. They extended the critique of traditional methods to include biases in the features of the female world studied by criminologists and deviance researchers (see Daly and Chesney-Lind 1988; Daly 1994; Chesney-Lind and Shelden 2004). Radical critics chastise criminologists for ignoring "upperworld" crime and the differential enforcement of laws by social class. Feminist critics argue that female crime has been ignored and that many observed patterns are products of differential law enforcement by gender. They also argue that theories developed to explain male crime and delinquency ignore dimensions of the female world and female experiences that are relevant to the explanation of low rates for violence and serious property crime as well as survival strategies such as prostitution and running away.

Some critics of traditional emphases in the sociology of deviance have proposed that the subject matter should be conduct and social arrangements that violate "the historically determined rights of individuals" (Schwendinger and Schwendinger 1975). Rather than studying "nuts," "sluts," and "perverts" (Liazos 1972:132), radical critics of the normative definitions of deviance invoke a specific set of norms defining justice or "rights" as the most "objective" and "universal" standard for judging the severity of problematic behavior. Such definitions invoke notions of natural law in which humans have rights that can be used to determine justice and injustice, and such standards are viewed as universal. The range of situations encompassed by their rights perspective includes characteristics of social systems as well as individual conduct. For example, a social system in which punishment is affected by the power and resources that people or organizations have would be considered deviant from a rights perspective. If members of a social system are defined as having "rights" to a living wage, a social system where that right is ignored would be deviant. Those advocating a rights or justice perspective often emphasize inalienable, self-evident, or universal rights, and such rights may be defined as including nonhuman life.

PROPOSED INNOVATIONS

This brief introduction to major features of the sociology of deviance reveals a sociological specialty characterized by widely shared themes as well as continuity between classic versions of theories and more contemporary applications. There are often heated debates about the strengths and weaknesses of different concepts, methodologies, and key subject matter, but these features can be found for any area of specialization in sociology. Yet there are claims that the field is dying. Colin Sumner (1994) subtitled his overview of *The Sociology of Deviance* as "An Obituary," and Joel Best (2004:ix) provides evidence that the use of the concept of deviance in general sociology journals has been declining since its peak in the 1970s. Goode (2004) proposes that concerns about "political correctness" have led many scholars to avoid the term *deviance* because it has become a public concept used to stigmatize and "pathologize" certain forms of conduct. Goode also states that he is "convinced that the field of the sociology of deviance is not as theoretically innovative as it once was and that "fewer influential 'big' ideas are being generated within its ranks" (p. 114).

Although there is no way to discern whether recent proposals will succeed as influential "big ideas," three attempts to be theoretically innovative in the sociology of deviance in recent years will be outlined here because they deal with the scope of the concept of deviance and propose new or modified conceptions of deviance: (1) proposed expansion of the concept of deviance to include "admired deviance" and "positive deviance," (2) Tittle and Paternoster's (2000) elaboration of deviance as violations of "middle-class norms," and (3) Tittle's development of a "control-balance" theory encompassing a wide range of forms of deviance.

Positive Deviance, Admired Deviance, and Negative Deviance

Deviance textbooks routinely note that behavior that might be considered as conforming to social norms (e.g., striving for recognition, working hard, trying to please others) can result in expressions of disapproval and negative labels (nerd, geek, egghead, rate-buster, brown nose, etc.). Attempts to abide by norms governing appropriate appearance can move into the realm of deviance (e.g., eating disorders, steroid use, obsessions with cleanliness).

When forms of behavior, appearance, or expression that are socially approved take on properties or qualities that are disapproved or worthy of social condemnation, then they fall within the realm of topics encompassed by the study of deviance. Moreover, conduct that violates normative standards may be admired by certain audiences (e.g., clever con operations).

Recognition that conduct that is consistent with normative standards can be reacted to negatively and that conduct that appears deviant may be reacted to positively has become a central tenet in arguments for expanding the sociology of deviance to include "positive deviance" and "admired deviance." Heckert and Heckert (2004) propose that "positive deviance" is "overconformity that is responded to in a confirmatory fashion" such as saints and Congressional Medal of Honor winners, and "deviance admiration" occurs when people positively evaluate deviance (e.g., outlaws, social bandits, Robin Hood). They argue that the category a person falls in will vary among groups with teachers admiring "gifted" students and peers regarding them as "rate busters." They also propose that "it is important to analyze why underconformity or nonconformity can result in positive evaluations (deviance admiration) or negative evaluations, depending on the era, place, or social group involved" and that "the same is true for over-conformity" (p. 213).

Although the attempt to create a new typology in which evaluations are independent of "deviance" is clearly "innovative," the concept of positive deviance has yet to be widely accepted as an advancement in the field for several reasons. First, Best (2004) argues that the wider the range of people and activities encompassed under the concept of deviance, the more difficult it will be to identify any common principles that would justify a sociology of deviance (p. 34). Second, the key questions that are raised as examples of the heuristic utility of such a typology, including admired and positive deviance, have been asked without such concepts. The fact that the same behaviors are reacted to differently by different groups is central to the shared theme of "relativity." Conduct can be defined negatively but still be admired if there are other collective standards governing the way in which it is violated. Limiting deviance as a concept to disapproved behavior or norm-violating behavior eliciting negative reactions does not preclude asking why some forms of approved behavior can come to be disapproved by certain groups in certain situations. Nor does it preclude asking how some forms of conformity can elicit positive evaluations from certain groups while others elicit negative evaluations. Third, the designation of positive deviance as overconformity that is positively evaluated and deviance admiration as underconformity or nonconformity that is positively evaluated leaves an important question unanswered. How are conformity, nonconformity, and underconformity to be determined? Heckert and Heckert appear to be reintroducing the statistical deviation conception of deviance that has been so widely rejected by sociologists. Determination of "over-" and "under-" conformity requires some sort of "social evaluation" unless they are to be determined in purely statistical terms. The meaning of "over" when attached to "conformity" is determined by evaluative standards or negative reactions, which places it under the traditional designation of deviance.

Another argument introduced as part of the rationale for the concept of positive deviance is the widely cited notion that deviance can serve positive functions. Deviance textbooks routinely draw on Durkheim's arguments and Dentler and Erickson's (1959) article on the functions of deviance in groups to highlight the irony that bad events can have "good" (functional) consequences. Crime is used as an example in that a criminal event can bring people together and enhance group solidarity. However, the logic of such arguments is rarely scrutinized and becomes part of an unquestioned academic folklore of the sociology of deviance. The sole exception is "The Function of Crime Myth," in which Bob Roshier (1977) stresses the importance of maintaining distinctions between sociological concepts of deviance and social control. He proposes that the functions attributed to "deviance" turn out to be the functions of "social control." The typical argument that crime or deviance serves functions in bringing the community together, enhancing solidarity, is a claim about the *rejection* of deviance (a form of social control), not the functions of deviance as defined independent of that reaction. It is the recurring response to a threat that is functionally explained, not the threat itself (see Jensen 1988).

"Middle-Class" Norms

Because "norms" are central to definitions of deviance as norm-violating behavior, there is considerable merit to recent attempts to more precisely define the standards that are violated. Such standards seem obvious when the focus is on serious crimes, killing of one's self, use of harmful substances, and some forms of bizarre behavior indicative of mental illness. However, there has been little attention paid to delineating the types of norms violated. A major step in that direction is Tittle and Paternoster's (2000) work on *Social Deviance* where they attempt to delineate "middle-class" norms and the behaviors that violate these norms. They propose 10 dominant norms: group loyalty, privacy, prudence, conventionality, responsibility, participation, moderation, honesty, peacefulness, and courtesy.

Their interpretation of each norm cannot be specified here, but the merits and problems in such a list should be addressed. One of the merits is that such a list facilitates recognition of the complications involved in determining whether specific instances of behavior fit in a category of normative violations. For example, group loyalty may call for behaviors that conflict with other "norms" such as honesty, conventionality, and responsibility. The sociology of deviance would benefit from a grounded specification of societal norms and their application to different situations.

The problem with such an attempt at this point in time is that no methodology for determining such normative standards has been attempted or proposed. Tittle and Paternoster (2000) do not provide any research data of any kind to justify their list. Moreover, they note that the lower class shares many, if not most, of these norms but provide no data to support any particular social distribution, nor any specific reason for calling them "middle class." How do these "norms" compare with other normative systems such as Elijah Anderson's (1999) *Code of the Street? Code of the Street* includes prohibitions against ratting and expectations for group loyalty as well as expectations that youth will physically defend themselves from affronts to their personal honor. Which "middle-class norms" are shared by males and females, blacks and whites, the advantaged and disadvantaged? Categorizing them as "middle class" will strike many sociologists as rather arbitrary.

Control Balance Theory

A feature of Merton's typology of types of deviance that is often overlooked is that he defined *conformity* as goal-oriented compliance with prescribed standards. Conformity to prescribed standards when no rational end appeared to be served was a form of deviance, "ritualism." People who rigidly adhere to rules even when such conformity has little purpose (e.g., rigid adherence to bureaucratic rules, obsessive cleanliness, some forms of "mental illness") fell in a "deviant" category. "Real" conformity was purposive behavior.

Charles Tittle (1995) has adopted a similar strategy in that he proposes six types of deviance that can be contrasted with "conscious recognition of the rules with studied obedience" (conformity): submission, defiance, predation, exploitation, plunder, and decadence. He argues that people are least likely to be deviant when their "control ratio" is balanced, that is, when the amount of control they wield is in balance with the amount of control wielded over them. Hence, when a person has no freedom of action and no way to exert control, deviance takes the form of "submission." Submission is viewed by Tittle as deviance because the individual is not willfully obedient (e.g., battered wives who submit). In contemporary American society, submission is likely to be negatively evaluated.

Those people who are moderately controlled by others but have a small amount of autonomy are likely to be "defiant," to express anger about their circumstances, or to willfully attempt to escape. Predatory deviance (e.g., theft, rape, assault) is more likely among those who are less subject to control but have some autonomy. All three of these (submission, defiance, and predation) occur among people with control deficits. In contrast, people who have power surpluses also engage in deviance, but it takes different forms. Those with small surpluses exploit others, those with modest surpluses plunder others, and those with the largest surpluses adopt decadent lifestyles.

Tittle supports his theory with examples and attempts to apply the theory to explaining variations among sociodemographic groups in types of deviance. At this point in time, appropriate operationalization of the concepts has not been established nor have the techniques for identifying covert forms of deviance such as submission been specified. However, Tittle's theory does address issues that distinguish control-balance theory from theories of crime in that different forms of deviance are proposed to be generated by different combinations of the same underlying mechanisms.

DIRECTIONS FOR THE FUTURE

The themes, theories, and issues discussed above provide the background for several proposals that the author believes will reinvigorate the sociology of deviance in the twenty-first century. The author believes that the best tactics for a revitalization include the following: (1) a "properties of deviant phenomena" approach to conceptions of deviance; (2) empirical demonstrations that the study of noncriminal deviance improves understanding of criminal conduct; (3) a more precise elaboration and application of basic sociological concepts, forces, and processes that justified the invention of a sociology of deviance; (4) expanded efforts to bridge specialties within sociology; and (5) a careful assessment of the qualitative-quantitative tensions in the field through an organized dialogue about methodology accurately representing both positivistic and qualitative approaches.

Properties of Deviant Phenomena

To this point, several different conceptions of "deviance" have been introduced, including statistical deviation, behavioral violations of norms, labeled people and conduct, violations of rights, positively and negatively evaluated over-, non-, and underconformity, and violations of middle-class norms. Although sociologists do not intend for the concept to be an expression of personal disapproval, the fact that the public has come to use the term as a derogatory label has led some critics to question the value of the concept. Among sociologists, statements that a form of conduct violates widely shared norms are not intended to be an endorsement of public derogation and censure.

Unfortunately, many sociologists have contributed to the reification of the concept as a derogatory public term rather than a scholarly concept. A typical opening discussion in textbooks on "deviance" or "deviant behavior" approaches the concept not as a theoretical or organizing concept central to a scholarly field of study but as a reified term in popular culture. For example, one of the most popular textbooks on deviant behavior begins with an example of a badly overweight woman and asks whether she "is deviant for being overweight." The question is answered by noting that "some people would say yes, but others would say no" and that "some would say that it is her

tormentors . . . who are deviant" (Thio 2004:3). Such statements are lead-ins to the common observation that there is "a great deal of disagreement among people as to what they consider deviant" (p. 4). Such introductions can be traced back at least as far as J. L. Simmons's (1969) work, where he reported the results of a study where he asked, "Who is deviant?" He found so many different answers that he concluded, "So deviance, like beauty, is in the eyes of the beholder" (pp. 3–4). Of course, to fully qualify as a form of deviance as defined by sociology, the phenomena so designated has to violate a widely shared social norm (i.e., there has to be more than one "beholder"). Direct questions about what is "deviant" reify the concept as a public category and ignore its scholarly origins.

Such initiations of students into the study of deviants, deviance, or deviant behavior are popular because they facilitate discussions of the wide range of people and behaviors that are disapproved or stigmatized by different "publics" and highlight the "relativity" of deviance. However, as a guide for the development of the sociology of deviance in the twenty-first century, the first recommendation to be made in this section is to reassert the disciplinary origins of the concept and to initiate a new discussion of relationship among different scholarly depictions of deviance. At a minimum, the study of public use of the term should be distinguished from sociological use.

Because some scholarly conceptions of deviance were generated in critical evaluations of deficiencies in the normative definition, different conceptions are viewed as competing with one another. For example, the "reactive" conception of deviance is depicted as "a property *conferred upon* that behavior by the people who come into direct or indirect contact with it" (Erickson 1966:6).

The focus is not on what offenders are "doing" or have done but on how people and conduct come to be defined or labeled in certain ways. This conception does lead sociologists to pay attention to issues that are ignored when the normative definition is the exclusive definition. The important subject matter is the invention, selection, and manipulation of beliefs that define conduct as bad, sinful, criminal, or the like and the selection of people into those categories. On the other hand, audiences are likely to confer some form of public label based on learned normative standards. The emphasis may be shifted, but normative standards cannot be dismissed as part of the process.

Instead of debating the "best" or most useful definition of deviance, it should be recognized that each conception highlights distinct issues and questions about properties of deviant phenomena. One of the most consequential advances in the physical sciences was the recognition that light can be analyzed as either waves or particles. Similarly, the phenomena encompassed under diverse conceptions of deviance have several distinct and variable properties. Reactivists and constructionists point to the types of group conflicts, negotiations, and decisions that are made in the process of designating episodes, events, behaviors, and people as instances of some type of deviance such as crime, sin, or evil. This "reactive" component of deviant phenomena can obey its own principles quite independent of the behavioral component. A normative perspective directs attention to a behavioral foundation in that actual conduct in violation of legal or social norms is one of the best predictors for designations of people as criminal by different audiences, and activities that violate widely shared norms as well as beliefs about rights have a long history of prohibition in legal codes. Yet the variable nature of legal and social norms as well as legal designations of rights precludes a stable yardstick for evaluating good and evil, justice and injustice. Self-evident human rights might provide a more universal standard for such decisions, but that approach does not eliminate disagreement on the exact nature of those self-evident standards nor on the proper adjudication among conflicting standards when rights are in conflict. Using the traditional definition of deviance (disapproved violations of shared norms) as an anchor, a variety of important questions can be asked without demanding a newer or broader definition of deviance. For example, instead of creating new categories of positive deviance or admired deviance, the focus should be on identifying the specific normative standards that define otherwise conforming behavior as inappropriate or lead to admiration of otherwise "deviant" conduct. Rather than creating a "typology," sociologists should be asking how behavior that appears to conform to normative standards can come to be disapproved and should be seeking to discern the norms that are violated when people "over conform."

One direction for research on the normative foundation for designations of deviant phenomena is a delineation of a specific category of norms that dominates public evaluations of social arrangements and personal experiences, "rights" or "justice norms." The notion of "rights" as the foundation for defining the appropriate subject matter of the study of deviance and social problems does not negate the value of the traditional definition. In fact, the basic questions asked from a rights perspective do not require a new vocabulary. The view that there is a set of justice norms defining rights that are widely shared in human societies is an empirical question as is the suspicion that they vary systematically among categories of people and over time. Variations in the extension of such rights to nonhuman life have yet to be established.

Questions about the link between purely "statistical" deviation or variation and deviance as violations of shared normative standards can be asked without introducing any new definition. For example, most youth have shoplifted at some time, but are still likely to define such behavior as a violation of widely shared property norms. Yet there has been very little discussion or research on how norms are sustained when the vast majority of members of a system violate them. In their work on "Techniques of Neutralization," almost half a century ago, Sykes and Matza (1957) proposed specific "situational excuses" that

moderated or "neutralized" the constraining influence of more general norms. Their theory is one of the few that recognizes normative complexity and conflicting norms as important features of a widely shared cultural landscape. The delineation of the mechanisms that allow people to violate standards that they appear to share has received very little attention in more contemporary work. Similarly, the normative standards that transform statistically rare behavior at the "positive" pole of variation into disapproved behavior are yet to be investigated.

Bridging Forms of Deviance

Criminology has flourished as a distinct discipline because it focuses on behaviors that are defined by legal statutes and where there is considerable consensus on their "deviant" qualities. However, the sociology of deviance encompasses a wide range of behaviors and characteristics that are not encompassed by law and where there are quite variable opinions. Moreover, many of those noncriminal, but deviant behaviors, have their own "specialists." In view of such specialization, the major task confronting the sociology of deviance is the development of theories that apply across types and/or the specification of the circumstances that structure the forms that deviance can take. In short, proponents of a sociology of deviance have to demonstrate that knowledge or information across types matters.

This argument is far from new and, in fact, was central to the classic founding scholarship in the sociology of deviance, Émile Durkheim's ([1897] 1951) *Suicide.* Durkheim's basic arguments about suicide have been modified and applied in one form or another to "deviance" in general and to crime in particular. The most cited work in criminology in the twentieth century was Hirschi's (1969) *Causes of Delinquency,* and Hirschi drew heavily on Durkheimian ideas about the deviance-inhibiting consequences of moral and social integration. Merton (1938) also drew on Durkheim in the development of his structural-strain theory of deviance, and Agnew (1992) and Messner and Rosenfeld (1997) continue to build on a Mertonian framework.

However, such applications have been made without recognizing that Durkheim proposed that the explanation of some forms of deviance were caused by contrary circumstances. He specifically argued that homicide was generated by the circumstances that were the opposite of those generating suicide. Yet his ideas on suicide were extended to property crime, violence, and a variety of forms of force and fraud with no attempt to address the fact that he proposed contrary causal conditions.

The only sociologists who have followed Durkheim's lead on this issue are various "stream" theorists who have proposed hypotheses about the "direction" of lethal violence (see Unnithan et al. 1994; Batton and Ogles 2003). Such ideas have not been central to criminology for the simple reason that self-directed lethal violence is not illegal. Yet if Durkheim's speculation is correct, rates of homicide may not be independent of rates of suicide. Were that shown to be the case, then criminological models of murder would need to address other forms of noncriminal deviance to adequately explain homicide.

How might this reintegration and demonstration of the vitality of a sociology of deviance as an integrating discipline be accomplished? Given the enduring accolades of the Durkheimian tradition, one tactic would be to build on the basic framework suggested by his stream analogy. What forms of deviance flow together, and which represent separate streams? If they flow from a common source, what diverts them into separate streams? This analysis could begin with suicide and homicide since there is already a body of research literature dealing with this issue. How do the two forms of lethal violence relate to one another in modern times? What are the features of social systems that structure different rates of lethal violence? Is Durkheim's speculation about religious passion as a source of high homicide rates but low suicide rates correct? By focusing on specific issues involving distinct forms of deviance, the importance of an integrated study of "disparate" forms of deviance may be revealed a few steps at a time.

The fact that a wide range of phenomena can be categorized under the same conceptual rubric does not mean that the explanations will be the same or that the forms of deviance will all be positively correlated with one another. Conceptual similarity does not mandate causal isomorphism. Consider two forms of "deviance" where the causal mechanisms at work would appear to be quite disparate, such as serial murder and suicide. They are both included in Tittle and Paternoster's chapter on "individualized deviance." Murder was categorized under violations of privacy in their violations of middle-class norms, and suicide was categorized under violations of norms of "participation." Yet when constructing specific chapters in their book on social deviance, serial murder and suicide are categorized together because they are both instances of individualized deviance. There may be several theoretical and empirical reasons for dealing with these types of deviance in the same chapter but only one similarity is noted, and the relevance of their normative scheme for identifying communalities is never discussed. Other than their designation as "individualized," possibilities of shared and distinct features of these different forms of deviance are not specified.

When shared properties of disparate forms of deviance are addressed, however, interesting new ideas begin to emerge. Does serial murder share more in common with suicide than other forms of murder? "Normal murders" generated in social situations of interpersonal conflict, sexual competition, and/or defense of honor and territory differ markedly from "abnormal murders" carried out in secrecy with sequences of isolated victims. Is serial murder distributed across states differently than normal murder? Is its distribution more similar to suicide than normal

murder? Again, the sociology of deviance can reassert its independence and theoretical originality by addressing the relationships among different forms of deviance.

Specification and Application of Basic Sociological Concepts

One of the themes shared by all sociological perspectives on deviance whether positivistic, constructionist, or radical is that forms of disapproved conduct are shaped by variable socialization, social learning, and social control mechanisms among other forces. Such concepts are introduced rather casually, as if their specific meaning were firmly established. Yet "social control" is used to refer to Hirschi's social bond theory of deviance, "reactions to deviance" (see Black 1979), and Jack Gibbs's (1981, 1989, 1994) definition, in which social control refers to attempts by one or more individuals to manipulate the behavior of another individual or individuals by or through a third party (by means other than a chain of command).

Not only are there diverse conceptions of social control, but virtually no attention has been paid to distinguishing among the three "social" variables, *social*ization, *social* control, and *social* learning. In fact, "socialization" is the least discussed of the three in the sociology of deviance,

Since John DeLamater's 1968 discussion of the three forms of socialization and their relevance to distinct theories of deviance, there has been no attempt to clearly identify the meaning of the concept and how to distinguish it from other concepts. The concept can be more clearly specified, however, by adopting Gibbs's strategy for defining social control. If socialization refers to "attempts" to do "something," the key question becomes "What is being attempted?" Focusing on attempts to "socialize" someone else, a plausible definition would be that socialization refers to attempts to "teach" something to someone. A person may attempt to "learn" something from someone as well. Such attempts are social in two different senses. Just as social control refers to a type of interaction or relationship among people, socialization is "social" as well. However, socialization can be argued to be "doubly" social because it involves attempts to teach and/or learn something social as well.

Socialization refers to attempts to teach or learn the values and norms appropriate to social roles. Moreover, key social roles tend to be defined in terms of specific social institutions. For example, parents may attempt to teach a child how to be a "good" son or daughter, a "good" brother or sister, a "good" person, or a "good" citizen. Teachers attempt to teach students how to be a "good" student, a "good" citizen, and a "good" classmate. Ministers and religious personnel attempt to teach how to be a "good" Muslim, or a "good" Christian, a "good" Jew, and so on. The specific content of attempts to teach or learn role-related values and norms may differ or conflict with other role expectations. In addition, such attempts may not occur or/and some types of attempts may be more effective than others. Authoritarian parental teaching styles may be less effective than styles that allow two-way communication. Parents who engage their children in discussions of roles, norms, and values are likely to be more effective than those who demand unquestioning obedience.

If socialization is defined in such terms, then it can be distinguished from "social control" as defined by Gibbs, Hirschi, or Black, and from social learning as delineated by Akers. One of Gibbs's types of control is "referential" control, where one party attempts to influence a second party by invoking "reference" to shared normative authority. In fact, he argues that "referential" control attempts are most likely to be successful when there is consensus on a normative framework. If socialization refers to attempts to teach or learn that normative framework, then socialization can affect attempts at referential social control as well as their probability of success. Similarly, socialization would be linked to two of Hirschi's social bonds, "belief," which is measured as acceptance of conventional normative standards, and "commitment," which is measured in terms of pursuit of conventional value-laden goals. Finally, as defined here, socialization would be most specifically linked with Akers's normative learning mechanism in social learning theory.

Establishing Links with Other Sociological Specialties

In addition to the integration of specialties dealing with distinct forms of deviance and a more precise differentiation of sociological concepts, the sociology of deviance can be revived by reasserting its links to other specialties within sociology itself. In a review of the empirical status of social learning theory, Akers and Jensen (forthcoming) argue that the links between various theories of deviance and basic sociological concepts characterizing sociology in general have been lost. One reason for this loss is the tendency for contemporary criminologists to fall in one of two camps, one emphasizing variations over time and space among societies and social units at the aggregate level (sometimes called "nonreductionist") and the other gathering data from individuals, couching their theories as "social psychological." Continual warnings about the "ecological fallacy" (Robinson 1950), the erroneous extension of findings about variations at the ecological level to variations among individuals, have discouraged sociologists and criminologists from attempting to bridge those levels. Sociological variables and processes that may vary over time and space are treated as virtually irrelevant to understanding variation in behavior among individuals. At the individual level, researchers may measure "moral beliefs," or "social bonds" that explain variation in samples of individuals, while nonreductionists focus on aggregate properties of social systems such as inequality, welfare policies, and institutional weaknesses. There is virtually no effort by scholars operating in the two "traditions" to propose how transitions can be made between these levels,

and those advocating a nonreductionist approach give the impression that the two cannot be bridged.

One means of reintegration would be to combine the development of theories that demonstrate the relevance of knowledge about one form of deviance for fully understanding other forms with specific attention, theoretically and empirically, to related concepts in other specialties. For example, Nachman Ben-Yehuda (1981a, 1981b, 1985) points out that the European witch craze falls under the rubric of collective behavior (i.e., a "craze"). However, not only is there little discussion of what type of collective behavior it was (e.g., a "panic" versus a "craze"), but the fact that it was carried out through courts means that it takes on the properties of attempted social control through institutional machinery, characteristics that would disqualify it as a form of "collective behavior." On the other hand, when the relevance of concepts of deviance, social control, and collective behavior for understanding the early-modern search for witches are considered together, a new set of questions are likely to be asked. Can waves of court processing involve "paniclike" processes? Are such waves of processing responses to panic in the general public? Were the targets of attacks on witches women who engaged in witchcraft, women in competition with men, women who violated gender norms, or random victims? When such questions are asked, ideas from a wide range of sociological specialties need to be considered.

Bridging the Quantitative-Qualitative Divide

When the concept of a "panic" is introduced into the discussion of "deviance," it not only raises questions that require bridging sociological specialties but also leads to further discussion of *social constructionism*. One of the most common types of evidence used to highlight the constructionist position is any indication of a tenuous or fabricated "reality" as the impetus for defining a social problem, defining problematic people, or applying definitions and labels to specific people. In fact, the most impressive "deconstruction" of a problem from such a perspective is a demonstration that the alleged reality is a total fabrication or a dramatic distortion of some real-world events. Socially constructed myths can be exposed when information on the actual events that prompt the moral enterprise defining a problem can be shown to be an over-dramatization or an overreaction to those events.

A common research theme in constructionist research is to examine the role of the media or the use of the media by various interest groups in the invention or definition of a social problem. Social constructionists can make a strong case for the view that "*reality depends on perspective, and perspective is to a degree arbitrary*" by demonstrating disparities among measures of reality. For example, Shelden, Tracy, and Brown (2001) state that data on gang-related articles in newspaper and magazines "demonstrates that media reporting of events does not always conform to reality" (p. 3). The specific pattern leading to that conclusion was the decline in news coverage "in recent years," coupled with "steady growth in the number of gangs and the number of gang members" in "surveys of law enforcement agencies." The gang problem could be interpreted as declining in one source of subjective imagery while remaining constant, or even increasing, using data pertinent to an alternative "subjective" reality.

In fact, the concept of a "moral panic" was introduced by social constructionists to encompass situations where the public, political, and media reactions to a troublesome event or "problem" appears to far exceed the actual magnitude or any changes in the magnitude of the problem (Goode and Ben-Yehuda 1994a, 1994b). The rediscovery of the "gang problem" in the 1980s is depicted by McCorkle and Miethe (2002) under the rubric of *Panic: The Social Construction of the Gang Problem,* and their analysis emphasizes the fabrication of many aspects of the problem. News about cocaine use among athletes is depicted as a problem fabricated through media hype with little or no relation to actual drug use (Reinarman and Levine 1989). Similar arguments have been proposed for problems ranging from the search for Satanists and witches in preschools (Richardson, Best, and Bromley 1991) to child abuse data (Best 1990) to the "crack-baby panic" (Logan 1999).

Constructionists' positions can range from interpretations where the problem is a virtual fabrication to milder forms where variations in some "measurable" form of "real-world" phenomena are allowed to enter into the social construction of the social problem. For example, Ben-Yehuda (2001) proposes what he calls "contextual constructionism," a constructionist position that allows consideration of an "objective" foundation for deviance and social problems: Contextual constructionism argues that while deviance and social problems are the results of "claim-making" activities, the so-called objective dimension can be assessed and evaluated by an expert based on some form of scientific evidence (http://sociology.huji.ac.il/ben-yehuda).

This contextual approach does open the door for integrating two styles of research. Whenever a claim is made that a particular situation is a moral panic or a fabricated problem, it is incumbent on those making such claims to clearly demonstrate that there was no surge or wave of real-world events that prompted a panic. Similarly, it is incumbent on sociologists using positivist methods to ask to what degree a public or media reaction was an "over-reaction" to any discernible change in behavior. Both the claim that it was primarily a social construction as well as any counterclaim that there was sone form of "objective" foundation require attention to data of some kind.

SUMMARY

This chapter began with a reminder of basic sociological principles or themes shared by scholars with otherwise divergent perspectives on specific definitions and the appropriate subject matter for the sociology of deviance. Every textbook in the sociology of deviance highlights similar broad themes, identifies basic epidemiological perspectives, and introduces critical perspectives that challenge traditional theories. Indeed, the issues that were identified as "in need of" attention for progress in the sociology of deviance are academic and scholarly, and the discipline can survive quite well without addressing them.

However, there are features of the field that need attention to reinvigorate "sociological" interest in the specialty and generate new theoretical and research issues. Instead of debating about the best definition of deviance, the focus should be on interrelationships among properties of deviant phenomena when conceived of in different ways. Moreover, there has been far too little attention to basic sociological concepts, how they differ, and where they overlap. Similarly, specific attention to the relation between the properties of phenomena of interest to scholars in the study of deviance and their properties when viewed through conceptual lenses from other fields of sociology (e.g., collective behavior, social control) could reinvigorate sociological interest in the field.

Given the popularity and growth of criminology as an independent and interdisciplinary field of study, the findings that would reassert the importance of a sociology of deviance would be empirical demonstrations that a full understanding of crime requires an understanding of other forms of noncriminal deviance. Indeed, Gottfredson and Hirschi's general theory of crime is actually a general theory of deviance in that it proposes positive relationships between forms of noncriminal deviance or rule breaking and criminal force and fraud. The "latent trait" emphasized in their theory is a general propensity for rule breaking. Akers's social learning theory has been a general theory of deviance from its beginning, and Merton's theory was a theory of deviance as well. An exclusive focus on behaviors defined as criminal or delinquent is not consistent with the major theories.

Within the specialty, the most important issue for progress in the twenty-first century is a rapprochement between social constructionist perspectives and perspectives that assume some measure of real variation in forms of deviance over time and among people and territories. Whether this perspective is called "contextual constructionism" or some other term, the hypothesis that there are measurable "positivist" foundations for forms of conduct defined as problematic within a society should be part of a modified constructionist approach to the study of deviance. Instead of rejecting each other's methods as inadequate for a proper understanding of deviance, a cooperative dialogue between quantitative and qualitative researchers may yield the types of new ideas that prominent theorists believe to be in such short supply.

38

SEXUAL DEVIANCE

VALERIE JENNESS

GILBERT GEIS
University of California, Irvine

The subject of "sexual deviance" provides a particularly informative illustration of the application of the sociological imagination. Other fields of study and practice such as psychology, psychiatry, and law focus on sexual deviance as an act or a course of action, usually indulged in by a person, either alone or as part of a group. Such acts may be distinctive in the sense that they vary from a stipulated norm. In these nonsociological writings, the emphasis is placed on the behavior and on the person who is performing the act, not on those who judge it. Such approaches also focus on the consequences of the behavior. If a person is derogated as a sexual deviant, there will be a variety of possible outcomes. Sometimes he or she might be tolerated, with the toleration often carrying a taint of disapproving condescension and moral superiority. For others labeled as sexual deviants, the consequences may be degradation or isolation, punishment by the state, or voluntary or involuntary enlistment in programs of therapy or in other remedial regimens.

For sociologists, true to disciplinary doctrine, it is not the behavior of the individual that is of primary concern but the process by means of which the person and the behavior come to be regarded as deviant. A single individual might initiate the labeling, but to be effective, that person must convince others that affixing a derogatory designation onto individuals who behave in a certain manner is desirable. The label must satisfy the needs of those who affix it, and it may offer other rewards, perhaps bounties for identifying sexual miscreants, such as child abusers, recognition as an upright and responsible citizen, or affirmation that the wayward will suffer and the devout and dutiful will prosper, if not in this life than assuredly in the hereafter. Judgments of sexual deviance can become weapons employed by those who consider themselves upright to try to see that others following different paths are defamed. Some of those who are "good" come to believe that they suffer by comparison because those who are "bad" seem to be having a much better time and, perhaps, much greater success, such as when a casually promiscuous actress sleeps her way into juicy roles or a gay person files suit against a nasty boss on grounds of sexual discrimination while the straight person is debarred from a similar kind of action for other forms of harassment.

In his classic formulation of deviance, Howard Becker (1973) pointed out that deviance is not a quality of the act one commits but, rather, a consequence of the application to an "offender" by others of rules and sanctions. Therefore, the ultimate measurement of whether or not an act—sexual or otherwise—is deviant depends on how others who are socially significant in terms of power and influence define the act. Social acts and actors violating norms of society can be termed "rule-breaking behavior" and "rule breakers," respectively. However, the terms "deviant behavior" and "deviant" will be reserved for acts and actors labeled as such by a social audience. As John Kitsuse (1962), another well-known sociologist of deviance, made clear: Forms of behavior per se do not differentiate deviants from nondeviants; it is the response of the conventional and conforming members of the society who identify and interpret behavior as deviant that sociologically transforms rule-breaking behavior into deviance and persons who break rules or norms into deviants. Recently, Charles Tittle and Raymond Paternoster (2000) summarized the predominant ways in which sociologists have defined deviance and offered their own definition as follows: "Any type of behavior that the majority of a given group regards as unacceptable or that evokes a collective response of a negative type" (p. 13).

The "response of a negative type" is crucial to designations of deviance. Consider how the British social scientist Colin Summer (1994) summarizes the process by which a "deviant" label is pinned on someone and the implications of this labeling:

> Making someone deviant is indeed an active process warranting a verb. Deviance is not a self-evident category. It does not just float down from the skies applying itself to people who quite obviously are deviant. Deviance is a historical term and its application and/or adoption can create a status which dwarfs all others in its consequences for the individual's existence. Even the most deviant of all deviants just does not "happen": someone has to pass judgment, to portray, to stigmatize, to insult, to heap abuse, to exclude or to reject. (P. 223)

According to Erving Goffman (1968), making a deviant label stick to those so stigmatized is essentially a power play by "normals," an attempt to have one's own interpretations prevail in the marketplace of social life (for an application of this theme to deviant sexuality see Plummer [1975] and Salamon [1989]). In a pioneering article, Kai Erikson (1962) reinforced the idea that the label "sexual deviant" often tends to trump all other elements of a person's character and behavior. "Even a confirmed miscreant," Erikson points out, "conforms in most of his daily behavior—using the correct spoon at mealtime, taking good care of his mother, or otherwise observing the mores of the society" (p. 308).

Obviously, it is necessary to delimit the reach of the term "sexual deviance." Among other ways, it can be narrowed by use of a yardstick that declares deviant as anything not done by most other persons, a continuum that can range from the merely unconventional to the patently bizarre. How many others need to behave in a certain manner to make those who do not do so deviant is far from obvious. Nor is it clear whether behavior that is commonplace within a particular cultural group, and even is valued by that group, may be said to be deviant if the approving group is small (but how large does it need to be?) and the practice of which it approves is not regarded as "proper" by the rest of the society. The eminent social psychologist Leon Festinger (1951) warned of the fallacy of attributing deviant behavior or opinions to an individual when his or her group affiliations are not adequately understood.

Numerous theoretical frameworks have been developed by sociologists to explain the occurrences, forms, and consequences of deviance, including sexual deviance. One way to make sense of these frameworks is to organize them according to the degree to which they are designed to address one of two central questions in the study of deviance. First, normative theories focus on norm violations by asking, "Who violates norms and why?" Second, reactivist theories focus on reactions to norm violations by asking, "Why are certain types of norm violations and not others reacted to as deviant and result in the stigmatization of the rule-breaker?" Theories of deviance can be classified as macroscopic and microscopic. The former focus on societal and group structures and the latter on individuals and the interactional patterns in which they engage and to which they are subject.

WITCHCRAFT AS SEXUAL DEVIANCE

There probably is no better substantive material by means of which to illuminate the sociological approach to sexual deviance than through an examination of witchcraft persecutions and prosecutions. In witchcraft cases, we had communities charging individuals with sexual and other acts that no human being conceivably could have performed. Women, and it almost invariably was women (Hester 1992; Karlson 1987; Williams and Adelman 1992), were accused of having sexual intercourse with the devil, whose "member," for some uncertain reason, almost always was said to have been uncomfortably cold. The devil had crept into innumerable female beds for episodes of illicit intercourse, and there were alleged sabbats that involved orgies of unbridled sexuality (Monter 1976). The accused typically were widowed women without male offspring to defend them, and they often confessed to the infamous charges leveled against them (Macfarlane 1999). On the Continent, torture was instrumental in eliciting "admissions of guilt," but in England, torture was not countenanced (Langbein 1977).

Typical was the reported confession of Elizabeth Clarke, a widow living in Manningtree in East Anglia, who was interrogated in 1645 by a pair of self-appointed witch finders. She described the devil to her interrogator as "a tall, black haired gentleman, a properer man than yourself" (Gaskill 2005:50). Then, as Malcolm Gaskill (2005) reports,

> Clarke related fondly how she had first enjoyed "carnal copulation" with Satan six or seven years earlier. From that time he had been a regular visitor to her bedchamber, always presentable in his lace collar, and ready with his breathless plea, "Bess, I must lye with you." She had never refused and the love-making usually lasted half the night. (P. 50)

After a formal court trial, Clarke was found guilty of witchcraft and hanged.

There is no need to attempt to determine why what the women accused as witches did was condemned, since it is obvious that they had not carried out the stipulated behaviors; that is, Elizabeth Clarke had not had sexual intercourse with the devil. She may or may not have been having sexual business with a lover, although; if so, it might have been in her imagination and not in reality. The core issue that has engaged the handful of sociologists who have studied witchcraft fits neatly into major concerns of the discipline: Why did those attaching the label of witchcraft do so? "Crimes without Criminals" is the title of sociologist Elliott Currie's contribution: It could equally aptly have been "Deviants without Deviance" (Currie 1968; see also Erikson 1966).

To illustrate the major sociological perspective on sexual deviance, we can consider a few of the numerous explanations of the dynamics of labeling that underlay witchcraft accusations. Perhaps the most persuasive view, at least for England, inheres in the theological ethos of the times. Tragedy was common and death of children a constant threat. Such occurrences were regarded as signs of divine disapproval, and the thought of godly disapprobation, given the intensity of religious commitment, could be terrifying. The preeminent seventeenth-century jurist Matthew Hale expressed the ruling dogma well: "Afflictions," he proclaimed, "are most certainly effects and fruits of sin: and worldly crosses and calamities do as naturally flow from precedent sins, as the crop doth from the seed that is sown" (Thirlwall, 1805:346). But what better tactic to deflect such disapproval than to maintain that the calamity of a diseased or dead child was the consequence of witchcraft and not of parental failure? Social anthropologists often note the functional utility of scapegoating. "This book," Lucy Mair (1969) writes in her study of witchcraft in tribal societies, "starts with the premise that in a world where there are few assured techniques for dealing with everyday crises, notably sickness, a belief in witches or the equivalence of one, is not only not foolish, it is indispensable" (p. xx). The tactic seemingly is not chosen with malice aforethought: It merely provides a scapegoat, generally one with commonly acknowledged "antisocial" traits (Geis and Bunn 1997; Thomas 1971).

The sexual content of the witchcraft charges against the usually impoverished women apparently is to be found in the concomitant fear and fascination with sexual indulgence that was particularly prominent in a society marked by puritan prudence and prudery. On the Continent, witchcraft charges, also suffused with erotic narratives, more often would be pressed against members of the "better classes," who were identified by the Inquisition because the state would confiscate the holdings of those burned for their allegedly heretical actions (Russell 1972). Besides these situations, personal jealousies and motives of revenge for real or imagined slights played into the lodging of charges against vulnerable and typically powerless parties. It is notable that an unbridled outbreak of witch-hunting on the Continent let up only when, under torture, accused women began to name the wives of prominent persons of the community as members of their coven (Midelfort 1972).

SEXUAL DEVIANCE AND SOCIOLOGY

For sociologists, then, it basically is not the elements of the act being considered that render it "deviant" but the response of others to that act. Therefore, for sociologists (and, indeed, for most others), there is no reason for either "sexual" or "deviance" to be anchored firmly in the realm of unambiguous lexical meaning. Sociological textbooks on deviance may include chapters or segments on obesity, blindness, mental illness, and a host of other conditions that are deemed to be more or less "different." The result often becomes an attempt to provide information about these conditions rather than to enter into a very complex and perhaps redundant attempt to determine why a ruling social system or a powerful group within it might define such things as deviant.

Like sociologists and other social scientists, preachers, pundits, and the public also have not felt constrained to confine themselves to a roster of precise behaviors when they talk or write about "deviance," "sexuality," or "sexual deviance." On one extreme, there is the work of Sigmund Freud ([1905] 2000), who put forward the idea that most normative and nonnormative human actions are the consequence of sexual forces. The ubiquitous Oedipal conflict represents the lust of a young male for his mother, just as a son's hostility toward his father has its roots in sexual jealousy and in competition for the mother's favors. Shoplifting a fountain pen is interpreted as castration anxiety that is acted out as a desire to acquire a substitute phallus. For others, acts with a sexual element that are proscribed in the Bible are declared to be deviant, though other biblical sins calling for the death penalty, such as cursing one's parents, go unheeded. For still other persons, anything with an erotic tinge that they do not approve of is regarded as "sexual deviance" or, to use the historically common term, "perversion." Finally, on the far side of the continuum, where many sociologists rest their case, there are those who steadfastly maintain that nothing a human being does can sensibly be regarded as deviant or perverted because all behavior represents an expression of the actor's humanity and seeks to satisfy a human need or desire. Their mantra tends to be in accord with the words of sociologist Paul Tappan (1947): "It is unwise," he declared, "for the social scientist ever to forget that all standards of social normation are relative, impermanent, and variable" (p. 101).

Tappan's (1947) dictum accords with the working ethos of sociologists and other social scientists grappling with how to understand the social standing and the causes, manifestations, and consequences of nonnormative sexual behavior—sexual deviance. In the process of empirically documenting and theoretically explaining varying forms of sexual deviance, sociologists' struggles with definitional ambiguities have, in turn, produced conceptual disagreements; amassed a large body of empirical research on the social organization of stigmatized identities, behaviors, groups, and communities organized around sex and sexuality; and developed a plethora of theoretical frameworks.

ON DEFINITIONAL AMBIGUITY

Reading across the large body of literature on sexual deviance shows that sociologists have not been the major players in the field, especially when compared with psychiatrists, anthropologists, and psychologists. In the medical field, the first comprehensive taxonomy of sexual deviance, Herman Kaan's (1844) *Psychopathia Sexualis,* drew analogies between the sexuality of what he regarded as primitive human groups and children. The primitives were said to display humanity's unrefined sexuality. Later, Richard von Krafft-Ebbing ([1888] 1988) established what has remained medical suzerainty over at least the more unusual forms of sexual expression and entered on the record a litany of words, often with Greek and Latin roots, that were deemed to require medical attention, terms such as *coprolagnia* (obtaining sexual gratification from eating, smelling, throwing, or handling excrement), *frottage* (achieving sexual gratification from rubbing up against another person), *necrophilia* (sexual intercourse with corpses), *piquerism* (getting sexual satisfaction from cutting flesh and shedding blood), and *urolagnia* (associating sexual satisfaction with urine and urination).

Sociologists continue to question the value of treating sexual deviance as separate field of inquiry while, at the same time, increasingly joining forces with humanists to address questions related to the historical and cultural variability over time and in different settings of the two sides of the same coin: normative sexuality and sexual deviance. What was once sexually deviant can become normative (i.e., premarital sex) and what was once sexually normative can become deviant (i.e., virgin sacrifices). Thus, sexual deviance cannot be defined by identifying empirical realms in an absolutist fashion.

The definitional ambiguities surrounding the term "sexual deviance" invite questions about what fits into the category "sexual" and what constitutes "deviance" before the terms can be combined in a productive way. We will first address this issue, and then will examine homosexuality, a particularly controversial realm of sexual behavior. We do so to demonstrate how sociologists view the contours of sexual deviance in structural, cultural, and interactional terms. We also will look at how interest groups, such as religious conservatives and homosexuals themselves, use sociological and other scientific perspectives to advance the positions they favor. Our central thesis throughout this chapter is that the sociological study of sexual deviance has produced a rather narrow body of literature that nonetheless offers significant contributions to larger sociological inquiry by explaining some of the most basic social processes (e.g., symbolic interaction) and structures (e.g., norms) of interest to the discipline.

CONCEPTUALIZING SEXUAL, DEVIANCE, AND SEXUAL DEVIANCE

The Sexual Realm

Sex looms large in society. In *The History of Sexuality,* Michel Foucault (1990), perhaps the most cited contemporary analyst of human sexuality, deemed sex "the explanation for everything, our master key" (p. 33). Similarly, social historian Jeffrey Weeks (1990) proclaimed that "as sex goes, so goes society" (p. 37). Yet at least since the term "sexuality" first appeared in the English dictionary in the early nineteenth century, its connotations and denotations have shifted across time, culture, and community. Defining the parameters of sexuality, as well as the dynamics that underlie its performance, has been a central point of debate among scholars (see, e.g., Epstein 1987; Foucault 1990; Laumann et al. 1994; Singer 1993; Stanton 1995).

Sexual behavior in American society represents one of the most emotion-laden areas of life, and deep and sensitive feelings about it often serve to shunt aside dispassionate consideration of its organization and dynamics. With a puritan heritage as a cultural backdrop, Americans tend to be simultaneously attracted and repelled by different aspects of sexual behavior, without agreeing as to what constitutes sex, sexual, sexuality, and sexual desire (Birken 1988). The semantic dilemma associated with "sexual" can be explicated by revisiting the notorious interactions between Bill Clinton, then president of the United States, and Monica Lewinsky, a onetime intern in the White House who had been exiled from that post because of judgments about her predatory eroticism. When allegations were raised that Lewinsky had orally copulated Clinton, his initial response was that whatever he might have done did not constitute "sex," an interpretation, it later came to light, endorsed by Lewinsky, who regarded their behavior as nothing more than good fun. Some wondered what the reaction might have been had Lewinsky been discovered licking Clinton's kneecap, somewhat (but also rather different in terms of common interpretations) in the manner of one of Clinton's closest advisers—Dick Morris—who delighted in sucking the toes of a prostitute in rendezvous they held at a hotel near the White House. Perhaps it was the adulterous nature of the relationship that moved some of the interactions between Clinton and Lewinsky into the realm of sexual, deviance from the point of view of most Americans (Kalb 2001). Or perhaps in the Clinton-Lewinsky scandal, it was the interaction in which Lewinsky inserted a cigar into her vagina and then offered it to Clinton, whose judgment was, "It tastes good" (Starr 1998).

The role played by Hillary Clinton, now the junior senator from New York, in the Lewinsky affair offers a good deal of insight into some dynamics of sexual deviance. Despite long-standing and compelling evidence that his behavior was in accord with a pattern of sexual dalliance,

Ms. Clinton initially maintained that the allegations against her husband represented part of "a vast right-wing political conspiracy to undo the results of two elections." Subsequently, she changed course, now declaring that although her husband had to take personal responsibility for his infidelity, its manifestation was the result of "abuse" he suffered as a child because of "terrible conflict" between his mother and grandmother. She added that a psychiatrist had told her that being placed in the vortex of a storm between two women is the worst possible situation for a boy because of his desire to please them both. Her husband's behavior, Ms. Clinton said, was a "sin of weakness" rather than of "malice" (Geis 2002:27–28). A *New Yorker* cartoon lampooned such excusatory claims based on prior victimization. A woman is testifying in court: "I know he cheated on me because of his childhood abuse," she says, "but I shot him because of mine."

Regardless of how the Clinton-Lewinsky affair is regarded, it reinforces the conclusion that precise designation of what is "sexual" is not a simple matter that can be resolved unequivocally. Lewinsky's and Clinton's testimony aside, the question of the status of oral copulation, a common enough practice throughout the United States (Laumann et al. 1994), reveals that the sexual realm is—like all social realms—historically and culturally contingent as well as locally and situationally defined.

Sexuality takes many forms precisely because it can be imbued with a multiplicity of meanings depending on operative cultural codes (Seidman 1992), hegemonic systems of meaning (Foucault 1990), and the social location and status of those producing, managing, and receiving sexual meanings (Morrison and Tallack 2005). As John Gagnon and William Simon (1973) explain in *Sexual Conduct,* "underlying all human activity, regardless of the field or its stage of development, there exists metaphors or informing imageries" (p. 1). In the sexual realm, the authors highlight the existence of "scripts" that are involved in learning the meaning of internal states, organizing the sequence of specifically sexual acts, decoding novel situations, setting the limits on sexual responses, and linking the meaning of nonsexual aspects of life to specifically sexual experiences (Gagnon and Simon 1973:19). Kenneth Plummer (1992) has observed that acts, identities, and expressions are only rendered sexual via the attachment of some meanings and not others. Steven Epstein (1987) takes this relativistic doctrine to its extreme: "Sexual acts have no inherent meaning, and in fact, no act is inherently sexual," he writes (p. 14). At least the latter part of that sentence is, at best, arguable: To insist, for instance, that copulation is not a sexual act is a reductionist claim that deprives the word *sexual* of any possible meaning. Epstein's claim may make for resounding ideology, but it leaves scientific and common understanding in the lurch.

Nonetheless, sociologists generally agree that sexuality is not a biologically derived fact, though, as we shall see, clashes persist regarding whether homosexual activity is a free choice or a genetically ordained activity. There is near consensus that within the limits of their physical characteristics, human beings are capable of any type of sexual activity, thus sex and sexuality can take innumerable forms. In *Intimate Matters: A History of Sexuality in America,* historians John D'Emilio and Estelle Freedman (1988) provide a wide-angled view of macroshifts in sexuality by documenting how, during the past 375 years,

> the meaning and place of sexuality in American life have changed: from a family-centered, reproductive sexuality in the colonial era; to a romantic, intimate, yet conflicted sexuality in nineteenth-century marriage; to a commercialized sexuality in the modern period, when sexual relations are expected to provide personal identity and individual happiness apart from reproduction. (P. xii)

See Birken (1988) for an alternative view. As the meaning of sexuality has changed in America from a primary association with reproduction within families to a primary association with emotional intimacy and physical pleasure for individuals, the norms delimiting the boundaries between acceptable sexuality and "abnormal" sexuality have also shifted. In 1643, in colonial New England, James Britton and 18-year-old Mary Lanham were hanged for having committed adultery (Banner 2002:6). Today, many persons enthusiastically offer up intimate details of their own adulteries on television talk shows, in newspaper interviews, and autobiographies, apparently on the assumption, undoubtedly correct, that these confessions are marketable to a prurient public (Gamson 1999).

Despite the complexities of metaphors, scripts, and norms that inform varying understandings of the content of sexuality, at the heart of the matter is a focus on being stereotyped and distinguished by gender, a concern with erotic activity and desire, and an emphasis on real or imagined stimulation and attendant bodily sensation. This formulation moves well beyond the definition of sexual employed by Alfred Kinsey, Wardell Pomeroy, and Clyde Martin (1948) in their pioneering study of human sexual behavior. They elected to use orgasm as the measure of what was and what was not a sexual act because it offered a reasonably concrete measure. In contrast, sociological definitions allow for an endless array of behavior, expression, and identity that do not result in orgasm; they also incorporate an acknowledgment that subjective elements intrude into such determinations. With regard to subjective elements in determinations of sexuality, Gagnon and Simon (1973) observe the following:

> It is perhaps startling to consider that when we think about the sexual, nearly our entire imagery is drawn from physical activities of bodies. Our sense of normalcy derives from organs being placed in legitimate orifices. We have allowed the organs, the orifices, and the gender of the actors to personify or embody or exhaust nearly all of the meanings that exist in the sexual situation. (P. 5)

More recently, Mark Graham (2004) revisited and revised this formulation by declaring as follows:

> Sexuality is in danger of becoming a thing, if it has not already become one. Under its umbrella have been assembled a host of bodily practices, tastes, pleasures, desires, moral judgments, and much more. These disparate phenomena have imploded into the term, providing sexuality with a remarkable range of application and an exaggerated explanatory power. (P. 300)

Regardless of the range of phenomena under the umbrella of sexuality, our individual and collective sense of "normalcy" is inextricably tied to ideas about deviance, sexual and otherwise. Indeed, much philosophical and legal debate concerning sexual deviance centers on the word "normal." The well-known humorist Robert Benchley must have had some standard in mind when he quipped that his "sex life wasn't normal but it was interesting" (Kunkel 2000:283). So too must have Kobe Bryant, the basketball celebrity, when he sought to defend himself against a rape allegation that included the complainant's statement that when he had intercourse with her, he had held her "around the neck from behind." This was not an indication of the use of force, Bryant maintained. He used the same tactic with another woman with whom, unbeknownst to his wife, he had sexual congress: "Me and Michelle, that's what we do, we do the same thing," Bryant told his interrogators (Brennan 2004:6A). Presumably, this was an effort to portray his behavior as natural and normal——at least for him. The behavior was but a part of his usual heterosexual repertoire.

The Realm of Deviance

From Durkheim's (1958) study of suicide onward, sociology as a discipline has provided a home for the study of deviance. Sociologists have generated empirical studies of criminals, the mentally ill, drug users, alcoholics, welfare recipients, communists, people with physical and cognitive disabilities, homosexuals, dwarfs, giants, heretics, tramps, hippies, prostitutes, motorcycle gang members, abortionees and abortioners, nudists, topless barmaids, religious and racial/ethnic minorities, blackmailers, exotic dancers, rodeo groupies, cock fighters, pedophiles, and terrorists—to name just a few. Sociologist Jerry Simmons learned from a survey that respondents identified more than 200 different kinds of people as "deviants," including prostitutes, perpetual bridge players, girls who wear makeup, drug addicts, and prudes (cited in Thio and Calhoun 2001:1).

The term "deviance" typically carries a meretricious connotation, although in the sexual and other realms, the designation on occasion can be employed as a compliment, such as when someone is declared to deviate upward from the norm in terms of beauty or sexual equipment or performance. There is also a possibility that deviance, particularly of a sexual variety, may be correlative——or even a cause or consequence—of impressive intellectual performance. For example, Richard Feynman, a Nobel Prize-winning physicist, who taught at Cal Tech, was wont to spend a good deal of time in a topless bar in Pasadena, saying that the ambiance fed his creative juices (Feynman 1985; Gleick 1993). Likewise, Kary Mullis, a biochemistry Nobelist, has been described as "a creative nonconformist verging on the lunatic." Among his antics was the display during class lectures of nude slides of his girlfriends surrounded by multicolored fractal patterns (Mullis 1998). Speaking more academically, leading scholars specializing in deviance, for example, Jack Katz (1988) and cultural criminologists (Ferrell and Sanders 1995) have encouraged sociological colleagues to recognize that deviance can be fun and exciting, perhaps even creative and artistic. Nonetheless, almost always "deviance" is used as a negative judgment, implying a lesser degree of adequacy and orthodoxy than is acceptable or should be permissible.

In simple terms, deviance can be defined as nonnormative behavior that, if detected, can be subject to informal or formal sanctions. Deviants are those who engage in behavior that deviates from norms in a disapproved direction in sufficient degree to exceed the tolerance limits of a discernable social group such that the behavior is likely to illicit a negative sanction if detected.

Sexual Deviance

As Erich Goode (2005) indicates,

> When the words "sexual deviant" are used to describe someone, the image that comes to mind is someone who is impelled to act as a result of uncontrollable, unfathomable, and distinctly abnormal motives—someone whose behavior is freakish, fetishist, and far-out. (P. 237)

Goode's alliterative prose captures the mindset of a large segment of the population; however, that mind-set lacks the nuances that enter into sociological judgments about what might be considered the full range of what could be called "sexual deviance."

Drawing on the conceptualization of sexuality and the conceptualization of deviance provided above, we can formally define sexual deviance as any erotic activity, identity, or expression with a focus on real or imagined stimulation and attendant bodily sensation that, if detected, can be subject to formal or informal sanctions. Defined in this manner, deviant sexuality can take many forms. Most commonly, sociologists who study sexual deviance have focused analytic attention on diverse types of people— homosexuals, prostitutes, exotic dancers, topless barmaids, nudists, masturbators, sodomites, sex offenders, and pedophiles who break historical, cultural, and group-specific sexual norms.

At the same time, other forms of sexual deviance have escaped sociological attention. For example, William

Heirens, a student at the University of Chicago, committed more than 300 burglaries and admitted achieving orgasm by the act of entering strange residences. When interrupted during his burglaries, Heirens three times killed the females he encountered and on each occasion lingered at the scene to carefully wash the bodies of his victims. He also left a message, written with lipstick in large letters on one living room wall where he had just murdered a woman: CATCH ME BEFORE I KILL MORE I CANNOT CONTROL MYSELF (Freeman 1955). Other examples include the so-called crush freaks, who are aroused by the sight of an insect exploded beneath a human foot (Biles 2004); wetlocks, who have an inclination to wear wet clothing and to obtain sexual pleasure by viewing other people wearing such clothing (Börstling 2000); zoophiles and bestialists, who have erotic interactions with animals, usually mammals (Beetz 2000; Beirne 1997); and people who engage in "bug chasing" (i.e., HIV-negative gay men who seek out relations with infected partners to take the risk of becoming infected with the deadly virus that causes AIDS) (Gauthier and Forsyth 1999); and cybersex (Daneback, Cooper, and Månsson 2005).

As with all sociological phenomena, sexual deviance can be subdivided into several broad categories (see, e.g., Gagnon and Simon 1968). First, there are acts that are deviant if consent is not present, such as forcible rape. Rape is a very difficult event to adjudicate because the essential elements of the behavior itself are routine, and it becomes uncommonly demanding to rebut a defense that insists that the complainant did not consent to what happened. The interplay of deviance and social norms is highlighted in the consistent research finding that the likelihood of a successful prosecution increases dramatically if the alleged rape victim has an impeccable sexual and personal background (LaFree 1989). Second, there are acts that are deemed wrongful because of the nature of the sexual object; these can include incest and can embrace marriage with close kin. Bestiality—that is, sexual relations with an animal—also comes under this heading, and in earlier days, not only the human but also the animal was executed for such behavior (Evans 1906). Third, sexual deviance also inheres in acts that are performed in a setting that is not regarded as proper for the behavior: Exhibitionism in places where genital exposure is regarded as inappropriate falls into this category. Heterosexual copulation at high noon in a crowded public square would also be seen as wayward and deviant. But each of these classifications admits to many variations in the characteristics of the persons involved and the particular form the behavior takes (Hensley and Tewksbury 2003:7–8; Wheeler 1960).

HOMOSEXUALITY

More than any other type of sexual deviance, sociologists have most consistently directed analytic attention to homosexual behavior. An entire chapter generally was devoted to the topic in most sociology of deviance textbooks, and discussion of homosexuality historically loomed large in chapters on "deviance" in introductory textbooks. More recently, however, writers have become skittish about grouping "homosexuality" and "deviance," since doing so might offend a not inconsiderable number of those assigning or reading the books. Today, sociology textbook discussions of homosexuality are likely to be subsumed in chapters with titles such as "Sexuality and Gender" (see, e.g., Giddens, Duneier, and Applebaum 2003).

The Humphreys Heritage

The classic study by sociologist Laud Humphreys of restroom homosexual activity in a public park provides a particularly informative example of sociological contributions to the study of sexual deviance. Humphreys (1970), an ordained Episcopal minister, had undertaken graduate work at Washington University in St. Louis, and his dissertation, published as *Tearoom Trade,* offered graphic accounts of homosexual encounters in the restrooms, most involving men from a considerable variety of social backgrounds who stopped there on the way home from work. Humphreys tells readers that he gathered his data by volunteering to serve as a lookout. He does not address the question of why the behavior he was exploring was considered sexually deviant, nor what its roots might be. Rather, he was concerned with the process, with what went on. Particularly notable for Humphreys was his finding that the restroom transactions were almost always carried out without verbal communication between the participants: In only 15 of the 50 episodes he observed were any words spoken. Instead, participants relied on a set of body movements that proclaimed their desire to engage in a transient homosexual liaison.

The Humphreys investigation is particularly notable for three matters, all concomitants of its focus on sexual deviance. The first was a quarrel between two preeminent sociologists regarding the propriety of Humphreys's work. Alvin Gouldner, the sociology department's chair, called Humphreys a "peeping parson" and told his dissertation chair, Lee Rainwater, who later would join the Harvard faculty, that the study was a shameless piece of voyeurism. Gouldner also pushed and kicked Humphreys in the belief that he was posting caricatures of him on departmental bulletin boards (Galliher, Brekhus, and Keys 2004). The dispute was seen as significant enough to merit a news story in the *New York Times* ("Sociology Professor" 1968).

The second issue involved Humphreys's taking down the license numbers of the cars driven by those who participated in the restroom sexual encounters and then using a law enforcement source to learn the names and addresses of these men. Thereafter, he changed his appearance and visited most of them, pretending that he was collecting information as part of a health survey. Among other things, Humphreys learned that by and large the men were married. Nicholas von Hoffman, a nationally syndicated columnist, thought that Humphreys's behavior was unethical, an unwarranted intrusion on the privacy of the men, and perhaps a threatening invasion if they were to recognize their visitor (von Hoffman 1975). Humphreys insisted that nobody he later interviewed connected him to the role of lookout that he took in the initial phase of the study. Today, of course, no university human subjects committee would approve Humphreys's research blueprint.

Finally, Humphreys only later disclosed that he himself was a gay man, leading critics to believe that he might well have misled them with regard to his actual role in the study. This view was reinforced by John Galliher and his colleagues (2004), who discovered that the restroom windows were small and covered with opaque glass and metal grillwork. It is arguable if up-front disclosure of Humphreys' sexual preference should have been mandatory, but the controversy that the issue aroused indicates how highly charged field inquiries about sexual deviance can become.

The Social Construction of Homosexuality

Sociologists, historians, anthropologists, and psychologist alike have been studying homosexuality since the invention of the term in 1869 by Hungarian physician Karl Maria Benkert (Halperin 1990:155). Benkert described homosexuality in the following terms:

> In addition to the normal sexual urge in man and woman, Nature in her sovereign mood has endowed at birth certain male and female individuals with the homosexual urge, thus placing them in a sexual bondage which renders them physically and psychically incapable—even with the best of intention—of normal erection. This urge creates in advance a distinct horror of the opposite [sex] and the victim of this passion finds it impossible to suppress the feeling which individuals of his own sex exercise upon him. (quoted in Hirschfeld 1936:322)

This picaresque hodgepodge of intuition, folklore, prescience, and patronization presages a large part of the full range of viewpoints that would be expressed over subsequent years about homosexual activity.

Beginning with sociologist Mary McIntosh's (1968) now classic article "The Homosexual Role," which argued against then prevailing medical opinions, sociologists have taken the position that homosexuality is first and foremost a social construction. In sharp contrast to essentialist approaches to homosexuality, which treat homosexuality as a biological force and consider homosexual identities to be cognitive realizations of genuine, underlying differences, constructionists stress that homosexuality as a social construct belongs to the world of culture and meaning, not biology (Epstein 1987). Accordingly, social constructionist approaches understand homosexuals as a type of person and homosexuality as a type of behavior to be social creations born of social arrangements, cultural

shifts, and social movements (see, e.g., Conrad and Schneider 1992; Stein 1997; Taylor and Whittier 1992); sexual behavior as conduct ultimately bound by cultural scripts (Laumann et al. 1994); and individual desire and choice as fundamentally defined by larger social narratives and ideologies that influence the stories people tell about themselves (Esterberg 1997; Plummer 1996; Stein 1997). Combined, these approaches to understanding homosexuality in sociological terms have reacted to essentialist themes running through prior published works by historians, psychologists, clinicians, and journalists to assert that sexualities of all sorts, including nonnormative sexualities, are informed by and products of historical moments, structural arrangements, cultural milieus, situational imperatives, and individual psychologies and biographies.

Much macrosociological work on homosexuality situates the study of same-sex desire and behavior within specific historical contexts to demonstrate the fluidity of sexuality in general and homosexuality in particular as a social construct across time and space. For example, in their work on the medicalization of deviance, Peter Conrad and Joseph Schneider (1992) demonstrate how dominant understandings of homosexuality as a sin were medicalized in the eighteenth century so that homosexuality came to be understood as a sickness and homosexuals were envisioned as diseased. As they explain, "From its origins as primarily a religious transgression, a sin, same-sex conduct had become by the end of the medieval period, a matter of state control, a crime, and ultimately was redefined in modern society as a sickness" (Conrad and Schneider 1992:172). More recent work has continued in this vein by demonstrating that contemporary understandings of same-sex desire and conduct are envisioned as a "sexual orientation" or "sexual preference" with consequences for legal standing, community affiliation, and lifestyle practices. Quite apart from empirical foci on different eras, this type of work shares a commitment to revealing the historical complementarity and continuity of religious, medical, and legal definitions of homosexuality that inevitably inform any understanding of same-sex desires and behaviors.

Toward a Nondeviant Status for Homosexuality

Politically and ideologically, the sociological stance often conflicts with what individuals with a preference for homosexual relationships and groups that support them believe is a more accurate and, assuredly, a more politically powerful set of assumptions about the etiology of homosexuality. They look to genetic elements rather than social situations to explain why some persons prefer members of their own gender as sexual partners. Typically, there is considerable reliance on anecdotal evidence: "I knew from an early age that I was much more attracted to other males (or other females) than I was to members of the opposite sex." But there also is a thriving industry in studies that seek to locate physiological differences between persons who engage in homosexual and those who participate in heterosexual encounters. The *New York Times* is wont to run such stories on its first page despite their invariably inconclusive, albeit suggestive nature.

In mid-2005, for instance, the newspaper offered a lengthy report about the use of a brain imaging technique that led Swedish neuroscientists to conclude that homosexual men respond to odors in the same way as women, but differently than heterosexual males (Savic, Berglund, and Lindstrom 2005; Wade 2005). The odors were those of a testosterone derivative found in men's sweat and an estrogen-like compound found in women's urine. Steven Pinker (2005), a Harvard professor of cognitive science, scoffed at the results, observing that "when people want to be titillated or to check out a prospective partner, most seek words or pictures, not dirty laundry" (p. A25). For Pinker, the biological puzzle inherent in homosexuality was that "any genetic tendency to avoid heterosexual tendencies should have been selected out long ago" (p. A25).

Wherever the truth might lie, genetic explanations have provided powerful ammunition in the drive to remove homosexuality from the roster of sexually deviant behavior and thereby to disarm those who insist that the behavior is a free and willful choice to violate prevailing codes of propriety. The success of such efforts was dramatically on display when the American Psychiatric Association removed homosexuality from consideration in the most recent edition of its *Diagnostic and Statistical Manual of Mental Disorders* (*DSM-IV*). It has been noted that

> homosexual activists lobbied hard . . . to have homosexuality rediagnosed. Commandeering the nomenclature committee, threatening violence at the national convention . . . the activists managed to secure a vote from the psychiatrists to remove homosexuality from the list of diagnostic disorders. (Knight 1998:47)

A pro-gay writer grants that the APA decision "was not a conclusion based on an approximation of the scientific truth as dictated by reason, but was instead an action demanded by the ideological temper of the times" (Bayer 1981:3–4). This development supplies evidence of the wisdom of the sociological approach to sexual deviance: Determination of the status is not a reflection of behavior per se but rather a negotiable matter, mediated by the power to prevail in a struggle over defining labels.

Public Opinion and Sexual Deviance

Public opinion polls taken in the latter part of the twentieth century show that judgments about homosexuality as sexual deviance are largely negative but that they have been shifting in significant ways. Lydia Saad (2005), a member of the Gallup organization, summarized the current situation well:

> Most Americans believe homosexuals should have equal rights in the workforce. But the public's underlying belief that homosexual relations are immoral seems to prevail in attitudes about expanding those rights to gay marriage, which a majority opposes. Barely half consider homosexuality a culturally acceptable lifestyle. While public tolerance of gays has increased considerably over the past three decades, there has been little change in the last few years, and support for homosexuals serving as teachers or in the clergy has actually declined. (P. 1)

Beginning in the latter part of the twentieth century, psychologists and sociologists alike began to enumerate sets of sequences by means of which people come to engage in homosexual behavior and how they make sense of the label "homosexual" (Dank 1971; Jenness 1992; Ponse 1978). Psychologists rely almost exclusively on theories of psychosexual development, whereas sociologists will commonly depend on a symbolic interactionist framework. Both approaches focus on the intersection between personal experiences, key interactions, and the historical moment that provide the social constructs that serve as the basis for self-evaluation. Personal testimony to the salience of this view appears in the introspective thoughts of a gay writer who reminisces about a particular episode in his youth:

> One weekend, when I was in college in Ann Arbor she [his girlfriend] came to visit me and we kissed passionately and undressed, but I was impotent. Today, there are pills for that, and behavioristic exercises. I sometimes wonder whether, if I'd been able to perform then and with other women, I would be married today. And, if so, would I be happier than I am now? (White 2005:129)

A clear message emanates from sociological research on homosexuality. There is an empirical and theoretical difference between "doing" behaviors associated with homosexuality and "being" homosexual; that is, there is a gap between same-sex behaviors, imputations of homosexuality, and the adoption of a homosexual/gay/lesbian identity. Carol Smith-Rosenberg (1975) illustrates this point by documenting the way in which romantic female friendships were comparatively common in the nineteenth century, but attributions of lesbianism and sexual deviance were absent with regard to these relationships. They were understood as compatible with heterosexual marriage. In the modern era, Laumann et al.'s (1994) work has revealed a high degree of variability in the ways that differing elements of homosexuality, especially desire, identity, and behavior, are distributed for both women and men.

The sociological focus on subjectivities and on attendant interpretations of sexual behavior has been used to make sense of everything from virginity loss (Carpenter 2005) to stigmatized sadomasochism (Weinberg, Williams, and Moser 1984; cf., Chancer 1992). With regard to homosexuality in particular, this line of research has documented the continuities and changes in identities, sexualities, and narratives emerging within and outside of homosexual communities embedded in discernable historical and cultural moments (Stein 1992). Plummer (2003) argues that we are living in a time characterized by "new sexual stories" and that we are witnessing the advent of the sexual citizen who refuses to be marginalized on account of his or her sexuality. What was once characterized as "sexual deviance" now entails new sexual subjectivities that demand recognition and respect—the antithesis of deviance.

DISCUSSION AND CONCLUSION

Stepping back from the details of the literature reported in this chapter, one thing is clear: Sociologists who study deviant sexuality have documented the plethora of ways in which sex, sexuality, and sexual desire are social products. By drawing analytic attention to nonnormative forms of sexuality, they have rendered vivid innumerable links between the social organization of sexuality, social processes, and social structures. Moreover, they have demonstrated that changes in the designation of "normalcy" and "sexual deviance" reflect larger changes in social institutions, especially the family, the economy, the law, and religion. Far from conceiving of sexuality, deviant or otherwise, as a private matter, sociologists have demonstrated that it is a public, political, and social fact. By focusing on nonnormative sexualities, sociologists have shown how social facts, orthodoxies, and social control come into being and get transformed and institutionalized as well as what they mean for our individual and collective lives. These contributions have come as a result of sociologists using studies of sexual deviance to refute assumptions about sexuality promulgated by psychologists, clinicians, journalists, and others both historically and in modern times. This refutation has been institutionalized via the inauguration of a Sexualities section in the American Sociological Association and the publication of a number of specialty journals devoted to the study of sexuality that adopt a broad, interdisciplinary perspective covering the social sciences, cultural history, cultural anthropology, and social geography, as well as feminism, gender studies, cultural studies, and lesbian and gay studies.

Sexual deviance as a powerful political item was highlighted during the 2004 presidential election in the United States when the term "moral issues" emerged on the political radar. Exit polls at election sites found that "moral values" was the item most often selected as the prime consideration in voters' choice of a presidential candidate. Republicans, particularly those on the far right, interpreted this to mean that the electorate had resonated to the party's stand against abortion and in favor of a constitutional ban on gay marriages. Democrats, counterpunching, pointed out that there were other "moral values" besides those with a sexual content, things such as the environment and health care. Neutral observers had little trouble adjudicating this dispute: It was matters touching on the hot-button topic of sexual deviance that had been in play to the advantage of the incumbent candidate.

What does the future hold for the study of sexual deviance? Medical specialists report that they "are concerned about the rate of progress of this field in the foreseeable future" (Laws and O'Donohue 1997:9). They observe that the subject area is becoming increasingly litigious, in part because of lawsuits based on incorrect predictions and problematic treatment modalities. They also bemoan the fact that funding for the research is becoming more precarious. It is claimed that "the picture is grim" and that "researchers need to bootstrap resources to meet minimal design requirements" (Laws and O'Donohue 1997:9). The sociological crystal ball is cloudier, but there are no strong supportive signs of future substantive or theoretical breakthroughs regarding sexual deviance. Some feminists are distressed that studies of sexual deviance tend to favor, even glamorize, underdog deviants and to ignore the victimization of women by male violence (Rodmell 1981). There is also a belief that the major sociological insight into the processes by which persons pin deviant labels on others have taken us as far as we are likely to go. On the other hand, undergraduate sociology courses in Social Problems and Social Deviance have always been particularly popular with students, and often help escalate departmental enrollments and thereby allow less consumer-attractive instruction to be carried on. The continuing search for up-to-date information on sexual deviants to undergird these courses will undoubtedly encourage further and better research and theorizing about sexual deviance.

39

CRIMINOLOGY

DAVID F. LUCKENBILL

KIRK MILLER
Northern Illinois University

Criminology is the body of knowledge regarding crime as a social phenomenon. In an early analysis, Edwin Sutherland (1947) observed that criminology examines the processes of making laws, breaking laws, and reacting to the breaking of laws.

> These processes are three aspects of a somewhat unified sequence of interactions. Certain acts which are regarded as undesirable are defined by the political society as crimes. In spite of this definition, some people persist in the behavior and thus commit crimes; the political society reacts by punishment or other treatment or by prevention. This sequence of interactions is the object-matter of criminology. (P. 1)

Accordingly, criminology can be divided into three branches: the study of law making, the study of law breaking, and the study of reactions to law breaking. Because the subjects of law making and reactions to law breaking are considered elsewhere in this *Handbook,* we will focus on the second branch, law breaking.

With respect to crime, sociologists have pursued several lines of investigation. They have sought to determine the patterns of crime—the manner in which criminal behavior is distributed along dimensions of time and space as well as social structure. They have endeavored to explain crime, determining the conditions that not only differentiate criminals from noncriminals but also account for the occurrence of crime. And they have explored the manner in which crime can be prevented. We will discuss these lines of inquiry in turn. Before we take up the distribution of crime, though, we need to consider its measurement.

MEASURING CRIME

A basic question of any intellectual discipline is "How do we know what we know?" Criminology is an empirical discipline and therefore relies on the scientific method to observe and document crime. Researchers rely on a variety of methods to measure the nature and extent of crime phenomena. Most of the scientific methods that criminologists use are quantitative, seeking to count the number and type of crimes and the correlates of crime. Researchers use two main types of quantitative data: secondary data generated from official sources and primary data generated from self-reports of offending and victimization.

The most important source of information used to measure the nature and extent of crime is official data drawn from police records. Since 1930, the Federal Bureau of Investigation has sponsored a nationwide program to compile a statistical description of crime in the United States. Today, more than 17,000 police agencies participate each year in this data collection and reporting program, known as the Uniform Crime Report (UCR). The UCR contains information about crimes that are known to police and crimes that have been cleared by police, commonly through arrest. Criminologists often use UCR data to construct a crime rate based on crimes reported to police or arrests made by police. A crime rate is preferable to a crime count because the rate takes into account the population of the area being described. For example, in the United States, UCR data for 2003 show a total of 16,503 murders known to police, a seemingly large number.

However, given the size of the nation's population—nearly 280 million people—the murder rate in 2003 was 5.7 murders per 100,000 people, among the lowest in the past four decades (Federal Bureau of Investigation 2004). The UCR provides information about crime by region, community type, and locality. Information regarding the age, race, and sex of criminals is limited to crimes known to police that have been cleared by arrest.

Until recently, the UCR classified serious crimes as "Index" or Part I crimes and less serious crimes as Part II crimes. Eight crimes are catalogued as index crimes: murder and nonnegligent manslaughter, forcible rape, robbery, aggravated assault, burglary, larceny-theft, motor vehicle theft, and arson. Criminologists, policymakers, and the media have traditionally relied on index crime data to track changes in serious crime over time and across space. Index data are a composite that belie large differences in the frequency of any particular offense. For example, the least serious offense, larceny-theft, accounts for more than 60 percent of Part I crimes as a group (Federal Bureau of Investigation 2004). Thus, fluctuations in more serious crimes, such as murder and rape, may be masked by the sheer volume of property crimes, like larceny. Crime researchers have recognized this fact and typically divide index crimes into two categories: violent crimes and property crimes.

The FBI is currently implementing a new data collection program, called the National Incident Based Reporting System (NIBRS). The NIBRS is designed to improve on the UCR by including more-detailed information about criminal events—the circumstances of the offenses and characteristics of the participants—that become known to police. This is a new approach in two respects. First, the NIBRS uses incidents as the primary unit of analysis. Second, it expands on the UCR by providing more detail about the nature and types of specific offenses in each crime incident, including information about the victim(s) and offender(s) involved in the incident, the type and value of property stolen, and the characteristics of those arrested.

Although the UCR and NIBRS contain a wealth of information, official records are problematic. Perhaps the most significant problem is that a substantial proportion of all crime goes unreported to police. Unreported crimes represent the so-called "dark figure" of crime because their nature and extent are unknown. Another weakness of official records is that they are collected, recorded, and reported by persons other than researchers and thus are secondary data. As Thorsten Sellin (1931) stated, each layer of administration in the collection of official crime data increases the potential for distortion, bias, or error, simultaneously decreasing the value of the data. Data derived from police records have also been criticized as political artifacts that reflect the interests and internal operational logics of law enforcement agencies. Furthermore, UCR data collection guidelines employ a decision rule, known as the hierarchy rule of classification, which

sacrifices information about criminal episodes involving more than one crime. It is frequently the case when a crime occurs that several laws are broken. However, the hierarchy rule means that police report to the FBI only the most serious crime in the incident. The rule systematically biases UCR data downward. A final weakness is that official records provide limited information about the correlates of crime, such as victim and offender relationship, sex by race composition of offender and victim, and offender drug and alcohol use. The NIBRS is designed to improve official records with regard to the last two criticisms—namely, the hierarchy rule and the limited correlates of crime.

Largely in response to concern about the validity of official data, researchers have devised other methods of collecting information about crime. Chief among these are self-report surveys. The advantage of survey methodology is that researchers are directly involved in collecting primary data from participants in crime. This provides researchers with more control over data collection and facilitates hypothesis testing. Self-report surveys typically come in two forms. One type asks participants to report on their own offending. The other type asks participants to report on their victimization experiences.

A self-report survey of offending asks a sample of individuals whether and how often they have engaged in any of a number of offenses during a particular period of time. Thornberry and Krohn (2000) trace the advent of self-report methodology to Sutherland's (1940) observation that respectable, middle-class people are likely to commit crimes but unlikely to wind up in police records. Perhaps inspired by Sutherland's observation, Porterfield's work (1946) was the first to employ the self-report method in studies of criminal and delinquent behavior. His work demonstrated the utility of self-reports for studies of crime and delinquency. The research of Short and Nye (1958) is most responsible for establishing self-reports as a methodological pillar of criminology. Over the years, criminologists have invested substantial resources in improving the self-report method by developing techniques to increase both the validity and the reliability of self-reported crime and delinquency (Hindelang, Hirschi, and Weis 1981).

Self-report surveys of offending can be distinguished by their substantive focus and sample design. A common approach has been to survey adolescents by using schools as sampling points. Among the most prominent examples of this is the Monitoring the Future project, an annual survey regarding drug use conducted with a nationally representative sample of 8th, 10th, and 12th graders (Johnston, O'Malley, and Bachman 1996). Other survey approaches employ general population samples in an effort to survey criminal or delinquent behavior. One of the major national surveys of delinquency is the National Youth Survey (NYS) (Elliott 1983). The NYS uses a national probability sampling design to sample over 1,700 youth ages 11–17 and questions respondents about their delinquent involvement as well as matters reflecting a variety of attitudinal and experiential issues. Like many other self-report surveys, the NYS provides criminologists with data that enable them to address etiological questions. Further, the NYS employs a panel design, allowing researchers to follow youth into adulthood.

The other type of self-report survey is the victimization survey. Here, researchers ask a sample of individuals whether and how often they have been the victims of particular criminal acts during a particular period of time. The best-known victimization survey is the National Crime Victimization Survey (NCVS), which began in 1973. This is a national household survey that is conducted twice a year. Unlike self-report surveys of offending, which were inspired by the empirical limitations associated with the police focus on crimes of the lower classes, the NCVS was motivated by concern about the failure of citizens to report crimes to police. Approximately 85,000 households and over 150,000 respondents participate each year, yielding the best estimate of actual crime committed in the United States. Unlike the UCR, the NCVS provides information about crimes that people have experienced as victims, whether or not the offenses were reported to police. Questions cover crimes suffered by individuals and their household, whether the crimes were reported to police, as well as characteristics of the victim, the household, and the offenders in personal crimes. Questions also cover the respondents' attitudes about the criminal justice system and their reasons for reporting or not reporting crimes to police. By and large, victimization surveys are restricted to the more conventional and readily recognized crimes against persons and property. They do not cover "victimless" crimes, such as drug use and gambling, and they ignore crimes committed on behalf of corporations, such as fraudulent advertising and price-fixing.

Both types of self-report surveys share certain advantages over official crime data and are an important source of information on crime. They can access a wide variety of offenses, from serious violations to petty offenses that are unlikely to be reported to police. Furthermore, by measuring the personal and social characteristics of offenders and/or victims, they can provide a rich source of data with which to assess theories of crime. Both types of self-reports also share certain limitations that are characteristic of the self-report method. The primary weaknesses of self-report surveys are a function of the adequacy of the sample and the accuracy of measurement. The issues bearing on the adequacy of a survey's sample are ensuring representative participation and receiving cooperation throughout the survey questionnaire. Measurement accuracy is an outcome of asking questions correctly and respondent candor and

memory. Although it appears that respondents are generally truthful in reporting their experiences as offenders and victims, there is evidence that underreporting is a threat to validity for self-report studies of both offending (Hindelang et al. 1981) and victimization (Murphy and Dodge 1981). Respondents may not reveal some of their criminal experiences out of embarrassment or a concern for privacy. In addition, respondents do not always remember the violations they committed or the violations committed against them, and they may remember crimes as more recent or more distant than they really were.

Statistics on crime are vital to the criminological enterprise. They help establish the basic social facts of crime, and these facts constitute the objects of explanation and provide evidence for the assessment of explanations. Unfortunately, crime statistics are among the most unreliable and difficult of all statistics on social phenomena. It is impossible to determine accurately the amount of crime in any given place at any given time. As indicated above, many crimes go undetected; others are detected but not reported, either to police or to researchers; still others are reported but not officially recorded. Thus, any record of crimes can be considered at most an index of the crimes actually committed. This fact has spurred both caution about sources of crime data and further inquiry to validate and improve empiricism in the field. A common solution is to compare the "behavior" of crime indexes across multiple data sources. Figure 39.1 illustrates how victimization data compare with official data since 1973. Although it

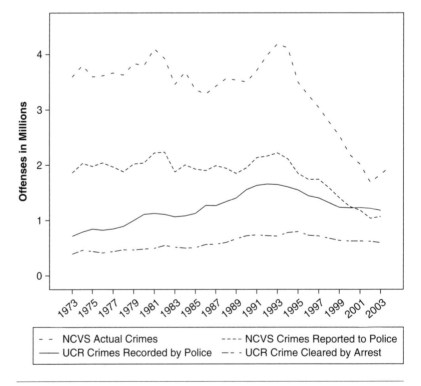

Figure 39.1 Comparing Four Measures of Violent Crime, 1973 to 2003

SOURCE: National Crime Victimization Surveys and Uniform Crime Reports. Adapted from Maston and Klaus (2005).

appears that victimization data provide a better measure of the true extent of crime, both data sources yield indexes that behave (increasing and decreasing) similarly during this time period.

PATTERNS OF CRIME

Criminologists endeavor to document patterns of crime in order to understand the nature and extent of crime. While the public regards many crimes as random acts, criminological inquiry shows that crime is not randomly distributed across individuals or groups. Criminological research on the patterns of crime focuses on the relationship of criminal behavior to dimensions of time and space and dimensions of social structure. One important insight in documenting patterns of crime is that crime tends to be an "intrastatus" activity. For a large proportion of crime, the statuses that describe offenders also describe victims. Criminology has paid close attention to a variety of contextual and structural dimensions that underlie the basic patterns of crime. These include the temporal and spatial distribution of crime as well as the age, sex, race, and social class of the participants.

Time and Space

Criminologists have long been interested in the social contexts that shape criminal offending. Social context is defined in terms of the temporal and spatial features that are correlated with crime. Criminologists have been concerned with at least three metrics of time: annual patterns, seasonal patterns, and daily patterns. Historical studies of crime in the United States suggest that serious crime increased in the decades prior to the Civil War and continued to increase following the war. Except for the years before and after World War I, reported crime experienced a general decline from about 1880 until the 1930s. Since this time, serious crime has generally grown slowly, with a more rapid increase beginning in the late 1960s (Gurr 1981). It peaked in 1981 and again in 1991 but declined in the middle and late 1990s and has been declining steadily ever since (see Figure 39.2).

Apart from annual changes, which reveal historical fluctuations, criminologists have determined that crime varies by other units of time. For example, crimes tend to increase around the time of the month that most people receive their paychecks, typically the beginning of the month. Crimes occur most frequently in the warmer months of summer, when youths are out of school and people spend longer periods of time outside, away from their homes. Murder tends to occur in the

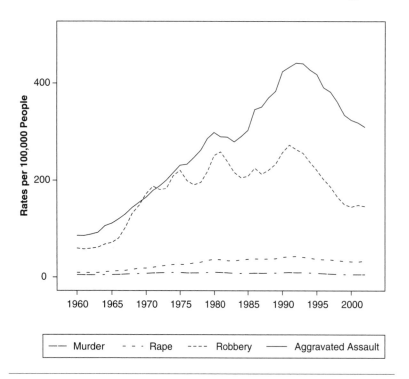

Figure 39.2   Violent Crimes Known to Police, 1960 to 2002

SOURCE: Federal Bureau of Investigation (2003, 2005).

evening, when more people are at leisure, and residential burglary tends to occur during the day, when more people are at work or school and less able to monitor their homes.

Criminologists also have sought to document the spatial patterns of crime. Researchers have determined that the rate of serious crime tends to increase with the size of the community. In general, urban areas have higher crime rates than suburban areas, and suburban areas have higher crime rates than rural areas. Consistently, victimization and self-report data show that crime is concentrated in large cities (Sutherland, Cressey, and Luckenbill 1992:176–81). However, it is noteworthy that in the United States, the extent to which the urban crime rate exceeds the rural rate varies over time. There is reason to expect that as improved communication and transportation have reduced the differences between urban and rural areas, the differences in the crime rates of the two areas have decreased and that rural and suburban crime rates have increased more rapidly than the urban rate. Within local communities, crime tends to be concentrated in neighborhoods that are marked by social deprivation. High-crime neighborhoods tend to possess higher-than-average rates of poverty, rental and vacant properties, single-parent households, and population mobility, all of which inhibit neighborhood organization to prevent crime.

Age

Crime is a young person's activity. Indeed, researchers have observed that age is the best predictor of criminal behavior. The relationship between age and crime is curvilinear. Criminal activity increases with age into adolescence, peaks in late adolescence or early adulthood, and then declines fairly quickly with age and continues to decline more slowly to death. This pattern generally holds regardless of sex, race, and class, as well as across time periods and places, leading some to argue that the age-crime relationship is invariant (Gottfredson and Hirschi 1986) (see Figure 39.3).

Criminologists have used the term "desistance" to describe the termination of criminal behavior as age increases past the peak offending years in late adolescence or early adulthood (Laub and Sampson 1993). Although most offenders "age out" of crime by early adulthood, a small percentage continues to offend over the life course. This observation has sparked interest in the role that age plays in distinguishing between different types of offenders. Contrary to the age invariance position, research on the effects of age at first offense and the trajectory of crime over the life course suggests the existence of distinct types of criminal careers that vary in terms of onset, duration, and intensity. Individuals who become involved in crime at an early age and those who have contact with the legal system earlier in adolescence are more likely to become chronic offenders or "life-course persisters." Laub and Sampson (1993) have shown that even among early-onset and chronic offenders, desistance from crime is possible. Research in this realm has also verified that the most common type of criminal career is "adolescent limited," meaning that criminal behavior is generally confined to the adolescent and early adult years, at which point desistance rapidly occurs.

Sex

Males have a higher rate of crime than females. Comparisons of sex-specific criminal behavior are frequently reported as a ratio of the frequency or rate of male offenses to female offenses. Although the gap in the sex ratio of offending varies for different types of crime, it is greatest for more serious types of crime. In the United States, for example, the sex ratio in arrests for murder in any given year is about eight male arrests to one female arrest. In contrast, the sex ratio in arrests for larceny, among the least serious crimes, is two male arrests for each female arrest. Self-report data confirm that males are more likely to be involved in crime than females, though these data tend to reveal less disparity in the sex ratio of criminal offending than official data, especially for less serious crimes (Triplett and Myers 1995). Some criminologists have argued that the discrepancy between arrest statistics and self-reports is related to the chivalrous approach criminal justice authorities take when females become the focus of law enforcement (Steffensmeier 1993).

Race

Official data paint a striking portrait of criminal activity in terms of racial status. Although whites account for the vast majority of all arrests, African Americans are much more likely to experience an arrest than whites. For example, African Americans account for over 40 percent of arrests for serious violent crimes and more than 25 percent for serious property crimes but represent just 13 percent of the population of the United States (Federal Bureau of Investigation 2004). Whites, in contrast, are disproportionately arrested for certain Part II crimes, such as alcohol and driving under the influence crimes. Recently, the size of the racial disparity in arrests for serious crime has declined, though race-specific risk of arrest is much larger for African Americans than for whites (see Figure 39.4).

Some criminologists have argued that racial discrimination in criminal justice may explain much of the race disparity observed in official data (Tonry 1995). Others have claimed that the justice system and its agents are reasonably objective in processing defendants, suggesting that racial disparity in official statistics reflect actual racial differences in crime (Wilbanks 1987). One way in which criminologists have attempted to settle this debate is by using self-report and victimization data to examine race-specific involvement in criminal behavior. The evidence from self-report studies of delinquency by African American and white youth suggests that race differences are much smaller than arrest statistics indicate (Elliott and Ageton 1980).

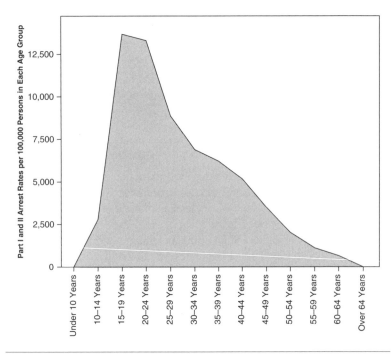

Figure 39.3   Distribution of Age-Specific Arrests, 2003

SOURCE: Federal Bureau of Investigation (2004, adapted from table 38, pp. 280–81).

Social Class

Criminologists have long assumed a negative correlation between social class and crime: Those at the lower end of the class system are more likely to be involved in crime than those at the upper end. Official statistics confirm that lower-class status is associated with greater involvement in crime. For example, residents of impoverished neighborhoods have the highest arrest rates, and those convicted of crime and sentenced to prison are more likely to be poor, unemployed, or underemployed.

Despite such evidence, criminologists have argued that the relationship between class and crime is less certain than official statistics indicate. The first criminologist to question the class-crime connection was Sutherland (1940). He observed that white-collar crimes—crimes committed by persons of respectability and high social status in the course of their occupations—are common though usually ignored in official crime statistics. Sutherland's insight has led to many criticisms of those who assume a negative correlation between class and crime.

Conclusions about the class-crime connection may reflect the source of information employed. Studies using self-report data tend to show that juveniles from all socio-economic backgrounds engage in delinquent behavior (Tittle, Villamez, and Smith 1978). However, these studies have been criticized for failing to clearly conceptualize class status (Braithwaite 1979) and for confusing delinquency with serious crime (Farnworth, Thornberry, Krohn, and Lizotte 1994).

In summary, criminologists have invested considerable effort in documenting the patterns of crime. These patterns are meaningful for policymakers in evaluating and planning societal responses to crime. These patterns are also meaningful for criminologists because correlating crime across dimensions of social context (time and space) and social structure (age, sex, race, and social class) reveals the empirical facts that theory must explain.

EXPLAINING CRIME

Over the past two centuries, various schools of criminology have flourished. A school of criminology is a system of thought that consists of a theory of crime causation integrated with policies of control implied in the theory. One of the first schools of criminology was the classical school, which developed in Europe during the eighteenth century through the efforts of Cesare Beccaria and Jeremy Bentham. The classical school views crime as a rational means for maximizing self-interest. Individuals are seen as hedonistic, pursuing pleasure and avoiding pain, and rational, calculating the pleasures and pains of alternative actions and choosing those actions that promise the greatest pleasure and least pain. It follows that individuals will choose to engage in crime when they determine that crime offers the most pleasure and least pain relative to other courses of action. It also follows that to control crime, the state need only convince people that crime will entail more pain than pleasure, and it can accomplish this by increasing the punishment of crime. When people realize that crime is less pleasurable, they will choose to engage in more satisfying actions. The positive school of criminology developed during the nineteenth century largely through the work of Cesare Lombroso and his followers. Grounded in the physical sciences, the positive school views crime as the product of personal defects or disorders. It maintains that the physical constitution influences behavior and that defects in biological structure or processes engender criminal behavior. The positive school insists that punishment will not control crime, because criminals do not calculate the pleasures and pains of alternative actions and choose those that maximize pleasure. Rather, it contends that the only reasonable way to control crime is to discover and manipulate its causes. Given that crime is the product of a personal defect or disorder, it follows that the best way to control crime is to treat that defect or disorder. This school fell from favor in the early twentieth century with the rise of the sociological school, which views crime as a function of the social environment. The sociological school has evolved over the course of the twentieth century, and it has come to dominate scholarly efforts to explain crime.

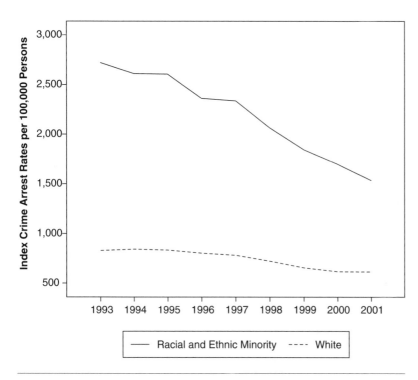

Figure 39.4　　Race-Specific Arrest Rates, 1993 to 2001

SOURCE: Federal Bureau of Investigation (2003:55–57).

The sociological school developed primarily in the United States. In the late nineteenth century, criminology was accepted as a field of study by the growing university departments of sociology, and since that time systematic studies of crime and criminals have been made mostly by sociologists. A survey conducted in 1901 revealed that criminology and penology were among the first courses offered under the title of sociology in American colleges (Tolman 1902–1903), and the *American Journal of Sociology* included articles and book reviews on criminology when it was first published in 1895. At the same time, though, American sociologists were impressed by many of the arguments advanced by the positive school. It was not until about 1915, after Charles Goring's *The English Convict* (1913) was published, that a strong environmentalist position was cultivated. It was probably this trend that prompted John Gillin (1914) to observe,

> The longer the study of crime has continued in this country, the greater has grown the number of causes of crime which may be described as social. This is the aspect in the development of American criminology which has given to that study in this country the title of "The American School." (P. 53)

The central thesis of the sociological school is that criminal behavior results from the same conditions and processes as other types of social behavior. Analyses of these conditions and processes as they pertain to crime have taken two forms. First, criminologists have sought to relate variations in crime rates to variations in social organization. A number of social conditions have been examined in relation to variations in the crime rates of societies and units of societies, including social and economic inequality, political and economic ideologies, and culture and normative conflict. In an early sociological investigation, Clifford Shaw (1929) used the Chicago School's ecological approach, an approach drawing heavily on Durkheim's analogy of society as an organism, to understand the distribution of delinquency across the urban landscape. He discovered that delinquency was concentrated in certain areas of the city and explained this fact in terms of social disorganization. He viewed delinquency as a pathology characteristic of blighted areas of the city, not the people who reside there. These areas featured substantial mobility, heterogeneity, and conflict, conditions that engendered social disorganization, a state in which traditional forms of social control are weak and people are free to participate in delinquent behavior. Durkheim's functionalist ideas about the nature and consequences of change in social solidarity informed strain theories of crime, notably exemplified in Robert Merton's (1938) anomie theory. In a pivotal statement, Albert Cohen (1955) argued that variation in the access of social classes to legitimate means for achieving success is related to variation in their rates of delinquency. In American society, lower-class children are encouraged to pursue the same goals as middle-class children, and they are judged by the same standards as middle-class children. Yet they lack the cultural and economic capital needed to compete effectively with middle-class children. As a result, many lower-class children experience failure, and they may respond by developing and participating in delinquent subcultures. These two arguments—that high rates of crime can be explained in terms of a breakdown of social organization and that high rates can be explained in terms of a strain between culturally induced aspirations and structurally limited opportunities— have figured in much contemporary theorizing at the macro level.

Second, criminologists have sought to identify the processes by which individuals become criminals. In general, their analyses relate criminality to variations in socialization. One line of thought, promoted by Travis Hirschi (1969) under the banner of control theory, maintains that criminality results from a breakdown of socialization. From this point of view, criminal behavior is an expression of natural impulses. When an individual's bond to society is weak, he or she is unlikely to internalize the values and norms of society or be sensitive to the wishes and expectations of others. The individual is uncontrolled and thereby free to engage in criminal behavior. Another line of thought, advanced by Edwin Sutherland (1947) and extended by Ronald Akers (1998), holds that criminality is a product of social learning. From this point of view, criminal behavior is not an expression of natural impulses. Rather, an individual learns to engage in criminal behavior in much the same way that he or she learns to engage in noncriminal behavior. It is the content of learning, not the process itself, that determines whether an individual becomes a criminal. These arguments—that criminality flows from a breakdown of socialization and that criminality is a product of socialization—continue to dominate thinking about crime at the micro level.

Over the past few decades, criminologists have pursued other forms of analysis. In the 1960s and early 1970s, some criminologists began to question the central assumptions and issues around which criminology had been organized. They observed that criminality is not an inherent property of a given act and that the violation of a criminal law does not necessarily result in an offender's apprehension and punishment. Rather, an act is criminal because lawmakers have created a law that makes it criminal, and those who violate the law are selectively apprehended and punished (Becker 1963). From this perspective, interest shifts from the criminal to the processes of defining and reacting to troublesome behavior (Quinney 1964; Turk 1969). Accordingly, criminologists increasingly turned their attention to patterns of selective law enforcement, asking what kinds of offenses and offenders are likely to be dealt with as crimes and criminals and why such offenses and offenders are subjected to such reactions. Further, in the course of demystifying the legal system, criminologists considered the consequences of being labeled and dealt with as a criminal, arguing that stigmatization reduces an individual's legitimate opportunities for success and alters the individual's identity and thus facilitates chronic criminality (Kitsuse 1962; Lemert 1972:62–92).

In the 1980s and 1990s, a number of criminologists sought to build integrated theories of crime. Traditionally, criminologists have assessed theories by subjecting two or more to what may be called "theory competition" (Akers and Sellers 2004:267). Recognizing that little is gained from such competition, criminologists have increasingly endeavored to devise more powerful explanatory models that fuse elements of two or more distinct theories of crime. For example, John Braithwaite (1989) drew on elements of control theory, social learning theory, and labeling theory in developing a theory of reintegrative shaming, and Charles Tittle (1995) combined elements of control theory, social learning theory, strain theory, and Marxist theory in building a control balance theory of deviance. Although integrative efforts are important, care must be exercised in this enterprise. As Akers (1989:24) aptly noted, the integration of theories, if done without regard to their incompatibilities, can result in useless "theoretical mush."

PREVENTING CRIME

Over the years, three methods for preventing crime have been used: punitive, defense, and interventionist. Punitive methods are based on the assumption that criminality and crime rates can be reduced by making people so fearful of being punished for committing crimes that they will refrain from doing so. The idea is that inflicting severe pain on offenders both reforms those who are punished (specific deterrence) and prevents others from committing crimes (general deterrence). Much of the legislation aimed at doing something dramatic about a crime problem is simply an attempt to increase the severity or certainty of punishment (Beckett and Sasson 2004). Defense methods are based on the assumption that crime can be reduced by making it hard for people to carry out crimes. Lighting streets, locking doors, and storing valuables in safes exemplify these methods (Felson 2002:144–64). The segregation of criminals by putting them behind bars so that they cannot victimize outsiders also illustrates defensive measures. Interventionist methods are based on the idea that punishment and defense are not enough. Rather, the assumption is that criminality and crime rates can be effectively reduced by determining the conditions that produce them and changing those conditions. Treatment methods based on the idea that offenders lack basic interpersonal skills try to develop their competence in empathy, problem solving, impulse control, and anger management, and methods based on the idea that offenders have learned to commit crime try to teach them lawful forms of behavior (Cullen 2002). More generally, interventionist methods assume that high crime rates are a product of economic, political, and social organization and that it is foolish to leave this organization intact and hope to reduce crime

rates by punishing criminals produced by it or defending against them. Instead, the idea is to modify the economic, political, or social order so as to reduce crime rates (Currie 1998).

There is considerable evidence that intervention is, or could be, the most effective system for reducing crime (Cullen 2002; MacKenzie 2000). As more is learned about crime, we will have a better basis for interventionist policies. If implemented consistently, these policies would protect society from crime in three ways.

First, they would secure the segregation of persons who have demonstrated their dangerousness by chronic involvement in serious crime. Although segregation will not reform these offenders, it will protect society both by incapacitating them and by expressing disapproval of serious deviation from the law. At present, we can neither change some chronic offenders nor significantly modify the social situations that spawn them. We can only defend ourselves from this small category of dangerous persons.

Second, interventionist policies would integrate into law-abiding society a larger proportion of citizens, including the majority of those who have committed crime but have not demonstrated dangerousness. It is generally acknowledged that social control stems from the rewards secured by lawful conduct rather than from direct fear of punishment. The effective deterrent is not the fear of legal sanctions as such but the fear of loss of status (Grasmick and Bursik 1990). But it is not really fear that inhibits criminal behavior. Rather, the law-abiding citizen is one who feels that doing certain things, such as stealing from a neighbor and assaulting a coworker, is unthinkable. The policies for crime prevention must, therefore, if they are to be effective, give more people a stake in conformity to the laws that prohibit criminal behavior.

Third, interventionist policies would define the social situations from which crimes are most likely to issue and make it possible to attack and eliminate those situations. But rather than trying to eliminate the economic, political, and social attitudes, conditions, and injustices that generate crime, political leaders have generally preferred to rely on fear of punishment (Currie 1998). Punishment seems to be cheaper, but it is not. Further, the emphasis on punishment distracts from the need for developing the conditions necessary for domestic tranquility. If shared attitudes of appreciation for certain values could be developed, punitive laws relating to those values would be unnecessary. If, for example, members of a society acquired an equal stake in the concept of private property, then trying to terrorize people into respecting property rights would become obsolete.

In summary, crime would be reduced by absorbing those criminals who can be absorbed, segregating for defense those who cannot be absorbed, and eliminating the conditions that are most conducive to crime and thus bring about the need to absorb some criminals and segregate others. Vigorous implementation of such policies would be evidence of social disapproval of crime as much as punishment would be. It is approbation and disapprobation rather than punishment of criminals that forestall crime among the majority of citizens, including the majority of the poor and powerless, from whose ranks most criminals come.

CONCLUSION

Our understanding of crime is rudimentary. To be sure, we have a sense of how crime is distributed along a number of structural, temporal, and spatial dimensions; we have a sense of the principal variables that affect the occurrence of crime and development of criminality and the general ways in which these variables operate to produce crime and criminality; and we have a sense of the kinds of methods that seem to work in controlling crime. Nevertheless, greater energy must be expended before we have a solid understanding of crime.

As we think about criminology in the twenty-first century, we see the field moving in several directions. We see sustained efforts to construct and improve the methodological tools for documenting crime, testing theories of crime, and assessing programs to control crime. We also see sustained efforts to formulate integrated theories of crime, theories that draw not only on elements at the sociological level of analysis but also on elements at multiple levels, including the biological and psychological. Integrated theory is moving criminology along a course that may ultimately define it as an interdisciplinary field of inquiry rather than a uniquely sociological specialty. These two tracks—one methodological and the other theoretical—will be increasingly intertwined. For example, the analytical state of the art allows for a wider and more rigorous variety of theory-testing endeavors, which encourages the further refinement of theory. Finally, we see continuing efforts to use criminological knowledge to enhance social welfare—to reduce levels of first crime and repeated crime and to do so in ways that are just to offenders, victims, and the larger community. These lines of development are not unique to the criminological enterprise. Indeed, they parallel trends in sociology where scholars strive to improve methodologies, devise integrated theories, and apply research to inform public policy and enrich collective life.

40

THE SOCIOLOGY OF GAMBLING

BO JASON BERNHARD

JAMES H. FREY
University of Nevada, Las Vegas

The size and scope of legalized gambling—to put aside its illegal manifestations for a moment—are simply mind-boggling. In America, for instance, more money is legally spent on gambling than is spent on movie tickets, theme parks, sports events, and music events combined (Morais 2002). Of course, sociologists have spent a substantial amount of productive research time examining the vast sociocultural impacts of Hollywood's movies, and the field has developed an impressively broad literature on the sociology of leisure and sport. Furthermore, sociologists of popular culture have studied the sociological reach of a music culture that today encompasses everything from Mozart to MTV.

Meanwhile, the gambling industry now dwarfs these more familiar sociological subjects, at least in the economic sense. Gambling also constitutes a formidable political entity: As of this writing, 48 of the 50 U.S. states offer some form of legalized gambling (Utah and Hawaii stand as the lone holdouts). Just as strikingly, a somewhat similar proportion of international jurisdictions are also embracing legalized gambling (or considering doing so).

Of course, gambling activity has probably been around as long as human groups have been around (the phrase "rolling the bones" harkens back to an era when playing dice games meant exactly that). Nor are the activity's intimate linkages with government new: In the United States, for instance, lotteries were legalized in the colonies by 1750. City governments, churches, jails, public utilities, road repair, and institutions of higher education, including many Ivy League schools, were financed by these lotteries (Rosecrance 1988).

However, at no time in human history have more types of gambling been more widely available to more human beings than they are today. In light of these observations, it would seem that sociologists everywhere might devote their tools to help advance our understanding of those of us who wager money on events whose outcomes are in doubt.

THE DEVELOPMENT OF SOCIOLOGICAL PERSPECTIVES ON GAMBLING

Some of the earliest writings on gambling were not specifically sociological, but they certainly invoked themes familiar to today's sociologists. For instance, because gambling was seen as undermining the very foundations of the Protestant ethic, it threatened those who were passionately protective of the latter in predictable ways. In 1883, Anthony Comstock warned that "the promise of getting something for nothing, of making a fortune without the slow plodding of daily toil, is one of Satan's most fascinating snares" (p. 56). For many, gambling's insidiousness offended social and moral sensibilities more than other scourges of the day such as alcohol.

In his pioneering study, Edward Devereux (1949) lamented that sociologists had neglected the study of gambling, given its ubiquity and institutionalization. Devereux viewed gambling within the context of functionalist theory, suggesting that wagering behavior had societal implications beyond the individualistic and pathological approaches that seemed to dominate then—and indeed, continue to dominate studies of gambling behavior today. Given the sociological frameworks popular in his time, it was perhaps predictable that Devereux explored the act as a safety valve that relieved stress and strain generally emanating from the restraints and rationality of a capitalistic system. In addition, Devereux also felt that dominant values were reinforced with admonitions against gambling and other deviant behaviors (p. 946).

Of course, it was recognized that gambling can also be dysfunctional, as Bloch (1951) pointed out, creating problems for family, work, and personal life. Much of the early nonsociological work on gambling behavior focused on the dysfunctional effects that gambling has on both the gambler as well as those close to him or her. This perspective coalesced in the field of psychology into a vast literature exploring treatments for gambling pathologies. Even sociologists were not immune to this impulse: Herman's (1967) study of racetrack betting used this more or less pathological framework for his analysis, as did Zola's (1963) research on offtrack betting.

In the early days of the field, legalized gambling was rare, and illegal gambling was widespread. As such, many of the first studies of the gambling act tended to employ a more or less criminological framework to interpret these behaviors. For instance, Tec's (1964) study of football betting in Sweden found that bettors were more likely to be employed, upwardly mobile, and motivated to achieve. They did not appear to be alienated or detached—contrary to what anomie theorists would predict. Other analysts presented evidence to support opportunity theory and anomie, demonstrating that those with available avenues of advancement and lower levels of status frustration were less likely to gamble (Li and Smith 1976). Studies by Light (1977) and Newman (1968) did not find that relative deprivation motivated gambling activity, particularly within the lower class. Instead, gambling was interpreted as a communal or shared activity with important cultural meanings. Downes et al. (1976) found that gambling was not peculiar to the lower class but was found across all categories of the social structure—that is, across racial, class, and occupational divides.

Not all studies of gambling focused on the financial "losers" who constitute the majority of gamblers. One interesting sociological research piece explored the familial, social, and professional changes confronted by lottery winners—a scenario that many of us have no doubt contemplated (Kaplan 1978). This was the first systematic study of gambling's "winners"—all of whom had come away with a prize of one million dollars or more. In his work, Kaplan found that relationships transformed in significant and unforeseen ways, and that many winners found that they could not maintain their prior institutional or organizational affiliations.

Against this background, the sociologist Henry Lesieur's work emerged as a pioneering contribution to our understanding of the ways in which social networks and communities affect gamblers' lives. Lesieur (1977) sought sociological explanations for problem gambling in his groundbreaking study of the career of racetrack and sports bettors—a work that established him as a pioneer of this emerging area of sociological inquiry.

In fact, Lesieur's work was so influential that despite his background as a sociologist, he was asked to play a central role in defining the American Psychiatric Association's criteria for pathological gambling (see American Psychiatric Association 1994). Lesieur observed that many problem gamblers found themselves entangled in an effort to try to win back losses—or "chasing"—a characteristic that has since served as a central feature of the diagnostic literature (Lesieur and Custer 1984:149–50; American Psychiatric Association 1994). Later, Lesieur served as the founding editor of the first specialty journal in the field, the *Journal of Gambling Behavior,* later renamed the *Journal of Gambling Studies.* Today, he is widely recognized in mental health circles as one of the founding figures in the field of pathological gambling studies.

CURRENT SOCIOLOGICAL PERSPECTIVES ON GAMBLING

The sociologists Smith and Abt (1984) argued for a shift from concern with the problematic aspects of gambling to a focus on understanding the activity as "play." In their view, gambling reinforces capitalistic and materialistic American values of self-reliance, risk taking, decision making, and skill enhancement. Furthermore, much like other games, gambling provides an outlet for socialization and cultural learning: From marbles to baseball card flipping, games of chance prepare children for games at a higher level and for participation in American life.

As Goffman (1967) noted before Smith and Abt, character is demonstrated through rituals—including gambling rituals. Thus, gambling might be seen as functional for social order by providing an escape from everyday life while reinforcing existing cultural norms (Smith and Abt 1984; Abt, Smith, and McGurrin 1985:64.)

Today, gambling has "normalized" and may be understood via lenses currently used to study other late-emerging capitalist industries. Reith (2003) points out that

> the gambling industry itself is increasingly owned by a limited number of multinational corporations, concentrated in an oligopolistic market. It is organized in a similar way to other major industries, with market research and advertising strategies designed to identify and target niche groups . . . Modern consumers have a variety of products and experiences to choose from, and an ever-larger and more powerful industry to supply them. (Pp. 19–20)

This "new" gaming industry has attracted a growing number of professional observers, primarily in the United States, Canada, Australia, New Zealand, and Europe. Most sociological perspectives have employed familiar tools of the field and applied them to our understanding of the spread of gambling. As the Australian sociologist Jan McMillen attests, gambling has not been exempt from trends commonly associated with the spread of globalization. McMillen (2003) points out that gambling has succumbed to

> the homogenizing forces of globalization: economic dominance of transnational corporations, often American; the acceptance of certain governing rules and economic tendencies; and standardization of products and consumer behavior . . . this new globalization is a largely cultural phenomenon, whatever its economic base. Nowhere is this better seen than in the transformation of gambling into one of the world's most rapidly expanding consumer activities. (P. 51)

More generally, it would seem that the development of the global *tourism* industry—one that, by many accounts, has evolved into the world's largest—has provided the macro-economic backdrop for the development of a global *gaming* industry. And as this industry becomes a truly global one, scholars of the globalizing gaming industry—like scholars of globalization as a whole—might begin to focus on homogenizing forces as well as those forces that highlight local differences.

For instance, gambling locations in North America, Australia, and Europe are largely dominated by a relatively similar collection of machine games developed by a handful of multinational corporations. In a postindustrial "deforestation effect," the overall portrait on the casino floor is one of machines replacing wooden tables, which are being hauled off to storage.

In Asia, meanwhile, these machine games have not proven as popular. In Asian casinos, these games are usually relegated to peripheral spaces within the gambling environment, as table-oriented games of chance predominate. Gamblers, for their part, "play" in an environment that is notably more serious than settings in Western societies. Were we to insist on a one-size-fits-all theoretical or methodological model for understanding such disparate sociocultural locales, our approaches might well prove to be deficient.

In some more-developed regions of the globalizing world, we are observing signs of a shift from social problems of deficiency to social problems of excess: for instance, starvation becomes less of a problem, only to be replaced by obesity. Both starvation and obesity, of course, are shaped by sociological as well as psychological and biological factors—as is certainly the case with gambling problems as well. In this context, it would seem that the "individual" problem we now call problem gambling may in fact be characterized as a quintessentially twenty-first-century "social problem"—one that is profoundly affected by macrolevel factors and that predictably involves an overindulgence (rather than an underindulgence).

Of course, professional views of those with gambling problems have not always been nuanced or multidimensional.

For years, the experts who tackled the task of understanding and explaining the lives of those who "gambled too much" spoke from church pulpits (rather than academic podiums) and located the problem in morality. In a sermon delivered on April 19, 1835, Samuel Hopkins tells us exactly how we are to "treat" the problem gambler:

> Let the gambler know that he is watched, and marked; and that, as a gambler, he is loathed. Let the man who dares to furnish a resort for the gambler know that he is counted a traitor to his duty, a murderer of all that is fair, and precious, and beloved among us. Let the voice of united, incensed remonstrance be *heard*—heard till the ears of the guilty tingle. (Pp. 17–18)

Unfortunately for problem gamblers, these kinds of historical perspectives have not been forgotten. This is why problem gamblers—who now are labeled by psychological institutions as "sick"—still self-diagnose as "evil" many years after these kinds of sermons were delivered.

This is a classic illustration of how a sociological imagination can help people understand the nuances of what "ails" them. A problem gambler might wonder, "If pathological gambling is a medical problem, then why is it that my friends treat me like a moral one?" The sociological answer is this: because the older religious interpretations of problem gamblers have generated far more momentum and power than the relatively youthful medical interpretations have. In the social battlefields of public discourse, 20 years or so of medical interpretations do not somehow magically eliminate the inertia of hundreds of years of influential religious interpretations. No matter how much we hail the recent advances of problem gambling science and medicine, they have not yet captured the public's intellectual and emotional imagination in the way that earlier moral-religious understandings have (Bernhard, forthcoming-b).

In his book *Pathological Gambling: The Making of a Medical Problem*, Brian Castellani (2000) concludes that the field is careening carelessly down a decidedly medical pathway at the expense of more multidimensional perspectives. Drawing on the insights of Foucault, Castellani argues that medical experts have dominated the problem gambling discourse for too long and that it is time for those representing a wider range of discourses to be included in the construction of knowledge about this social problem. Castellani argues for an approach that explores how medical discourses collide with those emanating from moral or policy quarters. What remains to be seen is whether these kinds of sociological perspectives can contribute to the popular view of gambling in the way that moral and then psychological ones have.

RESEARCHING GAMBLING IN THE 21ST CENTURY

The British sociologist Gerda Reith recently developed a thoughtful critique of the ways in which sociology should engage gambling as a subject of sociological inquiry. Noting that sociologists have long focused on the immorality or the sickness of those who gamble too much, Reith (2003) seeks instead to focus on the vast majority of gamblers who engage in gambling for recreation and fun.

In her work, Reith (2003) skillfully contemplates how an "age of chance" has emerged and engaged an age of reason. Long ago, of course, very little that occurred was attributed to mere chance—the gods, after all, controlled virtually every imaginable outcome. In the current context, chance has become accepted—and even commodified—by capitalist economies in the Western world. Looking to the future, Reith senses that a peculiar affection for chance will continue to develop, noting that "at the start of the twenty-first century, life *does* seem to be increasingly insecure," citing market fluctuations, transformations in work life, environmental doomsday scenarios, and the postmodern grappling with truth and certitude as evidence (pp. 182–83). Against these sociological backdrops, Reith astutely notes that gambling serves as "a conduit for chance: an arena in which (chance) appears in an intensified and, more importantly, controlled form" (p. 183). Hence, gambling provides a unique outlet for the impulses that accompany this era. From this perspective, gambling seems less a deviant act than a distilled one: It serves as a microcosm for much that is characteristic of our times.

Methodologically, the field continues to grapple with a variety of issues that are common in many relatively young areas of inquiry. Summarizing the methodological state of the field, Eadington (2003) notes that "it remains difficult to fully comprehend what the evidence is telling us" (p. 32) and later argues that "benefit/cost analysis applied to . . . gaming activities is still a relatively primitive science, primarily because of the difficulties in conceptualizing, observing, and measuring social costs" (p. 46).

Notably, it is a sociologist, Rachel Volberg, who has served as the problem gambling field's leading prevalence methodologist and researcher. Volberg (1996), whose tool of choice for determining problem gambling rates has been the telephone survey, nevertheless insists that multiple methods are preferable to any single one:

> Many of the questions now being asked about gambling and problem gambling cannot be answered by single surveys . . . As we move forward, it will be important to use a variety of methods to provide insights that no single approach can yield. Since all scientific methods contain biases, multiple research techniques (including experimental, clinical, historical, ethnographic and survey approaches) are needed to resolve puzzles and discrepancies as well as to provide a much-needed depth of perception to the field of gambling studies. (P. 126)

Today, it appears that even the medically and psychologically oriented researchers in the field of gambling studies are embracing these broader approaches to theory and method. For instance, a group of influential scholars—all trained in psychology—recently put forth a call to embrace a more macrolevel "public health" approach to the study of gambling behavior. Interestingly, this public health approach strikes a chord familiar to sociologists, because it advocates multiple levels of analysis, including those that focus on the individual, group, organizational, and institutional levels (Blaszczynski, Ladouceur, and Shaffer 2004).

GAMBLING AND PUBLIC POLICY

From a policy perspective, what makes gambling different from more conventional industries is the peculiar relationship between government entities and gambling businesses. As Eadington (2003) notes, "Gambling is one of the largest industries whose fundamental economic characteristics are substantially determined by political decisions" (p. 45). To this, we might add that state lotteries exist in a way that allows the government to sell products to its constituency directly and not via a generous tax break or other subsidy. Because of these relationships, government bodies may well find themselves with conflicting interests: On the one hand, they have an interest in maximizing gambling revenues (to sponsor government programs); on the other, they have an obligation to protect the public (some of whom may consume excessive amounts of lottery tickets).

In the United States, the government has been largely content to allow individual states to enforce and regulate gambling within their borders (Frey 1998). In other jurisdictions, national and provincial governments have entered into unique agreements with gaming business operators to offer gambling to native and tourist populations. In some cases, as with Canada, the government serves as a sort of "owner-operator" of casinos. As Rosecrance (1988) envisioned, gambling's widespread acceptance and its partnership with public entities has resulted in its mainstreaming and legitimization—and also its decriminalization.

Recently, gambling has enjoyed unprecedented support from a wide variety of public figures. Especially in more conservative political environments, where uttering the "t word" (taxation) is a sure way to get voted out of office, gambling is often seen as a "voluntary tax" willingly donated to state coffers by participants, who in exchange for their donation receive an entertainment benefit.

At the same time, in jurisdictions across Canada and Australia, for instance, public clamor has resulted in growing efforts among government entities to mitigate the costs associated with this "entertainment." Social movement organizations—most of which are affiliated with religious organizations in some manner—have once again emphasized the downside of gambling, and some jurisdictions have moved to address these critiques. To wit, the Canadian jurisdiction of Nova Scotia recently unveiled a test study of "responsible gaming devices" that have been attached to all gambling machines provincewide. These devices allow gamblers to check the amount of money they have won or lost over given periods of time (a sort of gambling "bank statement") as well as set monetary limits and/or time limits for their play.

With each technological leap forward, however, we must also be on guard against falling into traps that some of sociology's most famous voices have articulated. Bernhard and Preston (2004) point out that these policy interventions have a way of backfiring, as Robert Merton famously warned. As it turns out, several of the policies implemented in an effort to mitigate problem gambling have had unintended consequences, and a few have actually harmed those whom the policies ostensibly target. For instance, some jurisdictions have slowed down the speed of machine gambling games (thinking that this would help slow down the progression of gambling addicts), but research emerged that suggested that addicts actually played for *longer* periods of time when this policy was implemented. It would seem that in the twenty-first century, sociologists may well continue to rest their analyses on the able shoulders of the field's twentieth-century giants.

LINKAGES WITH OTHER SOCIOLOGICAL PERSPECTIVES

Some of sociology's favorite tools and perspectives can help illuminate a variety of aspects of gambling behavior. Robert Putnam's (2000) popular work *Bowling Alone,* for instance, argues that many of our recreational activities have become decidedly less social over the past few generations. Putnam's fundamental argument is that Americans are engaging in fewer social activities than in the past, and that this reduction in "social capital" can have potentially deleterious—even disastrous—consequences. Most germane to our discussion, in developing his argument, Putnam laments the decline of traditional game playing (such as bridge games) and the expansion of machine-based gambling:

> Substitutes for card playing have emerged, of course, everything from computer and video games to casino gambling. Like cards, these pastimes provide the spice of chance. Unlike card playing, however, these successors are distinguished by their solitary nature. My informal observation of Internet-based bridge games suggests that electronic players are focused entirely on the game itself, with very little social small talk, unlike traditional card games. Even fanatics of Microsoft Solitaire rarely play in a group, and any visitor to the new megacasinos that dot the land has chilling memories of acres of lonely "players" hunched in silence over one-armed bandits. Bridge, poker, gin rummy, and canasta are not being replaced by some equally "schmoozable" leisuretime activity. (Pp. 104–105)

For Putnam, the recent gambling mania is symptomatic of far larger social ills. Beyond Putnam's perspectives, there is much that is sociologically rich about the "social capital" (or lack thereof) of problem gamblers. For many problem gamblers, earlier in their "career," gambling activity was decidedly unproblematic and heavily social—a way to socialize and enjoy and evening with friends. Later in their career, many problem gamblers find themselves gambling in social situations less often and gambling alone more often. By the time they reach what the 12-step groups call "bottom," very few are gambling with anyone else—their social capital, it seems, has been reduced to nearly zero. Interestingly, their "recovery" embraces a dramatic reversal of this trend: Many turn to organized groups (such as professional therapy groups or Gamblers Anonymous) and reconnect with social worlds that they had abandoned. Whereas once they gambled alone, they eventually heal together (Bernhard, forthcoming-a).

For sociologists, obviously, group life has long been accepted as a foundational element of sociological inquiry. For gamblers with problems, an enhanced understanding of the nature and power of group life can perhaps deliver what Mills's (1959) sociological imagination once promised. As Bernhard (forthcoming-b) argues, gamblers with problems can recognize, as all of us can, that "individual" problems can in fact be better understood by exploring the sociological backdrops on which they are projected.

Other books that are familiar to sociologists touch on gambling as well. The cultural critic Neil Postman (1985) begins his seminal work *Amusing Ourselves to Death* by talking about the American "city symbols" that captured the essence of a variety of periods—Boston in the colonial days, for instance, or New York in the Ellis Island immigration era. In this work, which is remarkable for how well it continues to resonate 20 years later, Postman suggests that in our current age, the ultimate city-symbol of the times may well be found in Las Vegas. For Postman, this is not necessarily a positive development:

> For Las Vegas is a city entirely devoted to the idea of entertainment, and as such proclaims the spirit of a culture in which all public discourse increasingly takes the form of entertainment. Out politics, religion, news, athletics, education and commerce have been transformed into congenial adjuncts on show business, largely without protest or even much popular notice. The result is that we are a people on the verge of amusing ourselves to death. (Pp. 3–4)

Following Postman's lead, other analysts engaged in research that might be called a "sociology of Las Vegas." The work of Gottdiener, Collins, and Dickens (1999) presents an urban sociological perspective on Las Vegas—one that emphasizes the need to understand what might be called the first postindustrial city. After all, unlike Detroit or Pittsburgh, Las Vegas produces little that is physical in nature. Instead, the city "produces" experience for the nearly 40 million people who visit it annually.

Drawing on the sociospatial approach, these authors continue by arguing that we have seen a "Las Vegasization" of the rest of America and a simultaneous "Americanization" or "normalization" of Las Vegas. This convergence effect means that Las Vegas is no longer the deviant case study it once was—in fact, quite the contrary, it may well be a model laboratory for urban sociological inquiry.

The sociological study of gambling also shares affinities with the sociological study of "risk" (see, e.g., Frey 1991). Risk is a cultural construct that is shaped by the perceptions and evaluations of risk that individuals and societies assign to certain activities (including, presumably, gambling). More recently, some scholars have used this framework to better understand gambling's effects on societies. Invoking the term "risk society," Kingma (2004) observes that the liberalization of gambling laws, the growing perception of gambling as a legitimate economic and recreational pursuit, and the subsequent development of mechanisms to deal with gambling addiction are natural outcomes of the modernization process.

Risk analysis may well provide us with a framework for understanding the pros and cons of a variety of social influences. Social processes, as Short (1984) notes, have benefits as well as negative impacts on the "social fabric" (Giddens 1990, meanwhile, focuses on the term *social order* in his analysis). Wildavsky (1988) claims that risk is inherent in all activities, and seeking a "zero-risk" society—where all is safe and secure—leads only to stagnation.

Thus, as with all development, opportunities arise in some sectors, but costs too rear their heads. In policy and social research contexts, this means that gambling's potential benefits as a recreational, employment, and economic resource must be considered against the potential costs of addiction, crime, and personal/familial disruption. Risk management is the exercise of alerting individuals and societies to these adverse conditions (Short 1984).

Finally, gambling as risk was also examined by Erving Goffman (1967), who actually assumed the role of a dealer for several months in a Las Vegas casino. He was not studying gambling per se but rather used the gambling setting to study patterns of social interaction. Goffman was interested in the choice individuals made to place themselves in settings where there was personal or property risk at stake. In these settings, individuals seek "action," pursuing risky activities even when the risk is avoidable. Later, Frey (1984) applied this concept to gambling: "Action activities are consequential and fateful in that something of value can be won or lost on the outcome, and, by committing something of value, players indicate their seriousness.

The greater the consequences, the more fateful the enterprise becomes" (p. 113).

TECHNOLOGY, CHANGE, AND THE FUTURE

Like so many forces that ensnare our sociological attention, technology will certainly continue to shape gambling activities in the twenty-first century. Already, a variety of newer technologies can double as a gambling device, including cell phones and computers. In the United States, attorneys for the Bush administration have decided that Internet wagering is illegal under the 1961 Wire Act, which prohibited phone bets that took place across state lines. Of course, the Internet is more amorphous than the phone lines of the 1960s were, revealing the complexities inherent in regulating and monitoring acts that take place in virtual rather than brick-and-mortar worlds. Despite this presidential interpretation, millions of Americans (and many more bettors internationally) wager billions of dollars on sites that operate in jurisdictions that allow operators to flourish. Few Internet gamblers, it is safe to say, are fully aware of the legal status of the act—an oversight that is understandable, perhaps, given the widespread and increasing acceptance of gambling in general.

Other familiar technologies will also continue to shape the gambling landscape. Television has recently wielded its powerful cultural force, contributing significantly to the gambling boom by televising events such as celebrity poker and an ever-growing number of fictional and reality tales set in Las Vegas. With all this sociological momentum, it is difficult to envision a twenty-first century in which gambling becomes increasingly less important as a sociological force.

In closing, however, we should note that the history of gambling is hardly a tale of linear expansion: The activity has experienced spikes in popularity as well as occasional bouts with prohibition. To wit, even the state of Nevada has legalized gambling on three separate occasions (and banned it twice). When it comes to gambling, if we take the long sociological view, it seems prudent to bet on both growth *and* backlash as we look ahead to the twenty-first century.

41

ALCOHOL ABUSE AND ALCOHOLISM

PAUL M. ROMAN

University of Georgia, Athens

For those sociologists who have had the motivation and opportunity to study alcohol-related issues, the topic can prove compelling, often capturing the commitment of an entire career. Despite these implicit attractions, an examination of sociology journals and of the major emphases of academic departments of sociology suggests that the corpus of sociological work on alcohol use, alcohol abuse, and alcoholism is quite small. Indeed, Robert Straus (1973), an early and multigenerational contributor to the specialty, observed that relatively few social scientists are attracted to studying alcohol issues because of the stigma associated with the subject matter. The measure of "how much" sociological interest of effort is concentrated on a particular subject matter is more elusive than it might appear. Thus, an alternative view is that there is a substantial influence of sociological theory and research design within alcohol studies, but it is in many ways "hidden" in places other than sociology departments because of the peculiar organization of scientific research in the United States. For example, as an indirect result of sociological research on the behavior of what they are labeled "problem drinkers" (Room and Cahalan 1974), the medical definition of alcoholism is fundamentally sociological. Within official diagnostic manuals, alcohol dependence (alcoholism) is almost exclusively defined in terms of individuals' social role performance and others' definition of the extent to which this performance, due to repeated episodes of drinking, fails to meet social expectations. The centrality of a sociological model within a medical definition would seem to be an indicator of notable influence, yet most sociologists are probably unaware of the content of the definition or the sociological research that helped shape it.

The status of alcohol studies within sociology is a question within the sociology of science and a more complex challenge than it might appear (Wiener 1981). This issue is not limited to alcohol studies and converges on contemporary concerns about the importance of interdisciplinary research versus the "silos" within which academic disciplines tend to operate. The central assertion in this chapter is that there is great opportunity for the application of sociological theory and methods to issues around alcohol and the problems that its use creates. The location of both past and ongoing work of this nature is not highly visible within what might be called the sociological mainstream.

In this chapter, a sampling of some of the work in this specialty is provided, together with an analysis of how this specialty has developed and been shaped over time. The discussion here is largely limited to the United States. Although there is a range of sociological activity worldwide, the patterns of scholarly interaction tend to stay within national borders, largely because of the unique policies, service delivery systems, and research support structures that guide sociological work in different nations. The worldwide sociological study of alcohol issues is of great importance but is beyond the scope of the present discussion.

The chapter opens with an overview of the historical emergence of sociological interest in alcohol issues, and three different themes are described. This is followed by several examples of research that characterize each of the three thematic areas and a discussion of possible directions that may occur in the future.

THE ORGANIZATION OF THE SOCIOLOGY OF ALCOHOL-RELATED ISSUES

Since the early 1990s, the American Sociological Association (ASA) has had a section on the Sociology of Alcohol and Drugs, recently renamed to include research interest in tobacco use. More notable as a hub for sociological activity over the long term, the Society for the Study of Social Problems (SSSP) launched a Committee for Research on Drinking Behavior in 1955. This has since been modified to include research interest in drugs. Finally, a small but vibrant organization involving a range of international social science interests, including sociology, the Kettil Bruun Society (named in honor of the research contributions of a deceased Finnish sociologist), meets every other year at rotating venues that include the United States.

Despite these organizational structures, the actual scope of research and writing activity directed toward alcohol issues that is identifiably within sociology is relatively minimal. In a review article in an outlet central to alcohol studies, a sociological leader in the specialty (and cofounder of the ASA section), Helene R. White (1993), observes that the specialty has

> a low status in the discipline of sociology. An examination of three major journals in sociology (*Social Forces, American Journal of Sociology* and *American Sociological Review*) revealed that out of 1,600 articles published during the 1995-2004 period, there were three, none and three articles, respectively, that dealt with alcohol use or alcoholism. Thus, less than one percent of all articles published in these major sociology journals in the entire decade were directly related to drinking behavior. (P. 8)

One might add more data to this observation by noting that relatively little of the underlying research activity occurs within settings that are explicitly identified with sociology. A review of the research grants funded between 1972 and 2005 by the National Institute on Alcohol Abuse and Alcoholism (NIAAA, a part of the National Institutes of Health [NIH]) reveals fewer than 20 investigators who have been based within academic departments of sociology.

Sociologists' involvement in research and writing on alcohol issues is, however, partially masked by the organizational contexts in which it occurs. Much of the research and writing about alcohol (and drugs) takes place in interdisciplinary centers that are commonly based in medical centers or schools of public health. Notable are centers such as those at Rutgers University, University of Michigan, University of Washington, University of Texas, University of California at Los Angeles, University of Georgia, University of Kentucky, University of Connecticut, the University at Buffalo, and the University of Oklahoma. There is also a substantial amount of research activity that occurs in independent free-standing

organizations, both nonprofit and for-profit, such as the Research Triangle Institute, RAND Corporation, Pacific Institutes for Research and Evaluation, and Westat, Inc.

Those with sociological backgrounds working in settings as members of interdisciplinary teams are not readily identified as sociologists, nor is their work usually published in sociological outlets. Instead, it appears in numerous specialty outlets focused on substance abuse or in journals more broadly focused on psychiatry, general medicine, public health, or health services research.

Some of these publication outlets in turn represent specialized research organizations such as the Research Society on Alcoholism, the College of Problems of Drug Dependence, the Academy of Health Services Research, the American Society of Addiction Medicine, and the American Public Health Association. Participation in these organizations keeps sociologists involved in alcohol studies in contact with peers from other disciplines, who may be studying similar issues. Such interaction is important in building and sustaining reputations and prestige, as well as providing access to new research and publishing opportunities.

These networks in turn include persons selected as peer reviewers for research grant applications by the NIAAA, the National Institute on Drug Abuse (NIDA), and other funding agencies within the NIH. Sociologists and other network members also sit on the editorial boards of the specialty journals, such as *Addiction, Journal of Studies on Alcohol, American Journal of the Addictions, Journal of Substance Abuse Treatment, Substance Abuse and Misuse,* and many others, publication in which is central to peer interaction and part of the expectations associated with receiving grant and contract awards. Moreover, the funding agencies, principally within the NIH, are oriented toward alcoholism and the health and social consequences of alcohol abuse and are thus unlikely to provide favorable reviews or high priority to research aimed at fundamental sociological questions.

THE EMERGENCE OF THE SOCIOLOGY OF ALCOHOL-RELATED ISSUES

Alcohol issues became prominent in American culture in the 1830s, with the launching of the Temperance movement, substantially predating the emergence of American sociology. The social and organizational activity swirled around alcohol issues into the first quarter of the twentieth century, culminating in national Prohibition (Clark 1976; Rumbarger 1989). While the prohibition of alcohol manufacture and distribution in the United States would seem to have offered sociologists a great opportunity for commentary and perhaps criticism of this social policy, as well as opportunity for analyzing the emergence of the policy despite popular ambivalence, an examination of the content of the *American Journal of Sociology* and the *Journal of Social Forces,* the two extant sociological journals published during the period of Prohibition (enacted in 1918, enforcement began in 1920, repeal in 1933), finds almost no interest in the topic.

The sociological study of alcohol issues in the United States had its origins in the repeal of Prohibition in 1933. The enactment of Prohibition in 1920 marked the culmination of an 80-year period of prominence for a two-pronged set of efforts to remove drinking from American society, the Women's Christian Temperance Union and the Anti-Saloon League (Gusfield 1963; Clark 1976; Rumbarger 1989). The fundamental ideology of these overlapping but separate movements was that the manufacture, distribution, and use of alcohol are destructive to both social structure and social order. Drinking was said to have especially undermining effects on the family and the workplace through adult male drinking habits, highly visible in the relatively short-lived social institution of the saloon.

The development of two streams of sociological study can be traced back to the post-Prohibition period. Each of these flowed "naturally" from other events involving changes in social policy. A third stream was launched quite deliberately several years later but has developed in a quite limited fashion and at present appears to be dormant. These three streams can also be characterized by their typical foci: (1) alcohol abuse, or behavior which produces social costs and problems; (2) alcohol dependence and alcoholism; and (3) normative drinking behavior and the roles that the use of alcohol plays in social structure and social institutions.

The first stream is easily understood for its continuity with portions of the ideology of Prohibition and the Temperance movement in its focus on the problematic consequences of alcohol use. This research includes the relationships between drinking and a variety of undesirable social outcomes such as crime, unemployment, and family instability. This stream of research also focuses on the problematic drinking patterns of certain social groups, such as college students or the elderly.

Researchers aligned with this perspective rarely advocate a return to Prohibition but are strongly identified with both supply and demand reduction in the form of preventive education about the risks associated with drinking and increased controls on the availability of alcoholic beverages. In a traditional sociological sense, this is the "social problems" perspective on alcohol. From a broad perspective, this orientation today is closely aligned with the field of public health.

The second stream flowed from fascinating social changes that began in the 1930s and continue to evolve until the present day. Temperance ideology was coupled with the notion that alcohol consumption offered the potential of unmanageable habituation to anyone who drank. The best analogy to understanding is contemporary ideas about heroin use in American culture, namely, that the drug's effects are so potent and seductive that any user

is at high risk of becoming an addict. The repeal of Prohibition occurred for a complex set of political, economic, and social reasons that did not include a social "embrace" of alcohol as the "Good Creature of God" as it had been labeled in the eighteenth century. Drinking in American society is not seen as an expectation or a right but as a privilege or a necessary evil. However, repeal effectively undermined the perspective that alcohol use created a marked risk of loss of control and addiction. Another conception was needed.

Although some changes were almost immediate, the 20 years following the repeal of Prohibition led to a greatly modified vision of the social location of the alcohol problem, namely, the rejuvenation, rearticulation, alteration, and attempted widespread diffusion of the idea of the disease of alcoholism (Levine 1978; Schneider 1978). This was the first and central ingredient of this stream of research, and it opened the way for American society to reaccept the legal presence of alcohol because alcoholism occurs among relatively few people. Specifically, this disorder, characterized by a progression to loss of control over one's drinking, is posed to affect a relatively small proportion of alcohol users. Its definition specifically excludes the excessive use of alcohol as a cause of alcoholism and draws a distinction between this disease condition and deviant drinking behaviors. The deviant drinker has chosen to break laws and social norms and may be punished for this behavior, whereas alcoholics are driven by a compulsion that is supposedly out of their control.

The disease model could not be nurtured in a vacuum. The available organizational context was centered on the replacement of the "moral" approach to alcohol by a scientific or "rational" approach. The debate over right and wrong involving alcohol was to yield to objective and comprehensive understanding of the substance's nature and effects. This in turn would guide social policies based on reason instead of emotion. Through happenstance or predestination, the rapid success of this transformation was greatly enhanced by the emergence of the first scientific center of studies on alcohol at one of the most distinguished and respected centers of thought in the United States, Yale University.

The Laboratory of Applied Physiology, established many years earlier, included eclectic leaders such as Dr. Howard Haggard and Dr. Yandell Henderson, the latter having authored scientific articles about the relative harmlessness of beer consumption, data that may have added impetus to the repeal movement. Following repeal, a section on Alcohol Studies appeared in the Laboratory and eventually emerged as a full-scale Center of Alcohol Studies.

The scientific orientation was attractive to a number of prominent scientists outside Yale, who had been repelled by the Prohibition experiment and its irrational features. They formed the Research Council on Problems of Alcoholism as a means of garnering interest and support for the emerging specialty of scientific alcohol studies and were closely aligned with the activities at Yale. This council enhanced its linkage with scientific imagery by becoming affiliated with the American Association for the Advancement of Science (Beauchamp 1980). This group initially received some modest support from the alcohol beverage production industry, as well as from other sources, but it did not attract governmental support for research.

Almost simultaneous with the disease model and the superceding of moralism by the scientific approach was the rise of a fascinating solution to the newly defined disease, namely, the invention, codification, and diffusion of the fellowship of Alcoholics Anonymous (AA). Originally defined as a "cure" for alcoholism (later the ideology shifted to "once an alcoholic, always an alcoholic"), AA evolved from the Oxford Group concepts popular in the 1920s and 1930s. In order to open the way for full reentry into society, AA essentially embraced the disease model of alcoholism, although its referent has always been that the loss of control is traced to an "allergy."

While working informally and without a name for several years after its founding in 1935, AA came to national attention with an article in the then popular magazine the *Saturday Evening Post*. The AA program came to be articulated into a series of 12 steps. These steps include experiences of surrender to a higher power, self-examination, repentance, confession, meditation, and finally, service to others attempting to deal with their drinking problems. Membership in the fellowship requires only a sincere commitment to stop drinking. Passage through the steps, which is not mandatory and does not confer status, is reinforced by peer support, by attendance at regular meetings where members shared their "stories" of alcoholic defeat, and by sponsorship of an experienced AA member, who is available around the clock to provide advice and support.

The scientific approach, the disease concept, and AA constituted a mutually supportive and interdependent system that gave impetus to a substantial amount of research and promotional activity that brought the notion of alcoholism as a treatable illness into mainstream American culture. An illustrative capstone event of this integral process was the offer in 1954 of an honorary doctorate by Yale University to William G. Wilson, the cofounder of AA. Wilson refused the honor on the basis that it would set a precedent for individuals receiving personal recognition for the activities of AA (Hartigan 2000).

This core of the disease model of alcoholism, nested in a scientific approach, and the treatment of alcoholism with a logical, inexpensive, lay-based yet supportive of the disease concept is the home of the second stream of sociological research. It is notably interdisciplinary, and the unique contributions of sociology are not always clearly evident. This stream might be seen as a subfield of medical sociology, although it is not organized as such within sociology. The stream embodies social psychological studies, epidemiology, and health services research. It is, however, more closely aligned with medicine than with public health.

The third stream was intended to be within the sociological mainstream, but its development has become minimal and marginal to the mainstream of sociology. More than 60 years ago, a sociologist laid out a plan for using alcohol as the platform for a major endeavor in advancing sociological understanding of groups, communities, institutions, cultures, and societies (Bacon 1943). Selden Daskam Bacon was a Yale Ph.D. in sociology who studied under Albert Keller, who had been a student of William Graham Sumner. From the platform of the Yale Center and its emphasis on the scientific approach, Bacon saw distinctive roles for the social sciences assuming that the moral perspective on alcohol was relegated to the past.

In this treatise, Bacon saw both the history of alcohol in human societies and its pervasive presence in many realms of social institutional life as descriptive of its interconnections with the formation and deterioration of social norms and values. He recognized the fact that the apparent control of a potent drug flowing freely in adult society offered the potential for understanding the workings of basic processes of social control. Bacon's call included attention to all the "normal" and integrative uses of alcohol, in addition to expected sociological concerns with alcohol-related and alcohol-fueled conflict and deviant behavior.

While Bacon's plan never came to fruition, or is yet to be discovered by those who will develop it, he himself became a mainstream figure in the interdisciplinary research field of alcohol studies and, clearly identifying himself as a sociologist, became the first Director when Alcohol Studies achieved Center status at Yale. It should be noted that the relationship of the Center with Yale ended in 1962, when amidst a swirl of controversy, Yale president Kingman Brewster terminated the Center on the grounds that its interests were outside the University's central stream of basic research and education (Wiener 1981). With support from the only philanthropist who has ever given substantial resources to the field of alcohol studies and practice, R. Brinkley Smithers, and with support from the National Institute of Mental Health (where the minimal federal interest in alcohol-related research was located prior to the establishment of NIAAA), the Center on Alcohol Studies was successfully relocated to Rutgers University, where it remains today.

The remainder of this chapter reviews examples of sociological ideas and research about the broad notions of alcohol abuse and alcoholism. Rather than offering an abbreviated catalog of the entire body of this work, focus is on several illustrative samples in each stream.

THE FIRST STREAM: SOCIOLOGY, ALCOHOL ABUSE, AND SOCIAL PROBLEMS

Beginning with what has been referred to as the first stream of sociological research, the definition of alcohol abuse is distinctively sociological, based on deviation from the norms of acceptable drinking. If one's drinking is deviant in the eyes of another, then it may be said that an event of alcohol abuse has occurred. This becomes consequential when the defining other is more powerful than the drinker and decides to take action. Thus, a 12-year-old caught drinking a tiny amount from a bottle in her parents' liquor cabinet would likely be defined as an alcohol abuser by an observing parent. Later in her life, when she is a college student, the same female may be observed by her peers drinking a copious amount of beer through a funnel, and the behavior is not defined as abuse.

A narrower definition emerges when social reactions are considered, for there are far more incidents of alcohol abuse than there are incidents that generate significant social reactions. These reactions may include screening for people whose drinking exceeds legal levels, such as that which occurs commonly on highways and less commonly in workplaces. Or the reactions may be triggered by social impacts, costs, and damages that are associated with the presence of alcohol abuse. In some such situations, the alcohol use is defined as abuse regardless of its level, with the consequences being the determining factors.

An illustration of this approach to analysis is a social problem that is the result of technological change, namely, the emergence of motor vehicles of all types as primary modes of human transportation. There has been a highly effective diffusion of the idea that alcohol consumption is the leading cause of highway accidents and related injuries and fatalities. In many respects, this logic is continuous with the "demonization" themes so common during the Temperance movement. Importantly, motor vehicles had not achieved prominence in the period from 1840 to 1918, when the gradual movement toward alcohol prohibition was under way. Thus, the theme of drinking's impact on highway safety had no relevance to the Temperance and Anti-Saloon movements.

The alcohol linkage may be seen as "ecological (Roman 1981b)." Five "ingredients" are present when a drinking-driver casualty occurs: alcohol in bloodstream + driver + automobile + highway + crash event. Testing for alcohol in the bloodstream and/or other evidence of alcohol consumption is at the forefront of the investigation. If alcohol is found to be present in an adequate amount, it is typically concluded that it was the "cause" of the event. It takes precedence over other possible causal explanations that may not be considered.

As examples, the possibility that other conditions affecting the driver could have "caused" the accident, such as lack of sleep, physical exhaustion, or emotional preoccupations, are ruled out by default. Only recently has there been awareness that "groups drive cars," although resulting regulations about the composition of the passenger population in a given vehicle are limited to those under age 21.

Likewise, unless blatantly obvious conditions are observed, defects in the physical functioning of the automobile itself are not considered as a possible cause of the accident.

Similarly, while sometimes considered as a contributing factor, highway conditions are rarely, if ever, attributed as a primary cause of an accident when alcohol is found to be present.

Sociological studies have advanced four interrelated factors that account for the dominance of drinking-related explanations. First, there has been a well-organized social movement, Mothers Against Drunk Driving (MADD), that forcefully and effectively brought this linkage to public attention (Reinarman 1988) and led to spin-off organizations such as Students Against Drunk Driving (SADD). Rather than using scientific evidence about the linkage between drinking and vehicular accidents, MADD adopted two icons that were prominent in the Temperance movement, the innocent child and the irresponsible drunken male adult. The founders of MADD were mothers of children who had been killed or injured by a driver who had been found to be drinking. The meaning of the group's acronym lies in maternal anger over the light penalties imposed on the drunken drivers, and the all-too-common stories that these individuals had retained their driver's licenses. Thus, MADD pushed for heavier penalties and more extensive enforcement of drinking and driving laws, all based on the causal linkage between drinking and highway crashes.

A second contributing factor is the relative ease of generating explanatory evidence. Blood alcohol levels detected through breath or blood tests are objective indicators that are relatively easily measured and understood. By contrast, the location of other causes may involve subjectivity and set the stage for conflicting interpretations.

Third, along with much of the industrialized world, the causal linkage in the United States between drinking as a cause of vehicular accidents is an institutionalized explanation that goes without challenge. In the United States, such causal statements appear on every container of alcohol sold through a retail outlet. Another institutional marker of this causal belief is a set of "dram shop laws," which can hold individual servers or retail outlets responsible for the material consequences of intoxication. The alcohol production and distribution industry does not challenge this explanation and in fact cooperates in campaigns to promote nondrinking "designated drivers" and to make servers of alcohol sensitive to the potential driving-related consequences of excessive alcohol consumption.

Fourth, alternative explanations that focus on defects in cars or on highway design may be seen as challenging vested interests and creating liabilities that may prove problematic for manufacturers and/or public officials who design and maintain highways. By contrast, there are no defenders of drunk drivers. Persons who desire to drink and drive or who do so routinely have not organized themselves into interest groups to promote these opportunities. To argue in today's society that it is a person's right to drive with a blood alcohol level of .08 or greater is patently absurd on its face.

It is of interest that this singular causal theory has not been diluted by a parallel movement to impugn illegal drug use as a significant contributor to highway accidents. Considering the elements reviewed above, there is no trace of a social movement to address drugs and driving, and it is clear that measurement of drug use in an "onsite" fashion as is done with alcohol offers considerable technical challenges. The highway and the motor vehicle are, however, part of a different drug-related drama that echoes the Prohibition era, namely, the pursuit and apprehension of "suspicious" drivers and vehicles that are found to be carrying quantities of illegal drugs.

A similar set of social constructions can be found to prevail in a very different circumstance, namely, the consumption of alcohol by pregnant women (Armstrong 2003; Golden 2005). Drinking during pregnancy is imputed as the cause of a set of psychophysiological impairments observed in childhood known as the fetal alcohol syndrome (FAS), with milder forms of the symptoms referred to as fetal alcohol effects (FAE). The linkage of maternal drinking to these outcomes is ambiguous, as are the diagnoses of the disorders. Nevertheless, warnings about the effects of drinking on developing fetuses are universally diffused in the United States, including warning labels on alcoholic beverage containers and posted warnings in retail settings where alcoholic drinks are sold. Presumably, a woman who is noticeably pregnant and observed to be drinking would be stigmatized as irresponsible, perhaps in the extreme.

There are a number of problematic implications of this emergent normative structure (Armstrong 2003). First is the fact that when cases of apparent FAS and FAE have been closely examined, there is a strong association with poverty and general disorganization in the lives of the mothers. It appears likely that the outcomes of FAS and FAE stem from combinations of behaviors resulting in malnutrition, negligence of prenatal care, and heavy drinking. By focusing exclusively on maternal drinking behavior as the etiological agent, broader social conditions and life chances of the mothers and their offspring are effectively ignored.

Second, the ambiguous association between maternal drinking and FAS/FAE is used to impose social controls on pregnant women while effectively ignoring the drinking behaviors of fathers. Fathers' drinking may lead to the conditions of negligence and poverty that are important agents in the outcomes that have been labeled FAS/FAE. Likewise, the powerful indictment of drinking as a harmful agent draws attention away from nutritional factors and maternal behaviors such as tobacco smoking.

Third, the causal linkage is a mechanism for attributing blame solely to the mother and her behavioral choices. This may be seen as another mechanism whereby women's control over the reproductive process is curbed by the imposition of rules via simplistic interpretation of scientific data and through reasoning that easily crosses the border from science into morality.

Proscribed maternal drinking is remarkable in its simplicity in that it parallels the rules surrounding drinking and driving. Warning labels and signs are used to remind not only pregnant women of possibly damaging behavior but also bystanders of what pregnant women should and should not be doing. As with drinking and driving, there is no counteradvocacy group suggesting that pregnant women should be allowed to drink in moderation or that the research evidence about this linkage should be challenged.

That ambiguous data have been accepted as the basis for institutionalized rules that affect a significant portion of the population is another indicator of the lack of positive support for alcohol consumption in American culture and the absence of advocacy for the privilege of drinking. The overall attitude toward drinking during pregnancy, as with drinking before or during the experience of operating a motor vehicle, is "better safe than sorry," despite the possibilities that the causes of the adverse outcomes lie in something other than drinking.

Sociologists have long been attracted to the association between alcohol and crime, a direct heritage from the Temperance and Prohibition ideologies. One of the most thorough investigations has centered on alcohol and homicide (Parker 1996). It is clear that there is no direct causal linkage between drinking and violent behavior, but that the presence of drinking can be a facilitating factor in crime (Roman 1981a). This possibility is especially underlined when it is established that the victims of crime have frequently been drinking as well as the perpetrators, or that drinking by a crime victim created a particular vulnerability to victimization by a nondrinking perpetrator. This association has recently been examined extensively surrounding the issue of "date rape," of particular concern among college students (Abbey 2002).

There are a multitude of other social problems where data indicate an association with drinking, but where causality is difficult to discern. An example is homelessness, where drinking and alcohol abuse are complex correlates but hardly a singular cause. An emergent issue of the past decade has been "binge drinking" among college students, supposedly a set of risky and destructive behaviors affecting students who are naive about alcohol's dangers, their nondrinking peers, and the communities in which colleges are located. The imagery of risks associated with binge drinking by college students has been painted in broad strokes (Perkins 2002a) and, in the case of one highly effective moral entrepreneur, has been escalated to be associated with frequent fatalities (Wechsler and Wuethrich 2003). On the other side of the risk model, several sociologists have been active in the effort to develop interventions that will curb these behaviors (DeJong 2002; Perkins 2002b).

THE SECOND STREAM: SOCIOLOGY AND THE CAUSES OF ALCOHOLISM

Turning to the second stream of research, the overview now turns to studies that are primarily concerned with the disease of alcoholism and its treatment. Research in the twentieth century had strong suggestions of social factors in the etiology of alcohol dependence. Trice (1966) offered a theory of individually rewarding drinking experiences followed by selective and sequential associations with drinking groups within which increasingly heavy and chronic alcohol use was socially accepted. Individuals who became alcoholic were surmised to "drift" through structures of social tolerance, where they found social acceptance but eventually ended up at "the bottom," or on skid row.

Building on the work of other researchers who had examined homeless and disaffiliated alcoholics, Wiseman (1970) uncovered social patterns and social structure in the lives and interactions within these groups rather than anomie and normlessness. Later, the same author (Wiseman 1991) documented patterns of social interaction in couples where the husband was a recovering alcoholic, strongly suggesting that social role relationships could develop around a spouse's chronic alcoholism and can serve to prolong it; by contrast, the adjustments necessary for the couple to relate in the context of sobriety is more complex than might be assumed.

Bacon (1973) used role theory to describe how individuals used alcohol to "ease" their entry into social situations where they felt uncomfortable with their performance. This in turn was seen as creating risks of thwarted role learning when alcohol became an agent of "pampering" accompanied by a broader repertoire of alcohol use in conjunction with potentially uncomfortable social performances. This was later developed further into an explanation for why "social stars" seem at high risk for developing alcohol and drug problems (Roman and Blum 1984).

Akers (1992) developed a straightforward model based on learning theory, describing patterned rewards in social interaction wherein alcohol dependence could develop. Mulford (1984) used both data-based observations and experience as an alcoholism treatment program director to develop a theory of how the process of recovery from alcoholism actually begins during periods of one's heaviest drinking, looking closely at responses to the reactions of one's social audience. Norman Denzin (1987) developed a detailed and complex description of the construction of the alcoholic self, which followed an earlier monograph that described the emergence of a transformed self through the processes of alcoholism treatment and recovery (Denzin 1986). An outstanding ethnography by a sociologist provides a rich description of processes associated with the struggle for recovery within AA (Rudy 1986).

Despite considerable promise, these studies did not lead to programmatic research, largely because they did not attract research support. This lack of interest is largely explained by the intense support that came to surround the explanation of etiology within a biomedical model of causation, indicating possible variations in alcohol metabolism across individuals and often including suggestions of genetic origins of these behavior patterns.

THE SECOND STREAM: SOCIOLOGY AND THE TREATMENT OF ALCOHOLISM

Within the second stream of sociological research and writing, a new generation of sociologists has moved away from criticism of the disease model and attempts to supplant it with models based on social interaction and has instead implicitly embraced it through treatment and health services research. Following is an example of such sociological analysis, tracing the macroorganizational forces that affected growth and change in the alcoholism treatment industry.

Contemporary alcoholism treatment has its most direct lineage from the postrepeal social movement discussed earlier. Launched by enthusiastic members of AA, who recovered through its program during its first decade of existence, the National Council for Alcoholism Education (later the National Council on Alcoholism [NCA] and now the National Council on Alcoholism and Drug Dependence [NCADD]) was founded in 1943, its mission being to "mainstream" into the health care system the treatment of the disease of alcoholism. The fledgling organization was originally based at the alcohol studies center at Yale University, and thus attempted to build its image via a symbolic association with science and medicine.

Public treatment for inebriates has a long history, with several large-scale asylums established in the second half of the nineteenth century (Baumohl and Room 1990). These centers could accomplish little except to keep their patients away from alcohol for the duration of their stay. By the early twentieth century, they were largely abandoned and replaced by drunk farms and county poorhouses, where little in the form of treatment was attempted. NCA's first departure from this model was the "Yale Plan Clinics" (Bacon 1947). These clinics were based on the AA approach, administered independently from the state hospital system, and their suggested design implicitly pointed toward inclusion of middle-class alcoholics, a notable departure from the caricature of drunkards at the bottom of the social class pyramid within Temperance ideology.

These clinics did not diffuse widely, and thinking shifted by the 1960s toward the idea that structured inpatient care for a brief period of time is necessary for successful treatment of alcoholism. Furthermore, inpatient care was more consistent with medicalizing alcoholism as a serious disorder. What emerged was an approach eventually referred to as "the Minnesota Model"; the inpatient treatment regimen was designed to last four weeks, and was expected to be followed by lifelong affiliation with AA. In addition to group AA experiences, patients also received individual counseling and education about the impact of alcohol on the human organism.

Parallel to these developments, NCA leadership undertook a major campaign for the decriminalization of the public inebriate. This symbolic change was seen as necessary for elevating the status of alcoholism to "a disease like any other." The transformation of the alcoholic from "bad" to "sick" through the legislative process was viewed as highly significant at the time. NCA was successful in promoting this legislation. Inadvertently, perhaps, this accomplishment tended to reify the image of the alcoholic as a socially marginal, nonproductive public inebriate, a stereotype persisting from the Temperance movement. Thus, decriminalization was a limited and perhaps limiting organizational achievement relative to the movement's mainstreaming goal. It was especially limiting in that it did not build either advocacy or an appropriate constituency to promote NCA's goals.

Through the 1960s, NCA leadership slowly evolved the vision of locating alcoholism at all levels of social strata (Roman and Blum 1987). If alcoholism was a biological disorder, it should be widely dispersed within the population. Thus, the target of concern in the mainstreaming campaign moved from the highly visible, socially marginal public inebriate to the nearly invisible, socially integrated "hidden alcoholic."

Responding to its own definitions, NCA leadership became focused on the mechanisms to most effectively reach the vast bulk of American alcoholics who were not on skid row. In retrospect, a four-pronged campaign can be inferred (Roman and Blum 1987).

First, the public must be convinced that alcoholism was pernicious and pervasive and could be found anywhere in the social structure, from which it follows that the majority of alcoholics are indeed "hidden" and not receiving treatment.

Second, mechanisms must be made available for treating these "respectable" alcoholics, facilities clearly not represented by those that had been envisioned to serve the goal of decriminalization.

Third, to make treatment for alcoholism accessible, its costs must be covered like the costs for treatment of other disorders, leading to the clear need for the extension of health insurance coverage to include alcoholism.

Fourth, means must be established to identify and motivate the vast group of hidden alcoholics in the direction of treatment. Given the contrast in the apparent level of social integration between hidden alcoholics and the public inebriates that had previously been the primary target of treatment, it was clear that the workplace had great potential for serving this purpose. Workplace interventions, ultimately refined into employee assistance programs, were visible in a small but distinguished set of American corporations and were promoted as the mechanism that would provide the patients for a new system of treatment (Roman 1981a).

These goals came to be implemented through the establishment of NIAAA (see Wiener 1981; Olson 2003 for a detailed analysis of the political processes preceding NIAAA's emergence). As a new organization desiring to build a constituency, NIAAA worked closely with NCA. It moved on each of these four fronts to promote the idea that everyone was at risk for alcoholism, that a new system of privately based treatment should be established

and supported by health insurance coverage. The NIAAA also enthusiastically embraced workplace interventions, which had been previously developed and promoted by NCA (Roman 1981a).

Entrepreneurs from many backgrounds, including AA recovery, were attracted to build a national network of private alcoholism treatment centers. These centers enjoyed growth, development, and apparently substantial income approximately from the late 1970s to the late 1980s. The centers opening during this period almost universally followed the Minnesota Model. Local, regional, and national advertising emerged to diffuse the concept of inpatient treatment, and the mass media gave considerable attention to the experiences of alcoholism and recovery among celebrated personalities.

However, during the decade of the 1980s and into the 1990s, two major and interrelated challenges to the centers' financial and organizational health emerged. First was a challenge to the relative efficacy of the residential treatment services that were the sole or central activity of most of these centers. A federally commissioned study (Saxe 1983) indicated that there was no evidence of advantages of this mode of treatment over other types. The eventual conclusion was that the residential experience was far more elaborate and expensive than was needed to produce the rate of successful client outcomes that could be inferred from research data.

The second challenge supported the first, namely, the costs of alcoholism treatment. Beginning in the early 1980s, most employers were experiencing rising costs of health insurance coverage for their employees. Employers' concerns were also the concerns of third-party insurers, whose profits and competitive positions were adversely affected by rising costs. The combination of concerns by employers and insurers eventually spread to managers in the public sector responsible for managing public payments for eligible clients receiving private health care. All these factors accumulated toward the health care reform crisis of the early 1990s and the rise of managed care.

Residential inpatient care services provided by the relatively new set of private alcoholism treatment centers were thus under attack from two directions, and each attack was more or less bolstered by the other. On the one hand, it was argued that less expensive services (e.g., community-based outpatient care) could produce the same or better results in treating alcoholism. Furthermore, these treatment centers were especially vulnerable to strong and severe challenges to reduce the costs of services. Several features of private alcoholism treatment centers describe their weak buffers to these challenges to organizational survival.

1. The costs of inpatient care for alcoholism for 28 days were not large relative to the costs of care in a general hospital setting. But private residential alcoholism treatment was a new arrival on the health care scene, and employers and insurers had not had these costs previously. Because of

its newness, this system of treatment was far from being institutionalized within the larger culture's expectations and norms about appropriate medical care. There is little evidence of widespread acceptance of the importance or even the propriety of this treatment within the surrounding public culture.

2. Because of their newness, uniqueness, and tendency to be freestanding, alcoholism treatment centers had not established interdependent relationships with other parts of the health care system. Such interdependencies could act as buffers in the face of environmental challenges, with other service units that either sent or received referrals from alcoholism treatment centers coming to their aid and advocating for their value. Such potential interfaces include primary care physicians and hospital emergency rooms, but partly because of the short organizational life of these centers and other aspects of the "liability of newness" (i.e., the essentially nonmedical nature of alcoholism treatment), there is very little evidence of the development of such interdependencies.

3. Also related to newness, the treatment centers had not developed a collective identity that was manifest in a trade association or other lobbying group that could defend its unique interests. This is in part due to the variation in organizational sponsorship from which the centers were established (i.e., general hospitals, emergent nonprofit boards, and profit-making companies).

4. Most alcoholism treatment centers have little in their regimen that can "mystify" the external observer. The apparent simplicity of their core technology, as well as the strong spiritual emphases, made them especially vulnerable to external challenges to their value. The processes that go on in residential treatment programs appear as "just talk" readily comprehensible to the external observer, bearing no resemblance to medical care. This encourages criticism by outsiders of the "unnecessary" extent of group meetings or the "luxurious" nature of recreational facilities.

A field research study focused on 126 private treatment centers initiated in 1986 (Block 1990; Roman, Blum, and Johnson 2000) revealed that within a sample of these private centers, almost perfect isomorphism could be found, following patterns of 28-day inpatient treatment, using 12-step principles as the foundation for treatment design, and targeting services toward clienteles with appropriate health insurance coverage (Block 1990; Roman et al. 2000). Just as the growth of the population of these centers was spectacular, their transformation has occurred with almost equal rapidity. As the first study moved toward completion, a dramatic number of closures in the original population of centers were documented, with these organizational deaths clearly indicating environmental conditions that were failing to support the centers' existence. There was a nearly a 20 percent fatality rate in the sample of centers between 1989 and 1991 (Roman et al. 2000).

Continuing research indicates that inpatient care and the "Minnesota Model" have become increasingly rare as treatment facilities have been forced to expand their services and modify their treatment ideologies in an effort to adapt to the turbulent environment created by managed care (Johnson and Roman 2002; Roman and Johnson 2002). What were initially separate systems for treating alcohol and drug problems have become integrated. Survival of treatment programs appears increasingly dependent on diversification and seeking new markets for care, such as providing services to special population groups and integrating treatment for co-occurring disorders such as psychiatric illness, eating disorders, and compulsive gambling.

This analysis of a portion of the treatment system for alcoholism is typical of health services research on alcohol issues conducted by sociologists. It makes use of organizational approaches to understanding the growth and development of social systems. Related studies are focused on the adoption of innovations in substance abuse treatment systems and the role of specialized occupations in treating substance abuse problems. Other research has focused on the use of the workplace for identifying employees with alcohol problems and providing them with constructive assistance via the structures available in work organizations (Roman 1990).

THE THIRD STREAM: SOCIOLOGY AND SOCIAL INTEGRATION

The third stream examines an array of "normal" drinking and considers the potentially integrative role of alcohol in multiple sectors of society. There is an extensive anthropological record of the worldwide variations in the social patterns of alcohol use (Heath 2000), much of it emphasizing the socially integrative functions served by alcohol consumption. Several sociological studies follow in this tradition, although most of them tend to include questions about alcohol abuse and alcoholism as well.

Early in this tradition was a study by Robert Freed Bales (1946) of Irish drinking behavior. Looking at drinking in rural Ireland, Bales linked the observed patterns with social and cultural organization. The rules of primogeniture resulted in the oldest son inheriting the farm, with the remaining brothers staying on as farm laborers, but without the wherewithal to marry and raise their own families. Bales argued that heavy drinking had emerged as a functional substitute for sexual outlets among these men in puritanical Irish society and that it eventually diffused as a social acceptance of heavy drinking by men.

Charles Snyder (1958) completed his doctoral work at Yale with an extensive study of drinking among Orthodox Jews, attempting to understand how a culture could have a near-zero rate of abstinence and yet have few problems with alcohol. His conclusions centered on the social meanings of drinking as symbolic and supportive of family and religious life, with drinking typically present when at ceremonial events underlining the importance of family and of religion. Excessive drinking also had a negative association with non-Jewish outsiders, including memories of events when drunken anti-Semites would attack Jewish communities, particularly in Eastern Europe.

This work was revisited by Glassner and Berg (1980), who conducted research to establish the resilience of the minimal level of alcohol problems as Jewish communities moved away from Orthodox isolation and became more integrated with non-Jewish cultures. Their research revealed four factors: the continuing cultural association of alcohol abuse with non-Jews, the integration of moderate drinking into family-based rituals, tending to drink with other moderate-drinking Jewish family members and friends, and developing repertoires for avoiding the common pressures to drink heavily in social settings.

Other research that has considered the integrative effects of alcohol has suggested that drinking may be an important socialization rite of passage for youth and young adults (Maddox and McCall 1960). This conclusion is, of course, in sharp contrast to the current obsession with drinking among college students, and the symbolic association of death and injury with "binge drinking," a term effectively invented and diffused to precipitate a degree of moral panic (Wechsler and Wuethrich 2003).

Other studies have examined the settings of drinking and have generated some fascinating ethnographies of cocktail lounges, bars, and after-hours clubs (Cavan 1966; Spradley and Mann 1975; Roebuck and Frese 1976). One such ethnography provides a rich examination of the lives of blue-collar men in one community who centered much of their social life surrounding tavern-based drinking (LeMasters 1976).

However, not only is there no sociology of drinking in the mainstream of contemporary sociology, but also it is quite clear that relatively few sociologists include the use or misuse of alcohol in their research or writing. There can be little doubt that in the United States as well as around the world, alcohol issues are marginal to mainstream sociology. Perhaps this attention will change during the twenty-first century.

Robin Room (1976), a polymath sociologist who has explored and written about nearly every aspect of alcohol social history, policy, and epidemiology, wrote a brilliant but neglected essay on American ambivalence toward alcohol and its consequences. Within the social and historical context of American society, it is easy to see how the appreciative stance on alcohol could wither away from lack of social support. The current cultural context has been characterized as a "drug panic," and in such a setting, receptivity to discussions about the virtues and values of alcohol is likely to be low. However, in line with Room's observations, this does not mean that drinking will disappear or even significantly diminish. What it does mean is that talking about drinking and addressing deviant drinking in families or social settings through direct confrontation will both continue as taboo topics and taboo behaviors within this culture.

Looking only at American society, there is, however, little on the horizon to suggest that change in the pattern of sociological attention and investigation will occur. Despite the potential for their development, there are few tensions or conflicts to be observed among the constituent groups surrounding alcohol, these including consumers, the specialized medical care system's for alcohol dependence, the criminal justice system management of alcohol-related deviance, and the alcohol production and distribution industries.

Alcohol use is, however, an increasingly global phenomenon, and alcohol manufacture and distribution is an aggressively growing worldwide industry, replacing in many locations systems of indigenous alcohol production that have usually been accompanied by socially and culturally integrated customs of drinking. For example, the spread of alcohol availability is accompanied by the introduction of Western-style systems of work organization (Roman 2002). This presents two sets of potential problems. First are those where much more extensive use of alcohol develops among those with the newly acquired wherewithal to obtain it, coupled with employed persons' responses to advertising that much more extensive drinking than was known in the past is part of the new normative order. Second are the effects of wider availability of alcohol and attractive promotions in settings where the intermingling of drinking and work has been casually tolerated for centuries. In either case, the problems are not likely to be easily tractable, and an understanding of how to effectively deal with normative and organizational change emanating from sociological research could be potentially valuable. Thus, direct sociological attention to alcohol issues could come to flourish in the twenty-first century and beyond.

42

THE SOCIOLOGY OF DRUG USE

ERICH GOODE

The University of Maryland, College Park

Pharmacologists refer to substances that have an impact on thinking, feeling, mood, and perception as *psychoactive.* Humans have always ingested psychoactive substances. Higher organisms are neurologically hardwired to derive pleasure from the action of certain chemical substances. Psychoactive drugs, some powerfully so, activate pleasure centers of the brain, thereby potentiating continuing drug-taking behavior. People take drugs to experience the effects that come with their mind-active properties.

The neurological/pharmacological factor addresses how and why drug-taking behavior got started, but it does not address the most sociologically relevant issues: differences in drug-taking behavior between and among societies, social categories, and individuals in the population, as well as among drug types. In addition, the predisposition to use is a *necessary but not sufficient* explanation of use. Use also presupposes the *availability* or supply of, or opportunity to take, a given drug. Without a predisposition to use, drug use will not take place; without availability, it cannot take place.

Moreover, substances are defined as "drugs" in a variety of ways. Indeed, most substances referred to as drugs do not influence the mind at all—that is, they are not psychoactive. Many have medicinal or therapeutic value: Antibiotics, antacids, and antitussives offer ready examples. Why people take such drugs can be answered by addressing medical motives. Other drugs influence perception, mood, cognitive processes, and emotion. Alcohol clearly qualifies in this respect, as do methamphetamine and PCP. Hence, the recreational motive—getting high—factors into the explanatory equation. Still other substances, such as LSD,

marijuana, and heroin, are illegal or illicit—their possession and sale are controlled by law. Hence, their legal status is implicated in why—or, more accurately, why not—some people use them. The medical, psychoactive, and illegal categories overlap: LSD is both psychoactive and a controlled substance, and morphine is both psychoactive and used as medicine, as well as illegal for nonmedical or recreational purposes.

Medical sociologists are interested in the use of drugs in therapy. Criminologists study drugs as illegal substances. Economists look at drugs as an exchange commodity, bought, sold, and distributed according to patterns both similar to and different from those of legal products. Anthropologists conduct research on the consumption of psychoactive plant products by tribal and agrarian peoples; here, cultural factors in drug use predominate. Policy analysts examine the feasibility of specific drug policies. Pharmacologists consider the effects of drug substances on the physical organism; psychologists and psychopharmacologists study their effects on the brain—that is, the mind. In this chapter, I will focus on the use of drugs that are both psychoactive and illicit. In fact, drugs that strongly influence the mind tend to become criminalized. In the United States, aside from tobacco, which generates a "low-key" high, and alcohol, the only psychoactive substances that are not illegal for recreational purposes are those that are not widely used and have not yet become publicized as recreational drugs.

The task of sociologists has always been and remains establishing a distinctive voice in the din of competing perspectives and disciplines investigating drug use. Their focus is on what makes drug use a specifically *social* activity, how socialization, culture, social interaction, social inequality, deviance, and group membership play a central role in the use of psychoactive substances; what people do under the influence; and what societies do about the control of—or why they tolerate or accept—drug use and distribution.

EARLY SOCIOLOGICAL RESEARCH ON DRUG USE

People have been writing about psychoactive drug use and drug effects for at least 6,000 years, but it was not until little more than a century ago that the pathological or harmful side of substance abuse proved to be the major theme in texts on drug use. Surveys on rates of and dependence on medical opium and morphine were conducted in the United States as early as 1877 (Courtwright 1982:10). During a brief period following 1884, the medical profession dubbed cocaine "a miracle of modern science" (Spillane 2000:7–24), but within a decade, physicians began recognizing danger lurking in the unregulated use of the drug, specifically for causing overdoses, or what was then referred to as "cocaine poisoning," and dependence, or developing the "cocaine habit" (pp. 25–42). With respect to drugs, the second half of the nineteenth century witnessed a shift from a completely tolerant, laissez-faire or "hands off" legal policy to one that favored increasingly strict controls over their distribution and sale. By 1900, the unregulated medical consumption of drugs was drawing to a close, while users who sought recreation and intoxication loomed increasingly larger in the drug picture. By the 1920s, the intellectual context that surrounded drug use was saturated with the view that medical use is often, and recreational use is by its very nature, dangerous, harmful, and pathological.

Hence, most of the early sociological researchers found themselves challenging the dominant, conventional view. None of them questioned the idea that nonmedical drug use *could be* or *was often* harmful; the view they challenged was that such harm was *intrinsic* to the activity itself and was *unmediated* by social forces or factors. Moreover, these early sociologists suggested that the cure for the drug problem, namely, the drug laws and their enforcement, may be more harmful than drug use itself.

The first systematic sociological research on the subject of drug use grew out of the research on deviance, delinquency, and crime that was conducted in the 1920s by the faculty and graduate students of the Department of Sociology at the University of Chicago. These early Chicago sociologists located the cause of such untoward behavior in the social disorganization of certain neighborhoods, which they characterized by high residence density, poverty, transience, and dilapidation, conditions that generate moral cynicism among residents, increased opportunities for crime and deviance, and diminished social control.

During the 1920s, intellectuals, along with society's more enlightened wealthier citizens, abandoned the idea of a laissez-faire program of letting problems take care of themselves and began to see their role as one of progressive stewardship—that is, they saw themselves as having "a moral obligation to further the betterment of society." The early Chicago sociologists saw themselves as part of this emerging liberal, enlightened, reformist perspective, seeking solutions to "such social problems as crime, mental disorders, family breakdown, and alcoholism" (Pfohl 1994:184–85). It was out of this sociohistorical context that the sociology department's focus on social disorganization and the problematic behaviors it spawned was born.

Bingham Dai

The first systematic, full-scale sociological study of drug addiction in the Chicago tradition was conducted in the 1930s by Bingham Dai (1937) and was published as *Opium Addiction in Chicago*. While a tradition of medical and legal writings existed when he began his research, Dai argued that the sociological approach represented a contribution because the addict is "a member of society and a carrier of culture" (p. v). Moreover, sociology attempts to trace out the etiological or causal factors related to addiction. Dai examined data on 2,500 addicts from a psychiatric hospital, more than 300 nonaddict drug dealers, and 118 female addicts, for the period from 1928 to 1934. In addition, he conducted interviews and summarized 25 of them as "case studies" in his book.

The lives of these addicts, nearly all above the age of 20, were marked by irregular employment, poverty, weak or nonexistent family ties, and high rates of property crime after they became addicted. Dai (1937) characterized the neighborhoods in which his sample lived by a low level of community spirit and weak or absent "primary group associations" among residents, a high percentage of unattached males, many transients, physical deterioration, and cheap rental units. His drug addicts, he said, lived in an environment of high levels of "family disorganization, crime, vice, alcoholism, insanity and suicide" (p. 189). Such neighborhoods tolerated, gave license to, or encouraged deviant and criminal behavior—and drug addiction fit comfortably within this constellation of social problems.

Dai (1937) did, however, stress that opiate addicts were psychologically normal, did not commit crime prior to their addiction, and tended to commit property crimes rather than crimes of violence and, most important, that opiates did not have a medically harmful or "deteriorating effect" on the body (p. 72). Moreover, Dai's social disorganization approach emphasized an important truth that can be found in much sociological writing: Aside from their "unfortunate spatial location in the natural ecology of a changing society," the perspective "asks us to imagine" that drug addicts, like deviants in general, "are people like ourselves" (Pfohl 1994:209). In short, in most respects, Dai challenged the pathology orientation of the writings on drug use that were current at that time.

Alfred Lindesmith

Alfred Lindesmith also studied drug addiction, but unlike Dai, whose work fit squarely within the social disorganization tradition, made very little use of the Chicago School's focus on communities and neighborhoods. Lindesmith's dissertation devised and tested a micro-interactionist theory of opiate addiction. In *Opiate Addiction,* Lindesmith (1947, 1968) argued that in the initial stage of narcotic use, pleasure dominates as a motivating force. Because of the body's growing tolerance to narcotics, the user, to continue receiving pleasure, is forced to increase the dose of the drug—eventually to a point at which a physical dependence takes place. If use is discontinued because of arrest, disrupted supply, insufficient funds, or attempts at abstinence—or for any reason whatever—painful withdrawal symptoms wrack the addict's body. When the addict administers a dose of a narcotic and recognizes that it alleviates the anguish of withdrawal, an intense *craving* is generated for the drug. Hence, the addict does not become addicted voluntarily "but is rather trapped 'against his [or her] will' by the hook of withdrawal" (Lindesmith 1968:9). Lindesmith saw addicts as basically normal people ensnared in a compulsive habit over which they have no control. The crimes they commit are strictly to maintain their habits. Moreover, he argued, addicts derive no pleasure from opiates. Interestingly, Lindesmith's formulation begs the question of what it was that led the addict to experiment with opiates initially.

The political and policy implications of Lindesmith's (1965) conclusions were profound, conclusions that he developed in considerable detail in *The Addict and the Law.* If addiction is a direct consequence of the conjunction of a biophysical mechanism (withdrawal distress) and a cognitive process (recognizing that a dose of an opiate relieves withdrawal), then the addict cannot be held responsible for his or her condition. Like Dai's addicts, who were caught up in the tangle of community disruption, Lindesmith's addicts were innocents caught up in the uncontrollable impulse to avoid a relentless pharmacological process. Consequently, he reasoned, addiction should not be a crime, and addicts should not be locked up for attempting to relieve what is in effect a medical condition. Moreover, Lindesmith emphasized, the effects of the opiates are not medically harmful, adding further fuel to the fire of his criticism of the drug laws. As a consequence of his findings, Lindesmith became a staunch critic of American drug policy. Indeed, from the 1930s until the early 1960s, Lindesmith was one of the few critical voices speaking out against the government's war on drugs. Lindesmith's impact on the sociology of drug use has been enormous.

Howard S. Becker

Howard S. Becker earned his way through graduate school by playing the piano for jazz bands. His musical experience led to acquaintances with other musicians, most of whom used one or another illicit, controlled substance, mainly marijuana. Just as Lindesmith had raised the question of how someone becomes an opiate addict, Becker's research posed the issue of how one becomes a marijuana smoker. The intersection of the physiology of marijuana's effects and three social/cognitive processes—namely, learning how to use it, learning to perceive its effects, and learning to enjoy its effects—provides the mechanism that accounts for its use. Once one enjoys the effects of marijuana, to continue using it, one needs to nullify the forces of social control that conventional society exercises to prohibit this behavior—namely, maintain a supply of the drug, ensure a measure of secrecy about its use, and reorganize the sense of morality so that definitions of the deviance of use are neutralized. Becker's (1953, 1955) two articles on marijuana use, published in the 1950s, were later incorporated as chapters into his treatise, *Outsiders: Studies in the Sociology of Deviance* (Becker 1963).

Becker's analysis departed even more radically than did Dai's and Lindesmith's from the dominant "pathology" perspective: Dai's addicts were a product of a negative condition (community disruption), and Lindesmith regarded addiction as a medical condition, much like an illness, in need of treatment. But Becker's marijuana smokers—and his depiction of marijuana use—were normal in every imaginable way. Users had no pathological characteristics that impelled them to take the drug. There is no hint that the effects of marijuana are harmful. Even more striking, Becker's intellectual problem is not how users stop their use of this drug, it is precisely the reverse: He asks how people manage to *continue* using marijuana. And like Dai and Lindesmith, Becker staked out the distinctively sociological factors that influence the lineaments of drug use.

Edwin Schur

Edwin Schur (1962) compared the British policy of narcotic control versus the American policy. Since 1914, when the Harrison Narcotic Act was passed, and especially during the 1920s, when it came to be enforced, the dominant stance toward drug use in the United States has been *punitive.* And in the United States, Schur explained, because of this punitive policy, narcotics are extremely expensive and can be purchased regularly only if the user resorts to a life of crime. Hence, the connection between drug use and crime is extremely intimate: Nearly all addicts engage in money-making crimes. A large and vigorous addict subculture flourishes that serves to continually entice fresh, young recruits into the world of addiction. And the population of addicts in the United States is enormous—in the late 1950s, as many as a million, according to the estimate of "some authorities" (Schur 1962:44). Clearly, the punitive drug policy that prevailed in the 1950s—and still prevails today—has failed to curb drug addiction.

In contrast, the British system in the 1950s regarded narcotic addiction as a disease in need of treatment. Drugs were not then—and are not now—"legalized" in the United Kingdom. The dispensation of narcotics for recreational purposes was a crime, punishable by a prison sentence. Physicians could use narcotics for "ministering to the strictly medical" needs of their patients. But what this includes was fairly broadly construed. It included administering narcotics in the following situations: in diminishing doses for the purpose of gradual withdrawal; where it is medically unsafe to withdraw the patient from narcotics because of the severity of withdrawal; and when the patient leads a normal life maintained on narcotics but is incapable of doing so when withdrawn. There was the recognition "that in some cases prolonged prescribing of drugs may be necessary" (Schur 1962:205). In short, during the 1950s, the policy that prevailed in the United Kingdom was *medical* rather than punitive. Law enforcement did not interfere with a medical judgment that maintaining an addict on narcotics may be necessary. Under the British program, Schur argues, doses of narcotics were very cheap, addicts engaged in little criminal behavior, there was no addict subculture, there was no recruitment of novices by addicts, there was almost no diversion of drugs into the black market, there were very few addict-sellers, and the number of narcotic addicts in the United Kingdom was extremely low (fewer than 500 registered addicts). In sum, concluded Schur (1962), this "medically oriented approach seems to work very well" (p. 205).

Schur was interested in the contrasts between the British medical approach and the American punitive approach to addiction for both policy and theoretical reasons. From a policy standpoint, he wanted to convince authorities in the United States that their war on drugs was a failure and that the British system was a "humane and workable" program that had much to teach them about how to deal with the problem of addiction. Of theoretical interest, Schur critiqued the view that drug effects alone, or the predisposition to engage in deviance alone, could account for engaging in deviant behavior. In Britain, he explained, addicts—a population customarily thought of as highly predisposed to engage in crime and deviance—were taking narcotics, a behavior associated elsewhere with engaging in crime and deviance, but engaging in *very little* deviance and crime. Clearly, addiction per se does not generate high rates of crime and deviance.

To explain the low rates of deviant behavior in the United Kingdom, Schur employed the work of the early deviance theorists Edwin Lemert (1951) and Cloward and Ohlin (1960). Addicts in Britain were not labeled as deviants, Schur explained, and hence, neither developed a deviant identity nor became "secondary" deviants—that is, their lives did not revolve around their addiction, as Lemert's theory would predict, had they been stigmatized. And widespread illicit drug trafficking did not exist in the United Kingdom because no social structure of illicit drug distribution existed there, supporting Cloward and Ohlin's

insights on the importance of opportunity in criminal behavior.

However, beginning in the late 1960s, recreational drug use *exploded* in Britain, as it did elsewhere in the Western world. According to a BBC broadcast (March 24, 2002), there are 540 times as many registered narcotic addicts in the early twenty-first century in the United Kingdom as there were in the 1960s. There exists a huge black market there in heroin, as well as in all other illicit drugs, in addition to a vigorous, vibrant drug subculture. According to surveys conducted in Britain (Ramsay et al. 2001) and the European Union (European Monitoring Centre for Drugs and Drug Addiction 2004), the recreational use of illicit drugs, heroin included, in the United Kingdom is at the high end of use of other Western European countries and is only slightly below that of the United States. Moreover, in some ways, the drug policy in the United States is less punitive than it was in the late 1950s. For instance, there are 150,000 addicts in methadone maintenance programs here, and most first- or second-time nonviolent drug offenders end up in treatment programs, through the drug courts, rather than jail or prison. Hence, Schur's analysis is no longer as applicable today as it was in the late 1950s. The implications of these developments are now being debated by researchers and other observers.

IMPLICATIONS OF EARLY SOCIOLOGICAL INSIGHTS

These early sociologists of drug use imparted their distinctively sociological vision to the behavior they studied. The perspective on drug addiction, abuse, and consumption that prevailed at the time they wrote were overwhelmingly pathology oriented: Either the drug created out of whole cloth a new and fearsome creature, impelling the user against his or her will to engage in behavior totally alien and uncharacteristic, or users were psychopaths, their consumption of psychoactive substances a manifestation of their abnormal personalities. Sociologists challenged both versions of this pathology perspective, arguing that the social structure in which users interacted mediated and shaped their drug-taking and the impact that drugs had on their behavior. Neighborhood, cognitive processes, culture and subculture, laws and politics, all played a role in shaping why drugs are used and what impact they have on the lives of users as well as the society at large. The early research on drug use carved out a specialty where none had previously existed and placed its distinctive mark on future research.

If a single theme could be isolated out of the work of the pioneers of drug use, it would be that illicit drug use, abuse, and addiction are normative violations—that is, a form of deviance. Dai recognized that his drug addicts lived in disorganized neighborhoods, in which crime, delinquency, mental disorder, and suicide prevailed—drug addiction was in fact yet another variety of the deviant behavior that so abundantly thrived in such communities. Lindesmith's research was dedicated to the proposition that his addicts were not mentally ill, not inherently or intrinsically mentally aberrant or criminal, but that their criminality was a function of their legal status and their addiction, their association with the world of crime, the deviant and criminal label *imposed* on them and their inevitable, forced, subsequent subcultural associations. Becker's marijuana smokers struggled to neutralize the exercise of social control. Indeed, his work on drugs fit so neatly into the deviance paradigm that it provided chapters and case studies in a treatise on the sociology of deviance (Becker 1963). And Schur compared the impact of defining drug addiction as a crime and a form of deviance (as it was in the United States) with defining it as an illness (as it was in the United Kingdom) and found that criminalizing and stigmatizing the user here exacerbated the social and medical problems associated with addiction, while not doing so there minimized them. In short, these early researchers positioned the field of illicit drug use squarely within the context of the emerging field of the sociology of deviance.

THEORIES OF DRUG USE

The field of drug use studies has devised a substantial number of theories to explain or account for drug use. Most address predisposition only; very few attempt to explain availability or supply. In this section, I summarize a few of the more sociologically relevant theories of drug use. None of these theories is sufficient in itself to account for all drug use; instead, each argues that the condition or factor it focuses on makes drug use *more likely* than would be the case without it. Moreover, the validity of one of these theories should not imply that any of the others is false; for the most part, each of these theories complements rather than invalidates the others.

As with the efforts of the pioneers, current sociological theories depict illicit drug use as a subtype of deviant, non-normative, and criminal behavior—that is, current theories account for the consumption of psychoactive substances with the same theory used to explain the violation of society's laws and norms. As the authors of the "general theory of crime" point out (Gottfredson and Hirschi 1990), nearly all theories of crime and deviance—and the same applies to theories of drug use—are theories of motivation or *predisposition*. But a predisposition to behave a certain way is not a complete explanation. When it comes to drug use, predisposition alone is incomplete. Opportunity has not been fully incorporated into theories of drug use. The availability of a disposable income for the age cohort most likely to use drugs, a development that did not begin until well into the twentieth century, and the globalization of drug distribution, which did not begin in earnest until the 1970s, must be counted among those structural factors that expanded opportunities for persons so disposed to use drugs. A full exposition of the role of opportunity in illicit drug use awaits later research.

Social Control

Social control theory assumes that violations of society's norms are natural, understandable, and not in need of an explanation. What needs to be explained, its proponents argue, is why people conform to society's norms. If left to our own devices, we would all break the law and indulge in any manner of criminal behavior and normative violations. And what *explains* law-abiding behavior and conformity to society's norms, they say, is attachment (or "bonds") to conventional people, beliefs, institutions, and activities (Hirschi 1969). To the extent that we are bonded to our parents, to an education, to marriage and children, to a legal job and career, and to mainstream religion, we do not want to threaten or undermine our "investment" in them by engaging in deviant or criminal behavior—and that includes recreational, especially illicit, drug use. Hence, we see the patterning in drug use discussed in the following; that is, adolescents with college plans or persons who are religious, married, and/or have children are less likely to use drugs, while those with no college plans or who are irreligious, unmarried, and/or childless are more likely to do so. Drug use is "contained" by bonds with or adherence to conventional people, institutions, activities, and beliefs. To social control theorists, it is the *attachment* of people to conventionality that explains abstention from drugs; it is the *absence* or *weakness* of such attachments that explains drug use.

In support of social control theory, it is clear that criminal offending, illicit drug use included, varies enormously by involvement with conventional institutions and conventional others, *independent* of any stable, underlying traits or characteristics. For instance, men are less likely to commit crime, all other factors being held constant, when they are stably married and living with a wife. The same applies when persons are attending school. Both are independently related to the consumption of illegal psychoactive substances, and drug use, independent of any other factors, is related to criminal behavior (Horney, Osgood, and Marshall 1995). In short, "meaningful short-term change in involvement in crime"—and substance abuse as well—"is strongly related to variation in life circumstances" (p. 655). Marriage and school constitute social bonds that "contain" or inhibit deviant and criminal behavior, illicit drug use included.

Self-Control

Self-control theory agrees that it is conformity that needs to be explained, not normative violations or illegal behavior. But its explanation is very different, pushing its key factor, as it does, back to childhood. The factor that accounts for deviance and crime—drug use included—self-control theory argues, is low self-control. And its answer to the question of what accounts for low self-control is poor, inadequate parenting. Children who grow up in a household in which their parents are unable or unwilling to monitor and control their untoward behavior early on will develop a pattern of engaging in uncontrolled, impulsive, hedonistic, high-risk, and, ultimately, short-term, rewarding behavior that includes crime and drug use. People who lack self-control tend to be insensitive, self-centered, reckless, careless, short-sighted, nonverbal, inconsiderate, intolerant of frustration, and pleasure oriented. They are grabbers, cheats, liars, thieves, and exploiters. They act with no concern for the long-range consequences of their actions.

Drug use is simply one of many manifestations of their orientation to life, and that is to do whatever you want, whatever feels good, regardless of whether that causes harm to others or even, in the long run, to oneself. There is no need to explain the connection between drug use and crime, self-control theorists argue, because they are the same behavior, two sides of exactly the same low self-control behavior. The usual controls that keep most individuals in check are inoperative in the lives of drug users. And according to the proponents of this theory, low self-control can be traced back to bad parenting (Gottfredson and Hirschi 1990). The impulse to use drugs does *not* have to be learned, this perspective argues; hence, all learning theories of drug use—as well as all learning theories of crime and deviance—are in error. It is *abstention* from drugs that needs to be explained.

The "strong relationship" between criminal behavior and the use of psychoactive drugs has been shown to hold "regardless of age, race, gender, or country" (Uihlein 1994:149). Self-control theory argues that "they are consequences of common causal factors," that the age curve for both follows the same trajectory, that both drug use and delinquency are relatively stable over time, that drug use, like delinquency and crime, is versatile rather than specialized, that "drug use" and "crime" variables "appear indistinguishable from one another" (Uihlein 1994:151, 153–54), and that both can be traced to poor, inadequate parenting. Since the "logical structure" of drug use and that of criminal behavior are identical—both being the "manifestations of an underlying tendency to pursue short-term, immediate pleasure"—it follows that "crime and drug use are the same thing" and that research "designed to determine the causal relationship" between them "is a waste of time and money" (Gottfredson and Hirschi 1990:42, 93, 233–34).

Social Learning

Social learning theory emphatically disagrees with the control theories, arguing that people are not "naturally" predisposed to committing crimes or using drugs; instead, they have to specifically *learn* the positive value of nonnormative behaviors. The earliest sociological version of learning theory applies specifically to crime and is referred to as the theory of differential association (Sutherland 1939).

Learning theory argues that youngsters associate differentially with certain groups or social circles that provide "social environments for exposure" to definitions of correct or incorrect behavior, models of behavior to imitate, and opportunities to engage in certain kinds of behavior. These environments may discourage or encourage drug use. Family definitions, models, and opportunity are important in defining drug use one way or the other, but of course, they tend to discourage rather than encourage use. Additional agents of learning or socialization include other family members, neighbors, religious figures, teachers, and the mass media, each of whom has "varying degrees of effect on use and abstinence." Typically, however, peers are most influential, the family is a distant second, and the other socializing agents trail far behind (Akers 1998:171–72).

Learning theory argues that the probability of the use of psychoactive substances increases to the extent that someone (a) is exposed to persons, especially peers, who use rather than abstain from drugs; (b) hears definitions favorable rather than unfavorable to use; and (c) finds such use pleasurable rather than neutral or unpleasant. In addition, use escalates to the extent that a person associates with heavier users and with parties who define heavier use in positive terms and who develop a pattern of heavy use that is reinforcing or pleasurable (Akers 1998:175–76).

Conflict

Conflict theory argues that *inequality* is the root cause of drug use, at least the heavy, chronic abuse of and dependence on "hard" drugs such as crack cocaine and heroin. Such abuse, proponents of this theory argue, is strongly related to social class, income, power, and neighborhood. A significantly higher proportion of lower- and working-class inner-city residents abuse the hard drugs than is true of more affluent members of the society. More important, this is the case because of the impact of a number of key structural conditions that have their origin in economics and politics (Hamid 1990; Levine 1991; Bourgeois 1995).

The conflict perspective argues that drug dealing is more likely to take root and flourish in poor, powerless, socially disorganized communities than in more affluent, powerful, organized communities. Where residents cannot mobilize the relevant political forces to act against undesirable activities in their midst, open, organized, and widespread drug dealing is extremely likely. In addition, in communities in which poverty is entrenched, the economic structure has never developed or has decayed and collapsed, and a feeling of hopelessness, depression, and anomie is likely to take hold, making drug abuse especially appealing and attractive, providing a means of "escaping from a dreadful condition into one that seems, temporarily at least, more pleasant" (Levine 1991:4). For some, getting high—and getting high frequently—has become an oasis of excitement, pleasure, and fantasy in lives that would otherwise feel psychically impoverished and alienated. Most of the residents of deteriorated communities resist such blandishments. But sufficient numbers succumb to drug abuse to make the lives of the majority unpredictable, insecure, and dangerous. A drug subculture flourishes in response to what some residents have come to see as the hopelessness and despair of the reality of their everyday lives. And it is poverty that generates these feelings. In the words of Harry Gene Levine (1991), "The three most important things to understand about the sources of long-term crack and heroin abuse are: poverty, poverty, poverty" (p. 3).

A crucial assumption of the conflict approach to drug abuse is that there are two overlapping but conceptually distinct forms or varieties of drug use. The first, which makes up the vast majority of illegal users, is "casual" or "recreational" use. It is engaged in by a broad spectrum of the class structure, the middle and upper-middle class included. This type of use ranges from experimental and episodic to regular but controlled use. Such users rarely become a problem for the society except insofar as they are regarded as a problem by others. "Middle class status," says Harry Gene Levine (1991), "with its benefits and stability, tends to immunize people *not against drug use, but against long-term, hard drug use*" (p. 4).

The second type of drug use is abuse—compulsive, chronic, or heavy use—drug use that often escalates to dependence and addiction. It is typically accompanied by social and personal harm. Chronic abuse is motivated by despair, alienation, poverty, and community disintegration. Experts argue that moving from the first type of drug use (recreational) to the second (abuse) is more likely to take place among the impoverished than among the affluent and to be indulged in by residents of disorganized rather than intact communities (Levine 1991).

PATTERNS IN DRUG USE

Two of the largest, most nationally representative, and most valid drug use surveys are conducted in the United States: the National Survey on Drug Use and Health, based on a sample of the population as a whole (SAMHSA 2004), and the Monitoring the Future surveys, based on eighth, tenth, and twelfth graders, college students, and adults not in college of age 19 to 45. The results of these two yearly surveys, verified by others conducted in other countries, support the following generalizations or patterns in drug use.

The first pattern is that for all illicit drugs, *experimental use is the rule.* Most of the people who try a given illicit drug do not use it regularly; most in fact discontinue its use. The circle circumscribed by the universe of everyone who has ever taken a given drug at least once in their lives is much larger than the circle circumscribed by everyone who has taken it during the previous month.

The second pattern is that for all illicit drugs, *irregular, episodic, occasional use is more common than heavy, chronic, compulsive abuse.* The circle circumscribed by everyone who has used a given drug, say, less frequently than once a week in the past year is larger than the circle circumscribed by everyone who has used that drug more than 20 times a month—that is, more than 240 times in the past year.

The third pattern is that *the use of the legal drugs,* alcohol and tobacco, *is vastly greater than the use of the illegal drugs.* According to the most recent (2003) National Survey on Drug Use and Health, half of all Americans had consumed at least one alcoholic drink in the past month (50.1 percent) and a quarter had smoked one or more tobacco cigarettes (25.4 percent). But only 8 percent had used marijuana in the past 30 days, and just over one-half of 1 percent had used cocaine (0.6 percent).

Moreover—and this is the fourth pattern—the "loyalty" rate, the rate at which onetime users continue to use a drug, and use it regularly, is much greater for the legal drugs than for the illegal drugs. Six persons in 10 who ever drank alcohol (60.2 percent) had done so in the past month, and a third of persons who ever smoked a tobacco cigarette had done so in the past month (37.0 percent). But only one person in seven who had used marijuana at least one time in their lives (15.2 percent), and only 6.5 percent of those who had used cocaine one or more times in their lives did so in the past month. The comparable figures for PCP (0.8 percent) and LSD (0.5 percent) were much lower (SAMHSA 2004:188, 202). The more illicit the drug, the lower the continuance or loyalty rate it attracts among users.

The fifth pattern is that *the correlation between the use of legal and illegal drugs is extremely strong.* People who use alcohol and tobacco are much more likely to use any and all illicit drugs than people who do not do so. Moreover, the *more* they use the legal drugs, the *greater* is the likelihood that they use illegal drugs. Youths ages 12 to 17 who are both smokers and heavy drinkers are 20 times more likely to have used one or more illicit drugs (72.4 percent) than are youths who neither drink nor smoke (3.7 percent). Youths who drink heavily are 100 times more likely to have used cocaine in the past month (10.6 percent) than are nondrinkers (0.1 percent). The same generalizations prevail for all age groups, all drugs, legal and illegal, and all levels of use. The impulse to alter one's consciousness with one substance—whether legal or illegal—is strongly related to altering it with other substances.

The sixth pattern is this: *The use of psychoactive substances is strongly related to a person's age.* Drug use rises sharply from age 12 (the age at which most surveys begin asking respondents such questions) through adolescence, reaches a peak at about age 20, and then declines, year by year, after that. According to the 2003 National Survey on Drug Use and Health, only 2.7 percent of 12-year-olds say that they have used any illegal drug (excepting alcohol) in the past month. This rises to 24 percent for 20-year-olds and declines throughout the 20s and subsequently. It is 13.4 percent for persons in their late 20s (26–29); 8.4 percent for those in their late 30s (35–39); 6.8 percent for those in their late 40s (45–49); and only 2 percent for those in their late 50s. Only 0.6 percent of persons aged 65 or more said that they had used an illicit drug in the past month. For alcohol consumption, this curve is much flatter; the peak in consumption is reached between ages 21 and 22; use declines very slowly until age 60, and drops off more precipitously after that (SAMHSA 2004:193, 207).

The remaining patterns are the following. In addition to the young, and persons who use alcohol and smoke cigarettes, the categories in the population who have significantly higher-than-average likelihoods of using psychoactive substances include males (SAMHSA 2004:194); the unmarried, especially persons who cohabit without being married (Bachman et al. 2002:211–12); adolescents whose plans for the future do not include college (Johnston et al. 2004:452); and the unemployed (SAMHSA 2004:197). The categories in the population whose use of psychoactive substances is lower than the average include females (SAMHSA 2004:194); the married; women who are pregnant and couples with children; and persons who consider religion important in their lives and who frequently attend religious services. Persons who perceive great risks in drug use are more likely to disapprove of it and are less likely to indulge in drug use than are persons who do not perceive great risks in use (Bachman et al. 2002:121–55, 208–209, 211–12, 214–15).

These patterns, taken together, draw a consistent, coherent picture that provides a small number of generalizations about drug use as a form of behavior.

First generalization: Most people tend to be fairly cautious and temperate about their consumption of psychoactive substances. Heavy use is the exception, moderate use is the rule. This moderation extends to the relative avoidance of illicit drugs. Whether it is fear of arrest, the stigma of illegality, its deviant status, the inability to locate a dealer, or fear of physical harm, compared with alcohol and tobacco, the use of illegal drugs is relatively unpopular. And the more "illegal" and more *deviant* the use of the drug, the rarer its use is, and the less "loyal" users are to its use. The least stigmatized, the least deviant—and the least "criminal"—of the illicit drugs, marijuana, is *by far* the most popular, and the one users are most likely to "stick with" the longest. For the great majority of Americans—the same applies to the residents of the other countries in which drug surveys have been conducted—illicit drugs have less seductive appeal than do licit drugs.

And the second and closely related generalization: Unconventionality explains much of what we want to know about drug use. (An obvious but crucial point: Unconventionality is a matter of degree; it can be plotted along a continuum.) Unconventionality includes a broad range of associated and cognate characteristics, including experience and sensation seeking, low self-control,

impulsivity, and the tendency to take risks. Most people do not take serious risks; hence, most people do not use illicit drugs that are perceived to be dangerous and harmful, and even fewer use them regularly. The minority who do so tend to be more unconventional than the majority who do not. Drug use is an aspect or manifestation of unconventionality. The dimension of unconventionality begs the question of causal origin; unconventionality has a variety of origins, and indeed, stressing its importance is consistent with all the theories spelled out in the foregoing. Certain social statuses foster or engender unconventionality. Their members have relatively few responsibilities, weak ties to conventional society, and few agents of social control monitoring and controlling their behavior, and hence there are relatively few harmful social consequences to the negative aspects of risk-taking. Hence, they are more likely to engage in unconventional, high-risk behavior than are persons in statuses or positions encumbered by stronger conventional social bonds. And people relatively slipped from the bonds of conventionality tend to congregate, thereby increasing the likelihood that they will violate the norms of society.

The late teens to the early 20s represents the peak years of drug use; it is the exact point of the trajectory combining diminished levels of parental supervision and as-yet low levels of adult responsibilities. Males are more likely to have been socialized to take greater risks and to violate the conventional norms of the society; hence, it should come as no surprise that they exhibit consistently higher levels of illicit drug use and heavy alcohol consumption. The unmarried tend to be less bonded to responsibility and convention than the married, and when children appear in the lives of the married, this difference widens—hence, the differences we observe in their illicit drug use. And persons who live together are already more unconventional compared with persons who are legally married; this unconventionality manifests itself in their higher rates of drug use. Adolescents with no college plans have less to lose through risky behavior than do those with plans to attend college—thus, their higher rates of drug use (although this difference decreases the closer the youngster is to actually attending college). The college experience itself generates a large, dense congregation of young people, and thus, college students have similar, or even slightly higher, rates of drug use than do young people who do not attend college, even though the former are more invested in the future than the latter. The more alienated people are from traditional religion, the greater the likelihood is that they use drugs; the more they attend religious services and say that religion is very important in their lives, the lower that likelihood is. Again, unconventionality rears its head in the drug picture. And last, perceived risk is not only a measure of rationality but of unconventionality as well: People who see greater risk in specific activities tend to be more unconventional than those who see less. And the perception of risk—or the lack thereof—is *strongly* related to drug use.

CONTEMPORARY
ISSUES AND CONCERNS

The study by sociologists of drug use has become a substantial scholarly endeavor. More broadly, drug use constitutes a large conceptual and topical umbrella that attracts a collection of researchers with extremely diverse interests and concerns. The study of drug use is one of the more diffuse and incoherent fields in existence. Most of its researchers are not sociologists or even social scientists, and much of its data collection was not conducted for theoretical purposes. Drug-use surveys are extremely expensive to conduct, and hence, policy rather than theory tends to guide their direction. Many sociologists currently conducting research on drug use are members of a team made up of specialists working in other fields. Usually, sociologists offer methodological rigor to clinically oriented specialists. Even sociologists working on their own depend on the findings of research conducted by a scattering of nonsociological fields to a degree perhaps unprecedented in any subfield of sociology—these fields include pharmacology and psychopharmacology, medicine, psychiatry, epidemiology, the policy sciences, political science, history, anthropology, criminology, economics, cultural studies, and journalism. Sociologists are in a distinct minority among drug-use researchers. Many of the issues and questions that preoccupy contemporary sociologists of drug use are shaped outside their parent field.

In 2005, I mailed a questionnaire to the 120 members of the Society for the Study of Social Problems (SSSP), the majority of whom are sociologists, who list Drinking and Drugs as one of their division specialties, asking them about the topics that sociologists of drug use are most likely to investigate. Exactly half (60 members or 50 percent) responded. The topics respondents checked as most commonly investigated include the following.

Policy and Legal Issues

More than half of the respondents of the survey said that policy-related issues are among the most frequently studied topics among sociologists of drug use. This finding is consistent with the work of MacCoun and Reuter (2001), who address much of the research on policy and legal issues. These issues include the consequences of imprisoning drug users and sellers; what other countries are doing about the drug problem; alternatives to strict prohibition; whether and to what extent the "war on drugs" is working, prohibition is causing more problems than it solves, some form of legalization can work; policy alternatives; whether strict prohibition is the best way of dealing with the problems posed by drug abuse; and learning about how to deal with suppressing drug abuse (MacCoun and Reuter 2001). More than half of the respondents (32 out of 60) said that policy-related issues are among the most frequently studied topics among sociologists of drug use.

Epidemiology and Etiology

At least from as far back as the 1930s, the causes of drug use and the distribution of drug use in the population have been a mainstay of sociological research on the abuse of psychoactive substances. Thirty-five of the 60 respondents said that the issues of who uses which drugs and why (Johnston et al. 2004) continue to engage sociological researchers.

Drug Use and Crime

Goldstein's (1985) tripartite "drugs-violence nexus" has stimulated an enormous volume of commentary and research on the topic. In 2001, the National Institute of Justice (NIJ) invited three dozen experts to participate in a symposium titled "Toward a Drugs and Crime Research Agenda for the Twenty-First Century"; the presentations were published in 2003 (www.ojp.usdoj.gov/nij/pub-sum/194616.htm). Although much work has been conducted in the area, the participants agreed that the drugs-and-crime link is unresolved and needs further research. In spite of the vagaries of funding, roughly three-quarters of SSSP drug researchers (46 out of 60) believe that the drugs-crime nexus remains a central sphere of research attention for researchers.

Drug Use and the Community

Consistent with previous efforts of Hamid (1990), Bursik and Grasmick (1993), and Bourgeois (1995), 40 percent of the SSSP survey respondents believe the impact of drug use and extensive drug dealing on the viability of a community and whether and to what extent some communities are more vulnerable to the penetration of drug sellers into their midst offers a major topic of interest to sociologists and urban anthropologists who engage in drug research. "Drugs and the Community" is a specifically and distinctly sociological topic, one that has been on the subfield's agenda for much of the past century.

The Effectiveness of Treatment Programs

Many researchers believe that a reliance on imprisonment is ineffective and counterproductive; hence, the research on alternatives, mainly drug treatment programs. The federal government has sponsored three waves of studies on drug treatment, the Drug Abuse Reporting Program (DARP), 1969 to 1972; the Treatment Outcome Prospective Study (TOPS), 1979 to 1981; and the Drug Abuse Treatment Outcome Study (DATOS), 1991 to 1993. These surveys, based on nationally representative samples, indicate that drug treatment is an effective means of addressing drug abuse and addiction. Currently, scores of smaller studies of treatment programs are ongoing. Sociologists continue to play a central role in conducting a substantial portion of these studies, a fact asserted by half

(30 out of 60) of the survey respondents. In addition, preventing drug use, mainly by means of educational programs, is on the agenda of some researchers.

The Methodology of Surveying Drug Use

Research methods have been on the sociologist's agenda since the field's birth, and the study of drug use, which poses special methodological problems, exemplifies this principle, as asserted by a third of the respondents (19 out of 60). The best means of studying drug use and abuse, whether researchers get honest answers when asking respondents about their illicit, deviant behaviors, how the researcher addresses problems of validity and reliability, and how to conduct research among dangerous informants and subjects and access "hidden" populations of users and sellers are major topics that engage the field (Harrison and Hughes 1997; Dunlap and Johnson 1999; Wish et al. 2000).

The Dynamics of Drug Markets

The predisposition to use drugs does not explain use; it is a necessary but not sufficient condition for use. The availability of drugs is another precondition. How drugs are distributed, how drugs get from Point A to Point B, what is distinctive about buying and selling illicit products, and what the "social world" of the drug seller is like are frequently studied topics among sociologists and urban anthropologists engaged in studying drug use (Williams 1992; Bourgeois 1995; Jacobs 1999). These and related topics have offered intriguing strategic research issues to the drug researcher, a fact attested to by not quite half of our respondents (28 out of 60).

Other Topics

In addition to the forced-choice alternatives I offered, topics the survey respondents spontaneously wrote that attracted current sociological research interest include women and drug use; mothering and drug use; drugs and the family; HIV/AIDS; controlled or "functional" users of illicit drugs; the use of tobacco, especially by teenagers; drugs and health; the dangers of prescription and over-the-counter drugs; and cultural differences in drinking patterns.

THE FUTURE OF THE SOCIOLOGY OF DRUG USE

Most of the SSSP/Drinking and Drugs Division respondents believe that the topics mentioned in the foregoing will remain on the subfield's agenda. Furthermore, most respondents who answered the question specified their focus. Policy and legal questions will continue to engage sociologists of drug use, especially the decriminalization of marijuana; medical marijuana; the cost and impact of the "war on drugs," especially on minorities; drug courts; the efficacy of harm reduction strategies; devising a "saner" drug policy; and control over the legal drug industry. Etiology remains central to the field, especially the impact of inadequate parenting on drug abuse. The effectiveness of drug treatment will continue to be studied, especially early intervention and drug education. The study of drug markets will remain important, including the diffusion of heroin and other narcotics into rural areas and the globalization of drug distribution.

Additional topics that will loom large in the twenty-first century include women and drug use; abuses by the pharmaceutical industry; teenagers and alcohol consumption; narcoterrorism; the spread of HIV/AIDS; the impact of drug abuse on the family; the use of performance-enhancing drugs; the use of drugs at work; drugs and health care; the use of medications and the development of neurological stimulation as a means of controlling deviant behavior; the reentry of released inmates into the general population; the misuse of prescription drugs; and smoking behavior and policies designed to control it.

Regardless of whether these predictions of future research enterprises will be borne out, the small, extremely eclectic field of the sociology of drug use will remain a dynamic component of drug-use research. Moreover, in the future, as in the present and the past, policy issues will influence the direction that research takes. In addition, sociologists of drug use will continue to be influenced by drug researchers in other disciplines more than they influence the field of sociology. A policy-oriented focus, theoretical eclecticism, interdisciplinary research, and the image of narrow specialization are the price the sociologist of drug use has to pay for conducting research on one of the most fascinating—and distinctively sociological—of human behaviors.

43

JUVENILE DELINQUENCY

CLEMENS BARTOLLAS

University of Northern Iowa

Juvenile delinquency—crimes committed by young people—constitute, by recent estimates, nearly one-fifth of the crimes against people and one-third of the property crimes in the United States. The high incidence of juvenile crime makes the study of juvenile delinquency vital to an understanding of American society. *The Uniform Crime Reports,* juvenile court statistics, cohort studies, self-report studies, and victimization surveys are the major sources of data used to measure the extent and nature of delinquent behavior. These forms of examination have generally agreed on the following findings:

- Juvenile delinquency is widespread in the United States.
- The majority of youths have committed some form of delinquency during their adolescent years.
- Three out of four juvenile arrests are arrests of males.
- Lower-class youths tend to commit more frequent and serious offenses than do higher-class youths.
- Minority youths, especially African American, tend to commit more serious delinquent acts than do white youths.

The number of juvenile homicides has been going down since the mid-1990s. Philip J. Cook and John Laub (1998) found that a changing context, as well as a more limited availability of guns, helped explain the reduced rate of juvenile homicides. Cook and Laub predicted that this changing context would continue to decrease youth homicides in the immediate future. Cook and Jens Ludwig (2004) and Anthony A. Braga (2003) also identified the high correlation between gun ownership and juvenile homicides.

The study of juvenile delinquency is full of conflicting positions. There are those who believe that this area of study should be limited to the theories of why juveniles become involved with crime. Others contend that the study of delinquency also ought to include the environmental influences on juvenile crime, such as the family, school, peer and gang participation, and drug involvements. Still others conclude that the study of delinquency should include the social control of juvenile crime, as well as causation theories and environmental influences.

The study of delinquency has clearly changed over the years. Throughout the twentieth century, delinquency studies became more interdisciplinary, more concerned about the integration with other theories, more methodologically sophisticated, and more focused on long-term follow-up of juveniles, sometimes for several decades. The importance of human agency and delinquency across the life course, both of which rose in theoretical importance during the 1990s, are generating considerable excitement in the early years of the twenty-first century.

The main concerns of this chapter are the origins of the study of delinquency; the emergence of sociological theory; the environmental influences on delinquency; the biological, psychological, and sociological theories that have influenced the field of delinquency; the interdisciplinary theories that are affecting the study of juvenile delinquency; and the prospects for future developments.

ORIGINS OF THE STUDY OF JUVENILE DELINQUENCY

What to do with wayward juveniles has long been a concern of American society. Before the end of the eighteenth century, the family was believed to be the source of cause of deviancy, and therefore, the idea emerged that perhaps the well-adjusted family could provide the model for a correctional institution for children. The house of refuge, the first juvenile institution, reflected the family model wholeheartedly; it was designed to bring the order, discipline, and care of the family into institutional life. The institution was to become the home, the peers, the siblings, the staff, and the parents (Rothman 1971).

Juveniles Placed in Institutions

The New York House of Refuge, which opened on January 1, 1825, with six girls and three boys, is generally acknowledged as the first house of refuge. Over the next decade, Bangor, Boston, Chicago, Cincinnati, Mobile, Philadelphia, and Richmond followed suit in establishing houses of refuge. Twenty-three schools were chartered in the 1830s and another 30 in the 1840s. Some houses of refuge were established by private agencies, some by state governments or legislatures, and some jointly by public authorities and private organizations (Rothman 1971).

One of the changes in juvenile institutions throughout the remainder of the nineteenth century was the development of the cottage system. Eventually called "training schools" or "industrial schools," these institutions would house smaller groups of youths in separate buildings, usually no more than 20–40 youths per cottage. House parents, typically a man and his wife, constituted the staff in these cottages. Early cottages were log cabins; later cottages were constructed from brick or stone.

Barbara M. Brenzel's (1983) study of the State Industrial School for Girls in Lancaster, Massachusetts, the first state reform school for girls in the United States, revealed the growing disillusionment in the mid- to late nineteenth century regarding training schools. Intended as a model reform effort, Lancaster was the first "family-style" institution in the United States and embodied new theories about the reformation of youths. However, an "examination of a reform institution during the second half of the nineteenth century reveals the evolution from reformist visions and optimistic goals at mid-century to pessimism and 'scientific' determinism at the century's close" (p. 1). Brenzel added that "the mid-century ideal of rehabilitative care changed to the principle of rigid training and custodial care by the 1880s and remained so into the early twentieth century" (pp. 4–5).

Creation of the Juvenile Court

During the final decades of the nineteenth century, the Progressive Reformers viewed childhood as a period of dependency and exclusion from the adult world. To institutionalize childhood, they enacted a number of "child saving" laws, including child labor and compulsory school attendance laws. The juvenile court was viewed as another means to achieve unparalleled age segregation of children (Feld 1999). The following are a number of contextual factors that influenced the creation of this court.

Legal Context

The juvenile court was founded in Cook County (Chicago), Illinois, in 1899, when the Illinois legislature passed the Juvenile Court Act, and later that year was established in Denver, Colorado. The *parens patriae* doctrine provided a legal catalyst for the creation of the juvenile court, furnishing a rationale for use of informal procedures for dealing with juveniles and for expanding state power over the lives of children.

Political Context

In the *Child Savers,* Anthony Platt (1977) developed the political context of the origin of the juvenile court. He stated that the juvenile court was established in Chicago and later elsewhere because it satisfied several middle-class interest groups. He saw the juvenile court as an expression of middle-class values and of the philosophy of conservative political groups. In denying that the juvenile court was revolutionary, Platt charged that

the child-saving movement was not so much a break with the past as an affirmation of faith in traditional institutions. . . . What seemingly began as a movement to humanize the lives of adolescents soon developed into a program of moral absolutism through which youths were to be saved from movies, pornography, cigarettes, alcohol, and anything else which might possibly rob them of their innocence. (Pp. 98–99)

Economic Context

Platt (1977) argued that the behaviors that the child savers selected to be penalized—such as roaming the streets, drinking, fighting, engaging in sex, frequenting dance halls, and staying out late at night—were found primarily among lower-class children. Accordingly, juvenile justice from it inception, he contended, reflected class favoritism that resulted in the frequent processing of poor children through the system while middle- and upper-class children were more likely to be excused.

Sociocultural Context

The social conditions that were present during the final decades of the nineteenth century were the catalysts that led to the founding of the juvenile court. One social condition was that citizens became increasingly incensed by the treatment of children, especially the policy of jailing children with adults. Another social condition was that the higher status given middle-class women made them interested in exerting their newfound influence to improve the lives of children (Faust and Brantingham 1974).

Influence of Positivism

These pressures for social change took place in the midst of a wave of optimism that swept through the United

States during the Progressive Era, the period from 1899 to 1920. The emerging social sciences assured reformers that their problems with delinquents could be solved through positivism. According to positivism, youths were not responsible for their behavior and required treatment rather than punishment.

The concept of the juvenile court spread rapidly across the United States; by 1928, only two states did not have a juvenile court statute. In Cook County, the amendments that followed the original act brought the neglected, the dependent, and the delinquent together under one roof. The "delinquent" category comprised both status offenders and actual violators of criminal law.

Urban juveniles courts, especially, had clinics that provided psychological services for those youths referred to them by the juvenile court. Those who provided such services in the clinics were psychiatrists, clinical psychologists, or psychiatric social workers. The treatment modality that was frequently used was various versions of Freudian psychoanalysis. Typically, in a one-to-one relationship with a therapist, youths in trouble were encouraged to talk about past conflicts that caused them to express emotional problems through aggressive or antisocial behavior. The insights that youths gained from this psychotherapy were intended to help them resolve the conflicts and unconscious needs that drove them to crime. As a final step of psychotherapy, youths would become responsible for their behaviors.

THE EMERGENCE OF SOCIOLOGICAL THEORY

From the second decade of the twentieth century, the Chicago School of Sociology developed a sociological approach to delinquency that differed greatly from that found in psychological positivism. The intellectual movement of social disorganization theory came out of this Chicago school. To William I. Thomas and Florian Znaniecki (1927), social disorganization reflected the influence of an urban, industrial setting on the ability of immigrant subcultures, particularly parents, to socialize and effectively control their children. S. P. Breckinridge and Edith Abbott (1970) contributed the idea of plotting "delinquency maps." Frederick M. Thrasher (1927) viewed the youth gang as a substitute socializing institution whose function was to provide order, or social organization where there was none, or social disorganization.

Clifford R. Shaw and Henry D. McKay extended social disorganization by focusing specifically on the social characteristics of the community as a cause of delinquency. Their pioneering investigations established that delinquency varied in inverse proportion to the distance from the center of the city, that it varied inversely with socioeconomic status, and that delinquency rates in a residential area persisted regardless of changes in racial and ethic composition of the area (Reiss 1976).

Shaw and McKay viewed juvenile delinquency as resulting from the breakdown of social control among the traditional primary groups, such as the family and the neighborhood, because of the social disorganization of the community. Urbanization, rapid industrialization, and immigration processes contributed to the disorganization of the community. Thus, delinquent behavior became an alternative mode of socialization through which youths who grew up in disorganized communities were attracted to deviant lifestyles (Finestone 1976).

Shaw and McKay turned to ecology to show this relationship between social disorganization and delinquency. Shaw (1929) reported that marked variations of school truancy, juvenile delinquency, and adult criminality existed among different areas in Chicago. Shaw found that the nearer a given locality was to the center of the city, the higher its rates of delinquency and crime. Shaw further found that areas of concentrated crime maintained their high rates over a long period, even when the composition of the population changed markedly. Shaw and McKay (1931), in a study performed for the National Commission on Law Observance and Enforcement, reported that this basic ecological finding was also true for a number of other cities.

In their classic work *Juvenile Delinquency and Urban Areas,* Shaw and McKay (1942) developed these ecological insights in greater scope and depth. They studied males who were brought into the Cook County juvenile court on delinquency charges in 1900–1906, 1917–1923, and 1927–1933. Over this 33-year period, they discovered that the vast majority of the delinquent boys came from either an area adjacent to the central business and industrial areas or along two forks of the Chicago River. Then, applying Burgess's concentric zone hypothesis of urban growth, they measured delinquency rates by zone and by areas within the zone. They found that in all three periods, the highest rates of delinquency were in Zone I (the central city), the next highest in Zone II (next to the central city), in progressive steps outward to the lowest in Zone V. Significantly, although the delinquency rates changed from one period to the next, the relationship among the different zones remained constant, even though in some neighborhoods the ethnic compositions of the population changed totally.

Shaw and McKay eventually refocused their analysis from the influence of social disorganization of the community to the importance of economics on high rates of delinquency. They found that the economic and occupational structure of the larger society was more influential in the rise of delinquent behavior than was the social life of the local community. They concluded that the reason members of lower-class groups remained in the inner-city community was less a reflection of their newness of arrival and their lack of acculturation to American institutions than it was a function of their class position in society (Finestone 1976).

ENVIRONMENTAL INFLUENCES ON JUVENILE DELINQUENCY

The importance of the Shaw and McKay tradition of the environment and community has long remained in the study of delinquency. An examination of the relationship between the family and delinquency, school performance and delinquency, drug use and delinquency, and participation in gangs and delinquency are generally found in studies of environmental influences on delinquency.

The Family

In the midst of conflicting findings about the relationship between delinquency and the family, the following observations have received wide support:

- Family conflict and poor marital adjustment are more likely to lead to delinquency than the structural breakup of the family (Loeber and Stouthamer-Loeber 1986).
- Children who have delinquent siblings or criminal parents seem to be more prone to delinquent behavior than those who do not (Lauritsen 1993).
- Rejected children appear to be more prone to delinquent behavior than those who have not been rejected. Children who have experienced severe rejection are more likely to become involved in delinquent behavior than those who have experienced a lesser degree of rejection (Loeber and Stouthamer-Loeber 1986).
- Consistency of discipline within the family appears to be important in deterring delinquent behavior (McCord, McCord, and Zola 1959).
- The rate of delinquency seems to increase with the number of unfavorable factors in the home. Thus, multiple handicaps within the family are associated with a higher probability of juvenile delinquency than are single handicaps (Loeber and Stouthamer-Loeber 1986).

The School

Studies have found that the school is a critical context, or arena, of learning delinquent behavior. For example, Eugene Maguin and Rolf Loeber's (1996) meta-analysis found that "children with lower academic performance offended more frequently, committed more serious and violent offenses, and persisted in their offending" (p. 15).

The extent of delinquency in the school, including vandalism, violence, gangs, and the use of drugs, has received considerable examination (Bartollas 2006). The consequences of dropping out of school have also been investigated (Jarjoura 1993). In addition, there have been a number of efforts to improve the quality of the school experience. The development of alternative schools, the process of designing effective school-based violence-prevention programs, and the process of developing more positive school-community relationships have been three of the most promising intervention strategies in the school setting (Bartollas 2006).

Peers and Gangs

Researchers usually agree that most delinquent behavior, particularly more violent forms, takes place in groups, but they disagree on the quality of relationships within delinquent groups and on the influence of groups on delinquent behavior (Breckinridge and Abbott 1970; Piper 1985). There is still debate on several theoretical questions about groups and delinquency: How do delinquent peers influence each other? What causes the initial attraction to delinquent groups? What do delinquents receive from these friendships that result in continuing them?

Youth gangs represent one of the most serious forms of delinquency groups. Frederick Thrasher's (1927) definition of gangs is still one of the best definitions:

> A gang is an interstitial group originally formed spontaneously and then integrated through conflict. It is characterized by the following types of behavior: meeting face to face, milling, movement through space as a unit, conflict and planning. The result of this collective behavior is the development of tradition, unreflective, internal structure, esprit de corps, solidarity, morale, group awareness, and attachment to local territory. (P. 57)

Juveniles are involved in urban street gangs, where they are typically a minority of the membership. However, they make up nearly the total membership of emerging gangs that spread across the United States in the late 1980s and early 1990s. What has received considerable documentation is that law-violating behaviors increase with gang activities, that core members are involved in more serious delinquent acts than are fringe members, and that gang activities contribute to a pattern of violent behavior (Wolfgang, Thornberry, and Figlio 1987; Battin-Pearson et al. 1998; Miller 2001; Miller and Decker 2001).

The Use of Drugs and Its Relationship to Delinquent Behavior

Drug and alcohol use and juvenile delinquency have been identified as the most serious problem behaviors of juveniles. The good news is that substance abuse among adolescents has dropped significantly since the late 1970s. The bad news is that drug use has significantly increased among high-risk youths and is becoming commonly linked to juvenile delinquency (Centers for Disease Control and Prevention 2004; Johnston et al. 2004). In addition, more adolescents are selling drugs than ever before in the history of this nation. Moreover, the spread of AIDS within populations of drug users and their sex partners promises to make the problem of substance abuse even more difficult to control.

THE BIOLOGICAL, PSYCHOLOGICAL, AND SOCIOLOGICAL THEORIES THAT HAVE INFLUENCED THE FIELD OF DELINQUENCY

A number of theoretical answers have been given to the continually raised question: Why do juveniles commit crime? Early in the twentieth century, biological and psychological causes of delinquent behavior received more attention. In the last two-thirds of the twentieth century, sociological explanations to delinquency behavior received greater support with students of delinquency.

Biological Explanations of Delinquent Behavior

The belief in a biological explanation for criminality has a long history. Early approaches attempted to pinpoint the source of criminality in physical anomalies (Lombroso-Ferrero 1972), genealogical deficiencies (Shah and Roth 1974), and theories of human somatotypes or body types (Glueck and Glueck 1956; Cortes 1972). More recently, research has stressed the interaction between the biological factors within an individual and the influence of the particular environment. Supporters of this form of biological positivism claim that what produces delinquent behavior, like other behaviors, is a combination of genetic traits and social conditions. Recent advances in experimental behavior genetics, human population genetics, knowledge of the biochemistry of the nervous system, experimental and clinical endocrinology and neurophysiology, and other related areas have led to more sophisticated knowledge of the way in which the environment and human genetics interact to affect the growth, development, and functioning of the human organism (Shah and Roth 1974; Fishbein 1990).

Psychological Explanations of Delinquent Behavior

Psychological factors have long been popular in the positivist approach to the cause of juvenile delinquency because the very nature of *parens patriae* philosophy requires treatment of youths who are involved in various forms of delinquency. Psychoanalytic (Freudian) theory was first used with delinquents, but more recently other behavioral and humanistic schools of psychology have been applied to the problem of the illegal behaviors of juveniles. For example, some researchers in the 1980s and 1990s addressed the relationship between sensation seeking and crime (White, Labouvie, and Bates 1985; Fishbein 1990). Jack Katz's (1988) *Seductions of Crime* conjectures that when individuals commit crime, they become involved in "an emotional process—seductions and compulsions that have special dynamics" (p. 9). It is this "magical" and "transformative" experience that makes crime "sensible," even "sensually compelling." James Q. Wilson and Richard Herrnstein's (1985) *Crime and Human Nature* is another example of the influence of psychological factors on criminal or delinquent behaviors. They consider potential causes of crime and noncrime within the context of reinforcement theory, that is, the theory that behavior is governed by its consequent rewards and punishments, as reflected in the history of the individual. The rewards of crime, according to Wilson and Herrnstein (1985), are found in the form of material gain, revenge against an enemy, peer approval, and sexual gratification. The consequences of crime include pangs of conscience, disapproval of peers, revenge by the victim, and, most important, the possibility of punishment.

Sociological Explanations of Delinquent Behavior

Sociological theories related to delinquency causation have been grouped in a number of ways; the following sections will group them in structural theories of delinquency causation, process theories of delinquency causation, reaction theories of delinquency causation, and integrated theories of delinquency causation.

Structural Theories of Delinquency Causation

The setting for delinquency, as proposed by social structural theories, is the social and cultural environment in which juveniles grow up or the subcultural groups in which they choose to become involved. Using official statistics as their guide, these analysts claim that such forces as social disorganization, cultural deviance, status frustration, and social mobility are so powerful that they induce youths, especially lower-class ones, to become involved in delinquent behavior. Strain theory is a structural theory that has been widely applied to explaining delinquent behavior. Robert K. Merton's theory of anomie, Albert K. Cohen's theory of delinquent subcultures, and Richard A. Cloward and Lloyd E. Ohlin's opportunity theory are the most widely cited strain theories. Merton (1957) examined how deviant behavior is produced by different social structures. His primary aim was to discover how some social structures exerted pressure upon individuals in the society to engage in nonconforming rather than conforming behavior. Cohen's (1955) thesis in his book *Delinquent Boys: The Culture of the Gang* was that lower-class youths are actually protesting against the goals of middle-class culture, but they experience status frustration, or strain, because they are unable to attain these goals. Cloward and Ohlin (1960) conceptualized success and status as separate strivings that can operate independently of each other. They portrayed delinquents who seek an increase in status as striving for membership in the middle class, whereas other delinquent youths try to improve their economic post without changing their class position.

Social Process Theories of Delinquency Causation

Social process theories of delinquency causation examine the interactions between individuals and the environment that influence them to become involved in delinquent behaviors. Differential association, drift, and social control theories became popular in the 1960s because they provided a theoretical mechanism for the translation of environmental factors into individual motivation. Edwin H. Sutherland's (1947) formulation of differential association theory proposes that delinquents learn crime from others. His basic premise was that delinquency, like any other form of behavior, is a product of social interaction. In developing the theory of differential association, Sutherland contended that individuals are constantly being changed as they take on the expectations and points of view of the people with whom they interact in small, intimate groups. The process of becoming a delinquent, David Matza (1964) says, begins when an adolescent neutralizes himself or herself from the moral bounds of the law and drifts into delinquency. Drift, according to Matza, means that "the delinquent transiently exists in limbo between convention and crime, responding in turn to the demands of each, flirting now with one, now the other, but postponing commitment, evading decision. Thus he drifts between criminal and conventional action" (p. 28). Walter C. Reckless's (1961) control theory is based on the assumption that strong inner containment and reinforcing external containment provide insulation against deviant behavior. Travis Hirschi's (1967) *Causes of Delinquency* linked delinquent behavior to the quality of the bond an individual maintains with society, stating that "delinquent acts result when an individual's bond to society is weak or broken" (p. 16). He argues that humans' basic impulses motivate them to become involved in crime and delinquency unless there is reason for them to refrain from such behavior.

Social Reaction Theories of Delinquency Causation

Labeling theory, symbolic interactionst theory of delinquency, and conflict theory can be viewed as social reaction theories of delinquency causation because they focus on the role that social and economic groups and institutions have in producing delinquent behavior. The labeling perspective, whose peak of popularity was in the 1960s and 1970s, is based on the premise that society creates deviance by labeling those who are different from other individuals, when in fact they are different merely because they have been tagged with a deviant label part played by social audiences and their responses to the norm violations of juveniles (Tannenbaum 1938; Lemert 1951; Becker 1963; Triplett and Jarjoura 1994). Ross L. Matsueda (1992) and Karen Heimer (1995) have developed a symbolic interactionist theory of delinquency. This interactionist perspective "presupposes that the social order is the product of an ongoing process of social interaction and communication" (Matsueda 1992:1580). What is "of central importance is the process by which shared meanings, behavioral expectations, and reflected appraisals are built up in interaction and applied to behavior" (p. 1580). The conflict perspective views social control as an outcome of the differential distribution of economic and political power in society; thus, laws are seen as creation by the powerful for their own benefit (Shichor 1980). Conflict criminology has a great deal of variation; some theories emphasize the importance of socioeconomic class, some focus primarily on power and authority relationships, and others emphasize group and cultural conflict.

Integrated Theory

The theoretical development of integrated explanations of delinquency in the 1980s and 1990s has made a significant contribution to the understanding of delinquent behavior. Theory integration usually implies the combination of two or more existing theories on the basis of their perceived commonalities. Three of the better-known integrated theories are Michael R. Gottfredson and Travis Hirschi's (1990) general theory of crime; Delbert S. Elliot, Suzanne A. Ageton, and Rachelle J. Canter's (1979) integrated social process theory; and Terence P. Thornberry's (1987) interactional theory.

In *A General Theory of Crime,* Gottfredson and Hirschi (1990) define lack of self-control as the common factor underlying problem behaviors. Thus, self-control is the degree to which an individual is "vulnerable to the temptations of the moment." The other pivotal construct in this theory of crime is crime opportunity, which is a function of the structural or situational circumstances encountered by the individuals (Grasmick et al. 1993).

Elliott et al. (1979) offer "an explanatory model that expands and synthesizes traditional strain, social control, and social learning perspectives into a single paradigm that accounts for delinquent behavior and drug use" (p. 11). They argue that all three theories are flawed in explaining delinquent behavior. Integrating the strongest features of these theories into a single theoretical model, Elliott and colleagues theorize that there is a high probability of involvement in delinquent behavior when bonding to delinquent groups is combined with weak bonding to conventional groups. In Thornberry's interaction theory of delinquency, the initial impetus toward delinquency comes from a weaning of the person's bond to conventional society, represented by attachment to parents, commitment to school, and belief in conventional values. Associations with delinquent peers and delinquent values make up the social settling in which delinquency, especially prolonged serious delinquency, is learned and reinforced. These two variables, along with delinquent behavior itself, form a mutually reinforcing casual loop that leads toward increasing delinquency involvement over time (Thornberry 1987, 1989; Thornberry et al. 2003) (Table 43.1).

Table 43.1   Summary of Sociological Theories of Delinquency

	Theory	*Cause of Crime Identified in the Theory*	*Supporting Research*
Cultural Deviance Theory	Shaw and McKay	Delinquent behavior becomes an alternative mode of socialization through which youths who are part of disorganized communities are attracted to delinquent values and traditions.	Moderate
Strain Theory	Merton	Social structure exerts pressure on individuals who cannot attain the cultural goal of success, leading them to engage in nonconforming behavior.	Moderate
	Cohen	Lower-class boys are unable to attain the goals of middle-class culture, and therefore they become involved in nonutilitarian, malicious, and weak negative behavior.	
Opportunity Theory	Cloward and Ohlin	Lower-class boys seek out illegitimate means to attain middle-class success goals if they are unable to attain them through legitimate means, usually through one of three specialized gang contexts.	Moderate
Differential Association Theory	Sutherland	Criminal behavior is to be expected of individuals who have internalized a preponderance of definitions favorable to law violations.	Moderate
Drift Theory	Matza	Juveniles neutralize themselves from the moral bounds of the law and drift into delinquent behavior.	Moderate
Containment Theory	Reckless	Strong inner containment and reinforcing external containment provide insulation against criminal behavior.	Moderate
Social Control Theory (Bonding Theory)	Hirschi	Criminal acts result when an individual's bond to society is weak or broken.	Strong
Labeling Theory	Lemert and Becker	Society creates deviants by labeling those who are apprehended as different from other individuals, when in reality they are different only because they have been tagged with a deviant label.	
Symbolic Interactionist Theory	Matsueda and Heimer	This theory focuses on how the role-taking process can lead to delinquency or crime.	Moderate
Conflict Theory		This theory views social control as an outcome of the differential distribution of economic and political power in society. Some of these theorists emphasize the importance of socioeconomic class, some focus on power and authority relationships, and others emphasize group and cultural conflict.	Moderate
Integrated Theory	Gottfredson and Hirschi's general theory of crime	Self-control is defined as the common factor underlying problem behaviors. Self-control is the degree to which an individual is vulnerable to the temptations of the moment.	Strong
	Elliott et al.'s integrated social process theory	There is a high probability of involvement in delinquent behavior when bonding to delinquent groups is combined with weak bonding to conventional groups.	Moderate
	Thornberry's interactional theory	This theory views delinquency as the result of events that occur in a developmental fashion.	Moderate

IS DELINQUENT BEHAVIOR RATIONAL?

In the 1970s and 1980s, a variety of academic areas, including the sociology of deviance, criminology, economics, and cognitive psychology, began to view crime as the outcome of rational choices and decisions. The ecological tradition in criminology and the economic theory of markets, especially, have applied the notion of rational choice to crime.

Rational choice theory, borrowed primarily from the utility model in economics, was one area of intense interest during the 1980s and 1990s, especially within criminology, sociology, political science, and law. Rational choice theory, an extension of the deterrence doctrine of the classical school, includes incentives as well as deterrents and focuses on the calculation of payoffs and costs before delinquent and criminal acts are committed (Cornish and Clarke 1986; Akers 1990).

An analysis of delinquent behavior leads to the conclusion that antisocial behavior often appears rational and purposeful. Some delinquents clearly engage in delinquent behavior because of the low cost or risk of such behavior. The low risk comes from the *parens patriae* philosophy that is based on the presumption of innocence for the very young, as well as of reduced responsibility for those up to their midadolescence. Thus, in early adolescence, the potential costs of all but the most serious forms of delinquent behavior are relatively slight.

PROSPECTS FOR THE 21ST CENTURY

The development of both sociology and juvenile delinquency was influenced by the rise of the Chicago School of Sociology early in the twentieth century. With this common background, it is not surprising that juvenile delinquency has been so closely related to the discipline of sociology. Juvenile delinquency has been taught in the majority of sociology departments, as well as in many criminology or criminal justice programs in university settings and community colleges. The study of juvenile delinquency is further indebted to sociology because so many of the theories of delinquency causation are sociological theories of crime. Even though the study of juvenile delinquency has become interdisciplinary, sociological principles and theories remain critical in understanding the field of delinquency. Indeed, the new trends in delinquency, such as human agency and delinquency across the life course, are adapted from theoretical and empirical contributions largely taken from the field of sociology.

The prospects for the study of delinquency in the twenty-first century are vibrant and exciting.

Some of the emphases that will guide the study of delinquency are the examination of the development paths of delinquent behavior, a continued examination of human agency and delinquency across the life course, an investigation of the ways in which gender affects the study of delinquency, and a renewed search for more effective means of delinquency prevention.

Developmental Paths of Delinquency

One of the most exciting aspects about the study of juvenile delinquency today is the increasing number of developmental studies that have followed youth cohorts for a few years or even decades. One of the most widely respected of these studies is the research done by Terrie E. Moffitt and colleagues. For example, Moffitt, Donald R. Lynam, and Phil A. Silva's (1994) examination of the neuropsychological status of several hundred New Zealand males between the ages of 13 and 18 found that poor neuropsychological scores "were associated with early onset of delinquency" but were "unrelated to delinquency that began in adolescence" (p. 277). Moffitt's (1993) developmental theory views delinquency as proceeding along two developmental paths. On one path, children develop a lifelong path of delinquency and crime as early as age 3. They may begin to bite and hit shoplift and be truant at age 10, sell drugs and steal cars at age 16, rob and rape at age 22, and commit fraud and child abuse at age 30. These "life-course-persistent" (LCP) delinquents, according to Moffitt, continue their illegal acts throughout the conditions and situations they face. During childhood, they may also exhibit such neuropsychological problems as deficit disorders or hyperactivity and learning problems in schools.

On the other path, the majority of delinquents begin offending during the adolescent years and desist from delinquent behaviors around the 18th birthday. Moffitt refers to these youthful offenders as "adolescent-limited" (AL) delinquents. The early and persistent problems found with members of the LCP group are not found with the AL delinquents. Yet the frequency of offending and even the violence of offending during the adolescent years may be as high as the LCP. Moffitt notes that the AL antisocial behavior is learned from peers and sustained through peer-based rewards and reinforcements. AL delinquents continue in delinquent acts as long as such behaviors appear profitable or rewarding to them, but they have the ability to abandon those behaviors when prosocial styles become more rewarding (Moffitt 1993; Moffitt et al. 2001).

Human Agency and Delinquency across the Life Course

This enormous database of these developmental studies has contributed to the examination of such subjects as the importance of human agency in the lives of youths and later when they become adults and to delinquency or crime across the life course. Human agency refers to the importance given to juveniles who are not only acted upon by social influence and structural constraints but who make choices and decisions based on the alternatives that they see before them. Symbolic interactionism and life history studies have long acknowledged the importance of agency and rationality, and rational choice and routine activities research have more recently placed an importance on rationality in delinquent and criminal behavior. However, it has been the increased attention given to the life course in both sociology and delinquency studies that has sparked a dramatic resurgence of interest in agency in contemporary research.

The various perspectives on the life course relate individuals to their broader social context, but within the constraints of their world, individuals make choices among options that are available to them. It is these decisions that are so important in constructing their life course.

Delinquency across the life course has been examined extensively by Robert J. Sampson and James H. Laub's reanalysis of the Gluecks' data (Sampson and Laub 1993; Laub and Sampson 2003). This perspective of delinquency and crime across the life course has been employed in studies of the effects of youth gangs, faulty family relationships, poor performance in school, drug use, and gender variations in youth offending (Bartollas 2006).

Moreover, this interactive process develops over the person's life cycle. During early adolescence, the family is the most influential factor in bonding the youngster to conventional society and reducing delinquency. But as the youth matures and moves through middle adolescence, the world of friends, school, and youth culture becomes the dominant influence over behavior. Finally, as the person enters adulthood, commitment to conventional activities, and to family, especially, offers new avenues to reshape the person's bond to society and involvement with delinquent behavior (Thornberry 1987; Krohn et al. 2001).

Gender and Delinquent Behavior

The study of delinquency has been traditionally shaped by male experiences and understanding of the social world (Daly and Chesney-Lind 1988). Carol Smart (1976) and Dorie Klein (1995) were two early criminologists to suggest that a feminist criminology should be formulated because of the neglect of the feminist perspective in classical delinquency theory. Feminist criminologists have been quick to agree that adolescent females have different experiences compared with adolescent males. They generally support that females are more controlled than males, enjoy more social support, are less disposed to crime, and have fewer opportunities for certain types of crimes (Mazerolle 1998).

However, feminist criminologists disagree on how the male-oriented approach to delinquency should be handled. One approach focuses on the question of generalizability. In research on samples that include males and females, a routine strategy for those who emphasize cross-gender similarities is to test whether the given theoretical constructs account for the offending of both groups and to pay little attention to how gender itself might intersect with other factors to create different meanings in the lives of males and females. Those who support this gender-neutral position have generally examined such subjects as the family, social bonding, social learning, delinquent peer relationships, and, to a lesser degree, deterrence and strain (Daly 1995).

In contrast, other feminist theorists argue that new theoretical efforts are needed to help us understand female delinquency and women's involvement in adult crime. Eileen Leonard (1995), for example, questioned whether anomie, differential association, labeling, and Marist theories can be used to explain the crime patterns of women. She concluded that these traditional theories do not work for explaining female offending. Meda Chesney-Lind's (1989, 1995) application of the male-oriented theories to female delinquency has argued that existing delinquency theories are inadequate to explain female delinquency. She suggested that there is a need for a feminist model of delinquency, because a patriarchal context has shaped the explanations and handling of female delinquents and status offenders. What this means is that adolescent females' sexual and physical victimizations at home and the relationship between these experiences and their crimes have been systematically ignored.

Delinquency Prevention

Delinquency prevention has a long but somewhat disappointing history. The best-known models of delinquency prevention have included the Boston's Mid-city Project, Cambridge-Somerville Youth Study in Massachusetts, Chicago Area Projects, La Playa de Ponce in Puerto Rico, New York City Youth Board, and Walter C. Reckless and Simon Dinitz's self-concept studies in Columbus, Ohio. A number of studies have examined the effectiveness of these delinquency-prevention programs and have generally found that few studies showed significant results (Lundman, McFarlane, and Scarpitti 1976; Lundman and Scarpitti 1978).

Beginning in the 1980s and continuing to the present, a number of new delinquency-prevention efforts have been established. The Blueprints for Violence Prevention, developed by the Center for the Study and Prevention of Violence at the University of Colorado–Boulder and supported by the Office of Juvenile Justice and Delinquency Prevention, identified 11 model programs, as well as a number of promising violence-prevention and drug abuse programs. The identified model programs were Big Brothers Big Sisters of America; Bully Prevention Program; Functional Family Therapy (FFT); Incredible Years: Parent, Teacher, and Child Training Series; Life Skills Training; Midwestern Prevention Project; Multidimensional Treatment Foster Care (MTFC); Multisystemic Therapy (MST); Nurse-Family Partnership; Project Towards No Drug Abuse; and Promoting Alternative Thinking Strategies (Mihalic et al. 2004).

The popularity of delinquency-prevention programs, of course, is found in the realization that the most desirable strategy is to prevent delinquent behavior before it can occur. Even though delinquency-prevention programs have generally fallen short of controlling youth crime, there is every reason to believe that renewed efforts will be continued throughout the twenty-first century.

44

THE SOCIOLOGY OF CORRECTIONS

RICHARD TEWKSBURY

University of Louisville, Kentucky

LINDA G. SMITH

Research Consultant

The component of the criminal justice system that is responsible for carrying out sentences mandated by the court and for carrying out executions of individuals sentenced to the death penalty is corrections. The corrections component also has the responsibility of monitoring the location and behaviors of individuals charged with crimes while these individuals are processed through the system. Jails, prisons, halfway houses, probation, parole, prerelease, and supervised/conditional release are considered corrections.

THE RELATIONSHIP OF SOCIOLOGY AND CORRECTIONS

A sociological approach to corrections is important for understanding the ways correctional organizations, institutional practices, and employees serve the needs of society as one important component of social control. Additionally, sociological approaches always emphasize understanding the basic culture of groups and organizations and the ways individuals interact with and are influenced by social structures. Exploring correctional institutions from a sociological perspective provides an understanding of what corrections is, how it operates, why it is structured and operated in the way that it is, and to what degree and under what conditions this fundamental

component of the American justice system achieves its goals.

A sociological perspective of corrections provides understandings of both the facts of the organizations, structures, tasks, clients, staff, and goals of corrections. This perspective also provides insights about the way that correctional institutions and programs develop and maintain a culture. In turn, analysts of corrections explore the ways that cultural values, beliefs, and norms influence the tasks and outcomes of correctional efforts.

The American public tends to think that corrections should be about punishment and rehabilitation (Cullen, Fisher, and Applegate 2000). But policymakers believe that the public is most interested in punishment, especially strong and harsh punishment (Tonry 2004; Whitman 2003). Whatever its goal, as one of the primary aspects of social control efforts and the final component of the American criminal justice system, corrections depends on the courts for the administrative, structural, and procedural aspects of its work.

Since the advent of the prisoner's rights movement starting in the 1960s, judicial decisions have played a major role in establishing minimum standards for the physical facilities, social programs and contexts, staffing requirements, and medical and psychological treatment provided in correctional facilities. Corrections includes a wide range of activities and structures, ranging from the operation of jails and prisons, supervision of convicted offenders in the community, to mandatory program participation for individuals convicted of criminal offenses. In many ways, every detail about the design, operations, resources, and activities of a correctional institution or program is guided by judicial decisions.

Detaining persons in a secure facility where they cannot leave and where their activities are monitored and restricted is the centerpiece of corrections. All incarcerated persons, with the exception of some persons in jails, are imprisoned under court order for having been convicted of criminal acts. Execution and incarceration are the punishments that accompany the most serious forms of crime in our society.

Corrections also is charged with the task of providing treatment to individuals under its supervision for purposes of changing their behavior, keeping them healthy, maintaining their mental capacities, and/or providing them with tools and skills to be law-abiding citizens. The treatment components of corrections are interwoven into the incarceration component and are usually seen as a complement to other tasks, not a set of tasks that stand alone (Wright 2003). Inmates should be encouraged to enroll in educational programs, psychological counseling, job training, socialization skills training, and substance abuse counseling. Research has shown that each of these areas hold some promise in reducing recidivism (Cecil et al. 2000; Smith 2003; Wilson, Gallagher, and MacKenzie 2000).

THE GOALS OF CORRECTIONS

Four goals guide corrections: (1) rehabilitation, (2) retribution, (3) deterrence, and (4) incapacitation. Rehabilitation is intended to correct criminal offenders. The rehabilitation model is based on the assumption that offenders can be restored to law-abiding ways and that through treatment criminal behavior can be eliminated and the offender transformed into a productive, law-abiding individual.

Rehabilitation was the primary ideological position guiding American correctional efforts during the 1960s and early 1970s. However, in 1974, an influential review of research evaluating the effectiveness of correctional treatment programs proclaimed that "nothing works" (Martinson 1974). This idea was quickly and widely adopted by leading lawmakers, politicians, and correctional administrators to eliminate many rehabilitation programs.

Retribution is based on the idea that criminal offenders should be punished. Rather than working to "fix" something, retribution is to punish offenders even under harsh conditions, deprive them of luxuries, and provide some form of community supervision that is sufficiently negative so that offenders suffer similar to those they victimized.

Deterrence is intended to dissuade future crime by offenders and others. Punishment is to deter an offender from committing more criminal acts; in contrast, general deterrence is intended to dissuade others from engaging in criminal activity. The deterrence goal not only promotes the idea that offenders should be punished but also teaches offenders a lesson. That is, punishment is intended to discourage criminals from committing crime in the future.

Deterrence has many commonsense aspects; the idea is that when a crime is committed, the offender will subsequently be punished. Offenders learn that if they again engage in criminal activity, they will again be punished. To be effective, however, punishments must be swift, certain, and (to a lesser extent) severe. These ideas have long been recognized, having first been proposed by Cesare Beccaria ([1764] 1963). However, contrary to most popular assumptions and ongoing changes to policies, the severity of a punishment is the least important condition for deterrence to be achieved. Based on the utilitarian principle of Jeremy Bentham, punishment must be more severe to outweigh any gains received by engaging in criminal behavior but ideally should only minimally outweigh any gains realized from the offense (Burns and Hart 1996).

Research has not confirmed the commonly held belief that imprisonment or lengthy sentences have a deterrent effect on crime (e.g., Lippke 2002). In fact, harsh and undesirable prisons may have the exact opposite effect. Indeed, some researchers report sanctions based on the premise that prison deters people from committing crimes in the future may be misguided. McGuire (2002), for example, has shown that specific deterrence does not work if all that is done is place an offender in prison. To simply lock someone up does not lead to a reduction in their subsequent criminal behavior.

Similarly, the death penalty does not have a deterrent effect on homicide. While the specific offender who is executed will not commit further criminal acts, one of the primary arguments regarding capital punishment is that it will deter others (e.g., Cameron 1994; Erlich 1975, 1977). Some research, however, has not only failed to support the thesis that executions lead to lower homicide rates but, in fact, may have the exact opposite effect. Referred to as the "brutalization thesis," when the government condemns people to death, citizens view life as less valuable and violence as socially acceptable. Support for the brutalization effect is found in research that shows that in the aftermath of an execution, homicide rates actually increase (Cochran, Chamlin, and Seth 1994; Stack 1994). A pattern of racial discrimination in determining who will receive a sentence of death was reported by Baldus, Woodworth, and Pulaski (1990), and this research was critical in the 1972 U.S. Supreme Court decision of *Furman v. Georgia,* a landmark case that served as the basis for reevaluating as unconstitutional the death penalty laws across the United States.

The fourth purpose of American corrections is incapacitation. Incapacitation through incarceration is intended to remove offenders from society so that they do not have opportunities to commit criminal offenses. Taking incapacitation one step further is the idea of selective incapacitation where imprisonment is used for repetitive or violent offenders (Allen, Simonsen, and Latessa 2004).

Selective incapacitation is the doctrine used for mandatory sentencing laws.

Goals have changed over time and vary across jurisdictions. At various times in history, corrections has been considered a primary means for rehabilitating criminal offenders; at other times, the emphasis has been on showing offenders that crime "does *not* pay." Most recently, the focal concern of corrections has been punishment and incapacitation of inmates. While most correctional workers believe that all the ideologies have importance, when reporting what they believe to be the primary goal of corrections, clear patterns emerge (Tewksbury and Mustaine 2005). Custodial, programming, and support staff believe that public safety through incapacitation is the primary goal of corrections. Administrators, however, strongly support the rehabilitation model. And, when examining what the general public believes the goals of corrections should be, rehabilitation is ranked at or near the top in public opinion polls (Cullen et al. 2000), especially among women (Applegate, Cullen, and Fisher 2002). When juveniles are considered, rehabilitation is clearly identified as the most important goal (Moon, Cullen, and Wright 2003).

HISTORICAL BACKGROUND AND THE CHANGING PANORAMA OF CORRECTIONS

As the colonists settled in America during the 1600s, the punishments administered for individuals who committed both minor and serious crimes included public humiliation through the use of stocks, whipping, mutilation, branding, and hanging (for a more complete discussion of the historical development of American corrections, see Morris and Rothman 1995). The gallows were used for several offenses, not just murder. Slaves suffered even more severe punishments in the colonies in the South.

The severity of the punishments in colonial America emanated from the criminal code of England sometimes referred to as the "bloody code" of England. Appalled by the inhumane and often unjust punishments, the Quakers, particularly those in the province of Pennsylvania under the leadership of William Penn, advocated the use of incarceration as an alternative punishment. In 1682, William Penn wrote the "Great Law" or Quaker code that advocated a more humane treatment for criminal offenders. The Quaker code was in force until 1718 when it was repealed and replaced by the harsh codes of England originally adopted in this country.

Despite the fact that the earlier Quaker effort was repealed, they continued to work for humane treatment and abolishment of harsh punishment for criminal offenders and formed the first true penitentiary in 1790, the Walnut Street Jail in Philadelphia. As a new idea, the penitentiary was designed as an alternative to corporal punishment. An effort to improve conditions at the Walnut Street Jail spawned the creation of the Eastern State Penitentiary

(also in Philadelphia), which was finished in 1829. This larger-scaled prison, which represented a model of punishment that came to be known as the Pennsylvania system, used a system of solitary confinement without work. Other states also began development of their own prisons, but the New York State Prison at Auburn (which began the system known as the Auburn system), which opened in 1819, became the prototype for other states. The Auburn system ended up being more popular than the Pennsylvania system, primarily because it was more economic. In the Auburn system, inmates worked and produced a variety of types of goods, which were then sold.

The 1800s saw not only the development of several state prison systems but also the concept of probation and parole. John Augustus, known as the father of probation, worked voluntarily with the courts in Boston requesting temporary suspension of sentences of offenders who he would then provide supervision of. In 1878, Massachusetts passed the first probation statute paving the way for widespread use of probation for adults and juveniles. Parole, however, grew from the efforts of England's Captain Alexander Maconochie and Ireland's Sir Walter Crofton. The concept of indeterminate sentencing with the possibility of parole was implemented in the United States in 1876 and is still used in several states today, although at the end of the twentieth century, many states began to abolish parole and returned to determinate sentencing.

While a great deal of reform was occurring in corrections during the 1800s, the end of the Civil War brought about a dark time in corrections in the southern states. With most southern prisons destroyed or severely damaged due to the war, southern states were forced to use a system known as convict leasing. This was a practice whereby prisoners were turned over to private entrepreneurs for both safekeeping and work. Leased prisoners were commonly subjected to brutality and harsh conditions that brought about sickness, corruption, and frequently death for leased convicts. The use of convict labor was finally declared illegal in the early 1900s.

The 1900s saw the development of a changing set of guiding philosophies for corrections. The move was from one of punishment and reformation to one of rehabilitation. As a result of this philosophical shift, treatment and education programs were developed and administered inside prisons. Additionally, alternatives to incarceration (such as halfway houses) and more common use of probation and parole came to characterize American correctional efforts. A federal correctional system also emerged with the establishment of the Federal Bureau of Prisons in 1930. State prison industry programs were developed and became a driving force in corrections around this time as well. In the 1960s, the Supreme Court handed down numerous key decisions protecting the rights of offenders and prisoners.

In the 1970s, rehabilitation efforts once again gave way to increasingly harsher sentences and prisons operating with fewer programs. By the 1990s, many prisons and jails were struggling to keep inmate programs in place and faced severe budget cuts for these programs. Lawmakers believed (despite a large body of research to the contrary) that the public wanted harsher punishments and fewer amenities for inmates. Now in the early 2000s, the United States has the highest incarceration rate of any country in the Western, developed world, and prisons and jails continue to experience cutbacks in programming and treatment for offenders.

CONTEMPORARY CORRECTIONS

Contemporary corrections are based on two approaches—namely, institutional corrections and community corrections. Institutional corrections include any instance of incarceration, usually in a prison or jail. Community corrections, which are larger in terms of the number of criminal offenders served, involve wide-ranging programs and activities for criminal offenders who live and are supervised in the community. The most common forms of community corrections are probation and parole. Community corrections also include programs, usually referred to as "intermediate sanctions," that lie between incarceration and probation in their degree of restrictions and supervision.

Institutional Corrections

Institutional corrections refer to all units in which criminal offenders are incarcerated in a secure facility and where their activities are restricted and subject to continuous monitoring. These primary places of incarceration are prisons and jails. Prisons house same-sex individuals convicted of felonies and sentenced by a court of law to a period of confinement. Jails house men and women in separate spaces and include individuals who have been convicted of criminal offenses, individuals yet to be convicted, and civil commitments. Other types of correctional institutions include detention centers for juvenile offenders, temporary holding facilities operated by law enforcement agencies, detention facilities for immigration and customs violators, and some government-operated psychiatric and medical hospitals.

Prisons

Prisons exist in a wide range of degrees of security and restrictions on inmates. Prison "levels" include maximum-security facilities where inmates are housed behind walls or multiple layers of special fences and have their every activity closely supervised and restricted. Medium- and minimum-security facilities have decreasing levels of supervision and micro-activity-level restrictions. Other, more open institutions include prison camps, ranches, or medical facilities. Prisons also vary in their architectural design, their purpose, their size, and their culture. Most prisons operating in the early twenty-first century hold between 500 and 2,000 inmates, but some large facilities house 5,000 or more inmates.

Most prisons offer a number of treatment and education programs. The most common programs include substance abuse treatment, sex offender therapy, violence prevention, cognitive skills training, career planning, employment preparation, victim awareness, reentry and prerelease planning, and a variety of education and vocational training programs. These programs are designed to change offender behavior with the expectation of reducing recidivism and increasing employment opportunities after release from prison.

Jails

In contrast to prisons, jails hold those who are sentenced to one year or less as well as individuals charged with a criminal offense but not yet tried in a court of law (Stephan 2001). Many jails also hold "overflow" inmates from other state facilities as well as prison inmates returning to the local community for court appearances. In some cases, jails house people who are there for civil commitments such as contempt of court for not paying child support. Because jails house inmates of all security levels, it is more difficult to classify or separate inmates as rigorously as prisons. However, some jails separate inmates based on whether they are convicted or not.

Jails also differ from prisons in that they have very rapid and frequent turnover in their inmate population. More than 13 million people pass through American jails in a year, yet only 1.4 million of these individuals are imprisoned (Harrison and Beck 2005). Most jail inmates are incarcerated for one week or less, meaning that the culture, relationships between inmates or between inmates and staff, and dynamics of daily life change constantly. Two of the important consequences of this rapid turnover are that efforts to involve inmates in treatment efforts or any type of ongoing programs are difficult, and because the inmate population changes so quickly, there is little opportunity for an institutional culture to develop. Rather, jail inmates typically have very unstructured days in which their idleness leads to the possibility of misconduct and violence. However, some jails include educational, social, recreational, mental health, substance abuse treatment, and other forms of programming for inmates as do prisons. Perhaps the most important services provided are educational programs; numerous studies have shown that jail-based education programs produce lower rates of recidivism for inmate participants (Smith and Silverman 1994; Tewksbury 1994). Jail administrators believe that when programming is offered, facilities operate more smoothly with less violence.

Community Corrections

Community corrections involve the supervision of offenders while they are in the community. The most common form of community corrections, and in fact the most common form of criminal sentence in the United States, is probation. Other forms of community corrections include parole, home incarceration, halfway houses, day reporting centers, and work release centers. While the type and degree of supervision of offenders varies across each of these sanctions, what they all have in common is that offenders live in the community while having restrictions placed on their movements.

Probation is a sentence imposed by a court for which an offender has a sentence of incarceration suspended. While on probation, a probation officer monitors their activities, meets the offender periodically, and may administer drug or alcohol tests or impose other monitoring requirements on the offender. An offender who violates the conditions of probation receives a technical violation. If a probationer is found to be in violation, a judge will decide to either reinstate probation with additional restrictions or revoke the probation status and incarcerate the offender. If found to have committed another crime, the offender's probation is generally revoked.

Parole is the supervision of an offender in the community following early release from incarceration. Parolees are also subject to conditions that restrict their activities and are subject to both technical and new crime violations, both of which could result in reincarceration for the remaining time on the original prison sentence.

Home incarceration (also known as house arrest), as the name suggests, is essentially imprisonment in one's home. Typically, an offender sentenced to home incarceration is allowed to leave his or her home for only a limited list of reasons, including work, attending school and church, doctor's appointments, and limited shopping. Most home incarceration programs monitor offenders through electronic monitoring or the placement of an ankle bracelet that connects to a receiver in the offender's home. If the offender wanders too far from the receiver, the signal connection is broken and an alarm is activated in the monitoring office. A violation of the conditions of home incarceration subjects the offender to possible revocation and incarceration.

Some home incarceration programs have gone a step further with monitoring an offender's whereabouts through the addition of global positioning satellite monitoring of offenders (Johnson 2002). This technology allows officials to monitor the exact location of an offender at all times. This type of monitoring is considered most useful with offenders whose contact with specified individuals is prohibited.

Some forms of community corrections also involve temporary or periodic placement of offenders in institutions. Halfway houses, day reporting centers, and work release centers all require offenders to spend time in a residential setting while also interacting through work and school in the community. Halfway houses are residential institutions for offenders who are released from prison, probationers or parolees who violate the conditions of their supervision and are provided a second chance prior to being revoked (Munden, Tewksbury, and Grossi 1998), or for some offenders involved in intensive substance abuse treatment programs. Day reporting center programs require offenders to report to the treatment programs during the day and then return to their own residences. Work release centers are residential facilities that house offenders who are allowed to leave to go to jobs or school.

PRISON AND JAIL MILIEU AND SUBCULTURES

The prison environment and the demographics of both inmates and staff create a setting that is conducive to the development of subcultures. These subcultures represent a way of coping with confinement and the deprivation of liberty with rules that don't normally exist in mainstream society.

Prison and Jail Milieu

Prison inmates represent all segments of society although, as a whole, inmates are disproportionately people of color, poor, undereducated, and likely to be substance users and abusers (Harrison and Beck 2005; Mumola 1999). These common social demographics of prison inmates point to some important facts about crime, justice, and corrections in the United States. The economically, socially, and educationally disadvantaged are more likely to be identified as criminal offenders, processed through the criminal justice system, and sentenced to a period of incarceration. As a result, most correctional facilities currently hold a majority of inmates who are African American and Latino (Harrison and Beck 2005).

Many prisons are considered by interested observers to be intense and ripe for violence. One common explanation for this is that a prison is a closed environment devoid of individual privacy where prisoners are forced to interact with other inmates from a wide range of cultural, economic, and experiential backgrounds. This is the perfect setting for cultural clashes and violence among inmates and between inmates and staff workers. Although it is commonly believed that violence among inmates is based on issues of race (Carroll 1974), more recent research disputes this belief. For example, Trulson and Marquart (2002) demonstrate that when inmates are segregated by race, there is actually a higher level of violence than when inmates are integrated.

The milieu in jails is generally quite different from that found in prisons. Because they have recently entered from the streets, jail detainees are more likely than prison inmates to have more frequent and more serious health, behavioral, and mental health problems, and less controlled behavior. In this regard, jails are generally more chaotic and present serious short-term challenges for correctional officers. Jail inmates are also more likely than prison inmates to attempt suicide (Stephan 2001; Stephan and Karberg 2003) and to engage in violence. The risk of suicide in jail is especially acute during the first 72 hours of incarceration (Tahir 2003) and declines sharply after one week (Mumola 2005). The risk of suicide is also highest for novice inmates who have not been in jail previously. This is usually explained as a reaction to the shock of being incarcerated. This fact also contributes to the research finding showing that the suicide rate in small (i.e., 50 or fewer beds) jails is five times higher than in larger jails (Mumola 2005). For individuals in smaller communities, being arrested and jailed may be a more "public" event, lead to greater embarrassment and stigma, and lead inmates to see their situation as more desperate than for persons in larger cities. Jail inmates who attempt/commit suicide are typically middle-class individuals who find being in jail as stigmatizing, shocking to their sense of self, and they are often persons who are jailed while intoxicated or under the influence of drugs. While suicide is more common in jail than prison—in fact, it is the second leading cause of deaths among jail inmates—it is still not a "common" event. Approximately 320 jail inmates commit suicide annually (Stephan 2001).

Prison and Jail Subcultures

One of the interesting sociological insights about prisons is that there is a prison subculture, including norms, values, beliefs, and predictable patterns of behaviors. This subculture has been recognized by scholars since the early days of American corrections, but it is only in recent decades that it has also become widely acknowledged that there is no singular "prison culture" or experience. Rather, sometimes wide variations in norms, values, beliefs, and patterns of behavior may exist across prisons, and cultural components change over time (Hensley, Wright, and Tewksbury 2003; Hunt et al. 1993; Terry 2003). Therefore, it is important to consider the number, types, and relationships among inmates in a prison, as well as outside cultural issues that may be brought into prison, when considering how an institution operates and is experienced.

There are two basic approaches to understanding how a culture is established in prison. First is the idea that what is found inside a prison is a direct reflection of what inmates knew and experienced on the outside; this is the idea of importation of culture (Irwin and Cressey 1963). Such culture and behaviors represent aspects of "street culture," including norms, values, and beliefs that focus on violence and drug use and abuse. In short, what is imported is based on opposition to authority and represents criminal thinking and behavior. This, in turn, establishes the culture of the institution and creates an environment in which violence and resistance to authority are likely to be primary.

An alternative view suggests that prison culture develops in response to the loss of freedom, the lack of autonomy, broken relationships, and sense of insecurity (Clemmer 1940; Sykes 1958). Because incarceration represents denial of individual rights, inmates initially experience an anomic environment. When the behaviors, values, norms, and beliefs that inmates have known in the community do not apply to life on the inside, they must adjust to this reconstructed social world. As a result, new norms, values, beliefs, and behaviors are internalized in response to the loss and denial experienced during incarceration. Whereas importation theory suggests that prisons reflect the world as it was known by the inmates on the outside (see, e.g., John Irwin's *Prisons in Turmoil*), in this view, a new culture develops inside the prison.

Moreover, prison employees are primarily white, and many come from rural backgrounds since most prisons are located in rural rather than urban areas. Inmates, however, are not only likely to be persons of color, but they are also primarily from urban settings (Steurer, Smith, and Tracy 2001). Racial and ethnic minorities and urban poor inmates have little social capital and find the power of correctional staff to be oppressive. Because of their varied cultural backgrounds, inmates bring life experiences that are quite different from prison staff. As a result, the subcultural differences between the prison staff and the inmates can be quite distinct.

Jails, on the other hand, largely preclude the development of a stable culture and social structure because of the constant flow of people. As a result, jails are less organized than prisons, have fewer informal social controls to guide the activities and behaviors of inmates, and consequently are more volatile, more dangerous, and more chaotic environments than prisons. Jails also include individuals who have been in and out of jail many times and many first-time inmates, all of whom approach their incarceration in very different ways. As Garofalo and Clark (1985) have shown, experienced inmates know what to expect, how to best manage their stay, and how to make their time in confinement as comfortable as possible; newcomers, however, are highly unlikely to "learn" a jail culture. And when newly arriving jail inmates are mentally ill, injured, physically ill, or going through withdrawal from addiction, the likelihood of a culture developing—including norms, shared values, common attitudes, and recognized, known roles for those involved—is unlikely to occur.

CORRECTIONAL JURISDICTIONS

U.S. correctional institutions and community corrections are administered at three levels of government—the federal, state, and community levels. Definitions of criminal behavior are determined by all three levels of government, and just as law enforcement and judicial systems operate at these levels of government so too must the punishment/ enforcement activities operate. When convicted of violating a criminal statute, as defined by a particular level of government, that government entity is responsible for overseeing the sentence imposed on the offender.

Federal

The federal government, through the Bureau of Prisons and United States Probation office, oversees individuals who are charged with the violation of federal statutes. The federal government has not always operated prisons or other correctional programs, however. The first federal prison in the United States began operation in 1895 at Fort Leavenworth, Kansas, but a centralized administration overseeing federal prisons or prisoners was not created until creation of the Bureau of Prisons in 1930. The federal government is also involved in correctional activities through Immigration and Customs Enforcement, which operates detention facilities for illegal immigrants and others who violate customs laws, and most Native American tribes rely on the federal correctional system although some Native American tribes have functional criminal justice systems on their reservations, including correctional institutions. In addition, the U.S. military operates a correctional system.

State

All 50 states have an operating correctional system generally called the Department or Division of Corrections (in Ohio, it is called the Department of Rehabilitation and Correction). This system may have a secretary or director who is a member of the governor's cabinet, or it may be a subsystem under Public Safety. States operate both prisons and probation services for persons convicted of violating state felony criminal statutes. In those states where indeterminate sentencing is operating, states also administer parole. State correctional jurisdictions may be large as in Texas where at year-end in 2004, 168,105 offenders were in prison and more than 500,000 offenders were on probation or parole, or small as in New Hampshire where at year-end in 2004, 2,448 offenders were incarcerated and a little more than 5,000 offenders were on probation or parole (Glaze and Palla 2004). It should be noted that persons charged with crimes at the state level and who await their judicial processing while incarcerated will almost always be found in local jails.

Community

Jails function at the community level and are generally under the jurisdiction of the local sheriff, although some jails operate independently from law enforcement and answer directly to a local body of government such as a county commission. As mentioned previously, jails house both sentenced and unsentenced offenders and those who have been committed under civil statutes. Probation and even parole may be administered at the community level in the same manner as it is administered at the state level although for much shorter periods of supervision.

PRIVATIZATION

While governments have legal responsibilities for identifying, arresting, prosecuting, and imposing sentences/sanctions on criminal offenders, in some instances governments contract the management of correctional institutions and programs to private companies. The U.S. privatization movement, which began during the 1980s, has seen numerous correctional systems at all levels of government turn over all or some aspects of supervising criminal offenders to privately operated companies. Some of these private groups function as nonprofit groups, such as the Salvation Army or Volunteers of America, while others are for-profit corporations.

Private corrections provide all levels of governments with solutions to overcrowding of institutions often at lower costs. When an offender is incarcerated or supervised by a private entity, they are responsible for all aspects of security, custody, programming, care, and supervision. The privatization of corrections is heralded by advocates as less expensive to operate (Moore 1998) and delivering high-quality service compared with government-operated institutions. Critics, however, question both the cost savings argument (Perrone and Pratt 2003; Pratt and Maahs 1999) and the contention that private corrections actually provide an equal quality of facility, programs, and staff (Camp, Gaes, and Saylor 2000).

The privatization of prisons issue introduces some interesting sociological questions about power and structures of social institutions. If private corporations operate prisons, jails, and community corrections programs, who, then, is actually in charge of restricting the activities, legal rights, and freedoms of criminal offenders? For many observers, the following questions arise: Who owns these private companies? Is it correct and proper for one group of private individuals, who have not been elected or otherwise selected "by the people," to control another group? Answers to these questions are interwoven with issues of economics and the effort of all levels of government to reduce the costs of incarceration.

CURRENT CORRECTIONAL POPULATIONS

The current correctional populations say a great deal about American society in terms of where we stand on issues of punishment. According to Mauer (2003:2), the United States leads the world in the use of imprisonment. At mid-year 2004, the estimated correctional population was approximately 7 million with a total of 1,410,404 persons in state and federal prisons, 713,990 persons in local jails, more than 4.1 million persons on probation, and more than 775,000 persons on parole in the United States (Glaze and Palla 2004; Harrison and Beck 2005; Pastore and Maguire 2005). With more than 7 million American adults under some form of correctional supervision, and the U.S. Bureau of the Census reporting that in 2004, the United States had a population of approximately 223 million adults, about one in every 32 American adults was under some form of correctional supervision (U.S. Bureau of the Census 2006).

The demographics of the U.S. prison population as noted earlier in this chapter emphasizes the sociological impact of incarceration and harsh punishments on people of color, the undereducated, and those with low socioeconomic status (Harrison and Beck 2005; Mauer 2003). The current U.S. incarceration rate is also affecting communities, especially African American communities, and has long-term effects on such factors as neighborhood order, family structure, and child development. If the current incarceration trend continues, money for important social services will be diverted to house prisoners and will continue to tax budgets at all levels of government. Clearly, it is time to examine U.S. policies regarding crime and imprisonment to determine if the social and economic costs are justified to maintain current practices.

SOCIOLOGY AND CORRECTIONS IN THE 21ST CENTURY

Although sociology may have given way to analysts interested primarily in criminal justice programming, the sociological approach to corrections continues to represent the study and understanding of American society in a controlled and bounded milieu that serves as a microcosm of the larger American society. Indeed, the sociological perspective is important to understanding the system of corrections. Central to its operation are issues relating to culture and society, relationships between individuals and organizations, and the social structures of communities. All these directly affect corrections. During the twenty-first century, a sociological perspective on American corrections must be broad in focus and should take into consideration the diverse and wide-ranging social influences at both the micro and macro levels that create and sustain the culture. Research on organization, purpose, and functioning of what have become an important and ever growing institution, and the application of sociological concepts in the corrections milieu should continue to offer information that will prove useful to policymakers. Indeed, the American corrections system provides many diverse opportunities to see sociology in action through the continued use of the discipline's theories and insightful concepts.

PART IX

LOCALITY AND SOCIAL LIFE

45

HUMAN ECOLOGY

STEPHEN J. APPOLD

National University of Singapore

Ecology is defined as "the science of the economy of animals and plants; that branch of biology which deals with the relations of living organisms to their surroundings, their habits and modes of life, etc." (Oxford English Dictionary 2000). The first half of that definition implies an impulse toward efficient interdependence. Applied to humans, the second half of that definition implies much more than what is usually meant by the term *human ecology,* however. A consideration of the relations of individuals to their surroundings, their habits, and modes of life would include almost all aspects of what are now seen as "contextual effects." It would include some aspects of developmental psychology (e.g., Barker and Wright 1954) and much of environmental psychology (Bechtel 1997). These are part of what is sometimes called *autoecology* (treating organisms individually as opposed to *synecology,* the study of collectivities), a field of inquiry that is perhaps part of ecology but not what is usually included under the term. That definition would also include studies, such as Gerth and Mills's (1953) *Social Structure and Character,* among many others, that examine how a changing social structure affects the mode of life of a particular population. In contrast, sociological human ecology has been most concerned with investigating what are now termed *aggregation effects,* that is, how people, living together, create social organization. A reciprocal relationship between an individual or collectivity and its environment is posited. Human ecology is, therefore, concerned with

the nature and process of community development (Hawley 1950).

A BRIEF OUTLINE OF THE EARLY DEVELOPMENT OF HUMAN ECOLOGICAL THEORY

The term *ecology* was coined by the German botanist Ernst Haeckel in 1868, reviving much older concerns. The term *human ecology* may have been first used by J. Paul Goode, a University of Chicago geographer, at the 1907 meeting of the Association of American Geographers in describing an introductory university course. By 1920, Barrington Moore (1920), president of the Ecological Society of America, characterized geography as "human ecology" in his presidential address, and the journal *Ecology* reviewed Ellsworth Huntington and Sumner W. Cushing's *Principles of Human Geography* under the title "Human Ecology" the following year. In 1922, Harlan Barrows, concerned about the continuing relevance of the field as the era of discovery neared its end, accepted the attribution as the new and future identity for geography in his presidential address to the Association of American Geographers. Anthropologists showed an interest in the relation of their field to ecology as early as 1903, but the term *human ecology* does not appear to have been used by them until the 1930s. Today, human ecological theory may be most intensively discussed by anthropologists.

AUTHOR'S NOTE: I'd like to thank John D. Kasarda and Dennis L. Peck for comments and helpful suggestions on earlier drafts of this chapter.

Robert Park's 1915 essay "The City: Suggestions for the Investigation of Human Behavior in the City Environment" is sometimes thought to be the origin of ecological thought in sociology, but neither does Park mentions the term nor are the outlines of ecological theory visible. (The 1925 republication of that essay includes a substantially rewritten introduction including the term.) Ecology does not play a large role in his 1921 essay on "Sociology and the Social Sciences" either. That three-part essay roots sociology firmly in history, links collective phenomena to interaction, and outlines a program for research. Park did discuss human ecology in his 1925 presidential address to the American Sociological Society, but it was not until 1936 that Park addressed ecological theory systematically. Nevertheless, Hawley (1950:8) attributed the origin of human ecology in sociology to pages 161 to 216 in Park and Burgess's ([1921] 1969) *Introduction to the Science of Sociology.*

Park and Burgess's ([1921] 1969) monumental 1,000-page text is a comprehensive attempt at understanding social phenomena. Beginning with a discussion of the place of sociology among the social sciences (including the 1921 journal essay) and ending with a treatise on the nature of progress, the argument builds from human nature to society and the group. Connections are drawn between social contact and isolation, interaction and social forces, and four types of social relationships—competition, conflict, accommodation, and assimilation—to arrive at the forms of social control and collective action. Competition for ultimately limited resources and the connections engendered played a central role in the argument laid out in the text. These were classified as presocial because competition does not necessarily entail contact. Conflict implies a mutual awareness of the competing parties. Accommodation implies patterned adjustments of behavior, while assimilation implies a despecialization in behavioral patterns and a dissolution of social demarcation.

The range of issues and thought considered by Park and Burgess is impressive. A total of more than 180 collected edited contributions representing the work of more than 100 authors were introduced, reworked, and discussed by the authors. Park authored 14 of the included readings. Simmel was responsible for 10. Charles Darwin, Albion Small, and William Graham Sumner each had four readings included. Five authors, including John Dewey and W. I. Thomas, had three. Durkheim, Smith, Spencer, Le Bon, and 11 others each had two pieces, and 97 authors, including Comte, Cooley, Galton, Giddings, Gras, William James, Rousseau, Santayana, Schopenhauer, Sombart, Toennies, and Lester Ward, each made one contribution to the book. The large number of topics and breadth of authors suggests the diversity of intellectual sources that early American sociology drew on.

Despite the discussion of ecological concepts in one of the chapters of that work, a systematic discussion of human ecology was left to Roderick McKenzie in his 1924 essay "The Ecological Approach to the Study of the Human Community" and his 1927 article on "The Concept of Dominance and World-Organization." The outlines of contemporary human ecological theory become visible in these two works. In the first work, McKenzie stated the basic claim that competition, selection, and accommodation determine the size and organization of human communities before identifying four types of communities, enumerating the basic factors behind community growth and decline, specifying the relationship between resources, population, and organization, and discussing the relationship between the basic ecological mechanisms and the internal structure of communities. In the second work, McKenzie provided a broad road map to the development of Asia over the seven or eight decades since the work appeared. He discussed the relationship between transportation technology and European colonial expansion, pointing out that the separation of communication from transportation has permitted the concentration of control as it allowed the decentralization of operations, and he outlined the changes in patterns of production and trade brought about by the expansion process. The application of ecological theory to the world system was refined and expanded in a subsequent book chapter (McKenzie 1933). The outlines of contemporary human ecological methodology become visible in his 1933 book, *The Metropolitan Community,* where social demography, geographic mapping, and summary analysis of spatial movements were used to support arguments about social organization (McKenzie [1933] 1997). The spatial implications of the process of ecological succession on intra-urban residential patterns, in the form of the concentric zone model, was laid out by Burgess in 1925. This work, so well known to students of urban development today, did not figure prominently in the then contemporary theoretical debates.

Each of the three main founders of sociological human ecology was a part-time theorist. Park, who came to Chicago as a part-time, practice-track lecturer in 1914 from the Tuskegee Institute and left in 1932 for Fisk University devoted much of his time to studying the role of newspapers in what is now sometimes called the "public sphere." Burgess showed more sustained interest in the family than in the city. McKenzie, who apparently developed an interest in sociology after first becoming a classicist of some accomplishment, had his productive life cut short by illness. There was remarkably little systematic theoretical work advancing sociological human ecology before 1950. Human ecology was perhaps more extensively defined by its critics (e.g., Alihan [1938] 1964; Firey 1947) than by its proponents.

Ecological ideas were "in the air," however. E. Warming's *Oecology of Plants* appeared in 1909, Frederic Clements's *Plant Succession* in 1916. Both extended the work of Charles Darwin. Frederic Le Play's research on the relationship between family structure and the social environment in the mid-nineteenth century was known (Zimmerman and Frampton 1935). Galpin (1915) performed research on rural areas that had an impact on ecologically minded sociologists. J. Arthur Thomson, a biologist, and Patrick Geddes, one of the founders of modern city planning (Geddes 1915), collaborated on a book-length work of human ecology (1931) that extended earlier work. Herbert G. Wells, Julian Huxley, and George P. Wells published a three-volume comprehensive overview of ecology, with much of the last volume being devoted to human ecology, in 1934, which followed H. G. Wells's major survey of history (1921). J. W. Bews (1935), a botanist, offered a statement of human ecology that was extensively reviewed. The work of N. S. B. Gras (1922) and Adna Weber (1899) had an impact on the theorizing in human ecology. This was an era of sweeping generalization and the "big work," but there were many big ideas current at the time, and comparisons between humans and other species was only one of them.

Amos Hawley produced the first book-length statement of human ecology in 1950 and the first one that provided a systematic treatment of the theory, integrating social mechanisms and morphological outcomes. This has become the central statement of ecological theory. Hawley gave new prominence to the intricacies of human-commensal relations (discussed by Park and Burgess ([1921] 1969) but subsequently downplayed). That statement gave human ecology its contemporary form by codifying and extending the ecological thought of McKenzie and illustrating the resulting theory with the type of data and application in McKenzie's *Metropolitan Community*. Shortly before the appearance of Hawley's book, Donald Bogue published a study of metropolitan dominance (1949). Otis Dudley Duncan (1951) examined the question of optimal city size. Duncan (1959, 1964) later codified the thinking about the ecological complex and developed ecological theory and methods to study inter-urban dependences and patterns of development (Duncan et al. 1960; see also Vance and Smith 1954). Until about 1950, the illustrations used in ecological theorizing were not particularly urban in orientation even if all the protagonists had long-standing interests in cities as a social formation. Countering the urban preoccupation, Gibbs and Martin (1959) argued that the proper focus of human ecology was sustenance (subsistence) organization. Hawley's (1986) refined statement of ecological theory de-emphasized spatially delimited communities. Much of the recent theoretical advance has been in applying the ecological approach to studies of formal organizations (Bidwell and Kasarda 1985), industry structure and entrepreneurship (Carroll and Hannan 2000), cultural institutions (Blau 1989; Wuthnow 1987), and voluntary organizations (McPherson 1983).

This review is too narrow, however. While human ecology is not always well integrated into the theory, since the 1920s and continuing into the present, it has provided theoretical guidance for researchers investigating many types of behaviors that are not coordinated by a centralized authority. Park's contention that social distance would be reflected in spatial distance provides a holistic framework for understanding the patterned nature of noninstitutionalized behavior from crime and vice to voting and religious affiliation. Ecology's population perspective on social phenomena guides much research on stratification processes, including residential sorting and labor markets, family formation, and marriage. Despite the relative paucity of theoretical work, Quinn (1940) was able to find 347 pieces of ecological literature in 1940, and, a decade later, Quinn (1950) had found enough human ecology to fill 23 chapters in a 500-page review. The contributions in Micklin and Poston (1998) provide an extensive survey of human ecological theory and research. Berry and Kasarda's (1977) book includes a review of the history of sociological human ecology in addition to an application of the theory to urban issues. Given the placement and purpose of this chapter, the discussion will focus on territorially delimited communities.

UNDERSTANDING THE DEVELOPMENT OF ECOLOGICAL THOUGHT

Some of the early theoretical works in human ecology (Hollingshead 1940; Wirth 1945) and other disciplines were part of a boundary-making activity as factions of academics competed for recognized expertise over particular areas, but they were also symptomatic of a search for direction. Much of the early work in ecological theory must be seen as tentative first approximations of a theory—and more recent thought perhaps only a second approximation. In sociology's exploratory context, a theory with predictive power may be beyond reach. A theory capable of generating post hoc interpretations is useful, and one that is incorrect in informative ways can lead to successively more powerful formulations.

> Our coordinated knowledge which in the general sense of the term is Science, is formed by the meeting of two orders of experience. One order is constituted by the direct, immediate discriminations of particular observations. The other order is constituted by our general way of conceiving the Universe. They will be called, the Observational Order, and the Conceptual Order. The first point to remember is that the observational order is invariably interpreted in terms of the concepts supplied by the conceptual order.... We inherit an observational order, namely types of things which we do in fact discriminate; and we inherit a conceptual order, namely a rough system of ideas in terms of which we do in fact, interpret. (Whitehead 1933:198)

The quote, repeated by different authors who developed biological and sociological ecological theory, apparently captures the situation of sociologists in the first half of the twentieth century. They were searching for a methodology that would allow sociologists to adequately characterize the ways people lived together, and at the same time they were searching for ways of conceptualizing and understanding how that was accomplished. They were also searching for ways of bringing the observational and conceptual orders together, adjusting each in the process.

The following quote exemplifies the observational order that sociologists felt they needed to understand a century ago. Because Chicago played such a central role in the development of American sociology, an observation of that city is cited.

> Chicago is one of the most incredible cities. By the lake there are a few comfortable residential districts, mostly with stone houses, and right behind them there are little old wooden houses. Then come the "*tenements*" of the workingmen and absurdly dirty streets which are unpaved, or there is miserable macadamization. In the "*city,*" among the "*skyscrapers,*" the condition of the streets is utterly hair-raising. And they burn soft coal. In broad daylight one can see only three blocks ahead—everything is haze and smoke, the whole lake is covered by a huge pall of smoke in which the sails of the ships putting to sea quickly disappear.
>
> It is an endless human desert. From the city one travels into the endless distance, past blocks with Greek inscriptions and then past others with Chinese taverns, Polish advertisements, German beer parlors, until one gets to the "*stockyards.*" For as far as one can see from the clock tower of the firm Armour & Co. there is nothing but herds of cattle, lowing, bleating, endless filth. But on the horizon all around—for the city continues for miles and miles, until it melts into the multitude of suburbs—there are churches and chapels, grain elevators, smoking chimneys, and houses of every size.
>
> All hell had broken loose in the "*stockyards*": an unsuccessful strike, masses of strikebreakers; daily shootings with dozens of dead; a streetcar was overturned and a dozen women were squashed because a "*non-union man*" had sat in it; dynamite threats against the "*Elevated Railway,*" and one of its cars was actually derailed and plunged into the river. Right near our hotel a cigar dealer was murdered in broad daylight—all in all, a strange flowering of culture.
>
> There is a mad pell-mell of nationalities: Up and down the streets the Greeks shine the Yankees' shoes for 5 cents. The Germans are their waiters, the Irish take care of their politics, and the Italians of their dirtiest ditch digging. With the exception of the better residential districts, the whole tremendous city is like a man whose skin has been peeled off and whose intestines are seen at work. One can see everything—in the evening the prostitutes are placed in a show window with electric light and the prices are displayed! A characteristic thing is the maintenance of a specific Jewish-German culture. Theaters present in Yiddish *The Merchant of Venice* (with Shylock prevailing, however) and their own Jewish plays.
>
> Everywhere one is struck by the tremendous intensity of work—most of all in the "*stockyards*" with their "ocean of blood." From the moment when the unsuspecting bovine enters the slaughtering area, is hit by a hammer and collapses, it is in constant motion but [is] always (in the rhythm of work) tied to the machine that pulls the animal. One sees an absolutely incredible output in this atmosphere of steam, muck, blood, and hides.
>
> When they finish work, people often must travel for hours to get home. The streetcar company is bankrupt and hence does not purchase any new cars. The old ones break down every few moments. Around 400 people are killed or crippled in accidents every year. The company has calculated that those 400 indemnities cost it less than the required precautions, so it does not bother to introduce them. (Excerpted from Max Weber's (1975:285–87) letters, written during his 1904 visit to the United States)

Weber is known for, among his other accomplishments, theoretical writings on cities. His main work on the topic (1958) was, appropriately enough, originally titled "Illegitimate Domination." Yet his own work focused not on these observations but the power relationships and social contracts among the burghers of Medieval European cities in the absence of charisma or tradition as a legitimating force for social hierarchy.

With only minor revision, this was the situation a few years later, when McKenzie, Park, and later, Burgess arrived in Chicago. An American sociologist in Chicago observed what Weber saw, unfiltered by the interpretation of historians. If there was order here, it was not obviously one born out of social contract, much less of moral consensus. A social theory based on such agreement would be out of place. If the state had a role in creating order, its reach was seriously limited, and whatever the factors guiding behavior, they were not written into law. A theory stressing the importance of institutionalized authority would lack explanatory power. Individual and class interests probably motivated behavior but may not have determined the observed outcomes. An overly "organicist" conception of order would just as obviously have been out of place. In spite of the high level of apparent disorder, with individuals working at cross-purposes, somehow this social formation managed to survive. People continued arriving, and prosperity, at least most of the time, increased.

Searching for a way of conceptualizing what they were observing, Park (1936) and several others looked to the ecologist's "web of life" and cited Darwin's example of the cats and the clover to illustrate the binding factor in social arrangements.

> [Darwin] found . . . that humblebees were almost indispensable to the fertilization of the heartsease, since other bees do not visit this flower. The same thing is true with some kinds of clover. Humblebees alone visit red clover, as other bees cannot reach the nectar. The inference is that if the humblebees became extinct or very rare in England, the heartsease and red clover would become very rare, or wholly disappear. However, the number of humblebees in any district depends in a great measure on the number of field mice, which destroy their combs and nests. It is estimated that more than two-thirds of them are thus destroyed all over England. Near villages and small towns the nests of humblebees are more numerous than elsewhere and this is attributed to the number of cats that destroy the mice. Thus next year's crop of purple clover in certain parts of England depends on the number of humblebees in the district; the number of humblebees depends upon the number of field mice, the number of field

mice upon the number and the enterprise of the cats, and the number of cats as someone has added—depends on the number of old maids and others in neighboring villages who keep cats. (P. 2)

The image of cooperation without direct communication with its many indirect and surprising connections has captured the imagination of many sociologists. Competition was evident in cities a century ago but not a war of all against all. "Competitive cooperation," a sociological idea that was pressed into biological service, seemed to capture the basis of human community. According to Park and Burgess ([1921] 1969:507), "competition invariably tends to create an impersonal social order in which each individual, being free to pursue his own profit, and, in a sense, is compelled to do so, makes every other individual a means to that end." In other words, competition pushes people to cooperate. It has been difficult to keep both aspects of the concept simultaneously in focus, however, with some sociologists perhaps overemphasizing just one aspect of the concept. The ecological model allowed for a very populist image of human society wherein each person had an effect on others (even if unequal) and allowed for the possibility of a civil society and public sphere that did not exist in the shadow of the state—ideas that run throughout Park's work (e.g., Park [1904] 1972).

The biology was, to some extent, used as a loose analogy or trope, and the early human ecologists made no attempt to press the point. Human ecologists' efforts were frequently directed toward understanding exactly how the plant and animal analogy fell short, leading to much of the future development of the theory. Two points of divergence stand out. First, humans are better able to communicate and plan than are plants or animals. Relationships among them are thus more complex because coalitions can emerge from the competition, leading to conflict and possibly accommodation and assimilation in addition to specialization and segregation. Second, the different types of humans produced, to use Mills's ([1959] 1967) phrase, are not species. They are capable of geographic and social movement, leading to a concern for patterns of social mobility. Despite the biological connotations of the term, human ecology is essentially interactionist sociology. Ecology, as Hawley (1944:399–400) pointed out, is a social science whether applied to plants, animals, or humans (with some then contemporary books carrying titles such as *Plant Sociology*). Human ecology, with its observation that patterns of behavior are more variable than biological structure across species and its stress on adaptation to the social and physical environment, has often served as an antidote to explanations for social and cultural differences based on population genetics.

Park's 1921 essay on sociology and social science suggested that following periods of sociology as a philosophy of history and as schools attempting to define a point of view, a period of investigation and research was beginning,

and some of the subsequent debate was over the correct way of observing social phenomena. Much of the effort at the University of Chicago during the first third of the twentieth century went to community studies. McKenzie's dissertation on Columbus, Ohio, neighborhoods was a multimethod attempt to create an adequate "observational order" characterizing social organization. Early human ecologists referred quite positively to the work of the "social survey movement," including Booth (1920) in his landmark study of London. Several of the community studies performed during that era, such as Lynd and Lynd's (1929) *Middletown,* had selected relatively small, stable communities for study. Larger cities, having differentiated into multiple social worlds, were obviously too extensive for any one participant or observer to adequately observe directly, leading to a crisis in methodology. Homans (1949) and Coleman (1990), among others, rued the disappearance of community studies with an encompassing view of social organization. The use of quantitative analysis and secondary sources emerged in the 1930s and 1940s as a method of performing a naturalistic study while maintaining a holistic view. While some commentators have suggested that quantitative analysis was a strategy for gaining scientific legitimacy, by 1950 the claim to that legitimacy was more strongly made by sample surveys and small-group laboratory research, both of which sacrificed holism.

HUMAN ECOLOGY DISTILLED

The fundamental contention of human ecology is that community (social organization) arises through the interaction of a population and its physical and social environment. Ecology assumes a collective tendency to maximize life that is, however, limited by the repertoire of tools, techniques, and information (technology) available. That simple statement carries many implications. Because every living organism requires access to the biophysical environment for food and water, environmental dependence, however indirect, is an ever-present fact of life. The ultimate dependence of all humans on the biophysical environment implies that social organization is not purely a social construction emerging out of interaction. The social construction is thereby anchored. Because individuals are time bound, economizing on time is a significant factor in the maximization of life. Because interdependence is a means of maximizing life by allowing environmental access while economizing on time, it forms the basis for social relations. Because the intrinsic limitation on the behavioral variability of humans is indeterminate, interdependence can take many—sometimes simple, sometimes complex—forms.

Competition for resources among individuals plays a critical role in social organization. Competition can have at least three general types of effects on community (Schnore 1958), however, with the path of least resistance possibly prevailing. Demographic responses, a decline in births or increase in mortality, are one possible response to competition for resources (Hannan and Freeman 1977). Technological responses, the more efficient use of resources through conservation or the enlargement of the resources base, are a second collective response to competition (Boserup 1966; Hawley 1950:203; Schumpeter 1950). Organizational responses are a third type of response to competition. As Cooley (1930a:164) has suggested, "If 'all the world's a stage' [competition] is a process that distributes the parts among the players" (quoted in Hawley [1950:201]). It even helps create those roles. Competition leads to specialization and, therefore, differentiation. Differentiation results in a hierarchy of activities when the most productive activity is in most direct contact with the environment, resulting in its becoming a dominant or key function defining the conditions under which others will operate, creating sometimes intricate patterns of cooperation in which the participants might not even experience competition per se.

Activities are performed by people, leading to a process of matching individuals and activities and creating social stratification. The competition for resources that creates differentiation encourages the formation of coalitions to gain and protect such resources. The possible bases for coalitions are nearly endless, including even eye color. The salience of particular characteristics for such purposes depends on the ease and effectiveness with which they can be mobilized as a basis for action (Nielson 1985; Olzak 1986). Competition creates the impetus to form coalitions, and the success of the various efforts creates social categories that become the basis for commensal relations. While in some cases the categoric basis for recruitment is easily measured, in other cases difficult-to-measure criteria apply, such as the nature of a personnel director's university education (Useem 1989) or the neighborhood in which a person resides. The sometimes excessive credentialing requirements for particular occupations, selecting on parental income, could also be included among the commensal mechanisms of resource allocation. None of the bases are primordial.

The resulting social organization is composed of two interweaving, but distinct, types of interdependence relations: symbiotic and commensal. Symbiotic relations imply a degree of mutual interdependence among complementary and, therefore, functionally differentiated and specialized units, such as the different species in the "web of life" example above. Commensal relations, arising among those who engage in similar activities in a symbiotic web, imply common, parallel actions. Being built on the basis of similarity, they imply both a degree of competition for resources and cooperation to protect access to them. This mix of interests leads to restrictions on individual actions, providing a basis for understanding the structural bases of action. Despite focusing on the morphology of social organization, human agency in all its varied manifestations is essential to the ecological

theoretical framework. The human "balance of nature" can be attained only when life expands to the maximum attainable under prevailing conditions. The disparate aims, attempts, and projects of many individuals imply that the collective response to an environment is not simply a result of an individual's action writ large nor merely a cultural schema made real.

The "balance of nature" may be elusive, existing mainly in the minds of researchers, however (Park 1936:5, quoting Charles Enid). That equilibrium may be affected by any event that upsets the relationship between population (a set of individuals), organization (a set of direct and indirect social relations created by interrelated efforts at sustaining life), environment (a set of direct and indirect resources), and technology (a set of tools, techniques, and information), resulting in a population problem that becomes an impetus for social change that can be resolved in the three general ways outlined.

CHANGES IN SOCIAL ORGANIZATION

If the human "balance of nature" is essentially a matter of matching persons with activities, anything that disturbs that balance leads to social change. Changes in the productivity of sustenance technology have had a major impact on social organization, increasing the aggregate population that could be supported and the degree of hierarchical placement. Over the past century or so, communication and transportation technologies have clearly had substantial implications, increasing the scope of social integration. Each of these has directly or indirectly affected the size of the population compared with the set of activities. Technology, in all its various forms, is central to theories of large-scale social organization because it is a mechanism that stabilizes social relations despite changing actors, beliefs, and interests (Latour 1991). Human ecologists have explored some implications of the basic model more extensively compared with others, however.

Technological Change

Advances in subsistence technology are a necessary precondition for any significant increase in the size or complexity of any social formation (Nolan and Lenski 1999:65). Those technologies have evolved from hunting and gathering to horticultural to agricultural to industrial. Over the last century or so, that has resulted in a shift from farm to factory to office in the United States and other countries. The Industrial Revolution was due, in part, to the increasing efficiency of agricultural production, and the growth of service employment rests on increasing manufacturing efficiency (Baumol, Blackman, and Wolff 1989). The spatial distribution of population has changed as particular industries have expanded or contracted as new cities grew on the basis of specific products (Duncan and Lieberson 1970).

Subsistence technology influences social stratification by affecting the volume of surplus wealth and by influencing the bargaining power of all involved. Rewards (the product of labor) will be shared to the extent required to insure the survival and continued productivity of those others whose actions are necessary or beneficial to themselves (Lenski 1966). Recall that competition tends to create a social order wherein individuals are compelled to use others as means to their own ends (Park and Burgess 1921:507). But since each technology requires a different set of human resources for maximum output, the outcomes of the process of bargaining vary with the methods of production available. In the simplest societies, which generate small surpluses, such as hunter-gatherer bands, goods will be distributed largely on the basis of need. Across types of society, from those based on hunting and gathering to those based on agriculture, inequality grew as power differentials based on the degree of centrality in a network of interdependence increased. That historical trend reversed with the appearance of mature industrial societies because the greater complexity of functional interdependences gave those with specializations that supported the key function increased bargaining power. In agricultural societies, for example, 90 to 95 percent of the population was involved in the same basic function, leaving many individuals with little bargaining power and a few with central coordinating roles. The division of labor is substantially more complex in industrial societies, and individual functions are significantly more tightly integrated—with the automobile assembly line being the ideal typical example of each participant having veto power over production at any one moment. An increased ability to communicate, sometimes aided by proximity, gave those performing similar functions greater ability to solidify commensal relations, with those being often institutionalized in the form of labor unions, professional organizations, and industry groups.

Communication Technology and Ecological Expansion

A concern for communication and transportation technologies stems from human ecology's roots in interactionist sociology (Park 1921:13, 17). The unity of social formations is built on interaction. Thus, any development that extends the reach of communication, whether writing and newspapers (Park 1923) or railroads and automobiles (Ogburn 1946; Ullman 1980), theoretically affects the size and structure of human communities. Over the past century or so, improvements in transportation and communication technologies have changed unusually rapidly, and their impact on social organization has been pervasive. Both material and nonmaterial aspects of these technologies have been important, and their development is closely intertwined. Large firms, for example, are communication technologies facilitating and channeling interaction. These technologies have allowed the size and geographic scope

of organizational units to expand, giving rise to, at the largest scale, globalization.

Face-to-face exchange is the basic form of social interdependence. Urban planners sometimes use a radius of a five-minute walk in defining and planning neighborhoods (Leccese and McCormick 1999). The maximum distance people are willing to commute daily over long periods is approximately one hour each way, and the reach of daily delivery trips appears to delimit regions (Hawley 1950). Temporal rhythms combined with existing transportation technology, by affecting the frequency of interaction, helps form the texture of social organization. The extent of interaction is limited by the costs of carrying out interactions and the anticipated benefits to completing the interaction. Therefore, social innovations enhancing the ability to interact expanded the maximum possible size, differentiation, and hierarchy of populations. Improvements in the technology of transportation have expanded the range of interaction.

Each mode of interaction has its own characteristics, having to do with the relative costs of movement and of loading and unloading and with the democracy of destination. Navigation is limited to water, and river transportation is constrained by the course of water flow, leading to a long, thin settlement pattern, such as that along the ancient Nile. Sea navigation is less constrained but is focused by the location of natural harbors. Singapore, for example, owes its status as a busy port (and its prosperity) to its favorable location, Chicago to a river link between the Great Lakes and the Mississippi Valley. The development of railroads allowed the growth of large inland cities, with the railroad yards often within sight of the central business district. Atlanta and Columbus rose at railroad intersections. Both ships and railroads have relatively high terminal costs but low transportation costs, privileging distant relative to moderately near locations for interaction while concentrating activities at particular points of transfer. These seemingly trivial factors have had large effects on large-scale social organization.

Three inventions, all emerging within a short period of history, the wireless radio (1895), the automobile (1986), and the airplane (1903), revolutionized communication and travel because of the greater distances that could be covered and because of the greater democracy in their movement. The telegraph had already begun divorcing communication from transportation by 1840. Before that time, all communication required travel by a person (Pred 1966). The radio freed the transmission of information from the constraints of wires. More recently, airports have developed as centers for interaction (Irwin and Kasarda 1991). These centers may have been based on earlier settlements, but air transport further opened internal sites for further population growth. In the United States, air transport helped Denver grow, and the emerging freight transfer belt reaching from Louisville through Memphis and beyond may follow.

There is a tendency for population and wealth to collect at breaks or interruptions in routes of transportation

(Cooley [1894] 1930b). Mechanical breaks in movement resulting from a change in mode of transport have led to commercial breaks resulting from a change of ownership. Freight must be unloaded from one carrier and placed aboard another, and often it must be stored until a second carrier is ready or until an exchange is completed. Terminal facilities must, therefore, include warehousing and space for support functions such as repair and the administration of trade. That implies workers to handle the cargo and its administration, which, in turn, calls for their own support in the form of housing, food supply, and even entertainment. The accretion of personnel and physical structure at the point of interruption is cumulative; each new addition or elaboration entails others, and ultimately a large and complexly organized settlement unit takes form (Hawley 1950:243).

Some of the costs of interaction are purely social in nature, and as the frequency of various types of exchange increased, the attendant negotiations were regularized and the extent of interaction grew. The development of writing and, in stages, printing were milestones in the development of the technology of communication, each having a major social impact through preserving information over time and diffusing it through space. The gradual institutionalization of interaction in associational units, such as business firms and other bureaucracies, in the form of behavioral templates for negotiation also allowed the extent of interaction to increase. Large business firms are, in part, communication technologies (Beniger 1986) and, in part, templates or algorithms for social activity (Berlinski 2000). Internal economies of scale not being a sufficient condition, the growth of large firms was closely related to the need to coordinate activities over long distances, with the railroad companies themselves being among the earliest large firms and those that coordinated buying, production, and sales over long distances rapidly following (Chandler 1977). Appearing only in the second half of the nineteenth century in industry, by the 1920s, they were the most influential nongovernmental organizations. Such formal organizations emerged when the volume of exchange was sufficiently large and steady to routinize the transactions, lowering their costs, allowing them to schedule the flow of goods more closely than markets could.

Mismatches and Surplus Populations

The railroad, the automobile, the airplane, and the large organization have continued to radically, but not completely, shrink space. Near the end of the nineteenth century, streetcars and electric trains extended the reach of daily movement, particularly for those who could afford the transportation, allowing homes to be further separated from workplaces. Such separation allowed some workplaces to expand, facilitating the functional integration of a larger population. The combination of physically and socially expanding social systems created a physical and social path for new in-migrants: As the established population gained a more elevated position in the functional hierarchy and moved to more desirable residences more distant from the city center, a physical and social place was created for the new arrivals. Ecological expansion set in motion a process of physical and social succession that allowed for upward mobility. Put prosaically, as some people got better jobs and moved to the suburbs, occupational and residential space was created for others. Ecological expansion facilitated residential succession. Maintaining a balance between the number and type of people and the number and type of activities is an important ongoing social process, and the mechanisms of allocation are a central concern for human ecologists (Duncan 1965; Logan 1996; Stewman and Konda 1983). The processes of adjustment between population and activities is rarely smooth or efficient, leading to "surplus populations" that are themselves impetuses for social change.

The surprises induced by the many mismatches in social and geographic location, such as the slum just outside the "Gold Coast" (Zorbaugh 1929), the hobo's "main stem" near the business district (Anderson 1923), or the artist colony in a city of commerce, add a sense of dynamism to community life. Artists and literary writers do not necessarily require an urban location, however. They have little need to interact directly with the city around them. Indeed, many artistic communities have emerged in out-of-the-way locations such as Black Mountain, North Carolina. Nevertheless, the process of ecological expansion, outlined above, has often created underutilized space in the older centers of many cities, and artists have sometimes gathered in such urban zones-in-transition. The abandonment of Greenwich Village by the well-to-do at the beginning of the twentieth century for more efficient, uptown residences created a convenient, low-cost location for literary people, who were not closely integrated with the financial, commercial, and manufacturing activities surrounding them (Coser 1965). Deviance has been interesting to sociologists both as a social problem and, because of its theoretical relationship to social change, as a sociological issue. Certain types of crime and "vice" once collected in urban zones-in-transition, not because of any direct relationship between population density and crime but because such locations were the sites of least resistance.

The ecological expansion that allowed many people to move to higher-quality suburban housing and artists to congregate in central cities also created spaces for those whose proximity was also not required by nearby productive activities but who did not have the social power to be elsewhere. Ecological expansion, combined perhaps with the operation of commensal relations in the allocation of resources, has led to the segregation of population by firm, occupation, and residential area. As an extreme case, the diffusion of automobile transportation plus a "declining significance of race" in determining residence (Wilson 1978) has ironically led to residential hypersegregation along racial, educational, and income lines in the United States (Massey and Denton 1993). Employment in occupations and firms remains racially and gender segregated to a degree that cannot be explained by the qualifications of the respective groups (Jacobsen 1997; Petersen and Morgan 1995; Reskin and Cassirer 1996). Such hypersegregation may have led to the creation of an underclass—a set of people who are not just poor but effectively cut off from economic opportunities for themselves and their children. This situation can be seen in the spatial employment mismatches that still plague many U.S. cities. These mismatches are not merely spatial phenomena. They are intensified by commensal relations in the form of local governments that, under some conditions, may effectively undermine the educational opportunities for central-city residents (Kasarda 1989).

Sometimes, whole cities and regions have been made redundant by the industrial restructuring brought about by ecological expansion. Even so, the expansion process was not purely a matter of technological advance. Surplus population in rural areas and the U.S. South helped attract employment as transportation improvements allowed dispersion. Similarly, the declining mortality rates in what used to be called the Third World created a shift in the global locus of population. In 1950, two-thirds of the non-agricultural labor force in the world was found in the then industrialized countries. By 2000, fully two-thirds of a much larger nonagricultural labor force was to be found in the previously less-industrialized countries. (It is difficult to remember that a few short decades ago, labor shortages were so acute in Europe and North America that migrants were actively recruited and full employment was seen as a realistic policy goal.) As the technical and organizational aspects of transportation and communication technologies developed to the extent that close integration was possible, a surplus population was waiting for opportunities (Frobel, Heinrichs, and Kreye 1980).

HUMAN ECOLOGY IN PERSPECTIVE

Human ecology could be classified along with a larger family of theories that seek the explanation for patterns of social organization in the attempts of people to solve everyday problems. Several of the ecological postulates are, therefore, shared by other theoretical approaches in sociology. The assumption that social relations are rooted in biological needs is fundamental to the theories developed by Mead (1934), for example. The view of social organization as a set of exchanges of resources can be found in Blau (1964), among many others. The idea that social organization can be characterized as a complex pattern of relationships is developed by Nadel (1957) and others. Similarly, a division of social relationships into those that are directly concerned with productive work and those that are in reaction to the conditions of productive work is maintained by Homans (1950) and others. Human

ecology differs from other approaches to social organization perhaps in its focus on the holistic implications of these postulates, examining social organization as a population characteristic, rather than individual behavior or cultural meaning.

Human ecology's holistic stance is justified on the basis of the equifinality of micromotives. Becker (1976), for example, provided a dramatic demonstration to show that three very different decision rules—utility maximization, tradition-bound behavior, and random decisions—all produce the same aggregate patterns of behavior. Accordingly, Coleman (1990), White (1992), and Collins (2004) have each recently published comprehensive theoretical works examining how individual motivations and behavior aggregate into large-scale social organization. Each of those authors relied on very different assumptions and mechanisms to explain similar outcomes. By providing a broad overview of social process, macrosociology has much to contribute to the understanding of contemporary social organization.

One important aspect of that overview would be human ecology's perspective on power, disconnecting outcomes from actions and intentions. The ecological conception of dominance is somewhat broader than the concept of interpersonal power. Interpersonal power is usually defined in terms of person A compelling person B to act in accord with person A's will against B's own will for A's benefit. An ecological sense of power includes all that affects daily rhythms, the course of lives, occupational and residential distribution, and so on—that is, dominance is defined in terms of effect—the influencing of behavior—rather than in terms of intention or benefit. Often political institutions lack the means to overcome diffuse forces (Mann 1986). Ecology does not make assumptions about the stability of a set of actors either. In any form of large-scale social organization, there is likely to be a changing set of people and a changing set of role relations, and the connections between actions and outcomes is tenuous (March and Olsen 1976; Suttles 1990). By sampling on cities that were in some way successful, some of the literature on growth coalitions misinterprets the presence of particular types of actors for the causes of outcomes, overestimating the power of a small elite to determine events (Logan and Crowder 2002).

Because community is defined "not [by] like-mindedness, but [by] corporate action" (Park and Burgess 1921:42), the ecological approach to social organization informs the psychological, cultural, and moral aspects of human experience. The sociology of knowledge, for example, attempts to relate beliefs, attitudes, and values to social position (Mannheim 1936). Consequently, David Riesman (1950) based his division of tradition-directed, inner-directed, other-directed character types on the social positions and demographic rates linked to ecological organization. Important aspects of contemporary culture can be understood in the light of ecological expansion and the attendant population mismatches (Harvey 1989). More important, examining social relations from the perspective of functional integration allows for an understanding of moral ambiguity and cultural conflict in ways that theories based on a consensus normative order cannot (Alexander 1982:108). Such theories do not account for how values and norms are formed or for the reasons for conflict. A simple model positing that (1) in equilibrium "rule and action are one and the same" (Hawley 1986), (2) an occupational and demographic shift was induced by ecological expansion, and (3) a cultural lag exists (Ogburn 1964) appears to be quite useful in understanding many contemporary moral dilemmas (Hochschild 1989).

Today, we are increasingly tightly linked in a web of interdependences, yet many feel a loss of community. Browsing through the architecture and planning sections of a library or bookstore turns up many books suggesting that making our streets a little narrower, our settlements a bit more dense, our land uses somewhat more integrated, and our parking lots smaller would somehow rebuild community. Others suggest that living in central cities, perhaps in apartments instead of split-levels, traveling by foot or bus instead of automobile, and spending more time in coffee shops or bars instead of in living rooms would somehow heal our psyches. These books are full of drawings and photographs of buildings and streetscapes. They are largely empty of information on how the residents and users of the depicted spaces use their time and interact with others. Ecological theory suggests that such physical arrangements would produce, at best, simulacra of community. Human ecology shifts attention from the layout of buildings to the symbiotic and commensal relations that constitute community.

PATHS TO THE FUTURE

Human ecology posits that individuals adapt to their environments by forming symbiotic and commensal relationships of varying degrees of strength and pattern. It further postulates a collective tendency for the emergent pattern to maximize life to environmental limits, given the available technologies for subsistence and interaction. The heart of human ecology lies in understanding the web of life created by those relationships and how it is affected by particular changes. The process of ecological expansion has intertwined with population-activity mismatches to produce social change. Drawn by public interest and driven by intellectual comparative advantage, sociologists have explored human ecology in some directions and ignored others. Today, sociological human ecology could be characterized as a set of loose congeries of researchers, some of whom have independently rediscovered the basic ecological insights with no common research agenda (Freese 2001). It may be time for a new systematic synthesis. This chapter will close with just three questions for urban research—each, so far, only partially explored—that ecological theory may help address.

What effect do multilocational firms have on urban development? The present level of spatial integration probably owes as much to the consequent efforts to standardize products and procedures (as exemplified by the diverse activities of the International Standards Organization, which now goes so far as to specify standards for management methods) as to the jet plane and Internet themselves. Such possibilities suggest that cross-cutting forms of social organization—functionally integrated formal organizations and spatially delimited regions—have substantially changed the nature of spatial development. Physical break-in-bulk points were once also change-in-ownership points, requiring inspection, administration, and storage. To the extent that the former no longer implies the latter, the number of personnel required at break-in-bulk points diminishes (relative to what it otherwise would have been). Administration and goods movement may become progressively further decoupled from each other. Moreover, to the extent that the movement of goods is closely coordinated, the need for warehousing and other support facilities may be diminished. It is, for example, possible for a truck to arrive at a container port or airport just in time to whisk away or deliver a cargo, diminishing the functional importance of agglomeration. Cities are a collective method of economizing on time—but only one of several.

What will be the role of the so-called world cities as the global economy continues to expand? A handful of cities appear to be powerful command and control centers, based on finance and innovation in an expanding global economy. Power in the global system has proved to be ambiguous, however. Structural equivalence in trade and financial networks reduces the benefits of centrality. Trade surpluses in manufacturing goods have given "peripheral" countries considerable financial power. New York City has long ceased to be the primary center of scientific and technical innovation envisioned by Vernon (1960, 1966). Technological innovation occurs within a broad and expanding zone of indifference within wealthy societies. Research and development activities and other higher-order services appear to be relatively free of locational constraints. Attracting such activities has become an area of much tension for localities, indicating that research and development are not necessarily bound to particular places and that the locational factors are not well understood. Major multinational corporations are now headquartered in relatively small, seemingly remote towns with no apparent attenuation in accessibility. Much as some U.S. cities have become empty cores surrounded by prospering suburbs, the world system may develop in much the same way, with no clear role for the "world cities."

What is driving gentrification? Over the past several decades, there has been a small but perceptible flow of highly educated, mostly childless adults to a few select cities. Some have suggested that this is an expression of a "new class" or evidence of an exogenous culture change. Another possible explanation for this small migratory counterflow is based on the effects of the difficulties of matching people to jobs, which has led to progressively longer periods of education. In many countries, the surplus of educated labor has resulted in the externalization of employment ("boundaryless careers"), weak wages, and flat career trajectories, much as an oversupply of manufacturing capability in some sectors has led to the externalization of many activities (Piore and Sabel 1984). In some countries, a surplus of population has led to a pattern of inequality where the income variation within education, experience, and gender categories accounts for an increasing degree of total income equality. Some of those relatively underpaid service workers, unable to afford increasingly expensive suburban housing or to start families, may be congregating in a subset of American cities. From the point of view of the cities, this appears as gentrification, but from a larger point of view, it may be an expression of a "fear of falling" (Ehrenreich 1989).

46

THE SOCIOLOGY OF COMMUNITY

W. RICHARD GOE

Kansas State University

SEAN NOONAN

Harper College

As a sociological concept, community has been used to refer to a range of social phenomena. In a critical analysis of the concept, Joseph Gusfield (1975:xv–xvi) contended that there are two major usages of community. First, the concept is used to refer to a physical territory, or geographic area, where human beings reside and/or work. Second, community is used to refer to the quality or character of human relationships that bind persons to each other to form a social group. Many sociological studies of community focus on one of these definitions, while others have combined both usages. As will be described below, other studies have used a different definition of community altogether. Because of the diversity of definitions of community that have been developed, there has never been extensive agreement within the discipline of sociology on the precise meaning of the concept.

THE CONCEPTION OF COMMUNITY IN CLASSICAL SOCIAL THEORY

The origins of community as a sociological concept extend back to the birth of sociology as a discipline. In the nineteenth century, the ongoing development and spread of industrial capitalism in the European continent was prompting extensive social change. Gaining an understanding of the changes being wrought by this revolutionary economic system provided an important focus for the inquiries and writings of what are now known as the "classical" social theorists (see, e.g., Kumar 1978). Arguably the most important early social theorist in advancing the concept of community was the German sociologist Ferdinand Tönnies. A key observation of Tönnies ([1893] 1957) was that the development of industrial capitalism was associated with a change in the basis of social cohesion in society—that is, "the sentiments and motives which draw people to each other, keep them together, and induce them to joint action. . . . which resulting therefrom, make possible and sustain a common existence" (p. 237). The classic statement of these ideas was Tönnies's book *Gemeinschaft und Gesellschaft,* first published in 1887. In English, *Gemeinschaft und Gesellschaft* was literally translated as *Community and Society.*

For Tönnies ([1893] 1957), the basis of social cohesion was termed the *collective will* (analogous to group norms), which sets behavioral expectations and governs social relationships among individuals forming a social group. Tönnies contended that the basis of social cohesion was undergoing a transition from *Gemeinschaft* (community) to *Gesellschaft* (society). These concepts were developed as ideal types. Community represented the traditional basis of social cohesion, characterized by what Tönnies termed the "natural will." Simply put, social relationships guided by the natural will were characterized by emotional attachment, sentiment, intimacy, and shared characteristics such as kinship or religious beliefs. In contrast, society was viewed by Tönnies as the emergent basis of social cohesion characterized by the "rational will." Social relationships guided by the rational will were characterized by indifference, rational calculation, competition, and self-interest. Tönnies contended that with the development and advance of capitalism, social relationships based on community were declining and becoming subordinate to the rational will as the primary basis of social cohesion.

This dimension of Tönnies's ([1893] 1957) work reflects two important themes that would shape later developments in community sociology. The first was the view of community as representing a particular quality of social relationships among members of a social group involving emotional attachment, intimacy, and sentiment. Later theorists equated social relationships in community, or "communal relations" (see, e.g., Fischer 1977:8; Nisbet 1966:47), as being consistent with Charles Horton Cooley's (1909) concept of a primary group characterized by close, intimate, face-to-face interaction or Mark Granovetter's (1973) concept of strong interpersonal ties among a group of social actors. A second theme was that community was declining, or in the process of being "lost" (see, e.g., Nisbet 1966; Fischer 1977; Wellman 1979)—that is, the decline of community represented an important dimension of social change in industrial nations that had developed capitalist market economies.

Given that the *Gemeinschaft-Gesellschaft* dichotomy was developed as an ideal type, Tönnies ([1893] 1957) also discussed ideal prototypes of social forms that were "*Gemeinschaft*-like" or "*Gesellschaft*-like." In his discussion of social organizations and corporate bodies (pp. 257–259), Tönnies stated that the ideal *Gemeinschaft* prototype was the rural, agrarian village. In contrast, the ideal *Gesellschaft* prototype was the city. This dimension of Tönnies's work helped set the precedent for viewing community as a location, or geographic area of human settlement. However, it simultaneously advanced the view that communities must be small in size with members living in close geographic proximity to one another. Whether or not these represent necessary conditions for community later became a point of debate in community sociology (see, e.g., Wellman 1979).

In large part, the conceptions of community developed by other classical theorists were consistent with that of Tönnies ([1893] 1957). For example, Max Weber (1978:40–43) defined communal relationships as being based on tradition, or the affectual and emotional feelings of the parties involved. In his discussion of "political communities," Weber (1978:901–904) also recognized the territorial or geographic dimension of community. Building on the early conceptions of community, Georg Simmel ([1902–1903] 1950) examined the impersonal and calculative nature of social relationships found in the metropolis, which contrasted deeply with those found in small-town and rural life. The classical conceptions of community framed much of the debate in community sociology over the course of the twentieth century.

SIGNIFICANT DEVELOPMENTS IN COMMUNITY SOCIOLOGY DURING THE 20TH CENTURY

1920 to 1950

During the first several decades of the twentieth century in the United States, the classical conceptions of community developed by European sociologists influenced the early development of what eventually became more broadly construed as urban and community sociology. Highly influential in this process were the theoretical conceptions of and empirical research conducted by sociologists at the University of Chicago, which were primarily focused on understanding the causes, processes, and consequences of urbanization. This was highly significant at this time because America had undergone several decades of rapid urbanization and had evolved into an urban society.

Human Ecology and the Chicago School

Adapting concepts from plant and animal ecology, members of the Chicago School of urban sociology developed the theoretical framework of human ecology. Within this framework, the human community was conceived as a response by human beings to their need to secure resources from the environment and ensure their survival. As described by Roderick McKenzie ([1925] 1967),

> The human community has its inception in the traits of human nature and the needs of human beings. Man is a gregarious animal: he cannot live alone; he is relatively weak and needs not only the company of other human associates but shelter and protection from the elements as well. (P. 65)

Of particular concern was how the human community was organized and structured across geographic space. A key proposition of human ecology was that the human community was characterized by the ecological processes of competition, dominance, and succession (Park 1936). It was contended that human beings compete to determine how space in the community will be used. Through competition, a community is divided into a mosaic of "natural areas" characterized, or dominated, by particular population groups and/or land use patterns. This conception not only placed emphasis on the community as a physical territory but also extended it to encompass a system of social units (e.g., organizations, groups) through which specific human populations secure the resources needed to sustain their survival.

While members of the Chicago School extended further the theoretical ideas about the differences in human relationships in the context of a city versus a rural village (see, e.g., Wirth 1938), the ecological conception of the human community shifted emphasis away from community as a particular quality of social relationships involving emotional attachment, intimacy, and sentiment. Moreover, in regard to the territorial dimension, the human community was not limited to small villages with members living in close propinquity. Nor was it necessarily circumscribed by the defined geopolitical boundaries of a village or even a city. Rather, the geographic size of the ecological community was based on how the structure of organizations and institutions used by a specific population for sustenance was distributed across geographic space. In subsequent work, proponents of human ecology contended that the geographic scope of the human community was evolving beyond the city to encompass metropolitan areas or regions (see, e.g., McKenzie 1933; Bogue [1949] 1961).

Community Studies

While human ecology was rising to prominence as an approach to analyzing the human community, another important research tradition was being developed that became known as the community study (Bell and Newby 1971). At a basic level, community studies have typically employed a conception of community as a geographic territory, although other conceptual dimensions of community may be analyzed as well. Simply put, in conducting a community study, a particular town, village, neighborhood, city, or suburb is selected as a site for case study. A combination of research methods is then used to perform an in-depth analysis of social life within the community. These methods typically include field research and ethnography. Aspects of social life within the territory of the community that are studied may include (a) the nature of social relations among community members; (b) local organizations, institutions, and aspects of culture that are important for sustaining community members; (c) the local stratification system or class structure, including the distribution of wealth and power, race or ethnicity; (d) community boundaries; and (e) the psychosocial characteristics of community members, among others.

Credit for the community study has been given to Robert and Helen Lynd (1929) in their pioneering study of Muncie, Indiana, which was conducted in the 1920s and published under the pseudonym *Middletown* (Bell and Newby 1971:82–83). However, members of the Chicago School of urban sociology also contributed to this approach through a series of in-depth studies of "natural areas" (Zorbaugh [1926] 1961) within the city of Chicago (see, e.g., Thrasher 1927; Wirth 1928; Shaw et al. 1929; Zorbaugh 1929). These studies have been followed by an ongoing series of community studies that have focused on analyzing social life in cities, smaller subareas of cities such as neighborhoods, and small towns and rural villages (for an overview, see Bell and Newby 1971). The community study approach also became prominent in the subdiscipline of rural sociology, which placed more emphasis on finding applied solutions to problems faced by rural towns and villages in the United States and abroad (Wilkinson 1991:41–51). Over the long term, the community study

became an institutionalized method within the sociological study of community that continues to be used in the contemporary era (see, e.g., Anderson 1990; Duncan 1999; Salamon 2003; Small 2004).

1951 to 1990

By the middle of the twentieth century, the composite knowledge base of classical social theory, human ecology, community studies, and community research in rural sociology provided a plethora of different definitions of the concept of community. The lack of consensus over the meaning of the concept prompted George Hillery (1955) to conduct a content analysis of community definitions that had been used in 94 previous studies to determine if there were areas of agreement. Hillery found that 90 of the 94 studies agreed that community consisted of a group of persons engaging in social interaction, 73 of the 94 studies agreed that community consisted of a group of persons engaging in social interaction who have a "common tie or ties," and 70 of the 94 studies agreed that community consisted of a geographic area.

Taken together, 69 of the 94 studies agreed that community consisted of a group of persons (a) engaging in social interaction, (b) within a geographic area, and (c) having a common tie or ties. Hillery (1955) used the term *common tie* to refer to a wide range of phenomena, including a common lifestyle, culture, work, and beliefs; kinship; "consciousness of kind" (as elaborated below, a common psychological identification with a group); shared norms, values, or goals; and the use of shared institutions. Among the set of studies examined, the definitions of community employed by the human ecologists were found to differ the most (p. 119).

Taken together, the areas of agreement identified by Hillery (1955) represented a much less restrictive conception of community than that advanced by Tönnies ([1893] 1957) about half a century earlier. First, the relationships among the group of persons engaged in interaction did not have to consist of strong, primary ties based on emotional attachment, intimacy, and sentiment as specified by Tönnies. Rather, community members could be more loosely attached through sharing common lifestyles, beliefs, work, goals, or institutions, for example. Second, the size of the geographic territory of a community was unrestricted. Communities were not limited to a small agrarian village with persons living in close proximity to one another as specified by Tönnies. Over the next several decades, several important theoretical paradigms in sociology provided the basis for the development of new applications to the sociological study of community.

Structural Functionalism

Twentieth-century developments in structural-functionalist theory contributed to the development of several important theoretical approaches to the analysis of community. The first of these was a reformulation of human ecology theory by Amos Hawley. The initial statement of Hawley's (1950) reformulation was first published under the title *Human Ecology: A Theory of Community Structure*. After several decades of research and critique, interest in the human ecology framework developed by the Chicago School had waned (Schwab 1982:23–25). Hawley resolved problematic aspects of the original theory by employing a structural-functionalist approach and helped regenerate interest in using human ecology as a framework for community and urban research. In his restatement of the theory, Hawley (1950) defined community as "the structure of relationships through which a localized population provides its daily requirements" (p. 180). The community was conceived as a structure of functionally differentiated strata, comprised of connected communal units that perform functions contributing toward the sustenance of a localized population and its adaptation to the environment. Functional interdependence was viewed as providing the integrative force and basis for social cohesion in the community (p. 209).

Like the traditional ecological theory developed by members of the Chicago School, Hawley's (1950) restatement of the theory viewed community as consisting of a structured system of social units through which a human population adapts to the environment and secures the resources required for its survival. However, one key difference was that he de-emphasized the role of competition in influencing the structure of the community, choosing instead to focus on the functional interdependencies that developed among social units comprising the community (Berry and Kasarda 1977:12). Later termed *contemporary ecology* (see, e.g., Berry and Kasarda 1977), Hawley's reformulation contributed toward the maintenance of human ecology as a central theoretical paradigm in urban sociology.

A second important development related to structural functionalism was the application of Talcott Parsons's (1951) social systems theory to the analysis of community. Parsons defined a social system as

> a plurality of individual actors interacting with each other in a situation which has at least a physical or environmental aspect, actors who are motivated in terms of a tendency to the "optimization of gratification" and whose relation to their situations, including each other, is defined and mediated in terms of a system of culturally structured and shared symbols. (Pp. 5–6)

In applying this to a community, the notion of interaction among a plurality of "actors" was extended to include interaction among organizations and other social groups. The community was defined as a geographic territory that contained a social system. As conceived by Charles P. Loomis and J. Allan Beegle (1957), "The community may be defined as a social system encompassing a territorial unit within which members carry on most of the day-to-day activities necessary in meeting common needs" (p. 22).

Within the social systems framework, the community was conceived as a constituent system of the larger inclusive macrosystems of society. Roland L. Warren was one of the key proponents of this approach. Warren's ([1963] 1978) seminal work *The Community in America* defined a community as "that combination of social units and systems that perform the major social functions having locality relevance" (p. 9). Stated more clearly, the community system serves to provide people with "daily local access to those broad areas of activity (i.e. functions) that are necessary in day-to-day living" (p. 9).

Warren ([1963] 1978:163) used the term "vertical pattern" of the community to refer to the structural and functional relations of its various social units and subsystems to social systems exogenous to the territorial boundaries of the community. In contrast, he used the term "horizontal pattern" to refer to the structural and functional relations of the social units and subsystems comprising the community to each other (p. 164). Reflecting a different variant on the "community lost" thesis first posited by Tönnies ([1893] 1957), Warren ([1963] 1978) contended that as a result of a set of social change processes he termed "The Great Change," U.S. communities were losing their local autonomy in controlling the key functions that sustain the lives of their members and becoming increasingly dependent on the vertical pattern of the community to sustain the local population (pp. 52–95).

In addition to having a foundation in structural functionalism, a common thread between contemporary human ecology and the social systems approach to community is the view of community as consisting of a structured system of systemically linked social units that perform interdependent functions required to sustain the lives of people within a bounded geographic territory. In contrasting Hawley's (1950) reformulation of human ecology with Loomis and Beegle's (1957) or Warren's ([1963] 1978) social systems perspective, one difference is that social systems theorists appear to accept Tönnies's ([1893] 1957) restrictive view that community must consist of a small territorial settlement with necessary external resources being acquired through vertical systemic linkages. In contrast, Hawley's conception appears to place less restriction on the geographic scope of the community, which is viewed as capable of expanding to incorporate the social units to which the community became vertically linked.

Symbolic Interactionism

The twentieth-century development of symbolic interactionism as an important theoretical paradigm in sociology (for a collection of central works, see Manis and Meltzer 1967) also found application in the analysis of community. In general, studies of community employing concepts drawn from symbolic interactionism contend that a community is socially constructed by a group of individuals who identify themselves as members of a group with which they share common characteristics and have specific rights and obligations. This approach is exemplified by Joseph Gusfield (1975:44, 51), who contended that the classical theorists treated a community as a fixed social object that automatically impinged on the individual. Gusfield contended that community must instead be viewed as a process by which individuals symbolically construct identities as members of a group.

Drawing on the notion of "consciousness of kind" developed by Franklin Giddings (1922) and later referenced by Hillery (1955) (also termed *community sentiment* or *community attachment*—for a review, see Poplin 1979:18–22), community represents a psychosocial entity that is symbolically constructed and reconstructed over time by a group of individuals who define themselves as group members. Identification with the community group is facilitated by the emergence of group symbols such as a group name, a particular appearance or mode of dress, or other distinguishing characteristics. The symbolic construction of a community promotes a sense of participating in a shared history among members and creates awareness that members have particular rights and obligations in how they act in relation to other members compared to nonmembers (Gusfield 1975:23–52).

Symbolic identification of an individual with a community group aligns with the less restrictive definition of community deduced from Hillery's (1955) analysis discussed above. Gusfield (1975:32, 43) notes that although residing in proximity within a small territory can help promote the development of symbolically constructed communities, such communities also exist at broader geographic scales (e.g., national identities). Furthermore, symbolically constructed communities do not necessarily require face-to-face interaction and close, primary ties among members. Rather, such a community requires only that individuals identify themselves as group members. Even in the absence of strong primary ties with other members, attachment to symbolically constructed communities by the individual may become "primordial" (Geertz 1963; Fischer 1977), where the needs and the will of the individual become subordinate to the needs and the will of the collective (Gusfield 1975:49). This represents one way in which community can impose social order and control over the pursuit of individual self-interest.

Marxism and Political Economy

During the 1970s, a movement to examine community through a broadly Marxian and/or institutional political-economy framework began to gather momentum. Analyses of community taking this approach have typically employed the definition of community as a geographic territory. The focus is then placed on how the growth of the community and the spatial configuration of the community are influenced by the process of capital accumulation. As part of this process, special emphasis is typically given to the role of the state, class relations, and business cycles in the capitalist market economy.

Exemplifying this approach, Gordon (1977) illustrated the role of industrialists in drawing central city and suburban city boundaries in such a manner as to escape the social costs of production (pollution, etc.) and, crucially, operate to reduce possible worker resistance via a repertoire of spatial-political strategies. Castells (1977, 1983) emphasized the differential dynamics at work in the consumption norms of elites and the working class in cities. Additionally, Castells posited a structural contradiction between the need to increase profits for capital and the need to reproduce labor within cities. In highlighting this contradiction, Castells brought attention to the role of the welfare state, urban planning, subsidized housing, public education, and recreation as efforts to reconcile this inherent contradiction at work in the fabric of urban places under capitalism.

David Harvey provides an important exemplar of what could be called "classical" Marxian community studies. Working within a political-economy-of-place model, Harvey (1982, 1985, 1990) identifies the interactions between the multiple circuits of capital accumulation and the specific geographic-spatial features in the built environment of urban places. For Harvey, the built environment experiences waves of growth and decline as capital investment shifts between the productive, built environment, and state/tertiary circuits of capital. Harvey deploys a fairly traditional Marxist political-economy model to explain the circulation of capital between production, consumption, and the state. Then, Harvey adds a spatial-geographic component and theorizes the movement of capital across places in response to the fluctuations in the rate of profit. In essence, cities, towns, and neighborhoods rise and fall as capital moves from place to place seeking out a geographic innovation or "spatial fix" that operates alongside technological innovations and financial innovations of capitalist restructuring of spatial and social relations in the pursuit of profit (Harvey 1982, 1985).

Operating under a more ecumenical framework that built on human ecology and neo-Marxian approaches to place, Molotch (1976) and Logan and Molotch (1987) focus on the strategies of different social actors as they variously organize, cooperate, and compete in the social construction of places. For example, residents and workers tend to see place in terms of concrete, heterogeneous, use value as homes, parks, places of work, and places of worship. In contrast, developers, realtors, business owners, and finance capitalists tend to see place in terms of abstract, homogeneous exchange value as real estate, as property, and as places in which to capture profits. The dominant form of place-based, political-economic organization in urban communities are growth machines, which Logan and Molotch define as "an apparatus of interlocking pro-growth associations and governmental units" (p. 37).

The specific composition of actual growth machines varies from case to case but usually includes local government, real estate developers, local media, bankers, construction firms, and, occasionally, industrial capitalists. Most often, growth machines are united behind an ideological doctrine of free-market land use. As such, growth machines operate to legitimate and facilitate profitable real estate investment, which in turn will have secondary cumulative effects in the local real estate market, corporate investment, and labor markets. Growth machines work to secure rents from changing land use patterns and, in doing so, have the effect of spatially (re)organizing urban communities in such a way that place entrepreneurs are able to internalize the benefits of urban growth while externalizing the social, cultural, and political costs of that same growth to ordinary residents of the wider community. Recent studies in growth machine research have investigated the applicability of the model to more contemporary situations, suburban communities, and urban communities in the United Kingdom; Orange County, California; and Israel (Jonas and Wilson 1999; Logan and Crowder 2002).

CONTEMPORARY TRENDS AND DEVELOPMENTS IN COMMUNITY SOCIOLOGY

Over the past several decades, community research has continued to represent an important focus within sociology and related fields. As such, empirical and theoretical work engaging the various forms of community has both contributed to and reflected many of the important developments within the discipline. Key areas of interest in contemporary community sociology include the Internet and online communities; the communitarian movement; race-ethnicity-gender and community; and the relationship(s) between culture, consumption, and the development of urban communities.

Liberated and Online Communities

Over the past several decades, the theory and methods of social network analysis have been applied to the study of community. With this approach, community is viewed as a social network of primary relationships among a set of social actors. An important proponent of this approach has been Barry Wellman (1979), who employed a social network approach to examine what he termed "the community question." In essence, the community question seeks to understand how industrialization, urbanization, and bureaucratization have affected the structure and organization of communal networks (pp. 1201–1202).

The conception of community first advanced by Tönnies ([1893] 1957) implied that communal social relations were predominant only in small, agrarian villages. His description of these villages suggested that they were characterized by densely knit, solidary networks of communal social relations among residents who were connected on the basis of kinship, religion, and work. Simultaneously, Tönnies advanced the "community lost" argument (Wellman 1979:1204) that such communities were declining with the growth of industrial capitalism and urbanization. In contradiction to this thesis, community research conducted during the twentieth century found that dense, solidary networks of communal relationships persisted within small, territorial areas (e.g., neighborhoods) of large cities (see, e.g., Gans 1962; Liebow 1967; Suttles 1968). In effect, this presented the "community saved" argument (Wellman 1979:1205–206) in that such communal networks persisted with capitalist development and could be found in large cities as well as small towns and villages. In either case, close geographic proximity was assumed to be essential to the maintenance and formation of communal networks.

In contrast to these perspectives, Wellman (1979:1206–208) advanced the "community liberated" argument, which contended that as a result of the spatial separation of residence, workplace, and kinship; the increasing scale of urban communities; high rates of residential mobility; and low-cost, proficient communications and transportation technologies, communal networks are increasingly characterized by sparsely knit, interconnected networks of primary ties that are dispersed across geographic space. Thus, community has been liberated because close geographic proximity is no longer essential to the formation and maintenance of communal relationships.

If the automobile, airplane, and telephone facilitated the emergence of the liberated community, then the development of the Internet during the 1990s has accelerated the development of this social form and prompted the transition from group-based to networked societies (Castells 1996). Wellman and others (see, e.g., Wellman et al. 1996; Wellman 2001; Wellman and Haythornthwaite 2002) have documented the growth and maturation of the Internet. Hampton and Wellman (2002) contend that Internet communities are important social networks but not particularly special or separate from other aspects of social life. Rather, group-based solidarities are progressively being replaced by an Internet- (and other information technology) mediated matrix of networked individualism. Shared community, neighborhoods, and face-to-face interactions are being subsumed by multiple, partially personalized, geographically dispersed, and computer-mediated networks.

Within this model, Hampton and Wellman (2002) suggest an emerging spatial configuration that mixes global and local factors, a kind of "glocalization." Castells suggests that businesses (1996), organized crime syndicates (1998), and social movements of both the left and the right (1997) have used information technology and the dynamics of networked relationships to go global in both the scale and the scope of their activities.

The Communitarian Movement

The concept of community was central to a political movement that gathered momentum in the United States during the 1990s. Called the "communitarian movement," an important focus was to address the decline in civility in American social life. A key voice in the movement was Amitai Etzioni, who founded the Communitarian Network in 1993. In his 1995 presidential address to the American Sociological Association, Etzioni (1996) outlined his communitarian perspective. Community was defined as a network of affect-laden relationships among a group of individuals that is characterized by a high density of acquaintanceship (Freudenburg 1986) and a commitment to a set of shared values, norms, and meanings and a shared history and identity (i.e., consciousness of kind or communal attachment) (Etzioni (1996:5).

One of Etzioni's (1996) key propositions was that community is defined by a third criterion, "responsiveness"—that is, to be "authentic," a community must be highly responsive in meeting the "true" needs of *all* community members, both in the substance of its core values and in its social formation (pp. 1–5). In contrast, a community that responds to and meets the true needs of some members or groups but not others is termed a "partial" community. The partial community, therefore, represents an imposed social order on those members whose true needs are not met.

Etzioni (1996:5–9) contended that communities command centripetal forces that seek to induce members to act on behalf of the community (e.g., perform community service). In contradiction to such forces are centrifugal forces that seek to induce members to act on behalf of their self-interest. Both these forces vie with one another for dominance and are inversely related. If centripetal forces become too dominant, then the order imposed by the community will become too restrictive and will not allow the true needs of individual community members to be met, thereby resulting in unhappiness and misery. If centrifugal forces become too dominant, then the community will decline, and anarchy and conflict will reign as individuals attempt to benefit their self-interest at the expense of the interests of other individuals. Etzioni contended that in meeting the true needs of all community members, the authentic community balances the two forces, thereby providing for a more civil society.

In attempting to influence public policy and political beliefs, the communitarian movement has not been strongly embraced by either side of the political spectrum. On the one hand, the communitarian platform has been excoriated by the left, in part because it de-emphasizes the important role of the state in redressing inequality and injustice and other social problems created by a capitalist market economy. Instead, this responsibility is shifted to the community level and aligns with the principle of "devolution" favored by the conservative right. On the other hand, the communitarian platform has also been criticized by the right because of its emphasis on inhibiting and subordinating the pursuit of individual self-interest to the needs of the community. The notion that individuals have a social responsibility to the community that may take precedence over their own wants and desires aligns with the ideology of liberalism. Because of its discordance with both sides of the political spectrum, the platform of the communitarian movement has thus far not achieved a strong degree of influence in guiding political discourse and policy making in the United States.

Race, Ethnicity, Gender, and Community

Although interest in the interface between race, ethnicity, and community can be traced back to both the Chicago School and community study scholars, recent efforts in the area have been especially fruitful in examining the combined vectors of identity, interaction, institutions, and place-based territorial communities. Duneier (1999) uses the interaction codes of identity that social actors deploy in face-to-face encounters on the street to illuminate the micro-macro linkages at work in the environs of urban communities. He examines the lives of "unhoused" street vendors working in Lower Manhattan, New York. Key themes that emerge from Duneier's research include the role of local government in shaping regulation and repression; the emergent norms that shape vendor-to-vendor relations; and the layering of race, class, and gender in anonymous street interactions. Duneier describes how homeless panhandlers are able to engage in public harassment and "interactional vandalism" of women *as women* irrespective of the woman's class position.

Operating at a more macro and cross-cultural level, Spain (1992) shows how community spaces are gendered (and most often segregated), resulting in male privilege and lowered status for women. The dichotomies of public/private, work/home, market/family, and masculine/feminine intersect and overlap in a web of spatial power relations. In an engaging longitudinal ethnography, Naples (1998) has examined the experiences of women community workers in New York and Philadelphia from 1964 to 1974. Naples's study found that women involved in community-based antipoverty programs provided important paid and unpaid work for their communities. Additionally, Naples suggests that this work constituted a kind of "activist-mothering" that broadens and links the concepts of family and community together in a continuum of relations that include family, neighbors, neighborhood, and local schools.

Anderson (1990) describes how black-white interactions in public settings involve a variety of symbolic exchanges involving racial stereotyping and symbolic border work. Anderson (1990, 2000) also traces the vectors of racism, poverty, drugs, violence, and gentrification that plague poor urban African American communities. Logan and Stearns (1981), Logan and Schneider (1984), and Logan and Crowder (2002) have examined racial segregation, racial change, and ethnic enclaves in American suburbs from the 1960s until the present. In a similar vein, Massey and Denton (1993) argue that high and persistent levels of residential racial segregation play a crucial role in keeping disproportionate numbers of people of color mired in communities characterized by unemployment, poverty, and generalized social exclusion. Portes and Stepik (1993) and Bobo (2000) examined the specific racial-ethnic configurations at work in Miami and Los Angeles, respectively. In both cases, the development of these communities has been crucially shaped by immigrant groups from Asia, the Caribbean region, and Central and South America, with multidimensional ramifications that affect the economy, culture, and polity of these cities. However, immigrant groups have been more successful in capturing political and economic power in Miami than they have been in Los Angeles (cf. Portes and Stepik 1993; Bobo 2000).

Culture, Consumption, and the Development of Communities

An important line of contemporary community research has focused on the role of culture and cultural industries in economic development at the community level and in determining where development takes place. Sharon Zukin (1982, 1991, 1995) has examined how cultural industries have become increasingly important in the economies of U.S. urban communities, reflecting a shift of urban landscapes away from processes of production to an emphasis on the organization of consumption. As a consequence of new innovations in technology, finance, and business organization, Zukin argues that the relationship of market and place has become delinked. Capital now flows and circulates from place to place with increasing velocity. Cities emphasizing production (such as Detroit and Pittsburgh) have declined, while other cities oriented toward culture and consumption (e.g., Los Angeles and Miami) have risen to become leading exemplars of contemporary urbanism.

Change in the urban landscape is now driven by the appropriation of vernacular cultural forms by market forces. Urban factories are being replaced by trendy lofts, gentrification, as well as bohemian, new-wave, and niche consumer subcultures. At the same time, Disneyland (and by extension, Los Angeles) has appropriated the folklore, fantasy, and archetypes of mythic Americana and has transformed them from popular vernacular discourses into symbolic facades for power (Zukin 1991). Furthermore, the changing modalities of ludic consumption also reflect these same dynamics. Zukin contrasts the now defunct social-compact populism of Fordist or Keynesian Coney Island in the mid-twentieth century with the more recent growth of Las Vegas as a freewheeling artifice of spectacle under the logic of a more flexible and privatized free-market moment in the development of capitalism.

Research by Terry Nichols Clark contends that cultural amenities are the driving force of how and where people work, invest, accumulate, and aggregate, resulting in urban communities becoming entertainment machines (Lloyd

and Clark 2001; Clark 2004). For Clark (2004) and Richard Florida (2002, 2005), cultural amenities such as coffee shops and pubs, bookstores and music venues, film houses and theater districts, ethnic diversity and queer communities act as magnets for highly skilled, autonomous, and creative people. In turn, the availability of creative people (termed the *creative class* by Florida) influences where economic growth takes place and drives urban and regional growth. The research by Florida (2002, 2003, 2005) suggests that the creative class values a conception of community that is moving away from the more traditional notion of community characterized by strong primary ties of family, kin, and neighborhood. In its place, the creative class is seeking out places where community relationships are characterized by weaker ties and quasi-anonymous inclusiveness, openness, diversity, tolerance, and individuality (Florida 2005:30–31, 43–44).

THE RELEVANCE OF COMMUNITY IN 21ST CENTURY SOCIAL LIFE

As a central topic during the nascent stages of the development of sociology, community has been a topic of research and discourse for over two centuries (Bell and Newby 1971:21). In addition to sociology, and the related subdiscipline of rural sociology, concern with the concept of community has extended across disciplinary boundaries to include specialized fields such as community planning, social work, community health, and community development. As illustrated in this essay, there has been a lack of precision in how the concept has been defined by sociologists because it has been used to reference a range of different behavioral phenomena. As sociology enters the twenty-first century, it is useful to assess whether the concept of community remains relevant to the study of contemporary social life.

Defined as a geographic territory, community is clearly relevant to social life in the twenty-first century because humans still predominantly tend to settle in politically bounded, geographic spaces. At issue is whether communities must be limited to small territories as initially specified by Tönnies ([1893] 1957) in his identification of an empirical prototype of the concept. If so, then community truly is declining. While small agrarian villages broadly similar to those found in Tönnies's time are more prevalent in underdeveloped nations, they continue to disappear in number as urbanization progresses, either growing into larger towns and cities or stagnating and declining in population and size. Twentieth-century sociologists adapted the notion of the territorial community to include cities, subsections of cities such as neighborhoods, extensions of cities such as suburbs, and entire metropolitan areas. Assuming that these larger territorial settlements are indeed communities, it would appear that territorial communities are thriving in the early years of the twenty-first century.

In the developed nations, particularly the United States, a key change during the twentieth century was the ongoing growth in the size and geographic scale of territorial communities through suburban sprawl and the outward expansion of metropolitan communities. In highly urbanized areas, consolidated metropolitan areas have been formed from the outward growth of contiguous metropolitan areas with little to no undeveloped space in between. No matter what their size, human territorial settlements are virtually always overseen by some form of local, territorially bound government. The territorial community represents a key focus of public policy as local governments attempt to regulate and control local social conditions, including such issues as zoning and the construction of the built environment, education, crime, public health, and the development of the economy.

Defined as a network of intimate, primary relationships between humans involving emotional attachment and sentiment, community continues to be relevant to contemporary social life. It has been argued that the feelings of belonging and unity with one's fellow human beings and the feelings of social support, emotional attachment, trust, and intimacy that come from a network of communal relationships are an essential human need that influences the well-being of the individual (see, e.g., Stueve and Gerson 1977:79; Keller 2003:3–11). For this reason alone, the need to form and maintain communal relationships is just as relevant in the twenty-first century as in previous historical eras. One facet of communal networks that has ostensibly changed at the end of the twentieth century is the extent to which the formation and maintenance of communal relationships is limited by geographic proximity.

The research of Wellman and his colleagues (Wellman 1979, 2001; Wellman et al. 1996; Wellman and Haythornthwaite 2002) suggests that personalized communal networks that are geographically dispersed and mediated through information technology are becoming increasingly prevalent. This trend is likely to continue in the twenty-first century as the technology is further refined and becomes increasingly accepted as a mode for conducting human exchange. However, despite the growing prevalence of online relationships, propinquity and face-to-face interaction are likely to continue to be important in the formation and/or maintenance of communal relationships. This is because the degree of intimacy and familiarity allowed by online relationships is limited due to the constraints of the technology. While residing in close proximity for extended periods of time may no longer be an essential feature of communal networks, the greater intimacy and familiarity provided by face-to-face interaction, for however limited a period of time, is likely to continue to be important to communal relationships.

Defined as a structured system of social units that functions to provide necessary resources to sustain a human population or group, community also remains relevant to social life in the twenty-first century. A key change that has occurred over the past several decades is that the geographic scale of these systems has expanded and become increasingly international in scope as part of the process of "globalization." Theoretical conceptualizations of this form of community developed by human ecologists and social systems theorists did not explicitly address the fact that within these communal systems, resources are predominantly allocated through markets within the context of a capitalist market economy (see, e.g., Logan and Molotch 1987:5). Contemporary research on global "commodity chains" or "value chains" can be viewed as empirically describing subcomponents of communal systems for populations in the United States. This research documents how these systems have become global in scale as U.S. firms have shifted manufacturing and services to China, India, and other nation states in an effort to increase profits and increase their competitive advantage (see, e.g., Gereffi 1994; Dossani and Kenney 2003; Gereffi et al. 2005).

An important implication of this process is that the success of international-scale systems in allocating resources to human populations in the United States is dependent on stable trade relationships and international political stability. The critical issue concerns how easily the capacity to produce goods and services required to sustain the U.S. populace can be re-created within the United States, particularly if large-scale political instability does ensue at some future point. In effect, while globalization may increase economic efficiency, it comes with the risk of disruption to the communal systems that sustain the U.S. population.

Defined as a process by which individuals symbolically construct identities as members of a group, community still has relevance to twenty-first-century social life. It is reasonable to assume that within the social context of the contemporary world, individuals define themselves as belonging to multiple symbolically constructed communities that may or may not be restricted in geographic scale. Furthermore, membership of these communities helps compose an individual's self-identity. Some of these may be loose affiliations that impose few obligations on community members and are relatively benign in terms of their effect on social life (e.g., membership in the national community of Chicago Cubs fans). Others may represent stronger affiliations that involve extensive obligations and impose a strong social order on members, perhaps involving primordial attachment (Geertz 1963; Fischer 1977), where the self-interest of the individual becomes subordinate to the interests of the group (e.g., the community of fundamentalist Christians or the community of fundamentalist Muslims). These two symbolically constructed communities, in particular, have had significant impacts on social life in the United States and around the world in the initial years of the twenty-first century.

In closing, all the social phenomena that have been abstracted from social life and defined under the concept of community continue to have relevance for understanding social life at the beginning of the twenty-first century.

Human beings continue to predominantly settle in politically bounded, geographic territories; they continue to need and seek to establish intimate, primary ties with others; they continue to organize systems to extract, produce, and allocate resources needed to ensure the survival of the species; and they continue to identify and affiliate themselves with social groups. Despite the lack of precision as a social-scientific concept, community, in all its forms, continues to be relevant to the study of social behavior in the twenty-first century.

47

RURAL SOCIOLOGY

LINDA LOBAO
The Ohio State University

Rural sociology is a unique field. Woven into its development are attributes that many sociologists now recognize as central to disciplinary advancement. These attributes include a tradition of cross-disciplinary linkages, strong public policy influence, concern with social justice and public sociology, and interest in geographic space. Another unique feature is that rural sociology's institutional development leaves it perhaps the most independent of all sociological subfields. In fact, some analysts see it as a distinct discipline.

In this chapter, I trace rural sociology's development, discuss the resulting knowledge base, and consider its future prospects. The substantive scope of rural sociology is large and varied. One way of understanding the field is through the lens of geographic space. Attention to social life outside the spatial settings conventionally studied in sociology is the central element linking the diverse concerns of rural sociologists.

ORIGINS OF RURAL SOCIOLOGY

The roots of rural sociology are firmly tied to U.S. historical events and policy interventions. As Bertrand (1982) notes, rural sociology "has the distinction of being a truly American invention" (p. xi). The institutional infrastructure for establishing rural sociology was formed with the Morrill Land-Grant Act, signed by President Lincoln in 1862. The act set aside federal land in each state for building public colleges for the study of "agriculture and the mechanical arts," for extending the university system beyond elite private or religiously based institutions. Related legislation added other components. Research infrastructure, including access to federal funding pipelines, was established through the Agricultural Experiment Stations created in each state by the Hatch Act of 1887. Public outreach—bringing academic research directly into public use—was institutionalized through the Cooperative Extension Service, created by the Smith Lever Act of 1914. The Second Morrill Act of 1890 created 17 historically black land-grant colleges, and in 1994, 29 Native American tribal colleges were given land-grant status. Today, 105 land-grant institutions award one-third of all U.S. bachelor's degrees and 60 percent of all doctorates (Jischke 2004:3). This mix of public infrastructure is important not only in how rural sociology emerged but also in how it operates as a field of study and profession today.

In the first decade of the last century, more than a third of the U.S. population lived on farms, making it a key constituency for social movements and politicians. Farmers were also a strategic population for broader national interests. Cheap food was important for the profitability of large agribusiness interests and for urban employers who wanted to keep workers' wages low. Furthermore, a low-cost, steady supply of food was critical to the nation's capacity to make war, of escalating concern given Europe's engagement in World War I. As new immigrants swelled U.S. cities, domestic out-migration from rural to urban areas was thought to exacerbate urban social problems. Thus, there was federal interest in keeping farmers on the

AUTHOR'S NOTE: I thank Joseph Donnermeyer, William Flinn, Jeff Sharp, and Don Thomas for their comments. Any review article on rural sociology needs further to acknowledge Frederick Buttel, who transformed the field and inspired generations of rural sociologists.

465

land even as farm families themselves continued to out-migrate from rural areas.

Rural sociology was born into this era of concern with farm families and a federal goal of stemming rural out-migration. Its origins are usually traced to the creation of the County Life Commission in 1908 by President Theodore Roosevelt (Bertrand 1982; Hooks and Flinn 1981). The commission launched a nationwide investigation documenting the difficulties faced by farm families. It conducted surveys of farm families and compiled other information, leading to a report that formed the basis for subsequent national policy. The commission downplayed structural determinants of farmers' hardships (Hooks and Flinn 1981). Instead, it focused on individuals' human capital, cultural values, and weaknesses of rural schools and churches. Upgrading rural people's presumed social deficits was thus emphasized over addressing fundamental inequalities in power and economic resources.

In the wake of this widespread public attention, sociologists became increasingly interested in rural people, taking a social-problems approach that differed from the discipline's standard social-philosophical approach. Bertrand (1982) notes that they "called themselves rural sociologists and defined their professional effort as the development and application of concepts and theoretical models for the express purpose of improving the life and well-being of rural people" (p. xi). The first course in rural sociology was taught at the University of Chicago in 1894 (Nelson 1969:32). The first text, John Gillette's *Constructive Rural Sociology,* was published in 1913 (Olsen 1991:1). Broad recognition of the new field was conferred when George Vincent was elected president of the ASA (then called the American Sociological Society). He selected "The Sociology of Rural Life" as the focus of the annual meeting held in Columbus, Ohio, in 1916 (Hooks and Flinn 1981:98). In 1922, the Rural Section was established (Larson and Zimmerman 2003:2). It was the ASA's first section (Goudy 2005:24).

Meanwhile, within the nation's land-grant university system, rural sociology was further institutionalized. Rural sociology was formally recognized as a separate field of study with the passage of the Purnell Act in 1925 (Goudy 2005:25), which provided federal funds to support rural sociological research, teaching, and outreach (Rogers et al. 1988:18). The act itself grew out of concern with the agricultural depression, which began in the 1920s, a sharp contrast with urban America's boom (Stanton 1991:3).

Government funding lines provided an institutional home for rural sociology within the agricultural colleges, where mainly biologically related disciplines were located. Thus, rural sociology was pulled into an academic milieu that was more interdisciplinary but also increasingly segmented from its parent discipline. Some universities created separate departments of rural sociology, the first at Cornell in 1915 (Larson and Zimmerman 2003:13). Others housed rural sociologists with other sociologists in single departments but with faculty sorted by appointment into two different colleges, agriculture (for the rural sociologists) and liberal arts/sciences (for general sociologists). Last, rural sociologists were housed in multidisciplinary departments within colleges of agriculture. Individual rural sociologists and sometimes entire rural-sociology programs were placed in human ecology departments or in joint units with agricultural education. However, joint departments with agricultural economics, the second social science established by the Purnell Act, were the most common arrangement. Agricultural economists claimed the farm economy to be their area of expertise. While early rural sociologists were concerned with farming, the academic division of labor left them to focus more on the residual, nonfarm aspects of rural life, such as settlement patterns, social organization, and well-being. It was not until the agricultural restructuring of the 1970s that rural sociologists returned more to the study of the farm economy. The academic division of labor seen in distinct departmental arrangements and funding lines for positions provided via colleges of agriculture continues to this day and particularly differentiates rural sociology from general sociology.

As a result of this diverse system of institutional supports, early rural sociologists had their professional footing in several doors—the land-grant universities, federal government, and the ASA. Examples are seen in the careers of two of rural sociology's founders, Charles Galpin and Carl Taylor. Both were heads of the USDA's Division of Farm Population and Life, Bureau of Economic Analysis, and actively promoted rural sociological research (Stanton 1991:5). Galpin was elected vice president of the ASA in 1932 and published along with two leading sociologists, Pitirim Sorokin and Carle Zimmerman, the three-volume *A Systematic Source Book in Rural Sociology* (Larson and Zimmerman 2003). Taylor was elected president of the RSS (Rural Sociological Society) in 1939 and president of the ASA in 1946 (Larson and Zimmerman 2003). These and other early rural sociologists' social justice interests in farm laborers and other marginalized populations often put them at odds with vested interests. Taylor, for example, in challenging segregationist practices, saw his university position abolished by the Board of Trustees at North Carolina State (Larson and Zimmerman 2003:27).

With expanding interest in the field, the Rural Section in ASA decided to publish its own journal, *Rural Sociology.* The first issue appeared in 1936. In December 1937, the Rural Section went further, voting to establish a separate professional organization, the Rural Sociological Society (RSS). The separation occurred because rural sociology had grown large and varied and some felt limited by ASA (Nelson 1969:130–31). While most members of the Rural Section were college sociologists, the field interested agricultural and home economists and staff of farm and government organizations. Some were concerned that prospective interest in rural sociology would dampen since those having no desire to join the ASA were required to be ASA members. Furthermore, participation at ASA meetings was limited to one paper, tending to restrict involvement into a single section. With a new society, members retained a primary focus on rural sociology but were freer to present papers and join ASA sections. The organizational split signaled that rural sociologists saw themselves as occupying a separate field, with specialty areas within it, not simply as a specialty area within sociology. In 1938, the membership in RSS stood at 206 but rose steadily. In 1966, it reached 840 (Nelson 1969:133), hovering at around 1,000 since then.

DISTINCT ATTRIBUTES OF THE FIELD

The founding of rural sociology set in place a series of defining attributes and axes of tension that have influenced its subsequent development, including the contemporary work of rural sociologists. One attribute pervading rural sociology from its inception is a focus on settings where development has played out unevenly and tended to leave people and places in more marginal positions. Elsewhere, I have argued that rural sociology is a sociology of the geographic periphery (Lobao 1996)—that is, rural sociologists focus on the places and populations with the least resources and the greatest social structural impediments to higher incomes, employment, and access to state social provisions. These settings vary from the advanced industrialized and urban areas conventionally studied by sociologists. Thus, there is a stable thread on the types of places on which rural sociologists have always focused—rural areas within developed nations and, as rural sociology later progressed, the developing nations of the globe with large, rural, and agriculturally dependent populations.

A second attribute early established was a varied substantive focus, with periodic tensions as to the saliency of certain topics. As noted in the foregoing, as the academic division of labor evolved, rural sociologists moved away from attention to agriculture, toward general topics such as family, community, and settlement patterns. Furthermore, since rural sociology began as a field spanning sociology's body of knowledge, it incorporated basically the same substantive content as general sociology, thus making for an array of specialties within it. For example, specialties include "rural crime," "rural health," "rural women," the "rural family," and so forth. Of the current, 13 substantively oriented interest group sections within RSS, all but the sociology of agriculture have counterpart sections within the ASA.

Given the varied topics studied, periodic tension has emerged over whether rural sociology has a defining substantive focus. Much of this tension has involved the saliency of attention to agriculture and the broader rural economy versus attention to nonagricultural or noneconomic aspects of rural life. When many rural sociologists re-embraced the study of agriculture in the 1970s period onward, there were calls to view the sociology of agriculture as the defining focus of the "new rural sociology"

(Friedland 1991; Newby 1983). Attention to the broader rural economy developed in the 1980s and 1990s, with rural restructuring epitomizing the "new rural sociology" of that period (Falk 1996; Tickamyer 1996). More recently, a view that much rural sociological research can be captured under the banner of spatial inequality has been offered (Lobao 2004; Lobao and Saenz 2002). In this view, seemingly disparate traditions within rural sociology, such as those of rural economic structure, inequality research, and agricultural and environmental sociology, are seen as linked through their attention to geographic space.

A third attribute early established is interest in applied research, often aimed at pressing social issues and involving direct outreach to rural people. This has sometimes created tension between those advocating the importance of applied work and those who view the field as lacking theoretical robustness (Sewell 1965). In reality, of course, the applied-basic division with regard to any research question may be virtually seamless. And contemporary rural sociologists tend to see their field as strengthened by giving weight to both. The point is, however, that tension about whether the field is overly applied has been discussed for many decades (Falk 1996; Ford 1985; Sewell 1965).

A fourth attribute is that rural sociologists typically navigate between established, often-elite stakeholders and broader public interests. Although the institutional setting of rural sociology provides access to added federal and state support, it comes with strings attached. Rural sociologists are subject to organizational pressures not typical for other sociologists (Friedland 1982; Sewell 1965). A primary goal of colleges of agriculture is to serve clientele beyond students. While this once included most rural people, today's clientele are narrower interest groups, many outside direct farming, such as agribusiness corporations. While agricultural economists largely embraced catering to agribusiness interests, rural sociologists by and large remained faithful to their roots. They have always taken as their clientele the rural poor, minorities, small farmers, and the public at large. Sometimes this focus has come at the expense of their own careers, when their research or outreach efforts challenged elite interests.

Fifth, rural sociology has always been interdisciplinary oriented. This is partly because of its subject material, which, being varied and attending to ecological aspects of social life, connects it to other disciplines, including the biological sciences. It also stems from the field's institutional location in land-grant universities. Here rural sociologists often work on multidisciplinary research teams and are housed in units with other disciplines. Addressing applied social issues also calls for interdisciplinary approaches.

Sixth, rural sociology has always had a strong public policy presence. Rural sociologists have directed major federal agencies, routinely testified before Congress, and contributed to major legislation, including federal farm bills. Decennial volumes edited by the presidents of the

Rural Sociological Society are produced to highlight key public policy issues in the coming decade for government officials as well as for social scientists (Brown and Swanson 2003; Dillman and Hobbs 1982; Flora and Christenson 1991).

Finally, given its distinct institutional status, early separation from the ASA, and broad substantive focus, perhaps the field's capstone tension is captured in the question, To what degree is rural sociology different from general sociology? This perennial question has engendered a range of answers. Books on the field characterize it as an independent discipline (Bertrand 1982:xi; Stanton 1991:1). As such, since its founding, some have viewed rural sociology as more allied with agricultural economics than with sociology (Olsen 1991). Nelson (1969) takes a middle point, arguing that it is an "enclave" within sociology, "not a truly specialized field of interest comparable to the family, population, methodology, or the community . . . [but] as broad in its content as sociology itself" (p. 130). Others see little difference from the parent discipline. John Gillette, author of the first textbook on rural sociology, noted in 1916, "it has been said of rural sociology, 'There ain't no such animal.' It is asserted that there is but one sociology, and that is the general science of sociology" (Nelson 1969:35). More recently, Falk (1996) notes, "Rural sociologists are simply general sociologists who have a particular focus in their work . . . things rural always play some part in what we do" (p. 164).

Tension about the disciplinary status of rural sociology is not merely ontological but has real outcomes for practice of the profession. Professional identity as a separate entity or part of sociology figures in job searches, grant competitions, and journal article submissions. Within the RSS, debates repeatedly occur over the location of annual meetings, with those—based on professional identity—arguing for or against annual meeting locations close to the ASA.

The issues and tensions above often appear as new to each succeeding generation of rural sociologists. Yet they were built early into the field. Rural sociologists are remarkably introspective about these issues. This relatively small field has generated numerous articles taking stock of its disciplinary status, strengths, and shortcomings. Keeping in mind that the issues noted above continually pervade rural sociology, I provide an overview of research in the early stages of the field and then focus in more detail on the contemporary knowledge base. My discussion centers on U.S.-generated literatures, which continue to form the bulk of the work.

RURAL SOCIOLOGICAL RESEARCH: THE FIRST FIVE DECADES

The substantive focus, theory, and methodological approaches of rural sociological research in its first 50 years are captured in a number of review articles. Two companion articles delineate substantive foci of research.

Sewell (1965) takes stock of three eras: the Depression and World War II (1936–1945) and the early (1946–1955) and late postwar periods (1956–1965). Christenson and Garkovich (1985) focus on the period from 1966 to 1985. Both studies examine articles published in *Rural Sociology* and use the same categories to classify research topics. The substantive categories delineated are the following: social organization (including family, education, religion, stratification, community), social change, social psychology, population, social welfare and policy, methodology, and issues related to the profession. In the list of topics, little appears to differentiate the field from general sociology. However, distinctiveness remains in the application of these topics to the rural population, a segment the parent discipline neglected as it assumed that urban-based mass society was to wash over all people.

The importance of the topics above ebbs and flows with the decades, appearing to follow both trends in general sociology and rural sociologists' interests in the social problems of rural people. Interest in social welfare and policy (a category that includes housing, level of living, poverty, minorities, and social problems) peaks during the Depression, with about one-third of *Rural Sociology* articles attending to that topic. Concern with the conditions of farm labor also peaks during the Depression era (Sewell 1965:433), with a small uptake occurring in the late 1970s (Christenson and Garkovich 1985). Topics addressing social psychology exhibit consistent growth. While interest in social psychology followed general disciplinary trends, it also reflected growing research on the diffusion of innovations, a topic that gave rural sociologists a key niche in agricultural colleges. This body of work was directed to assessing individuals' attitudes and behaviors related to adoption of agricultural technologies produced in the post–World War II period (Rogers 1971). Much of this work was later highly critical of the inequality-producing effects of these technologies. Finally, topics involving social organization and population (largely urban-rural trends) remained consistent topics of research throughout the entire 50-year period. In the last decade (1976–1985) studied, Christenson and Garkovich (1985:512) report that the four major topical areas, with their respective proportion of articles produced, were social psychology (31 percent), social organization (24 percent), population (12 percent), and social change (11 percent).

Theoretical approaches are also addressed in review articles. Companion pieces by Picou, Wells, and Nyberg (1978) and Falk and Zhao (1989) focus, respectively, on the 1965 to 1976 and 1976 to 1985 periods. Sewell (1965) addresses the 1936 to 1965 period. All analyze articles published in *Rural Sociology*. They report that rural sociological research is generally more applied and less theoretical than general sociology. The paradigmatic stance was largely "social facts" (e.g., deductive traditions ranging from functionalism to Marxism), with 92 percent of articles taking this stance from 1965 to 1976 and 76 percent from 1976 to 1985 (Falk and Zhao 1989:591). Articles in the social definition (e.g., Meadian tradition) paradigm constituted 6 percent of those published from 1965 to 1976 and 9 percent from 1976 to 1985, while articles classified as a "mixed" paradigmatic perspective made up 1 percent of those published from 1965 to 1976 and 14 percent from 1976 to 1985 (Falk and Zhao 1989:591). In terms of specific theories, rural sociologists appear to follow the parent discipline. For example, Falk and Zhao (1989) note the rise of neo-Marxian approaches in rural sociology in the late 1970s.

Reviews assessing research methodology are found in Sewell (1965), Stokes and Miller (1985), and Falk and Zhao (1989). These authors indicate that early work tended to be descriptive and centered on local populations to which rural sociologists had easy access. As the field evolved, the methodology became more rigorous and quantitative. The vast majority of articles published in *Rural Sociology* from 1936 to 1985 used primary data from surveys and secondary data, with surveys the most common (Stokes and Miller 1985). While individuals thus were mainly the unit of observation, there was continual interest in geographic space. About 30 percent of articles produced between 1936 and 1985 used ecological units as the unit of observation.

U.S. rural sociology led to the field's growth elsewhere. The European Society for Rural Sociology (ESRS) was established in 1957. Christenson and Garkovich (1985) note that European rural sociology emerged from liberal arts–type settings and tends to be more theoretical and philosophical than U.S. rural sociology. However, they point out that the differences are also a function of the divides between general U.S. and European sociology, the former itself being more empirical and quantitative. RSS and ESRS joined in efforts to create the International Rural Sociological Association (IRSA), established in 1966. In 1969, the Latin American Rural Sociological Association was formed, followed later by the Australia and Oceania Network and the Asian Rural Sociological Association. All these member societies make up the IRSA today.

RURAL SOCIOLOGICAL RESEARCH: THE CONTEMPORARY PERIOD

While a flurry of articles assessed the status of rural sociology over its first 50 years, the more recent period is met by less systematic scrutiny. Still, edited volumes delineate the substantive scope of research (Brown and Swanson 2003; Flora and Christenson 1991; Goreham 1997), and review articles of specific topics exist (Buttel 2002; Lobao and Meyer 2001). I provide an overview of the research and then distinguish substantive bodies of work.

Rural sociology's diverse substantive scope remains in topical areas overlapping with those of general sociology. Research-related interest groups in the RSS highlight the present diversity: education and work, family and household, community, natural resources, population, health, poverty, policy, racial/ethnic groups, gender, applied/extension sociology, the sociology of agriculture, and, until recently, international development. In comparing rural sociology's first 50 years with the 1986 to 1995 period, Garkovich and Bell (1995) report a movement away from research on social psychology and social organization and toward social change and stratification (social welfare and policy), a pattern following general sociology.

With regard to theory, little suggests that previous patterns are altered: Rural sociologists build from sociology using theories germane to substantive areas above (Falk 1996). At the same time, they maintain an interest in applied and policy-related research, where conventional sociological theory is less transferable. Within certain substantive areas, rural sociologists have developed their own theoretical perspectives rather independent of sociology, with these sometimes challenging conventional views of the parent discipline. Such independent theorizing is seen particularly within the sociology of agriculture (Lobao and Meyer 2001).

With regard to methods, rural sociologists follow trends in sociology (Falk 1996). However, the distinct subject matter addressed by rural sociologists, coupled with the need for data on specific populations, often means conventional secondary data have limited usefulness (Tickamyer 1996). Rural sociologists thus have to rely perhaps more than other sociologists on independent data-collection activities. Finally, rural sociologists are at the forefront of sociology in their use of spatial analytical methods and geographic information systems (GIS) (Voss et al., forthcoming).

In the following, I discuss the major branches of contemporary research. Rural sociologists are leading contributors to the research on community, environmental sociology, and international development. As these fields are addressed elsewhere in this volume, I give particular attention to the sociology of agriculture and rural inequality research, areas more specific to rural sociology. It should be noted that any research area is porous, and individual researchers straddle the following areas.

The Sociology of Agriculture

The sociology of agriculture focuses on an economic sector that general sociology has long neglected. Its theoretical orientation also developed quite independent of the parent discipline. A recent review of much of this work is found in Lobao and Meyer (2001). As noted previously, in the late 1970s, rural sociologists recognized massive changes occurring in farming and turned to critical political-economic analysis of that sector. Seminal publications documenting this turn include Buttel and Newby (1980), Newby (1983), and Friedland, Barton, and Thomas (1991). Several overlapping topics have occupied researchers: agricultural change, including development of local and global food systems; effects of agricultural change on communities, families, and women; and issues of agricultural science, technology, and sustainable agriculture.

Farming and Agrifood Systems

In contemporary research, three types of agricultural change have been of particular interest. First are changes in the demography of farming, seen in the declining number of farms and farm population (Albrecht and Murdock 1990). Rural sociologists historically addressed this topic as a broad, national issue. More recent focus is on the sustainability of farming in particular localized settings at the urban-rural interface, or where large metro areas meet the countryside (Jackson-Smith 2003; Salamon 2003).

The second change entails farm structure and the relative growth of "industrialized farms" and decline of family or moderate-size farms. The persistence of family farming and the form it takes as capitalism advances is debated (Mann 1990). Since the late 1990s, particular attention has been given to the industrializing of livestock production (Thu and Durrenberger 1998).

Last, rural sociologists move beyond the farm gate to study agrofood systems at the global and local scales. This research also moves beyond focus on the production aspects of agriculture to consumption (Fine 2004; Goodman 2002). The global commodity chains literature connects capital, labor, and resources needed in different stages of the production process to geographic regions; and it considers how global commodity production/consumption markets are created through state and macroeconomic processes (Bonanno et al. 1994; Friedland 2001; Friedland et al. 1981). A similar topic is addressed at the local scale: Researchers are interested in networks among farmers, consumers, processors, and retailers and how these might sustain local food systems (Allen 2004; Lyson 2004). Rural sociologists not only study local food systems but also facilitate their development through outreach programs.

For researchers studying these three changes, conventional theories from economic sociology are of limited use since they miss the path of development of agriculture. Researchers draw from and extend critical, Marxist-oriented frameworks and, more recently, postmodern, actor-network, and civic society perspectives to theorize these changes.

Farm Communities and Families

Another body of work centers on the impacts of farm change on communities and households. Walter Goldschmidt's research (1978) catapulted interest in the topic of farming and communities. His case study of two California towns originally conducted in the 1930s found that large-scale, industrialized farms (as compared with smaller, family farms) had detrimental impacts on community well-being. From the 1970s onward, rural sociologists have tested variants of this finding, known as the "Goldschmidt hypothesis." Numerous subsequent studies, conducted across the nation at different time periods, support aspects of this hypothesis, but often with qualification.

For reviews, see Lobao (1990) and Swanson (1988). This research shows that even in a postindustrial economy, farming affects community well-being, although certainly not as much as nonfarm industries. Furthermore, family farming appears to be a marker of a strong local civic society (Lyson 2004; Tolbert, Lyson, and Irwin 1998). Research on the topic continues to evolve in accordance with changes in farming. Since the 1990s, analysts have turned to the industrialization of livestock farming and its impacts on communities' economic, social, and environmental conditions (Thu and Durrenberger 1998). Research in this area has been used for policy and public sociology purposes. A recent example is South Dakota's constitutional amendment regulating absentee-owned corporate farms, where rural sociologists' research showing potential detrimental community effects of such farms was used in federal court cases in 2001 and 2003.

Rural sociologists also examine the more microimpacts of agricultural change on the household, including gender roles (see Lobao and Meyer 2001). While this topic always interested rural sociologists, it took on renewed interest in the 1980s and 1990s with the lingering farm crisis (Lasley et al. 1995). Researchers examined household survival strategies, again arguing that general sociology's focus on urban populations made invisible the spectrum of work and survival strategies used by rural people (Sachs 1996; Tickamyer 1996). The gender division of labor was studied (Barlett 1993; Lobao and Meyer 1995). While researchers expected the gender division of labor to shift, with women performing more work in direct farming, this did not appear to occur in the wake of financial hardship. The emotional well-being of farm men and women was related to financial hardship (Ramirez-Ferrero 2005). Researchers also studied family resiliency. Elder and Conger (2000) documented that farm life for children had beneficial effects on their emotional health and educational attainments, despite financial hardship.

Agricultural Sciences and Technology

A third research area centers on agricultural sciences and technology. Research on adoption-diffusion of agricultural technologies has long been a part of rural sociology, although this tradition waned in the post-1970s. It was resurrected in the 1990s as sociologists studied the new wave of biotechnologies in crops such as corn, cotton, and soybeans and in dairying (Buttel 1997). In contrast to earlier work, current rural sociologists take a more critical stance in analyzing why certain technologies and products come into use and the risks they may pose to society (Busch et al. 1991; DuPuis 2002; Molnar and Kinnucan 1989). Focus has also turned to indigenous knowledge about farm technologies and practices. Here researchers are concerned with sustaining local knowledge about farming and how this knowledge can be harnessed to create a more sustainable, socially just system (Bell 2004).

Rural Inequality Research

Rural sociology contains a large body of research on stratification grounded in different literatures. These literatures overlap substantively and conceptually, making up a general inequality tradition. Much of the work explores comparative urban-rural differences in economic opportunities and other life chances for various social groups. In that sense, it is concerned with spatial inequality at the subnational or regional scale (Lobao 2004). This research is a unique contribution to sociology for two reasons: Until recently, sociologists studying stratification largely neglected "space"; and when space was brought in to study stratification, it was typically at the scale of the city and neighborhood or, conversely, at the cross-national scale. Rural sociology's middle, subnational scale of focus distinguishes it from other sociological fields. This research often employs counties, labor market areas, or regions either as units of analysis directly or as multilevel measures of context surrounding households and individuals. I divide these literatures according to focus on general inequalities, race/ethnicity, and gender.

General Inequalities: Rural Poverty, Rural Labor Markets, and Demographic Research

Rural Poverty. A large literature exists on poverty in rural regions, which contrasts with sociology's urban-poverty literature, Rural-poverty rates are historically higher than urban-poverty rates, making the topic of particular concern (Jensen, McLaughlin, and Slack 2003). Poverty among working families is also higher in rural areas, indicating deficiencies in rural-employment structures. The Rural Sociological Task Force on Persistent Rural Poverty consolidated and pushed forward this work in a seminal 1993 volume. In addition to numerous articles on the topic, the books include Billings and Blee (2000), Duncan (1999), Fitchen (1991), and Lyson and Falk (1993). Much of this literature focuses on persistently poor rural regions. Conceptual approaches also exist to understand general subnational patterns of poverty (Lobao 2004).

Rural Labor Markets. This literature represents a unique contribution, for it addresses the conceptualization of and empirical issues involved in studying work and inequality at the subnational scale, across urban-rural regions and communities. It addresses how the spatial context of economic structure (industries, firms, and employment) shapes earnings, incomes, and other indicators of well-being (Falk, Schulman, and Tickamyer 2003; Singelmann and Deseran 1993). Another innovation is attention to conceptualization and measurement of both "labor markets" and "work" from a rural standpoint. Arguing that conventional labor market areas were too small to capture rural work-residence relationships, Killian and Tolbert (1993) developed ecological units to reflect this new labor market geography, now used widely. Because official statistics often miss work activities of rural people, researchers have turned to conceptualizing and collecting primary data on the informal sector (Falk et al. 2003; Tickamyer 1996). Rural labor markets research challenges traditional neoclassical human capital explanations of inequality. In giving primary attention to structural determinants of inequality, this research shows how economic returns to individuals' human capital attributes such as education vary by urban-rural context, with rural workers receiving lower returns (Cotter 2002; Tigges and Tootle 1990).

Sociodemographic Inequalities. Demographers have a large presence in rural sociology and many study stratification. Their research moves beyond economic inequalities, to address a variety of well-being indicators such as migration, fertility, mortality, and family formation. Demographers also cast a wider net with regard to determinants of inequality, giving attention to both economic structure and sociodemographic factors, such as marriage and family structure (Fosset and Seibert 1997; Lichter and McLaughlin 1995). Last, they point out complexities in analyzing inequality due to the considerable variation within and between urban-rural regions (Brown and Lee 1999).

Although the three previous literatures remain distinct, there is a greater blending of them at present. They all show that economic structure is a main determinant of urban-rural variations in inequality. Rural areas are slower growing and lack employment opportunities, and existing jobs are poorly remunerated. Recent work finds that a weaker civil society (Tolbert et al. 1998, 2002) and local state (Dewees, Lobao, and Swanson 2003; Tickameyer et al. 2000; Warner and Hebdon 2001) also contribute to poorer well-being. Interest in welfare reform is linking researchers from all three of these traditions (Weber, Duncan, and Whitener 2002; Zimmerman 2002). Due to poorer economic conditions and less local government capacity to administer devolved social programs, rural areas tend to fare worse under welfare reform.

The Rural Racial/Ethnic Segregation Tradition. Rural sociology has a rich tradition addressing racial and ethnic segregation at the regional, subnational level that sets it apart from sociology's conventional focus on the inner city. Regional patterns of racial/ethnic segregation and concentration are examined through attention to Native American reservations, the Southern Black Belt, Mexican American boarder enclaves, and communities with newer ethnic in-migration (Falk 2004; Saenz 1997; Snipp 1996; Wimberley and Morris 2002). This literature goes beyond the urban segregation literature in its breadth of territorial scale and depth of historical analysis. Researchers consider how ethnic stratification of regions develops, such as through past political economic forces and public policies that may date back for centuries.

Rural Gender Inequality. Large literatures on rural gender issues have existed since the 1980s. These mainly focus on women's work and well-being (Haney 1997; Tickamyer and Henderson 2003). As feminist and political economy perspectives filtered into rural sociology in the 1980s, the study of farm women's work was elevated to a distinct topical area with explicit theorizing (Sachs 1983, 1996). Rural poverty and labor market researchers also have specific interest in women (Rural Sociological Task Force on Persistent Rural Poverty 1993; Tickamyer and Henderson 2003). These researchers address work and socioeconomic inequalities between rural women and men as well as urban-rural differences between women. Gender segregation across industries and occupations is spatialized, with rural women facing fewer quality employment opportunities than their urban counterparts. Rural women are particularly likely to engage in informal sector activities to piece together family livelihoods. The poverty rates of rural women are higher than those of urban women, and there is some evidence that rural women fare worse under welfare reform (Ticakmyer and Henderson 2003). Finally, a "rural masculinities" literature is emerging (Campbell, Bell, and Finney, 2006). While this research tends to be concerned with identity formation and cultural representation, some studies attend to men's emotional well-being and changing work statuses (Ramirez-Ferrero 2005).

Community Studies

Rural sociology has a strong community tradition overlapping that of urban sociology. A large literature addresses the conceptual and methodological issues in defining and studying the rural "community" (see Liepens 2000). Community ethnographies and surveys are common methodologies. Here I discuss four features of rural sociology's variant of community studies.

First, community settings studied tend to be small, remote, and less affluent, which are characteristics of rural places nationally. These places typically have limited social, economic, and governmental resources, which creates barriers to adapting to changes.

Second, much research centers on the rural community as a social system (Wilkinson 1991) and analyzes the manner in which communities adapt to changes brought about by external economic and social forces. For example, researchers often study industrial restructuring due to globalization and other shifts, with this work providing an important corrective to urban-based industrial restructuring literature (Anderson 2000; Winson 1997). Rural communities tend to be more vulnerable to the effects of global competition and trade policies such as NAFTA in part because of their greater dependence on labor-intensive industries or agricultural products (e.g., corn in the case of Mexican communities). They are hit hard by business downturns as they tend to have a less varied industrial mix, fewer options of other employment, poorer-quality jobs, and a less-educated workforce (Anderson 2000).

Suburbanization processes and their impacts have also become a major topic of study (Salamon 2003). Alternatively, some analysts are concerned with communities' resiliency, studying the manner in which social capital networks and other "social infrastructure" allow progressive adaptation to economic and other changes (Flora and Flora 2003; Flora et al. 1997; Luloff and Bridger 2003; Sharp 2001).

Third, rural sociologists also treat the community as a site of social solidarity, place sentiments, and local culture (Bell 1994; Liepens 2000). While past work studying community in this way took a functionalist approach, recent work often blends critical and interpretive perspectives. For example, Falk (2004) examines how a sense of place developed among poor African Americans who lived through the pre-Civil Rights era of segregation in a southern community.

Last, rural sociologists contribute to community development from the standpoint of research, policy, and practice. The volumes by Brown and Swanson (2003) and Flora and Christenson (1991) contain articles highlighting this work. Green (2003) reviews the research on economic development in small communities. Rural sociologists are well represented in the Community Development Society, an association of practitioners and researchers.

Environment and Natural Resources Sociology

The study of the environment is central to modern rural sociology. As this large field exists independently and is addressed elsewhere in this volume, I briefly focus on its rural-sociological variants. Rural sociologists' contributions to environmental sociology are given a detailed discussion by Buttel (1996, 2002) and Field and Burch (1988). They were among the founders of environmental sociology, and many leading environmental sociologists are rural sociologists, as seen in research by Buttel (1996), Dunlap et al. (2002), Field and Burch (1988), and Freudenberg and Gramling (1994).

Rural sociologists' research spans three bodies of work, environmental sociology, natural resources sociology, and social impact assessment, with the two latter traditions particular to the field. Buttel (2002) provides an excellent comparison of environmental and natural resources sociology. Natural resources sociology was established as a research group within rural sociology by the mid-1960s, predating general sociology's interest in the environment (Buttel 2002:206). It grew out of the institutional setting of U.S. government and colleges of agriculture in land-grant universities, tends to focus on communities and regions, and has a more applied focus on policy, resource management, and conflict resolution. By contrast, environmental sociology grew out of a liberal arts tradition, focuses more on the nation-state and urban areas, and is often highly theoretical.

Natural resource sociologists are often concerned with the impacts of the extractive sector, particularly mining and forestry in resource-dependent regions in developed and less-developed countries. This research tradition treats places, people, and economic sectors that general sociology typically neglects. Populations such as miners, loggers, peasants, indigenous people, and the rural poor are often a focus. Development processes involving the extractive sector work out in ways different from those of manufacturing or services, with boom-and-bust cycles producing greater swings in economic well-being over time (Bunker 1985; Fruedenberg and Gramling 1994). A related focus is the environmental and social impacts of general industrial development processes, such as the production of hazardous waste and other pollution (Murdock, Krannich, and Leistritz 1999). In both sets of topics, issues of environmental justice are usually of concern, as poor populations are typically located in more at-risk settings.

Social impact assessment grew out of public policy interest in documenting the impacts of extractive and potentially environmentally degrading industries. This research entails conceptual and methodological approaches for studying these impacts and treats a broad scope of outcome indicators, such as environmental and economic conditions, and social problems, such as community stress and crime (Burdge 1999; Freudenberg 1986).

Other Areas of Research

Two research areas, rural demography and international development, should be mentioned due to their long history in rural sociology. Rural demographers, in addition to attending to spatial inequalities, have produced a large body of work charting urban-rural differences in settlement patterns and significant national trends in population growth and decline. For example, researchers found a 1970s-decade "nonmetro turnaround," when the rural population grew and the net migration from urban to rural areas increased, and a 1980s-decade reversion back to older, historical trends of net rural to urban migration (Fuguitt, Brown, and Beale 1989). The past decade reflects a "rural rebound" or modest growth in the nonmetro population (Johnson and Fuguitt 2000). Demographers are also concerned with developing new census classifications to tap urban-rural differences in postindustrial economies (Champion and Hugo 2004).

International development has long been a field of study in rural sociology. However, it is probably safe to say that rural sociologists do not compartmentalize this topic as much as general sociologists do. Contemporary rural sociologists tend to have their foot in both U.S. and global research. Most of the topics discussed previously are examined in both international and domestic settings. Any one rural sociologist often has ongoing research projects in the United States as well as in other nations. Populations of interest to rural sociologists, the rural poor, farmers, and those engaged in natural resource extraction tend to characterize developing nations. Most of the developing world remains rural. Colleges of agriculture have long engaged in international development activities funded by federal agencies and have extensive ties with international universities and governments. Rural sociologists thus are located in institutional settings that give them many opportunities to conduct research across the globe. Attention to peripheral settings globally tends to make rural sociologists recognize and build from both domestic and international literatures addressing theory, research, policy, and public outreach.

Last, other bodies of research characterize the field. A good view of recent topical issues engaging rural sociologists is provided by Brown and Swanson's edited volume (2003).

FUTURE DEVELOPMENT OF RURAL SOCIOLOGY

What does the future hold for rural sociology? I consider rural sociology's distinct niche in sociology, new topics of research, and institutional issues in sustaining the field.

Rural sociology provides a unique window on social life, whose importance appears to be increasingly recognized. Attention to the spatial dimensions of social life is the central element linking rural sociology's diverse concerns. Rural sociologists study the people, places, and economic sectors (agriculture and natural resource industries) that characterize spatial settings typically overlooked by general sociologists. Their long-standing interest in exploring urban-rural variations has led them to focus on a distinct scale of social life—the subnational scale—located between the city and nation-state. This spatial scale of focus and related substantive topics of study will continue to create a distinct niche for rural sociology.

In addition, there is reason to think that rural sociology will have a broader influence in the future because the topical areas it encompasses are of growing interest to social scientists at large. Over the past decade, there has been widespread sociological interest in the spatial aspects of social life. Rural sociologists have long addressed conceptual, substantive, and methodological issues in studying space, and their subnational scale of focus has no counterpart elsewhere in sociology. As sociology becomes further spatialized, the visibility of rural sociological research is bound to increase. Interest in space also is connecting rural sociology to disciplines such as geography and regional science. Researchers from these disciplines increasingly attend each other's meetings and participate in broad initiatives to spatially integrate the social sciences.

Similarly, rural sociologists are at the forefront of research addressing other issues of rising concern to sociologists. For some time, they have studied consumption issues, largely through research on the food system and, more recently, on use aspects of rural landscapes. They have also long studied the treatment of animals and farm animal welfare. Consumption study is an emerging research area in sociology, and "Animals and Society" is the ASA's newest section. Buttel (2002) also sees rural sociology's natural resource tradition as increasingly relevant to broader environmental sociology. This tradition has amassed a wealth of empirical studies on places, populations, and environmental practices that can inform and move forward the more abstract, national, and urban-oriented environmental literature.

Within the branches of research discussed previously, a few examples of topical areas that should continue to engage rural sociologists may be noted. The study of spatial inequality appears to be growing as rural sociologists increasingly address work inequality issues from a comparative spatial vantage. Furthermore, the topic bridges a number of specialty areas within rural sociology and links rural sociology itself to other disciplines (Lobao 2004).

The sociology of agriculture remains vibrant. Buttel (2003) notes that the contemporary period has ushered in a number of topics that should engage rural sociologists. These include global long-distance commodity production/consumption chains; global neoliberalism of agriculture, where public interests and those of small farmers are becoming subordinate to corporate interests; industrialization of the livestock industry; and use of biotechnologies. Conversely, Buttel (2003) argues for the need to scrutinize countervailing forces, such as protest and consumer movements, that might mediate these trends and create a more socially just agricultural system. To this list of topics, one might add the study of local food systems and civic agriculture (Lyson 2004); the relentless suburbanization of farming areas; and consumption issues of all types, from food to rural landscapes. Last, researchers can be expected to increasingly address nutrition, obesity, and food choice issues, topics that link rural sociology to the biological sciences.

In the post-2000 period, a new wave of policy-relevant research has emerged, a trend that can be expected to continue (Swanson 2001). The trend is reflected in the policy-related volume produced by two past RSS presidents, David Brown and Louis Swanson (2003), in recent RSS efforts to produce policy briefs for government and nongovernmental officials and in the RSS membership in the Consortium of Social Science Association (COSSA), which brings social science research to bear on federal policy. Rural development policy, farm policy, rural poverty, and welfare reform are topics often addressed.

Last, it is worth noting three areas where research gaps remain to be filled. First, in the face of widespread changes in the food and agricultural system, environment, and rural regions, rural sociologists need to take greater stock of theory. These changes are interrelated and require more holistic theoretical approaches that go beyond and link the respective branches of research. They entail questions such as, How does the development of capitalism proceed—and what will be the role of rural places in this development? How are inequalities related to poverty, food and

nutrition, environmental conditions, and other life chances reproduced? Theoretical development of rural sociology is needed to answer these questions and to create a more coherent field. Second, rural sociologists have not devoted much attention to the meaning and significance of the 2000 and 2004 presidential elections, which are related in part to the limited theorizing about the role of rural areas in national development. These elections challenged rural sociologists' views that urban-rural social beliefs and political gaps were closing. Is there a new spatial logic to politics, where rural areas increasingly reflect the sentiments of two sets of residents—nonfarm, long-time rural residents historically neglected by government and antigovernment, socially conservative newcomer urban populations? Third, as Tickamyer (1996) noted some time ago, gaps in the quality and quantity of available data need to be addressed. Methodologies and measures to collect data tailored to rural populations should be given attention.

One question sometimes asked is, Can rural sociology remain relevant in the face of the declining rural population? First, given the uneven nature of capitalism, there will always be places that remain marginalized, left behind historically or in the course of different rounds of development. Second, rural environments persist due to their social construction and are constantly reproduced. People believe "rural" social life and settings to be real and act on this belief. For example, families and corporations make decisions about moving into rural locations on the basis of their preconceived views about these places. People construct "rural environments" in urban settings, such as those seen in community gardens and in regulations protecting urban wildlife. Last, there are numerous, objective indicators that continue to differentiate people and places by degree of rurality: poverty rates, employment opportunities, educational attainments, access to health care, local government resources, and so forth. The 2000 and 2004 presidential elections are a powerful reminder of these continuing differences.

I have noted the continuing importance of rural sociology as a field and that there will always be a "rurality" to study in the future. However, in the future, the institutional support system is likely to look different from what it does today. Since the 1980s, agricultural colleges have undergone dramatic changes in regard to federal and state support. This has led to slow or no growth in the faculty of most disciplines in these colleges. At the same time, there appears to be rising interest in topics addressed by the field, such as food, farming, rural inequality, and environment, among sociologists located in liberal arts settings. Furthermore, since public concerns about food, farming, and the environment continue to increase, the presence of rural sociologists in nongovernmental and governmental institutions can be expected to grow. Thus, likely there will be continuity in the research undertaken by rural sociologists, but there will be some change in the institutional settings where this work is conducted.

Issues addressed by rural sociologists pertaining to farming, food, environmental conditions, and rural poverty are among the most important public concerns today. Moreover, these issues offer distinct empirical and theoretical challenges for sociology as a discipline. In the past, rural sociology's broad scope and historical institutional location too often left rural sociologists looking inward and separated from the parent discipline. The institutional changes noted in the foregoing, coupled with the centrality of issues addressed by rural sociologists, may produce a back-to-the future scenario, where rural sociology once again becomes more closely linked and engaged with the parent discipline.

48

URBAN SOCIOLOGY IN THE 21ST CENTURY

SASKIA SASSEN

University of Chicago

Identifying critical issues confronting an urban sociology of the twenty-first century entails a decision and a judgment, both in turn inevitably derived from an interpretation of history in the making. The enterprise is, thus, partial and positioned. Developing analytical and empirical elements (and I emphasize elements) for an urban sociology focused on the early twenty-first century does not override existing sociological tools nor the rich scholarship on cities. Indeed, the trends this chapter focuses on do not necessarily encompass the prevailing features of the urban condition today. Most of social life in cities probably still corresponds to older continuing and familiar trends. That is why much of urban sociology's traditions and well-established subfields will remain important and continue to constitute the heart of this discipline. At the same time, if one were confined to traditional concepts of urban sociology, one would overlook or underestimate critical aspects of major new trends coming together in a growing number of cities. And while there are good reasons why most of urban sociology has not quite engaged these issues, notably the deficiencies of current data sets to address trends at the level of the city, we need to push forward. Already in the 1980s and 1990s, we have seen important contributions to this forward-looking task in urban sociology (e.g., Friedmann and Wolff 1982; Sassen-Koob 1982; Gottdiener 1985; Rodriguez and Feagin 1986; Castells 1989; King 1990; Zukin 1991; Abu-Lughod 1994; Lash and Urry 1994; Smith 1995, to cite but a few) as well as in other urban disciplines. But current trends also signal the beginning of a whole new research and theorization agenda.[1]

Large cities around the world are today the terrain where some of the novel conditions marking the twenty-first century hit the ground: Multiple globalization processes assume concrete localized forms, electronic networks intersect with thick environments (whether financial centers or activist meetings), and new subjectivities arise from the encounters of people from all around the world. Thus, today's large cities have emerged as a strategic site for a whole range of new types of operations, some pertaining to the global economy (e.g., Globalization and World Cities Study Group and Network [GaWC]; Fainstein and Judd 1999; Scott 2001; Abrahamson 2004; Gugler 2004; Rutherford 2004; Amen, Archer, and Bosman 2006; Harvey, 2007) and others to political, cultural, and subjective domains (e.g., Abu-Lughod 1994; Clark and Hoffman-Martinot 1998; Allen, Massey, and Pryke 1999; Watson and Bridges 1999; Glaeser 2000; Cordero-Guzman, Smith, and Grosfoguel 2001; Krause and Petro 2003; Lloyd 2005; Brenner and Keil 2006; and Barlett 2007).

Some of these trends are urban, but others are not and merely find in the city one of the sites for their enactment. Either way, it suggests that cities are a type of place where we can carry out detailed ethnographies, surveys, or other types of empirical studies about several of today's major processes that are global at least in some of their dimensions. It is one of the nexuses where the new types of trends materialize and assume concrete forms that can be constituted as objects of study.

The effort in this chapter is to discuss the scholarship that has sought to capture these trends in their urban shape. The chapter is thus not a comprehensive examination of the vast scholarship on urban sociology, mostly focused on more familiar conditions, but an attempt to detect novel trends becoming evident in cities as we enter the twenty-first century. Following a brief introduction, the first half of this chapter examines a series of major economic dynamics that carry significant urban implications and hence call for the development of novel analytic elements. The second half follows the same logic but in this case focuses on a variety of transnational political and cultural processes.

THE CITY AS AN OBJECT OF STUDY

As an object of study, the city has long been a debatable construct in sociology and in the social sciences generally, whether in earlier writings (Castells 1972; Harvey 1985; Timberlake 1985; Logan and Molotch 1987; Lefebvre [1974] 1991) or in more recent ones (Taylor 1995; Brenner 1998; Dear 2001; Thrift and Amin 2002; Veltz 2005; Short 2006). The concept of the city is complex, imprecise, and charged with specific historical and thereby variable meanings (e.g., Park, Burgess, and McKenzie 1967; Castells 1972; Harvey 1985; Sennett 1994; Wellman 1999; Paddison 2001). Today's major trends further add to these debates and complexity.

We can identify two major trends that lie behind this variety of conditions and that organize this chapter. One is a major shift in state policy toward targeting particular subnational spaces for development and resource allocation—and away from the promotion of convergence in national territorial development. Particular types of cities and advanced high-tech industrial districts are two of the main targets, with global cities and "silicon valleys" the most extreme instances. This shift toward privileging particular subnational spaces partly arises from globalization and the new information technologies. To this we can add a second critical trend associated and enabled by globalization and the expanding presence of the new information technologies in all domains of social life: the emergence of new cultural forms that cannot be contained exclusively within national framings, such as global imaginaries and cultural transnationalisms. Cities have turned out to be important spaces for enacting some of these novel cultural elements. These two major trends have significant implications for our analysis and theorization of cities at the dawn of the twenty-first century. While these trends today may hold especially for major cities, they are directly or indirectly affecting a rapidly growing range of diverse types of cities.

Today's conditions bring to the fore the fact that major cities are nodes, where a variety of economic, political, and subjective processes intersect in particularly pronounced concentrations. In the context of globalization, many of these processes not only operate at a global scale but also materialize in the concrete environments of cities. Thus, cities emerge as one territorial or scalar moment in a variety of transurban dynamics. This is, however, not the city as a bounded unit, but the city as a complex location in a grid of cross-boundary processes. Furthermore, this

type of city is not simply one step in the ladder of the traditional scalar hierarchy that puts cities above the neighborhood and below the national, regional, and global levels. Rather, it is one of the spaces of the global, and it engages the global directly, often bypassing the national. Some cities may have had this capacity long before the current era (e.g., King 1990; several chapters in Gugler 2004), but today these conditions extend to a growing number of cities and to a growing number of sectors within cities. This can be read as a qualitatively different phase. Furthermore, insofar as the national as container of social process and power is cracked (Taylor 1995; Wellman 1999; Abu-Lughod 2000; Beck 2000; Brenner 2004; Orum and Chen 2004), it opens up possibilities for a geography of politics that links subnational spaces across borders. This points to the formation of a new type of transnational politics that localizes in these cities (e.g., Bhachu 1985; Valle and Torres 2000; Chinchilla and Hamilton 2001; Cordero-Guzman et al. 2001), and to the possibility that the emergent global civil society posited by a growing number of scholars (e.g., see chapters in Glasius, Kaldor, and Anheier 2002; Beck 2006; Bartlett 2007; Nashashibi 2007) is actually partly enacted in a network of cities.

This type of perspective reintroduces place in the analysis of major nonurban dynamics, more precisely, the challenge of recovering place in the context of globalization, the new information technologies, and the intensifying of transnational and translocal dynamics. But it also reintroduces place in the study of cities. An obvious tradition of scholarship that comes to mind in this regard is the old school of ecological analysis (Park et al. 1967; Suttles 1968; see also Duncan 1959; Anderson 1990). One might ask if their methods could be particularly useful in recovering the category place under current conditions. Robert Park and the Chicago School conceived of "natural areas" as geographic areas determined by unplanned, subcultural forces. Some of the best studies in urban sociology were produced using fieldwork within a framework of human ecology—mapping detailed distributions and assuming functional complementarity among the diverse "natural areas" identified in Chicago.[2]

I would argue that detailed fieldwork is a necessary step in capturing many of the new aspects in the urban condition, including those having to do with the major trends focused on in this article. But assuming complementarity brings us back to the notion of the city as a bounded space and to notions of functional ecologies. Instead, today we need to see the city as one site, albeit a strategic one, where multiple transboundary processes intersect and produce distinct sociospatial formations. So one could say that recovering place can only partly be met through the techniques of research of the old Chicago School of urban sociology. I do think that we need to go back to the school's depth of engagement with urban areas and the effort toward detailed mappings. The type of ethnographies done by Duneier (1999), the scholars Burawoy et al. (1991),

Klinenberg (2003), Lloyd (2005), and McRoberts (2005) are excellent examples, using many of the techniques yet working within a different set of assumptions.

To some extent, it is the major cities in the highly developed world that most clearly display the processes discussed here, or best lend themselves to the heuristics deployed. However, increasingly these processes are present in cities in developing countries as well (Santos, De Souze, and Silveira 1994; Knox and Taylor 1995; Cohen et al. 1996; Stren 1996; Parnreiter 2002; Parsa and Keivani 2002; Schiffer Ramos 2002; Gugler 2004; several chapters in Amen et al. 2006). Their lesser visibility is often due to the fact that they are submerged in the megacity syndrome. Sheer population size and urban sprawl create their own orders of magnitude (e.g., Dogan and Kasarda 1988; Gugler 2004; Kerbo 2005); and while they may not alter much the power equation that I describe, they do change the weight, and the legibility, of some of these properties (e.g., Portes and Lungo 1992a, 1992b; Cohen et al. 1996; Stren 1996; Marcuse and van Kempen 2000; Roberts and Portes 2006).

In the next few sections, I examine these issues through the lens of the urban economy in a global digital age. In the second half of the chapter, I do so through the lens of politics and culture.

CITIES IN A GLOBAL ECONOMY

The meaning of cities in a global and increasingly digitized age is one of the subjects we confront as we enter the new century (Friedmann 1986; Castells 1989; Short and Kim 1999; Valle and Torres 2000; Sassen [1991] 2001; Thrift and Amin 2002; Drainville 2004). Yet the understandings and the categories that still dominate mainstream discussions about the future of advanced economies imply that in a global digital age, the city has become obsolete for leading economic actors; this would also imply the obsoleteness of the city as a site for researching major nonurban dynamics. We need to subject these notions to critical examination. There are at least two sets of issues that need to be teased out if we are to understand the role of cities in a global information economy and, further, the capacity of urban research to produce knowledge about that economy. One of these concerns the extent to which these new types of electronic formations, such as electronic financial markets, are indeed disembedded from social contexts. The second set of issues concerns the role of place for global firms and global markets.

In the late twentieth century, massive developments in telecommunications and the ascendance of information industries led analysts and politicians to proclaim the end of cities. Cities, they told us, would become obsolete as economic entities. The growth of information industries allows firms and workers to remain connected no matter where they are located. The digitizing of services and trade shifts many economic transactions to electronic networks, where they can move instantaneously around the globe or within a country. Indeed, from the 1970s onward, we saw large-scale relocations of offices and factories to less congested and lower-cost areas than central cities, and we saw the growth of computerized workplaces that could be located anywhere—in a clerical "factory" in the Bahamas or in a home in the suburbs. Finally, the emergent globalization of economic activity seemed to suggest that place—particularly the type of place represented by cities—no longer mattered much for advanced sectors.

All these trends are happening, and they are becoming more intense. But they are only half of the story of today's global and digital age. Alongside the well-documented spatial dispersal of economic activities and the digitizing of growing parts of the sphere of consumption and entertainment, we are seeing in a growing number of cities a growing concentration of a wide range of highly specialized professional activities, top-level management and control operations, and, perhaps most unexpectedly, a multiplication of low-wage jobs and low-profit economic sectors. More analytically, we might think of these trends as the development of novel forms of territorial centralization amidst rapidly expanding economic and social networks with global span.

Given the generalized trends toward dispersal—whether at the metropolitan or global level—and the widespread conviction that this is the future, what requires explaining is that at the same time, we see this growth of centralized territorial nodes. What the evidence is increasingly showing is that firms and markets that operate in multisited national and global settings require central places where the top-level work of running global systems gets done. Furthermore, information technologies and industries designed to span the globe actually require a vast physical infrastructure containing strategic nodes with hyperconcentrations of very material facilities. Finally, even the most advanced information industries, such as global finance and the specialized corporate legal and accounting services, have a "production" process that is partly place bound (see, generally, Sassen [1991] 2001.

Once these place-centered processes are brought into the analysis of the new global and electronic economy, funny things happen. It turns out to be not only the world of top-level transnational managers and professionals but also that of their secretaries and that of the janitors cleaning the buildings where the new class works. Furthermore, it also turns out to be the world of a whole new workforce, often increasingly immigrant and minoritized citizens, who take on the functions once performed by the mother or wife of the older middle classes: Nannies, domestic cleaners, and dog walkers also hold jobs in the new globalized sectors of the economy. So do truck drivers and industrial service workers. We see the emergence of an economic configuration very different from that suggested by the concept of information economy. We recover the material conditions, production sites, and place boundedness that are also part of globalization and the information economy. To understand the new globalized economic sectors, we actually need detailed examinations of a broad range of urban activities, firms, markets, and physical infrastructures that go beyond the images of global electronic networks and the new globally circulating professional classes. (See, e.g., Samers 2002; Ehrenreich and Hochschild 2003; Lloyd 2005; but see also, e.g., Ruggiero and South 1997; Hagedorn 2006.)

These types of detailed examinations allow us to see the actual role played by cities in a global economy. They help us understand why when the new information technologies and telecommunications infrastructures were introduced on a large scale in all advanced industries beginning in the 1980s, we saw sharp growth in the central business districts of the leading cities and international business centers of the world—New York, Los Angeles, London, Tokyo, Paris, Frankfurt, São Paulo, Hong Kong, Sydney, Toronto, among others. For some cities, this took off in the 1980s and for others, in the 1990s. But all experienced some of their highest growth in decades in the actual area covered by state-of-the-art office districts; the related high-end shopping, hotel, and entertainment districts; high-income residential neighborhoods; and the numbers of firms located and opening up in these downtown areas. These trends in major cities go against what should have been expected according to models emphasizing territorial dispersal; this is especially true when one considers the high cost of locating in a major downtown area. Complicating understanding and often getting most of the attention from the media and commentators was the considerable number of large banks and insurance firms and the administrative headquarters of large firms moving out in the 1980s even as the number of smaller, highly specialized and high-profit firms was beginning to grow rapidly in the downtowns of major cities. This shows us that the growth trends taking shape in central cities beneath the aggregate data about losses were part of a new type of economic configuration that could not be captured through standard categories.

THE INTERSECTION OF GLOBAL PROCESSES AND CITIES

These trends raise a series of questions about cities that begin with larger, not necessarily urban issues. How are the management, financing, and servicing processes of internationalization actually constituted in cities that function as regional or global nodes in the world economy? And what is the actual part of the larger work of running the global operations of firms and markets that gets done in these cities?

The answers to these two questions help us understand the new or sharply expanded role of a particular kind of city in the world economy that took off in the mid-1980s. At the heart of this development lie two intersecting processes that are critical to the current economic phase and have received little attention—either empirical or conceptual—from urban sociology, except in the scholarship on world and global cities.

The first process is the sharp growth in the globalization of economic activity. Economic globalization has raised the scale and the complexity of international transactions, thereby feeding the growth of top-level multinational headquarter functions and the growth of services for firms, particularly advanced corporate services. It is important to note that even though globalization raises the scale and complexity of these central functions, these trends are also evident at smaller geographic scales and lower orders of complexity, as would be the case with firms that operate regionally or nationally; central functions also become more complex in these firms as they run increasingly dispersed operations, even though not global, notably setting up chains (often by buying up the traditional single-owner shops) to sell flowers, food, and fuel, or to run chains of hotels and a growing range of service facilities. Although operating in simpler contexts, these firms also need to centralize their control, management, and specialized servicing functions. National and regional market firms need not negotiate the complexities of international borders and the regulations and accounting rules of different countries, but they do create a growing demand for corporate services of all kinds, feeding economic growth in second-order cities.

The second process we need to consider, and one that has received little if any attention from urban sociology, is the growing service intensity in the organization of all industries (see Sassen [1991] 2001, chap. 5; for a comprehensive overview, see Bryson and Daniels 2006). While it partly overlaps with the first process, it is important to recognize that this development has contributed to a massive growth in the demand for services by firms in all industries, from mining and manufacturing to finance and consumer services. Cities are key sites for the production of services for firms. Hence, the increase in service intensity in the organization of all industries has had a significant growth effect on cities beginning in the 1980s. It is important to recognize that this growth in services for firms is evident in cities at different levels of a nation's urban system. Some of these cities cater to regional or subnational markets, others cater to national markets, and yet others cater to global markets. In this context, the specific effect of globalization can be conceived of as one of scale and added complexity.

The key process from the perspective of the urban economy is the growing demand for services by firms in all industries and across market scale—global, national, or regional.

As a result of these two intersecting processes, we see in cities the formation of a new urban economic core of high-level management and specialized service activities that comes to replace the older, typically manufacturing-oriented office core. In the case of cities that are major international business centers, the scale, power, and profit levels of this new core suggest that we are seeing the formation of a new urban economy. This is so in at least two regards. First, even though many of these cities have long been centers for business and finance, since the mid-1980s there have been dramatic changes in the structure of their business and financial sectors, as well as sharp increases in the overall magnitude and weight of these sectors in the urban economy (Sassen [1991] 2001, chaps. 5–7; Abrahamson 2004; Madigan 2004; Bryson and Daniels 2006). Second, the ascendance of the new finance and services complex, particularly in international finance, engenders what may be regarded as a new economic regime; that is, although this sector may account for only a fraction of the economy of a city, it imposes itself on that larger economy. Most notably, the possibility for superprofits in finance has the effect of devalorizing manufacturing insofar as the latter cannot generate the superprofits typical in much financial activity.

This is not to say that everything in the economy of these cities has changed. On the contrary, they still show a great deal of continuity and many similarities with cities that are not global. Rather, the implantation of global processes and markets has meant that the internationalized sector of the economy has expanded sharply and has imposed a new valorization dynamic—that is, a new set of criteria for valuing or pricing various economic activities and outcomes. This has had devastating effects on large sectors of the urban economy. High prices and profit levels in the internationalized sector and its ancillary activities, such as top-of-the-line restaurants and hotels, have made it increasingly difficult for other sectors to compete for space and investments. Many of these other sectors have experienced considerable downgrading and/or displacement; for example, neighborhood shops tailored to local needs are replaced by upscale boutiques and restaurants catering to the new high-income urban elite.

Although at a different order of magnitude, these trends also took off in the early 1990s in a number of major cities in the developing world that have become integrated into various world markets: São Paulo, Buenos Aires, Bangkok, Taipei, and Mexico City are only a few examples. Also in these cities, the new urban core was fed by the deregulation of financial markets, the ascendance of finance and specialized services, and integration into the world markets. The opening of stock markets to foreign investors and the privatization of what were once public sector firms have been crucial institutional arenas for this articulation. Given the vast size of some of these cities, the impact of this new core on their larger urban area is not always as evident as in central London or Frankfurt, but the transformation is still very real.

NATIONAL AND TRANSNATIONAL URBAN SYSTEMS

The trends described in the preceding sections point to the emergence of a new kind of urban system, one operating at the global and transnational regional levels. This is a system wherein cities are crucial nodes for the international coordination and servicing of firms, markets, and even whole economies that are increasingly transnational. And these cities emerge as strategic places in an emergent transnational political and cultural geography. Most cities, however, including most large cities, are not part of these new transnational urban systems, a subject I address briefly in the next section. Typically, urban systems are coterminous with nation-states, and most cities exist within these national geographies. Correspondingly, with rare exceptions (Chase-Dunn 1984; Timberlake 1985; Sassen [1991] 2001), studies of city systems have until recently assumed that the nation-state is the unit of analysis. While this is still the most common view, there is now a growing scholarship that allows for the possibility that intercity networks can cross national borders directly, bypassing the interstate system. This novel focus is partly a function of actual changes in the international sphere, notably the formation of global economic processes discussed in the preceding section and the accompanying deregulation and opening up of national systems.

A rapidly growing and highly specialized research literature began to focus in the 1980s on different types of economic linkages binding cities across national borders (Noyelle and Dutka 1988; Castells 1989; Daniels 1991). Today, this has emerged as a major issue of interest to a variety of disciplines (see, e.g., the growing number of entries in the GaWC Web site [www.lboro.ac.uk/gawc]; Graham and Marvin 1996; Simmonds and Hack 2000; Scott 2001; Smith and Timberlake 2002; Gugler 2004; Taylor 2004; Amen et al. 2006), even though the data are partial and often problematic. Prime examples of such linkages are the multinational networks of affiliates and subsidiaries typical of major firms in manufacturing and specialized services. The internationalization and deregulation of various financial markets is yet another, very recent development that binds cities across borders. An increasing number of stock markets around the world now participate in a global equities market. There are also a growing number of less directly economic linkages, notable among which are a variety of initiatives launched by urban governments that amount to a type of foreign policy by and for cities. In this context, the long-standing tradition of designating sister cities (Zelinsky 1991) has been reactivated since the 1980s, taking on a whole new meaning in the case of cities eager to operate internationally without going through their national governments.

There is good evidence that the development of transnational corporate service firms was associated with the needs of transnational firms for global servicing capabilities (Sassen [1991] 2001, chap. 5; Ernst 2005). One of the best data sets at this time on the global networks of affiliates of leading firms in finance, accounting, law, and advertising is the Globalization and World Cities Study Group and Network, usually referred to as GaWC. Recent

GaWC research shows that the network of affiliates in banking/finance and law firms closely follows the relative importance of world cities in those two sectors. The transnational banking/finance or law firm, therefore, can offer global finance and legal services to a specific segment of potential customers worldwide. Furthermore, global integration of affiliates and markets requires making use of advanced information and telecommunications technology that can come to account for a significant share of costs—not just operational costs but also, and perhaps most important, research and development costs for new products or advances on existing products.

So much of social science is profoundly rooted in the nation-state as the ultimate unit for analysis that conceptualizing processes and systems as transnational is bound to create much controversy (Giddens 1990; Beck 2000). Even much of the literature on world or global cities does not necessarily proclaim the existence of a transnational urban system: In its narrowest form, this literature posits that global cities perform central place functions at a transnational level. But that leaves open the question of the nature of the articulation among global cities. If we accept that they basically compete with each other for global business, then they do not constitute a transnational system, and studying several global cities simply falls into the category of traditional comparative analysis. If, on the other hand, we posit that in addition to competing with each other, global cities are also the sites for transnational processes with multiple locations, then we can begin to explore the possibility of a systemic dynamic binding these cities.

Elsewhere (Sassen [1991] 2001), I have argued that in addition to the central place functions performed by these cities at the global level as posited by Hall (1966), Friedmann and Wolff (1982), and Sassen-Koob (1982), these cities relate to one another in distinct systemic ways. For example, already in the 1980s I found that the interactions between New York, London, and Tokyo, particularly in terms of finance and investment, consisted partly of a series of processes that can be thought of as the "chain of production" in finance. Thus, in the mid-1980s, Tokyo was the main exporter of the raw material we call money, while New York was the leading processing center in the world. It was in New York that many of the new financial instruments were invented and that money either in its raw form or in the form of debt was transformed into instruments aimed at maximizing the returns on that money. London, on the other hand, was a major *entrepôt* that had the network to centralize and concentrate small amounts of capital available in a large number of smaller financial markets around the world, partly as a function of its older network for the administration of the British Empire. This is just one example suggesting that these cities do not simply compete with each other for the same business. There is an economic system that rests on the distinct types of locations and specializations each city represents. Furthermore, it seems likely that the strengthening of

transnational ties among the leading financial and business centers is accompanied by a weakening of the linkages between each of these cities and its hinterland and national urban system. Cities such as Detroit, Liverpool, Manchester, Marseilles, the cities of the Ruhr, and now increasingly Nagoya and Osaka have been affected by the territorial decentralization of many of their key manufacturing industries at the domestic and international levels.

Finally, one of the major trends globally is the growth of megacities in the developing world. The figures and the trends are familiar.

GLOBALIZATION AND NATIONAL URBAN SYSTEMS IN THE GLOBAL SOUTH

What is the impact of economic globalization on national urban systems? Does the globalization of major industries, from auto manufacturing to finance, have distinct effects on different types of national urban systems? Many regions in the world—Latin America, the Caribbean, large parts of Asia, and (to some extent) Africa—have long been characterized by urban primacy as an older scholarship has established (Hardoy 1975; Linn 1983; Dogan and Kasarda 1988; Stren and White 1989; Feldbauer et al. 1993). Primate cities account for a disproportionate share of population, employment, and gross national product (GNP).

Primacy is not simply a matter of absolute size, nor is large size a marker of primacy. Primacy is a relative condition that holds within a national urban system. Some of the largest urban agglomerations in the world do not necessarily entail primacy: New York, for example, is among the 20 largest cities in the world, but it is not a primate city, given the multipolar nature of the urban system in the United States. Furthermore, primacy is not an exclusive trait of developing countries, even though its most extreme forms are to be found in the developing world: Tokyo and London are primate cities. Finally, the emergence of the so-called megacities may or may not be associated with primacy. The 20 largest urban agglomerations by 2003 (and the foreseeable future) include some cities that are not necessarily primate, such as New York, Los Angeles, Tianjin, Osaka, Calcutta, and Shanghai, and others that can be characterized as having low levels of primacy, such as Paris and Buenos Aires.

Primacy and megacity status are clearly fed by urban population growth, a process that is expected to continue. But they combine in multiple patterns; there is no single model. The evidence worldwide points to the ongoing urbanization of the population, especially in developing countries. As in the developed countries, one component of urban growth in those countries is the suburbanization of growing sectors of the population. The higher the level of development, the higher the urbanization rate is likely to be. Thus, a country like Argentina had an urbanization rate of 90.1% by 2003, which is quite similar to that of highly developed countries, although it is to some extent a function of the primacy of Buenos Aires in the national urban system. In contrast, Algeria's urbanization rate of 59% and Kenya's 39% differ sharply from the urbanization level in developed countries. Finally, there are countries such as India and China that have vast urban agglomerations, notwithstanding their very low rate of urbanization. Vast population size can trump the fact of having many very large cities. As a result, the information conveyed by an indicator such as the urbanization rate in these countries differs from that of countries with more average population sizes.

Given the considerable variability across the global south, in what follows the focus is especially on Latin America and the Caribbean, areas that have received much attention in the scholarship and have also been profoundly affected by the world economy. On the subject of primacy, the literature about Latin America shows considerable convergence in the identification of major patterns, along with multiple interpretations of these patterns. Many studies in the late 1970s and early 1980s found sharper primacy rather than the emergence of the more balanced national urban systems forecast by *modernization* theory (for critical evaluations, see El-Shakhs 1972; Roberts 1976; Smith 1985; Walters 1985). The disintegration of rural economies, including the displacement of small landholders by expanding large-scale commercial agriculture, and the continuing inequalities in the spatial distribution of institutional resources are generally recognized as key factors strengthening primacy (Regional Employment Program for Latin America and the Caribbean [PREALC] 1987; Kowarick, Campos, and de Mello 1991; for an examination of current conditions generally in the global South, see Kerbo 2006).

Less widely known and documented is that in the 1980s there was a deceleration in primacy in several, although not all, countries in Latin America. This trend will not eliminate the growth of megacities, but it is worth discussing in some detail because it resulted in part from specific aspects of economic globalization—concrete ways in which global processes implant themselves in particular localities. The overall shift in growth strategies toward export-oriented development and large-scale tourism enclaves created growth poles that emerged as alternatives to the primate cities for rural to urban migrations (Landell-Mills, Agarwala, and Please 1989; Portes and Lungo 1992a, 1992b; Gilbert 1996; Roberts and Portes 2006). This shift was substantially promoted by the expansion of world markets for commodities and the foreign direct investments of transnational corporations, both in turn often stimulated by World Bank and International Monetary Fund programs.

One of the best sources of information on the emergence of these patterns in the 1980s is a large, collective, multicity study directed by Portes and Lungo (1992a, 1992b) that focused on the Caribbean region, including

Central America. The Caribbean has a long history of urban primacy. Portes and Lungo studied the urban systems of Costa Rica, the Dominican Republic, Guatemala, Haiti, and Jamaica, countries that clearly reflect the immense variety of cultures and languages in this region. These countries represent a wide range of colonization patterns, ethnic compositions, economic development, and political stability. In the 1980s, export-oriented development, a cornerstone of the Caribbean Basin Initiative, and the intense promotion of tourism began to draw workers and firms. Expanded suburbanization has also had the effect of decentralizing population in the primate cities of the Caribbean, while adding to the larger metropolitan areas of these cities. The effect of these trends can be seen clearly in Jamaica, for example, where the primacy index declined from 7.2 in 1960 to 2.2 in 1990, largely as a result of the development of the tourism industry on the northern coast of the island, the revival of bauxite production for export in the interior, and the growth of satellite cities at the edges of the broader Kingston metropolitan area.

In some Caribbean countries, however, the new growth poles have had the opposite effect. Thus, in Costa Rica, a country with a far more balanced urban system, the promotion of export manufacturing and tourism has tended to concentrate activities in the metropolitan area of the primate city of San José and its immediate surrounding cities, such as Cartago. Finally, in the case of Guatemala, export manufacturing and tourism are far less developed, largely because of the extremely violent political situation until the 1990s. Development of export-oriented growth remains centered in agriculture. Guatemala has one of the highest levels of urban primacy in Latin America because alternative growth poles have been rare. Only in the 1990s did efforts to develop export agriculture promote some growth in intermediate cities, with coffee and cotton centers growing more rapidly than the capital, Guatemala City.

At the same time, deregulation and the associated sharp growth of foreign direct investment since the early 1990s has further strengthened the role of the major Latin American business centers, particularly Mexico City, São Paulo, and Buenos Aires; Buenos Aires has had sharp ups and downs—a sharp downturn in 2001 due to Argentina's massive crisis and a resurgence in 2005. Privatization has been a key component of this growth. Foreign direct investment, via privatization and other channels, has been associated with deregulation of financial markets and other key economic institutions. Thus, the central role played by the stock market and other financial markets in these increasingly complex investment processes has raised the economic importance of the major cities where these institutions are concentrated. Because the bulk of the value of investment in privatized enterprises and other, often related investments has been in Mexico, Argentina, and Brazil, the impact of vast capital inflows is particularly felt in the corporate and financial sectors in their primate cities—Mexico City, Buenos Aires, and São Paulo. We see in these cities the emergence of conditions that resemble patterns evident in major Western cities: highly dynamic financial markets and specialized service sectors; the over-valorization of the output, firms, and workers in these sectors; and the devalorization of the rest of the economic system (Ciccolella and Mignaqui 2002; Parnreiter 2002; Shiffer Ramos 2002; Buechler 2007).

In brief, economic globalization has had a range of impacts on cities and urban systems in Latin America and the Caribbean. In some cases, it has contributed to the development of new growth poles outside the major urban agglomerations. In others, it has actually raised the weight of primate urban agglomerations, in that the new growth poles were developed in these areas. A third case is that represented by the major business and financial centers in the region, several of which saw a sharp strengthening in their linkages with global markets and with the major international business centers in the developed world. Production zones, centers for tourism, and major business and financial centers are three types of sites for the implantation of global processes. Beyond these sites is a vast terrain containing cities, towns, and villages that is either increasingly unhinged from this new international growth dynamic or is part of the low-profit end of long chains of production. The character of the articulation or dissociation is not simply a question of city size, since there exist long subcontracting chains connecting workers in small villages to the world markets. It is, rather, a question of how these emergent transnational economic systems are articulated, how they connect specific localities in less-developed countries with markets and localities in highly developed countries (see, e.g., Bonacich et al. 1994; Gereffi, Humphrey, and Sturgeon 2005). The implantation of global processes seems to have contributed to sharpening the separation between cities, or sectors within cities, that are articulated with the global economy and those that are not. This is a new type of interurban inequality, one not predicated on old hierarchies of city size. The new inequality differs from the long-standing forms of inequality present in cities and national urban systems because of the extent to which it results from the *implantation* of a global dynamic, be it the internationalization of production and finance or international tourism.

A NEW TRANSNATIONAL POLITICAL GEOGRAPHY

The incorporation of cities into a new cross-border geography of centrality also signals the emergence of a parallel political geography. What we are seeing is a set of specific and partial rather than all-encompassing dynamics. It is not only the transmigration of capital that takes place in this global grid but also that of people, both rich (i.e., the new transnational professional workforce) and poor (i.e., most migrant workers); and it is a space for the transmigration of cultural forms, the reterritorialization of "local" subcultures.

Using a variety of methodologies and conceptual framings, a growing scholarship is beginning to document these trends, signaling that major cities have emerged as a strategic site not only for global capital but also for the transnationalization of labor and the formation of translocal politics, communities, and identities or subjectivities (e.g., Boyd 1989; Basch, Glick-Schiller, and Blanc-Szanton 1994; Mahler 1995; Smith 1995; Bonilla et al. 1998; Skillington 1998; Body-Gendrot 1999; Yuval-Davis 1999; Cordero-Guzman et al. 2001; Levitt 2001; Smith and Guarnizo 2001; Hagedorn 2006; Bartlett, 2007). In this regard, cities are a site for new types of political operations. The centrality of place in a context of global processes makes possible a transnational economic and political opening for the formation of new claims and hence for the constitution of entitlements, notably rights to place. At the limit, this could be an opening for new forms of "citizenship" (e.g., Holston 1996; Dawson 1999; Torres et al. 1999). The emphasis on the transnational and hyper-mobile character of capital has contributed to a sense of powerlessness among local actors, a sense of the futility of resistance. But an analysis that emphasizes place suggests that the new global grid of strategic sites is a terrain for politics and engagement (Abu-Lughod 1994; Dunn 1994; King 1996; Brenner and Theodore 2002; Sandercock 2003; Drainville 2004; see, generally, Brenner and Keil 2006; Bartlett 2007).

If we consider that large cities concentrate both the leading sectors of global capital and a growing share of disadvantaged populations—immigrants, many of the disadvantaged women, people of color generally, and in the megacities of developing countries, masses of shanty dwellers—then we can see that cities have become a strategic terrain for a whole series of conflicts and contradictions (Sennett 1990; Massey and Denton 1993; Wilson 1997; Allen et al. 1999; Body-Gendrot 1999; Isin 2000; Soja 2000; Drainville 2004; Sassen 2004). We can then think of cities also as one of the sites for the contradictions of the globalization of capital (see Katznelson 1992 on Marx and cities).

Foreign firms and international businesspeople have increasingly been entitled to do business in whatever country and city they chose—entitled by new legal regimes, by the new economic culture, and through progressive deregulation of national economies. They are among the new city users. The new city users have made an often immense claim on the city and have reconstituted strategic spaces of the city in their image. Their claim to the city is rarely contested, even though the costs and benefits to cities have barely been examined. They have profoundly marked the urban landscape. For Martinotti (1993), they contribute to change the social morphology of the city; the new city of these city users is a fragile one, whose survival and successes are centered on an economy of high productivity, advanced technologies, and intensified exchanges (Martinotti 1993). It is a city whose space consists of airports, top-level business districts, top-of-the-line hotels and restaurants, in brief, a sort of urban glamour zone.

Perhaps at the other extreme are those who use urban political violence to make their claims on the city, claims that lack the de facto legitimacy enjoyed by the new "city users." These are claims made by actors struggling for recognition, entitlement, claiming their rights to the city (Fainstein 1993; Wacquant 1997; Wright 1997; Body-Gendrot 1999; Hagedorn 2006). These claims have, of course, a long history; every new epoch brings specific conditions to the manner in which the claims are made. The growing weight of "delinquency" (e.g., smashing cars and shop windows; robbing and burning stores) in some of these uprisings over the last decade in major cities of the developed world is perhaps an indication of the sharpened socioeconomic zone and the urban war zone (Body-Gendrot 1993, 1999). The extreme visibility of the difference is likely to contribute to further brutalization of the conflict: the indifference and greed of the new elites versus the hopelessness and rage of the poor.

In the next two sections, I focus on two particular features of this emergent transnational political geography centered largely in intercity networks. These capture at least two important features of the larger dynamic discussed in this section that need to be addressed by an urban sociology of the early twenty-first century. They are the shift in diasporic networks away from an exclusive orientation to the homeland and toward other diasporic groups across the globe, and second, the emergence of a globally networked politics enacted by often powerless and resource-poor individuals and groups focused on issues that are deeply local but recur in localities across the globe.

GLOBAL CITIES AND DIASPORIC NETWORKS

There has been rapid growth in the variety of networks concerned with transboundary issues such as immigration, asylum, international women's agendas, antiglobalization struggles, and many others (e.g., Poster 1997; Mele 1999; Mills 2002; Yang 2003; Lustiger-Thaler and Dubet 2004). While these are not necessarily urban in their orientation or genesis, their geography of operations is partly inserted in a large number of cities (e.g., Riemens and Lovink 2002; Yang 2003). The new network technologies, especially the Internet, ironically have strengthened the urban map of these transboundary networks (for a critical examination of key features of these technologies, see, e.g., Wajcman 2002; Van de Donk et al. 2005; Dean, Anderson, and Lovink, 2006). It does not have to be that way, but at this time cities and the networks that bind them function as an anchor and an enabler of cross-border transactions and struggles. Global cities, especially, already have multiple intercity transactions and immigrants from many different parts of the world. These same developments and conditions also facilitate the globalizing of terrorist and trafficking networks.

Global cities and the new strategic geographies that connect them and partly bypass national states are becoming one factor in the development of globalized diasporic networks (e.g., Ong and Nonini 1997; Axel 2002). This is a development from the ground up, connecting a diaspora's multiple groups distributed across various places. In doing so, these networks multiply the transversal transactions among these groups and destabilize the exclusive orientation to the homeland typical of the older radial pattern. Furthermore, an even partial reorientation away from national homeland politics can partly lead such a group to transact with other diasporas in a city, as well as with nondiasporic groups involved in other types of transnationalism. In such developments, in turn, lies the possibility that at least some of these networks and groups can become part of the infrastructure for global civil society rather than being confined to deeply nationalistic projects (Sassen 2004). These dynamics can then be seen as producing a shift toward globalizing diasporas by enabling transversal connections among the members of a given diaspora flung across the world, and by intensifying the transactions among diverse diasporic and nondiasporic groups within a given city.

Cities are thick enabling environments for these types of activities, even though the networks themselves are not urban per se. In this regard, these cities enable the experience of participation in global nonstate networks. We might say that global civil society gets enacted partly in the microspaces of daily life rather than on some putative global stage. Groups can experience themselves as part of a globalized diaspora even when they are in a place where there might be few conationals and the term "diaspora" hardly applies. In the case of global cities, there is the added dimension of the global corporate economy and its networks and infrastructures enabling cross-border transactions and having the effect of partly denationalizing urban space.

Both globalization and the international human rights regime have contributed to create operational and legal openings for nonstate actors to enter international arenas once exclusive to national states. Various, often as yet very minor developments signal that the state is no longer the exclusive subject for international law or the only actor in international relations. Other actors—from nongovernmental organizations and First Nation peoples to immigrants and refugees who become subjects of adjudication in human rights decisions—are increasingly emerging as subjects of international law and actors in international relations. That is to say, these nonstate actors can gain visibility as individuals and as collectivities, and come out of the invisibility of aggregate membership in a nation-state exclusively represented by the state.

The key nexus in this configuration is that the weakening of the exclusive formal authority of states over national territory facilitates the ascendance of sub- and transnational spaces and actors in politico-civic processes. The national as container of social process and power is cracked, enabling the emergence of a geography of politics and civics that links subnational spaces. Cities are foremost in this new geography. The density of political and civic cultures in large cities and their daily practices roots, implants, and localizes global civil society in people's lives. Insofar as the global economic system can be shown to be partly embedded in specific types of places and partly constituted through highly specialized cross-border networks connecting today's global cities, one research task for those of us who want to understand how this all intersects with immigrants and diasporas is, then, to know about the specific contents and institutional locations of this multiscalar globalization. Furthermore, it means understanding how the emergence of global imaginaries changes the meaning of processes that may be much older than the current phase of globalization, but that today are inscribed by the latter. Immigrant and diasporic communities are much older than today's globalization. But that does not mean that they are not altered by various specific forms of globalization today.

The space constituted by the worldwide grid of global cities, a space with new economic and political potentialities, is perhaps one of the most strategic spaces for the formation of transnational identities and communities. This is a space that is both place-centered in that it is embedded in particular and strategic cities, and it is transterritorial because it connects sites that are not geographically proximate yet intensely connected to each other.

A POLITICS OF PLACES AND GLOBAL CIRCUITS

The cross-border network of global cities is a space where we are seeing the formation of new types of "global" politics of place. These vary considerably: They may involve contesting corporate globalization or they may involve homeland politics. The demonstrations by the antiglobalization network have signaled the potential for developing a politics centered on places understood as locations on global networks. Some of the new globalizing diasporas have become intensive and effective users of the Internet to engage in these global politics of place around issues that concern them. This is a place-specific politics with global span. It is a type of political work deeply embedded in people's actions and activities but made possible partly by the existence of global digital linkages (Meyer 1997; Espinoza 1999; Miller and Slater 2000; Riemens and Lovink 2002; Van de Donk et al. 2005; Dean et al. 2006).

Furthermore, it is a form of political and institution-building work centered in cities and networks of cities and in nonformal political actors. We see here the potential transformation of a whole range of "local" conditions or institutional domains (such as the household, the community, the neighborhood, the local school, and health care entities) into localities situated on global networks. From being lived or experienced as nonpolitical, or domestic, these places are transformed into "microenvironments with global span." What I mean by this term is that technical connectivity will create a variety of links with other similar local entities in other neighborhoods in the same city, in other cities, and in neighborhoods and cities in other countries. A community of practice can emerge that creates multiple lateral, horizontal communications, collaborations, solidarities, and supports. This can enable local political or nonpolitical actors to enter into cross-border politics.

The space of the city is a far more concrete place for politics than that of the national state system. It becomes a place where nonformal political actors can be part of the political scene in a way that is much more difficult at the national level. Nationally, politics needs to run through existing formal systems: whether the electoral political system or the judiciary (taking state agencies to court). Nonformal political actors are rendered invisible in the space of national politics. The city accommodates a broad range of political activities—squatting, demonstrations against police brutality, fighting for the rights of immigrants and the homeless, the politics of culture and identity, gay and lesbian and queer politics, and the homeland politics that many diasporic groups engage in. Much of this becomes visible on the street. Much of urban politics is concrete, enacted by people rather than dependent on massive media technologies. Street-level politics make possible the formation of new types of political subjects that do not have to go through the formal political system. These conditions can be critical for highly politicized diasporic groups and in the context of globalization and Internet access, can easily lead to the globalizing of a diaspora. The city also enables the operations of illegal networks.

The mix of focused activism and local/global networks represented by the variety of organizations involved creates conditions for the emergence of at least partly transnational identities. The possibility of identifying with larger communities of practice or membership can bring about the partial unmooring of identities and thereby facilitate a globalizing of a diaspora and a weakened radial structure with the homeland at the center of the distribution of the groups of a given diaspora. While this does not necessarily neutralize attachments to a country or national cause, it does shift this attachment to include translocal communities of practice and/or membership.

Beyond the impact on immigrants and diasporas, the network of cities becomes a crucial building block for an architecture of global civil society that can incorporate both the micropractices and microobjectives of people's political passions without diluting the former. The possibility of transnational identities emerging as a consequence of this thickness of micropolitics is crucial for strengthening global civil society; the risk of nationalism and fundamentalism is, clearly, present in these dynamics as well.

CONCLUSION

The processes examined in this chapter call for the development of specific analytic categories. The transnationalization of economic activity is evident in a variety of the conditions examined here: the growth of global markets for finance and specialized services, the need for transnational servicing networks in response to sharp increases in international investment, the reduced role of the government in the regulation of international economic activity, and the corresponding ascendance of other institutional arenas, notably global markets and corporate headquarters. There is an emergent scholarship in urban sociology that has been focusing on these issues through the lens of global and world cities, discussed in this chapter. But there are key questions that require more research. One of these, on which there is little agreement, is whether this multiplication of intercity transactions may be contributing to the formation of transnational urban systems, which might eventually partly bypass national states, especially in a context of globalization, deregulation, and privatization.

These types of dynamics bring about a rather profound transformation in the character of the city as an object of study and in the character of the urban as a designator. For instance, the pronounced orientation to the world markets evident in such cities raises questions about the articulation with their hinterlands and nation-states. Cities typically have been and still are deeply embedded in the economies of their region, indeed often reflecting the characteristics of the latter. And urban systems are meant to be national and to secure the territorial integration of a country. But cities that are strategic sites in the global economy tend, in part, to disconnect from their region and their national urban systems, thereby undermining a key proposition in traditional scholarship about urban systems—namely, that these systems promote the territorial integration of regional and national economies.

A second bundle of issues examined in this chapter are the tendencies contributing to new forms of inequality among cities and within cities. Both of these types of inequality have been part of the character of cities since their very beginning. But today's conditions are sharpening these cross-border geographies of centrality constituted through the growing articulation among the advanced economic sectors and high-level professional classes of an increasing number of cities. On the other hand, cities and areas outside these new geographies of centrality tend to become peripheralized, or become more so than they had been. Similarly, within cities we are seeing a sharpening of divisions and new types of conflicts.

A third set of issues concerns the emergence of a broad set of cross-border networks involving poor and generally disadvantaged or powerless actors. This is in turn producing a whole series of new and newly invigorated intercity geographies for both practices and subjective operations. This trend undermines a critical assumption about the urban poor—their lack of connection to larger networks and their lack of social capital.

These are just some of the challenges that urban sociology confronts as we enter the twenty-first century. As I indicated at the beginning of this chapter, most cities and urban populations are not affected by these trends, and hence much of the rich scholarship in urban sociology can handle vast stretches of urban reality. But we do also need to recognize the emergence of new foundational dynamics that while minor in the larger urban landscape do nonetheless call for our scholarly attention.

49

THE SOCIOLOGY OF MIGRATION

ZAI LIANG

State University of New York, Albany

Migration is an old story. For thousands of years, people have migrated to search for food, survive, conquer frontiers, colonize new territories, escape from war zones or political turmoil, and look for new and more rewarding and exciting opportunities. Originating from Africa, the modern *Homo sapiens* arrived in Eurasia at least 40,000 years ago and in North and South America more than 20,000 years ago (Davis 1974; Diamond 1997; Hirschman 2005). In a broad sense, the history of the world is a history of human migration and settlement. As a country of immigrants, the United States is perhaps the best example in this regard. Sociologists have long been interested in theorizing about different types of societies—from Ferdinand Tönnies's dichotomy of "community" and "society" to Émile Durkheim's "mechanic solidarity" and "organic solidarity." The former, being the more traditional society, is characterized by more intimate relations among members—that is, people in the group know each other well. Decisions in these communities were often made by village or clan leaders rather than collectively. In contrast, in modern societies, it is impossible to know all the people in the community, and decisions concerning the welfare of community members are more likely to be made jointly in one way or another. The typology of the founding fathers of sociology clearly captures the major trends of social change and transformation over time; what was not made explicit was that underlying this transition from a traditional to a modern society, there is also a story of migration. As cities become centers of economic activities, there is also an increase in rural to urban migration. Urban communities are commonly much larger than villages, and anonymity is a major feature of urban society. Likewise, migration is also dealt with in some of Karl Marx's writings. For example, Marx wrote, "In the sphere of agriculture, modern industry has a more revolutionary effect than elsewhere, for this reason, it annihilates the peasant, that bulwark of the old society, and replaces him by the wage-labourer" (quoted in Tucker 1978:416). More often than not, the wage laborers in England that Marx was referring to then were migrants from rural areas.

The main purpose of this chapter is to review sociological studies of migration and highlight some of the most important contributions that sociologists have made to the field of migration studies. In doing so, we plan to cover international migration as well as internal migration. Given the vast scope of the literature on migration and the continuing expansion of the field, this review has to be highly selective. We end the chapter by discussing the future prospects of research on migration.

MIGRATION AS A MULTIDISCIPLINARY FIELD OF STUDY

Migration attracted scholars from multiple disciplines from the very beginning. Given the large body of literature on migration contributed by scholars from different fields—economics, demography, anthropology, history, geography, and sociology—it is impossible to discuss all

AUTHOR'S NOTE: This chapter is supported, in part, by a grant from the National Science Foundation (SES-0138016).

the major practitioners in the field. Therefore, instead of providing an exhaustive list of scholars in these disciplines who study migration, I will highlight the most important contributions by practitioners from two major disciplines (geography and economics) to the field of migration studies. In fact, one of the earliest scholarly papers on migration was written by a geographer, Ravenstein (1889) using census data from England, in which he outlined several laws of migration. Naturally, geographers are concerned with migration because migration inevitably involves crossing geographical boundaries and changes the spatial distribution of the population (within and across countries). Some of the most well-known and influential geographers who work on migration issues include Wilbur Zelinsky and Andrei Rogers. In an attempt to develop a parallel theory of migration similar to the theory of demographic transition, Zelinsky (1971) proposed the theory of mobility transition, in which he outlined five stages of mobility associated with different stages of development. One of the significant insights from Zelinsky's theory is that he recognized a relationship between technological changes and forms/types of migration/mobility. For example, as modes of transportation (i.e., high-speed trains and the popular use of automobiles) improve, people are more likely to engage in circular migration or commuting to cities from suburban areas.

Likewise, based on the idea of the model fertility schedule and on fundamental regularities of migration by age, Rogers and his colleagues developed a model migration schedule (Rogers and Willekens 1986). This approach begins with the observation that like fertility and mortality, migration is an age-dependent social behavior—that is, patterns of migration are closely related to age. To construct a model migration schedule, Rogers and colleagues identified three stages/components of migration associated with the individual life cycle: pre–labor force component, labor force component, and post–labor force component. There are two sets of parameters used to estimate such models: one associated with the profile of migration and the other associated with the level of migration. *Profile* describes how migration propensity varies by age and *level* depicts the magnitude of migration. The most important insight from this line of research is that, typically, countries share a strikingly similar profile of migration and differ only by level. In other words, the age pattern of migration is nearly universally similar (at least based on the data available to Rogers and his colleagues), and the difference in migration between countries lies only in the level of migration (some countries have higher levels of migration and others have low levels of migration).

More recently, the increasing application of geographical information system (GIS) in many fields (including migration) reflects the unique contribution of geographers, who have revolutionized our understanding of spatial patterns of migration and population distribution. Here, we discuss just three ways in which GIS helps researchers study migration behavior. First, GIS allows us to visualize patterns of migration that can take several characteristics into account. Second, GIS technology can allow us to model explicitly how the spatial location of a community affects the prevalence of certain behaviors, such as migration or fertility, among individuals in the community (Weeks 2004). For example, Community A is already established as a migrant-sending community. If Community B (not a migrant-sending community) is located near Community A, we can model the extent to which this spatial linkage between Community A and Community B can influence the migration behavior of individuals in Community B. This analysis is often under the rubric of the analysis of diffusion patterns. Third, migrants (both internal and international) are often difficult to capture in national surveys. In the United States, for example, some of the immigrants are undocumented, and they usually try to avoid any contact with people from formal organizations. In China, most of the migrants are not registered at their destinations. Thus, a survey that uses registered population will miss a substantial number of migrants. Recently, Landry and Shen (2005) have used the spatial sampling technique to increase the coverage of China's migrant population. Their results suggest that the coverage of migrant populations has improved significantly.

Economists have also made important contributions to the field of migration studies. Larry Sjaastad (1969) established the foundation of the micro-economic theory of human migration, which has proved to be helpful to migration researchers. The central idea is that based on cost-benefits calculation, individuals choose to move to places where they can be most productive. In contrast, economists in the neoclassical macro-economic tradition would pay more attention to wage differentials between regions (countries) (Todaro 1976). The wage in turn is determined by supply of and demand for labor in each region. Another economist whose work has drawn attention recently is Oded Stark (1991), who, along with his associates, has popularized the so-called new economics of migration. There are at least two significant insights in Stark's work. One is the notion that migration decisions are not made by isolated individuals but rather by families or households. Second, unlike the neoclassical macro-economic theory of migration, which assumes that higher wage rates at migrant destinations (compared with migrant origins) drive migrant flows, the new economics of migration rejects this assumption and only assumes that economic conditions in the migrant-sending and -receiving regions are negatively or weakly associated (Massey et al. 1998). This departure from the narrow focus on wage differentials has important implications. For instance, within the framework of the new economics of migration, even if the wage gap between the United States and Mexico remains the same or is even reduced, international migration from Mexico to the United States can still continue if social and political changes in Mexico increase the degree of uncertainty or risks involved in living there.

In the field of international migration, among economists, George Borjas (1999) probably has done the most research on immigration issues. One of the most important findings of his work is his thesis of the "declining quality of immigrants"—that is, over time, there has been a significant decline in the relative education of immigrants entering the U.S. labor market. Further, this decline in the quality of immigrants coincides with change in the source countries of immigration, from Europe to Latin America and Asia. However, Borjas's results are inconclusive. As Alba and Nee (2003) have pointed out, by using formal education as the yardstick of the quality of immigrants, Borjas probably understated the pace of assimilation of recent immigrants due to on-the-job learning and adult education. Borjas's (1999) results are also confounded by the possibility of emigration of successful immigrants. Moreover, in a recent paper using cohorts, derived from administrative data, of people who had immigrated in the 1970s, 1980s, and 1990s, Jasso (2004) casts further doubt on the thesis of declining quality of immigrants. For example, Jasso (2004) found no evidence of declining quality of immigrants among female immigrants.

Having provided an overview of major contributions by scholars in other social science fields, we now turn to discussion of the relationship between migration studies and the development of American sociology and focus on contributions made by sociologists in migration studies.

MIGRATION STUDIES AND AMERICAN SOCIOLOGY

The University of Chicago was the first to have a sociology department in the United States, which was founded in 1892 (Bulmer 1984). The turn of the twentieth century was a significant time in the immigration history of the United States. This was a period when the country witnessed one of the largest immigrant flows, mainly characterized by immigration from Southern and Eastern European countries. Over the period from 1891 to 1930, nearly 23 million immigrants arrived in the United States. Most of the immigrants who came from Eastern and Southern European countries settled in major metropolitan areas. For example, in 1910, 70 percent of the population in the city of Chicago consisted of immigrants and their children (Steinberg 1989). One of the University of Chicago sociologists, W. I. Thomas, wrote that "immigration was a burning question . . . this was mainly the new immigration, from southern and eastern Europe. The larger groups were Poles, Italians, and Jews" (cited in Bulmer 1984:46). Given this statement, it was not surprising that W. I. Thomas went on to conduct a major project on the Polish immigrants. This project culminated in a landmark book with his Polish collaborator Florien Znaniecki, *The Polish Peasants in Europe and America* (Thomas and Znaniecki 1984).

One of the innovations of the book was the use of life histories of immigrants so that scholars could study "changes of attitude over time." Thomas and Znaniecki (1984) also used letters and diaries from immigrants. But perhaps the most profound impact the book had on the sociology of immigration was that it opened up a new research methodology: life history method in the study of immigrant life. When applied to a large and representative sample of immigrants, the technique is powerful in making statements and generalizations about the life of immigrants. For example, in the Mexican Migration Project, directed by Douglas S. Massey and Jorge Durand, systematic life history data were collected on migration history, marriage history, fertility history, and labor history (Massey et al. 1987). As a result, the project allowed researchers to explore a variety of topics related to the immigration process, such as migration networks, wages, gender consequences of migration, and the impact of immigration on source communities. The second main contribution of this book was the explicit attention to migrant-receiving as well as migrant-sending communities. This recognition led to the authors' efforts to collect data at both migrant origin and migrant destination. This method of linking migrant origin with destination proved to have a long-lasting influence in the field of migration studies (Landale et al. 2000; Massey et al. 1987).

While W. I. Thomas was studying the Polish peasants, his other colleagues at the University of Chicago were busy studying other aspects of immigrant life, again using Chicago as a social laboratory. Among them, two of the most influential sociologists, Robert Park and Ernest Burgess, proposed the idea of assimilation to describe the experience of immigrants and minorities. According to Park and Burgess (1969),

> assimilation is a process of interpenetration and fusion in which persons and groups acquire the memories, sentiments, and attitudes of other persons and groups and, by sharing their experience and history, are incorporated with them in a common cultural life. (P. 735)

This assimilation paradigm has long been the dominant perspective in understanding the trajectories of successive generations of immigrants. The paradigm has been significantly expanded and elaborated by Milton Gordon (1964).

Long a paradigm for the study of immigrants and various ethnic groups, the assimilation thesis has recently met some challenges when applied to the situation with post-1965 nonwhite immigrants (Zhou 1999). In light of evidence that is not entirely consistent with the assimilation perspective, Portes and Zhou (1993) proposed an alternative theoretical paradigm, known as "segmented assimilation." The key insight of segmented assimilation is that the assimilation process will not be the same for all contemporary immigrant groups. The assimilation process is segmented because of possible divergent paths for different immigrant groups. Some will follow the time-honored path of rapid acculturation and joining the mainstream white middle class. Others will experience socioeconomic mobility but will preserve the immigrant community's values and maintain some degree of ethnic culture and tradition. The third possibility is that some immigrant groups (mainly West Indians) actually experience downward mobility, merging with the native-born African American population in inner cities (Zhou 1999). Although scholars agree on these divergent paths of mobility for immigrants, no one declares that the assimilation paradigm from the Chicago School of Sociology is dead.

In a recent book, Richard Alba and Victor Nee (2003) make the most forceful defense of the assimilation paradigm. Examining evidence on language, socioeconomic mobility, and intermarriage, they show that assimilation continues to be a dominant force that characterizes today's immigrants and their children. In defending the assimilation perspective, Alba and Nee also remind us of two important facts. One is that today's immigrants and their children live in a favorable social environment as a result of institutional changes brought about by the civil rights movement. Second, the experience of earlier generations of European immigrants tells us that in the process of becoming Americans, immigrants also changed American society. Ultimately, it is also an empirical question whether the assimilation paradigm will continue to hold for the new immigrants and their children in the twenty-first century.

MIGRATION AND ECONOMIC DEVELOPMENT: MYTH AND REALITY

There is a reciprocal relationship between migration and development. Migration is driven by economic development. Economic development in urban areas generates demand for labor, but economic development in rural areas makes many peasants redundant. As a result, a large number of peasants move to cities to work in the burgeoning manufacturing sectors. In the case of European countries, during the period of the Industrial Revolution, Massey (1988) argues that "the processes of capital accumulation, enclosure, and market creation weaken individuals' social and economic ties to rural communities, making large-scale migration possible" (p. 392). Some of the migrants went to cities in Europe, and others chose to migrate to the United States. As a result, in the period from 1885 to 1914, 55 million international migrants from Europe arrived in the United States (Hatton and Williamson 1998).

At first, it may seem to be straightforward to appreciate the idea that marketization and economic development give rise to rural to urban migration. However, sometimes the logic may be misunderstood by policymakers and the general public when facing concrete policy decisions. Take the case of international migration from Mexico to the United States, for example. The common perception is that Mexicans want to come to the United States because their country is poor. Thus, the argument goes that if we help Mexicans develop their economy, it would stem the tide of migration from Mexico. While this is certainly the case in the long run, in the short run, economic development increases migration rather than reduces it (Massey 1988). The large increase in migration during the Industrial Revolution in Europe is a classic example of how economic development can increase international migration (Hatton and Williamson 1998; Massey 1988).

The same logic also applies to internal migration. Similar forces have been operating to stimulate migration in developing countries (see Brockerhoff 2000; Caldwell 1973 for African countries; Massey 1988 for the case of Mexico; and Liang 2001 for the case of China). Perhaps the most notable country for migration in the last two decades is China. Since the late 1970s, China has been in the process of transition to a market-oriented economy, which has provided a major impetus for a large volume of internal migration, mainly from rural to urban areas. Even by conservative estimates, China's intercountry migrant population reached nearly 80 million in 2000 (Liang and Ma 2004). The fundamental changes in the Chinese countryside are the institutional changes in the mode of production: the adoption of a household responsibility system. Essentially, it is a transition from a system of production team (consisting of many households) to household-based farming, which greatly improved the efficiency of agricultural production. At the same time, market reforms in urban China, as manifested in an increasing flow of foreign capital to coastal regions and gradually reduced barriers for migrants, paved the way for a large number of rural migrants. The lesson is that not anticipating the demographic consequences of market transition often leaves the government ill prepared for the sudden rise in the migrant population.

MIGRATION NETWORKS, CUMULATIVE CAUSATION, AND PERPETUATION OF MIGRATION

There is a consensus among students of migration that migrant networks play a very important role in the migration process. According to Massey et al. (1993), "migration networks are sets of interpersonal ties that connect migrants, former migrants, and nonmigrants in origin and destination areas through kinship, friendship, and shared community origin" (p. 728). The existence of such migration networks is important in lowering the costs of migration and consequently increasing its benefits. Migrants who are from community origins provide the best channel of information about potential destinations and in the case of undocumented international migration, the best route for crossing the borders. Migration networks are equally important once migrants arrive at destination areas in terms of providing information on jobs, housing, and other potential service needs for new arrivals. Students of migration from different fields have demonstrated the importance of migration networks in a variety of settings. In some cases, migration networks were seen as "chain migration," and in other cases, "family and friends" have an influence in the context of both internal and international migration (McDonald and McDonald 1974; Tilly and Brown 1967; Walker and Hannan 1989).

China presents a good example of internal migration. In Beijing, the formation of Zhejiang village is a testimony to the importance of province-based ethnicity and migration networks (Liang 2001; Ma and Xiang 1998). Zhejiang village (Zhejiang *cun*) is located several miles south of Tiananmen Square and is a place where people from Zhejiang province (mainly the Wenzhou area) converge to conduct a variety of businesses (primarily garment workshops and shops). Similarly, China's coastal regions, with a large number of joint-venture enterprises (such as shoe factories and toy-manufacturing factories), have attracted a great number of internal migrants from the inner provinces. Fieldwork in some of the factories in coastal China suggests clear patterns of chain migration: Migrants from the same province tend to go to the same factories where previous migrants from the province work (Liang and Morooka 2005). One foreman in a Taiwanese-owned factory helps recruit over 300 workers from her hometown in Sichuan province in central China. From the factory's management point of view, they also like this recruitment strategy because it is easy to manage, employee turnover is low, and the workforce is likely to be stable.

Similar systematic studies have also been conducted on the settlement patterns of international migrants in the United States. Using pooled cross-sectional time series data, Walker and Hannan (1989) studied the settlement patterns of migrants and demonstrated the role of migrant stock and lagged migration in the settlement patterns of immigrants in U.S. metropolitan areas.

The simple idea of migration networks has been further developed in other directions. One is to generate innovative hypotheses such as mechanisms for changes in educational selectivity (Massey et al. 1994). Students of migration have long realized the socioeconomic selectivity of migration. Lee (1966), for example, argued that migrants who move primarily because of "pull" factors at the place of destination are likely to be positively selected from the population at their place of origin. This positive selection includes individuals with higher education. What is less clear is whether migration selection will diminish or increase over time. In a recent study of international migration from Mexico to the United States, Massey et al. (1994) noted some apparent discrepancies in terms of the relationship between migration and socioeconomic selectivity across different communities. For example, some studies found that migrants were mainly landless workers, and others suggested that migrants were mainly landowners. Massey et al. argued that what appears to be an inconsistency in the socioeconomic selectivity of migration actually has some internal logic once we take a comparative perspective

across communities and over time. They further argued that in the initial stage of migration, it is always the people who are in the middle of the socioeconomic hierarchy who are likely to move. This is because migration is a risky and costly enterprise; thus, poor people may find it too costly to move, while rich people do not have much incentive to move.

Massey et al. (1994) further stated that "social capital, however, plays a powerful role in mitigating these costs and risks, and its accumulation over time tends to reduce the selectivity of migration" (p. 1495). In other words, in the initial stage of the migration process, migration is likely to be positively selective of individuals from higher socioeconomic strata. Over time, as more and more individuals participate in the migration process, it will reach a point where it is likely that a potential migrant would know someone (either a friend or family member) who is a migrant in a destination community. Because of the utility of this social capital, finding jobs and housing for a potential migrant is a lot easier, and thus, the costs of migration are likely to fall and migration selectivity diminishes. In sum, this literature on migration suggests the following hypothesis: Over time, migration will become less selective in the socioeconomic background of migrants. Even though Massey et al. (1994) illustrate this rationale using the example of international migration from Mexico to the United States, research on the great South to North migration in the United States conducted by Tolnay (1998) led to similar conclusions. Using the Integrated Public Use Microdata Series of the U.S. Census Bureau, Tolnay (1998) showed that during the period from 1940 to 1990, the positive selection of migration from the South declined appreciably.

This decline in education selectivity has some implications for migrants and policy. From the perspective of potential migrants, this declining educational selectivity means that as a vehicle of social mobility, migration becomes more accessible to a much broader segment of the population in a community. From the perspective of the migrant-receiving community, the implication is that the "quality" (as measured by education) of migrants is likely to decline over time. Of course, we need to note that this decline in educational selectivity is true only when we hold access to educational opportunity constant over time. The reality is likely to be much more complex because in many migrant-sending communities, expansion of educational opportunities will change the educational composition of the community population over time.

Migration network theory initially deals with factors at the individual level alone. Many empirical studies have documented the evidence that having a family member already a migrant or having a migrant friend significantly increases the probability of migration for other family members. In recent years, migration network theory has been further expanded and elaborated to consider the impact of migration in the community context. This is commonly known as the "cumulative causation theory of migration." According to this perspective, "causation is cumulative in that each act of migration alters the social context within which subsequent migration decisions are made, typically in ways that make additional movement more likely" (Massey et al. 1993:451).

Scholars have identified several mechanisms operating at the community level that sustain the momentum of migration. Here, we highlight three of them. First, migration will change the distribution of income in the migrant-sending community. The major idea here is the thesis of relative deprivation. In sociology, the concept of relative deprivation has been invoked to study mobility and rebellion (Gurr 1969; Tilly 1978) as well as military morale during World War II (Stouffer 1949–1950). In the migration field, some people migrate to increase their absolute income and wealth, and others might increase their relative income in the community of origin. Prior to initiation of migration, income distribution in these communities tends to be relatively equal; everybody is probably equally poor. Once people start migrating, and especially when remittances are sent home, income distribution in the community changes. Those who are otherwise content now think that they are more deprived because they see their neighbors' income rising sharply. This sense of relative deprivation stimulates more people to think about ways to increase their income, very often by migration.

This sense of relative deprivation is manifested in other ways as well. One of the most important assets for households is housing. In all migrant communities across the globe, we find that one of the high priorities for migrants once they accumulate enough money is to build a house or add more amenities to their houses. This is particularly the case with international migrants, where the income from migration can be highly lucrative. Liang and Zhang (2004) documented that in China's Fujian province, where there has been a major immigration flow to the New York metropolitan area, a large portion of remittances has been devoted to building big mansions, sometimes big mansions where few people actually reside. It is impossible to build these luxury houses for households whose members work in the community. These houses are symbols of migrants' success. However, for other households, viewing these luxury houses on a daily basis, it naturally creates feelings of relative deprivation, which may lead them to consider migrating internationally as well. This thesis of relative deprivation has been tested systematically by Stark and Taylor (1988) in the context of Mexican migration to the United States.

Second, migration also affects the organization of agricultural production. Because of the availability of more disposable income, migrant households are more likely to use capital-intensive methods (the use of machines and fertilizers and good-quality seeds) than nonmigrant households for agricultural production. The use of capital-intensive methods reduces the demand for agricultural labor and thus creates more impetus for migration. However, we should note that the empirical evidence is more complicated than

what is presented in this view. In China, during the last two decades, internal and international migrations have had a major impact on migrant-sending communities. The typical pattern of change in agricultural production for households with migrants is not only to use capital-intensive methods but also to hire people to work on the land assigned to the household. Some of the people hired are local peasants, and others are from remote and poor provinces. To the extent that some local peasants are hired, migration actually generates a demand for labor in agricultural production, which has the potential of discouraging further migration.

Third, perhaps the most important impact of migration on the migrant-sending community is the creation of a "culture of migration." Over time, migration changes values and perceptions in the migrant-sending communities and consequently reshapes and redefines what is considered to be normative behavior among young people. This is the case in many communities where migration is prevalent, that migration becomes the rite of passage and the thing to do for young people. In fact, negative sanctions often accompany people who are not willing to leave. In migrant-sending communities of Fujian province in southern China, young people who are not willing to leave are often considered *mei chuxi* (with no great future).

This culture of migration also has an impact on school-age children; some of them see their future in a foreign destination and pay less attention to schoolwork. In sum, migration network theory and cumulative causation of migration suggest behavioral changes at the individual level and the impact of migration at the community level, all of which lead to the increase and perpetuation of migration. One important implication is that because of these changes at the individual and community levels, migration becomes more and more a self-feeding process and independent of the original socioeconomic forces that led to it in the first place. Therefore, migration becomes more and more difficult to control.

MIGRATION, RACE, AND POVERTY

One of the most important topics in migration research in the context of the United States is the migration and residential mobility of African Americans. The topic is important because migration often leads to social mobility because of new jobs and opportunities. Second, because of the history of racial discrimination in the United States, migration is also a barometer to measure the nature of race relations and degree of discrimination, especially in housing markets.

The "Great Migration" of African Americans from the South is perhaps one of the most important demographic events of twentieth-century America and has stimulated many sociological studies to identify its causes and consequences. As a result of this migration, by 1980, over 4 million southern-born blacks lived outside that region (Tolnay 2003). A critical factor in the initiation of black migration from the South was the enactment of more restrictive immigration policies (with the intention of limiting immigrants from Eastern and Southern European countries) in the 1920s (Collins 1997). This in some ways provides a unique opportunity to conduct two major comparative studies. One is to compare African Americans who moved from the South to the North with the Eastern and Southern European immigrants. Stanley Lieberson took advantage of this opportunity to conduct such a study. Lieberson (1980) found, for example, that there was clearly an occupational queue, with blacks (both northern born and southern born) located in the lowest strata with unskilled and semiskilled occupations. Immigrants from Southern and Eastern Europe and native-born whites were above blacks in the occupational queue and enjoyed advantages in getting desirable jobs.

The second comparative study was the study of southern-born blacks with northern-born blacks. This comparison arrived at very intriguing results regarding family patterns and socioeconomic attainment. Earlier work by Lieberson and Wilkinson (1976) found that southern-born blacks were more likely than northern-born blacks to be married and to reside with their spouse. Recent studies (Tolnay 2003; Tolnay and Crowder 1999; Wilson 2001) further suggest that compared with northern-born blacks, southern-born blacks were less likely to have children out of wedlock, and their children were more likely to reside with both parents. Other intriguing findings suggest that southern migrants were more likely to be employed, had higher incomes, and were less likely to be on public assistance (Long 1974; Tolnay 2003). Although scholars have offered a variety of explanations for the different outcomes for southern migrants and northern-born blacks, Tolnay (2003) states that "for the most part the reasons behind the economic and family advantages enjoyed by southern migrants over northerners remain a mystery" (p. 220).

So far we have discussed internal migration of African Americans from the South to the North. We now turn to another aspect of migration for African Americans: residential mobility. It is well established that African Americans experience the most extreme residential segregation among all minority groups, and Massey and Denton (1993) went so far as to characterize African Americans' residential experience as "hyper-segregation." Although scholars have devoted substantial efforts to document residential patterns among different groups, relatively few studies have actually looked at the dynamics of residential mobility or lack of it for African Americans, which presumably plays a major role in the patterns of residential segregation. In addition, residential mobility is important because mobility is believed to lead to better neighborhoods that often enhance employment and educational prospects or neighborhoods with a greater variety of services and facilities (South and Crowder 1997). Combining census data with longitudinal data from the Panel Study of Income Dynamics, South and Crowder (1997) examined the effect of the sociodemographic characteristics of

individuals as well as the community on residential mobility—namely, from poor neighborhoods to better neighborhoods. They found that compared with whites, blacks are less likely to move out of poor neighborhoods and much more likely to move into them, even when socioeconomic status variables are controlled. This underscores the disadvantage that African Americans face in residential mobility.

Residential mobility for African Americans has also been considered as one of the underlying reasons for the concentrated poverty facing African Americans (Wilson 1987). In his highly acclaimed book *The Truly Disadvantaged,* William Julius Wilson (1987) developed an argument and presented evidence to explain the concentrated poverty in urban America. One of the major forces identified by Wilson (1987) was migration of middle-class African Americans away from mixed-income neighborhoods to suburban locations where the majority of whites reside. However, scholars have contested the evidence, whether it is sufficient to support Wilson's argument. In one of the first papers to test this "black middle-class flight" hypothesis, Massey et al. (1994) used data from the Panel Study on Income Dynamics to show that poor blacks are moving out of poor neighborhoods at higher rates than nonpoor blacks, which is not consistent with Wilson's argument. Quillian (1999) argues that Massey et al.'s (1994) method is not well suited for capturing change over time. Using a method that he believed was better at capturing changes over time, Quillian (1999) shows results that are supportive of Wilson's (1987) argument—that is, blacks, and especially poor blacks, move into white nonpoor neighborhoods more often than they move out. Thus, the debate on the black middle-class flight hypothesis has not yet been settled. Overall, the most interesting aspect of studying race and migration/residential mobility sociologically is to place migration issues in the larger context of race relations in American society.

THE FUTURE OF MIGRATION RESEARCH

Several scholars have characterized the current period as the age of migration. According to the latest report from the United Nations, there are currently 175 million people who reside in countries outside their countries of birth (World Commission on Social Dimension of Globalization 2004). Globalization and growth in international trade are likely to stimulate further international migration in the years to come. At the same time, it is also projected that sometime in this century, for the first time, the world will see over 50% of the population residing in urban areas. Most of this increase in urbanization will be achieved through rural to urban migration. This is clearly the best of times for students of migration. Sid Goldstein (1976) once said that "migration is the stepchild in the field of demography." But times have changed. In the fields of both international and internal migration, we have witnessed major developments and progress in the last two decades. In this chapter, we have reviewed some of these major developments, but obviously this review cannot do justice to the vast literature on migration (international migration and internal migration). For example, in the United States, the large wave of post-1965 immigration has been accompanied by a great wave of studies on immigrant entrepreneurship, assimilation, and intermarriage; the initiation and perpetuation of immigration; the issues confronting second-generation immigrants; immigration and gender; transnationalism in the new migration era; the economic impact of immigration; and, more recently, religion and immigration. In the remainder of the chapter, we discuss some of the potentially fruitful areas for future research. The list is, of course, highly selective and reflects the author's bias. But it does identify some of the potential areas of migration research that are likely to be important in the years to come. In some cases, the research is concerned with international migration or internal migration; in other cases, it may be concerned with both.

First, more comparative studies of immigration are needed. As a field of study, we have accumulated a lot of knowledge about international migration for each country of destination, but we need more studies to take a comparative perspective. For example, as Massey et al. (1994) stated, "Far too much research is centered in Mexico, which because of its unique relationship to the United States may be unrepresentative of broader patterns and trends" (p. 739). Over the years, Massey and his associates have studied many aspects of Mexican migration to the United States, including the impact of migration networks, the changing educational selectivity of immigrants, the comparison of wage rates between undocumented immigrants and documented immigrants, and the impact of immigration on migrant-sending communities. It is important that we carry out similar studies for immigrant groups from other countries to see if the findings from the Mexican case can be generalizable to other groups of immigrants and countries of migrant origin. Of course, it is not enough to simply carry out similar studies for different groups or countries of origin. To the extent that different findings emerge, we need to identify the potential reasons behind them, which could stimulate further theoretical development of international migration. Another kind of comparative study design is to study similar immigrant groups in many immigrant destinations. Essentially, we hold migrant group characteristics constant (people with the same language, culture, and religion, etc.) to see how they behave and fare in different host country contexts. This would allow researchers to examine how host country characteristics, such as immigration policies, the context of reception, and history of immigration, affect the adaptation process of the immigrant group. Along this direction, Richard Alba (2005) has done some pioneering work examining assimilation and exclusion among second-generation immigrants in France, Germany, and the United States.

Still another comparative study could be to examine a particular community of origin to study how people choose different migration destination countries. We know that immigrants from Peru have gone to different countries: Japan, the United States, and some European countries. We know relatively little about the forces behind the decision to choose one country of destination over another. China's Fujian province is a particularly good example in this regard. There has been a major flow of international migrants from the Fujian province to the New York metropolitan area over the last two decades. The New York–bound immigrants are for the most part from eastern Fujian. It is interesting that people from northern Fujian choose to migrate to European countries such as Italy and Hungary. Systematic studies are clearly needed to explore the different patterns of migration for people from different parts of the Fujian province.

Second, although we know a lot about migration and its consequences, we have limited knowledge on return migration. Return migration may be very high in some cases. Previous studies of return migration suggest that in other countries, it may account for upward of one-third of the migrant flow (Gmelch 1980; Warren and Kraly 1985). Jasso and Rosenzweig (1982) estimate that as high as 56% of the 1971 cohort of legal Mexican immigrants may have left the United States by 1979. In addition, the nature of return migration has important theoretical implications for the subsequent study of migrant adaptation in the host destination (Gmelch 1980). If, for example, the return migrants are positively selected on socioeconomic characteristics, the current literature on migrant adaptation at the place of destination may be biased in terms of underestimating the effect of assimilation. In the case of immigrants in the United States, a better understanding of the selectivity of return immigrants has the potential to resolve the controversy surrounding the thesis of declining quality of immigrants, as argued by Borjas (1999).

Moreover, return migration is also important because return migrants often bring back the remittances (i.e., financial capital) in addition to human capital in terms of acquired skills and work experience, factors that are crucial for economic development in the place of origin. Furthermore, return migration has important health consequences, as evidenced during the recent global severe acute respiratory syndrome (SARS) outbreak. In addition to contagious or infectious diseases like SARS or avian flu, return migration also poses serious concerns for public health in terms of sexually transmitted diseases because of the high likelihood that migrants are engaging in unprotected/unsafe sex and subsequently transmitting the disease to their spouses or new partners on return (Yang 2002). Therefore, the magnitude and direction of return migration have implications for the public health of migrants as well as their spouses/partners and family members. Last, return migration is also closely linked to the idea of transnationalism, an area of research that has also received more attention from scholars in recent years. Return migrants are likely to remigrate or travel back and forth between countries (and communities). Understanding the nature of return migration may provide new insights into transnational activities.

Third, the field of migration should take advantage of recent developments in research methodology. For example, multilevel modeling is now a standard statistical technique to examine the impact of context/community on individual behavior. Recent studies on the impact of social context on fertility behavior have taken full advantage of state-of-the-art technology in modeling contextual effects (Axinn and Yabiku 2001). Students of migration should find this kind of modeling useful because most of our theoretical ideas emphasize the context of migration (at the village, province, and country levels). The community-level characteristics include socioeconomic conditions, employment opportunities, and measures of income inequality. We can even test some of the ideas concerning migration networks (Liang and Morooka 2005). Within the multilevel model framework, testing of interaction effects between community-level variables and individual-level variables can be easily performed. For example, we can examine whether educated individuals are more likely to use migration networks in the initiation of migration. A recent paper on immigrants' employment in 18 countries (using contextual-level variables at the country level) is also in this direction (Van Tubergen et al. 2004).

So far, we have discussed research areas in international and internal migration. Research on residential mobility in developing countries is also lacking. A quick search of the sociological abstracts on residential mobility in the last 10 years turns out 317 articles on developed countries and 20 on developing countries. The international comparisons on residential mobility often focus on developed countries. Data availability may be the reason for this. We should note, however, that the magnitude of residential mobility in developing countries can be enormous. Data from the Chinese 2000 census show that nearly 40 million people made intracounty moves (residential mobility) (Liang and Ma 2004). Another demographic giant, India, may be in a similar position. As developing countries become more and more urbanized and with the middle-class population increasing in many parts of the developing world, the time may be right to turn our attention to the study of residential mobility in developing countries as well.

50

THE SOCIOLOGY OF DEVELOPMENT

CORNELIA BUTLER FLORA

JAN L. FLORA
Iowa State University

Development can be viewed as "organized social change" (McMichael 2000). Social change has long been a topic for social theorists and sociological studies. But viewing it as influenced by the intentionality of external actors is relatively recent and refers primarily to the economic performance of the global South[1] (Elliott 1994:10).

The development era and the modernization project began in the 1940s as the United States became the undisputed military and economic power in the capitalist world and the Soviet Union emerged as its chief military and economic rival. Through the establishment of multilateral institutions at the end of World War II, in which the United States held primacy, and through the development of bilateral aid institutions and economic, political, and military relationships, the United States sought to improve conditions, first in Europe and then in the global South, and to tie nations in Asia Minor, the Middle East, and the South in general to the capitalist camp. The Soviet Union, through close integration with its client states in Eastern Europe and military, economic, and political ties to selected countries in the South, competed with the United States for influence. While one system was capitalist with varying degrees of *market economies* and the other state socialist with *command economies,* both pursued modernization projects. Ultimately, the promise of modernization was what each superpower dangled before nations of the global South. This chapter is about the modernization project of the surviving capitalist system. Whether the United States–led modernization project itself succeeded is the

question addressed. We seek to answer this question through the lens of the sociology (and economics) of development.

There are few areas of sociology where theory is so closely linked to changes in the global landscape than in the sociology of development, which takes as given that the causes of underdevelopment are linked to its "cure." Development theories have been used to justify a set of policies consistent with the modernization project that support capital accumulation. That use has impelled other sociologists, practitioners, and activists to provide countertheories with different causal models of how to, first, get to the modernization goal, then expand that goal, and ultimately reject it. The study of the organization of development efforts, the degree to which development can be intentional, the very definitions of development, whether it is unidimensional or multidimensional, and the actors involved (global, national, regional, local) make the sociology of development a highly contested and potentially influential realm of sociology.

To understand this contextual and contrapuntal relationship between competing development theories, we will look at different stages and turning points in the world economy and political situation in relation to the global North's dominant assistance paradigms in relation to industrial and agrarian developments and characterize the South's responses to them. Thus, we will address each time period by looking at the global context, the particular modernization project applied in that context (both industrial and agricultural manifestations), the response of the South, and the alternative development theories used to respond to the modernization project. We will sum up with an assessment regarding future directions of the sociology of development.

THE MODERNIZATION PROJECT AS IT GREW OUT OF WORLD WAR II

Economic and Political Context

Discourses of underdevelopment and development emerged in the 1940s and became institutionalized in the context of decolonization, the Cold War, and the United States' struggle for hegemony. A specific blueprint for planned social change (modernization overcoming traditionalism), shaped by Western notions of social evolution, was promoted by the North, adopted by elites in the South, and underpinned the newly established global institutions. These included the United Nations, the development institutions established by the Bretton Woods Agreement signed in July 1944, which became operational in 1946 (the World Bank, made up of the International Bank for Reconstruction and Development and the International Development Association, and the International Monetary Fund [IMF]), and the General Agreement on Tariffs and Trade (GATT). That blueprint was articulated around the notion that Third World[2] countries would "catch up" with the First World through economic growth, technological transfer, and Westernization. Thus, a series of bilateral development assistance programs were set up, increasingly supplemented by multilateral foreign assistance efforts.

The devastation of Europe and Japan in World War II marked the end of the empire, opening the floodgates for new nation-states to emerge in Africa, Asia, and the Caribbean. Thus, decolonialization preceded modernization, as the emerging Cold War demanded that attention be paid to stopping regimes hostile to Northern interests from coming to power. Development aid was one positive sanction for directing Southern countries toward the Northern modernization project. Covert military intervention was a negative sanction. In some places, these two efforts were linked.

The United States did not attempt to mobilize a major foreign economic assistance program until near the end of World War II. The Marshall Plan, with its large capital investments in Europe's productive infrastructure, was the initial bilateral commitment to development assistance (Morss and Morss 1982:19). The Marshall Plan attempted to block communist political and military initiatives and prevent Russia from gaining ground in a war-ravaged Europe. It also ensured that the United States would have important trading partners.

The immediate and striking success of the Marshall Plan in Europe and the heightened fear of communist influence in developing countries inspired U.S. planners to attempt a similar operation in the South. However, the Marshall Plan contrasted markedly with the subsequent focus of aid to developing countries. Financial capital and physical infrastructure were the limiting factors in rebuilding Western Europe and Japan. Institutional structures that favored industrial production had been in place, only temporarily interrupted by the war. A highly educated population was able to provide the management and skilled labor necessary for moving from reconstruction immediately into production. Market channels had merely to be revitalized, not invented. Reconstruction was carried out by the private sector, with financing from the public sector. In contrast, in the South, education and technical knowledge (human capital), as well as institutional capacity, were lacking. Modernizing the South was a much more daunting task.

Modernization in Theory and Practice

The modernization project was synonymous with development after World War II. McMichael (2000) sees the development/modernization project as "linking human development to national economic growth" (p. 25). Modernization would take place through the nation-state, and economic growth was the motive force for improvements in the standard of living of citizens of each country. Thus, traditionalism, localism, and "excessive" display of ethnic interests were negative; modernization was positive. The Western or capitalist version of modernization involved what Parsons (1951) termed the pattern variables: achievement rather than ascription, specificity rather than diffuseness, universalism rather than particularism, and orientation toward self rather than the collective. Economists linked these modern pattern variables of social action to economic growth (Rostow 1951, 1952).

Dominant Assistance Paradigms

The initial model of economic development that directed the post–World War II efforts of the United States has been referred to as the resource-constraint model. Walter Rostow (1951, 1964) was the best-known proponent of this model. The 15 years that followed World War II were typified by efforts to increase national output and by investments to increase capital stock. Morss and Morss (1982) refer to this as the "big lever" approach to development.[3]

The Point IV Program, announced by President Harry Truman in his inaugural address on January 20, 1949, laid out the rationale for a plan to provide economic and technical assistance to help people in developing countries produce more, eschewing the colonial model of exporting raw materials from and importing manufactured goods to colonies. In 1950, Commonwealth foreign ministers met in Colombo and launched the Colombo Plan, which provided aid to South and Southeast Asia for economic development. In both cases, decolonization was linked to development (McMichael 2000:23).

During the late 1940s and 1950s, most Northern countries gave foreign aid multilaterally through the United Nations or, in the case of British Commonwealth countries, Plan Colombo. Japanese overseas development assistance was initially in the form of reparations. For example, it was only in 1959 that the Canadian Department of Trade and Commerce set up an Economic and Technical Assistance Bureau to look after developing countries' growing needs for international assistance. Australia's International Aid program began in 1974, although the Australian government provided development assistance to Papua New Guinea since 1946. Japan's Official Development Assistance began in 1954 when it joined the Colombo Plan, an organization set up in 1950 to assist Asian countries in their socioeconomic development.

In the 1950s and 1960s, the United States dominated the global economy from a technological standpoint and continued its bilateral stance on foreign assistance. It was reassuring to U.S. citizens that the United States not only led in patents granted and productivity per worker but also in lawn mowers and televisions per capita (Lipton 1984). Thus, there seemed an obligation to send the kind of assistance that remade the South in the North's image.

Dominant Agrarian Paradigms

The Green Revolution began during this period. Scientists trained in the United States and Europe were successful in creating new cultivars adaptable to Mexican commercial farming.

While efforts at selecting and breeding corn were relatively unsuccessful in terms of increased production, the wheat program, led by Norman Borlaug, resulted in widespread adoption and large production increases. The new "miracle varieties" required a substantial increase in inputs, including water, fertilizer, and later pesticides, but they allowed two blades to grow where only one was there before. It can be argued that the difference in the impact of the two programs was due less to research results than to differences in the users of the products. Wheat farmers in Mexico were more like U.S. farmers than were the Mexican corn farmers. The wheat farmers were commercial farmers, while the corn farmers were subsistence farmers (Myren 1969).

Responses from the South

Latin American states, particularly the larger ones—Brazil, Mexico, and Argentina—having profited from stimulation of industrial production for the war effort, were prepared to continue expansion of industrial production. The UN Economic Commission for Latin America articulated an import substitution industrialization strategy (Prebisch 1950), which from the mid-1950s on, involved, first, fomenting domestically owned consumer goods and light industry and, later, heavy industry (Gereffi 1994:39). Only at the beginning of the 1970s did the failure to markedly expand the middle class result in the stagnation of this policy.

Alternative Development Paradigms

Certain writings that came out of the European/ African experiences with colonialism and decolonization rejected Westernization. At the same time, Vatican II (1962–1965) and the following encyclical, Populorum Progressio (1967) and meeting of the Council of Bishops in Medellin, Colombia (1968), inspired Liberation Theology in the South, particularly Latin America (Gutiérrez 1973). A number of the influential priests active in the Liberation Theology movement were sociologists, such as Camilo Torres in Colombia (Torres 1965).

Membership in the United Nations increased during the 1950s and 1960s, as countries in Africa, Asia, and the Caribbean gained independence. As members of the United Nations, these nations had a heightened concern for economic development and general skepticism of the Westernized modernization model for achieving it. They agitated for change in the market (trade policies) and state (development policies) as means toward modernization. Julius Nyerere, the first president of Tanzania, redefined development as "increasing peoples' freedom and well-being" (Snyder 2004:34).

There was a definite conflict between the economic resource-constraint initiative (modernization), which favored advantaged classes and a trickle-down approach, and the political participation initiative, which was concerned about distributional issues. It was often convenient to abandon the efforts aimed at increasing participation. The rationale for abandonment was not to note the inconvenience and political sensitivity of this approach but to label participation a failure (Holdcroft 1978).

THE "REVOLUTIONARY" 1960s

Economic and Political Context

Politically, the 1960s can be characterized as a period of revolutionary movements or, with respect to U.S. development efforts, of efforts to contain those movements. The 1960s began on January 1, 1959, with the triumph of the Cuban Revolution. The Cuban Revolution, the Bay of Pigs debacle (1961), and the Cuban missile crisis (1962) colored U.S. development efforts in Latin America throughout the 1960s and even into the 1980s, as the specter of the Cuban revolution haunted the Central American revolutions and was used to justify U.S. support of Central American counterinsurgency in the Reagan era. Similarly, the war in Vietnam, heating up in the early 1960s, affected development approaches in Asia and beyond. As United States Agency for International Development (USAID) states in its brief history on its Web site:

> In Asia, USAID's first emphases were on countering the spread of communism, particularly the influence of the People's Republic of China. This quickly ballooned into a large program of assistance based on counter-insurgency and democratic and economic development in Vietnam, which lasted until the withdrawal of American troops in 1975. In Africa, USAID focused on such initiatives as the education of the leadership of the newly-independent countries and meeting other economic and social imperatives. (USAID 2005)

Perhaps more important for understanding the unfolding sociology of development, the intellectual impacts of the anti-Vietnam War movement in the United States and in Europe generated new intellectual currents, as did the foment around land reform and movements against *el imperialismo yanqui*[4] in Latin America and in other parts of the South.

Modernization in Theory and Practice

In the late 1950s and early 1960s, a new generation of modernization sociologists began filling in empirical underpinnings for Parsons's (1951) pattern variables of achievement, specificity, universalism, and individualism. David McClelland (1964) was a noted early modernization sociologist who used projection techniques to assess individuals' achievement motivation or need for achievement and analyzed the content of popular literature to get at national entrepreneurial qualities. Alex Inkeles (1964) conducted cross-national surveys with individuals in different walks of life to determine their location on a modernity scale, which he found to be cross-nationally valid and which correlated to the degree of modernity of the country. A modern man (women were not prominent subjects in the modernization project) was open to new experiences, was independent of authority figures, believed in science, was oriented to social mobility, planned ahead, and was active in local civic life. Bellah's (1957) study of the origins of industrialism in Tokugawa Japan was a more nuanced and culturally sensitive modernization study (see So 1990, chap. 3, for a discussion of these and other modernization theorists' work).

Dominant Assistance Paradigms

The Alliance for Progress was established in 1961 in direct response to the Cuban revolution of 1959. It recognized that some of the constraints to progress in the hemisphere stemmed from more than a lack of resources and knowledge. Land reform, an issue Smith (1947) was loath to address in the 1940s, became a salient issue in the 1960s.

In 1962, USAID was created under the Kennedy administration, bringing together a number of previously dispersed foreign aid programs: the International Cooperation Administration, the Development Loan Fund, the Food for Peace (P.L. 480) program, and local currency-lending activities of the Export-Import Bank. The new organization was perceived as a permanent agency, unlike its predecessors, which had been created to deal with particular international problems (Tendler 1975:15). The new agency was established for the following reasons:

> The new directions most emphatically stressed were a dedication to development as a long-term effort requiring country-by-country planning and a commitment of resources on a multi-year, programmed basis. The new focus of development was to achieve economic growth and democratic, political stability in the developing world to combat both the perceived spread of ideological threats such as communism and the threat of instability arising from poverty. The economic development theory of W. W. Rostow [1951], which posited "stages of economic development," most notably a "takeoff into growth" stage, provided the premise for much of the development planning in the newly-formed U.S. Agency for International Development. (USAID 2005)

While World Bank loans and USAID assistance were aimed at moving countries into a capitalist mode of production and thus the Western geopolitical camp, the Soviet Union's foreign assistance included loans repaid in local currency or traditional exports combined with technical assistance supporting countries doing central planning and public ownership. Setting the development agenda became a key strategy in the Cold War and the North's modernization project, whether capitalist or socialist.

Dominant Agrarian Paradigms

From the U.S. perspective, foreign aid was to become a lever for convincing governments to make policy changes, including land reform, needed to diminish a perceived communist threat. The major landowners were fearful of expropriation if their land continued to be exploited in the traditional extensive manner, so they began to intensify production, investing in the capital improvements and technological inputs necessary to produce such crops as sugar and cotton for the world market. The newly created national research institutions emphasized the crops grown by these modernizing operators, for it was the large farmers who had political influence over the state.

Responses from the South

Partly aided by post–World War II land reforms that sharply reduced inequality and the large amounts of aid from the United States in the 1950s, South Korea and Taiwan, which along with the city-states of Singapore and Hong Kong, made great leaps forward in export-oriented industrialization (EOI), steadily raising the standards of living of their people. These advances were made in relation to strong direction from the state (Gereffi 1994), and in the case of Korea, a militant labor movement helped guarantee that benefits accrued to workers as well as to industrialists (Berberoglu 1992:61–64). In the 1960s, industrialization in these two countries focused on light, labor-intensive industries, but in the 1970s, they expanded into petrochemicals, steel, automobiles, and ship building. Gereffi (1994:38) argues that in the 1970s, there was a degree of convergence of these Asian economies with those of the larger Latin American countries. Both groups of countries diversified their industrial activities to include both import substitution industrialization and EOI.

Perhaps what is important about the advances made by the East Asian "tigers" (Korea, Taiwan, Singapore, and Hong Kong) is that in the 1980s, and even today, neo-conservatives hold them up as shining examples of how open economies of the South can move forward dramatically on the path of development; they fail to take into account the fact that they were shepherded through the various stages of industrialization by strong states that regulated the private sector and, unlike the Latin American countries, instituted policies that sharply limited growth in inequalities (Schnitz 1984).

While there was a great deal of popular mobilization around breaking up the large estates and distributing the land among peasants in Latin America during the 1960s and 1970s, the concern for land reform among liberal Latin American leaders was less a concern for social justice and more a desire to modernize large estates and increase productivity as a way to deflect peasant agitation for land (Barsky and Cosse 1981). The latter objective was effectively accomplished in most countries in South America during this period (Thiesenhusen 1995).

Alternative Development Paradigm

By the mid-1960s, sociologists, particularly in the South, questioned the causal assumptions behind the modernization model, although they did not question the modernization goal. They insisted that underdevelopment could not be understood without examining the legacy of colonialism. Dependency (Chilcote 1974; Cardoso and Faletto 1979) and world-systems theories (Wallerstein 1974; Chirot and Hall 1982) were the main challenges to modernization theories in the 1960s and 1970s. Even scholars from more traditional economic and sociological backgrounds questioned the enduring inequalities (Boserup 1970; Snyder 1972) that remained as the modernization model was applied. With the work of Esther Boserup, the macroanalysis of regional inequality was coupled with mezzoanalysis of continuing gender, ethnic, and class inequality.

Dependency theorists responded to the modernization theorists, first, on the basis of the *causes* of underdevelopment and, second, on the actual impact of the interventions aimed at reducing it. While the modernization approach represented the North, dependency theory came from the South (Blomstrom and Hettne 1984). Thus, the historical relationships between North and South had to be examined and specified (Cardoso and Faletto 1979).

Alvin So (1990) sees dependency theory arising in Latin America "as a response to the bankruptcy of the program of the U.N. Economic Commission for Latin America (ECLA) in the early 1960s" (p. 91). Neither orthodox Marxism nor the modernization model provided adequate explanatory power or viable action agenda (Dos Santos 1973). Andre Gunder Frank (1968) brought Northern attention to this perspective in discussions of neocolonialism and the creation of dependency in his book *Development and Underdevelopment in Latin America.* Dos Santos laid out three historical forms of dependency: colonial dependence, financial-industrial dependence, and technological-industrial dependence. The modernization model created technological-industrial dependence. Amin (1976) stressed that the peripheral formation of capitalism was quite different from what had occurred in the Northern countries; the Southern social and economic base was characterized by extremely uneven production, disarticulation, and the economic domination of the center. Dependency theorists, a very heterogeneous group, did not deny the modernization project's goal of economic growth. But they demanded that it be broadened to include all those living in the periphery. Thus, they concluded that there was a need for decreased contact with the core rather than the transfer of technology and structures from the core to the periphery. Perhaps the greatest weakness of classical dependency theory was its overspecification, leading to what in retrospect was an increasingly unlikely solution—revolutionary decoupling from the North.

THE 1970S: COMMODITY BOOM AND INDUSTRIAL STAGNATION

Economic and Political Context

U.S. trade imbalances and an outflow of foreign exchange during the Lyndon Johnson presidency of "guns and butter" (1963–1969) led to President Richard Nixon's negotiation of the Smithsonian agreement in May 1973, which replaced the Bretton Woods agreement. The "dirty float" was instituted, which allowed currency values to fluctuate worldwide. According to Allen and Laney (1982),

> the advent of floating exchange rates signaled a decline in the role of central banks in establishing exchange rates, and, to an extent, interest rates, opening the door for market forces to prevail as capital controls were reduced and cross-country banking restrictions were eased. (P. 36)

Capital, always more mobile than other factors of production, became even more mobile.

For developing countries, introduction of the "floating peg" was propitious. Many of them had pegged their currency to the U.S. dollar and thus became more competitive vis-à-vis European producers. Furthermore, the expanding Middle Eastern markets—and speculation by oil-producing states in the commodities markets—allowed for rapid expansion of exports, including agricultural products, without pressure from established suppliers who saw their market share threatened. The United States and Western European nations did feel threatened. They responded with increased protectionism.

Modernization in Theory and Practice

Mainstream development theorists focused on the notion of dual economies, where traditional agricultural sectors diverted resources from industry, dampening accumulation. However, Theodore Schultz (1964) and others wrote about the rationality of the peasantry in the face of highly risky contexts.

In the 1970s, world-systems theories (Wallerstein 1974, 1986; Chirot and Hall 1982) were added to dependency theory as a challenge to modernization theories, but not necessarily to the modernization project. While dependency theory focused particularly on U.S. neo-imperialism and increasing international inequality, world-systems theory arose in an attempt to provide a more complete analysis of the forces at work in the development process (Berberoglu 1992). World-systems theory linked unequal development in capitalist agriculture to the origins of the European world economy in the sixteenth century (Wallerstein 1974, 1979). That analysis of particular kinds of market and state relationships stresses the historical roots of underdevelopment.

World-systems theory, like dependency theory, looked at internal as well as international inequalities. It provides a useful frame for sociologists to examine gender, inequality, and development (Ward 1984).

While dependency theory focuses on the core and the periphery, world-systems theories see the world as more complex, moving from a bimodal system to a trimodal one: core, semiperiphery, and periphery. Wallerstein (1979:70) sees semiperipheral countries serving to buffer the economic and political crises brought about by increasing accumulation in the core countries. Gereffi's (1994) analysis of industrialization in the South is an excellent example of the application of world-systems theory.

Dominant Assistance Paradigms

In 1971, the Senate rejected the foreign assistance bill for the two succeeding fiscal years. This was the first time that either House had rejected foreign aid authorization since approval of the Marshall Plan in 1948. According to USAID's (2005) publicly presented history, the Senate rejected the bill for multiple reasons: (1) opposition to the Vietnam War; (2) concern that aid was too focused on short-term military considerations; and (3) concern that aid, particularly development aid, was a giveaway program producing few foreign policy gains for the United States.

The House Committee on Foreign Affairs took the lead in reforming foreign assistance by introducing the concept of "basic human needs" for aiding the "poorest of the poor" in Southern nations and focused on more direct assistance to those groups by replacing

> the old categories of technical assistance grants and development loans with new functional categories aimed at specific problems such as agriculture, family planning, and education. The aim of bilateral development aid was to concentrate on sharing American technical expertise and commodities to meet development problems, rather than relying on large-scale transfers of money and capital goods, or financing of infrastructure. The structure of the FAA [Foreign Assistance Act, first passed in 1962] remains today pretty much the way it was following these 1973 amendments. (USAID 2005)

The decade of the 1970s was also a period of reorientation by the World Bank. Johnson named Robert McNamara, who had prosecuted the Vietnam War as U.S. Secretary of Defense in Lyndon Johnson's cabinet, to the presidency of the World Bank in 1968, but the full implementation of McNamara's reforms did not occur until his second term as bank president. The new focus was on poverty reduction and basic human needs, necessitated, according to Ayres (1983), by the failure of the trickle-down approach to have any impact on poverty. The change in focus was announced in McNamara's speech to the World Bank Board of Governors in Nairobi on September 24, 1973. Prior to McNamara's tenure, the World Bank was

> a remarkably conservative institution. It was basically a project lender. The projects it financed were quite traditional as it shunned riskier sectors in the borrowing nations.
> The objective was growth, and growth could be technocratically orchestrated regardless of the political systems in the countries that were the recipients of Bank loans . . . The Bank in the pre-McNamara years avoided a role as a *development agency* in favor of the more traditional role of *bank*. (Ayres 1983:3–4)

Between the first half of the 1960s to 1975, more than three-fourths of the bank's lending was for electric power and transportation, 6 percent was for agricultural development, and 1 percent was for social services. By the time McNamara left the bank in 1981, lending for agriculture and rural development had grown to 31 percent of the total, with three-fourths of the agricultural and rural development loans having a small farmer component. And the World Bank's total loan portfolio had quadrupled in McNamara's tenure. Lending for industrial development with more attention to small industry, significant investment in primary and informal education, in health, and in urban housing also showed remarkable growth during his tenure. Power, transportation, and telecommunications, while growing in absolute amount, declined from 57 percent of the total in 1968 to 39 percent in 1981 (Ayres 1983:4–6).

Dominant Agrarian Paradigm(s)

At the same time U.S. Secretary of Agriculture Butz (1971–1976) urged U.S. farmers to plant fencerow to fencerow, secretaries of agriculture in developing countries encouraged conversion of forests and prairie into cropland. While colonization schemes allowed fulfillment of individual desires for land, they also furthered national goals of expanding export earnings and securing borders in remote areas. That they required expensive infrastructure was no problem: Credit was readily available as both public and private banks scurried to recycle petrodollars. The fact that these investments rapidly degraded the environment and exploited the colonists who first cleared the land, then were forced to sell out to large landowners, was generally ignored (Flora 1990).

Integrated rural development projects (IRDPs) established during the 1970s continued efforts to extend the Green Revolution to farmers with key resources, such as flat land, the ability to purchase fertilizer, and to access irrigation water. The desire for quick results over potential long-term gains heavily influenced where IRDPs were located.

Declining foreign assistance activity by U.S. universities in the mid-1970s (less than half the contracts that were in place in 1970) corresponded with both a decline in total USAID funding and the redirection of development activities. Land-grant universities were able to mobilize their considerable political clout to argue that the emphasis on capital transfer over institution building was inappropriate. Stressing the continuing world food problem, the universities presented themselves as uniquely able to combat famine and reduce hunger in the developing world by applying the research-teaching-extension model to increase productivity.

The result was the passage in 1974 of Title XII of the Foreign Assistance Act.[5] In effect, Title XII gave foreign aid a domestic constituency—the land-grant system, which, Tendler (1975:38–39) argued, it previously had lacked.

During the 1970s, modernization theory was attacked as increasing inequality and failing to increase economic development, and the modernization project was on the defensive following the U.S. defeat in Southeast Asia by relatively ill-equipped guerrilla fighters whose most important weapon was nationalism (not Chinese support), public disclosure of CIA covert operations and FBI spying on domestic dissidents, and by Watergate.

Responses from the South

The 1970s, with the increased flow of petrodollars, was also a decade of building roads and other infrastructure. Changing terms of trade for raw commodities, beginning with oil, and the increased prices they commanded led to high inflation and a surplus of capital—ideal for development loans for massive infrastructural investments. Southern countries, because of favorable real interest rates

that were sometimes negative, borrowed from both private domestic and international banks. Those expenditures were justified by the slogan "reaching the poorest of the poor." It was reasoned that the poor could not be reached if there were no roads and no decent water to drink (Nicholson 1979:225). Large-capital projects suddenly became fashionable, led in rural areas by such programs as colonization, integrated rural development, and massive water projects. World Bank investment in infrastructure was thus often hidden in rural development and social programs. Government planners of the South sought out capital-intensive projects and borrowed the money to implement them. Modernization theory urged the adoption of technology, and the lenders and borrowers took this to mean that the more massive and expensive the technology, the better.

Alternative Development Paradigm

By the 1970s, theorists and practitioners of development, particularly in Latin America and Africa, increasingly questioned the modernization blueprint and terms of debate. They were greatly influenced by the context of economic crisis, environmental crisis, and—in the 1980s—the increasing burden of debt. These crises were triggered by the changed terms of trade in 1973 when the price of oil—and all commodities—rose steeply in world markets, increasing the amount of capital in circulation and thus the need (particularly by oil-exporting nations) to lend it out at interest.

Questioning the Modernization Goals

As Europe was recovering economically, the donors who supported the participatory model became bilateral donors in the mid-1970s. For example, Germany organized its semiautonomous bilateral aid agency, GTZ, in 1975. Previous development aid from Germany was through political parties or through the United Nations. The Norwegians, Swedes, and Danes became active foreign assistance donors in the 1970s. As highly participatory societies concerned with social equity, they brought that model to development practice, with an emphasis on the poor, particularly women and indigenous peoples.

As structural adjustment increased exclusionary tendencies, excluded groups became mobilized. These social movements, in turn, influenced scholarship and institutional structures.

Women in both the North and the South became increasingly concerned as the imposition of modernization further disadvantaged women (Tinker and Bramsen 1980; Charlton, Everett, and Staudt 1989; Tinker 1990). Organizing politically in Northern countries, they brought world attention to the situation of women in the South during the International Women's Decade (1975–1985) (Snyder 1972, 2004). In the United States, the passage of the Percy Amendment to the Foreign Assistance Act of 1973 required that women be specifically addressed in foreign development assistance and led to the establishment of the Office of Women in Development in USAID (Staudt 1985; Frazier and Tinker 2004).

THE DEBT CRISIS, STRUCTURAL ADJUSTMENT, AND SHRINKING THE STATE

Economic and Political Context

Credit, Weber tells us (1947:180), is a plan based on expectations about the future. Nations that borrowed, counting on the continuing decrease in the value of the dollar, now had to repay in more expensive dollars. Real interest rates in the early 1980s were double the interest rates of the 1970s (Watkins 1986; World Bank 1988).

In the early 1980s, the heavy indebtedness of the governments in the South led to a severe fiscal crisis (Schnitz 1984). In Latin America, the 1980s are referred to as "the lost decade."

The belief in technology—particularly *big* technology in huge infrastructure projects in the 1970s—on the part of both international bankers and ministers of finance left Southern governments with huge debts.

Development Theory and Practice

Development practitioners decided that the state was inefficient as a modernizing entity and turned to market and civil society for solutions. The slogan was to substitute trade for aid. And the "failed states" had to reform. Structural adjustment meant cutting social programs to focus on exports.

The "Chicago boys," who were instrumental in setting up the neoliberal regime in Chile after the overthrow of the democratically elected government of Salvador Allende on September 11, 1973, gained theoretical hegemony during the 1980s. The thrust of development was on hastening entrance into the market economy (Friedman 1973). In part, this was making virtue of necessity, because of the huge indebtedness of Southern economies. Income-generation projects for rural women were coupled with projects aimed at linking peasant men to international markets (Flora 1987).

Dominant Assistance Paradigms

During the 1980s and into the 1990s, international lenders, particularly the IMF, the lender of last resort, required countries to restructure their economies through policies of fiscal austerity and free trade that theoretically would generate the capital necessary to reduce external debt and foster internal growth. Loan write-downs, interest rate reduction, and continued capital flow were not forthcoming for most developing countries. Instead, Northern

bankers and politicians urged governments in the South, often with less internal legitimacy than governments in the North, to institute policies they themselves were unwilling to institute at home because of the political protest such policies inevitably generate (George 1988).

Northern donor countries and multilateral lenders rejected the import substitution focus of the early theories of modernization. Rather, they urged Southern countries to seek their comparative advantage. The drive to open markets began. Structural adjustment, aimed at facilitating debt repayment, led to disinvestment in social infrastructure and safety nets that sociologists of development argued was critical for national development. Vulnerability of the poorest populations increased. In response, countermovements, consisting of feminists, environmentalists, and indigenous and other rural peoples, further challenged dominant development strategies, including the goals stressing increase in foreign exchange and gross domestic product.

The "New Orthodoxy" in foreign assistance introduced in the 1980s stressed "food self-reliance" over "food self-sufficiency." Developing countries stressed production for export if exports produce foreign exchange to buy food grains from the United States. The goal was to reach the market-responsive farmer rather than the limited-resource farmer.

Moving from a modernization to a political economy lens, such strategies reinforced the existing relations of dependency through which the North dominated the South.

Dominant Agrarian Paradigms

Because of the demand to increase exports to provide foreign exchange, export crops were supported, which meant support for research in these areas, undergirded by schemes to bring more lands into production. Small farmers were to be better linked to the market through appropriate technologies, spurred by a number of projects aimed at increasing small-farm efficiency. Increasingly, these strategies were informed by an understanding that small farmers did what they did not out of ignorance but out of rational choice in the face of risky environments. Thus, at least a portion of aid was aimed at small farmers and farming systems. But the goal was to increase production to increase market penetration.

Responses from the South

Protests against structural adjustment grew in the South as safety nets and basic services previously offered by the state were dramatically reduced. The IMF was the focus of a great deal of this protest.

Alternative Development Paradigm

The increasing concern for inequalities that seemed an integral part of the modernization project mobilized a number of scholars to address both the means and the ends of modernization (Staudt 1991). Women and indigenous groups gained voice during the 1980s, demanding that their values and worldview were not the negative half of the traditional-modern dualism, but instead a vital part of real development.

In the 1980s and into the 1990s, reducing poverty, rural and urban, emerged as the key development issues (as opposed to the key fiscal issues of generating foreign exchange for debt repayment and cutting internal expenditures), shifting the unit of analysis from the nation-state to regions within states. The Food and Agriculture Organization (FAO) of the United Nations terms sustainable livelihoods, *gestion de terroir,* and farming systems as "people centered approaches" (Baumann et al. 2004). Both scholars and development professionals increasingly recognized the need for programs targeted to excluded populations, particularly women (Moser 1993; Frazier and Tinker 2004); building on the Work of International Women's Year, pro-Women in Development legislation passed first in Europe and then in the United States in the 1970s.

While locally based, these approaches turned to institutional rather than individual actors for change. Robert Chambers (1983) stressed the importance of local knowledge and the need for the outside agents of change to learn from local people. He called for reversals in learning and in management. Implicit in these ideas was an acceptance of the destructive nature of outside influence and particularly cultural and economic penetration.

Norman Uphoff (1986) was an early proponent of local agency through local institutions. International development should support those institutions in achieving more sustainable natural resources management, rural infrastructure, primary health care, agricultural production, and nonagricultural enterprises. While there was discussion with the local institution-building approach on whether to build on existing institutions or create new ones, the importance of local institutions in the global setting was stressed. The shift toward a focus on civil society began.

THE 1990s

Economic and Political Context

Economies of the South followed those of the North in the economic boom of the mid-1990s, reinforcing the pressures for further liberalization of trade. But in 1997, the "miracle" economies of Asia suffered a financial crisis, greatly devaluing their currency and their stock markets. China and India, with state-controlled banking sectors, grew rapidly and were not affected by the Asian crisis. Sachs (2005) points to strict monetary and contractory fiscal policies implemented by the governments at the advice of IMF in the wake of the crisis. Banerjee (2005) points out that "many countries felt their fiscal rectitude was not adequately rewarded by increased growth" (p. 142).

In other parts of the South, ethnic cleansing and civil wars showed that the transition to capitalism and democracy was difficult and required serious institutional attention.

Modernization in Theory and Practice

The failure of the neoliberal modernization project and the growing negotiating power of nongovernmental organizations (NGOs) (Carroll 1992) led to new theories of development in the 1990s, including the importance of social capital for poverty reduction (Evans 1996; Woolcock 1998; Narayan 1999) and actor network theories of development (Murdock 2000; Long 2001). These theories were partially adopted by binational and multinational state actors, with some redirection of resources for development assistance.

The sociology of development incorporates both structural and actor perspectives (Long 2001). The most interesting theories and practice struggle with the different epistemologies of the two perspectives and the intellectual and political space available.

These approaches were in part a response to the declining ability of the public sector to invest in modernization efforts and in part from a questioning of the modernization project itself. Unlike the structural theories, which conceptualize development as a product of external forces, empowerment theories of development view development as resulting from internal processes. While some of these theories accepted the structural damage caused by the intrusion of capitalism on traditional societies, all of them required a redefinition of the goals of development (Black 1991).

Dominant Assistance Paradigms

By 1995, the World Bank under President Wolfensohn began to mainstream social concerns as part of the development agenda (World Bank Operations Evaluation Department 2005). People-centered approaches (Korten and Klaus 1984) were only partially able to counter the negative effects of privatization urged by the North and the abdication by nation-states of the South of their roles in providing a safety net for the majority of their citizens.

USAID shifted from a focus on agriculture to a focus on natural resources. Natural resource management in developing countries required local participation and community, not just individual, engagement (Bromley 1991). Community-based natural resource management schemes were supported in Asia, Africa, and Latin America, with an emphasis on indigenous knowledge as an important complement to scientific ecosystem knowledge (Mazur and Titilola 1992).

At the same time, there was a strong push for privatization of not only state but also communal resources.

As the central state was both impoverished and ineffective, development programs and conditions stressed decentralization and devolution (Cohen and Peterson 1999). There was, in general, "renewed emphasis on the importance of . . . institutions—ranging all the way from property rights, to civil service reform, to financial systems" (Ranis 2005:130).

Dominant Agrarian Paradigm(s)

Two paradigms dominated agrarian change. On the one hand, natural resource conservation gained in importance as the destruction of the rain forests and the increase in endangered species raised serious public concern. Particularly in marginal areas, conservation, from reforestation to sustainable watershed management, was to modify traditional agricultural systems. And on more fertile lands, technology should be used to maximize production. Finally, as the antidrug war increased in political saliency in the United States, programs to substitute nontraditional agricultural crops for coca and poppies were heavily funded.

Responses from the South

Southern resistance to policy-based loans and conditionality increased. Southern scholars focused on the negative impacts of structural adjustments, including increases in infant mortality and decreases in life expectancy. NGOs vigorously attacked the inequalities exacerbated by structural adjustment and privatization programs. The calls for growth with equity increased.

Alternative Development Paradigm

By the end of the 1990s, alternative approaches, which included participatory development, microcredit, and empowerment, were part of the international development portfolio. However, indigenous people increasingly organized themselves and allies to claim/reclaim their languages, their governance structures, and their germplasm.

THE NEW MILLENNIUM

Economic and Political Context

By the early twenty-first century, the induced fiscal crisis of the state in many countries of the North, coupled with strategies of homeland security and increasing internal strife in the South, further reduced and redirected international development investments. As globalization has exacerbated inequality among nations, across subnational regions, and among individuals and households, development has become a global enterprise (McMichael 2000:15). The modernization project became the cultural and economic integration of the world. The market, rather than the state, is assumed to be the dominant actor, and international institutional intervention shifted from United Nations organizations, such as the United Nations Development Program (UNDP) and the FAO, to the GATT

and then the World Trade Organization (WTO). The civil society countermovements to this modernization project are an important component of the sociology of development (Flora 2003).

Modernization in Theory and Practice

Free trade as the solution to underdevelopment still has strong proponents as the WTO seeks to lower the barriers to the flow of capital, goods, and services. Development loans still have conditionality that includes decreasing tariffs and decreasing price supports.

Dominant Assistance Paradigms

Empowerment, "the expansion of assets and capabilities of poor people to participate in, negotiate with, influence, control and hold accountable institutions that affect their lives" (Narayan 2002:xviii), at least gets lip service in most development programs (Baumann et al. 2004). Gross domestic product is no longer the major indicator of development success. The Millennium Development Goals (MDGs) are now stated as the object of development, to be sought for themselves and not assumed to come with increased incomes.

There are eight millennium development goals, and all have targets and indicators.[6]

There are four pillars of UNDP's strategy in support of the goals:

- Integrating the MDGs into all aspects of the UN system's work at the country level, including creating new guidelines for country assessments and national development frameworks.
- Assisting developing countries in preparing MDG reports that chart progress toward the goals, in cooperation with other UN agencies, the World Bank, the IMF, civil society, and other partners.
- Supporting the Millennium Project, led by Professor Jeffrey Sachs of Columbia University, and the Millennium Campaign to build global support for the goals.
- Supporting advocacy and awareness-raising efforts based on national strategies and national needs. Developed countries focus on trade, aid, technology, and other support needed to reach the MDGs, while in developing countries, the aim is to build coalitions for action and help governments set priorities and use resources more effectively (UNDP 2005b).

A critical aspect of the dominant development paradigm is monitoring and accountability. Not only are there nonmonetary goals, there are concrete indicators.

Responses from the South

Southern countries, particularly on the African continent, link meeting the MDGs with debt forgiveness. While the world's richest countries discussed these issues at the July 2005 G-8 meeting, the willingness to invest in development is limited, particularly in the United States.

Sociology of development is now more concerned with globalization than with development practice. Yet there is a continuing need to theorize development processes and practices to deal with the major role of international development—reducing poverty, which includes increasing income, increasing livelihood stability, and increasing voice among the poor so that those most concerned about poverty can be involved in its reduction. This is particularly urgent, given the counterforces to development: the constant pressure for modernization that the current pressures for globalization represent.

PART X

THE QUANTIFICATION OF SOCIAL LIFE

51

Demography

Dudley L. Poston Jr.

Texas A&M University

Michael Micklin

Center for Scientific Review, National Institutes of Health

Amanda K. Baumle

University of Houston

This chapter defines, circumscribes, and reviews the field of demography, providing insight into the breadth of issues covered by this interdisciplinary specialization. Attention is first directed to the discipline of demography, its definition, and conceptual and methodological character,[1] while later sections focus specifically on the various resources of demography. In addition to describing the resources and issues encompassed by the field, the chapter also identifies what the authors believe to be three research areas requiring future attention. Finally, unlike many of the sociological specializations discussed in this *Handbook*, demography has not always been viewed primarily as a subfield of sociology. This issue is also explored in this chapter.

WHAT IS DEMOGRAPHY?

When professors introduce demography and its subject matter in their graduate and undergraduate courses, many find useful what Bogue (1969) has proposed as the three basic demographic questions: (1) How large (or small) is the population? (2) How is the population composed in terms of the demographic characteristics of age and sex, and two additional characteristics closely aligned to demography, namely, race and marital status? and (3) How is the population distributed spatially? Answers to these questions are typically formulated in terms of the effects of the three demographic processes of fertility, mortality, and migration/mobility. A consideration of these materials leads to defining demography generally as *the scientific study of the size, composition, and spatial distribution of human populations, and the changes that occur in these phenomena through the processes of fertility, mortality, and migration* (Poston 2000).

The subject matter of demography is often divided into formal or mathematical demography and social demography or population studies (Hauser and Duncan 1959a). Formal demography may be distinguished from social demography by the substantive foci of the independent and dependent variables. Both approaches endeavor to model dependent variables that are demographic in nature; that is, they are concerned with one of the demographic processes of fertility, mortality, or migration or one of the demographic characteristics of age and sex. However, the independent variables of formal demography are also demographic, whereas those of social demography are nondemographic.

To illustrate, a formal demographer might examine among populations the influence of age composition on the birth rate or, alternately, the influence of the birth rate on age composition. Another illustration of a formal demographic exercise would be an analysis among cities of the effects of the sex composition of in-migrants on city death rates. In contrast, a social demographer might study the influence of a sociological independent variable, such as social class, on the death rate; or the effects of a social psychological variable, such as attitudes about motherhood, on desired and intended fertility; or the effects of a geographic variable, such as annual rainfall, on population density; or the influence of an economic variable, such as economic or livelihood opportunities, on the migration rate (Kammeyer and Ginn 1986). Social demography is necessarily broader in scope and orientation than formal demography. As Preston (1993) has written, it includes "research of any disciplinary stripe on the causes and consequences of population change" (p. 593).

Schofield and Coleman (1986) have brought these two approaches together, as follows:

> The subject matter of demography may be imagined as being arranged within a sphere with a hard mathematical core and a softer socio-economic and biological rind. The core represents the specific technical property of demography; the mathematical theory which deals with statics and dynamics of population; vital rates in relation to the age structure, dynamics, growth and their perturbations, and all the techniques of measurement, analysis and substitution that follow. . . . But this hard core of demography does not touch the surface of the real world directly, except through measurement and reconstruction. It does so only when the population is made specific. An outer structure of theory and fact is then necessary to explain and predict that population's response, through the specific agencies of independent biological, social and economic causes and consequences of population trends. In this outer region of demography, the numerical techniques and ideas of demography act as an interdisciplinary common currency. Demography, which deals with the hardest (biological) facts in social science, enables material from one subject to be used in conjunction with material drawn from another. This permits the risks of the fundamental human events of birth and death to be analyzed interchangeably by ideas which may draw on sociology, geography, history, biology and other subjects. (P. 5)

Demographers, however, do not always agree about the boundaries and restrictions of their field. Caldwell (1996) states the problem succinctly as follows:

> What demography is and what demographers should be confined to doing remains a difficult area in terms not only of the scope of professional interests, but also of the coverage aimed at in the syllabuses for students and in what is acceptable for journals in the field. (P. 305)

In the United States, most graduate training programs in demography are located in departments of sociology, although this is not the case in many other countries. Some U.S. demographers thus argue that demography is best treated as a subdiscipline or specialization of sociology owing to this organizational relationship (Moore 1959:833). The late Kingsley Davis (1948), who served at different times as president of both the Population Association of America and the American Sociological Association, wrote in 1948 in his classic sociology textbook, *Human Society,* that "the science of population, sometimes called demography, represents a fundamental approach to the understanding of human society" (p. 551). The relationship between sociology and demography is hence a fundamental one: "Society is both a necessary and sufficient cause of population trends" (pp. 553–54).

Others subscribe to a broader purview of the discipline, particularly social demography, claiming that demography is not a specialization of sociology, or of any discipline, but a discipline in its own right. Consider the definition of demography in today's most popular demography textbook, *Population: An Introduction to Concepts and Issues,* by John Weeks (2005), now in its ninth edition: "Demography is concerned with virtually everything that influences, or can be influenced by population size, distribution, processes, structures, or characteristics" (p. 5). It is no wonder that J. M. Stycos (1987) observed that "as a field with its own body of interrelated concepts, techniques, journals and professional associations, demography is clearly a discipline" (p. 616). J. C. Caldwell (1996) also reached this conclusion, but more for methodological reasons:

> Demography will remain a distinct discipline because of its approach: its demand that conclusions be in keeping with observable and testable data in the real world, that these data be used as shrewdly as possible to elicit their real meanings, and that the study should be representative of sizable or significant and definable populations. (P. 333)

Earlier in this chapter, demography was defined as the scientific study of the size, composition, and spatial distribution of human populations and the changes that occur in these phenomena through the processes of fertility, mortality, and migration. How this activity, the study of population, is carried out and the results it produces depend on a set of disciplinary resources (Micklin and Poston 2005). These resources are important for the operation of most, if not all, of the topics discussed in this *Handbook.*[2]

Demographic theories and models are statements of the evident or hypothesized course, causes, and/or consequences of demographic phenomena at varying levels of aggregation (Coale and Trussell 1996; Coleman and Schofield 1986; Hauser and Duncan 1959b). *Demographic methods* comprise a body of procedures and techniques for collecting, evaluating, adjusting, estimating, and analyzing demographic data, while *demographic materials* consist of the sources of raw data such as censuses, vital registration systems, population registers, and sample surveys (Hauser and Duncan 1959a; also see Siegel and Swanson 2004). The *infrastructure of demography* consists of the professional organizations, modes of disseminating ideas and research findings, and institutional sources of research support that influence the kinds of work done under the banner of the discipline and how the results are portrayed and received. Finally, *demographic praxis* refers to the use of demographic data and research findings by governments, businesses, and other organizations for predicting, planning, monitoring, and evaluating a wide range of demographic and nondemographic conditions, events, and trends (Siegel 2002). Each of these resources is discussed in detail in the next section.[3] This will serve as a further introduction to the subject matter of demography and how demographic research is carried out.

THE RESOURCES OF DEMOGRAPHY

Demographic Theories and Models

In the last 50 years or so, a variety of views have been presented about the nature and status of demographic theory. In 1952, demographer Rupert Vance lamented the "poverty" of theory in demography. A decade later Robert Gutman (1960) wrote "in defense" of population theory, contending that "demography . . . continues to offer illuminating theoretical statements which organize knowledge, lead to the acquisition of new knowledge, and help in the solution of population problems" (p. 333). Hauser and Duncan (1959b) identified several important population theories, including those derived from Malthus, optimum population theory, demographic transition theory, and psychosocial theories of fertility. But they concluded by stating that "demographers in general may have much to gain from additional allocation of energy to deliberate efforts directed toward theory-construction in conjunction with the conduct of empirical research" (p. 104).

Recent assessments of the discipline of demography are less ambivalent about the adequacy of population theories. Writing in 1979, Charles Nam argued,

> The issues of demographic journals today are replete with theoretically based articles, in stark contrast to those of the past. We no longer fall behind our fellow disciplines in theoretical development, and a merging of lower-order propositions into a theoretical whole is now as conceivable in demography as in any of the social sciences. (Pp. 490–91)

Yet a decade and a half later Eileen Crimmins (1993) stated that "although our theoretical approaches are considerably more complex now than in the past, demography still has highly developed theories in only a few areas. Fertility behavior is the exception" (p. 587). Other population scientists point to demographic transition theory as the theoretical staple of the discipline (Caldwell 1997; Kirk 1996; Lee 2003).

Although a variety of new or reformulated population theories have been proposed in recent decades, their clarification and evaluation remain a challenge for the field. On the other hand, demography has such an abundance of both formal theory and discursive theory that its theoretical accomplishments rival those of any of the other social sciences. Regarding formal theory, one need only consider, for instance, the richness and precision of stable population theory. Regarding discursive theory, few social sciences may claim as much theory as one finds in, say, the study of fertility. Prominent theories to explain fertility behavior include demographic transition theory, wealth flows theory, human ecological theory, political economic theory, feminist theory, proximate determinants theory, biosocial theory, relative income theory, and diffusion theory (see Caldwell 1997; Hirschman 1994). Any view among nondemographers that demography is void of theory was incorrect in the past and is incorrect today.

Demographic Methods

There is agreement among demographers about the significant advances that have occurred in the past 50 years in methods of data collection and analysis. In their systematic review of this topic, Hauser and Duncan (1959a) covered standard census procedures, vital registration systems, the sample survey, rudimentary data processing, and several types of administrative record systems. They also discussed techniques for evaluating, adjusting, estimating, and analyzing demographic data.

In the past half-century, improvements have been forthcoming in each of the techniques, partly through the application of advances in electronic information systems. National census taking is increasingly based on statistical sampling theory and techniques, resulting in more efficient and accurate data collection.

In recent decades, the uncertain quality and availability of demographic data have led to the development of a variety of techniques for evaluating, adjusting, estimating, and projecting population parameters (Ahlburg and Lutz 1998; Ahlburg, Lutz, and Vaupel 1998; Brass 1996; Coale and Demeny 1968; Keyfitz 1975, 1981; Siegel and Swanson 2004). Although the results of many of these exercises, particularly population forecasts, are notoriously inaccurate, their use continues.

Demographic Materials

This set of basic disciplinary resources may be divided into *primary data sources* and *data compendia*, for example, data banks. The most comprehensive and generalizable primary data source is the national population census. National census coverage has improved considerably since the end of World War II, largely through assistance provided to developing countries by the United Nations and a few other organizations. Among 94 developing countries with a population in the mid-1990s of at least

1 million, only 49 conducted a national population census in the decade of the 1950s, by the 1990s, that figure had risen to 71 countries (Cleland 1996). The content, completeness, and accuracy of information collected through censuses vary widely from one country to the next. Overall, the situation has surely improved worldwide.

Another important source of demographic information is the civil registration system, which typically collects information on demographic events such as births, deaths, and changes of civil status as they occur. Although not 100 percent accurate and complete, vital registration in the more developed nations is far better than in the poor nations. Cleland (1996) contends that although civil registration systems in developing countries are "seriously defective, it would not be correct that the data are of little value to demographers" (p. 435). Techniques have been developed for data adjustment and analysis, yielding a rough notion of trends and differentials in vital events.

Beginning in the 1970s, coordinated cross-national surveys emerged as an important source of demographic information. Between 1974 and 1986, sample surveys of reproductive behavior and related social and psychological indicators were conducted in 62 countries, representing 40 percent of the world's population, under the auspices of the World Fertility Survey (Cleland and Hobcroft 1985; Cleland and Scott 1987). This effort was succeeded by another coordinated international program of research, the Demographic and Health Surveys, with 170 sample surveys carried out in 69 developing countries between 1986 and 2003. The obvious advantage of these surveys was the opportunity for comparative analysis and generalization of findings beyond a single population.

Less ambitious demographic surveys, typically focusing on a single country or community, have been a part of the demographer's repertoire for decades. Early studies of fertility include the Indianapolis study (Kiser 1953; Kiser and Whelpton 1953), the Princeton study (Westoff, Potter, and Sagi 1963; Westoff et al. 1961), and surveys of family and reproductive behavior carried out in Puerto Rico (Hill, Stycos, and Back 1959; Stycos 1955). The number of demographic surveys has grown steadily over the years. Examples in the United States include the monthly Current Population Survey, the weekly health interview survey, and the various rounds of the National Survey of Family Growth (NSFG) carried out by the National Center for Health Statistics, the most recent being Cycle 6 conducted in 2002. Another important source of demographic information is the Adolescent Health Survey, which was started in the early 1990s by the Carolina Population Center at the University of North Carolina.

In short, in the past five decades, there has been an enormous increase in the availability of primary demographic data. The various sources differ in terms of data quality, but the trend has been toward better coverage and reduced error in census enumeration and collection of survey data. Moreover, the development of techniques to estimate missing values or reduce measurement error has increased the utility of these sources of demographic information.

Another welcome addition to the disciplinary resources of demography is the growing availability of repositories for demographic data. Some of these collections are longstanding and others are of more recent vintage (for discussion, see Micklin and Poston 2005).

Overall, the volume of demographic and population-related information resources has grown dramatically, particularly over the last two decades. The research-oriented demographer has a virtually unlimited access to multiple data banks and statistical yearbooks, many of them via the Internet (see below). Used judiciously, this rapidly increasing set of resources provides a means of examining linkages between population conditions and trends and a wide range of societal phenomena.

The Infrastructure of Demography

The development of any scientific discipline depends to an increasing extent on its organizational infrastructure, which includes several components. In the case of demography, these are four: (1) professional and affiliated organizations; (2) professional journals that serve as outlets for the results of demographic research; (3) Internet sites that facilitate communication among demographers, access to research ideas and reports, and retrieval of demographic data; and (4) the application of knowledge produced to resolve societal problems. Each of these infrastructure components is now discussed.

With respect to the first component, professional organizations, the oldest professional association of population scientists is the International Union for the Scientific Study of Population (IUSSP). The Union was founded officially in Paris in 1928 and in 1947 was reorganized as an association of 147 individual members representing 32 countries. By 2005, the IUSSP had grown to nearly 2,000 members, approximately one-third from developing nations. The IUSSP publishes a set of monographs covering diverse topics related to population; many are the result of scientific meetings sponsored by the IUSSP. The full meetings of the IUSSP are held every four years.

Shortly after the launch of the IUSSP, the Population Association of America (PAA) was organized in 1931 with 38 original members. By 1955, membership numbered 430, and as of the date of its 68th annual meeting in 2005, the organization had approximately 3,000 members. Annual meetings of the PAA are devoted to presentation and discussion of research reports and theoretical papers, some of which are published in the PAA's official quarterly journal, *Demography*.

In 1983, the European Association for Population Studies (EAPS) was founded. EAPS organizes conferences, seminars, and workshops; disseminates population-related information; and publishes the *European Journal of Population*.

The Southern Demographic Association (SDA) is a scientific and educational society of demographers that was first organized in 1971 as the Southern Regional Demographic Group. The SDA has approximately 200 members and publishes a journal, *Population Research and Policy Review.*

These professional associations certainly do not exhaust those that exist worldwide. Their descriptions here are intended to illustrate the variety of activities undertaken by such organizations and to suggest that while not as large as many scientific disciplines, demography is a viable and flourishing profession.

In addition to the above-mentioned professional associations, there are many affiliated organizations that are more or less loosely linked with professional demographic organizations and with the discipline as a whole. They contribute to the activities of demographers via several functions, including (1) the funding of demographic research, (2) the public advocacy of important demographic and population-related issues and/or policy concerns, (3) the dissemination of demographic data and research findings, (4) the provision of population education, and (5) the delivery of services to address population problems and improve population health (see Micklin and Poston 2005 for more discussion).

Another component of infrastructure is demographic periodicals. In the 1950s, demographers had few specialized outlets for their work. Most demographic research was published in journals of sociology and economics. The only demographic journals available were the Italian journal *Genus* (1934), the *Population Index* (1935) (which was devoted primarily to bibliographic references), the Population Reference Bureau's *Population Bulletin* (1945), the British journal *Population Studies* (1947), and the Indian journal *Population Review* (1957). There was a slow but steady increase in the 1960s in periodicals devoted to demography. *Studies in Family Planning,* published by the Population Council, made its appearance in 1963. A year later, the first issue of the official journal of the PAA, *Demography,* appeared along with the initial publication of the *International Migration Review.* In 1969, the Alan Guttmacher Institute issued the first volume of *Family Planning Perspectives* and followed it in 1975 with the *International Family Planning Digest* (which would later be called *International Family Planning Perspectives*). The Population Council's creation of the *Population and Development Review* in 1975 was a major addition to demography's journal repertoire. Later debuts of demographic journals included *Population and Environment* (1978), *Population Research and Policy Review* (1981), the *European Journal of Population* (1985), *Journal of Population* Economics (1987), the English edition of the French journal *Population* (1989), *Demographic Research* (1999), and *Applied Population and Policy* (2004). Demographers today have many more opportunities to publish results of their research in discipline-friendly periodicals.

Another infrastructure component is Internet sites that facilitate communication among demographers, access to research ideas and reports, and retrieval of demographic data. Considering the case of demography, one cannot help but be impressed with changes in the infrastructure of the discipline resulting from Internet access (see Gryn 1997). However, given the rate of change of Web site addresses and the addition of new sites, it would be futile here to devote a great deal of space to site references. However, several useful sites will be mentioned that have a likelihood of stability.

The United Nations operates a Population Information Network (POPIN) at http://www.un.org/popin/. POPIN includes a list of relevant publications from the UN and affiliated organizations as well as a list of journals and newsletters with population content. The Population Reference Bureau operates a site (POPNET) (http://www.popnet.org/) that includes links to a wealth of organizational sources (international, nongovernmental, university centers, associations, directories, "listservs," and databases). The Office of Population Research of Princeton University provides access to its *Population Index* site (http://popindex.princeton.edu/index.html) with regular coverage of 400 journals. Finally, the Committee for International Cooperation in National Research in Demography (CICRED) offers access to a wide range of information.

Demographic Praxis

Here the concern is with the applications of demographic knowledge. In recent decades there have been considerable advances in this particular resource of demography. Applied demography is a thriving enterprise, providing employment for a sizeable number of demographers (Micklin 1992; Siegel 2002). Three specific examples of applied demographic activity will be mentioned.

First, demographers serve as advisors, witnesses, and technicians on matters of political apportionment and redistricting. Over time, populations become redistributed within political jurisdictions. Periodically, the decision is made to reassess the correspondence between population distribution and voting districts. In such cases, demographic expertise is invaluable.

Second, the increased size and rate of population growth as well as population density have been linked to environmental deterioration, particularly in less developed nations (Shi 2003; United Nations 2001; York, Rosa, and Dietz 2003). Demographers are frequently called to participate in multidisciplinary teams given the responsibility of developing a plan to halt the environmental damage.

Third, demographers are often asked to provide various types of population forecasts in conjunction with community development programs. Large-scale expansion of transportation facilities and construction of residential structures are likely to change patterns of population growth, distribution, and perhaps composition. Officials need research data to estimate the extent of disruption that will occur.

RESEARCH CHALLENGES

There are three areas of demographic research that the authors of this chapter deem to be particularly relevant and important for research in future years.[4] These are areas that to date have received insufficient attention by demographers and, moreover, are areas many consider to be preeminent in terms of their actual or potential contribution to the state of demographic knowledge. They are (1) male fertility, (2) biosocial models of demography, and (3) sexual orientation. This is a short and selective listing. But these are areas that have impressed the authors of this chapter as important, relevant, and challenging. It is not known whether other demographers will agree with the selection.

Male Fertility

Why are males not included in the study of fertility? In discussions in both the scholarly and popular literatures, the methods and numbers pertaining to fertility rates almost always apply only to females but are referred to as fertility rates and fertility numbers, not as female fertility rates and female fertility numbers. In the development and testing of fertility theories in the demographic and social science literatures, the explanations are implicitly based on females but are referred to as fertility theories, not as female fertility theories.

But as everyone knows, biology requires that females and males must both intimately be involved in the production of children. Fertility is not a process that involves only women. So, why have males been ignored in conventional demographic studies of fertility? The answer is not because female and male fertility rates are the same. Although some might believe they should be, in fact they are not, and this is shown below.

It is not at all an understatement that until the past few years virtually all conventional demographic research on fertility has been devoted to analyses of women. Until recently, meetings of the PAA and the IUSSP seldom included sessions on the male side of fertility. Indeed, it has only been since the late 1990s that articles and book chapters on male fertility have started to appear in the demographic literature. In 1998, the journal *Demography* published a special issue on the topic of male reproduction. In 2000, a major paper appeared in the journal *Population and Development Review* (Greene and Biddlecom 2000) that evaluated current research and suggested directions for future research on male reproductive roles. And also in 2000, a monograph was published on *Fertility and the Male Life-Cycle in the Era of Fertility Decline* (Bledsoe, Lerner, and Guyer 2000) based in large part on the papers presented at a 1995 conference of the IUSSP.

POPLINE was consulted a few years ago for a review of the literature on the topic of fertility. The POPLINE search reported more than 75,000 fertility studies conducted between 1950 and 2000. Of these, only 381 dealt with fertility and reproduction behaviors involving males, two-thirds of which were biological and medical in orientation, focusing on such issues as spermatogenesis (e.g., Aitken et al. 1986) and medical and biological aspects of fertility regulation (Singh and Ratnam 1991). The other one-third mainly comprises papers investigating family planning policies (e.g., Adamchak and Adebayo 1987) and fertility regulation (Mbizvo and Adamchak 1992), male attitudes toward fertility and family planning (Micklin 1969), and economic considerations and cultural factors that shape male fertility (Muvandi 1995). Most of the fertility analyses uncovered in the POPLINE search that included males (often along with females) were published in the 1990s.

So, why has conventional demographic research in fertility concentrated largely, if not exclusively, on women? Seven specific reasons may be proposed to justify excluding males from fertility studies (Poston et al. 2005:871–72). First, Greene and Biddlecom (2000) write that the (1) "most important barrier to the inclusion of men in demographic research was normative and reflected the socialization of influential demographers and the research course they set" (p. 83). Men were regarded principally as breadwinners, and "as typically uninvolved in fertility except to impregnate women and to stand in the way of their contraceptive use" (p. 83). This is a gender-related perspective and focuses significantly on the social construction of the male gender role. The reasoning is biological, not sociological. This is hardly a satisfactory justification for ignoring males in fertility studies.

Keyfitz (1977) notes (although does not necessarily endorses) four more reasons. Two of them are that (2) data on parental age at the birth of a child are more frequently collected on registration certificates for the mothers than for the fathers; and (3) when such data are obtained for mothers and fathers, there are a greater number of instances of unreported age data for fathers, and this is especially the situation for births occurring outside marriage.

While it is true that demographic surveys have tended to focus more on women than on men, this situation has improved significantly in recent years. Also, birth registration certificates, particularly in the developed world, now typically include data on both parents. Certificates for births occurring outside marriage, however, occasionally still do omit data on fathers. Finally, Coleman (2000:43) notes that as of 1995, 15 countries in the industrialized world have published, at one or more times in recent years, data and/or rates on male fertility in their demographic yearbooks or related publications.

The next two reasons mentioned by Keyfitz (1977) are (4) the fecundity, and hence, the childbearing years of women occur in a more sharply defined and narrower range (15–49) than they do for men (15–79); and (5) "both the spacing and number of children are less subject to variation among women; a woman can have children only at intervals of 1 or 2 years, whereas a man can have hundreds" (p. 114). The fourth point is true theoretically, and indeed "in polygamous populations a man's fertility can remain high well into his fifties and sixties; . . . [however], in controlled fertility societies, it peaks . . . with a mode in the mid-twenties" (Coleman 2000:41). This is due in part to low fertility norms in Western societies, as well as to a small average age difference of about two to three years between men and women in first marriages. Regarding the fifth point, Guyer (2000) observes that although biologically a man has the potential for siring dozens more children than a woman, this large difference in number of children ever born only occurs in a few societies and "amongst a tiny minority of the population" (p. 64).

Another reason is that (6) female fertility rates are thought to be more fundamental because they are more physiological; that is, they are more bound by biological limitations, and hence are more influenced by the proximate determinants than are male rates. Indeed, several of the proximate determinants are virtually "man-free" (Coleman 2000:31) and thus less tractable. Also "mothers remember events such as miscarriages and deaths in early childhood more clearly than fathers do, and there is no ambiguity as to whether a child is theirs or not" (Greene and Biddlecom 2000:85). The fact that births are more tractable to mothers than to fathers cannot be ignored. But this fact makes it all the more necessary to include males in fertility studies, if for the only reason that by including males, one would then be able to estimate the degree of false paternity in a population, a subject about which little is known. Moreover, Greene and Biddlecom (2000) observe that "since demographers do not limit themselves to counting but also attempt to explain and predict fertility behavior, this methodological justification is patently weak" (p. 85).

The last reason proposed to justify the exclusion of men in studies of fertility is (7) the incompatibility of male and female fertility rates. Unless the population is closed and has a stable age distribution, the rates will likely be different. The differential rates are due to a host of causes that are well known to demographers, some of which are that more males are born than females, males have higher age-specific death rates than females, males marry at older ages than females, males remarry more quickly than females, and emigration and immigration both are often sex selective. These and other factors act together to produce male and female fertility rates that are not the same.

The United Nations (2002) has assembled a natality database that includes age-specific fertility rates (ASFRs) for males and females for various years in the 1990s. Poston, Baumle, and Micklin (2005) have calculated male and female total fertility rates (TFRs) for 19 countries for 1994. They report that most countries have male TFRs that are actually larger than their female TFRs. For instance, Tunisia and Panama show male TFRs that are 623 and 674 births, respectively, larger than their female TFRs. Among those few countries with larger female TFRs than male TFRs, Australia and the United States show the greatest differences, with female TFRs that are 915 and 201 births, respectively, larger than their male TFRs. Only a few countries, namely, Singapore, Canada, and Denmark, have male and female TFRs that are near equal (see Poston et al. 2005:873 for a similar analysis of the counties of Taiwan).

The fact that male and female fertility rates are not the same makes it all the more important and necessary to analyze male fertility along with female fertility. The factors causing the differentials vary over time in their magnitude and effects on the male and female fertility rates. In some cases, they may well be sex specific and will not be realized or understood empirically unless both male and female rates are investigated.

Biosocial Models of Demography

Biosocial models of demography combine biological variables (e.g., hormonal levels and genetic factors) with social variables to predict demographic outcomes, in particular, those outcomes or processes that are biological in nature, that is, fertility and mortality. Aside from demographic studies of the proximate determinants of fertility, the incorporation of biological variables into explanatory models of demographic processes is not an activity to which demographers have devoted even a modest amount of attention. It is likely that there are proportionally more sociologists than demographers developing and testing biosocial models of human behavior. For whatever reasons, demographers have avoided such developments.

Casterline (1995) is one of a handful of demographers who recognize the importance of incorporating biological thinking into our theories of demography. He observes that demographers "can no longer run away from biosocial models . . . It requires either extraordinary blindness or exceptional stubbornness to fail to recognize that fertility and mortality . . . are determined in part by biological variables" (p. 359).

Casterline (1995) argues that after 1994, the "passive avoidance of biosocial models [among demographers] is no longer an option . . . [owing to Udry's presidential address in 1994 to the Population Association of America] challenging demographers to take biosocial models seriously" (p. 360). In his address, Udry (1994) reported research showing that "one-fourth of the variance in women's 'gendered' behavior" is accounted for by a model comprising "prenatal and adult androgen measures and their interaction" (p. 520). This research (Udry, Morris, and Kovenock 1995) concludes that "gendered behavior is not entirely socially constructed, but partly built on a biological foundation" (p. 367).

Udry is a demographer who, over the years, has developed and tested biosocial models of demographic outcomes. He has published several papers introducing "biosocial models of adolescent sexuality that combine traditional sociological models with models derived from a biological theory of hormone effects" (1988:709; see also Udry, Talbert, and Morris 1986). Weller (1995) notes that just because Udry claims that a "behavior has biological foundations [does not mean he believes] it does not also have social foundations" (p. 281).

Here is a hypothetical equation, proposed by Casterline (1995:360):

$$D_i = hB_i + sS_i + c(B_i * S_i) + e_i$$

where D is some demographic outcome, B is a vector of biological variables, S is a vector of social variables, h and s are vectors of parameters to be estimated indicating the effects of the biological and social variables, e is a disturbance, and the subscript i refers to individuals.

In the first place, much of demography assumes the parameter h not to be significantly different from zero. But Casterline (1995) counters that the

> denial of the existence of parameter h . . . [is] now amply refuted by empirical scientific evidence . . . Scientists . . . must acknowledge that a substantial and solid body of evidence supports the proposition that individual variation in many behaviors is biologically driven . . . The challenge for scientists is to determine the magnitude of parameter h. (P. 361)

In Casterline's equation, the biological and social variables may be considered as additive and as interacting. The $B_i * S_i$ interaction would posit that the "effect of biological variables is conditioned by the level of social variables" (Casterline 1995: 361), a point made also by Udry (1994; see also Udry 1995).

Casterline (1995) and Udry (1994, 1996) both admit that biosocial models will have no role in certain demographic studies. Casterline (1995) observes that "a large fraction of the central research questions in social demography concerns secular change and or macro/societal variation, and hence it is not clear that much attention need be given [in such analyses] to biological variables" (p. 368). The role of biosocial models in demography thus depends greatly on the demographic outcome being investigated. Given the results of Udry and several others regarding the empirical importance of biological variables as predictors of certain types of demographic outcomes, it is concluded that demographers can no longer afford to ignore the potential of biological predictors of them.

Sexual Orientation

Policymakers are increasingly focusing attention on issues concerning the gay and lesbian community. This recent surge in interest may be attributed partly to judicial decisions seen as victories for homosexuals, including the Supreme Court's decision striking down Texas's law against same-sex sodomy, and the Massachusetts Supreme Court's ruling that the state constitution requires the state to give same-sex couples marriage rights equal to those of opposite-sex couples (*Goodridge et al. v. Department of Public Health* 2003; *Lawrence et al. v. Texas* 2003). In coming years, policymakers are likely to look to demographers and other social scientists to provide information on the homosexual community to aid them in constructing arguments for or against certain policies. Presently, however, there has been little demographic work done in the area of sexual orientation; many questions are just beginning to be explored, and some remain virtually untouched.

The demography of sexual orientation is underdeveloped due in large part to a lack of representative data sets with samples of sufficient size to answer many of the questions that researchers would like to ask about the homosexual community. Many of the larger surveys conducted of the homosexual population were surveys of convenience, such as those drawn from readership of magazines or newspapers (see the discussion of Black et al. 2000). U.S. researchers seeking representative samples of the gay and lesbian population must rely on the General Social Survey (GSS), the National Health and Social Life Survey (NHSLS), the NSFG—Cycle 6, and the census to explore research questions. Studies conducted using the GSS, the NHSLS, or the NSFG are limited due to the small number of individuals captured in these surveys who either identify as homosexual or who report having engaged in sexual activity with a same-sex partner. In the NHSLS, for instance, the sample consists of 3,432 American men and women but includes only 12 women and 27 men who identify as homosexual. And it includes only 32 women and 45 men who either identify as homosexual and/or had exclusively same-sex sex partners in the past year. The numbers in the NSFG are almost twice as large. However, sample sizes such as these are far too small to conduct many analyses of the homosexual population of interest to demographers, such as their distributions across cities, states, or occupations.

Beginning in 1990, however, the U.S. Census Bureau introduced a change on the long-form questionnaire that resulted in the creation of a large data set of same-sex individuals. The bureau offered respondents the option of identifying individuals living in the household as unmarried partners, after studies indicated the increasing number of opposite-sex and same-sex individuals living in marriage-like relationships in the United States (Baumle, Compton, and Poston, forthcoming; Black et al. 2000). The unmarried-partner category permits unmarried heterosexual and homosexual couples to identify themselves as a couple.

In the 2000 U.S. Census, 1,188,782 individuals identified themselves as being in same-sex unmarried partner households on the census, 605, 052 males and 586,730 females (Simmons and O'Connell 2003). The addition of this category to the census has opened the door for social scientists to explore a number of issues relating to homosexuals that were previously out of reach due to the paucity of data.

Census data on same-sex partners are limited, however, in that only individuals who choose to identify asunmarried partners on the census questionnaire are captured. Thus, individuals who prefer not to self-identify are not counted. Furthermore, the census question allows data to be collected only for same-sex partners living in the same household, leaving homosexuals who are single unaccounted for. Nonetheless, the advantages of the census data over other data sources renders the census an attractive source for research on homosexuals, and studies attempting to quantify the extent of possible bias have concluded that the problem is not so severe as to warrant abstaining from using census data.

Surprisingly, however, little research has been conducted in this area to date, despite the availability of census data for both 1990 and 2000. And the work that has been done has been dominated by economists rather than demographers. There are a number of important areas of research in the area of sexual orientation, however, in which demographers and other social scientists can and should play an important role in the coming years.

One of the primary concerns of policymakers in both formulating policy goals and determining their impacts will center on the places in which gays and lesbians are located within the country. Data from the 1990 and 2000 U.S. Censuses indicate that there are concentrations of gays and lesbians in virtually all the metropolitan areas of the country. However, with but a few exceptions (Baumle et al., forthcoming; Black et al. 2000, 2002; Gates and Ost 2004; Walther and Poston 2004), there has been little effort among social scientists at indexing these concentrations among the metropolitan areas of the United States and examining the extent to which the indexes are associated with the social, ecological, and political characteristics of the areas. Preliminary research using 2000 data indicate that in most metropolitan areas, the levels of concentrations of partnered lesbians are higher than those of partnered gays. San Francisco is an outlier with many more partnered gays per 1,000 never-married males than partnered lesbians per 1,000 never-married females. Most metropolitan areas show the opposite. Limited research also indicates that ecological characteristics of metropolitan areas reflecting amenities of interest to both homosexuals and heterosexuals are more associated with the levels of homosexual prevalence than are characteristics pertaining to factors important only for homosexuals (Baumle et al., forthcoming; Black et al. 2002). Even less quantitative research has been undertaken regarding the differential concentration of partnered gays and lesbians in the nonmetropolitan and rural areas of the United States (Baumle et al., forthcoming).

Another area of homosexual demography in which there is a major research void is residential segregation. Demographers have paid virtually no attention to patterns of residential segregation of homosexuals from married and unmarried heterosexuals (for an exception, see Baumle et al., forthcoming). Preliminary research indicates that levels of segregation of homosexuals (gays and lesbians treated separately) from unmarried and married heterosexuals are sizable, that lesbians are less segregated from heterosexuals than are gays, and that gays and lesbians are segregated from each other. Extensive demographic research on racial residential segregation of black and Hispanic minorities from the white majority indicates that the segregation is largely involuntary. Early research on the segregation of homosexuals from heterosexuals suggests that the segregation is both involuntary and voluntary, but considerable work remains to be done that would sort out these differences and estimate statistical models to explain them.

For decades, U.S. politicians have been proposing the adoption of a federal law prohibiting discrimination in employment on the basis of sexual orientation. Policymakers might turn to social science research to answer important questions in assessing whether such a law is necessary: Do homosexuals earn less than heterosexuals? Are homosexuals segregated into different occupations than heterosexuals? The majority of studies examining homosexuality and work have focused on the relationship between sexual orientation and income. Once controls are introduced for individual characteristics, most research finds that gay men earn less than heterosexual men (Badgett 1995; Baumle et al., forthcoming; Black et al. 2003; Klawitter and Flatt 1998). Findings about the earnings of lesbians are mixed (Badgett 1995; Baumle et al., forthcoming; Klawitter and Flatt 1998). Research is ongoing concerning income differences between homosexuals and heterosexuals, but there is no clear consensus as to the cause of the income differences if they do exist.

Badgett (1995) finds that occupational differences account for some of the income differences between homosexuals and heterosexuals. Occupational segregation, therefore, is another area in which future research needs to be conducted in assessing whether inequalities exist in the workplace between homosexuals and heterosexuals. Baumle et al. (forthcoming) have explored the manner in which homosexuals and heterosexuals are segregated in professional occupations. They find that partnered homosexuals are overrepresented in the professions as a whole and appear to be concentrated within fields that are focused on creativity, psychology/counseling, and law/social work. Partnered homosexuals are underrepresented primarily in the engineering and teaching professions. Additional research needs to be conducted to determine the cause of such occupational segregation, as well as to examine segregation in occupations outside the professions.

Finally, the debate concerning the legal right of homosexual couples to marriage is one that is virtually global (Merin 2002). There are few places in which homosexuals have been granted marriage rights equal to those of heterosexuals, and family rights vary widely both within and between countries. To provide guidance to legislators in formulating marriage and family laws, demographers must develop a literature about the family practices of homosexuals. What is the average length of a homosexual relationship? How prevalent is childrearing among lesbian and gay couples? Do lesbian and gay couples predominantly adopt or raise their own children? These questions, and others, are important to address if demographers and policymakers are to understand the manner in which laws and social policies are to be constructed to address the needs of the homosexual population.

In the above and last section of this chapter, three broad areas of demographic research have been proposed requiring major conceptual and methodological advances. They represent challenges to demographers. They require demographers to not undertake fertility analyses that are based only on females, to not estimate demographic models that are based only on social variables, and to not restrict their investigations, implicitly or explicitly, to heterosexuals. According to Horton (1999), an important characteristic of "critical demography," as opposed to "conventional demography," is the posing of "questions that challenge the prevailing social order" (p. 365). In some ways, demographic research in the areas outlined above may well challenge existing demographic paradigms.

Also, the issues and topics presented here comprise a short and very selective list. There are certainly many other areas of research requiring the future attention of demographers.

CONCLUSION

Over the past 50 years, the field of demography has changed substantially (see Hauser and Duncan 1959c; Poston and Micklin 2005). First, the theoretical base of the field has expanded considerably in terms of the subject matter incorporated and its links to other disciplines. Demographic theories now encompass phenomena other than the standard variables reflected in the demographic equation (population size, composition, and distribution, and fertility, mortality, and migration). This is because demographic research has shown that fuller explanation of population conditions, trends, and events requires that theories and models incorporate nondemographic variables and that the effects of demographic conditions and trends extend to nearly all dimensions of human societies and their natural environments. As the substantive concerns of demographers have grown, so has their reliance on concepts, theories, and methods developed in other disciplines such as economics, political science, social psychology, and cultural anthropology. In short, the scope of the field of demography—the "demographer's ken"—has widened considerably.

A second way in which demography has changed over the past half-century is the enormous expansion in the availability of demographic materials, including both primary and secondary data sources. The frequency, coverage, and accuracy of basic demographic data collection systems, for example, census and vital registration procedures, have increased worldwide, although there is still sizeable variation among countries and regions. Such improvements increase the likelihood that routine demographic activities such as population counts, estimates, and

projections will become more accurate and, therefore, more useful for social, political, and economic planning.

Perhaps the most significant changes in the field of demography are seen in its infrastructure. Examples include a growing number of professional organizations, the expanded number and variety of outlets for distributing research findings, an enormous variety of Internet sites that provide demographic information or discussions of topics of demographic interest, and the continuing spread of efforts to use demographic information to inform and influence local, regional, national, and international practices and policies.

Throughout this chapter, we have suggested that the scope of demographic theories and research now extends throughout the social and behavioral sciences. Readers should not interpret these comments to mean that demography and population studies are any less significant for the discipline of sociology than they were decades earlier. Indeed, several features of the sociological perspective all but guarantee that demography will remain an integral component of sociological theory and research. First, a sizeable number of sociologists continue to show a primary interest in the standard demographic variables of population size, composition, and distribution and the processes that influence changes in these variables—that is, fertility, mortality, migration, and social mobility. The continued strong interest and enrollment in the Sociology of Population section in the American Sociological Association is indirect testimony to this contention. Second, much of sociology is concerned with human groups and aggregates, including such varied forms as peer and kinship groups, formal organizations, residential communities, and nation-states. Even those sociologists who focus their attention on individual conduct or personal characteristics tend more often than not to interpret these individual variables in terms of features of the group or collective context in which they are embedded. Questions about contextual effects are often raised in demographic terms, for example, various indicators of group size, composition, and/or distribution. Third, the discipline of sociology grew out of a problem-oriented concern with the quality of life in human societies, and this concern is still a vibrant force. Demographers, many of them sociologists, have continued this concern, raising questions about the effects of population size and growth on the sustainability of social and economic development, particularly in the poorer societies and regions of the world, and on medium- to long-term effects on natural resource supplies and environmental quality.

The examples presented above are intended only to whet the reader's appetite to think more about the integral connections between sociology and demography. There is much conceptual, theoretical, and empirical territory to be explored. One conclusion, however, is clear: The study of population is a key component of twenty-first-century sociology.

52

THE SOCIOLOGY OF SOCIAL INDICATORS

KENNETH C. LAND

Duke University, North Carolina

ABBOTT L. FERRISS

Emory University

Social indicators are statistical time series "used to monitor the social system, helping to identify changes and to guide intervention to alter the course of social change" (Ferriss 1988:601). Examples include unemployment rates, crime rates, estimates of life expectancy, health status indices, school enrollment rates, average achievement scores, election voting rates, and measures of subjective well-being with life as a whole. This chapter begins with a review of the historical development of the field, and then defines the main types of social indicators in use today. This is followed by a section on the uses of social indicators, including a description of a sociological model of social change that includes social indicators. A concluding section describes the prospects for future developments in social indicators.

THE HISTORICAL DEVELOPMENT OF THE FIELD OF SOCIAL INDICATORS

Social Indicators in the 1960s

The term *social indicators* was given its initial meaning in an attempt, undertaken in the early 1960s by the American Academy of Arts, to detect and anticipate the nature and magnitude of the second-order consequences of the space program for American society (Land 1983:2; Noll and Zapf 1994:1). Frustrated by the lack of sufficient data to detect such effects and the absence of a systematic conceptual framework and methodology for analysis, some members of the Academy project attempted to develop a system of social indicators—statistics, statistical series, and other forms of evidence to detect and anticipate social change as well as to evaluate specific programs and their impact. The results of this part of the Academy project were published in a volume (Bauer 1966) bearing the name *Social Indicators*.

Generally, the sharp impulse of interest in social indicators in the 1960s grew out of the movement toward collection and organization of national social, economic, and demographic data that began in Western societies during the seventeenth and eighteenth centuries and accelerated in the twentieth century (Carley 1981:14–15). The work of sociologist William F. Ogburn and his collaborators at the University of Chicago in the 1930s and 1940s on the theory and measurement of social change is more proximate and sociologically germane (Land 1975). As chairman of President Herbert Hoover's Research Committee on Social Trends, Ogburn supervised production of the two-volume *Recent Social Trends* (President's Research Committee on Social Trends 1933), a path-breaking contribution to social reporting. Ogburn's ideas about the measurement of social change influenced several of his students—notably Albert D. Biderman, Otis Dudley Duncan, Albert J. Reiss, Jr., and Eleanor Bernert Sheldon, who played major roles in the emergence and development of the field of social indicators in the 1960s and 1970s. Another historical origin in sociology is the work of Howard W. Odum (1936) at the University of North Carolina, who published *Southern Regions of the United States*. This volume brought together indicators under an institutional framework, revealing regional disparities in welfare, and demonstrating the need for more definitive data. Involved in the study was Margaret Jarman Hagood, who developed one of the first indices of well-being, a level of living index of farm families (Ferriss 2004).

The appearances of these studies were not isolated events. Several other influential analysts commented on the lack of a system for charting social change. They advocated that the U.S. government establish a "system of social accounts" that would facilitate a cost-benefit analysis of more than the market-related aspects of society already indexed by the National Income and Product Accounts (see, e.g., National Commission on Technology, Automation and Economic Progress 1966; Sheldon and Moore 1968). The need for social indicators also was emphasized by the publication of the 101-page *Toward a Social Report* (U.S. Department of Health, Education, and Welfare 1969) on the last day of the Johnson administration in 1969. Conceived of as a prototypical counterpart to the annual economic report of the president, each of its seven chapters addressed major issues of social concern, namely, health and illness; social mobility; the physical environment; income and poverty; public order and safety; learning, science, and art; and participation and alienation, and each assessed prevalent conditions. The *Report* established the linkage of social indicators to the systematic reporting on social issues for the purpose of public enlightenment but did not elaborate on policy implications of the findings, as some scholars had advocated.

Social Indicators in the 1970s and 1980s

At the end of the 1960s, the enthusiasm for social indicators was sufficiently strong and broad-based for Duncan (1969:1) to write of the existence of a Social Indicators Movement. In 1972, the National Science Foundation supported the Social Science Research Council Center for Coordination of Research on Social Indicators in Washington, D.C. The Russell Sage Foundation supported the publication of several major efforts to define and develop a methodology for the measurement of indicators of subjective well-being as measures of the quality of life (QOL) (Campbell and Converse 1972; Andrews and Withey 1976; Campbell, Converse, and Rodgers 1976). The federal government initiated a series of comprehensive social indicator chart books showing trends in a variety of social forces with limited analyses and few policy implications (U.S. Office of Management and Budget 1974, 1978; U.S. Bureau of the Census 1981). Policy implications, however, were outlined in a series of issues of *The Annals of the American Academy of Political and Social Sciences* (Gross 1967; Taeuber 1978, 1981).

Social scientists recognized the need for more comprehensive data, especially in time series. This led to establishing several important surveys, sponsored by the federal government (Ferriss 1979), that provide important indicators today: the National Opinion Research Center's (NORC) General Social Survey, begun in 1972, the Bureau of Justice Statistics' annual National Crime Victimization Survey, and later, the Survey of Income and Program Participation.

Under editorship of Alex Michalos, the first volume of the international journal *Social Indicators Research* appeared in 1974, providing a medium for exchange of research findings. At the same time, the United Nations Organization for Economic Cooperation and Development stimulated the issuance of national social reports based on social indicators. This led to the initiation of social surveys and the improvement of other data-gathering efforts internationally. This also was promoted by the Statistical Commission of the United Nations and United Nations Educational, Scientific, and Cultural Organization (UNESCO). Many nations continue to issue annual or biennial social reports, such as *Donnes Sociales* (France), *Datenreport* (Germany), *Inequality in Sweden,* and *Social Trends* (United Kingdom).

In contrast to the 1970s, social indicators activities slowed in the 1980s, because reductions in funding or nonrenewals led, for example, to the closing of the Center for Coordination of Research on Social Indicators (Social Science Research Council 1983); the discontinuation of related work at several international agencies; the termination of government-sponsored social indicators reports in some countries, including the United States; and the reduction of statistical efforts to monitor various aspects of society. Several explanations have been given for this turnabout (Rockwell 1987; Andrews 1990; Bulmer 1990; Ferriss 1990b; Innes 1990; Johnston 1990; Rose 1990). Certainly, politics and the state of national economies in the early 1980s are among the most identifiable proximate causes. Owing to faltering economies and budget deficits, governments reduced spending. In addition, many perceived that social indicators were not fulfilling their initial promise of contributing to public policy making. This was due, in part, to an overly simplistic view of how and under what conditions knowledge influences policy.

Social Indicators in the 1990s and 2000s

The 1980s ended with the question of "What Ever Happened to Social Indicators?" (Rose 1990) and the mistaken conclusion that the field had faded away. Shortly afterward, however, interest in social indicators revived, and since the mid-1990, the field has been expanding.

The revival of interest became vividly apparent in the 1990s (Land 1996, 2000) owing to the widespread political, popular, and theoretical appeal of the quality-of-life (QOL) concept. This concept emerged and became part of the Social Indicators Movement in the late 1960s and early

1970s as social scientists in highly developed Western industrial societies raised doubts about economic growth as the major goal of societal progress (Noll and Zapf 1994:1–2). They cited the "social costs" of economic growth and raised doubts about whether "more" should be equated with "better." Their discussion posed QOL as an alternative to the more and more questionable concept of the affluent society, and they incorporated QOL in discussions of social policy and politics as a new, but more complex, multidimensional goal. As a goal of social and economic policy, QOL encompasses many or all domains of life and subsumes, in addition to individual material and immaterial well-being, such collective values as freedom, justice, and the guarantee of natural conditions of life for present and future generations (Cummins 1996; Diener and Suh 1997; Ferriss 2001). The political use of the QOL notion is paralleled in the private sector by the widespread use and popularity of numerous rankings—based on weighted scales of multiple domains of well-being—of the "best" places to live, work, do business, and play be they cities, states, regions, or nations.

The theoretical appeal of the QOL concept as an integrating notion in the social sciences and related disciplines is, in part, due to the perceived importance of measuring individuals' subjective assessments of their satisfaction with various life domains and with life as a whole. For instance, QOL has become a concept that bridges the discipline of marketing research and strategic business policy with social indicators. Marketing is an important social force—with far-reaching direct and indirect impacts on the prevailing QOL in a society—through consumer satisfaction (Samli 1987; Sirgy and Samli 1995) and its impact on satisfaction with life as a whole. The intersection of marketing research with social indicators through the QOL concept led to the organization in the mid-1990s of the multidisciplinary International Society for Quality-of-Life Studies (http://www.isqols.org).

In addition to the widespread appeal of the QOL concept, another key development in the field of social indicators in the 1990s and early 2000s is evident: The field has entered a new era of the construction of composite or summary social indicators. Often these indices are used to summarize indicators (objective and/or subjective) of a number of domains of life into a single index of the QOL for the population or society as a whole or for some significant segment thereof (e.g., children and youth, the elderly, racial and minority groups, cities and states or regions within the nation). Many of the pioneers of the Social Indicators Movement in the 1960s and 1970s backed away from the development of summary indices, instead concentrating on basic research on social indicators, measuring the QOL and developing a richer social data base. Today, however, researchers attempt to answer one of the original questions motivating the Social Indicators Movement: How are we doing overall in terms of the QOL? With respect to our past? With respect to other comparable units (e.g., cities, states, regions,

nations)? Responses to these questions are encouraging and include the following examples: (1) at the level of the broadest possible comparisons of nations with respect to the overall QOL, the *Human Development Index* (United Nations Development Programme 2004), Diener's (1995) *A Value Based Index for Measuring National Quality of Life* and Estes's (1988, 1998) *Index of Social Progress;* (2) at the level of comparisons at the national level over time in the United States, the *Fordham Index of Social Health* (Miringoff and Miringoff 1999) and the *Genuine Progress Indicator* (Redefining Progress 1995), and for a specific subpopulation, the *Child Well-Being Index* developed by Land, Lamb, and Mustillo (2001, 2004; Land 2004).

TYPES OF SOCIAL INDICATORS

Policy/Welfare/Criterion Indicators

Based on the premise that social indicators should relate directly to social policy-making considerations, an early definition by economist Mancur Olson, the principal author of *Toward a Social Report,* characterized a social indicator as a "statistic of direct normative interest which facilitates concise, comprehensive and balance judgments about the condition of major aspects of a society" (U.S. Department of Health, Education, and Welfare 1969:97). Olson went on to state that such an indicator is, in all cases, a direct measure of welfare and is subject to the interpretation that if it changes in the "right" direction, while other things remain equal, things have gotten better, or people are better off. Accordingly, by this definition, statistics on the number of doctors or police officers could not be social indicators, whereas figures on health or crime rates could be.

In the language of policy analysis (Fox 1974:120–123), social indicators are "target" or "output" or "outcome" or "end-value" variables, toward changes in which some public policy (program, project) is directed. Such a use of social indicators requires (Land 1983:4) that (a) members of a society agree about what needs improving, (b) it is possible to decide unambiguously what "getting better" means, and (c) it is meaningful to aggregate the indicators to the level of aggregation at which the policy is defined.

In recognition of the fact that various other meanings have been attached to the term *social indicators,* the tendency among recent authors is to use a somewhat different terminology for the class of indicators identified by Olson. For instance, Land (1983:4) termed this the class of *normative welfare indicators.* Building on the Olson approach, MacRae (1985:5) defined *policy indicators* as "measures of those variables that are to be included in a broadly policy-relevant system of public statistics." With a meaning similar to that of MacRae, Ferriss (1990b:416) used the felicitous term *criterion indictors.*

As an example, Land et al. (2001, 2004) developed a composite child well-being index consisting of 28 social indicator time series for the United States grouped into seven domains: material well-being, health, security/ behavioral concerns, educational attainments, a place in the community, social relationships, and emotional/ spiritual well-being. This index is computed annually based on the most recent data available for the component indicators (see http://www.soc.duke.edu/~cwi/). It can be considered a criterion indicator for changes (improve- ments, deteriorations) in the QOL or well-being of children and youth in American society compared with base-year values of the component indicators.

Life Satisfaction and/or Happiness Indicators

Another class of social indicators has its roots in the work of Angus Campbell and Philip E. Converse in the early 1970s. In *The Human Meaning of Social Change* (1972), they argued that the direct monitoring of key social-psychological states (attitudes, expectations, feel- ings, aspirations, and values) in the population is necessary for an understanding of social change and the QOL. In this approach, social indicators seek to measure psychological satisfaction, happiness, and life fulfillment by using survey research instruments that ascertain the subjective reality in which people live. The result may aptly be termed *life sat- isfaction, subjective well-being,* or *happiness indicators.*

The Campbell-Converse approach led to two major methodological studies in the 1970s (Andrews and Withey 1976; Campbell, Converse, and Rodgers 1976) and a subsequent edited volume (Andrews 1986) exploring the use of various survey and analytic techniques for mapping individuals' feelings of satisfaction with aspects ("domains") of their experiences. These studies examine domains ranging from the highly specific (house, family, etc.) to the global (life as a whole). A number of other stud- ies and applications of these concepts and techniques have appeared over the past three decades (for reviews, see Diener 1994; Veenhoven 1996; Diener et al. 1999) and continue to appear. One or more studies of subjective well-being indicators can be found in almost any issue of the journal *Social Indicators Research* and the *Journal of Happiness Studies.* Research on the related concept of happiness as an index of well-being was surveyed by Veenhoven (1984).

Social indicators literature has established firmly the principle that the linkage between objective conditions and subjective well-being (defined in terms of response to sam- ple survey or interview questions about happiness or satis- faction with life as a whole) is sometimes paradoxical. This leads to the conclusion that subjective as well as objective states should be monitored. However, numerous studies of the measurement and psychodynamics of sub- jective well-being over the past three decades have led to a better understanding of this construct (see, e.g., Cummins 1995, 1998; Cummins, Gullone, and Lau 2002). Research continues, however, and it would be incorrect to say that the debates have been settled. It appears that this construct may have both *traitlike* (i.e., a durable psychological condition that differs among individuals and contributes to stability over time and consistency across situations) and *statelike* (i.e., a condition that is reactive to situational differences) *properties* (see, e.g., Veenhoven 1994, 1998; Stones et al. 1995).

With respect to the statelike properties of subjective well-being, Davis (1984) used an accumulated sample from several years of NORC General Social Surveys to document the responsiveness of happiness with life as a whole to (a) "new money" (recent changes in respondents' financial status as opposed to current income level), (b) "an old man or lady" (being married or having an intimate living partner), and (c) "two's company" (a household size of two as compared with living alone or families of three or more). Numerous other studies have found additional factors that are more or less strongly associated with variations in subjective well-being. But the relevance of intimate living conditions/family status almost always is replicated. The connection of subjective well-being to income levels has been a particularly intriguing problem for social indicators researchers ever since Easterlin's (1973) finding that income differences between nations predicted national differences in happiness but that the association of happiness with income within countries was much weaker (for reviews of this research literature, see Ahuvia and Friedman 1998; Diener and Biswas-Diener 2002). Recently, however, Davis's finding of a positive relationship of "new money" or recent income changes to happiness has been replicated by Schyns (2001), using data from a panel study conducted in Russia from 1993 to 1995. Studies of the relationship of subjective well-being or happiness indices to income and other social, demo- graphic, economic, and cultural factors continue to be a lively area of research interest.

Descriptive Social Indicators

Building on the Ogburn legacy of research on social trends, a third approach to social indicators focuses on social measurements and analyses designed to improve our understanding of what the main features of society are, how they interrelate, and how these features and their relationships change (Sheldon and Parke 1975:696). This produces *descriptive social indictors*—indexes of the state of society and changes taking place therein. Although descriptive social indicators may be more or less directly (causally) related to the well-being goals of public policies or programs and thus include policy or criterion indicators, they are not limited to such uses. For instance, in the area of health, descriptive indicators might include preventive indicators such as the percent of the population that does not smoke cigarettes, as well as criterion indicators such as the number of days of activity limitations in the past month or an index of self-reported satisfaction with health. Ferriss (1990a) gave a compilation of descriptive indicators for the United States at the end of the 1980s. Regularly published national social indicator compilations for other nations similarly contain numerous examples. An example: Speed, social and geographic mobility, single-person households, and materialistic acquisitions are treated in a volume that charts visible and invisible changes in the United States and speculates on the future (Kane 2001).

The various statistical forms that descriptive social indicators can take are described by Land (1983:6). These can be ordered by degree of abstraction from those that require only one or two data series and little processing (e.g., an age-specific death rate) to those that involve more complicated processing into a single summary index (e.g., years of life expectancy at age x, years of active or disability-free life expectancy at age x). Descriptive social indicators can be formulated at any of these levels of abstraction. Moreover, as described in Juster and Land (1981), these indicators can, at least in principle, be organized into demographic- or time-budget-based systems of social accounts.

THE USES OF SOCIAL INDICATORS

The Enlightenment Function

The Social Indicators Movement was motivated by the principle that it is important to *monitor changes over time* in a broad range of social phenomena that extend beyond the traditional economic indicators and that include *indicators of QOL* (Andrews 1990:401; Noll and Zapf 1994:5). Many organized actors in contemporary society—including government agencies, organizations and activists interested in social change programs, scholars, and marketing researchers interested in market development and product innovations—monitor indicators in which they have a vested interest and want to see increase or decline (Ferriss 1988:603).

A second principle that has been part of the Social Indicators Movement from the outset (e.g., Biderman 1970; Land 1996) is that a critically important role of social indicators in contemporary democratic societies is *public enlightenment through social reporting.* In brief, modern democracies require social reporting to describe social trends, explain why an indicator series behaves as it does and how this knowledge affects interpretation, and highlight important relationships among series (Parke and Seidman 1978:15).

It is also important to document the consequences that are reasonably attributable to changes in a series. This includes the systematic use of social indicators to *forecast trends in social conditions and/or turning points therein* (Land 1983:21). To be sure, the area of projection or forecasting is filled with uncertainties. Techniques range from the naïve extrapolation of recent trends to futuristic scenario construction to complex model building with regression, time series, or stochastic process techniques. Moreover, there appear to be intrinsic limits to the accuracy of forecasts in large-scale natural and social systems

(Land and Schneider 1987). But demands for the anticipation of the future (at a minimum, for the description of "what will happen if present trends continue"), for foresight and forward thinking in the public and private sectors, and for the assessment of critical trends (Gore 1990) appear to be an intrinsic part of contemporary postindustrial societies. Thus, it is prudent to expect that the "anticipation" task will become an increasingly important part of the enlightenment function of social indicators.

As the decades of the 1990s and 2000s unfolded, the model of a comprehensive national social report in the tradition pioneered by Ogburn and Olson clearly had faltered in the United States, at least in the sense of federal government sponsorship and/or production. But the key ideas of monitoring, reporting, and forecasting were evident to greater or lesser extents in the production of continuing, periodic subject matter-specific publications by various federal agencies, including *Science Indicators* (published by the National Science Foundation) *The Condition of Education, Youth Indicators* and *Educational Indicators* (published by the Department of Education), the *Report to the Nation on Crime and Justice* (published by the Department of Justice), *Health USA* (published by the Department of Health and Human Services), and numerous Bureau of the Census publications. Special topics involving groups of federal agencies also receive attention from time to time. For instance, the Federal Interagency Forum on Child and Family Statistics began in 1997 an annual publication, *America's Children: Key National Indicators of Well-Being.* In addition, the United States has numerous private research organizations, policy institutes, and scholars that continue to produce reports, monographs, and books interpreting social trends and developments in various areas of social concern. Caplow et al. (1991) published a privately generated, comprehensive social report on the United States. The report follows a framework that was employed for several other countries (France, Germany, Italy, and others). These social reports provided the basis for a study of the comparative social change in the several Western countries.

In contrast to the situation in the United States, comprehensive social reports/social indicators compendiums continue to be published periodically in several other countries. Examples are the *Social Trends* series published annually since 1970 by the United Kingdom's Central Statistical Office, the *Datenreport* series published biennially since 1983 by the Federal Republic of Germany, the *Social and Cultural Report* published biennially by the Social and Cultural Planning Office of The Netherlands, and *Australian Social Trends* published annually by the Australian Bureau of Statistics. Citations and summary reviews of these and other social indicators/social reports publications can be found in the quarterly newsletter and review of social reports, *SINET: Social Indicators Network News* (www.soc.duke.edu/resources/sinet/index.html).

The difference in the organization of social indicators and social reporting work in the United States as compared with that in other countries is, in part, attributable to the lack of a central statistical office responsible for the coordination of all federal statistical activities in the United States. More generally, despite the invention of the ideas of social indicators and comprehensive social reporting in the United States, the sector reports on science, health, education, crime, and housing are all that remain of official federal reporting systems. While U.S. administrations have issued reports that attempt to review national social conditions (U.S. President's National Goals Research Staff 1970; U.S. President's Commission for a National Agenda for the Eighties 1980), the U.S. Congress has proposed but never finally mandated a social report on the nation.

Whether a new round of legislative effort will eventually create the necessary institutional base for a national social report remains to be seen. Perhaps marking a turning point and indicative of things to come is Public Law 100-297, enacted April 28, 1988, which requires an annual education indicators report to the president and Congress. Another possibility centers on an effort by the U.S. General Accounting Office (2003), acting at the behest of a Congressional committee, to develop a social indicator system for the United States (see also www .keyindicators.org).

The Policy Analysis Function

Policy analysts distinguish various ways of guiding or affecting public policy, including *problem definition, policy choice and evaluation of alternatives,* and *program monitoring* (MacRae 1985:20–29). In the formative days of social indicator development, Bertram M. Gross advocated the application of social indicators to policy evaluation and development (Gross and Springer 1967). The social reporting/public enlightenment approach to social indicators centers on the first of these, namely, the use of social indicators in problem definition and the framing of the terms of policy discourse. Indeed, studies of the actual use of social indicators suggest that this is precisely the manner in which they have affected public action (Innes 1990).

But policy analysts always have hoped for more from social indicators, namely, the shaping of public policy and planning through the policy choice process. At a minimum, this requires the identification of key variables that determine criterion indicators and changes therein (i.e., causal knowledge). More generally, it requires the construction of elaborate causal models and forecasting equations (often in the form of a "computer model") that can be used to simulate "what would happen if" under a variety of scenarios about policies and actions. An example of this is the development of the National Cancer Institute model for the control and reduction of the incidence of cancer in the United States in the year 2000 (Greenwald and Sondik 1986). Various policy and action scenarios and their implications for cancer mortality were simulated and estimated with this computer model. These simulations led to a decision to allocate funds to prevention, education, screen-

ing, and treatment, and their implications for cancer mortality were simulated and estimated with this computer model. These simulations led to a decision to allocate funds to a prevention program rather than to additional clinical treatment.

A SOCIOLOGICAL MODEL FOR THE USES OF SOCIAL INDICATORS

Ferriss (2002a) noted that the following *model for directed social change* emerged during the 1990s in such areas as health, education, and the welfare of children and youth in the United States: (a) *Identify trends in criterion indicators,* the direction or rate of change of which should be changed. (b) *Gather together intelligence* from experiments, field research, or theory that suggests what should be done to bring about the desired change. (c) *Launch a decentralized program to effect change in specific criterion indicators* by specific amounts, to be attained by a target date. (d) *Monitor progress* by periodically assessing trends on the specific indicators, modifying strategies as needed. (e) As initial goals are reached, *set new goals* for continued progress. The model adds social indicators to the conceptual scheme for processes of social change, beginning with cultural values, set forth by Robin M. Williams, Jr. (1967). Land and Ferriss (2002) developed a more complete articulation of this scheme in the form of a sociological model that accommodates both the enlightenment and the policy analysis functions of social indicators.

These functions may encompass the setting of goals for future change. Identifying such goals and setting about altering their direction or rate of change is a process called *telesis,* which means "progress that is intelligently planned and directed; the attainment of the desired ends by the application of intelligent human effort to the means" (*Webster's New Collegiate Dictionary* 1977; Ward 1903 used the term in a broader sense; see also Commager 1967). Land and Ferriss (2002) recently described several interrelated telic conceptual schemes for the use of social indicators in large, complex societies such as the United States.

Figure 52.1 presents an overview of telesis, identifying the principal elements of the model, with social indicators as the central feature. Figure 52.2 identifies relationships in detail of the teleological process. The following paragraphs describe the components of the model and introduce illustrative examples.

Values of society, cultural values, are the starting point in the initiation of social change, as illustrated in Figure 52.1. The following values have been ranked among the top five in surveys of the American public: "A world at peace (free of war and conflict); family security (taking care of loved ones); freedom (free choice, independence); happiness (contentedness); and self-respect (self-esteem)" (Inglehart 1990:119). Cultural values such as these define the desires (wants) of people in society. For example,

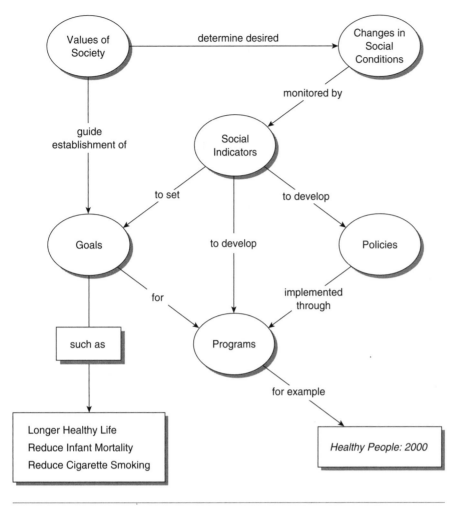

Figure 52.1   Overview of Telesis

SOURCE: Land, K. C., & Ferris, A. L., "Conceptual models for the development and use of social indicators," in Glatzer, W., Habich, R., & Mayer, K. U. (eds.), *Sozialer Wandel und gesellschafliche Dauerbeobactung*, copyright © 2002. Reprinted with permission of Verlag fuer Socialwissenschaften.

"family security" translates into the need, among other things, to preserve life and to live free from harm, and identifies the goal of "longer healthy life," as shown in Figure 52.1. This value was central to the program of the Surgeon General in 1964 to reduce cigarette smoking in order to reduce illness and extend life expectancy (U.S. Department of Health and Human Services 1990).

Values determine desired changes in conditions, such as tobacco consumption. Social indicators identify the current status of the practice. For example, in 1990, 25.3 percent of persons 20 years of age and older smoked cigarettes. Health authorities set 15 percent as the goal for 2000. While the goal was not realized, 23.1 percent smoking in 2000, nevertheless, there had been some reduction. During this period, the length of life, 73.7 years at birth in 1980, rose to 77.0 years. Mortality rates declined 16 percent. Thus, the status of the condition in the population as identified by social indicators led to the development of policies to be implemented through programs to reach the goal.

Social indicators help establish the discrepancy between the actual and desired conditions. Trends in

indicators reveal the direction of change, whether improving or declining. That a gap exists in social conditions relative to the desired is a call to action. The pattern of optimism that change is possible must also be present.

When the goal and policy are set, the teleological process begins (see Figure 52.2). Knowledge of the sequences of actions that will bring about the desired effect is needed. This knowledge must arise from experiments, observations, practical experience, demonstrations, and tests. For example, in the case of the development of the *Healthy People* (U.S. Department of Health and Human Services 1990) program to reduce cigarette smoking, many prior studies—as many as 7,000—had proved the adverse health consequences of cigarette smoking and others had shown that stopping the habit led to improved health (Centers for Disease Control and Prevention 1989). Such information about causes and effects helped establish the goal of reducing cigarette consumption.

The next problem was to determine what programs held promise to effect change in the indicator. In the case of cigarette smoking, it was initially thought that the secession of cigarette smoking could be prompted through clinical advice of physicians to their patients. It was soon evident that this approach was inadequate. Broader effort, eventually involving labeling and restrictive legislation, proved to be more effective.

Lester Ward, the early-twentieth-century sociologist who first employed the concept of telesis in social affairs, believed that change could most effectively be accomplished through legislative initiatives (Ward 1906; Commager 1967). Legislation, especially by state legislatures, in the late 1970s, pushed the nonsmoking movement toward success. Whether through legislation or through private initiatives, resources—money, workers, cooperation of actors, and so on—are required. As with any social movement, the generation of public interest and support is necessary. Dependence on governmental support is one approach, as *Healthy People* illustrates. Private interests can also be successful, as the KIDS COUNT program (http://www.aecf.org/kidscount) illustrates. Without resources of funds and manpower, the telic process will falter.

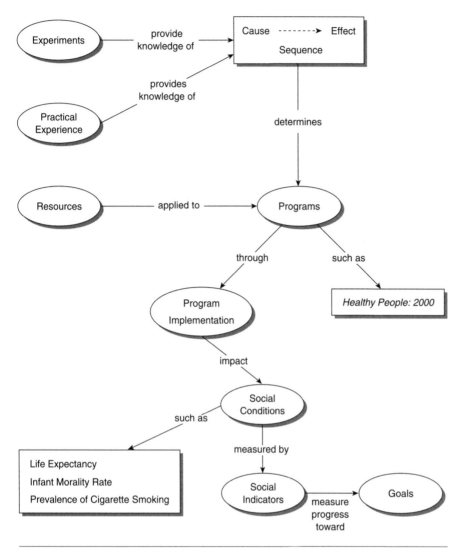

Figure 52.2   The Teleological Process

SOURCE: Land, K. C., & Ferris, A. L., "Conceptual models for the development and use of social indicators," in Glatzer, W., Habich, R., & Mayer, K. U. (eds.), *Sozialer Wandel und gesellschafliche Dauerbeobactung,* copyright © 2002. Reprinted with permission of Verlag fuer Socialwissenschaften.

progress during the 1990s in 8 of the 10 indicators that it monitors (Ferriss 2002b). Knowledge, state by state, of effective procedures that generated the changes would enable future efforts to select more efficient interventions. O'Hare and Lamb (2004) described the variation in the progress of the several states in the change process.

Not all segments of the population may welcome a proposed change. In fact, those whose livelihood depends on continuing the status quo may resist change. In the case of reduction in cigarette smoking, the tobacco industry, including the farmers, reluctantly entered into the change process, and inducements for their participation were advanced. The movement to establish a vegetarian diet in place of the diet predominately based on meat and dairy products offers another example of forces resisting change. Advocates of the vegan diet have presented evidence that it can reduce rates of death and disability from heart disease, cancer, diabetes, osteoporosis, autoimmune conditions, and other illnesses. They cite evidence from nutrition and epidemiological studies, particularly *The China Study.* A description of the sizable active forces opposed to such change to a vegan diet is ably described in Campbell (2005).

Social indicators provide evidence of change or lack thereof. Monitoring progress should lead to an evaluation of the interventions attempted. With various programs in place in the several U.S. states, natural experiments in effective/ineffective interventions would yield evidence of effective approaches. With such evaluations, revision of the program may be initiated and new goals set.

Monitoring progress involves identifying these changes not only in the aggregate but also with respect to sectors of a target population. Segments of the population differ in prevalence rates. Attention must be directed toward the most critically affected segments. If progress is not being realized, interventions should then be evaluated for their effectiveness and, if found lacking, new steps initiated.

Study of effective interventions is needed to establish the more economically feasible pathway to change. As an example, the KIDS COUNT program to improve the well-being of children in the United States observed

PROSPECTS FOR THE FUTURE

We modestly anticipate that social indicators will continue to serve the enlightenment function for societies and their citizens and politicians. We expect that policymakers will find many more applications in the future of social indicators to policy choice and evaluation. In particular, such applications will probably occur in three areas. The first is the additional development of well-grounded, theoretically informed, and policy-relevant indicators and models for national- and/or regional-level analyses within particular fields, such as health, education, crime, and science (Bulmer 1990). In such applications, the phenomena to be included are definable and delimited, and the limitations of the data on which the indicators are based are known. The health field, particularly, may be expected to pursue change sequences, as evident in the pages of *Health USA.*

We also expect the use of social indicators to expand in the field of social impact assessment (Finsterbusch 1980; Land 1982). Social impact assessment has arisen as part of environmental impact assessment legislation and attempts to anticipate the social effects of large-scale public projects (e.g., dams, highways, nuclear waste disposal facilities) as well as to assess the damage of both natural and human-made disasters (e.g., earthquakes, oil spills, nuclear plant accidents). The use of QOL measures, now quite reliably measured, would enhance evaluation of public intervention efforts, such as the program of the Appalachian Regional Commission and the Delta Regional Authority, now evaluated by less precise methods (Ferriss 2004). This application of social indicators in impact assessments brings the field back full circle to its point of origination in the American Academy effort of the 1960s.

Finally, and not of least importance, we expect that the many times series of indicators now available will increasingly be used by sociologists to assess theories, hypotheses, and models of social change, thus bringing social indicators data to bear on core issues in sociology, namely, understanding social change. With a tremendous increase in the richness of social data available for many societies today as compared with two or three decades ago, a new generation of social indicators researchers has returned to the task of constructing summary indices. Thus, the field of social indicators will probably see several decades of such index construction and competition among various indices—with a corresponding need for careful assessments to determine which indices have substantive validity for which populations in the assessment of the QOL and its changes over time and social space.

PART XI

COLLECTIVE BEHAVIOR
AND SOCIAL MOVEMENTS

53

THE SOCIOLOGY OF COLLECTIVE BEHAVIOR

BENIGNO E. AGUIRRE

University of Delaware, Newark

HISTORICAL OVERVIEW OF THE FIELD

The field of collective behavior is coterminous with the analysis of social dynamics. Before the emergence of the specialty, there was a concern with social change and societal transformation in the form of well-known and celebrated commentary about society and culture, such as Thucydides' account of the Peloponnesian War and Niccolo Machiavelli's advice to the prince. Abramson (1961:47–95) (see also Nye 1975; Rule 1988:91–118) provides a succinct account of origins, which by convention, are traced to Gustave LeBon, for he above all other Europeans writing at the end of the nineteenth century and the first decades of the twentieth captured the imagination of the public with his book titled *The Crowd,* which is both a compilations of the ideas of writers who opposed the ideals of the French Revolution and democracy—most prominently those of Edmund Burke, Hippolyte Taine, Scipio Sighele, Pasquale Rossi, and Gabriel Tarde—and an effective vehicle for conceptions of how people acted together that had and continue to have influence, as shown in Sigmund Freud's social psychology and in some of Robert E. Park's views of collective behavior.

Tarde's (1969) influence was particularly important. He identified the characteristics of collective behavior as involving a set of psychic and mental interactions of people who are aware of each other, possess similarities of beliefs and goals, share a conviction and passion for what they believe that is relatively new or previously unexpressed, and act in concert. For Tarde, collective behavior was, as was true of all other forms of social behavior, the result of imitative behavior diffusing outward from an initial point of interaction (see his influence on Faris 1926). Imitation came about through contagion. People first imitate the ideas of the new advanced by their social superiors. Crowds occurred earlier than publics in social evolution. In the crowd, imitation is associated with physical proximity and face-to-face interaction. In the public, interaction takes place through newspapers and thus exhibits a spiritual or mental contiguity not limited by space or number of participants. People in publics, contrary with what is the case in crowds, can belong to a number of publics (Steigerwalt 1974).

LeBon employed the racist ideas of his time to describe collective behavior in terms of psychological regression and contagion. People, particularly lower-class individuals, when acting together in a crowd, lost their individuality and regressed to what he presumed they had in common: their race and national origins. The effect of socialization on personality was a thin patina easily removed under the hypnotic influence and emotional interstimulation of the mob. These simple ideas were expressed in scientific-sounding principles such as the law of the mental unity of the crowd. The crowd was capable of acts of heroism and savage horror; it all depended on chance events and the sway of symbols and suggestions. There is also in LeBon a theory of history, although this is not as prominent, in which crowds served a useful purpose of destroying the useless practices of the past and facilitating the emergence of the new; periods of intense and

AUTHOR'S NOTE: The author would like to acknowledge, with thanks, E. L. Quarantelli and Joel Best's many comments and suggestions, which improved the manuscript. All remaining shortcomings are his own.

concentrated crowd activity mark the end and the beginning of historical epochs. The ambivalence is never resolved in his writings: The crowd both destroyed individual personality and brought about social change and the possibility of progress.

THE AMERICAN CONTEXT

Collective behavior as an area of sociological specialization starts in the United States with the pioneering efforts of Robert E. Park (Turner 1967), who in 1899 traveled to Germany, where he studied at the Universities of Berlin, Strasbourg, and Heidelberg. His doctoral dissertation (Park [1904] 1972) is titled *Crowd and Public*—it reflects many of the ideas in vogue at the time in Europe. Particularly noteworthy is his use of G. Tarde's concept of the public to identify a collective behavior form quite different from the crowd, in which deliberative and rational discussion and assessment of alternative viewpoints and interests were seen as the foundation of collective behavior and decision making. Later on, in his classic statement appearing as a chapter in his textbook coauthored with Ernest Burgess titled *Introduction to the Science of Sociology* (Park and Burgess 1921), Park laid out the contours of the field of specialization. Here we see the enduring characteristics of his scholarship. Reflecting the ideas in vogue at the time, Park to varying extents borrows from LeBon's view of the crowd as irrational and dominated by psychological regression. But this is never the dominant form of collective behavior in his writings, which advanced the field considerably by identifying a multiplicity of forms and by arranging these forms in a continuum of institutionalization, from elementary forms of collective behavior, to mass behaviors and social movements, to the emergence of institution. It is a natural sequence approach to social change. Institutions fail to satisfy human needs, and people who are affected by their failures become dissatisfied. Thus, there is first a stage of individual unrest, which is the foundation of social unrest, which then provides the grievance base for the possible occurrence of collective behavior, which in turn is the possible basis for the institutions that exist in the society, both as providing reasons to change them and as sources of ideas and resources for the direction of the change that is sought. Collective behavior becomes the mechanism for change and social adjustment of institutions. In its optimism and pragmatism, it is a quintessential American view of the mechanics of social change very different from the pessimism and reactionary perspective of LeBon and the European intellectual tradition he represented.

Psychological Strands

A psychological tradition to the study of collective behavior also exists (Locher 2002; Rule 1988:200–24). For Floyd Allport (1924), individual predispositions explained the phenomena of collective behavior, understood as an aggregate of individual cognitions. People previously interested in the same sort of activities converged to specific places to satisfy their interests. He also incorporated some of LeBon's ideas, arguing that once in a crowd, people expressed impulses that otherwise they would not be willing or able to acknowledge. Neil Miller and John Dollard (1941) also presented an individual-level explanation of collective behavior in their learning theory of human behavior: People learn similar responses to similar situations or stimuli and thus respond in a similar fashion to them. In crowds, they also experience heightened stimulation, caused in part by human density, anonymity, and the impact of the crowd leader. McPhail (1991) provides a critical summary of this tradition.

DIVERGING PERSPECTIVES IN THE COLLECTIVE BEHAVIOR TRADITION

Many scholars studied under R. E. Park and later with Herbert Blumer at the University of Chicago and then at Berkeley and with Talcott Parsons at Harvard University (for a brief account of Parsons' sociological contributions, see http://www.hewett.norfolk.sch.uk/curric/soc/PARSONS/ Parsons.htm) and carried out the traditions of the field. Some of the most renowned members of these second and third generations are Neil Smelser, John Lofland, Gary Marx, David Snow, Joseph Gusfied, Kurt and Gladys Engel Lang, Ralph Turner, Lewis Killian, E. L. Quarantelli, Norris Johnson, William Feinberg, Bert Useem, Anthony Oberschall, and Orrin Klapp.

Herbert Blumer (1939, 1969), Park's student at the University of Chicago, early on in his career repeated in his writings many of the ideas initially advanced by Park and developed a view of collective behavior that had the unwelcome effect of helping to marginalize it from mainstream sociology, for he created a distinct social psychology for it. In his view, collective behavior was characterized by circular interaction rather than by symbolic interaction: People participating in instances of collective behavior did not evaluate and then respond to the acts of others but responded automatically and emotionally to them (Zygmunt 1986). There are other criticisms of Blumer's scholarship (McPhail 1991), but these do not mention the many other conceptual breakthroughs and lasting contributions he made. Among them are his understanding of social problems as collective behavior (Blumer 1971), his criticisms of public opinion polling (Blumer 1948), and his empirical analysis of fashion (Blumer 1969). In these other writings, Blumer used symbolic interaction to make sense of the social life he was explaining.

Herbert Blumer's analysis of social problems was one of the pioneering efforts that provided the basis for the current dominant view of social problems as social constructions. From its perspective, the acceptance of a claim as a social problem is the outcome of a set of stages in which many of the claims presented by collective actors are discouraged. Throughout it is characterized as a complex political process in which the outcome of any claim is uncertain and is very often determined by established interests, the effect of differential social power, and access to centers of public persuasion such as the mass media and government agencies.

Similarly, his criticism of public opinion polling emphasized that such polling often conveys the erroneous impression that every opinion counts equally in the setting of the public agenda. Instead, Blumer pointed out that this is the case only if the link between the opinion and the outcome is unmediated by social organization. In instances in which public opinion is vulnerable to the effect of structures of power and control, the opinions of persons central to institutions in which this power resides are much more important and influential than others in affecting outcomes. Blumer's statement on fashion continues to be one of the key articles in the study of this form of collective behavior. Based on months of observation and conversations with members of fashion houses in Paris, France, he pointed out the cultural fields in which fashion was prone to occur and the specific practices that accompanied the setting of fashion, in what he characterized as a process of cultural selection that negotiated the paradox of continuity and discontinuity of popular tastes.

In the case of H. Blumer and N. Smelser, as well as other scholars included in this review, it is possible to underestimate their scholarship to build up our own arguments and theories. It is more useful, however, to recognize the situated nature of all knowledge and the strengths and weaknesses of their contributions in the light of present-day understanding in the discipline. To go back to Park, his institutionalization continuum allows us to appreciate the fabricated nature of some collective behavior, in which centers of social power such as the corporation and the state construct instances of collective behavior and social movement organizations (SMOs) as part of their increasing sophisticated efforts to control culture and politics. It is no longer collective behavior on one side and institution on the other but their mixing that must be assumed nowadays. Park never examined these matters but pointed to the link between the two.

Other Writers

The Chicago tradition of collective behavior established by Park and Blumer, and to a lesser extent the strands of structural functionalist theorizing from Harvard, was used by a number of other important contributors to develop often-divergent scholarly contributions. Most of their writings combined an abiding interest in versions of symbolic interaction with historical, complex organizational, and other structural emphases.

Kurt and Gladys Lang (1961), in their textbook on social dynamics, continued the ways of thinking about collective behavior found in Blumer's earlier writings,

defining collective dynamics as "those patterns of social action that are spontaneous and unstructured inasmuch as they are not organized and are not reducible to social structure." Collective dynamics are marked by transformations of social systems, or the emergence of a collective definition, the undermining of expectations and trust on established definitions of the situation, anxieties, mass conversion or changes in values, and the crystallization of new forms of social life. Particularly problematic for more recent understanding of the subject matter of the specialty is their emphasis on spontaneity and contagion, and the separation of collective behavior from the institutions of society. They also wrote a number of monographs on mass communications, politics, and symbols (Lang 1983) and have shown a particular interest in the study of the interface of generations and social change (Roberts and Lang 1985).

Different from the Langs is Richard LaPiere (1938), who sponsored a radical nominalist social psychological perspective on collective behavior, defined as the "interaction which occurs between two or more socialized human beings for the duration of the particular situation in which the interaction occurs" (p. 3). He then classified social interactions in terms of origin and function, the members in the situation, the relationship between overt behavior and covert feelings, and the elements of leadership (pp. 45–46). Elsewhere (LaPiere and Farnsworth 1936: 465–84), he makes the distinction between normal and abnormal forms of collective behavior: fads, booms, crazes, and fashion are presumably normal; the *audience fanatique,* lynching mobs, uncoordinated riots, panic, mobs or coordinated riots, and revolutions are abnormal. These conceptual boundaries, definitions, and types, with an emphasis on momentary interaction, create an idiosyncratic understanding of collective behavior that stands apart from most other conceptualizations.

Quite different from both the Langs and LaPiere is Orrin Klapp (1962, 1964, 1969), who made important and unique contributions to the specialty of collective behavior. For Klapp, social life is dramaturgical, theaterlike, and can be understood using symbolic interaction. He located collective behavior in the post–World War II period. He argued that dramatic improvements in mass communication created breakdowns in meanings and deficits in social recognition. It was predominantly one-way communication from the mass media to the individual. In this context, he identified collective behavior as a solution to alienation and anxiety in modern society. According to Klapp (1970), collective identity is a system of reference group identifications people need to have a satisfactory conception of selves. Those who lack them are identity seekers, people searching for new selves. Pervasive shortcomings in meaning lead to collective identity searches such as style rebellions.

Klapp's approach is a type of convergence explanation: Identity seekers have predispositions that make them participate in collective acts. Some of his most provocative writings are his identification of style search as a form of collective behavior—a collective search for a distinctive expression of mass identity via personal appearance and life style. Symbolic leaders are charismatic people whose public gestures and styles represent an identity solution to seekers. The identity solution is through what Klapp called an open symbolic transaction in which values and meanings are not all known in advance and into which parties enter expecting bargaining, a dialectic, carrying off roles. The chief way symbolic transaction is done is through anonymous interpersonal communication, or communication from an unidentified source, a network not defined, or from people the person does not control and who are strangers. Klapp also devoted attention to social types, such as the fool, the villain, and the hero. For example, his major classification of heroes includes winners, splendid performers, heroes of social acceptability, independent heroes, and group servants, each composed of subcategories. Even though mass society theory of collective behavior is not in vogue nowadays, and even as we disagree with Klapp's notion that collective behavior takes place among strangers, it is still the case that he dealt with very important forms of collective behavior that go mostly unrecognized nowadays. As one example among many, Edelman's (1988) and other social science literature on the spectacle owes much to Klapp's pioneering efforts.

David Snow also combined symbolic interaction and drama. He was among the first to use Erving Goffman's dramatist theory to examine a victory celebration to excellent effect. He and his collaborators (Snow, Zurcher, and Peters 1981) used the metaphor of the theater to identify the various groups of actors in the celebration, their on-stage and off-stage behavior, and the effect of distant spectators, such as merchants, in the eventual cessation of the activities, as they exerted pressure on the police to stop what they eventually came to perceive as a public nuisance. Subsequently, he and his collaborators have also shown greater interest in the study of SMOs, particularly of homeless people (Anderson, Snow, and Cress 1994; Cress and Snow 2000). Borrowing the concept of frame from Goffman but favoring a hierarchical view of power and influence, they have advanced a widely used perspective on types of movement frames as rhetorical mechanisms used for resource acquisition and mobilization (Benford and Snow 2000; Snow et al. 1986).

Joseph Gusfield (1986) examined status politics in his study of the temperance movement. He understood it as an organized reaction of native-born, Protestant, small-town, and rural folks to the reality of industrialization, immigration, and urbanism in the post-Civil War period. Prohibition legislation, the main goal of the movement, was a cultural affirmation of their claims for continued cultural preeminence and control of the state. Important in this work is not only his attempt to understand the importance of symbols in the struggle for control of state institutions but also his conception of moral passage, based on Émile Durkheim's ([1897] 1951, [1893] 1997) approach to public morality, which allowed him to recognize the ebb and flow in interpretations of behavior as either legal or illegal and to link them to the struggles by mobilized collectivities. Later on, Gusfield and his colleagues wrote on the characteristics of new social movements (Larana, Johnston, and Gusfield 1994).

Anthony Oberschall's (1973, 1993) approach is even more different from the others' and similar to Gusfield's, in that his sociology is imbued with a profound sense of history. He has studied social conflict, particularly opposition movements, riots, and rebellions. He has examined opposition movements, stressing their rational components of choice and decision making as well as emotional outrage, misconceptions, and anger. Social conflicts occur in episodes with elements of action and reaction during which large groups of people express grievances, voice demands, and organize marches, demonstrations, and other collective behaviors. He examined the process of mobilization of aggrieved people in pursuit of collective goals, and how central organization, ideology, and leadership are central to the production of mobilization as well as to its cessation. Oberschall examined the patterns of diffusion in the civil rights movement (Oberschall 1989a, 1989b) and the processes that marked its quiescence (Oberschall 1978), developed an important analysis of witchcraft epidemics of deviance, and wrote monographs on social movements. His structural explanation of the witchcraft epidemic ties the practice to the emergence of rationality in the West, which in his view facilitated the increased severity of the sanctions attached to the deviance and the number of people punished; in the Middle Ages, prior to the rise of science, people expected miracles and supernatural acts, among them witchcraft. In another very worthwhile paper, Oberschall (1978) argues that the decline of the 1960s social movements (student, antiwar, and civil rights movements) did not come about from government efforts to suppress them. Instead, it was the outcome of the internal disorganization and chronic conflict and division among the movements, and the eventual disinterest of the mass media as other public concerns emerged, such as environmental degradation and the condition of women. Without the media attention and without effective internal organization, the movement collapsed. Most recently (Oberschall 1994), he has carried out extensive research in Eastern European countries to provide explanations to the patterns of collective behaviors that marked their transitions to postcommunist political systems.

E. L. Quarantelli is another of the writers included in this review who, while he was influenced by symbolic interaction, has developed a lifelong interest in the study of social organization and its transformations during moments of crises. He wrote a number of papers on collective behavior topics. In work coauthored with Hundley (Quarantelli and Hundley 1969), he tested Smelser's theory of collective behavior and pointed out that the omnipotence of protesters, a key characteristic that presumably made up their hostile generalized belief, could not be confirmed. In another paper, Quarantelli (1974) wrote about the lack of a critical mass of trained scholars in the specialty as an important structural impediment to its maturity as a field of specialization in sociology. He found that there was an insufficient degree of consensus among practitioners about the definition of the field and what it contained and about the key analytical and empirical challenges it faced. Yet in another paper, he and Weller (Weller and Quarantelli 1973) amended and expanded Turner and Killian's theory of emergent norm to argue for the inclusion in it of emergent social relations—it is not just culture but social relations that must be considered in a theory of collective behavior. More recently, he and his collaborators helped clarify the characteristics of cycles of fads, which, contrary to common assumptions, are not inconsequential social behavior without histories and lasting effects and whose diffusion cannot be predicted (Aguirre, Quarantelli, and Mendoza 1988). One of his most important contributions, explored elsewhere in this review, is his lifelong attempt to understand disaster phenomena using his own perspective of collective behavior mediated by social organization.

John Lofland (1966) also mixed symbolic interaction with the analysis of social organization of religious social movements and the dynamics of religious conversion. He resurrected the examination of dominant emotions in instances of collective behavior (Lofland 1985) as involving, to varying degrees, the emotions of fear, hostility, and joy. Unfortunately, to this day the study of collective behavior has not profited from the sustained attention of specialists in the sociology of emotion, an increasingly important field in the discipline. He also developed an analytical model of collective behavior as types of surges (Lofland 1993a) that can be used to understand fads and other forms of collective behavior. More recently, Lofland (1996) offered a comprehensive inventory of key empirical generalizations about the most important analytical issues in the study of social movements.

Gary Marx and Bert Useem are well known for their abiding interest in the study of formal social control and the action of the state. Marx (1974) contributed a classic analysis of the ways government infiltrates SMOs and encourages them to break the law and wrote about issueless riots (Marx 1970). He has also examined the increasingly institutionalized practices that undermine privacy and make people vulnerable to government surveillance (for a near complete list of his publications, see web .mit.edu/gtmarx/www/garyhome.html). Also emphasizing the effect of social control is Bert Useem. He and his collaborators have developed what is arguably the best-known explanation of prison riots in the breakdown model of social control in prisons (Useem 1985, 1998; Useem and Kimball 1989). In it, they argue, based on comparisons of prison reforms in different states, that the action of state bureaucracies, particularly prison administrators and state

and national governments, can create the conditions under which social order breaks down or is restored; attempts to improve prisons can have the unintended consequence of disrupting the established order of the prison and facilitating riots. Useem has published on a number of other subjects, to include the dynamics of movements and countermovements (Zald and Useem 1987).

Different from the works of other scholars included in this review are Norris Johnson and William Feinberg's pioneering efforts to construct computer simulations of crowd behavior. They have used computer simulations to examine "intra and inter group interaction resulting in individual and group responses to cues for action" (Feinberg and Johnson 1989) and understand the effect of outside agitators in crowds (Feinberg and Johnson 1988), the effects of ambiguity on crowds (Feinberg and Johnson 1990) and the emergence of consensus in crowds (Feinberg and Johnson n.d.). They have developed Firescap (Feinberg and Johnson 1995), a computer simulation model that simulates the behavior of crowds reacting to a fire hazard, and have made a number of contributions to fire science (Feinberg and Johnson 1997a, 1997b, 1998), such as examining the effect of the number of exits on the emergency evacuation behavior of computer-simulated crowds. The importance of this work is that it is one of the few approaches to simulation that incorporates accurate assumptions regarding collective behavior of emergency egress. They have also used documents, interviews, and other information to study how people behave in these situations and have documented the pro-social nature of collective behavior in instances previously characterized as panic. This research has had a profound effect on current understandings of these situations of collective anxiety and crisis (for a review of the panic literature, see Aguirre 2005).

Emergent Norm

The Chicago tradition, as developed in part by H. Blumer's symbolic interactionism, provided the foundation to R. Turner and L. Killian's (1987) theory of emergent norm. Emergent norm theory (ENT) is based on a symbolic interaction conceptualization that emphasizes the importance of norms and social relations. It posits that nontraditional, collective behavior emerges from a normative crisis brought about by a precipitating event that, depending on how the event is collectively perceived and interpreted by the participants, destroys, neutralizes, or no longer allows the preexisting normative guidelines, division of labor, power, and other social arrangements to be collectively defined as appropriate guides for action to respond to the crisis. The crisis creates a sense of uncertainty and urgency forcing people to act, and participants are forced to create a new, emergent normative structure to guide their behavior in the crisis. They mill about as they attempt to define the situation, propose cues for appropriate action, evaluate their relevant skills in terms of the new demands of the situation, and try out alternate schemes to solve the problem. Forced by the crisis to abandon their previously established social relationships, statuses, and normative guidelines regarding legitimate ways of acting, people engage in collective behavior to solve the problems created by the crisis, in the most extreme case (Weller and Quarantelli 1973) in effect reconstituting groups and social relationships. ENT theory assumes the presence of heterogeneous actors with different backgrounds, relevant skills, perceptual abilities, and motives about what is going on, what should be done to respond to the crisis, and who is responsible to do what and when. ENT assumes that collective behavior is not irrational but social, normative behavior.

Subsequent research has pointed out problems with ENT, which, while not invalidating it, still must be addressed. Quarantelli and Weller (see also Levy 1989; Neil and Phillips 1988) observed that emergence is not only normative and cultural but is also socially relational. McPhail has argued that the emergent norm cannot explain the on-and-off nature of participation of people in the stationary demonstrations and rallies he has studied; ENT does not tell us much about the longitudinal dimensions of emergent norms and about how they change. Marx and McAdam (1994) solved it in a little-noted contribution that addressed the lack of specificity that scholars had identified in the concept of the emergent norm. These analysts specified the characteristics not of the emergent norm but of the emergent situation that is typical of instances of collective behavior (Marx and McAdam 1994). From this perspective, it is no longer a norm but a series of dimensions, including norms, that typifies sociocultural emergence, such as whether or not the culture specifies who are the members, how they are going to assemble and disassemble, the emotive and linguistic practices that are expected, the extent of regularity in the occurrence of the event, its purpose, its division of labor, and its connection to broader patterns of social life, to name some of the most important dimensions. It is possible to extend this insight into a view of collective behavior as involving institutionalization and deinstitutionalization (see the following).

Yet another issue that has become apparent is that in a large gathering typically there are multiple groups that have divergent and at times conflicting perspectives orienting their collective action. ENT does not incorporate an explicit understanding of the ecological elements of the social organization of collective behavior, such as multiple groups trying to come to some coordinated collective action. Instead, its focus is on social interaction in a collectivity of people. Key to understanding riots and emergency evacuations, to name only two collective behaviors, are the multiple collectivities sharing multiple ecological settings. Part of these problems could be addressed by incorporating Goffman's (1963) dramatistic view of social life. Following Goffman (for an excellent review, see Brown and Goldin 1973, chap. 8), crises—what in Goffman's term are topics for focused interaction in

encounters—disrupt culturally specified occasions in specific physical settings. There is an occasion and the gathering of people enacting it. Such gatherings are composed of single individuals and of small groups. Then there is the crisis, the precipitating event that starts focused interaction in an encounter and the period of the mobilization and collective behavior. For Goffman, interactions in these encounters are face-to-face, rich in meaning, revealing, rapidly changing, augmenting "attention to detail, an intensification of mutual dependence, and an absorption in the interactive moment" (as cited in Brown and Goldin 1973:154), with people moving about, facilitating information dissemination.

Goffman argues that encounters develop two types of norms that regulate them and permit their continuation through time and space. These are rules of irrelevance and of transformation. The first helps people engaged in reconstituting their groups to identify what is relevant and irrelevant about their situation, what they must attend to; the second help people incorporate into their social organizations extraneous items in such a way that the encounter is preserved (as cited in Brown and Goldin 1973:155–56). Still in need of research is the process of proselytizing of groups in instances of collective behavior as they attempt to convince others to accept their viewpoints about what is going on and what needs to be done. There is some evidence that in evacuating collectivities the existence of multiple groups slows down the process of decision making of groups (Aguirre, Wenger, and Vigo 1998).

Value Added

Neil Smelser's (1963; see also 1968, 1992) value-added approach to collective behavior has also been influential in the specialty (see, e.g., Adamek and Lewis 1973; Cilliers 1989; Lewis 1989; McAllister 2002; Weeber and Rodeheaver 2003). It provides a drastically different perspective on collective behavior. It is derived from Talcott Parson's (1971) structural functionalism, starting with the analysis of the components of social action and their hierarchical relationships (facilities, motivation, norms, and values) and then developing the concept of strain among the components in the context of a set of five broad determinants of collective behavior also arranged from the most to the least inclusive. It defines collective behavior as behavior by people attempting to resolve inappropriately the strains under the influence of a generalized belief that is, in Smelser's view, akin to a magical belief. It claims that there is a short-circuiting effect, so that resources of the components are misused and misapplied. This is perhaps the most controversial part of the theory. Still, there are other, more positive elements, such as the insight that comes from considering the notion of structural conduciveness. Other worthwhile aspects are (a) that it circumscribes all collective behavior to a finite and rather small set of forms and associates each form with specific generalized beliefs, (b) the value of the description of the characteristics of the precipitating events, and (c) the theory's distinction of pre- and postmechanisms of social control. Subsequent writings that do not mention Smelser still develop concepts, such as repertoires of contention by C. Tilly (1978), that are vaguely reminiscent of Smelser's ideas. More recent writings by Smelser (in Alexander et al. 2004: chap. 2 and epilogue) use the logic of parallels to apply insights from Sigmund Freud (1938) and other writers concerned with the structure and dynamics of the personality system to study social and cultural systems. This is most apparent in his recent analysis of cultural trauma in the aftermath of the 2001 terrorist attack of the World Trade Center complex and the Pentagon.

THE REACTION

Starting in the late 1970s and early 1980s, collective behavior as a specialty experienced its own form of a fad of collective reproach. It was a surge characterized by the use by scientists of established concepts in a new way, a form of cultural emergence; a prevailing locus of interaction revolving around a professional ideology; the prevalence of the emotion of hostility; and an international arena of discourse occurring over a period of years and bounded by class-professional identities (for cults in sociology, see Martin 1974; for a surge in the sustainable development discourse, see Aguirre 2002; on the postmodernist fad, see Best 1995).

The surge was in part facilitated by the rapid social change that occurred during the 1960 to 1980 period in the United States and that contrasted rather sharply with the relative absence of social movement activity in the 1950s. The civil rights, antiwar, women's, and environmentalist movements mobilized the sympathy of sociologists and provided the experiences and historical context for the reaction in the specialty, which at the extreme considered anything other than explicit political social movement activity inconsequential and not worth studying (Aguirre and Quarantelli 1983). Even as a critical mass of practitioners emerged that established the study of social movements on firm grounds, this was not the case for collective behavior. The opposite was more nearly true; the surge discouraged the emergence of a critical mass of scholars interested in its study.

The surge ignored the many strands of scholarship in the specialty and grouped most collective behaviorists as LeBonians and irrationalists (see, e.g., Melucci 1988; more extensive criticisms of the surge in Aguirre 1994). Despite a number of voices counseling restraint (Aguirre 1994; Killian 1980, 1984, 1994; Lofland 1993b; Rule 1989; Smelser 1970; Turner 1981), it brought about a much greater emphasis on models of rationality and formal organization, as typified by the writings of Olson (1971), which established the conundrum of the free rider in collective action (or the idea that people are motivated to maximize profits and minimize costs and that if they can get individual profit from collective efforts without contributing to the effort, they will do so). Also part of this emphasis was Granovetter's (1978) threshold model of collective action, which argued that participation was determined by the distribution of thresholds to participate in collective action in a population of would-be participants rather than by the willingness to participate of the individuals. Marwell and Oliver's (1993) theory of the critical mass added a very worthwhile correction and specification to Olson's theory, while more marginally, Berk's (1974) attempted to identify rational principles in crowd behaviors and Gamson (1990) argued for the importance of complex organizational features such as centralization as predictors of successful efforts of SMOs. The surge provided ideological support to the resource mobilization approach (RMA) to social movements and its variants (McCarthy and Zald 1977).

The surge, in what has come to be known as the collective action school, has received extensive critical attention (see, e.g., Buechler and Cylke 1997; Ferree and Miller 1985; Piven and Cloward 1979, 1991). It was dominant during the late 1970s, 1980s, and early 1990s in American sociology and was only recently challenged by the cultural turn in the discipline. The same is not true of Continental sociology, which continued to show an appreciation of collective behavior scholarship, as shown by efforts to understand football stadia disasters in the United Kingdom (Elliott and Smith 1993; Lewis 1982, 1986, 1987), hooliganism in Belgium (De Vreese 2000), and public disorder and riot in England and Canada. Particularly noteworthy is the research of Waddington and his collaborators, centered on the flashpoints model (Waddington 1992; Waddington, Jones, and Critcher 1987; see also Lebeuf and Soulliere 1996 and Drury and Reicher's [1999] social identity model of crowd behavior).

The Social Behavioral Interactional Perspective

McPhail's (1991; see also www.soc.uiuc.edu/people/CVPubs/cmcphail/CV.pdf) is perhaps the most sophisticated statement of the collective action formulation. He proposes what is known as the social behavioral-interactional (SBI) perspective. In it, collective action is conceptualized in terms of the organization of convergent activity or the number of people marching, and the degree to which they do things in common, such as jumping, moving sideways in the same direction at the same speed, gesticulating in the same way, and raising their arms. These are some of the behavioral elements. The symbolic elements are the instructions people receive to act collectively that they use to adjust their behavior to the behavior of others in the gathering. There are many types of instructions identified in the theory. The theory borrows from Goffman's emphasis on the gathering, examining not only what happens in the gathering but also the assembling or convergence behavior that makes it possible as well as the stage of dispersal. SBI examines the subunits acting in the gathering, the most common of which are small groups of friends and others forming clusters and semicircles.

McPhail and his collaborators (McPhail and Tucker 2003) deny the usefulness of the concept of collective behavior and emergence. They have developed a cybernetic model to account for the behavior of people doing things together and taking others into account as they behave. This cybernetic model has had very limited use so far, for it does not predict the collective behavior presumably at the center of SBI interests. Despite its rejection of sociocultural emergence, other aspects of McPhail's SBI model are valuable, particularly its emphasis on looking at what people do together in gatherings and instances of collective behavior. Such data are worth collecting in any case, as shown by Wright's (1978) earlier examinations of crowds and riots; Seidler, Meyer, and Gillivray's (1976) approach to collecting data in gatherings (see also Meyer and Seidler 1978); the analysis of the riot process by Stark et al. (1974); and studies of the effects of crowd size (Milgram, Bickman, and Berkowitz 1969; Newton and Mann 1980).

CONTINUED RELEVANCE OF THE APPROACH

Despite its undeniable impact in the discipline of American sociology in downgrading the scholarship that had taken place in the specialty and in blocking the creation of a critical mass of scholars interested in the study of collective behavior, the surge did not succeed entirely in wiping out the collective behavior tradition. In a curious turn, other disciplines in the social, natural, and physical sciences, while not showing a unified set of theoretical ideas and a program of research that would generate cumulative knowledge among them, nevertheless continued to study subject matter that could be understood as examples of collective behavior. This is true, for example, of research on robotics (Baldassarre, Nolfi, and Parisi 2003), ecology (Ward, Gobet, and Kendall 2001), fire science (Santos and Aguirre 2005), structural engineering, disaster studies, the economics of market crashes (Kaizoji 2000; Mann, Nagel, and Dowling 1976; Prechter 2001; Sornette 2003; Spotton Visano 2002), the impact of the new electronic technology on convergence behavior and politics (Rheingold 2002; see also Rafael 2003), group-level cognition in philosophy (Wilson 2001), expressive voting (Schuessler 2000), social control and policing of gatherings of various types (De Biasi 1998; Schweingruber 2000; Stott and Reicher 1998a, 1998b), the sociology of religious and political movements (Davis and Boles 2003; Eyerman and Jamison 1998; Mattern 1998), the history of rioting in the United States (Gilje 1999), epidemics of deviance (Goode and Ben-Yehuda 1994), public opinion (van Ginneken 2003), studies of relative deprivation (Walker and Smith 2002), and the examination of urban legends, to name some of the most relevant, which consider the

emergence and impact of group-level effects and ask questions outside the cost-benefit calculus of the free rider.

In anthropology, the writings of Clifford Geertz, Victor Turner, and their students on ceremonies and celebrations of various types are traditions of scholarship through which the study of collective behavior has continued (for a summary of this literature, see Mukerji and Schudson 1986). This is also true of recent writings by Brass (1996, 1997; see also Tambiah 1997), a political scientist, in which he uses Smelser's value-added model to construct a model of an institutionalized riot system. He identifies a set of structured interests such as those of political parties and candidates for elected offices in India, as well as the chronic corruption of the police, to understand the production by riot specialists of ethnic, communal, and racial riots. These are people who profit from riots and who have access to the resources needed to make them happen; often riots are mistakenly attributed to ancestral hatreds. Similarly, the scholarship that attempts to understand the Eastern European revolutions marking the end of the Soviet Union is based on carefully constructed, nuanced accounts of the personalities, institutions, organizations, and historical events that participated in the transition that is reminiscent of previous efforts to understand social change in the collective behavior tradition. Among the best works of this scholarship are the analyses by Jadwiga Staniszkis (Gross 1984), Piotr Sztompka (1993), Timothy Garton Ash (1990), Mate Szabo (1996), and Jan Pakulski (1986).

A review of a field with which I am well acquainted, disaster studies, shows that many aspects of disasters continue to be understood from a collective behavior perspective. This is particularly true of the scholarship produced by the Disaster Research Center (DRC) founded by E. L. Quarantelli and Russell R. Dynes (www.udel.edu/DRC) and by other social scientists studying disasters, in which institutional change in moments of collective behavior—the continuity and discontinuities between structure and social dynamics during these crises—is profitably examined. Group emergence, convergence of material and people to the site of the disaster, the often unplanned and yet effective coordination and cooperation that takes place among responding organizations, the unofficial volunteering collective behavior that typifies most disaster response and search-and-rescue activities, these and many other topics of investigation continue to be understood using collective behavior formulations (for some of DRC's publications, see http://dspace.udel.edu). The sociology of disasters is perhaps the exception to the rule, in that it has developed a critical mass of practitioners who apply collective behavior formulations to understanding the social aspects of disasters. In turn, the social science of disasters is increasingly recognized as an important field by the National Science Foundation and other disciplines such as fire science, in which computer simulation models of building evacuations are incorporating much of the knowledge accumulated in the social sciences of disasters to render their calculations of time to evacuate and the behavior of evacuating units more valid and thus more useful to the engineer and architect designing for the safety of the built environment.

SYNTHESIS AND PROSPECTS FOR THE 21ST CENTURY

There is value in attempting to provide an answer to the question of what is collective behavior. A number of critics have argued that there is no established conceptual boundary to this field of specialization and no growth of cumulative scientific knowledge in it because of the plethora of processes and forms of social organizations that are included in it; in the words of one of these critics, "it is a miscellany, a heap of odds and ends that we choose to classify under one heading" (Professor Joel Best, personal correspondence, July 2005). Contrary to this view, it is possible to synthesize elements from a number of conceptualizations available in this literature to make explicit its underlying unity. Irrespective of the often-heard assertion about the presence of seemingly irreconcilable differences in some of these writings, many existing approaches in fact can be fruitfully assembled together to bring coherence to the specialty area.

It is useful to recognize, as did Park and Burgess at the inception of the study of collective behavior in the United States (Park and Burgess 1921), that many types of social behavior take place in collectivities of people and yet are not collective behavior in the sense of the rubric and practice of the profession, for they do not represent sociocultural emergence. Furthermore, as Herbert Blumer (1946) advised us, the behavior of small groups is different from collective behavior, for in small groups, patterns of social interaction and social control are more immediate. Small groups are the most frequently found constituents of gatherings, which may, if the necessary conditions are met, be the foundation of most instances of collective behavior. Finally, present in the work of these and other contributors to the specialty are the insight that all forms of collective behavior and action are enmeshed in social control systems. Collective behavior and action is inextricably linked to the systems of institutions and cannot be understood outside these contexts.

Key Dimensions

A static view of the key dimensions that identify the boundaries of the field of collective behavior involves the following.

The units of social organization that are found in instances of collective behavior: Taking a cue from the seminal typology-centered work of R. E. Park (see Turner 1967), it can be assumed that there are three master units that may be present to a greater and lesser extent in all empirical cases of collective behavior. They are small groups, associational networks of individuals and complex organizations, and SMOs.

The cultural and socio-organizational features of instances of collective behavior: As initially discussed by Gary Marx and later published in his book (Marx and McAdam 1994:1–17), these cultural features are to be understood as arranged in a continuum of emergence and institutionalized relevant cultural elements such as norms, power arrangements, division of labor, and social relationships in instances of collective behavior. This dimension of sociocultural emergence, partly emphasized in the writings of Turner and Killian (1987) and Weller and Quarantelli (1973), and with roots in the seminal contributions of Park and Burgess (1921) and Blumer (1946), is an important defining characteristic of collective behavior, allowing the differentiation of collective behavior and action from institutionalized social life. Marx and McAdam argue that there is no collective behavior and action in the absence of such emergence, irrespective of the unit of social organization present in the situation. Nevertheless, all conceptions of role playing extant in the social sciences acknowledge the universality of sociocultural emergence in social life (Strauss 1993). Thus, it is a matter of degree rather than kind; a significantly greater amount of sociocultural emergence must occur that will allow us to differentiate collective behavior from institutionalized patterns of social life.

The third and final element in the definition of collective behavior is the concept of dominant emotion. As argued by N. Smelser (1963:67–130) and more recently formalized by John Lofland (1985:35–88), who rescues emotion from the link to irrationality present in G. LeBon, among others, three prevailing emotions are present to varying extents in all instances of collective behavior. They are fear, hostility, and joy. Unfortunately, at the present time not much research exists on this dimension. A lot more research attention placed on the reception and understanding of emotions during instances of collective behavior such as their presence, manipulation, effects, transformation, and their uses during precipitating events, the mobilization of participants, and the rhetorical explanations of social action is needed.

Emergence Embedded in Institutionalization

Collective behavior is part of the process of institutionalization (and deinstitutionalization) that takes place in society. Institutions consist of acts that are objective, repeatable by others, and exterior, defined by many people in similar ways so that they constitute part of the reality of their lives. They are both objective and exterior to the actor. The term *institutionalization* captures the procession, the flow that either strengthens or transforms these structured realities. In the words of Zucker (1977), "institutionalization is both a process and a property variable. It is the process by which individual actors transmit what is socially defined as real and. . . . (a) more or less taken-for-granted part of social reality" (p. 728). Acts that are institutionalized are more uniform and easily shared, more capable of resisting change, and easier to transmit (p. 729). As stated earlier, the actors in collective behavior are individuals, small groups, social networks of individuals and complex organizations, and SMOs acting in compact gatherings or in diffuse collectivities of people. Collective behavior is not small-group behavior but rather is the behavior of large collectivities of people. Collective behavior in the context of institutionalization means emergent behavior that takes place both in terms of culture and social relations; the large size of acting collectivity and sociocultural emergence that is part of the social change of the institutions of society is the essential characteristic of collective behavior.

Further Clarifications

The dramaturgical view of collective behavior (Brown and Goldin 1973) complements the emphasis on sociocultural emergence. It is based on the use of the metaphor of the theater to make sense of instances of collective behavior, allowing for the systematic examination of its contents and the effects of power and social control in it. Moreover, broadly defined and shared preoccupations revolving around current-day master categories of age, race/ethnicity, class/occupation, gender/sex, and ethnocentrism/nationalism also provide the context for most instances of collective behavior taking place today.

Instances of collective behavior and action differ in their time and space coordinates. Attention to time and space allows the differentiation of instances of collective behavior in terms of their relative complexity, in what is a morphological analysis of forms of increasing complexity (Lofland 1993a; McPhail 1991). It includes in its spatial referent a continuum from the microspace to local, regional, national, and international arenas of interaction. Temporally, it is also a continuum from the fleeting instance of collective behavior and action of less than one hour or a few hours to those that occur over a period of weeks, months, and even years. However, there are also social space and time (Sorokin and Merton 1937) associated with institutional processes that are of great importance to the specialty, the so-called institutional rhythms whose changes are associated with the occurrence of institutional transformations and instances of collective behavior.

It is useful in this context to also make the parallel division that the RMA (McCarthy and Zald 1977) makes between social movement organization and social movement as preference structure toward social change in a population, to provide a theoretically meaningful connection between the study of social movements and the study of collective behavior. Thus, the field of collective behavior, as Tarde recognized, is concerned with two ideal-type spheres of social action: compact gatherings and diffuse collectivities. The first type would include a number of collective behavior forms such as marches, protest demonstrations, emergency egress behavior, and convergence

behavior in the aftermath of disasters, and rallies, in which participants share space and time and are potentially available to each other by sight and sound. The other ideal type would be represented by forms of collective behavior in which participants are diffuse in time and space, such as fads, fashion, rumors, and urban legends. These are social forms that reflect topics of interest to segments of public opinion, such as leisure, music, and styles of consumption. Empirically, these two ideal-type collective behavior spheres are interdependent. For example, mass migrations are characterized by compact gatherings and also by currents of public opinions, rumors, and collectively shared evaluations of places of destination of the would-be immigrants; fashion is created, as Blumer pointed out, by fashion houses and yet adopted and enacted by a broad category of men and women; mass rallies in Nazi Germany developed symbols and images that helped in creating hatred against Jews among a large proportion of the population of the country; more recently, the xenophobic acts of skinheads keep alive hatreds of aliens (Watts 2001). The relationship between these two master types of collective behaviors should be the topic of sustained scientific research efforts in the future.

Examination of diffuse collectivities focuses attention on the social organizational mechanisms that participate in the creation of concerted action among dispersed people. The mass media immediately come to mind, both the traditional types of mass media and present-day changes in the industry, such as the Internet, cyberspace, and other communication technologies that are transforming the manifestations of collective behavior even as they are changing other aspects of social life. An example is music sharing in the Internet, a new form of collective behavior that is based on emergent definitions of what constitute nondeviant behavior. Moreover, there are other mechanisms that inform diffuse collectivities and create social life, bringing about collective reactions such as the networks of complex organizational activities of organized religion, political parties, and the interconnected instrumentalities of the state.

A very important topic for future research is the determination of the key elements of compact gatherings that are relevant to understanding their transformation into collective behavior forms, as well as greater scientific understanding of the structure and dynamics of a finite number of collective behavior forms. What is needed is a tradition of scholarship on these forms that would come about from the work of a critical mass of scholars interested in them.

Boundaries

The aforementioned conceptual dimensions would constitute the boundaries of the specialty area of collective behavior at present. It is useful to think of them as forming a multidimensional space composed of different regions in which different forms of collective behavior can be placed. They summarize a large amount of research and theorizing in the specialty area of collective behavior and point to needed research. When considered together, they remind us of the great variability of forms and contents in empirical instances of collective behavior, of their fluid, unstable, transformation-prone nature, and of their connectedness and continuity with institutionalized social life. The dimensions help us identify the prototypical cases of collective behavior while reminding us of the difficult problem of identification at the margins and of the embeddedness of instances of collective behavior in institutionalized arrangements in society and culture that they seek to transform.

The scheme does not give a priori preference to the study of avowedly political instances of collective behavior, for reasons presented elsewhere (Aguirre and Quarantelli 1983). Instead, it is a catholic understanding of the field of specialization, which would reintegrate to it topics of research that are increasingly marginalized from it, such as the study of religious movements and religious effervescence, and of publics and public opinion. It also recognizes the limited use of the concept of the crowd and the mass as the prototype forms of collective behavior. Its starting point is different, namely, the presence of people in concentrated gatherings and diffused collectivities—an understanding central to the writings of E. Goffman, John Lofland, and Clark McPhail, among other scholars. As modern scholarship attests, the so-called crowds are in most times and places aggregations of small groups of kin, neighbors, acquaintances, and friends that are differentially impacted by the characteristics of the precipitating event and the outcome of proselytizing among small groups in the gatherings (Brown and Goldin 1973).

SMOs are recognized in the proposed synthesis as one of the basic units of social organization that may act in instances of collective behavior. General social movements often bring about episodes of collective behavior and the collective action of SMOs. Likewise, instances of collective behavior are often found at the inception of social movements and SMOs. Attention to the social movement–collective behavior interface and its iterativeness may help bring about the much-needed reintegration of the study of collective behavior/action and social movements while preserving the distinct features of both.

Not all collective actions of SMOs are relevant to the proposed synthesis. Rather, only a certain type of collective action of SMOs and voluntary organizations showing sociocultural emergence would interest collective behaviorists. Similarly, most actions of states and corporations would not be germane to the specialty. Nevertheless, the collective action of corporate entities that represent the manufacture of instances of collective behavior and SMOs would indeed be of interest, apart from the collective behavior that takes place inside corporations (Zald and Berger 1971). A case in point is the creation, organization, and mobilization by the tobacco industry in the United States of pro-corporate activism from small groups of smokers to attempt to discredit the opposition to smoking

(Santos 2004); similar efforts by corporations to attempt to discredit the environmental movement; and the organizational and interorganizational emergence that takes place in the immediate aftermath of disasters during search-and-rescue efforts and in other efforts to help stricken communities. This corporate activity becomes much more frequent in the increasingly state- and corporate-directed cultures of advanced capitalism and are key processes of interest to collective behaviorists. Thus, for example, the Stalinist purges would be fertile ground for investigations, as is the creation and use by governments throughout the world of SMOs and instances of collective behavior (Aguirre 1984). The 2004 U.S. presidential election political campaigns are another case in point.

The concept of prevailing emotion in instances of collective behavior (Lofland 1985) is useful for describing instances of collective behavior and is thus incorporated into the proposed scheme, although complex sociocultural events made up of both collective behavior and institutionalized social life occurring in many places over comparatively long periods of time are often typified by more than one dominant emotion. The World Trade Center's September 11, 2001, terrorist attack is an example in which multiple instances of institutionalized action and collective behavior took place, dominated at various stages by both fear and hostility. Chronologically and anecdotally, they ranged from the anxiety and fear of the evacuees of the doomed towers and the first responders to the dread and sorrow typifying the search and rescue and the convergence of assistance and sympathy from throughout the country and the world, to the nationwide hostile public opinion, mass anger, and war preoccupations that followed the attack and that eventuated in the U.S. assault on Afghanistan. Still to be understood are the shifts of dominant emotion over time in these complex events.

Theoretical Inclusiveness

The proposed scheme does not conflict with the substantive emphases of the two models of the citizen surge and of loosely structured collective action forms, respectively advanced by John Lofland (1993a) and Anthony Oberschall (1980), or with Waddington et al.'s (1987:158–63) model of "flashpoint" events, with its emphasis on structural, political/ideological, cultural, contextual, situational, and interaction levels of analysis of disorders. It can also accommodate moral panics of the type Goode and Ben-Yehuda (1994) discuss, such as satanic scares—a collective behavior form suffused by fear and hostility, concerned with a behavior, satanism, enacted by all units of social organizations, regional and national in scope, bounded by class, lasting for months if not years. It can also accommodate financial panics and panics in crowded places such as theaters, the latter involving crowds, fear, emergent sociocultural and social relational elements, behavior centered, localized in time and space and the former involving diffuse behavior, conventionalized, object centered—money, national and international, limited both by time and class boundaries. Similarly, the Red Scare of the 1950s involved ethnocentrism/nationalism, was nationwide, deeply affected by the political institutions of the American state, lasted for years, was dominated by hostility and fear, with both emergent and conventionalized cultural and relational elements, and all units of social organization participated in it. Episodes of hysteria typically are of two subtypes. One involves a circumscribed place, is short lived, age and gender related, in which small groups evince either fear or hostility. The other subtype is more diffuselike, dominated by more complex features such as multiple acting units and bigger space and time referents.

The framework could facilitate the accumulation of consistently gathered information about instances of collective behavior. This is particularly true if in the future a critical mass of specialists were to develop, for as Quarantelli (1974) documented, to this day there is an insufficient number of scientists working on such matters. What is needed for fads, fashion, rumors, and the other manifestations of collective behaviors is what has taken place in the study of SMOs, in which an international scientific community has emerged and created a tradition of scholarship and a base of shared knowledge about the subject matter of interest to it. Perhaps, once this critical mass came about, the framework offered here could facilitate the understanding of forms of collective behavior as belonging to common sense and scientific genres, as these are understood in the methodology advocated by Wendy Griswold (1987) to study cultural objects, which would make it amenable to historical-cultural documentation and comparative analysis. The cumulative effects would be to increase the professional interest of social scientists in the study of collective behavior, helping identify analytical questions and empirical issues that are unknown or that have not received much attention at present, with the end result of developing a richer understanding of social change.

Precis

This chapter reviewed the origins and the controversies in the specialty of collective behavior and identified directions for its future. It also offered a synthesis of key ideas to identify the boundaries of the field. Such identification is useful, particularly for a field that has experienced so much controversy and soul-searching during its recent past. In its terms, collective behavior incidents are suffused by sociocultural emergence, are inextricably dramaturgical in nature, exhibit a limited range of dominant emotions, are carried out by a limited number of social units, and are located both in time and space and in social spaces reflecting issues associated with the master categories of age, race/ethnicity, class/occupation, gender/sex, and ethnocentrism/nationalism. The proposed synthesis has attempted to provide a coherent sense of the existing scholarship and to encourage interested scholars to join with others in locating fruitful areas of research and theorizing and thus fill the many lacunas in our knowledge base. It is only a preliminary first step, for typological exercises, while important, are only precursors to the development of theory; if adopted by others, it will serve to organize and orient research in collective behavior and to facilitate the disciplined accumulation of scientific findings in the specialty, a program of research that will eventually permit the identification of genres of instances of collective behavior, their comparative treatment as cultural objects, and their elucidation following established methodologies for the study of culture (see Griswold 1987). So far, the scheme has proven to be useful in understanding the surge of sustainable development (Aguirre 2002).

54

Social Movements

David S. Meyer

Kelsy Kretschmer
University of California, Irvine

In the summer of 1999, three women entered the Lilith Fair, a rock concert organized by and for women musicians and singers, wearing gags and shirts with the phrase "Peace Begins in the Womb." They walked to a line of information booths representing various women's causes and interests, ultimately standing next to the booths of the National Organization for Women (NOW) and Planned Parenthood Federation of America. The three protesters, members of Feminists for Life, a group organized around the claim that opposition to abortion is the most authentically feminist position, had applied for booth space at the Lilith Fair that year and had been denied. The activists wore gags to convey what they saw as their forced marginalization in the feminist movement as punishment for their efforts against abortion. NOW and Planned Parenthood, larger organizations that supported abortion rights, had both been granted booth space, and the members of Feminists for Life bought concert tickets to stage their demonstration and silently protest their exclusion ("Meet FFL Activists" 2002).

It doesn't really matter that the rock concert, organized for several years by popular musician and songwriter Sarah McLachlan, was not explicitly feminist. It provided a venue in which to contest the very definition of the identity "feminist." An extremely successful commercial endeavor to prove that women did not need to tour with male musicians to sell tickets, McLachlan described the tour environment as inspired by feminist values. In this spirit, promoters granted space to organizations supporting women's causes from rape and incest help lines to cancer research foundations. The groups used their tables to display information and promote themselves and their causes. It's not clear whether there were any large long-term effects from this gag protest; Feminists for Life showed up at only one concert on the tour and Lilith did not change any of its concert policies. The Lilith concerts continue, reaching a distinct audience. Feminists for Life also continues, reaching a much smaller one, and still tries to contest the definition of feminism while opposing abortion rights.

The story, however, underscores a few distinct points about social movements that we will explore in this chapter. First, although social movements make expressly political claims on matters of public policy, in this case abortion rights, they are not limited to the policy process; social movements are always about more than their explicit claims, including components of culture and values. Second, social movements are vehicles that express a constructed social and political identity, in this case feminism, one often, as in this case, contested. Third, social movements such as American feminism have deep roots and long legacies that are not easily bounded in time. Note that the American feminist movement, expressed most strongly in two distinct waves separated by roughly 50 years (prior to suffrage, in 1920, and as one of several important movements commencing in the 1960s) (Rupp and Taylor 1987; Banaszak 1996; Sawyers and Meyer 1999), continues to influence both American culture and politics. Finding discrete beginnings and endings of social movements is difficult.

Fourth, social movements consist of both interested individuals and established organizations that coordinate much of a movement's efforts. These groups and individuals agree on some aspects of politics or values but differ on other issues, such as preferred organizational forms, decision making, and values. Groups cooperate, to some degree, in the service of shared goals, but factions within them compete for both prominence and support. Fifth, while social movements establish distinct spaces and cultures, they are not divorced from mainstream politics and culture; they draw ideas, support, and grievances from the larger society and contribute the same back to it.

In this chapter, we examine the phenomenon of social movements, beginning with a brief discussion of the historical importance of the topic in sociology. We outline the interactions within movements, between movements, and with the environment outside of the movement, including both the government and the rest of society. We then offer a working definition of "social movement" identifying key issues in understanding the origins, development, and ultimate impact of social movements.

SIGNIFICANCE OF SOCIAL MOVEMENTS IN SOCIOLOGY

The study of various forms of social movements, collective expressions of values, grievances, and identities that spill over the boundaries of conventional politics, is deeply rooted in sociology. Predictably, from the outset, scholars have defined social movements in accord with their larger vision of how societies function and/or change. Marx, as a critical example, saw social movements as the expression of material interests that organized class conflict and ultimately propelled social and political change. In contrast, Durkheim ([1933] 1979, [1951] 1997) viewed social movements as the collective expression of aggregate psychological dysfunction and anomie, representing a society's failure to integrate diverse social constituencies. Following this line in focusing on crowd behavior, Le Bon (1977) saw movements as a collective phenomenon that represents the loss of individual identity and conscience.

Such visions remain and continue to inform, albeit in nuanced ways, more contemporary treatments of social movements. In broad terms, social movements can be seen as the rational employment of less conventional means to achieve political gains unlikely to be won otherwise and can also be seen as the expressed frustration of a constituency unsuccessful in winning acceptance or accommodation from mainstream society. Historically, such evaluations have often turned on the particular social movement under scrutiny and the normative concerns of the analyst. As might be expected, scholarly focus has shifted in response to perceived gaps in the latest wave of scholarship, such that research has moved back and forth between studies that look at movements from the outside in, starting with the context in which movements emerge

and develop, and those that look at movements from the inside out, which focus on the dynamics, processes, and meanings of individual mobilization within social movements.

As sociology is the study of both how societies function and how societies change, social movements offer a rich ground for empirical study of both these phenomena. Social movement actors, while envisioning a better world, fight in this one. The progression of a social movement offers a vision of how society and state work (the world they fight in) and how societies change (when activists can achieve some portion of their goals).

The first large wave of scholarship on movements, following World War II and set in the context of an expanding American role in the world, focused on the heinous movements that had led to the war, particularly Nazism. Understandably, analysts viewed the Nazi movement, which emphasized mass mobilization and emotion, as a symptom and consequence of a society gone mad. Contrasted with more moderate and conventional means of politics, such as interest associations and political parties, scholars saw movements as the product of societal dysfunction. Following Durkheim, both scholars and popular analysts (e.g., Hoffer 1951; Kornhauser 1959; Smelser 1962; Lipset and Raab 1970) contended that movements were irrational, dysfunctional, and ultimately dangerous. They occurred in societies that didn't offer sufficient number and variety of integrating institutions, including social clubs and advocacy groups. In short, movements were the province of the disconnected.

This "collective behavior" approach to social movements took deep root even as the world around was undermining its very tenets. As the civil rights movement, commencing in the 1950s, and a broad range of 1960s movements (antiwar, antinuclear, student, ethnic identity, feminist, environmental) emerged, the basic template of social dysfunction proved to be of extremely limited value.

At an aggregate level, particularly in light of the Cold War, the United States defined the sort of open democratic polity filled with the intermediary associations that would preempt the development of social movements. The movements of the 1950s and 1960s belied the notion that such associations would prevent social movements. Rather than being a futile gesture of exasperation, analysts found that protest often led to real political gains (e.g., Lipsky 1968; Piven and Cloward 1971, 1977; Gamson 1990). At the individual level, empirical studies of student activist leaders showed them to be relative models of emotional health: Compared with their less active colleagues, the student leaders were better connected with a variety of social organizations, displayed more developed and integrated personalities, and even enjoyed better relationships with their parents (Keniston 1968). The notion of movements as the product of social dysfunction mostly gave way over time to a view of social protest as an augmentation of more conventional politics, a sensible strategy—particularly for those badly positioned to make claims effectively in other ways (Lipsky 1968; McCarthy and Zald 1977). Protest and social movement activity was increasingly seen as less a rejection of more conventional politics than an addition to it.

Scholars' analytic focus turned from the social and political factors that promoted protest movements to the purposive efforts of organizers to generate social protest. Assuming a continual sufficiency of grievances, McCarthy and Zald (1977) pointed to the logistical achievement of applying a range of resources, including money, expertise, and public support, to the production of organizational growth and protest activity. Scholars devoted a great deal of attention to the "free-rider problem," that is, the predisposition of individuals to benefit from collective action without participating in it (Olson 1965).

Influenced by this "resource mobilization" perspective (Jenkins 1983), scholars pointed out that the free-rider problem was less an absolute constant than an elastic tendency that responded to external circumstances (Meyer and Imig 1993). Returning to look at the context in which movements emerge, scholars within the "political process" or "political opportunity" perspective (e.g., Eisinger 1973; Tilly 1978; McAdam 1982; Kitschelt 1986; Tarrow 1989; Meyer 1990, 2004) emphasized that the external world affected the issues, tactics, and ultimate influence of social movements.

More recently, critics have charged (e.g., Goodwin and Jasper 2003) that the political process approach had flattened political agency out of the study of social movements, imposing a rigid deterministic framework on the interpretation of collective action. These criticisms have spurred a vigorous debate and encouraged the injection of culture, emotion, and narrative to the study of social movements.

DEFINING SOCIAL MOVEMENTS

Social scientists collectively grapple with defining social movements depending on what they want to rule in or rule out. As a result, definitional disputes over the past few decades developed over whether to include or exclude such phenomena as civic advocacy groups, riots, revolutions, religious sects, and artistic innovations (e.g., Snow 2005). Tarrow's (1998) succinct definition of movements as "collective challenges, based on common purposes and social solidarities, in sustained interaction with elites, opponents, and authorities" (p. 4) provides a useful starting point. This definition is broad enough to be very inclusive, but others nonetheless emphasize the need to extend conventional analytical boundaries to include, for example, the pursuit of cultural change (e.g., Gamson and Meyer 1996; Rochon 1998), a range of authorities who might be challenged (Snow 2005), desperate political rebellions (Einwohner 2003), the distinct worldview within social movements (Whittier 1995), and resistance to repression in authoritarian settings (Boudreau 2004). The real challenge for scholars is less to develop a strict taxonomy that consensually categorizes diverse phenomena than to develop strong analytical tools that can be useful for understanding those phenomena (see McAdam, Tarrow, and Tilly 2001). Such a focus on tools and processes will allow for the accumulation of knowledge while avoiding the trap of generalizing from selective cases, no matter how interesting (see McAdam et al. 2005).

We can view social movements not only as continuous with other social and political behavior but also as including something more. We can start by thinking about the claims that social movements express, recognizing the critical importance of political context. For large numbers of people to engage in ongoing challenges to mainstream politics and culture, they must believe that their efforts are necessary and, at least, *potentially* successful. In the absence of the belief of necessity, most people will confine themselves to personal pursuits and more conventional, and less costly or risky, political action. In the absence of the belief in potential efficacy, most people will not want to waste their efforts. This is not to say that there are not dedicated individuals and organizations who will pursue their vision of social goods regardless of the political environment and their judgment of likely efficacy (e.g., see Nepstad 2004), only that such individuals and groups will remain politically marginal without the support of others who are not normally engaged in social action. Therefore, social movements are partly distinguished by their interaction with mainstream politics and culture, drawing individuals and ideas from the mainstream and targeting at least some of their activities toward that mainstream.

Although social movement challenges are generally typed by one cause or claim, say, supporting civil rights or opposing taxes, those involved with such movements frequently agree on much more than those expressed claims. This agreement includes both a variety of political ideas and softer cultural norms, such as aesthetic choices about music, literature, and presentation of self (Taylor and Whittier 1992). Thus, while the most visible element of a social movement, its claims on policies, tends to be simple, the reality underneath that demand, the metaphoric nine-tenths of the iceberg, is broader. A critical question for scholars is to establish why a particular side of that iceberg, that is, a defined set of critical issues, becomes ascendant at one time or another.

Social movement activity contains elements of spontaneity, but these occur around a structure provided by established groups. Depending on the political setting, these groups can be covert, as were the *samizdat* networks in the former Soviet Union, or very visible and recognized by the government, as we see in the range of advocacy organizations that define interest group politics in the United States (Clemens and Minkoff 2004). While individuals join in social movements as they grow, and operate autonomously in the service of shared convictions, formal organizations provide a bulwark for mobilizing and interpreting collective action.

For most movements, several organizations are engaged in shared efforts to mobilize support and effect change. These organizations, however, operate with conflicting concerns. On the one hand, cooperation with groups that share some goals enhances the prospects for political efficacy. At the same time, organizations seek to survive, particularly groups that have established professional positions whose occupants earn their living from the organization (Staggenborg 1988; Wilson 1995). Cooperation with other groups entails risks for social movement organizations; sharing the spotlight may mean losing control of an organization's public presentation of itself, can compromise credibility by affiliation with tainted allies, and can risk individual identity by obscuring individual organizations' efforts in the service of a larger goal. The opportunities of politics encourage cooperation while the exigencies of organizational survival demand securing a distinct identity, a niche in the larger universe of groups, so as to ensure the continued flow of resources (Rochon and Meyer 1997). Organizers must balance these competing pressures and the ways by which they affect the dynamics of social movements.

By definition, the peak of social movement activity is limited in time. The unusual mobilization of groups and individuals in the service of collective goals changes through the interaction of challengers with the world they challenge. States and societies manage social movement challenges to minimize disruption and uncertainty. The most obvious management strategies include repressing activism through harsh punishment, acquiescing to political claims through policy reform, or recognizing social movement actors and affording them less difficult and disruptive means of making claims; in liberal polities, such as the United States, management strategies often include all three strategies, unraveling a social movement coalition in the process (Meyer and Tarrow 1998). We can think of this process as *institutionalization of dissent,* which doesn't decisively resolve the claims or concerns of a social movement but undermines its capacity to disrupt day-to-day life.

DEVELOPMENT OF SOCIAL MOVEMENTS

Although some scholars have offered models of social movement activism that assume fixed patterns of mobilization and demobilization based on constants such as personal disappointment (Hirschman 1982) or inevitable collective disappointment in the face of the unavoidable intractability of social problems (Downs 1972), it makes more sense to see social movement trajectories as contingent and as intimately tied to the larger political context. We can gain analytical leverage on the emergence of social movements by thinking about an individual's decision to engage in movement activity. If most people are unlikely to join protest movements unless they believe their efforts are necessary and possibly successful, we need to understand when those beliefs will become widespread. Organizers' tactics and rhetoric are important in conveying such beliefs, as discussed below, but understanding the ebbs and flows of collective action begins with an analysis of the circumstances in which these beliefs take root. Scholars focusing on the emergence, development, and ultimate impact of social movements describe the world around a social movement as "political opportunities."

External factors go a long way in defining the costs, risks, and potential outcomes of collective action. The first articulation of the concept of political opportunities focused on the comparative openness to political participation of urban governments in the 1960s. Peter Eisinger (1973) found that urban riots were most likely in cities that had what he described as a combination of "open" and "closed" political opportunities. Tilly (1978) expanded this finding to national politics and refined it theoretically. His claim was that political regimes that actively invited conventional political participation preempted protest by offering potentially effective alternatives. At the same time, regimes could limit protest through repression, essentially raising the costs and risks of social movement participation while minimizing the apparent prospects of efficacy. Social movements, then, take place in an atmosphere of some tolerance and openness, but without full inclusion—when activists can believe that protest might be both necessary and potentially effective. Changes in opportunities encourage activists to take to the streets, through either increased tolerance and safety or enhanced threats and provocation.

Empirical studies of social movements over long periods of time (see, especially, McAdam 1982; Costain 1992) emphasized governmental openings and limited repression as precursors for social movements, essentially focusing on one side of the curve. But some studies have emphasized the importance of threat in provoking mobilization (Meyer 1990; Smith 1996; Almeida 2003). How can we reconcile these apparently contradictory findings? We believe that the key is to recognize differential opportunities facing different constituencies. While some constituencies who are generally excluded from meaningful participation can be drawn into social movements by expanded tolerance, others who normally enjoy routine access to the political process will turn to social movements only in response to threats or exclusion (Meyer 2004).

The recognition of differential opportunities also throws analytic light on the process of demobilization. When authorities respond to social movements, they shape the context in which challenges continue or not. Faced with harsh repression, most activists will retreat, waiting for better times and perhaps organizing for them. Offered chances for apparently meaningful consultation on matters of policy or viable political participation, activists will emphasize less costly, more routine means of politics at the expense of social protest. Either response can mark the end of a period of high mobilization by diminishing the attractions of protest as a political strategy.

Polities have preferred strategies for dealing with dissent that reflect both the nature of political institutions and the developed culture of dissent and governance. Thus, many smaller parliamentary democracies, for example, the Scandinavian countries, offer extensive opportunities for dissident factions to present their ideas and to compete for parliamentary representation, providing numerous routes for communication, if not political efficacy. In doing so, they diminish the attractiveness of protest. In contrast, more authoritarian contexts, including state communist governments such as China in 1989 or the Roman Catholic Church (Katzenstein 1998), respond decisively to protest efforts, rejecting claims and often sanctioning protesters harshly. These authorities diminish the attractiveness of protest by undermining hopes of efficacy.

Larger liberal polities can offer mixed receptions to both movements and differential responses to various parties within a movement coalition, welcoming some claims and claimants into mainstream politics while repressing or ignoring others. Such differential responses diminish the volatility of social movements by facilitating the breakup of movement coalitions (Sawyers and Meyer 1999). Policy reforms, for example, can diminish the urgency of action for some activists; even if they do not satisfy all members of a coalition, they can rob a movement of the capacity to command public attention.

The nature of the challenged authority affects the shape and claims of the dissenting coalition that mounts a social movement. In authoritarian settings, people with a wide range of grievances can unite around basic civil liberties and simple procedural issues of inclusion. In Eastern Europe before the end of the Cold War, for example, all reformers had a common interest in political openness. In contrast, in liberal polities with a range of potentially viable political issues and venues for action, activists choose not only whether to engage political and social mobilization but also what claims to make, where, how, and with whom. When the state offers readily accessible, relatively low cost, and essentially no-risk means of participation—such as voting or political campaigning—to choose protest movement activity is not obviously natural, and the increasingly common forms of protest politics are those that are the least disruptive, such as petitions and demonstrations rather than riots or other violent action (Meyer and Tarrow 1998).

The issue of which claims to make or what issues to pursue is, perhaps paradoxically, most difficult in liberal politics. In such settings, it is possible to engage on a broad spectrum of political issues. Organizers press their preferred claims, trying to link them to potential activists' concerns. Issue activists try to launch new campaigns, but only periodically do their entreaties reach responsive audiences in the political mainstream and threaten to alter the normal conduct of politics. Although it is easiest analytically to focus on their efforts, attributing success or failure to the tactics or rhetoric of appeals for mobilization, this is fundamentally mistaken. External political realities alter the risks or costs that citizens are willing to bear in making decisions about whether to engage in political activism and what issues are viable for substantial challenges. It makes sense to be more concerned about nuclear war, for example, when the president of the United States suggests that it may be inevitable and survivable and increases spending on nuclear weapons; it also makes sense to distrust the more conventional styles of politics that produced such a president (Meyer 1990). Similarly, it seems more reasonable to organize for women's rights when the state establishes a commission on women, formally prohibits discrimination, and suggests that it may play a role in combating it (Costain 1992). Activists are not ineluctably linked to one set of issues. An American activist concerned with social justice may protest against nuclear testing in 1962, for voting rights in 1964, against the war in Vietnam in 1967, for an Equal Rights Amendment (ERA) in 1972, and against corporate globalization at the end of the century, without dramatically altering his perception of self or justice. Rather, he will be responding to the most urgent, or the most promising, issues that appear before him. In this way, the issues that activists mobilize around are those the state sets out as challenges and opportunities.

The important point is that movements arise within a particular constellation of social and political factors. Movements do not decline because they run out of gas, recognize their failures, or because adherents get bored and move on to something else. Rather, protest movements decline when the state effects some kind of new arrangement with at least some activists or sponsors. Such arrangements can include repression, incorporating new claims or constituencies in mainstream institutions, and policy reform. Protest campaigns dissipate when activists no longer believe that a movement strategy is possible, necessary, or potentially effective. Repression inhibits the perception of possibility. In contrast, when established political institutions such as parties and interest groups take up some of the claims of challenging social movements, the perception that extrainstitutional activity is necessary erodes.

Mobilization: Constructing Political Opportunity

Regardless of the objective conditions of political alignments, potential participation, or public policy, movements do not emerge unless substantial numbers of people are invested with a subjective sense of both urgency and efficacy. The job of the organizer is to persuade significant numbers of people that the issues they care about are indeed *urgent,* that alternatives are *possible,* and that the constituencies they seek to mobilize can in fact be invested with *agency* (Gamson and Meyer 1996).

The process of building activism is a function of successfully building on shared cultural understandings to generate a new vision of change in which political mobilization is necessary. Scholars have described the rhetorical dimension of this process as "framing," that is, providing a cognitive structure of interpretation that links personal political choices with larger social conditions (Gamson 1992; Snow and Benford 1992). Organizers convey collective action frames through their own organizational materials, through speeches, stories, and songs, and mediate through reports in the range of mass media (Ryan 1991; Rohlinger 2002).

Of course, organizers do not construct these interpretations in a vacuum nor do potential activists interpret each new appeal solely on its own terms. Both operate in a larger political environment, a crucible in which their values are honed. Critical to the successful emergence of protest movements is a positive feedback loop through which well-positioned elites reinforce both an alternate position on issues and the choice of protest as a strategy. In the case of civil rights in the United States, for example, the Supreme Court's 1954 decision *Brown v. Board of Education* legitimated criticism of segregation and offered the promise of federal government intervention as a powerful ally against southern state and local governments. The decision suggested new possibilities for social organization.

Organizers recognize, then, that to promote and then sustain activism they need to build and reinforce not only a shared understanding of a social problem but also a sense of community among potential activists. The sources of community and the struggles for change understandably differ across movements and across contexts. Successful labor organizers in Poland built unions around the shared experiences of their members, both at the workplace and at home, addressing the range of concerns in both spheres (Osa 2003). East German dissidents organized in the Protestant Church, while the intellectuals in Czechoslovakia who spearheaded the revolution of 1989 found political space in the now famous Magic Lantern theater. The first step in launching any effective political campaign is searching out and filling available free spaces, nurturing in embryo the social values activists want to see expressed in the larger society. Even in a repressive state with an underdeveloped civil society, social movement mobilization is the activity of the organized, *en bloc,* rather than a mystical melding of atomized individuals.

What Movements Do

Organizers, established groups, sympathizers, zealots, outsiders, opponents, and bystanders, both inside and outside government, can engage in the life of a social movement, mobilized in different ways for overlapping goals. Whereas organizers spend a great deal of effort in crafting demands, fashioning slogans and arguments, and devising strategy, they rarely enjoy complete control of even their own side of a social movement's efforts, much less the critical responses of government and mobilized opponents (Meyer and Staggenborg 1996). Because most movement organizations are constant in actively seeking to mobilize new supporters and stage new actions, movements have porous and blurry boundaries. Indeed, a key dilemma for activists is how broadly to draw the lines of alliances within a movement: More supporters means more diversity and less control; narrower, sharper coalitions of action afford greater clarity, more control, and likely less influence (Meyer 2007).

Organizations mobilize action in accord with both established practices within an institutional context (e.g., voting, lobbying, strikes, petitions) and in accord with their own established scripts of action. Charles Tilly (1993) has observed that the astonishing thing about what he describes as the "repertoire of contention" is how limited the actual range of tactics employed is. In contemporary settings, with the social movement a well-established form of organization and political claims-making, resorting to well-known strategies for influence, for example, the mass demonstration, minimizes the costs and risks for those involved, allowing easy access to mobilization and the prospect for sustained efforts.

Much movement activity surrounds the promotion of ideas. Organizers write and post analyses of social problems and potential solutions, as do individuals with no necessary connection with movement organizations. They assemble different versions of their arguments, some designed to generate outside, perhaps even extranational, support (e.g., Keck and Sikkink 1998), others directed to closer policymakers and political figures, and still others, in short form, designed to mobilize mass support. It's hard to overstate the diversity of ways to communicate movement ideas, ranging from long manifestos, sometimes published as books (think of Betty Friedan's *Feminine Mystique*), to bumper stickers and buttons. East German peace and democracy activists, for example, devised a patch depicting a statue given to the United Nations by the Soviet Union, depicting swords beaten into plowshares. When the government rightly interpreted the patch as an attack on its own policies and existence, activists took to wearing blank patches, developing a symbolic politics based on a sort of irony (Tismaneanu 1989). Organizers can file lawsuits on behalf of their concerns or constituencies, seeking to mobilize allies within the government. These kinds of communication range from developed and documented arguments to symbolic shorthand.

Activists also engage in actions to draw attention to themselves and their ideas. Sometimes, this involves using well-established means of political participation in new ways or for new causes. They circulate petitions, engage in referenda or electoral campaigns, lobby elected officials, and—where and when they can—vote. They can try to reach potential supporters by going door to door or more efficiently appearing at events and organizations that might support their effort—in other words, finding locations where they might reach a number of likely supporters, such as church services, union meetings, theater groups, professional associations, or community picnics. Supporters can sign, mark a box, make financial contributions, talk to neighbors, feed activists, or even quietly smile when they learn of activist efforts.

Somewhat more dramatically, organizers can stage demonstrations, which often feature large assemblies of people united in the service of a few clear demands. People cheer and chant, listen to speakers and music, hold signs, talk to other demonstrators, yell at counterdemonstrators, and return to their homes knowing that many more people agree with them. The demonstration becomes a symbol for a broader range of activities, both representing and punctuating a movement campaign that always includes much more over a longer period of time.

In addition to mass demonstrations, activists have devised still more dramatic means of showing numbers, commitment, and endorsing their ideas. Activists engage in vigils, sometimes fasting, strike, organize boycotts, and establish semipermanent camps in support of their cause. Sometimes they dress in costumes, in the hope of attracting the attention of the mass media; recently, activists against cruelty to animals paraded naked as a costume. Farmers drove tractors to Washington, D.C., to protest foreclosure policies, and environmental activists often ride boats or bicycles to demonstrate their concerns. Gay and lesbian activists staged "kiss-ins" in the 1980s, in efforts to boost their political and social visibility.

And sometimes, some activists break laws or employ violence to promote their ideas and undermine policies with which they disagree. Civil rights activists in the United States willfully violated local segregation laws, asking to borrow books in segregated libraries; they also violated orders not to march or demonstrate, sometimes suffering harsh punishment from police. Antiabortion activists assemble outside clinics that perform abortions, trying to talk or yell young women out of entering the clinics. On occasion, they assemble in large numbers to try to block all access to the clinic. Some zealots shoot doctors or bomb buildings and may alienate as many potential supporters as they mobilize in the process. Radical and disruptive tactics, such as civil disobedience or violence, then can serve as a double-edged sword, generating visibility, demonstrating commitment, and potentially provoking a backlash.

The inventory of tactics above is hardly complete. The point is that movements are characterized by a tremendous diversity of activity, all seen to be in the service of common purposes. Just as activists in the same movement have a diversity of opinions and concerns, people generate a broad range of actions to support their ideas, and partisans on all sides argue about who is actually "in" or "out" of the social movement of the moment.

THE EFFECTS OF SOCIAL PROTEST MOVEMENTS

Activists, authorities, and their opponents all act as if social movements matter, but the when and how they do is a matter of considerable uncertainty and debate. Because the conditions that promote social movements also promote alternative solutions for redress, disentangling the relative effects of movements and institutional actors is no easy matter (Amenta 1998; Meyer 2005). Beyond this, the diversity of claims and tactics within a social movement, often occurring simultaneously, make it virtually impossible to tease out which group or event had what effect. Furthermore, the effects of social movements often play out over a very long time and generate consequences far beyond the imagination, much less the intentions, of activists, authorities, and opponents. Activists virtually never get *all* they demand and may not get credit for what concessions they do get; they also may produce outcomes that they do not explicitly call for but that are nonetheless of great consequence.

For heuristic purposes, we can identify distinct levels of influence that social movements can affect. Social movements challenge current public policies and sometimes they also alter governing alliances and public policy. Because movement activists aspire to change not only specific policies but also broad cultural and institutional structures, they therefore can affect far more than their explicitly articulated targets. The organizations that activists establish for a particular political struggle generally outlive that battle and continue to engage in politics, often on different issues and in different ways. Movements also change the lives of those who participate in them in ways that can radically reconstruct subsequent politics, including subsequent social protest movements. Movements build communities of struggle and communities that can sustain themselves and also change in unanticipated ways. We can see the influence of protest movements in four distinct but interdependent areas: public policy, political organizations, culture, and participants (Meyer and Whittier 1994). Each of these is important not just for its impact on the larger society but also for its direct and indirect effects on other social movements.

Public Policy

Movements generally organize and mobilize around specific policy demands ranging from ending drunk driving to toppling a government. Activists seek to represent their concerns and their claimed constituencies within mainstream political institutions, to speak for those who protest, and often to attract notice of external actors, broadening the scope of the political struggle (Schattschneider 1960). Social protest can set agendas for government, giving political life to issues otherwise ignored. It can embolden supporters within government, giving them inspiration or cover for political reforms, partly by at least implicitly promising future support for politicians who prove to be allies.

Scholarship on social movement impact on policy derives generally from the pioneering work of William Gamson (1990), who traced the political and policy outcomes of 53 challenging groups in America before World War II. Gamson identified two kinds of positive responses—recognition as legitimate actors and policy concessions—that did not necessarily come together. Gamson identified the organizational attributes such as size, resources, and disruptiveness that seemed to come with success but didn't examine how groups achieved influence. A number of other scholars have conducted case studies of particular movements or issues, finding the ways in which social protest percolates through the political system to produce some changes.

Because public policy includes symbolic and substantive components, policymakers can make symbolic concessions to try to avoid granting the aggrieved group's substantive demands or giving it new power. Elected officials can offer combinations of rhetorical concessions or attacks, in conjunction with symbolic policy changes, to respond to or preempt political challenges (Edelman 1971). Visible appointments to high-level positions, rhetorical flourishes, and symbolic policy changes may quiet, at least momentarily, a challenging movement demanding substantive reforms. Both symbolic and substantive concessions in response to pressure from one social movement change the context in which other challengers operate. They open or close avenues of influence, augment or diminish the pressure a movement can bring to bear, or raise or lower the costs of mobilization. Thus, movements can alter the structure of political opportunities they and others face in the future.

And sometimes this influence, shrouded in apparent defeat, has longer-term consequences. One clear response to the American movement against the Vietnam War was the end of the draft, even as President Nixon publicly announced that the broad movement would have no impact on his conduct of the war. (Politicians are understandably loath to credit protests for influencing their views or policies, given the obvious risks of appearing weak, manipulated, or of encouraging others to protest.) The end of the draft, in conjunction with the domestic political fallout of the war, created a policy consensus within the military and among strategic experts that minimized large-scale American participation in extended wars for roughly 30 years. This is not what demonstrators sought in 1969, but it is hardly insignificant.

Advocacy Organizations

Strong social movements spur the creation of new advocacy groups, which generally continue even well after the peak of mobilization has passed (Minkoff 1995; Wilson 1995). NOW, for example, established in the early part of the second wave of American feminism, has continued in good and bad times for the movement, preserving a vision of feminist ideals, advocating and educating on matters of policy, and serving as a resource for subsequent mobilization campaigns. Green parties that developed in advanced industrialized countries during the early 1980s as the extension of social movements, such as the peace, feminist, community, and environmental movements,

continued to exist in most countries. Sometimes members even entered parliaments or government. They have taken on new issues and tried to compete for new constituencies, becoming a relatively stable part of the political reality in several European countries.

Sometimes organizations stick with a relatively narrow range of issues, but just as frequently, they respond to new political challenges. In the movement against the American war in Iraq, for example, Meyer and Corrigall-Brown (2005) note the presence of numerous organizations whose primary concerns are not in foreign policy or peace but instead in women's rights, civil rights, or the environment. A clear legacy of social movements is the establishment of organizations that can fight on related causes through a variety of means in the future.

Culture

Social movements struggle on a broad cultural plane where state policy is only one parameter (Fantasia 1988; Whittier 1995). Movements must draw from mainstream public discourse and symbols to recruit new activists and advance their claims, yet they must also transform those symbols to create the environment they seek. Symbols, meanings, and practices forged in the cauldron of social protest often outlive the movements that created them. The familiar peace symbol, for example, designed to support the British Campaign for Nuclear Disarmament in the 1950s, migrated to the United States during its antiwar movement, back to Europe in the 1980s, and to Asia as a rallying point for prodemocracy movements in the 1990s.

Indeed, in the absence of concrete policy successes, movements are likely to find culture a more accessible venue in which to work, building support for subsequent challenges on matters of policy. In the late 1970s and 1980s, Eastern European dissidents chose explicitly "antipolitical" strategies of participation, in a deliberate attempt to create a "civil society," that is, a set of social networks and relationships independent of the state. Publication of *samizdat* literature, production of underground theater, and appropriating Western rock music to indigenous political purposes were all important political work for democratic dissidents. This battle, in the least promising of circumstances, proved to be critical in precipitating and shaping the end of the Cold War.

Thomas Rochon (1998) contends that while the explicit political struggle takes up a large share of activist attention, it is the cultural changes that are both more likely and more lasting. Citing the example of the women's movement in the United States, Rochon notes that while activists lost in their campaign for ratification of the ERA, they effected large-scale changes in the way women were viewed in a variety of venues, including the family, the workplace, and politics. We might note that in responding to ERA advocates, opponents frequently laid out a list of all the aspects of gender equity they supported (Mansbridge 1987; Sawyers and Meyer 1999). The area of cultural effects of movements is underdeveloped both theoretically and empirically, but it promises to be an area for important work in the future.

Participants

Social movements also affect those who participate in them, sometimes dramatically and forever. People who participate in movements step into history as actors, not simply as victims, and this transformation is not easily reversible. Movement activists forge new identities in struggle, identities that carry on beyond the scope of a particular campaign or movement. Someone who has forged a sense of self and values through collective action and tried to exercise political power through membership in a community of struggle will not readily submit to being acted on by distant authorities in the future.

Activists come to see themselves as members of a group that is differentiated from outsiders. They interpret their experiences in political terms and politicize their actions in both movement contexts and everyday life. Collective identities constructed during periods of peak mobilization endure even after protest dies down. Onetime movement participants continue to see themselves as progressive activists even as organized collective action decreases, and they make personal and political decisions in light of this identity (Taylor and Whittier 1992; Whittier 1995). Veterans of Freedom Summer, for example, became leading organizers in the peace and student movements of the 1960s, the feminist and antinuclear movements of the 1980s, and beyond (McAdam 1988). By changing the way individuals live, movements contribute to broad cultural change, but beyond that they seed mainstream politics and society with activists, organizations, and issues that animate change in the future.

In summary, movements can influence not only the terrain on which subsequent challengers struggle but also the resources available to challengers and the general atmosphere surrounding the struggle. In changing policy and the policy-making process, movements can alter the structure of political opportunity new challengers face. By producing changes in culture, movements can change the values and symbols used by both mainstream and dissident actors. They can expand the tactical repertoire available to new movements. By changing participants' lives, movements alter the personnel available for subsequent challenges.

FUTURE PROSPECTS FOR THE FIELD

Academic inquiry on social movements has advanced substantially over the past few decades through a process of oscillation, emphasizing first context, then activists, then context again. On almost parallel tracks, scholarship has also shifted over the decades from emphasizing emotions, then rationality, then emotions again. Increasingly, however, scholars have come to read—and write—across constricting paradigms, working toward synthetic approaches that adapt to the analytic problem at hand. This is a promising development, one that is likely to aid in the development of robust concepts, often organized around questions of *how* activists translate opportunities into mobilization and *how* institutional politics processes and manages the challenges of protest mobilization.

Scholars have also responded to the new movements of our time, extending the analytical frame of social movements to consider a broader geographic diversity of cases, transnational activism, fundamentalism, and terrorism. Underlying such studies is the notion that concepts and methods developed in the study of a relatively limited set of cases can be developed to cope with a broader range of phenomena. These developments make the study of social movements an especially promising, and potentially important, field of study.

55

MASS COMMUNICATIONS

VINCENT MOSCO

Queen's University, Canada

This chapter begins by taking up two major challenges facing a sociological analysis of mass communications. One is to define and specifically to set boundaries on precisely what constitute mass communications and the other is to specify what constitutes sociological research on mass communications, when much of what should be included in the literature is produced by people who are not sociologists. The chapter then addresses the origins of mass communications research because these roots, particularly concerns about propaganda and an interest in using mass communications for commercial purposes, have had an enormous influence on the development of the field.

Following an overview of the history, the chapter takes up the three primary coordinates for examining the sociology of mass communications: content, communicators, and audiences. The content of mass communications has been examined from two major approaches encompassing varieties of content analysis and discourse analysis. Content analysis has been favored by those who see the interpretation of content as less problematic than those who adopt a discourse analysis approach, which takes into account the subjective nature of texts and the likelihood of multiple readings. Research focusing on media communicators includes analysis of the industry, where the problem of concentrated ownership and control has occupied considerable attention. It also takes up the organization of mass communication activities, with scholars here calling attention to the impact of work practices and organizational routines on media content. Finally, mass communicator research also examines the profession of mass communications and specifically the tensions between professional and worker values and identities. The third element of mass communications research focuses on audiences or the receivers and users of what the media produce. Research here encompasses the nature of the audience, particularly the extent of its active involvement in media interpretation and use, and the relationship of the audience concept to more traditional sociological categories such as social class, status, race, and gender. The chapter concludes by raising questions about the future of mass communications and the challenges that current transformations are posing to sociological research and to communication policy.

WHAT IS THE SOCIOLOGY OF MASS COMMUNICATIONS?

There are numerous useful definitions of communication, starting with the technical meaning provided by Shannon and Weaver (1949). Although the authors begin with the rather ethereal view of communication as the ways in which one mind can affect another, they concentrate on the process by which a communicator or encoder sends a message or signal through a transmitter in such a way as to minimize noise and reach a recipient or decoder. Various forms of this definition have proved to be popular, including the colloquial but useful "who says what to whom for what purpose." I have offered a version that is explicitly sociological and resists the labeling of senders and receivers: Communication is a social process of exchange whose content is the measure or mark of a social relationship (Mosco 1996).

The meaning of communication is debatable, but it is less of a problem than determining what *mass* means. In general, to distinguish it from interpersonal communication or the exchange of messages between two or a few people, mass communications refers to the process of sending messages from one or a few sources to many receivers. The difficulty is determining just when interpersonal becomes mass communications and when mass communications becomes popular communication. At the heart of mass communications are forms defined by their technical means of communication, primarily newspapers, radio and television broadcasting, and cinema. The definitional challenges arise when it is a small group of people producing a newspaper, setting up a small radio network, or making a documentary for another small group of people. Are these forms of mass communication because they are intended for more people than produce it and because they use means of communication that are typically associated with mass communications? Or are they interpersonal communication because of the small scale of the sender-receiver relationship? Or are they examples of another form of communication, what Mattelart (1983) has called *popular communication* to refer to communication that grows out of the grass roots and is intended to expand the power of the masses? There is no fine line to separate interpersonal from mass communications or mass from popular communication. However, the distinctions are useful as long as they are not too sharply drawn. Mass communications relate to message transmission from a small group of people with more power than the large group of people to whom they communicate. Interpersonal communication also involves power but tends to be more horizontal and includes fewer people. Finally, popular communication tends to emanate from the ground up and may include a few or many communicators and a large or small audience.

In addition to the challenge of specifying mass communications, there is the difficulty of defining the community of scholars who carry out research in the field. Sociologists have made significant contributions to all facets of mass communications scholarship from the pioneering methodological strategies of Paul Lazarsfeld and Patricia Kendall (1948) to the analysis of how mass communications work is organized and produced in Gaye Tuchman's (1990) and Herbert Gans's (2004) work, on through the study of social movements and industry power in the research of Todd Gitlin (2003). Nevertheless, there is as much or even more work that takes up key points of interest for the sociology of mass communications produced by people who are not sociologists. Address only the work of those trained in sociology, and you would likely produce a well-integrated map of the sociology of mass communications, but it would be far less than complete, particularly in important areas where sociology meets historical and political economic analysis. Consequently, this chapter takes a more expansive approach to the field by defining broadly the kind of work that fits within the arena of mass communications and by addressing the work of scholars that bears centrally on the sociology of mass communications, regardless of whether these scholars are defined or define themselves as sociologists.

ORIGINS: PROPAGANDA AND ADVERTISING

The process of sending messages from one person or a small group to many people is not new. From antiquity, large organizations such as states and religious organizations depended on steady flow of mass communications. However, it is not after the arrival of the printing press in the fifteenth century that we begin to see an acceleration in the speed and in the reach of mass communications. Nevertheless, mass communications still depended for centuries on the speed of transportation that would be needed to physically carry messages, in whatever print form, to their destination. As Carey (1992) and more recently Starr (2004) have described, the arrival of the telegraph broke the connection between communication and transportation by permitting messages to be sent electronically over ever-increasing distances. Schudson (1978) and Schiller (1981) have documented just how crucial this was in the expansion of the mass-circulation newspaper in the late nineteenth and early twentieth centuries. Prior to the telegraph, newspapers reached large numbers of people but only after their news made the long and costly journey over land or sea, taking weeks or months to deliver the results of an election or other major news event. The mass-circulation newspaper also raised the fears of those who worried about the power such forms of mass communications could display and encouraged the hopes of those who saw opportunities to expand commerce.

These fears and hopes grew with the telephone, although it is more the icon of expanded interpersonal communication, and they grew even more with the rise of radio and later television broadcasting. Radio came along in the 1920s at a time of growing tension among states and growing interest in expanding commercial markets. The former led to the worry that foreign states might make use of the new means of communication to penetrate distant societies and use propaganda to accomplish their goals of conquest without having to resort to military invasion. There were also domestic fears among many that their own governments would use radio to expand internal propaganda and thereby shout down the alternative voices that lacked the power to reach the masses but that were necessary to strengthen democracy. For those who feared the growth of fascism, the skilled use of the microphone by early electronic propagandists such as Goebbels was more than just worrisome. But Americans who opposed what they felt was the bigotry of religious zealots such as Father Coughlin or who opposed the New Deal and the "fireside chats" that President Roosevelt used to advance the cause were also deeply troubled. As Barnouw (1966, 1968) demonstrated in his social history of broadcasting in the

United States, serious scholarship on how mass communications work began partly in response to the perceived threat of propaganda. Buxton's research (1994) is important because it demonstrates the pivotal role of the Rockefeller foundation in supporting the early research of scholars such as Lazarsfeld and Cantril into the propaganda power of mass communications. As a result, serious academic attention was paid to understanding the power of specific media events such as the broadcast of Orson Welles's dramatization of *War of the Worlds,* which many interpreted to be a news account of an alien invasion and others saw as a surrogate for what would happen if the United States were attacked by foreign forces.

Mass communications research also got started because business saw enormous opportunities to expand the reach of advertising. Mass advertising began with the newspaper and other forms of print material. The arrival of a medium that permitted mass circulation of audio communication created opportunities to significantly expand mass advertising. But there were many unanswered questions. Would people welcome, or even tolerate, an uninvited voice into the living room? Initial reluctance led to regulations limiting radio advertising to the identification of a product. What forms of advertising would reduce listener resistance and actually sell products? Would it take unvarnished information or entertaining jingles and vignettes? To answer these questions, soap companies and a host of others hired social scientists to carry out experimental and survey research, enabling them to pioneer approaches that would become the mainstays of mass communications research when television came along. The earliest self-conscious and systematic academic studies of mass communications were conducted by researchers such as Paul Lazarsfeld, Wilbur Schramm, and others affiliated with commercial research initiatives, such as those supported by the Princeton Radio Research Project. A number of academic studies conducted throughout the late 1930s and early 1940s frequently engaged in analyses of radio audiences, simultaneously, as Buxton (1994) notes, "accepting the framework of commercial broadcasting as a given" (p. 148). Gitlin (1978), in his critique of early mass communications research, argues that an "administrative" agenda derived from the needs of commercial broadcasters drove much of this research, and thus these needs in a sense are responsible for determining much of the so-called dominant paradigm of mass communications studies.

Quantitative and qualitative knowledge of the radio audience became a central concern to both broadcasters and academics during the 1940s. It is here, in this historically important period, that the commercial orientation of much early mass communications research is readily apparent. Indeed, Lazarsfeld and Kendall (1948:82) explicitly call for a connection between the research activities of both commercial media and academic researchers. A concrete example of this is given by Eaman (1994), who cites the participation in 1935 of Lazarsfeld, then professor at Columbia University and director of the Bureau of

Applied Social Research, along with Frank Stanton, the first head of CBS's research department, in the development of the CBS Program Analyzer, a device designed to gauge audience reactions to specific CBS programs.

Building on this foundation, the state and the corporation would continue to have an intimate relationship with mass communications research, helping to fund its development and refine its methodologies and also contributing to tensions between the pure and applied advocates in the field.

CONTENT

There is no ideal way of carving up the research terrain in mass communications, but one useful approach is to distinguish between the study of content, production, and reception. In practice, it is not easy to separate the three since the structure of production has an influence on content, as does audience response. But as long as one keeps in mind the mutual constitution of all three, it is heuristically valuable to address each one. Perhaps prompted by the fear of propaganda or taken by the opportunities to sell, the initial response from casual observers to scholars was to believe that mass communications had a direct and powerful impact on audiences, the equivalent of what some liked to call a hypodermic needle that could inject influence into the societal bloodstream and thereby shape public attitudes and values, whether that meant which political party to support or which perfume to buy. The results of this research were mixed, revealing that indeed mass communications did have an impact but the process by which it worked was complex. An early and influential attempt to document the effects of media content on viewers was conducted between 1929 and 1932 through the Payne Foundation. Known as the Payne Fund studies, these investigations responded to the popularly held belief that violent and sexually suggestive movie content contributed to juvenile delinquency and other social ills. According to Lowery and DeFleur (1995), these studies had two main objectives:

> In one category, the goals are to assess the content of the films and to determine the size and content of their audiences. The second category attempts to assess the effects on those audiences of their exposures to the themes and messages of motion pictures. (P. 24)

These studies concluded that media content did indeed have an effect on audiences, a conclusion that served to reinforce public perceptions of the dangers of uncontrolled media content, but that there were mediating factors.

Notions of audience activity came quickly after the academics entered mass communications studies. The early focus on ratings research was not sufficient to sustain prolonged academic investigation. Likewise, the deepening debate over the approach to questions of media effects required theories that would have to go beyond simple quantitative and passive models of the audience. Yet the focus on audiences remained, even as we see a rise in theoretical perspectives stressing the active nature of audiences and the relative lack of power of media texts and hence of broadcasters.

One of the earliest of this type of theoretical perspective was the "two-step flow" model of communication offered by Katz and Lazarsfeld (1955) in 1948. This model introduced the intervening variable of the "opinion leader" to help explain why media texts do not necessarily have the desired, direct effect. While the merits of this approach have been widely debated and critiqued, the important feature is that for the first time people were seen as playing an active, albeit institutionally circumscribed, role in the consumption of media texts. This broke somewhat with the history of "audience" as a numerically defined entity, transforming what was essentially a statistical entity into an organic and reflexive social grouping. The political significance of this was not only to theoretically diminish the power of the mass media but to further elevate the audience to the status of a legitimate feature of social life. Changes in attitudes and values were more likely to take place when the mass communications process was mediated by what came to be called opinion leaders or respected members of the relevant community. With their support of a particular message, these political, business, or community leaders would strengthen the message by giving it a personal touch of legitimacy that would, it was found, overcome the reluctance to internalize a message sent by a more impersonal voice. As a result, the two-step flow approach to understanding mass communications replaced approaches that relied on direct-injection models. This also strengthened the sociological purchase on mass communications research because it gave added weight to the view that, however sophisticated the technology, communication, even mass communications, remained a distinctly social process.

The early research also had important methodological implications. The initial perspective on mass communications gave support to a straightforward analysis of media content, which amounted to different versions of content analysis. If media messages directly influenced a mass public, then one could read the impact directly from the messages themselves. Given the recognition that, at the very least, opinion leaders could shape the process of media reception, leading to acceptance or rejection, and to a strong or a weak response, then it was necessary to examine the structure of social relations involving transmission and reception along with the assessment of content. This was important because it contributed to the inclusion of social structural analysis in mass communications studies and, perhaps even more important, to the inclusion of mass communications as a component in the study of all sorts of social and political movements and organizations. This did not mean that content analysis completely gave way to a more mediated approach.

The rise of television and its perceived power created a new wave of interest in content analysis particularly in the study of problem areas such as violence, advertising, and pornography. One of the primary centers for this work, especially for the study of televised violence, was the Annenberg School of Communication, which used the support of the Annenberg Foundation and government funding to carry out content analyses of televised violence as well as of commercial advertising (Gerbner and Gross 1980). This research was widely followed by activists and policymakers who used the results on what they perceived to be extensive televised violence, commercialism, and explicit depictions of sexuality to promote regulation and to pressure broadcasters. The research and its influence gave new life to content analysis, and it has remained a leading approach to examining media content. But content analysis has also come under criticism, not only because it neglected the role of opinion leaders and other important social actors but because it neglected to account for the interpretive powers of audiences.

Discourse analysis provided the major alternative in the study of content. This approach drew heavily from cultural studies that extended its influence across the social sciences and humanities in the 1970s. Cultural studies is a broad-based intellectual movement that concentrates on the constitution of meaning in texts, defined broadly to include all forms of social communication. It has grown from many strands, including one based on the drive to oppose academic orthodoxies, particularly the tendency to organize knowledge in disciplinary canons such as English literature. The approach now contains numerous currents and fissures that provide considerable ferment from within as well as without. From the beginning, especially in the British context, cultural studies have been strongly influenced by Marxian perspectives, including the tendency to see culture as intimately connected to social relations, particularly as organized around class, gender, and race, with a focus on their asymmetries and antagonisms. Furthermore, Marxian concerns with power, particularly the power to define and realize needs and interests, influenced the development of cultural studies, as is evidenced, for example, in the work of Thompson (1963) and Willis (1977), which brought to the fore the cultural construction of class relations. Marxian concerns are also exemplified in the work at the Centre for Contemporary Cultural Studies in Birmingham, prominent in the research of Hall (1982). This concentrated on the view that culture is neither independent nor externally determined but rather is best viewed as the site of social difference, struggle, and contestation. Indeed, commentators have noted that one of the significant differences between the British and American approaches to cultural studies is that the former has adopted a more explicitly Marxian and generally political position. Cultural studies in the United States also contain numerous divisions, but one can safely conclude that there is a greater tendency for them to draw inspiration from a pluralist conception of society and politics that sees power as widely dispersed, from functionalist anthropology and sociology, which concentrate on how cultural practices maintain order and harmony in social life, and from symbolic interactionist social psychology, which uses the language of ritual and drama to examine the production and reproduction of symbolic communities (Carey 1979).

Discourse analysis drew from cultural studies a broad conception of media content as embedded in texts and subject to multiple readings and interpretations—that is, texts are polysemic. Two main directions characterized the approach. The first emphasized the polysemic nature of texts and concentrated on the ability of receivers to interpret and make use of communication to satisfy various instrumental and emotional needs. Communication may be purposive, but even the interpretation and behavioral consequences of propaganda are unpredictable. Some discursive analyses would go so far as to view receivers and audiences as co-constituting or producing texts. From this perspective, audiences author their own texts and do so in a multiplicity of ways. One cannot read an audience from the content analysis of texts, but one can understand interpretations through in-depth readings of texts and by engaging the audience that creates its own meanings (Schiffrin, Tannen, and Hamilton 2001). Another approach to discourse analysis emphasized the power of texts as sent and, while accepting the potential for multiple readings, including oppositional and alternative ones; this approach made more room for the ability of original creators to set the agenda for a narrow range of interpretations. For these analysts, texts become part of a dominant ideology or hegemony that forms the taken-for-granted "common sense" within which interpretation would have to be fit for it to be accepted as legitimate (Abercrombie, Hill, and Turner 1980; Abercrombie and Longhurst 1998).

COMMUNICATORS

Sociological research has examined communicators in three primary ways. It has analyzed the industry mainly through political economic research. It has examined the structure of media production primarily by using an organizational sociology approach. Finally, sociological studies of the occupational dimension of communication have been carried out largely through a sociology of professions and a labor studies approach. The development of the media industry has not differed sharply from that of other industries. One of the critical differences is that the media industry has been the subject of regulation, particularly in the broadcasting and related sectors dependent on the use of scarce electromagnetic spectrum. Nevertheless, the secular trend is toward larger corporations controlling more sectors in the communication industry. Specifically, early research on the media industry demonstrated that one or a few companies dominated their specific sectors. For example, in the 1930s, concerns were raised about the

power of RCA to control radio through outright ownership of stations, affiliation agreements with other stations, and control over sources of information and entertainment. This research prompted government inquiries and some regulatory controls (McChesney 1994). Later research found companies such as RCA and CBS branching out from radio and music into television through the ownership of networks and stations and through affiliate agreements with local stations. This change in industry structure, referred to as cross-ownership control or media concentration, was fueled by opportunities to profit from the ability to leverage power in one medium to assert control over another (McChesney 1999). This was easier to accomplish in the mass communications business because of the ease with which its products could be reproduced after their initial production. Current research focuses on the ability of a handful of media conglomerates to extend cross-media ownership across the full range of print, broadcasting, cable television, film, and video, on to newer Web-based media. Many of these are U.S.-based firms such as Time Warner; General Electric, which owns NBC; Viacom, which owns CBS; and Disney, the owner of ABC. However, research has demonstrated that media conglomeration is now a global phenomenon, with firms such as Rupert Murdoch's News Corporation, Germany-based Bertelsmann, and the Sony Corporation joining the dominant tier of mass communications powers (Bagdikian 2004).

There is little disagreement in the literature over the structure of the media industry, but there is intense debate over the significance of media concentration. On the one side are concerns that industry structure restricts the free flow of information and entertainment, limiting diversity and biasing the news to support the interests of corporate owners and their advertising partners. Drawing from a broad neo-Marxian perspective, Herman and Chomsky (2002) go so far as to consider this a new form of propaganda, a way of manufacturing consent. Others whose focus is critical sociological theory (Garnham 2000; Murdock 2000) and political economy (Murdock and Golding 2000; Schiller 1999) argue that media concentration is a threat to democracy and an extension of imperialism or neocolonialism through the control over media and new technologies. These views would lead to support for a variety of policy measures, including breaking up media monopolies to promote competition, deepening regulation of large media firms to insist that they support a diversity of media voices, and strengthening public and community media.

Alternatively, some argue that there is less to worry about. Drawing on neoclassical economic theory, Compaine (2000) has questioned the extent of media concentration and the power of companies to translate their organizational control into control over the content produced by media professionals. According to this view, large media companies succeed because they meet the demands of audiences as registered in the marketplace.

This leads Compaine to promote less government involvement in the marketplace to free companies to better serve their diverse audiences. Starting from postmodern and postcolonial theory, Featherstone (2003) challenges the view that media conglomerates have the ability to shape minds worldwide. Much of this work updates policy debates that began in the 1960s and 1970s about media imperialism and the need to support or oppose the development of a New World Information and Communication Order that would rectify imbalances in global flows of communication (Schiller 1992). Today, the policy debates are about things such as the global digital divide and the need to develop global movements for cultural diversity or, on the other hand, to support global free trade as the primary means of advancing economic development with the means of communication (Compaine 2001; Klein 2002; Mosco and Schiller 2001; Murdock and Golding 2004; Servon 2002).

Research on mass communications has also addressed communicators from the perspective of organizational theory, specifically by assessing the process of producing mass communications. Rather than focus on the broad sweep of political economy that informs so much of the work that examines the industry, this perspective concentrates on the narrower view that the content of mass communications is heavily influenced by bureaucratic considerations, organizational routines, and work rules. Initially, this research focused on newspapers and concluded that news organizations set up schedules and routines that regularized the process of news gathering and production to meet the need to fill a news hole of a certain size every day. Coverage of scheduled events such as government meetings and the assignment of reporters to news beats (e.g., crime and sports) provided a defense against the uncertainty inherent in producing a product with unpredictable content. Making the job as predictable and routine as possible, Tuchman (1990) and Fishman (1990) argued, helped to explain the content of newspapers. This work has been extended to the study of broadcasting and film, where predictability and routine are argued to matter just as much whether the end result is news or entertainment (Gans 2004; Wasko 2003).

More recently, organizational research has begun to address a different but equally interesting question. How can bureaucratic organizations, with their beats and routines, meet the challenge of the Internet, where bloggers, independent musicians, and amateur video makers count on a culture that is increasingly infused with the view that communication is free (Lessig 2004)? Can media bureaucracies survive in a networked world (Boczkowski 2004)? Some argue that they can by changing key elements of the old bureaucratic routines, including adopting the post-Fordist practices that accept more uncertainty but have independent contractors and strategic partners take on the risk (Wayne 2003). They are also aiming to do so by pressing strongly for intellectual property protections that, if applied worldwide, would make it more difficult to treat information and entertainment as public goods (Vaidhyanathan 2004). Finally, following a historical pattern, large bureaucratic media organizations are actively co-opting their competitors by hiring bloggers, producing low-cost music downloading services that feature independent artists, and developing a strong Internet presence (Boczkowski 2004; Lessig 2004). The key research question remains how to control uncertainty. The difference today is that the uncertainty emanates more powerfully from a global networked world.

In addition to having an interest in industry and organizational processes, scholars have addressed the roles and identities of direct media producers, including professionals and technicians responsible for creating news and entertainment for the masses. Those who make media have experienced a conflicted identity because they share some characteristics, including advanced education/training and the independence born of skills and certification, but they lack the power enjoyed by more guildlike professions such as law and medicine. Moreover, because their work is often highly regimented and precarious and because they are often organized in trade unions with long histories of collective bargaining and some militancy, they have a lot in common with the working class. This is especially the case, as McKercher (2002) has demonstrated, because they are increasingly subjected to the processes of automation and de-skilling, which were once limited to industrial occupations. Moreover, with Reuters shipping newswire jobs to Bangalore, Disney sending animation work to Asia, and Hollywood turning to Canada for what the Screen Actors Guild calls low-wage "runaway production," media workers are increasingly threatened by outsourcing (Elmer and Gasher 2005; Mosco 2005).

Two questions are particularly prominent in this area of research. Drawing on the literature in the sociology of the professions and on labor process research, how do media workers respond to their conflicting identities as professionals and as workers? The answer to this question takes up historical research on the evolution of media professions, the changing social composition of media professions, and changes in the relative status of media work in society (Ewen 1976, 1998; Schudson 1978, 1984; Tunstall 1981). The second question asks how media workers are responding to the changes in work, including automation, de-skilling, and outsourcing. This area of research takes up the reorganization of traditional labor unions and the development of new sources of social movement organization. In the United States, Canada, and Europe, labor organizations have built large unions that represent workers across the full range of communication activities. In the United States, the Communication Workers of America now bills itself as a "trade union for the information age" because it represents workers in print, broadcasting, telecommunications, and information technology sectors. In Canada, the Communication, Energy and Paperworkers union is a similarly convergent organization of communication and knowledge workers. In Europe, Union Network

International is a federation made up largely of media and information labor. These efforts represent a response to the changing communication landscape that supporters claim provides opportunities to present a united front against media conglomerates. Additionally, workers in hard-to-organize sectors such as computer communication, and those in a workforce with little union knowledge or experience such as the computer game industry, have established social movement labor organizations that do not negotiate contracts but defend workers rights in a variety of areas. Good examples include the National Writers Union and the Washington Alliance of Technology workers, an organization that represents Microsoft workers. Research on convergent trade unions and social movement organizations draws from labor studies to determine whether these represent a genuine return of labor power in a fast-growing industry or just evidence of the failure of trade unions using more traditional forms of organization (Mosco 2005).

THE AUDIENCE

The *audience* concept is one of the fundamental ideas of mass communications and also one of the most hotly contested. Even scholars providing a critical view of the idea acknowledge its importance. In a widely cited assessment of the term, Allor (1988) concluded that "the concept of the audience . . . is the underpinning prop for the analysis of the social impact of mass communications in general" (p. 217). As Meehan (1990) has demonstrated, audience research goes back to the early days of radio. Other mass media such as print and film could rely on circulation numbers and box-office receipts, respectively, to tell them how large their audience was. But the anonymity of radio broadcasting necessitated a different approach, one that would call for systematic research techniques. This need to determine how many people were listening was one shared by commercial (primarily American) and public service broadcasters (notably British and Canadian). While the underlying rationales of public service and commercial broadcasting may differ, the impetus behind audience research remained the same: Broadcasters needed to know that their programming was reaching people. Given the financial stakes in the media business, it is not surprising that the techniques of survey research were finely honed by the ratings services to determine the size of audiences and their responses to programs and to advertising. The growing investment in radio and television broadcasting can be attributed in part to the certainty, sometimes reasonable and sometimes not, that people were listening and watching and that research could quantify the value of placing investment bets on a particular station or program.

The implicit, and sometimes explicit, perspective underlying this research is that the audience is an important but largely passive component in the mass communications system. This idea fit well with those who leaned to a mass society perspective, a view that industrial society created not only a labor force but also a mass of largely docile consumers who carried out their role as passive recipients of products and messages without disturbing the social fabric. The notion of the audience as a passive mass recurs throughout the history of mass communications studies. The propaganda function of the commercial mass media posited by Marxist cultural theorists, such as those of the Frankfurt School, often assumes a passive, consuming role for the audience by emphasizing the relative power of ideologically loaded media content. Mass society theorists make similar assumptions, arguing that media content reinforces the existing social order and that people are generally resigned to this fate (McQuail 1983). But for others, the *audience* was a strange concept, largely a marketing term with no lineage in the corpus of sociological concepts. These would rather deal with social class, race, ethnicity, and gender, and with social organization and social movement, because these concepts are embedded in classical and contemporary theoretical traditions (Abercrombie and Longhurst 1998; Butsch 2000).

Whether or not they used the term *audience,* scholars also grew uncomfortable with the view that audiences were passive recipients of media messages and began to develop research programs that documented the active nature of audiences. Much of this work arose out of cultural studies and the increasing sociological interest in agency (Hagen and Wasko 2000; Ross and Nightingale 2003). Audiences were active agents, if not authors of their own texts, and sociological studies increasingly examined the nature and extent of this activity. Some of this research went to the other extreme by claiming that the process of cheering for or complaining about a television show constituted audience resistance and demonstrated that the media space produced by large media conglomerates was far from hegemonic. Nevertheless, this marked a maturing of sociological research on audiences because it moved the question from how we measure audiences to better service the commercial side of the business to how we understand the behavior of audiences and their role in contributing to the production of meaning in media texts. Assisted by the growing field of audience history research (Butsch 2000), scholars began to move the audience from a statistical category to a complex force made up of many tendencies and numerous social identities.

Research informed more by political economy than by cultural studies reasserted the value of thinking about the audience as a significant category for understanding how mass communications work. Much of this work drew from Smythe's (1977) view that the audience was a marketable commodity whose activity or labor was sold to advertisers. Other work has taken on a more sociological character and has been produced by scholars who believe that one way out of the audience morass was to consider alternative approaches to the interpretation of media consumption, approaches that decline to accept audience status as a fundamentally determinant social relation. One such example is provided by Press (1991; see also Meehan and Riordan 2002), who situates the experience of television viewing within the wider social relations of gender, class, and age. The analysis of media effects remains the focus here, but it does not treat women as a specific audience, constituted by their relationship to television. Rather, what is important is the lived experiences women bring to television viewing, and how these experiences help one to interpret the social relations of media activity.

Press acknowledges that the process of media reception is complicated, and her approach avoids the extreme conclusions that viewers are passive in the face of dominant media ideology and that viewer interpretation is automatically valorized. Using ethnographic research on women's television use, she argues that not only does gender influence media consumption and interpretation, but class and generational affiliations also further shape such media habits. When approached along these lines, the fact that different groups of viewers interpret media content differently is not altogether surprising. In a sense, she could be said to be documenting an "active audience." However, Press's approach has the conceptual strength to sidestep this intellectual dead end and ask the questions that deal with why such differences emerge. Lived experiences such as gender, class, and age are what constitute people as human beings, and it is these experiences that are brought to the act of watching television.

Long (1994) provides another useful example in her project that confronts the image of the solitary reader, reconceptualizing this cultural act as a fundamentally social one. Her research entails an examination of women's reading groups, analyzing how these groups have allowed women to come together to determine meaning from media texts and how this social activity has served to transform their own image of women's role in society. As with Press, Long's approach allows her to move beyond a simplistic conception of women as audiences for reading materials, instead seeing how they actively constitute themselves in relation to the media. By focusing on the reading groups themselves, Long provides us with a close understanding of how specific collections of people organize themselves into specific audiences. This approach also leaves room for class and race considerations, and for how these identities play a part in the choice of texts to be read, how interpretation is achieved collectively, and what, if any, political and social agenda is behind such activities.

Long (1994) also exhorts us to pay attention to what she terms the "social infrastructure of reading." This consideration has two basic dimensions. First, we need to remember "that reading must be taught, and that the socialization into reading always takes place within specific social relationships" (pp. 192–93). This is an important reminder for those who study mass communications. Applying this observation, we can say that one's socialization into viewing also takes place within specific social relationships, be they familial, gendered, racial, generational, or otherwise. Long leads us, as does Press, to consider the social relations that

constitute us as social human beings prior to our membership in any particular audience. The second dimension of this social infrastructure Long refers to as the "social base" (p. 193), comparing this to the physical infrastructure required for transportation systems. This consideration is vitally important because it directs us to the spheres of production and distribution, reminding us that what is available for consumption is often institutionally circumscribed, something that political economists, among others, have long argued. Audience "activity," however conceptualized, is constrained both by factors of socialization and what fundamentally amounts to the institutional distribution of power.

A final example of an intellectual approach that transcends the traditional treatment of the audience is offered by folklore scholar Susan Davis (1986), who provides us with an analysis of the uses of parades and street theatre in antebellum Philadelphia. Spectacles such as these can be considered precursors of twentieth-century media texts. Parades offered an essential form of public communication, and their organization also reflected social status and power relations. For instance, parades celebrating civic occasions were often organized by those in the upper classes, such as up-and-coming industrialists, wealthy merchants, and skilled artisans. The excessive pageantry of these parades was meant not only as a celebration but also as a display of social power and an attempt to legitimize the existing social hierarchy. Parades from those of the lower classes, such as the Mummers or striking workers, typically lacked such excessive displays of wealth and formal organization and were meant as a challenge to the existing social order.

This observation reminds us that the processes of production involve an attempt, whether implicit or explicit, to construct meaning. Audience members' relations to such spectacles often depended on the meanings implicit in each particular parade, and their responses often depended on their position in the social hierarchy. One of Davis's most interesting findings is that the role of the audience varied according to the parade itself. Excessive pageantry, garish displays of wealth, and quasi-militaristic order worked to keep audience members from participating, instead relegating them to the sidelines while visions of the legitimate social order promoted by the dominant class flowed past. Working-class parades, on the other hand, tended to have far less formal organization and at times actively encouraged parade watchers to march and otherwise participate in the event. This observation leads us again to consider the institutional limitations of the production process. Audience members exist not only in relation to the media text itself but are also constituted out of the entire set of social relations.

FUTURE DIRECTIONS

The chapter concludes by discussing how important challenges to the *mass* in mass communications are having, and will likely continue to have, a significant influence on the direction of research in the field. The means of mass communications have always held the potential to break down the mass, enabling many to actively communicate. In the early days of each wave of new media, this has typically been the case. Radio developed from the work of many amateurs whose home-based "stations" led many to believe that genuine two-way wireless communication was at hand. But eventually, large commercial interests and governments dashed these opportunities by taking the scarce frequencies that amateurs used (McChesney 1994). Nevertheless, the hope remained to establish more democratic means of communication, realizing what Bertolt Brecht held out as the potential for every receiver to also serve as a transmitter. While it is true that each new technology makes this promise and that there is little especially new in the promises made by advocates of digital media, there are some signs that new media can turn audiences into full-fledged communicators or at least give them greater control than what they enjoyed in the era of passive mass communications (Mosco 2004). We are now beginning to see this in television, with the massive expansion in the number of channels available along with technologies such as TiVo, which allow viewers to record programs for later playback. The opportunity to control the program schedule and eliminate commercials is upsetting the economic and structural control that large broadcasters once enjoyed. This alone requires scholars to rethink the nature of the mass in this area of mass communications.

Questioning the mass is even more central with the arrival of the Internet and more generally of network-based modes of social interaction and communication (Castells 2001). Widespread access to high-speed services provides people with greater choice of information and entertainment sources and enables them to produce more of their own communication. This has already eroded the circulation of the traditional daily newspaper and is cutting into the amount of time spent viewing television. The rapid spread of online publishing, from personal diaries and news accounts included in blogs and podcasts to longer audio and video productions, raises more questions about a potential shift from mass to networked, community-based, or even individualized communication systems. These developments provide fresh challenges to scholars who might need to rethink the fundamental categories of mass and audience and to consider the extent to which this heralds the arrival of more genuinely democratic communication.

Traditional communicators acknowledge these challenges, and scholars who might be prone to seeing revolutionary transformations in the arrival of a digital world need to pay increasing attention to their attempts to retain commercial advantage. One way for media conglomerates to maintain and perhaps even to strengthen their power is to expand across the range of mass communications products and leverage each against the other to fend off more localized competition. Specifically, ownership of newspapers, magazines, and book-publishing firms provides conglomerates with massive amounts of material for online information products. Ownership of entertainment companies offers similar opportunities. All of this is substantially enhanced by the nature of the product, digital communication, because of the ease with which it can be reproduced, reconstituted, and distributed internationally. Furthermore, information technology-based flexible systems of production allow big companies to operate with less labor and to draw from a global workforce. One of the vital areas for scholarly attention in this attempt to retain key elements of the traditional mass communications system is the ability of firms to expand their control over intellectual property (Lessig 2004).

The ability to turn communication into a marketable commodity has always been a challenge because so much of communication is freely circulated. The question of whether communication is a commodity or a public good has been a fundamental challenge for scholars and policymakers (Starr 2004). On the one hand, computer-based systems facilitate the process of commodification by making it easier to measure and to monitor, to package and repackage communication products in a marketable form. But they also make it easier for people to communicate and to freely circulate what companies would like to market commercially. The conflicts over intellectual property, including primarily copyright and patent and trademark issues, will occupy scholars and policymakers for some time. Policymakers are often torn between the pressure to support commercial use of intellectual property and the need to promote access to information. The former recognizes that communication and information are now engines of economic growth, the latter that they are essential for advancing democracy. Overly restrictive intellectual property laws in the name of economic growth can shrink access and stifle the diversity of sources and content necessary to promote widespread participation in the political process. But the absence of protections for the creators of intellectual property can erode the incentive to invest in new forms of communication and information content.

These issues have already moved from the national to the international stage because they are connected with the aspirations of societies, including less-developed ones, to develop their own communication and information systems and to use them for economic and social development (Zhao 2001). One of the central policy issues of our time is how to extend the call, first heard in the 1950s, for a new international economic order, to the communication and information arena. Specifically, this means providing access to the means of communication to the less-developed world, a majority of whose citizens have yet to make a telephone call. Indeed, current policy discussions, most recently carried on in a series of international policy meetings called the World Summit on the Information Society, have examined ways of implementing the right to communicate as a basic human right. Again, global companies and some governments in the developed world balk at the prospect of renewed government regulation, but supporters of the right to communicate maintain that international regulation, perhaps, including a role for the United Nations through UNESCO and the International Telecommunications Union, is essential for extending access to the less-developed world. How these issues are resolved will go a long way in setting the pattern for evolving systems of global and local communication, including whether the term *mass communications* remains essential to the work of sociology.

PART XII

SOCIETY IN MOTION

56

SOCIAL CHANGE

STEPHEN K. SANDERSON

Boulder, Colorado

Since its very beginning, sociology has had an abiding interest in social change, as the classical contributions of Comte, Spencer, Marx and Engels, Weber, and even Durkheim attest. But the study of social change has been, and indeed can only be, interdisciplinary. Anthropologists and archaeologists have long been interested in social change. They have formulated numerous evolutionary theories of society intended to fill in details of the broad outline of human social evolution over the past 10,000 years. Such study must also take into account the work of historians, and especially general theories of history.

In this chapter, I look at forms of social change under the following headings: theories of social evolution, the course of long-term evolution, social evolutionism and historical sociology, revolutions and state breakdowns, social movements, the development of the modern world-system and the institutions of modernity, globalization and economic development, and late modernity and postmodernity.

THEORIES OF SOCIAL EVOLUTION

Social evolution is a process of social change that exhibits some sort of directional sequence. In the second half of the nineteenth century, there were many well-known evolutionary theorists in both sociology and anthropology, including Herbert Spencer, Lewis Henry Morgan, Edward Burnett Tylor, L. T. Hobhouse, William Graham Sumner, Albert Galloway Keller, and Edward Westermarck, among others. Outside sociology and anthropology, Karl Marx

and Friedrich Engels also developed an evolutionary model of society based on economics and the class struggle (Sanderson 2007).

After a period of several decades in which evolutionary theories were heavily criticized, in the 1930s and 1940s evolutionism revived in the work of V. Gordon Childe (1936, 1951), Leslie White (1943, 1959), and Julian Steward (1955). Childe and White emphasized technological development as a critical force behind social evolution and developed broad evolutionary schemes. Steward focused on ecological determinants of cultural evolution and stressed that most evolution moved along a series of paths rather than one grand path. After 1960, a new generation of anthropologists and sociologists built on the work of these three thinkers. Elman Service (1970) developed an evolutionary typology based on a society's sociopolitical organization: bands, tribes, chiefdoms, and states. Robert Carneiro (1970) developed a famous theory of the evolution of the state that stressed population growth, warfare, and environmental circumscription. Circumscribed environments are those in which areas of fertile land are surrounded by natural barriers that impede the movement of people out of the area. Warfare is the result of population growth and resource scarcity, and when land is plentiful, people may be able to respond to war by simply moving away. But in circumscribed environments, land is eventually filled up, and the solution to more population pressure and resource scarcity becomes political conquest and, ultimately, state formation.

About the same time, sociologist Gerhard Lenski (1966) developed an evolutionary theory of stratification. The key to the rise of stratification, according to Lenski, was technological advancement and increasing economic productivity. Once societies start to produce an economic surplus, competition and conflict over its control emerge, and as surpluses grow larger, struggles intensify and stratification systems become more elaborate. Later, Lenski (1970, 2005) expanded this theory to go beyond stratification. In both his early and later works, Lenski distinguished five major evolutionary stages: hunting and gathering, simple horticulture, advanced horticulture, agrarianism, and industrialism. As societies progress through these stages, a wide range of evolutionary consequences follow.

Sociologist Talcott Parsons (1966, 1971) developed an evolutionary theory that concentrated on the evolution of ideas and social institutions. He formulated the concept of an *evolutionary universal* to describe and explain how a society achieves a new stage of evolutionary adaptation and thereby improves its level of functional efficiency.

One of the most important theories of social evolution of this period was developed by Marvin Harris (1977), who saw the tendency of societies to deplete their environments as the result of population growth as the engine of social evolution. When populations grew, pressure on resources intensified and standards of living declined. At some point, people had no choice but to advance their technologies so as to make their economies more productive. Thus, farming replaced hunting and gathering, and then later farming with the use of the plow replaced farming with the use of simple hand tools. But technological change itself leads to further population growth and greater environmental degradation, and so a new wave of technological change eventually becomes necessary. For Harris, social evolution, at least in preindustrial societies, is a process in which people have been running as hard as they can just to avoid falling farther and farther behind.

Stephen Sanderson (1994a, 1995a, 1995b, 1999a, 1999b, 2007) has built on the evolutionary ideas of Harris. He has formalized, extended, and to some extent modified them by developing a comprehensive theory that he calls *evolutionary materialism*. The theory is laid out in terms of a detailed set of axioms, postulates, and propositions dealing with the nature of social evolution, the basic causal forces in social evolution (demography, ecology, technology, and economics), similarities and differences between biological and social evolution, the role of agency and structure in social evolution, and the tempo and mode of evolution. Sanderson uses evolutionary materialism as a general framework with which to understand three great evolutionary transformations: the origins of agriculture, the rise of the state, and the transition to modern capitalism.

Another sociological contributor to a theory of social evolution is Jonathan Turner (1995, 2003), whose theory focuses on social differentiation. According to Turner, the ultimate force setting social evolution in motion is population growth; population growth generates increased logistical loads, which in turn generate selection pressures for new social structures to handle these increasing demands.

Population growth increases the values of four macrosocial forces—production, distribution, regulation, and reproduction—and as the values of these forces escalate, institutional differentiation occurs.

THE COURSE OF SOCIAL EVOLUTION

Virtually all social evolutionists agree that the first great social transformation was the Neolithic Revolution, which introduced plant and animal domestication. This began about 10,000 years ago in Southwest Asia, but the transition to communities based on agriculture occurred more or less independently at later times in Southeast Asia, China, Mesoamerica, South America, and North America (agriculture came to Europe by migrations from the East). The transition to agriculture led to settled and more densely populated communities that for a while remained relatively egalitarian but that eventually gave way to stratified societies organized into chiefdoms (Sanderson 1999b:20–52).

By about 5,000 years ago, in several parts of the world societies that had evolved into chiefdoms were beginning to make the transition to a state level of political organization, or to what many scholars call *civilization*. This occurred first in Mesopotamia and Egypt, and then later in China, the Indus valley in northern India, parts of Europe, and Mesoamerica and Peru. Most civilizations have been agrarian societies, thus cultivating the land with plows and draft animals and intensively fertilizing the soil. Like the Neolithic Revolution, the transition to civilization and the state was a process of independent parallel evolution in several parts of the world (Sanderson 1999b:53–95).

From the time of the emergence of the first states, it was to take several thousand years before a shift to a qualitatively new mode of social organization occurred. Most sociologists argue that it was the *Industrial Revolution* of the late eighteenth century that introduced a qualitatively new form of social life, industrial society. However, in recent years some sociologists have moved this transformation back in time to the sixteenth century (Wallerstein 1974a, 1974b). The qualitative shift is, then, considered to be the transition to a *capitalist world-economy*. Capitalism—selling goods in a market to earn a profit—in some form or another has existed for thousands of years, but after the sixteenth century, it began to replace earlier, precapitalist forms of social life. From this perspective, the Industrial Revolution was simply part of the logic inherent in the advance of capitalism. Although most scholars treat the rise of capitalism as Europe's decisive contribution to the world, at about the same point in history Japan began to undergo a capitalist transition of its own (Sanderson 1994b).

There have been many attempts to explain this transition (Sanderson 1999b:155–168; Emigh 2005), such as Weber's ([1904] 1958) famous Protestant ethic theory, which Robert Bellah (1957) applied to the case of Japan.

Randall Collins (1997) has applied Weberian thinking in a different way, pointing mainly to the role of Buddhist monasteries in medieval Japan in stimulating entrepreneurship. Different types of Weberian arguments have been presented by Chirot (1985, 1986) and Mann (1986). Various Marxian theories, emphasizing either a "crisis of feudalism" (Dobb [1947] 1963; Wallerstein 1974a, 1974b) or the revival of trade in medieval Europe (Sweezy [1950] 1976), have also been formulated.

A world-system interpretation has been proposed by Andre Gunder Frank and Barry Gills (1993). They reject the notion that a qualitative shift to a capitalist mode of production occurred in sixteenth-century Europe and emphasize a much longer process of quantitative economic growth that has been occurring on a world level for some 5,000 years. In a more recent work, Frank (1998) argues that Asia, and especially China, was more advanced than Europe until the eighteenth century. Similar arguments for the equal if not greater economic power of Asia have been made by Pomeranz (2000) and Hobson (2004).

Sanderson (1994b, 1999b:168–78) has offered a synthetic theory that is intended to apply equally to the cases of Europe and Japan. He points to five major similarities between late-feudal Europe and Tokugawa Japan that served as important preconditions stimulating capitalist development in both regions: small size, location on large bodies of water, temperate climate, population growth, and highly decentralized feudal politicoeconomic regimes. Sanderson stresses that these preconditions operated within the context of a very long-term evolutionary trend, expanding world commercialization, which had been occurring since about 5,000 years ago and which created a kind of critical economic mass that provided the basis for the development of capitalism.

Currently, there is no real consensus on which of these many and varied theories work best. Perhaps all that can be reasonably concluded at this point is that this continues to be one of the most important issues in the sociological study of major social transformations and is likely to remain so in the years to come.

EVOLUTIONISM AND HISTORICAL SOCIOLOGY

In the 1970s, sociology experienced a "comparative-historical revolution," and the study of large-scale historical change, a fundamental part of classical sociology, revived. With a few notable exceptions, historical sociologists have not been friendly to evolutionary theories of social change. Two of the earliest recent historical sociologists were S. N. Eisenstadt and Barrington Moore, Jr. Eisenstadt's (1963) *The Political Systems of Empires* made use of Parsonian neoevolutionary assumptions, as did his more general theoretical essay "Social Change, Differentiation, and Evolution" (1964). Barrington Moore Jr.'s (1966) *Social Origins of Dictatorship and Democracy,*

perhaps the most important work in the initial revival of historical sociology, identified three major historical trajectories that led to modernity: a capitalist and democratic path (England, France, and the United States), a capitalist and initially democratic path but with a temporary reversion to fascism (Germany and Japan), and a Communist path (Russia and China). Moore explained these outcomes in loosely Marxian terms, arguing that where capitalist forces were strongest and landlord forces weakest, the outcome was democratic, but where capitalist forces were weakest and landlord forces strongest, the outcome was the most undemocratic.

Perry Anderson (1974a, 1974b) was more explicitly Marxist in his orientation. Anderson traced out the crisis of Roman antiquity and identified the conditions under which it was replaced by feudalism. He then traced out the crisis of this new mode of production many centuries later and showed how it led to the centralized bureaucratic states that formed in Europe between the fifteenth and the nineteenth centuries.

Michael Mann's (1986) *The Sources of Social Power* was an attempt to look at world history from a largely Weberian perspective. The main thesis of this book was that there are four major types of social power—ideological, economic, military, and political—which are relatively autonomous realms of social life.

Randall Collins (1986, 1995) has also taken a Weberian approach to historical sociology. In his work on geopolitics, he identified a particular type of society, the agrarian-coercive society, that is constantly seeking to expand the territory under its control. But as the territories of such societies grow larger, these societies become increasingly costly to maintain. Failure in war becomes increasingly common, and this, combined with the rising economic costs of maintaining the state apparatus, leads to a crisis and ultimately a collapse. Collins applied this geopolitical model not only to preindustrial states but also to predict the eventual collapse of the Soviet Union.

Immanuel Wallerstein (1974a, 1974b, 1979, 1980, 1989) created a revolutionary new paradigm in historical sociology, *world-systems analysis* (WSA). WSA is based on the assumption that societies are not independent entities but are embedded in larger intersocietal networks—world-systems—that are usually organized in a hierarchical fashion. Wallerstein postulated that a specifically capitalist world-system had begun to form in Europe and elsewhere around 1450. This world-economy consisted of an economically and politically dominant segment, or *core;* a highly subordinated and exploited segment used by the core for cheap labor, access to important resources, and the production of raw materials for export, or *periphery;* and an intermediate zone that was both exploiter and exploited, or *semiperiphery.*

WSA is evolutionary in the sense of specifying a long-term directional trend in the history of the world-system. This trend is the *deepening of capitalist development,* which is essentially the extension of the logic of commodity production to the entire economic sphere and even beyond it. Societies evolve only as parts of the world-system. Chase-Dunn and Hall (1997) have tried to give the evolutionary character of WSA much more historical depth. They argue that there have been world-systems of various types for thousands of years and identify three major types of world-systems in world history: kin-based world-systems, tributary world-systems, and the modern world-system. The authors explain the transition from one type of world-system to another largely in cultural materialist terms. Their model can be summarized approximately as follows: population growth → environmental degradation → population pressure → emigration → circumscription → conflict, hierarchy formation, and intensification. (For a much more detailed summary and critique of WSA, see Sanderson 2005b.)

REVOLUTIONS AND STATE BREAKDOWNS

An especially important form of change in recent centuries is that of revolution and state breakdown. Theda Skocpol (1979) distinguishes between *social revolutions* and *political revolutions* and defines social revolutions as "rapid, basic transformations of a society's state and class structures [that are] accompanied and in part carried through by class-based revolts from below" (p. 4). Political revolutions involve only the transformation of state structures, there being no corresponding transformation of class or social structures. Goldstone (1991) has used the alternative term *state breakdown,* which occurs when a society's government undergoes a crisis so severe that its capacity to govern is crippled. Only some state breakdowns become actual revolutions. Many state breakdowns lead to only limited political changes, ones that are not dramatic enough to warrant the label revolution.

Perhaps the most dramatic revolutions have been the French Revolution of 1789, the Russian Revolution of 1917, and the Chinese Revolution that began in 1911 and culminated in 1949. To these may be added other social revolutions in the Third World, such as the Cuban Revolution in 1959, which replaced the corrupt Batista regime with a socialist regime; the Islamic Revolution in Iran in 1979, which ushered in rule by Islamic theocrats; the Nicaraguan Revolution of the same year; and the more recent revolutions against Communist rule in Eastern Europe and the Soviet Union. During 1989, in East Germany, Czechoslovakia, Poland, Hungary, Romania, and Bulgaria, there were major political transformations toward more democratic and open political regimes. In 1990, Yugoslavia splintered into several separate states, most of which shifted more toward democracy and capitalism (Sanderson 2005a).

Numerous theories of revolution have been proposed (Sanderson 2005a:61–106). Well-known older theories include the rising expectations theory of James Davies (1962) and the relative deprivation theory of Ted Robert Gurr (1970). Probably the most famous theory of revolution is Marx's, which emphasizes the socioeconomic order and class struggle (Marx and Engels [1848] 1978). In Marx's formulation, as capitalism advanced, the working class would expand in size and the capitalist class, through the gradual concentration of capital, would shrink. Ultimately, a huge working class would confront a tiny bourgeoisie. There would also occur an economic polarization and intensifying conflict between the two classes. With the continuing advance of capitalism, the working class would become better organized and at some point would rise up and overthrow the capitalist class and usher in a socialist society.

Marxian theory has not, for the most part, been supported by the historical events of the past century. No advanced capitalist society has experienced a socialist revolution. On the contrary, such revolutions have occurred in overwhelmingly agrarian societies, first in Russia in 1917, and then later in China and Cuba and other parts of the Third World. And it has been the peasantry rather than the working class that has been most central to revolutionary change. Where the Marxian theory falls short is in its failure to take into account the political realm. More recent Marxian theories focusing on Third World revolutions have emphasized the disruption of peasant life by the spread of capitalist market relations (Wolf 1969) and the kinds of economic situations that make Third World peasants most likely to revolt (Paige 1975).

The major alternative to Marxian theories emphasizes the political side of social life. *State-centered theorists* make an important distinction between revolutionary *attempts* and revolutionary *outcomes.* Marxian theories identify economic conditions that lead to discontent and thus revolutionary attempts, but these have not been successful in predicting revolutionary outcomes. The state-centered theory developed by Skocpol (1979) was designed to explain the three Great Revolutions. Skocpol's theory holds that the Great Revolutions resulted from a coming together of two overpowering circumstances, a massive crisis within the state organizations of France, Russia, and China, and widespread rebellion among the lower classes, especially the peasantry. State crises result, according to Skocpol, from severe international political and military pressures and from economic difficulties that produce widespread dissatisfaction among the peasant population.

Jack Goldstone's (1991) state-centered theory attempts to explain four cases of state breakdown: the English Revolution of the mid-seventeenth century, the French Revolution of the last decade of the eighteenth century, the Anatolian rebellions of the 1600s in the Ottoman Empire, and the fall of China's Ming Dynasty in 1644. Goldstone argues that state breakdowns have been cyclical phenomena that have occurred in two major waves, one peaking in the mid-seventeenth century and the other in the mid-nineteenth century. Goldstone's *demographic/structural model* considers how population growth leads to widespread social and economic dissatisfaction and subsequently a state crisis. When populations grow, prices increase while tax revenues lag, which means that states must increase taxes. Because it is difficult to increase taxes enough to maintain fiscal stability, a state fiscal crisis normally ensues. Population growth also has a negative effect on social and economic elites, because it increases the number of competitors for elite positions, leading in turn to occupational frustrations within the elite. Population growth also drives down wages. With higher prices and lower wages, both rural and urban misery increase, precipitating food riots and wage protests. The result of this combination of unfortunate circumstances is widespread state crisis and, ultimately, a state breakdown.

Wickham-Crowley's (1992) state-centered theory is designed to explain Latin American revolutions. In the second half of the twentieth century, successful revolutions occurred in only two Latin American countries, Cuba in 1959 and Nicaragua in 1979. Cuba and Nicaragua shared several features that were critical for the formation and success of revolutionary movements, the most important of which was a distinctive type of state, a *neopatrimonial regime.* Such a regime has a highly corrupt ruler who turns the state into his own personal property; he personally controls the military, suppresses political parties, and dispenses rewards and favors in a highly personalized manner. In short, he dictatorially controls the state and bends it to his whims. It is precisely this type of regime, Wickham-Crowley argues, that is most vulnerable to overthrow because the dictator eventually alienates virtually all major social groups, thus creating an opportunity for these groups to form a revolutionary coalition despite their opposing interests.

The Great Revolutions and the Third World revolutions were "revolutions from below" created by a combination of revolt by subordinate classes in conjunction with state weakness. However, the revolutions against Communism were what have been called "revolutions from above," or revolutions made by one segment of the political elite against another (Sanderson 2005a). When Mikhail Gorbachev rose to power in the Soviet Union in 1985, he inaugurated the economic and political reforms known as *perestroika* and *glasnost,* which were intended to move the Soviet Union in a more market-oriented and democratic direction. Gorbachev also changed the relationship of the Soviet Union to its Eastern European satellites (Kumar 2001). By 1989, Gorbachev had made it clear that the Soviet Union would no longer intervene in the affairs of Eastern Europe, where social discontent and protest against the Communist regimes intensified. In fact, there is evidence that the Soviet leadership actually encouraged revolt (Kumar 2001). Without Soviet support, these regimes could not survive.

Within the Soviet Union, the revolution was a classic example of revolution from above (Hahn 2002). Mass action was negligible or nonexistent, and the regime was brought down by infighting within the political elite,

which was severely divided on the direction the country should take. The elite divisions themselves seemed to be primarily the result of the severe economic problems of Soviet society. Gorbachev's economic reforms were designed to deal with these problems, which became especially serious after the mid-1970s. But the economic and political reforms unleashed political forces over which Gorbachev eventually lost control, resulting in the Soviet collapse (Hahn 2002).

SOCIAL MOVEMENTS

Social movements are organized campaigns by segments of the public to press some claim or achieve some political goal. In some instances, they shade into, and may be scarcely distinguishable from, revolutionary organizations, but most social movements have much more moderate and limited aims than revolutionary groups. Like revolutions, social movements are modern political phenomena. The first social movements may have begun in London in the late eighteenth century, but they were not common until the 1820s or 1830s, when there were large and highly effective mobilizations devoted to such things as the rights of workers, the emancipation of Catholics, and parliamentary reforms. In France, the full complement of social movement claim making began to be seen in the mid-nineteenth century (Tilly 2004).

The nineteenth century saw a major expansion in the number and range of social movements. A sampling of social movements in the United States during this time would include the American Anti-Slavery Society, the Grand Eight Hour Leagues, the International Workingmen's Association, and the American Federation of Labor (Gamson 1990; Tilly 2004). By late in the century, social movements had begun to represent a wider range of interests, and there was a notable decline in violence, probably as a result of the expansion of political rights. In the twentieth century, and especially in its second half, the social movement had become commonplace. As Tilly (2004) points out, the year 1968 saw a sudden surge in movement activity. In May of that year, French students and workers collaborated in an attack on the de Gaulle regime, the Dubček regime in Czechoslovakia launched a liberalization campaign, and there was a great flurry of movement activity in the United States: accelerating protests against the Vietnam War, collective violence in black neighborhoods in more than a hundred American cities, the radical student movement at Columbia University, and a Poor People's March on Washington. Then, in 1989, there were the numerous outbreaks of popular protest against Communism in Eastern Europe (Tilly 2004).

Over this entire period, social movements became increasingly internationalized. In just the first two months of 2001, for example, there were protests of various types in the Philippines, Nigeria, Ethiopia, Argentina, and

Mexico, not to mention the activities of antiglobalization forces protesting at the meeting of the World Trade Organization in Porto Allegre, Brazil, as well as at meetings of the World Economic Forum in Davos, Switzerland, and Cancun, Mexico (Tilly 2004).

In a sense, the causes of social movements are just the opposite of the causes of revolutions. Whereas revolutions are most likely where states are highly repressive but also weak and vulnerable, social movements are much more likely to emerge in highly democratic societies. Social movements have accelerated in direct proportion to increased democratization, and nothing much resembling a social movement can be found today in such undemocratic states as Kazakhstan, Belarus, or the People's Republic of China (Tilly 2004). Democracy promotes social movements for several reasons. For example, it broadens and equalizes rights and it expands protections for citizens against arbitrary government action (Tilly 2004). And just as democratization promotes social movements, social movements generally promote democratization. Social scientists used to consider social movements "outsiders," but it has become increasingly clear that there is often a very fine line between social movements and regular government activity (Goldstone 2003).

But why do *certain types* of movements emerge *in certain places* and *at certain times?* McAdam, McCarthy, and Zald (1996) speak of a growing consensus that three sets of factors working together determine the emergence and nature of social movements: political opportunities, mobilization of resources, and "framing." In his *resource mobilization theory,* Tilly (1978) emphasized the first two sets of resources. *Political opportunities* involve the extent to which a political environment is favorable to social movement activity. For example, if a group making claims has formal or informal power, and if the government against which the claims are being made is unlikely or unable to engage in repression, then a favorable political environment exists. Both American and European students of social movements have sought to understand how a nation's political environment has affected the form, extent, and degree of success of social movements (McAdam et al. 1996).

Mobilization of resources concerns the extent to which the members of a group share common needs and interests, have built up a network of ties that gives them some degree of unification, and control important resources that give them the capability of pursuing their joint aims. The particular nature and extent of these various resources shape social movement outcomes. Finally, there is *framing,* an idea borrowed from Erving Goffman's notion of "frames" (Snow and Benford 1992). Framing involves the shared meanings and social definitions that people build up regarding their situation: what they feel aggrieved about and how they imagine that redress of their grievances can best be brought about. In the emerging consensus of which McAdam et al. (1996) speak, framing is considered a crucial mediating factor between opportunities, resources, and actions.

THE WORLD-SYSTEM AND THE INSTITUTIONS OF MODERNITY

The modern world was ushered into existence in the sixteenth century with the transition from a feudal to a more capitalist economy. Wallerstein, as we have seen, saw this as a transition to a *capitalist world-economy.* In the first phase of its development (about 1450–1640) (Wallerstein 1974a), capitalist agriculture and early forms of industrial production prevailed, and the leading core powers were Holland, Great Britain, and northern France. A capitalist periphery formed in Eastern Europe and Iberian America and a semiperiphery in Southern Europe.

A "second era of great expansion of the capitalist world-economy" began in the 1760s (Wallerstein 1989). It was marked by the beginnings of the Industrial Revolution in Britain in the mid-eighteenth century, the spread of industrialization to other parts of Western Europe and to North America in the nineteenth century, and the enormous embarkation of the most powerful European states on a process of massive colonization. In the twentieth century, the United States emerged as the great core power, but later challenges to U.S. supremacy have come from East Asia, first from Japan and more recently from China. The center of the world-economy has been tilting eastward, and it is likely that within half a century much of East Asia, centered on China, will be dominant in the world-economy.

The development of the world-economy has been paralleled in the political realm by the rise of an *interstate system* and its new national states, which were much larger in scale and much more centrally coordinated than the feudal states that preceded them. It actually took several hundred years for these states to form. Germany, for example, was not a unified nation-state until after 1871, and in the Italian peninsula there were several hundred small city-states that came together in the nineteenth century to form what is now Italy (Tilly 1990).

The past two centuries have witnessed the rise of modern social structures and institutions. First, there was a shift from largely rural, agricultural societies to highly urbanized and industrialized societies. As these changes proceeded, the old class structure of nobles, retainers, merchants, peasants, and a large "lumpenproletariat" gave way to a new class structure centered on capitalists, industrial managers, and factory workers. This class structure has in the past century or so changed even further with the formation of a large middle class, a moderately sized class of learned professionals, and a rapidly expanding class of service workers. Sociologists have tried to map this class structure in various ways and with varying degrees of success (e.g., Wright 1985, 1997; Rossides 1990). Daniel Bell (1973) has argued that in recent decades a further change has occurred in the class structure with the shift from industrial to "postindustrial" societies. The dominant class in postindustrial societies is no longer a capitalist class, but a "social intelligentsia," or a class of highly educated persons whose dominance is based on their possession of advanced forms of theoretical knowledge (cf. Kumar 1995).

Three other major changes of the past century have been the rise of democratic governments, the emergence and expansion of mass education, and the formation of welfare states. Democracies—governments with legislative bodies, free elections, mass suffrage, and individual rights and liberties—emerged earliest in the settler colonies that hived off from Britain, in the most developed societies of Western Europe, and in Japan (Rueschemeyer, Stephens, and Stephens 1992; Sanderson 2004). Democracy came much later to the less-developed world, but a major new wave of democratization began in the 1980s (Kurzman 1998; Green 1999).

The first system of mass education formed in Germany in 1763, but these systems began mostly in the nineteenth century, and by the end of the century mass primary education was in place throughout Western Europe and North America. Mass secondary education came much later, beginning only in the late nineteenth century in the United States and not until the twentieth in Western Europe. University education has become widespread only since the middle of the twentieth century. The less-developed world lags behind, but it has been following a very similar developmental path (Meyer et al. 1977; Shofer and Meyer 2005).

Welfare states have been products of the twentieth century, and three main types can be identified (Esping-Andersen 1990). *Liberal* welfare states have been characteristic of England and her settler colonies, the United States, Canada, Australia, and New Zealand. Here, the state provides citizens meager to modest income support. *Conservative* welfare states, found primarily in Austria, Germany, France, and Italy, provide much greater benefits, but the distributional system is highly status-differentiated, with benefit structures being very different for middle- and working-class families. The *social democratic* welfare state provides very high levels and many types of benefits to all citizens regardless of class or status. These regimes are most characteristic of Denmark, Norway, Sweden, and to some extent the Netherlands.

Other changes associated with the rise of modernity include transformations in gender roles, the family, and forms of intimacy. There have been enormous transformations in gender relations in the past four decades, with women moving out of the home and into the workplace in unprecedented numbers. They occupy positions of high status and authority everywhere and increasingly dominate the educational world. For example, over 55 percent of undergraduate students are now women, and professional and graduate students are increasingly female. Half of the new admittees to medical and law schools in the United States are women, and about half of new Ph.D.s in biology are granted to women. In such fields as psychology, sociology, and anthropology, 70 percent or more of new Ph.D.s go to women (Browne 2002, 2005).

These transformations in gender relations, along with other changes, have had enormous consequences for personal life and intimate relationships. The family has been forced to endure a set of enormous shocks. The divorce rate has skyrocketed, as have the number of single-parent families, most of which are headed by women. The family has largely lost its old function as an economic institution and even much of its function as a reproductive institution (Tiger 1999). People increasingly marry for love, and this has created almost unbearably high expectations for intimate relationships (Collins 1985). In the words of Stephanie Coontz (1992, 2005), love has destroyed the traditional family.

GLOBALIZATION AND ECONOMIC DEVELOPMENT

In recent years, there has been constant and ubiquitous talk of *globalization,* which can be defined as "the widening, deepening, and speeding up of worldwide interconnectedness in all aspects of contemporary social life" (Held et al. 1999:2). There are essentially three main forms of globalization. *Economic globalization* involves the extent of international trade, capital flows, and migration and is best measured in terms of the ratio of world trade to world output. Global interconnectedness via trade has been growing faster than the world-economy itself. In 1990, the ratio of world trade in goods and services to world gross domestic product was 19 percent, but by 2000 it had increased to 29 percent. Another important indicator of economic globalization is change in the ratio of cross-border capital flows to world output. The amount of capital flowing across international borders has been growing faster than the world-economy itself (World Bank 2002). A third indicator is the increasing flow of people across international borders. The number of international migrants is growing considerably faster than world population itself (International Organization for Migration 2003). In the 1990s, the rate of increase in the ratio of growth in migrants relative to world population was roughly three times that experienced in the period between 1975 and 1990.

Political globalization involves not only a growing interconnectedness between nation-states in the interstate system but also an increasing connectedness between supra-, sub-, and nonstate actors (Meyer et al. 1997; Beckfield 2003). Growth of intergovernmental organizations (IGOs) (e.g., the United Nations, the European Union, and the North Atlantic Treaty Organization) is a good indicator of political globalization. In 1960, the average country belonged to 18 such organizations, but by 2000 the average country was a member of 52 (Beckfield 2003). Another good indicator of political globalization is the growth of international nongovernmental organizations (INGOs) (e.g., the International Red Cross, Greenpeace, and the International Chamber of Commerce). In 1960, the average country had within it private individuals or organizations who were members of 141 INGOs, but by 2000 the average country was tied to 984 (Beckfield 2003).

Sociocultural globalization involves the emergence of a "world culture." This is evidenced in processes of cultural and institutional consolidation and in the increasingly cosmopolitan character of cultural consumption, as cultural products, knowledge, and lifestyles diffuse across national boundaries. For example, McDonald's has tens of thousands of restaurants in 118 countries, the world's 20 biggest-grossing films of 2002 were all produced by a Hollywood studio, and CNN is available in nearly every country with a cable or satellite television system. Sociocultural globalization is also indicated by such things as a dramatic surge in international tourism, a major increase in international telephone traffic, and the stupendous growth of the Internet and people's reliance on it.

Whether globalization is preponderantly good or preponderantly bad for human well-being, especially the well-being of people in the less-developed world, has been a hotly debated issue (e.g., Singer 2002; Stiglitz 2003). On the positive side, considerable evidence shows major increases in life expectancy in the less-developed world in recent decades, much of which is due to sharply plummeting rates of infant and child mortality (Lomborg 2001; Singer 2002), and since 1970 there has been a sharp reduction in the proportion of the world's population said to be starving.

Based on these figures, things seem to be improving rather than deteriorating. Yet critics of globalization insist that even if there has been some sort of absolute improvement for the world's worst-off populations, globalization has nonetheless led to an increase in global inequality. The United Nations' 1999 *Human Development Report* showed that in 1960, the ratio of the richest quintile of the world's population to the poorest quintile was approximately 30:1, but by 1997 this had increased to 74:1 (see also Korzeniewicz and Moran 1997). However, studies that measure world income inequality using purchasing power parity (PPP) income estimates (e.g., Goesling 2001; Firebaugh 2003) find that the level of world inequality has remained essentially the same since the early 1960s, or perhaps even declined slightly (Firebaugh and Goesling 2004).

It is often pointed out that these improvements in living conditions are *average* improvements, and that there are still many people whose lives have not been improved, or may actually have deteriorated, because of globalization. Although globalization has benefited hundreds of millions of people, for millions of others globalization has not been good. There are still some segments of many underdeveloped societies that lead an extremely marginal and unpleasant existence. Tens of millions of people still live in crowded shantytowns in extremely flimsy makeshift housing, areas that contain open sewers and that are disease infested. (For an extensive discussion of the evidence pro and con on globalization, see Sanderson and Alderson 2005:225–38.)

The bulk of the evidence reviewed above seems to call into question some of the basic assumptions of dependency and world-system theories of underdevelopment (e.g., Bornschier, Chase-Dunn, and Rubinson 1978; Bornschier and Chase-Dunn 1985). These theories claim that the development of the most advanced countries has led to the underdevelopment of the least developed. Although this may have been the case in earlier historical periods (see Mahoney 2003), it does not seem to be the case any longer. In the current period, foreign investment from developed countries in less-developed countries appears to be beneficial rather than harmful (e.g., Firebaugh 1992), and there has been much more development taking place than dependency and world-system theories allow for. Even the most recent sophisticated tests of these theories by their erstwhile supporters (e.g., Kentor and Boswell 2003) show that, at a minimum, they require serious revision. (For an extensive summary of the findings of these studies, see Sanderson 2005b.)

None of this means that we must return to some sort of modernization theory, such as the classical theory of Rostow (1960) or the more recent theory of Landes (1998). These theories also leave a lot to be desired. Perhaps there should be a reconsideration of the Marxian versions of modernization theory developed some years ago by Szymanski (1981) and Warren (1980), who resurrected Marx's thoughts on the role of imperialism in the developmental trajectories of the less-developed world. Szymanski and Warren claim that Marx took the view that imperialism would create conditions in less-developed countries that would lead them along the same developmental path as the imperialist countries.

LATE MODERNITY AND POSTMODERNITY

The tempo and character of social change in the past few decades have been extraordinary. As Anthony Giddens (1990) has argued, the modern world has witnessed a set of changes heretofore unprecedented in human history. These changes involve the *pace of change,* the *scope of change,* and the *specific nature of modern social institutions.* The pace of change in today's world is not only extreme but also constantly accelerating. The scope of change is enormous, as indicated by the previous discussion of globalization. And there are specific features of modern institutions that have never been seen before, such as "the wholesale dependence of production upon inanimate power sources, or the thoroughgoing commodification of products and wage labor" (Giddens 1990:6). In Ben Agger's (2004) terms, we live in an era of "fast capitalism," which is rapidly becoming "faster and faster capitalism."

Giddens identifies the master trend of human history as *time-space distanciation,* or a "stretching out" of time and space. In the early twenty-first century, this process has reached extreme proportions, and as a result, "living in the modern world is more like being aboard a careening juggernaut . . . rather than being in a carefully controlled and well-driven motor car" (Giddens 1990:53). According to Giddens (2002), we are already living in a "runaway world" that will continue to run away faster and faster as time goes by. Other astute observers of the contemporary scene, such as David Harvey (1989), see a world marked by a *condition of postmodernity*. Harvey argues that increasing globalization has led to a continual shrinking of the psychological experience of time and space, a phenomenon he calls *time-space compression*. This is in a sense the mirror image of Giddens's time-space distanciation. In recent centuries, Harvey argues, there have been several periods of time-space compression. Harvey sees the latest episode as having begun in the 1970s, and like the earlier episodes, this one has had profoundly psychologically destabilizing consequences for the individuals who have been experiencing it, especially changes in personal life of a very disruptive nature. For Harvey, two consequences stand out in particular. The first has been the accentuation of the "volatility and ephemerality of fashions, products, production techniques, labour processes, ideas and ideologies, values and established practices. The sense that 'all that is solid melts into air' has rarely been more pervasive" (Harvey 1989:285–86). Second, there has been an increasing emphasis on

> the values and virtues of instantaneity (instant and fast foods, meals, and other satisfactions) and of disposability (cups, plates, cutlery, packaging, napkins, clothing, etc.). . . . It meant more than just throwing away produced goods, but also being able to throw away values, life-styles, stable relationships, and attachments to things, buildings, places, people, and received ways of doing and being. (P. 286)

If Harvey is on target in his identification of the nature and sources of a major social transformation, then the implications for the future seem ominous. Since time-space compression is inherent in the very logic of capitalist development, the pace of production, consumption, and social life will continue to increase. Future waves of time-space compression would be expected to be even more intense, and as such would likely produce even more severe forms of psychological destabilization. If this were to occur, then the time-space compression of the early twenty-first century may in retrospect seem relatively mild, a prospect that is scarcely enticing.

FUTURE PROSPECTS

The study of social change, so critical a part of classical sociology, became something of a poor stepchild during the middle decades of the twentieth century, but in the past 30 years it has been tremendously revitalized. Comparative-historical sociology has become a major branch of sociology and is, in fact, one of sociology's most vigorous and sophisticated branches. The study of revolutions has become a major area of focus of comparative-historical sociologists, and more recently, new life has been breathed into the study of social movements. And sociologists continue to study social evolution in numerous ways. Even the study of the family and gender relations has become more historical, and thus more devoted to change.

If the past three decades are any indication, then future prospects in the study of change look very bright. It is to be expected that the study of evolution, revolution, social movements, globalization, and modernity will not only continue but also expand and branch out. Indeed, as the pace of modern social life continues to accelerate, sociologists, always concerned with recent social trends, will devote even more energy to describing and explaining it, as well as to predicting where we may be headed.

57

Dynamic Systems Theory

Tom R. Burns

University of Uppsala, Sweden

with Philippe R. DeVillé

In sociology, there is no single systems theory.[1] There are several theories, some diverging substantially from one another, for instance, in the degree to which human agency, creativity, and entrepreneurship are assumed to play a role in system formation and re-formation; the extent to which conflict and struggle are taken into account; the extent to which power and stratification are part and parcel of the theory; and the extent to which structural change and transformation—and more generally, historical developments—are taken into account and explained. What the various systems theories have in common is a concern with the complex and varied interconnectedness and interdependencies of social life. Multiple structures, their interrelationships, and their historical development hold center stage. Systems are also more than the sum of their parts. Attention is focused on the different parts and levels of a system and their interrelationships, for instance, between institutions, collective and individual agents, and interaction processes in multilevel complexes.

This chapter provides a brief overview and assessment of those sociological systems theories that focus on the dynamics and transformation of social systems with particular attention to capitalist systems.[2] Drawing on these systems approaches, it provides a synthesis of theorizing about capitalism and points for future research. The chapter also suggests the value and place in sociological theory of dynamic systems theories.

MULTIPLE APPROACHES

Three established dynamic system theoretic approaches can be identified that develop a socioeconomic approach to analyzing capitalist systems and their evolution: the Marxian systems approach, the world systems approach, and the actor-oriented dynamic systems approach (inspired by Walter Buckley's work but also incorporating Marxian and Weberian elements). These three systems approaches are methodologically holistic (Gindoff and Ritzer 1994) but with varying degrees of attention to human agency and microprocesses.

Historical, Political Economic Systems Theory

The historical approach of Marx ([1867] 1967, 1973a, 1973b; see Mandel 1993) and van Parijs (1993), among others, conceives of all societies as evolving in a series of stages. Each stage is characterized by a particular structure,

AUTHOR'S NOTE: This chapter was written while the author was a visiting scholar at the Center for Environmental Science and Policy, Stanford University. He is grateful to the Center for providing a cordial and intellectually challenging milieu. Several of the ideas on capitalist development in the chapter were presented by the author and DeVillé at the World Congress of the International Institute of Sociology, Beijing, People's Republic of China, July 2004. They are grateful to Joseph Berger, Mark Granovetter, Mark Jacobs, Helena Flam, D. L. Peck, Walter Powell, and Ros Sydie for their comments and suggestions during the preparation of this chapter.

a certain mode of production, as well as other structures, the "superstructure" of politics, ideology, and culture derived from and dependent on the economic base or structure of production. Human beings generate these structures through their own actions but not always under the conditions of their own choosing or in the ways they intend. Marx and Marxists focused their theoretical and empirical research on capitalist systems and their emergence and transformation.

Because of contradictions between structures—between, for instance, the "forces of production" (among other things, new knowledge, techniques, and scientific developments that contribute to generating such forces) and the "relations of production" (e.g., the private ownership of the means of production or systems of management and control)—the capitalist system undergoes crises, leading eventually to transformation. Also, modern capitalism accomplishes the production of larger and larger quantities of goods, but such effective abundance is threatened by insufficient demand from consumers (wage earners). Producers are faced with declining profits, some or many going bankrupt. This leads to consolidation and sets the stage for future, often more encompassing, crises.

According to Marx, advances in technology and knowledge, increasing the size of production units, contribute to changes in the mode of production and hence redistribute power among classes over time. And the changing power distributions cause changes in political and cultural institutions[3]—that is, the superstructure. Those with growing power under emerging conditions increase their influence over institutional conditions.

Systems of Production: An Expansive Production System. Capitalists pursue profits. Profits gained are reinvested, expanding productive facilities, productive output, and profits. In other words, this is a system that generates profits and leads to economic expansion. And in the Marxist scheme, profitability and expansion are based on the exploitation of workers.

In the Marxian conception, capitalism is also a system of social reproduction. Material goods essential for continued production are reproduced. The production processes also reproduce class relations, capitalists, and workers. And these social groups through their structured interactions and productive activities also reproduce the economy. The dominant social class maintains and reproduces the state as its instrument, which upholds the property system, contracts, and banks, among other major institutions. That is, the state contributes to the maintenance and reproduction of the capitalist system with its structures of class domination, distribution of gains (surplus value) unequally between capitalists and workers, and the accumulation of capital.

The expansion of productive capacity is accompanied by the replacement of workers by labor-saving technologies. This combined with the reduction of wages to an absolute minimum (that is, a level of subsistence) would, in the Marxian conception, reduce demand for production.

A crisis of overproduction would result. Such a crisis drives some capitalists into bankruptcy. There is consolidation—a tendency to oligopoly and monopoly, a development that occurred over and over again, particularly for many manufacturing sectors as well as for banking and some commercial sectors. According to Marx, crises would deepen and eventually lead to a revolution, whereby capitalism would be replaced by socialism.

The critique of Marxist theory has been diverse, sustained, and of varying quality (Collins 1988). The theory (or family of theories) has been relatively weak and inconsistent in conceptualizing and taking into account human agency as well as fully developing relevant theories of institutions and cultural formations. There was a persistent failure, even among many of those who made use of Marxian theorizing much later (for instance, after World War II), to overlook or neglect the role of the state and democratization in regulating and stabilizing capitalism—for instance, in addressing overproduction, unemployment, and other recurrent problems of capitalism. Also, the development of systematic and practical economic knowledge facilitated regulation of the economy and dealing with some of its (many) instabilities and failures (see later). Marx's prediction of the demise and eventual overthrow of capitalism has definitely not been realized, even partly, thus far. Many capitalist systems proved themselves robust, particularly in countries that developed democracy, and state agencies were willing and able to regulate and stabilize capitalist development.

In spite of its limitations, Marxist theorizing continues to inspire and develop. For instance, (1) there has emerged within neo-Marxist research a more complex view of politics and the state as agent (with greater autonomy and readiness to pursue its own interests, which might diverge from those of the capitalists [Burawoy and Skocpol 1982; Burawoy and Wright 2001; O'Connor 1973; Poulantzas 1978; Przeworski 1985; Wright, Levine, and Sober 1992, among others] playing a key role in the regulation and stabilization of capitalism; (2) greater attention has been paid to human agency, individual and collective, especially the variety of different agents and (3) to ideational and cultural factors and the production of knowledge and normative orders (Anderson 1976; Burawoy and Skocpol 1982; Lockwood 1964; van Parijs 1993; Wright et al. 1992); and (4) world systems theory (WST) places the evolution of capitalist systems in a global and comparative perspective, addressing matters of imperialism and economic dependency among nations (see below). In sum, recent developments in neo-Marxist theorizing (which rejects simplistic materialism) have overcome some of the earlier deficiencies. It continues to have much to contribute to sociology and the other social sciences in spite of the general demise of interest and engagement in Marxian theorizing.

World Systems Theory

Drawing selectively on Marxist theory, WST (Bergesen 1983; Chase-Dunn 1997; Chase-Dunn and Grimes 1995;

Chase-Dunn and Hall 1993; Hopkins and Wallerstein 1982; Wallerstein 1974, 2004) has focused on dependency among nations and imperialism and put the evolution of capitalist systems in a global and comparative perspective. It shared the Marxian historical perspective paying close attention to economics but shifted the focus from a single state to a global world economic system linked by economic trade. However, greater attention was paid to market and trade expansion than to modes of production.

Concretely, the theory conceptualizes the ways in which competing states are linked together into a global system in the context of an interlinked economic (trading) system and the way they have an impact on one another, engage in unequal exchange, and are differentiated as core (rich, developed, and powerful) and periphery (poor, underdeveloped, and relatively weak). The former dominates the latter, yet the functioning of each part affects the other's internal structure. Wealth and other gains take place in the core; peripheral areas are systematically underdeveloped. Core states compete and may engage in wars that are economically motivated. This leads to rising military and governmental expenditures, which in turn generates taxation pressures and, ultimately, domestic resistance; however, booty and resources gained through conquest might bring in sufficient resources and reinforce capabilities to pacify domestic populations and establish stabilizing institutional arrangements (Collins 1988:96).

Core economies have military power because they have the greater material resources. Their labor is free and well paid. There is high demand as well as intensive consumption. The core is characterized by substantial profitability, high wage levels, and high-skill economies producing diverse and advanced goods and services. In the core, profitability is achieved without brutal exploitation of labor. The periphery is characterized by low profitability, low wages, and the production of less advanced goods and services. Labor tends to be more extremely exploited.

From around 1450, the world empire model (as found, e.g., in the Chinese, Ottoman, or Spanish empires) was replaced by the world economy model (these are ideal types) (Collins 1988). The latter system corresponds to global or world capitalism. It is a historically established system defined by the priority of an endless accumulation of capital. Systems of exchange based on center-periphery differentiation in the global trading system result in unequal exchange (differential gains of surplus value). There is oligopolistic production (with high profits, high wages, multiple benefits, and positive developments) in the center as opposed to competitive production (low profits, low wages, negative developments) in the periphery—therefore, expansion in the center, stagnation and blockage in the periphery. In a word, center-periphery is relational.

The system is also characterized by nation-states—that is, political structures, within a larger economic structure, a network of societies. In the WST perspective, forces operating on the world system level are more significant for development (in scale and direction) than forces operating on the national or enterprise level. States are institutions created by the operation of the world economy (Wallerstein 2004). The system also organizes capitalists and workers into particular global relationships.

The importance of WST for the development of historical sociology cannot be overemphasized. In addition, by conceptualizing positions of societies in a matrix of global trade and diplomacy, WST contributed to breaking out of the tendency among most sociologists, including Marxists, to study individual societies in isolation from one another (Chirot and Hall 1982:102). WST has also developed and applied a variety of systemic concepts and analyses, such as structures of domination, center-periphery relationships, semiperipheral regions (halfway between center and periphery in terms of economic structure and power), periphery in the center and center in the periphery, unequal exchange and accumulation, and antisystemic movements. As in the case of other dynamic systems theories, multiple structures and their historical development hold center stage.

Critique of WST has been substantial (Chirot and Hall 1982; Collins 1988; Janowitz 1977; Skocpol 1977, among others) as in the case of other systems theories including Marxian (and Parsonian) variants.

1. WST is a functionalist theory that assumes but fails to prove that capitalism is largely dysfunctional. Developed countries (DCs) and less-developed countries (LDCs) are viewed as homogeneous classes of the same world system, whereas there are major differences among DCs and among LDCs in that they have different sociocultural and political contexts and their socioeconomic development logics and functional potentialities differ (see later).

2. Like Marxism, WST has been relatively weak and inconsistent in conceptualizing and taking into account human agency as well as theorizing and developing relevant institutional and cultural theories. In the "longue duree," there is relatively little agency according to Wallerstein (2004). As opposed to the "industrial proletariat" or "political man" or "rational actor," WST "lacks a central actor" (p. 21). For WST, actors are "not primordial atomic elements, but part of a systemic mix out of which they emerged and upon which they act . . . their freedom is constrained by their biographics and the social prisons of which they are a part" (p. 21).

3. There is a neglect of social relationships associated with modes of production and technological developments and an overemphasis on unequal exchange and circulation.

4. Mechanisms of exploitation are not clear, and conclusions about such matters appear ad hoc and arbitrary. The criticism of Chirot and Hall (1982) still applies:

> World-system theory's transposition of Marx to an international plane has been accompanied by an assertation that, on the whole, economically peripheralized people are being continuously immiserized. That is why a world

revolution against the "bourgeois" is expected. Wallerstein believes that capitalist economic growth is a zero-sum game. Countries that develop do so at the expense of others that lose. Since only a few grow, most decline. The widening gap in per capita GNP between rich and poor countries, then, is not an anomaly but a natural result of capitalist growth. Only socialism can change this. (P. 100)

5. There is an all too general (and relatively untheorized) treatment of cultural formations and institutions. In due course, there has been increasing attention to ideological and cultural factors—in contrast to WST's early development, which was largely "materialistic." The most recent formulation of WST, WST-II (Wallerstein 2004), concerns itself with the production and consumption of culture—for instance, knowledge production, science production, production of norms and cultural artifacts, policy processes, ethics and morality.

Actor-Oriented, Dynamic Systems Theories

Some of these theories are Buckley's (1967, 1998) modern systems theory; Archer's (1995) morphogenetic theory; Baumgartner, Burns, and DeVillé's theory of actor-system dynamics (ASD) (Baumgartner, Burns, and DeVillé 1986; Burns, Baumgartner, and DeVillé 1985); and Geyer and van der Zouwen's (1978) sociocybernetics. This family of theories, inspired to a great extent by Buckley, is nonfunctionalist. Complex, dynamic social systems are analyzed in terms of stabilizing and destabilizing mechanisms. The structural and cultural properties of society are carried by, transmitted, and reformed through individual and collective actions and interactions. Structures such as institutions and cultural formations are temporally prior and relatively autonomous yet possessing causal powers, constraining and enabling people's social actions and interactions. Agents through their interactions generate structural reproduction, elaboration, and transformation. So one is concerned not only with the identification and development of social structures but also with the specification of the concrete mechanisms—including feedback processes that entail both stabilizing, equilibrating features (morphostasis) and structure-elaborating or disorganizing and transforming features (morphogenesis). In such terms, institutional structures help to create and re-create themselves in an ongoing developmental process in which human agents in the context of sociocultural systems play constructive as well as transformative/destructive roles. Such an approach enables one to identify and analyze the complex mechanisms of stable reproduction as well as of the transformation of structures and the genesis of new forms (morphostasis vs. morphogenesis). Active agents with their distinctive characteristics, motivations, and powers interact and contribute to the reproduction and transformation of structure: establishing and reforming structures such as institutions, sociotechnical systems, and physical and ecological structures, but always within given constraints and opportunities and not in

precisely the ways the agents intend. Internal selection and structuring processes that reproduce, modify, or transform are based on power distributions among societal agents and populations of organizations as well as individuals. These theories (especially in the work of Archer and ASD) theorize institutions and sociocultural formations in their own right, identifying and explaining the real and variegated structures that have emerged historically and are elaborated and developed in ongoing social processes. ASD has drawn, in particular, on Weber and Marx (DeVillé was personally acquainted with the Marxist Ernest Mandel in Belgium) but redefining key concepts in modern sociological terms (e.g., through institutional and cultural theorizing): concepts such as class, power, domination, exploitation, conflict and struggle, and unequal exchange and accumulation. Conceptual models of production, reproduction, and transformation as well as revolution have been elaborated. A part of the theoretical work has extended Marxist theory through theorizing about social agents (individuals and collective), institutions, and culture and their role in processes of reproduction and transformation. Some of the characteristic features of ASD are as follows:

1. In addition to consideration of capital and capital accumulation (as one of the driving forces of the system), ASD pays particular attention to the accumulation of knowledge, skills, techniques, and technology (including organizational and managerial knowledge, techniques, and skills)—in a word, *multiple processes of accumulation* (Baumgartner 1978). There is also infrastructural accumulation as well as natural resource accumulation (and destruction). There is typically loss and destruction of key resources as well. And there is unequal access to and control over the resources or "wealth" of these accumulation processes, reflecting the power relations of modern society.

2. Because capitalism is characterized by market failures and unexpected destabilization, systematic regulation and stabilization strategies are essential for the stability of modern capitalism (see later). There has been sustained development of more or less effective regulatory mechanisms and the partial stabilization of capitalist systems in developed parts of the world (classical Marxism exaggerated the power of capitalists to impose conditions on the nation-state benefiting them).

3. Everyday, "nonrevolutionary" democratic politics has played a major role in the emergence of welfare and economic regulatory regimes and contributed to the "refutation" of the Marxian prediction of the demise of capitalism (or possibly, simply the postponement of its demise). The logic of democratic politics is often noneconomic in character, connected, for instance, with gaining and maintaining the loyalty of citizens, not only to ensure system functioning but also to predispose them to pay taxes, obey laws, and be prepared to make other sacrifices such as

fighting in wars. In general, ASD emphasizes the complex, ironic nature of democratic politics (Burns and Kamali 2003). It has also identified a "new politics" (Burns 1999), in which nongovernmental organizations (NGOs) and experts play key roles, which establishes new forms of regulation based on enterprise concern about reputation and goodwill (e.g., inducing the adoption of business ethical codes, ethical audits, and related internal regulatory arrangements). These processes take place also on the global level (see later).

4. Substantial attention has been paid to the politics and formation and re-formation of international economic institutions and development: on one level, the economic relationships between countries, on another level, that of international economic institutions dealing with markets, trade, banking, and technological development (Baumgartner, Burns, and DeVillé 1975, 1986). There is also a long history of countries using political and military power to gain favorable trade conditions (England was a master at this in relation to countries such as Portugal, Egypt, India, and Kenya [under colonial rule], as well as other countries). ASD also examined the morphogenesis of international frameworks of trade, banking, setting of standards, institution building, and reform.

SUMMING UP

The convergent tendencies among the three approaches—particularly in incorporating and developing contemporary institutional and cultural analysis—are an important part of their further development.[4] Of course, one might ask, why not simply concentrate on developing institutional and cultural theories and abandon dynamic systems theorizing as such? The immediate answer is that structures and structural mechanisms are *more* than institutional and cultural processes. In particular, the interplay of physical structures, sociocultural and institutional systems, and interaction orders cannot be properly conceptualized, described, and analyzed on the basis of purely institutional and cultural theorizing. Emergent as well as purely technical and "natural" system linkages must be accounted for and analyzed for theoretical as well as practical reasons.

For instance, among the major subtypes of interstructural problems are incompatibilities between structures of the social system, on the one hand, and structures in the environment, on the other—that is, a particular type of interstructural problem (see later). Social system structures and outputs/performances may not fit and be sustainable in the system's environment (as in the Easter Island phenomenon, where the indigenous population developed institutional arrangements and practices that could not be sustained in the Easter Island physical environment; this led to an ecological and eventually social order collapse and the disappearance of most of the population). In general, complex feedback loops between societal orders

and their environments generate under certain conditions forms of destabilizing and nonsustainable developments. Histories of the salination (and declining production) of agricultural land, desertification, deforestation, ozone depletion, and global warming, among other negative developments, point to the role of human communities in the destruction of their natural resource bases. This is part of the materiality of socioeconomic life, with which these theories of capitalism have been concerned.

As explained more fully later, the often-exaggerated critique of system theorizing in sociology has been unfortunate, since these theories have much to contribute to sociology and other social sciences not only on a purely theoretical level but also on the empirical level of describing and analyzing the complexity and dynamics of capitalist systems, including contemporary global capitalism.

CAPITALIST SYSTEMS: TOWARD A NEW SYNTHESIS

Capitalism is triumphant in most parts of the world. The theories discussed in this chapter have addressed the complexity and dynamics of capitalism, predicting the long-term demise of classical capitalism, but for substantially different reasons. This section outlines a synthesis based on the contributions of the three approaches. It examines selected aspects of the functioning (and malfunctioning) of capitalist systems, their conditions for sustained growth and expansion, their persistent tendencies to instability and crisis, and the mechanisms that produce and reproduce economic inequalities and power within and among capitalist societies.

Systematic investigations of capitalism show that a complex of core institutions and cultural formations make up its structural and normative order. This order incites and legitimizes, among other things, acquisitiveness (greed), competition, accumulation of wealth and economic power, and substantial social inequality. Property rights enable, for instance, appropriation of gains and legitimize accumulation; they also reinforce incentives to pursue such gains and to use economic power and wealth (as well as other powers) to make further gains and to defend as well as develop capitalist institutions.

Capitalism is a powerful system not only for producing and distributing goods and services, wealth, and innovations in products and means of production but also for producing a spectrum of negative consequences: inequalities, exploitation, damages to third parties, social and psychological disruptions, depletions of natural resources, and environmental destruction, among others. Powerful agents (including capitalists and their managers) react to some of the consequences, judging them to be negative and trying in some instances to correct them or to limit their impact. Such countervailing actions—affecting the functioning and development of capitalism—become much more elaborate and vigorous in the context of democratic politics. A far greater range of agents can and do make demands for reform and regulation of capitalism. As a result, under conditions of democracy, there is a substantial *politics of capitalism* and capitalist developments. A variety of proposals for reform are introduced, and a spectrum of regulating systems is established and elaborated. In this way, some (but, of course, not all) of the negative consequences of capitalism, including class and other conflicts, are addressed (although not usually fully corrected). Because capitalist institutional arrangements and their core processes along with countervailing movements and systems of regulation are socially embedded, there emerge *multiple capitalisms* differentiated by their diverse forms of functioning, regulation, performance, and dynamics. Such a sociological conception of capitalism is spelled out in the following sections.

Defining Cultural and Structural Properties

Modern capitalism is a powerful engine of change, generating revolutionary powers and transforming the conditions of life: economic, technological, social, and environmental. Dynamic capitalism is characterized not only by its freedoms (or minimalist constraints) and its acquisitive spirit (the pursuit of economic interests and gains) but also by its capacity to accommodate and symbiosize with diverse interests and values, the opportunities it provides for "positive-sum games," its effective forms of power and control, and its competitive mechanisms. A brief description of these characteristics is given below.

1. *Multiple freedoms:* There is not only the decentralized freedom to trade and to initiate new products and forms of production or to commodify new goods and services and to penetrate new areas and establish markets but also the freedom to create and adapt new forms of extended cooperation and organization (e.g., joint stock company, joint ventures, and franchises) and the freedom to compete (which is otherwise highly constrained in many groups and communities). Also, under capitalism the constraints on the accumulation of wealth and power are minimalized, hence the substantial tendencies to monopoly or oligopoly in many areas of production and distribution.

2. *The acquisitive spirit and more:* Substantial numbers of societal agents (individuals as well as collectives) are motivated and possess the resources to invest in new opportunities and projects, hoping to realize profits and to multiply their wealth (a form of generalized power). Capitalist institutional arrangements provide opportunities to pursue multiple interests that far exceed the mere interest to pursue wealth—for instance, the interest in sociability and cooperation with others (or in competition with others); in exercising power and control over others; in

doing something useful, such as producing a valuable good or service or creating a new good or service; in trying out an idea or starting a project with others; in providing jobs and opportunities for others; or in generating wealth for good causes. That is, *capitalist forms can accommodate an extraordinary range of material and ideal interests.* And, indeed, the wealth generated by capitalism may support many values necessary or important to human existence, including family and community life, welfare, education, music, art, religious institutions, and spirituality. Nonetheless, the strongest value—which is built into its institutions, for instance, its accounting systems (see Note 14)—is money value; its power and control mechanisms are mainly directed at gaining and expanding monetary wealth and accumulation. But as emphasized below, there are other countervailing forces, concerns, and movements.

3. *Complex institutional arrangements:* Modern capitalism consists of a *complex of core social institutions* for organizing production, exchange, and distribution. In particular, there are relatively *free markets* for raw materials such as land and energy, goods and services, capital, and labor. *Property rights and contracts* provide a systematic basis for knowing who owns what and who are creditors and debtors. They distinguish groups and populations in society in terms of differential control over economic resources and the means of production.[5] *Money* has multiple functions—as a medium of exchange, as a standard or measure of value, and as the basis for initiating economic projects and enterprises and expanding productive capacity and economic power, that is, capital.[6] *Firms operate as decentralized systems of institutionalized domination* over human and material resources,[7] innovating, producing, distributing, and exchanging in the pursuit of profit and economic power ("the acquisitive principle"). Their bureaucratic and other forms of control are based largely on private property rights,[8] which enable differential access to and control over resources. Superordinates (owners/managers) not only command their employees but also have the power to establish and reform relevant rules of action, to judge and to sanction, and to allocate resources.[9] *Systems are developed to mobilize and apply in a systematic way expert knowledge*—scientific, technical, and practical knowledge as well as the organizational capability to produce and distribute. A type of essential knowledge system is *accounting* (the basis of strict calculation in economic rationalization), which focus on and quantify the essentials of costs, prices, and profits and enable calculability and the rational pursuit of profit and economic power.

4. *Power and control:* Capitalism through enterprises, contracts, franchises, and other legal forms provides a high degree of control and regulatory potential. Substantial power can be exercised over human beings and resources in organizing and directing production. Knowledge and expertise can be mobilized to innovate in creating new technologies, techniques, and forms of cooperation and

organization. The wealth generated by capitalist endeavors (as well as the knowledge and organizational capacities) is of interest to states and can be used to influence policy and politics as well as other domains of society (Baumgartner, Burns, and DeVille 1979). Through its generation of wealth and its freedom to innovate in technologies, techniques, and strategies, capitalism is capable of not only dramatically changing societal conditions but also circumventing or breaking out of many of the constraints imposed by regulative regimes such as those established by the national state (see later discussion). It is not only based on but also generates unequal power structures.

5. *Institutionalized competition:* Competition, in which particular actors struggle more or less openly for power, is one of the major mechanisms driving social innovation and change in capitalist systems—but not, of course, according to a program, plan, or design. Weber (1951) generally stressed the importance of such "competitive processes" in social change, under conditions where there is no clear-cut domination structure. Thus, Europe as a system of interconnected states in competition with one another operated to drive the transformative process of rationalization. There was no unified empire, as, for example, in China. Weber (1951) argued, "Just as competition for markets compelled the rationalization of private enterprise, so competition for political power compelled the rationalization of state economy and economic policy in the Occident and in the China of the Warring States" (p. 61). According to Weber (1951:61), during the periods of the "Warring States," "the very stratum of state prebendaries (or local honoratiores) who blocked administrative rationalization in the Empire became its most powerful promoters and change agents. In the private economy, cartellization weakens rational calculation, which is the soul of capitalism; among states, power monopoly prostrates rational management in administration, finance, and economic policy". Weber suggested that in the Orient, it took military or religious revolutions to bring about transformations: to shatter the firm structure of *prebendary interests,* thus creating completely new power distributions and, in turn, new economic conditions. Rationalization concerned not only administration but also taxation and budgeting, as well as military and diplomatic areas. Attempts at internal innovation in China through reforms were wrecked time and time again by the opposition of officialdom. In sum, *lack of competition tends to inhibit or restrain innovation and transformative processes.*

Competitive processes may be constrained to varying degrees. Some social orders have elaborate institutionalized systems for regulating competition and resolving conflicts. Others have few such arrangements; or the arrangements collapse under the pressures of crisis or transformative conditions, when key actors or groups no longer adhere to or accept the arrangements.

Core Mechanisms and the Logic of Capitalist Functioning

Of interest for our purposes here are several of the core mechanisms underlying the functioning and dynamics of capitalism. A brief description of these is given below:

1. *The complex of capitalist institutions* organizes the processes of socioeconomic production, distribution, and exchange in particular ways, generating multiple socioeconomic outcomes and developments. The latter include not only diverse effects in the sphere of economic production and market exchange ("spin-offs") but also unintended and unpredictable effects ("spillovers") in other spheres, such as the social, environmental, and political. Thus, *capitalism is not a purely economic undertaking but political and cultural as well.* Some goods and services, profitability (or loss), capital accumulation (or its failure), knowledge, new techniques, class relations, interests, and political mobilization and struggle are not usually confined to one sphere or segment of society but spread their effects throughout society (and multiple societies).

The productive base of a modern, capitalist society rests on a *complex of powers* ("resources" or "wealths") and the accumulation of these powers: capital in the form of money—that is, generalized power to acquire or control resources and to motivate action; physical or material capital (in the form of machinery, buildings, land, other natural resources); human capital or "resources" (knowledge, value structures and commitments, skills, health); regulatory and governance structures; infrastructures (transport systems, including roads, railroads, waterways, air transport); communication systems (telephone, radio, television, and the World Wide Web [WWW]); natural resources (water, air, energy, minerals, and ecosystems). When considering accumulation as well as reproduction or sustainability, this complex of powers must be the focus of analysis, not just capital in the form of money wealth.

2. *Actors or classes of actors have different positions of power and control in the system* based on their roles in the division of labor and on their differential possession of property and other control rights. The different social positions have qualitatively and quantitatively different linkages to, and claims over, the gains of multiple outcomes and developments (spin-offs and spillovers); they also have differential linkages and disclaimers with respect to costs or burdens and risks. Historically, the owners and managers of capitalist enterprises have been in a position on average to maintain profitability in spite of legal and normative pressures to maintain wages above subsistence levels and to incorporate the costs of externalities (e.g., addressing environmental damages). This fact and the "general interest" of many economic as well as noneconomic elites in the viability and sustained development of capitalism(s) constrain the pressures and tendencies to internalize the costs of externalities and to alter the profitability equation. Still, there is a secular trend, as pointed

out earlier, to constrain and redirect capitalist functioning, especially in the context of democratic conditions (see later discussion).

3. *Class and center-periphery differentiations:* The capitalist institutional arrangements generate not only unequal acquisition but also sustained unequal accumulation of capabilities, resources, and social powers among different actors or classes of actors with their differentiated positions in relation to the processes and outcomes of production, distribution, and exchange. In general, the distribution of benefits and costs under capitalist institutional arrangements is unequal and tends to increase inequality over time. The more promising entrepreneurs, enterprises, sectors, expansive regions, and nations tend to gain access to and attract additional resources and investments; the stagnant, marginal agents and areas lose access to such resources. *In the absence of effective regulation, extreme concentrations of economic power and wealth are generated, because power attracts and begets economic as well as other power(s) (knowledge, skills, techniques, managerial and governance capabilities, political mobilization opportunities).*

The inequalities lead, in turn, to systematically differential capacities to take advantage of and shape productive opportunities as well as to avoid or overcome burdens and cost traps and vicious circles of stagnation and decline (see below). In general, power differences and uneven development capabilities tend to be reproduced and elaborated, other things being equal. A basic structure of inequality is maintained at the same time that there is some mobility of nations, sectors, enterprises, and groups upward as well as downward.

4. *Unanticipated and unintended consequences in a complex system:* ASD provided a systematic basis for identifying and explaining some of the unintended consequences of capitalism as a complex, dynamic system (such a notion was also articulated earlier in the work of Karl Marx, Friedrich Hayek, and Robert Merton, among others). Complex systems operate, in a certain sense, autonomously from human intentions and concrete actions—the effects produced cannot be inferred from the effects intended. Of particular interest are unintended consequences arising from hierarchies—a class of systemic properties—related to social power relations between individuals, groups, classes, and system parts—for example, domination relations between classes or between core sectors and peripheral sectors. Some unintended consequences lead to unexpected dynamic properties (e.g., when conflicts generated by power struggles lead to escalating conflicts); system functioning and development may be highly destabilizing and unpredictable—a situation that challenges the basic assumption of the "rational expectations" school in economics. ASD has contributed to making unintended consequences and related developments explicit, identifiable, and thus subject to analysis and the formulation of possible policy recommendations.

In sum, capitalism like any complex social system generates unanticipated and unintended spin-offs and spillovers, many of which cannot be known or predicted beforehand. This is due to bounded human knowledge or modeling capacity as well as limited regulatory capabilities with respect to such complex systems. Some unintended spin-offs and spillovers operate to destabilize or undermine capitalist effectiveness, institutional functioning, and legitimacy.

5. *Capitalist crises:* Historically, capitalist systems, in both their national and their international forms, have experienced a number of economic and political crises that destabilized them. Many diverse types of crises have occurred and continue to occur: Crises of overproduction—ameliorated to some extent by government fiscal and credit policies—is one type. Others are, for instance, deep socioeconomic depression or hyperinflation; powerful speculative runs on a currency; extreme exchange rate volatility; disruptive cycles of investment and disinvestment; shifts in market boundaries leading to local or regional depression; failure or inability of the state or the industry associations to protect or stabilize the conditions of key economic sectors; escalating capital-labor conflicts as well as other conflicts among industrial groups, between debtors and creditors, or between producers and consumers; major sociopolitical movements aimed at radically transforming capitalism or even eliminating it; other political crises due to ethnic, religious, or ideological conflicts that are difficult to address effectively within the existing political/administrative system; regulatory failures and crises in banking and finance; and government deficit growing in the context of rigidities (for instance, entitlements combined with political or socioeconomic power conditions that make it difficult for the state to increase taxes or government revenues).[10] Many of these developments in a capitalist system, if uncontrolled or unregulated, would severely disrupt its functioning and threaten its sustainability.

6. *Discontent and protest:* Actors or groups of actors adversely affected by the operation or development of capitalism may under conditions such as a functioning democracy articulate their deprivations and disadvantages, for example, with reference to norms and values about "rights," "distributive justice," "fairness," or even "efficiency and rationality." Some mobilize to try to reform the institutional setup or at least certain (for them) undesirable features of it. Such activities usually bring them into conflict with those having an interest in, or a commitment to, the established institutional arrangements. Beginning in the nineteenth century, labor movements challenged and struggled to transform and even to replace capitalism. This resulted in the politics of capitalism and led to substantial regulation and welfare developments in a number of countries ("taming the capitalist dragon") (Jaeger 1994). But there have been not only labor movements but also environmental, religious, and status groups mobilizing and

pressuring for change. The idea of constructing and reconstructing the system has become an established organizing principle. A great variety of movements and pressure groups operate on all levels in opposition to some capitalist developments.

The general pattern is that capitalist concentration of power, uneven development, and negative spin-offs and spillovers tend to evoke discontent and antisystemic movements—or the threat of such movements—to constrain or regulate the negative features of capitalist functioning and development. While labor and other social movements are prominent examples of such social pressure, it is worth recalling that the farmer, small business, and consumer groups have also played a prominent role—and in some instances continue to play an influential role—in the opposition to tendencies toward massive concentration of wealth and economic power in capitalist development. Although they do not challenge the principles of private property rights, they oppose excessive power concentration and systems of credit, distribution, and government policy making that appear to favor economic domination. This has been particularly the case in societies with well-established democratic norms and institutions, a strong labor movement, as well as other social movements concerned with the struggle of particular status groups (ethnic, religious, gender, elderly, professions).

Such reactions (or even their potential) have led in numerous instances to the establishment of institutional arrangements to regulate the concentration and functioning of capitalist power. Regulation in practice has to a greater or lesser extent (at least in Organization for Economic Cooperation and Development [OECD] countries) constrained some misuses and abuses of economic power and some of its immediate economic, social, and environmental impacts; typically, however, it has not blocked or prevented the uneven accumulation of economic wealth and power and the capacity of powerful capitalist agents to shape future developments in technology, production, and distribution. This pattern continues on the global level (see later).

7. *Regulatory development:* The history of modern capitalism is characterized by innovative attempts to create and develop state as well as private regulatory mechanisms designed to counteract or overcome its failures and instabilities (some attempts were also aimed at replacing capitalism with another system, such as socialism or communism). In dealing with crises, many capitalist societies have shown a remarkable capacity to promote policy strategies and to design regulatory processes operating to reduce negative impacts and to maintain or reinforce capitalism's stability and legitimacy. Public regulatory institutions and policies were established in as early as the 1800s to limit capitalist instability and substantial concentration and abuse of a economic power in the hands of relatively few. The imposition of public constraints is the result in some cases of enlightened self-interest and in other cases, the result of political movements and pressures. The constraints

are observable in the form of financial and monetary controls, antitrust laws, labor legislation, land use regulation, regional development policies, pollution controls, and other environmental and social restrictions; these often entail substantial sanctions, including fines and prison sentences. Such measures have been designed, at least in part, to prevent or reduce the excessive negative consequences of capitalist functioning and development, in particular the extremes of inequality, the abuse and misuse of economic power, intense social conflicts, socioeconomic instability, and environmental destruction. In general, governments of most advanced countries (e.g., OECD countries) have more or less successfully regulated several (of course, not all) of the negative impacts of capitalist functioning. Elaborate regulatory frameworks are to a large extent state organized or sanctioned but with substantial private interest involvement.

This regulatory conception of capitalist development applies also to addressing social conflict. Class tensions and struggles as well as other conflicts (among producers, between producers and consumers, between creditor and debtor interests) are a persistent fact, arising from the institutionalized differences in power, the conflicting interests and commitments, and the uneven development of socioeconomic capabilities. For instance, enterprise power relations translate into major decisions of owners/managers with respect to, for instance, transforming or closing a workplace, determining the type and level of production and employment, introducing particular forms of technology and work organization, determining directly and indirectly the qualitative and quantitative aspects of the work environment, and allocating resources and profits. Workers (and their labor unions if they exist) may react in various ways to the subordination to capitalist power. Different forms of power struggle and conflict between owners/managers and workers over the conditions and terms of employment have been characteristic features of capitalist relations of production. These conflictive tendencies take a variety of forms and are not easily suppressed under democratic conditions. Attempts are also made to establish and maintain a reasonable level of cooperation and productivity (for instance, with minimum levels of strikes, slowdowns, and other forms of labor-capital unrest) in the face of inherent conflict. The lengthy and continuing formulation of factory and workplace acts and labor market legislation is well known. Parallel to this has been the establishment and sanctioning of various arrangements to facilitate communication, negotiation, and conflict settlements between capital and labor.

Modern societies are characterized by substantial differences in values and lifestyles, endowments, powers, and wealth. How is social agreement—and social equilibrium—achieved, if at all, under conditions of conflicting perspectives and interests? Barring systematic coercion, found in many peripheral economies, there are several established institutional arrangements (Baumgartner, Buckley, and Burns 1975; Burns and Roszkowska, forthcoming). Conciliation, mediation, and arbitration and their normative and institutional prerequisites have been outstanding mechanisms for reducing the intensity and violence of societal conflict, including class conflict. Welfare systems are another major institutional arrangement to ensure widespread support and legitimacy for capitalist arrangements, in part by providing economic security in the face of capitalism's tendency to generate insecurity. Where these routines of relationship are established, group conflict loses its sting and becomes an institutionalized pattern of social life (Dahrendorf 1959:20). But class conflict is not the only source of tension and potential destabilization of modern capitalism. Concerns with the environment, animal rights (e.g., the use of animals in testing of products), disruption of communities, impact on marginal or weak groups, and impact on poor regions of the world are other major areas of contention.

Effective regulation depends on the development of models for describing and assessing the state of the system, identifying problematic developments, choosing appropriate solutions, and evaluating the success of selected strategies (Burns and Carson 2005). One particular class of models essential to capitalism are accounting systems—that is, coherent sets of numerical data collected, organized, and used in the assessment and regulation of socioeconomic systems such as business firms, government agencies, and nations. This is a major aspect of *systematic self-reflectivity*. Accounting systems provide "limited" or *bounded* representations and reflectivity of socioeconomic systems such as business enterprises, government agencies, and nation-states. There are always "uncharted territories." This is currently the case for values related to issues such as biodiversity, aesthetic aspects of landscape, tranquility, leisure (in the sense of free time) or their opposites. Historically, one can observe a dialectic relationship between the use of established accounting models, the emergence of new problems and issues, critical self-reflection and innovation, and the construction of new accounting approaches. One strand of this dialectic has been to construct new accounting approaches for increasingly more encompassing levels (Burns et al. 2002).

But, in general, regulatory mechanisms never encompass the entire social system; invariably, there will be gaps and unanticipated developments (Burns and DeVillé 2003; see also Note 14). Not only can potential *external* factors (natural forces, "unexpected" disasters) disrupt capitalist system functioning and reproduction, but also *internal* (endogenous) factors and processes can generate systemic changes. Indeed, regulatory mechanisms themselves are often transformative in character—they change perceptions, modify practices, evoke new strategies, create new power relations, and so on. Most important, policies ultimately redistribute material power (wealth) as well as symbolic power among social actors with conflicting interests; they may contribute to the emergence of new value orientations, models, or strategies so that the overall stability of the system is undermined or threatened, contrary to intentions.[11]

In sum, regulatory institutional arrangements address a variety of capitalist failures and instabilities, resolve or prevent major conflicts, and overcome substantial loss of confidence in, or opposition to, the capitalist system. A minimum level of acceptance, if not satisfaction (reinforced by ideology) with capitalism, has been accomplished in most OECD countries. Conditions of the laboring classes and the general population have improved on the national level in these countries as well as in some LDCs. On the other hand, in many LDCs (with relatively resource-poor, corrupt, and/or authoritarian regimes that ignore or neglect the diverse problems and externalities produced by capitalist functioning), capitalist agents are not subject to the same degree of regulation as in OECD countries.

8. *Socioeconomic diversity and multiple capitalisms:* The notion of a single, almost homogeneous global economy is a myth. The world economy is dominated by the triad of Europe, Japan, and the United States. Moreover, the capacities to exploit opportunities for gains and avoid burdens and losses are very unequally distributed. Given the substantial variation in institutional and cultural conditions, it is not surprising that a variety of different, but more or less effective and expansive, capitalist arrangements have been developed; there are also a variety of failed capitalisms. A corollary to this is that nations differ in their capacity and readiness to effectively regulate and stabilize capitalist functioning and development, explaining in part some of the differences in capitalist performance, for example, between DCs and LDCs, and also the variations within each of these categories (see later).

Thus, capitalism has taken significantly different forms in countries and regions such as Argentina, Austria, Brazil, Canada, Chile, England, France, Germany, Italy, Japan, South Korea, Russia, Sweden, Taiwan, and the United States. This variation is captured by the notion of the social embeddedness or contextualization of economic processes (Baugartner et al. 1986; Granovetter 1985; Hollingsworth and Boyer 1997). Production complexes and processes of capital accumulation tend to vary substantially: Socioeconomic accumulation is associated in some cases with the development of innovative production systems—for instance, through investment in R&D (research and development)—and the realization of new knowledge and techniques for improving production processes and products; in other instances, it is associated with petroleum extraction, as in the case of oil-rich countries like Saudi Arabia and Kuwait; and in still other instances, with international banking and finance (Switzerland, Luxembourg). Similarly, sources of disruption or blockage of production, market processes, and capital accumulation may differ substantially: in one case, civil war; in another case, runaway inflation; in yet another, a dictator overtaxing and constraining entrepreneurial activity; or various combinations of these (see later discussions).

A theory of multiple capitalisms derives from and compels attention to *the sociocultural and political contexts of capitalist processes and evolution.* Not only does such a conceptualization help us better understand the different development patterns of some DCs and LDCs, including those LDCs that manage some upward mobility (see below), but it also helps one to identify and understand some of the emerging differences between two obvious central "complexes," the European Union (EU), on the one hand, and the United States, on the other. The emerging conception of a "social capitalism" in the EU is differentiated from the more "unfettered capitalism" in the United States, suggesting the different sociocultural and political contexts of capitalist development in the two areas: differences in the conception of regulation (more acceptable and expected in Europe, less so in the United States); welfare considered as central to modern society and as more or less compatible with capitalist development (the EU) versus welfare as a burden, possibly a necessary one but a constraint on effective capitalist expansion (the United States); the environment to be protected even at the expense of burdening capitalism (the EU) versus the notion of minimizing costs of environmental protection (the United States); technology development approached with caution in the EU versus more optimism and risk taking in the United States. There is often less difference in practice than is expressed in the rhetoric of public statements and postures.

9. *Complexity, contradictions, and multiple sources of crisis:* As a complex, dynamic system, capitalism is only partially understood, even with the most elaborate scientific models and modeling efforts and accomplishments. Two general classes of problem situations can make for instability and malperformance and lead potentially to systemic crisis (Burns and Carson 2005). The following is inspired in part by the work of Lockwood (1964) and Archer (1995).[12]

- Systemic imbalances (overproduction or insufficient demand, excessive money or credit expansion); instability (price or demand volatility, speculative fevers); malfunctioning processes and subsystems (regulatory failures, blockage or collapse of key transport and communication systems); vicious or destructive feedback processes
- Social problems, intergroup conflicts and struggle, or disruptive opposition, especially under conditions where the instruments of conflict regulation and settlement are weak or inappropriate

Typically, problem situations become crises if they substantially and persistently disrupt the core processes essential for capitalist order: production and market activities, profit making, capital accumulation, and maintenance and reproduction of key institutions.

A common thread in the approach of dynamic systems theories has been the conceptualization and analysis of interstructural relations and the instabilities and problems to which they give rise. Multiple, incompatible structures

cause performance failures, instability, and disorder at the same time that they are associated with social conflict and struggle between societal groups and classes. Several major areas of crisis relating to systemic and interstructural problem situations can be identified.

10. *Disorder from systemic lags:* One may speak of institutional lag between established institutions, on the one hand, and new relations of development, on the other hand. The emergent "forces" clash with institutional constraints. There are contradictions between established structures and emergent structures (such as new technologies and strategies, new forms of competition). For instance, knowledge and technical or technological developments lead to conditions exposing the limitations of existing institutions and regulatory machinery. There are costly negative developments or clashes with ideals or strong moral principles. Thus, in the area of contemporary information technologies, established legal regimes concerning intellectual property rights have proven inadequate, setting the stage for reform initiatives. Institutional incentives perversely block creative, fruitful developments or allow for extreme forms of unacceptable deviance. In the latter case, for instance, the introduction and development of the WWW resulted in many fruitful and important accomplishments but also enabled its exploitation for commercial pornography, racial music markets, and extremist political and racist homepages, among other problems. And such developments led to demands for increased and new regulation,

11. *Multisegment disorder* (e.g., contradictions between capitalist and democratic values and institutional arrangements): Through its unintended impact on other spheres of social life, capitalism generates disorder and dissatisfaction, which provoke movements of opposition and nonacceptance. That is, agents in its social and political context may turn against it. This is due to its many impacts, including negative ones on populations, communities, and the environment; it is systematically destabilizing and destructive. Hence, the importance of some form of monitoring and opportunities to voice and to point out problems and express discontent: a relatively free press, scientific professions, and public participation. Systemic counterparts to capitalist arrangements—such as democratic political structures in one form or another—are also essential to its effectiveness and sustainability.

But as indicated earlier, democracy itself is destabilizing for capitalism, especially when the consequences of capitalist expansion, technological development, and capitalist accumulation are not immediately clear, so that reactions may follow long after, when problem situations have reached a crisis state, and major demands and conflicts ensue. It is also important to bear in mind that the egalitarianism of democracy clashes with capitalism's exclusiveness and concentration of wealth and the power to decide future developments.

12. *Integrative disorder:* There is a lack of social integration (sufficient organization, social cohesion, or solidarity) as a basis to regulate, stabilize, or solve critical problems associated with the complex systemic interdependencies of capitalism. The problem of the relationship between system interdependencies and social fragmentation is particularly acute at the global level today (although there are currently movements and institutional developments that point toward partial solutions, as discussed later). This can be understood as the lack of global governance and the fragmentation of states making up the context of global capitalism. Some (Burns and DeVillé 2003, DeVillé and Burns 2004; Martinelli 2005) see emerging norms, community formations, international government organizations, and NGOs developing a regulatory context (but one that is highly uneven and incomplete). But the problem of growing "system interconnectedness" typically develops faster than the establishment of forms of cultural and political integration for purposes of constraining and regulating global capitalism. Where future developments will lead remains, in the final analysis, to be seen.[13]

A related problem is that of disorder from *improper or perverse social integration* with respect to system interdependencies (instead of a lack altogether of social integration for problem solving and regulation). Regulatory models and institutions are inappropriate and ineffective (possibly counterproductive), although they may have been appropriate and effective in the past. Regulatory regimes, which provided solutions earlier, often become problems and destabilizing factors in themselves. Regulatory institutions and policies ostensibly designed to limit or overcome particular destabilizing conditions of capitalism produce instead unintended consequences. This reflects incompatibilities between the regulatory system and capitalist development, arising from the fact that the regulatory system is designed to deal with relationships and processes of an *earlier, somewhat different capitalist system.* Invariably, the regulatory system is itself transformed.

The fact that regulatory apparatuses have never completely succeeded in preventing or controlling system instability and group conflict in capitalist societies is demonstrated by the occurrence of strikes, demonstrations, absenteeism, and complaints and symptoms of stress and "burnout" even in highly developed welfare societies such as those of the EU and North America (or, more generally, OECD countries). New types of problems and demands continue to emerge—for instance, problems regarding the quality of the work environment, participatory demands, and ecological considerations.

In general, the regulatory processes, while stabilizing the system temporarily to a greater or lesser extent, may create conditions for the emergence of new institutional problems and social conflicts and set the stage for intensified instability. For instance, in the area of money, what were conceived of as stabilizing measures—a single national currency and a central bank in the United States in the nineteenth century—themselves became new destabilizing factors, as when the Federal Reserve System (the central bank of the United States) contributed through its policies and regulatory arrangements to deepening and prolonging the Great Depression of 1929 and its aftermath (Burns and DeVillé 2003).

13. *Reflexive disorder:* A fundamental contradiction in the capitalist system is the requirement of order and predictability in a system that produces disorder and unpredictability. This is a robust contradiction, as we argue briefly below. Capitalist owners/managers as well as regulators require stability and predictability to make decisions and govern their production activities in rational terms. At the same time, capitalist agents, regulators, and other groups generate instability and unpredictability through innovations in strategies, techniques, and technologies. They are driven to do this particularly under conditions of competition and conflict. Capitalist agents in competition with one another—or anticipating future competition—innovate. They bring about changes in products, production processes, and distribution. Some of these changes have unintended consequences.

Also, democratic conditions themselves enable opposition to capitalist development (or certain aspects of it) and potential destabilization of capitalist functioning and development. Competitors, societal groups, and state agents respond to some of the many externalities generated intentionally and unintentionally in the context of capitalist functioning (including the expansion of existing projects and the launching of new ones). In general, the multiple responses are typically uncoordinated. For instance, NGOs may demonstrate against and, in other ways, draw media attention to diverse capitalist externalities. Or a government—anticipating the demands of citizen groups or responding to pressures from such groups affected negatively by past, current, or anticipated capitalist development—may introduce new policies, instruments, and strategies of regulation. Even when there are attempts to avoid disruptions, changes in regulations have unintended, quite often disruptive, consequences in a complex system.

In sum, capitalist agents as well as regulators require stability and predictability to make rational decisions and govern their production activities at the same time that they and others (including the opponents to capitalism) generate instability, unpredictability, and disorder through their very actions and interactions. This systemic contradiction makes for unending crises.

The Future of Globalizing Capitalism

The failure of Marx's prediction of the collapse of capitalism as a result of declining profits and the failure to sustain capital accumulation can be understood in terms of the robustness of the system, given proper regulatory conditions. This robustness was particularly characteristic of those systems where capitalism was apparently most ripe for revolution, namely, the advanced capitalist societies. One explanation of Marx's failure (if we assume that there might be some truth in his claim) to predict correctly has been offered by WST—namely, the exploitation of peripheral producers by those in the center, enabling center countries to sustain high levels of profitability and capital accumulation. Another explanation (which does not exclude the first) is that the successful establishment and elaboration of regulatory regimes in most OECD countries and some LDCs have stabilized capitalist functioning to a greater or lesser extent and at the same time have mediated class and other conflicts. The package of regulatory measures ensured capital as well as other key accumulation and development processes.

The regulatory complex as well as substantial reallocation of resources can limit or correct the development of extreme inequality and uneven development capabilities among regions, sectors, and occupational groups. Part of the corrective adjustment has been the development of modern welfare state societies in the West. *Unfortunately, such regulation is almost totally lacking at the international level.* Nor do such regulative regimes exist in most Third World countries to the same extent as in DCs (such as the OECD countries). Many of the earlier problems of capitalist system instability and sociopolitical confrontation have reappeared in new forms. For instance, there has emerged a new global politics of capitalism, as illustrated in protests since around 2000 against the World Trade Organization in Seattle, Washington; the G8 meetings in Prague, the Czech Republic, and Genoa, Italy; the World Economic Forum meeting in Davos, Switzerland; as well as the EU meetings in Nice, France, and Gothenburg, Sweden. Such protests are directed to some extent against global capitalist institutional arrangements and practices; they generate uncertainties and the risk of disruption of, and constraint on, capital accumulation and development. This sets the stage for a growing global politics of capitalism and the articulation of demands for increased regulation and even major restructuration of its arrangements.

In any analysis of *globalization* as a major elaboration and restructuring of, among other things, capitalist arrangements, it is essential to differentiate between an elaboration of older patterns and the emergence of entirely new patterns, mentalities, and strategies. Globalization is scarcely a new phenomenon if by globalization is meant the systematic and rapid increase in trade or even in foreign direct investment. Some forms of globalization date far back, which WST deserves much credit for highlighting. Others are more recent—for instance, the highly developed globalization prior to World War I as a result of the development of railroads and steamships. What is largely new today are the transnational and oligopolistic arrangements in a wide spectrum of markets. Also important is the overall predominance of financial regulation of productive activities. The latter pattern results, in part, from the increased liberalization of capital flows and the speculative dynamics that characterize much of this flow. These two fundamental processes have contributed to a declining effectiveness of national policies and regulation and imply, according to some, the "end of economic or capitalist politics." One would advise caution against such simple causality. While the world system has given capitalist agents opportunities to avoid national state regulation (which has been emphasized by WST), one can observe the emergence of several limited forms of international regulation (International Monetary Fund, WTO, standards organizations) and NGOs as effective pressure groups.

In other words, there is indeed an obvious question about the relevance and role of national democracy and state institutions as an effective vector for regulation and development of capitalism. Nevertheless, one finds new forms of collective organizations (e.g., many NGOs) that push for new policies and new forms of social organization. The "antiglobalization" movement will probably discover itself as not so much against globalization as against the hegemonic nature of capitalism as a system of social organization and power. Certainly, contemporary politics is no longer the usual "democratic representative processes" within a state framework (and its constitution) (Burns 1999). Politics has become a multitude of diversified, often decentralized modes of social organization and social action at local as well as more global levels, dealing with the *praxis* of social (including, of course, economic) life and attempting to invent alternative structures and strategies. To what extent there will emerge from the multiple experiments a coherent, more macrosocial model for capitalism remains to be seen. But there is no doubt that such evolution has already become sufficiently pronounced that it will sooner or later have major macrosocial and economic consequences.

In those national contexts with a well-functioning democracy, constraints have in the past been imposed on capitalist development (and forms of exploitation). Such a process may or may not emerge on the global level. But it is unlikely in the foreseeable future that regulation will be accomplished by a world state (a successor, e.g., to the United Nations); rather, one would expect intermediation through associations and networks of diverse actors: corporate interests and NGOs as stakeholders characterized by issue and situation specificity. Moreover, the ultimate constraints on capitalist development are arguably material limitations: pollution, resource depletion, and climate change, among others. In some cases, one or more key factors in the productive base are declining or threatened with substantial decline in the foreseeable future. Long-term sustainability will not be possible. Historically, such nonsustainability has occurred but was limited in scope— that is, more local in character. Currently, there are more encompassing erosions but also more attention, greater mobilization, and sustained pressures to bring about reform and restructuring. More recently, new pressures and conflicts are driving innovations and efficiencies in areas neglected by earlier capitalists and their managers, who largely concerned themselves with labor-saving and labor-controlling innovations. Now more attention is being given to innovations in energy use, pollution control, renewal of resources, recycling, hydrocarbon fuel replacement, and resource use generally. Whether this development is sufficient to realize the long-term sustainability of capitalist systems remains highly uncertain.

CONCLUDING REMARKS

The discussion in this chapter draws attention to several of the instabilities of capitalism—both as an economic system per se and as a force generating sociopolitical instability and environmental deterioration. It argues that appropriate regulation is essential for stabilizing capitalist systems and facilitating their effective functioning. The effective regulation and functioning of capitalism require not only appropriate institutional arrangements but also social agents who have the competence and motivation to lead and realize in practice the institutional arrangements under varying circumstances and to effectively adapt and reform them in response to operational failures and environmental changes. Such regulation also depends on political authority to introduce and implement regulative frameworks.[14]

Modern societies have developed and continue to develop revolutionary powers—driven to a great extent by dynamic capitalism—at the same time that they have bounded knowledge of these powers and their consequences. Unintended consequences abound: Social as well as ecological systems are disturbed, stressed, and transformed. But new social agents and movements form and react to these conditions, developing new strategies and critical models and providing fresh challenges and opportunities for institutional innovation and transformation. Consequently, modern capitalist societies—characterized by their core arrangements as well as the many and diverse opponents to some or many aspects of capitalist development—are involved not only in a global struggle but also in a largely uncontrolled experiment (or, more precisely, a multitude of experiments). The capacity to monitor and assess such experimentation remains strictly bounded (see "Core Mechanisms," para. 7). The current capacity to constrain and regulate global capitalism is also severely

limited, as pointed out earlier. How, then, is the powerful class of global capitalists to be made responsible and accountable for their actions? What political forms and procedures might link the new politics suggested above to the global capitalist economy? These are important research and policy questions. Theories that investigate and analyze capitalism and its evolution in more holistic ways—such as the theories presented in this chapter—have an important role to play in explaining capitalist dynamics and in developing suitable policies.

The dynamic systems theories outlined in this chapter clearly point to sociologically important phenomena: the material conditions of social life, social class, stratification, the conditions that affect group mobilization and political power, conflict processes, and the reproduction and transformation of capitalist systems. They have also incorporated a number of key concepts of mainstream sociology in constructive and useful ways: for instance, institutional, cultural, and normative conceptualizations; networks and movements; diverse types of social relationships and roles; social systems in relation to one another and to the natural environment; reproductive and transformative loops; and sustainability issues.[15] These approaches shift the focus from single-factor explanations of capitalist dynamics and development patterns to structural and interstructural considerations in the spirit of Max Weber (1976, 1981) (for another multifactor approach to the analysis of capitalism, see Hollingsworth and Boyer 1997).

The theories presented here perform an important function within sociology and among the social sciences and humanities: They contribute to a common language, conceptualization, and theoretical integration in the face of extreme fragmentation among the social sciences as well as within sociology itself. The latter suffers especially as a result of the institutionalized concentration on midlevel empirical and theoretical research—that is, "middle-range theorizing." On a practical level, there remains the venerable challenge to establish and develop sociology and a social science complex that can readily and systematically put pieces of specialized knowledge together to address major contemporary problems, in particular, understanding and taming global capitalism.

VOLUME ONE NOTES

PART I: THE DISCIPLINE OF SOCIOLOGY

Chapter 2. The History of Sociology: The European Perspective

1. However, as parallel and further research showed, the problem of understandability, that is, controlling bi- and multivariate relationships by regularities of human conduct, remained an unsolved problem. For example, Le Play (1806–1882) tried, without much success, to break the limits of Quetelet's secondary statistics by creating suitable data for research problems. His method of building a "monography" forms a small *N* qualitative observation. His overconservative empiricism saw the family as the basic institution of society. Other early "qualitative" designs include the analysis of autobiographies (see Kern 1982:102ff.).

2. For an early discussion of this practical understanding of causality in Weber's methodological writings, see Goldenweiser (1938). Turner and Factor (1994) present a discussion on the legal origins of Weber's concept of causality. For the influence of Edmund Husserl's phenomenology on Weber, see Muse (1981).

PART II: INTERNATIONAL PERSPECTIVES

Chapter 5. Asian Sociology

1. For example, the first encyclopedia of sociology, published in 1944, contained the work of 72 Japanese scholars (Takemura 1999). On the development of sociology prior to World War II in English, see Kawamura (1994), Koyano (1976), Odaka (1950), and Tominaga (1993). Japanese sources include Kawamura (1973). Five sociological references have been published in Japan since 1944: Morioka, Shiobara, and Honma (1993), which includes 1,726 pages with 55 Japanese sociologists; Mita, Kurihara, and Tanaka (1988), which includes the work of 100 sociologists; Kitagawa (1984); Fukutake, Hidaka, and Takashi (1958), spanning 977 pages and including 53 Japanese scholars; and Shinmei (1944), including work by 72 Japanese sociologists.

2. For example, in 1947, there were 11 social science journals, of which 4 were published in English. In addition, Chinese and non-Chinese scholars conducted a number of community studies and published abroad (King 1978:38). Significant studies include Li Ching-han's study of village family life comparing his earlier and later studies in 1926 and 1956 and Fei Hsiao-tung's analysis of villages in the Yangtse Delta in 1936 and 1956 (King 1978:54).

3. The first Social Stratification and Social Mobility (SSM) research was carried out under the leadership of Kunio Odata of the University of Tokyo in collaboration with the International Sociological Association. The 1965 SSM was led by Saburo Yasuda of Tokyo Kyoiku University. The 1975 SSM was led by Kein'ichi Tominaga of the University of Tokyo. The 1985 SSM was led by Atsushi Naoi of Osaka University. The 1995 SSM was led by Kazuo Seiyama of the University of Tokyo.

4. The Center for the Study of Social Stratification and Inequality (CSSI) pursues development of new theories and methodologies on social stratification and inequality. It focuses on "new types of inequality" or new disparities in affluent societies in which basic equality has been realized and in which these inequalities have become urgent social problems. Social stratification research in Japan has developed many empirical studies, and the CSSI attempts to develop more theorizing ones. Another COE program is titled "Social Research for the Enhancement of Human Well-being." With a team of 19 researchers, it aims to build a center for international comparative research focusing on the distinctive cultural diversity of Japan and Asia.

5. After several attempts to create national data archives failed in the 1980s, some individual Japanese researchers made their electronic data available to academic circles, including public opinion surveys and a panel study on consumer attitudes. Two universities opened data archives in the early 1990s.

6. In fact, Japanese professors do not circulate their working papers for comments and criticisms as American counterparts do. Except for a few journals that are peer reviewed, Japanese academics publish their papers without much peer input and revision (S. Yazawa, personal communication, June 3, 2005).

Chapter 6. Sociology in Canada

1. This information on the early development of qualitative sociology in Canada is based in large part on the excellent research done on this topic by Fatima Camara and Richard Helmes-Hayes (2003) in an unpublished conference paper.

Chapter 7. European Sociology

1. For Germany, a detailed, complete, Internet-based data set of all German professors of sociology and their life courses exists (Hillmert 2002). However, as many Western countries went along a comparable pattern of educational expansion in the 1960s, there is good reason to believe that a similar situation applies to other European sociologies as well. Undoubtedly, there will be a generational break during the next 10 years, which may considerably change the way sociology is understood and practiced. As Hillmert shows, German professors undergo a long phase of professional qualification until they receive their first call for a chair. Average age at dissertation thesis is 31 years, at habilitation thesis 38 years, and at first call 40 years. On a longitudinal basis, Hillmert estimates that only between 24% and 35% of all those who qualify manage to become professor. Mobility on the way to a chair is high and goes down dramatically once a chair is received. There is no clear pattern of certain schools dominating the distribution of chairs. Current professors are much older than the German population (mean 56.6, $n = 315$). Until 2012, 66% of the current incumbents of a professorship will retire. As the sociology of sociology shows, some of the old controversies will be equally forgotten as will important stocks of knowledge. Therefore, this generational break holds both great chances and risks for advancing research.

2. For more detailed discussions of the national sociological traditions *within* Europe, see Genov (1989), Nedelmann and Sztompka (1993), the four volumes of Boudon, Cherkaoui, and Alexander (1997), Torrance (1976), Halliday (1968), Kultygin (2003), Weiss (1989), and several entries in Borgatta (2000).

3. Important European "Durkheimians" are among others: Maurice Halbwachs (1925), Marcel Mauss (1950), Célestin Bouglé (1899).

4. Scholars have accused Giddens of "reinventing the wheel" concerning the role of structures in sociological theory and of structuralism in general. See Clark, Modgil, and Modgil (1990). See Badcock (1975) for the sociological significance of structuralism.

5. Early surveys not covered in our presentation include the English social surveys (1830–1850), the "enquête ouvrière" in France, and the "younger historical school" in Germany (Kern 1982:79ff.).

6. For European research in elites, see Pareto (1968), Mosca (1939), and Djilas (1983).

7. The scheme now includes 11 occupational classes. See Brauns, Steinmann, and Haun (2000) for the foundations of the CASMIN scheme based on the German microcensus, the British Labour-Force Surveys, and the French Enquête sur l'Emploi.

8. See Bulmer (1975) and Thompson (1980) for studies on class culture. See Bernstein's (1975) study in class-specific linguistic codes.

PART III: THE SCIENTIFIC APPROACH TO THE STUDY OF SOCIETY

Chapter 9. Qualitative Methodology

1. Qualitative research has separate and distinguished histories in education, social work, communications, psychology, history, organizational studies, medical science, anthropology,

and sociology. This chapter builds on and extends arguments in Denzin (1997, 2003), Denzin and Lincoln (2000, 2005), and Lincoln and Denzin (2000).

2. Definitions: *structuralism*: any system is made up of a set of oppositional categories embedded in language; *semiotics*: the science of signs or sign systems—a structuralist project; *poststructuralism*: language is an unstable system of referents, making it impossible to ever completely capture the meaning of an action, text, or intention; *postmodernism*: a contemporary sensibility, developing since World War II, that privileges no single authority, method, or paradigm; *hermeneutics*: an approach to the analysis of texts that stresses how prior understandings and prejudices shape the interpretive process; *phenomenology*: a complex system of ideas associated with the works of Husserl, Heidegger, Sartre, Merleau-Ponty, and Alfred Schutz; *cultural studies*: a complex, interdisciplinary field that merges with critical theory, feminism, and poststructuralism.

3. This section draws on and reworks Denzin and Lincoln (2000:18–19).

4. Olesen (2000) identifies three strands of feminist research: mainstream empirical, standpoint and cultural studies, and poststructural, postmodern, placing Afrocentric and other models of color under the cultural studies and postmodern categories.

PART V: SOCIAL AGGREGATIONS

Chapter 15. The Sociology of Social Structure

1. As can be seen, these matters cover some of the central themes of sociology. An exhaustive review of these problems is not possible within the framework of this chapter. Our presentation will, therefore, be necessarily selective.

2. If we go far enough on this path and construct broad categories of social positions, we reach the classic tradition of social stratification studies (Kerbo 2000).

3. In addition, Kontopoulos (1993) considers two other intermediate strategies that we will not consider here because they would complicate the discussion. These two additional strategies are "heterarchy," or moderate emergence, and "hierarchy," or strong emergence.

4. As Kontopoulos (1993) observes in his works before and after the quoted articles, Collins situates himself more along the lines of conflict theory and includes macrostructural factors and processes in his explanatory models such as the inheritance of resources, the distribution of power, and a society's level of technological development. These factors cannot be directly reduced to repeated microinteractions.

5. The model of the classic rational actor suggests that the subject has a purpose, exhaustively determines the means available to achieve it, and chooses the best among them.

Chapter 20. The Sociology of Social Networks

1. For contemporary network theorists, these ideas continue to be central. Social networks constitute social spaces among identities and provide the structure that links social interaction and society (Stryker 1980; White 1992:70). Coser (1991:25) echoes this and Simmel's original ideas by arguing that multiple

statuses essentially enrich social worlds by granting individuals greater autonomy.

2. First, actors were to be partitioned into sets of relationships that depended on more than the *presence* of social ties. Second, following from this, the *absence* of ties was pivotal to understanding the structure of social networks. Third, to get at this structure, many different types of ties (e.g., advice, authority, friendship), rather than one, would be preferable. Fourth, the nature of those ties would be inferred from clustering individuals with similar patterns of both the presence and the absence of ties. Finally, the search for structure would focus on the identification of *zero blocks,* clusters defined by the absence of ties. Thus, in their approach, the role of negative spaces helped solve analytical problems and led to the development of important concepts (e.g., "structural holes"; Burt 2001).

3. An earlier and more specific version of these principles addressing the challenge of illness and disability appears in Pescosolido (1991).

4. Given the dynamic nature of social networks and concerns that some may be fleeting or based only on weak bonds of affiliation (Granovetter 1982), a major concern in pursuing the network research agenda has been whether reports of social network ties are accurate and can be measured with reasonable scientific precision (see Marsden 2005 on these issues).

5. According to Cederman (2005), such agent-based modeling allows for experimentation within which agents interact and create social environments (see also Robins and Pattison 2005).

Chapter 21. Work and Occupations

1. While all efforts were made to assemble a comprehensive bibliography, there are limitations to all such efforts and debates on what is correct to include. My focus was on case studies of work and occupations in the Hughesian tradition, what is now referred to as work ethnography. I concentrated on the leading journals of sociology, and significant edited collections, generating a list of just under300 citations. As I continue this research, I continue to add titles to the bibliography, so my claims about the distribution and development of topics should be seen as tentative.

Part VI: Social Distinctions and Diversity

Chapter 24. The Sociology of Gender

1. For example, Durkheim ([1897] 1951) believed that although there was little differentiation between males and females, over the course of evolution, differentiation between the sexes produced profound physiological and psychological differences between them such that modern women were quite "unable to fulfill the same functions in society as man" (p. 385) and that she "recalls . . . certain characteristics of primitive natures" (Durkheim [1893] 1984:247). For Weber ([1915] 1946), despite his wife's feminism, women remained governed by their biologically natural, sensual constitutions in contrast to the more ethical and intellectual abilities of men (p. 345). Spencer ([1899] 1969) believed that educating women was racial suicide because

"absolute or relative infertility was generally produced in women by mental labour carried to excess" (p. 486). And Pareto ([1916] 1935) was particularly scathing about nineteenth-century feminists, calling them hysterical women "in want of a mate" (p. 696), an observation that was often attributed to second-wave feminists of the 1960s.

These views did not go unchallenged. There were some feminist precursors, such as Marianne Weber, Charlotte Perkins Gilman, Beatrice Webb, and the first woman sociologist, Harriet Martineau, who anticipated much of Durkheim's methodological writings and whose qualified endorsement of Comte was exceptionally influential in establishing sociology in the English-speaking world.

2. The provision of feminist demands for such practical matters as equal pay and parental leaves did not alter the basic economic inequities in the work world, and feminist debates within the academy did not fundamentally change either institutional structures or theoretical paradigms (Stacy and Thorne 1985, 1996).

3. This complaint still has resonance, as the Nairobi prostitutes, who have been the subjects of AIDS research because they seem to have an immunity to the disease, demonstrate. Most of them have seen few advantages in over a decade of Western study other than free health care and drugs, and most, some in their sixties, still need to prostitute themselves so that they and their dependants can survive.

4. Sociology has not totally ignored the issue of the body, as Goffman's work as well as that of Smith, Hochschild, Mauss, and Douglas illustrate. In recent years, there has been considerable interest in exploring body issues in more branches of "mainstream" sociology—for example, in sports sociology, medical sociology, masculinity studies, and gerontology. But in many cases, the focus has been theoretically abstract as well as maintaining a commitment to foundationalism. Finally, early feminists did not ignore the significance of the body, especially in relation to medical practices and women's rights to sexual pleasure, as the important collection *Our Bodies, Ourselves* (Boston Women's Health Book Collective 1971) illustrates.

Part IX: Locality and Social Life

Chapter 48. Urban Sociology in the 21st Century

1. See, for example, the effort in this direction by the National Academy of Sciences Panel on Cities in 2003.

2. We can see this in early works such as *The Taxi Dance Hall* and *The Gold Coast and the Slum.*

Chapter 50. The Sociology of Development

1. South refers to countries, primarily in the southern hemisphere, that have low levels of per capita income. The term is viewed as preferable to "underdeveloped countries," "developing countries," or "Third World counties," all of which represent specific eras of development discourse, theory, and practice.

2. During the Cold War, the First World was defined as the developed capitalist world; the Second World, the socialist nations; and the Third World, the less-developed nations that were essentially up for grabs in terms of their alignment with

either the First or Second Worlds. Following the demise of the Soviet Bloc, the dichotomy of North and South (which is really a continuum) is in more frequent usage. We will use the latter terminology throughout this chapter.

3. Characterized by

- A focus on increasing aggregate production.
- Macroeconomic planning to identify constraints to increasing aggregate production.
- A view that output growth was primarily constrained by inadequate technology investment.
- Foreign assistance to eliminate investment shortages and foreign assistance not tied to specific project activities but directed at the use of Western equipment and technologies, including community development and traditional agricultural extension techniques; large-scale infrastructural investments; education through technical assistance and foreign schooling for students from developing nations; and institution building (Morss and Morss 1982:22–23).

4. Yankee imperialism.

5. Under Title XII, activities were to: Be directly related to the food and agricultural needs of developing countries. Be carried out within the developing countries. Be adapted to local circumstances. Provide for the most effective interrelationship between research, education, and extension in promoting agricultural development in developing countries. Emphasize the improvement of local systems for delivering the best available knowledge to the operators of small farms in such countries.

6. Eight millennium development goals:

1. Eradicate extreme poverty and hunger. Target for 2015: Halve the proportion of people living on less than a dollar a day and those who suffer from hunger.

2. Achieve universal primary education. Target for 2015: Ensure that all boys and girls complete primary school.

3. Promote gender equality and empower women. Targets for 2005 and 2015: Eliminate gender disparities in primary and secondary education preferably by 2005, and at all levels by 2015.

4. Reduce child mortality. Target for 2015: Reduce by two-thirds the mortality rate among children less than five years.

5. Improve maternal health. Target for 2015: Reduce by three-quarters the ratio of women dying in childbirth.

6. Combat HIV/AIDS, malaria, and other diseases. Target for 2015: Halt and begin to reverse the spread of HIV/AIDS and the incidence of malaria and other major diseases.

7. Ensure environmental sustainability. Targets:

- Integrate the principles of sustainable development into country policies and programs and reverse the loss of environmental resources.
- By 2015, reduce by half the proportion of people without access to safe drinking water.
- By 2020, achieve significant improvement in the lives of at least 100 million slum dwellers.

8. Develop a global partnership for development. Targets:

- Develop further an open trading and financial system that includes a commitment to good governance, development, and poverty reduction—nationally and internationally.
- Address the least developed countries' special needs, and the special needs of landlocked and small island developing states.
- Deal comprehensively with developing countries' debt problems.
- Develop decent and productive work for youth.

- In cooperation with pharmaceutical companies, provide access to affordable essential drugs in developing countries.
- In cooperation with the private sector, make available the benefits of new technologies—especially information and communications technologies (UNDP 2005a).

PART X: THE QUANTIFICATION OF SOCIAL LIFE

Chapter 51. Demography

1. The first section of this chapter draws on materials in Poston (2000).

2. See Abbott (2001) for a discussion of the context and social structure of scientific disciplines, although he is more interested in relations among disciplines than in the kinds of resources that make disciplinary activity possible.

3. This section draws on and is adapted from materials in Micklin and Poston (2005).

4. This section is adapted from materials in Poston (2000) and Poston et al. (2005).

PART XII: SOCIETY IN MOTION

Chapter 57. Dynamic Systems Theory

1. In the most abstract terms, a system is a set of objects together with relationships between the objects. Such a concept implies that a system has properties, functions, and dynamics distinct from its constituent objects and relationships. A systems approach is not unique to sociology. Many of the major theorists have belonged to other disciplines, including mathematics, with concerns and conceptual and analytic challenges rather different from those facing sociologists and social scientists.

2. Elsewhere, we consider systems theories such as Parsons's (1951, 1966) functionalist systems theory. Functionalist-type theories share commonalities with Marxian systems theory (Burns forthcoming; Collins 1988; Stinchcombe 1968).

3. An institution or institutional arrangement organizes people in a complex of relationships, roles, and norms that constitute and regulate recurring interaction processes among participants. Institutions are exemplified by family, a business organization or government agency, markets, democratic associations, and educational and religious communities.

4. Collins (1988) criticizes Marxian and world systems theories (but his remarks apply to ASD as well) for not being concerned with "the origins of capitalism." This is an important question. But so are questions such as the current functioning (or malfunctioning), the key regulatory controls, and the problematic development of capitalism.

5. Modern capitalism provides forms that enable agents to realize gains from complex transactions and those that take place over long periods of time, for instance, institutional arrangements that establish secure title or rights to property and to mortgage property. Ultimately, in case of disputes, one has access to impartial courts that enforce contracts, but one also has the opportunities (rights) to create new forms of extensive cooperation and

organization, such as joint stock companies, franchises, and joint ventures (Olson 2000).

6. These different uses and functions of money in a modern capitalist economy are, in part, contradictory and a source of instability. For instance, the stability of money as a measure of value is persistently threatened by the use of money as a continual source of funds for capitalist investment, development, and further accumulation. Monetary and financial authorities establish and regulate the highly complex and potentially unstable money systems (Burns and DeVillé 2003).

7. This system of domination ("class relations" for Marx and Weber) emerged as a twofold historical process through which sizeable population groups were separated from the means of production, while other groups had or gained control over and concentrated these means in their own hands (Burns and Flam [1987] 1990).

8. Ownership of the means of production is, in large part, private or if not fully private, highly independent, in the ideal case, from political or religious decision making and controls.

9. The extremes for Karl Marx were the owners and controllers of the means of production, on the one hand, and the propertyless laborers, on the other. The latter were the subjects and objects of economic development in a certain sense. Of course, this model ignored other bases of social power and control such as the political in democratic societies or the emerging power of knowledge and expertise.

10. Mountains of public and private debts characterize—and threaten the stability of—several advanced states, most notably the contemporary United States.

11. Fully developed modern capitalism is not likely to be "the end of history"—that is, where there is no viable alternative to the capitalist market system (cf. Fukuyama 1992). The question remains (as we will discuss later), Where do the dynamics of the capitalism system lead? And what is the place of "politics" in such an evolution? One must recognize the incompleteness of knowledge and regulatory controls and the contradictory nature of sociopolitical actions and institutional arrangements.

12. Earlier (in Summing Up) we drew attention to the potential incompatibility between a socioeconomic order and the natural environment on which it depends for resources, which is yet another type of critical problem situation.

13. Even at the national level, there is typically a lack of systematic overview of the functioning and impacts of the multitude of interventions, and this tends to produce disorders and instability in its own right. Effective overall stabilization requires some degree of coordination and balancing. The challenge is amplified in the context of globalization and its multiple contradictory developments and impacts.

14. Part of this process entails the development of knowledge and accounting systems to control these and other new problem areas. It is a major contemporary challenge to develop information and accounting systems cutting across the economic, social, and material spheres. This is related to the emergence of the "triple bottom line" concept.

15. For example, in the case of Marxist theorizing, see Anderson (1976), Burawoy and Skocpol (1982), Burawoy and Wright (2001), Collins (1988), Moore (1966), van Parijs (1993), and Wright et al. (1992); for the development of WST, see Chase-Dunn (1997) and Wallerstein (2004); with respect to ASD, see Burns and Carson (2002, 2005) and Burns and Flam ([1987] 1990).

VOLUME ONE REFERENCES

PART I: THE DISCIPLINE OF SOCIOLOGY

Chapter 1. The Sociological Perspective

Beck, Bernard. 1999. "The Future of Sociology." *Sociological Inquiry* 69:121–29.

Berger, Peter L. 1963. *Invitation to Sociology: A Humanistic Perspective.* Garden City, NY: Anchor Books.

Bernard, L. L. and Jessie Bernard. 1943. *Origins of American Sociology.* New York: Thomas Y. Crowell.

Best, Joel. 2001. *Damned Lies and Statistics: Untangling Numbers from the Media, Politicians, and Activists.* Berkeley: University of California Press.

Best, Joel. 2003. "Killing the Messenger: The Social Problems of Sociology." *Social Problems* 50:1–13.

Black, Timothy. 1999. "Going Public: How Sociology Might Matter Again." Special Section: Saving Sociology (Part II) *Sociological Inquiry* 690:257–75.

Bramson, Leon. 1961. *The Political Context of Sociology.* Princeton, NJ: Princeton University Press.

Burawoy, Michael. 2005. "For Public Sociology." *American Sociological Review* 70:4–28.

Calhoun, Arthur W. 1919. *A Social History of the American Family: From Colonial Times to the Present.* Vol. 3. Cleveland, OH: Arthur H. Clark.

Crothers, Charles. 2001. "History of Sociology." Pp. 1550–52 in *Reader's Guide to the Social Sciences,* edited by J. Michie. Chicago, IL: Fitzroy Dearborn.

Derber, Charles. 2003. *The Wilding of America: Money, Mayhem, and the New American Dream.* New York: Worth.

Eisenstadt, Shmuel N. 1968. "The Development of Sociological Thought." Pp. 23–36 in *International Encyclopedia of the Social Sciences,* edited by D. L. Sills. New York: Macmillan/Free Press.

Fine, Gary Alan. 2006. "The Chaining of Social Problems: Solution, and Unintended Consequences in the Age of Betrayal." *Social Problems* 53:3–17.

Frickel, Scott and Neil Gross. 2005. "A General Theory of Scientific/Intellectual Movements." *American Journal of Sociology* 70:204–32.

Friedrichs, Robert W. 1970. *A Sociology of Sociology.* New York: Free Press.

Gans, Herbert J., ed. 1990. *Sociology in America.* Newbury Park, CA: Sage.

Goudsblom, J. and J. Heilbron. 2001. "History of Sociology." Pp. 14574–80 in *International Encyclopedia of the Social & Behavioral Sciences,* edited by N. J. Smelser and P. B. Baltes. Amsterdam: Elsevier.

Gouldner, Alvin W. 1970. *The Coming Crisis in Western Sociology.* New York: Basic Books.

Gusfield, Joseph R. 1990. "Sociology's Effects on Society." Pp. 31–46 in *Sociology in America,* edited by H. J. Gans. Newbury Park, CA: Sage.

Harris, Catherine and Michael Wise. 1998. "Grassroots Sociology and the Future of the Discipline." *American Sociologist* Winter:29–47.

Hollander, Paul. 1999. "Saving Sociology?" *Sociological Inquiry* 69:130–47.

Homans, George C. 1967. *The Nature of Social Science.* New York: Harcourt, Brace & World.

Jacobs, Jerry A. 2004. "ASR: Yesterday, Today, Tomorrow." *American Sociological Review* 69:v–vi.

Kuhn, Thomas S. [1962] 1970. *The Structure of Scientific Revolutions.* 2d ed. Chicago, IL: University of Chicago Press.

Kurtz, Lester R. 1986. *Evaluating Chicago Sociology.* Chicago, IL: University of Chicago Press.

Lecuyer, Bernard and Anthony R. Oberschall. 1968. "The Early History of Social Research." Pp. 36–52 in *International Encyclopedia of the Social Sciences,* edited by D. L. Sills. New York: Macmillan/Free Press.

Lee, Alfred McClung. 1978. *Sociology for Whom?* New York: Oxford University Press.

Lengermann, Patricia Madoo and Jill Niebrugge-Brantley. 1998. *The Women Founders: Sociology and Social Theory, 1830–1930.* Boston, MA: McGraw-Hill.

Lewis, Michael. 1999. "Introduction: Saving Sociology (Part I)." *Sociological Inquiry* 69:106–109.

Lundberg, George A. 1947. *Can Science Save Us?* New York: David McKay.

MacIver, R. M. 1934. "Sociology." Pp. 232–46 in *Encyclopedia of the Social Sciences,* edited by E. R. A. Seligman and A. Johnson. New York: Macmillan.

Madge, John. 1962. *The Origins of Scientific Sociology.* New York: Free Press.

Martineau, Harriet. 1836/1837. *Society in America.* London, England: Saunders & Otley.

Martineau, Harriet. 1838. *How to Observe Morals and Manners.* London, England: Charles Knight.

Merton, Robert K. [1957] 1968. *Social Theory and Social Structure*. New York: Free Press.

Mills, C. Wright. 1959. *The Sociological Imagination*. New York: Oxford University Press.

Myrdal, Gunnar. 1969. *Objectivity in Social Research*. New York: Pantheon Books.

Nisbet, Robert A. 1966. *The Sociological Tradition*. New York: Basic Books.

Noble, David F. 1999. *The Religion of Technology*. New York: Penguin Putnam.

Odum, Howard W. 1951. *American Sociology: The Story of Sociology in the United States through 1950*. New York: Longmans, Green.

Odum, Howard W. [1927] 1965. *American Masters of Social Science*. Port Washington, NY: Kennikat Press.

O'Neill, William L. 1967. *Divorce in the Progressive Era*. New Haven, CT: Yale University Press.

Peck, Dennis L. 1982. "Future Prospects for Sociology(ists): Observations of a Non-Rural Sociologist." *The Rural Sociologist* 2:315–21.

Reiss, Albert J. 1968. "Sociology: The Field." Pp. 1–22 in *International Encyclopedia of the Social Sciences*, edited by D. L. Sills. New York: Macmillan/Free Press.

Ross, E. A. 1936. "Some Contributions of Sociology to the Guidance of Society." *American Sociological Review* 1:29–32.

Rossi, Peter H. 1999. "Saving Academic Sociology." *Sociological Inquiry* 69:110–20.

Shahidian, Hammed. 1999. "Saving the Savior." *Sociological Inquiry* 69:303–27.

Small, A. W. 1895. "The Era of Sociology." *American Journal of Sociology* 1:1–15.

Smelser, Neil J. 1990. "External Influences on Sociology." Pp. 49–60 in *Sociology in America*, edited by H. J. Gans. Newbury Park, CA: Sage.

Talbot, Marion. 1896. "Sanitation and Sociology." *American Journal of Sociology* 2:74–81.

Touraine, Alain. 1990. "American Sociology Viewed from Abroad." Pp. 239–52 in *Sociology in America*, edited by H. J. Gans. Newbury Park, CA: Sage.

Turner, Jonathan H. 2001. "Sociology, Survey." Pp. 1538–50 in *Reader's Guide to the Social Sciences*, edited by J. Michie. Chicago, IL: Fitzroy Dearborn.

Turner, Stephen and Alan Sica. 2006. "Two Scholars Examine Golden Decade's Imprint on Today's Sociologists." *Footnotes* 34(2):4.

Volkart, E. H. 1968. "Thomas, W. I." Pp. 1–6 in *International Encyclopedia of the Social Sciences*, vol. 16, edited by D. L. Sills. New York: Macmillan/Free Press.

Ward, Lester A. 1896. "Contributions to Social Philosophy. IX. The Purpose of Sociology." *American Journal of Sociology* 2:446–60.

Wharton, Amy S. 2006. "Letter from the Editor." *Social Problems* 59:1–2.

Whitt, Hugh P. 2001. "The Moral Statisticians" Pp. 229–35 in *Encyclopedia of Criminology and Deviant Behavior, Historical, Conceptual, and Theoretical Issues*, vol. 1, edited by P. A. Adler, P. Adler, and J. Corzine. Philadelphia, PA: Brunner-Routledge.

Wright, Carroll D. 1895. "Contributions of the United States Government to Social Science." *American Journal of Sociology* 1(3):241–75.

Wrong, Dennis H. 1990. "Sociology's Effects on America." Pp. 19–30 in *Sociology in America*, edited by H. J. Gans. Newbury Park, CA: Sage.

Chapter 2. The History of Sociology: The European Perspective

Abbott, Andrew. 1998. "The Causal Devolution." *Sociological Methods & Research* 27(2):148–81.

Ajzen, Icek and Martin Fishbein. 1980. *Understanding Attitudes and Predicting Social Behavior*. Englewood Cliffs, NJ: Prentice Hall.

Alexander, Jeffrey. 1982. *Theoretical Logic in Sociology*. Vols. 1–4. Berkeley: University of California Press.

Aristotle. 1943. *Aristotle's Politics*. Translated by Benjamin Jowett. New York: Modern Library.

Blalock, Hubert M. 1982. *Conceptualization and Measurement in the Social Sciences*. Beverly Hills, CA: Sage.

Blumer, Herbert. 1954. "What Is Wrong with Social Theory?" *American Sociological Review* 19:3–10.

Bond, Rod and Peter Saunders. 1999. "Routes of Success: Influences on the Occupational Attainment of Young British Males." *British Journal of Sociology* 50(2):S217–49.

Breen, Richard and John H. Goldthorpe. 1999. "Class Inequality and Meritocracy: A Critique of Saunders and an Alternative Analysis." *British Journal of Sociology* 50:S1–27.

Coser, Lewis A. 1956. *The Functions of Social Conflict*. New York: Free Press.

Dahrendorf, Ralf. 1958. "Toward a Theory of Social Conflict." *Journal of Conflict Resolution* 2(June):170–83.

Dahrendorf, Ralf. 1959. *Class and Class Conflict in Industrial Society*. Stanford, CA: Stanford University Press.

Desrosières, Alain. 1993. *La Politique des grands nombres (The Politics of Great Numbers)*. Paris, France: La Découverte.

Diewald, Martin. 2001. "Unitary Social Science for Causal Understanding: Experiences and Prospects of Life Course Research." *Canadian Studies in Population* 28(2):219–48.

Duncan, Otis D. 1984. *Notes on Social Measurement*. New York: Russell Sage.

Durkheim, Émile. 1938. *The Rules of Sociological Method*. Chicago, IL: University of Chicago Press.

Durkheim, Émile. 1952. *Suicide*. London, England: Routledge & Kegan Paul.

Durkheim, Émile. 1984. *The Division of Labor in Society*. New York: Free Press.

Ferguson, Adam. 1773. *An Essay on the History of Civil Society*. London, England: Caddel.

Garfinkel, Harold. 1967. *Studies in Ethnomethodology*. Englewood Cliffs, NJ: Prentice Hall.

Giddens, Anthony. 1984. *The Constitution of Society. Outline of the Theory of Structuration*. Cambridge, England: Polity Press.

Goffman, Erving. 1959. *The Presentation of Self in Everyday Life*. New York: Doubleday.

Goffman, Erving. 1961. *Asylums*. New York: Anchor Books.

Goldenweiser, Alexander. 1938. "The Concept of Causality in the Physical and Social Sciences." *American Sociological Review* 3:624–36.

Goldthorpe, John H., with Catriona Llewellyn and Clive Payne. 1980. *Social Mobility and Class Structure in Modern Britain*. Oxford, England: Clarendon Press.

Goldthorpe, John H. 2000. *On Sociology: Numbers, Narratives, and the Integration of Research and Theory.* Oxford, England: Oxford University Press.

Hegel, Georg W. F. 2005. *Philosophy of Right.* Mineola, NY: Dover.

Heider, Fritz. 1958. *The Psychology of Interpersonal Relations.* New York: Wiley.

Hobbes, Thomas. 1904. *Leviathan; or, the Matter, Forme & Power of a Commonwealth, Ecclesiasticall and Civill.* Cambridge, England: Cambridge University Press.

Jahoda, Marie, Paul F. Lazarsfeld, and Hans Zeisel. [1933] 2002. *Marienthal: The Sociography of an Unemployed Community,* with a new introduction by Christian Fleck. New Brunswick, NJ: Transaction.

Kalberg, Stephen. 2005. "A Cross-National Consensus on a Unified Sociological Theory? Some Inter-Cultural Obstacles." *Soziologie* 34(1):40–53.

Kern, Horst. 1982. *Empirische Sozialforschung: Ursprünge, Ansätze, Entwicklungslinien (Social Research: Origins, Approaches, Development).* Munich, Germany: C. H. Beck.

Kluegel, James R., David S. Mason, and Bernd Wegener, eds. 1995. *Social Justice and Political Change: Public Opinion in Capitalist and Post-Communist States.* New York: Aldine de Gruyter.

Kluegel, James R. and Eliot R. Smith. 1986. *Beliefs about Inequality.* New York: De Gruyter.

Krebs, Dagmar and Peter Schmidt, eds. 1993. *New Directions in Attitude Measurement.* Berlin, Germany: De Gruyter.

Lazarsfeld, Paul F. and Anthony Oberschall. 1962. "Max Weber and Empirical Social Research." *American Sociological Review* 30:185–99.

Lazarsfeld, Paul F. and Morris Rosenberg, eds. 1955. *Language of Social Research.* Glencoe, IL: Free Press.

Lenzer, Gertrud, ed. 1998. *Auguste Comte and Positivism: The Essential Writings.* New Brunswick, NJ: Transaction.

Luhmann, Niklas. 1990. "Meaning as Sociology's Basic Concept." Pp. 21–79 in *Essays on Self-Reference.* New York: Columbia University Press.

Luhmann, Niklas. 1995. *Social Systems.* Stanford, CA: Stanford University Press.

Mayer, Karl Ulrich. 2000. "Promises Fulfilled? A Review of 20 Years of Life-Course Research." *Europäisches Archiv für Soziologie* 41(2):259–82.

Mead, George Herbert. 1936. *Movements of Thought in the Nineteenth Century,* edited by Merritt M. Moore. Chicago, IL: University of Chicago Press.

Montesquieu, Charles de. 1999. *Considerations on the Causes of the Greatness of the Romans and Their Decline.* Indianapolis, IN: Hackett.

Muse, Kenneth R. 1981. "Edmund Husserl's Impact on Max Weber." *Sociological Inquiry* 51:99–104.

Oberschall, Anthony. 1972. "The Institutionalization of American Sociology." Pp. 182–251 in *The Establishment of Empirical Sociology,* edited by Anthony Oberschall. New York: Harper & Row.

Ogburn, William F. and Meyer F. Nimkoff. 1964. *A Handbook of Sociology.* London, England: Routledge & Kegan Paul.

Parsons, Talcott. 1937. *The Structure of Social Action.* New York: McGraw-Hill.

Parsons, Talcott. 1951. *The Social System.* Glencoe, IL: Free Press.

Quah, Stella R. and Arnaud Sales, eds. 2000. *The International Handbook of Sociology.* London, England: Sage.

Rousseau, Jean-Jacques. 1972. *Du Contrat Social* (edited with an introduction and notes by Ronald Grimsley). Oxford, England: Clarendon Press.

Schütz, Alfred and Talcott Parsons. 1977. *Zur Theorie sozialen Handelns: Ein Briefwechsel (The Theory of Social Action: An Exchange of Letters).* Frankfurt am Main, Germany: Suhrkamp.

Silverman, David, ed. 2004. *Qualitative Research: Theory, Method and Practice.* London, England: Sage.

Smith, Adam. 1963. *An Inquiry into the Nature and Causes of the Wealth of Nations.* Homewood, IL: R. D. Irwin.

Smith, Adam. 1971. *The Theory of Moral Sentiments.* New York: Garland.

Spinoza, Benedictus de. 1899. *Ethic Demonstrated in Geometrical Order.* London, England: Duckworth.

Stigler, Stephen M. 1986. *The History of Statistics: The Measurement of Uncertainty before 1900.* Cambridge, MA: Harvard University Press.

Strasser, Hermann. 1976. *The Normative Structure of Sociology: Conservative and Emancipatory Themes in Social Thought.* London, England: Routledge & Kegan Paul.

Strauss, Anselm, ed. 1956. *George Herbert Mead on Social Psychology.* Chicago, IL: University of Chicago Press.

Turner, Jonathan H. 1989. "Sociology in the United States: Its Growth and Contemporary Profile." Pp. 220–42 in *National Traditions in Sociology,* edited by N. Genov. London, England: Sage.

Turner, Stephen P. and Regis A. Factor. 1994. *Max Weber: The Lawyer as Social Thinker.* London, England: Routledge.

Weber, Max. 1949. *The Methodology of the Social Sciences.* Translated by E. Shils and H. Finch. New York: Free Press.

Weber, Max. [1922] 1968. *Economy and Society.* Berkeley: University of California Press.

Weber, Max. 1981. "Some Categories of Interpretive Sociology." *Sociological Quarterly* 22:151–80.

Weber, Max. 2001. *The Protestant Ethic and the Spirit of Capitalism.* Los Angeles, CA: Roxbury.

Wright, Erik Olin. 1997. *Class Counts: Comparative Studies in Class Analysis.* New York: Cambridge University Press.

Chapter 3. The History of Sociology: The North American Perspective

Abraham, J. H. 1977. *The Origins and Growth of Sociology.* New York: Penguin.

Acland, Charles R. and William J. Buxton, eds. 1999. *Harold Innis in the New Century: Reflections and Refractions.* Montréal, Québec, Canada: McGill-Queen's Press.

American Sociological Association. Webpage: www.asanet.org. Source of data on trends in ASA membership statistics, sociology enrollment, and degrees awarded in U.S. colleges and universities.

Barnes, Harry Elmer, ed. 1948. *An Introduction to the History of Sociology.* Chicago, IL: University of Chicago Press.

Bernard, L. L. and Jessie Bernard. [1943] 1965. *Origins of American Sociology: The Social Science Movement in the United States.* New York: Russell & Russell.

Blasi, Anthony J. 2004. "The Ph.D. and the Institutionalization of American Sociology." *The American Sociologist* 35:37–45.

Blasi, Anthony J., ed. 2005. *Diverse Histories of American Sociology.* Leiden, The Netherlands: Brill.

Bottomore, Tom and Robert Nisbet, eds. 1978. *A History of Sociological Analysis.* London, England: Heinemann.

Brym, Robert J., with Bonnie J. Fox. 1989. *From Culture to Power: The Sociology of English Canada.* Toronto, Canada: Oxford University Press.

Bulmer, Martin. 1984. *The Chicago School of Sociology: Institutionalization, Diversity, and the Rise of Sociological Research.* Chicago, IL: University of Chicago Press.

Coser, Lewis. 1956. *The Functions of Social Conflict.* Glencoe, IL: Free Press.

Coser, Lewis. 1971. *Masters of Sociological Thought: Ideas in Historical and Social Context.* New York: Harcourt Brace Jovanovich.

Coser, Lewis. 1978. "American Trends." Pp. 287–320 in *A History of Sociological Analysis,* edited by T. Bottomore and R. Nisbet. London, England: Heinemann.

Deegan, Mary Jo. 1988. *Jane Addams and the Men of the Chicago School, 1892–1918.* New Brunswick, NJ: Transaction Books.

Deegan, Mary Jo, ed. 1991. *Women in Sociology: A Bio-Bibliographical Sourcebook.* New York: Greenwood Press.

Deegan, Mary Jo. 2002. *Race, Hull House, and the University of Chicago: A New Conscience against Ancient Evils.* Westport, CT: Praeger.

Falardeau, Jean-Charles. 1967. *The Rise of Social Sciences in French Canada.* Québec, Canada: Department of Cultural Affairs.

Fine, William F. 1976. *Progressive Evolutionism and American Sociology, 1890–1920.* Ann Arbor, MI: UMI Research Press.

Goetting, Ann and Sarah Fenstermaker, eds. 1995. *Individual Voices, Collective Visions: Fifty Years of Women in Sociology.* Philadelphia, PA: Temple University Press.

Haskell, Thomas. 1977. *The Emergence of Professional Social Science: The American Social Science Association and the Nineteenth Century Crisis of Authority.* Urbana: University of Illinois Press.

Hill, Michael R. 2005a. *Centennial Bibliography on the History of American Sociology.* Washington, DC: American Sociological Association.

Hill, Michael R. 2005b. "Jesse Lawson and the National Sociological Society of 1903, pp. 127–140 in *Diverse Histories of American Sociology,* edited by Anthony J. Blasi. Leiden, The Netherlands: Brill.

Hill, Michael R. and Susan Hoecker-Drysdale. 2001. *Harriet Martineau: Theoretical and Methodological Perspectives.* London, England: Routledge.

Hinkle, Roscoe C. and Gisela J. Hinkle. 1954. *The Development of Modern Sociology: Its Nature and Growth in the United States.* New York: Random House.

Hoecker-Drysdale, Susan. 1990. "Women Sociologists in Canada: Three Careers." Pp.152–76 in *Despite the Odds: Essays on Canadian Women and Science,* edited by M. Gosztonyi Ainley. Montréal, Québec, Canada: Véhicule Press.

Hoecker-Drysdale, Susan. 1992. *Harriet Martineau: First Woman Sociologist.* Oxford, England: Berg Publishers.

Hoecker-Drysdale, Susan. 1996. "Sociologists in the Vineyard: The Careers of Everett Cherrington Hughes and Helen Macgill Hughes." Pp. 220–31 in *Creative Couples in the Sciences,* edited by H. Pycior, N. Slack, and P. Abir-Am. New Brunswick, NJ: Rutgers University Press.

Hoecker-Drysdale, Susan. 2002. "Harriet Martineau." Pp. 41–68 in *The Blackwell Companion to Major Social Theorists,* edited by G. Ritzer. Malden, MA: Blackwell.

House, Floyd Nelson. 1936. *The Development of Sociology.* New York: McGraw-Hill.

Laslett, Barbara and Barrie Thorne, eds. 1997. *Feminist Sociology: Life Histories of a Movement.* New Brunswick, NJ: Rutgers University Press.

Lengermann, Patricia and Jill Niebrugge-Brantley. 1998. *The Women Founders: Sociology and Social Theory, 1830–1930.* Boston, MA: McGraw-Hill.

Levine, Donald N. 1995. *Visions of the Sociological Tradition.* Chicago, IL: University of Chicago Press.

Lipset, Seymour Martin and Neil J. Smelser, eds. 1961. *Sociology: The Progress of a Decade.* Englewood Cliffs, NJ: Prentice-Hall.

Lundberg, George. 1947. *Can Science Save Us?* New York: Green Publishers.

Lynd, Robert. 1939. *Knowledge for What? The Place of Social Science in American Culture.* Princeton, NJ: Princeton University Press.

Martineau, Harriet. 1853. *The Positive Philosophy of Auguste Comte.* Freely translated and condensed by H. Martineau. 2 vols. London, England: John Chapman.

Martineau, Harriet. 1989. *How to Observe Morals and Manners.* Edited by M. R. Hill. New Brunswick, NJ: Transaction Books.

Martineau, Harriet. 2004. *Harriet Martineau: Studies of America, 1831–1868.* Edited by S. Hoecker-Drysdale. 8 vols. Bristol: Thoemmes Continuum.

Maus, Heinz. 1962. *A Short History of Sociology.* New York: Philosophical Library.

McDonald, Lynn. 1993. *The Early Origins of the Social Sciences.* Montreal, Canada: McGill-Queen's University Press.

McDonald, Lynn. 1994. *The Women Founders of the Social Sciences.* Ottawa, Canada: Carleton University Press.

McDonald, Lynn, ed. 1998. *Women Theorists on Society and Politics.* Waterloo, Ontario, Canada: Wilfrid Laurier Press.

Mead, George Herbert. 1934. *Mind, Self, and Society.* Edited by Charles W. Morris. Chicago, IL: University of Chicago Press.

Mead, George Herbert. 2001. *Essays in Social Psychology.* Edited by Mary Jo Deegan. New Brunswick, NJ: Transaction Publishers.

Nichols, Lawrence T., ed. 2002. "Thematic Issue: Canadian Sociology." *The American Sociologist* 33.

Odum, Howard W. 1951. *American Sociology: The Story of Sociology in the United States through 1950.* Westport, CT: Greenwood Press.

Park, Robert E., Ernest W. Burgess, and Roderick D. McKenzie. 1925. *The City.* Chicago, IL: University of Chicago Press.

Platt, Jennifer. 1996. *A History of Sociological Research Methods in America, 1920–1960.* Cambridge, England: Cambridge University Press.

Reinharz, Shulamit. 1992. *Feminist Methods in Social Research.* New York: Oxford University Press.

Reinharz, Shulamit, ed. 1993. *A Contextualized Chronology of Women's Sociological Work.* Waltham, MA: Brandeis University Press.

Rhoades, Lawrence J. 1981. *A History of the American Sociological Association 1905–1980.* Washington, DC: American Sociological Association.

Rosich, Katherine J. 2005. *A History of the American Sociological Association 1981–2004.* Washington, DC: American Sociological Association.

Ross, Dorothy. 1991. *The Origins of American Social Science.* Cambridge, England: Cambridge University Press.

Shore, Marlene. 1987. *The Science of Social Redemption: McGill, the Chicago School, and the Origins of Social Research in Canada.* Toronto, Canada: University of Toronto Press.

Small, Albion W. 1916. "Fifty Years of Sociology in the United States." *American Journal of Sociology* 21:721–864.

Small, Albion W. 1924. *Origins of Sociology.* Chicago, IL: University of Chicago Press.

Small, Albion W. and George Vincent. 1894. *An Introduction to the Study of Society.* New York: American Book.

Smelser, Neil. 2003. "Sociology: Spanning Two Centuries." *The American Sociologist* 34:5–19.

Turner, Stephen P. and Jonathan H. Turner. 1990. *The Impossible Science: An Institutional Analysis of American Sociology.* Newbury Park, CA: Sage.

Ward, Lester. 1883. *Dynamic Sociology.* New York: D. Appleton.

Zeitlin, Irving M. 2001. *Ideology and the Development of Sociological Theory.* 7th ed. Englewood Cliffs, NJ: Prentice-Hall.

Chapter 4. Sociological Theory in the 21st Century

Adorno, Theodor. [1966] 1973. *Negative Dialectics.* New York: Seabury.

Alexander, Jeffrey C., ed. 1985. *Neofunctionalism.* Beverly Hills, CA: Sage.

Alexander, Jeffrey C. 2004. "Cultural Pragmatics: Social Performance between Ritual and Strategy." *Sociological Theory* 22:527–73.

Alexander, Jeffrey C. and Paul Colomy. 1985. "Toward Neofunctionalism." *Sociological Theory* 3:11–23.

Alexander, Jeffrey C. and Philip Smith. 2001. "The Strong Program in Cultural Theory." Pp. 135–50 in *Handbook of Sociological Theory,* edited by J. H. Turner. New York: Kluwer Academic.

Althusser, Louis. 1965. *For Marx.* New York: Pantheon.

Baudrillard, Jean. 1981/1994. *Simulacra and Simulation.* Ann Arbor: University of Michigan Press.

Blumer, Herbert. 1969. *Symbolic Interactionism.* Englewood Cliffs, NJ: Prentice Hall.

Bourdieu, Pierre. 1977. *Outline of a Theory of Practice.* Cambridge, England: Cambridge University Press.

Burawoy, Michael and Erik Olin Wright. 2001. "Sociological Marxism." Pp. 459–86 in *Handbook of Sociological Theory,* edited by J. H. Turner. New York: Kluwer Academic.

Burke, Peter J. 1991. "Identity and Social Stress." *American Sociological Review* 56:836–49.

Burke, Peter J., ed. 2006. *Contemporary Social Psychological Theories.* Stanford, CA: Stanford University Press.

Burke, Peter J., Timothy J. Owens, Richard Sherpe, and Peggy A. Thoits, eds. 2003. *Advances in Identity Theory and Research.* New York: Kluwer Academic.

Carroll, Glenn R., ed. 1988. *Ecological Models of Organizations.* Cambridge, MA: Ballinger.

Chase-Dunn, Christopher. 1998. *Global Formation: Structures of the World Economy.* 2d ed. Lanham, MD: Rowman & Littlefield.

Chase-Dunn, Christopher. 2001. "World Systems Theory." Pp. 589–612 in *Handbook of Sociological Theory,* edited by J. H. Turner. New York: Kluwer Academic.

Chase-Dunn, Christopher and Thomas D. Hall. 1997. *Rise and Demise: Comparing World Systems.* Boulder, CO: Westview.

Collins, Randall. 1975. *Conflict Sociology: Toward an Explanatory Science.* New York: Academic Press.

Collins, Randall. 1981. "On the Micro-Foundations of Macro-Sociology." *American Journal of Sociology* 86:984–1014.

Collins, Randall. 1986. *Weberian Sociological Theory.* Cambridge, England: Cambridge University Press.

Collins, Randall. 2004. *Interaction Ritual Chains.* Princeton, NJ: Princeton University Press.

Comte, Auguste. [1830–1842] 1896. *The Positive Philosophy of Auguste Comte.* Translated by H. Martineau. London, England: George Bell & Sons.

Cook, Karen S. and Eric R. W. Rice. 2001. "Exchange and Power." Pp. 699–721 in *Handbook of Sociological Theory,* edited by J. H. Turner. New York: Kluwer Academic.

Cosmides, Leda. 1989. "The Logic of Social Exchange." *Cognition* 31:187–276.

Cosmides, Leda and John Tooby. 1989. "Evolutionary Psychology and the Generation of Culture." *Ethology and Sociobiology* 10:51–97.

Dahrendorf, Ralf. 1958. "Out of Utopia: Toward a Reorientation of Sociological Analyses." *American Journal of Sociology* 64:120–28.

Dahrendorf, Ralf. 1959. *Class and Class Conflict in Industrial Society.* Stanford, CA: Stanford University Press.

Dawkins, Richard. 1976. *The Selfish Gene.* New York: Oxford International.

de Saussure, Ferdinand. [1915] 1966. *Course in General Linguistics.* New York: McGraw-Hill.

Durkheim, Émile. [1893] 1947. *The Division of Labor in Society.* New York: Free Press.

Durkheim, Émile. [1912] 1947. *The Elementary Forms of the Religious Life.* New York: Free Press.

Foucault, Michel. 1972. *The Archaeology of Knowledge.* London, England: Tavistock.

Frank, Andre Gunder. 1969. *Capitalism and Underdevelopment in Latin America.* New York: Monthly Review Press.

Frisbie, Parker and John D. Kasarda. 1988. "Spatial Processes." Pp. 86–98 in *Handbook of Sociology,* edited by N. J. Smelser. Newbury Park, CA: Sage.

Garfinkel, Harold. 1967. *Studies in Ethnomethodology.* Englewood Cliffs, NJ: Prentice Hall.

Gergen, Kenneth J. 1991. *The Saturated Self.* New York: Basic Books.

Giddens, Anthony. 1984. *The Constitution of Society.* Cambridge, England: Polity Press.

Goffman, Erving. 1959. *The Presentation of Self in Everyday Life.* Garden City, NY: Doubleday.

Goffman, Erving. 1967. *Interaction Ritual: Essays in Face-to-Face Behaviors.* Garden City, NY: Anchor Books.

Goldstone, Jack. 1991. *Revolution and Rebellion in the Early Modern World.* Berkeley: University of California Press.

Gramsci, Antonio. [1928] 1971. *Selections from Prison Notebooks.* New York: International Publishers.

Habermas, Jurgen. 1981/1984. *The Theory of Communicative Action.* 2 vols. Boston, MA: Beacon Press.

Hannan, Michael T. and John Freeman. 1977. "The Population Ecology of Organizations." *American Journal of Sociology* 89:929–64.

Harvey, David. 1989. *The Conditions of Postmodernity.* Oxford, England: Blackwell.

Hawley, Amos. 1986. *Human Ecology: A Theoretical Essay.* Chicago, IL: Chicago University Press.

Heise, David. 1979. *Understanding Events: Affect and the Construction of Social Action.* Cambridge, England: Cambridge University Press.

Horkheimer, Max. [1947] 1972. *Dialectic of Enlightenment.* New York: Herder and Herder.

Horkheimer, Max. [1947] 1974. *Eclipse of Reason.* New York: Oxford University Press.

Horne, Christine. 2004. "Values and Evolutionary Psychology." *Sociological Theory* 22:477–503.

Hoyt, Homer. 1939. *The Structure and Growth of Residential Neighborhoods in American Cities.* Washington, DC: Federal Housing Administration.

Husserl, Edmund. [1913] 1969. *Ideas: General Introduction to Pure Phenomenology.* London, England: Collier-Macmillan.

Jakobson, Roman. 1962–1971. *Selected Writings 1, 2.* The Hague, The Netherlands: Mouton.

Jameson, Fredric. 1984. *The Postmodern Condition.* Minneapolis: University of Minnesota Press.

Kellner, Douglas. 1995. *Media Culture; Cultural Studies, Identity and Politics between the Modern and Postmodern.* London, England: Routledge.

Lamont, Michèle. 1999. *The Territories of Race: Black and White Boundaries.* Chicago, IL: University of Chicago Press.

Lash, Scott and John Urry. 1987. *The End of Organized Capitalism.* Madison: University of Wisconsin Press.

Lawler, Edward J. 2001. "An Affect Theory of Social Exchange." *American Journal of Sociology* 107:321–52.

Lenski, Gerhard. 1966. *Power and Privilege: A Theory of Social Stratification.* New York: McGraw-Hill.

Lévi-Strauss, Claude. [1958] 1963. *Structural Anthropology.* New York: Basic Books.

Lévi-Strauss, Claude. 1979. *Myth and Meaning.* New York: Schocken.

Li, Rebecca S. K. and Jonathan H. Turner. 1998. "Conflict Theories in Historical-Comparative Perspective." Pp. 194–213 in *The Structure of Sociological Theory,* 6th ed. Belmont, CA: Wadsworth.

Lopreato, Joseph. 2001. "Sociobiological Theorizing." Pp. 405–34 in *Handbook of Sociological Theory,* edited by J. H. Turner. New York: Kluwer Academic.

Lopreato, Joseph and Timothy Crippen. 1999. *Crisis in Sociology: The Need for Darwin.* New Brunswick, NJ: Transaction.

Luhmann, Niklas. 1982. *The Differentiation of Society.* Translated by S. Holmes and C. Larmore. New York: Columbia University Press.

Lukács, György. [1922] 1968. *History and Class Consciousness.* Cambridge: MIT Press.

Lyotard, Jean-Francois. 1979. *The Postmodern Condition.* Minneapolis: University of Minnesota Press.

Machalek, Richard and Michael W. Martin. 2004. "Sociology and the Second Darwinian Revolution." *Sociological Theory* 22:455–76.

Malinowski, Bronislaw. [1944] 1964. *A Scientific Theory of Culture.* London, England: Oxford University Press.

Marx, Karl. [1867] 1967. *Capital: A Critical Analysis of Capitalist Production.* Vol. 1. New York: International Publishers.

Marx, Karl and Friedrich Engels. [1847] 1970. *The Communist Manifesto.* New York: International Publishers.

McCall, George P. and J. L. Simons. 1978. *Identities and Interactions.* New York: Free Press.

Mead, George Herbert. 1934. *Mind, Self, and Society.* Chicago, IL: University of Chicago Press.

Moore, Barrington. 1966. *Social Origins of Dictatorship and Democracy.* Boston, MA: Beacon Press.

Münch, Richard. 1987. *Theory of Action: Toward a New Synthesis Going beyond Parsons.* London, England: Routledge.

Münch, Richard. 2001. *The Ethics of Modernity: Formation and Transformation in Britain, France, Germany, and the United States.* Lanham, MD: Rowman & Littlefield.

Nolan, Patrick and Gerhard Lenski. 2004. *Human Societies.* Boulder, CO: Paradigm Press.

Paige, Jeffrey. 1975. *Agrarian Revolution.* New York: Free Press.

Park, Robert E. 1936. "Human Ecology." *American Journal of Sociology* 42:1–15.

Parsons, Talcott. 1951. *The Social System.* Glencoe, IL: Free Press.

Parsons, Talcott. 1966. *Societies: Evolutionary and Comparative Perspectives.* Englewood Cliffs, NJ: Prentice Hall.

Parsons, Talcott. 1978. *Action Theory and the Human Condition.* New York: Free Press.

Parsons, Talcott, Robert F. Bales, and Edward A. Shils. 1953. *Working Papers in the Theory of Action.* New York: Free Press.

Parsons, Talcott and Neil J. Smelser. 1956. *Economy and Society.* New York: Free Press.

Radcliffe-Brown, A. R. 1952. *Structure and Function in Primitive Society.* New York: Free Press.

Rorty, Richard. 1979. *Philosophy and the Mirror of Nature.* Princeton, NJ: Princeton University Press.

Runciman, W. G. 1989. *A Treatise on Social Theory.* Vol. 2. Cambridge, England: Cambridge University Press.

Sacks, Harvey. 1992. *Lectures on Conversation.* Oxford, England: Blackwell.

Sanderson, Stephen K. 1995. *Social Transformations: A General Theory of Historical Development.* Oxford, England: Blackwell.

Sanderson, Stephen K. 1999. *Macrosociology: An Introduction to Human Societies.* 4th ed. New York: Longman.

Savage, Joanne and Satoshi Kanazawa. 2004. "Social Capital and the Human Psyche: Why Is Social Life Capital?" *Sociological Theory* 22:504–24.

Scheff, Thomas. 1988. "Shame and Conformity: The Deference-Emotion System." *American Sociological Review* 53:395–406.

Schegloff, Emanuel. 2001. "Accounts of Conduct in Interaction." Pp. 287–321 in *Handbook of Sociological Theory,* edited by J. H. Turner. New York: Kluwer Academic.

Schütz, Alfred. [1932] 1967. *The Phenomenology of the Social World.* Evanston, IL: Northwestern University Press.

Simmel, Georg. [1907] 1990. *The Philosophy of Money.* Translated by T. Bottomore and D. Frisby. Boston, MA: Routledge.

Skinner, B. F. 1938. *The Behavior of Organisms.* New York: Appleton-Century-Crofts.

Skocpol, Theda. 1979. *States and Social Revolutions.* New York: Cambridge University Press.

Smith, Adam. [1776] 1976. *An Inquiry into the Causes of the Wealth of Nations.* Oxford, England: Clarendon.

Smith-Lovin, Lynn and David R. Heise. 1988. *Analyzing Social Interaction.* New York: Gordon & Breach.

Snow, David A. and Robert D. Benford. 1988. "Ideology, Frame Resonance, and Participant Mobilization." *International Social Movement Research* 1:197–217.

Spencer, Herbert. [1874–1896] 1898. *The Principles of Sociology.* 3 vols. New York: Appleton-Century.

Stryker, Sheldon. 1980. *Symbolic Interactionism.* Menlo Park, CA: Benjamin-Cummings.

Stryker, Sheldon. 2001. "The Road to Identity Theory." Pp. 211–31 in *Handbook of Sociological Theory,* edited by J. H. Turner. New York: Kluwer Academic.

Summer-Effler, Erika. 2002. "The Micro Potential for Social Change." *Sociological Theory* 20:41–60.

Summer-Effler, Erika. 2004a. "Defensive Strategies." *Advances in Group Processes* 21:309–25.

Summer-Effler, Erika. 2004b. "A Theory of Self, Emotion, and Culture." *Advances in Group Processes* 21:273–308.

Tilly, Charles. 1978. *From Mobilization to Revolution.* Reading, MA: Addison-Wesley.

Tilly, Charles. 1993. *European Revolutions, 1492–1992.* Oxford, England: Blackwell.

Turner, Jonathan H. 1975. "A Strategy for Reformulating the Dialectical and Functional Theories of Conflict." *Social Forces* 53:433–44.

Turner, Jonathan H. 1994. "The Ecology of Macrostructure." *Advances in Human Ecology* 3:113–37.

Turner, Jonathan H. 1995. *Macrodynamics: Toward a Theory on the Organization of Human Populations.* New Brunswick, NJ: Rutgers University Press.

Turner, Jonathan H. 2002. *Face-to-Face: Toward a Sociological Theory of Interpersonal Behavior.* Stanford, CA: Stanford University Press.

Turner, Jonathan H. and David E. Boyns. 2001. "The Return of Grand Theory." Pp. 353–78 in *Handbook of Sociological Theory,* edited by Jonathan H. Turner. New York: Kluwer Academic.

Turner, Jonathan H. and Alexandra Maryanski. 1979. *Functionalism.* Menlo Park, CA: Benjamin-Cummings.

Turner, Jonathan H. and Alexandra Maryanski. 1988. "Is Neofunctionalism Really Functional?" *Sociological Theory* 6:110–21.

Turner, Jonathan H. and Jan E. Stets. 2005. *The Sociology of Emotions.* Cambridge, England: Cambridge University Press.

Turner, Ralph H. 1968. "Social Roles: Sociological Aspects." In *International Encyclopedia of the Social Sciences.* New York: Macmillan.

Turner, Ralph H. 2001. "Role Theory." Pp. 233–54 in *Handbook of Sociological Theory,* edited by Jonathan H. Turner. New York: Kluwer Academic.

Turner, Ralph H. and Lewis M. Killian. 1987. *Collective Behavior.* Englewood Cliffs, NJ: Prentice Hall.

Turner, Stephen Park and Jonathan H. Turner. 1990. *The Impossible Science.* Newbury Park, CA: Sage.

van den Berghe, Pierre. 1981. *The Ethnic Phenomenon.* New York: Elsevier.

Wallerstein, Immanuel. 1974. *The Modern World System.* New York: Academic Press.

Watson, John B. 1913. "Psychology as the Behaviorist Views It." *Psychological Review* 20:158–77.

Weber, Max. [1905] 1958. *The Protestant Ethic and the Spirit of Capitalism.* New York: Scribners.

Weber, Max. [1922] 1968. *Economy and Society.* Translated by G. Roth and C. Wittich. New York: Bedminister.

Williams, George C. 1966. *Adaptation and Natural Selection.* Princeton, NJ: Princeton University Press.

Wilson, Erik Olin. 1975. *Sociobiology: The New Synthesis.* Cambridge, MA: Harvard University Press.

Wright, Erik Olin. 1997. *Class Counts.* Cambridge, England: Cambridge University Press.

Wuthnow, Robert. 1987. *Meaning and Moral Order: Explorations in Cultural Analyses.* Berkeley: University of California Press.

PART II: INTERNATIONAL PERSPECTIVES

Chapter 5. Asian Sociology

Aoi, Kazuo and Keiko Wakabayashi. 1993. "Chinese Sociology" (in Japanese). Pp. 1566–68 in *New Encyclopedia of Sociology,* edited by Kiyomi Morioka, Tsutomu Shiobara, and Yasuhei Honma. Tokyo, Japan: Yuhikaku.

Fei, Xiaotung. 1984. *Small Town, Big Problem* (in Chinese). Nanjing, China: Jiangsu People's Press.

Fukutake, Tadashi, Rokuro Hidaka, and Akira Takashi, eds. 1958. *Shakaigaku jiten (Encyclopedia of Sociology).* Tokyo, Japan: Yuhikaku.

Gerlach, Michael. 1992. *Alliance Capitalism: The Social Organization of Japanese Business.* Berkeley: University of California Press.

Granovetter, Mark. 1994. "Business groups." Pp. 453–75 in *The Handbook of Economic Sociology,* edited by J. N. Smelser and R. Swedberg. Princeton, NJ: Princeton University Press.

Iwai, Noriko. 2004. "Japanese General Social Survey: Beginning and Development." ZA Information 55 (Published in November 2004 by the Central Data Archive Empirical Social Research, University Cologne at http://www.gesis.org/en/za/index.htm).

Kawamura, Nozomu. 1973. *Nihon shakaigakushi kenkyu* (A study of the history of sociology in Japan). Tokyo, Japan: Nihon Shakaigaku Kenkyu.

Kawamura, Nozomu. 1994. *Sociology and Society in Japan.* New York: Kegan Paul International.

Khondker, Habibul Haque. 2004. "Glocalization as Globalization: Evolution of a Sociological Concept." *Bangladesh e-Journal of Sociology* 1(2):1–9. Retrieved March 15, 2005 (http://64.233.161.104/search?q=cache:vr0c0fjQa04J:www.bangladeshsociology.org/Habib%2520–2520ejournal%2520Paper%2520GlobalizationHHK,%2520PDF.pdf+Khondker+glocalization+as+globalization&hl=en).

King, Ambrose Yeo-Chi. 1978. "The Development and Death of Chinese Academic Sociology: A Chapter in the Sociology of Sociology." *Modern Asian Studies* 12:37–58.

Kitagawa, Ryukichi, ed. 1984. *Gendai shakaigaku jiten* (Modern Encyclopedia of Sociology). Tokyo, Japan: Yushindo.

Koyano, Shogo. 1976. "Sociological Studies in Japan: Prewar, Postwar and Contemporary Stages." *Current Sociology* 24:1–195.

Li, Hanlin, Fang Ming, Wang Ying, Sunbingyao, and Qi Wang. 2001. "Chinese Sociology, 1898–1968." *Social Forces* 65:612–40.

Lie, John. 1996. "Sociology of Contemporary Japan." *Current Sociology* 44(1):1–101.

Matsui, Hiroshi. 1997. "Plans for Data Archives at the Information Center for Social Science Research on Japan." *Social Science Japan* 10(August):9–10.

Merle, Aurore. 2004. "Towards a Chinese Sociology for 'Communist Civilisation' in Peking." *Perspectives Chinoises* 52:1–12. Retrieved February 13, 2005 (http://www.cefc.com.hk/uk/pc.articles/art_ligne.php?num_art_ligne=5201).

Mita, Munesuke, Akira Kurihara, and Yoshihisa Tanaka, eds. 1988. *Shakaigaku jiten* (Encyclopedia of Sociology). Tokyo, Japan: Kobundo.

Morioka, Kiyomi, Tsutomu Shiobara, and Yasuhei Honma, eds. 1993. *Shin shakgaku jiten* (New Encyclopedia of Sociology). Tokyo, Japan: Yuhikaku.

Morioka, Kiyomi and Yazawa, Shujiro. 1993. "Gendai Shakaigaku no Kokusaiteki Tenkai" (Internationalization of Sociology). Pp. 1543–47 in *Shin shakgaku jiten* (New Encyclopedia of Sociology), edited by Kiyomi Morioka, Tsutomu Shiobara, and Yasuhei Honma. Tokyo, Japan: Yhikaku.

Nakao, Keiko. 1998. "Sociological Work in Japan." *Annual Review of Sociology* 24:499–516.

Odaka, Kunio. 1950. "Japanese Sociology: Past and Present." *Social Forces* 28:400–409.

Robertson, Roland. 1992. *Globalization: Social Theory and Global Culture.* London, England: Sage.

Sasaki, Masamichi. 2000. "Japanese Sociology." Pp. 1477–83 in *Encyclopedia of Sociology,* edited by Edgar Borgatta. New York: Macmillan.

Shinmei, Masamichi, ed. 1944. *Shakaigaku jiten* (Encyclopedia of Sociology). Tokyo, Japan: Kawade Shobo.

Smith, Tom W., Jibum Kim, Achim Koch, and Alison Park. 2005. "The GSS Model of Social-Science Research." *ZUMA—Nachrichten* 56(29):68–77.

Social Science Japan Data Archive. 2005. Retrieved April 5, 2005 (http://ssjda.iss.u-tokyo.ac.jp/en/da_about.html).

Takemura, Hideki. 1999. "Literature on Modern Japanese Sociologists." *Tsushin* 5(2):6. Fall Newsletter published by the Reischauer Institute of Japanese Studies. Retrieved December 10, 2004 (http://www.fas.harvard.edu/~rijs/DCJArt_Sociols_v5n2_1999.html).

Tanioka, Ichiro and Noriko Iwai. 2003. "JGSS Project: Its Origin and Background" (in Japanese). *Statistics* October:47–54.

Tominaga, Ken'ichi. 1993. *Nihon shakai no nyu webu.* Tokyo, Japan: University of Tokyo Press.

U.S. Library of Congress. 2003. "Country Studies U.S." Retrieved December 20, 2004 (http://www.countrystudies.us/china/69.htm).

Whyte, Martin. 2000. "China Studies." Pp. 297–304 in *Encyclopedia of Sociology,* edited by Edgar F. Borgatta. London, England: Macmillan.

Xueguang, Zhou and Pei Xiaomei. 1997. "Chinese Sociology in a Transitional Society." *Contemporary Sociology* 26(5):569–72.

Yazawa, Shujiro. 2000. "Introduction: Japanese Sociology Bibliography of Japanese Sociological Literature in Foreign Languages." (Published in *Japan Sociological Society,* July 1998, and updated in February 2000.) Retrieved December 10, 2004 (http://www.members.aol.com/ShuYazawa/bib2.htm).

Chapter 6. Sociology in Canada

Abrams, Philip. 1968. *The Origins of British Sociology: 1834–1914.* Chicago, IL: University of Chicago Press.

Albas, Daniel and Cheryl Albas. 1984. *Student Life and Exams: Stresses and Coping Strategies.* Dubuque, IA: Kendall-Hunt.

Alford, Robert. 1998. *The Craft of Inquiry: Methods, Theories and Evidence.* Oxford, England: Oxford University Press.

Andersen, Robert, James Curtis, and Edward Grabb. 2006. "Trends in Civic Association Activity in Four Democracies: The Special Case of Women in the United States." *American Sociological Review* 71:376–400.

Armstrong, Pat. 2001. *Women and Health Care Reform in Canada.* Aurora, Ontario, Canada: Garamond Press.

Armstrong, Pat and Hugh Armstrong. 1978. *The Double Ghetto: Canadian Women and Their Segregated Work.* Toronto, Ontario, Canada: McLelland and Stewart.

Armstrong, Pat and Hugh Armstrong. 2003. *Wasting Away: The Undermining of Canadian Health Care.* Toronto, Ontario, Canada: Oxford University Press.

Armstrong, Pat, Hugh Armstrong, and Claudia Fegan. 1998. *Universal Health Care: What the United States Can Learn from the Canadian Experience.* New York: New Press.

Atkinson, Michael. 2003. *Tattooed: The Sociogenesis of a Body Art.* Toronto, Ontario, Canada: University of Toronto Press.

Baber, Zaheer. 1996. *The Science of Empire: Scientific Knowledge, Civilization, and Colonial Rule in India.* Albany: State University of New York Press.

Baer, Douglas. 1990. "Socialization into Dominant vs. Counter Ideology Among University-Educated Canadians." *Canadian Review of Sociology and Anthropology—Revue Canadienne De Sociologie Et D'Anthropologie* 27:487–504.

Baer, Douglas. 2005. "On the Crisis in Canadian Sociology: Comment on McLaughlin." *Canadian Journal of Sociology* 30:491–502.

Baer, Douglas, J. Curtis, and E. Grabb. 2001. "Has Voluntary Association Activity Declined? Cross-National Analyses for Fifteen Countries." *Canadian Review of Sociology and Anthropology—Revue Canadienne De Sociologie Et D'Anthropologie* 38:249–74.

Baer, Douglas, E. Grabb, and W. Johnston. 1990. "The Values of Canadians and Americans: A Critical Analysis and Reassessment." *Social Forces* 68:693–713.

Baer, Douglas, E. Grabb, and W. Johnston. 1993. "National Character, Regional Culture, and the Values of Canadians and Americans." *Canadian Review of Sociology and Anthropology—Revue Canadienne De Sociologie Et D'Anthropologie* 30:13–36.

Baehr, Peter. 2002. *Founders, Classics, Canons: Modern Disputes Over the Origins and Appraisal of Sociology's Heritage.* New Brunswick, NJ: Transaction Publishers.

Béland, Daniel and John Myles. 2003. *Stasis Amidst Change: Canadian Pension Reform in an Age of Retrenchment.* Hamilton, Ontario, Canada: SEDAP Research Program, McMaster University.

Boyd, Monica. 1979. *Rank and Salary Differentials in the 1970s: A Comparison of Male and Female Full-time Teachers in Canadian Universities and Colleges.* Ottawa, Ontario, Canada: Association of Universities and Colleges of Canada.

Boyd, Monica, John Goyder, Frank Jones, Hugh McRoberts, Peter C. Pineo, and John Porter, eds. 1985. *Ascription and Achievement: Studies in Mobility and Status Attainment in Canada.* Ottawa, Ontario, Canada: Carleton University Press.

Boyd, Monica and D. Thomas. 2001. "Match or Mismatch? The Employment of Immigrant Engineers in Canada's

Labour Force." *Population Research and Policy Review* 20(1–2):107–133.

Breton, Raymond. 1989. "Québec Sociology: Agendas from Society or from Sociologists?" *Canadian Review of Sociology and Anthropology* 26:557–70.

Breton, Raymond. 1990. *Ethnic Identity and Equality: Varieties of Experience in a Canadian City*. Toronto, Ontario, Canada: University of Toronto Press.

Breton, Raymond and J. Reitz. 2005. *Ethnic Relations in Canada: Institutional Dynamics*. Montréal, Québec, Canada: McGill-Queen's University Press.

Bryant, Joseph. 1996. *Moral Codes and Social Structure in Ancient Greece: A Sociology of Greek Ethics from Homer to the Epicureans and Stoics*. Albany: State University of New York Press.

Brym, Robert. 1980. *Intellectuals and Politics*. London, England: Allen & Unwin.

Brym, Robert. 1987. "The Political Sociology of Intellectuals: A Critique and Proposal." Pp. 199–209 in *Intellectuals in Liberal Democracies,* edited by A. G. Gagnon. New York: Praeger.

Brym, Robert. 1988. "Structural Location and Ideological Divergence: Jewish Marxist Intellectuals in Turn-of-the-Century Russia." Pp. 359–79 in *Social Structures: A Network Approach,* edited by B. Wellman and S. D. Berkowitz. Cambridge, England: Cambridge University Press.

Brym, Robert. 2001. "Intellectuals, Sociology of." Pp. 7631–35 in *International Encyclopedia of the Social and Behavioral Sciences,* vol. 11, edited by N. J. Smelser and P. B. Baltes. Oxford, England: Elsevier Science.

Brym, Robert. 2003. "The Decline of the Canadian Sociology and Anthropology Association." *Canadian Journal of Sociology* 28:411–16.

Brym, Robert and Bonnie Fox. 1989. *From Culture to Power: The Sociology of English Canada*. Toronto, Ontario, Canada: Oxford University Press.

Brym, Robert and John Myles. 1989. "Social Science Intellectuals and Public Issues in English Canada." *University of Toronto Quarterly* 58:442–51.

Brym, Robert and Celine Saint-Pierre. 1997. "Canadian Sociology." *Contemporary Sociology* 26:543–46.

Budros, Art. 2004. "Social Shocks and Slave Social Mobility: Manumission in Brunswick County, Virginia, 1782–1862." *American Journal of Sociology* 110:539–79.

Burawoy, Michael. 2004. "Public Sociologies: Contradictions, Dilemmas, and Possibilities." *Social Forces* 82:1603–18.

Burawoy, Michael. 2005a. "Provincializing the Social Sciences." Pp. 508–25 in *The Politics of Method in the Human Sciences: Positivism and Its Epistemological Others,* edited by George Steinmetz. Durham, NC: Duke University Press.

Burawoy, Michael. 2005b. "2004 Presidential Address: For Public Sociology." *American Sociological Review* 70:4–28.

Buxton, William. 1985. *Talcott Parsons and the Capitalist Nation-State: Political Sociology as a Strategic Vocation*. Toronto, Ontario, Canada: University of Toronto Press.

Buxton, William and Charles Acland. 1999. *Harold Innis in the New Century: Reflections and Refractions*. Montreal, Québec, Canada: McGill-Queen's University Press.

Camara, Fatima and Richard Helmes-Hayes. 2003. "Tracing the Historical Development of Symbolic Interactionism in Canada: A Proposal for the Examination of Communication Networks in the SI Community." Paper presented at the 20th Qualitative Analysis Conference, May 21–24, Carleton University, Ottawa, Ontario, Canada.

Carroll, Michael P. 1986. *The Cult of the Virgin Mary: Psychological Origins*. Princeton, NJ: Princeton University Press.

Carroll, Michael P. 1989. *Catholic Cults and Devotions: A Psychological Enquiry*. Kingston, Ontario, Canada: McGill-Queen's University Press.

Carroll, Michael P. 2005. "Who Owns Democracy? Explaining the Long Running Debate over Canadian/American Value Differences." *Canadian Review of Sociology and Anthropology* 42:267–82.

Carroll, William K. 1986. *Corporate Power and Canadian Capitalism*. Vancouver: University of British Columbia Press.

Carroll, William K. 1992a. *Fragile Truths: Twenty-Five Years of Sociology and Anthropology in Canada*. Ottawa, Ontario, Canada: Carleton University Press.

Carroll, William K. 1992b. *Organizing Dissent: Contemporary Social Movements in Theory and Practice: Studies in the Politics of Counter-Hegemony*. Toronto, Ontario, Canada: Garamond Press.

Carroll, William K. 2004. *Corporate Power in a Globalizing World: A Study in Elite Social Organization*. Don Mills, Ontario, Canada: Oxford University Press.

Clairmont, Donald and Dennis W. Magill. 1974. *Africaville: The Life and Death of a Canadian Black Community*. Toronto, Ontario, Canada: McClelland and Stewart.

Clark, Samuel. 1995. *State and Status: The Rise of the State and Aristocratic Power in Western Europe*. Kingston, Ontario, Canada: McGill-Queen's University Press.

Clark, S. D. 1948. *Church and Sect in Canada*. Toronto, Ontario, Canada: University of Toronto Press.

Clark, S. D. 1959. *Movements of Political Protest in Canada, 1640–1840*. Toronto, Ontario, Canada: University of Toronto Press.

Clark, S. D. 1976. *Canadian Society in Historical Perspective*. Toronto, Ontario, Canada: McGraw-Hill Ryerson.

Clement, Wallace. 1975. *The Canadian Corporate Elite: An Analysis of Economic Power*. Toronto, Ontario, Canada: McClelland and Stewart.

Clement, Wallace. 1977. *Continental Corporate Power: Economic Elite Linkages between Canada and the United States*. Toronto, Ontario, Canada: McClelland and Stewart.

Clement, Wallace. 1986. *The Struggle to Organize: Resistance in Canada's Fishery*. Toronto, Ontario, Canada: McClelland and Stewart.

Clement, Wallace. 2001. "Canadian Political Economy's Legacy for Sociology." *Canadian Journal of Sociology* 26(3):405–20.

Clement, Wallace and John Myles. 1994. *Relations of Ruling: Class and Gender in Postindustrial Societies*. Montreal, Québec, Canada: McGill-Queen's University Press.

Clement, Wallace and Leah F. Vosko. 2003. *Changing Canada: Political Economy as Transformation*. Montreal, Québec, Canada: McGill-Queen's University Press.

Collins, Randall. 1998. *The Sociology of Philosophies: A Global Theory of Intellectual Change*. Cambridge, MA: Belknap Press of Harvard University Press.

Cormier, Jeffrey. 2004. *The Canadianization Movement: Emergence, Survival and Success*. Toronto, Ontario, Canada: University of Toronto Press.

Coser, Lewis. 1965. *Men of Ideas: A Sociologist's View*. New York: Free Press.

Coser, Lewis. 1984. *Refugee Scholars in America: Their Impact and Their Experiences*. New Haven, CT: Yale University Press.

Creighton, D. G. 1957. *Harold Adams Innis: Portrait of a Scholar.* Toronto, Ontario, Canada: University of Toronto Press.

Curtis, Bruce. 2001. *The Politics of Population: State Formation, Statistics, and the Census of Canada, 1840–75.* Toronto, Ontario, Canada: University of Toronto Press.

Curtis, Bruce and Lorna Weir. 2005. "Crisis Talk: Comments on McLaughlin's Canada's Impossible Science." *Canadian Journal of Sociology* 30(4):503–11.

Davies, Scott. 1995. "Leaps of Faith: Shifting Currents in Critical Sociology of Education." *American Journal of Sociology* 100:1448–78.

Davies, Scott and Neil Guppy. 1997. "Fields of Study, College Selectivity, and Student Inequalities." *Social Forces* 73:131–51.

Eichler, Margarit. 1988. *Families in Canada Today: Recent Changes and Their Policy Consequences.* 2d ed. Toronto, Ontario, Canada: Gage.

Eichler, Margarit. 2001. "Women Pioneers in Canadian Sociology: The Effects of a Politics of Gender and a Politics of Knowledge." *Canadian Journal of Sociology—Cahiers Canadiens De Sociologie* 26:375–403.

Eichler, Margarit. 2002. "Feminism and Canadian Sociology." *American Sociologist* 33:27–41.

Ericson R. V. and P. M. Baranek. 1982. *The Ordering of Justice: A Study of Accused Persons as Dependants in the Criminal Process.* Toronto, Ontario, Canada: University of Toronto Press.

Ericson, R. V., P. M. Baranek, and J. B. L. Chan. 1987. *Visualizing Deviance: A Study of News Organizations.* Toronto, Ontario, Canada: University of Toronto Press.

Fong, Eric. 2003. "American Diversity: A Demographic Challenge for the Twenty-First Century." *Social Forces* 82:432–34.

Fong, Eric. 2004. "Destination Canada: Immigration Debates and Issues." *International Migration Review* 38:334–36.

Fong, Eric and R. Wilkes. 2003. "Racial and Ethnic Residential Patterns in Canada." *Sociological Forum* 18:577–602.

Fournier, Marcel. 2001. "Québec Sociology and Québec Society: The Construction of a Collective Identity." *Canadian Journal of Sociology* 26:333–47.

Fournier, Marcel. 2002. "Québec Sociology: A Discipline of Its Objects." *American Sociologist* 33:42–54.

Fox, Bonnie. 1993. *Family Patterns, Gender Relations.* Toronto, Ontario, Canada: Oxford University Press.

Fox, John and Michael Ornstein. 1986. "The Canadian State and Corporate Elites in the Postwar Period." *Canadian Review of Sociology and Anthropology—Revue Canadienne De Sociologie Et D'Anthropologie* 23:481–506.

Frank, Arthur W. 1995. *The Wounded Storyteller: Body, Illness, and Ethics.* Chicago, IL: University of Chicago Press.

Frank, Arthur W. 2004. *The Renewal of Generosity: Illness, Medicine, and How to Live.* Chicago, IL: University of Chicago Press.

Fuller, Steve. 2000. "A Very Qualified Success, Indeed: The Case of Anthony Giddens and British Sociology." *Canadian Journal of Sociology* 25:507–16.

Galliher, John F. and James Galliher. 1995. *Marginality and Dissent in Twentieth-Century American Sociology: The Case of Elizabeth Briant Lee and Alfred McClung Lee.* Albany: State University of New York Press.

Gartner, Rosemary. 1991. "Family-Structure, Welfare Spending, and Child Homicide in Developed Democracies." *Journal of Marriage and the Family* 53:231–40.

Gartner, Rosemary and R. MacMillan. 1995. "The Effect of Victim-Offender Relationship on Reporting Crimes of Violence against Women." *Canadian Journal of Criminology* 37:393–429.

Gartner, Rosemary and B. McCarthy. 1991. "The Social Distribution of Femicide in Urban Canada, 1921–1988." *Law and Society Review* 25:287–311.

Gieryn, Thomas F. and Richard F. Hirsch. 1983. "Marginality and Innovation in Science." *Social Studies of Science* 13:87–106.

Goffman, Erving. 1959. *The Presentation of Self in Everyday Life.* Garden City, NY: Anchor Books.

Gouldner, Alvin. 1965. *Enter Plato: Classical Greece and the Origins of Social Theory.* New York: Basic Books.

Gouldner, Alvin. 1970. *The Coming Crisis of Western Sociology.* New York: Basic Books.

Grabb, Edward, Douglas Baer, and James Curtis. 1999. "The Origins of American Individualism: Reconsidering the Historical Evidence." *Canadian Journal of Sociology—Cahiers Canadiens De Sociologie* 24:511–33.

Grabb, Edward and James Curtis. 1988. "English Canadian-American Differences in Orientation Toward Social Control and Individual Rights." *Sociological Focus* 21:127–40.

Grabb, Edward and James Curtis. 2005. *Regions Apart: The Four Societies of Canada and the United States.* Toronto, Ontario, Canada: Oxford University Press.

Grabb, Edward, J. Curtis, and D. Baer. 2000. "Defining Moments and Recurring Myths: Comparing Canadians and Americans After the American Revolution." *Canadian Review of Sociology and Anthropology—Revue Canadienne De Sociologie Et D'Anthropologie* 37:373–419.

Grabb, Edward, J. Curtis, and D. Baer. 2001. "On Accuracy and Big Pictures: Reply to Lipset." *Canadian Review of Sociology and Anthropology—Revue Canadienne De Sociologie Et D'Anthropologie* 38:101–103.

Haas, Jack and William Shaffir. 1991. *Becoming Doctors: The Adoption of a Cloak of Competence.* Greenwich, CT: JAI Press.

Hagan, John. 1989a. "Comparing Crime and Criminalization in Canada and the USA." *Canadian Journal of Sociology* 14:361.

Hagan, John. 1989b. "Enduring Differences: Further Notes on Homicide in Canada and the USA." *Canadian Journal of Sociology* 14:490.

Hagan, John. 1991. "Destiny and Drift: Subcultural Preferences, Status Attainments, and the Risks and Rewards of Youth." *American Sociological Review* 56:567–82.

Hagan, John. 2001. *Northern Passage: American Vietnam War Resisters in Canada.* Cambridge, MA: Harvard University Press.

Hagan, John and Holly Foster. 2001. "Youth Violence and the End of Adolescence." *American Sociological Review* 66:874–99.

Hagan, John and Jeffery Leon. 1977. "Rediscovering Delinquency: Social History, Political Ideology and the Sociology of Law." *American Sociological Review* 42:587–98.

Hagan, John, Ross MacMillan, and Blair Wheaton. 1996. "New Kid in Town: Social Capital and the Life Course Effects of Family Migration on Children." *American Sociological Review* 61:368–85.

Hagan, John and B. McCarthy. 1997. *Mean Streets: Youth Crime and Homelessness.* New York: Cambridge University Press.

Hagan, John and B. Wheaton. 1993. "The Search for Adolescent Role Exits and the Transition to Adulthood." *Social Forces* 71:955–980.

Hall, John A. 1986. *Rediscoveries: Some Neglected Modern European Political Thinkers.* Oxford, England: Oxford University Press.

Hall, John A. 1988. *Liberalism: Politics, Ideology and the Market.* Chapel Hill: The University of North Carolina Press.

Hall, John A. 1994. *Coercion and Consent: Studies on the Modern State.* Cambridge, England: Polity Press.

Hall, John A. 1996. *International Orders.* Cambridge, England: Polity Press.

Hannigan, John. 1998. *Fantasy City: Pleasure and Profit in the Postmodern Metropolis.* London, England: Routledge.

Helmes-Hayes, Richard. 2002. "John Porter: Canada's Most Famous Sociologist." *American Sociologist* 33:79–104.

Helmes-Hayes, Richard C. and James E. Curtis. 1998. *The Vertical Mosaic Revisited.* Toronto, Ontario, Canada: University of Toronto Press.

Helmes-Hayes, Richard and Dennis Wilcox-Magill. 1993. "A Neglected Classic—Marsh, Leonard Canadians in and Out-of-Work." *Canadian Review of Sociology and Anthropology—Revue Canadienne De Sociologie Et D'Anthropologie* 30:83–109.

Hiller, Harry. 1982. *Society and Change: S. D. Clark and the Development of Canadian Sociology.* Toronto, Ontario, Canada: University of Toronto Press.

Hughes, Everett C. 1943. *French Canada in Transition.* Chicago, IL: University of Chicago Press.

Innis, Harold. 1923. *History of the Canadian Pacific Railway.* London, England: P. S. King.

Innis, Harold. 1927. *The Fur Trade in Canada.* Toronto, Ontario, Canada: Oxford University Press.

Innis, Harold. 1930. *Problems of Staple Production in Canada.* Toronto, Ontario, Canada: Ryerson Press.

Innis, Harold. 1946. *Political Economy in the Modern State.* Toronto, Ontario, Canada: Ryerson Press.

Innis, Harold. 1950. *Empire and Communications.* Oxford, England: Clarendon Press.

Johnston, Josée. 2005. "The 'Second Shift' of Canadian Sociology: Setting Sociological Standards in a Global Era." *Canadian Journal of Sociology* 30:513–27.

Kauppi, Niilo. 1996. *French Intellectual Nobility: Institutional and Symbolic Transformations in the Post-Sartrian Era.* Albany: State University of New York Press.

Kemple, Thomas M. 1995. *Reading Marx Writing: Melodrama, the Market, and the "Grundrisse."* Stanford, CA: Stanford University Press.

Klapp, Orrin. 1962. *Heroes, Villains, and Fools: The Changing American Character.* Englewood Cliffs, NJ: Prentice Hall.

Klapp, Orrin. 1964. *Symbolic Leaders: Public Dramas and Public Men.* Chicago, IL: Aldine.

Kowalchuk, Lisa. 2003a. "Asymmetrical Alliances, Organizational Democracy and Peasant Protest in El Salvador." *Canadian Review of Sociology and Anthropology* 40(3): 291–309.

Kowalchuk, Lisa. 2003b. "Peasant Struggle, Political Opportunities and the Unfinished Agrarian Reform in El Salvador." *Canadian Journal of Sociology* 28:309–40.

Kroker, Arthur. 1984. *Technology and the Canadian Mind: Innis/McCluhan/Grant.* Montreal, Québec, Canada: New World Perspectives.

Kumar, Krishan. 2001. "Sociology and the Englishness of English Social Theory." *Sociological Theory* 19:41–64.

Lamont, Michele. 1987. "How to Become a Dominant French Philosopher: The Case of Jacques Derrida." *American Journal of Sociology* 95:584–622.

Lamont, Michele. 2000. "Meaning-Making in Cultural Sociology: Broadening Our Agenda." *Contemporary Sociology—A Journal of Reviews* 29:602–607.

Laxer, Gordon. 1989. *Open for Business: The Roots of Foreign Ownership in Canada.* Toronto, Ontario, Canada: Oxford University Press.

Laxer, Gordon. 1991. *Perspectives on Canadian Economic Development: Class, Staples, Gender, and Elites.* Toronto, Ontario, Canada: Oxford University Press.

Lepenies, Wolfe. 1988. *Between Literature and Science.* Cambridge, England: Cambridge University Press.

Leroux, Robert. 2001. "La Nation and the Québec Sociological Tradition (1890–1980)." *Canadian Journal of Sociology* 26:349–73.

Li, Peter S. 1996. *The Making of Post-War Canada.* Toronto, Ontario, Canada: Oxford University Press.

Li, Peter S. 1998. *The Chinese in Canada.* Toronto, Ontario, Canada: Oxford University Press.

Li, Peter S. 2003. *Destination Canada: Immigration Debates and Issues.* Don Mills, Ontario, Canada: Oxford University Press.

Luxton, Meg. 1980. *More Than a Labour of Love: Three Generations of Women's Labour in the Home.* Toronto, Ontario, Canada: Women's Educational Press.

MacGregor David. 1984. *The Communist Ideal in Hegel and Marx.* Toronto, Ontario, Canada: University of Toronto Press.

MacGregor David. 1992. *Hegel, Marx, and the English State.* Boulder, CO: Westview Press.

Marchak, M. Patricia. 1983. *Green Gold: The Forest Industry in British Columbia.* Vancouver: University of British Columbia Press.

Marchak, M. Patricia. 1991. *The Integrated Circus: The New Right and the Restructuring of Global Markets.* Montreal, Québec, Canada: McGill-Queen's University Press.

Marchak, M. Patricia. 1995. *Logging the Globe.* Montreal, Québec, Canada: McGill-Queen's University Press.

Marchak, M. Patricia. 1996. *Racism, Sexism, and the University: The Political Science Affair at the University of British Columbia.* Montréal, Québec, Canada: McGill-Queen's University Press.

Marchak, M. Patricia, Scott L. Aycock, and Deborah M. Herbert. 1999. *Falldown: Forest Policy in British Columbia.* Vancouver, British Columbia, Canada: David Suzuki Foundation.

Marsh, Leonard. 1940. *Canadians In and Out of Work: A Survey of Economic Classes and Their Relation to the Labour Market.* Toronto, Ontario, Canada: Oxford University Press.

Marsh, Leonard. 1943. *Report on Social Security for Canada.* Advisory Committee for Reconstruction, Ottawa, Ontario, Canada.

Marshall, Barbara. 1994. *Engendering Modernity: Feminism, Social Theory, and Social Change.* Boston, MA: Northeastern University Press.

Marshall, Victor W. 1980. *The Last Chapters: A Sociology of Aging and Dying.* Monterey, CA: Brooks/Cole.

McDonald, Lynn. 1993. *The Early Origins of the Social Sciences.* Montréal, Québec, Canada: McGill-Queen's University Press.

McDonald, Lynn. 1994. *The Women Founders of the Social Sciences.* Ottawa, Ontario, Canada: Carleton University Press.

McDonald, Lynn. 1998. *Women Theorists on Society and Politics.* Waterloo, Ontario, Canada: Wilfrid Laurier University Press.

McLaughlin, Neil. 1998. "How to Become a Forgotten Intellectual: Intellectual Movements and the Rise and Fall of Erich Fromm." *Sociological Forum* 13:215–46.

McLaughlin, Neil. 2001. "Optimal Marginality: Innovation and Orthodoxy in Fromm's Revision of Psychoanalysis." *Sociological Quarterly* 42:271–88.

McLaughlin, Neil. 2005. "Canada's Impossible Science: Historical and Institutional Origins of the Coming Crisis in Anglo-Canadian Sociology." *Canadian Journal of Sociology—Cahiers Canadiens De Sociologie* 30:1–40.

McLaughlin, Neil. 2006. "Whither the Future of Canadian Sociology? Thoughts on Moving Forward." *The Canadian Journal of Sociology-Cahiers Canadiens De Sociologie* 31:107–130.

McLuhan, Marshall. 1994. *Understanding Media: The Extensions of Man.* Cambridge: MIT Press.

Merton, Robert K. 1949. *Social Theory and Social Structure.* Glencoe, IL: Free Press.

Miall, Charlene and Andrew Miall. 2003. "The Exxon Factor: The Roles of Corporate and Academic Science in the Emergence and Legitimation of a New Global Model of Sequence Stratigraphy." *Sociological Quarterly* 43:307–34.

Mills, C. W. 1967. *The Sociological Imagination.* London, England: Oxford University Press.

Murphy, Raymond. 2005. "Prejudice and Pride: A Commentary on 'Canada's Impossible Science.'" *Canadian Journal of Sociology* 30:529–32.

Myles, John. 1984. *Old Age in the Welfare State: The Political Economy of Public Pensions.* Lawrence, KS: University of Kansas Press.

Nakhaie, Reza. 1992. "Class and Voting Consistency in Canada—Analyses Bearing on the Mobilization Thesis." *Canadian Journal of Sociology—Cahiers Canadiens De Sociologie* 17:275–99.

Nakhaie, Reza. 1996. "The Reproduction of Class Relations by Gender in Canada." *Canadian Journal of Sociology—Cahiers Canadiens De Sociologie* 21:523–58.

Nakhaie, Reza. 1997. "Vertical Mosaic Among the Elites: The New Imagery Revisited." *Canadian Review of Sociology and Anthropology—Revue Canadienne De Sociologie Et D'Anthropologie* 34:1–24.

Nakhaie, Reza. 2002. "Gender Differences in Publication Among University Professors in Canada." *Canadian Review of Sociology and Anthropology—Revue Canadienne De Sociologie Et D'Anthropologie* 39:151–79.

Nakhaie, Reza and Robert Brym. 1999. "The Political Attitudes of Canadian Professors." *Canadian Journal of Sociology—Cahiers Canadiens De Sociologie* 24:329–53.

Ogmundson, Richard. 1994. "Beyond Lipset and his Critics." *Canadian Review of Sociology and Anthropology* 31:196–99.

Ogmundson, Richard. 2002. "Neglected Research Opportunities." *American Sociologist* 33(1):55–78.

Ogmundson, Richard. 2005. "Does It Matter if Women, Minorities and Gays Govern? New Data Concerning an Old Question." *Canadian Journal of Sociology—Cahiers Canadiens De Sociologie* 30:315–24.

Ogmundson, Richard and M. Doyle. 2002. "The Rise and Decline of Canadian Labour, 1960 to 2000: Elites, Power, Ethnicity and Gender." *Canadian Journal of Sociology—Cahiers Canadiens De Sociologie* 27:413–54.

O'Neill, John. 1976. *On Critical Theory.* New York: Seabury.

Ornstein, Michael. 1986. "The Political-Ideology of the Canadian Capitalist Class." *Canadian Review of Sociology and Anthropology—Revue Canadienne De Sociologie Et D'Anthropologie* 23:182–209.

Ornstein, Michael. 1988. "Corporate Involvement in Canadian Hospital and University Boards, 1946–1977." *Canadian Review of Sociology and Anthropology—Revue Canadienne De Sociologie Et D'Anthropologie* 25:365–88.

Ornstein, Michael. 1989. "The Social-Organization of the Canadian Capitalist Class in Comparative Perspective." *Canadian Review of Sociology and Anthropology—Revue Canadienne De Sociologie Et D'Anthropologie* 26:151–77.

Pinard, Maurice and Richard Hamilton. 1984. "The Class Bases of the Québec Independence Movement: Conjectures and Evidence." *Ethnic and Racial Studies* 7:19–54.

Polster Claire. 2001. "A Break from the Past: Impacts and Implications of the Canada Foundation for Innovation and the Canada Research Chairs Initiatives." *Canadian Review of Sociology and Anthropology* 39:275–99.

Porter, John. 1965. *The Vertical Mosaic: An Analysis of Social Class and Power in Canada.* Toronto, Ontario, Canada: University of Toronto Press.

Prus, Robert. 1989a. *Pursuing Customers: An Ethnography of Marketing Activities.* Newbury Park, CA: Sage.

Prus, Robert. 1989b. *Making Sales: Influence as Interpersonal Accomplishment.* Newbury Park, CA: Sage.

Prus, Robert. 1996. *Symbolic Interaction and Ethnographic Research: Intersubjectivity and the Study of Human Lived Experience.* New York: State University of New York Press.

Prus, Robert. 1997. *Subcultural Mosaics and Intersubjective Realities: An Ethnographic Research Agenda for Pragmatizing the Social Sciences.* New York: SUNY Press.

Prus Robert and S. Irini. 1980. *Hookers, Rounders and Desk Clerks: The Social Organizaiton of the Hotel Community.* Salem, WI: Sheffield.

Prus, Robert and C. R. D. Sharper. 1977. *Road Hustler: The Career Contingencies of Professional Card and Dice Hustlers.* Lexington, MA: Lexington Books.

Reitz, Jeffrey. 1980. *The Survival of Ethnic Groups.* Toronto, Ontario, Canada: McGraw-Hill Ryerson.

Reitz, Jeffrey. 1998. *Warmth of the Welcome: The Social Causes of Economic Success for Immigrants in Different Nations and Cities.* Boulder, CO: Westview Press.

Seidman, Steven. 1994. *Contested Knowledge: Social Theory in the Postmodern Era.* Cambridge, England: Blackwell.

Shaffir, William. 1974. *Life in a Religious Community: The Lubavitcher Chassidim in Montreal.* Toronto, Ontario, Canada: Holt, Rinehart & Winston.

Shore, Marlene. 1987. *The Science of Social Redemption: McGill, The Chicago School, and the Origins of Social Research in Canada.* Toronto, Ontario, Canada: University of Toronto Press.

Sinclair, Peter. 1985. *From Traps to Draggers: Domestic Commodity Production in Northwest Newfoundland, 1850–1982.* St. John's: Institute of Social and Economic Research, Memorial University of Newfoundland.

Sinclair, Peter. 1988. *A Question of Survival: The Fisheries and Newfoundland Society*. St. John's: Institute of Social and Economic Research, Memorial University of Newfoundland.

Slaughter, Sheila and Larry L. Leslie. 1999. *Academic Capitalism: Politics, Policies and the Entrepreneurial University*. Baltimore, MD: Johns Hopkins University Press.

Smith, Dorothy E. 1975. "What It Might Mean to Do a Canadian Sociology—Everyday World As Problematic." *Canadian Journal of Sociology—Cahiers Canadiens De Sociologie* 1(3):363–76.

Smith, Dorothy E. 1987. *The Everyday World as Problematic: A Feminist Sociology*. Toronto, Ontario, Canada: University of Toronto Press.

Smith, Dorothy E. 1995. *The Conceptual Practices of Power: A Feminist Sociology of Knowledge*. Toronto, Ontario, Canada: University of Toronto Press.

Smith, Dorothy E. 1999. *Writing the Social: Critique, Theory, and Investigations*. Toronto, Ontario, Canada: University of Toronto Press.

Staggenborg, Suzanne. 1986. "Coalition Work in the Pro-Choice Movement: Organizational and Environmental Opportunities and Obstacles." *Social Problems* 33:375–90.

Staggenborg, Suzanne. 1988. "The Consequences of Professionalization and Formalization in the Pro-Choice Movement." *American Sociological Review* 53:585–605.

Staggenborg, Suzanne. 1989. "Organizational and Environmental Influences on the Development of the Pro-Choice Movement." *Social Forces* 68:204–40.

Staggenborg, Suzanne. 1998. "Countermovement Dynamics in Federal Systems: A Comparison of Abortion Movements in Canada and the United States." *Research in Political Sociology* 8:209–40.

Staggenborg, Suzanne. 2001. "Beyond Culture versus Politics: A Case Study of a Local Women's Movement." *Gender and Society* 15:505–28.

Stebbins, Robert. 1984. *The Magician: Career, Culture and Social Psychology in a Variety Art*. Toronto, Ontario, Canada: Clark Irwin.

Stebbins, Robert. 1987. *Canadian Football: The View from the Helmet*. London: University of Western Ontario, Centre for Social and Humanistic Studies.

Stebbins, Robert. 1990. *The Laugh Makers: Stand-up Comedy as Art, Business and Life-Style*. Montreal, Québec, Canada: McGill-Queen's University Press.

Stebbins, Robert. 1995. *Tolerable Differences: Living with Deviance*. 2d ed. Whitby, Ontario, Canada: McGraw-Hill Ryerson.

Stebbins, Robert. 2004. *Between Work and Leisure: The Common Ground of Two Separate Worlds*. New Brunswick, NJ: Transaction Publishers.

Stehr, Nico. 1992. *Practical Knowledge: Applying the Social Sciences*. London, England: Sage.

Stehr, Nico. 1994. *Knowledge Societies*. New York: Sage.

Sydie, R. A. 1987. *Natural Women, Cultured Men: A Feminist Perspective on Sociological Theory*. Toronto, Ontario, Canada: Methuen.

Sydie, R. A. 1994. "Sex and the Sociological Fathers." *Canadian Review of Sociology and Anthropology—Revue Canadienne De Sociologie Et D'Anthropologie* 31:117–38.

Sydie, R. A. 2005. "Response to Neil McLaughlin's 'Canada's Impossible Science: Historical and Institutional Origins of the Coming Crisis in Anglo-Canadian Sociology.'" *Canadian Journal of Sociology* 30:533–36.

Tanner, Julian. 2001. *Teenage Troubles: Youth and Deviance in Canada*. Toronto, Ontario, Canada: Nelson Thomson Learning.

Tindall, D. B. and B. Wellman. 2001. "Canada as Social Structure: Social Network Analysis and Canadian Sociology." *Canadian Journal of Sociology—Cahiers Canadiens De Sociologie* 26:265–308.

Ungar, Sheldon. 1994. "Apples and Oranges—Probing the Attitude-Behavior Relationship for the Environment." *Canadian Review of Sociology and Anthropology* 31:288–304.

Ungar, Sheldon. 1998. "Bringing the Issue Back In: Comparing the Marketability of the Ozone Hole and Global Warming." *Social Problems* 45:510–27.

Ungar, Sheldon. 2000. "Knowledge, Ignorance and the Popular Culture: Climate Change versus the Ozone Hole." *Public Understanding of Science* 9:297–312.

Veltmeyer, Henry. 1997. "Latin America in the New World Order." *Canadian Journal of Sociology—Cahiers Canadiens De Sociologie* 22:207–42.

Wellman, Barry. 1979. "The Community Question: The Intimate Networks of East Yorkers." *American Journal of Sociology* 84:1201–31.

Wellman, Barry. 1999. *Networks in the Global Village: Life in Contemporary Communities*. Boulder, CO: Westview Press.

Wolf, Daniel. 1991. *The Rebels: A Brotherhood of Outlaw Bikers*. Toronto, Ontario, Canada: University of Toronto Press.

Wolfe, Alan. 1998. *Marginalized in the Middle*. Chicago, IL: University of Chicago Press.

Woolgar, Steve and Dorothy Pawluch. 1985. "Ontological Gerrymandering: The Anatomy of Social Problems Explanations." *Social Problems* 32:214–27.

Wrong, Dennis H. 1998. *The Modern Condition: Essays at Century's End*. Stanford, CT: Stanford University Press.

Chapter 7. European Sociology

Abbott, Andrew. 1998. "The Causal Devolution." *Sociological Methods & Research* 27:148–81.

Adorno, Theodor W. and Max Horkheimer. 1972. *Dialectic of Enlightenment*. New York: Seabury Press.

Badcock, C. R. 1975. *Lévi-Strauss: Structuralism and Sociological Theory*. London, England: Hutchinson.

Beck, Michael and Karl-Dieter Opp. 2001. "Der faktorielle Survey und die Messung von Normen (The Factorial Survey and the Measurement of Norms)." *Kölner Zeitschrift für Soziologie und Sozialpsychologie* 53:283–306.

Beck, Ulrich. 1992. *Risk Society*. London, England: Sage.

Berger, Peter L. and Thomas Luckmann. 1966. *The Social Construction of Reality. A Treatise in the Sociology of Knowledge*. New York: Doubleday.

Bernstein, Basil. 1975. *Class, Codes, and Control. A Theoretical and Empirical Analysis, with Special Reference to Education*. London, England: Routledge & Kegan Paul.

Bond, Rod and Peter Saunders. 1999. "Routes of Success: Influences on the Occupational Attainment of Young British Males." *British Journal of Sociology* 50:217–49.

Borgatta, Edgar F., ed. 2000. *Encyclopedia of Sociology*. New York: Macmillan.

Borkenau, Franz. 1973. *Der Übergang vom feudalen zum bürgerlichen Weltbild* (The Transition from the Feudal to the Bourgeois World View). Darmstadt, Germany: Wissenschaftliche Buchgesellschaft.

Boudon, Raymond. 1974. *Education, Opportunity and Social Inequality.* New York: Wiley.

Boudon, Raymond, Mohamed Cherkaoui, and Jeffrey Alexander, eds. 1997. *The Classical Tradition in Sociology. The European Tradition,* 4 vols. London, England: Sage.

Bouglé, Célestin. 1899. *Les idées égalitaires.* Paris, France: Alcan.

Bourdieu, Pierre. 1984. *Distinction: A Social Critique of the Judgement of Taste.* Cambridge, MA: Harvard University Press.

Bourdieu, Pierre. 1990. *The Logic of Practice.* Stanford, CA: Stanford University Press.

Brauns, Hildegard, Susanne Steinmann, and Dietmar Haun. 2000. "The Construction of Class Schemes According to Erikson, Goldthorpe and Portocarero with Reference to National Data Sources from Germany, Great Britain and France." *ZUMA-Nachrichten* 46:7–63.

Braverman, Harry. 1974. *Labour and Monopoly Capital: The Degradation of Work in the Twentieth Century.* London, England: Monthly Review Press.

Breen, Richard and John H. Goldthorpe. 1999. "Class Inequality and Meritocracy: A Critique of Saunders and an Alternative Analysis." *British Journal of Sociology* 50:1–27.

Brüderl, Josef and Andreas Diekmann. 1994. "Bildung, Geburtskohorte und Heiratsalter." *Zeitschrift für Soziologie* 23:56–73.

Bulmer, Martin. 1975. *Working-Class Images of Society.* London, England: Routledge.

Clark, Jon, Celia Modgil, and Soi-Ian Modgil, eds. 1990. *Anthony Giddens: Consensus and Controversy.* London, England: Falmer Press.

Crozier, Michel and Erhard Friedberg. 1980. *Actors and Systems: The Politics of Collective Action.* Chicago, IL: University of Chicago Press.

Dahrendorf, Ralf. 1959. *Class and Class Conflict in an Industrial Society.* London, England: Routledge.

Diekmann, Andreas and P. Preisendörfer. 1998. "Environmental Behavior. Discrepancies between Aspirations and Realities." *Rationality and Society* 10:79–102.

Diewald, Martin. 2001. "Unitary Social Science for Causal Understanding: Experiences and Prospects of Life Course Research." *Canadian Studies in Population* 28:219–48.

Djilas, Milovan. 1983. *The New Class: An Analysis of the Communist System.* San Diego, CA: Harcourt Brace Jovanovich.

Durkheim, Émile. [1895] 1982. *The Rules of Sociological Method.* New York: Free Press.

Durkheim, Émile. 1897. *Suicide: A Study in Sociology.* New York: Free Press.

Elias, Norbert. [1937] 1978/1982. *The Civilizing Process.* Vols. 1 and 2. New York: Urizen (Vol. 1); Oxford, England: Blackwell (Vol. 2).

Erbslöh, Barbara, Thomas Hagelstange, Dieter Holtmann, Joachim Singelmann, and Hermann Strasser. 1988. "Klassenstruktur und Klassenbewusstsein in der Bundesrepublik Deutschland" (Class Structure and Class Consciousness in the FR Germany). *Kölner Zeitschrift für Soziologie und Sozialpsychologie* 40:245–61.

Esser, Hartmut. 2002. "In guten wie in schlechten Tagen? Das Framing der Ehe und das Risiko zur Scheidung. Eine Anwendung und ein Test des Modells der Frame-Selektion" (In Good Times and in Bad? The Framing of Marriage and the Risk of Divorce. An Application and a Test of the Model of Frame-selection). *Kölner Zeitschrift für Soziologie und Sozialpsychologie* 54:27–63.

Evans, Geoffrey and C. Mills. 1998. "Identifying Class Structures. A Latent Class Analysis of the Goldhorpe Class Schema." *European Sociological Review* 14:87–106.

Gadamer, Hans-Georg. 1975. *Truth and Method.* New York: Seabury.

Genov, Nikolai, ed. 1989. *National Traditions in Sociology.* London, England: Sage.

Giddens, Anthony. 1976. *New Rules of Sociological Method. A Positive Critique of Interpretative Sociologies.* London, England: Hutchinson.

Giddens, Anthony. 1984. *The Constitution of Society. Outline of the Theory of Structuration.* Cambridge, England: Polity Press.

Goldenweiser, Alexander. 1938. "The Concept of Causality in the Physical and Social Sciences." *American Sociological Review* 3:624–36.

Goldthorpe, John H. 1997. "Rational Action Theory for Sociology." *British Journal of Sociology* 49:167–92.

Goldthorpe, John H. (in collaboration with Catriona Llewellyn and Clive Payne). 1980. *Social Mobility and Class Structure in Modern Britain.* Oxford, England: Clarendon Press.

Goldthorpe, John H. 2000a. *On Sociology. Numbers, Narratives, and the Integration of Research and Theory.* Oxford, England: Oxford University Press.

Goldthorpe, John H. 2000b. "Rent, Class Conflict, and Class Structure: A Commentary on Sørensen." *American Journal of Sociology* 106:1572–82.

Grusky, David and Jesper B. Sørensen. 1998. "Can Class Analysis be Salvaged?" *American Journal of Sociology* 103:1187–234.

Habermas, Jürgen. [1985] 1988. *The Philosophical Discourse of Modernity.* Cambridge, England: Polity Press.

Habermas, Jürgen. [1992] 1996. *Between Facts and Norms: Contributions to a Discourse Theory of Law and Democracy.* Cambridge: MIT Press.

Halbwachs, Maurice. 1925. *Les cadres sociaux de la mémoire.* Paris, France: F. Alcan.

Halliday, R. J. 1968. "The Sociological Movement, the Sociological Society and the Genesis of Academic Sociology in Britain." *Sociological Review* 16:377–98.

Hedström, Peter and Richard Swedberg. 1996. "Rational Choice, Empirical Research, and the Sociological Tradition." *European Sociological Review* 12:127–46.

Hedström, Peter and Richard Swedberg. 1998. "Rational Choice, Situational Analysis, and Empirical Research." Pp. 70–87 in *Rational Choice and Large-Scale Data Analysis,* edited by H.-P. Blossfeld and G. Prein. Boulder, CO: Westview Press.

Heider, Fritz. 1958. *The Psychology of Interpersonal Relations.* New York: Wiley.

Hillmert, Jürgen. 2002. "Altersstruktur und Karrierewege der Professorinnen und Professoren in der deutschen Soziologie" (Age Structure and Careers of Professors in German Sociology). *Kölner Zeitschrift für Soziologie und Sozialpsychologie* 54:116–35.

Husserl, Edmund. 1931. *Ideas: General Introduction to Pure Phenomenology.* New York: Macmillan.

Inglehart, Ronald. 1977. *The Silent Revolution. Changing Values and Political Styles among Western Publics.* Princeton, NJ: Princeton University Press.

Jahoda, Marie, Paul F. Lazarsfeld, and Hans Zeisel. 2002. *Marienthal: The Sociography of an Unemployed Community.* New Brunswick, NJ: Transaction Publishers.

Kaase, Max. 1998. "Datenzugang und Datenschutz" (Data Access and Data Protection). Pp. 101–11 in *Handwörterbuch zur Gesellschaft Deutschlands (Dictionary of the German Society)* edited by B. Schäfers and W. Zapf. Opladen, Germany: Leske+Budrich.

Kern, Horst. 1982. *Empirische Sozialforschung. Ursprünge, Ansätze, Entwicklungslinien* (Social Research. Origins, Approaches, Development). Munich, Germany: C. H. Beck.

Klingemann, Ute and Jürgen Falter. 1993. "Hilfe für Juden während des Holocaust. Sozialpsychologische Merkmale der nichtjüdischen Helfer und Charakteristika der Situation" (Help for Jews during the Holocaust. Social Psychological Features of Non-Jewish Helpers and Characteristics of the Situation). Pp. 115–16 in *Mut zur Menschlichkeit. Hilfe für Verfolgte während der NS-Zeit,* edited by G. B. Ginzel. Cologne, Germany: Rheinland Verlag.

Kultygin, Vladimir Pavlovich. 2003. "Universal Content and National Forms in the Development of Sociological Knowledge: The View of a Russian Sociologist." *Current Sociology* 51:671–87.

Lazarsfeld, Paul and A. Oberschall. 1962. "Max Weber and Empirical Social Research." *American Sociological Review* 30:185–99.

Lockwood, David. 1956. "Some Remarks on *The Social System.*" *British Journal of Sociology* 7(2):134–45.

Lockwood, David. 1966. "Sources of Variation in Working Class Images of Society." *Sociological Review* 14:244–67.

Luhmann, Niklas. 1973. "Die Zurechnung von Beförderungen im öffentlichen Dienst" (The Attribution of Promotions among Civil Servants). *Zeitschrift für Soziologie* 2(4):326–51.

Luhmann, Niklas, ed. 1990. "Meaning as Sociology's Basic Concept." Pp. 21–79 in *Essays on Self-Reference.* New York: Columbia University Press.

Luhmann, Niklas. 1995. *Social Systems.* Stanford, CA: Stanford University Press.

Luhmann, Niklas. 1997. *Die Gesellschaft der Gesellschaft* (The Society of the Society), 2 vols. Frankfurt, Germany: Suhrkamp.

Marcuse, Herbert. 1969. *Reason and Revolution; Hegel and the Rise of Social Theory.* Boston, MA: Beacon Press.

Marsh, Catherine. 1982. *The Survey Method.* London, England: Allen & Unwin.

Marshall, Gordon. 1997. *Repositioning Class. Social Inequality in Industrial Societies.* London, England: Sage.

Marx, Karl. 1859. *Contribution to the Critique of Political Economy.* Moscow, Russia: Progress.

Mauss, Marcel. 1950. *Sociologie et Anthropologie.* Paris, France: PUF.

McCarthy, Thomas. 1986. "Komplexität und Demokratie—die Versuchungen der Systemtheorie" (Complexity and Democracy—The Temptations of Systems Theory). Pp. 177–215 in *Kommunikatives Handeln. Beiträge zu Jürgen Habermas' "Theorie des kommunikativen Handelns,"* edited by A. Honneth and H. Joas. Frankfurt, Germany: Suhrkamp.

Mosca, Gaetano. 1939. *The Ruling Class.* New York: McGraw-Hill.

Nassehi, Armin and Gerd Nollmann, eds. 2004. *Bourdieu und Luhmann. Ein Theorienvergleich* (A Comparison of Theories). Frankfurt, Germany: Suhrkamp.

Nedelmann, Birgitta and Piotr Sztompka, eds. 1993. *Sociology in Europe. In Search of Identity.* New York: Walter de Gruyter.

Nollmann, Gerd and Hermann Strasser. 2002. "Individualisierung als Deutungsmuster sozialer Ungleichheit. Zum Problem des Sinnverstehens in der Ungleichheitsforschung" (Individualization as an Interpretive Scheme of Inequality. The Problem of Understanding in Stratification Research). *Österreichische Zeitschrift für Soziologie* 3:1–37.

Opp, Karl-Dieter. 1998. "Can and Should Rational Choice Theory Be Tested by Survey Research?" Pp. 204–230 in *Rational Choice Theory and Large-Scale Data Analysis,* edited by H.-P. Blossfeld and G. Prein. Boulder, CO: Westview Press.

Opp, Karl-Dieter and Jürgen Friedrichs. 1996. "Brückenannahmen, Produktionsfunktionen und die Messung von Präferenzen" (Bridge Hypotheses, Production Functions, and the Measurement of Preferences). *Kölner Zeitschrift für Soziologie und Sozialpsychologie* 48(Suppl.):546–59.

Ossowski, Stanislaw. 1963. *Class Structure in the Social Consciousness.* New York: Free Press.

Pakulski, Jan and Malcolm Waters. 1996. *The Death of Class.* London, England: Sage.

Pareto, Vilfredo. 1968. *The Rise and Fall of the Elites.* Totowa, NJ: Bedminster Press.

Pareto, Vilfredo. [1916] 1980. *Trattato di Sociologia Generale* (The Mind and Society). Minneapolis: University of Minnesota Press.

Renner, Karl. 1953. *Wandlungen der modernen Gesellschaft* (Social Change in Modern Society). Wien, Germany: Verlag der Wiener Volksbuchhandlung.

Schütz, Alfred. 1932. *The Phenomenology of the Social World.* London, England: Heinemann.

Schütz, Alfred. 1967. *Collected Papers I: The Problem of Social Reality,* edited by M. Natanson. The Hague, Netherlands: Martinus Nijhoff.

Schütz, Alfred and Talcott Parsons. 1977. *Zur Theorie sozialen Handelns. Ein Briefwechsel* (The Theory of Social Action. An Exchange of Letters). Frankfurt, Germany: Suhrkamp.

Simmel, Georg. 1908. *Soziologie: Untersuchungen über die Formen der Vergesellschaftung* (Sociology: Inquiries into the Forms of Socialization). Leipzig, Germany: Duncker & Humblot.

Simmel, Georg. [1897] 1983. Rosen. Eine soziale Hypothese (Roses. A Social Hypothesis). Pp. 169–72 in *Schriften zur Soziologie,* edited by H.-J. Dahme and O. Rammstedt. Frankfurt, Germany: Suhrkamp.

Sombart, Werner. [1913] 2001. "The Origins of the Capitalist Spirit." Pp. 33–54 in *Werner Sombart: Economic Life in the Modern Age,* edited by N. Stehr and R. Grundmann. New Brunswick, NJ: Transaction.

Sørensen, Aage B. 2000. "Toward a Sounder Basis for Class Analysis." *American Journal of Sociology* 106:1523–58.

Sorokin, Pitirim A. 1937/1941. *Social and Cultural Dynamics.* New York: American Book Company (Vols. 1–3); New York: Bedminster Press (Vol. 4).

Spencer, Herbert. 1898. *First Principles.* New York: D. Appleton.

Thompson, Edward P. 1980. *The Making of the English Working Class.* London, England: Gollancz.

Tönnies, Ferdinand [1887] 1957. *Gemeinschaft und Gesellschaft* (Community and Society). East Lansing: Michigan State University Press.

Torrance, John. 1976. "The Emergence of Sociology in Austria, 1885–1935." *Archives Européennes de Sociologie* 17:185–219.

Touraine, Alain. 1969. *La société postindustrielle.* Paris, France: Editions Denoel.

Touraine, Alain. 1983. *Production de la société.* Paris, France: Seuil.

Tucker, William T. 1965. "Max Weber's Verstehen." *Sociological Quarterly* 157–65.

Weber, Max [1905] 1930. *The Protestant Ethic and the Spirit of Capitalism.* London, England: Allen & Unwin.

Weber, Max [1904] 1949. *The Methodology of the Social Sciences.* Glencoe, IL: Free Press.

Weber, Max. 1968. *Economy and Society.* Berkeley: University of California Press.

Weber, Max. 1981. "Some Categories of Interpretive Sociology." *Sociological Quarterly* 22:151–80.

Weiss, Johannes. 1989. "Sociology in the Federal Republic of Germany." Pp. 100–17 in *National Traditions in Sociology,* edited by N. Genov. London, England: Sage.

Wright, Erik Olin. 1997. *Class Counts: Comparative Studies in Class Analysis.* New York: Cambridge University Press.

Wright, Erik Olin. 2000. "Class, Exploitation, and Economic Rents: Reflections on Sørensen's 'Sounder Basis.'" *American Journal of Sociology* 106:1559–71.

Young, Michael. 1958. *The Rise of Meritocracy.* London, England: Tames and Hudson.

Chapter 8. British Sociology

Abercrombie, Nicholas, Stephen Hill, and Bryan S. Turner. 1980. *The Dominant Ideology Thesis,* London, England: George Allen & Unwin.

Ameli, Saied R. and Arzu Merali. 2004. *British Muslims' Expectations of the Government. Dual Citizenship: British, Islamic or Both?* Wembley, England: Islamic Human Rights Commission.

Anderson, Perry. 1964. "The Origins of the Present Crisis." *New Left Review* 23:26–53.

Barbalet, Jack. M. 1998. *Emotion, Social Theory and Social Structure. A Macrosociological Approach.* Cambridge, England: Cambridge University Press.

Barratt, Michele. 1992. *The Politics of Truth. From Marx to Foucault.* Cambridge, England: Polity Press.

Bauman, Zygmunt. 1993. *Postmodern Ethics.* Oxford, England: Blackwell.

Beck, Ulrich. 1992. *Risk Society. Towards a New Modernity.* London, England: Sage.

Berger, Peter and Thomas Luckmann. 1967. *The Social Construction of Reality.* New York: Doubleday.

Bernstein, Basil B. 1971. *Class, Codes and Control.* London, England: Routledge & Kegan Paul.

Bourdieu, Pierre. 1984. *Distinction. A Social Critique of the Judgement of Taste.* London, England: Routledge & Kegan Paul.

Cohen, Percy. 1968. *Modern Social Theory.* London, England: Heinemann.

Dahrendorf, Ralph. 1959. *Class and Class Conflict in an Industrial Society.* London, England: Routledge & Kegan Paul.

Dawe, Alan. 1970. "The Two Sociologies." *British Journal of Sociology* 21(2):207–18.

Dennis, Norman, Fernando M. Henriques, and Clifford Slaughter. 1962. *Coal Is Our Life.* London, England: Eyre and Spottiswoode.

Durkheim, Émile. [1912] 1954. *The Elementary Forms of the Religious Life.* London, England: Allen & Unwin.

Durkheim, Émile. [1893] 1960. *The Division of Labor in Society.* Glencoe, IL: Free Press.

Edmunds, June and Bryan S. Turner. 2002. *Generations, Society and Culture.* Buckingham, England: Open University Press.

Featherstone, Mike. 1991. *Consumer Culture and Postmodernism.* London, England: Sage.

Featherstone, Mike, Mike Hepworth, and Bryan S. Turner, eds. 1991. *The Body. Social Process and Cultural Theory.* London, England: Sage.

Giddens, Anthony. 1971. *Capitalism and Modern Social Theory.* Cambridge, England: Cambridge University Press.

Giddens, Anthony. 1984. *The Constitution of Society. Outline of a Theory of Structuration.* Cambridge, England: Polity Press.

Giddens, Anthony. 1990. *The Consequences of Modernity.* Cambridge, England: Polity Press.

Giddens, Anthony. 1998. *The Third Way.* Cambridge, England: Polity Press.

Giddens, Anthony and Gavin MacKenzie, eds. 1982. *Social Class and the Division of Labour: Essays in Honour of Ilya Neustadt.* Cambridge, England: Cambridge University Press.

Gilroy, Paul. 1987. *There Ain't No Black in the Union Jack.* London, England: Routledge.

Goldthorpe, John H., David Lockwood, Frank Bechhofer, and Jennifer Platt. 1969. *The Affluent Worker in the Class Structure.* Cambridge, England: Cambridge University Press.

Hall, Stuart and Martin Jacques, eds. 1983. *The Politics of Thatcherism.* London, England: Lawrence and Wishart.

Hall, Stuart and Thomas Jefferson. 1976. *Resistance through Rituals. Youth Cultures in Postwar Britain.* London, England: Hutchinson.

Halsey, A. H. 1957. *Social Class and Educational Opportunity.* London, England: Heinemann.

Hirst, Paul. 2001. *War and Power in the 21st Century.* Cambridge, England: Polity Press.

Hoggart, Richard. 1957. *The Uses of Literacy.* Harmondsworth, England: Penguin Books.

Lockwood, David. 1958. *The Blackcoated Worker.* London, England: Allen & Unwin.

Lovell, Terry. 2000. "Feminisms of the Second Wave." Pp. 299–324 in *Blackwell Companion to Social Theory,* edited by B. S. Turner. Oxford, England: Blackwell.

Loyal, Steven. 2003. *The Sociology of Anthony Giddens.* Cambridge, England: Polity Press.

MacIntyre, Alasdair. 1967. *Secularization and Moral Change.* Oxford, England: Oxford University Press.

MacIntyre, Alasdair. 1968. *Marxism and Christianity.* Harmondsworth, England: Penguin Books.

Mann, Michael. 1973. *Consciousness and Action in the Western Working Class.* London, England: Macmillan.

Mann, Michael. 1987. "Ruling Class Strategies and Citizenship." *Sociology* 2:339–54.

Marshall, Thomas H. 1950. *Citizenship and Social Class and Other Essays.* Cambridge, England: Cambridge University Press.

Miliband, Ralph. 1969. *The State in Capitalist Society.* London, England: Weidenfeld & Nicolson.

Mitchell, Juliet. 1966. "Women: The Longest Revolution." *New Left Review* 40:10–30.

Mumford, Lewis. 1948. "Patrick Geddes, Victor Banford and Applied Sociology in England: The Social Survey, Regionalism, and Urban Planning." Pp. 677–695 in *An Introduction to the History of Sociology,* edited by H. E. Barnes. Chicago, IL: University of Chicago Press.

Oakley, Ann. 1974. *The Sociology of Housework.* London, England: Martin Robertson.

Parsons, Talcott and Neil J. Smelser. 1956. *Economy and Society. A Study in the Integration of Economic and Social Theory.* London, England: Routledge & Kegan Paul.

Plummer, Ken. 2000. "Symbolic Interactionism in the Twentieth Century." Pp. 193–222 in *The Blackwell Companion to Social Theory,* edited by B. S. Turner. Oxford, England: Blackwell.

Poulantzas, Nicos. 1969. "The Problems of the Capitalist State." *New Left Review* 58:67–78.

Rex, John. 1961. *Key Problems in Sociological Theory.* London, England: Routledge & Kegan Paul.

Rex, John. 1970. *Race Relations in Sociological Theory.* London, England: Weidenfeld & Nicolson.

Rex, John. 1973a. *Discovering Sociology. Studies in Sociological Theory and Method.* London, England: Routledge & Kegan Paul.

Rex, John. 1973b. *Race, Colonialism and the City.* London, England: Routledge & Kegan Paul.

Rex, John. 1974a. *Approaches to Sociology.* London, England: Routledge & Kegan Paul.

Rex, John. 1974b. *Sociology and the Demystification of the Modern World.* London, England: Routledge & Kegan Paul.

Rex, John. 1981. *Social Conflict: A Conceptual and Theoretical Analysis.* London, England: Longman.

Rex, John. 1986. *Race and Ethnicity.* Milton Keynes, England: Open University Press.

Rex, John and Robert Moore. 1967. *Race Community and Conflict: A Study of Sparkbrook.* London, England: Oxford University Press.

Rex, John and Sally Tomlinson. 1979. *Colonial Immigrants in a British City.* London, England: Routledge & Kegan Paul.

Rojek, Chris and Bryan S. Turner. 2000. "Decorative Sociology: Towards a Critique of the Cultural Turn." *The Sociological Review* 48(4):629–48.

Runciman, W. G. 1966. *Relative Deprivation and Social Justice.* London, England: Routledge & Kegan Paul.

Shields, Rob, ed. 1992. *Lifestyle Shopping. The Subject of Consumption.* London, England: Routledge.

Spencer, Baldwin and Francis J. Gillen. 1997. *The Northern Tribes of Central Australia.* London, England: Routledge/ Thoemmes Press.

Spencer, Herbert. 1884. *The Man versus the State.* New York: Appleton.

Tawney, Richard H. 1926. *Religion and the Rise of Capitalism.* London, England: John Murray.

Taylor, Ian, Paul Walton, and Jock Young. 1973. *The New Criminology, for a Social Theory of Deviance.* London, England: Routledge & Kegan Paul.

Titmuss, Richard. 1962. *Income Distribution and Social Change, a Study in Criticism.* London, England: George Allen & Unwin.

Townsend, Peter and Nigel Davidson. 1982. *Inequalities in Health.* Harmondsworth, England: Penguin Books.

Turner, Bryan S. 1984. *The Body & Society. Explorations in Social Theory.* Oxford, England: Blackwell.

Turner, Bryan S. 1986. *Citizenship and Capitalism. The Debate about Reformism.* London, England: Allen & Unwin.

Turner, Bryan S. 1990. "Ideology and Utopia in the Formation of an Intelligentsia: Reflections on the English Cultural Conduit." *Theory Culture & Society* 9(1):183–210.

Turner, Bryan S., ed. 1993. *Citizenship and Social Theory.* London, England: Sage.

Turner, Bryan S. and Peter Hamilton, eds. 1994. *Citizenship. Critical Concepts,* 2 vols. London, England: Routledge.

Turner, Bryan S. and Chris Rojek. 2001. *Society & Culture. Principles of Scarcity and Solidarity.* London, England: Routledge.

Urry, John and John Wakeford, eds. 1973. *Power in Britain: Sociological Readings.* London, England: Heinemann.

Williams, Raymond. 1958. *Culture and Society 1780–1950.* London, England: Chatto & Windus.

Williams, Raymond. 1989. *What I Came to Say.* Lonon, England: Hutchinson Radius.

Willis, Paul. 1977. *Learning to Labour.* Farnborough, England: Saxon House.

Wilmott, Peter and Michael Young. 1960. *Family and Class in a London Suburb.* London, England: Routledge & Kegan Paul.

Wilson, Bryan. 1967. *Patterns of Sectarianism. Organization and Ideology in Social and Religious Movements.* London, England: Heinemann.

Worcester, Kent. 1996. *C. L. R. James. A Political Biography.* Albany: State University of New York Press.

Part III: The Scientific Approach to the Study of Society

Chapter 9. Qualitative Methodology

Agger, Ben. 2000. *Public Sociology: From Social Facts to Literary Acts.* New York: Rowman & Littlefield.

Atkinson, Elizabeth. 2004. "Thinking outside the Box: An Exercise in Heresy." *Qualitative Inquiry* 10(1):111–29.

Atkinson, Paul, Amanda Coffey, and Sara Delamont. 2001. "Editorial: A Debate about Our Canon." *Qualitative Research* 1:5–21.

Atkinson, Paul and Martyn Hammersley. 1994. "Ethnography and Participant Observation." Pp. 248–61 in *Handbook of Qualitative Research,* edited by N. K. Denzin and Yvonna S. Lincoln. Thousand Oaks, CA: Sage.

Bateson, Gregory. 1972. *Steps to an Ecology of Mind.* New York: Ballantine.

Becker, Howard S. 1986. *Doing Things Together.* Evanston, IL: Northwestern University Press.

Becker, Howard S. 1996. "The Epistemology of Qualitative Research." Pp. 53–71 in *Ethnography and Human Development,* edited by R. Jessor, A. Colby, and R. A. Schweder. Chicago, IL: University of Chicago Press.

Becker, Howard S., Blanche Geer, Anselm Strauss, and Everett Hughes. 1961. *Boys in White.* Chicago, IL: University of Chicago Press.

Bishop, Russell. 1998. "Freeing Ourselves from Neo-Colonial Domination in Research: A Maori Approach to Creating

Knowledge." *International Journal of Qualitative Studies in Education* 11:199–219.

Bloch, Marianne. 2004. "A Discourse That Disciplines, Governs, and Regulates: On Scientific Research in Education." *Qualitative Inquiry* 10(1):96–110.

Bruner, Edward. 1993. "Introduction: The Ethnographic Self." Pp. 1–26 in *Anthropology and Literature,* edited by P. Benson. Urbana: University of Illinois Press.

Cannella, Gaile S. and Yvonna S. Lincoln. 2004. "Dangerous Discourses II: Comprehending and Countering the Redeployment of Discourses (and Resources) in the Generation of Liberatory Inquiry." *Qualitative Inquiry* 10(2):165–74.

Carey, James W. 1989. *Culture as Communication.* Boston, MA: Unwin Hyman.

Clough, Patricia T. 1998. *The End(s) of Ethnography.* 2d ed. New York: Peter Lang.

Delamont, Sara, Amanda Coffey, and Paul Atkinson. 2000. "The Twilight Years?" *International Journal of Qualitative Studies in Education* 13:223–38.

Denzin, Norman K. 1997. *Interpretive Ethnography.* Thousand Oaks, CA: Sage.

Denzin, Norman K. 2003. *Perrformance Ethnography: Critical Pedagogy and the Politics of Culture.* Thousand Oaks, CA: Sage.

Denzin, Norman K. and Yvonna S. Lincoln. 2000. "Introduction: The Discipline and Practice of Qualitative Research." Pp. 1–29 in *Handbook of Qualitative Research,* 2d ed., edited by N. K. Denzin and Y. S. Lincoln. Thousand Oaks, CA: Sage.

Denzin, Norman K. and Yvonna S. Lincoln. 2005. "Introduction: The Discipline and Practice of Qualitative Research." Pp. 1–42 in *Handbook of Qualitative Research,* 3d ed., edited by N. K. Denzin and Y. S. Lincoln. Thousand Oaks, CA: Sage.

Dilthey, W. L. [1900] 1976. *Selected Writings.* Cambridge, England: Cambridge University Press.

Flick, Uwe. 1998. *An Introduction to Qualitative Research.* London, England: Sage.

Freire, Paulo. 1998. *Pedagogy of Freedom.* New York: Roman & Littlefield.

Guba, Egon G. 1990. "The Alternative Paradigm Dialog." Pp. 17–30 in *The Paradigm Dialog,* edited by E. C. Guba. Newbury Park, CA: Sage.

Guba, Egon G. and Yvonna S. Lincoln. 2000. "Paradigmatic Controversies, Contradictions, and Emerging Confluences." Pp. 163–88 in *Handbook of Qualitative Research,* 2d ed., edited by N. K. Denzin and Y. S. Lincoln. Thousand Oaks, CA: Sage.

Heshusius, Lous. 1994. "Freeing Ourselves from Objectivity: Managing Subjectivity or Turning toward a Participatory Mode of Consciousness." *Educational Researcher* 23:15–22.

Howe, Kenneth R. 2004. "A Critique of Experimentalism." *Qualitative Inquiry* 10(1):42–61.

Huber, Joan. 1995. "Centennial Essay: Institutional Perspectives on Sociology." *American Journal of Sociology* 101:194–216.

Kincheloe, Joe L. and Peter McLaren. 2000. "Rethinking Critical Theory and Qualitative Research." Pp. 279–314 in *Handbook of Qualitative Research,* 2d ed., edited by N. K. Denzin and Y. S. Lincoln. Thousand Oaks, CA: Sage.

Kong, Travis S., Dan Mahoney, and Ken Plummer. 2002. "Queering the Interview." Pp. 239–58 in *Handbook of Interview Research,* edited by J. F. Gubrium and J. A. Holstein. Thousand Oaks, CA: Sage.

Ladson-Billings, Gloria. 2000. "Racialized Discourses and Ethnic Epistemologies." Pp. 257–76 in *Handbook of Qualitative Research,* 2d ed., edited by N. K. Denzin and Y. S. Lincoln. Thousand Oaks, CA: Sage.

Lather, Patti. 2004. "This Is Your Father's Paradigm: Government Intrusion and the Case of Qualitative Research in Education." *Qualitative Inquiry* 10(1):15–34.

Lincoln, Yvonna S. and Norman K. Denzin. 2000. "The Seventh Moment: Out of the Past." Pp. 1047–1065 in *Handbook of Qualitative Research,* 2d ed., edited by N. K. Denzin and Y. S. Lincoln. Thousand Oaks, CA: Sage.

Lopez, Gerardo R. 1998. "Reflections on Epistemology and Standpoint Theories: A Response to a Maori Approach to Creating Knowledge." *International Journal of Qualitative Studies in Education* 11:225–31.

Maxwell, Joseph A. 2004. "Reemergent Scientism, Postmodernism, and Dialogue across Differences." *Qualitative Inquiry* 10(1):35–41.

Olesen, Virgina. 2000. "Feminisms and Qualitative Research at and into the Millennium. Pp. 215–56 in *Handbook of Qualitative Research,* 2d ed., edited by N. K. Denzin and Y. S. Lincoln. Thousand Oaks, CA: Sage.

Popkewitz, Thomas S. 2004. "Is the National Research Council Committee's Report on Scientific Research in Education Scientific? On Trusting the Manifesto." *Qualitative Inquiry* 10(1):62–78.

Rosaldo, Renato. 1989. *Culture & Truth.* Boston, MA: Beacon.

Ryan, Katherine E. and Lisa K. Hood. 2004. "Guarding the Castle and Opening the Gates." *Qualitative Inquiry* 10(1):79–95.

Seale, Clive, Giampietro Gobo, Jaber F. Gubrium, and David Silverman. 2004. "Introduction: Inside Qualitative Research." Pp. 1–11 in *Qualitative Research Practice,* edited by C. Seale, G. Gobo, J. F. Gubrium, and D. Silverman. London, England: Sage.

St. Pierre, Elizabeth A. 2004. "Refusing Alternatives: A Science of Contestation." *Qualitative Inquiry* 10(1):130–39.

Stacey, Judith. 1988. "Can There Be a Feminist Ethnography?" *Women's Studies International Forum* 11(1):21–27.

Strauss, Anselm and Juliet Corbin. 1999. *Basics of Qualitative Research.* 2d ed. Thousand Oaks, CA: Sage.

Teddlie, Charles and Abbas Tashakkori. 2003. "Major Issues and Controversies in the Use of Mixed Methods in the Social and Behavioral Sciences." Pp. 3–50 in *Handbook of Mixed Methods in Social and Behavioral Research,* edited by A. Tashakkori and C. Teddlie. Thousand Oaks, CA: Sage.

Tillman, Linda C. 1998. "Culturally Specific Research Practices: A Response to Bishop." *International Journal of Qualitative Studies in Education* 11:221–24.

Weinstein, Matthew. 2004. "Randomized Design and the Myth of Certain Knowledge: Guinea Pig Narratives and Cultural Critique." *Qualitative Inquiry* 10(2):246–60.

Chapter 10. Quantitative Methodology

Abell, Peter. 1971. *Model Building in Sociology.* New York: Schocken Books.

Abell, Peter. 2004. "Narrative Explanation: An Alternative to Variable Centered Explanation." *Annual Review of Sociology* 30:287–310.

Allison, Paul D. 1984. *Event History Analysis: Regression for Longitudinal Event Data.* Beverly Hills, CA: Sage.

Allison, Paul D. 2005. *Fixed Effects Regression Methods for Longitudinal Data Using SAS.* Cary, NC: SAS.

Bailey, Kenneth D. 1973. "Monothetic and Polythetic Typologies and Their Relationship to Conceptualization, Measurement, and Scaling." *American Sociological Review* 38:18–33.

Bailey, Kenneth D. 1974a. "Interpreting Smallest Space Analysis." *Sociological Methods and Research* 3:3–29.

Bailey, Kenneth D. 1974b. "Cluster Analysis." Pp. 59–128 in *Sociological Methodology 1975,* edited by D. R. Heise. San Francisco, CA: Jossey-Bass.

Bailey, Kenneth D. 1994a. *Typologies and Taxonomies: An Introduction to Classification Techniques.* Thousand Oaks, CA: Sage.

Bailey, Kenneth D. 1994b. *Methods of Social Research.* 4th ed. New York: Free Press.

Bailey, Stanley R. 2004. "Group Dominance and the Myth of Racial Democracy: Antiracism Attitudes in Brazil." *American Sociological Review* 69:728–47.

Blalock, Hubert M., Jr. 1960. *Social Statistics.* New York: McGraw-Hill.

Blalock, Hubert M., Jr. 1969. *Theory Construction: From Verbal to Mathematical Formulations.* Englewood Cliffs, NJ: Prentice Hall.

Blalock, Hubert M., Jr. 1971. *Causal Models in the Social Sciences.* Chicago, IL: Aldine.

Blalock, Hubert M., Jr. 1979. *Social Statistics.* Rev. 2d ed. New York: McGraw-Hill.

Blalock, Hubert M., Jr. 1982. *Conceptualization and Measurement in the Social Sciences.* Beverly Hills, CA: Sage.

Bridgman, Percy W. 1948. *The Logic of Modern Physics.* New York: Macmillan.

Cole, Stephen, ed. 2001. *What's Wrong with Sociology?* New Brunswick, NJ: Transaction.

Coleman, James S. 1964. *Introduction to Mathematical Sociology.* New York: Free Press.

Davis, James A. 2001. "What's Wrong with Sociology." Pp. 99–119 in *What's Wrong with Sociology,* edited by S. Cole. New Brunswick, NJ: Transaction.

Doreian, Patrick, Vladimir Batagelj, and Anuska Ferligoj. 2005. *Generalized Blockmodeling.* Cambridge, England: Cambridge University Press.

Duncan, Otis D. 1966. "Path Analysis: Sociological Examples." *American Journal of Sociology* 72:1–16.

Durkheim, Émile. [1938] 1964. *Rules of the Sociological Method.* New York: Free Press.

Edling, Christofer R. 2002. "Mathematics in Sociology." *Annual Review of Sociology* 28:197–220.

Fararo, Thomas J. 1973. *Mathematical Sociology: An Introduction to Fundamentals.* New York: Wiley.

Fararo, Thomas J. 1989. *The Meaning of General Theoretical Sociology: Tradition and Formalization.* Cambridge, England: Cambridge University Press.

Goode, William J. and Paul K. Hatt. 1952. *Methods in Social Research.* New York: McGraw-Hill.

Griffin, Larry J. 2004. "'Generations and Collective Memory' Revisited: Race, Region, and Memory of Civil Rights." *American Sociological Review* 69:544–57.

Guo, Guang and Hongxin Zhao. 2000. "Multilevel Modeling for Binary Data." *Annual Review of Sociology* 26:441–62.

Hagle, Timothy M. 2004. "Pseudo R-squared." Pp. 878–79 in *The Sage Encyclopedia of Social Science Research Methods,* vol. 3, edited by M. Lewis-Beck, A. E. Bryman, and T. F. Liao. Thousand Oaks, CA: Sage.

Harknett, Kristen and Sara S. McLanahan. 2004. "Racial and Ethnic Differences in Marriage after the Birth of a Child." *American Sociological Review* 69:790–811.

Hollister, Matissa N. 2004. "Does Firm Size Matter Anymore? The New Economy and Firm Size Wage Effects." *American Sociological Review* 69:659–76.

Iverson, Gudmund R. 2004. "Quantitative Research." Pp. 896–97 in *The Sage Encyclopedia of Social Science Research Methods,* vol. 3, edited by M. Lewis-Beck, A. E. Bryman, and T. F Liao. Thousand Oaks, CA: Sage.

Jahoda, Marie, Morton Deutsch, and Stuart W. Cook. 1951. *Research Methods in Social Relations.* New York: Holt, Rinehart & Winston.

Joyner, Kara and Grace Kao. 2005. "Interracial Relationships and the Transition to Adulthood." *American Sociological Review* 70:563–81.

Kemeny, John G. and J. Laurie Snell. 1962. *Mathematical Models in the Social Sciences.* New York: Blaisdell.

Knoke, David and Michael Hout. 1974. "Social and Demographic Factors in American Political Party Affiliation, 1952–72." *American Sociological Review* 39:700–13.

Land, Kenneth C. 1968. "Principles of Path Analysis." Pp. 1–37 in *Sociological Methodology 1969,* edited by E. F. Borgatta. San Francisco, CA: Jossey-Bass.

Lazarsfeld, Paul F., ed. 1954. *Mathematical Thinking in the Social Sciences.* Glencoe, IL: Free Press.

Lee, Cheol-Sung. 2005. "Income Inequality, Democracy, and Public Sector Size." *American Sociological Review* 70:158–81.

Lewis-Beck, Michael, Alan E. Bryman, and Tim F. Liao. 2004. *The Sage Encyclopedia of Social Science Research Methods.* Thousand Oaks, CA: Sage.

Lundberg, George A. 1939. *Foundations of Sociology.* New York: Macmillan.

Lundberg, George A. 1947. *Can Science Save Us?* New York: Longmans, Green.

Macy, Michael W. and Robert Willer. 2002. "From Factors to Actors: Computational Sociology and Agent-Based Modeling." *Annual Review of Sociology* 28:143–66.

McKinney, John C. 1966. *Constructive Typology and Social Theory.* New York: Appleton-Century-Crofts.

McLeod, Jane D. and Karen Kaiser. 2004. "Childhood Emotional and Behavioral Problems and Educational Attainment." *American Sociological Review* 69:636–58.

Marsh, Lawrence C. and David R. Cormier. 2001. *Spline Regression Models.* Thousand Oaks, CA: Sage.

Meeker, Barbara F. and Robert K. Leik. 2000. "Mathematical Sociology." Pp. 1786–92 in *Encyclopedia of Sociology,* edited by E. F. Borgatta and R. J. V. Montgomery. 2d ed. New York: Macmillan.

Messner, Steven F., Eric P. Baumer, and Richard Rosenfeld. 2004. "Dimensions of Social Capital and Rates of Criminal Homicide." *American Sociological Review* 69:882–903.

Monette, Duane R., Thomas J. Sullivan, and Cornell R. DeJong. 2005. *Applied Social Research.* 6th ed. Belmont, CA: Brooks/Cole.

Raftery, Adrian E. 2005. "Quantitative Research Methods." Pp. 15–39 in *The Sage Handbook of Sociology,* edited by C. Calhoun, C. Rojek, and B. Turner. Thousand Oaks, CA: Sage.

Rudner, Richard. 1966. *The Philosophy of the Social Sciences.* Englewood Cliffs, NJ: Prentice Hall.

Stevens, S. S. 1951. "Mathematics, Measurement, and Psychophysics." Pp. 1–49 in *Handbook of Experimental Psychology,* edited by S. S. Stevens. New York: Wiley.

Torche, Florencia. 2005. "Social Mobility in Chile." *American Sociological Review* 70:422–49.

Tubergen, Frank van, Ineke Maas, and Henk Flap. 2004. "The Economic Incorporation of Immigrants in 18 Western Societies: Origin, Destination, and Community Effects." *American Sociological Review* 69:704–27.

Uggen, Christopher and Amy Blackstone. 2004. "Sexual Harassment as a Gendered Expression of Power." *American Sociological Review* 69:64–92.

Weber, Max. 1949. *The Methodology of the Social Sciences.* Translated by E. A. Shils and H. A. Finch. Glencoe, IL: Free Press.

White, Harrison C. 1963. *An Anatomy of Kinship: Mathematical Models for Structures of Cumulated Roles.* Englewood Cliffs, NJ: Prentice Hall.

White, Harrison C. 1970. *Chains of Opportunity: System Models of Mobility in Organizations.* Cambridge, MA: Harvard University Press.

Yamaguchi, Kazuo. 1983. "Structure of Intergenerational Occupational Mobility; Generality and Specificity in Resources, Channels, and Barriers." *American Journal of Sociology* 88:718–45.

Chapter 11. Comparative Historical Sociology

Abrams, Philip. 1982. *Historical Sociology.* Ithaca, NY: Cornell University Press.

Abu-Lughod, Janet. 1989. *Before European Hegemony.* Oxford, England: Oxford University Press.

Almond, Gabriel and G. Bingham Powell. 1966. *Comparative Politics: A Developmental Approach.* Boston, MA: Little, Brown.

Anderson, Perry. 1974. *Lineages of the Absolutist State.* London, England: New Left Books.

Arendt, Hannah. 1951. *The Origins of Totalitarianism.* New York: Harcourt Brace.

Ariès, Philippe. 1981. *The Hour of Our Death.* New York: Alfred A. Knopf.

Arrighi, Giovanni. 1994. *The Long Twentieth Century: Money, Power, and the Origins of Our Times.* London, England: Verso.

Arrighi, Giovanni. 1997. "Capitalism and the Modern World-System: Rethinking the Non-Debates of the 1970s." Retrieved May 24, 2005 (http://fbc.binghamton.edu/gaasa96.htm).

Bergquist, Charles. 1986. *Labor in Latin America: Comparative Essays on Chile, Argentina, Venezuela, and Colombia.* Stanford, CA: Stanford University Press.

Bonacich, Edna, Lucie Cheng, Norma Chinchilla, Nora Hamilton, and Paul Ong, eds. 1994. *Global Production: The Apparel Industry in the Pacific Rim.* Philadelphia, PA: Temple University Press.

Brenner, Robert. 1977. "The Origins of Capitalist Development: A Critique of Neo-Smithian Marxism." *New Left Review* 104:25–92.

Burawoy, Michael. 1972. *The Colour of Class on the Copper Mines: From African Advancement to Zambianization.* Manchester, England: Manchester University Press.

Burawoy, Michael. 1981. "The Capitalist State in South Africa: Marxist and Sociological Perspectives on Race and Class." *Political Power and Social Theory* 2:279–335.

Burawoy, Michael. 1989. "Two Methods in Search of Science: Skocpol versus Trotsky." *Theory and Society* 18:759–805.

Calhoun, Craig. 1996. "The Rise and Domestication of Historical Sociology." Pp. 305–37 in *The Historical Turn in the Human Sciences,* edited by T. McDonald. Ann Arbor: University of Michigan Press.

Calhoun, Craig. 1998. "Explanation in Historical Sociology: Narrative, General Theory, and Historically Specific Theory." *American Journal of Sociology* 104:846–71.

Candland, Christopher and Rudra Sil, eds. 2001. *The Politics of Labor in a Global Age: Continuity and Change in Late-Industrializing and Post-Socialist Economies.* Oxford, England: Oxford University Press.

Canel, Eduardo. 1997. "New Social Movement Theory and Resource Mobilization Theory: The Need for Integration." Pp. 189–221 in *Community Power and Grassroots Democracy: The Transformation of Social Life.* London, England: Zed Books.

Cohen, Jean. 1985. "Strategy or Identity: New Theoretical Paradigms and Contemporary Social Movements." *Social Research* 52:663–716.

Collier, Ruth and David Collier. 1991. *Shaping the Political Arena: Critical Junctures, the Labor Movement, and Regime Dynamics in Latin America.* Princeton, NJ: Princeton University Press.

Comninel, George. 2003. "Historical Materialist Sociology and Revolutions." Pp. 85–95 in *Handbook of Historical Sociology,* edited by G. Delanty and E. F. Isin. Thousand Oaks, CA: Sage.

Deflem, Mathieu. 2000. "On the Methodology of Comparative Historical Sociology: Scattered Notes." Retrieved June 23, 2005 (http://www.cas.sc.edu/socy/faculty/deflem/zhistory.htm).

Eder, Klaus. 2003. "Social Movements and Democratization." Pp. 276–86 in *Handbook of Historical Sociology,* edited by G. Delanty and E. F. Isin. Thousand Oaks, CA: Sage.

Eisenstadt, Shmuel N. 1966. *Modernization: Protest and Change.* Englewood Cliffs, NJ: Prentice Hall.

Evans, Peter. 1985. "Transnational Linkages and the Economic Role of the State: An Analysis of Developing and Industrialized Nations in the Post-World War Two Period." Pp. 192–226 in *Bringing the State Back In,* edited by P. Evans, D. Rueschemeyer, and T. Skocpol. Cambridge, England: Cambridge University Press.

Farhi, Farideh. 1990. *States and Urban-based Revolutions: Iran and Nicaragua.* Urbana: University of Illinois Press.

Frank, Andre Gunder and Barry Gills. 1993. *The World System: Five Hundred Years or Five Thousand?* New York: Routledge.

Frenkel, Stephen, ed. 1993. *Organized Labor in the Asia-Pacific Region: A Comparative Study of Trade Unionism in Nine Countries:* Ithaca, NY: ILR Press.

Giddens, Anthony. 1971. *Capitalism and Modern Social Theory.* Cambridge, England: Cambridge University Press.

Giddens, Anthony. 1987. *The Nation State and Violence.* Vol. 2, *A Contemporary Critique of Historical Materialism.* Berkeley: University of California Press.

Gills, Dong-Sook S. and Nicole Piper, eds. 2002. *Women and Work in Globalising Asia.* London, England: Routledge.

Goldstone, Jack. 2003. "Comparative Historical Analysis and Knowledge Accumulation in the Study of Revolutions." Pp. 41–90 in *Comparative Historical Analysis in the Social*

Sciences, edited by J. Mahoney and D. Rueschemeyer. Cambridge, England: Cambridge University Press.

Goldthorpe, John. 1982. "On the Service Class, Its Formation and Future." Pp. 162–85 in *Social Class and the Division of Labour. Essays in Honour of Ilya Neustadt,* edited by A. Giddens and G. Mackenzie. Cambridge, England: Cambridge University Press.

Goldthorpe, John. 1991. "The Uses of History in Sociology: Reflections on Some Recent Tendencies." *British Journal of Sociology* 42:211–30.

Goodwin, Jeff. 1997. "State-Centered Approaches to Social Revolutions: Strengths and Limitations of a Theoretical Tradition." Pp. 11–37 in *Theorizing Revolutions,* edited by J. Foran. New York: Routledge.

Gough, Ian. 1979. *The Political Economy of the Welfare State.* London, England: Macmillan.

Habermas, Jurgen. 1973. *Legitimization Crisis.* Boston, MA: Beacon Press.

Haydu, Jeffrey. 1988. *Between Craft and Class: Skilled Workers and Factory Politics in the United States and Britain, 1890–1922.* Berkeley: University of California Press.

Hobsbawm, Eric. 1965. "The Crisis of the Seventeenth Century." Pp. 5–58 in *Crisis in Europe, 1560–1660: Essays from Past and Present,* edited by T. Aston. London, England: Routledge & Kegan.

Huber, Evelyne and Frank Stafford, eds. 1995. *Agrarian Structure and Political Power: Landlord and Peasant in the Making of Latin America.* Pittsburgh, PA: University of Pittsburgh Press.

Huntington, Samuel. 1997. *The Clash of Civilizations and the Remaking of World Order.* New York: Touchstone.

Hutchison, Jane and Andrew Brown. 2001. *Organizing Labour in Globalizing Asia.* London, England: Routledge.

Immergut, Ellen M. 1992. *Health Policies: Interests and Institutions in Western Europe.* Cambridge, England: Cambridge University Press.

Jessop, Bob. 2001. "Bringing the State Back In (Yet Again): Reviews, Revisions, Rejections, and Redirections." *International Review of Sociology* 11:149–73.

Katzenstein, Peter J. 1984. *Corporatism and Change: Austria, Switzerland and the Politics of Industry.* Ithaca, NY: Cornell University Press.

Katzenstein, Peter J. 1985. *Small States in World Markets.* Ithaca, NY: Cornell University Press.

Kimeldorf, Howard, 1988. *Reds or Rackets?: The Making of Radical and Conservative Unions on the Waterfront.* Berkeley: University of California Press.

King, Desmond. 1992. "The Establishment of Work-Welfare Programmes in the United States and Britain: Politics, Ideas, and Institutions," Pp. 217–50 in *Structuring Politics: Historical Institutionalism in Comparative Analysis,* edited by S. Steinmo, K. Thelen, and F. Longstreth. New York: Cambridge University Press.

Kiser, Edgar and Michael Hechter. 1991. "The Role of Theory in Comparative-Historical Sociology." *American Journal of Sociology* 97:1–30.

Mahoney, James. 2002. *The Legacies of Liberalism: Path Dependence and Political Regimes in Central America.* Baltimore, MD: Johns Hopkins University Press.

Mahoney, James. 2003. "Knowledge Accumulation in Comparative Historical Research: The Case of Democracy and Authoritarianism." Pp. 131–74 in *Comparative Historical Analysis in the Social Sciences,* edited by

J. Mahoney and D. Rueschemeyer. Cambridge, England: Cambridge University Press.

Mahoney, James and Dietrich Rueschemeyer, eds. 2003. *Comparative Historical Analysis in the Social Sciences.* Cambridge, England: Cambridge University Press.

Mann, Michael. 1986. *The Sources of Social Power.* Vol 1. Cambridge, England: Cambridge University Press.

Mann, Michael. 1993. *The Sources of Social Power.* Vol. 2. Cambridge, England: Cambridge University Press.

Matlock, Jack F., Jr. 1999. "Can Civilizations Change." *Proceedings of the American Philosophical Society* 143(3):428–39. Retrieved May 20, 2005 (http://www .aps-pub.com/proceedings/1433/Matlock.pdf).

Melucci, Alberto. 1980. "The New Social Movements." *Social Science Information* 19(2):199–226.

Melucci, Alberto. 1985. "The Symbolic Challenge of Contemporary Movements." *Social Research* 52:789–816.

Mies, Maria. 1986. *Patriarchy and Accumulation on a World Scale: Women and the International Division of Labour.* London, England: Zed Books.

Miliband, Ralph. 1969. *The State in Capitalist Society.* New York: Basic Books.

Moore, Barrington. 1966. *The Social Origins of Dictatorship and Democracy.* Boston, MA: Beacon Press.

Murillo, Maria Victoria. 2001. *Labor Unions, Partisan Coalitions, and Market Reforms in Latin America.* Cambridge, England: Cambridge University Press.

Myles, John and Adnan Turegun. 1994. "Comparative Studies in Class Structure." *American Review of Sociology* 20:103–24.

O'Connor, James. 1973. *The Fiscal Crises of the State.* New York: St. Martin's Press.

Offe, Claus. 1973. "The Abolition of Market Control and the Problem of Legitimacy, Part 1." *Kapitalstate* 1:109–16.

Offe, Claus and Volker Ronge. 1975. "Notes: Theses on the Theory of the State," *New German Critique* 6:137–47.

Orloff, Ann Shola. 1993. *The Politics of Pensions: A Comparative Analysis of Britain, Canada, and the United States, 1880–1940.* Madison: University of Wisconsin Press.

Parsons, Talcott. 1966. *Societies: Evolutionary and Comparative Perspectives.* Englewood Cliffs, NJ: Prentice-Hall.

Parsons, Talcott. 1969. *Politics and Social Structure.* New York: Free Press.

Parsons, Talcott. 1971. *The System of Modern Society.* Englewood Cliffs, NJ: Prentice-Hall.

Paige, Jeffery. 1997. *Coffee and Power: Revolution and the Rise of Democracy in Central America.* Cambridge, MA: Harvard University Press.

Paige, Jeffery. 1999. "Conjecture, Comparison, and Conditional Theory in Macrosocial Inquiry." *American Journal of Sociology* 105:781–800.

Pierson, Paul. 1994. *Dismantling the Welfare State?: Reagan, Thatcher and the Politics of Retrenchment.* Cambridge, England: Cambridge University Press.

Pierson, Paul. 2000. "Increasing Returns, Path Dependency, and the Study of Politics." *American Political Science Review* 94:251–67.

Polanyi, Karl. 1944. *The Great Transformation.* New York: Octagon Books.

Poulantzas, Nicos. 1975. *Classes in Contemporary Capitalism.* London, England: New Left Books.

Ragin, Charles. 1987. *The Comparative Method: Moving Beyond Qualitative and Quantitative Strategies.* Berkeley: University of California Press.

Rostow, Walt. 1960. *Politics and Stages of Growth*. Cambridge, England: Cambridge University Press.

Reuschemeyer, Deitrich and Peter Evans. 1985. "The State and Economic Transformation: Towards an Analysis of the Conditions Underlying Effective Intervention." Pp. 44–76 in *Bringing the State Back In,* edited by P. Evans, D. Rueschemeyer, and T. Skocpol. Cambridge, England: Cambridge University Press.

Silver, Beverly J. 2003. *Forces of Labor: Workers' Movements and Globalization since 1870*. Cambridge, England: Cambridge University Press.

Skocpol, Theda. 1979. *States and Social Revolutions*. Cambridge, England: Cambridge University Press.

Skocpol, Theda. 1985. "Bringing the State Back In: Strategies of Analysis in Current Research." Pp. 3–37 in *Bringing the State Back In,* edited by P. Evans, D. Rueschemeyer, and T. Skocpol. Cambridge, England: Cambridge University Press.

Skocpol, Theda. 1992. *Protecting Soldiers and Mothers*. Cambridge, MA: Harvard University Press.

Smelser, Neil J. 1968. *Essays in Sociological Explanation*. Englewood Cliffs, NJ: Prentice-Hall.

Sombart, Werner. [1902] 1928. *Der moderne Kapitalismus*. Munich: Duncker & Humblot.

Spengler, Oswald. 1926. *The Decline of the West*. New York: A. A. Knopf.

Stepan-Norris, Judith and Maurice Zeitlin. 2002. *Left Out: Reds and America's Industrial Unions*. Cambridge, England: Cambridge University Press.

Steinmo, Sven. 1993. *Taxation and Democracy: Swedish, British and American Approaches to Financing the Modern State*. New Haven, CT: Yale University Press.

Stinchcombe, Arthur. 1978. *Theoretical Methods in Social History*. New York: Academic Press.

Taylor, Andrew. 1989. *Trade Unions and Politics: A Comparative Introduction*. New York: Macmillan.

Tilly, Charles. 1975. *The Rebellious Century, 1830–1930*. Cambridge, MA: Harvard University Press.

Tilly, Charles. 1978. *From Mobilization to Revolution*. Reading, MA: Addison-Wesley.

Tilly, Charles. 1981. *As Sociology Meets History*. New York: Academic Press.

Tilly, Charles. 1984. *Big Structures, Large Processes, Huge Comparisons*. New York: Russell Sage Foundation.

Tilly, Charles. 1985. "War Making and State Making as Organized Crime." Pp. 169–91 in *Bringing the State Back In,* edited by P. Evans, D. Rueschemeyer, and T. Skocpol. Cambridge, England: Cambridge University Press.

Thompson, E. P. 1963. *The Making of the English Working Class*. New York: Vintage Books.

Tolliday, Stephen and Jonathan Zeitlin, eds. 1985. *Shop Floor Bargaining and the State: Historical and Comparative Perspectives*. Cambridge, England: Cambridge University Press.

Toynbee, Arnold J. 1934. *A Study of History*. London, England: Oxford University Press.

Voss, Kim. 1993. *The Making of American Exceptionalism: The Knights of Labor and Class Formation in the Nineteenth Century*. Ithaca, NY: Cornell University Press.

Wallerstein, Immanuel. 1974. *The Modern World-System,* vol. 1, *Capitalist Agriculture and the Origins of the European World-Economy in the Sixteenth Century*. New York: Academic Press.

Wallerstein, Immanuel. 2000. "From Sociology to Historical Social Science. Prospects and Obstacles." *British Journal of Sociology* 51:25–35.

Weber, Max. 1949. "'Objectivity' in Social Science and Social Policy." Pp. 50–113 in *The Methodology of the Social Sciences,* edited by E. Shils and H. Finch. Glencoe, IL: The Free Press of Glencoe.

Weber, Max. [1919] 1958. "Politics as a Vocation." Pp. 77–128 in *From Max Weber: Essays in Sociology,* edited by H. H. Gerth and C. Wright Mills. New York: Oxford University Press.

Weber, Max. 1975. *Roscher and Knies: The Logical Problems of Historical Economics*. New York: The Free Press.

Weber, Max. [1930] 2001. *The Protestant Ethic and the Spirit of Capitalism*. New York: Routledge.

Wickham-Crowley, Timothy. 1991. *Exploring Revolution: Essays on Latin American Insurgency and Revolutionary Theory*. Armonk, NY: M. E. Sharpe.

Wickham-Crowley, Timothy. 1992. *Guerrillas and Revolution in Latin America: A Comparative Study of Insurgents and Regimes since 1956*. Princeton, NJ: Princeton University Press.

Wright, Eric Olin. 1978. *Class, Crises and the State*. London, England: New Left Books.

Zysman, John. 1983. *Governments, Markets, and Growth: Financial Systems and Politics of Industrial Change*. Ithaca, NY: Cornell University Press.

PART IV: THE FABRIC OF SOCIAL LIFE

Chapter 12. The Sociology of Culture

Alexander, Jeffery C. 1990. "Analytical Debates: Understanding the Relative Autonomy of Culture." Pp. 1–27 in *Culture and Society: Contemporary Debates,* edited by J. C. Alexander and S. Seidman. Cambridge, England: Cambridge University Press.

Alexander, Jeffery C. 2003. *The Meaning of Social Life: A Cultural Sociology*. New York: Oxford University Press.

Alexander, Jeffery C. and Phillip Smith. 1993. "The Discourse of American Civil Society: A New Proposal for Cultural Studies." *Theory and Society* 22(2):151–207.

Allan, Kenneth. 1998. *The Meaning of Culture: Moving the Postmodern Critique Forward*. Westport, CT: Praeger.

Althusser, Louis. 1971. *Lenin and Philosophy and Other Essays*. Translated by B. Brewster. London, England: New Left Books.

Althusser, Louis and Etienne Balibar. 1970. *Reading Capital*. London, England: New Left Books.

Appadurai, Arjun. 1997. *Modernity at Large: Cultural Dimensions of Globalization*. Minneapolis: University of Minnesota Press.

Archer, Margaret S. 1988. *Culture and Agency: The Place of Culture in Social Theory*. New York: Cambridge University Press.

Arendt, Hannah. [1954] 1968. *Between Past and Future: Eight Exercises in Political Thought*. Enlarged edition. New York: Penguin Books.

Arendt, Hannah. 1958. *The Human Condition*. Chicago, IL: University of Chicago Press.

Baudrillard, Jean. [1981] 1994. *Simulacra and Simulation*. Translated by S. F. Claser. Ann Arbor: University of Michigan Press.

Bell, Daniel. 1976. *The Cultural Contradictions of Capitalism*. New York: Basic Books.

Bellah, Robert. 1970. *Beyond Belief: Essays on Religion in a Post-Traditional World.* New York: Harper & Row.

Bellah, Robert. 1975. *The Broken Covenant.* New York: Seabury Press.

Bellah, Robert, Richard Madsen, William M. Sullivan, Ann Swidler, and Steven M. Tipton. 1985. *Habits of the Heart.* Berkeley: University of California Press.

Bergesen, Albert. 1993. "The Rise of Semiotic Marxism." *Sociological Perspectives* 36:1–22.

Biernacki, Richard. 1999. "Method and Metaphor after the New Cultural History." Pp. 62–92 in *Beyond the Cultural Turn: New Directions in the Study of Society and Culture,* edited by V. E. Bonnell and L. Hunt. Berkeley: University of California Press.

Bilimoria, Purushottama. 2003. "What is the 'Subaltern' of the Comparative Philosophy of Religion?" *Philosophy East & West* 53:340–66.

Bonnell, Victoria E. and Lynn Hunt, eds. 1999. *Beyond the Cultural Turn: New Directions in the Study of Society and Culture.* Berkeley: University of California Press.

Brantlinger, Patrick. 1990. *Crusoe's Footprints: Cultural Studies in Britain and America.* London, England: Routledge.

Bourdieu, Pierre. 1977. *Outline of a Theory of Practice.* Translated by R. Nice. Cambridge, England: Cambridge University Press.

Camic, Charles and Neil Gross. 1998. "Contemporary Developments in Sociological Theory: Current Prospects and Conditions of Possibility." *Annual Review of Sociology* 24:453–76.

Cerulo, K. 1988. "Analyzing Cultural Products: A New Method of Measurement." *Social Science Research* 17:317–52.

Cerulo, K. 1995. *Identity Designs: The Sights and Sounds of a Nation.* New Brunswick, NJ: Rutgers University Press.

Chakravorty-Spivak, Gayatri. [1985] 1988. "Can the Subaltern Speak?" Pp. 271–313 in *Marxism and the Interpretation of Culture,* edited by C. Nelson and L. Grossberg. Urbana: University of Illinois Press.

Clifford, James. 1986. "Introduction: Partial Truths." Pp. 1–26 in *Writing Culture: The Poetics and Politics of Ethnography,* edited by J. Clifford and G. E. Marcus. Berkeley: University of California Press.

Coleman, J. and T. Fararo, eds. 1992. *Rational Choice Theory: Advocacy and Critique.* Newbury Park, CA: Sage.

Davies, Ioan. 1995. *Cultural Studies and Beyond: Fragments of Empire.* London, England: Routledge.

de Man, Paul. 1979. *Allegories of Reading: Figural Language in Rousseau, Nietzsche, Rilke, and Proust.* New Haven, CT: Yale University Press.

de Saussure, Ferdinand. 1960. *Course in General Linguistics.* London, England: Peter Owen.

Derrida, Jacques. 1974. *Of Grammatology.* Translated by G. Chakravorty-Spivak. Baltimore, MD: Johns Hopkins University Press.

Dilthey, Wilhelm. 1976. "The Construction of the Historical World in the Human Studies." Pp. 168–245 in *Wilhelm Dilthey: Selected Writings,* edited by H. P. Rickman. London, England: Cambridge University Press.

Dirks, Nicholas B. 1996. "Is Vice Versa? Historical Anthropologies and Anthropological Histories." Pp. 17–51 in *The Historic Turn in the Human Sciences,* edited by T. J. McDonald. Ann Arbor: University of Michigan Press.

Durkheim, Émile. [1895] 1938. *The Rules of Sociological Method,* edited by G. E. Catlin. Translated by S. A. Solovay and J. H. Mueller. Glencoe, IL: Free Press.

Durkheim, Émile. [1915] 1965. *The Elementary Forms of the Religious Life.* Translated by J. W. Swain. New York: Free Press.

Eisenstadt, Shmuel. 1989. "Culture and Social Structure in Recent Sociological Analysis." Pp. 5–11 in *Social Structure and Culture,* edited by H. Haferkamp. New York: Walter de Gruyter.

Elteren, Melvan. 2003. "U.S. Cultural Imperialism Today: Only a Chimera?" *SAIS Review* 23:169–88.

Farganis, James, ed. 2004. *Readings in Social Theory: The Classic Tradition to Post-Modernism.* Boston, MA: McGraw-Hill.

Feierman, Steven. 1999. "Colonizers, Scholars, and the Creation of Invisible Histories." Pp. 182–216 in *Beyond the Cultural Turn: New Directions in the Study of Society and Culture,* edited by V. E. Bonnell and L. Hunt. Berkeley: University of California Press.

Filmer, Paul. 1998. "Theory/Practice." Pp. 227–45 in *Core Sociological Dichotomies,* edited by C. Jenks. London, England: Sage.

Foucault, Michel. 1980. *Power/Knowledge,* edited by C. Gordon. New York: Pantheon Books.

Gallagher, Charles. 1979. "Introduction." Pp. 1–7 in *Modernization, Economic Development, and Cultural Values: A Bellagio Conference.* New York: Rockefeller Foundation.

Geertz, Clifford. 1973. *Interpretation of Cultures.* New York: Basic Books.

Geertz, Clifford. 1983. *Local Knowledge: Further Essays in Interpretive Anthropology.* New York: Basic Books.

Gramsci, Antonio. 1971. *Selections from the Prison Notebooks.* New York: International Publishers.

Greer, Scott. 1969. *The Logic of Social Inquiry.* Chicago, IL: Aldine.

Griswold, Wendy. 1987. "A Methodological Framework for the Sociology of Culture." *Sociological Methodology* 17:1–35.

Griswold, Wendy. 1993. "Recent Moves in the Sociology of Literature." *Annual Review of Sociology* 19:455–67.

Grossberg, Lawrence. 1998. "The Victory of Culture. Part I: Against the Logic of Mediation." *Angelaki* 3:3–29.

Habermas, Jurgen. 1992. "Further Reflections on the Public Sphere." Pp. 421–61 in *Habermas and the Public Sphere,* edited by C. Calhoun. Cambridge: MIT Press.

Hall, John R. and Mary Jo Neitz. 1993. *Culture: Sociological Perspectives.* Engelwood Cliffs, NJ: Prentice Hall.

Hall, Stuart. 1992. "Cultural Studies and Its Theoretical Legacies." Pp. 277–94 in *Cultural Studies,* edited by L. Grossberg, C. Nelson, and P. A. Treichler. New York: Routledge.

Huntington, Samuel P. 1996. *The Clash of Civilizations and the Remaking of World Order.* New York: Simon & Schuster.

Jenks, Chris. 2005. *Culture.* London, England: Routledge.

Kane, Ann. 1991. "Cultural Analysis in Historical Sociology: The Analytic and Concrete Forms of the Autonomy of Culture." *Sociological Theory* 9(1):53–69.

Kaplan, David. [1965] 1968. "The Superorganic: Science or Metaphysics." Pp. 20–31 in *Theory in Anthropology: A Sourcebook,* edited by R. A. Manners and D. Kaplan. Chicago, IL: Aldine.

Kroeber, Alfred and Clyde Kluckhohn. [1952] 1963. *Culture: A Critical Review of Concepts and Definitions.* New York: Vintage Books.

Kulchyski, Peter. 1997. "From Appropriation to Subversion: Aboriginal Cultural Production in the Age of Postmodernism." *American Indian Quarterly* 21:605–21.

Laclau, Ernesto. 1988. "Metaphor and Social Antagonisms." Pp. 249–57 in *Marxism and the Interpretation of Culture,* edited by C. Nelson and L. Grossberg. Urbana: University of Illinois Press.

Laclau, Ernesto and Chantal Mouffe. 1985. *Hegemony and Socialist Strategy: Toward a Radical Democratic Politics.* London, England: Verso.

Lévi-Strauss, Claude. 1966. *The Savage Mind.* Chicago, IL: University of Chicago Press.

Lewandowski, Joseph D. 2001. *Interpreting Culture: Rethinking Method and Truth in Social Theory.* Lincoln: University of Nebraska Press.

Linstead, Stephen. 1993. "From Postmodern Anthropology to Deconstructive Ethnography." *Human Relations* 46:97–118.

Marcus, G. 1998. *Ethnography through Thick and Thin.* Princeton, NJ: Princeton University Press.

Marx, Karl. [1904] 1959. "Excerpts from *A Contribution to the Critique of Political Economy.*" Pp. 42–46 in *Marx & Engels: Basic Writings on Politics and Philosophy,* edited by L. S. Feuer. Garden City, NY: Anchor Books.

McDonald, Terrence J. 1996. "Introduction." Pp. 1–13 in *The Historic Turn in the Human Sciences,* edited by T. J. McDonald. Ann Arbor: University of Michigan Press.

Milner, Andrew. 1994. *Contemporary Cultural Theory: An Introduction.* London, England: UCL Press.

Mohr, John W. 1998. "Measuring Meaning Structures." *Annual Review of Sociology* 24:345–70.

Mouffe, Chantal. 1979. *Gramsci and Marxist Theory.* London, England: Routledge & Kegan Paul.

Mouffe, Chantal. 1988. "Hegemony and New Political Subjects: Toward a New Concept of Democracy." Pp. 89–181 in *Marxism and the Interpretation of Cultures,* edited by C. Nelson and L. Grossberg. Urbana: University of Illinois Press.

Norris, Christopher. 1991. *Deconstruction: Theory and Practice.* London, England: Routledge.

Parsons, Talcott. 1951. *The Social System.* London, England: Routledge & Kegan Paul.

Peterson, Richard A. 1979. "Revitalizing the Culture Concept." *Annual Review of Sociology* 5:137–66.

Poulantzas, N. 1973. *Political Power and Social Classes.* London, England: New Left Books.

Poulantzas, N. 1974. *Classes in Contemporary Capitalism.* London, England: New Left Books.

Poulantzas, N. 1978. *State, Power and Socialism.* London, England: New Left Books.

Radcliffe-Brown, A. R. 1957. *A Natural Science of Society.* Glencoe, IL: Free Press.

Rose, Sonya O. 1999. "Cultural Analysis and Moral Discourses: Episodes, Continuities, and Transformations." Pp. 217–38 in *Beyond the Cultural Turn: New Directions in the Study of Society and Culture,* edited by V. E. Bonnell and L. Hunt. Berkeley: University of California Press.

Roseberry, William. 1982. "Balinese Cockfights and the Seduction of Anthropology." *Social Research* 49:1013–28.

Said, Edward. [1978] 1995. *Orientalism.* Harmondsworth, England: Penguin.

Saukko, Paula. 2003. *Doing Research in Cultural Studies: An Introduction to Classical and New Methodological Approaches.* London, England: Sage.

Schatzki, Theodore R., Karin Knorr Cetina, and Eike von Savigny. 2001. *The Practice Turn in Contemporary Theory.* New York: Routledge.

Schutz, Alfred. [1953] 1963. "Common-Sense and Scientific Interpretation of Human Action." Pp. 302–46 in *Philosophy of the Social Sciences: A Reader,* edited by M. Natanson. New York: Random House.

Schutz, Alfred. [1954] 1963. "Concept and Theory Formation in the Social Sciences." Pp. 231–49 in *Philosophy of the Social Sciences: A Reader,* edited by M. Natanson. New York: Random House.

Schwartz, Stephen Adam. 2000. "Every Man an Ubermensch: The Culture of Cultural Studies." *Substance* 29:104–38.

Seidman, Stephen. 1990. "Substantive Debates: Moral Order and Social Crisis—Perspectives on Modern Culture." Pp. 217–35 in *Culture & Society: Contemporary Debates,* edited by J. C. Alexander and S. Seidman. Cambridge, England: Cambridge University Press.

Sewell, William H., Jr. 1992. "A Theory of Structure: Duality, Agency, and Transformation." *American Journal of Sociology* 98:1–29.

Sewell, William H., Jr. 1997. "Geertz, Cultural Systems, and History: From Synchrony to Transformation." *Representations* 59:35–75.

Sewell, William H., Jr. 1999. The Concept(s) of Culture." Pp. 35–61 in *Beyond the Cultural Turn: New Directions in the Study of Society and Culture,* edited by V. E. Bonnell and L. Hunt. Berkeley: University of California Press.

Somers, Margaret R. 1999. "The Privatization of Citizenship: How to Unthink a Knowledge Culture." Pp. 121–61 in *Beyond the Cultural Turn: New Directions in the Study of Society and Culture,* edited by V. E. Bonnell and L. Hunt. Berkeley: University of California Press.

Swidler, Ann. 1986. "Culture in Action: Symbols and Strategies." *American Sociological Review* 51:273–86.

Swidler, Ann. 2001. "What Anchors Cultural Practices." Pp. 74–92 in *The Practice Turn in Contemporary Theory,* edited by T. R. Schatzki, K. K. Cetina, and E. von Savigny. New York: Routledge.

Thompson, E. P. 1963. *The Making of the English Working Class.* London, England: Gollancz.

Tilly, Charles. 1997. "Parliamentarization of Popular Contention in Great Britain, 1758–1834." *Theory and Society* 26:245–73.

Tudor, Andrew. 1999. *Decoding Culture: Theory and Method in Cultural Studies.* London, England: Sage.

Turner, Stephen. 1994. *The Social Theory of Practices: Tradition, Tacit Knowledge, and Presuppositions.* Chicago, IL: University of Chicago Press.

Vaillancourt, Pauline Marie. 1986. *When Marxists Do Research.* New York: Greenwood Press.

Walsh, David W. 1998. "Subject/Object." Pp. 275–98 in *Core Sociological Dichotomies,* edited by C. Jenks. London, England: Sage.

Weber, Max. [1904] 1949. *The Methodology of the Social Sciences.* Translated and edited by E. A. Shils and H. A. Finch. New York: Free Press.

Weber, Max. [1915] 1958. "The Social Psychology of the World Religions." Pp. 267–301 in *From Max Weber: Essays in Sociology.* Translated and edited by H. H. Gerth and C. Wright Mills. New York: Oxford University Press.

White, Hayden. 1973. *Metahistory: The Historical Imagination in Nineteenth-Century Europe.* Baltimore, MD: Johns Hopkins University Press.

White, Leslie A. [1954] 1968. "On the Concept of Culture." Pp. 15–20 in *Theory in Anthropology: A Sourcebook,* edited by R. A. Manners and D. Kaplan. Chicago, IL: Aldine.

Williams, Raymond. 1981. *The Sociology of Culture.* New York: Schocken Books.

Wuthnow, Robert. 1987. *Meaning and Moral Order: Explorations in Cultural Analysis.* Berkeley: University of California Press.

Wuthnow, Robert and Marsha Witten. 1988. "New Directions in the Study of Culture." *Annual Review of Sociology* 14:49–67.

Chapter 13. The Sociology of Socialization

Acock, Alan C. and Vern L. Bengtson. 1978. "On the Relative Influence of Mothers and Fathers: A Covariance Analysis of Political and Religious Socialization." *Journal of Marriage and the Family* 40(3):519–30.

Adler, Patricia A. and Peter Adler. 1998. *Peer Power.* New Brunswick, NJ: Rutgers University Press.

Anderson, Elijah. 1976. *A Place on the Corner.* Chicago, IL: University of Chicago Press.

Anderson, Elijah. 1990. *Streetwise: Race, Class, and Change in an Urban Community.* Chicago, IL: University of Chicago Press.

Arkin, William and Lynne R. Dobrofsky. 1978. "Military Socialization and Masculinity." *Journal of Social Issues* 34(1):151–68.

Arnett, Jeffrey J. 1995. "Adolescents' Use of Media for Self-Socialization." *Journal of Youth and Adolescence* 25(5):519–33.

Bachman, Jerald G., Peter Freedman-Doan, David R. Segal, and Patrick M. Malley. 2000. "Distinctive Military Attitudes among U.S. Enlistees, 1976–1997: Self-Selection versus Socialization." *Armed Forces and Society* 26(4):561–85.

Bandura, Albert. 1969. "Social Learning Theory of Identificatory Processes." Pp. 213–62 in *Handbook of Socialization Theory and Research,* edited by D. A. Goslin. Chicago, IL: Rand McNally.

Bandura, Albert. 1977. *Social Learning Theory.* Englewood Cliffs, NJ: Prentice Hall.

Barnes, Grace M., Michael P. Farrell, and Allen Cairns. 1986. "Parental Socialization Factors and Adolescent Drinking Behaviors." *Journal of Marriage and the Family* 48(February):27–36.

Baron, Stephan W. and David B. Tindall. 1993. "Network Structure and Delinquent Attitudes within a Juvenile Gang." *Social Networks* 15:255–73.

Barretti, Marietta. 2004a. "The Professional Socialization of Undergraduate Social Work Students." *Journal of Baccalaureate Social Work* 9(2):9–30.

Barretti, Marietta. 2004b. "What Do We Know about the Professional Socialization of Our Students?" *Journal of Social Work Education* 40(2):255–83.

Bernard, Luther L. 1924. *Instinct.* New York: Holt, Rinehart & Winston.

Bernstein, Basil. 1965. "A Socio-Linguistic Approach to Social Learning." Pp. 144–68 in *Penguin Survey of the Social Sciences,* edited by J. Gould. New York: Penguin Books.

Bernstein, Basil. 1977. *Class, Codes, and Control,* vol. 3. London, England: Routledge & Kegan Paul.

Biafora, Frank A., George J. Warheit, Rick S. Zimmerman, Andres G. Gil, Eleni Apospori, Dorothy Taylor, et al. 1993. "Racial Mistrust and Deviant Behaviors among Ethnically Diverse Black Adolescent Boys." *Journal of Applied Social Psychology* 23:891–910.

Bourdieu, Pierre. 1974. "The School as a Conservative Force." Pp. 32–46 in *Contemporary Research in the Sociology of Education,* edited and translated by J. Eggleston. London, England: Methuen.

Bourdieu, Pierre. 1977. "Cultural Reproduction and Social Reproduction." Pp. 487–511 in *Power and Ideology in Education,* edited by J. Karabel and A. H. Halsey. New York: Oxford University Press.

Bourdieu, Pierre and Jean-Claude Passeron. 1977. *Reproduction in Education, Society and Culture.* London, England: Sage.

Bourne, Peter G. 1967. "Some Observations on the Psychosocial Phenomena Seen in Basic Training." *Psychiatry* 30(2):187–96.

Bowles, Samuel. 1977. "Unequal Education and the Reproduction of the Social Division of Labor." Pp. 137–53 in *Power and Ideology in Education,* edited by J. Karabel and A. H. Halsely. New York: Oxford University Press.

Bowles, Samuel and Herbert Gintis. 1976. *Schooling in Capitalist America.* New York: Basic Books.

Bowles, Samuel and Herbert Gintis. 2002. "Schooling in Capitalist America Revisited." *Sociology of Education* 75:1–18.

Brega, Angela G. and Lerita M. Coleman. 1999. "Effects of Religiosity and Racial Socialization in African-American Adolescents." *Journal of Adolescents* 22:233–42.

Brooks-Gunn, Jeanne, Greg J. Duncun, and Lawrence Aber, eds. 1997. *Neighborhood Poverty, vol. 1: Context and Consequences for Children.* New York: Russell Sage.

Cain, Leonard D., Jr. 1964. "Life Course and Social Structure." Pp. 272–309 in *Handbook of Modern Sociology,* edited by R. E. Lee Faris. Chicago, IL: Rand McNally.

Carlson, Joseph R., George Thomas, and Richard H. Anson. 2004. "Cross-Gender Perceptions of Correction Officers in Gender-Segregated Prisons." *Journal of Offender Rehabilitation* 39(1):83–103.

Chodorow, Nancy. 1978. *Reproduction of Mothering: Psychoanalysis and the Sociology of Gender.* Berkeley: University of California Press.

Clark, Kenneth. 1965. *Dark Ghetto: Dilemmas of Social Power.* New York: Harper & Row.

Clausen, John A. 1968. "A Historical and Comparative View of Socialization Theory and Research." Pp. 18–72 in *Socialization and Society,* edited by J. A. Clausen. Boston, MA: Little, Brown.

Collins, Randall. 1977. "Some Comparative Principles of Educational Stratification." *Harvard Educational Review* 47(1):5–9.

Collins, Randall. 1979. *The Credential Society: An Historical Sociology of Education.* New York: Academic Press.

Constantine, Madonna G. and Sha'kema M. Blackmon. 2002. "Black Adolescents' Racial Socialization Experiences: Their Relations to Home, School, and Peer Self-Esteem." *Journal of Black Studies* 32(3):322–35.

Cookson, Peter W., Jr. and Caroline Hodges Persell. 1985. *Preparing for Power: America's Elite Boarding Schools.* New York: Basic Books.

Cooley, Charles Horton. [1902] 1964. *Human Nature and the Social Order.* New York: Schocken Books.

Cooper, Virginia W. 1985. "Women in Popular Music: A Quantitative Analysis of Feminine Images." *Sex Roles* 13(9–10):499–506.

Coser, Lewis. 1974. *Greedy Institutions: Patterns of Undivided Commitment.* New York: Free Press.

Crittenden, Paul. 1990. *Learning to Be Moral: Philosophical Thoughts About Moral Development.* Atlantic Heights, NJ: Humanities Press International.

Darwin, Charles. [1872] 1966. *On the Origin of Species.* Cambridge, MA: Harvard University Press.

Davies, Bronwyn. 1991. *Frogs and Snails and Feminist Tales.* Sydney, Australia: Allen & Unwin.

Denzin, Norman K. 1977. *Childhood Socialization.* San Francisco, CA: Jossey-Bass.

Dietz, Tracy L. 1998. "An Examination of Violence and Gender Role Portrayals in Video Games: Implications for Gender Socialization and Aggressive Behavior." *Sex Roles* 38(5/6):425–42.

Donohew, Lewis, Richard R. Clayton, William F. Skinner, and Susan Colon. 1999. "Peer Networks and Sensation Seeking: Some Implications for Primary Socialization Theory." *Substance Abuse & Misuse* 34(7):1013–23.

Downs, William R. 1987. "A Panel Study of Normative Structure, Adolescent Alcohol Use, and Peer Alcohol Use." *Journal of Studies on Alcohol* 48(2):167–75.

Durkheim, Émile. [1895] 1964. *The Rules of Sociological Methods.* New York: Free Press.

Durkheim, Émile. [1915] 1965. *The Elementary Forms of the Religious Life.* New York: Free Press.

Durkheim, Émile. 1973. *Moral Education: A Study in the Theory and Application of the Sociology of Education.* New York: Free Press.

Edin, Kathryn and Laura Lein. 1997. *Making Ends Meet: How Single Mothers Survive on a Welfare Check.* New York: Russell Sage.

Elder, Glen H., Jr. 1974. *Children of the Great Depression: Social Change in Life Experience.* Chicago, IL: University of Chicago Press.

Elder, Glen H., Jr. 1975. "Age Differentiation in the Life Course." *Annual Review of Sociology* 1:165–90.

Elder, Glen H., Jr. 1994. "Time, Human Agency, and Social Change: Perspectives on the Life Course." *Social Psychology Quarterly* 57(1):4–15.

Elder, Glen H., Jr. 1998. "The Life Course and Human Development." Pp. 939–91 in *Handbook of Child Psychology,* vol. 1, edited by W. Damon and R. M. Lerner. New York: Wiley.

Elkin, Frederick and Gerald Handel. 1984. *The Child and Society: The Process of Socialization.* 4th ed. New York: Random House.

Erickson, Erik H. 1959. "Identity and the Life Cycle." In *Psychological Issues* (Monograph) 1, 1. New York: International Universities Press.

Ex, Caroline T. G. M and Jam M. A. M. Janssens. 1998. "Maternal Influences on Daughters' Gender Role Attitudes." *Sex Roles* 38:171–86.

Faludi, Susan. 1991. *Backlash: The Undeclared War against Women.* New York: Crown.

Faris, John H. 1975. "The Impact of Basic Combat Training: The Role of the Drill Sergeant in the All-Volunteer Army." *Armed Forces and Society* 2(1):115–27.

Fischer, Ann R. and C. M. Shaw. 1999. "African Americans' Mental Health and Perceptions of Racist Discrimination: The Moderating Effects of Racial Socialization Experiences and Self-Esteem." *Journal of Counseling Psychology* 46(3):395–407.

Fordham, Signithia. 1988. "Racelessness as a Factor in Black Students' School Success: Pragmatic Strategy or Pyrrhic Victory?" *Harvard Educational Review* 58:54–84.

Fordham, Signithia and John U. Ogbu. 1986. "Black Students' School Success: Coping with the 'Burden of Acting White.'" *Urban Review* 18:176–206.

Franke, Volker C. 2000. "Duty, Honor, Country: The Social Identity of West Point Cadets." *Armed Forces and Society* 26(2):175–202.

Freud, Sigmund. 1923. *The Ego and the Id.* London, England: Hogarth.

Freud, Sigmund. 1946. *The Ego and the Mechanism of Defense.* New York: International Universities Press.

Freud, Sigmund. 1949. *An Outline of Psychoanalysis.* New York: W. W. Norton.

Furnham, Adrian and Nadine Bitar. 1993. "The Stereotypical Portrayal of Men and Women in British Television Advertisements." *Sex Roles* 29(3–4): 297–310.

Garfinkel, Harold. 1956. "Conditions of Successful Degradation Ceremonies." *American Journal of Sociology* 61(2):420–24.

Gelman, Susan A., Marianne G. Taylor, and Simone P. Nguyen. 2004. "Mother-Child Conversations about Gender." *Monographs of the Society for Research on Child Development* (Serial No. 275) 69, 1.

Glascock, Jack. 2001. "Gender Roles on Prime-Time Network Television: Demographics and Behaviors." *Journal of Broadcasting and Electronic Media* 45(Fall):656–69.

Glaser, Barney G. and Anselm L. Straus. 1971. *Status Passage: A Formal Theory.* Chicago, IL: Aldine-Atherton.

Goertzel, Ted and Acco Hengst. 1971. "The Military Socialization of University Students." *Social Problems* 19(2):258–67.

Goffman, Erving. 1961. *Asylums: Essays on the Social Situation of Mental Patients and Other Inmates.* Chicago, IL: Aldine.

Goldberg, Susan and Michael Lewis. 1969. "Play Behavior in the Year Old Infant: Early Sex Differences." *Child Development* 40(March):21–31.

Gomez-Mejia, Luis R. 1983. "Sex Differences during Occupational Socialization." *Academy of Management Journal* 26(3):492–99.

Goslin, David A., ed. 1969. *Handbook of Socialization Theory and Research.* Chicago, IL: Rand McNally.

Gottfredson, Michael and Travis Hirschi. 1990. *A General Theory of Crime.* Stanford: University of California Press.

Hadaway, Kirk C. and Wade C. Roof. 1979. "Those Who Stay Religious 'Nones' and Those Who Don't: A Research Note." *Journal of the Scientific Study of Religion* 18(June):194–200.

Hallinan, Maureen T. 1994. "Tracking: From Theory to Practice." *Sociology of Education* 67(April):79–84.

Hammond, Phillip E., Mark A. Shibley, and Peter M. Solow. 1994. "Religion and Family Values in Presidential Voting." *Sociology of Religion* 55(3):277–90.

Handel, Gerald, ed. 1988. *Childhood Socialization.* New York: Aldine de Gruyter.

Hartup, Willard. 1999. "Constraints on Peer Socialization: Let Me Count the Ways." *Merrill-Palmer Quarterly* 45(1):172–83.

Hayes, Bernadette C. 1995. "The Impact of Religious Identification and Political Attitudes: An International Comparison." *Sociology of Religion* 56(2):177–94.

Heinz, Walter R. and Victor Marshall. 2003. *Social Dynamics of the Life Course: Transitions, Institutions, and Interrelations.* Hawthorne, NY: Aldine de Gruyter.

Henley, N. M. 1989. "Molehill or Mountain? What We Know and Don't Know about Sex Bias in Language." Pp. 59–78 in *Gender and Thought: Psychological Perspectives,* edited by M. Crawford and M. Gentry. New York: Springer-Verlag.

Himmelfarb, Harold. S. 1980. "The Study of American Jewish Identification: How It Is Defined, Measured, Obtained, Sustained and Lost." *Journal for the Scientific Study of Religion* 19(1):48–60.

Hirschi, Travis. 1969. *Causes of Delinquency.* Berkeley: University of California Press.

Hoffman, Lois W. 1977. "Changes in Family Roles, Socialization, and Sex Differences." *American Psychologist* 42(August):644–57.

Hughes, Diane. 2003. "Correlates of African American and Latino Parents' Messages to Children about Ethnicity and Race: A Comparative Study of Racial Socialization." *American Journal of Community Psychology* 31(1–2):15–33.

Hughes, Diane and Deborah Johnson. 2001. "Correlates in Children's Experiences of Parents' Racial Socialization Behaviors." *Journal of Marriage and Family* 63(November):981–95.

Hunsberger, Bruce. 1980. "A Reexamination of the Antecedents of Apostasy." *Review of Religious Research* 21(2):158–70.

Hunsberger, Bruce. 1983. "Apostasy: A Social Learning Perspective." *Review of Religious Research* 25(1):21–38.

Hunsberger, Bruce and Laurence B. Brown. 1984. "Religious Socialization, Apostasy, and the Impact of Family Background." *Journal for the Scientific Study of Religion* 23(3):239–51.

Inkeles, Alex. 1969. "Social Structure and Socialization." Pp. 615–632 in *Handbook of Socialization Theory and Research,* edited by D. A. Goslin. Chicago, IL: Rand McNally.

Jelen, Ted G. and Marthe A. Chandler. 1996. "Patterns of Religious Socialization: Communalism, Associationalism, and the Politics of Lifestyle." *Review of Religious Research* 38(2):142–58.

Kaplan, Howard B., Steven S. Martin, and Cynthia A. Robbins. 1984. "Pathways to Adolescent Drug Use: Self-Derogation, Peer Influence, Weakening of Social Controls and Early Substance Use." *Journal of Health and Social Behavior* 25(3):270–89.

Karner, Tracy X. 1998. "Engendering Violent Men: Oral Histories of Military Masculinity." Pp. 197–232 in *Masculinities and Violence,* edited by L. H. Bowker. Thousand Oaks, CA: Sage.

Katz, Pearl. 1990. "Emotional Metaphors, Socialization, and Roles of Drill Sergeants." *Ethos* 18(4):457–80.

Keister, Lisa A. and Stephanie Moller. 2000. "Wealth Inequality in the United States." *Annual Review of Sociology* 26:63–81.

Kelly, Kathleen and Lewis Donohew. 1999. "Media and Primary Socialization." *Substance Abuse & Misuse* 34(7):1033–45.

Kilgore, Sally B. 1991. "The Social Organizational Context of Tracking in Schools." *American Sociological Review* 56(April):189–203.

Kolbe, Richard H. and Carl D. Langefeld. 1993. "Appraising Gender Role Portrayals in TV Commercials." *Sex Roles* 28(7–8):393–417.

Kohlberg, Lawrence. 1969. "Stage and Sequence: The Cognitive-Developmental approach to Socialization." Pp. 347–480 in *Handbook of Socialization Theory and Research,* edited by D. Goslin. Chicago, IL: Rand McNally.

Kozol, Jonathan. 1991. *Savage Inequalities: Children in America's Schools.* New York: Crown.

LeVine, Robert A. 1969. "Culture, Personality, and Socialization: An Evolutionary View." Pp. 503–42 in *Handbook of Socialization Theory and Research,* edited by D. A. Goslin. Chicago, IL: Rand McNally.

Levy, Edna. 2000. "Fresh Mattresses: Sexuality, Fertility and Soldiering in Israeli Public Culture." *Race, Gender & Class* 7(1):71–90.

Lifton, Robert J. 1993. *The Protean Self: Human Resilience in an Age of Fragmentation.* New York: Basic Books.

Lombroso, Cesare. 1911. *Crime: Its Causes and Remedies.* Translated by H. P. Horton. Boston, MA: Little, Brown.

Lorber, Judith. 1993. *Paradoxes of Gender.* New Haven, CT: Yale University Press.

MacLeod, Jay. 1995. *Ain't No Makin' It: Aspirations & Attainment in a Low-Income Neighborhood.* Boulder, CO: Westview Press.

Marshall, Victor W. and Margaret M Mueller. 2003. "Theoretical Roots of the Life-Course Perspective." Pp. 3–32 in *Social Dynamics of the Life Course,* edited by W. Heinz and V. Marshall. Hawthorne, NY: Aldine de Gruyter.

Martin, Todd F., James M. White, and Daniel Perlman. 2003. "Religious Socialization: A Test of the Channeling Hypothesis of Parental Influence on Adolescent Faith Maturity." *Journal of Adolescent Research* 18(2):169–87.

McBroom, James R. 1994. "Correlates of Alcohol and Marijuana Use among Junior High School Students: Family, Peers, School Problems, and Psychosocial Concerns." *Youth and Society* 26(1):54–68.

McKay, Mary M., Marc S. Atkins, Tracie Hawkins, Catherine Brown, and Cynthia J. Lynn. 2003. "Inner-City African American Parental Involvement in Children's Schooling: Racial Socialization and Social Support from the Parent Community." *American Journal of Community Psychology* 32(1–2):107–14.

McWhorter, John. 2001. *Losing the Race: Self-Sabotage in Black America.* New York: Perennial.

Mead, Margaret. 1930. *Growing Up in New Guinea.* New York: Morrow.

Mead, George Herbert. 1934. *Mind, Self, and Society.* Chicago, IL: University of Chicago Press.

Melia, Kath M. 1984. "Student Nurses' Construction of Occupational Socialization." *Sociology of Health and Illness* 6(2):132–51.

Merton, Robert K. 1968. *Social Theory and Social Structure.* New York: Free Press.

Miller, David B. and Randall MacIntosh. 1999. "Promoting Resilience in Urban African American Adolescents: Racial Socialization and Identity as Protective Factors." *Social Work Research* 23(3):159–69.

Mortimer, Jaylan and Roberta G. Simmons. 1978. "Adult Socialization." *Annual Review of Sociology* 4:421–54.

Oetting, Eugene R. and Josheph F. Donnermeyer. 1998. "Primary Socialization Theory: The Etiology of Drug Use and Deviance. I. *Substance Use & Misuse* 33(4):995–1026.

Oetting, Eugene R., Joseph F. Donnermeyer, and Jerry L. Deffenbacher. 1998. "Primary Socialization Theory: The Influence of the Community on Drug Use and Deviance. III. *Substance Use & Misuse* 33(8):1629–65.

Ogbu, John U. 1978. *Minority Education and Caste: The American System in Cross-Cultural Perspective.* New York: Academic Press.

Ogbu, John U. 1983. "Minority Status and Schooling in Plural Societies." *Comparative Education Review* 27:168–90.

Okamoto, Dina and Paula England. 1999. "Is there a Supply Side to Occupational Sex Segregation?" *Sociological Perspectives* 42(4):557–82.

Ontai-Grzebik, Lenna L. and Marcela Raffaelli. 2004. "Individual and Social Influences on Ethnic Identity among Latino Young Adults." *Journal of Adolescent Research* 19(5):559–75.

Pearce, Lisa D. and William G. Axinn. 1998. "The Impact of Family Religious Life and the Mother-Child Relationship." *American Sociological Review* 63(6):810–28.

Perlow, Leslie A. 1997. *Finding Time: How Corporations, Individuals, and Families Can Benefit from New Work Practices.* Ithaca, NY: ILR Press.

Peters, John F. 1985. "Adolescents as Socialization Agents to Parents." *Adolescence* 20(80):921–33.

Peters, John F. 1994. "Gender Socialization of Adolescents in the Home: Research and Discussion." *Adolescence* 29(116):913–34.

Peters, Marie F. 1985. "Racial Socialization of Young Black Children." Pp. 159–73 in *Black Children: Social, Educational, and Parental Environments,* edited by H. P. McAdoo and J. L. McAdoo. 2d ed. Newbury Park, CA: Sage.

Piaget, Jean. 1950. *The Psychology of Intelligence.* London, England: Reutledge & Kegan Paul.

Piaget, Jean. 1954. *The Construction of Reality in the Child.* New York: Basic Books.

Piaget, Jean and Barbel Inhelder. 1969. *The Psychology of the Child.* New York: Basic Books.

Powell-Dahlquist, Joel and Lee G. Vigilant. 2004. "Way Better Than Real: Manga Sex to Tentacle Hentai." Pp. 91–103 in *Net.seXXX: Readings on Sex, Pornography, and the Internet,* edited by D. D. Waskul. New York: Peter Lang.

Purcell, Piper and Lisa Stewart. 1990. "Dick and Jane in 1989. *Sex Roles* 22(3–4):177–85.

Rainwater, Lee. 1970. *Behind Ghetto Walls: Black Families in a Federal Slum.* Chicago, IL: Aldine-Atherton.

Ramirez-Valles, Jesus, Marc A. Zimmerman, and Lucia Juarez. 2002. "Gender Differences of Neighborhood and Social Control Processes: A Study of the Timing of First Intercourse among Low-Achieving, Urban, African American Youth." *Youth and Society* 33(3):418–41.

Regnerus, Mark D. 2000. "Shaping School Success: Religious Socialization and Educational Outcomes in Metropolitan Public Schools." *Journal for the Scientific Study of Religion* 39(3):363–70.

Riley, Matilda White. 1979. "Introduction: Life-Course Perspectives." Pp. 3–13 in *Aging from Birth to Death,* edited by M. W. Riley. Boulder, CO: Westview Press.

Risman, Barbara J. 1998. *Gender Vertigo: American Families in Transition.* New Haven, CT: Yale University Press.

Ritzer, George. 1993. *The McDonaldization of Society: An Investigation into the Changing Character of Contemporary Life.* Thousand Oaks, CA: Pine Forge Press.

Ritzer, George. 1998. *The McDonaldization Thesis: Explorations and Extensions.* Thousand Oaks, CA: Sage.

Roof, Wade C. and Dean R. Hoge. 1980. "Church Involvement in America: Social Factors Affecting Membership and Participation." *Review of Religious Research* 21(4):405–26.

Rosow, Irving. 1974. *Socialization to Old Age.* Berkeley: University of California Press.

Saks, Alan M. and Blake E. Ashforth. 1997. "Organizational Socialization: Making Sense of the Past and Present as a Prologue for the Future." *Journal of Vocational Behavior* 51:234–79.

Sanders, Mavis G. 1997. "Overcoming Obstacles: Academic Achievements as a Response to Racism and Discrimination." *Journal of Negro Education* 66(1):83–93.

Sanders-Thompson, Vetta L. 1994. "Socialization to Race and its Relationship to Racial Identification among African Americans." *Journal of Black Psychology* 20(2):175–88.

Schein, Edgar H. 2004. "Learning When and How to Lie: A Neglected Aspect of Organizational and Occupational Socialization." *Human Relations* 57(3):260–73.

Scott, Lionel D., Jr. 2003. "The Relation of Racial Identity and Racial Socialization to Coping with Discrimination among African American Adolescents." *Journal of Black Studies* 33(4):520–38.

Segal, Mady W. 1986. "The Military and the Family as Greedy Institutions." *Armed Forces and Society* 13(1):9–38.

Shapiro, Thomas M. 2004. *The Hidden Cost of Being African American: How Wealth Perpetuates Inequality.* New York: Oxford University Press.

Shatan, Chaim F. 1977. "Bogus Manhood, Bogus Honor: Surrender and Transformation in the United States Marine Corps." *The Psychoanalytic Review* 64(4):585–610.

Signorielli, Nancy. 1989. "Television and Conceptions about Sex Roles: Maintaining Conventionality and the Status Quo." *Sex Roles* 21(5–6):341–60.

Simmel, Georg. 1950. *The Sociology of Georg Simmel.* Translated and edited by K. H. Wolff. Glencoe, IL: Free Press.

Stepan, Nancy L. 1991. *The Hour of Eugenics: Race, Gender, and Nation in Latin America.* Ithaca, NY: Cornell University Press.

Stevens, Gwendolyn, Fred M. Rosa, and Sheldon Gardner Jr. 1994. "Military Academies As Instruments of Value Change." *Armed Forces and Society* 20(3):473–84.

Stevenson, Howard C. 1994. "Validation of the Scale of Racial Socialization for African American Adolescents: Steps toward Multidimensionality." *Journal of Black Psychology* 20(4):445–68.

Stevenson, Howard C., Jocelyn Reed, and Preston Bodison. 1996. "Kinship Social Support and Adolescent Racial Socialization Beliefs: Extending the Self to Family." *Journal of Black Psychology* 22(4):498–508.

Sutherland, Edwin H., Donald R. Cressey, and David F. Luckenbill. 1992. *Principles of Criminology.* 11th ed. Dix Hills, NY: General Hall.

Thomas, Murray R. 1999. *Human Development Theories.* Thousand Oaks, CA: Sage.

Thompson, Patricia C., Louis P. Anderson, and Roger A. Bakeman. 2000. "Effects of Racial Socialization and Racial Identity on Acculturative Stress in African American College Students." *Cultural Diversity and Minority Psychology* 6(2):196–210.

Toennies, Fredinand. [1887] 1988. *Community and Society (Gemeinschaft und Gesellschaft).* New Brunswick, NJ: Transaction.

Van Evra, Judith. 1998. *Television and Child Development.* 2d ed. Mahwah, NJ: Lawrence Erlbaum.

Ward, Janie. V. 2000. *The Skin We're In: Teaching Our Children to Be Emotionally Strong, Socially Smart, Spiritually Connected.* New York: Free Press.

Watson, John B. 1924. *Behavior.* New York: Norton.

Weitzman, Lenore. 1979. *Sex Role Socialization.* Palo Alto, CA: Mayfield.

Weitzman, Lenore, Deborah Eifler, Elizabeth Hokada, and Catherine Ross. 1972. "Sexual Socialization in Picture Books for Preschool Children." *American Journal of Sociology* 77(6):1125–50.

Westerhoff, John H., III. 1973. "A Changing Focus: Toward an Understanding of Religious Socialization." *Andover Newton Quarterly* 14(2):118–29.

Whitbeck, Les B. 1999. "Primary Socialization Theory: It All Begins with the Family." *Substance Use & Abuse* 34(7):1025–32.

Wilcox, Bradford W. 1998. "Conservative Protestant Childrearing." *American Sociological Review* 63(6):796–809.

Wilcox, Clyde and Ted G. Jelen. 1990. "Evangelicals and Political Tolerance." *American Politics Quarterly* 18:25–46.

William, Terry M. and William Kornblum. 1990. *Growing Up Poor.* Lexington, MA: D. C. Heath.

Willis, Paul. 1976. *Learning to Labor.* London, England: Routledge & Kegan Paul.

Wilson, Edward O. 1975. *Sociobiology: The New Synthesis.* Cambridge, MA: Harvard University Press.

Wilson, James Q. and Richard J. Herrnstein. 1985. *Crime and Human Nature.* New York: Simon & Schuster.

Wilson, William J. 1987. *The Truly Disadvantaged: The Inner City, the Underclass, and Public Policy.* Chicago, IL: University of Chicago Press.

Wilson, William J. 1996. *When Work Disappears: The World of the New Urban Poor.* Chicago, IL: University of Chicago Press.

Windermiller, Myra, Nadine Lambert, and Elliot Turiel. 1980. *Moral Development and Socialization.* Boston, MA: Allyn & Bacon.

Worden, Alissa P. 1993. "The Attitudes of Women and Men in Policing: Testing Conventional and Contemporary Wisdom." *Criminology* 31(2):203–41.

Wrong, Dennis. 1961. "The Oversocialized Conception of Man in Modern Sociology." *American Sociological Review* 26(April):183–93.

Chapter 14. Social Psychology

Allport, Floyd Henry. 1924. *Social Psychology.* Boston, MA: Houghton Mifflin.

Asch, Solomon E. 1956. "Studies of Independence and Conformity: A Minority of One against a Unanimous Majority." *Psychological Monographs* 70(9) (Whole No. 416).

Becker, Howard S. 1963. *Outsiders.* New York: Free Press.

Berger, Joseph, M. Hamit Fisek, Robert Z. Norman, and David G. Wagner. 1985. "The Formation of Reward Expectations in Status Situations." Pp. 215–61 in *Status, Rewards, and Influence,* edited by J. Berger and M. Zelditch. San Francisco, CA: Jossey-Bass.

Berger, Joseph, M. Hamit Fisek, Robert Z. Norman, and Morris Zelditch. 1977. *Status Characteristics and Social Interaction.* New York: Elsevier.

Berger, Joseph, Cecilia L. Ridgeway, M. Hamit Fisek, and Robert Z. Norman. 1998. "The Legitimation and Delegitimation of Power and Prestige Orders." *American Sociological Review* 63:379–405.

Berger, Joseph, Susan J. Rosenholtz, and Morris Zelditch. 1980. "Status Organizing Processes." *Annual Review of Sociology* 6:479–508.

Berger, Joseph and Morris Zelditch, eds. 1985. *Status, Rewards, and Influence.* San Francisco, CA: Jossey-Bass.

Berger, Peter L. and Thomas Luckmann. 1966. *The Social Construction of Reality.* Garden City, NY: Doubleday.

Blass, Thomas, ed. 2000. *Obedience to Authority: Current Perspectives on the Milgram Paradigm.* Mahwah, NJ: Lawrence Erlbaum.

Blau, Peter M. 1964. *Exchange and Power in Social Life.* New York: Wiley.

Blau, Peter M. 1977. *Inequality and Heterogeneity.* New York: Free Press.

Blumer, Herbert. 1969. *Symbolic Interactionism: Perspective and Method.* Englewood Cliffs, NJ: Prentice Hall.

Brim, Orville G. and Stanton Wheeler. 1966. *Socialization after Childhood: Two Essays.* New York: Wiley.

Brisett, Dennis and Charles Edgley, eds. 1990. *Life as Theatre: A Dramaturgical Source Book.* New York: Aldine de Gruyter.

Burke, Peter J. 1991. "Identity Processes and Social Stress." *American Sociological Review* 56:836–49.

Burke, Peter J. and Jan E. Stets. 1999. "Trust and Commitment through Self-Verification." *Social Psychology Quarterly* 62:347–66.

Cohen, Elizabeth G. 1993. "From Theory to Practice: The Development of an Applied Research Program." Pp. 385–415 in *Theoretical Research Programs,* edited by J. Berger and M. Zelditch Jr. Stanford, CA: Stanford University Press.

Cohen, Elizabeth G. and Rachel A. Lotan. 1997. "Operation of Status in the Middle Grades: Recent Complications." Pp. 222–40 in *Status, Network, and Structure: Theory Development in Group Processes,* edited by J. Szmatka, J. Skvoretz, and J. Berger. Stanford, CA: Stanford University Press.

Cohen, Elizabeth G. and Susan Roper. 1972. "Modifications of Interracial Interaction Disability: An Application of Status Characteristics Theory." *American Sociological Review* 37:643–57.

Cook, Karen S. 1977. "Exchange and Power in Networks of Interorganizational Relation." *Sociological Quarterly* 18:62–82.

Cook, Karen S. and Richard M. Emerson. 1978. "Power, Equity and Commitment in Exchange Networks." *American Sociological Review* 43:721–39.

Cook, Karen S., Gary Alan Fine, and James S. House. 1995. *Sociological Perspectives on Social Psychology.* Boston, MA: Allyn & Bacon.

Corsaro, William A. 1997. *The Sociology of Childhood.* Thousand Oaks, CA: Pine Forge Press.

Corsaro, William A. and Donna Eder. 1990. "Children's Peer Cultures." *Annual Review of Sociology* 16:197–220.

Delamater, John, ed. 2003. *Handbook of Social Psychology.* New York: Kluwer Academic/Plenum.

Elder, Glen H., Jr. 1985. *Life Course Dynamics: Trajectories and Transitions, 1968–1980.* Ithaca, NY: Cornell University Press.

Elder, Glen H., Jr. 1998. *Children of the Great Depression.* 25th anniversary ed. New York: Harper & Collins.

Elder, Glen H., Jr. and Avshalom Caspi. 1988. "Human Development and Social Change: An Emerging Perspective on the Life Course." Pp. 77–113 in *Persons in Context,* edited by N. Bolger, A. Caspi, G. Downey, and M. Moorehouse. New York: Cambridge University Press.

Emerson, Richard M. 1962. "Power-Dependence Relations." *American Sociological Review* 27:31–41.

Emerson, Richard M. 1972a. "Exchange Theory, Part I: A Psychological Basis for Social Exchange." Pp. 38–57 in *Sociological Theories in Progress,* vol. 2, edited by J. Berger, M. Zelditch, and B. Anderson. Boston, MA: Houghton-Mifflin.

Emerson, Richard M. 1972b. "Exchange Theory, Part II: Exchange Relations and Networks." Pp. 58–87 in *Sociological Theories in Progress,* vol. 2, edited by J. Berger, M. Zelditch, and B. Anderson. Boston, MA: Houghton-Mifflin.

Emerson, Richard M. 1976. "Social Exchange Theory." *Annual Review of Sociology* 2:335–62.

Emerson, Richard M. 1981. "Social Exchange Theory." Pp. 30–65 in *Social Psychology: Sociological Perspectives,* edited by M. Rosenberg and Ralph H. Turner. New York: Basic Books.

Festinger, Leon. 1957. *A Theory of Cognitive Dissonance.* Palo Alto, CA: Stanford University Press.

Fisek, M. Hamit, Joseph Berger, and Robert Z. Norman. 1991. "Participation in Heterogeneous and Homogeneous Groups: A Theoretical Integration." *American Journal of Sociology* 97:114–42.

Fiske, Susan T. and Shelley E. Taylor. 1991. *Social Cognition.* 2d ed. New York: McGraw-Hill.

Foschi, Martha. 1989. "Status Characteristics, Standards and Attributions." Pp. 58–72 in *Sociological Theories in Progress,* edited by J. Berger, M. Zelditch, and B. Anderson. Newbury Park, CA: Sage.

Foschi, Martha. 2000. "Double Standards for Competence: Theory and Research." *Annual Review of Sociology* 26:21–42.

Freese, Lee. 1974. "Conditions for Status Equality in Formal Task Groups." *Sociometry* 37:177–88.

Garfinkel, Harold. 1967. *Studies in Ethnomethodology.* Englewood Cliffs, NJ: Prentice Hall.

Gilbert, Daniel T., Susan T. Fiske, and Gardner Lindzey. 1998. *The Handbook of Social Psychology.* Vols. 1 & 2, 4th ed. Boston, MA: McGraw-Hill.

Goffman, Erving. 1959. *The Presentation of Self in Everyday Life.* New York: Doubleday/Anchor.

Goffman, Erving. 1961. *Asylums: Essays on the Social Situation of Mental Patients and Other Inmates.* New York: Doubleday.

Goffman, Erving. 1963. *Stigma: Notes on the Management of Spoiled Identity.* Upper Saddle River, NJ: Prentice Hall.

Goffman, Erving. 1967. *Interaction Ritual: Essays on Face-to-Face Behavior.* Garden City, NY: Doubleday/Anchor.

Goffman, Erving. 1971. *Relations in Public: Microstudies of the Public Order.* New York: Basic Books

Goffman, Erving. 1974. *Frame Analysis: An Essay on the Organization of Experience.* New York: Harper & Row.

Goffman, Erving. 1976. *Gender Advertisements.* New York: Harper Colophon.

Goffman, Erving. 1983. "The Interaction Order." *American Sociological Review* 48:1–17.

Gordon, S. L. 1990. "Social Structural Effects on Emotions." Pp. 145–79 in *Research Agendas in the Sociology of Emotions,* edited by T. D. Kemper. Albany: State University of New York Press.

Haney, Craig, W. Banks, and Philip Zimbardo. 1973. "Interpersonal Dynamics in a Simulated Prison." *International Journal of Criminology and Penology* 1:69–97.

Hardin, Garret. 1968. "The Tragedy of the Commons." *Science* 162:1243–48.

Harmon-Jones, Eddie and Judson Mills. 1999. *Cognitive Dissonance: Progress on a Pivotal Theory in Social Psychology.* Washington, DC: American Psychological Association.

Heider, Fritz. 1958. *The Psychology of Interpersonal Relations.* New York: Wiley.

Heise, David R. 1977. "Social Action as the Control of Affect." *Behavioral Science* 22:163–77.

Heise, David R. 1979. *Understanding Events: Affect and the Construction of Social Action.* Cambridge, England: Cambridge University Press.

Heise, David R. 2002. *Affect Control Theory.* Retrieved June 22, 2006 (www.indiana.edu/~socpsy/ACT/).

Hirschi, Travis. 1969. *Causes of Delinquency.* Los Angeles: University of California Press.

Hochschild, Arlie R. 1983. *The Managed Heart: Commercialization of Human Feeling.* Berkeley: University of California Press.

Homans, George C. 1958. "Social Behavior as Exchange." *American Journal of Sociology* LXII:597–606.

Homans, George C. 1961. *Social Behavior and Its Elementary Forms.* New York: Harcourt, Brace & World.

Homans, George C. 1964. "Bringing Men Back In." *American Sociological Review* 19:809–18.

Homans, George C. 1974. *Social Behavior and Its Elementary Forms.* New York: Harcourt, Brace & World.

House, James S. 1977. "The Three Faces of Social Psychology." *Sociometry* 40:161–177.

Hovland, Carl I., Irving K. Janis, and Harold H. Kelley. 1953. *Communication and Persuasion.* New Haven, CT: Yale University Press.

Howard, Judith A. 1995. "Social Cognition." Pp. 90–117 in *Sociological Perspectives on Social Psychology,* edited by K. S. Cook, G. A. Fine, and J. S. House. Boston, MA: Allyn & Bacon.

Johansson, Anna C. and Jane Sell. 2004. "Sources of Legitimation and Their Effects on Group Routines: A Theoretical Analysis." Pp. 89–116 in *Legitimacy Processes in Organizations,* edited by C. Johnson. Amsterdam: Elsevier/JAI Press.

Johnson, Cathryn, ed. 2004. *Legitimacy Processes in Organizations. Research in the Sociology of Organizations.* Vol. 22. Amsterdam: Elsevier/JAI Press.

Jones, Edward E. and K. E. Davis. 1965. "From Acts to Dispositions: The Attribution Process in Person Perception." Pp. 219–66 in *Advances in Experimental Social Psychology,* vol. 2, edited by L. Berkowitz. New York: Academic Press.

Kelley, Harold H. 1967. "Attribution Theory in Social Psychology." Pp. 192–241 in *Nebraska Symposium on Motivation,* edited by D. Levine. Lincoln: University of Nebraska Press.

Kemper, Theodore D. 1987. "How Many Emotions Are There? Wedding the Social and Autonomic Components." *American Sociological Review* 93:263–89.

Kemper, Theodore D. 1991. "Predicting Emotions from Social Relations." *Social Psychology Quarterly* 54:330–42.

Knottnerus, J. David. 1997. "The Theory of Structural Ritualization." Pp. 257–79 in *Advances in Group Processes,* vol. 14, edited by B. Markovsky, M. J. Lovaglia, and L. Troyer. Greenwich, CT: JAI Press.

Knottnerus, J. David. 2002. "Agency, Structure and Deritualization: A Comparative Investigation of Extreme Disruptions of Social Order." Pp. 85–106 in *Structure, Culture and History: Recent Issues in Social Theory,* edited by S. C. Chew and J. D. Knottnerus. Lanham, MD: Rowman & Littlefield.

Knottnerus, J. David. 2005. "The Need for Theory and the Value of Cooperation: Disruption and Deritualization" (presidential address, Mid-South Sociological Association, Baton Rouge, LA, 2003). *Sociological Spectrum* 25:5–19.

Knottnerus, J. David and Jian Guan. 1997. "The Works of Peter M. Blau: Analytical Strategies, Developments and Assumptions." *Sociological Perspectives* 40:109–28.

Knottnerus, J. David and Frederique Van de Poel-Knottnerus. 1999. *The Social Worlds of Male and Female Children in the Nineteenth Century French Educational System: Youth, Rituals and Elites.* Lewiston, NY: Edwin Mellen Press.

Kohn, Melvin L. and Carmi Schooler, with the collaboration of Joanne Miller, Karen A. Miller, Carrie Schoenbach, and Ronald Schoenberg. 1983. *Work and Personality: An Inquiry into the Impact of Social Stratification.* Norwood, NJ: Ablex.

Kollock, Peter. 1994. "The Emergence of Exchange Structures: An Experimental Study of Uncertainty, Commitment, and Trust." *American Journal of Sociology* 100:313–45.

Kuhn, Manford H. and Thomas S. McPartland. 1954. "An Empirical Investigation of Self-Attitudes." *American Sociological Review* 19:68–76.

Lawler, Edward J. and Shane R. Thye. 1999. "Bringing Emotions into Social Exchange Theory." *Annual Review of Sociology* 25:217–44.

Lawler, Edward J. and J. Yoon. 1996. "Commitment in Exchange Relations: Test of a Theory of Relational Cohesion." *American Sociological Review* 61:89–108.

Lewin, Kurt. 1943. "Psychology and the Process of Group Living." *Journal of Social Psychology, SPSSI Bulletin* 17:113–31.

Lovaglia, Michael J., Elizabeth A. Mannix, Charles D. Samuelson, Jane Sell, and Rick K. Wilson. 2005. "Conflict, Power and Status in Groups." Pp. 139–84 in *Theories of Small Groups: Interdisciplinary Perspectvies,*

edited by M. S. Poole and A. B. Hollingshead. Thousand Oaks, CA: Sage.

MacKinnon, Neil. 1994. *Symbolic Interaction as Affect Control.* Albany: State University of New York Press.

Maines, David. 1977. "Social Organization and Social Structure in Symbolic Interactionist Thought." *Annual Review of Sociology* 3:235–59.

Manis, Jerome and Bernard N. Meltzer, eds. 1978. *Symbolic Interactionism: A Reader in Social Psychology.* Boston, MA: Allyn & Bacon.

Markovsky, Barry, Le Roy F. Smith, and Joseph Berger. 1984. "Do Status Interventions Persist?" *American Sociological Review* 49:373–82.

Markovsky, Barry, David Willer, and Travis Patton. 1988. "Power Relations in Exchange Networks." *American Sociological Review* 5:101–17.

Maynard, Douglas W. 2003. *Bad News, Good News: Conversational Order in Everyday Talk and Clinical Settings.* Chicago, IL: University of Chicago Press.

Maynard, Douglas W. and Steven. E. Clayman. 1991. "The Diversity of Ethnomethodology." *Annual Review of Sociology* 17:385–418.

Maynard, Douglas W. and Anssi Perakyla. 2003. "Language and Social Interaction." Pp. 233–57 in *Handbook of Social Psychology,* edited by J. Delamater. New York: Kluwer Academic/Plenum.

McCall, George J. and Jerry L. Simmons. 1966. *Identities and Interactions.* New York: Free Press.

McDougall, William. 1908. *An Introduction to Social Psychology.* London, England: Methuen.

Mead, George Herbert. 1934. *Mind, Self, and Society.* Chicago, IL: University of Chicago Press.

Merton, Robert K. and Alice S. Rossi. 1950. "Contributions to the Theory of Reference Group Behavior." Pp. 40–105 in *Continuities in Social Research: Studies in the Scope and Method of 'The American Soldier,'* edited by R. K. Merton and P. F. Lazarsfeld. Glencoe, IL: Free Press.

Messick, David M. and Marilynn B. Brewer. 1983. "Solving Social Dilemmas: A Review." Pp. 11–44 in *Review of Personality and Social Psychology,* vol. 4, edited by L. Wheeler and P. Shaver. Beverly Hills, CA: Sage.

Milgram, Stanley. 1965. "Some Conditions of Obedience and Disobedience to Authority." *Human Relations* 18:57–76.

Milgram, Stanley. 1974. *Obedience to Authority: An Experimental View.* New York: Harper & Row.

Mirowsky, John and Catherine Ross. 1989. *Social Causes of Psychological Distress.* New York: Aldine de Gruyter.

Molm, Linda. 1997. *Coercive Power in Social Exchange.* Cambridge, England: Cambridge University Press.

Molm, Linda D., Nobuyuki Takahashi, and Gretchen Peterson. 2000. "Risk and Trust in Social Exchange: An Experimental Test of a Classical Proposition." *American Journal of Sociology* 105:1396–427.

Mortimer, Jeylan T. and Roberta G. Simmons. 1978. "Adult Socialization." *Annual Review of Sociology* 4:421–54.

Olson, Mancur. 1965. *The Logic of Collective Action: Public Goods and the Theory of Groups.* Cambridge, MA: Harvard University Press.

Ostrom, Elinor, Roy Gardner, and James Walker. 1994. *Rules, Games, and Common-Pool Resources.* Ann Arbor: The University of Michigan Press.

Owens, Timothy J. 2003. "Self and Identity." Pp. 205–32 in *Handbook of Social Psychology,* edited by J. Delamater. New York: Kluwer Academic/Plenum.

Parsons, Talcott. 1951. *The Social System.* New York: Free Press.

Prendergast, Christopher and J. David Knottnerus. 1993. "The New Studies in Social Organization: Overcoming the Astructural Bias." Pp. 158–85 in *Interactionism: Exposition and Critique,* 3d ed., edited by L. T. Reynolds. Dix Hills, NY: General Hall.

Retzinger, Suzanne and Thomas J. Scheff. 2000. "Emotion, Alienation, and Narratives: Resolving Intractable Conflicts." *Mediation Quarterly* (Fall):71–86.

Reynolds, Larry T. 1993. *Interactionism: Exposition and Critique.* 3d ed. Dix Hills, NY: General Hall.

Reynolds, Larry T. 2003. "Intellectual Precursors." Pp. 39–58 in *Handbook of Symbolic Interactionism,* edited by L. T. Reynolds and N. J. Herman-Kinney. Lanham, MD: AltaMira Press/Rowman & Littlefield.

Reynolds, Larry T. and Nancy J. Herman-Kinney, eds. 2003. *Handbook of Symbolic Interactionism.* Lanham, MD: AltaMira Press/Rowman & Littlefield.

Ridgeway, Cecilia L. 1987. "Nonverbal Behavior, Dominance, and the Basis of Status in Task Groups." *American Sociological Review* 52:683–94.

Ridgeway, Cecilia L. 1991. "The Social Construction of Status Value: Gender and Other Nominal Characteristics." *Social Forces* 70:367–86.

Ridgeway, Cecilia L. 2001. "Inequality, Status, and the Construction of Status Beliefs." Pp. 323–40 in *Handbook of Sociological Theory,* edited by J. H. Turner. New York: Kluwer Academic/Plenum.

Ridgeway, Cecilia L. and James Balkwell. 1997. "Group Processes and the Diffusion of Status Beliefs." *Social Psychology Quarterly* 60:14–31.

Ridgeway, Cecilia L. and Joseph Berger. 1986. "Expectations, Legitimation, and Dominance Behavior in Groups." *American Sociological Review* 51:603–17.

Ridgeway, Cecilia L. and Cathryn Johnson. 1990. "What is the Relationship between Socioemotional Behavior and Status in Task Groups?" *American Journal of Sociology* 95:1189–212.

Ridgeway, Cecilia L., Cathryn Johnson, and David Diekema. 1994. "External Status, Legitimacy, and Compliance in Male and Female Groups." *Social Forces* 72:1051–1077.

Rosenberg, Morris and H. Ralph Turner, eds. 1981. *Social Psychology: Sociological Perspectives.* New York: Basic Books.

Ross, E. A. 1908. *Social Psychology: An Outline and Source Book.* New York: Macmillan.

Sacks, Harvey. 1992a. *Lectures on Conversation.* Vol. 1, *Fall 1964–Spring 1968.* Oxford, England: Basil Blackwell.

Sacks, Harvey. 1992b. *Lectures on Conversation.* Vol. 2, *Fall 1968–Spring 1972.* Oxford, England: Basil Blackwell.

Scheff, Thomas J. 1990. *Microsociology: Discourse, Emotion, and Social Structure.* Chicago, IL: University of Chicago Press.

Scheff, Thomas J. 1994. *Bloody Revenge: Nationalism, War, and Emotion.* Boulder, CO: Westview Press.

Scheff, Thomas J. 1997. *Emotions, the Social Bond, and Human Reality: Part/Whole Analysis.* Cambridge, England: Cambridge University Press.

Schegloff, Emanuel A. 1991. "Reflections on Talk and Social Structure." Pp. 44–70 in *Talk and Social Structure,* edited by D. Boden and D. H. Zimmerman. Berkeley: University of California Press.

Sell, Jane. Forthcoming. "Social Dilemma." In *Blackwell Encyclopedia of Sociology,* edited by G. Ritzer. Oxford, England: Blackwell.

Sell, Jane, Zeng-yin Chen, Pam Hunter-Homes, and Anna Johansson. 2002. "A Cross-Cultural Comparison of Public Good and Resource Good Settings." *Social Psychology Quarterly* 65:285–97.

Sell, Jane, J. David Knottnerus, Christopher Ellison, and Heather Mundt. 2000. "Reproducing Social Structure in Task Groups: The Role of Structural Ritualization." *Social Forces* 79:453–75.

Sell, Jane and Rick K. Wilson. 1999. "The Maintenance of Cooperation: Expectations of Future Interaction and the Trigger of Group Punishment." *Social Forces* 77:1551–70.

Shelley, Robert K. 2001. "How Performance Expectations Arise from Sentiments." *Social Psychology Quarterly* 64:72–87.

Sherif, Muzafer. 1936. *The Psychology of Social Norms.* New York: Harper.

Simpson, Brent and David Willer. 2002. "Applications of Elementary Theory to Social Structures of Antiquity." Pp. 231–54 in *Structure, Culture, and History: Recent Issues in Social Theory,* edited by S. C. Chew and J. D. Knottnerus. Lanham, MD: Rowman & Littlefield.

Skinner, B. F. 1976. *About Behaviorism.* New York: Vintage.

Smith-Lovin, Lynn and David Heise, eds. 1988. *Analyzing Social Interaction: Research Advances in Affect Control Theory.* New York: Gordon & Breach.

Sorensen, Glorian and Jeylan T. Mortimer. 1988. "Implications of the Dual Roles of Adult Women for Their Health." Pp. 157–200 in *Work Experience and Psychological Development through the Life Span,* edited by J. T. Mortimer and K. M. Borman. Boulder, CO: Westview.

Stets, Jan E. 2003. "Emotions and Sentiments." Pp. 309–35 in *Handbook of Social Psychology,* edited by J. Delamater. New York: Kluwer Academic/Plenum.

Stets, Jan E. and Peter J. Burke. 2002. "A Sociological Approach to Self and Identity." Pp. 128–52 in *Handbook of Self and Identity,* edited by M. R. Leary and J. P. Tangney. New York: Guilford Press.

Stolte, John R. and Richard M. Emerson. 1977. "Structural Inequality: Position and Power in Network Structures." Pp. 117–38 in *Behavioral Theory in Sociology,* edited by R. L. Hamblin and J. H. Kunkel. New Brunswick, NJ: Transaction.

Stouffer, Samuel A., Edward A. Suchman, Leland C. DeVinney, Shirley A. Star, and Robin M. Williams Jr. 1949. *The American Soldier.* Vols. 1 & 2. Princeton, NJ: Princeton University Press.

Stryker, Sheldon. 1980. *Symbolic Interactionism: A Social Structural Version.* Menlo Park, CA: Benjamin Cummings.

Stryker, Sheldon. 2001. "Traditional Symbolic Interactionism, Role Theory, and Structural Symbolic Interactionism: The Road to Identity Theory." Pp. 211–31 in *Handbook of Sociological Theory,* edited by J. H. Turner. New York: Kluwer Academic/Plenum.

Stryker, Sheldon and Kevin D. Vryan. 2003. "The Symbolic Interactionist Frame." Pp. 3–28 in *Handbook of Social*

Psychology, edited by J. Delamater. New York: Kluwer Academic/Plenum.

Sudnow, David. 1967. *Passing On: The Social Organization of Dying.* Upper Saddle River, NJ: Prentice Hall.

Thoits, Peggy. 1990. "Emotional Deviance: Research Agendas." Pp. 180–203 in *Research Agendas in the Sociology of Emotions,* edited by T. D. Kemper. Albany: State University of New York Press.

Turner, Jonathan H. 1986. *The Structure of Sociological Theory.* 4th ed. Chicago, IL: Dorsey Press.

Turner, Jonathan H. 2002. *Face-to-Face: Towards a Sociological Theory of Interpersonal Behavior.* Stanford, CA: Stanford University Press.

Wagner, David G. and Joseph Berger. 1993. "Status Characteristics Theory: The Growth of a Program." Pp. 23–63 in *Theoretical Research Programs: Studies in the Growth of Theory,* edited by J. Berger and M. Zelditch. Stanford, CA: Stanford University Press.

Walker, Henry A., Larry Rogers, and Morris Zelditch. 2002. "Acts, Persons, Positions, and Institutions: Legitimating Multiple Objects and Compliance with Authority." Pp. 323–39 in *Structure, Culture, and History: Recent Issues in Social Theory,* edited by S. C. Chew and J. D. Knottnerus. Lanham, MD: Rowman & Littlefield.

Webster, Murray and Martha Foschi. 1988. *Status Generalization: New Theory and Research.* Stanford, CA: Stanford University Press.

Webster, Murray and Joseph M. Whitmeyer. 1999. "A Theory of Second-Order Expectations and Behavior." *Social Psychology Quarterly* 62:17–31.

Whalen, M. and Donald H. Zimmerman. 1987. "Sequential and Institutional Contexts in Calls for Help." *Social Psychology Quarterly* 50:172–85.

Whitmeyer, Joseph and Karen S. Cook. 2002. "Social Structure and Social Exchange." Pp. 271–302 in *Structure, Culture, and History: Recent Issues in Social Theory,* edited by S. C. Chew and J. D. Knottnerus. Lanham, MD: Rowman & Littlefield.

Willer, David, ed. 1999. *Network Exchange Theory.* Westport, CT: Praeger.

Willer, David and Bo Anderson, eds. 1981. *Networks, Exchange and Coercion.* New York: Elsevier/Greenwood.

Wilson, Rick K. and Jane Sell. 1997. "Cheap Talk and Reputation in Repeated Public Goods Settings." *Journal of Conflict Resolution* 41:695–717.

Yamagishi, Toshio. 1995. "Social Dilemmas." Pp. 311–35 in *Sociological Perspectives on Social Psychology,* edited by K. Cook, G. A. Fine, and J. S. House. Boston, MA: Allyn & Bacon.

Zelditch, Morris, William Harris, George M. Thomas, and Henry A. Walker. 1983. "Decisions, Nondecisions, and Metadecisions." Pp. 1–32 in *Research in Social Movements, Conflicts and Change,* vol. 5, edited by L. Kriesberg. Greenwich, CT: JAI Press.

Zelditch, Morris and Henry A. Walker. 1984. "Legitimacy and the Stability of Authority." *Advances in Group Processes* 1:1–25.

Zimbardo, Philip G., Christina Maslach, and Craig Haney. 2000. "Reflections on the Stanford Prison Experiment: Genesis, Transformations, Consequences." Pp. 193–237 in *Obedience to Authority: Current Perspectives on the Milgram Paradigm,* edited by T. Blass. Mahwah, NJ: Lawrence Erlbaum.

Zimmerman, Donald H. and Diedre Boden. 1991. "Structure-in-Action: An Introduction." Pp. 3–21 in *Talk and Social Structure,* edited by D. Boden and D. H. Zimmerman. Cambridge, England: Polity Press.

PART V: SOCIAL AGGREGATIONS

Chapter 15. The Sociology of Social Structure

Aron, Raymond. 1971. *Dix-huit leçons sur la société industrielle.* Paris, France: Gallimard.

Blau, Peter M. 1976a. "Introduction: Parallels and Contrasts in Structural Inquiries." Pp. 1–20 in *Approaches to the Study of Social Structure,* edited by P. M. Blau. London, England: Open Books.

Blau, Peter M. 1976b. "Parameters of Social Structure." Pp. 220–53 in *Approaches to the Study of Social Structure,* edited by P. M. Blau. London, England: Open Books.

Blau, Peter M. 1977a. *Inequality and Heterogeneity: A Primitive Theory of Social Structure.* New York: Free Press.

Blau, Peter M. 1977b. "A Macrosociological Theory of Social Structure." *American Journal of Sociology* 83:26–54.

Blau, Peter M. 1980. "A Fable about Social Structure." *Social Forces* 58:777–88.

Blau, Peter M. 1981. "Diverse Views of Social Structure and Their Common Denominator." Pp. 1–23 in *Continuities in Structural Inquiry,* edited by P. M. Blau and R. K. Merton. Beverly Hills, CA: Sage.

Blau, Peter M. 1994. *Structural Context of Opportunities.* Chicago, IL: University of Chicago Press.

Boudon, Raymond. 1968. *A quoi sert la notion de "structure"?* Paris, France: Gallimard.

Boudon, Raymond. 1981. *The Logic of Social Action.* Boston, MA: Routledge & Kegan Paul.

Boudon, Raymond. 1986. *Theories of Social Change: A Critical Appraisal.* London, England: Basil Blackwell/Polity Press.

Bourdieu, Pierre. 1989. *Le sens practique.* Paris, France: Les Editions de Minuit.

Brinton, Mary C. and Victor Nee, eds. 1998. *The New Institutionalism in Sociology.* New York: Russell Sage.

Coleman, James. 1990. *Foundations of Social Theory.* Cambridge, MA: Belknap Press of Harvard University Press.

Collins, Randall. 1981. "On the Microfoundations of Macrosociology." *The American Journal of Sociology* 5:984–1014.

Collins, Randall. 1988. *Theoretical Sociology.* Orlando, FL: Harcourt Brace Jovanovich.

Dahrendorf, Ralf. 1972. *Class and Class Conflict in Industrial Society.* London, England: Routledge & Kegan Paul.

DiMaggio, Paul. 1994. "Culture and Economy." Pp. 27–57 in *The Handbook of Economic Sociology,* edited by N. J. Smelser and R. Swedberg. Princeton, NJ: Princeton University Press.

Durkheim, Émile. [1895] 1938. *The Rules of Sociological Method.* Chicago, IL: University of Chicago Press.

Durkheim, Émile. [1893] 1964. *The Division of Labor in Society.* New York: Free Press.

Elster, Jon. 1989. *Nuts and Bolts for the Social Sciences.* Cambridge, England: Cambridge University Press.

Gambetta, Diego. 1987. *Were They Pushed or Did They Jump? Individual Decision Mechanism in Education.* Cambridge, England: Cambridge University Press.

Giddens, Anthony. 1984. *The Constitution of Society: Outline of the Theory of Structuration.* Oxford, England: Polity Press.

Granovetter, Mark. 2005. "The Impact of Social Structure on Economic Outcomes." *Journal of Economic Perspectives* 19:33–50.

Hamilton, Peter. 1983. *Talcott Parsons.* London, England: Tavistock.

Homans, Georges C. 1967. *The Nature of Social Science.* New York: Harcourt, Brace & World.

Homans, Georges C. 1974. *Social Behavior: Its Elementary Forms.* New York: Hartcourt Brace Jovanovich.

Homans, Georges C. 1976. "What Do We Mean by Social 'Structure'?" Pp. 53–65 in *Approaches to the Study of Social Structure,* edited by P. M. Blau. London, England: Open Books.

Homans, Georges C. 1987. "Behaviorism and After" Pp. 58–81 in *Social Theory Today,* edited by A. Giddens and J. H. Turner. London, England: Polity Press.

Kerbo, Harold R. 2000. *Social Stratification and Inequality: Class Conflict in Historical, Comparative and Global Perspective.* New York: McGraw-Hill.

Kontopoulos, Kyriacos M. 1993. *The Logics of Social Structure.* Cambridge, England: Cambridge University Press.

Lévi-Strauss, Claude. [1949] 1968. *Structural Anthropology.* London, England: Penguin.

López, José and John Scott. 2000. *Social Structure.* Buckingham, England: Open University Press.

Lin, Nan. 2001. *Social Capital: A Theory of Social Structure and Action.* New York: Cambridge University Press.

Marx, Karl. [1859] 1936. "Preface to *A Contribution to the Critique of Political Economy.*" Pp. 354–59 in *Karl Marx, Selected Works,* vol. 1. New York: International Publishers.

Merton, Robert K. 1976. "Structural Analysis in Sociology." Pp. 21–52 in *Approaches to the Study of Social Structure,* edited by P. M. Blau. London, England: Open Books.

Murdock, George P. 1949. *Social Structure.* New York: Macmillan.

Nadel, Siegfried F. 1957. *The Theory of Social Structure.* Glencoe, IL: Free Press.

Parsons, Talcott. 1951. *The Social System.* New York: Free Press.

Perrow, Charles. 1986. *Complex Organizations.* New York: Random House.

Piaget, Jean. 1970. *Structuralism.* New York: Basic Books.

Prendergast, Christopher and J. David Knottnerus. 1994. "Recent Developments in the Theory of Social Structure." *Current Perspectives in Social Theory* S1:1–26.

Radcliffe-Brown, Alfred R. 1940. "On Social Structure." *Journal of the Royal Anthropological Society of Great Britain* 70:1–12.

Roemer, John, ed. 1986. *Analytical Marxism.* Cambridge, England: Cambridge University Press.

Rytina, Steve. 1992. "Social Structure." Pp. 1970–76 in *Encyclopedia of Sociology,* vol. 4, edited by E. F. Borgatta and M. L. Borgatta. New York: Macmillan.

Sewell, William H., Jr. 1992. "A Theory of Structure: Duality, Agency, and Transformation." *American Journal of Sociology* 1:1–29.

Simmel, Georg. [1908] 1950. *The Sociology of George Simmel.* Glencoe, IL: Free Press.

Simmel, Georg. [1908] 1955. *Conflict and the Web of Group-Affiliations.* Glencoe, IL: Free Press.

Simon, Herbert. 1982. *Models of Bounded Rationality.* Cambridge: MIT Press.

Smelser, Neil J. 1992. "Social Structure." Pp. 103–29 in *Handbook of Sociology,* edited by N. J. Smelser. Newbury Park, CA: Sage.

Weber, Max. [1921] 1968. *Economy and Society,* 3 vols. Totowa, NJ: Bedminster Press.

Wellman, Barry and Stephen D. Berkowitz. 1988. "Introductions: Studying Social Structures." Pp. 1–14 in *Social Structures: A Network Approach,* edited by B. Wellman and S. D. Berkowitz. New York: Cambridge University Press.

Chapter 16. The Sociology of Group Dynamics

Adams, J. Stacy. 1965. "Inequity in Social Exchange." *Advances in Experimental Social Psychology* 2:267–99.

Arrow, Holly, Kelly Bouas Henry, Marshall Scott Poole, Susan Wheelan, and Richard Moreland. 2005. "Traces, Trajectories, and Timing: The Temporal Perspective on Groups." Pp. 313–67 in *Theories of Small Groups: Interdisciplinary Perspectives,* edited by M. S. Poole and A. B. Hollingshead. Thousand Oaks, CA: Sage.

Axelrod, R. 1984. *The Evolution of Cooperation.* New York: Basic Books.

Bales, Robert F. 1950. *Interaction Process Analysis: A Method for the Study of Small Groups.* Chicago, IL: University of Chicago Press.

Bell, Richard, Henry A. Walker, and David Willer. 2000. "Power, Influence, and Legitimacy in Organizations: Implications of Three Theoretical Research Programs." *Research in the Sociology of Organizations* 17:131–77.

Berger, Joseph, Thomas L. Conner, and M. Hamit Fisek. 1974. *Expectation States Theory: A Theoretical Research Program.* Cambridge, MA: Winthrop. Reprint, Lanham, MD: University Press of America, 1982.

Berger, Joseph, M. Hamit Fisek, Robert Z. Norman, and David G. Wagner. 1985. "Formation of Reward Expectations in Status Situations." Pp. 215–61 in *Status, Rewards and Influence,* Edited by J. Berger and M. Zelditch Jr. San Francisco, CA: Jossey-Bass.

Berger, Joseph, M. Hamit Fisek, Robert Z. Norman, and Morris Zelditch Jr. 1977. *Status Characteristics and Social Interaction: An Expectation-Status Approach.* New York: Elsevier.

Berger, Joseph, Cecilia L. Ridgeway, M. Hamit Fisek, and Robert Z. Norman. 1998. "The Legitimation and Delegitimation of Power and Prestige Orders." *American Sociological Review* 63:379–405.

Berger, Joseph, David G. Wagner, and Morris Zelditch Jr. 1992. "A Working Strategy for Constructing Theories: State Organizing Processes." Pp. 107–23 in *Metatheorizing: Key Issues in Sociological Theory,* vol. 6, edited by G. Ritzer. Newbury Park, CA: Sage.

Berger, Joseph, Morris Zelditch Jr., Bo Anderson, and Bernard P. Cohen. 1972. "Structural Aspects of Distributive Justice, a Status Value Formulation." Pp. 119–46 in *Sociological Theories in Progress,* vol. 2, edited by J. Berger, M. Zelditch Jr., and B. Anderson. New York: Houghton Mifflin.

Bienenstock, Elisa J. and Phillip Bonacich. 1993. "Game Theory Models for Exchange Networks: Experimental Results." *Sociological Perspective* 36:117–35.

Blau, Peter M. 1964. *Exchange and Power in Social Life.* New York: Wiley.

Borgatta, Edgar F. and Robert F. Bales. 1953. "Interaction of Individuals in Reconstituted Groups." *Sociometry* 16:302–20.

Brann, Peter and Margaret Foddy. 1987. "Trust and the Consumption of a Deteriorating Common Resource." *Journal of Conflict Resolution* 31:615–30.

Brewer, Marilynn and Roderick M. Kramer. 1986. "Choice Behavior in Social Dilemmas: Effects of Social Identity, Group Size and Decision Framing." *Journal of Personality and Social Psychology* 50:543–49.

Burke, Peter J. 2003. "Interactions in Small Groups." Pp. 363–88 in *Handbook of Social Psychology,* edited by J. Delamater. New York: Kluwer Academic/Plenum.

Cohen, Elizabeth G. 1982. "Expectation States and Interracial Interaction in School Settings." *Annual Review of Sociology* 8:209–35.

Cohen, Elizabeth G. 1993. "From Theory to Practice: The Development of an Applied Research Program." Pp. 385–415 in *Theoretical Research Programs: Studies in the Growth of Theory,* edited by J. Berger and M. Zelditch Jr. Stanford, CA: Stanford University Press.

Cohen, Elizabeth G. and Susan Roper. 1972. "Modifications of Interracial Interaction Disability: An Application of Status Characteristics Theory." *American Sociological Review* 37:643–65.

Cook, Karen S. and Richard M. Emerson. 1978. "Power, Equity, and Commitment in Exchange Networks." *American Sociological Review* 43:721–39.

Cook, Karen S., Richard M. Emerson, Mary R. Gillmore, and Toshio Yamagishi. 1983. "The Distribution of Power in Exchange Networks: Theory and Experimental Results." *American Journal of Sociology* 89:275–305.

Correll, Shelley J. and Cecilia L. Ridgeway. 2003. "Expectation States Theory." Pp. 29–51 in *Handbook of Social Psychology,* edited by J. Delamater. New York: Kluwer Academic/Plenum.

Coser, Lewis. 1956. *The Functions of Social Conflict.* New York: Free Press.

Coser, Lewis. 1967. *Continuities in the Study of Social Conflict.* New York: Free Press.

Crawford, Sue E. S. and Elinor Ostrom. 1995. "A Grammar of Institutions." *American Political Science Review* 89:582–600.

Dawes, Robyn M. 1980. "Social Dilemmas." *Annual Review of Psychology* 31:169–93.

Dornbusch, Sanford and W. Richard Scott. 1975. *Evaluation and the Exercise of Authority.* San Francisco, CA: Jossey-Bass.

Emerson, Richard M. 1962. "Power-Dependence Relations." *American Sociological Review* 27:31–41.

Emerson, Richard M. 1964. "Power-Dependence Relations: Two Experiments." *Sociometry* 27:282–98.

Emerson, Richard M. 1972. "Exchange Theory, Part I: A Psychological Basis for Social Exchange." Pp. 58–87 in *Sociological Theories in Progress,* vol. 2, edited by J. Berger, M. Zelditch Jr., and B. Anderson. Boston, MA: Houghton Mifflin.

Evan, William M. and Morris Zelditch Jr. 1961. "A Laboratory Experiment on Bureaucratic Authority." *American Sociological Review* 26:883–93.

Freese, Lee and Bernard P. Cohen. 1973. "Eliminating Status Generalization." *Sociometry* 36:177–93.

Friedkin, Noah. 1992. "An Expected Value Model of Social Power: Predictions for Selected Exchange Networks." *Social Networks* 14:213–29.

Goar, Carla and Jane Sell. 2005. "Modifying Racial Inequality in Task Groups through Task Definition." *Sociological Quarterly* 46:525–43.

Hardin, Garrett. 1968. "The Tragedy of the Commons." *Science* 162:1243–48.

Hare, R. Paul, Edgar F. Borgatta, and Robert F. Bales, eds. 1965. *Small Groups in Social Interaction.* Rev. ed. New York: Alfred A. Knopf.

Hegtvedt, Karen A. and Jody Clay-Warner. 2004. "Linking Legitimacy and Procedural Justice: Expanding on Justice Processes in Organization." Pp. 213–37 in *Research in Sociology of Organizations: Legitimacy Process in Organizations,* edited by C. Johnson. London, England: Elsevier.

Hegtvedt, Karen A. and Barry Markovsky. 1995. "Justice and Injustice." Pp. 257–80 in *Sociological Perspectives on Social Psychology,* edited by K. Cook, G. Alan Fine, and J. House. Boston, MA: Allyn & Bacon.

Hegtvedt, Karen A. and Cathryn Johnson. 2000. "Justice Beyond the Individual: A Future with Legitimation." *Social Psychology Quarterly* 63:298–311.

Homans, George C. 1950. *The Human Group.* New York: Harpers.

Homans, George C. 1958. "Social Behavior as Exchange." *American Journal of Sociology* 63:597–606.

Homans, George C. 1961. *Social Behavior: Its Elementary Forms.* New York: Harcourt Brace Jovanovich.

Homans, George C. 1974. *Social Behavior: Its Elementary Forms.* Rev. ed. New York: Harcourt Brace Jovanovich.

Humphreys, Paul and Joseph Berger. 1981. "Theoretical Consequences of the Status Characteristics Formulation." *American Journal of Sociology* 86:958–83.

Hwang, Kwang-kuo. 1987. "Face and Favor: The Chinese Power Game." *American Journal of Sociology* 92:944–74.

Jasso, Guillermina. 1980. "A New Theory of Distributive Justice." *American Sociological Review* 45:3–32.

Jasso, Guillermina. 1988. "Principles of Theoretical Analysis." *Sociological Theory* 6:1–20.

Jasso, Guillermina. 2001. "Formal Theory." Pp. 37–68 in *Handbook of Sociological Theory,* edited by J. H. Turner. New York: Kluwer Academic/Plenum.

Johansson, Anna C. and Jane Sell. 2004. "Sources of Legitimation and their Effects on Group Routines: A Theoretical Analysis." Pp. 89–116 in *Research in the Sociology of Organizations: Legitimacy Processes in Organizations,* edited by C. Johnson. Oxford, England: Elsevier.

Kerr, N. L. and C. M. Kaufman-Gilleland. 1994. "Communication, Commitment, and Cooperation in Social Dilemmas." *Journal of Personality and Social Psychology* 66:513–29.

Knottnerus, J. David. 1997. "The Theory of Structural Ritualization." Pp. 257–79 in *Advances in Group Processes,* vol. 14, edited by B. Markovsky, M. J. Lovaglia, and L. Troyer. Greenwich, CT: JAI Press.

Knottnerus, J. David and Frederique Van de Poel-Knottnerus. 1999. *The Social Worlds of Male and Female Children in the Nineteenth Century French Educational System: Youth, Rituals and Elites.* Lewiston, NY: Edwin Mellon Press.

Kollock, Peter. 1994. "The Emergence of Exchange Structures: An Experimental Study of Uncertainty, Commitment, and Trust." *American Journal of Sociology* 100:313–45.

Kollock, Peter. 1998. "Social Dilemmas: The Anatomy of Cooperation." *Annual Review of Sociology* 24:183–214.

Kopelman, Shirli, J. Mark Weber, and David M. Messick. 2002. "Factors Influencing Cooperation in Common Dilemmas: A Review of Experimental Psychological Research." Pp. 113–56 in *The Drama of the Commons,* edited by E. Ostrom, T. Dietz, N. Dolšak, P. C. Stern, S. Stonich, and E. U. Weber. Washington, DC: National Academy Press.

Lawler, Edward J. 1975. "An Experimental Study of Factors Affecting the Mobilization of Revolutionary Coalitions." *Sociometry* 38:163–79.

Lawler, Edward J. 1986. "Bilateral Deterrence and Conflict Spiral: A Theoretical Analysis." Pp. 107–30 in *Advances in Group Processes,* vol. 3, edited by E. J. Lawler. Greenwich, CT: JAI Press.

Lawler, Edward J. 2001. "An Affect Theory of Social Exchange." *American Journal of Sociology* 107:321–52.

Lawler, Edward J., Rebecca Ford, and Mary A. Blegen. 1988. "Coercive Capability in Conflict: A Test of Bilateral Deterrence versus Conflict Spiral Theory." *Social Psychology Quarterly* 51:93–107.

Lawler, Edward J., Cecilia Ridgeway, and Barry Markovsky. 1993. "Structural Social Psychology and the Micro-Macro Problem." *Sociological Theory* 11:268–90.

Lawler, Edward J. and M. E. Thompson. 1978. "Impact of a Leader's Responsibility for Inequity on Subordinate Revolts." *Social Psychology Quarterly* 41:264–68.

Lawler, Edward J., Shane Thye, and Jeongkoo Yoon. 2000. "Emotion and Group Cohesion in Productive Exchange." *American Journal of Sociology* 106:616–57.

Lawler, Edward J. and Jeongkoo Yoon. 1993. "Power and the Emergence of Commitment Behavior in Negotiated Exchange." *American Sociological Review* 58:465–81.

Lawler, Edward J. and Jeongkoo Yoon. 1996. "Commitment in Exchange Relations: Test of a Theory of Relational Cohesion." *American Sociological Review* 61:89–108.

Lawler, Edward J. and Jeongkoo Yoon. 1998. "Network Structure and Emotion in Exchange Relations." *American Sociological Review* 63:871–94.

Lewin, Kurt, Ronald Lippitt, and Ralph White. 1939. "Patterns of Aggressive Behavior in Experimentally Created 'Social Climates.'" *Journal of Social Psychology* 10:271–99.

Lovaglia, Michael J. and Jeffrey Houser. 1996. "Emotional Reactions and Status in Groups." *American Sociological Review* 61:867–83.

Lovaglia, Michael J., Jeffrey W. Lucas, Jeffrey A. Houser, Shane Thye, and Barry Markovsky. 1998. "Status Processes and Mental Ability Scores." *American Journal of Sociology* 104:195–228.

Lovaglia, Michael J., Elizabeth A. Mannix, Charles D. Samuelson, Jane Sell, and Rick K. Wilson. 2005. "Conflict, Power and Status in Groups." Pp. 139–84 in *Theories of Small Groups: Interdisciplinary Perspectives,* edited by M. S. Poole and A. B. Hollingshead. Thousand Oaks, CA: Sage.

Lovaglia, Michael J., John Skvoretz, David Willer, and Barry Markovsky. 1995. "Negotiated Exchanges in Social Networks." *Social Forces* 74:123–55.

Lucas, Jeffrey W., C. Wesley Younts, Michael J. Lovaglia, and Barry Markovsky. 2001. "Lines of Power in Exchange Networks." *Social Forces* 80:185–214.

Markovsky, Barry. 1985. "Toward a Multilevel Distributive Justice Theory." *American Sociological Review* 50:822–39.

Markovsky, Barry, John Skvoretz, David Willer, Michael J. Lovaglia, and Jeffrey Erger. 1993. "The Seeds of Weak Power: An Extension of Network Exchange Theory." *American Sociological Review* 58:197–209.

Markovsky, Barry, David Willer, and Travis Patton. 1988. "Power Relations in Exchange Networks." *American Sociological Review* 53:220–36.

Martin, Michael W. and Jane Sell. 1985. "The Effect of Equating Status Characteristics on the Generalization Process." *Social Psychology Quarterly* 48:178–82.

Martin, Michael W. and Jane Sell. 1986. "Rejection of Authority: The Importance of Type of Distribution Rule and Extent of Benefit." *Social Science Quarterly* 67:855–68.

McCabe, Kevin, Daniel Houser, Lee Ryan, Vernon Smith, and Theodore Trouard. 2001. "A Functional Imaging Study of Cooperation in the Two-Person Reciprocal Exchange." *Proceedings of the National Academy of Sciences of the United States of America* 98:11832–35.

Mead, George Herbert. 1934. *Mind, Self, and Society.* Chicago, IL: University of Chicago Press.

Messick, D. M. and M. B. Brewer. 1983. "Solving Social Dilemmas: A Review." Pp. 11–44 in *Review of Personality and Social Psychology,* vol. 4, edited by L. Wheeler and P. Shaver. Beverly Hills, CA: Sage.

Mintz, A. 1951. "Non-adaptive Group Behavior." *Journal of Abnormal Social Psychology* 46:150–59.

Molm, Linda D. 1990. "Structure, Action and Outcomes: The Dynamics of Power in Exchange Relations." *American Sociological Review* 55:427–47.

Molm, Linda D. 1994. "Is Punishment Effective? Coercive Strategies in Social Exchange." *Social Psychology Quarterly* 57:76–94.

Molm, Linda D. 1997a. *Coercive Power in Social Exchange.* Cambridge, England: Cambridge University Press.

Molm, Linda D. 1997b. "Risk and Power Use: Constraints on the Use of Coercion in Exchange." *American Sociological Review* 62:113–33.

Molm, Linda D., Nobuyuki Takahashi, and Gretchen Peterson. 2000. "Risk and Trust in Social Exchange: An Experimental Test of a Classical Proposition." *American Journal of Sociology* 105:1396–427.

Moore, Barrington. 1978. *Injustice: The Social Bases of Obedience and Revolt.* White Plains, NY: M. E. Sharpe.

Olson, Mancur. 1965. *The Logic of Collective Action: Public Goods and the Theory of Groups.* Cambridge, MA: Harvard University Press.

Orbell, John M., Alphons J. C. van de Kragt, and Robyn M. Dawes. 1988. "Explaining Discussion-Induced Cooperation." *Journal of Personality and Social Psychology* 54:811–19.

Ostrom, Elinor, James Walker, and Roy Gardner. 1992. "Covenants with and without a Sword: Self-Governance Is Possible." *American Political Science Review* 86:404–17.

Pugh, Meredith D. and Ralph Wahrman. 1983. "Neutralizing Sexism in Mixed-Sex Groups: Do Women Have to Be Better Than Men?" *American Journal of Sociology* 88:746–62.

Read, Peter B. 1974. "Sources of Authority and the Legitimation of Leadership in Small Groups." *Sociometry* 37(2):189–204.

Ridgeway, Cecilia L. 1991. "The Social Construction of Status Value: Gender and Other Nominal Characteristics." *Social Forces* 70:367–86.

Ridgeway, Cecilia L. 1997. "Where Do Status Beliefs Come from? New Developments." Pp. 137–58 in *Status, Network, and Structure,* edited by J. Szmatka, J. Skvoretz, and J. Berger. Stanford, CA: Stanford University Press.

Ridgeway, Cecilia L. and Kristan Glasgow Erickson. 2000. "Creating and Spreading Status Beliefs." *American Journal of Sociology* 106:579–615.

Ridgeway, Cecilia L., Kathy J. Kuipers, Elizabeth Heger Boyle, and Dawn T. Robinson. 1998. "How do Status Beliefs Develop? The Roles of Resources and Interactional Experience." *American Sociological Review* 62:218–35.

Robinson, Dawn T., Christabel L. Rogalin, and Lynn Smith-Lovin. 2004. "Physiological Measures of Theoretical Concepts: Some Ideas for Linking Deflection and Emotion to Physical Responses During Interaction." *Advances in Group Processes* 21:77–115.

Sally, D. 1995. "Convention and Cooperation in Social Dilemmas: A Meta-Analysis of Experiments from 1958 to 1992." *Rationality and Society* 7:58–92.

Samuelson, Charles D. and D. M. Messick. 1995. "Let's Make Some New Rules: Social Factors That Make Freedom Unattractive." Pp. 48–68 in *Negotiation as a Social Process,* edited by R. Kramer and D. M. Messick. Thousand Oaks, CA: Sage.

Sato, Kaori. 1987. "Distribution of the Cost of Maintaining Common Resources." *Journal of Experimental Social Psychology* 31:19–31.

Scharlemann, John P., Catherine C. Eckel, Alex Kacelnik, and Rick W. Wilson. 2001. "The Value of a Smile: Game Theory with a Human Face." *Journal of Economic Psychology* 22:617–40.

Sell, Jane, Zeng-yin Chen, Pam Hunter-Holmes, and Anna Johansson. 2002. "A Cross-Cultural Comparison of Public Good and Resource Good Settings." *Social Psychology Quarterly* 65:285–97.

Sell, Jane, J. David Knottnerus, Christopher Ellison, and Heather Mundt. 2000. "Reproducing Social Structure in Task Groups: The Role of Structural Ritualization." *Social Forces* 79:453–75.

Sell, Jane, Michael J. Lovaglia, Elizabeth A. Mannix, Charles D. Samuelson, and Rick K. Wilson. 2004. "Investigating Conflict, Power, and Status within and among Groups." *Small Group Research* 35:44–72.

Sell, Jane and Michael W. Martin. 1983. "The Effects of Group Benefits and Type of Distribution Rule on Non-Compliance to Legitimate Authority." *Social Forces* 61:1168–85.

Sell, Jane and Yeongi Son. 1997. "Comparing Public Goods with Common Pool Resources: Three Experiments." *Social Psychology Quarterly* 60:118–37.

Sell, Jane and Rick K. Wilson 1999. "The Maintenance of Cooperation: Expectations of Future Interaction and the Trigger of Group Punishment." *Social Forces* 77:1551–70.

Sewell, William H., Jr. 1992. "A Theory of Structure: Duality, Agency, and Transformation." *American Journal of Sociology* 98:1–29.

Simmel, Georg. [1907] 1971. *On Individuality and Social Forms,* edited by D. N. Levine. Chicago, IL: University of Chicago Press.

Son, Yeongi and Jane Sell. 1995. "Are the Dilemmas Posed by Public Goods and Common Pool Resources the Same?" Pp. 69–88 in *Advances in Human Ecology,* vol. 4, edited by L. Freese. Greenwich, CT: JAI Press.

Tammivaara, J. S. 1982. "The Effects of Task Structure on Beliefs about Competence and Participation in Small Groups." *Sociology of Education* 55:212–22.

Thibaut, John W. and Harold H. Kelley. 1959. *The Social Psychology of Groups.* New York: Wiley.

Thomas, George M., Henry A. Walker, and Morris Zelditch Jr. 1986. "Legitimacy and Collective Action." *Social Forces* 65:378–404.

Wagner, David G., Rebecca S. Ford, and Thomas W. Ford. 1986. "Can Gender Inequalities Be Reduced?" *American Sociological Review* 51:47–61.

Walker, Henry A., Larry Rogers, and Morris Zelditch Jr. 2002. "Acts, Persons, and Institutions: Legitimating Multiple Objects and Compliance with Authority." Pp. 323–39 in *Structure, Culture, and History: Recent Issues in Social Theory,* edited by S. C. Chew and J. D. Knottnerus. Oxford, England: Rowman & Littlefield.

Walker, Henry A., George M. Thomas, and Morris Zelditch Jr. 1986. "Legitimation, Endorsement and Stability." *Social Forces* 64(3):620–43.

Walker, Henry A., Shane R. Thye, Brent Simpson, Michael J. Lovaglia, David Willer, and Barry Markovsky. 2000. "Network Exchange Theory: Recent Development and New Directions." *Social Psychology Quarterly* 63:324–37.

Walster, Elaine, George W. Walster, and Ellen Berscheid. 1978. *Equity: Theory and Research.* Boston, MA: Allyn & Bacon.

Weber, Max. [1924] 1978. *Economy and Society,* vols. 1 and 2, edited by G. Roth and C. Wittich. Berkeley: University of California Press.

Webster, Murray, Jr. 1977. "Equating Characteristics and Social Interaction: Two Experiments." *Sociometry* 40:41–50.

Webster, Murray, Jr. and Martha Foschi. 1988. "Overview of Status Generalization." Pp. 1–20, 477–78 in *Status Generalization: New Theory and Research,* edited by M. Webster Jr. and M. Foschi. Stanford, CA: Stanford University Press.

Webster, Murray, Jr. and Stuart J. Hysom. 1998. "Creating Status Characteristics." *American Sociological Review* 63:351–78.

Webster, Murray, Jr. and LeRoy F. Smith. 1978. "Justice and Revolutionary Coalitions: A Test of Two Theories." *American Journal of Sociology* 84:267–92.

Willer, David. 1987. *Theory and the Experimental Investigation of Social Structures.* New York: Gordon & Breach.

Willer, David, ed. 1999. *Network Exchange Theory.* Westport, CT: Praeger.

Willer, Robert B., Lisa Troyer, and Michael J. Lovaglia. 2001. "Using Power to Elevate Status: Observers of Power Use." Presented at the annual meeting of the American Sociological Association, August, Washington, DC.

Wilson, Rick K. and Jane Sell. 1997. "Cheap Talk and Reputation in Repeated Public Goods Settings." *Journal of Conflict Resolution* 41:695–717.

Yamagishi, Toshio. 1988. "The Provision of a Sanctioning System in the United States and Japan." *Social Psychology Quarterly* 51:265–71.

Yamagishi, Toshio. 1995. "Social Dilemmas." Pp. 311–35 in *Sociological Perspectives on Social Psychology,* edited by K. Cook, G. A. Fine, and J. S. House. Boston, MA: Allyn & Bacon.

Zelditch, Morris, Jr. 2001. "Processes of Legitimation: Recent Developments and New Directions." *Social Psychology Quarterly* 64:4–17.

Zelditch, Morris, Jr. and Henry A. Walker. 1984. "Legitimacy and the Stability of Authority." *Advances in Group Processes* 1:1–25.

Chapter 17. The Sociology of Organization

Albrow, Martin. 1970. *Bureaucracy.* New York: Praeger.

Aldrich, Howard E. and Jeffrey Pfeffer. 1976. "Environments of Organizations." *Annual Review of Sociology* 2:79–105.

Barnard, Chester. 1938. *The Functions of the Executive.* Cambridge, MA: Harvard University Press.

Biggart, Nicole. 2002. *Readings in Economic Sociology.* Malden, MA: Blackwell.

Blau, Peter and Marshall Meyer. 1987. *Bureaucracy in Modern Society.* New York: Random House.

Campbell, John L. and Leon N. Lindberg. 1990. "Property Rights and the Organization of Economic Activity by State." *American Sociological Review* 55:634–47.

Castells, Manuel. 1996. *The Rise of the Network Society.* Malden, MA: Blackwell.

Child, John. 1972. "Organizational Structure, Environment, and Performance: The Role of Strange Choice." *Sociology* 6:1–22.

Colignon, Richard. 1997. *Power Plays: Critical Events in the Institutionalization of the Tennessee Valley Authority.* Albany: State University of New York Press.

Colignon, Richard and Chikako Usui. 2003. *Amakudari: The Hidden Fabric of Japan's Economy.* Ithaca, NY: Cornell University Press.

Cyert, Richard and James March. 1963. *A Behavioral Theory of the Firm.* Upper Saddle River, NJ: Prentice Hall.

Davis, Gerald and Doug McAdam. 2000. "Corporations, Classes, and Social Movements after Managerialism." *Research in Organizational Behavior* 22:193–236.

Dill, William R. 1958. "Environment as an Influence on Managerial Autonomy." *Administrative Science Quarterly* 2:409–43.

DiMaggio, Paul. 1988. "Interest and Agency in Institutional Theory." Pp. 3–21 in *Institutional Patterns and Organizations: Culture and Environment,* edited by L. Zucker. Cambridge, MA: Ballinger.

DiMaggio, Paul. 1991. "Introduction." Pp. 267–92 in *The New Institutionalism in Organizational Analysis,* edited by W. Powell and P. DiMaggio. Chicago, IL: University of Chicago Press.

DiMaggio, Paul, ed. 2003. *The Twenty-First Century Firm: Changing Economic Organization in International Perspective.* Princeton, NJ: Princeton University Press.

DiMaggio, Paul J. and Walter W. Powell. 1983. "The Iron Cage Revisited: Institutional Isomorphism and Collective Rationality in Organizational Fields." *American Sociological Review* 48:147–60.

Dobbin, Frank. 1994. *Forging Industrial Policy: The U.S., Britain, and France in the Railway Age.* New York: Cambridge University Press.

Donaldson, Lex. 1996. "The Normal Science of Structural Contingence Theory." Pp. 57–76 in *Handbook of Organization Studies,* edited by S. Clegg, C. Hardy, and W. Nord. Thousand Oaks, CA: Sage.

Dore, Ronald. 1984. "Goodwill and the Spirit of Market Capitalism." *British Journal of Sociology* 34:459–82.

Emery, Fred E. and E. L. Trist. 1965. "The Causal Texture of Organizational Environments." *Human Relations* 18:21–32.

Fligstein, Neil. 1987. "The Intraorganizational Power Struggle: Rise of Financial Personnel to Top Leadership in Large Corporations, 1919–1979." *American Sociological Review* 52:44–58.

Fligstein, Neil. 1996. "Markets as Politics: A Political-Cultural Approach to Market Institutions." *American Sociological Review* 61:656–73.

Fligstein, Neil. 2001. *The Architecture of Markets: An Economic Sociology of Twenty-First-Century Capitalist Societies.* Princeton, NJ: Princeton University Press.

Galaskiewicz, Joseph. 1985. "Interorganizational Relations." *Annual Review of Sociology* 11:281–304.

Gerlach, Michael. 1992. *Alliance Capitalism: The Social Organization of Japanese Business.* Berkeley: University of California Press.

Gerth, Hans and C. Wright Mills, trans. and eds. 1946. *From Max Weber: Essays in Sociology.* New York: Oxford University Press.

Granovetter, Mark. 1985. "Economic Action and Social Structure: The Problem of Embeddedness." *American Journal of Sociology* 85:481–510.

Guillen, Mauro. 2003. "The Economic Sociology of Markets, Industries, and Firms." *Theory and Society* 32:505–15.

Hall, Richard H. and Pamela S. Tolbert. 2005. *Organizations: Structures, Processes, and Outcomes.* Upper Saddle River, NJ: Pearson Prentice Hall.

Hamilton, Gary and Nicole W. Biggart. 1988. "Market, Culture, and Authority: A Comparative Analysis of Management and Organization in the Far East." *American Journal of Sociology* 94(Suppl.):S52–94.

Hannan, Michael T. and Glenn R. Carroll. 1995. "An Introduction to Organizational Ecology." Pp. 17–31 in *Organizations in Industry: Strategy, Structure and Selection,* edited by G. Carroll and M. Hannan. New York: Oxford University Press.

Hannan, Michael T. and John H. Freeman. 1977. "The Population Ecology of Organizations." *American Journal of Sociology* 82:929–64.

Jepperson, Ronald L. 1991. "Institutions, Institutional Effects, and Institutionalism." Pp. 143–63 in *The New Institutionalism in Organizational Analysis,* edited by W. Powell and P. DiMaggio. Chicago, IL: University of Chicago Press.

March, James G., ed. 1965. *Handbook of Organizations.* Chicago, IL: Rand McNally.

Martin, John L. 2003. "What Is Field Theory?" *American Journal of Sociology* 109:1–49.

Meyer, John W. and Brian Rowan. 1977. "Institutionalized Organizations: Formal Structure as Myth and Ceremony." *American Journal of Sociology* 83:340–63.

Michels, Robert. [1911] 1962. *Political Parties.* New York: Collier.

Mill, John S. 1861. *Considerations on Representative Government.* London, England: Parker, Son, and Bourn.

Mosca, Gaetano. [1895] 1939. *Elementi di Scienza Politica.* Translated as *The Ruling Class* by H. Kahn, edited and revised by A. Livingston. New York: McGraw-Hill.

Nohria, Nitin and Robert G. Eccles. 1992. *Networks and Organizations: Structure, Form and Action.* Cambridge, MA: Harvard Business School Press.

Perrow, Charles. 1986. *Complex Organizations: A Critical Essay.* New York: Random House.

Perrow, Charles. 2002. *Organizing America: Wealth, Power, and the Origins of Corporate Capitalism.* Princeton, NJ: Princeton University Press.

Pfeffer, Jeffrey. 1982. *Organizations and Organization Theory.* Boston, MA: Pittman.

Pfeffer, Jeffrey. 1997. *New Directions for Organizational Theory: Problems and Prospects.* New York: Oxford University Press.

Pfeffer, Jeffrey and Gerald R. Salancik. 1978. *The External Control of Organizations: A Resource Dependence Perspective.* New York: Harper & Row.

Podolny, Joel M. and Karen L. Page. 1998. "Network Forms of Organizations." *Annual Review of Sociology* 24:57–76.

Powell, Walter. 1990. "Neither Market nor Hierarchy: Network Forms of Organization." Pp. 295–336 in *Research in Organizational Behavior,* vol. 12, edited by L. L. Cummings and B. Straw. Greenwich, CT: JAI Press.

Powell, Walter W. and Laurel Smith-Doerr. 1994. "Networks and Economic Life." Pp. 368–402 in *The Handbook of Economic Sociology,* edited by N. Smelser and R. Swedberg. New York: Russell Sage.

Romanelli, Elaine. 1991. "The Evolution of New Organizational Forms." *Annual Review of Sociology* 17:79–103.

Roy, William. 1998. *Socializing Capital: The Rise of the Large Industrial Corporation in America.* Princeton, NJ: Princeton University Press.

Saxenian, Annalee. 1996. *Regional Advantage: Culture and Competition in Silicon Valley and Route 128.* Cambridge, MA: Harvard University Press.

Scott, W. Richard. 1975. "Organizational Structure." *Annual Review of Sociology* 1:1–20.

Scott, W. Richard. 2003. *Organizations: Rational, Natural, and Open Systems.* Englewood Cliffs, NJ: Prentice Hall.

Selznick, Philip. 1943. "An Approach to the Theory of Bureaucracy." *American Sociological Review* 8:47–54.

Selznick, Philip. 1948. "Foundations of a Theory of Organizations." *American Sociological Review* 13:25–35.

Selznick, Philip. 1949. *TVA and the Grass Roots.* Berkeley: University of California Press.

Simon, Herbert. 1957. *Administrative Behavior.* New York: Macmillan.

Stark, David. 1996. "Recombinant Property in East European Capitalism." *American Journal of Sociology* 101(4): 993–1027.

Swartz, David. 1997. *Culture and Power.* Chicago, IL: University of Chicago Press.

Swedberg, Richard. 2003. *Principles of Economic Sociology.* Princeton, NJ: Princeton University Press.

Tolbert, Pamela and Lynne Zucker. 1996. "The Institutionalization of Institutional Theory." Pp. 175–90 in *Handbook of Organization Studies,* edited by S. Clegg, C. Hardy, and W. Nord. Thousand Oaks, CA: Sage.

Uzzi, Brian. 1996. "The Sources and Consequences of Embeddedness for Economic Performance of Organizations: The Network Effect." *American Sociological Review* 60: 674–98.

Warren, Roland. 1967. "The Interorganizational Field as a Focus for Investigation." *Administrative Science Quarterly* 12:396–419.

Weick, Karl. 1995. *Sensemaking in Organizations.* Thousand Oaks, CA: Sage.

Weber, Max. 1958. *The Protestant Ethic and the Spirit of Capitalism.* New York: Scribner.

Weber, Max. 1968. *Economy and Society: An Outline of Interpretive Sociology.* Edited by G. Roth and C. Wittich. New York: Bedminster Press.

Weber, Max. 1981. *General Economic History.* New Brunswick, NJ: Transaction.

Williamson, Oliver. 1975. *Markets and Hierarchies: Analysis and Antitrust Implications.* New York: Free Press.

Williamson, Oliver. 1981. "The Economics of Organization: The Transaction Cost Approach." *American Journal of Sociology* 87:548–77.

Chapter 18. Industrial Sociology

Adler, Paul and Robert Cole. 1993. "Designed for Learning: A Tale of Two Auto Plants." *Sloan Management Review* 34(Spring):85–94.

Berggren, Christian. 1992. *Alternatives to Lean Production: Work Organization in the Swedish Auto Industry.* Ithaca, NY: ILR Press.

Berggren, Christian. 1994. "NUMMI versus Uddevalla." *Sloan Management Review* 35(Winter):37–45.

Blauner, Robert. 1964. *Alienation and Freedom: The Factory Worker and His Industry.* Chicago, IL: University of Chicago Press.

Bluestone, Barry and Bennett Harrison. 1982. *The Deindustrialization of America: Plant Closings, Community Abandonment, and the Dismantling of Basic Industry.* New York: Basic Books.

Blumberg, Paul. 1968. *Industrial Democracy: The Sociology of Participation.* New York: Schocken Books.

Boraiko, Allen A. 1985. "Storing Up Trouble: Hazardous Waste." *National Geographic,* March, pp. 318–51.

Braverman, Harry. 1974. *Labor and Monopoly Capital: The Degradation of Work in the Twentieth Century.* New York: Monthly Review Press.

Brown, Lester R. 1981. *Building a Sustainable Society.* New York: W. W. Norton.

Brown, Murray. 1966. "Toward an Endogenous Explanation of Industrialization." *Social Research* 33(2):295–313.

Budiansky, Stephen. 1994. "10 Billion for Dinner, Please." *U.S. News & World Report,* September 12, pp. 57–60.

Campbell, Colin. 1987. *The Romantic Ethic and the Spirit of Modern Consumption.* Oxford, England: Basil Blackwell.

Carey, Alex. 1967. "The Hawthorne Studies: A Radical Criticism." *American Sociological Review* 32:403–16.

Catton, William R., Jr. 1993. "Carrying Capacity and the Death of a Culture: A Tale of Two Autopsies." *Sociological Inquiry* 63(2):202–23.

Chang, Clara and Constance Sorrentino. 1991. "Union Membership Statistics in 12 Countries." *Monthly Labor Review* 114(12):46–53.

Charlton, Michael. 1986. "The Revolution of Necessity." Episode 4 of the video series *Out of the Fiery Furnace,* produced by Robert Raymond. Melbourne, Australia: Magnum Opus Films.

Chedd, Graham. 1980. *The Chaco Legacy,* produced by Michael Ambrosino. Boston, MA: Odyssey Series.

Chinoy, Ely. 1955. *Automobile Workers and the American Dream.* Boston, MA: Beacon Press.

Ciccantell, Paul S. and Stephen G. Bunker. 2004. "The Economic Ascent of China and the Potential for Restructuring the Capitalist World-System." *Journal of World-Systems Research* 10(3):565–89.

Clawson, Dan and Mary A. Clawson. 1999. "What Has Happened to the US Labor Movement? Union Decline and Renewal." *Annual Review of Sociology* 25:95–119.

Cole, Robert E. 1971. *Japanese Blue-Collar: The Changing Tradition.* Berkeley: University of California Press.

Daily, Gretchen, Anne H. Ehrlich, and Paul R. Ehrlich. 1994. "Optimum Human Population Size." *Population and Environment: A Journal of Interdisciplinary Studies* 15(6):469–75.

Daly, Herman E. 1973. "The Steady-State Economy: Toward a Political Economy of Biophysical Equilibrium and Moral Growth." Pp. 149–74 in *Toward a Steady-State Economy,* edited by H. E. Daly. San Francisco, CA: W. H. Freeman.

Deane, Phyllis. 1965. *The First Industrial Revolution.* Cambridge, England: Cambridge University Press.

Diamant, A. 1977. "Democratizing the Workplace: The Myth and Reality of *Mitbestimmung* in the Federal Republic of Germany." Pp. 25–48 in *Worker Self-Management in Industry: The West European Experience,* edited by G. D. Garson. New York: Praeger.

Diamond, Jared. 2005. *Collapse: How Societies Choose to Fail or Succeed.* New York: Penguin Group.

Dobkowski, Michael N. and Isidor Wallimann. 2002. "Introduction: On the Edge of Scarcity." Pp. xxi–xxxi in *On the Edge of Scarcity: Environment, Resources, Population, Sustainability, and Conflict,* edited by M. N. Dobkowski and I. Wallimann. Syracuse, NY: Syracuse University Press.

Dobyns, Lloyd and Clare Crawford-Mason. 1991. *Quality or Else: The Revolution in World Business.* Boston, MA: Houghton Mifflin.

Economic Report of the President, 1994. 1994. February. Washington, DC: Council of Economic Advisors.

Fantasia, Rick, Dan Clawson, and Gregory Graham. 1988. "A Critical View of Worker Participation in American Industry." *Work and Occupations* 15:468–88.

Farber, Henry S. and Alan B. Krueger. 1993. "Union Membership in the United States: The Decline Continues." Pp. 105–34 in *Employee Representation: Alternatives and Future Directions,* edited by Bruce E. Kaufman and Morris M. Kleiner. Madison, WI: Industrial Relations Research Association.

Firebaugh, Glenn and Brian Goesling. 2004. "Accounting for the Recent Decline in Global Inequality." *American Journal of Sociology* 110(2):283–312.

Form, William. 1976. *Blue-Collar Stratification: Auto Workers in Four Countries.* Princeton, NJ: Princeton University Press.

Form, William and Kyu Han Rae. 1988. "Convergence Theory and the Korean Connection." *Social Forces* 66(3):618–44.

Franke, Richard H. and James D. Kaul. 1978. "The Hawthorne Experiments: First Statistical Interpretation." *American Sociological Review* 43(5):623–43.

Freeman, Richard B. and James L. Medoff. 1984. *What Do Unions Do?* New York: Basic Books.

Frege, Carola. 2003. "Transforming German Workplace Relations: Quo Vadis Cooperation." *Economic and Industrial Democracy* 24(3):317–47.

Freyssenet, Michel. 1998. "Reflective Production: An Alternative to Mass Production and Lean Production?" *Economic and Industrial Democracy* 19(1):91–117.

Friedman, Thomas L. 2005. *The World Is Flat: A Brief History of the Twenty-first Century.* New York: Farrar, Straus & Giroux.

Furstenberg, Friedrich. 1977. "West German Experience with Industrial Democracy." *Annuals of the American Academy of Political and Social Science* 431(May):44–53.

Geoghegan, Thomas. 1991. *Which Side Are You On? Trying to Be for Labor When It Is Flat on Its Back.* New York: Plume.

Gern, Jean-Peirre. 1995. "Economic Globalization and Growing Anomie." *International Journal of Sociology and Sociology Policy* 15:8–10, 65–76.

Gersuny, Carl. 1981. *Work Hazards and Industrial Conflict.* Hanover, NH: University Press of New England for the University of Rhode Island.

Ginsbourger, Francis. 1981. "Japan's Dark Side," *World Press Review* (July):32–33.

Goldman, Paul and Donald R. Van Houten. 1981. "Bureaucracy and Domination: Managerial Strategy in Turn-of-the-Century American Industry." Pp. 89–216 in *Complex Organizations: Critical Perspectives,* edited by M. Zey-Ferrell and M. Aiken. Glenview, IL: Scott Foresman.

Gordon, David M. 1978. "Up and Down the Long Roller Coaster." Pp. 22–35 in *U.S. Capitalism in Crisis,* prepared by the Crisis Reader Editorial Collective. New York: Union for Radical Political Economics.

Gottfried, Heidi. 1998. "Whither Taylorism?" *Work, Employment, and Society* 12(3):545–49.

Graham, Laurie. 1993. "Inside a Japanese Transplant: A Critical Perspective." *Work and Occupations* 20(2):147–73.

Graham, Laurie. 1995. *On the Line at Subaru-Isuzu: The Japanese Model and the American Worker.* Ithaca, NY: ILR Press.

Grenier, Guillermo. 1988. *Inhumane Relations: Quality Circles and Anti-Unionism in American Industry.* Philadelphia, PA: Temple University Press.

Guest, Robert H. 1957. "Job Enlargement: A Revolution in Job Design." *Personnel Administration* 20:9–16.

Guest, Robert H. 1987. "Industrial Sociology: The Competitive Edge." *Footnotes,* January, pp. 5, 8.

Harrington, Michael. 1977. *The Vast Majority: A Journey to the World's Poor.* New York: Simon & Schuster.

Harris, Marvin. 1977. *Cannibals and Kings: The Origins of Cultures.* New York: Random House.

Harrison, Bennett and Barry Bluestone. 1988. *The Great U-Turn: Corporate Restructuring and the Polarizing of America.* New York: Basic Books.

Harvey, Edward B. 1975. *Industrial Society: Structures, Roles, and Relations.* Homewood, IL: The Dorsey Press.

Hill, Stephen. 1981. *Competition and Control at Work: The New Industrial Sociology.* Cambridge: MIT Press.

Hodson, Randy. 1996. "Dignity in the Workplace under Participative Management: Alienation and Freedom Revisited." *American Sociological Review* 61(5):719–38.

Hodson, Randy, Sandy Wessh, Sabine Rieble, Cheryl Sorenson Jamison, and Sean Creighton. 1993. "Is Worker Solidarity Undermined by Autonomy and Participation? Patterns from the Ethnographic Literature." *American Sociological Review* 58(June):398–416.

Horn, Patricia. 1993. "Paying Top Lose Our Jobs: The U.S.'s Job Export Strategy." *Dollars and Sense,* March, pp. 10–11, 20–21.

Howes, Candice. 1993. *Japanese Auto Transplants and the U.S. Automobile Industry.* Washington, DC: Economic Policy Institute.

Inkeles, Alex. 1960. "Industrial Man: The Relation of Status to Experience, Perception, and Value." *American Journal of Sociology* 66(1):1–31.

Inkeles, Alex and Peter H. Rossi. 1961. "National Comparisons of Occupational Prestige." Pp. 506–16 in *Sociology*, edited by S. M. Lipset and N. J. Smelser. Englewood Cliffs, NJ: Prentice Hall.

Johnson, Ana Gutierrez and William F. Whyte. 1977. "The Mondragon System of Worker Production Cooperatives." *Industrial and Labor Relations Review* 31(1):18–30.

Johnson, Christopher H. 2002. "Introduction: De-Industrialization and Globalization." *International Review of Social History*, 47(Suppl. 10, December):3–33.

Johnson, William B. 1991. "Global Work Force 2000: The New World Labor Market." *Harvard Business Review* 69(March–April):115–27.

Jones, Stephen R. G. 1992. "Was There a Hawthorne Effect?" *American Journal of Sociology* 98(3):451–68.

Kamala, Bonala K. 1998. *Globalization: The Perils for Vulnerable Groups*. International Sociological Association.

Kanter, Rosabeth M. 1977. *Men and Women of the Corporation*. New York: Basic Books.

Kanter, Rosabeth M. 1983. *The Change Masters: Innovation & Entrepreneurship in the American Corporation*. New York: Simon & Schuster.

Kanter, Rosabeth M. 1989. *When Giants Learn to Dance*. New York: Simon & Schuster.

Kanter, Rosabeth M. 1991. "Transcending Business Boundaries: 12,000 World Managers View Change." *Harvard Business Review* 69(May–June):151–64.

Kanter, Rosabeth M. 1995. *World Class: Thriving Locally in the Global Economy*. New York: Touchstone.

Kanter, Rosabeth M. and Richard I. Corn. 1994. "Do Cultural Differences Make a Business Difference? Contextual Factors Affecting Cross-Cultural Relationship Success." *Journal of Management Development* 13(Winter):5–23.

Kappel, Robert. 1995. "Core and Periphery in the Global Order: Globalization, Tripolarity and Marginalization" (in German). *Peripherie* 15(December):59–60, 79–117.

Kasmir, Sharryn. 1996. *The Myth of Mondragon: Cooperatives, Politics, and Working-Class Life in a Basque Town*. Albany: State University of New York Press.

Kassalow, Everett M. 1984. "The Future of American Unionism: A Comparative Perspective." *Annals of the American Association of Political and Social Scientists* 73(May):52–63.

Kerbo, Harold R. 2006. *Social Stratification and Inequality: Class Conflict in Historical, Comparative, and Global Perspective*. 6th ed. New York: McGraw-Hill.

Kimeldorf, Howard and Judith Stephan-Norris. 1992. "Historical Studies of Labor Movement in the United States." *Annual Review of Sociology* 18:495–517.

Knights, David and David Collinson. 1985. "Redesigning Work on the Shop Floor: A Question of Control and Consent." Pp. 197–226 in *Job Redesign: Critical Perspectives on the Labor Process*, edited by D. Knights, H. Willmott, and D. Collinson. Aldershot, England: Gower.

Kornbluh, Hy. 1984. "Work Place Democracy and Quality of Work Life: Problems and Prospects." *Annals of American Academy of Political and Social Science* 473(May):88–95.

Lenssen, Nicholas. 1992. "Confronting Nuclear Waste." Pp. 46–65 in *State of the World, 1992*, edited by Lester R. Brown. New York: Norton.

Lewis, Chris H. 2002. "Global Industrial Collapse: The Necessary Collapse." Pp. 16–29 in *On the Edge of Scarcity:*
Environment, Resources, Population, Sustainability, and Conflict, edited by M. N. Dobkowski and I. Wallimann. Syracuse, NY: Syracuse University Press.

Main, Jeremy. 1994. *Quality Wars: The Triumphs and Defeats of American Business*. New York: Free Press.

Marsh, Robert M. 1984. "Whither the Comparative Study of Modernization and Development?" Pp. 81–106 in *Work, Organizations, and Society*, edited by M. B. Brinkerhoff. Westport, CT: Greenwood Press.

Marsh, Robert M. and Hiroshi Mannari. 1976. *Modernization and the Japanese Factory*. Princeton, NJ: Princeton University Press.

McGinnis, James B. 1979. *Bread and Justice: Toward a New International Economic Order*. New York: Paulist Press.

Meadows, Donella H., Dennis L. Meadows, Jorgen Randers, and William W. Behrens III. 1974. *The Limits to Growth*. 2d ed. New York: Potomac Associates Books.

Meadows, Donella H., Dennis L. Meadows, and Jorgen Randers. 1992. *Beyond the Limits*. Post Hills, VT: Chelsea Green.

Michalowski, Raymond J. and Ronald C. Kramer. 1987. "The Space between Laws: The Problem of Corporate Crime in a Transnational Context." *Social Problems* 34(1):34–53.

Miller, Delbert C. 1984. "Whatever Will Happen to Industrial Sociology." *Sociological Quarterly* 25(Spring):251–56.

Mondragon Corporacion Cooperativa. 2003. [Home page]. Retrieved January 2007, 2003 (www.mondragon.mcc.es/ing/index.asp).

Mondragon Corporacion Cooperativa. 2005. *Frequently Asked Questions: Corporation*. Retrieved March 28, 2005 (www.mcc.coop/ing/.contacto/faqs6.html).

Naoi, Atsushi and Carmi Schooler. 1985. "Occupational Conditions and Psychological Functioning in Japan." *American Journal of Sociology* 90(4):729–52.

Parker, Mike. 1985. *Inside the Circle: A Union Guide to QWL*. Boston, MA: South End.

Parker, Mike and Jane Slaughter. 1988. *Choosing Sides: Unions and the Team Concept*. Boston, MA: South End.

Parshall, Gerald. 1992. "The Great Panic of '93." *U.S. News & World Report*, November 2, pp. 70, 72.

Pencavel, John. 2001. *Worker Participation: Lessons from the Worker Co-Ops of the Pacific Northwest*. New York: Russell Sage Foundation.

Pennsylvania State University and WQED. 1993. "The Collapse." Program #8 of *Out of the Past*. Burlington, VT: Annenberg/CPB Collection.

Perrucci, Robert. 1994. *Japanese Auto Transplants in the Heartland*. Hawthorne, NY: Aldine de Gruyter.

Perry, Stewart E. 1978. *San Francisco Scavengers: Dirty Work and the Pride of Ownership*. Berkeley: University of California Press.

Peters, Tom. 1987. *Thriving on Chaos: Handbook for a Management Revolution*. New York: HarperPerennial.

Pimentel, David, Rebecca Harman, Matthew Pacenza, Jason Pecarsky, and Marcia Pimentel. 1994. "Natural Resources and an Optimum Human Population." *Population and Environment: A Journal of Interdisciplinary Studies* 15(5):347–69.

Postel, Sandra and Christopher Flavin. 1991. "Reshaping the Global Economy." Pp. 170–88 in *State of the World: 1991*, edited by L. R. Brown. New York: W. W. Norton.

Putman, John J. 1977. "West Germany: Continuing Miracle." *National Geographic*, August, pp. 151–81.

Ramsay, H. 1977. "Cycles of Control: Worker Participation in Sociological and Historical Perspective." *Sociology* 11:481–506.

Reich, Robert. 1991. *The Work of Nations: Preparing Ourselves for 21st Century Capitalism.* New York: Knopf.

Roethlisberger, Fritz J. and William J. Dickson. 1939. *Management and the Worker: An Account of a Research Program Conducted by the Western Electric Company, Hawthorne Works, Chicago.* Cambridge, MA: Harvard University Press.

Ross, Robert J. S. and Kent C. Trachte. 1990. *Global Capitalism: The New Leviathan.* Albany: State University of New York.

Rothstein, Frances and Michael L. Blim, eds. 1992. *Anthropology and the Global Factory: Studies of the New Industrialization in the Late Twentieth Century.* New York: Bergin & Garvey.

Rowley, R. Kent. 1977. "A Skeptical View of the West German Model." Pp. 219–21 in *Industrial Democracy Today,* edited by G. Sanderson and F. Stapenhurst. Toronto, Ontario, Canada: McGraw-Hill.

Roy, Donald. 1952. "Quota Restriction and Goldbricking in a Machine Shop." *American Journal of Sociology* 57:427–42.

Roy, Donald. 1954. "Efficiency and the Fix: Informal Intergroup Relations in a Piece-Work Machine Shop." *American Journal of Sociology* 60:255–66.

Roy, Donald. 1958. "Banana Time: Job Satisfaction and Informal Interaction." *Human Organization* 18:158–68.

Safizadeh, M. Hossein. 1991. "The Case of Workgroups in Manufacturing Operations." *California Management Review* 33(4):61–82.

Sallaz, Jeffrey J. 2004. "Manufacturing Concessions: Attritionary Outsourcing at General Motor's Lordstown, USA Assembly Plant." *Work, Employment and Society* 18(4):687–708.

Sass, Robert. 2000. "Agricultural "Killing Fields": The Poisoning of Costa Rica Banana Workers." *International Journal of Health Services* 30(3):491–514.

Schumacher, E. F. 1973. *Small Is Beautiful: Economics as if People Mattered.* New York: Harper & Row.

Simon, Julian L. 1981. *The Ultimate Resource.* Princeton, NJ: Princeton University Press.

Simpson, Ida H. 1989. "The Sociology of Work: Where Have the Workers Gone?" *Social Forces* 67(3):563–81.

Sorge, A. 1976. "The Evolution of Industrial Democracy in the Countries of the European Community." *British Journal of Industrial Relations* 14:274–94.

Statistical Abstract of the United States, 1997: The National Data Book. 1997. Washington, DC: U.S. Bureau of the Census.

Statistical Abstract of the United States, 2004–2005: The National Data Book. 2004. Washington, DC: U.S. Bureau of the Census.

Stover, Ronald G., Melodie L. Lichty, and Penny W. Stover. 1999. *Industrial Societies: An Evolutionary Perspective.* Englewood Cliffs, NJ: Prentice Hall.

Storm, Servaas and J. Mohan Rao. 2004. "Market-Led Globalization and World Democracy: Can the Twain Ever Meet?" *Development and Change* 35(3):567–81.

Tainter, Joseph A. 1988. *The Collapse of Complex Societies.* New York: Cambridge University Press.

Taylor, Frederick W. 1911. *Scientific Management.* New York: Harper & Row.

Taylor, Lee. 1968. *Occupational Sociology.* New York: Oxford University Press.

Thomas, Robert J. 1985. "Quality and Quantity: Worker Participation in the U.S. and Japanese Automobile Industries." Pp. 162–88 in *Technological Change and Worker Movements,* edited by M. Dubofsky. Beverly Hills, CA: Sage.

Thorne, Alan. 1989. "The Feathered Serpent" episode. *Man on the Rim: Peopling the Pacific.* Falls Church, VA: Landmark Films.

Thurow, Lester C. 1987. "A Surge in Inequality." *Scientific American* 256(5):30–37.

Thurow, Lester C. 1992. *Head to Head: The Coming Economic Battle Among Japan, Europe, and America.* New York: William Morrow.

Troy, Leo. 1990. "Is the U.S. Unique in the Decline of Private Sector Unionism?" *Journal of Labor Research* 11(2): 111–43.

Turner, Lowell. 1991. *Democracy at Work: Changing World Markets and the Future of Labor Unions.* Ithaca, NY: Cornell University Press.

U.S. Bureau of Labor Statistics. 2005a. *Labor Force Statistics from the Current Population Survey.* Retrieved December 7, 2005 (ftp.bls.gov/pub/suppl/empsit.ceseeb16.txt).

U.S. Bureau of Labor Statistics. 2005b. *Union Members Summary.* USDL 05–112. Retrieved December 6, 2005 (www.bls.gov/news.release/unioin2.nro).

Walker, Charles R. 1950. *Steeltown: An Industrial Case History of the Conflict Between Progress and Security.* New York: Harper.

Walker, Charles R. and Robert H. Guest. 1952. *The Man on the Assembly Line.* Cambridge, MA: Harvard University Press.

Walker, Charles R., Robert H. Guest, and Arthur N. Turner. 1956. *The Foreman on the Assembly Line.* Cambridge, MA: Harvard University Press.

Watkins, T. H. 1993. *The Great Depression: America in the 1930s.* New York: Little, Brown.

Weil, Simone. 1962. "Factory Work." Pp. 452–57 in *Man, Work, and Society: A Reader in the Sociology of Occupations,* edited by S. Nosow and W. Form. New York: Basic Books.

Weiler, Paul C. 1993. "Governing the Workplace: Employee Representation in the Eyes of the Law." Pp. 81–104 in *Employee Representation: Alternatives and Future Directions,* edited by Bruce E. Kaufman and Morris M. Kleiner. Madison, WI: Industrial Relations Research Association.

Wilkinson, Richard G. 1973. *Poverty and Progress: An Ecological Perspective on Economic Development.* New York: Praeger.

Whyte, William F. 1968. "Elton Mayo." Pp. 82–83 in *The International Encyclopedia of the Social Sciences.* New York: Macmillan.

Whyte, William F. and Kathleen K. Whyte. 1991. *Making Mondragon: The Growth and Dynamics of the Worker Cooperative Complex.* Ithaca, NY: ILR Press.

Wolf, Jamie. 2005. *Globalization in the Steel Industry: The Market and Commodity Chain Transitions from Industrial to Post-Industrial Capitalism.* Charlotte, NC: Southern Sociological Society.

Womack, James P., Daniel T. Jones, and Daniel Roos. 1990. *The Machine That Changed the World.* New York: Rawson Associates.

Zwerdling, Daniel. 1978a. "Intro." Pp. 1–8 in *Democracy at Work: A Guide to Workplace Ownership, Participation, &*

Self-Management Experiments in the United States & Europe, edited by D. Zwerdling. Washington, DC: Association for Self-Management.

Zwerdling, Daniel. 1978b. "Cooperative Central." Pp. 101–11 in *Democracy at Work: A Guide to Workplace Ownership, Participation, & Self-Management Experiments in the United States & Europe,* edited by D. Zwerdling. Washington, DC: Association for Self-Management.

Chapter 19. The Sociology of Voluntary Associations

Baer, Douglas E., James E. Curtis, and Edward G. Grabb. 2001. "Has Voluntary Association Activity Declined? Cross-National Analyses for Fifteen Countries." *Canadian Review of Sociology and Anthropology* 38:249–74.

Betz, Michael and Bennett Judkins. 1975. "The Impact of Voluntary Association Characteristics on Selective Attraction and Socialization." *Sociological Quarterly* 16:228–40.

Brown, Richard D. 1973. "The Emergence of Voluntary Associations in Massachusetts, 1760–1830." *Journal of Voluntary Action Research* 2:64–73.

Cassel, Carol A. 1999. "Voluntary Associations, Churches, and Social Participation Theories of Turnout." *Social Science Quarterly* 80:504–17.

Christerson, Brad and Michael Emerson. 2003. "The Costs of Diversity in Religious Organizations: An In-Depth Case Study." *Sociology of Religion* 64:163–81.

Cohen, Jean L. and Andrew Arato. 1992. *Civil Society and Political Theory.* Cambridge: MIT Press.

Curtis, James E., Douglas E. Baer, and Edward G. Grabb. 2001. "Nations of Joiners: Explaining Voluntary Association Membership in Democratic Societies." *American Sociological Review* 66:783–805.

Curtis, James E., Edward G. Grabb, and Douglas E. Baer. 1992. "Voluntary Association Membership in Fifteen Countries: A Comparative Analysis." *American Sociological Review* 57:139–52.

Curtis, James E., Ronald D. Lambert, Steven D. Brown, and Barry J. Kay. 1989. "Affiliating with Voluntary Associations: Canadian–American Comparisons." *Canadian Journal of Sociology* 14:143–61.

Cutler, Stephen J. 1976. "Age Differences in Voluntary Association Memberships." *Social Forces* 55:43–58.

Cutler, Stephen J. 1981. "Voluntary Association Participation and Life Satisfaction: Replication, Revision, and Extension." *International Journal of Aging and Human Development* 14:127–37.

DeVall, William B. and Joseph Harry. 1975. "Associational Politics and Internal Democracy." *Journal of Voluntary Action Research* 4:90–97.

Dougherty, Kevin D. 2003. "How Monochromatic Is Church Membership? Racial–Ethnic Diversity in Religious Community." *Sociology of Religion* 64:65–85.

Edwards, Bob and Michael Foley. 1998. "Social Capital and Civil Society Beyond Putnam." *American Behavioral Scientist* 42:124–39.

Edwards, Bob and Michael Foley. 2001. "Much Ado about Social Capital." *Contemporary Sociology* 30:223–24.

Edwards, Michael. 2004. *Civil Society.* Cambridge, England: Polity Press.

Eisenstadt, Shmuel N. 1972. "The Social Conditions of the Development of Voluntary Association: A Case Study of Israel." *Journal of Voluntary Action Research* 1:2–13.

Ellison, Christopher G. and Bruce London. 1992. "The Social and Political Participation of Black Americans: Compensatory and Ethnic Community Theories Revisited." *Social Forces* 70:681–701.

Erickson, Bonnie H. and T. A. Nosanchuk. 1998. "Contact and Stereotyping in a Voluntary Association." *Bulletin de Methodologie Sociologique* 60:5–33.

Etzioni, Amitai. 2001. "Is Bowling Together Sociologically Lite?" *Contemporary Sociology* 30:223–24.

Fischer, Lucy R. and Kay B. Schaffer. 1993. *Older Volunteers.* Newbury Park, CA: Sage.

Gordon, C. Wayne and Nicholas Babchuk. 1959. "A Typology of Voluntary Associations." *American Sociological Review* 24:22–29.

Grabb, Edward and James Curtis. 1992. "Voluntary Association Activity in English Canada, French Canada, and the United States: A Multivariate Analysis." *Canadian Journal of Sociology* 17:371–88.

Gustafson, Kathleen, Alan Booth, and David Johnson. 1979. "The Effects of Labor Force Participation on Gender Differences in Voluntary Association Affiliation: A Cross-National Study." *Journal of Voluntary Action Research* 8:51–56.

Hendricks, Jon and Stephen J. Cutler. 2001. "The Effects of Membership in Church-Related Associations and Labor Unions on Age Differences in Voluntary Association Affiliations." *Gerontologist* 41:250–56.

Hougland, James G. 1982. "Voluntary Organizations and Attitudes Toward the Community." *Sociological Inquiry* 52:53–70.

Janoski, Thomas and John Wilson. 1995. "Pathways to Voluntarism: Family Socialization and Status Transmission Models." *Social Forces* 74:271–92.

Kaufman, Jason. 2002. "For the Common Good? American Civic Life in the Golden Age of Fraternity." New York: Oxford University Press.

Knoke, David. 1981. "Commitment and Detachment in Voluntary Associations." *American Sociological Review* 46:141–58.

Knoke, David. 1986. "Associations and Interest Groups." *Annual Review of Sociology* 12:1–21.

Ladd, Everett Carll. 1999. *The Ladd Report.* New York: Free Press.

Lipset, Seymour Martin. 1989. *Continental Divide: The Values and Institutions of the United States and Canada.* Washington, DC: Canadian–American Committee.

London, Bruce. 1975. "Racial Differences in Social and Political Participation: It's Not Simply a Matter of Black and White." *Social Science Quarterly* 56:274–86.

Lynd, Robert S. and Helen Merrell Lynd. 1929. *Middletown: A Study in Contemporary American Culture.* New York: Harcourt, Brace.

Mark, Noah. 1998. "Birds of a Feather Sing Together." *Social Forces* 77:453–85.

Mayhew, Bruce H. 1980. "Structuralism vs. Individualism. Part I—Shadowboxing in the Dark." *Social Forces* 59:335–75.

McPherson, Miller. 1982. "Hypernetwork Sampling: Duality and Differentiation among Voluntary Organizations." *Social Networks* 3:225–49.

McPherson, Miller. 1983. "An Ecology of Affiliation." *American Sociological Review* 48:519–32.

McPherson, Miller and Lynn Smith-Lovin. 1982. "Women and Weak Ties: Differences by Sex in the Size of Voluntary Organizations." *American Journal of Sociology* 87:883–904.

McPherson, Miller and Lynn Smith-Lovin. 1986. "Sex Segregation in Voluntary Associations." *American Sociological Review* 51:61–79.

McPherson, Miller, Lynn Smith-Lovin, and Matthew E. Brashears. 2006. "Social Isolation in America, 1985–2004." *American Sociological Review* 71:353–75.

McPherson, Miller, Lynn Smith-Lovin, and James M. Cook. 2001. "Birds of a Feather: Homophily in Social Networks." *Annual Review of Sociology* 27:415–44.

Mead, Karen. 2000. "Beneficent Maternalism: Argentine Motherhood in Comparative Perspective, 1880–1920." *Journal of Women's History* 12:120–45.

Mills, C. Wright. 1959. *The Sociological Imagination.* New York: Oxford University Press.

Monti, Daniel J., Colleen Butler, Alexandra Curley, Kirsten Tilney, and Melissa F. Weiner. 2003. "Private Lives and Public Worlds: Changes in Americans' Social Ties and Civic Attachments in the Late-20th Century." *City & Community* 2:143–63.

Olsen, Marvin E. 1982. *Participatory Pluralism: Political Participation and Influence in the United States and Sweden.* Chicago, IL: Nelson-Hall.

Palisi, Bartolomeo J. 1985. "Voluntary Associations and Well-Being in Three Metropolitan Areas: Cross-Cultural Evidence." *International Journal of Contemporary Sociology* 22:265–88.

Palisi, Bartolomeo J. and Bonni Korn. 1989. "National Trends in Voluntary Association Memberships: 1974–1984." *Nonprofit and Voluntary Sector Quarterly* 18:179–90.

Paxton, Pamela. 1999. "Is Social Capital Declining in the United States? A Multiple Indicator Assessment." *American Journal of Sociology* 105:88–127.

Popielarz, Pamela A. 1999. "(In)voluntary Association: A Multilevel Analysis of Gender Segregation in Voluntary Organizations." *Gender & Society* 13:234–50.

Popielarz, Pamela A. and Miller McPherson. 1995. "On the Edge or In Between: Niche Position, Niche Overlap, and the Duration of Voluntary Association Memberships." *American Journal of Sociology* 101:698–720.

Pugliese, Donato J. 1986. *Voluntary Associations: An Annotated Bibliography.* New York: Garland.

Putnam, Robert D. 1995. "Bowling Alone: America's Declining Social Capital." *Journal of Democracy* 6:65–78.

Putnam, Robert D. 2000. *Bowling Alone: The Collapse and Revival of American Community.* New York: Simon & Schuster.

Richmond, David, A. 2003. "Embeddedness in Voluntary Associations and the Timing of Geographic Moves." *Sociological Forum* 18:295–322.

Rietschlin, John. 1998. "Voluntary Association Membership and Psychological Distress." *Journal of Health and Social Behavior* 39:348–55.

Rose, Arnold M. 1956. *Sociology: The Study of Human Relations.* New York: Alfred A. Knopf.

Rotolo, Thomas. 1999. "Trends in Voluntary Association Participation." *Nonprofit and Voluntary Sector Quarterly* 28:199–212.

Rotolo, Thomas. 2000. "A Time to Join, a Time to Quit: The Influence of Life Cycle Transitions on Voluntary Association Membership." *Social Forces* 3:1133–61.

Rotolo, Thomas and John Wilson. 2003. "Work Histories and Voluntary Association Memberships." *Sociological Forum* 18:603–19.

Salamon, Lester. 2002. "The Resilient Sector: The State of Nonprofit America." Pp. 3–64 in *The State of Nonprofit America,* edited by L. Salamon. Washington, DC: Brookings Institute Press.

Schulman, Daniel C. 1978. "Voluntary Organization Involvement and Political Participation." *Journal of Voluntary Action Research* 7:86–105.

Shapiro, Robert Y. 2000/2001. "Review of 'Bowling Alone: The Collapse and Revival of American Community.'" *Political Science Quarterly* 115:618–20.

Smith, Constance E. and Anne Freedman. 1972. *Voluntary Associations: Perspectives on the Literature.* Cambridge, MA: Harvard University Press.

Smith, David H. 1975. "Voluntary Action and Voluntary Groups." *Annual Review of Sociology* 1:247–70.

Stoll, Michael A. 2001. "Race, Neighborhood Poverty, and Participation in Voluntary Associations." *Sociological Forum* 16:529–57.

Thomas, William I. and Florian Znaniecki. 1927. *The Polish Peasant in Europe and America.* New York: Alfred A. Knopf.

Tocqueville, Alexis de. [1835] 2000. *Democracy in America.* Translated by H. C. Mansfield and D. Winthrop. Chicago, IL: University of Chicago Press.

Warde, Alan, Gindo Tampubolon, Mark Tomlinson, Kath Ray, Brian Longhurst, and Mike Savage. 2003. "Trends in Social Capital: Membership of Associations in Great Britain, 1991–98." *British Journal of Political Science* 33:515–34.

Watson, Roy E. L. 1982. "The Adjustment of a National Voluntary Association to Change in Its Environment: The Case of the Canadian Mental Health Association." *Canadian Public Policy* 8:586–95.

Whyte, William Foote. 1943. *Street Corner Society: The Social Structure of an Italian Slum.* Chicago, IL: University of Chicago Press.

Wilson, John. 2000. "Volunteering." *Annual Review of Sociology* 26:215–40.

Wilson, John. 2001. "Dr. Putnam's Social Lubricant." *Contemporary Sociology* 30:225–27.

Wilson, John and Thomas Janoski. 1995. "Contribution of Religion to Volunteer Work." *Sociology of Religion* 56:137–52.

Chapter 20. The Sociology of Social Networks

Alderson, Arthur S. and Jason Beckfield. 2004. "Power and Position in the World City System." *American Journal of Sociology* 109:811–51.

Allison, Paul D. 1978. "Testing for Interaction in Multiple Regression." *American Journal of Sociology* 83:144.

Baker, Wayne E. 1990. "Market Networks and Corporate Behavior." *American Journal of Sociology* 96:589–625.

Barabasi, Albert-Laszlo. 2003. *Linked: How Everything Is Connected to Everything Else and What It Means.* New York: Plume.

Barley, S. R. 1986. "Technology as an Occasion for Structuring: Evidence from Observations of CT Scanners and the Social Order of Radiology Departments." *Administrative Science Quarterly* 31:78–108.

Barnes, John A. 1954. "Class and Committees in a Norwegian Island Parish." *Human Relations* 7:39–58.

Barnes, John A. 1972. "Social Networks." *Addison-Wesley Module in Anthropology* 26:1–29.

Barnland, Dean C. and Carrol Harlund. 1963. "Propinquity and Prestige as Determinants of Communication Networks." *Sociometry* 26:466–79.

Barrera, Manuel, Jr. 1986. "Distinctions between Social Support Concepts, Measures and Models." *American Journal of Community Psychology* 14:413–55.

Bearman, Peter S., James Moody, and Katherine Stovel. 2004. "Chains of Affection: The Structure of Adolescent Romantic and Sexual Networks." *American Journal of Sociology* 110:44–91.

Berkman, Lisa. 1986. "Social Networks, Support, and Health: Taking the Next Step Forward." *American Journal of Epidemiology* 123:559–62.

Blau, Judith 1993. *Social Contracts and Economic Markets.* New York: Plenum.

Blau, Peter M. 1974. "Presidential Address: Parameters of Social Structure." *American Sociological Review* 39:615–35.

Blau, Peter M. 1977. "A Macrosociological Theory of Social Structure." *American Journal of Sociology* 83:26–55.

Bott, Elizabeth. 1957. *Family and Social Network.* London, England: Tavistock.

Bourdieu, Pierre and Loic Wacquant. 1992. *An Invitation to Reflexive Sociology.* Chicago, IL: University of Chicago Press.

Breiger, Ronald L. 1976. "Career Attributes and Network Structure: A Blockmodel Study of a Biomedical Research Specialty." *American Sociological Review* 41:117–35.

Burt, Ronald S. 1976. "Positions in Networks." *Social Forces* 55:93–122.

Burt, Ronald S. 1980. "Models of Network Structure." *Annual Review of Sociology* 6:79–141.

Burt, Ronald S. 1992. *Structural Holes: The Social Structure of Competition.* Cambridge, MA: Harvard University Press.

Burt, Ronald S. 2001. "Structural Holes versus Network Closure as Social Capital." Pp. 31–56 in *Social Capital: Theory and Research,* edited by N. Lin, K. S. Cook, and R. S. Burt. New York: Aldine de Gruyter.

Campbell, Karen E. and Rachel A. Rosenfeld. 1985. "Job Search and Job Mobility: Sex and Race Differences." *Research in the Sociology of Work* 3:147–74.

Carrington, Peter J., John Scott, and Stanley Wasserman. 2005. *Models and Methods in Social Network Analysis.* Cambridge, England: Cambridge University Press.

Caspi, Avshalom, Joseph McClay, Terrie E. Moffitt, Jonathan Mill, Judy Martin, Ian W. Craig, Alan Taylor, and Richie Poulton. 2002. "Role of Genotype in the Cycle of Violence in Maltreated Children." *Science* 297:851–54.

Castells, Manuel. 2000. "Toward a Sociology of the Network Society." *Contemporary Sociology* 29:693–99.

Cederman, Lars-Erik. 2005. "Computational Models of Social Forms: Advancing Generative Process Theory." *American Journal of Sociology* 110:864–95.

Cohen, Sheldon and Thomas A. Wills. 1985. "Stress, Social Support, and the Buffering Hypothesis." *Psychological Bulletin* 98:310–57.

Coleman, James S. 1990. *Foundations of Social Theory.* Cambridge, MA: The Belknap Press of Harvard University.

Collins, Randall. 1988. *Theoretical Sociology.* New York: Harcourt Brace Jovanovich.

Coser, Rose L. 1991. *In Defense of Modernity: Role Complexity and Individual Autonomy.* Stanford, CA: Stanford University Press.

Deffuant, Guillaume, Sylvie Huet, and Frédéric Amblard. 2005. "An Individual-Based Model of Innovation Diffusion Mixing Social Value and Individual Benefit." *American Journal of Sociology* 110:1041–69.

Doreian, Patrick, Vladimir Batagelj, and Anuska Ferligoj. 2005. "Positional Analyses of Sociometric Data." Pp. 77–97 in *Models and Methods in Social Network Analysis,* edited by P. J. Carrington, J. Scott, and S. Wasserman. New York: Cambridge University Press.

Dozier, Mary. 1993. "Tailoring Clinical Case Management: The Role of Attachment." Pp. 41–58 in *Case Management for Mentally Ill Patients,* edited by M. Haris and H. E. Bergman. Longhorne, PA: Harwood.

Dozier, Mary, Kelly L. Cue, and Lara Barnett. 1994. "Clinicians as Caregivers: Role of Attachment Organization in Treatment." *Journal of Consulting & Clinical Psychology* 62:793–800.

Durkheim, Émile. 1951. *Suicide.* New York: Free Press.

Edwards, Bob and Michael W. Foley. 2001. "Much Ado about Social Capital." *Contemporary Sociology* 30:227–30.

Eguiluz, Victor M., Dante R. Chialvo, Guillermo A. Cecchi, Marwan Baliki, and A. Vania Apkarian. 2005. "Scale-Free Brain Functional Networks." *Physical Review Letters* 94(1):018102.

Elder, Glen H., Jr. 1985. "Perspectives on the Life Course." Pp. 23–49 in *Life Course Dynamics: Trajectories and Transitions,* edited by G. H. Elder Jr. Ithaca, NY: Cornell University Press.

Elder, G. H., Jr. 1998a. "The Life Course and Human Development." Pp. 939–91 in *Handbook of Child Psychology,* vol. 1, *Theoretical Models of Human Development,* edited by R. M. Lerner and W. Damon. New York: Wiley.

Elder, Glen H., Jr. 1998b. "The Life Course as Developmental Theory." *Child Development* 69:1–12.

Elder, Glen H., Jr. and Lisa A. Pellerin. 1998. "Linking History and Human Lives." Pp. 264–94 in *Methods of Life Course Research: Quantitative and Qualitative Approaches,* edited by J. Z. Giele and G. H. Elder Jr. Thousand Oaks, CA: Sage.

Emirbayer, Mustafa and Jeff Goodwin. 1994. "Network Analysis, Culture, and the Problem of Agency." *American Journal of Sociology* 99:1411–54.

Entwisle, Doris R., Karl L. Alexander, and Linda Steffel Olson. 2005. "First Grade and Educational Attainment by Age 22: A New Story." *American Journal of Sociology* 110:1458–1502.

Erikson, Bonnie H. 1996. "Culture, Class, and Connections." *American Journal of Sociology* 102:217–51.

Etzioni, Amitai. 2001. "Is Bowling Together Sociologically Lite?" *Contemporary Sociology* 3:223–24.

Faber, Ashley D. and Stanley Wasserman. 2002. "Social Support and Social Networks: Synthesis and Review." Pp. 29–72 in *Social Networks and Health,* edited by J. A. Levy and B. A. Pescosolido. New York: Elsevier Science.

Fischer, Claude. 1982. *To Dwell among Friends.* Berkeley: University of California Press.

Fowler, James H. and Oleg Smirnov. 2005. "Dynamic Parties and Social Turnout: An Agent-Based Model." *American Journal of Sociology* 110:1070–94.

Freeman, Linton C. 2004. *The Development of Social Network Analysis: A Study in the Sociology of Science.* Vancouver, British Columbia, Canada: Empirical Press.

Freidson, Eliot. 1970. *Profession of Medicine: A Study of the Sociology of Applied Knowledge.* New York: Dodd, Mead.

Fremont, Allen M. and Chloe E. Bird. 2000. "Social and Psychological Factors, Physiological Processes, and Physical Health." Pp. 334–52 in *Handbook of Medical Sociology,* edited by C. E. Bird, P. Conrad, and A. M. Fremont. Upper Saddle River, NJ: Prentice Hall.

Galaskiewicz, Joseph. 1985. *Social Organization of an Urban Grants Economy: A Study of Business Philanthropy and Nonprofit Organizations.* New York: Academic Press.

Galaskiewicz, Joseph, Stanley Wasserman, Barbara Rauschenbach, Wolfgang Bielefeld, and Patti Mullaney. 1985. "The Influence of Corporate Power, Social Status, and Market Position on Corporate Interlocks in a Regional Network." *Social Forces* 64:403–31.

Giddens, Anthony. 1990. *The Consequences of Modernity.* Stanford, CA: Stanford University Press.

Giele, Janet Z. 2002. "Longitudinal Studies and Life-Course Research: Innovations, Investigators, and Policy Ideas." Pp. 15–36 in *Looking at Lives: American Longitudinal Studies of the Twentieth Century,* edited by E. Phelps, F. F. Furstenberg Jr., and A. Colby. New York: Russell Sage.

Granovetter, Mark. 1982. "The Strength of Weak Ties: A Network Theory Revisited." Pp. 105–30 in *Social Structure and Network Analysis,* edited by P. Marsden and N. Lin. Beverly Hills, CA: Sage.

Haines, Valerie A., John J. Beggs, and Jeanne S. Hurlbert. 2002. "Exploring the Structural Contexts of the Support Process: Social Networks, Social Statuses, Social Support, and Psychological Distress." Pp. 269–92 in *Social Networks and Health,* edited by J. A. Levy and B. A. Pescosolido. New York: Elsevier Science.

Harary, Frank, Robert Z. Norman, and Dorwin Cartwright. 1965. *Structural Models: An Introduction to the Theory of Directed Graphs.* New York: Wiley.

Hargens, Lowell L. 2000. "Using the Literature: Reference Networks, Reference Contexts and the Social Structure of Scholarship." *American Sociological Review* 65:846–65.

Helminen, Anneli, Tuomo Rankinen, Sari Vaisanen, and Rainer Rauramaa. 1997. "Social Network in Relation to Plasma Fibrinogen." *Journal of Biosocial Science* 29:129–39.

Holschuh, Jane and Steven P. Segal. 2002. "Factors Related to Multiplexity in Support Networks of Persons with Severe Mental Illness." Pp. 293–321 in *Social Networks and Health,* edited by J. A. Levy and B. A. Pescosolido. New York: Elsevier Science.

Homans, George C. 1951. *The Human Group.* London, England: Routledge & Kegan Paul.

Homans, George C. 1961. *Social Behavior: Its Elementary Forms.* New York: Harcourt, Brace & World.

House, James S. 1981. *Work Stress and Social Support.* Reading, MA: Addison-Wesley.

House, James S., Karl R. Landis, and Debra Umberson. 1988. "Social Relationships and Health." *Science* 241:540–45.

House, James S., Cynthia Robbins, and Helen L. Metzner. 1982. "The Association of Social Relationships and Activities with Mortality: Prospective Evidence from the Tecumseh Community Health Study." *American Journal of Epidemiology* 116:123–40.

Huckfeldt, Robert and John Sprague. 1987. "Networks in Context: The Social Flow of Political Information." *American Political Science Review* 81:1197–216.

Jennings, Helen H. 1943. *Leadership and Isolation: A Study of Personality in Interpersonal Relations.* New York: Longmans.

Jinnett, Kimberly, Ian Coulter, and Paul Koegel. 2002. "Cases, Context and Care: The Need for Grounded Network Analysis." Pp. 101–11 in *Advances in Medical Sociology,* vol. 8, *Social Networks and Health,* edited by J. A. Levy and B. A. Pescosolido. Oxford, England: Elsevier Science.

Kadushin, Charles. 1966. "The Friends and Supporters of Psychotherapy: On Social Circles in Urban Life." *American Sociological Review* 31:786.

Kahn, Robert L. and Toni C. Antonucci. 1980. "Convoys over the Life Course: Attachment, Roles, and Social Support." Pp. 253–86 in *Life Span Development and Behavior,* edited by P. B. Baltes and O. G. Brim. San Diego, CA: Academic Press.

Klovdahl, Alden S., Edward A. Graviss, and James M. Musser. 2002. "Infectious Disease Control: Combining Molecular Biological and Network Methods." Pp. 73–99 in *Social Networks and Health,* edited by J. A. Levy and B. A. Pescosolido. New York: Elsevier Science.

Knoke, David. 1990. *Political Networks.* New York: Cambridge University Press.

Koehly, Laura M. and Philippa Pattison. 2005. "Random Graph Models for Social Networks: Multiple Relations or Multiple Raters." Pp. 162–91 in *Models and Methods in Social Network Analysis,* edited by P. J. Carrington, J. Scott, and S. Wasserman. New York: Cambridge University Press.

Laumann, Edward O. and David Knoke. 1987. *The Organizational State: Social Choice in National Policy Domains.* Madison: University of Wisconsin Press.

Laumann, Edward O. and Franz U. Pappi. 1976. *Networks of Collective Action: A Perspective on Community Influence Systems.* New York: Academic Press.

Leik, Robert K. and Mary A. Chalkey. 1996. "On the Stability of Network Relations under Stress." *Social Networks* 19:63–74.

Leventhal, Howard, Elaine A. Leventhal, and Richard J. Contrada. 1997. "Self-Regulation, Health and Behavior: A Perceptual-Cognitive Approach." *Psychology and Health* 12:1–17.

Levy, Judith A. and Bernice A. Pescosolido. 2002. *Social Networks and Health.* New York: JAI Press.

Lin, Nan. 1999. "Building a Network Theory of Social Capital." *Connections* 22:28–51.

Lin, Nan. 2000. "Inequality in Social Capital." *Contemporary Sociology* 29:785–95.

Long, J. Scott. 1997. *Regression Models for Categorical and Limited Dependent Variables.* Thousand Oaks, CA: Sage.

Lysaker, Paul H., Morris D. Bell, J. G. Goulet, and R. M. Milstein. 1994. "Relationship of Positive and Negative Symptoms to Cocaine Abuse in Schizophrenia." *Journal of Nervous and Mental Disorders* 182:109–12.

Marsden, Peter. 2000. "Social Networks." Pp. 2727–35 in *Encyclopedia of Sociology,* 2d ed., edited by E. F. Borgatta and R. J. V. Montgomery. New York: Macmillan.

Marsden, Peter. 2005. "Recent Developments in Network Measurement." Pp. 8–30 in *Models and Methods in Social*

Network Analysis, edited by P. J. Carrington, J. Scott, and S. Wasserman. New York: Cambridge University Press.

Maryanski, Alexandra and Jonathan H. Turner. 1992. *The Social Cage: Human Nature and the Evolution of Society.* Stanford, CA: Stanford University Press.

Milgram, Stanley. 1967. "The Small-World Problem." *Psychology Today* 1:61–67.

Mitchell, J. Clyde. 1969. *Social Networks in Urban Situations: Analyses of Personal Relationships in Central African Towns.* Manchester, England: Institute for Social Research, University of Zambia, by Manchester University Press.

Moen, Phyllis, Julie Robison, and Donna Dempster-McClain. 1995. "Caregiving and Women's Well-Being: A Life Course Approach." *Journal of Health and Social Behavior* 36:259–73.

Monge, Peter R. and Noshir Contractor. 2003. *Theories of Communication Networks.* New York: Oxford University Press.

Moody, James, Daniel McFarland, and Skye Bender-deMoll. 2005. "Dynamic Network Visualization." *American Journal of Sociology* 110(4):1206–41.

Moore, Gwen. 1992. "Gender and Informal Networks in State Governments." *Social Science Quarterly* 73:46–61.

Moreno, Jacob L. 1934. *Who Shall Survive? Foundations of Sociometry, Group Psychotherapy, and Sociodrama.* Washington, DC: Nervous and Mental Disease.

Moreno, Jacob L. and Helen H. Jennings. 1938. "Statistics of Social Configurations." *Sociometry* 1:342–74.

Morgan, Myfanwy, Donald L. Patrick, and John R. Charlton. 1984. "Social Networks and Psychosocial Support among Disabled People." *Social Science and Medicine* 19:489–97.

Morin, R. C. and Edward Seidman. 1986. "A Social Network Approach and the Revolving Door Patient." *Schizophrenia Bulletin* 12:262–73.

Moss, Scott and Bruce Edmonds. 2005. "Sociology and Simulation: Statistical and Qualitative Cross-Validation." *American Journal of Sociology* 110:1095–131.

Newcomb, Theodore M. 1961. *The Acquaintance Process.* New York: Holt, Rhinehart & Winston.

Northway, Mary L. 1940. "A Method for Depicting Social Relationships Obtained by Sociometric Testing." *Sociometry* 3:144–50.

O'Reilly, Patrick. 1998. "Methodological Issues in Social Support and Social Network Research." *Social Science and Medicine* 26:863–73.

Orlinsky, David and Ken Howard. 1987. "A General Model of Psychotherapy." *Journal of Integrative and Eclectic Psychotherapy* 6:6–27.

Padgett, John F. and Christopher K. Ansell. 1993. "Robust Action and the Rise of the Medici, 1400–1434." *American Journal of Sociology* 98:1259–319.

Pagel, Mark D., William W. Erdly, and Joseph Becker. 1987. "Social Networks: We Get By with (and in Spite of) a Little Help from Our Friends." *Journal of Personality and Social Psychology* 53:793–804.

Pavalko, Eliza K. 1997. "Beyond Trajectories: Multiple Concepts for Analyzing Long-Term Process." Pp. 129–47 in *Studying Aging and Social Change: Conceptual and Methodological Issues,* edited by M. A. Hardy. Thousand Oaks, CA: Sage.

Paxton, Pamela. 2002. "Social Capital and Democracy: An Interdependent Relationship." *American Sociological Review* 67:254–77.

Pearlin, Leonard I. and Carol S. Aneshensel. 1986. "Coping and Social Supports: Their Functions and Applications." Pp. 417–37 in *Applications of Social Science to Clinical Medicine and Health Policy,* edited by D. Mechanic and L. H. Aiken. New Brunswick, NJ: Rutgers University Press.

Perry, Brea L. 2005a. "Disordered Minds, Disrupted Relationships? Social Network Instability and Serious Mental Illness." Indiana University, Bloomington. Unpublished manuscript.

Perry, Brea L. 2005b. "Pre-Disease Pathways: Integrating Biological, Psychological, and Sociological Perspectives on Health and Illness." Indiana University, Bloomington. Unpublished manuscript.

Pescosolido, Bernice A. 1990. "The Social Context of Religious Integration and Suicide: Pursuing the Network Explanation." *The Sociological Quarterly* 31:337–57.

Pescosolido, Bernice A. 1991. "Illness Careers and Network Ties: A Conceptual Model of Utilization and Compliance." Pp. 161–84 in *Advances in Medical Sociology,* edited by G. Albrecht and J. Levy. Greenwich, CT: JAI Press.

Pescosolido, Bernice A. 1992. "Beyond Rational Choice: The Social Dynamics of How People Seek Help." *American Journal of Sociology* 97:1096–138.

Pescosolido, Bernice A. 1994. "Bringing Durkheim into the 21st Century: A Social Network Approach to Unresolved Issues in the Study of Suicide." Pp. 264–95 in *Émile Durkheim: Le Suicide—100 Years Later,* edited by D. Lester. Philadelphia, PA: Charles Press.

Pescosolido, Bernice A., Carol Brooks-Gardner, and Keri M. Lubell. 1998. "How People Get into Mental Health Services: Stories of Choice, Coercion and 'Muddling Through' from 'First-Timers.'" *Social Science and Medicine* 46:275–86.

Pescosolido, Bernice A. and Beth A. Rubin. 2000. "The Web of Group Affiliations Revisited: Social Life, Postmodernism, and Sociology." *American Sociological Review* 65:52–76.

Pescosolido, Bernice A. and Eric R. Wright. 2002. "Sorry, I Forgot: The Role of Recall Error in Longitudinal Personal Network Studies." *Social Networks & Health* 8:113–29.

Pescosolido, Bernice A. and Eric R. Wright. 2004. "The View from Two Worlds: The Convergence of Social Network Reports between Mental Health Clients and Their Ties." *Social Science & Medicine* 58:1795–806.

Pescosolido, Bernice A., Eric R. Wright, Maggie Alegria, and Mildred Vera. 1998. "Social Networks and Patterns of Use among the Poor with Mental Health Problems in Puerto Rico." *Medical Care* 36:1057–72.

Pescosolido, Bernice A., Eric R. Wright, and W. Patrick Sullivan. 1995. "Communities of Care: A Theoretical Perspective on Care Management Models in Mental Health." Pp. 37–80 in *Advances in Medical Sociology,* edited by G. Albrecht. Greenwich, CT: JAI Press.

Portes, Alejandro. 1998. "Social Capital: Its Origins and Applications in Modern Sociology." *Annual Review of Sociology* 24:1–24.

Powell, Walter W., Douglas R. White, Kenneth W. Koput, and Jason Owen-Smith. 2005. "Network Dynamics and Field Evolution: The Growth of Interorganizational Collaboration in the Life Sciences." *American Journal of Sociology* 110:1132–205.

Putnam, Robert D. 1995. "Bowling Alone: America's Declining Social Capital." *Journal of Democracy* 6:65–78.

Rahn, Wendy M. 2004. "Feeling, Thinking, Being, Doing: Public Mood, American National Identity, and Civic Participation." Presented at the annual meeting of the Midwest Political Science Association, April 17, Chicago, IL.

Robins, Garry and Philippa Pattison. 2005. "Interdependencies and Social Processes: Dependence Graphs and Generalized Dependence Structures." Pp. 192–214 in *Models and Methods in Social Network Analysis,* edited by P. J. Carrington, J. Scott, and S. Wasserman. New York: Cambridge University Press.

Rogers, Everett M. 1971. *Communication of Innovations.* New York: Free Press.

Rosenfield, Sarah and Suzanne Wenzel. 1997. "Social Networks and Chronic Mental Illness: A Test of Four Perspectives." *Social Problems* 44:200–16.

Rumbaut, Ruben G. 1977. "Ties That Bind: Immigration and Immigrant Families in the United States." Pp. 3–45 in *Immigration and the Family: Research and Policy on U.S. Immigrants,* edited by A. Booth, A. C. Crouter, and N. Landale. Mahwah, NJ: Erlbaum.

Shonkoff, Jack P. and Deborah A. Phillips. 2000. *From Neurons to Neighborhoods: The Science of Early Childhood Development. Institute of Medicine Committee Report.* Washington, DC: National Academy Press.

Simmel, Georg. 1955. *Conflict and the Web of Group Affiliations.* New York: Free Press.

Snijders, Tom A. B. 1998. *Models for Longitudinal Social Network Data.* Groningen, The Netherlands: University of Groningen.

Snyder, David and Edward L. Kick. 1979. "Structural Position in the World System and Economic Growth 1955–1970: A Multiple-Network Analysis of Transnational Interactions." *American Journal of Sociology* 84:1096–126.

Stryker, Sheldon 1980. *Symbolic Interactionism.* Menlo Park, CA: Benjamin/Cummings.

Suchman, Edward A. 1964. "Sociomedical Variation among Ethnic Groups." *American Journal of Sociology* 70:319–31.

Suchman, Edward A. 1965. "Social Patterns of Illness and Medical Care." *Journal of Health & Human Behavior* 6:2–16.

Suitor, Jill J. and Karl Pillemer. 2002. "Gender, Social Support, and Experiential Similarity during Chronic Stress: The Case of Family Caregivers." *Advances in Medical Sociology: Social Networks and Health* 8:247–66.

Suitor, Jill J., Barry Wellman, and David L. Morgan. 1996. "It's About Time: How, Why, and When Networks Change." *Social Networks* 19:1–8.

Thoits, Peggy 1995. "Stress, Coping, and Social Support Processes: Where Are We? What Next?" *Journal of Health and Social Behavior* 36(Suppl. 1):53–79.

Tilly, Charles. 1984. *Big Structures, Large Processes, Huge Comparisons.* New York: Russell Sage.

Tolsdorf, C. C. 1976. "Social Networks, Support, and Coping: An Exploratory Study." *Family Process* 15:407–17.

Turner, R. Jay and F. Marino. 1994. "Social Support and Social Structure: A Descriptive Epidemiology." *Journal of Health & Social Behavior* 35:193–212.

Valente, Thomas W. 2005. "Network Models and Methods for Studying the Diffusion of Innovations." Pp. 98–116 in *Models and Methods in Social Network Analysis,* edited by P. J. Carrington, J. Scott, and S Wasserman. New York: Cambridge University Press.

Waldinger, Roger. 1995. "The "Other Side" of Embeddedness: A Case Study of the Interplay between Economy and Ethnicity." *Ethnicity and Racial Studies* 18:555–80.

Wasserman, Stanley. 2003. "Foreword: Multitheoretical, Multilevel—and Multianalytical." Pp. vii–x in *Theories of Communication Networks,* edited by P. R. Monge and N. S. Contractor. New York: Oxford University Press.

Wasserman, Stanley and Katherine B. Faust. 1994. *Social Network Analysis: Methods and Applications.* New York: Cambridge University Press.

Watts, Duncan J. 2003. *Six Degrees: The Science of a Connected Age.* New York: W. W. Norton.

Wellman, Barry. 1981. "Applying Network Analysis to the Study of Support." Pp. 171–200 in *Social Networks and Social Support,* edited by B. H. Gottlieb. Beverly Hills, CA: Sage.

Wellman, Barry. 1982. "Studying Personal Communities." Pp. 61–80 in *Social Structure and Network Analysis,* edited by P. Marsden and N. Lin. Beverly Hills, CA: Sage.

Wellman, Barry and Milena Gulia. 1999. "Net Surfers Don't Ride Alone: Virtual Communities as Communities." Pp. 331–66 in *Networks in the Global Village,* edited by B. Wellman. Boulder, CO: Westview.

Wellman, Barry, Renita Wong, David Tindall, and Nancy Nazer. 1996. "A Decade of Network Change: Turnover, Persistence and Stability in Personal Communities." *Social Networks* 19:27–50.

Werner, Emmy E. 2002. "Looking for Trouble in Paradise: Some Lessons Learned from the Kauai Longitudinal Study." Pp. 297–314 in *Looking at Lives: American Longitudinal Studies of the Twentieth Century,* edited by E. Phelps, F. F. Furstenberg Jr., and A. Colby. New York: Russel Sage.

White, Harrison C. 1992. *Identity and Control: A Structured Theory of Social Action.* Princeton, NJ: Princeton University Press.

White, Harrison C., Scott A. Boorman, and Ronald L. Brieger. 1976. "Social Structure from Multiple Networks. I. Blockmodels of Roles and Positions." *American Journal of Sociology* 88:135–60.

Wilson, John. 2001. "Review: Dr. Putnam's Social Lubricant." *Contemporary Sociology* 30:225–27.

Wilson, William J. 1987. *The Truly Disadvantaged: The Inner-City, the Underclass, and Public Policy.* Chicago, IL: University of Chicago Press.

Wilson, William J. 1996. *When Work Disappears: The World of the New Urban Poor.* New York: Knopf.

Wright, Eric R. 1997. "The Impact of Organizational Factors on Mental Health Professionals' Involvement with Families." *Psychiatric Services* 48:921–27.

Chapter 21. Work and Occupations

Alvesson, Mats. 1998. "Gender Relations and Identity at Work: A Case Study of Masculinities and Femininities in an Advertising Agency." *Human Relations* 51(8):969–1005.

Applebaum, Herbert A. 1981. *Royal Blue: The Culture of Construction Workers.* New York: Holt, Rinehart & Winston.

Applegate, Jeffrey S. and Lenard W. Kaye. 1993. "Male Elder Caregivers." Pp. 152–66 in *Doing "Women's Work": Men in Nontraditional Occupations,* edited by C. L. Williams. Newbury Park, CA: Sage.

Becker, Howard S. 1952. "The Professional Dance Musician and his Audience." *American Journal of Sociology* 57:136–44.

Becker, Howard S. 1982. *Art Worlds*. Berkeley: University of California Press.

Becker, Howard S. and Blanch Geer. 1958. "The Fate of Idealism in Medical School." *American Sociological Review* 23(1): 50–56.

Becker, Howard S., Blanche Geer, Everett Hughes, and Anselm Strauss. 1961. *Boys in White: Student Culture in Medical School*. Chicago, IL: University of Chicago Press.

Bell, Michael. 1976. "Tending Bar at Brown's: Occupational Role as Artistic Performance." *Western Folklore* 35:93–107.

Bittner, Egon. 1967. "The Police on Skid Row." *American Sociological Review* 32:699–715.

Bogdan, Robert. 1972. "Learning to Sell Door to Door." *American Behavioral Scientist* 16:55–64.

Brandt, Deborah. 2002. *Tangled Routes: Women, Work, and Globalization on the Tomato Trail*. Lanham, MD: Rowman & Littlefield.

Bryant, Clifton D., 1974a. "Socialization for Khaki-Collar Crime: Military Training as Criminalization Process," Pp. 35–36 in *Images of Crime: Offenders and Victims*, edited by T. P. Thornberry and E. Sagarin. New York: Praeger.

Bryant, Clifton D. 1974b. "Olive-Drab Drunks and G. I. Junkies: Alcohol and Narcotic Addiction in the U.S. Military." Pp. 129–45 in *Deviant Behavior: Occupational and Organizational Bases*, edited by C. D. Bryant. Chicago, IL: Rand McNally.

Bryant, Clifton D. and Kenneth B. Perkins. 1982. "Containing Work Disaffection: The Poultry-Processing Worker." Pp. 199–212 in *Varieties of Work*, edited by P. Stewart and M. Cantor. Beverly Hills, CA: Sage.

Burawoy, Michael. 1984. "Organizing Consent on the Shop Floor: The Game of Making Out." Pp. 231–40 in *Critical Studies in Organization and Bureaucracy*, edited by F. Fischer and C. Sirianni. Philadelphia, PA: Temple University Press.

Caplow, Theodore. 1954. *The Sociology of Work*. Minneapolis: University of Minnesota Press.

Chinoy, Eli. 1964. "Manning the Machines: The Assembly-Line Worker." Pp. 51–81 in *The Human Shape of Work*, edited by P. Berger. New York: Macmillan.

Collins, Jane. 2003. *Threads: Gender, Labor, and Power in the Global Apparel Industry*. Chicago, IL: University of Chicago Press.

Dabney, Dean A. and Richard C. Hollinger. 1999. "Illicit Prescription Drug Use Among Pharmacists." *Work and Occupations* 26:77–106.

Dant, Tim. 2004. "The Driver-Car." *Theory, Culture and Society* 21(4):61–79.

Davis, Fred. 1959. "The Cabdriver and His Fare." *American Journal of Sociology* 63:158–65.

Ditton, Jean. 1977. "Learning to Fiddle Customers: An Essay on the Organized Production of Part-Time Theft." *Work and Occupations* 4:427–49.

Engels, Frederick. [1845] 1973. *The Condition of the Working Class in England: From Personal Observation and Authentic Sources*. Moscow, Russia: Progress Publishers.

Faulkner, Robert R. 1973a. "Career Concerns and Mobility Motivations of Orchestra Musicians." *Sociological Quarterly* 14:334–49.

Faulkner, Robert R. 1973b. "Orchestra Interaction: Some features of Communication and Authority in an Artistic Organization." *Sociological Quarterly* 14:147–57.

Fine, Gary. 1985. "Occupational Aesthetics: How Trade School Students Learn to Cook." *Urban Life* 14:3–41.

Firestone, Juanita, Raymond Garza, and Richard Harris. 2005. "Protestant Work Ethic and Worker Productivity in a Mexican Brewery." *International Sociology* 20:27–44.

Fitzpatrick, J. 1980. "Adapting to Danger: A Participant Observation Study of an Underground Coal Mine." *Work and Occupations* 10:147–78.

Garot, Robert. 2004. "'You're Not a Stone': Emotional Sensitivity in a Bureaucratic Setting." *Journal of Contemporary Ethnography* 33:735–66.

Geer, Blanche, ed. 1972. *Learning to Work*. Beverly Hills, CA: Sage.

Groce, Stephen B. and Margaret Cooper. 1990. "Just Me and the Boys? Women in Local Level Rock and Roll." *Gender and Society* 4:220–29.

Haas, Jack. 1977. "Learning Real Feelings: A Study of Ironworkers' Reactions to Fear and Danger." *Work and Occupations* 4:147–70.

Haas, Jack and William Shaffir. 1982. "Ritual Evaluation of Competence: The Hidden Curriculum of Professionalization in an Innovative Medical School Program." *Work and Occupations* 9:131–54.

Haas, Jack and William Shaffir. 1984. "The 'Fate of Idealism' Revisited." *Urban Life* 13:63–81.

Haberstein, R. W. 1962. "Sociology of Occupations: The Case of the American Funeral Director." Pp. 225–46 in *Human Behavior and Social Processes*, edited by A. M. Rose. Boston, MA: Houghton Mifflin.

Hall, Oswald. 1948. "The Stages of a Medical Career." *American Journal of Sociology* 53:327–36.

Harper, Douglas. 1982. *Good Company*. Chicago, IL: University of Chicago Press.

Harper, Douglas. 1987. *Working Knowledge: Skill and Community in a Small Shop*. Chicago, IL: University of Chicago Press.

Heyl, Barbara. 1977. "The Madam as Teacher: The Training of House Prostitutes." *Social Problems* 24:545–55.

Hochschild, Arlie R. 1979. "Emotion Work, Feeling Rules, and Social Structure." *American Journal of Sociology* 85(3):551–75.

Hoff, T. J. 1999. "The Social Organization of Physician-Managers in a Changing HMO." *Sociology of Work and Occupations* 26(3):324–51.

Hughes, Everett C. [1952] 1971. "The Sociological Study of Work: An Editorial Foreword." Pp. 298–303 in *The Sociological Eye: Selected Papers*. Chicago, IL: Aldine.

Hughes, Everett C. 1959. "Prestige." *Annals of the American Academy of Political Sciences* 325:45–49.

Hughes, Everett C. 1960. "The Professions in Society." *Canadian Journal of Economics and Political Science* 26:54–61.

Hughes, Everett C. 1965. "Professions." *Daedalus: Journal of the American Academy of Arts and Sciences* 92(4):655–68.

Hughes, Everett C. 1970. "The Humble and the Proud: The Comparative Study of Occupations." *Sociological Quarterly* 11:147–56.

Hughes, Everett C. 1994. *On Work, Race, and the Sociological Imagination*, edited by Lewis A. Coser. Chicago, IL: University of Chicago Press.

Isaksen, Lise Widding. 2002. "Toward a Sociology of (Gendered) Disgust: Images of Bodily Decay and the Social Organization of Care Work." *Journal of Family Issues* 23:791–811.

Jackall, Robert. 1988. *Moral Mazes.* New York: Oxford University Press.

Jacobs, Jerry. 1969. "Symbolic Bureaucracy: A Case Study of a Social Welfare Agency." *Social Forces* 47:413–22.

Jurik, Nancy C. 1988. "Striking a Balance: Female Correction Officers, Gender Role Stereotypes, and Male Prisons." *Social Inquiry* 58:291–305.

Khleif, B. B. 1985. "Role Distance, Role Closeness, and Role Neutrality of Classroom Teachers." *Sociologia Internationalis* 23(1):101–11.

Kleinman, Sherryl. 1984. "Women in Seminary: Dilemmas of Professional Socialization." *Sociology of Education* 25:210–19.

Lawson, Helene. 1999. "Working on Hair." *Qualitative Sociology* 22(3):235–57.

Lembright, Muriel and J. Riemer. 1982. "'Women Truckers' Problems and the Impact of Sponsorship." *Work and Occupations* 9:457–74.

Lewis, Linda. 1997. "Female Employment and Elite Occupations in Korea: The Case of 'Her Honor' the Judge." *Korean Studies* 21:54–71.

Lively, Kathryn. 2001. "Occupational Claims to Professionalism: The Case of Paralegals." *Symbolic Interaction* 24(3):343–66.

Macias, Thomas. 2003. "The Changing Structure of Structural Assimilation: White-Collar Mexican Ethnicity and the Significance of Ethnic Identity Professional Organizations." *Social Science Quarterly* 84(4):946–55.

Mayo, Elton. 1945. *The Human Problems of an Industrial Civilization.* Salem, NH: Ayer.

Mulcahy, Susan D. and Robert Faulkner. 1977. "Work Individuation Among Women Machine Operators." *Sociology of Work and Occupations* 4:303–25.

Murray, Susan B. 1998. "Child Care Work: Intimacy in the Shadows of Family Life." *Qualitative Sociology* 21:149–68.

Murray, Suzan B. 2000. "Getting Paid in Smiles: The Gendering of Child Care Work." *Symbolic Interaction* 23:135–60.

Molstad, Clark. 1986. "Choosing and Coping with Boring Work." *Urban Life* 15:215–236.

Perakyla, Anssi. 1991. "Hope Work in the Care of Seriously Ill Patients." *Qualitative Health Research* 1:407–33.

Podmore, D. and A. Spencer. 1982. "Women Lawyers in England: The Experience of Inequality." *Work and Occupations* 9:337–61.

Riemer, J. W. 1977. "Becoming a Journeyman Electrician: Some Implicit Indicators in the Apprenticeship Process." *Work and Occupations* 4:87–98.

Roy, Donald. 1952. "Quota Restriction and Goldbricking in a Machine Shop." *American Journal of Sociology* 57:427–43.

Roy, Donald. 1953. "Work Satisfaction and Social Reward in Quota Achievement: An Analysis of Piecework Incentive." *American Sociological Review* 18(October):507–14.

Roy, Donald F. 1959–1960. "Banana Time: Job Satisfaction and Informal Interaction." *Human Organization* 18:158–68.

Sanders, Clinton R. 1974. "Psyching Out the Crowd: Folk Performers and Their Audiences." *Urban Life and Culture* 3:264–81.

Sanders, Clinton R. 1994. "Annoying Owners: Routine Interactions with Problematic Clients in a General Veterinary Practice." *Qualitative Sociology* 17:159–70.

Stebbins, R. A. 1969. "Role Distance, Role Distance Behavior, and Jazz Musicians." *British Journal of Sociology* 20:406–15.

Stone, R. 1946. "Status and Leadership in a Combat Fighter Squadron." *American Journal of Sociology* 51:388–95.

Taylor, Frederick Winslow. 1911. *The Principles of Scientific Management.* New York: Harper and Brothers.

Thompson, William E. 1983. "Hanging Tongues: A Sociological Encounter with the Assembly Line." *Qualitative Sociology* 6:215–37.

Thorlindsson, Thorolfur. 1994. "Skipper Science: A Note on the Epistemology of Practice and the Nature of Expertise." *Sociological Quarterly* 35:329–46.

Van Maanen, John. 1973. "Observations on the Making of Policemen." *Human Organization* 32:407–17.

Van Maanen, John. 1976. "Breaking In: Socialization to Work." Pp. 67–130 in *Handbook of Work, Organization and Society,* edited by R. Dubin. Chicago, IL: Rand McNally.

Vaught, Charles and David L. Smith. 1980. "Incorporation and Mechanical Solidarity in an Underground Coal Mine." *Work and Occupations* 7:159–87.

Whyte, William Foote. 1949. "The Social Structure of the Restaurant." *American Journal of Sociology* 54:302–10.

Wilson, Robert N. 1954. "Teamwork in the Operating Room." *Human Organization* 12:9–14.

PART VI: SOCIAL DISTINCTIONS AND DIVERSITY

Chapter 22. Social Stratification

Alderson, Arthur S. and Francois Nielsen. 1999. "Income Inequality, Development, and Dependence: A Reconsideration." *American Sociological Review* 64:606–31.

Alderson, Arthur S. and Francois Nielsen. 2002. "Globalization and the Great U-Turn: Income Inequality Trends in 16 OECD Countries." *American Journal of Sociology* 107:1244–99.

Aldrich, Howard and Jane Weiss. 1981. "Differentiation within the U.S. Capitalist Class: Workforce Size and Income Differences." *American Sociological Review* 46:279–89.

Blau, Peter and Otis Dudley Duncan. 1967. *The American Occupational Structure.* New York: John Wiley.

Bollen, Kenneth A. and Stephen J. Appold. 1993. "National Industrial Structure and the Global System." *American Sociological Review* 58:283–301.

Bornschier, Volker. 1995. *Western Society in Transition.* New Brunswick, NJ: Transaction Press.

Bornschier, Volker and Christopher Chase-Dunn. 1985. *Transnational Corporations and Underdevelopment.* New York: Praeger.

Bornschier, Volker, Christopher Chase-Dunn, and Richard Rubinson. 1978. "Cross-National Evidence of the Effects of Foreign Investment and Aid on Economic Growth and Inequality: A Survey of Findings and a Reanalysis." *American Journal of Sociology* 84:651–83.

Bornschier, Volker and Thank-Huyen Ballmer-Cao. 1979. "Income Inequality: A Cross-National Study of the Relationships between MNC-Penetration, Dimensions of the Power Structure and Income Distribution." *American Sociological Review* 44:487–506.

Bourdieu, Pierre. 1984. *Distinction: A Social Critique of the Judgement of Taste.* Cambridge, MA: Harvard University Press.

Bourdieu, Pierre. 1993. *The Field of Cultural Production: Essays on Art and Leisure.* New York: Columbia University Press.

Bourdieu, Pierre. 1996. *The State Nobility.* Palo Alto, CA: Stanford University Press.

Chase-Dunn, Christopher. 1975. "The Effects of International Economic Dependence on Development and Inequality: A Cross-National Study." *American Sociological Review* 40:720–38.

Chase-Dunn, Christopher. 1989. *Global Formation: Structures of the World-Economy.* Oxford, England: Basil Blackwell.

Chirot, Daniel. 1986. *Social Change in the Modern Era.* New York: Harcourt Brace College Publishers.

Clark, Terry Nichols and Seymour Martin Lipset, eds. 2001. *The Breakdown of Class Politics: A Debate on Post-Industrial Stratification.* Washington, DC: Woodrow Wilson Center Press.

Cuber, John and William Kenkel. 1954. *Social Stratification in the United States.* New York: Appleton-Century-Crofts.

Dahrendorf, Ralf. 1959. *Class and Class Conflict in Industrial Society.* Stanford, CA: Stanford University Press.

Danziger, Sheldon H. and Robert H. Haveman, eds. 2001. *Understanding Poverty.* Cambridge, MA: Harvard University Press.

Davis, Kingsley and Wilbert Moore. 1945. "Some Principles of Stratification." *American Sociological Review* 10:242–49.

de Soysa, Indra and John R. Oneal. 1999. "Boon or Bane?: Reassessing the Productivity of Foreign Direst Investment." *American Sociological Review* 64:766–82.

DiMaggio, Paul. 1982. "Cultural Capital and School Success: The Impact of Status Culture Participation on Grades of U.S. High School Students." *American Sociological Review* 47:189–201.

DiMaggio, Paul and John Mohr. 1985. "Cultural Capital, Educational Attainment, and Marital Selection." *American Journal of Sociology* 90:1231–61.

Durkheim, Émile. 1964. *The Division of Labor in Society.* New York: Free Press.

Erikson, Robert and John H. Goldthorpe. 1992. *The Constant Flux: A Study of Class Mobility in Industrial Societies.* Oxford, England: Clarendon Press.

Esping-Anderson, G. 1990. *The Three Worlds of Welfare Capitalism.* Princeton, NJ: Princeton University Press.

Evans, G., ed. 1999. *The End of Class Politics? Class Voting in Comparative Context.* Oxford, England: Oxford University Press.

Featherman, David and Robert Hauser. 1978. *Opportunity and Change.* New York: Academic Press.

Firebaugh, Glenn. 1992. "Growth Effects of Foreign and Domestic Investment." *American Journal of Sociology* 98:105–30.

Firebaugh, Glenn. 1996. "Does Foreign Capital Harm Poor Nations? New Estimates Based on Dixon and Boswell's Measures of Capital Penetration." *American Journal of Sociology* 102:563–78.

Firebaugh, Glenn and Frank D. Beck. 1994. "Does Economic Growth Benefit the Masses? Growth, Dependence, and Welfare in the Third World." *American Sociological Review* 59:631–53.

Frank, Andre Gunder. 1969. *Capitalism and Underdevelopment in Latin America.* New York: Monthly Review Press.

Frank, Andre Gunder. 1975. *On Capitalist Underdevelopment.* Bombay, India: Oxford University Press.

Frank, Andre Gunder. 1978. *Dependent Accumulation and Underdevelopment.* New York: Monthly Review Press.

Frank, Andre Gunder. 1998. *Reorient: Global Economy in the Asian Age.* Los Angeles: University of California Press.

Gerth, Hans and C. Wright Mills. 1946. *From Max Weber: Essays in Sociology.* New York: Oxford University Press.

Giddens, Anthony. 1973. *The Class Structure of the Advanced Societies.* New York: Harper & Row.

Goodin, R. E., B. Headey, R. Muffels, and H. Dirven. 1999. *The Real Worlds of Welfare Capitalism.* Cambridge, England: Cambridge University Press.

Gordon, Milton. 1963. *Social Class in American Sociology.* New York: McGraw-Hill.

Gouldner, Alvin. 1970. *The Coming Crisis in Western Sociology.* New York: Basic Books.

Harrison, Bennett and Barry Bluestone. 1988. *The Great U-Turn: Corporate Restructuring and the Polarizing of America.* New York: Basic Books.

Herkenrath, Mark and Volker Bornschier. 2003. "Transnational Corporations in World Development—Still the Same Harmful Effects in an Increasingly Globalized World Economy?" *Journal of World System Research* 9:105–39.

Hertz, Thomas. 2004. "Rags, Riches and Race: The Intergenerational Economic Mobility of Black and White Families in the United States." Pp. 165–91 in *Unequal Chances: Family Background and Economic Success,* edited by S. Bowles, H. Gintis, and M. Osborne. New York: Russell Sage.

Hewitt, Christopher. 1977. "The Effect of Political Democracy and Social Democracy on Equality in Industrial Societies: A Cross-National Comparison." *American Sociological Review* 42:450–63.

Hout, Michael. 1988. "More Universalism, Less Structural Mobility: The American Occupational Structure in the 1980s." *American Journal of Sociology* 93:1358–400.

Hunter, Floyd. 1953. *Community Power Structure: A Study of Decision Makers.* Chapel Hill: University of North Carolina Press.

Iceland, John. 2003. *Poverty in America.* Berkeley: University of California Press.

Jackman, Robert. 1975. *Politics and Social Equality: A Comparative Analysis.* New York: John Wiley.

Jencks, Christopher, Marshall Smith, Henry Acland, Mary Jo Bane, David Cohen, Herbert Gintis, et al. 1972. *Inequality: Reassessment of the Effect of Family and Schooling in America.* New York: Harper & Row.

Jenkins, Richard. 1992. *Pierre Bourdieu: Key Sociologists.* New York: Routledge.

Kentor, Jeffery. 2001. "The Long Term Effects of Globalization on Population Growth, Inequality, and Economic Development." *Social Problems* 48(4):435–55.

Kentor, Jeffrey and Terry Boswell. 2003. "Foreign Capital Dependence and Development: A New Direction." *American Sociological Review* 68:301–13.

Kerbo, Harold. 1981. "Characteristics of the Poor: A Continuing Focus in Social Research." *Sociology and Social Research* 65:323–31.

Kerbo, Harold. 2006a. *Social Stratification and Inequality: Class and Class Conflict in Historical and Comparative Perspective,* 6th ed. New York: McGraw-Hill.

Kerbo, Harold. 2006b. *World Poverty: Global Inequality and the Modern World System.* New York: McGraw-Hill.

Kerbo, Harold and Hermann Strasser. 2000. *Modern Germany: A Society in Transition: A Volume in the Comparative Societies Series.* New York: McGraw-Hill.

Kerbo, Harold and Juan Gonzalez. 2003. "Class and Nonvoting in Comparative Perspective: Possible Causes and Consequences for the United States." *Research in Political Sociology* 12:177–98.

Kerbo, Harold R. and John A. McKinstry. 1995. *Who Rules Japan? The Inner-Circles of Economic and Political Power.* Westport, CT: Praeger.

Kingston, Paul W. 2000. *The Classless Society.* Palo Alto, CA: Stanford University Press.

LeDuc, L., R. G. Niemi, and P. Norris, ed. 1996. *Comparing Democracies: Elections and Voting in Global Perspective.* Thousand Oaks, CA: Sage.

Lenski, Gerhard. 1966. *Power and Privilege.* New York: McGraw-Hill.

Lukes, Steven. 1973. *Émile Durkheim: His Life and Work: A Historical and Critical Study.* New York: Penguin Books.

Lynd, Robert and Helen Lynd. 1929. *Middletown.* New York: Harcourt Brace Jovanovich.

Lynd, Robert and Helen Lynd. 1937. *Middletown in Transition.* New York: Harcourt Brace Jovanovich.

Marx, Karl and Frederick Engles. 1964. *The Communist Manifesto.* New York: Verso.

Mills, C. Wright. 1956. *The Power Elite.* New York: Oxford University Press.

Mishel, Lawrence, Jared Bernstein, and John Schmitt. 1999. *The State of Working America, 1998–99.* Ithaca, NY: Cornell University Press.

Morgan, Laurie A. 1998. "Glass-Ceiling Effect or Cohort Effect? A Longitudinal Study of the Gender Earnings Gap for Engineers, 1982–1989." *American Sociological Review* 63:479–83.

Nolan, Patrick D. 1983. "Status in the World System, Income Inequality, and Economic Growth." *American Journal of Sociology* 89:410–19.

Page, Charles H. 1969. *Class and American Sociology.* New York: Schocken Books.

Pease, John, William Form, and Joan Huber. 1970. "Ideological Currents in American Stratification Literature." *American Sociologist* 5:127–37.

Perrucci, Robert and Earl Wysong. 2003. *The New Class Society: Goodbye American Dream?* 2d ed. New York: Rowman & Littlefield.

Pfautz, Harold. 1953. "The Current Literature on Social Stratification: Critique and Bibliography." *American Journal of Sociology* 58:391–418.

Pressman, Steven. 2001. "The Decline of the Middle Class: An International Perspective." Working Paper No. 280, Luxembourg Income Study, Luxembourg.

Rank, Mark Robert. 2004. *One Nation, Underprivileged: Why American Poverty Affects Us All.* New York: Oxford University Press.

Rubinson, Richard. 1976. "The World Economy and the Distribution of Income within States: A Cross-National Study." *American Sociological Review* 41:638–59.

Skocpol, Theda. 1979. *States and Social Revolutions: A Comparative Analysis of France, Russia, and China.* New York: Cambridge University Press.

Skocpol, Theda and Edwin Amenta. 1985. "Did Capitalists Shape Social Security?" *American Sociological Review* 50:572–75.

Smeeding, Timothy M. 1997. "Financial Poverty in Developed Countries: The Evidence from LIS." Working Paper No. 155, Luxembourg Income Study, Luxembourg.

Smeeding, Timothy M., Lee Rainwater, and Gary Burtless. 2001. "United States Poverty in a Cross-National Context." Pp. 162–89 in *Understanding Poverty,* edited by S. H. Danziger and R. H. Haveman. New York: Russell Sage.

Snyder, David and Edward Kick. 1979. "Structural Position in the World System and Economic Growth, 1955–1970: A Multiple Analysis of Transnational Interactions." *American Journal of Sociology* 84:1096–128.

Solon, Gary. 1992. "Intergenerational Income Mobility in the United States." *American Economic Review* 82:393–408.

Stack, Steven. 1978a. "The Effect of Direct Government Involvement in the Economy on the Degree of Income Inequality: A Cross-National Study." *American Sociological Review* 43:880–88.

Stack, Steven. 1978b. "Internal Political Organization and the World Economy of Income Inequality." *American Sociological Review* 42:271–72.

Stokes, Randall and David Jaffee. 1982. "Another Look at the Export of Raw Materials and Economic Growth." *American Sociological Review* 47:402–07.

Strasser, Hermann. 1976. *The Normative Structure of Sociology: Conservative and Emancipatory Themes in Social Thought.* London, England: Routledge & Kegan Paul.

Thernstrom, Stephen. 1964. *Poverty and Progress: Social Mobility in a Nineteenth Century City.* Cambridge, MA: Harvard University Press.

Thelen, Kathleen A. 1991. *Union of Parts: Labor Politics in Postwar Germany.* Ithaca, NY: Cornell University Press.

Treiman, Donald J. 1977. *Occupational Prestige in Comparative Perspective.* New York: Academic Press.

Turner, Lowell. 1991. *Democracy at Work: Changing World Markets and the Future of Labor Unions.* Ithaca, NY: Cornell University Press.

U.S. Bureau of the Census. 2004. *Income, Poverty, and Heath Insurance Coverage in the United States, 2003.* Washington, DC: Government Printing Office (www.census.gov).

Wallerstein, Immanual. 1974. *The Modern World-System.* New York: Academic Press.

Wallerstein, Immanual. 1977. "How Do We Know Class Struggle When We See It?" *Insurgent Sociologist* 7:104–106.

Wallerstein, Immanual. 1980. *The Modern World-System II: Mercantilism and the Consolidation of the European World Economy, 1600–1750.* New York: Academic Press.

Wallerstein, Immanual. 1989. *The Modern World-System III: The Second Era of Great Expansion of the Capitalist World-Economy, 1730–1840s.* New York: Academic Press.

Wallerstein, Immanual. 1999. *The End of the World As We Know It: Social Science for the Twenty-First Century.* Minneapolis: University of Minnesota Press.

Warner, W. Lloyd and Paul S. Lunt. 1941. *The Social Life of a Modern Community.* Yankee City Series, Vol. 1. New Haven, CT: Yale University Press.

Warner, W. Lloyd, and Paul S. Lunt. 1942. *The Status System of a Modern Community.* Yankee City Series, Vol. 2. New Haven, CT: Yale University Press.

Warner, W. Lloyd and Leo Srole. 1949. *The Social Systems of American Ethnic Groups.* Yankee City Series, Vol. 3. New Haven, CT: Yale University Press.

Weede, Erich. 1980. "Beyond Misspecification in Sociological Analysis of Income Inequality." *American Sociological Review* 45:497–501.

Western, Mark and Erik Olin Wright. 1994. "The Permeability of Class Boundaries to Intergenerational Mobility among Men in the United States, Canada, Norway, and Sweden." *American Sociological Review,* 59:606–29.

World Bank. 2000. *World Development Report.* New York: Oxford University Press.

Wright, Erik Olin. 1978a. *Class, Crisis and the State.* New York: Schocken Books.

Wright, Erik Olin. 1978b. "Race, Class, and Income Inequality." *American Journal of Sociology* 83:1368–88.

Wright, Erik Olin. 1997. *Class Counts: Comparative Studies in Class Analysis.* Cambridge, England: Cambridge University Press.

Wright, Erik Olin and Donmoon Cho. 1992. "The Relative Permeability of Class Boundaries to Cross-Class Friendships: A Comparative Study of the United States, Canada, Sweden, and Norway." *American Sociological Review* 57:85–102.

Wright, Erik Olin, Cynthia Costello, David Hachen, and Joey Sprague. 1982. "The American Class Structure." *American Sociological Review* 47:709–26.

Wright, Erik Olin and Bill Martin. 1987. "The Transformation of the American Class Structure, 1960–1980." *American Sociological Review* 93:1–29.

Wrong, Dennis. 1959. "The Functional Theory of Stratification: Some Neglected Considerations." *American Sociological Review* 24:772–82.

Wrong, Dennis. 1964. "Social Inequality without Social Stratification." *Canadian Review of Sociology and Anthropology* 1:5–16.

Zeitlin, Irving M. 1968. *Ideology and the Development of Sociological Theory.* Englewood Cliffs, NJ: Prentice Hall.

Chapter 23. The Sociology of Racial and Ethnic Relations

American Anthropological Association. 1998. *American Anthropological Association Statement on Race.* Arlington, VA: American Anthropological Association.

American Sociological Association. 2002. *Statement of the American Sociological Association on the Importance of Collecting Data and Doing Social Scientific Research on Race.* Washington, DC: American Sociological Association.

Blank, Rebecca. 2001. "An Overview of Trends in Social and Economic Well-Being, by Race." Pp. 21–39 in *America Becoming: Racial Trends and their Consequences,* vol. 1, edited by N. Smelser, W. J. Wilson, and F. Mitchell. Washington, DC: National Academy Press.

Blauner, Robert. 1972. *Racial Oppression in America.* New York: Harper & Row.

Bobo, Lawrence D. 2001. "Racial Attitudes and Relations at the Close of the Twentieth Century." Pp. 264–301 in *America Becoming: Racial Trends and Their Consequences,* vol. 1, edited by N. Smelser, W. J. Wilson, and F. Mitchell. Washington, DC: National Academy Press.

Carmichael, Stokely and Charles Hamilton. 1967. *Black Power: The Politics of Liberation in America.* New York: Random House.

Coleman. 1966. *Equality of Educational Opportunity.* Washington, DC: Department of Health, Education, and Welfare.

Coleman, James, Sarah Kelly, and John Moore. 1975. *Trends in School Segregation.* Washington, DC: Urban Institute.

Cox, Oliver C. 1948. *Caste, Class, and Race: A Study in Social Dynamics.* New York: Doubleday.

Davis, Allison, Burleigh Gardner, and Mary Gardner. 1941. *Deep South: A Social Anthropological Study of Caste and Class.* Chicago, IL: University of Chicago Press.

Denton, Nancy and Douglas Massey. 1989. "Residential Segregation of Blacks, Hispanics, and Asians by Socioeconomic Status and Gender." *Social Science Quarterly* 69:797–818.

Dollard, John. 1937. *Caste and Class in a Southern Town.* New Haven, CT: Yale University Press.

Farley, Reynolds. 1977. "Residential Segregation in Urbanized Areas of the U.S. in 1970: An Analysis of Social Class and Racial Differences." *Demography* 14:497–518.

Featherman, David and Robert Hauser. 1976. "Changes in the Socio-Economic Stratification of the Races, 1962–1973." *American Journal of Sociology* 82:621–49.

Fraser, Steven, ed. 1995. *The Bell Curve Wars: Race, Intelligence, and the Future of America.* New York: Basic Books.

Gans, Herbert. 1979. "Symbolic Ethnicity: The Future of Ethnic Groups and Cultures in America." *Ethnic and Racial Studies* 2(1):1–21.

Glazer, Nathan and Daniel Patrick Moynihan. 1970. *Beyond the Melting Pot: The Negroes, Puerto Ricans, Jews, Italians, and Irish of New York City.* Cambridge: MIT Press.

Gordon, Milton. 1964. *Assimilation in American Life.* New York: Oxford University Press.

Greeley, Andrew. 1974. *Ethnicity in the United States.* New York: John Wiley.

Hacker, Andrew. 1992. *Two Nations: Black and White, Separate, Hostile, Unequal.* New York: Ballantine Books.

Herrnstein, Richard and Charles Murray. 1994. *The Bell Curve: Intelligence and Class Structure in American Life.* New York: Free Press.

Iceland, John, Daniel Weinberg, and Erika Steinmetz. 2002. "Racial and Ethnic Segregation in the United States, 1980–2000." U.S. Census Bureau. Special Report Series, CENSR #3.

Jacoby, Russell and Naomi Glauberman, eds. 1995. *The Bell Curve Debate: History, Documents, Opinions.* New York: Times Books.

Kerbo, Harold. 2006. *Social Stratification and Inequality.* 6th ed. New York: McGraw-Hill.

Kluegal, James R. 1990. "Trends in Whites' Explanations of the Black-White Gap in Socioeconomic Status, 1977–1989." *American Sociological Review* 55:512–25.

Kluegal, James R. and Eliot R. Smith. 1986. *Beliefs about Inequality: Americans Views of What Is and What Ought to Be.* New York: Aldine de Gruyter.

Lieberson, Stanley. 1980. *A Piece of the Pie: Blacks and White Immigrants Since 1880.* Berkeley: University of California Press.

Lyman, Stanford. 1972. *The Black American in Sociological Thought: A Failure of Perspective.* New York: Capricorn Books.

MacIver, Robert M. 1948. *The More Perfect Union: A Program for the Control of Inter-Group Discrimination in the United States.* New York: Macmillan.

Massey, Douglas. 2001. "Residential Segregation and Neighborhood Conditions in U.S. Metropolitan Areas." Pp. 391–434 in *America Becoming: Racial Trends and Their Consequences,* vol. 1, edited by N. Smelser, W. J. Wilson, and F. Mitchell. Washington, DC: National Academy Press.

Massey, Douglas and Nancy Denton. 1993. *American Apartheid: Segregation and the Making of the Underclass.* Cambridge, MA: Harvard University Press.

McKee, James B. 1993. *Sociology and the Race Problem: The Failure of a Perspective.* Urbana: University of Illinois Press.

Merton, Robert. 1949. "Discrimination and the American Creed." Pp. 99–126 in *Discrimination and the National Welfare,* edited by R. W. MacIver. New York: Harper.

Moskos, Charles C. and John Sibley Butler. 1996. *All That We Can Be: Black Leadership and Racial Integration the Army Way.* New York: Basic Books.

Moynihan, Daniel P. 1965. *The Negro Family: The Case for National Action.* Washington, DC: Government Printing Office.

Myrdal, Gunnar. 1944. *An American Dilemma: The Negro Problem in Modern Democracy.* New York: Harper & Row.

National Advisory Commission on Civil Disorders. 1968. *Report of the National Advisory Commission on Civil Disorders.* New York. Bantam Books.

Oliver, Melvin and Thomas Shapiro. 1995. *Black Wealth/White Wealth: A New Perspective on Racial Inequality.* New York: Routledge.

Omi, Michael and Howard Winant. 1986. *Racial Formation in the United States: From the 1960s to the 1980s.* New York: Routledge & Kegan Paul.

Orfield, Gary. 2001. "Schools More Separate: Consequences of a Decade of Resegregation." Civil Rights Project, Harvard University.

Park, Robert E. 1930. "Social Assimilation." Pp. 281–83 in *Encyclopedia of the Social Sciences,* edited by E. R. A. Seligman and A. Johnson. New York: Macmillan.

Park, Robert E. [1939] 1950. "The Nature of Race Relations." Pp. 81–116 in *Collected Papers of Robert Ezra Park,* vol. 1, *Race and Culture,* edited by R. E. Park. Glencoe, IL: Free Press.

Pettigrew, Thomas F. and Kurt W. Back. 1967. "Sociology in the Desegregation Process: Its Use and Disuse." Pp. 692–724 in *The Uses of Sociology,* edited by P. Lazersfeld, W. Sewell, and H. Wilensky. New York: Basic Books.

Rainwater, Lee. 1967. *The Moynihan Report and the Politics of Controversy.* Cambridge: MIT Press.

Schuman, Howard, Charlotte Steeh, Lawrence Bobo, and Maria Krysan. 1997. *Racial Attitudes in America: Trends and Interpretations.* Rev. ed. Cambridge, MA: Harvard University Press.

Smith, James P. 2001. "Race and Ethnicity in the Labor Market: Trends Over the Short and Long Term." Pp. 52–97 in *America Becoming: Racial Trends and Their Consequences,* vol. 2, edited by N. Smelser, W. J. Wilson, and F. Mitchell. Washington, DC: National Academy Press.

Steinberg, Stephen. 1989. *The Ethnic Myth: Race, Ethnicity, and Class in America.* Boston, MA: Beacon Press.

Taeuber, Karl and Alma Taeuber. 1965. *Negroes in Cities: Residential Segregation and Neighborhood Change.* Chicago, IL: Aldine.

Van den Berghe, Pierre L. 1967. *Race and Racism: A Comparative Perspective.* New York: John Wiley.

Warner, W. Lloyd. 1936. "American Caste and Class." *American Journal of Sociology* 42:234–37.

Willie, Charles V. 1979. *The Caste and Class Controversy.* Dix Hills, NY: General Hall.

Willie, Charles V. 1995. "The Relativity of Genotypes and Phenotypes." *Journal of Negro Education* 64(3):267–76.

Wilson, Frank Harold. 1995. "For Whom Does the Bell Toll: Meritocracy, the Cognitive Elite, and the Continuing Significance of Race in Postindustrial America." *Journal of Negro Education* 64(3):253–66.

Wilson, Franklin, Marta Tienda, and Lawrence Wu. 1995. "Race and Unemployment: Labor Market Experiences of Black and White Men, 1968–1988." *Work and Occupations* 22(3):245–70.

Wilson, William Julius. 1978. *The Declining Significance of Race: Blacks and Changing American Institutions.* Chicago, IL: University of Chicago Press.

Wilson, William Julius. 1987. *The Truly Disadvantaged: The Inner City, the Underclass, and Public Policy.* Chicago, IL: University of Chicago Press.

Wilson, William Julius. 1996. *When Work Disappears: The World of the New Urban Poor.* New York: Alfred A. Knopf.

Wirth, Louis. 1928. *The Ghetto.* Chicago, IL: University of Chicago Press.

Yinger, John. 1998. "Housing Discrimination Is Still Worth Worrying About." *Housing Policy Debate* 9(4):893–928.

Young, Donald. 1932. *American Minority Peoples: A Study of Racial and Cultural Conflict in the United States.* New York: Harper.

Chapter 24. The Sociology of Gender

Acker, Joan. 1973. "Women and Social Stratification: A Case of Intellectual Sexism." *American Journal of Sociology* 78:936–45.

Balbus, Isaac. 1982. *Marxism and Domination: A Neo-Hegelian, Feminist, Psychoanalytic Theory of Sexual, Political and Technological Liberation.* Princeton, NJ: Princeton University Press.

Barash, David. 1977. *Sociobiology and Behavior.* New York: Elsevier.

Barrett, Michele. 1980. *Women's Oppression Today: Problems in Marxist Feminist Analysis.* London, England: Verso.

Bhavnani, Kum-Kum, ed. 2001. *Feminism and Race.* New York: Oxford University Press.

Blackwood, Evelyn. 1994. "Sexuality and Gender in Certain Native American Tribes: The Case of Cross-Gender Females." Pp. 301–15 in *Theorizing Feminism: Parallel Trends in the Humanities and Social Sciences,* edited by A. C. Herrman and A. J. Stewart. Boulder, CO: Westview Press.

Bordo, Susan. 1989. "The Cartesian Masculinization of Thought." *Signs* 11:439–56.

Boston Women's Health Book Collective. 1971. *Our Bodies, Ourselves.* New York: Simon & Schuster.

Braidotti, R. 1991. *Patterns of Dissonance.* Translated by E. Gould. Oxford, England: Polity Press.

Brod, Harry. 1987. *The Making of Masculinities.* Boston, MA: Unwin Hyman.

Brown, Wendy. 2003. "Gender in Counterpoint." *Feminist Theory* 4:365–68.

Butler, Judith. 1990. *Gender Trouble: Feminism and the Subversion of Identity.* New York: Routledge.

Butler, Judith. 1993. *Bodies That Matter.* New York: Routledge.

Butler, Judith and Joan W. Scott, eds. 1992. *Feminists Theorize the Political.* New York: Routledge.

Chafetz, Janet Saltzman. 1999. "The Varieties of Gender Theory in Sociology." Pp. 3–23 in *The Handbook of the Sociology of Gender,* edited by J. S. Chafetz. New York: Kluwer Academic/Plenum.

Chodorow, Nancy. 1978. *The Reproduction of Mothering.* Berkeley: University of California Press.

Clough, Patricia Ticineto. 2003. "Affect and Control: Rethinking the Body 'Beyond Sex and Gender.'" *Feminist Theory* 4:359–64.

Collins, Patricia Hill. 1990. *Black Feminist Thought.* Cambridge, England: Unwin.

Connell, R. W. 1987. *Gender and Power: Society, the Person and Sexual Politics.* Stanford, CA: Stanford University Press.

Connell, R. W. 2002. *Gender.* Cambridge, England: Polity Press.

Coontz, Stephanie and Peta Henderson. 1986. *Women's Work, Men's Property: The Origins of Gender and Class.* London, England: Verso.

Coward, Rosalind. 1983. *Patriarchal Precedents: Sexuality and Social Relations.* London, England: Routledge & Kegan Paul.

David, Deborah and Robert Brannon, eds. 1976. *The Forty-Nine Percent Majority.* Reading, MA: Addison-Wesley.

Dawkins, Richard. 1976. *The Selfish Gene.* Oxford, England: Oxford University Press.

Delphy, Christine. 1984. *Close to Home.* London, England: Hutchinson, in association with the Explorations in Feminism Collective.

Diamond, Irene and Lee Quinby, eds. 1988. *Feminism and Foucault: Reflections of Resistance.* Boston, MA: Northeastern University Press.

Dinnerstein, Dorothy. 1977. *The Mermaid and the Minotaur.* New York: Harper & Row.

Diprose, Rosalyn. 1994. *The Bodies of Women.* London, England: Routledge.

DuCille, Ann. 1994. "Occult of True Black Womanhood: Critical Demeanor and Black Feminist Studies." *Signs* 19:7591–629.

Durkheim, Émile. [1897] 1951. *Suicide: A Study in Sociology.* New York: Free Press.

Durkheim, Émile. [1893] 1984. *The Division of Labour in Society.* Translated by W. D. Halls. London, England: Macmillan.

Eichler, Margrit. 1980. *The Double Standard: A Feminist Critique of Feminist Social Science.* New York: St. Martin's Press.

Eisenstein, Zillah, ed. 1979. *Capitalist Patriarchy and the Case for Socialist Feminism.* New York: Monthly Review Press.

Elshtain, Jean B. 1982. *Public Man, Private Woman.* Princeton, NJ: Princeton University Press.

Engels, Friedrich. 1935. *Socialism: Utopian and Scientific.* New York: International Publishers.

Epstein, Steven. 1994. "A Queer Encounter: Sociology and the Study of Sexuality." *Sociological Theory* 12:188–202.

Farrell, Warren. 1975. *The Liberated Man.* New York: Random House.

Fausto-Sterling, Anne. 2005. "The Bare Bones of Sex: Part 1: Sex and Gender." *Signs* 30:1491–527.

Felski, Rita. 1997. "The Doxa of Difference." *Signs* 23:1–21.

Ferree, Myra, Judith Lorber, and Beth B. Hess, eds. 1999. *Revisioning Gender.* Thousand Oaks, CA: Sage.

Findlay, Deborah. 1995. "Discovering Sex: Medical Science, Feminism and Intersexuality." *Canadian Review of Sociology and Anthropology* 32:25–52.

Firestone, Shulamith. 1970. *The Dialectic of Sex.* New York: Bantam Books.

Foucault, Michel. 1976. *The History of Sexuality.* Vol. 1, *An Introduction.* New York: Vintage Books.

Foucault, Michel. 1980. *Power/Knowledge: Selected Interviews and Other Writings, 1971–1977.* Brighton, England: Harvester.

Fox, Bonnie. 1980. *Hidden in the Household.* Toronto, Ontario, Canada: Women's Press.

Fox Keller, Evelyn. 1989. "Holding the Center of Feminist Theory." *Women's Studies International Forum* 12:313–18.

Fraser, Nancy. 1989. *Unruly Practices: Power, Discourse, and Gender in Contemporary Social Theory.* Minneapolis: University of Minnesota Press.

Fraser, Nancy and Nancy A. Naples. 2003. "To Interpret the World and to Change It: An Interview with Nancy Fraser." *Signs* 29:1103–24.

Friedan, Betty. 1963. *The Feminine Mystique.* New York: Dell.

Giddens, Anthony. 1973. *The Class Structure of Advanced Societies.* London, England: Hutchinson.

Glenn, Evelyn Nakano. 1992. "From Servitude to Service Work: Historical Continuities in the Racial Division of Paid Reproductive Labor." *Signs* 18:1–43.

Gordon, Linda. 1994. *Pitied but Not Entitled: Single Mothers and the History of Welfare 1890–1935.* New York: Free Press.

Haraway, Donna J. 1991. *Simians, Cyborgs, and Women: The Reinvention of Nature.* New York: Routledge.

Hawkesworth, Mary. 1997. "Confounding Gender." *Signs* 22:649–85.

Hawkesworth, Mary. 2004. "The Semiotics of Premature Burial: Feminism in a Postfeminist Age." *Signs* 29:961–86.

Hearn, Jeff. 2004. "From Hegemonic Masculinity to the Hegemony of Men." *Feminist Theory* 5:49–72.

Hess, Beth B. and Myra M. Ferree, eds. 1987. *Analyzing Gender: A Handbook of Social Science Research.* Newbury Park, CA: Sage.

Heyes, Cressida. 2003. "Feminist Solidarity after Queer Theory: The Case of Transgender." *Signs* 28: 1093–120.

Hird, Myra. 2000. "Gender's Nature: Intersexuals, Transexualism and the 'Sex'/'Gender' Binary." *Feminist Theory* 1:347–64.

Hird, Myra. 2003. "Considerations for a Psycho-Analytic Theory of Gender Identity and Sexual Desire: The Case of Intersex." *Signs* 28:1067–1092.

Hird, Myra. 2004. *Sex, Gender and Science.* New York: Palgrave Macmillan.

Hirsch, Marianne. 1981. "Mothers and Daughters." *Signs* 7:200–22.

hooks, bell. 1981. *Ain't I a Woman: Black Women and Feminism.* Boston, MA: South End Press.

Huber, Joan. 2004. "Lenski Effects on Sex Stratification Theory." *Sociological Theory* 22:258–68.

Ingram, Chrys. 1994. "The Heterosexual Imaginary: Feminist Sociology and Theories of Gender." *Sociological Theory* 12:203–19.

Irigaray, L. 1974. *Speculum of the Other Woman.* Translated by G. C. Gill. New York: Cornell University Press.

Kessler, S. 1990. "The Medical Construction of Gender: Case Management of Intersex Infants." *Signs* 16:3–26.

Kessler, S. 1998. *Lessons from the Intersexed.* New Brunswick, NJ: Rutgers University Press.

Kimmel, Michael S. and Michael A. Messner. 1989. *Men's Lives.* New York: Macmillan.

Knaak, Stephanie. 2004. "On the Reconceptualizing of Gender: Implications for Research Design." *Sociological Inquiry* 74:302–17.

Kristeva, J. 1986. *The Kristeva Reader.* Edited by T. Moi. Oxford, England: Basil Blackwell.

Kuhn, A. and A Wolpe, eds. 1978. *Feminism and Materialism.* London, England: Routledge & Kegan Paul.

Laqueur, T. 1990. *Making Sex: Body and Gender from the Greeks to Freud.* Cambridge, MA: Harvard University Press.

Lerner, Gerda. 1986. *The Creation of Patriarchy.* Oxford, England: Oxford University Press.

Lorber, Judith. 1981. "On the Reproduction of Mothering: A Methodological Debate." *Signs* 6:482–514.

Lovell, Terry. 1996. "Feminist Social Theory." Pp. 307–39 in *The Blackwell Companion to Social Theory,* edited by B. S. Turner. Oxford, England: Blackwell.

Lowe, Marian and Ruth Hubbard, eds. 1983. *Woman's Nature: Rationalizations of Inequality.* New York: Pergamon.

Luxton, Meg. 1980. *More Than a Labour of Love.* Toronto, Ontario, Canada: Women's Press.

Maccoby, Eleanor E. and Carol N. Jacklin. 1975. *The Psychology of Sex Differences.* Stanford, CA: Stanford University Press.

MacKinnon, Catherine. 1982. "Feminism, Marxism, Method, and the State: An Agenda for Theory." *Signs* 7:515–44.

Marcus, Sharon. 2005. "Queer Theory for Everyone: A Review Essay." *Signs* 31:191–218.

Marshall, Barbara. 1994. *Engendering Modernity: Feminism, Social Theory and Social Change.* Boston, MA: Polity Press/Northeastern University Press.

Marshall, Barbara. 2000. *Configuring Gender: Explorations in Theory and Politics.* Peterborough, Ontario, Canada: Broadview Press.

Mihesuah, Devon A. 2000. "A Few Cautions at the Millennium on the Merging of Feminist Studies with American Indian Women's Studies." *Signs* 25:1247–51.

Millet, Kate. 1970. *Sexual Politics.* Garden City, NY: Doubleday.

Mitchell, Juliet. 1973. *Women's Estate.* New York: Vintage Books.

Mitchell, Juliet. 1975. *Psychoanalysis and Feminism.* New York: Vintage Books.

Modleski, Tania. 1991. *Feminism without Women.* London, England: Routledge.

Mohanty, Chandra Talpade. 1992. "Feminist Encounters: Locating the Politics of Experience." Pp. 74–92 in *Destabilizing Theory,* edited by M. Barrett and A. Phillips. Cambridge, England: Polity Press.

Money, J. and A. A. Ehrhardt. 1972. *Man and Woman, Boy and Girl.* Baltimore, MD: John Hopkins University Press.

Namaste, Ki. 1994. "The Politics of Inside/Out: Queer Theory, Poststructuralism and a Sociological Approach to Sexuality." *Sociological Theory* 12:220–31.

Nicholson, Linda. 1994. "Interpreting Gender." *Signs* 20:79–105.

Oakley, Ann. 1974. *The Sociology of Housework.* New York: Pantheon Books.

O'Brien, Mary. 1981. "Feminist Theory and Dialectical Logic." *Signs* 7:144–57.

O'Neill, John. 1985. *Five Bodies: The Human Shape of Modern Society.* Ithaca, NY: Cornell University Press.

Overall, C. 1989. *The Future of Human Reproduction.* Toronto, Ontario, Canada: Woman's Press.

Pareto, Vilfredo. [1916] 1935. *The Mind and Society.* Vol. 2. London, England: Jonathan Cape.

Parsons, Talcott. [1942] 1954. *Essays in Sociological Theory.* Glencoe, IL: Free Press.

Parsons, Talcott and Robert Bales. 1955. *Family, Socialization and Interaction Process.* New York: Free Press.

Pateman, Carole. 1988. *The Sexual Contract.* Cambridge, England: Polity Press.

Petchesky, Rosalind Pollack. 1980. "Reproductive Freedom: Beyond a Woman's Right to Choose." *Signs* 5:661–85.

Pleck, Joseph. 1981. *The Myth of Masculinity.* Cambridge: MIT Press.

Pringle, R. and S. Watson. 1992. "'Women's Interests' and the Poststructural State." Pp. 53–73 in *Destabilizing Theory,* edited by M. Barrett and A. Phillips. Stanford, CA: Stanford University Press.

Ramazanoglu, Caroline, ed. 1993. *Up against Foucault.* London, England: Routledge.

Rattansi, Ali. 1995. "Just Framing: Ethnicities and Racisms in a 'Postmodern' Framework." Pp. 250–86 in *Social Postmodernism,* edited by L. Nicholson and S. Seidman. Cambridge, England: Cambridge University Press.

Ricci, N. P. 1987. "The End/s of Woman." *Canadian Journal of Political and Social Theory* 11:11–27.

Rich, Adrienne. 1980. "Compulsory Heterosexuality and Lesbian Existence." *Signs* 5:631–60.

Rose, Jacqueline. 1986. *Sexuality in the Field of Vision.* London, England: Verso.

Rubin, Gayle. 1975. "The Traffic in Women: Notes on the 'Political Economy' of Sex." Pp. 157–210 in *Toward an Anthropology of Women,* edited by R. R. Reiter. New York: Monthly Review Press.

Sargent, Lydia, ed. 1981. *Women and Revolution.* Montreal, Québec, Canada: Black Rose Books.

Sawicki, Jana. 1999. "Disciplining Mothers: Feminism and the New Reproductive Technologies." Pp. 190–202 in *Feminist Theory and the Body,* edited by J. Price and M. Shildrick. Edinburgh, Scotland: Edinburgh University Press.

Sawicki, Jana. 1991. *Disciplining Foucault.* New York: Routledge.

Sayers, Janet. 1982. *Biological Politics.* London, England: Tavistock.

Schiebinger, L. 1993. *Nature's Body.* London, England: Pandora.

Scott, Joan. 1997. "Comment on Hawkesworth's 'Confounding Gender.'" *Signs* 22:697–702.

Seccombe, Wally. 1974. "The Housewife and Her Labor under Capitalism." *New Left Review* 83:3–34.

Sedgwick, Eva Kosofsky. 1990. *Epistemology of the Closet.* Berkeley: University of California Press.

Seidman, Steven. 1994. "Symposium: Queer Theory/Sociology: A Dialogue." *Sociological Theory* 12:166–77.

Shildrick, M. and J. Price, eds. 1998. *Vital Signs.* Edinburgh, Scotland: Edinburgh University Press.

Shildrick, M. 2004. "Genetics, Normativity and Ethics." *Feminist Theory* 5:149–65.

Smith, Barbara, ed. 1983. *Home Girls: A Black Feminist Anthology.* New York: Kitchen Table, Women of Color Press.

Smith, Dorothy. 1987. *The Everyday World as Problematic: A Feminist Sociology.* Toronto, Ontario, Canada: University of Toronto Press.

Smith, Dorothy. 2002. "Forward." Pp. ix–xii in *Doing Gender, Doing Difference,* edited by S. Fenstermaker and C. West. New York: Routledge.

Spelman, Elizabeth. 1988. *Inessential Woman: Problems of Exclusion in Feminist Thought.* Boston, MA: Beacon Press.

Spencer, Herbert. [1899] 1969. *The Principles of Sociology.* Vol. 3. New York: Macmillan.

Spivak, Gayatri Chakravorty. 1988. "Can the Subaltern Speak?" Pp. 271–313 in *Marxism and the Interpretation of Culture,* edited by C. Nelson and L. Grossberg. Urbana: University of Illinois Press.

Stacy, J. and B. Thorne. 1985. "The Missing Feminist Revolution in Sociology." *Social Problems* 32:301–16.

Stacy, J. and B. Thorne. 1996. "Is Sociology Still Missing Its Feminist Revolution?" *Perspectives: The ASA Theory Section Newsletter* 18:1–3.

Stoller, Robert. 1968. *Sex and Gender: On the Development of Masculinity and Femininity.* New York: Science House.

Sydie, R. A. 1987. *Natural Women, Cultured Men: A Feminist Perspective on Sociological Theory.* Toronto, Ontario, Canada: Methuen.

Thistle, Susan. 2000. "The Trouble with Modernity: Gender and the Remaking of Social Theory." *Sociological Theory* 18:275–88.

Walby, Sylvia. 1990. *Theorizing Patriarchy.* Oxford, England: Basil Blackwell.

Walton, Jean. 2001. *Fair Sex, Savage Dreams: Race, Psychoanalysis, Sexual Difference.* Durham, NC: Duke University Press.

Weber, Max. [1925] 1978. *Economy and Society.* Vol. 2, edited by G. Roth and C. Wittich. Berkeley: University of California Press.

Weber, Max. [1915] 1946. "Religious Rejections of the World and Their Directions." Pp. 323–59 in *From Max Weber: Essays in Sociology,* edited by H. Gerth and C. Wright Mills. New York: Oxford University Press.

West, Candace and Don Zimmerman. 1987. "Doing Gender." *Gender and Society* 1:125–51.

Wilson, Edward O. 1975. *Sociobiology: The New Synthesis.* Cambridge, MA: Harvard University Press.

Yeatman, Anna. 1986. "Women, Domestic Life and Sociology." Pp. 157–72 in *Feminist Challenges: Social and Political Theory,* edited by C. Pateman and E. Gross. Sydney, Australia: Allen & Unwin.

Young, Iris. 1981. "Beyond the Unhappy Marriage: A Critique of Dual Systems Theory." Pp. 43–69 in *Women and Revolution,* edited by L. Sargent. Montreal, Québec, Canada: Black Rose Books.

Young, Iris. 1994. "Gender as Seriality: Thinking about Women as a Social Collective." *Signs* 19:713–39.

Chapter 25. The Sociology of Sexuality

Amato, Paul. 2001. "The Consequences of Divorce for Children and Adults." Pp. 488–506 in *Understanding Families into the New Millennium: A Decade in Review,* edited by R. M. Milardo. Minneapolis, MN: National Council on Family Relations.

Andsager, Julie and Kimberly Roe. 2003. "'What's Your Definition of Dirty, Baby?' Sex in Music Video." *Sexuality and Culture* 7:79–97.

Bancroft, John, Debra Herbenick, and Meredith Reynolds. 2003. "Masturbation as a Marker of Sexual Development; Two Studies 50 Years Apart." Pp. 156–85 in *Sexual Development in Childhood,* edited by J. Bancroft. Bloomington: Indiana University Press.

Barak, Azy, William A. Fisher, Sandra Belfry, and Darryl R. Lashambe. 1999. "Sex, Guys, and Cyberspace: Effects of Internet Pornography and Individual Difference on Men's Attitudes towards Women." *Journal of Psychology and Human Sexuality* 11:63–91.

Barron, Martin and Michael Kimmel. 2000. "Sexual Violence in Three Pornographic Media: Toward a Sociological Explanation." *Journal of Sex Research* 37:161–68.

Berger, Peter and Thomas Luckmann. 1966. *The Social Construction of Reality.* New York: Doubleday.

Blumstein, P. and P. Schwartz. 1983. *American Couples.* New York: Morrow.

Bogaert, Anthony. 2004. "Asexuality: Prevalence and Associated Factors in a National Probability Sample." *Journal of Sex Research* 41:279–87.

Buss, David M. 1998. "Sexual Strategies Theory: Historical Origins and Current Status." *Journal of Sex Research* 35:19–31.

Bussey, K. and A. Bandura. 1999. "Social Cognitive Theory of Gender Development and Differentiation." *Psychological Review* 106:676–713.

Byers, Sandra E. 2005. "Relationship Satisfaction and Sexual Satisfaction: A Longitudinal Study of Individuals in Long-Term Relationships." *Journal of Sex Research* 42:113–18.

Collins, W. A. and L. A. Sroufe. 1999. "Capacity for Intimate Relationships: A Developmental Construction." Pp. 125–47 in *The Development of Romantic Relationships in Adolescence,* edited by W. Furman, B. B. Brown, and C. Feiring. Cambridge, England: Cambridge University Press.

Connolly, Jennifer, Wendy Craig, Adele Goldberg, and Debra Pepler. 2004. "Mixed-Gender Groups, Dating, and Romantic Relationships in Early Adolescence." *Journal of Research on Adolescence* 14:185–207.

Crawford, Mary and Danielle Popp. 2003. "Sexual Double Standards: A Review and Methodological Critique of Two Decades of Research." *Journal of Sex Research* 40:12–26.

Day, R. 1992. "The Transition to First Intercourse among Racially and Culturally Diverse Youth." *Journal of Marriage and the Family* 54:749–62.

DeLamater, John. 2005. "Values Trump Data: The Bush Administration Approach to Sexual Science." Paper presented at World Association of Sexual Health, July 12, Montreal, Québec, CA.

DeLamater, John and P. MacCorquodale. 1979. *Premarital Sexuality: Attitudes, Relationships, Behavior.* Madison: University of Wisconsin Press.

DeLamater, John and Morgan Sill. 2005. "Sexual Desire in Later Life." *Journal of Sex Research* 42:138–49.

DeLamater, John, and Sara Moorman. Forthcoming. "Social Behavior in Later Life." Under review.

Diamond, Lisa M. 2003. "Was It a Phase? Young Women's Relinquishment of Lesbian/Bisexual Identities Over a 5-Year Period." *Journal of Personality and Social Psychology* 84:352–64.

Farrar, Kirstie, Dale Kunkel, Erica Biely, Keren Eyal, Rena Fandrich, and Edward Donnerstein. 2003. "Sexual Messages During Prime-Time Programming." *Sexuality and Culture* 7:7–37.

Finkelhor, David, K. Mitchell, and J. Wolak. 2000. *Online Victimization: A Report on the Nation's Youth.* Washington, DC: National Center for Missing and Exploited Children.

Fisher, Deborah A., Douglas L. Hill, Joel W. Grube, and Enid L. Gruber. 2004. "Youth and Television: Examining Sexual Content across Program Genres." Paper presented at Society for Research on Adolescence, March, Baltimore, MD.

Foucault, Michel. 1998. *The History of Sexuality,* vol. 1, *The Will to Knowledge.* London, England: Penguin.

Gallmeier, Charles P., David Knox, and Marty E. Zusman. 2002. "Going Out or Hanging Out: Couple Dating and Group Dating in the New Millennium." *Free Inquiry in Creative Sociology* 30:221–25.

Gerbner, George, L. Gross, and M. Morgan. 2002. "Growing Up With Television: Cultivation Processes." Pp. 43–67 in *Media Effects: Advances in Theory and Research,* 2d ed., edited by J. Bryant and D. Zillman. Mahwah, NJ: Erlbaum.

Goldman, R. J. and J. D. Goldman. 1982. *Children's Sexual Thinking.* London, England: Routledge & Kegan Paul.

Gossett, Jennifer Lynn and Sarah Byrne. 2002. "'Click Here': A Content Analysis of Internet Rape Sites." *Gender & Society* 16:689–709.

Greenberg, Bradley S. and Rick Busselle. 1996. "What's Old, What's New? Sexuality on the Soaps." *SIECUS Report* 25(5):14–16.

Harper, Gary W., Christine Gannon, Susan E. Watson, Joseph E. Catania, and M. Margaret Dolcini. 2004. "The Role of Close Friends in African American Adolescents' Dating and Sexual Behavior." *Journal of Sex Research* 41:351–62.

Hicks, Thomas and Harold Leitenberg. 2001. "Sexual Fantasies about One's Partner vs. Someone Else: Gender Differences in Incidence and Frequency." *Journal of Sex Research* 38:43–50.

Hofferth, S. L. 1990. "Trends in Adolescent Sexual Activity, Contraception, and Pregnancy in the United States." Pp. 217–33 in *Adolescence and Puberty,* edited by J. Bancroft and J. Reinisch. New York: Oxford University Press.

Humphreys, L. 1970. *Tearoom Trade: Impersonal Sex in Public Places.* Chicago, IL: Aldine.

Hyde, Janet and John DeLamater. 2006. *Understanding Human Sexuality,* 9th ed. Boston, MA: McGraw-Hill.

Impett, Emily A. and Letitia A. Peplau. 2003. "Sexual Compliance: Gender, Motivational, and Relationship Perspectives." *Journal of Sex Research* 40:87–100.

Irvine, Janice M. 2003. "'The Sociologist as Voyeur': Social Theory and Sexuality Research, 1910–1978." *Qualitative Sociology* 26:429–56.

Jackson, P., N. Stevenson, and K. Brooks. 1999. "Making Sense of Men's Lifestyle Magazines." *Environment and Planning D: Society and Space* 17:353–69.

Kaiser Family Foundation. 1997. *National Survey of Teens: Teens Talk about Dating, Intimacy, and their Sexual Experiences.* Menlo Park, CA: Kaiser Family Foundation (www.kff.org).

Kinsey, Alfred C., Wardell Pomeroy, and C. Martin. 1948. *Sexual Behavior in the Human Male.* Philadelphia, PA: Saunders.

Kinsey, Alfred C., Wardell Pomeroy, and C. Martin. 1953. *Sexual Behavior in the Human Female.* Philadelphia, PA: Saunders.

Kuttler, Ami Flam and Annette M. La Greca. 2004. "Linkages among Adolescent Girls' Romantic Relationships, Best Friendships, and Peer Networks." *Journal of Adolescence* 27:395–414.

Lambert, Tracy A., Arnold S. Kahn, and Kevin J. Apple. 2003. "Pluralistic Ignorance and Hooking Up." *Journal of Sex Research* 40:129–33.

Lamberts, S. W. J., A. van den Beld, and A. J. van der Lely. 1997. "The Endocrinology of Aging." *Science* 278:419–24.

Laumann, Edward O., John Gagnon, Robert Michael, and Stuart Michaels. 1994. *The Social Organization of Sexuality.* Chicago, IL: University of Chicago Press.

Laumann, Edward O., Stephen Ellingson, Jenna Mahay, Anthony Paik, and Yoosik Youm. 2004. *The Sexual Organization of the City.* Chicago, IL: University of Chicago Press.

Lawson, A. 1988. *Adultery: An Analysis of Love and Betrayal.* New York: Basic Books.

Leitenberg, Harold and Kris Henning. 1995. "Sexual Fantasy." *Psychological Bulletin* 117:469–96.

Lindau, S., E. O. Laumann, W. Levinson, and L. Waite. 2003. "Synthesis of Scientific Disciplines in Pursuit of Health: The Interactive Biopsychosocial Model." *Perspectives in Biology and Medicine* 46:S74–S86.

Longmore, Monica A. 1998. "Symbolic Interactionism and the Study of Sexuality." *Journal of Sex Research* 35:44–57.

Machin, David and Joanna Thornborrow. 2003. "Branding and Discourse: The Case of *Cosmopolitan.*" *Discourse and Society* 14:453–71.

Marsiglio, William, John H. Scanzoni, and Kendal L. Broad. 2000. "Sexual Behavior Patterns." Pp. 2549–68 in *Encyclopedia of Sociology.* Vol. 4. 2d ed., edited by E. F. Borgatta and R. J. V. Montgomery. New York: Gale.

Martinson, F. M. 1994. *The Sexual Life of Children.* Westport, CT: Bergin and Garvey.

Masters, W. H., V. E. Johnson, and R. C. Kolodny. 1982. *Human Sexuality.* Boston, MA: Little, Brown.

McCleneghan, J. Sean. 2003. "Selling Sex to College Females: Their Attitudes about 'Cosmopolitan' and 'Glamour' Magazines." *Social Science Journal* 40:317–25.

Mitchell, Kimberly J., David Finkelhor, and Janis Wolak. 2003. "The Exposure of Youth to Unwanted Sexual Material on the Internet: A National Survey of Risk, Impact, and Prevention." *Youth & Society* 34:330–58.

Okami, Paul, Richard Olmstead, and Paul R. Abramson. 1997. "Sexual Experiences in Early Childhood: 18-Year Longitudinal Data from the UCLA Family Lifestyles Project." *Journal of Sex Research* 34:339–47.

Parents Television Council. 2000. *What a Difference a Decade Makes: A Comparison of Prime Time Sex, Language, and Violence in 1989 and 1999.* Special report. Retrieved July 20, 2005 (www.parentstv.org/publications/reports/Decadestudy/Decadestudy.html).

Raffaelli, Marcela and Lenna Ontai. 2004. "Gender Socialization in Latino/a Families: Results From Two Retrospective Studies." *Sex Roles* 50:287–99.

Ramey, James W. 1975. "Intimate Groups and Networks: Frequent Consequences of Sexually Open Marriage." *Family Coordinator* 24:515–30.

Reichert, Tom. 2002. "Sex in Advertising Research: A Review of Content, Effects, and Functions of Sexual Information in Consumer Advertising." *Annual Review of Sex Research* 13:241–73.

Risman, Barbara and Pepper Schwartz. 2002. "After the Sexual Revolution: Gender Politics in Teen Dating." *Contexts* 1:16–24.

Rosario, M., H. Meyer-Bahlburg, J. Hunter, T. Exner, M. Swadz, and A. Keller. 1996. "The Psychosexual Development of

Urban Lesbian, Gay, and Bisexual Youths." *Journal of Sex Research* 33:113–26.

Rostosky, Sharon Scales, Brian L. Wilcox, Margaret Laurie Comer Wright, and Brangy A. Randall. 2004. "The Impact of Religiosity on Adolescent Sexual Behavior: A Review of the Evidence." *Journal of Adolescent Research* 19:677–97.

Rubin, Arlene M. and James R. Adams. 1986. "Outcomes of Sexually Open Marriages." *Journal of Sex Research* 22:311–19.

Smith, Tom. 2003. *American Sexual Behavior: Trends, Sociodemographic Differences, and Risk Behavior.* GSS Topical Report No. 25, University of Chicago, National Opinion Research Center.

Soley, Lawrence C. and Gary Kurzbard. 1986. "Sex in Advertising: A Comparison of 1964 and 1984 Magazine Advertisements." *Journal of Advertising* 15(3):46–54.

Sprecher, Susan. 1998. "Social Exchange Theories and Sexuality." *Journal of Sex Research* 35:32–43.

Stack, S. and J. H. Gundlach. 1992. "Divorce and Sex." *Archives of Sexual Behavior* 21:359–68.

Taylor, Laramie D. 2005. "All For Him: Articles about Sex in American Lad Magazines." *Sex Roles: A Journal of Research* 52:153–63.

Teachman, J. D., L. M. Tedrow, and K. D. Crowder. 2000. "The Changing Demography of America's Families." Pp. 453–65 in *Understanding Families into the New Millenium: A Decade in Review,* edited by R. M. Milardo. Minneapolis, MN: National Council on Family Relations.

Thomsen, Steven R., Michelle M. Weber, and Lora Beth Brown. 2002. "The Relationship between Reading Beauty and Fashion Magazines and the Use of Pathogenic Dieting Methods among Adolescent Females." *Adolescence* 37(145):1–18.

Thorne, Barrie. 1993. *Gender Play: Girls and Boys in School.* New Brunswick, NJ: Rutgers University Press.

Tiefer, Leonore. 2004. *Sex Is Not a Natural Act and Other Essays.* 2d ed. Boulder, CO: Westview Press.

Treas, Judith. 2002. "How Cohorts, Education and Ideology Shaped a New Sexual Revolution on American Attitudes toward Nonmarital Sex, 1972–1998." *Sociological Perspectives* 45:267–83.

Trussel, J. and B. Vaughn. 1991. *Selected Results Concerning Sexual Behavior and Contraceptive Use from the 1988 National Survey of Family Growth and the 1988 National Survey of Adolescent Males.* Working Paper No. 91–12, Office of Population Research, Princeton, NJ.

Tyler, Melissa. 2004. "Managing between the Sheets: Lifestyle Magazines and the Management of Sexuality in Everyday Life." *Sexualities* 7:81–106.

Udry, J. R. 1988. "Biological Predispositions and Social Control in Adolescent Sexual Behavior." *American Sociological Review* 53:709–22.

United Nations. 2000. *Wall Chart on Marriage Patterns 2000.* Retrieved July 11, 2005 (www.un.org/esa/population/publications/worldmarriage).

Upchurch, Dawn M., Lene Levy-Storms, Clea A. Sucoff, and Carol S. Aneshensel. 1998. "Gender and Ethnic Differences in the Timing of First Sexual Intercourse." *Family Planning Perspectives* 30:121–27.

U.S. Bureau of the Census. 2004. "Estimated Median Age at First Marriage, by Sex: 1890 to Present." Retrieved July 11, 2005 (www.census.gov/population/socdemo/hh-fam/tabMS-2.pdf).

U.S. Bureau of the Census. 2005. *Statistical Abstract of the United States, 2004.* Washington, DC: Bureau of the Census.

Ventura, S. J., W. D. Mosher, S. A. Curtin, J. C. Abma, and S. Henshaw. 2001. "Trends in Pregnancy Rates for the United States, 1976–1997." *National Vital Statistics Reports* 49(4).

Wade, Lisa and John DeLamater. 2002. "Relationship Dissolution as a Life Stage Transition: Effects on Sexual Attitudes and Behaviors." *Journal of Marriage and the Family* 64:898–914.

Wikipedia. 2005. Polyamory. Retrieved July 13, 2005 (http://en.wikipedia.org/wiki/Polyamory).

World Association of Sexual Health (WAS). 2005. "Sexual Health in the Millennium." A declaration issued on July 15 (www.worldsexology.org/about_sexualrights.asp).

PART VII: SOCIAL INSTITUTIONS

Chapter 26. The Sociology of Love, Courtship, and Dating

Bailey, Beth. 1988. *From Front Porch to Back Seat: Courtship in Twentieth Century America.* Baltimore, MD: Johns Hopkins University Press.

Becker, Gary. 1974. "A Theory of Marriage. Part II." *Journal of Political Economy* 82(2):S11–26.

Benz, Joseph J., Mary K. Anderson, and Richard J. Miller. 1995. "Attributions of Deception in Dating Situations." *The Psychological Record* 55:305–14.

Berscheid, Ellen and Elaine H. Walster. 1978. *Interpersonal Attraction.* 2d ed. Reading, MA: Addison-Wesley.

Blackwell, Debra L. and Daniel T. Lichter. 2004. "Homogamy among Dating, Cohabiting, and Married Couples." *The Sociological Quarterly* 45:719–37.

Brown, Robert. 1987. *Analyzing Love.* New York: Cambridge University Press.

Bulcroft, K. and Margaret O'Conner. 1986. "The Importance of Dating Relationships on Quality of Life for Older Persons." *Family Relations* 35:397–401.

Buss, David M. 1988. "The Evolution of Human Intrasexual Competition: Tactics of Mate Attraction." *Journal of Personality and Social Psychology* 54:616–28.

Buss, David M., Todd K. Shackelford, Lee A. Kirkpatrick, and Randy J. Larsen. 2001. "A Half Century of Mate Preferences: The Cultural Evolution of Values." *Journal of Marriage and the Family* 63:491–503.

Cate, Rodney M. and Sally A. Lloyd. 1992. *Courtship. Sage Series on Close Relationships.* Newbury Park, CA: Sage.

Cere, Daniel. 2001. "Courtship Today: The View from Academia." *Public Interest* 143:53–72.

Clark, Catherine L., Phillip R. Shaver, and Matthew F. Abrahams. 1999. "Strategic Behaviors in Romantic Relationship Initiation." *Personality and Social Psychology Bulletin* 25:707–20.

Dickson, Fran C., Patrick C. Hughes, and Kandi L. Walker. 2005. "An Exploratory Investigation into Dating among Later-Life Women." *Western Journal of Communication* 69:67–82.

Groom, Carla J. and James W. Pennebaker. 2005. "The Language of Love: Sex, Sexual Orientation, and Language Use in Online Personal Advertisements." *Sex Roles* 52:447–61.

Hatfield, E. and R. L. Rapson. 1987. "Passionate Love: New Directions in Research." Pp. 109–39 in *Advances in Personal Relationships,* vol. 1, edited by W. H. Jones and D. Perlman. Greenwich, CT: JAI Press.

Hendrick, Susan S. and Clyde Hendrick. 1992. *Romantic Love. Sage Series on Close Relationships.* Newbury Park, CA: Sage.

Hovick, Shelly R. A., Renee A. Meyers, and C. Erik Timmerman. 2003. "E-mail Communication in Workplace Romantic Relationships." *Communication Studies* 54:468–82.

Hughes, Mikayla, Kelly Morrison, and Kelli Jean K. Asada. 2005. "What's Love Got to Do with It? Exploring the Impact of Maintenance Rules, Love Attitudes, and Network Support on Friends with Benefits Relationships." *Western Journal of Communication* 69:49–66.

Huyck, Margaret H. 2001. "Romantic Relationships in Later Life." *Generations* 25:9–17.

Jang, Su A., Sandi W. Smith, and Timothy R. Levine. 2002. "To Stay or to Leave? The Role of Attachment Styles in Communication Patterns and Potential Termination of Romantic Relationships Following Discovery of Deception." *Communication Monographs* 69:236–52.

Johnson, Michael P. and Kathleen J. Ferraro. 2000. "Research on Domestic Violence in the 1990s: Making Distinctions." *Journal of Marriage and Family* 62:948–63.

Kass, Amy A. and Leon R. Kass. 1999. *Wing to Wing, Oar to Oar: Readings on Courting and Marrying.* South Bend, IN: University of Notre Dame Press.

Kerckhoff, A. C. and K. E. Davis. 1962. "Value Consensus and Need Complementarity in Mate Selection." *American Sociological Review* 27:295–303.

Lee, John A. 1973. *The Colours of Love.* Toronto, Ontario, Canada: New Press.

Levin, Irene. 2004. "Living Apart Together: A New Family Form." *Current Sociology* 52:223–40.

Levine, Robert, Suguru Sato, Tsukasa Hashimoto, and Jyoti Verma. 1995. "Love and Marriage in Eleven Cultures." *Journal of Cross-Cultural Psychology* 26:554–71.

McElhany, L. J. 1992. "Dating and Courtship in the Later Years." *Generations* 16:21–23.

Mileham, Beatriz Lia Avila. 2003. "Online Infidelity in Internet Chat Rooms: An Ethnographic Exploration." University of Florida, Gainesville. Unpublished doctoral dissertation.

Murstein, Bernard I. 1970. "Stimulus-Value-Role: A Theory of Marital Choice." *Journal of Marriage and the Family* 32:465–81.

Neff, Lisa A. and Benjamin R. Karney. 2005. "To Know You Is to Love You: The Implications of Global Adoration and Specific Accuracy for Marital Relationships." *Journal of Personality and Social Psychology* 88:480–97.

Owens, Erica. 2005. "Does He Like Me, or Does He Like Me Like Me? Interpretive Work in the Dating World." Presented at the annual meeting of the Society for the Study of Symbolic Interaction, August 14, Philadelphia, PA.

Ponzetti, James J., Jr. 2005. "Family Beginnings: A Comparison of Spouses' Recollections of Courtship." *Family Journal* 13(2):132–38.

Reiss, Ira L. 1960. "Toward a Sociology of the Heterosexual Love Relationship." *Marriage and Family Living* 22:139–45.

Reiss, Ira L. 1980. *Family Systems in America.* 3d ed. New York: Holt, Rinehart & Winston.

Rowntree, S. C. 1989. "Johnny Loves Mary Forever": What Therapy Doesn't Know about Love. Pp. 31–53 in *Beyond Individualism: Toward a Retrieval of Moral Discourse in America,* edited by D. L. Gelpi. Notre Dame, IN: University of Notre Dame Press.

Simons, Ronald L., Kuei-Hsiu Lin, and Leslie C. Gordon. 1998. "Socialization in the Family of Origin and Male Dating Violence: A prospective Study." *Journal of Marriage and the Family* 60:467–78.

Singer, Irving. 1984. *The Nature of Love,* vol. 2, *Courtly and Romantic.* Chicago, IL: University of Chicago Press.

Sternberg, Robert J. 1986. "A Triangular Theory of Love." *Psychological Review* 93:119–35.

Sternberg, Robert J. 1998. *Love Is a Story: A New Theory of Relationships.* London, England: Oxford University Press.

Stone, Lawrence. 1980. *The Family, Sex, and Marriage in England 1500–1800.* New York: Harper & Row.

Tennov, Dorothy. 1979. *Love and Limerence: The Experience of Being in Love.* New York: Stein & Day.

Tjaden, Patricia and Nancy Thoennes. 1998. Prevalence, Incidence, and on Sequences of Violence against Women: Findings from the National Violence against Women survey, November, Washington, DC: National Institute of Justice/Centers for Disease Control and Prevention.

Tooke W. and L. Camire. 1991. "Patterns of Deception in Intersexual and Intrasexual Mating Strategies." *Ethology and Sociobiology* 12:345–64.

Van de Vate, Dwight, Jr. 1981. *Romantic Love: A Philosophical Inquiry.* University Park: Pennsylvania State University Press.

Vaughan, Diane. 1986. *Uncoupling: Turning Points in Intimate Relationships.* New York: Oxford University Press.

Waller, Willard. 1937. "The Rating and Dating Complex." *American Sociological Review* 2:727–34.

Waskul, Denis D. 2002. "The Naked Self: Being a Body in Televideo Cybersex." *Symbolic Interaction* 25:199–228.

Yancey, George. 2002. "Who Interracially Dates? An Examination of the Characteristics of Those Who Have Interracially Dated." *Journal of Comparative Family Studies* 33:179–90.

Chapter 27. Marriage and Divorce in the United States

Anderson, E. R. and S. Wolchik. 2001. "Divorce and Children's Development." Pp. 3807–10 in *International Encyclopedia of the Social & Behavioral Sciences,* vol. 6, edited by Neil J. Smelser and Paul B. Baltes. New York: Elsevier.

Andrews, Stephen Pearl. 1975. *Love, Marriage, and the Condition of Women.* Weston, MA: M & S Press.

Beale, Calvin L. 1950. "Increased Divorce Rates Among Separated Persons as a Factor in Divorce Since 1940." *Social Forces* 29:72–74.

Blake, Nelson Manfred. 1962. *The Road to Reno: A History of Divorce in the United States.* New York: MacMillan.

Calhoun, Arthur W. 1917. *Social History of the American Family.* Vol. 1. Cleveland, OH: Arthur H. Clark.

Calhoun, Arthur W. 1918. *Social History of the American Family.* Vol. 11. Cleveland, OH: Arthur H. Clark.

Calhoun, Arthur W. 1919. *Social History of the American Family.* Vol. III. Cleveland, OH: Arthur H. Clark.

Cavers, David F. 1937. "Migratory Divorce." *Social Forces* 1:96–107.

Cherlin, Andrew J. 1992. *Marriage, Divorce, and Remarriage.* Cambridge, MA: Harvard University Press.

Coontz, Stephanie. 1992. *The Way We Never Were: American Families and the Nostalgia Trap.* New York: Basic Books.

Coontz, Stephanie. 2000. *The Way We Never Were: American Families and the Nostalgia Trap* 2d ed. New York: Basic Books.

Coontz, Stephanie. 2005. *Marriage, a History: From Obedience to Intimacy or How Love Conquered Marriage.* New York: Viking.

Cuber, John F. and Peggy B. Harroff. 1966. *The Significant Americans.* New York: Appleton.

Dickinson, George E. and Michael R. Leming. 1990. *Understanding Families: Diversity, Continuity, and Change.* Boston, MA: Allyn & Bacon.

Dike, Samuel W. 1889. "Statistics on Marriage and Divorce." *Political Science Quarterly* 4:592–614.

Flexner, Eleanor and Ellen Fitzpatrick. [1908] 1996. *Century of Struggle: The Women's Rights Movement in the United States.* Cambridge, MA: Belknap Press.

Fournad, D. George. 1929. "Eugenics and Eugenic Marriages." *Journal of Educational Sociology* 3:171–80.

Furstenberg, Frank F., Jr. 1990. "Divorce and the American Family." *Annual Review of Sociology* 16:379–403.

Galston, William A. 1996. "Divorce American Style." *Public Interest.* 124:12–26.

Goode, William J. 1951. "Economic Factors and Marital Stability." *American Sociological Review* 16:802–12.

Hankins, Frank H. 1931. "Divorce." Pp. 177–84 in *Encyclopedia of the Social Sciences,* edited by E. R. A. Seligman. New York: Macmillan.

Harmsworth, Harry C. and Mhyra S. Minnis. 1955. "Non-Statutory Causes of Divorce: The Lawyers' Point of View." *Marriage and Family Living* 17:316–21.

Honigmann, John J. 1953. "A Comparative Analysis of Divorce." *Marriage and Family Living* 15:37–43.

Howard, George Elliott. 1904. *A History of Matrimonial Institutions,* vol. 3. Chicago, IL: University of Chicago Press, Callaghan.

Howard, George Elliott. 1909. "Is the Freer Granting of Divorce an Evil?" *American Journal of Sociology* 14:766–96.

Hurley, Dan. 2005. "Divorce Rate: It's Not as High as You Think." *New York Times,* April 19, p. D7.

Jacobson, Paul H. 1959. *American Marriage and Divorce.* New York: Rinehart.

Kirkpatrick, Clifford. 1968. "Disorganization and Dissolution." Pp. 313–22 in *International Encyclopedia of the Social Sciences,* edited by D. L. Sills. New York: Macmillan.

Kurz, D. 2001. "Divorce and Gender." Pp. 3810–14 in *International Encyclopedia of the Social and Behavioral Sciences,* edited by N. J. Smelser. New York: Elsevier.

Lamanna, Mary Ann and Agnes Riedmann. 1991. *Marriages and Families: Making Choices and Facing Change.* Belmont, CA: Wadsworth.

Lowie, Robert H. 1933. "Marriage." Pp. 146–54 in *Encyclopedia of the Social Sciences,* vol. 10, edited by E. R. A. Seligman and A. Johnson. New York: Macmillan.

Malveaux, Julianne and Deborah Perry. 2003. *Unfinished Business: The Ten Most Important Issues Women Face Today.* New York: Perigee.

Martin, Teresa Castro and Larry L. Bumpass. 1989. "Recent Trends in Marital Dissolution." *Demography* 26:37–51.

Monahan, Thomas P. 1951. "One Hundred Years of Marriages in Massachusetts." *American Journal of Sociology* 56:534–45.

Monahan, Thomas P. 1955. "Divorce by Occupational Level." *Marriage and Family Living* 17(4):322–24.

National Center for Health Statistics. 1991. *Monthly Vital Statistics Report* 40(4 Suppl.), August 26.

National Center for Health Statistics. 1992. *Monthly Vital Statistics Report* 40(13), September 30.

National Center for Health Statistics. 1993. *Monthly Vital Statistics Report: Annual Summary of Births, Marriages, Divorce, and Deaths: United States, 1992* 41(13), September 28.

National Center for Health Statistics. 2005a. *National Vital Statistics Reports, Births, Marriages, Divorces, and Deaths: Provisional Data for 2004* 53(21), June 28, Table A, Updated October 18, 2005.

National Center for Health Statistics. 2005b. *National Vital Statistics Reports* 54(7), December 22.

Newman, Samuel C. 1950. "Trends in Vital Statistics of Marriages and Divorces in the United States." *Marriage and Family Living* 12:89–90.

Nock, Steven L. and Paul W. Kingston. 1990. *The Sociology of Public Issues.* Belmont, CA: Wadsworth.

Norton, Arthur J. and Louisa F. Miller. 1992. "Marriage, Divorce, and Remarriage in the 1990's." *U.S. Bureau of the Census, Current Population Reports, P23–180.* Washington, DC: Government Printing Office.

Notestein, Frank W. 1968. "Willcox, Walter F." Pp. 553–55 in *International Encyclopedia of the Social Sciences,* edited by D. L. Sill. New York: Macmillan.

Ogburn, William Fielding. 1927. "Eleven Questions Concerning American Marriages." *Social Forces* 6:5–12.

Ogburn, William F. and M. F. Nimkoff. 1955. *Technology and the Changing Family.* Cambridge, MA: Riverside Press.

O'Neill, William L. 1967. *Divorce in the Progressive Era.* New Haven, CT: Yale University Press.

Peck, Dennis L. 1993. "The Fifty Percent Divorce Rate: Deconstructing a Myth." *Journal of Sociology and Social Welfare.* 20:135–44.

Riley, Glenda. 1991. *Divorce: An American Tradition.* New York: Oxford University Press.

Ruggles, Steven. 1997. "The Rise of Divorce and Separation in the United States, 1880–1990." *Demography* 34:455–66.

Saunders, John. 1988. *Basic Demographic Measures: A Practical Guide for Users.* Lanham, MD: University Press of America.

Schoen, Robert, Nan Marie Astone, Kendra Rothert, Nicola J. Standish, and Young J. Kim. 2002. "Women's Employment, Marital Happiness, and Divorce." *Social Forces* 81:643–62.

Scott, Jacqueline L. 2001. "Marriage." Pp. 1014–15 in *Reader's Guide to the Social Sciences,* vol. 2, edited by J. Michie. London, England: Fitzroy Dearborn Publishers.

Sears, David O., Letitia Anne Peplau, Jonathan L. Freedman, and Shelley E. Taylor. 1988. *Social Psychology* 6th ed. Englewood Cliffs, NJ: Prentice Hall.

Shively, Charles. [1853, 1889]. 1975 *Love, Marriage, and Divorce and the Sovereignty of the Individual: A Discussion between Henry James, Horace Greeley, and Stephen Pearl Andrews.* Weston, MA: M & S Press. (Originally published in 1853 and republished in 1889 in Boston, MA, by Benj. R. Tucker)

Statistical Office of the European Communities, Demographic Statistics. 1988–1990. "Marriage and Divorce Rates, Selected Countries: 1960–1988." *U.S. Department of Health and Human Services, National Center for Health Statistics. Monthly.* Retrieved January 23, 2003 (http://ed.gov/pubs/YouthIndicators/indtab05.html).

Strauss, William and Neil Howe. 1997. *The Fourth Turning: An American Prophecy.* New York: Broadway Books.

Thwing, Charles F. [1913] 1887. *The Family: An Historical and Social Study,* 2d ed. Boston, MA: Lee & Shepard.

U.S. Bureau of the Census. 1908. *Marriage and Divorce 1867–1906.* Part II, *General Tables, 1908.* Vital Statistics Division, Special Reports. Washington, DC: U.S. Government Printing Office.

U.S. Bureau of the Census. 1909. *Marriage and Divorce 1867–1906, Part I, Summary, Laws, Foreign Statistics.* Vital Statistics Division, Special Reports. Washington, DC: U.S. Government Printing Office.

U.S. Bureau of the Census. 1919. *Marriage and Divorce, 1916.* Washington, DC: U.S. Government Printing Office.

U.S. Bureau of the Census. 1926. *Marriage and Divorce, 1924.* Washington, DC: U.S. Government Printing Office.

U.S. Bureau of the Census. 1930. *Marriage and Divorce, 1928: Statistics of Marriages, Divorces, and Annulments of Marriage.* Seventh Annual Report. Washington, DC: U.S. Government Printing Office.

U.S. Bureau of the Census 1931. *Marriage and Divorce, 1929. Statistics of Marriages, Divorces, and Annulments of Marriage.* Eight Annual Report. Washington, DC: U.S. Government Printing Office.

U.S. Bureau of the Census. 1932. *Marriage and Divorce, 1930, Statistics of Marriages, Divorces, and Annulments of Marriage.* Ninth Annual Report. Washington, DC: U.S. Government Printing Office.

U.S. Bureau of the Census. 1934. *Marriage and Divorce, 1932, Statistics of Marriages, Divorces, and Annulments of Marriage.* Eleventh Annual Report. Washington, DC: Government Printing Office.

U.S. Bureau of the Census. 1940. *Statistical Abstract of the United States, 1939.* Washington, DC: U.S. Government Printing Office.

U.S. Bureau of the Census. 1941. *Statistical Abstract of the United States, 1940.* Washington, DC: U.S. Government Printing Office.

U.S. Bureau of the Census. 1942. *Statistical Abstract of the United States, 1941.* Washington, DC: U.S. Government Printing Office.

U.S. Bureau of the Census. 1947. *Statistical Abstract of the United States.* Washington, DC: U.S. Government Printing Office.

U.S. Bureau of the Census. 1975. *Historical Statistics of the United States, Colonial Times to 1970.* Bicentennial ed., Part 2. Pp. 49, 64.

U.S. Bureau of the Census. 1999. *Statistical Abstract of the United States, 1999,* Table 115, p. 110 (119th ed.) Washington, DC: U.S. Government Printing Office.

U.S. Bureau of the Census. 2001. *Statistical Abstract of the United States: 2001,* 121st ed. Washington, DC: U.S. Government Printing Office.

U.S. Bureau of the Census. 2004. *Statistical Abstract of the United States: 2004–2005,* 124th ed. Washington, DC: U.S. Government Printing Office.

U.S. Bureau of Foreign and Domestic Commerce. 1930. *Statistical Abstract of the United States, 1930.* Washington, DC: U.S. Government Printing Office.

U.S. Bureau of Statistics. 1911. *Statistical Abstract of the United States, 1910.* Washington, DC: Government Printing Office.

Vernier, Chester. 1935. *American Family Laws: A Comparative Study of the Family Law of the Forty-Eight American States, Alaska, the District of Columbia, and Hawaii.* Palo Alto, CA: Stanford University Press.

White, Lynn K. 1990. "Determinants of Divorce: A Review of Research in the Eighties." *Journal of Marriage and the Family* 52:904–12.

Willcox, Walter Francis. 1891. *The Divorce Problem: A Study in Statistics. Studies in History, Economics, and Public Law.* Vol. 1, No. 1. New York: Columbia College.

Willcox, Walter Francis. 1893. "A Study in Statistics." *Political Science Quarterly* 8:69–96.

Willcox, Walter Francis. 1897. *The Divorce Problem: A Study in Statistics.* New York: Columbia University.

Zellner, William W. 2001. *Extraordinary Groups: An Examination of Unconventional Lifestyles.* 7th ed. New York: Worth.

Chapter 28. Family Sociology in the 21st Century

Baca Zinn, Maxine and D. Stanley Eitzen. 2002. *Diversity in Families.* 6th ed. Boston, MA: Allyn & Bacon.

Bengston, Vern L., Alan C. Acock, Katherine R. Allen, Peggye Dilworth-Anderson, and David Klein, eds. 2005. *Sourcebook of Family Theory and Research.* Thousand Oaks, CA: Sage.

Benokraitis, Nijole V., ed. 2000. *Feuds about Families: Conservative, Centrist, Liberal and Feminist Perspectives.* Upper Saddle River, NJ: Prentice Hall.

Berardo, Felix. 1987. "The American Family: A Commentary." *Journal of Family Issues* 8:426–28.

Berardo, Felix M. and Constance L. Shehan. 1984. "Family Scholarship: A Reflection of the Changing Family?" *Journal of Family Issues* 5:577–98.

Berardo, Felix M. and Constance L. Shehan. 2004. "Family Problems in Global Perspective." Pp. 246–60 in *Handbook of Social Problems: A Comparative International Perspective,* edited by G. Ritzer. Thousand Oaks, CA: Sage.

Bernard, Jesse. 1972. *The Future of Marriage.* New York: Bantam.

Boss, Pauline G., William J. Doherty, Ralph LaRossa, Walter R. Schumm, and Suzanne K, Steinmetz, eds. 1993. *Sourcebook of Family Theories and Methods: A Contextual Approach.* New York: Plenum Press.

Burr, Wesley. 1979. *Contemporary Theories about the Family.* 2 vols. New York: Free Press.

Christensen, Harold T. 1964. *Handbook of Marriage and the Family.* Chicago, IL: Rand McNally.

Coleman, Marilyn and Lawrence Ganong, eds. 2003. *Points and Counterpoints: Controversial Relationship and Family Issues in the 21st Century.* Los Angeles, CA: Roxbury.

Coontz, Stephanie. 2000. "Historical Perspectives on Family Studies." *Journal of Marriage and the Family* 62:283–97.

Demo, David H., Katherine R. Allen, and Mark A. Fine, eds. 2000. *Handbook of Family Diversity.* New York: Oxford University Press.

Ferree, Myra Marx. 1990. "Beyond Separate Spheres: Feminism and Family Research." *Journal of Marriage and the Family* 52:866–84.

Fox, Greer L. and Velma M. Murry. 2000. "Gender and Families: Feminist Perspectives and Family Research." *Journal of Marriage and the Family* 62:1160–72.

Giddens, Anthony. 2005. "The Global Revolution in Family and Personal Life." Pp. 26–31 in *Families in Transition,* 13th ed., edited by A. Skolnick and J. H. Skolnick. Boston, MA: Pearson Education. (Originally published in *Runaway World: How Globalization Is Reshaping Our Lives,* edited by A. Giddens. New York: Routledge, 1999)

Glenn, Norval D. 1997. "A Critique of Twenty Family and Marriage and the Family Textbooks." *Family Relations* 46:197–208.

Goode, William J. 2005. "The Theoretical Importance of the Family." Pp. 14–25 in *Families in Transition,* 13th ed., edited by A. Skolnick and J. H. Skolnick. Boston, MA: Pearson Education. (Originally published in *The Family.* 2d ed. Englewood Cliffs, NJ: Prentice Hall, 1982)

Hill, Reuben. 1962. "Cross-National Family Research: Attempts and Prospects." *International Social Science Journal* 14:425–51.

Hill, Reuben and Donald A. Hansen. 1960. "The Identification of Conceptual Frameworks Utilized in Family Study." *Marriage and Family Living* 4:299–311.

Klein, David M. and Joan A. Jurich. 1993. "Metatheory and Family Studies." Pp. 51–67 in *Sourcebook of Family Theories and Methods,* edited by P. G. Boss, W. J. Doherty, R. LaRossa, W. R. Schumm, and S. K. Steinmetz. New York: Plenum Press.

Lopata, Helena Z. and Barrie Thorne. 1978. "On the Term 'Sex Roles.'" *Signs: Journal of Women in Culture and Society* 3:638–51.

Mann, Susan A., Michael D. Grimes, Alice Abel Kemp, and Pamela J. Jenkins. 1997. *Journal of Family Issues* 18:315–49.

Nye, F. Ivan and Felix M. Berardo. 1966. *Emerging Conceptual Frameworks in Family Analysis.* New York: Macmillan. (Reissued with new introduction by Praeger, New York, 1982)

Nye, F. Ivan and Felix M. Berardo. 1973. *The Family: Its Structure and Interaction.* New York: Macmillan.

Osmond, Marie W. and Barrie Thorne. 1993. "Feminist Theories: The Social Construction of Gender in Families and Society." Pp. 591–622 in *Sourcebook of Family Theories and Methods,* edited by P. Boss, W. Doherty, R. LaRossa, W. Schumm, and S. Steinmetz. New York: Springer.

Parsons, Talcott and Robert F. Bales. 1955. *Family, Socialization, and Interaction Processes.* Glencoe, IL: Free Press.

Ponzetti, James J., Jr. 2003. *International Encyclopedia of Marriage and Family.* 2d ed. New York: Macmillan Reference USA.

Popenoe, David. 1993. "American Family Decline, 1960–1990: A Review and Appraisal." *Journal of Marriage and the Family* 55:527–42.

Safilios-Rothschild, Constantina. 1969. "Family Sociology or Wives' Family Sociology? A Cross-Cultural Examination of Decision Making." *Journal of Marriage and the Family* 31:290–301.

Settles, Barbara. 2000. "Sociology of the Family: Global Advances and Challenges." Pp. 173–96 in *International Handbook of Sociology,* edited by S. Quan and A. Sales. Thousand Oaks, CA: Sage.

Sprey, Jetse, ed. 1990. *Fashioning Family Theory.* Newbury Park, CA: Sage.

Stacey, Judith. 1990. *Brave New Families: Stories of Domestic Upheaval in Late 20th Century America.* New York: Basic Books.

Sussman, Marvin B. and Suzanne K. Steinmetz, eds. 1987. *Handbook of Marriage and the Family.* New York: Plenum Press.

Thomas, Darwin I. and Jean E. Wilcox. 1987. "The Rise of Family Theory." Pp. 81–102 in *Handbook of Marriage and the Family,* edited by M. B. Sussman and S. K. Steinmetz. New York: Plenum Press.

Thompson, Linda and Alexis Walker. 1995. "The Place of Feminism in Family Studies." *Journal of Marriage and the Family* 57:847–65.

Thorne, Barrie and Marilyn Yalom. 1992. *Rethinking the Family: Feminist Questions.* Boston, MA: Northeastern University Press.

Vincent, Clark. 1966. "Familia Spongi: The Adaptive Function." *Journal of Marriage and the Family* 28:29–36.

White, James M. and David M. Klein. 2002. *Family Theories.* 2d ed. Thousand Oaks, CA: Sage.

Winton, Chester A. 1995. *Frameworks for Studying Families.* Guilford, CT: Dushkin.

Zetterberg, Hans. 1963. *On Theory and Verification in Sociology.* Totowa, NJ: Bedminster Press.

Chapter 29. The Sociology of Religion

Anonymous. [ca. 14th century] 1978. *The Cloud of Unknowing and Other Works.* Translated by C. Wolters. Reprint, London, England: Penguin Classics.

Bellah, Robert. 1970. *Beyond Belief: Essays on Religion in a Post-Traditional World.* New York: Harper & Row.

Berger, Peter. 1969. *The Sacred Canopy.* Garden City, NY: Anchor Books.

Bibby, Reginald and Merlin B. Binkerhoff. 1974. "When Proselytizing Fails: An Organizational Analysis." *Sociological Analysis* 35:189–200.

Bruce, Steve. 1996. *Religion in the Modern World.* Oxford, England: Oxford University Press.

Coleman, James William. 2001. *The New Buddhism: The Western Transformation of an Ancient Tradition.* New York: Oxford University Press.

Durkheim, Émile. [1915] 1965. *The Elementary Forms of Religious Life.* Translated by J. W. Swain, Reprint, New York: Free Press.

Finke, Roger and Rodney Stark. 1992. *The Churching of America, 1776–1990: Winners and Losers in Our Religious Economy.* New Brunswick, NJ: Rutgers University Press.

Freud, Sigmund. 1957. *The Future of an Illusion.* Translated by W. D. Robson-Scott. Garden City, NJ: Doubleday.

Iannaccone, Laurence R. 1994. "Why Strict Churches Are Strong." *American Journal of Sociology* 99:1180–211.

Kapleau, Philip. 1989. *Three Pillars of Zen.* Rev. ed. New York: Anchor.

Kurtz, Lester. 1995. *Gods in the Global Village: The World's Religions in Sociological Perspective.* Thousand Oaks, CA: Pine Forge.

Lofland, John. 1966. *Doomsday Cult: A Study of Conversion, Proselytization and Maintenance of Faith.* Englewood Cliffs, NJ: Prentice Hall.

Lofland, John and Norman Skonovd. 1981. "Conversion Motifs." *Journal for the Scientific Study of Religion* 3:294–308.

Marx, Karl. 1844. "Contribution to the Critique of Hegel's Philosophy of Right." Pp. 43–59 in *Early Writings,* edited by T. Bottomore. New York: McGraw-Hill.

Marx, Karl and Friedrich Engels. 1957. *On Religion.* New York: Schocken Books.

Merton, Robert K. 1957. *Social Theory and Social Structure.* Glencoe, IL: Free Press.

Niebuhr, H. Richard. 1957. *The Social Sources of Denominationalism.* New York: Meridian Books.

O'Dea, Thomas F. 1966. *The Sociology of Religion.* Englewood Cliffs, NJ: Prentice Hall.

Otto, Rudolf. 1923. *The Idea of the Holy.* Translated by J. W. Harvey. London, England: Oxford University Press.

Richardson, James T. and Mary Stewart. 1978. "Conversion Process Models and the Jesus Movement." Pp. 24–42 in *Conversion Careers: In and Out of the New Religions,* edited by J. T. Richardson. Beverly Hills, CA: Sage.

Roberts, Keith A. 2004. *Religion in Sociological Perspective.* 4th ed. Belmont, CA: Wadsworth/Thomson.

Snow, David A. and Cynthia Phillips. 1980. "The Lofland-Stark Model: A Critical Reassessment." *Social Problems* 27:430–47.

Stark, Rodney and William Simms Bainbridge. 1985. *The Future of Religion: Secularization, Revival, and Cult Formation.* Berkeley: University of California Press.

Tillich, Paul. 1967. *Systematic Theology.* Chicago, IL: University of Chicago Press.

Troeltsch, Ernst. 1931. *The Social Teachings of the Christian Churches.* Translated by O. Wyon. New York: Macmillan.

Warner, R. Stephen. 1993. "Work in Progress toward a New Paradigm for the Sociological Study of Religion in the United States." *American Journal of Sociology* 98:1044–93.

Weber, Max. 1930. *The Protestant Ethic and the Spirit of Capitalism.* Translated by T. Parsons. New York: Scribners.

Weber, Max. 1947. *The Theory of Social and Economic Organization.* Translated by A. M. Henderson and T. Parsons. New York: Oxford University Press.

Weber, Max. 1951. *The Religion of China.* Translated by H. H. Gerth. Glencoe, IL: Free Press.

Weber, Max. 1952. *Ancient Judaism.* Translated by H. H. Gerth. Glencoe, IL: Free Press.

Weber, Max. 1958. *The Religion of India.* Translated by H. H. Gerth and D. Martindale. Glencoe, IL: Free Press.

Weber, Max. 1963. *The Sociology of Religion.* Translated by E. Fiscshoff. Boston, MA: Beacon Press.

Yinger, Milton. 1970. *The Scientific Study of Religion.* New York: Macmillan.

Zetterberg, Hans. 1952. "The Religious Conversion as a Change of Social Roles." *Sociology and Social Research* 36:159–66.

Chapter 30. Political Sociology

Akard, Patrick J. 1992. "Corporate Mobilization and Political Power." *American Sociological Review* 57:597–615.

Alford, Robert R. 1963. *Party and Society.* Chicago, IL: Rand McNally.

Alford, Robert R. and Roger Friedland. 1985. *The Powers of Theory.* New York: Cambridge University Press.

Almeida, Paul D. 2003. "Opportunity Organizations and Treat-Induced Contention." *American Journal of Sociology* 109:345–400.

Almond, Gabriel and Sidney Verba. 1963. *The Civic Culture.* Princeton, NJ: Princeton University Press.

Alonso, William and Paul Starr, eds. 1987. *The Politics of Numbers.* New York: Russell Sage.

Althusser, Louis. 1978. *Lenin and Philosophy and Other Essays.* New York: Monthly Review Press.

Amenta, Edwin. 1998. *Bold Relief.* Princeton, NJ: Princeton University Press.

Amenta, Edwin and Yvonne Zylan. 1991. "It Happened Here." *American Sociological Review* 56:250–65.

Anderson, Margo and Stephen E. Fienberg. 1999. *Who Counts?* New York: Russell Sage.

Andrews, Kenneth T. 1997. "The Impacts of Social Movements on the Political Process." *American Sociological Review* 62:800–19.

Andrews, Kenneth T. 2001. "Social Movements and Policy Implementation." *American Sociological Review* 66:71–95.

Apter, David. 1965. *The Politics of Modernization.* Chicago, IL: University of Chicago Press.

Baran, Paul A. and Paul M. Sweezy. 1966. *Monopoly Capital.* New York: Monthly Review Press.

Barrow, Clyde W. 1993. *Critical Theories of the State.* Madison: University of Wisconsin Press.

Becker, Peter and Richard Wetzell, eds. 2005. *Criminals and Their Scientists.* New York: Cambridge University Press.

Beckett, Katherine. 1994. "Setting the Public Agenda." *Social Problems* 41:425–48.

Behrens, Angela, Christopher Uggen, and Jeff Manza. 2003. "Ballot Manipulation and the Menace of Negro Domination." *American Journal of Sociology* 109:559–605.

Bell, Daniel. 1960. *End of Ideology.* Glencoe, IL: Free Press.

Bell, Daniel. 1964. *The New American Right.* Garden City, NY: Doubleday.

Bendix, Reinhard. 1964. *Nation-Building and Citizenship.* New York: John Wiley.

Bendix, Reinhard, ed. 1968. *State and Society.* Boston, MA: Little, Brown.

Bendix, Reinhard and Seymour Martin Lipset. 1957. "Political Sociology." *Current Sociology* 6:79–99.

Benford, Robert D. and David A. Snow. 2000. "Framing Processes and Social Movements." *Annual Review of Sociology* 26:611–39.

Berelson, Bernard, Paul Lazarfeld, and William McPhee. 1954. *Voting.* Chicago, IL: University of Chicago Press.

Block, Fred. 1981. "The Fiscal Crisis of the Capitalist State." *Annual Review of Sociology* 7:1–27.

Block, Fred. 1987. *Revising State Theory.* Philadelphia, PA: Temple University Press.

Boies, John L. 1989. "Money, Business and the State." *American Sociological Review* 54:821–32.

Boli, John and George M. Thomas. 1997. "World Culture in the World Polity." *American Sociological Review* 62:171–90.

Brooks, Clem. 2000. "Civil Rights Liberalism and the Suppression of a Republican Political Realignment in the United States, 1971–1996. "*American Sociological Review* 65:483–505.

Brooks, Clem and Jeff Manza. 1997a. "The Social and Ideological Bases of Middle-Class Political Realignment in the United States, 1972–1992." *American Sociological Review* 62:191–209.

Brooks, Clem and Jeff Manza. 1997b. "Social Cleavages and Political Alignments in US Elections." *American Sociological Review* 62:937–46.

Brubaker, Rogers. 1992. *Citizenship and Nationhood in France and Germany.* Cambridge, MA: Harvard University Press.

Brubaker, Rogers. 1996. *Nationalism Reframed.* New York: Cambridge University Press.

Brustein, William. 1996. *The Logic of Evil.* New Haven, CT: Yale University Press.

Buechler, Steven M. 1995. "New Social Movement Theories." *Sociological Quarterly* 36:441–64.

Burris, Val. 1987. "Business Partisanship of American Business." *American Sociological Review* 52:732–44.

Burris, Val. 1991. "Interlocks and the Political Behavior of Corporations and Corporate Elites." *Social Science Quarterly* 72:537–51.

Burris, Val. 1992. "PACs, Interlocks and Regional Differences in Corporate Conservatism." *American Journal of Sociology* 97:1451–55.

Burstein, Paul. 1981. "The Sociology of Democratic Politics and Government." *Annual Review of Sociology* 7:291–319.

Burstein, Paul. 1998. "Bringing the Public Back In." *Social Forces* 77:27–62.

Burstein, Paul and April Linton. 2002. "The Impact of Political Parties, Interest Groups, and Social Movement Organizations on Public Policy." *Social Forces* 81:381–408.

Calavita, Kitty, Henry Pontell, and Robert Tillman. 1997. *Big Money Crime.* Berkeley: University of California Press.

Calhoun, Craig, ed. 1992. *Habermas and the Public Sphere.* Cambridge: MIT Press.

Campbell, Angus, Philip Converse, Warren Miller, and Donald Stokes. 1960. *The American Voter.* New York: John Wiley.

Campbell, John L. 1993. "The State and Fiscal Sociology." *Annual Review of Sociology* 19:163–85.

Campbell, John L. 2004. *Institutional Change and Globalization.* Princeton, NJ: Princeton University Press.

Campbell, John and Leon Lindberg. 1990. "Property Rights and the Organization of Economic Activity by the State." *American Sociological Review* 55:634–47.

Campbell, John L. and Ove K. Pedersen, eds. 2001. *The Rise of Neoliberalism and Institutional Analysis.* Princeton, NJ: Princeton University Press.

Castles, Francis G. and Deborah Mitchell. 1992. "Identifying Welfare State Regimes." *Governance* 5:1–26.

Castles, Francis G. and Deborah Mitchell. 1993. "Worlds of Welfare and Families of Nations." Pp. 93–128 in *Families of Nations,* edited by F. Castles. Brookfield, VT: Dartmouth.

Clark, Gordon and Michael Dear. 1984. *State Apparatus.* Boston, MA: Allen & Unwin.

Clawson, Dan and Mary Ann Clawson. 1987. "Reagan or Business?" Pp. 201–17, in *The Structure of Power in America,* edited by M. Schwartz. New York: Holmes and Meier.

Clawson, Dan and Alan Neustadtl. 1989. "Interlocks, PACs, and Corporate Conservatism." *American Journal of Sociology* 94:749–73.

Clawson, Dan, Alan Neustadtl, and James Bearden. 1986. "The Logic of Business Unity." *American Sociological Review* 51:797–81.

Clawson, Dan, Alan Neustadt, and Mark Weller. 1998. *Dollars and Votes.* Philadelphia, PA: Temple University Press.

Clawson, Dan and Tie Ting Su. 1990. "Was 1980 Special?" *Sociological Quarterly* 31:371–88.

Clemens, Elisabeth S. 1993. "Organizational Repertoires and Institutional Change." *American Journal of Sociology* 98:755–98.

Clemens, Elisabeth S. and James Cook. 1999. "Politics and Institutionalism." *Annual Review of Sociology* 25:441–66.

Converse, Phillip E. 1964. "The Nature of Belief Systems in Mass Publics." In *Ideology and Its Discontent,* edited by D. Apter. New York: Free Press.

Crozier, Michel J., Samuel P. Huntington, and Joji Watanuki. 1975. *The Crisis of Democracy.* New York: New York University Press.

Cutright, Phillips. 1963. "National Political Development." *American Sociological Review* 28:253–64.

Cutright, Phillips. 1965. "Political Structure, Economic Development and National Social Security Programs." *American Journal of Sociology* 70:537–50.

Dalton, Russell, Scott Flanagan, and Paul Beck, eds. 1984. *Electoral Change in Advanced Industrial Democracies.* Princeton, NJ: Princeton University Press.

Della Porta, Donnatella and H. Reiter, eds. 1998. *Policing Protest.* Minneapolis: University of Minnesota Press.

Deutsch, Karl W. 1966. *Nationalism and Social Communication.* Cambridge: MIT Press.

Diani, Mario. 1996. "Linking Mobilization Frames and Political Opportunities." *American Sociological Review* 61:1053–69.

Dixon, Marc and Vincent J. Roscigno. 2003. "Status, Networks, and Social Movement Participation." *American Journal of Sociology* 108:1292–327.

Dobbin, Frank R. 1992. "The Origins of Private Social Insurance." *American Journal of Sociology* 97:1416–50.

Dobbin, Frank R. 1994. *Forging Industrial Policy.* New York: Cambridge University Press.

Dobbin, Frank R. and Timothy Dowd. 2000. "The Market That Antitrust Built." *American Sociological Review* 65:631–58.

Dobratz, Betty, Timothy Buzzell, and Lisa Waldner. 2003. "Introduction." *Research in Political Sociology* 12:1–16.

Domhoff, G. William. 1967. *Who Rules America?* Englewood Cliffs, NJ: Prentice Hall.

Domhoff, G. William. 1970. *The Higher Circles.* New York: Random House.

Domhoff, G. William. 1974. *The Bohemian Grove and Other Retreats.* New York: Harper & Row.

Domhoff, G. William. 1978. *The Powers That Be.* New York: Vintage.

Domhoff, G. William, ed. 1980. *Power Structure Research.* Beverly Hills, CA: Sage.

Domhoff, G. William. 1983. *Who Rules America Now?* Englewood Cliffs, NJ: Prentice Hall.

Domhoff, G. William. 1990. *The Power Elite and the State.* New York: Aldine de Gruyter.

Downs, Anthony. 1957. *An Economic Theory of Democracy.* New York: Harper.

Earl, Jennifer, Sarah Soule, and John McCarthy. 2003. "Protest under Fire?" *American Sociological Review* 68:581–606.

Edelman, Murray. 1964. *The Symbolic Uses of Politics.* Urbana: University of Illinois Press.

Eliasoph, Nina. 1998. *Avoiding Politics.* New York: Cambridge University Press.

Ertman, Richard. 1997. *Birth of the Leviathan.* New York: Cambridge University Press.

Esping-Andersen, Gøta. 1990. *The Three Worlds of Welfare Capitalism.* Princeton, NJ: Princeton University Press.

Evans, Peter, Dietrich Rueschemeyer, and Theda Skocpol, eds. 1985. *Bringing the State Back In.* New York: Cambridge University Press.

Ferrara, Maurizio. 1996. "The 'Southern Model' of Welfare in Social Europe." *Journal of European Social Policy* 6:17–37.

Ferree, Myra Marx. 2003. "Resonance and Radicalism." *American Journal of Sociology* 109:304–44.

Ferree, Myra Marx, William Gamson, Jurgen Gerhards, and Dieter Rucht. 2002. "Four Models of the Public Sphere in Modern Democracy." *Theory and Society* 31:289–324.

Finegold, Kenneth and Theda Skocpol. 1995. *State and Party in America's New Deal.* Madison: University of Wisconsin Press.

Fligstein, Neil. 1996. "Markets as Politics." *American Sociological Review* 61:656–73.

Fligstein, Neil and Alec Sweet. 2002. "Constructing Polities and Markets." *American Journal of Sociology* 107:1206–43.

Fording, Richard C. 1997. "The Conditional Effect of Violence As a Political Tactic." *American Journal of Political Science* 41:1–29.

Foucault, Michel. 1986. "Governmentality." *Ideology and Consciousness* 6:5–21.

Frank, Andre Gunder. 1967. *Capitalism and Underdevelopment in Latin America.* New York: Monthly Review Press.

Gamson, William A. 1968. *Power and Discontent.* Homewood, IL: Dorsey Press.

Gamson, William A. 1975. *The Strategy of Social Protest.* Homewood, IL: Dorsey Press.

Gamson, William A. 1992. *Talking Politics.* New York: Cambridge University Press.

Gamson, William A. 1996. "Framing Political Opportunity." Pp. 291–311 in *Comparative Perspectives on Social Movements,* edited by D. McAdam, J. McCarthy, and M. Zald. New York: Cambridge University Press.

Gamson, William A. and Andre Modigliani. 1989. "Media Discourse and Public Opinion on Nuclear Power." *American Journal of Sociology* 95:1–37.

Gamson, William A. and Gadi Wolfseld. 1993. "Movements and Media as Interacting Systems." *Annals of the American Academy of Political and Social Science* 528:114–25.

Garland, David. 2001. *The Culture of Control.* Chicago, IL: University of Chicago Press.

Giddens, Anthony. 1987. *The Nation-State and Violence.* Berkeley: University of California Press.

Gilbert, Jess and Carolyn Howe. 1991. "Beyond 'State vs. Society.'" *American Sociological Review* 56:204–20.

Glasberg, Davita Silfan and Dan Skidmore. 1997. *Corporate Welfare Policy and the Welfare State.* New York: Aldine de Gruyter.

Goldstone, Jack A. 1991. *Revolution and Rebellion in the Early Modern World.* Berkeley: University of California Press.

Goldstone, Jack A., Ted Gurr, and Farrokh Moshiri, eds. 1991. *Revolutions of the Late Twentieth Century.* Boulder, CO: Westview Press.

Goodwin, Lawrence. 1976. *Democratic Promise.* New York: Oxford University Press.

Gornick, Janet and Jerry Jacobs. 1998. "Gender, the Welfare States, and Public Employment." *American Sociological Review* 63:688–710.

Grant, Donald Sherman, II. 1995. "The Political Economy of Business Failure across the American States, 1970–1985." *American Sociological Review* 60:851–73.

Grant, Donald Sherman, II and Michael Wallace. 1994. "The Political Economy of Manufacturing Growth and Decline across the American States, 1970–1985." *Social Forces* 73:33–63.

Gusfield, Joseph R. 1963. *Symbolic Crusade.* Urbana: University of Illinois Press.

Hall, John R., ed. 1997. *Reworking Class.* Ithaca, NY: Cornell University Press.

Hall, Peter. 1981. "Political Sociology." *Current Perspectives on Social Theory* 2:15–20.

Hall, Peter and David Soskice, eds. 2001. *Varieties of Capitalism.* New York: Oxford University Press.

Hecther, Michael. 2004. "From Class to Culture." *American Journal of Sociology* 110:400–45.

Hechter, Michael and Satoshi Kanazawa. 1997. "Sociological Rational Choice Theory." *Annual Review of Sociology* 23:191–214.

Hicks, Alexander M. 1995. "Is Political Sociology Informed by Political Science?" *Social Forces* 73:1219–29.

Hicks, Alexander M. 1999. *Social Democracy and Welfare Capitalism.* Ithaca, NY: Cornell University Press.

Hicks, Alexander, Thomas Janoski, and Mildred Schwartz. 2005. "Political Sociology in the New Millennium." Pp. 1–32 in *Handbook of Political Sociology,* edited by T. Janoski, R. Alford, A. Hicks, and M. Schwartz. New York: Cambridge University Press.

Hicks, Alexander and Lane Kenworthy. 1998. "Cooperation and Political Economic Performance in Affluent Democratic Capitalism." *American Journal of Sociology* 103:1631–72.

Hicks, Alexander M. and Duane H. Swank. 1983. "Civil disorder, relief mobilization, and AFDC Caseloads." *American Journal of Political Science* 27:695–716.

Hooks, Gregory. 1990a. "From an Autonomous to a Captured Agency." *American Sociological Review* 55:29–43.

Hooks, Gregory. 1990b. "The Rise of the Pentagon and U.S. State Building." *American Journal of Sociology* 96:358–404.

Hooks, Gregory. 1991. *Forging the Military-Industrial Complex.* Urbana: University of Illinois Press.

Hooks, Gregory. 1994. "Regional Processes in the Hegemonic Nation." *American Sociological Review* 59:746–72.

Hout, Michael, Clem Brooks, and Jeff Manza. 1995. "The Democratic Class Struggle in the United States, 1948–1992." *American Sociological Review* 60:805–28.

Huber, Evelyne, Charles Ragin, and John D. Stephens. 1993. "Social Democracy, Christian Democracy, Constitutional Structure and the Welfare State." *American Journal of Sociology* 99:711–49.

Huber, Evelyne and John D. Stephens. 2000. "Partisan Government, Women's Employment, and the Social Democratic Service State." *American Sociological Review* 65:323–42.

Huber, Evelyne and John D. Stephens. 2001. *Development and Crisis of the Welfare State.* Chicago, IL: University of Chicago Press.

Hunter, Floyd. 1953. *Community Power Structure.* Chapel Hill: University of North Carolina Press.

Huntington, Samuel P. 1968. *Political Order in Changing Societies.* New Haven, CT: Yale University Press.

Immergut, Ellen M. 1998. "The Theoretical Core of the New Institutionalism." *Politics and Society* 26:5–34.

Inglehart, Ronald. 1997. *Modernization and Postmodernization.* Princeton, NJ: Princeton University Press.

Inglehart, Ronald and Wayne E. Baker. 2000. "Modernization, Cultural Change, and the Persistence of Traditional Values." *American Sociological Review* 65:19–52.

Isaac, Larry and Lars Christiansen. 2002. "How the Civil Rights Movement Revitalized Labor Militancy." *American Sociological Review* 67:722–46.

Isaac, Larry and William R. Kelly. 1981. "Racial Insurgency, the State and Welfare Expansion." *American Journal of Sociology* 86:1348–86.

Iversen, Torben. 2001. "The Dynamics of Welfare State Expansion." Pp. 45–79 in *The New Politics of the Welfare State,* edited by P. Pierson. New York: Oxford University Press.

Iversen Torben and Thomas R. Cusack. 2000. "The Causes of Welfare State Expansion." *World Politics* 52:313–49.

Jacobs, David and Ronald E. Helms. 1996. "Toward a Political Model of Incarceration." *American Journal of Sociology* 102:323–57.

Jacobs, David and Richard Kleban. 2003. "Political Institutions, Minorities, and Punishment." *Social Forces* 82:725–55.

Janoski, Thomas. 1990. "Conflicting Approaches to Citizenship Rights." *Comparative Social Research* 12:209–38.

Janowitz, Morris. 1968. "Political Sociology." *International Encyclopedia of Social Science* 12:298–307.

Jenkins, J. Craig. 1983. "Resource Mobilization Theory and the Study of Social Movements." *Annual Review of Sociology* 9:527–53.

Jenkins, J. Craig and Barbara G. Brents. 1989. "Social Protest, Hegemonic Competition, and Social Reform." *American Sociological Review* 54:891–909.

Jenkins, J. Craig, David Jacobs, and Jon Agnone. 2003. "Political Opportunities and African American Protest, 1948–1997." *American Journal of Sociology* 109:277–303.

Jenkins, J. Craig and Charles Perrow. 1977. "Insurgency of the Powerless." *American Sociological Review* 42:249–68.

Jessop, Bob. 1982. *The Capitalist State.* New York: New York University Press.

Jessop, Bob. 1990. *State Theory.* University Park: Pennsylvania State University Press.

Jones, Catherine, ed. 1993. *Perspectives on the Welfare State in Europe.* New York: Routledge.

Kent, Stephanie and David Jacobs. 2004. "Social Divisions and Coercive Control in Advanced Societies." *Social Problems* 51:343–61.

Kertzer, David I. and Dominique Arel, eds. 2002. *Census and Identity.* New York: Cambridge University Press.

King, Desmond and Stewart Wood. 1999. "The Political Economy of Neoliberalism." Pp. 371–97 in *Continuities and Change in Contemporary Capitalism,* edited by H. Kitschelt, P. Lang, G. Marks, and J. Stephens. New York: Cambridge University Press.

Kiser, Edgar and Michael Hechter. 1991. "The Role of General Theory in Comparative Historical Sociology." *American Journal of Sociology* 97:1–30.

Kitschelt, Herbert B. 1986. "Political Opportunity Structures and the Political Protest." *British Journal of Political Science* 16:57–85.

Kitschelt, Herbert, Peter Lange, Gary Marks, and John D. Stephens, eds. 1999. *Continuity and Change in Contemporary Capitalism.* New York: Cambridge University Press.

Klandermans, Bert. 1984. "Mobilization and Participation." *American Sociological Review* 49:583–600.

Klandermans, Bert and Dirk Oegema. 1987. "Potentials, Networks, Motivations, and Barriers." *American Sociological Review* 52:519–31.

Kolko, Gabriel. 1963. *Triumph of Conservatism.* Chicago, IL: Quadrangle.

Koopmans, Ruud. 1993. "The Dynamics of Protest Waves." *American Sociological Review* 58:637–58.

Kornhauser, William. 1959. *The Politics of Mass Society.* New York: Free Press.

Korpi, Walter. 1978. *The Working Class and Welfare Capitalism.* New York: Routledge & Kegan Paul.

Korpi, Walter. 1983. *The Democratic Class Struggle.* New York: Routledge.

Korpi, Walter. 1989. "Power, Politics and State Autonomy in the Development of Social Citizenship." *American Sociological Review* 54:309–28.

Korpi, Walter. 2000. "Faces of Inequality: Gender, Class, and Patterns of Inequalities in Different Types of Welfare States. *Social Politics* 7:127–91.

Korpi, Walter. 2003. "Welfare-State Regress in Western Europe." *Annual Review of Sociology* 29:589–609.

Korpi, Walter and Joakim Palme. 1998. "The Paradox of Redistribution and Strategies of Equality." *American Sociological Review* 63:661–87.

Kourvetaris, George A. and Betty Dobratz. 1982. "Political Power and Conventional Political Behavior." *Annual Review of Sociology* 8:289–317.

Kourvetaris, George A. and Betty Dobratz. 1983. "An Analysis and Assessment of Political Sociology." *Micropolitics* 3:89–133.

Lachmann, Richard. 2003. "Elite Self-Interest and Economic Decline in Early Modern Europe." *American Sociological Review* 68:346–72.

Laraña, Enrique, Hank Johnson, and Joseph Gusfield, eds. 1994. *New Social Movements from Ideology to Identity.* Philadelphia, PA: Temple University Press.

Lane, Robert E. 1962. *Political Ideology.* New York: Free Press.

Lee, David and Bryan Turner, eds. 1996. *Conflicts about Class.* New York: Longman.

Lenski, Gerhard E. 1966. *Power and Privilege.* New York: McGraw-Hill.

Lieberman, Robert C. 1998. *Shifting the Color Line.* Cambridge, MA: Harvard University Press.

Lipset, Seymour Martin. 1959a. "Political Sociology." Pp. 81–114 in *Sociology Today,* edited by R. Merton, L. Bloom, and L. Cottrell. New York: Basic Books.

Lipset, Seymour Martin. 1959b. "Some Social Requisites of Democracy." *American Sociological Review* 53:71–85.

Lipset, Seymour Martin. 1960. *Political Man.* New York: Doubleday.

Lipset, Seymour Martin. 1963. *First New Nation.* New York: Basic Books.

Lipset, Seymour Martin, Martin Trow, and James Coleman. 1956. *Union Democracy.* New York: Free Press.

Lipsky, Michael. 1968. "Protest as a Political Resource." *American Political Science Review* 62:1144–58.

Lukes, Steven. 1974. *Power.* London, England: Macmillan.

Mann, Michael. 1987. "Ruling Class Strategies and Citizenship." *Sociology* 21:339–54.

Mann, Michael. 1988. *States, War and Capitalism*. Cambridge, MA: Basil Blackwell.

Mann, Michael. 1993. *The Sources of Social Power*. Vol. 2. New York: Cambridge University Press.

Manza, Jeff. 2000. "Race and the Underdevelopment of the American Welfare State." *Theory and Society* 29:819–32.

Manza, Jeff and Clem Brooks. 1997. "The Religious Factor in U.S. Presidential Elections, 1960–1992." *American Journal of Sociology* 103:38–81.

Manza, Jeff and Clem Brooks. 1998. "Gender Gap in U.S. Presidential Elections?" *American Journal of Sociology* 103:1235–66.

Manza, Jeff and Clem Brooks. 1999. *Social Cleavages and Political Change*. New York: Oxford University Press.

Manza, Jeff, Michael Hout, and Clem Brooks. 1995. "Class Voting in Capitalist Democracies Since World War II." *Annual Review of Sociology* 21:137–62.

Marwell, Gerald and Pamela Oliver. 1993. *The Critical Mass in Collective Action*. Cambridge, England: Cambridge University Press.

McAdam, Doug. 1982. *Political Process and the Development of Black Insurgency, 1930–1970*. Chicago, IL: University of Chicago Press.

McAdam, Doug. 1989. "The Biographical Consequences of Activism." *American Sociological Review* 54:744–60.

McAdam, Doug and Yang Su. 2002. "The War at Home." *American Sociological Review* 67:696–721.

McCarthy, John D., Clark McPhail, and Jackie Smith. 1996. "Images of Protest." *American Sociological Review* 61:478–99.

McCarthy, John D. and Mayer N. Zald. 1977. "Resource Mobilization and Social Movements." *American Journal of Sociology* 82:1212–41.

McNall, Scott, Rhonda Levine, and Rick Fantasia, eds. 1991. *Bringing Class Back In*. Boulder, CO: Westview Press.

Meyer, David S. and Debra C. Minkoff. 2004. "Conceptualizing Political Opportunity." *Social Forces* 82:1457–92.

Meyer, David S. and Suzanne Staggenborg. 1996. "Movements, Countermovements, and the Structure of Political Opportunity." *American Journal of Sociology* 101:1628–60.

Meyer, John W., John Boli, George Thomas, and Francisco Ramirez. 1997. "World Society and the Nation State." *American Journal of Sociology* 103:144–81.

Miliband, Ralph. 1969. *The State in Capitalist Society*. New York: Basic Books.

Miliband, Ralph. 1977. *Marxism and Politics*. New York: Oxford University Press.

Miliband, Ralph. 1982. *Class Power and State Power*. London, England: Verso.

Mills, C. Wright. 1956. *Power Elite*. New York: Oxford University Press.

Minkoff, Debra C. 1997. "The Sequencing of Social Movements." *American Sociological Review* 62:779–99.

Minkoff, Debra C. 1999. "Bending with the Wind." *American Journal of Sociology* 104:1666–703.

Mizruchi, Mark S. and Thomas Koenig. 1986. "Economic Sources of Corporate Political Consensus." *American Sociological Review* 51:482–91.

Moller, Stephanie, D. Bradley, E. Huber, F. Nielsen, and J. Stephens. 2003. "Determinates of Relative Poverty in Advanced Capitalist Nations." *American Sociological Review* 68:22–51.

Moore, Barrington, Jr. 1966. *Social Origins of Dictatorship and Democracy*. Boston, MA: Beacon.

Morris, Aldon D. 1981. "Black Southern Sit-In Movement." *American Sociological Review* 46:744–67.

Morris, Aldon D. 1992. "Political Consciousness and Collective Action." Pp. 351–73 in *Frontiers in Social Movement Theory*, edited by A. Morris and C. M. Mueller. New Haven, CT: Yale University Press.

Morris, Aldon D. 1993. "Birmingham Confrontation Reconsidered." *American Sociological Review* 58:621–36.

Mueller, Carol. 1997. "International Press Coverage of East German Protest Events." *American Sociological Review* 62:820–32.

Myers, Daniel J. and Schaefer Caniglia. 2004. "All the Rioting That's Fit to Print." *American Sociological Review* 69:519–43.

Nash, Kate. 2000. *Contemporary Political Sociology: Globalization, Politics and Power*. Malden, MA: Basil Blackwell.

Neuman, W. Lawrence. 1998. "Negotiated Meanings and State Transformation" *Social Problems* 45:315–35.

O'Connor, James. 1973. *The Fiscal Crisis of the State*. New York: St. Martin's.

O'Connor, James. 1984. *Accumulation Crisis*. New York: Basil Blackwell.

Oliver, Pamela E. and Gregory Maney. 2000. "Political Cycles and Local Newspaper Coverage." *American Journal of Sociology* 106:463–505.

Oliver, Pamela E. and Daniel J. Meyers. 1999. "How Events Enter the Public Sphere." *American Journal of Sociology* 105:38–87.

Olson, Marcur. 1965. *The Logic of Collective Action*. Cambridge, MA: Harvard University Press.

Opp, Karl-Dieter and Christiane Gern. 1993. "Dissident Groups, Personal Networks, and Spontaneous Cooperation." *American Sociological Review* 58:659–80.

Orloff, Ann Shola. 1993. "Gender and Social Rights of Citizenship." *American Sociological Review* 58:303–28.

Orloff, Ann Shola. 1996. "Gender in the Welfare State." *Annual Review of Sociology* 22:51–78.

Orloff, Ann Shola and Theda Skocpol. 1984. "Why Not Equal Protection?" *American Sociological Review* 49:726–50.

Orum, Anthony. 1966. "A Reappraisal of the Social and Political Participation of Negroes." *American Journal of Sociology* 72:32–46.

Orum, Anthony. 1996. "Almost a Half Century of Political Sociology." *Current Sociology* 44:132–51.

Paige, Jeffrey M. 1975. *Agrarian Revolution*. New York: Free Press.

Petras, James F. 1969. *Politics and Social Forces in Chilean Development*. Berkeley: University of California Press.

Pichardo, Nelson. 1997. "New Social Mobilizations." *Annual Review of Sociology* 23:411–30.

Pierson, Paul. 2001. "Coping with Permanent Austerity." Pp. 410–456 in *The New Politics of the Welfare State*, edited by P. Pierson. New York: Oxford University Press.

Piven, Frances Fox and Richard A. Cloward. 1971. *Regulating the Poor*. New York: Pantheon Books.

Piven, Frances Fox and Richard A. Cloward. 1977. *Poor People's Movements*. New York: Vintage.

Piven, Frances Fox and Richard A. Cloward. 2000. *Why Americans Still Don't Vote*. Boston, MA: Beacon.

Poulantzas, Nicos. 1973. *Political Power and Social Classes.* London, England: New Left Books.

Poulantzas, Nicos. 1974. *Fascism and Dictatorship.* London, England: New Left Books.

Poulantzas, Nicos. 1978. *State, Power, Socialism.* London. England: New Left Books.

Prechel, Harland. 1990. "Steel and the State." *American Sociological Review* 55:648–68.

Prechel, Harland. 1997. "Corporate Transformation to the Multilayered Subsidiary Form." *Sociological Forum* 12:405–39.

Prechel, Harland. 2000. *Big Business and the State.* Albany: State University of New York Press.

Prechel, Harland and John Boies. 1998. "Capital Dependence, Financial Risk, and Change from the Multidivisional to the Multilayered Subsidiary Form." *Sociological Forum* 13:321–62.

Quadagno, Jill. 1984. "Welfare Capitalism and the Social Security Act of 1935." *American Sociological Review* 49:632–48.

Quadagno, Jill. 1987. "Theories of the Welfare State." *Annual Review of Sociology* 13:109–28.

Quadagno, Jill. 1988. *The Transformation of Old Age Security.* Chicago, IL: University of Chicago Press.

Quadagno, Jill. 1990. "Race, Class and Gender in the U.S. Welfare State." *American Sociological Review* 55:11–28.

Quadagno, Jill. 1992. "Social Movements and State Transformation." *American Sociological Review* 57:616–34.

Quadagno, Jill. 1994. *The Color of Welfare.* New York: Oxford University Press.

Ramirez, Francisco, Yasemin Soysal, and Susanne Shanahan. 1997. "The Changing Logic of Political Citizenship." *American Sociological Review* 62:735–45.

Ransford, H. Edward. 1968. "Isolation, Powerlessness, and Violence." *American Journal of Sociology* 73:581–91.

Rasler, Karen. 1996. "Concessions, Repression, and Political Protest in the Iranian Revolution." *American Sociological Review* 61:132–52.

Roche, Maurice. 1992. *Rethinking Citizenship.* Cambridge, England: Polity Press.

Roy, William G. 1984. "Class Conflict and Social Change in Historical Perspective." *Annual Review of Sociology* 10:483–506.

Roy, William G. 1997. *Socializing Capital.* Princeton, NJ: Princeton University Press.

Rueschemeyer, Dietrich, Evelyne Huber Stephens, and John D. Stephens. 1992. *Capitalist Development and Democracy.* Chicago, IL: University of Chicago Press.

Rush, Gary. 1967. "Status Consistency and Rightwing Extremism." *American Sociological Review* 32:86–92.

Savelsberg, Joachim J. 1992. "Law That Does Not Fit Society." *American Journal of Sociology* 97:1346–415.

Savelsberg, Joachim J. 1994. "Knowledge, Domination and Criminal Punishment." *American Journal of Sociology* 99:911–43.

Savelsberg, Joachim, Lara Cleveland, and Ryan King. 2004. "Institutional Environments and Scholarly Work." *Social Forces* 82:1275–302.

Scott, James. 1998. *Seeing Like a State.* New Haven, CT: Yale University Press.

Segal, David. 1969. "Status Inconsistency, Cross Pressures, and American Political Behavior." *American Sociological Review* 34:352–58.

Segal, David and David Knoke. 1968. "Social Mobility, Status Inconsistency and the Partisan Realignment of the United States." *Social Forces* 47:154–47.

Shoup, Laurence H. and William Minter, 1977. *Imperial Brain Trust.* New York: Monthly Review Press.

Skerry, Peter. 2000. *Counting on the Census?* Washington, DC: Brookings Institution Press.

Skocpol, Theda. 1979. *States and Revolutions.* New York: Cambridge University Press.

Skocpol, Theda. 1985. "Bringing the State Back In." Pp. 3–43 in *Bringing the State Back In,* edited by P. Evans, D. Rueschemeyer, and T. Skocpol. New York: Cambridge University Press.

Skocpol, Theda. 1992. *Protecting Soldiers & Mothers: The Political Origins of Social Policy in the United States.* Cambridge, MA: Harvard University Press.

Skocpol, Theda and Edwin Amenta. 1985. "Did Capitalists Shape Social Security?" *American Sociological Review* 50:572–78.

Smelser, Neil. 1963. *The Theory of Collective Behavior.* New York: Free Press.

Snow, David A. and Robert D. Benford. 1992. "Master Frames and Cycles of Protest." Pp. 133–55 in *Frontiers in Social Movement Theory,* edited by. A. Morris and C. M. Mueller. New Haven, CT: Yale University Press.

Snow, David A., E. Burke Rochford Jr., Steven K. Worden, and Robert D. Benford. 1986. "Frame Alignment Processes, Micromobilization, and Movement Participation." *American Sociological Review* 51:464–81.

Snow, David A., Louis Zurcher Jr., and Sheldon Ekland-Olson. 1980. "Social Networks and Social Movements." *American Sociological Review* 45:787–801.

Somers, Margaret R. 1993. "Citizenship and the Place of the Public Sphere." *American Sociological Review* 58:587–620.

Soule, Sarah and Susan Olzak. 2004. "When Do Movements Matter?" *American Sociological Review* 69:473–97.

Soule, Sarah and Yvonne Zylan. 1997. "Runaway Train?" *American Journal of Sociology* 103:733–62.

Soysal, Y. N. 1994. *Limits of Citizenship.* Chicago, IL: University of Chicago Press.

Steinmetz, George, ed. 1999. *State/Culture.* Ithaca, NY: Cornell University Press.

Stephens, John D., E. Huber, and L. Ray. 1999. "The Welfare State in Hard Times." Pp. 164–93 in *Continuity and Change in Contemporary Capitalism,* edited by H. Kitschelt, P. Lange, G. Markes, and J. Stephens. New York: Cambridge University Press.

Stouffer, Samuel. 1955. *Communism, Conformity and Civil Liberties.* New York: Doubleday.

Stryker, Robin. 1989. "Limits on Technocratization of the Law." *American Sociological Review* 54:341–58.

Stryker, Robin. 1990. "Law, Science and the Welfare State." *American Journal of Sociology* 96:684–726.

Stryker, Robin. 1994. "Rules, Resources, and Legitimacy Processes." *American Journal of Sociology* 99:847–910.

Sutton, John R. 2000. "Imprisonment and Social Classification in Five Common-Law Democracies, 1955–1985." *American Journal of Sociology* 106:350–86.

Sutton, John R. 2004. "The Political Economy of Imprisonment in Affluent Western Democracies, 1960–1990." *American Sociological Review* 69:170–89.

Swank, Duane. 1992. "Politics and the Structural Dependence of the State in Democratic Capitalist Nations." *American Political Science Review* 86:38–54.

Swank, Duane. 2002. *Global Capital, Political Institutions, and Policy Change in Developed Welfare States.* New York: Cambridge University Press.

Tarrow, Sidney. 1994. *Power in Movement.* New York: Cambridge University Press.

Teixeira, Ruy A. 1992. *The Disappearing American Voter.* Washington, DC: Brookings.

Tilly, Charles, ed. 1975. *The Formation of National States in Western Europe.* Princeton, NJ: Princeton University Press.

Tilly, Charles. 1978. *From Mobilization to Revolution.* Reading, MA: Addison Wesley.

Tilly, Charles. 1990. *Coercion, Capital and European States.* Cambridge, MA: Basil Blackwell.

Tilly, Charles, ed. 1996. *Citizenship, Identity and Social History.* New York: Cambridge University Press.

Torpey, John. 2000. *The Invention of the Passport.* New York: Cambridge University Press.

Uggen, Christopher and Jeff Manza. 2002. "Democratic Contraction?" *American Sociological Review* 67:777–803.

Useem, Michael. 1984. *The Inner Circle.* New York: Oxford University Press.

Wallerstein, Immanuel. 1976. *The Modern World System.* New York: Academic Press.

Weinstein, James. 1968. *The Corporate Ideal in the Liberal State.* Boston, MA: Beacon.

Whittier, Nancy. 1997. "Political Generations, Micro-Cohorts, and the Transformation of Social Movements." *American Sociological Review* 62:779–99.

Wilensky, Harold. 1975. *The Welfare State and Equality.* Berkeley: University of California Press.

Wilensky, Harold L. and Charles N. Lebeaux. 1958. *Industrial Society and Social Welfare.* New York: Russell Sage.

Williams, William Applebaum. 1964. *The Great Evasion.* Chicago, IL: Quadrangle.

Wisler, Dominique and Marco Giugni. 1999. "Under the Spotlight." *Mobilization* 4:171–87.

Wolf, Eric R. 1969. *Peasant Wars of the Twentieth Century.* New York: Harper & Row.

Wolfe, Alan. 1973. *The Seamy Side of Democracy.* New York: David McKay.

Wright, Erik O. 1978. *Class, Crisis and the State.* London, England: New Left Books.

Wright, Erik O. 1997. *Class Counts.* New York: Cambridge University Press.

Zald, Mayer N. and Michael A. Berger. 1978. "Social Movements in Organizations." *American Journal of Sociology* 83:823–61.

Zeitlin, Maurice. 1967. *Revolutionary Politics and the Cuban Working Class.* Princeton, NJ: Princeton University Press.

Zeitlin, Maurice, W. Lawrence Neuman, and Richard E. Ratcliff. 1976. "Class Segments." *American Sociological Review* 41:1006–29.

Chapter 31. The Sociology of Education

Anyon, Jean. 1983. *Social Class and Gender in U.S. Education.* London, England: Routledge.

Bank, Barbara J. and Bruce J. Biddle. 1997. "Social Psychological Theories in Education." Pp. 32–42 in *International Encyclopedia of the Sociology of Education,* edited by L. J. Saha. New York: Elsevier.

Banks, Oliver. 1971. *The Sociology of Education.* 2d ed. London, England: Batsford.

Bernstein, Basil. 1977. *Class, Codes and Control.* Vol. 3, *Towards a Theory of Educational Transmission.* 2d ed. London, England: Routledge.

Bidwell, Charles E. 2005. "A Sociological Agenda for Research on Education." Pp. 15–36 in *The Social Organization of Schooling,* edited by L. V. Hedges and B. Schneider. New York: Russell Sage.

Bidwell, Charles E. and Noah E. Friedkin. 1988. "The Sociology of Education." Pp. 449–71 in *Handbook of Sociology,* edited by N. J. Smelser. Newbury Park, CA: Sage.

Bowles, Samuel and Herbert Gintis. 1976. *Schooling in Capitalist America: Educational Reform and the Contradictions of Economic Life.* London, England: Routledge.

Brown, David K. 2001. "The Sources of Educational Credentialism: Status Cultures, Labor Markets, and Organizations." *Sociology of Education* 74(extra issue):19–34.

Cohen, Elizabeth G. and Rachel A. Lotan, eds. 1997. *Working for Equity in Heterogenous Classrooms.* New York: Teachers College Press.

Collins, Randall. 1979. *The Credential Society.* New York: Academic Press.

Corwin, Ronald G. 1970. *Militant Professionalism.* New York: Appleton.

Dreeben, Robert. 2005. "Teaching and the Competence of Occupations." Pp. 51–71 in *The Social Organization of Schooling,* edited by L. V. Hedges and B. Schneider. New York: Russell Sage.

Durkheim, Émile. [1922] 1956. *Education and Sociology.* Glencoe, NY: Free Press.

Epstein, Joyce L. and Mavis G. Sanders. 2000. "Connecting Home, School, and Community: New Directions for Research." Pp. 285–306 in *Handbook of the Sociology of Education,* edited by M. T. Hallinan. New York: Kluwer.

Gamoran, Adam, Walter G. Secada, and Cora B. Marrett. 2000. "The Organizational Context of Teaching and Learning: Changing Theoretical Perspectives." Pp. 37–64 in *Handbook of the Sociology of Education,* edited by M. T. Hallinan. New York: Kluwer.

Giroux, Henry A. 1981. *Ideology, Culture, and the Process of Schooling.* London, England: Falmer.

Goffman, Erving. 1972. *Interaction Ritual.* London, England: Allen Lane.

Hallinan, Maureen T., ed. 2000a. *Handbook of the Sociology of Education.* New York: Kluwer.

Hallinan, Maureen T. 2000b. "On the Linkages between Sociology of Race and Ethnicity and Sociology of Education." Pp. 65–84 in *Handbook of the Sociology of Education,* edited by M. T. Hallinan. New York: Kluwer.

Hallinan, Maureen T. 2000c. "Introduction: Sociology of Education at the Threshold of the Twenty-first Century." Pp. 1–12 in *Handbook of the Sociology of Education,* edited by M. T. Hallinan. New York: Kluwer.

Hansen, Donald A. 1967. "The Uncomfortable Relation of Sociology and Education." Pp. 3–35 in *On Education: Sociological Perspectives.* New York: Wiley.

Hedges, Larry V. and Barbara Schneider, eds. 2005. *The Social Organization of Schooling.* New York: Russell Sage.

Ingersoll, Richard M. 2005. "The Anomaly of Educational Organizations and the Study of Organizational Control." Pp. 91–110 in *The Social Organization of Schooling,* edited by L. V. Hedges and B. Schneider. New York: Russell Sage.

Kerckhoff, Alan C. 2001. "Education and Social Stratification Processes in Comparative Perspective." *Sociology of Education* 74(extra issue):3–18.

Luke, Allan. 1997. "Critical Discourse Analysis." Pp. 50–57 in *International Encyclopedia of the Sociology of Education,* edited by L. J. Saha. New York: Elsevier.

McFarland, Daniel A. 2005. "Why Work When You Can Play? Dynamics of Formal and Informal Organization in Classrooms." Pp. 147–74 in *The Social Organization of Schooling,* edited by L. V. Hedges and B. Schneider. New York: Russell Sage.

Metz, Mary. 2000. "Sociology and Qualitative Methodologies in Education." *Harvard Educational Review* 70:60–74.

Natriello, Gary. 2001. "Bridging the Second Digital Divide: What Can Sociologists of Education Contribute?" *Sociology of Education* 74:260–65.

Persell, Caroline H. 2000. "Values, Control, and Outcomes in Public and Private Schools." Pp. 387–410 in *Handbook of the Sociology of Education,* edited by M. T. Hallinan. New York: Kluwer.

Riegle-Crumb, Catherine. 2005. "The Cross-National Context of the Gender Gap in Math and Science." Pp. 227–43 in *The Social Organization of Schooling,* edited by L. V. Hedges and B. Schneider. New York: Russell Sage.

Riehl, Carolyn. 2001. "Bridges to the Future: The Contributions of Qualitative Research to the Sociology of Education." *Sociology of Education* 74(extra issue):115–34.

Rosenbaum, James E. and Stephanie A. Jones. 2000. "Interactions between High Schools and Labor Markets." Pp. 411–36 in *Handbook of the Sociology of Education,* edited by M. T. Hallinan. New York: Kluwer.

Rosenthal, Robert and Lenore Jacobsen. 1982. *Pygmalion in the Classroom.* New York: Irvington.

Saha, Lawrence J. 1997a. "Preface." Pp. 1–8 in *International Encyclopedia of the Sociology of Education,* edited by L. J. Saha. New York: Elsevier.

Saha, Lawrence J. 1997b. "Sociology of Education: An Overview." Pp. 106–17 in *International Encyclopedia of the Sociology of Education,* edited by L. J. Saha. New York: Elsevier.

Saha, Lawrence J. and J. Zubrzycki. 1997. "Classical Sociological Theories of Education." Pp. 11–21 in *International Encyclopedia of the Sociology of Education,* edited by L. J. Saha. New York: Elsevier.

Schmid, Carol L. 2001. "Educational Achievement, Language-Minority Students, and the New Second Generation." *Sociology of Education* 74(extra issue):71–87.

Shain, Farzana and Jenny Ozga. 2001. "Identity Crisis? Problems and Issues in the Sociology of Education." *British Journal of Sociology* 22:109–20.

Suter, Larry E. 2001. "Suggestions for Future Directions for Research in Sociology of Education." *Sociological Focus* 34:459–61.

Turner, Jonathan H. and Douglas E. Mitchell. 1997. "Contemporary Sociological Theories of Education." Pp. 21–31 in *International Encyclopedia of the Sociology of Education,* edited by L. J. Saha. New York: Elsevier.

Tyre, Peg. 2006. "The Trouble with Boys." *Newsweek,* January 30, pp. 44–52.

Wagenaar, Theodore C. 1987. "What Do We Know about Dropping Out of High School?" Pp. 161–90 in *Research in Sociology of Education and Socialization,* edited by R. Corwin. Greenwich, CT: JAI Press.

Wagenaar, Theodore C. 1997. "What Characterizes Home Schoolers: A National Study." *Education* 117(3):440–44.

Waller, Willard. 1932. *The Sociology of Teaching.* New York: Wiley.

Walters, Pamela B. 2000. "The Limits of Growth: School Expansion and School Reform in Historical Perspectives." Pp. 241–61 in *Handbook of the Sociology of Education,* edited by M. T. Hallinan. New York: Kluwer.

Weick, Karl E. 1976. "Administering Education in Loosely Coupled Schools." *Phi Delta Kappan* 63:673–76.

Chapter 32. Economic Sociology

Adams, Julia. 1996. "Principals and Agents, Colonialists and Company Men: The Decay of Colonial Control in the Dutch East Indies." *American Sociological Review* 61(1):12–28.

Baran, Paul A. 1957. *The Political Economy of Growth.* New York: Monthly Review Press.

Baran, Paul A. and Paul M. Sweezy. 1966. *Monopoly Capital.* New York: Modern Reader.

Bendix, Reinhard. 1956. *Work and Authority in Industry: Ideologies of Management in the Course of Industrialization.* New York: John Wiley.

Biernacki, Richard. 1995. *The Fabrication of Labor: Germany and Britain, 1640–1914.* Berkeley: University of California Press.

Budros, Art. 1997. "The New Capitalism and Organizational Rationality: The Adoption of Downsizing Programs, 1979–1994." *Social Forces* 76:229–49.

Burawoy, Michael. 1979. *Manufacturing Consent: Changes in the Labor Process under Monopoly Capitalism.* Chicago, IL: University of Chicago Press.

Campbell, John L., J. Rogers Hollingsworth, and Leon N. Lindberg, eds. 1991. *Governance of the American Economy.* New York: Cambridge University Press.

Cardoso, Fernando Henrique and Enzo Faletto. 1979. *Dependency and Development in Latin America.* Berkeley: University of California Press.

Carruthers, Bruce. 1996. *City of Capital: Politics and Markets in the English Financial Revolution.* Princeton, NJ: Princeton University Press.

Chandler, Alfred D., Jr. 1977. *The Visible Hand: The Managerial Revolution in American Business.* Cambridge, MA: Harvard University Press.

Cumings, Bruce. 1987. "The Origins and Development of the Northeast Asian Political Economy: Industrial Sectors, Product Cycles, and Political Consequences." Pp. 44–83 in *The Political Economy of the New Asian Industrialism,* edited by F. C. Deyo. Ithaca, NY: Cornell University Press.

Davis, Gerald F., Kristina A. Diekmann, and Catherine H. Tinsley. 1994. "The Decline and Fall of the Conglomerate Firm in the 1980s: The Deinstitutionalization of an Organizational Form." *American Sociological Review* 59:547–70.

DiMaggio, Paul J. and Walter W. Powell. 1983. "The Iron Cage Revisited: Institutional Isomorphism and Collective Rationality in Organizational Fields." *American Sociological Review* 35:147–60.

Djelic, Marie-Laure. 1998. *Exporting the American Model: The Postwar Transformation of European Business.* New York: Oxford University Press.

Dobbin, Frank. 1994. *Forging Industrial Policy: The United States, Britain, and France in the Railway Age.* New York: Cambridge University Press.

Dobbin, Frank and Timothy Dowd. 2000. "The Market That Antitrust Built: Public Policy, Private Coercion, and Railroad Acquisitions, 1825–1922." *American Sociological Review* 65:635–57.

Dore, Ronald. 1973. *British Factory–Japanese Factory.* Berkeley: University of California Press.

Dore, Ronald. 2000. *Stock Market Capitalism: Welfare Capitalism: Japan and Germany versus the Anglo-Saxons.* New York: Oxford University Press.

Durkheim, Émile. 1933. *The Division of Labor in Society.* Translated by G. Simpson. New York: Free Press.

Evans, Peter. 1979. *Dependent Development: The Alliance of Multinational, State, and Local Capital in Brazil.* Princeton, NJ: Princeton University Press.

Evans, Peter. 1995. *Embedded Autonomy: States and Industrial Transformation.* Princeton, NJ: Princeton University Press.

Fligstein, Neil. 1990. *The Transformation of Corporate Control.* Cambridge, MA: Harvard University Press.

Fligstein, Neil. 2001. *The Architecture of Markets: The Economic Sociology of Twenty-first Century Capitalist Societies.* Princeton, NJ: Princeton University Press.

Fligstein, Neil and Linda Markowitz. 1993. "Financial Reorganization of American Corporations in the 1980s." Pp. 185–206 in *Sociology and the Public Agenda,* edited by W. J. Wilson. Newbury Park, CA: Sage.

Gao, Bai. 1997. *Economic Ideology and Japanese Industrial Policy: Developmentalism between 1931 and 1965.* New York: Cambridge University Press.

Gao, Bai. 2001. *Japan's Economic Dilemma: The Institutional Origins of Prosperity and Stagnation.* New York: Cambridge University Press.

Gereffi, Gary. 1983. *The Pharmaceutical Industry and Dependency in the Third World.* Princeton, NJ: Princeton University Press.

Gereffi, Gary and Miguel Korzeniewicz, eds. 1994. *Commodity Chains and Global Capitalism.* New York: Praeger.

Gorski, Philip S. 1993. "The Protestant Ethic Revisited: Disciplinary Revolution and State Formation in Holland and Prussia." *American Journal of Sociology* 99(2):265–316.

Granovetter, Mark. 1985. "Economic Action and Social Structure: The Problem of Embeddedness." *American Journal of Sociology* 91:481–510.

Guillén, Mauro F. 1994. *Models of Management: Work, Authority, and Organization in a Comparative Perspective.* Chicago, IL: University of Chicago Press.

Guillén, Mauro F. 2001. *The Limits of Convergence: Globalization and Organizational Change in Argentina, South Korea, and Spain.* Princeton, NJ: Princeton University Press.

Guthrie, Douglas. 1999. *Dragon in a Three-Piece Suit: The Emergence of Capitalism in China.* Princeton, NJ: Princeton University Press.

Hamilton, Gary G. and Nicole Woolsey Biggart. 1988. "Market, Culture, and Authority: A Comparative Analysis of Management and Organization in the Far East." *American Journal of Sociology* 94:S52–94.

Hofstede, Geert. 1980. *Culture's Consequences: International Differences in Work Values.* Beverly Hills, CA: Sage.

Johnson, Chalmers. 1982. *MITI and the Japanese Miracle: The Growth of Industrial Policy, 1925–1975.* Stanford, CA: Stanford University Press.

Kiser, Edgar and Joachim Schneider. 1995. "Bureaucracy and Efficiency: An Analysis of Taxation in Early Modern Prussia." *American Sociological Review* 59(2):187–204.

Konrád, George and Ivan Szelényi. 1979. *The Intellectuals on the Road to Class Power.* Brighton, England: Harvester Press.

Lenin, V. I. [1916] 1971. "Imperialism, the Highest Stage of Capitalism." Pp. 169–263 in *Lenin: Selected Works.* New York: International Publishers.

Lincoln, James R. and Arne L. Kalleberg. 1985. "Work Organization and Workforce Commitment: A Study of Plants and Employees in the U.S. and Japan." *American Sociological Review* 50:738–60.

Lincoln, James R. and Arne Kalleberg, with Mitsuyo Hanada and Kerry McBride. 1990. *Culture, Control and Commitment: A Study of Work Organization and Work Attitudes in the United States and Japan.* Cambridge, England: Cambridge University Press.

Marx, Karl. 1894. *Das Kapital,* 3 vols. New York: International Publishers.

Marx, Karl. [1852] 1963. *The Eighteenth Brumaire of Louis Bonaparte.* Reprint. New York: International Publishers.

Marx, Karl. 1971. *The Grundrisse.* Edited and translated by D. McLellan. New York: Harper & Row.

Marx, Karl. 1974. *The German Ideology.* New York: International Publishers.

Marx, Karl and Friedrich Engels. [1872] 1972. "Manifesto of the Communist Party." Pp. 331–362 in *The Marx-Engels Reader,* edited by R. Tucker. New York: Norton.

Meyer, John W. and Brian Rowan. 1977. "Institutionalized Organizations: Formal Structure as Myth and Ceremony." *American Journal of Sociology* 83:340–63.

Mintz, Beth and Michael Schwartz. 1985. *The Power Structure of American Business.* Chicago, IL: University of Chicago Press.

Mizruchi, Mark S. 1992. *The Structure of Corporate Political Action: Interfirm Relations and Their Consequences.* Cambridge, MA: Harvard University Press.

Nee, Victor. 1989. "A Theory of Market Transition: From Redistribution to Markets in State Socialism." *American Sociological Review* 54:663–81.

Nee, Victor. 1991. "Social Inequalities in Reforming State Socialism: Between Redistribution and Markets in China." *American Sociological Review* 56:267–82.

Nee, Victor. 1992. "Organizational Dynamics of Market Transition: Hybrid Forms, Property Rights, and Mixed Economy in China." *Administrative Science Quarterly* 37:1–27.

Nee, Victor. 1996. "The Emergence of a Market Society: Changing Mechanisms of Stratification in China." *American Journal of Sociology* 101:908–49.

Novak, Michael, ed. 1993. *The Catholic Ethic and the Spirit of Capitalism.* New York: Free Press.

Orrù, Marco, Nicole Woolsey Biggart, and Gary G. Hamilton. 1991. "Organizational Isomorphism in East Asia."

Pp. 361–389 in *The New Institutionalism in Organizational Analysis,* edited by W. Powell and P. DiMaggio. Chicago, IL: University of Chicago Press.

Ouchi, William G. 1981. *Theory Z: How American Business Can Meet the Japanese Challenge.* Reading, MA: Addison-Wesley.

Perrow, Charles. 1992. "Organizational Theorists in a Society of Organizations." *International Sociology* 3:371–80.

Perrow, Charles. 2002. *Organizing America: Wealth, Power, and the Origins of Corporate Capitalism.* Princeton, NJ: Princeton University Press.

Powell, Walter W. and Paul J. DiMaggio, eds. 1991. *The New Institutionalism in Organizational Analysis.* Chicago, IL: University of Chicago Press.

Roy, William G. 1997. *Socializing Capital: The Rise of the Large Industrial Corporation in America.* Princeton, NJ: Princeton University Press.

Sachs, Jeffrey. 1989. "My Plan for Poland." *International Economy* 3:24–29.

Scott, W. Richard. 1995. *Institutions and Organizations.* Thousand Oaks, CA: Sage.

Stark, David. 1992a. "Path Dependence and Privatization Strategies in East Central Europe." *East European Politics and Societies* 6:17–51.

Stark, David. 1992b. "From System Identity to Organizational Diversity: Analyzing Social Change in Eastern Europe." *Contemporary Sociology* 21:299–304.

Stark, David and Laszlo Bruszt. 1998. *Postsocialist Pathways: Transforming Politics and Property in East Central Europe.* Cambridge, England: Cambridge University Press.

Streeck, Wolfgang. 1992. *Social Institutions and Economic Performance: Studies of Industrial Relations in Advanced Capitalist Economies.* Newbury Park, CA: Sage.

Swedberg, Richard. 1998. *Max Weber and the Idea of Economic Sociology.* Princeton, NJ: Princeton University Press.

Swedberg, Richard. 2001. "Max Weber's Vision of Economic Sociology." Pp. 77–95 in *The Sociology of Economic Life.* Boulder, CO: Westview Press.

Szelényi, Iván. 1983. *Urban Inequalities under State Socialism.* New York: Oxford University Press.

Szelényi, Iván, with Robert Manchin, Pál Juhász, Bálint Magyar, and Bill Martin. 1988. *Socialist Entrepreneurs: Embourgeoisement in Rural Hungary.* Madison: University of Wisconsin Press.

Useem, Michael. 1984. *The Inner Circle.* New York: Oxford University Press.

Useem, Michael. 1996. *Investor Capitalism: How Money Managers Are Changing the Face of Corporate America.* New York: Basic Books.

Wallerstein, Immanuel. 1976. *The Modern World-System.* New York: Academic Press.

Wallerstein, Immanuel. 1980. *The Modern World System II.* New York: Academic Press.

Weber, Max. [1916] 1951. *The Religion of China; Confucianism and Taoism.* Glencoe, IL: Free Press.

Weber, Max. [1917] 1952. *Ancient Judaism.* Glencoe, IL: Free Press.

Weber, Max. [1916] 1958. *The Religion of India: The Sociology of Hinduism and Buddhism.* Glencoe, IL: Free Press.

Weber, Max. 1963. *The Sociology of Religion.* Translated by E. Fischoff, with and introduction by T. Parsons. Boston, MA: Beacon.

Weber, Max. 1978. *Economy and Society,* 2 vols. Edited by G. Roth and C. Wittich. Berkeley: University of California Press.

Weber, Max. 2002. *The Protestant Ethic and the Spirit of Capitalism.* Translated by S. Kalberg. Los Angeles, CA: Roxbury.

Westney, Eleanor. 1987. *Imitation and Innovation: The Transfer of Western Organizational Forms to Meiji Japan.* Cambridge, MA: Harvard University Press.

Whitley, Richard. 1992a. *Business Systems in East Asia: Firms, Markets, and Societies.* London, England: Sage.

Whitley, Richard, ed. 1992b. *European Business Systems: Firms and Markets in Their National Contexts.* London, England: Sage.

Whitley, Richard and Peer Hull Kristensen, eds. 1996. *The Changing European Firm: Limits to Convergence.* New York : Routledge.

Williamson, Oliver E. 1985. *The Economic Institutions of Capitalism.* New York: Free Press.

Zelizer, Viviana A. 1987. *Pricing the Priceless Child: The Changing Social Value of Children.* New York: Basic Books.

Chapter 33. Medical Sociology

Abbott, Andrew. 2000. "Reflections on the Future of Sociology." *Contemporary Sociology* 29:296–300.

Anderson, Odin W. 1952. "The Sociologist and Medicine." *Social Forces* 31:38–42.

Annandale, Ellen. 1998. *The Sociology of Health and Medicine: A Critical Introduction.* Cambridge, England: Polity Press.

Annandale, Ellen. 2003. *Feminist Theory and the Sociology of Health and Illness.* London, England: Routledge.

Becker, Howard, Blanche Geer, Everett C. Hughes, and Anselm L. Strauss. 1961. *Boys in White: Student Culture in Medical School.* Chicago, IL: University of Chicago Press.

Berger, Peter L. and Thomas Luckmann. 1966. *The Social Construction of Reality.* New York: Doubleday.

Best, Steven and Douglas Kellner. 1991. *Postmodern Theory: Critical Interrogations.* New York: Guilford Press.

Best, Steven and Douglas Kellner. 2001. *The Postmodern Adventure: Science, Technology, and Cultural Studies at the Third Millennium.* New York: Guilford Press.

Bilkey, W. J. 1996. "Confusion, Fear, and Chauvinism: Perspectives on the Medical Sociology of Chronic Pain." *Perspectives in Biology and Medicine* 39:270–80.

Blackwell, Elizabeth. 1902. *Essays in Medical Sociology.* London, England: Ernest Bell.

Bloom, Samuel W. 1986. "Institutional Trends in Medical Sociology." *Journal of Health and Social Behavior* 27:265–76.

Bloom, Samuel W. 2002. *The Word as a Scalpel: A History of Medical Sociology.* New York: Oxford University Press.

Bury, Michael. 2005. *Health and Illness.* Cambridge, England: Polity Press.

Capra, Fritjof. 1996. *The Web of Life.* New York: Anchor Books/Doubleday.

Capra, Fritjof. 2002. *The Hidden Connections: Integrating the Biological, Cognitive, and Social Dimensions of Life into a Science of Sustainability.* New York: Doubleday.

Carr-Saunders, A. M. and P. A. Wilson. 1928. *The Professions.* Oxford, England: Clarendon Press.

Castellani, Brian and Frederic W. Hafferty. 2006. "Professionalism and Complexity Science: A Preliminary Investigation." Pp. 3–23 in *Medical Professionalism: A Critical Review,* edited by D. Wear. New York: Springer.

Chard, J. A., R. J. Lilford, and B. V. Court. 1997. "Qualitative Medical Sociology: What Are Its Crowning Achievements?" *Journal of the Royal Society of Medicine* 90:604–609.

Chard, Jiri, Richard Lilford, and Derek Gardiner. 1999. "Looking Beyond the Next Patient: Sociology and Modern Health Care." *Lancet* 353:486–89.

Charmaz, Kathy and Debora Paterniti. 1999. *Health, Illness and Healing: Society, Social Context and Self: An Anthology.* Los Angeles, CA: Roxbury Publishing Company.

Chaska, N. L. 1977. "Medical Sociology for Whom?" *Mayo Clinic Proceedings* 52:813–18.

Christakis, Nicholas. A. 1995. "The Similarity and Frequency of Proposals to Reform U.S. Medical Education: Constant Concerns." *Journal of the American Medical Association,* 274:706–11.

Clarke, Adele E. and Virginia L. Olesen, eds. 1999. *Revisioning Women, Health and Healing: Feminist, Cultural, and Technoscience Perspectives.* New York: Routledge.

Cockerham, William. 2001. "Medical Sociology and Sociological Theory." Pp. 3–22 in *Medical Sociology,* edited by W. Cockerham. New York: Blackwell.

Cockerham, William. 2004. *The Blackwell Companion to Medical Sociology.* Malden, MA: Blackwell.

Collins, Randall and Michael Makowsky. 2004. *The Discovery of Society.* 7th ed. New York: McGraw-Hill.

Conrad, Peter. 2005. *Sociology of Health and Illness.* New York: Worth Publishers.

Cook, Clarissa. 2004. "'Who Cares About Marx, Weber and Durkheim?' Social Theory and the Changing Face of Medicine." *Health Sociology Review* 13:87–96.

Day, Robert Alan. 1981. "Toward the Development of a Critical, Sociohistorically Grounded Sociology of Sociology: The Case of Medical Sociology." Ph.D. dissertation, University of Missouri-Columbia, Columbia, MO.

Dolch, Norman A. 1990. "Perceptions from a Preceptor in an Applied Medical Sociology Internship Program." *Teaching Sociology* 18:298–302.

Fadem, Barbara. 2001. *High-Yield Behavioral Science.* 2d ed. New York: Lippincott, Williams & Wilkins.

Foucault, Michel. 1980. *Power/Knowledge: Selected Interviews and Other Writings 1972–1977.* New York: Pantheon Books.

Foucault, Michel. 1987. *The Ethical of Care for the Self as a Practice of Freedom: An Interview.* Translated by J. D. Gauthier. Cambridge: MIT Press.

Foucault, Michel. 1988. *Technologies of the Self: A Seminar with Michel Foucault,* edited by L. Martin, H. Gutman, and P. Hutton. Amherst: University of Massachusetts.

Fox, Nicholas. 1994. *Postmodernism, Sociology, and Health.* Toronto, Ontario, Canada: University of Toronto Press.

Fox, Renee C. 1985. "Reflections and Opportunities in the Sociology of Medicine." *Journal of Health and Social Behavior* 26:6–14.

Freeman, Linton. 2004. *The Development of Social Network Analysis: A Study in the Sociology of Science.* Vancouver, British Columbia, Canada: Booksurge.

Freidson, Eliot. 1961 "The Sociology of Medicine: A Trend Report and Bibliography." *Current Sociology* 10/11(entire issue).

Freidson, Eliot. 1970a. *Profession of Medicine: A Study of the Sociology of Applied Knowledge.* New York: Harper & Row.

Freidson, Eliot. 1970b. *Professional Dominance: The Social Structure of Medical Care.* New York: Atherton Press.

Freidson, Eliot. 2001. *Professionalism: The Third Logic.* Chicago, IL: University of Chicago Press.

Gabelko, Katrina and Alan McBride. 1991. "Teaching Applied Sociology: Development of a Graduate-Level Seminar in Clinical Medical Sociology." *Teaching Sociology* 19:372–78.

Gerhardt, Uta. 1989. *Ideas About Illness: An Intellectual and Political History of Medical Sociology.* London, England: Macmillan.

Glaser, Barney G. and Anselm L. Strauss. 1965. *Awareness of Dying.* Chicago, IL: Aldine.

Glaser, Barney G. and Anselm L. Strauss. 1967. *The Discovery of Grounded Theory: Strategies for Qualitative Research.* Chicago, IL: Aldine.

Glaser, Barney G. and Anselm L. Strauss. 1968. *Time for Dying.* Chicago, IL: Aldine.

Goffman, Erving. 1986. *Stigma: Notes of the Management of Spoiled Identity.* New York: Simon & Schuster.

Gravetter, Frederick J. and Larry B. Wallnau. 2003. *Statistics for the Behavioral Sciences.* 6th ed. Belmont, CA: Wadsworth.

Hafferty, Frederic W. 2000. "Medical Education." Pp 238–57 in *Handbook of Medical Education,* 5th ed., edited by C. Bird, A. Fremont, and P. Conrad. Upper Saddle River, NJ: Prentice Hall.

Hafferty, Frederic W. and Donald W. Light Jr. 1995. "Professional Dynamics and the Changing Nature of Medical Work." *Journal of Health and Social Behavior* (extra issue):132–53.

Hafferty, Frederic W. and John B. McKinlay. 1993. *The Changing Medical Profession: An International Perspective.* New York: Oxford University Press.

Hafferty, Frederic W. and Fredric D. Wolinsky. 1991. "Conflicting Characterizations of Professional Dominance." Pp. 225–49 in *Current Research on Occupations and Professions,* edited by J. Levy. Greenwich, CT: JAI Press.

Hall, Oswald. 1951. "Sociological Research in the Field of Medicine: Progress and Prospects." *American Sociological Review* 16:639–49.

Halsey, A. H. 2004. *A History of Sociology in Britain.* New York: Oxford University Press.

Haney, C. Allen, Margaret A. Zahn, and Jan Howard. 1983. "Applied Medical Sociology: Learning from Within." *Teaching Sociology* 11:92–104.

Harkess, Shirley. 2000. "The Impact of Feminism on Mainstream Medical Sociology: An Assessment." *Research in the Sociology of Health Care* 17:153–72.

Henderson, Gail, Nancy King, Ronald Strauss, and Sue Estroff. 1997. *The Social Medicine Reader.* Durham, NC: Duke University Press.

Henderson, Lawrence J. 1935. "Physician and Patient as a Social System." *New England Journal of Medicine* 212:819–23.

Hoppe, Sue K. and Judith K. Barr. 1990. "The Graduate Internship Program in Applied Medical Sociology." *Teaching Sociology* 18:291–97.

Iphofen, Ron and Fiona Poland. 1997. "Professional Empowerment and Teaching Sociology to Health Care Professionals." *Teaching Sociology* 25:44–56.

Jobling, Ray. 1979. "Editorial." *Sociology of Health & Illness* 1:i.

Kitto, Simon. 2004. "Strategies for Teaching the Sociological Imagination to Medical Students: The Role of Embodiment." *Health Sociology Review* 13:74–86.

Leigh, H. and M. F. Reiser. 1986. "Comparison of Theoretically Oriented and Patient-Oriented Behavioral Science Courses." *Academic Medicine* 61:169–74.

Levine, Sol. 1987. "The Changing Terrains in Medical Sociology: Emergent Concern with the Quality of Life." *Journal of Health and Social Behavior* 28:1–6.

Levine, Sol. 1995. "Time for Creative Integration in Medical Sociology." *Journal of Health and Social Behavior* (extra issue):1–4.

Link, Bruce. 2003. "The Production of Understanding." *Journal of Health and Social Behavior* 44:457–69.

Lupton, Deborah. 2003. *Medicine as Culture: Illness, Disease and the Body in Western Societies.* 2d ed. Thousand Oaks, CA: Sage.

McIntire, Charles. 1915. "The Expanse of Sociologic Medicine." *Journal of Sociological Medicine* 16:1–3.

McIntire, Charles. 1991. "The Importance of the Study of Medical Sociology." *Sociological Practice* 9:30–7.

Mechanic, David and David A. Rochefort. 1996. "Comparative Medical Systems." *Annual Review of Sociology* 22:239–79.

Merton, Robert K., Leo G. Reeder, and Patricia L. Kendall. 1957. *The Student-Physician: Introductory Studies in the Sociology of Medical Education.* Cambridge, MA: Harvard University Press.

Mirowsky, John and Catherine E. Ross. 2003. *Social Causes of Psychological Distress.* New York: Aldine de Gruyter.

Navarro, Vicente. 2002. *The Political Economy of Social Inequalities: Consequences for Health and Quality of Health.* Amityville, NY: Baywood.

Parsons, Talcott. 1951. *The Social System.* New York: Free Press.

Petersdorf, R. G. and A. R. Feinstein. 1981. "An Informal Appraisal of the Current Status of 'Medical Sociology.'" *Journal of the American Medical Association* 245:943–50.

Petersen, Alan and Robin Bunton. 1997. *Foucault, Health and Medicine.* New York: Routledge.

Reid, Margaret. 1979. "The Development of Medical Sociology in Britain." Discussion Papers in Social Research No. 13, University of Glasgow, Glasgow, Scotland.

Ruderman, F. A. 1981. "What Is Medical Sociology?" *Journal of the American Medical Association* 245:927–29.

Sahler, Olle and John Carr. 2003. *The Behavioral Science in Health Care.* Cambridge, MA: Hogrefe & Huber.

Scambler, Graham. 2003. *Sociology as Applied to Medicine.* 5th ed. London, England: W. B. Saunders.

Scott, John. 2000. *Social Network Analysis: A Handbook.* Thousand Oaks, CA: Sage.

Sengstock, Mary C. 2001. "Contributions of Clinical Sociology to the Medical Field." *Sociological Practice: A Journal of Clinical and Applied Sociology* 3:297–318.

Shilling, Chris. 2004. "Physical Capital and Situated Action: A New Direction for Corporeal Sociology." *British Journal of Sociology of Education* 25:473–87.

Stacey, Margaret and Hilary Homans. 1978. "The Sociology of Health and Illness: Its Present State, Future Prospects and Potential for Health Research." *Sociology* 12:281–307.

Starr, Paul E. 1982. *The Social Transformation of American Medicine: The Rise of a Sovereign Profession and the Making of a Vast Industry.* New York: Basic Books.

Stevens, Rosemary. 1971. *American Medicine and the Public Interest.* New Haven, CT: Yale University Press.

Straus, Robert. 1957. "The Nature and Status of Medical Sociology." *American Sociological Review* 22:200–204.

Strauss, Anselm L. and Barney G. Glaser. 1970. *Anguish: A Case History of a Dying Trajectory.* Mill Valley, CA: Sociology Press.

Taylor, Steve and David Field. 2003. *Sociology of Health and Health Care.* 3d ed. Malden, MA: Blackwell.

Thomas, Richard K. 2003. *Society and Health: Sociology for Health Professionals.* New York: Plenum Press.

Turner, Bryan S. 1990. "The Interdisciplinary Curriculum: From Social Medicine to Postmodernism." *Sociology of Health & Illness* 12:1–23.

Turner, Bryan S. 1992. *Regulating Bodies: Essays in Medical Sociology.* London, England: Routledge.

Turner, Bryan S. 1996. *Body and Society: Explorations in Social Theory.* 2d ed. London, England: Sage.

Warbasse, James P. 1909. *Medical Sociology: A Series of Observations Touching Upon the Sociology of Health and the Relations of Medicine to Society.* New York: D. Appleton.

Watts, Duncan. 2004. "The New Science of Networks." *Annual Review of Sociology* 30:243–70.

Weitz, Rose. 2003. *Sociology of Health, Illness, and Health Care.* Belmont, CA: Wadworth.

White, Kevin. 2002. *An Introduction to the Sociology of Health and Illness.* London, England: Sage.

Williams, Simon J. 2001. "Sociological Imperialism and the Profession of Medicine Revisited: Where Are We Now?" *Sociology of Health & Illness* 23:135–58.

Williams, Simon J. 2005. "Parsons Revisited: From the Sick Role to . . . ?" *Health* 9:123–44.

Chapter 34. The Sociology of Law

Agarwal, Bina. 1995. *A Field of One's Own: Gender and Land Rights in South Asia.* Cambridge, England: Cambridge University Press.

Albiston, Catherine. 1999. "The Rule of Law and the Litigation Process: The Paradox of Losing by Winning." *Law & Society Review* 33:869–910.

Albiston, Catherine. 2005. "Bargaining in the Shadow of Social Institutions: Competing Discourses and Social Change in Workplace Mobilization of Civil Rights." *Law & Society Review* 39:11–50.

Ayres, Ian and John Braithwaite. 1992. *Responsive Regulation: Transcending the Deregulation Debate.* Oxford, England: Oxford University Press.

Baldus, David, George Woodworth, David Zuckerman, Neil Alan Weinar, and Barbara Broffitt. 1998. "Racial Discrimination and the Death Penalty in the Post Forman Era: An Empirical and Legal Overview with Recent Findings from Philadelphia." *Cornell Law Review* 83:1638–737.

Black, Donald. 1976. *The Behavior of Law.* London, England: Academic Press.

Black, Donald. 1989. *Sociological Justice.* Oxford, England: Oxford University Press.

Bleich, Erik. 2003. *Race Politics in Britain and France: Ideas and Policymaking Since the 1960s.* Cambridge, England: Cambridge University Press.

Blumstein, Alfred, Jacqueline Cohen, and Daniel Nagin, eds. 1978. *Deterrence and Incapacitation. Estimating the Effects of Criminal Sanctions on Crime Rates.* Washington, DC: National Academy of Sciences.

Bohannan, Paul. 1965. "The Differing Realms of Law." *American Anthropologist* 67(6, pt. 2):33–42.

Boyle, Elizabeth. 2002. *Female Genital Cutting: Cultural Conflict in the Global Community.* Baltimore, MD: Johns Hopkins University Press.

Bumiller, Kristin. 1987. "Victims in the Shadow of the Law: A Critique of the Model of Legal Protection." *Signs* 12:421–34.

Burstein, Paul. 1991. "Legal Mobilization as a Social Movement Tactic: The Struggle for Equal Employment Opportunity." *American Journal of Sociology* 96:1201–25.

Carruthers, Bruce G., Sarah Babb, and Terence C. Halliday. 2001. "Institutionalizing Markets, or the Market for Institutions? Central Banks, Bankruptcy Laws, and the Globalization of Financial Markets." Pp. 194–226 in *The Rise of Neoliberalism and Institutional Analysis,* edited by John L. Campbell and Ove K. Pederson. Princeton, NJ: Princeton University Press.

Charrad, Mounira M. 2001. *States and Women's Rights: The Making of Postcolonial Tunisia, Algeria and Morocco.* Berkeley: University of California Press.

Chesler, Mark A., Joseph Sanders, and Debra S. Kalmuss. 1988. *Social Science in Court. Mobilizing Experts in the School Desegregation Cases.* Madison. University of Wisconsin Press.

Cole, David. 1999. *No Equal Justice: Race and Class in the American Criminal Justice System.* New York: New Press.

Conley, John M. and William M. O'Barr. 1990. *Rules versus Relationships: The Ethnography of Legal Discourse.* Chicago, IL: University of Chicago Press.

Cotterrell, Roger. 1995. *Law's Community: Legal Theory in Sociological Perspective.* Oxford, England: Oxford University Press.

Davis, F. James. 1962. "Law as a Type of Social Control." Pp. 39–61 in *Society and the Law: New Meanings for an Old Profession,* edited by F. James Davis, Henry H. Foster Jr., C. Ray Jeffrey, and E. Eugene Davis. New York: Free Press.

Dezalay, Yves and Bryant G. Garth. 1996. *Dealing in Virtue: International Commercial Arbitration and the Construction of a Transnational Legal Order.* Chicago, IL: University of Chicago Press.

Dezalay, Yves and Bryant G. Garth. 2002. *The Internationalization of Palace Wars: Lawyers, Economists, and the Contest to Transform Latin American States.* Chicago, IL: University of Chicago Press.

Dobbin, Frank and Timothy Dowd. 2000. "The Market That Antitrust Built: Public Policy, Private Coercion and Railroad Acquisitions, 1825–1922." *American Sociological Review* 65:635–57.

Dobbin, Frank and John Sutton. 1998. "The Strength of the Weak State: The Rights Revolution and the Rise of Human Resource Management Divisions." *American Journal of Sociology* 104:441–76.

Donahue, John J., III and James Heckman. 1991. "Continuous versus Periodic Change: The Impact of Civil Rights Policy on the Economic Status of Blacks." *Journal of Economic Literature* 29:1603–43.

Durkheim, Émile. [1893] 1933. *The Division of Labor in Society.* New York: Free Press.

Edelman, Lauren. 1992. "Legal Ambiguity and Symbolic Structures: Organizational Mediation of Civil Rights Law." *American Journal of Sociology* 97:1531–76.

Edelman, Lauren B. and Robin Stryker. 2005. "A Sociological Approach to Law and the Economy." Pp. 526–51 in *The Handbook of Economic Sociology,* 2d ed., edited by Neil J. Smelser and Richard Swedberg. Princeton, NJ: Princeton University Press.

Edelman, Lauren B. and Mark Suchman. 1997. "The Legal Environments of Organizations." *Annual Review of Sociology* 23:497–534.

Edelman, Lauren B., Christopher Uggen, and Howard S. Erlanger. 1999. "The Endogeneity of Law: Grievance Procedures as Rational Myth." *American Journal of Sociology* 105:406–54.

Erlich, Isaac. 1975. "The Deterrent Effect of Capital Punishment: A Question of Life and Death." *American Economic Review* 654:397–417.

Ewick, Patricia and Susan Silbey. 1998. *The Common Place of Law: Stories from Everyday Life.* Chicago, IL: University of Chicago Press.

Ewick, Patricia and Susan Silbey. 2003. "Narrating Social Structure: Stories of Resistance to Legal Authority." *American Journal of Sociology* 106:1328–72.

Ewing, Sally. 1987. "Formal Justice and the Spirit of Capitalism: Max Weber's Sociology of Law." *Law & Society Review* 21:487–512.

Farley, John E. 1998. *Sociology.* 4th ed. Upper Saddle River, NJ: Prentice Hall.

Feld, Barry. 1999. *Bad Kids: Race and the Transformation of the Juvenile Court.* New York: Oxford University Press.

Fligstein, Neil and Alec Stone Sweet. 2002. "Constructing Politics and Markets: An Institutionalist Account of European Integration." *American Journal of Sociology* 107:1206–43.

Forbath, William. 1991. *Law and the Shaping of the American Labor Movement.* Cambridge, MA: Harvard University Press.

Foucault, Michel. 1979. *Discipline and Punish: The Birth of the Prison.* Translated by Alan Sheridan. New York: Vintage Books.

Frederickson, George M. 1981. *White Supremacy. A Comparative Study in American and South African History.* Oxford, England: Oxford University Press.

Friedman, Lawrence M. 1989. "Law, Lawyers and Popular Culture." *Yale Law Journal* 98:1579–1604.

Friedman, Lawrence M. 1995. "Introduction." Pp. 1–18 in *Law & Society: Readings on the Social Study of Law,* edited by S. Macauley, L. M. Friedman, and J. Stookey. New York: W. W. Norton.

Friedman, Lawrence M. 2005. "Coming of Age: Law and Society Enters an Exclusive Club." *Annual Review of Law & Social Science* 1:1–16.

Frohman, Lisa. 1997. "Convictability and Discordant Locales: Reproducing Race, Class and Gender Ideologies in Prosecutorial Decision-Making." *Law & Society Review* 31:531–56.

Fuller, Sally Riggs, Lauren B. Edelman, and Sharon Matusik. 2000. "Legal Readings: Employee Interpretation and Enactment of Civil Rights Law." *Academy of Management Review* 25:200–16.

Galanter, Marc. 1974. "Why the Haves Come Out Ahead: Speculation on the Limits of Legal Change." *Law & Society Review* 8:95–160.

Garland, David. 1990. *Punishment in Modern Society: A Study in Social Theory.* Chicago, IL: University of Chicago Press.

Gibbs, Jack P. 1986. "Deterrence Theory and Research." Pp. 87–130 in *Law as a Behavioral Instrument,* edited by G. Melton. Lincoln: University of Nebraska Press.

Giddens, Anthony. 1984. *The Constitution of Society: Outline of the Theory of Structuration.* Berkeley: University of California Press.

Grasmick, Harold G. and Paul J. Bursick Jr. 1990. "Conscience, Significant Others and Rational Choice: Extending the Deterrence Model." *Law & Society Review* 24:837–86.

Grossman, Joel, Stewart Macauley, and Herbert Kritzer. 1999. "Do the Haves Still Come Out Ahead?" *Law & Society Review* 33:803–10.

Harper, Shannon and Barbara Reskin. 2005. "Affirmative Action at School and on the Job." *Annual Review of Sociology* 31:357–79.

Harris, Beth. 1999. "Representing Homeless Families: Repeat Player Implementation Strategies." *Law & Society Review* 33:911–39.

Heinz, John and Edward O. Laumann. 1983. *Chicago Lawyers: The Social Structure of the Bar.* New York: Russell Sage.

Hoffman, Elizabeth A. 2003. "Legal Consciousness and Dispute Resolution: Different Disputing Behavior at Two Similar Taxicab Companies." *Law & Social Inquiry* 28:691–716.

Holtzman, Mellisa K. 2003. *Theorizing Legal Change: Doctrinal Shifts in Custody Disputes Between Biological and Non-Biological Parents in the State of Iowa.* Ann Arbor: UMI Dissertation Services.

Hull, Kathleen. 2003. "The Cultural Power of Law and the Cultural Enactment of Legality: The Case of Same-Sex Marriage." *Law & Social Inquiry* 28:629–57.

Hyde, Alan. 1983. "The Concept of Legitimation in the Sociology of Law." *Wisconsin Law Review* 1983:379–426.

Jensen, Gary G., Maynard L. Erickson, and Jack P. Gibbs. 1978. "Perceived Risk of Punishment and Self-Reported Delinquency." *Social Forces* 57:57–78.

Kelly, Erin. 2003. "The Strange History of Employer Sponsored Childcare: Interested Actors, Ambiguity and the Transformation of Law in Organizational Fields." *American Journal of Sociology* 109:606–49.

Klein, L. R., B. Forst, and V. Filatov. 1978. "The Deterrent Effect of Capital Punishment: An Assessment of the Estimates." Pp. 336–60 in *Deterrence and Incapacitation: Estimating the Effects of Criminal Sanctions on Crime Rates,* edited by A. Blumstein, J. Cohen, and D. Nagin. Washington, DC: National Academy Press.

Kostiner, Idit. 2003. "Evaluating Legality: Toward a Cultural Approach to the Study of Law and Social Change." *Law & Society Review* 37:323–68.

Lanza-Kaduce, Lonn, Marvin D. Krohn, Marcia Radosevich, and Ronald L. Akers. 1979. "Law and Durkheimian Order: An Empirical Examination of the Convergence of Legal and Social Definitions of Law." Pp. 41–61 in *Structure, Law and Power: Essays in the Sociology of Law,* edited by Paul J. Brantingham and Jack M. Kress. Beverly Hills, CA: Sage.

Lempert, Richard. 1999. "A Classic at 25: Reflections on Galanter's 'Haves' Article and Work It Has Inspired." *Law & Society Review* 33:1099–1112.

Lempert, Richard and Joseph Sanders. 1986. *An Invitation to Law and Social Science: Desert, Disputes and Distribution.* New York: Longman.

Lind, E. Allen, Carol Kulick, and Maureen Ambrose. 1993. "Individual; and Corporate Dispute Resolution: Using Procedural Fairness as a Decision Heuristic." *Administrative Science Quarterly* 38:224–51.

Liska, Allen E. and Mark Tausig. 1979. "Theoretical Interpretations of Social Class and Racial Differentials in Legal Decision-Making for Juveniles." *Sociological Quarterly* 20:197–207.

Marshall, Anna-Maria. 2003. "Injustice Frames, Legality and the Everyday Construction of Sexual Harassment." *Law & Social Inquiry* 28:659–89.

McCammon, Holly J. 2001. "Labor's Legal Mobilization: Why and When Do Workers File Unfair Labor Practices?" *Work and Occupations* 28:143–75.

McCammon, Holly J. and Melinda Kane. 1997. "Shaping Judicial Law in the Post-World War II. Period: When Is Labor's Legal Mobilization Successful?" *Sociological Inquiry* 67:275–98.

McCann, Michael. 1998. "How Does Law Matter for Social Movements?" Pp. 76–108 in *How Does Law Matter?* Edited by Bryant G. Garth and Austin Sarat. Chicago, IL: Northwestern University Press.

McIntyre, Lisa J. 1994. *Law in the Sociological Enterprise: A Reconstruction.* Boulder, CO: Westview Press.

Meidinger, Errol. 1987. "Regulatory Culture: A Theoretical Outline." *Law & Policy* 9:355–85.

Melnick, Shep. 1983. *Regulation and the Courts: The Case of the Clean Air Act.* Washington, DC: Brookings Institution.

Merry, Sally Engle. 1985. "Concepts of Law and Justice Among Working Class Americans: Ideology as Culture." *Legal Studies Forum* 9:59–77.

Merry, Sally Engle. 1986. "Everyday Understandings of the Law in Working-Class America." *American Ethnologist* 12:253–70.

Moe, Terry. 1987. "Interests, Institutions and Positive Theory: The Politics of the NLRB." *Studies in American Political Development* 2:236–99.

Nielsen, Laura Beth. 2004. *License to Harass: Law, Hierarchy and Offensive Public Speech.* Princeton, NJ: Princeton University Press.

Paternoster, Raymond, Linda E. Saltzman, Theodore Chiricos, and Gordon P. Waldo. 1982. "Perceived Risk and Deterrence: Methodological Artifacts in Perceptual Deterrence Research." *Journal of Criminal Law and Criminology* 17:1238–58.

Paternoster, Raymond, Linda E. Saltzman, Gordon P. Waldo, and Theodore G. Chiricos. 1983. "Estimating Perceptual Stability and Deterrent Effects: The Role of Perceived Legal Punishment in the Inhibition of Criminal Involvement." *Journal of Criminal Law and Criminal Punishment* 74:270–297.

Pedriana, Nicholas. 2006. "From Protective to Equal Treatment: Legal Framing Processes and Transformation of the Women's Movement in the 1960s." *American Journal of Sociology* 111:1718–61.

Pedriana, Nicholas and Robin Stryker. 1997. "Political Culture Wars 1960s Style: Equal Opportunity-Affirmative Action Law and the Philadelphia Plan." *American Journal of Sociology* 103:633–91.

Pedriana, Nicholas and Robin Stryker. 2004. "The Strength of a Weak Agency: Enforcement of Title VII of the 1964 Civil Rights Act and the Transformation of State

Capacity, 1965–1971." *American Journal of Sociology* 110:709–60.

Piliavin, Irving, Rosemary Gartner, Craig Thornton, and Ross L. Matsueda. 1986. "Crime, Deterrence and Rational Choice." *American Sociological Review* 51:101–19.

Radelet, Michael L. and Marian J. Borg. 2000. "The Changing Nature of Death Penalty Debates." *Annual Review of Sociology* 26:43–61.

Reskin, Barbara. 1998. *The Realities of Affirmative Action.* Washington, DC: American Sociological Association.

Rogers, Joel. 1990. "Divide and Conquer: Further Reflections on the Distinctive Character of American Labor Laws." *Wisconsin Law Review* 1990:1–147.

Rose-Ackerman, Susan. 1992. *Rethinking the Progressive Agenda: The Reform of the American Regulatory State.* New York: Free Press.

Rosenberg, Gerald N. 1991. *The Hollow Hope: Can Courts Bring About Social Change?* Chicago, IL: University of Chicago.

Sabatier, Paul. 1975. "Social Movements and Regulatory Agencies: Toward a More Adequate—and Less Pessimistic— Theory of 'Clientele Capture.'" *Policy Sciences* 6:301–42.

Saguy, Abigail. 2003. *What Is Sexual Harassment? From Capitol Hill to the Sorbonne.* Berkeley: University of California Press.

Saltzman, Linda E., Raymond Paternoster, Gordon P. Aldo, and Thedore G. Chiricos. 1982. "Deterrent and Experiential Effects: The Problem of Causal Order in Perceptual Deterrence Research." *Journal of Research in Crime and Delinquency* 19:172–89.

Sampson, Robert J. and Janet L. Lauritsen. 1997. "Racial and Ethnic Disparities in Crime and Criminal Justice in the United States." Pp. 311–74 in *Ethnicity, Crime, and Immigration: Comparative and Cross-National Per-spectives,* edited by M. Tonry. Vol. 21 *of Crime and Justice: A Review of Research.* Chicago, IL: Chicago University Press.

Sarat, Austin. 1990. "The Law Is All Over: Power, Resistance and the Legal Consciousness of the Welfare Poor." *Yale Journal of Law and the Humanities* 2:343–79.

Sarat, Austin and Stuart Scheingold. 2001. *Cause Lawyering and the State in a Global Era.* Oxford, England: Oxford University Press.

Savelsberg, Joachim. 1992. "Law That Does Not Fit Society: Sentencing Guidelines as a Neoclassical Reaction to the Dilemmas of Substantivized Law." *American Journal of Sociology* 87:1346–81.

Savelsberg, Joachim. 2002. "Cultures of Control in Contemporary Societies." *Law & Social Inquiry* 27: 685–710.

Shapiro, Martin and Alec Stone Sweet. 2002. *On Law, Politics and Judicialization.* Oxford, England: Oxford University Press.

Southworth, Ann. 2005. "Conservative Lawyers and the Contest over the Meaning of 'Public Interest Law.'" *UCLA Law Review* 52:1224–78.

Spitzer, Stephen. 1975. "Punishment and Social Organization: A Study of Durkheim's Theory of Penal Evolution." *Law & Society Review* 9:613–35.

Steinberg, Marc W. 2003. "Capitalist Development, the Labor Process and the Law." *American Journal of Sociology* 109:445–95.

Stigler, George. 1971. "The Theory of Economic Regulation." *Bell Journal of Economic and Management Science* 2:3–21.

Stone, Katherine V. W. 2004. *From Widgets to Digits: Employment Regulation for a Changing Workplace.* Cambridge, England: Cambridge University Press.

Stryker, Robin. 1989. "Limits on Technocratization of the Law: The Elimination of the National Labor Relations Board's Division of Economic Research." *American Sociological Review* 54:341–58.

Stryker, Robin. 1994. "Rules, Resources and Legitimacy Processes: Some Implications for Social Conflict, Order and Change." *American Journal of Sociology* 99:847–910.

Stryker, Robin. 2000a. "Government Regulation." Pp. 1089–1111 in *Encyclopedia of Sociology,* 2d ed., vol. 2, edited by Edgar F. Borgatta and Rhonda J. V. Montgomery. New York: Macmillan.

Stryker, Robin. 2000b. "Legitimacy Processes as Institutional Politics: Implications for Theory and Research in the Sociology of Organizations." *Research in the Sociology of Organizations* 17:179–223.

Stryker, Robin. 2001a. "Legitimacy." Pp. 8700–8704 in *International Encyclopedia of the Social and Behavioral Sciences,* vol. 13, edited by Neil J. Smelser and Paul B. Baltes. Oxford, England: Elsevier Science.

Stryker, Robin. 2001b. "Disparate Impact and the Quota Debates: Law, Labor Market Sociology and Equal Employment Policies." *Sociological Quarterly* 42:13–46.

Stryker, Robin. 2003. "Mind the Gap: Law, Institutional Analysis and Socio-Economics. *Socio-Economic Review* 1:335–67.

Stryker, Robin. 2006. "Sociological Analysis of Labor Law." In *Encyclopedia of Law and Society: American and Global Perspectives,* edited by D. S. Clark. Thousand Oaks, CA: Sage.

Sutton, John R. 2001. *Law/Society: Origins, Interactions and Change.* Thousand Oaks, CA: Pine Forge Press.

Sutton, John R., Frank Dobbin, John W. Meyer, and W. Richard Scott. 1994. "The Legalization of the Workplace." *American Journal of Sociology* 99:944–71.

Swedberg, Richard. 2002. "The Case for an Economic Sociology of Law." Presented at Princeton Economic Sociology Conference, February 22–23, Princeton, NJ.

Trevino, A. Javier. 1996. *The Sociology of Law: Classical and Contemporary Perspectives.* New York: St. Martin's Press.

Trubeck, David. 1972. "Max Weber on Law and the Rise of Capitalism." *Wisconsin Law Review* 3:720–53.

Tyler, Tom R. 1990. *Why People Obey the Law.* New Haven, CT: Yale University Press.

Tyler, Tom R. 1994. "Governing Amid Diversity: The Effect of Fair Decision-Making on the Legitimacy of Government Procedures." *Law & Society Review* 28:809–31.

Tyler, Tom R., Jonathan D. Casper, and Bonnie Fisher. 1989. "Maintaining Allegiance toward Political Authorities: The Role of Prior Attitudes and the Use of Fair Procedures." *American Journal of Political Science* 33:629–52.

Weber, Max [1921] 1978. *Economy & Society.* Translated and edited by G. Roth. Berkeley: University of California Press.

Williams, Kirk R. and Richard Hawkins. 1986. "Perceptual Research on General Deterrence: A Critical Review" *Law & Society Review* 20:545–72.

Wilson, James Q. 1980. "The Politics of Regulation." Pp. 370–71 in *The Politics of Regulation,* edited by J. Q. Wilson. New York: Basic Books.

Vogel, Steven K. 1996. *Freer Markets, More Rules: Regulatory Reform in Advanced Industrial Countries.* Ithaca, NY: Cornell University Press.

Yeager, Peter C. 1990. *The Limits of Law: The Public Regulation of Private Pollution.* Cambridge, England: Cambridge University Press.

Yngvesson, Barbara. 1988. "Making Law at the Doorway: The Clerk, the Court, and the Construction of Community in a New England Town." *Law & Society Review* 22:409–48.

Zimring, Frank E. and Gordon Hawkins. 1973. *Deterrence: The Legal Threat in Crime Control.* Chicago, IL: University of Chicago Press.

Chapter 35. Military Sociology

Abbott, Andrew. 2002. "The Army and the Theory of Professions." Pp. 523–36 in *The Future of the Army Profession,* edited by D. M. Snyder and G. L. Watkins. Boston, MA: McGraw-Hill.

Bachman, Jerald G., John D. Blair, and David R. Segal. 1977. *The All-Volunteer Force: A Study of Ideology in the Military.* Ann Arbor: University of Michigan Press.

Bass, Bernard. 1998. *Transformational Leadership.* Mahwah, NJ: Lawrence Erlbaum.

Battistelli, Fabrizio. 1997. "Peacekeeping and the Postmodern Soldier." *Armed Forces & Society* 23:467–84.

Biderman, Albert D. 1967. "What Is Military?" Pp. 122–37 in *The Draft: A Handbook of Facts and Alternatives,* edited by S. Tax. Chicago, IL: University of Chicago Press.

Boene, Bernard. 2000. "Social Science Research, War, and the Military in the United States." Pp. 149–251 in *Military Sociology: The Richness of a Discipline,* edited by G. Kummel and A. Prufert. Baden-Baden, Germany: Nomos.

Bogart, Leo, ed. 1969. *Social Research and the Desegregation of the U.S. Army.* Chicago, IL: Markham.

Booth, Bradford, William W. Falk, David R. Segal, and Mady W. Segal. 2000. "The Impact of Military Presence in Local Labor Markets on the Employment of Women." *Gender & Society* 14:318–32.

Booth, Bradford, Meyer Kestnbaum, and David R. Segal. 2001. "Are Post-Cold War Militaries Postmodern?" *Armed Forces & Society* 27:319–42.

Booth, Bradford and David R. Segal. 2005. "Bringing Soldiers Back In." *Race, Class, & Gender* 12:34–57.

Bourg, Chris and Mady W. Segal. 1999. "The Impact of Family-Supportive Policies and Practices on Organizational Commitment to the Army." *Armed Forces & Society* 25:633–52.

Bowman, William, Roger Little, and G. Thomas Sicilia, eds. 1986. *The All-Volunteer Force after a Decade.* Washington, DC: Pergamon-Brassey's.

Bryant, Clifton D. 1979. *Khaki-Collar Crime: Deviant Behavior in the Military Context.* New York: Free Press.

Burk, James. 2001. "The Military's Presence in American Society, 1950–2000." Pp. 247–74 in *Soldiers and Civilians: The Civil-Military Gap and American National Security,* edited by P. D. Feaver and R. H. Kohn. Cambridge: MIT Press.

Clausen, John A. 1984a. "The American Soldier and Social Psychology." *Social Psychology Quarterly* 47:184–85.

Clausen, John A. 1984b. "Research on the American Soldier as a Career Contingency." *Social Psychology Quarterly* 47:207–13.

Coates, Charles H. and Roland J. Pellegrin. 1965. *Military Sociology: A Study of American Military Institutions and Military Life.* University Park, MD: Social Sciences Press.

Curry, C. David. 1985. *Sunshine Patriots: Punishment and the Vietnam Offender.* Notre Dame, IN: University of Notre Dame Press.

Dandeker, Christopher and Mady W. Segal. 1996. "Gender Integration and Armed Forces: Recent Policy Developments in the United Kingdom." *Armed Forces & Society* 23:29–47.

Durkheim, Émile. 1951. *Suicide.* New York: Free Press.

Ender, Morten G. and David R. Segal. 1998. "Race, Class, Gender, and New Media Use in the Military." Pp. 65–81 in *Cyberghetto or Cybertopia,* edited by B. Ebo. Westport, CT: Greenwood Press.

Feaver, Peter D. and Richard H. Kohn, eds. 2001. *Soldiers and Civilians: The Civil-Military Gap and American National Security.* Cambridge: MIT Press.

Friedman, Milton. 1967. "Why Not a Volunteer Army?" Pp. 200–207 in *The Draft: A Handbook of Facts and Alternatives,* edited by S. Tax. Chicago, IL: University of Chicago Press.

Ginzberg, Eli, James K. Anderson, Sol. W. Ginzberg, and John L. Herma. 1959. *The Ineffective Soldier: Lessons for Management and the Nation.* 3 vols. New York: Columbia University Press.

Haltiner, Karl. 1999. "The Definite End of the Mass Army in Western Europe?" *Armed Forces & Society* 25:7–36.

Hamilton, V. Lee, David Rohall, David R. Segal, and Mady W. Segal. 2001. "Downsizing the Russian Army: Consequences for Organizational Leavers, Survivors, and Spouses." *Journal of Political and Military Sociology* 29:73–91.

Helmer, John. 1974. *Bringing the War Home: The American Soldier in Vietnam and After.* New York: Free Press.

Hicks, Louis and Curt Raney. 2003. "The Social Impact of Military Growth in St. Mary's County, Maryland, 1940–1995." *Armed Forces & Society* 29:353–71.

Hill, Reuben. 1949. *Families under Stress: Adjustment to the Crises of War Separation and Reunion.* New York: Harper.

Hollingshead, August B. 1946. "Adjustment to Military Life." *American Journal of Sociology* 51:439–50.

Homans, George C. 1946. "The Small Warship." *American Sociological Review* 11:294–300.

Huntington, Samuel P. 1957. *The Soldier and the State.* Cambridge, MA: Harvard University Press.

Janowitz, Morris. 1960. *The Professional Soldier.* Glencoe, IL: Free Press.

Janowitz, Morris. 1964. *The Military in the Political Development of New Nations.* Chicago, IL: University of Chicago Press.

Kelty, Ryan D. 2005. "Civilianization of the Military: The Social-Psychological Effects of Integrating Civilian and Military Personnel." Ph.D. dissertation, Department of Sociology, University of Maryland, College Park, MD.

Kestnbaum, Meyer. 2002. "Citizen-Soldiers, National Service, and the Mass Army: The Birth of Conscription in Revolutionary Europe and North America." *Comparative Social Research* 20:117–44.

Lasswell, Harold D. 1941. "The Garrison State." *American Journal of Sociology* 46:455–68.

Lifton, Robert J. 1963. *Thought Reform and the Psychology of Totalism: A Study of "Brainwashing" in China.* New York: W. W. Norton.

Lindesmith, Alfred R. 1946. "Teachers in the Army Air Forces." *American Journal of Sociology* 51:404–07.

Little, Roger W. 1969. "Buddy Relations and Combat Performance." Pp. 195–223 in *The New Military,* edited by M. Janowitz. New York: W. W. Norton.

Lumsdaine, Arthur A. 1984. "Mass Communications Experiments in Wartime and Thereafter." *Social Psychology Quarterly* 47:198–206.

Malesic, Marjan, ed. 2003. *Conscription vs. All-Volunteer Forces in Europe.* Baden-Baden, Germany: Nomos.

Mills, C. Wright. 1956. *The Power Elite.* New York: Oxford University Press.

Moore, Brenda. 1996. *To Serve My Country, to Serve My Race.* New York: New York University Press.

Moore, Brenda. 2003. *Serving Our Country: Japanese American Women in the Military during World War II.* New Brunswick, NJ: Rutgers University Press.

Moskos, Charles C. 1973. "The American Dilemma in Uniform: Race in the Armed Forces." *Annals of the American Academy of Political and Social Science* 400:94–106.

Moskos, Charles C. 1976. *Peace Soldiers: The Sociology of a United Nations Military Force.* Chicago, IL: University of Chicago Press.

Moskos, Charles C. 1977. "From Institution to Occupation: Trends in Military Organization." *Armed Forces & Society* 4:41–50.

Moskos, Charles C. 2000. "Toward a Postmodern Military: The United States as a Paradigm." Pp. 14–31 in *The Postmodern Military: Armed Forces after the Cold War,* edited by C. C. Moskos, J. A. Williams, and D. R. Segal. New York: Oxford University Press.

Moskos, Charles C. and John Sibley Butler. 1996. *All That We Can Be: Black Leadership and Racial Integration the Army Way.* New York: HarperCollins.

Moskos, Charles C., John Allen Williams, and David R. Segal. 2000. *The Postmodern Military: Armed Forces after the Cold War.* New York: Oxford University Press.

Moskos, Charles C. and Frank R. Wood. 1988. *The Military: More Than Just a Job?* Washington, DC: Pergamon-Brassey's.

Munson, E. L. 1921. *The Management of Men.* New York: Henry Holt.

Phelps, Ruth H. and Beatrice J. Farr, eds. 1996. *Reserve Component Soldiers as Peacekeepers.* Alexandria, VA: U.S. Army Research Institute for the Behavioral and Social Sciences.

Reed, Brian J. and David R. Segal. 2000. "The Impact of Multiple Deployments on Soldiers' Peacekeeping Attitudes, Morale, and Retention." *Armed Forces & Society* 27:57–78.

Rose, Arnold M. 1946. "The Social Structure of the Army." *American Journal of Sociology* 51:361–64.

Sampson, Robert J. and John H. Laub. 1996. "Socioeconomic Achievement in the Life Course of Disadvantaged Men: Military Service as a Turning Point, circa 1940–1965." *American Sociological Review* 61:347–67.

Savage, Paul L. and Richard A. Gabriel. 1976. "Cohesion and Disintegration in the American Army." *Armed Forces & Society* 2:340–76.

Scott, Wilbur. 2004. *Vietnam Veterans Since the War. The Politics of PTSD, Agent Orange, and the National Memorial.* Norman: University of Oklahoma Press.

Scott, Wilbur and Sandra Carson Stanley, eds. 1994. *Gays and Lesbians in the Military: Issues, Concerns, and Contrasts.* New York: Aldine De Gruyter.

Segal, David R. 1986. "Measuring the Institutional/Occupational Change Thesis." *Armed Forces & Society* 12:351–76.

Segal, David R. 1989. *Recruiting for Uncle Sam: Citizenship and Military Manpower Policy.* Lawrence: University Press of Kansas.

Segal, David R. 1995. "Bridging the Gap: Implications for Army Personnel Quality from Contemporary Sociological Research." Pp. 311–28 in *Future Soldiers and the Quality Imperative,* edited by R. L. Phillips and M. R. Thurman. Fort Knox, KY: U.S. Army Recruiting Command.

Segal, David R. 2005. "Time, Race, and Gender Differences in the Effects of Military Service on Veteran Outcomes." Pp. 166–89 in *Historical Influences on Lives and Aging,* edited by K. W. Schaie and G. H. Elder. New York: Springer.

Segal, David R. and Nehama E. Babin. 2000. "Institutional Change in Armed Forces at the Dawning of the 21st Century." Pp. 218–35 in *International Handbook of Sociology,* edited by S. Quah and A. Sales. London, England: Sage.

Segal, David R. and Meyer Kestnbaum. 2002. "Professional Closure in the Military Labor Market: A Critique of Pure Cohesion." Pp. 441–58 in *The Future of the Army Profession,* edited by D. M. Snyder and G. L. Watkins. Boston, MA: McGraw-Hill.

Segal, David R. and Yuko Kurashina. Forthcoming. "New Missions, or Old Missions for New Actors?" *International Review of Sociology.*

Segal, David R., David E. Rohall, Joseph C. Jones, and Angela M. Manos. 1999. "Meeting the Missions of the 1990s with a Down-Sized Force." *Military Psychology* 11:149–67.

Segal, David R. and Mady W. Segal. 1993. *Peacekeepers and Their Wives: American Participation in the Multinational Force and Observers.* Westport, CT: Greenwood Press.

Segal, David R. and Mady W. Segal. 2004. "America's Military Population." *Population Bulletin* 59:1–40.

Segal, Mady W. 1986. "The Military and the Family as Greedy Institutions." *Armed Forces & Society* 14:559–85.

Segal, Mady W. 1995. "Women's Military Roles Cross-Nationally: Past, Present, and Future." *Gender & Society* 9:757–75.

Shibutani, Tamatsu. 1978. *The Derelicts of Company K.* Berkeley: University of California Press.

Shils, Edward A. and Morris Janowitz. 1948. "Cohesion and Disintegration in the Wehrmacht in World War II." *Public Opinion Quarterly* 12:280–315.

Smith, M. Brewster. 1984. "The American Soldier and Its Critics: Who Survives the Attack on Positivism?" *Social Psychology Quarterly* 47:192–98.

Spencer, Herbert. 1908. *The Principles of Sociology.* New York: Appleton.

Stanley, Jay, Mady W. Segal, and Charlotte J. Laughton. 1990. "Grass Roots Family Action and Military Policy Responses." *Marriage and Family Review* 15:207–23.

Stouffer, Samuel A., Arthur A. Lumsdaine, Marion Harper Lumsdaine, Robin M. Williams Jr., M. Brewster Smith, Irving L. Janis, Shirley A. Star, and Leonard S. Cottrell Jr. 1949. *The American Soldier: Combat and Its Aftermath.* Princeton, NJ: Princeton University Press.

Stouffer, Samuel A., Edward A. Suchman, Leland C. DeVinney, Shirley A. Star, and Robin M. Williams Jr. 1949. *The American Soldier: Adjustment during Army Life.* Princeton, NJ: Princeton University Press.

Taylor, William J., Roger L. Arango, and Robert S. Lockwood, eds. 1977. *Military Unions: U.S. Trends and Issues.* Beverly Hills, CA: Sage.

Trainor, Stephen C. 2004. "Differential Effects of Institutional Socialization on Value Orientations in Naval Academy Midshipmen." Ph.D. dissertation, Department of Sociology, University of Maryland, College Park, MD.

Weber, Max. 1968. *Economy and Society.* Totowa, NJ: Bedminster Press.

Williams, Robin M., Jr. 1984. "Field Observations and Surveys in Combat Zones." *Social Psychology Quarterly* 47:186–92.

Wong, Leonard and Jeffrey McNally. 1994. "Downsizing the Army: Some Policy Implications Affecting the Survivors." *Armed Forces & Society* 20:199–216.

Woodruff, Todd D. 2003. "Influence of the Life Course on the Development and Salience of Soldier Identity." M.A. thesis, University of Maryland, College Park, MD.

Woodruff, Todd, Ryan Kelty, and David R. Segal. 2006. "Propensity to Serve and Motivation to Enlist among American Combat Soldiers." *Armed Forces & Society* 32:353–66.

Wright, Quincy. 1942. *A Study of War.* Chicago, IL: University of Chicago Press.

Yerkes, Robert M., ed. 1921. *Psychological Examining in the U.S. Army.* Washington, DC: U.S. Government Printing Office.

Zeidner, Joseph and Arthur J. Drucker. 1983. *Behavioral Science in the Army: A Corporate History of the Army Research Institute.* Alexandria, VA: U.S. Army Research Institute.

PART VIII: SOCIETAL PROBLEMS AND DISAFFECTIONS

Chapter 36. Social Problems

Betz, Michael. 1974. "Riots and Welfare: Are they Related?" *Social Problems* 21:345–55.

Blau, Judith and Peter Blau. 1982. "The Cost of Inequality: Metropolitan Structure and Violent Crime." *American Sociological Review* 47:114–29.

Blumer, Herbert. 1971. "Social Problems as Collective Behavior." *Social Problems* 18:298–306.

Coleman, James William and Donald R. Cressey. 1980. *Social Problems.* New York: Harper & Row.

Coleman, James William and Donald R. Cressey. 1993. *Social Problems.* 5th ed. New York: HarperCollins.

Davies, James C. 1962. "Toward a Theory of Revolution." *American Journal of Sociology* 27:5–19.

Davies, James C. 1969. "The J-Curve of Rising and Declining Satisfactions as a Cause of Some Great Revolutions and a Contained Rebellion." Pp. 671–710 in *Violence in America,* edited by H. D. Graham and T. R. Gurr. New York: Signet Books.

Domhoff, G. William. 2006. *Who Rules America?* New York: McGraw-Hill.

Esping-Anderson, G. 1990. *The Three Worlds of Welfare Capitalism.* Princeton, NJ: Princeton University Press.

Fuller, Richard C. and Richard R. Myers. 1941. "The Natural History of a Social Problem." *American Sociological Review* 6:320–28.

Gans, Herbert. 1972. "Positive Functions of Poverty." *American Journal of Sociology* 78:275–89.

Galliher, John and James McCartney. 1973. "The Influence of Funding Agencies on Juvenile Delinquency Research." *Social Problems* 21:77–90.

Gallup, George H. 2004. *The Gallup Report.* Retrieved June 28, 2004 (http://www.gallup.com).

Garraty, John. 1978. *Unemployment in History: Economic Thought and Public Policy.* New York: Harper & Row.

George, Henry. [1883] 1939. *Social Problems.* New York: Robert Schalkenbach Foundation.

Goodin, R. E., B. Headey, R. Muffels, and H. Dirven. 1999. *The Real Worlds of Welfare Capitalism.* Cambridge, England: Cambridge University Press.

Gouldner, Alvin. 1970. *The Coming Crisis in Western Sociology.* New York: Basic Books.

Gurr, Ted. 1970. *Why Men Rebel.* Princeton, NJ: Princeton University Press.

Hofstader, Richard. 1955. *The Age of Reform: From Bryan to FDR.* New York: Knopf.

Hofstede, Geert. 1991. *Cultures and Organizations: Software of the Mind.* New York: McGraw-Hill.

Horton, Paul B. and Gerald R. Leslie. 1955. *The Sociology of Social Problems.* New York: Appleton-Century-Crofts.

Isaac, Larry and William Kelly. 1981. "Racial Insurgency, the State, and Welfare Expansion: Local and National Level Evidence from the Postwar United States." *American Journal of Sociology* 86:1348–86.

Julian, Joseph. 1973. *Social Problems.* Englewood Cliffs, NJ: Prentice Hall.

Julian, Joseph. 1977. *Social Problems.* 2d ed. Englewood Cliffs, NJ: Prentice Hall.

Kelley, William and David Snyder. 1980. "Racial Violence and Socioeconomic Changes among Blacks in the United States." *Social Forces* 58:739–60.

Kerbo, Harold. 1981. "Characteristics of the Poor: A Continuing Focus in Social Research." *Sociology and Social Research* 65:323–31.

Kerbo, Harold R. 1982. "Movements of 'Crisis' and Movements of 'Affluence': A Critique of Deprivation and Resource Mobilization Theories of Social Movements." *Journal of Conflict Resolution* 26:645–63.

Kerbo, Harold R. 2006a. *Social Stratification and Inequality: Class Conflict in Historical, Comparative, and Global Perspective.* 6th ed. New York: McGraw-Hill.

Kerbo, Harold R. 2006b. *World Poverty: Global Inequality and the Modern World System.* New York: McGraw-Hill.

Kerbo, Harold and Juan Gonzalez. 2003. "Class and Nonvoting in Comparative Perspective: Possible Causes and Consequences for the United States." *Research in Political Sociology* 12:177–98.

Kerbo, Harold and Hermann Strasser. 2000. *Modern Germany.* New York: McGraw-Hill.

Kuhn, Thomas. 1970. *The Structure of Scientific Revolutions.* 2d ed. Chicago, IL: University of Chicago Press.

Ladd, Everett Carll and Karlyn H. Bowman. 1998. *Attitudes toward Economic Inequality.* Washington, DC: AEI Press.

Mauss, Armand L. 1975. *Social Problems as Social Movements.* New York: Lippincott.

McCarthy, John D. and Mayer N. Zald. 1977. "Resource Mobilization and Social Movements: A Partial Theory." *American Journal of Sociology.* 82:1212–41.

McAdam, Doug. 1982. *Political Process and the Development of Black Insurgency: 1930–1970.* Chicago, IL: University of Chicago Press.

McLellan, David. 1973. *Karl Marx: His Life and Thought.* New York: Harper & Row.

Mead, George H. 1899. "The Working Hypothesis of Social Reform." *American Journal of Sociology* 5:404–12.

Merton, Robert K. and Robert Nisbet. 1971. *Social Problems.* 3d ed. New York: Harcourt Brace Jovanovich.

Merton, Robert K. and Robert Nisbet. 1976. *Social Problems.* 4th ed. New York: Harcourt Brace Jovanovich.

Mills, C. Wright. 1959. *The Sociological Imagination.* New York: Oxford University Press.

Nieuwbeerta, Paul. 2001. "The Democratic Class Struggle in Postwar Societies: Traditional Class Voting in Twenty Countries, 1945–1990." Pp. 121–36 in *The Breakdown of Class Politics: A Debate on Post-Industrial Stratification,* edited by T. N. Clark and S. M. Lipset. Washington, DC: Woodrow Wilson Center Press.

Paige, Jeffrey. 1975. *Agrarian Revolution.* New York: Free Press.

Parsons, Talcott. 1937. *The Structure of Social Action.* New York: Free Press.

Piven, Frances Fox and Richard Cloward. 1971. *Regulating the Poor: The Functions of Public Welfare.* New York: Basic Books.

Piven, Frances Fox and Richard Cloward. 1977. *Poor Peoples' Movements: Why They Succeed, Why They Fail.* New York: Pantheon Books.

Piven, Frances Fox and Richard Cloward. 1988. *Why Americans Don't Vote.* New York: Pantheon Books.

Piven, Frances Fox and Richard Cloward. 2000. *Why Americans Still Don't Vote: And Why Politicians Want It That Way.* Boston, MA: Beacon Press.

Ritzer, George. 2005. *Sociological Theory.* New York: McGraw-Hill.

Schwendinger, Herman and Julia R Schwendinger. 1974. *The Sociologists of the Chair: A Radical Analysis of the Formative Years of North American Sociology, 1883–1922.* New York: Basic Books.

Smeeding, Timothy M., Lee Rainwater, and Gary Burtless. 2001. "United States Poverty in a Cross-National Context." Pp. 162–92 in *Understanding Poverty,* edited by S. H. Danziger and R. H. Haveman. New York: Russell Sage.

Spector, Malcolm and John I. Kitsuse. 1973. "Social Problems: A Reformation." *Social Problems* 21:145–59.

Strasser, Hermann. 1976. *The Normative Structure of Sociology: Conservative and Emancipatory Themes in Social Thought.* London, England: Routledge & Kegan Paul.

Thelen, Kathleen A. 1991. *Union of Parts: Labor Politics in Postwar Germany.* Ithaca, NY: Cornell University Press.

Tocqueville, Alexis de. 1955. *The Old Regime and the French Revolution.* New York: Doubleday.

Useem, Michael. 1976a. "State Production of Social Knowledge: Patterns in Government Financing of Academic Social Research." *American Sociological Review* 41:613–29.

Useem, Michael. 1976b. "Government Influence on the Social Science Paradigm." *Sociological Quarterly* 17:146–61.

Verba, Sidney, Steven Kelman, Gary Orren, Ichiro Miyake, Joji Watanuki, Ikuo Kabashima et al. 1987. *Elites and the Idea of Equality.* Cambridge, MA: Harvard University Press.

Williams, Kirk. 1984. "Economic Sources of Homicide: Reestimating the Effects of Poverty and Inequality." *American Sociological Review* 49:283–89.

Chapter 37. The Sociology of Deviance

Agnew, Robert. 1992. "Foundation for a General Strain Theory of Crime and Delinquency." *Criminology* 10:47–87.

Akers, Ronald L. 1977. *Deviant Behavior.* Belmont, CA: Wadsworth.

Akers, Ronald L. 1998. *Social Structure and Social Learning: A General Theory of Crime and Deviance.* Boston, MA: Northeastern University Press.

Akers, Ronald L. and Gary F. Jensen, eds. 2003. *Social Learning and the Explanation of Crime. Advances in Criminological Theory.* Vol. 11. New Brunswick, NJ: Transaction.

Akers, Ronald L. and Gary F. Jensen. Forthcoming. "Empirical Status of Social Learning Theory of Crime and Deviance: The Past, Present, and Future." In *Taking Stock: The Status of Criminological Theory,* vol. 15, edited by F. T. Cullen, J. P. Wright, and K. R. Blevins. New Brunswick, NJ: Transaction.

Anderson, Elijah. 1999. *Code of the Street: Decency, Violence, and the Moral Life of the Inner City.* New York: W. W. Norton.

Batton, C. and R. Ogles. 2003. "'Who's It Gonna Be—You or Me?' The Potential of Social Learning for Integrated Homicide-Suicide Theory." Pp. 85–108 in *Social Learning and the Explanation of Crime,* edited by R. L. Akers and G. F. Jensen. New Brunswick, NJ: Transactions.

Ben-Yehuda, Nachman. 1981a. "The European Witch Craze of the 14th to 17th Centuries: A Sociologist's Perspective." *American Journal of Sociology* 86:1–30.

Ben-Yehuda, Nachman. 1981b. "Problems Inherent in Socio-Historical Approaches to the European Witch-Craze." *Journal for the Scientific Study of Religion* 20:326–38.

Ben-Yehuda, Nachman. 1985. *Deviance and Moral Boundaries.* Chicago, IL: University of Chicago Press.

Ben-Yehuda, Nachman. 2001. Academic staff statement at Web site for the Hebrew University of Jerusalem. Retrieved October 4, 2004 (http://sociology.huji.ac.il/ben-yehuda%20research.html).

Best, Joel. 1990. *Threatened Children: Rhetoric and Concern about Child Abuse.* Chicago, IL: University of Chicago Press.

Best, Joel. 2004. *Deviance: Career of a Concept.* Belmont, CA: Wadsworth/Thomson Learning.

Black, Donald. 1976. *The Behavior of Law.* New York: Academic Press.

Black, Donald. 1979. "Common Sense in the Sociology of Law." *American Sociological Review* 44:18–27.

Chambliss, William J. and Michel Mankoff, eds. 1976. *Whose Law? What Order?* New York: John Wiley.

Chesney-Lind, M. and R. G. Shelden. 2004. *Girls, Delinquency, and Juvenile Justice.* Belmont, CA: Wadsworth/Thomson Learning.

Daly, K. 1994. *Gender, Crime, and Punishment.* New Haven, CT: Yale University Press.

Daly, K. and M. Chesney-Lind. 1988. "Feminism and Criminology." *Justice Quarterly* 5:497–538.

DeLamater, J. 1968. "On the Nature of Deviance." *Social Forces* 46:445–55.

Dentler, Robert and Kai Erickson. 1959. "The Functions of Deviance in Groups." *Social Problems* 7(Fall):94–197.

Durkheim, Émile. [1897] 1951. *Suicide: A Study in Sociology.* Translated by J. A. Spaulding and G. Simpson. New York: Free Press.

Erickson, K. 1966. *The Wayward Puritans.* New York: Wiley.

Faris, Robert E. L. 1948. *Social Disorganization.* New York: Ronald Press.

Gibbs, Jack P. 1981. *Norms, Deviance, and Social Control.* New York: Elsevier.

Gibbs, Jack P. 1989. *Control: Sociology's Central Notion.* Urbana: University of Illinois Press.

Gibbs, Jack P. 1994. *A Theory about Control.* Boulder, CO: Westview Press.

Goode, Erich. 1994. *Deviant Behavior.* Englewood Cliffs, NJ: Prentice Hall.

Goode, Erich. 2004. "The 'Death' Macguffin Redux: Comments on Best." *Deviant Behavior* 25:493–509.

Goode, Erich and Nachman Ben-Yehuda. 1994a. *Moral Panics: The Social Construction of Deviance.* Oxford, England: Blackwell.

Goode, Erich and Nachman Ben-Yehuda. 1994b. "Moral Panics: Culture, Politics, and Social Construction." *Annual Review of Sociology* 20:149–71.

Gottfredson, Michael R. and Travis Hirschi. 1990. *A General Theory of Crime.* Stanford, CA: Stanford University Press.

Heckert, A. and D. Heckert. 2004. "Using a New Typology of Deviance to Analyze Ten Common Norms of the United States Middle-Class." *The Sociological Quarterly,* 45:209–28.

Hirschi, Travis. 1969. *Causes of Delinquency.* Berkeley: University of California Press.

Jensen, Gary F. 1988. "Functional Research on Deviance: A Critical Analysis and Guide for the Future." *Deviant Behavior* 9:1–18.

Liazos, Alex. 1972. "Nuts, Sluts, and Perverts: The Poverty of the Sociology of Deviance." *Social Problems* 20:103–20.

Logan, E. 1999. "The Wrong Race, Committing Crime, Doing Drugs and Maladjusted for Motherhood: The Nation's Fury over Crack Babies." *Social Justice* 26:115–38.

McCorkle, Richard C. and T. D. Miethe. 2002. *Panic: The Social Construction of the Street Gang Problem.* Upper Saddle River, NJ: Prentice Hall.

Merton, Robert K. 1938. "Social Structure and Anomie." *American Sociological Review* 3:672–82.

Messner, Steven and R. Rosenfeld. 1997. "Political Restraint of the Market and Criminal Homicide: A Cross-National Application of Institutional Anomie Theory." *Social Forces* 75:1393–416.

Platt, Anthony. 1975. "Prospects for a Radical Criminology in the USA." Pp. 95–112 in *Critical Criminology,* edited by I. Taylor, P. Walton, and J. Young. London, England: Routledge & Kegan Paul.

Quinney, Richard. 1975. "Crime Control in Capitalist Society: A Critical Philosophy of Legal Order." Pp. 181–202 in *Critical Criminology,* edited by I. Taylor, P. Walton, and J. Young. London, England: Routledge & Kegan Paul.

Reinarman, C. and H. Levine. 1989. "The Crack Attack: Politics and Media in America's Latest Drug Scare." Pp. 115–37 in *Images of Issues: Typifying Contemporary Social Problems,* edited by J. Best. New York: Aldine de Gruyter.

Richardson, J. T., J. Best, and D. G. Bromley. 1991. *The Satanism Scare.* New York: Aldine de Gruyter.

Robinson, W. S. 1950. "Ecological Correlations and the Behavior of Individuals." *American Sociological Review* 15:351–57.

Roshier, B. 1977. "The Function of Crime Myth." *Sociological Review* 25:309–23.

Rubington, Earl and M. Weinberg, eds. 2005. *Deviance: The Interactionist Perspective.* Boston, MA: Allyn & Bacon.

Schwendinger, Herman and Julia Schwendinger. 1975. "Defenders of Order or Guardians of Human Rights?" Pp. 113–47 in *Critical Criminology,* edited by I. Taylor, P. Walton, and J. Young. London, England: Routledge & Kegan Paul.

Sellin, Thorsten. 1938. *Culture, Conflict and Crime.* New York: Research Council.

Shelden, R., S. K. Tracy, and W. B. Brown. 2001. *Youth Gangs in American Society.* 2d ed. Belmont, CA: Wadsworth/ Thomson Learning.

Simmons, J. L. 1969. *Deviants.* Berkeley, CA: Glendessary Press.

Sumner, C. 1994. *The Sociology of Deviance: An Obituary.* New York: Continuum.

Sutherland, Edwin H. 1934. *Principles of Criminology.* Philadelphia, PA: J. B. Lippincott.

Sutherland, Edwin H. 1939. *Principles of Criminology.* Philadelphia, PA: J. B. Lippincott.

Sutherland, Edwin H. 1947. *Principles of Criminology.* Philadelphia, PA: J. B. Lippincott.

Sykes, Gresham M. and David Matza. 1957. "Techniques of Neutralization: A Theory of Delinquency." *American Sociological Review* 22:664–70.

Taylor, I., P. Walton, and J. Young. 1973. *The New Criminology.* New York: Harper & Row.

Taylor, I., P. Walton, and J. Young. 1975. *Critical Criminology.* London, England: Routledge & Kegan Paul.

Thio, Alex. 2004. *Deviant Behavior.* 7th ed. Boston, MA: Allyn & Bacon.

Tittle, C. R. 1995. *Control Balance: Toward a General Theory of Deviance.* Boulder, CO: Westview Press.

Tittle, C. R. and R. Paternoster. 2000. *Social Deviance and Crime.* Los Angeles, CA: Roxbury.

Thomas, William I. and Florian F. Znaniecki. 1927. *The Polish Peasant in Europe and America.* New York: Alfred A. Knopf.

Unnithan, N. P., Lynn Huff-Corzine, Jay Corzine, and Hugh Whitt. 1994. *The Currents of Lethal Violence: An Integrated Model of Suicide and Homicide.* Albany: State University of New York Press.

Warren, Carol A. B. and T. X. Karner. 2005. *Discovering Qualitative Methods.* Los Angeles, CA: Roxbury.

Chapter 38. Sexual Deviance

Banner, Stuart. 2002. *The Death Penalty: An American History.* Cambridge, MA: Harvard University Press.

Bayer, Ronald. 1981. *Homosexuality and American Psychiatry: The Politics of Diagnosis.* New York: Basic Books.

Becker, Howard S. 1973. *Outsides: Studies in the Sociology of Deviance.* New York: Free Press.

Beetz, Andrea M. 2000. "Human Sexual Contact with Animals." 5th Congress of the European Federation of Sexology, Berlin, Germany, June 29–July 2. Archive for Sexology.

Beirne, Piers. 1997. "Rethinking Bestiality: Toward a Concept of Interspecies Sexual Assault." *Theoretical Criminology* 1:317–40.

Biles, Jeremy. 2004. "I, Insect, or Bataille and the Crush Freaks." *James Head* 7:115–31.

Birken, Lawrence. 1988. *Consuming Desire: Sexual Science and the Emergence of a Culture of Abundance 1871–1914.* Ithaca, NY: Cornell University Press.

Börstling, Robert. 2000. "Wetlook Paraphilia: Aspects of Sexual Variation." 5th Congress of the European Federation of Sexology, Berlin, Germany, June 29–July 2. Archive for Sexology.

Brennan, Charlies. 2004. "Changed Story: Transcript Shows Tale Shifted as Cops Revealed Evidence." *Rocky Mountain News,* September 17, p. 6A.

Carpenter, Laura M. 2005. *Virginity Lost: An Intimate Portrait of First Sex in America.* New York: New York University Press.

Chancer, Lynn. 1992. *Sadomasochism in Everyday Life: The Dynamics of Power and Powerlessness.* New Brunswick, NJ: Rutgers University Press.

Conrad, Peter and Joseph W. Schneider. 1992. *Deviance and Medicalization: From Badness to Sickness.* Philadelphia, PA: Temple University Press.

Currie, Elliott. 1968. "Crimes without Criminals." *Law and Society Review* 3:7–32.

Daneback, Kristian, Al Cooper, and Sven-Axel Månsoon. 2005. "An Internet Study of Cybersex Participants." *Archives of Sexual Behavior* 34:321–28.

Dank, Barry M. 1971. "Coming Out in the Gay World." *Psychiatry: Journal for the Study of Interpersonal Process* 34:180–97.

D'Emilio, John and Estelle B. Freedman. 1988. *Intimate Matters: A History of Sexuality in America.* New York: Harper & Row.

Durkheim, Émile. 1958. *The Rules of Sociological Method.* Translated by S. A. Solovay and John H. Muller. Glencoe, IL: Free Press.

Epstein, Steven. 1987. "Gay Politics, Ethnic Identity: The Limits of Social Constructionism." *Socialist Review* 93:9–54.

Erikson, Kai. 1962. "Notes on the Sociology of Deviance." *Social Problems* 9:307–14.

Erikson, Kai. 1966. *Wayward Puritans: A Study in the Sociology of Deviance.* New York: Wiley.

Esterberg, Kristin G. 1997. *Lesbian and Bisexual Identities: Constructing Communities, Constructing Selves.* Philadelphia, PA: Temple University Press.

Evans, Edward P. 1906. *The Criminal Prosecution and Capital Punishment of Animals.* New York: E. P. Dutton.

Ferrell, Jeff and Clinton R. Sanders, eds. 1995. *Cultural Criminology.* Boston, MA: Northeastern University Press.

Festinger, Leon. 1951. "Informal Communication in Small Groups." Pp. 28–43 in *Groups, Leadership and Men,* edited by Harold Guetzkow. Pittsburgh, PA: Carnegie Press.

Feynman, Richard. 1985. "Surely You're Joking, Mr. Feynman?" Pp. in *Adventures of a Curious Character,* edited by Edward Hutchins. New York: W. W. Norton.

Foucault, Michel. 1990. *The History of Sexuality.* Vol. 3. Translated by Robert Hurley. New York: Vintage Books.

Freeman, Lucy. 1955. *Before I Kill More . . .* New York: Crown.

Freud, Sigmund. [1905] 2000. *Three Essays on the Theory of Sexuality.* Translated by James Strachey. New York: Basic Books.

Gagnon, John H. and William Simon. 1968. "Sexual Deviance in Contemporary America." *Annals of the American Academy of Political and Social Science* 376:106–22.

Gagnon, John H. and William Simon. 1973. *Sexual Conduct: The Social Sources of Human Sexuality.* Chicago, IL: Aldine.

Galliher, John F., Wayne H. Brekhus, and David P. Keys. 2004. *Laud Humphreys: Prophet of Homosexuality and Sociology.* Madison: University of Wisconsin Press.

Gamson, Joshua. 1999. *Freaks Talk Back: Tabloid Talk Shows and Sexual Noncomformity.* Chicago, IL: University of Chicago Press.

Gaskill, Malcolm. 2005. *Witchfinder: A Seventeenth-Century English Tragedy.* London, England: John Murray.

Gauthier, Deann K. and Craig J. Forsyth. 1999. "Bareback Sex, Bug Chasers, and the Gift of Death." *Deviant Behavior* 20:85–100.

Geis, Gilbert. 2002. "Victims." Pp. 15–31 in *Victims and Victimization: Essential Readings,* edited by David Schichor and Stephen G. Tibbetts. Prospect Heights, IL: Waveland.

Geis, Gilbert and Ivan Bunn. 1997. *A Trial of Witches: A Seventeenth-Century Witchcraft Prosecution.* London, England: Routledge.

Giddens, Anthony, Mitchell Duneier, and Richard P. Applebaum. 2003. *Introduction to Sociology.* New York: W. W. Norton.

Gleick, James. 1993. *Genius: Life and Science of Richard Feynman.* New York: Viking.

Goffman, Erving. 1968. *Stigma: Notes on the Management of Spoiled Identity.* Englewood Cliffs, NJ: Prentice Hall.

Goode, Erich. 2005. *Deviant Behavior.* 7th ed. Upper Saddle River, NJ: Pearson/Prentice Hall.

Graham, Mark. 2004. "Sexual Things." *GLQ: A Journal of Lesbian and Gay Studies* 10:299–303.

Halperin, David. 1990. *One Hundred Years of Homosexuality: And Other Essays on Greek Love.* New York: Routledge.

Hensley, Christopher and Richard Tewskbury, eds. 2003. *Sexual Deviance: A Reader.* Boulder, CO: Lynne Rienner.

Hester, Marianne. 1992. *Lewd Women and Wicked Witches: A Study of the Dynamics of Male Domination.* London, England: Routledge.

Hirschfeld, Magnus. 1936. *Encyclopaedia Sexualis.* New York: Dingwall-Rock.

Humphreys, Laud. 1970. *Tearoom Trade: Interpersonal Sex in Public Places.* Chicago, IL: Aldine.

Jenness, Valerie. 1992. "Coming Out: The Categorization Problem." Pp. 65–74 in *Modern Homosexualities: Fragments of Lesbian and Gay Experience,* edited by Kenneth Plummer. New York: Routledge.

Kaan, Heinrich. 1844. *Psychopathia Sexualis.* Leipzig, Germany: Leopold Voss.

Kalb, Marvin. 2001. *One Scandalous Story: Clinton, Lewinsky, and Thirteen Days That Tarnished American Journalism.* New York: Free Press.

Karlson, Carol F. 1987. *The Devil in the Shape of a Woman.* New York: W. W. Norton.

Katz, Jack. 1988. *Seductions of Crime: Moral and Sensual Attractions of Doing Evil.* New York: Basic Books.

Kinsey, Alfred C., Wardell B. Pomeroy, and Clyde E. Martin. 1948. *Sexual Behavior in the Human Male.* Philadelphia, PA: W. B. Saunders.

Kitsuse, John I. 1962. "Societal Reactions to Deviant Behavior: Some Conceptual Problems." *Social Problems* 9:247–57.

Knight, Ronald H. 1998. *Age of Consent: The Rise of Relativism and the Corruption of Popular Culture.* Dallas, TX: Spence.

Kunkel, Thomas, ed. 2000. *Letters from the Editor: The New Yorker's Harold Ross.* New York: Modern Library.

LaFree, Gary. 1989. *Rape and Criminal Justice: The Social Construction of Sexual Assault.* Belmont, CA: Wadsworth.

Langbein, John H. 1977. *Torture and the Law of Proof: Europe and England in the Ancient Régime.* Chicago, IL: University of Chicago Press.

Laumann, Edward O., John H. Gagnon, Robert T. Michael, and Stuart Michaels. 1994. *The Social Organization of Sexuality: Sexual Practices in the United States.* Chicago, IL: University of Chicago Press.

Laws, D. Richard and William O'Donohue. 1997. *Sexual Deviance: Theory, Assessment, and Treatment.* New York: Guilford.

Macfarlane, Alan. 1999. *Witchcraft in Tudor and Stuart England: A Regional and Comparative Study.* 2d ed. London, England: Routledge.

Mair, Lucy P. 1969. *Witchcraft.* New York: McGraw-Hill.

McIntosh, Mary. 1968. "The Homosexual Role." *Social Problems* 16:182–92.

Midelfort, H. C. Erik. 1972. *Witch Hunting in Southwestern Germany, 1562–1684.* Stanford, CA: Stanford University Press.

Morrison, Todd G. and Dani Tallack. 2005. "Lesbian and Bisexual Women's Interpretations of Lesbian and Ersatz Lesbian Pornography." *Sexuality & Culture* 9:3–30.

Monter, E. William. 1976. *Witchcraft in France and Switzerland: The Borderlands during the Reformation.* Ithaca, NY: Cornell University Press.

Mullis, Kary. 1998. *Dancing Naked in the Mind Field.* New York: Pantheon Books.

Pinker, Steven. 2005. "Sniffing Out the Gay Gene." *New York Times,* May 17, pp. A25.

Plummer, Kenneth. 1975. *Sexual Stigma: An Interactionist Account.* London, England: Routledge & Kegan Paul.

Plummer, Kenneth. 1992. *Modern Homosexualities: Fragments of Lesbian and Gay Experiences.* New York: Routledge.

Plummer, Kenneth. 1996. *Telling Stories: Power, Change, and Social Worlds.* New York: Routledge.

Plummer, Kenneth. 2003. *Intimate Citizenship: Private Decisions and Public Dialogues.* Seattle: University of Washington Press.

Ponse, Barbara. 1978. *Identities in the Lesbian World.* Westport, CT: Greenwood.

Rodmell, Sue. 1981. "Men, Women and Sexuality: A Feminist Critique of the Sociology of Deviance." *Women's Studies International Quarterly* 4:145–55.

Russell, Jeffrey B. 1972. *Witchcraft in the Middle Ages.* Ithaca, NY: Cornell University Press.

Saad, Lydia. 2005. "Gay Rights Attitudes a Mixed Bag: Broad Support for Equal Job Rights, but Not Gay Marriage." Retrieved July 1, 2005 (http://www.gallup.com/poll/content/login.aspx?ci=16402).

Salamon, Edna. 1989. "The Homosexual Escort Agency: Deviance Disavowel." *The British Journal of Sociology* 40:1–21.

Savic, Ivanka, Hans Berglund, and Per Lindstrom. 2005. "Brain Response to a Putative Phenomenes in Homosexual Men." *Proceedings of the National Academy of Sciences of the United States* 102:7356–61.

Seidman, Steven. 1992. *Embattled Eros: Sexual Politics and Ethics in Contemporary America.* New York: Routledge.

Singer, Linda. 1993. *Erotic Welfare: Sexual Theory and Politics in the Age of Epidemic.* New York: Routledge.

Smith-Rosenberg, Carol. 1975. "The Female World of Love and Ritual: Relations Between Women in the 19th Century." *Signs* 1:19–27.

"Sociology Professor Accused of Beating Student." 1968. *New York Times,* June 10, p. 25.

Stanton, Donna C. 1995. *Discourses of Sexuality: From Aristotle to AIDS.* Ann Arbor: University of Michigan Press.

Starr, Kenneth. 1998. *The Starr Report: The Findings of Independent Counsel Kenneth W. Starr on President Clinton and the Lewinsky Affair.* Washington, DC: Public Affairs.

Stein, Arlene. 1992. "Sisters and Queers: The Decentering of Lesbian Feminism." *Socialist Review* 22:33–55.

Stein, Arlene. 1997. *Sex and Sensibility: Stories of a Lesbian Generation.* Berkeley: University of California Press.

Sumner, Colin. 1994. *The Sociology of Deviance: An Obituary.* New York: Continuum.

Tappan, Paul W. 1947. "Who Is the Criminal?" *American Sociological Review* 12:95–102.

Taylor, Verta and Nancy Whittier. 1992. "Collective Identity in Social Movement Communities: Lesbian Feminist Mobilization." Pp. 104–29 in *Frontiers in Social Movement Theory,* edited by Aldon D. Morris and Carol McClurg Mueller. New Haven, CT: Yale University Press.

Thio, Alex and Thomas C. Calhoun. 2001. *Readings in Deviant Behavior.* Needham Heights, MA: Allyn & Bacon.

Thirlwall, Thomas. 1805. *The Works, Moral and Religious, of Sir Matthew Hale,* vol. 2. London, England: H. D. Symonds.

Thomas, Keith. 1971. *Religion and the Decline of Magic: Studies in Popular Beliefs in Sixteenth and Seventeenth Century England.* London, England: Weidenfeld and Nicolson.

Tittle, Charles and Raymond Paternoster. 2000. *Social Deviance and Crime: An Organizational and Theoretical Approach.* Los Angeles, CA: Roxbury.

von Hoffman, Nicholas. 1975. "Sociological Snoopers and Journalistic Moralizers," part 1. Pp. 177–81 in *Tearoom Trade: Impersonal Sex in Public Places,* 2d ed., edited by Laud Humphreys. Chicago, IL: Aldine.

von Krafft-Ebbing, Richard. [1888] 1988. *Psychopathia Sexualis: With Especial Reference to Contrary Sexual Instinct.* New York: Classics of Psychiatry and Behavioral Sciences Library.

Wade, Nicholas. 2005. "For Gay Men, Different Scent of Attraction." *New York Times,* May 10, pp. A1, A16.

Weinberg, Martin S., Colin J. Williams, and Charles Moser. 1984. "The Social Constituents of Sadomasochism." *Social Problems* 32:379–89.

Weeks, Jeffrey. 1990. "Sexuality and History Revisited." Pp. 37–40 in *State, Private Life, and Political Change,* edited by L. Jamieson and H. Corr. London, England: Macmillan.

Wheeler, Stanton. 1960. "Sex Offenses: A Sociological Critique." *Law and Contemporary Problems* 25:238–78.

White, Edmund. 2005. "My Women: Why I Love Some of Them." *New Yorker,* June 13, p. 115, and June 20, p. 133.

Williams, Selma R. and Pamela W. Adelman. 1992. *Riding the Nightmare: Women and Witchcraft from the Old World to Colonial Salem.* New York: Harper Perennial.

Chapter 39. Criminology

Akers, Ronald L. 1989. "A Social Behaviorist's Perspective on Integration of Theories of Crime and Deviance." Pp. 23–36 in *Theoretical Integration in the Study of Deviance and Crime,* edited by S. Messner, M. Krohn, and A. Liska. Albany: State University of New York Press.

Akers, Ronald L. 1998. *Social Learning and Social Structure.* Boston, MA: Northeastern University Press.

Akers, Ronald L. and Christine S. Sellers. 2004. *Criminological Theories.* 4th ed. Los Angeles, CA: Roxbury.

Becker, Howard S. 1963. *The Outsiders.* New York: Free Press.

Beckett, Katherine and Theodore Sasson. 2004. *The Politics of Injustice.* 2d ed. Thousand Oaks, CA: Sage.

Braithwaite, John. 1979. *Inequality, Crime and Public Policy.* London, England: Routledge.

Braithwaite, John. 1989. *Crime, Shame, and Reintegration.* Cambridge, England: Cambridge University Press.

Cohen, Albert K. 1955. *Delinquent Boys.* Glencoe, IL: Free Press.

Cullen, Francis T. 2002. "Rehabilitation and Treatment Programs." Pp. 253–89 in *Crime: Public Policies for Crime Control,* edited by J. Wilson and J. Petersilia. Oakland, CA: ICS Press.

Currie, Elliott. 1998. *Crime and Punishment in America.* New York: Henry Holt.

Elliott, Delbert S. 1983. *National Youth Survey.* Boulder, CO: Behavioral Research Institute.

Elliott, Delbert S. and Suzanne S. Ageton. 1980. "Reconciling Race and Class Differences in Self-Reported and Official Estimates of Delinquency." *American Sociological Review* 45:95–110.

Farnworth, Margaret, Terence P. Thornberry, Marvin D. Krohn, and Alan J. Lizotte. 1994. "Measurement in the Study of Class and Delinquency: Integrating Theory and Research." *Journal of Research in Crime and Delinquency* 31:32–61.

Federal Bureau of Investigation. 2003. *Age-Specific Arrest Rates and Race-Specific Arrest Rates for Selected Offenses 1993–2001.* Washington, DC: U.S. Department of Justice.

Federal Bureau of Investigation. 2004. *Crime in the United States, 2003.* Washington, DC: U.S. Department of Justice.

Federal Bureau of Investigation. 2005. *State and National Level Crime Trend Estimates.* Washington, DC: Federal Bureau of Investigation [producer]; Washington, DC: Bureau of Justice Statistics [distributor]. Retrieved December 1, 2005 (http://bjsdata.ojp.usdoj.gov/dataonline/Search/Crime/Stat/StatebyState.cfm).

Felson, Marcus. 2002. *Crime and Everyday Life.* 3d ed. Thousand Oaks, CA: Sage.

Gillin, John L. 1914. "Social Factors Affecting the Volume of Crime." Pp. 53–67 in *Physical Bases of Crime: A Symposium,* edited by the American Academy of Medicine. Easton, PA: American Academy of Medicine Press.

Goring, Charles. 1913. *The English Convict.* London, England: HMSO.

Gottfredson, Michael and Travis Hirschi. 1986. "The True Value of Lambda Would Appear to Be Zero: An Essay on Career Criminals, Criminal Careers, Selective Incapacitation, Cohort Studies, and Related Topics." *Criminology* 24:213–34.

Grasmick, Harold G. and Robert J. Bursik Jr. 1990. "Conscience, Significant Others, and Rational Choice: Extending the Deterrence Model." *Law and Society Review* 24:837–61.

Gurr, Ted R. 1981. "Historical Trends in Violent Crime: A Critical Review of the Evidence." *Crime and Justice* 3:295–353.

Hindelang, Michael J., Travis Hirschi, and Joseph G. Weis. 1981. *Measuring Delinquency.* Beverly Hills, CA: Sage.

Hirschi, Travis. 1969. *Causes of Delinquency.* Berkeley: University of California Press.

Johnston, Lloyd D., Patrick M. O'Malley, and Jerald G. Bachman. 1996. *National Survey Results on Drug Use from the Monitoring the Future Study, 1975–1995.* Rockville, MD: U.S. Department of Health and Human Services.

Kitsuse, John I. 1962. "Societal Reactions to Deviant Behavior: Problems of Theory and Method." *Social Problems* 9:247–56.

Laub, John and Robert J. Sampson. 1993. "Turning Points in the Life Course." *Criminology* 31:301–25.

Lemert, Edwin M. 1972. *Human Deviance, Social Problems, and Social Control.* 2d ed. Englewood Cliffs, NJ: Prentice Hall.

MacKenzie, Doris Layton. 2000. "Evidence-Based Corrections: Identifying What Works." *Crime and Delinquency* 46:457–71.

Maston, Kathy and Patsy Klaus. 2005. *Four Measures of Serious Violent Crime.* Washington, DC: U.S. Department of Justice, Bureau of Justice Statistics. Retrieved September 5, 2005 (http://www.ojp.usdoj.gov/bjs/glance/tables/4meastab.htm).

Merton, Robert K. 1938. "Social Structure and Anomie." *American Sociological Review* 3:672–82.

Murphy, L. R. and R. W. Dodge. 1981. "The Baltimore Recall Study." Pp. 16–21 in *The National Crime Survey: Working Papers,* vol. 1, *Current and Historical Perspectives,* edited by R. G. Lenhen and W. G. Skogan. Washington, DC: U.S. Government Printing Office.

Porterfield, Austin L. 1946. *Youth in Trouble.* Fort Worth, TX: Leo Potishman.

Quinney, Richard. 1964. "Crime in Political Perspective." *American Behavioral Scientist* 8:19–22.

Sellin, Thorsten. 1931. "The Basis of a Crime Index." *Journal of Criminal Law and Criminology* 22:335–56.

Shaw, Clifford R. 1929. *Delinquency Areas.* Chicago, IL: University of Chicago Press.

Short, James F., Jr. and F. Ivan Nye. 1958. "Extent of Unrecorded Juvenile Delinquency: Tentative Conclusions." *Journal of Criminal Law and Criminology* 49:296–302.

Steffensmeier, Darrell. 1993. "National Trends in Female Arrests, 1960–1990: Assessment and Recommendations for Research." *Journal of Quantitative Criminology* 9:413–41.

Sutherland, Edwin H. 1940. "White Collar Criminality." *American Sociological Review* 5:1–12.

Sutherland, Edwin H. 1947. *Principles of Criminology.* 4th ed. Philadelphia, PA: Lippincott.

Sutherland, Edwin H., Donald R. Cressey, and David F. Luckenbill. 1992. *Principles of Criminology.* 11th ed. Dix Hills, NY: General Hall.

Thornberry, Terence P. and Marvin D. Krohn. 2000. "The Self-Report Method for Measuring Delinquency and Crime." Pp. 38–84 in *Measurement and Analysis of Crime and Justice,* vol. 4, *Criminal Justice 2000,* edited by D. Duffee. Washington, DC: National Institute of Justice.

Tittle, Charles R. 1995. *Control Balance.* Boulder, CO: Westview Press.

Tittle, Charles R., Wayne J. Villamez, and Douglas A. Smith. 1978. "The Myth of Social Class and Criminality: An Assessment of the Empirical Evidence." *American Sociological Review* 43:643–56.

Tolman, Frank L. 1902–1903. "The Study of Sociology in Institutions of Learning in the United States." *American Journal of Sociology* 7:797–838; 8:85–121, 251–72, 531–58.

Tonry, Michael. 1995. *Malign Neglect.* New York: Oxford University Press.

Triplett, Ruth and Laura B. Myers. 1995. "Evaluating Contextual Patterns of Delinquency: Gender-Based Differences." *Justice Quarterly* 12:59–84.

Turk, Austin T. 1969. *Criminality and the Legal Order.* Chicago, IL: Rand McNally.

Wilbanks, William. 1987. *The Myth of a Racist Criminal Justice System.* Monterey, CA: Brooks/Cole.

Chapter 40. The Sociology of Gambling

Abt, Vicki, James F. Smith, and Martin C. McGurrin. 1985. "Ritual, Risk, and Reward: A Role Analysis of Race Track and Casino Encounters." *Journal of Gambling Behavior* 1(1):64–75.

American Psychiatric Association. 1994. *Diagnostic and Statistical Manual of Mental Disorders.* 4th ed. Washington, DC: American Psychiatric Association.

Bernhard, Bo J. Forthcoming-a. "On the Shoulders of Mills: A (Clinical) Sociological Imagination via a Bio-Psycho-Social-Sociological Model." *American Behavioral Scientist.*

Bernhard, Bo J. Forthcoming-b. "The Voices of Vices: Sociological Perspectives on the DSM-IV Pathological Gambling Entry." *American Behavioral Scientist.*

Bernhard, Bo J. and Frederick W. Preston. 2004. "On the Shoulders of Merton: Potentially Sobering Consequences of Problem Gambling Policy." *American Behavioral Scientist* 47(11):1395–1405.

Blaszczynski, Alex, Robert Ladouceur, and Howard J. Shaffer. 2004. "A Science-Based Framework for Responsible Gambling: The Reno Model." *Journal of Gambling Studies* 20(3):301–17.

Bloch, Herbert A. 1951. "The Sociology of Gambling." *American Journal of Sociology* 57:215–21.

Castellani, Brian. 2000. *Pathological Gambling: The Making of a Medical Problem.* Albany: State University of New York.

Commission on the Review of the National Policy toward Gambling. 1976. *Gambling in America.* Washington, DC: U.S. Government Printing Office.

Comstock, Anthony. 1883. *Traps for the Young.* New York: Funk & Wagnalls.

Conrad, Peter and Joseph W. Schneider. 1992. *Deviance and Medicalization: From Badness to Sickness.* Philadelphia, PA: Temple University Press.

Devereux, Edward C. 1949. "Gambling and the Social Structure: A Sociological Study of Lotteries and Horse Racing in America." Ph.D. dissertation, Harvard University, Cambridge, MA.

Downes, David M., B. P. Davies, M. E. David, and P. Stone. 1976. *Gambling, Work and Leisure.* London, England: Routledge & Kegan Paul.

Eadington, William R. 2003. "Values and Choices: The Struggle to Find Balance with Permitted Gambling in Modern Society." Pp. 31–48 in *Gambling: Who Wins? Who Loses?* edited by G. Reith. Amherst, NY: Prometheus.

Frey, James H. 1984. "Gambling: A Sociological Review." *Annals of the American Academy of Political and Social Science* 474:107–21.

Frey, James H. 1991. "Social Risk and the Meaning of Sport." *Sociology of Sport Journal* 8:136–45.

Frey, James H. 1998. "Federal Involvement in U.S. Gaming Regulation." *Annals of the American Academy of Political and Social Science* 556:138–52.

Giddens, Anthony. 1990. *The Consequences of Modernity.* Palo Alto, CA: Stanford University Press.

Goffman, Erving. 1967. *Interaction Ritual: Essays on Face-to-Face Behavior.* New York: Anchor.

Gottdiener, Marc, Claudia C. Collins, and David R. Dickens. 1999. *Las Vegas: The Social Production of an All-American City.* Malden, MA: Blackwell.

Herman, Robert K. 1967. "Gambling as Work: A Sociological Study of the Racetrack." Pp. 87–104 in *Gambling,* edited by R. K. Herman. New York: Harper & Row.

Hopkins, Samuel. 1835. *The Evils of Gambling: A Sermon.* Montpelier, VT: E. P. Walton.

Kaplan, H. Roy. 1978. *Lottery Winners: How They Won and How Winning Changed Their Lives.* New York: Harper & Row.

Kingma, Sytze. 2004. "Gambling and the Risk Society: The Liberalisation and Legitimation Crisis of Gambling in the Netherlands." *International Gambling Studies* 4:47–67.

Lesieur, Henry R. 1977. *The Chase: Career of the Compulsive Gambler.* Garden City, NY: Doubleday/Anchor.

Lesieur, Henry R. and Robert L. Custer. 1984. "Pathological Gambling: Roots, Phases and Treatment." *Annals of the American Academy of Political and Social Science* 474:146–56.

Li, Wen Lang and Martin Smith. 1976. "The Propensity to Gamble: Some Structural Determinants." Pp. 189–206 in *Gambling and Society,* edited by W. R. Eadington. Springfield, IL: Charles C Thomas.

Light, Ivan. 1977. "Numbers Gambling among Blacks: A Financial Institution." *American Sociological Review* 42:892–904.

McMillen, Jan, ed. 1999. *Gambling Cultures: Studies in History and Interpretation.* London, England: Routledge.

McMillen, Jan. 2003. "From Local to Global Gambling Cultures." Pp. 49–63 in *Gambling: Who Wins? Who Loses,* edited by G. Reith. Amherst, NY: Prometheus.

Mills, C. W. (1959). *The Sociological Imagination.* London, England: Oxford.

Morais, R. C. 2002. "Casino Junkies." *Forbes,* April 29, pp. 66–70.

Newman, Otto. 1968. "The Sociology of the Betting Shop." *British Journal of Sociology* 19:17–33.

Postman, Neil. 1985. *Amusing Ourselves to Death: Public Discourse in the Age of Show Business.* New York: Penguin.

Putnam, Robert D. 2000. *Bowling Alone: The Collapse and Revival of American Community.* New York: Simon & Schuster.

Reith, Gerda. 2003. "Pathology and Profit: Controversies in the Expansion of Legal Gambling." Pp. 9–28 in *Gambling: Who Wins? Who Loses?* edited by G. Reith. Amherst, NY: Prometheus.

Rosecrance, John. 1988. *Gambling without Guilt: The Legitimation of an American Pastime.* Pacific Grove, CA: Brooks/Cole.

Short, James F., Jr. 1984. "The Social Fabric at Risk: Toward a Social Transformation of Risk Analysis." *American Sociological Review* 49:711–25.

Smith, James F., Jr. and Vicki Abt. 1984. "Gambling as Play." *Annals of the American Academy of Political and Social Science* 474:122–32.

Tec, Nechama. 1964. *Gambling in Sweden.* Totowa, NJ: Bedminster Press.

Volberg, Rachel A. 1996. "Prevalence Studies of Problem Gambling in the United States." *Journal of Gambling Studies* 12(2):111–28.

Volberg, Rachel. 2001. *When the Chips Are Down: Problem Gambling in America.* New York: Century.

Wildavsky, Aaron. 1988. *Searching for Safety.* New Brunswick, NJ: Transaction.

Zola, I. K. 1963. "Observations on Gambling in a Lower Class Setting." *Social Problems* 10:353–61.

Chapter 41. Alcohol Abuse and Alcoholism

Abbey, A. 2002. "Alcohol Related Sexual Assault: A Common Problem Among College Students." *Journal of Studies on Alcohol* (Suppl. 14):118–28.

Akers, Ronald. 1992. *Drugs, Alcohol and Society.* Belmont, CA: Wadsworth.

Armstrong, Elizabeth M. 2003. *Conceiving Risk and Bearing Responsibility: Fetal Alcohol Syndrome and the Diagnosis of Moral Disorder.* Baltimore, MD: Johns Hopkins University Press.

Bacon, Selden Daskam. 1943. "Sociology and the Problems of Alcohol: Foundations for a Sociologic Study of Drinking Behavior." *Quarterly Journal of Studies on Alcohol* 4:402–45.

Bacon, Selden Daskam. 1947. "The Mobilization of Community Resources for the Attack on Alcoholism." *Quarterly Journal of Studies on Alcohol* 8:473–87.

Bacon, Selden Daskam. 1973. "The Process of Addiction to Alcohol: Social Aspects." *Quarterly Journal of Studies on Alcohol* 34:1–27.

Bales, Robert F. 1946. "Cultural Differences in the Rates of Alcoholism." *Quarterly Journal of Studies on Alcohol* 6:480–99.

Baumohl, J. and R. Room. 1990. "Inebriety, Doctors and the State: Alcoholism Treatment Organizations before 1940." Pp. 135–74 in *Recent Developments in Alcoholism,* vol. 5, edited by M. Galanter. New York: Plenum Press.

Beauchamp, D. 1980. *Beyond Alcoholism: Alcohol and Public Health.* Philadelphia, PA: Temple University Press.

Block, L. 1990. "Alcoholism Treatment Providers and the Workplace." Pp. 315–26 in *Alcohol Problems in the Workplace: Employee Assistance Programs and Strategic Alternatives,* edited by P. M. Roman. Westport, CT: Greenwood/Quorum Press.

Cavan, S. 1966. *Liquor License: An Ethnography of Bar Behavior.* New York: Aldine.

Clark, N. 1976. *Deliver Us From Evil: An Interpretation of American Prohibition.* New York: D. C. Heath.

DeJong, W. 2002. "The Role of Mass Media in Reducing High Risk Drinking Among College Students." *Journal of Studies on Alcohol* (Suppl. 14):182–92.

Denzin, Norman. 1986. *The Recovering Alcoholic.* Beverly Hills, CA: Sage.

Denzin, Norman. 1987. *The Alcoholic Self.* Newbury Park, CA: Sage.

Glassner, Barry and D. Berg. 1980. "How Jews Avoid Alcohol Problems." *American Sociological Review* 45:647–64.

Golden, J. 2005. *Message in a Bottle: The Making of Fetal Alcohol Syndrome.* Cambridge, MA: Harvard University Press.

Gusfield, Joseph. 1963. *Symbolic Crusade: Status Politics and the American Temperance Movement.* Champaign: University of Illinois Press.

Hartigan, F. 2000. *Bill W.: A Biography of Alcoholics Anonymous Co-Founder Bill Wilson.* New York: St. Martin's Press.

Heath, D. 2000. *Drinking Occasions.* New York: Brunner Mazel.

Johnson, J. A. and Paul M. Roman. 2002. "Predicting Closure of Private Substance Abuse Treatment Facilities." *Journal of Behavioral Health Services and Research* 29:115–125.

LeMasters, E. 1976. *Blue Collar Aristocrats: Life Styles at a Blue Collar Tavern.* Madison: University of Wisconsin Press.

Levine, H. 1978. "The Discovery of Addiction: Changing Conceptions of Habitual Drunkenness in American Society." *Journal of Studies on Alcohol* 39:143–74.

Maddox, G. and B. McCall. 1960. *Drinking among Teen-Agers: A Sociological Interpretation of Alcohol Use by High-School Students.* New Haven, CT: College and University Press.

Mulford, H. 1984. "Rethinking the Alcohol Problem: A Natural Process Model." *Journal of Drug Issues* 14:31–44.

Olson, N. 2003. *With a Lot of Help from Our Friends: The Politics of Alcoholism.* New York: Writers Club Press.

Parker, R. 1996. *Alcohol and Homicide.* Albany: State University of New York Press.

Perkins, W. 2002a. "Surveying the Damage: A Review of Research on Consequences of Alcohol Misuse in College Populations." *Journal of Studies on Alcohol* (Suppl. 14):91–100.

Perkins, W. 2002b. "Social Norms and the Prevention of Alcohol Misuse in Collegiate Contexts." *Journal of Studies on Alcohol* (Suppl. 14):164–72.

Reinarman, C. 1988. "The Social Construction of an Alcohol Problem: The Case of Mothers against Drunk Driving and Social Control in the 1980s." *Theory and Society* 17:91–120.

Roebuck, Julian and Wolfgang Frese. 1976. *The Rendezvous: A Case Study of an After-Hours Club.* New York: Free Press.

Roman, Paul M. 1981a. "From Employee Alcoholism to Employee Assistance: An Analysis of the De-Emphasis on Prevention and on Alcoholism Problems in Work-Based Programs." *Journal of Studies on Alcohol* 43:244–72.

Roman, Paul M. 1981b. "Situational Factors in the Relationship between Alcohol and Crime." Pp. 143–51 in *Alcohol and Crime,* edited by J. Collins, Jr. New York: Guilford Press.

Roman, Paul M., ed. 1990. *Alcohol Problems in the Workplace: Employee Assistance Programs and Strategic Alternatives.* Westport, CT: Greenwood/Quorum Press.

Roman, Paul M. 2002. "Missing Work: The Decline in Infrastructure and Support for Workplace Alcohol Intervention in the United States, with Implications for Developments in Other Nations." Pp. 197–210 in *Changing Substance Abuse through Health and Social Systems,* edited by W. Miller and C. Weisner. New York: Kluwer/Plenum.

Roman, Paul M. and T. Blum. 1984. "Alcohol, Pampering, and the Rise to Social Stardom." *Contemporary Drug Problems* 12:223–42.

Roman, Paul M. and T. Blum. 1987. "Notes on the New Epidemiology of Alcoholism in the USA." *Journal of Drug Issues* 17:321–32.

Roman, Paul M., T. Blum, and J. Johnson. 2000. "The Transformation of Private Alcoholism Treatment: Results of a National Study." Pp. 321–42 in *Research in Medical Sociology,* vol. 7, edited by J. Levy, D. McBride, and R. Stephens. Greenwich, CT: JAI Press.

Roman, Paul M. and J. Johnson. 2002. "Adoption and Implementation of New Technologies in Substance Abuse Treatment." *Journal of Substance Abuse Treatment* 22:1–8.

Room, Robin. 1976. "Ambivalence as Sociological Explanation: The Case of Cultural Explanations of Alcohol Problems." *American Sociological Review* 41:1047–65.

Room, Robin and D. Cahalan. 1974. *Problem Drinking in American Society.* New Brunswick, NJ: Center of Alcohol Studies at Rutgers University.

Rudy, D. 1986. *Becoming Alcoholic: Alcoholics Anonymous and the Reality of Alcoholism.* Carbondale: Southern Illinois University Press.

Rumbarger, J. 1989. *Profits, Power and Prohibition: Alcohol Reform and the Industrialization of America.* Albany: State University of New York Press.

Saxe, L. 1983. *The Effectiveness of Alcoholism Treatment in Partial vs. Inpatient Settings.* Health Technology Case Study 22. Washington, DC: U.S. Office of Technology Assessment.

Schneider, J. 1978. "Deviant Drinking as Disease: Alcoholism as a Social Accomplishment." *Social Problems* 25:361–72.

Snyder, Charles. 1958. *Alcohol and the Jews: A Cultural Study of Drinking and Sobriety.* New Haven, CT: Yale Center of Alcohol Studies.

Spradley, J. and B. Mann. 1975. *The Cocktail Waitress: Woman's Work in a Man's World.* New York: John Wiley.

Straus, R. 1973. "Alcohol and Society." *Psychiatric Annals* (whole issue)3.

Trice, H. 1966. *Alcoholism in America.* New York: McGraw-Hill.

Wechsler, H. and B. Wuethrich. 2003. *Dying to Drink: Confronting Binge Drinking on College Campuses.* Emmaus, PA: Rodale.

Weisner, C. and R. Room. 1984. "Financing and Ideology in Human Services: The Alcoholism Treatment System as a Case Study." *Social Problems* 33:167–88.

White, H. 1993. "Sociology, Ten Years of Progress." Pp. 8–28 in *Recent Developments in Alcoholism,* vol. 11, edited by M. Galanter. New York: Plenum Press.

Wiener, C. 1981. *The Politics of Alcoholism. Building an Arena around a Social Problem.* New Brunswick, NJ: Transaction Books.

Wiseman, J. 1970. *Stations of the Lost.* Englewood Cliffs, NJ: Prentice Hall.

Wiseman, J. 1991. *The Other Half: Wives of Alcoholics and Their Social-Psychological Situations.* New York: Aldine de Gruyter.

Chapter 42. The Sociology of Drug Use

Akers, Ronald L. 1998. *Social Learning and Social Structure: A General Theory of Crime and Deviance.* Boston, MA: Northeastern University Press.

Bachman, Jerald G., Patrick M. O'Malley, Lloyd D. Johnston, John E. Schulenberg, Alison B. Bryant, and Alicia C. Merline. 2002. *The Decline of Substance Use in Young Adulthood: Changes in Social Activities, Roles, and Beliefs.* Mahwah, NJ: Lawrence Erlbaum.

Becker, Howard S. 1953. "Becoming a Marijuana Smoker." *American Journal of Sociology* 59:235–42.

Becker, Howard S. 1955. "Marijuana Use and Social Control." *Social Problems* 3:35–44.

Becker, Howard S. 1963. *Outsiders: Studies in the Sociology of Deviance.* New York: Free Press.

Bourgeois, Phillipe. 1995. *In Search of Respect: Selling Crack in El Barrio.* Cambridge, England: Cambridge University Press.

Bursik, Robert J. and Harold G. Grasmick. 1993. *Neighborhoods and Crime: The Dimensions of Effective Community Control.* New York: Lexington Books.

Cloward, Richard and Lloyd Ohlin. 1960. *Delinquency and Opportunity: A Theory of Delinquent Gangs.* New York: Free Press.

Courtwright, David T. 1982. *Dark Paradise: Opiate Addiction in America before 1940.* Cambridge, MA: Harvard University Press.

Dai, Bingham. 1937. *Opium Addiction in China.* Shanghai, People's Republic of China: Commercial Press.

Dunlap, Eloise and Bruce D. Johnson. 1999. "Gaining Access to Hidden Populations: Strategy for Gaining Cooperation of Drug Sellers/Dealers and Their Families in Ethnographic Research." *Drugs and Society: A Journal of Contemporary Issues* 14:127–49.

European Monitoring Centre for Drugs and Drug Addiction. 2004. *Annual Report 2004: The State of the Drugs Problem in the European Union and Norway.* Lisbon, Portugal: EMCDDA.

Goldstein, Paul J. 1985. "The Drugs/Violence Nexus: A Tripartite Conceptual Framework." *Journal of Drug Issues* 15:493–506.

Gottfredson, Michael L. and Travis Hirschi. 1990. *A General Theory of Crime.* Stanford, CA: Stanford University Press.

Hamid, Ansley. 1990. "The Political Economy of Crack-Related Violence." *Contemporary Drug Problems* 17:31–78.

Harrison, Lana and Arthur Hughes, eds. 1997. *The Validity of Self-Reported Drug Use: Improving the Accuracy of Survey Estimates.* Rockville, MD: Department of Health and Human Services.

Hirschi, Travis. 1969. *Causes of Delinquency.* Berkeley: University of California Press.

Horney, Julie, D. Wayne Osgood, and Ineke Haen Marshall. 1995. "Criminal Careers in the Short-Term: Intra-Individual Variation in Crime and Its Relation to Local Life Circumstances." *American Sociological Review* 60:655–73.

Jacobs, Bruce A. 1999. *Dealing Crack: The Social World of Street-corner Selling.* Boston, MA: Northeastern University Press.

Johnston, Lloyd D., Patrick M. O'Malley, Jerald G. Bachman, and John E. Schulenberg. 2004. *Monitoring the Future: National Survey Results on Drug Use, 1975–2003,* vol. 1, *Secondary School Students.* Bethesda, MD: National Institute on Drug Abuse.

Lemert, Edwin M. 1951. *Social Pathology: A Systematic Approach to the Theory of Sociopathic Behavior.* New York: McGraw-Hill.

Levine, Harry Gene. 1991. "Just Say Poverty: What Causes Crack and Heroin Abuse." Presented at the annual meeting of the Drug Policy Foundation, November, Washington, DC.

Lindesmith, Alfred R. 1947. *Opiate Addiction.* Bloomington, IN: Principia Press.

Lindesmith, Alfred R. 1965. *The Addict and the Law.* Bloomington: Indiana University Press.

Lindesmith, Alfred R. 1968. *Addiction and Opiates.* Chicago, IL: Aldine.

MacCoun, Robert J. and Peter Reuter. 2001. *Drug War Heresies: Learning from Other Vices, Times, and Places.* Cambridge, England: Cambridge University Press.

Pfohl, Stephen. 1994. *Images of Deviance and Social Control: A Sociological History.* 2d ed. New York: McGraw-Hill.

Ramsay, Malcolm, P. Baker, C. Goulden, C. Sharp, and A. Sondhi. 2001. *Drug Misuse Declared in 2000: Results from the British Crime Survey.* London, England: Home Office Research.

SAMHSA (Substance Abuse and Mental Health Services Administration). 2004. *Results from the 2003 National Survey on Drug Use and Health: National Findings.* Rockville, MD: SAMHSA.

Schur, Edwin M. 1962. *Narcotic Addiction in Britain and America: The Impact of Public Policy.* Bloomington: Indiana University Press.

Spillane, Joseph F. 2000. *Cocaine: From Medical Marvel to Modern Menace in the United States, 1884–1920.* Baltimore, MD: Johns Hopkins University Press.

Sutherland, Edwin H. 1939. *Principles of Criminology.* 3d ed. Philadelphia, PA: Lippincott.

Uihlein, Carolyn. 1994. "Drugs and Alcohol." Pp. 149–57 in *The Generality of Deviance,* edited by T. Hirschi and M. R. Gottfredson. Brunswick, NJ: Transaction.

Williams, Terry. 1992. *Crackhouse: Notes from the End of the Line.* New York: Penguin.

Wish, Eric D., Thomas Gray, Jonathan Sushinsky, George S. Yacoubian Jr., and Nora Fitzgerald. 2000. "An Experiment to Enhance the Reporting of Drug Use by Arrestees." *Journal of Drug Issues* 30:55–76.

Chapter 43. Juvenile Delinquency

Akers, Ronald L. 1990. "Rational Choice, Deterrence, and Social Learning Theory in Criminology: The Path Not Taken." *Journal of Criminal Law and Criminology* 81:653–76.

Bartollas, Clemens. 2006. *Juvenile Delinquency.* 7th ed. Boston: Allyn & Bacon.

Battin-Pearson, Sara R., Terence P. Thornberry, J. David Hawkins, and Marvin D. Krohn. 1998. "Gang Membership, Delinquent Peers, and Delinquent Behavior." *Juvenile Justice Bulletin,* October.

Becker, Howard S. 1963. *Outsiders.* New York: Free Press.

Braga, Anthony A. 2003. "Serious Youth Gun Offenders and the Epidemic of Youth Violence in Boston." *Journal of Quantitative Criminology* 19:33–54.

Breckinridge, S. P. and Edith Abbott. 1970. *The Delinquent Child and the Home.* New York: Arno Press.

Brenzel, Barbara. 1983. *Daughters of the State.* Cambridge: MIT Press.

Centers for Disease Control and Prevention. 2004. *Youth Risk Behavior Surveillance-United States.* Washington, DC: U.S. Government Printing Office.

Chesney-Lind, Meda. 1989. "Girls, Crime and Women's Place." *Crime and Delinquency* 35:5–29.

Chesney-Lind, Meda. 1995. "Girls, Delinquency and Juvenile Justice: Toward a Feminist Theory of Young Women's Crime." Pp. 71–88 in *The Criminal Justice System and Women,* edited by B. R. Price and N. J. Sokoloff. New York: McGraw-Hill.

Cloward, Richard A. and Lloyd E. Ohlin. 1960. *Delinquency and Opportunity: A Theory of Delinquent Gangs.* Glencoe, IL: Free Press.

Cohen, Albert K. 1955. *Delinquent Boys: The Culture of the Gang.* Glencoe, IL: Free Press.

Cook, Philip J. and John Laub. 1998. "The Unprecedented Epidemic in Youth Violence." Pp. 27–64 in *Crime and Justice,* edited by M. H. Moore and M. Tonry. Chicago, IL: University of Chicago Press.

Cook, Philip J. and Jens Ludwig. 2004. "Does Gun Prevalence Affect Teen Gun Carrying After All?" *Criminology* 42:27–54.

Cornish, Derek and Ronald V. Clarke, eds. 1986. *The Reasoning Criminal: Rational Choice Perspectives on Offending.* New York: Springer.

Cortes, Juan B., with Florence M. Gatti. 1972. *Delinquency and Crime: A Biopsychosocial Approach; Empirical, Theoretical, and Practical Aspects of Criminal Behavior.* New York: Seminar Press.

Daly, Kathleen. 1995. "Looking Back, Looking Forward: the Promise of Feminist Transformation. Pp. 447–48 in *The Criminal Justice System and Women,* edited by B. R. Price and N. J. Sokoloff. New York: McGraw-Hill.

Daly, Kathleen and Meda Chesney-Lind. 1988. "Feminism and Criminology?" *Justice Quarterly* 5:497–538.

Elliott, Delbert S., Suzanne S. Ageton, and Rachelle J. Canter. 1979. "An Integrated Theoretical Perspective on Delinquent Behavior." *Journal of Research in Crime and Delinquency* 16:3–27.

Faust, Frederic and Paul J. Brantingham, eds. 1974. *Juvenile Justice Philosophy.* St. Paul, MN: West.

Feld, Barry. 1999. *Bad Kids: Race and the Transformation of the Juvenile Court.* New York: Oxford University Press.

Finestone, Harold. 1976. *Victims of Change: Juvenile Delinquents in American Society.* Westport, CT: Greenwood Press.

Fishbein, Diana. H. 1990. "Biological Perspectives in Criminology." *Criminology* 28:27–72.

Glueck, Nelson and Eleanor Glueck. 1956. *Physique and Delinquency.* New York: Harper & Row.

Gottfredson, Michael R. and Travis Hirschi. 1990. *A General Theory of Crime.* Palo Alto, CA: Stanford University Press.

Grasmick, Harold G., Charles R. Tittle, Robert J. Bursik Jr., and Bruce J. Arneklev. 1993. "Testing the Core Empirical Implications of Gottfredson and Hirschi's General Theory of Crime." *Journal of Research in Crime and Delinquency* 30:5–29.

Heimer, Karen. 1995. "Gender, Race, and the Pathways to Delinquency." Pp. 140–53 in *Crime and Inequality,* edited by J. Hagen and R. D. Peterson. Stanford, CA: Stanford University Press.

Hirschi, Travis. 1967. *Causes of Delinquency.* Berkeley: California University Press.

Jarjoura, G. Roger. 1993. "Does Dropping Out of School Enhance Delinquent Involvement? Results from a Large-Scale National Probability Sample." *Criminology* 31:149–71.

Johnston, L. D., P. M. O'Malley, J. G. Bachman, and J. E. Schulenberg. 2004. *Monitoring the Future: Monitoring the*

Future National Results on Adolescent Drug Use: Overview of Key Findings. Bethesda, MD: National Institute of Drug Abuse.

Katz, Jack. 1988. *Seductions of Crime: Moral and Sensual Attractions in Doing Evil.* New York: Basic Books.

Klein, Dorie. 1995. "The Etiology of Female Crime: A Review of the Literature." Pp. 30–53 in *The Criminal Justice System and Women,* edited by B. R. Price and N. J. Sokoloff. New York: McGraw-Hill.

Krohn, Marvin D., Terence P. Thornberry, Craig Rivera, and Marc Le Blanc. 2001. "Later Delinquency Careers." Pp. 67–93 in *Child Development,* edited by R. Loeber and D. P. Farrington. Thousand Oaks, CA: Sage.

Laub, James H. and Robert J. Sampson. 2003. *Shared Beginnings, Divergent Lives Delinquent Boys to Age 70.* Cambridge, MA: Harvard University Press.

Lauritsen, Janet L. 1993. "Sibling Resemblance in Juvenile Delinquency: Findings from a National Youth Survey." *Criminology* 31:387–409.

Lemert, Edwin M. 1951. *Social Pathology.* New York: McGraw-Hill.

Leonard, Eileen. 1995. "Theoretical Criminology and Gender." Pp. 55–70 in *The Criminal Justice System and Women,* edited by B. R. Price and N. J. Sokoloff. New York: McGraw-Hill.

Loeber, Rolf and M. Stouthamer-Loeber. 1986. "Family Factors as Correlates and Predictors of Juvenile Conduct Problems and Delinquency." Pp. 29–149 in *Crime and Justice: An Annual Review of Research,* edited by M. Tonry and N. Morris. Chicago, IL: University of Chicago Press.

Lombroso-Ferrero, Gina. 1972. *Criminal Man According to Classification of Cesare Lombroso.* Montclair, NJ: Patterson Smith.

Lundman, Richard J., Paul T. McFarlane, and Frank R. Scarpitti. 1976. "Delinquency Prevention: A Description and Assessment of Projects Reported in the Professional Literature." *Crime and Delinquency* 22:297–309.

Lundman, Richard J. and Frank R. Scarpitti. 1978. "Delinquency Prevention: Recommendations for Future Projects." *Crime and Delinquency* 24:207–20.

Maguin, Eugene and Rolf Loeber. 1996. "Academic Performance and Delinquency." Pp. 145–264 in *Crime and Justice: A Review of Research,* vol. 20, edited by M. Tonry. Chicago, IL: University of Chicago Press.

Matsueda, Ross. L. 1992. "Reflected Appraisals: Parental Labeling, and Delinquency: Specifying a Symbolic Interactionist Theory." *American Journal of Sociology* 97:1577–611.

Matza, David. 1964. *Delinquency and Drift.* New York: John Wiley.

Mazerolle, Paul. 1998. "Gender, General Strain, and Delinquency: An Empirical Examination." *Justice Quarterly* 15:65–91.

McCord, W. J., J. McCord, and Irvin Zola. 1959. *The Origins of Crime.* New York: Columbia University Press.

Merton. Robert K. 1957. *Social Theory and Social Structure.* 2d ed. New York: Free Press.

Mihalic, Sharon, Katerine Irwin, Abigail Fagan, Diane Ballard, and Delbert Elliott. 2004. *Blueprints for Violence Prevention.* Washington, DC: Office of Juvenile Justice and Delinquency Prevention.

Miller, Jody. 2001. *One of the Guys: Girls, Gangs, and Gender.* New York: Oxford University Press.

Miller, Jody and Scott Decker. 2001. "Young Women and Gang Violence: Gender, Street Offending, and Violent Victimization in Gangs." *Justice Quarterly* 18:115–39.

Moffitt, Terrie. 1993. "Adolescent-Limited and Life-Course-Persistent Antisocial Behavior: A Developmental Taxonomy." *Psychological Review* 100:674–701.

Moffitt, Terrie, Donald R. Lynam, and Phil A. Silva. 1994. "Neuropsychological Tests Predicted Persistent Male Delinquency." *Criminology* 32:277–300.

Moffitt, Terrie E., Avshalom Caspi, Michael Rutter, and Phil A. Silva. 2001. *Sex Differences in antisocial behavior.* Cambridge, England: Cambridge University Press.

Piper, Elizabeth S. 1985. "Violent Offenders: Lone Wolf or Wolfpack." Presented at the annual meeting of the American Society of Criminology, San Diego, CA.

Platt, Anthony. 1977. *The Child Savers.* 2d ed. Chicago, IL: Chicago University Press.

Reckless, Walter C. 1961. "A New Theory of Delinquency and Crime." *Federal Probation* 24:42–46.

Reiss, Albert J., Jr. 1976. "Setting the Frontiers of a Pioneer in American Criminology: Henry McKay." Pp. 64–88 in *Delinquency: Crime and Society,* edited by J. F. Short. Chicago, IL: University of Chicago Press.

Rothman, David J. 1971. *Discovery of the Asylum.* Boston, MA: Little, Brown.

Sampson, Robert J. and James H. Laub. 1993. *Crime in the Making: Pathways and Turning Points through Life.* Cambridge, MA: Harvard University Press.

Shah, Saleem A. and Loren H. Roth. 1974. "Biological and Psychophysiological Factors in Criminality." Pp. 101–73 in *Handbook of Criminology,* edited by D. Glaser. Chicago, IL: Rand McNally.

Shaw, Clifford R. 1929. *Delinquent Areas.* Chicago, IL: University of Chicago Press.

Shaw, Clifford R. and Henry D. McKay. 1931. *Social Factors in Juvenile Delinquency.* Washington, DC: National Commission on Law Observance and Enforcement.

Shaw, Clifford R. and Henry D. McKay. 1942. *Juvenile Delinquency and Urban Areas.* Chicago, IL: University of Chicago Press.

Smart, Carol. 1976. *Women, Crime and Criminology: A Feminist Critique.* Boston, MA: Routledge & Kegan Paul.

Shichor, David. 1980. "The New Criminology: Some Critical Issues." *British Journal of Criminology* 20:1–19.

Sutherland, Edwin H. 1947. *Principles of Criminology.* 10th ed. Philadelphia, PA: J. P. Lippincott.

Tannenbaum. Frank. 1938. *Crime and the Community.* New York: Columbia University Press.

Thomas, William I. and Florian Znaniecki. 1927. *The Polish Peasant in Europe and America.* 5 vols. New York: Knopf.

Thornberry, Terence P. 1987. "Toward an Interactional Theory of Delinquency." *Criminology* 25:863–91.

Thornberry, Terence P. 1989. "Reflections on the Advantages and Disadvantages of Theoretical Integration." Pp. 51–60 in *Theoretical Integration in the Study of Deviance and Crime: Problems and Prospects,* edited by S. Messner, M. Krohn, and A. Liska. Albany: State University of New York Press.

Thornberry, Terence P., Marvin D. Krohn, Alan J. Lizotte, Carolyn A. Smith, and Kimberly Tobin. 2003. *Gangs and Delinquency in Developmental Perspective.* Cambridge, England: Cambridge University Press.

Thrasher, Frederick. 1927. *The Gang: A Study of 1313 Gangs in Chicago.* Chicago, IL: University of Chicago Press.

Triplett, Ruth Ann and G. Roger Jarjoura. 1994. "Theoretical and Empirical Specification of a Model of Informal Labeling." *Journal of Quantitative Criminology* 10:241–76.

White, Herlene Raskin, Erich W. Labouvie, and Marsha E. Bates. 1985. "The Relationship between Sensation Seeking and Delinquency: A Longitudinal Analysis." *Journal of Research in Crime and Delinquency* 22:195–211.

Wilson, James Q. and Richard J. Herrnstein. 1985. *Crime and Human Nature.* New York: Simon & Schuster.

Wolfgang, E. Marvin, Terence P. Thornberry, and Robert F. Figlio. 1987. *From Boy to Man: From Delinquency to Crime.* Chicago, IL: University of Chicago Press.

Chapter 44. The Sociology of Corrections

Allen, Harry, Clifford E. Simonsen, and Edward J. Latessa. 2004. *Corrections in America.* Upper Saddle River, NJ: Prentice Hall.

Applegate, Brandon K., Francis T. Cullen, and Bonnie Fisher. 2002. "Public Views toward Crime and Correctional Policies: Is There a Gender Gap?" *Journal of Criminal Justice* 30:89–100.

Baldus, David C., George G. Woodworth, and Charles A. Pulaski Jr. 1990. *Equal Justice and the Death Penalty.* Boston, MA: Northeastern University Press.

Beccaria, Cesare. [1764] 1963. *On Crimes and Punishments.* Translated by H. Paolucci. Indianapolis, IN: Bobbs-Merrill.

Burns, J. H. and H. L. A. Hart. 1996. *An Introduction to the Principles of Morals and Legislation: An Authoritative Edition.* New York: Oxford University Press.

Cameron, Samuel. 1994. "A Review of the Econometric Evidence on the Effects of Capital Punishment." *Journal of Socio-Economics* 23:197–214.

Camp, Scott D., Gerald G. Gaes, and William G. Saylor. 2000. "Quality of Prison Operations in the U.S. Federal Sector: A Comparison with a Private Prison." *Punishment & Society* 4:27–53.

Carroll, Leo. 1974. *Hacks, Blacks and Cons.* Prospect Heights, IL: Waveland.

Cecil, Dawn K., Daniella A. Drapkin, Doris Layton MacKenzie, and Laura J. Hickman. 2000. "The Effectiveness of Adult Basic Education and Life-Skills Programs in Reducing Recidivism: A Review and Assessment of the Research." *Journal of Correctional Education* 51:207–26.

Clemmer, Donald. 1940. *The Prison Community.* New York: Rinehart.

Cochran, John K., Mitchell B. Chamlin, and Mark Seth. 1994. "Deterrence or Brutalization? An Assessment of Oklahoma's Return to Capital Punishment." *Criminology* 32:107–34.

Cullen, Francis T., Bonnie S. Fisher, and Brandon K. Applegate. 2000. "Public Opinion about Punishment and Corrections." Pp. 1–79 in *Crime and Justice: A Review of Research,* vol. 27, edited by M. Tonry. Chicago, IL: University of Chicago Press.

Erlich, Issac. 1975. "The Deterrent Effect of Capital Punishment." *American Economic Review* 65:397–98.

Erlich, Issac. 1977. "Capital Punishment and Deterrence." *Journal of Political Economy* 85:741–42.

Garofalo, James and Richard D. Clark. 1985. "The Inmate Subculture in Jails." *Criminal Justice and Behavior* 12(4):415–34.

Glaze, Lauren E. and Seri Palla. 2004. *Probation and Parole in the United States, 2003.* Washington, DC: Bureau of Justice Statistics.

Harrison, Paige M. and Allen J. Beck. 2005. *Prison and Jail Inmates at Midyear 2004.* Washington, DC: Bureau of Justice Statistics.

Hensley, Christopher, Jeremy Wright, and Richard Tewksbury. 2003. "The Evolving Nature of Prison Argot and Sexual Hierarchies." *The Prison Journal* 83(3):289–300.

Hunt, Geoffrey, Stephanie Riegel, Tomas Morales, and Dan Waldorf. 1993. "Changes in Prison Culture: Prison Gangs and the Case of the 'Pepsi Generation.'" *Social Problems* 40:389–409.

Irwin, John and Donald Cressey. 1963. "Thieves, Convicts and the Inmate Culture." *Social Problems* 10:142–55.

Johnson, Kathrine. 2002. "States' Use of GPS Offender Tracking Systems." *Journal of Offender Monitoring* 15:15, 21–22, 26.

Lippke, Richard L. 2002. "Crime Reduction and the Length of Prison Sentences." *Law & Policy* 24(1):17–35.

Martinson, Robert. 1974. "What Works? Questions and Answers about Prison Reform." *The Public Interest* 35:22–54.

Mauer, Marc. 2003. "Introduction: The Collateral Consequences of Imprisonment." *Fordham Urban Law Journal* 30(5):1491–500.

McGuire, James. 2002. "Criminal Sanctions versus Psychologically-Based Interventions with Offenders: A Comparative Analysis." *Psychology, Crime and Law* 8(2):183–208.

Moon, Melissa M., Francis T. Cullen, and John Paul Wright. 2003. "It Takes a Village: Public Willingness to Help Wayward Youth." *Youth Violence and Juvenile Justice* 1:32–45.

Moore, Adrian T. 1998. *Private Prisons: Quality Corrections at a Lower Cost.* Los Angeles, CA: Reason Public Policy Institute.

Morris, Norval and David J. Rothman. 1995. *The Oxford History of the Prison.* New York: Oxford University Press.

Mumola, Christopher. 1999. *Substance Abuse and Treatment, State and Federal Prisoners, 1997.* Washington, DC: Bureau of Justice Statistics.

Mumola, Christopher. 2005. *Suicide and Homicide in State Prisons and Local Jails.* Washington, DC: Bureau of Justice Statistics.

Munden, David, Richard Tewksbury, and Elizabeth Grossi. 1998. "Intermediate Sanctions and the Halfway Back Program in Kentucky." *Criminal Justice Policy Review* 9:431–49.

Pastore, Ann L. and Kathleeen Maguire, eds. 2005. *Sourcebook of Criminal Justice Statistics, 2003.* Washington, DC: U.S. Government Printing Office.

Perrone, Dina and Travis C. Pratt. 2003. "Comparing the Quality of Confinement and Cost-Effectiveness of Public versus Private Prisons: What We Know, Why We Do Not Know More, and Where to Go from Here?" *Prison Journal* 83(3):301–22.

Pratt, Travis C. and Jeff Maahs. 1999. "Are Private Prisons More Cost-Effective Than Public Prisons? A Meta-Analysis of Evaluation Research Studies." *Crime and Delinquency* 45:358–71.

Smith, Linda G. 2003. *Does Educating Incarcerated Offenders Work? Examining the Results of the OCE/CEA Three State*

Recidivism Study. Lanham, MD: American Correctional Association.

Smith, Linda G. and Mitchell Silverman. 1994. "Functional Literacy Education for Jail Inmates: An Examination of the Hillsborough County Jail Education Program." *Prison Journal* 73(4):414–32.

Stack, Steven. 1994. "Execution Publicity and Homicide in Georgia." *American Journal of Criminal Justice* 18:25–39.

Stephan, James J. 2001. *Census of Jails, 1999.* Washington, DC: Bureau of Justice Statistics.

Stephan, James J. and Jennifer Karberg. 2003. *Census of State and Federal Correctional Facilities, 2000.* Washington, DC: Bureau of Justice Statistics.

Steurer, Steven, Linda G. Smith, and Alice Tracy. 2001. *Final Report: Three-State Recidivism Study.* Washington, DC: U.S. Department of Education.

Sykes, Gresham. 1958. *The Society of Captives: A Study of a Maximum Security Prison.* Princeton, NJ: Princeton University Press.

Tahir, Laura. 2003. "Supervision of Special Needs Inmates by Custody Staff." *Corrections Today* 65:110.

Terry, Charles. 2003. "Managing Prisoners as Problem Populations and the Evolving Nature of Imprisonment: A Convict Perspective." *Critical Criminology* 12(1):43–66.

Tewksbury, Richard. 1994. Improving the Educational Skills of Jail Inmates: Preliminary Program Findings. *Federal Probation* 58:55–59.

Tewksbury, Richard and Elizabeth Ehrhardt Mustaine. 2005. "Correctional Orientations of Prison Staff." Presented at the annual meetings of the Academy of Criminal Justice Sciences, March 2005, Chicago, IL.

Tonry, Michael. 2004. *Thinking about Crime: Sense and Sensibility in American Penal Culture.* New York: Oxford University Press.

Trulson, Chad and James W. Marquart. 2002. "The Caged Melting Pot: Toward an Understanding of the Consequences of Desegregation in Prisons." *Law and Society Review* 36:743–81.

U.S. Bureau of the Census. 2006. Retrieved January 12, 2006 (http://www.census.gov).

Whitman, James Q. 2003. *Harsh Justice: Criminal Punishment and the Widening Divide between America and Europe.* New York: Oxford University Press.

Wilson, David B., Catherine A. Gallagher, and Doris L. MacKenzie. 2000. "A Meta-Analysis of Corrections-Based Education, Vocation, and Work Programs for Adult Offenders." *Journal of Research in Crime and Delinquency* 37:347–68.

Wright, Kevin. 2003. *Defining and Measuring Correctional Performance: Final Report.* Middletown, CT: Association of State Correctional Administrators.

PART IX: LOCALITY AND SOCIAL LIFE

Chapter 45. Human Ecology

Alexander, Jeffrey C. 1982. *Theoretical Logic in Sociology.* London, England: Routledge & Kegan Paul.

Alihan, Milla A. [1938] 1964. *Social Ecology: A Critical Analysis.* New York: Cooper Square.

Anderson, Nels. 1923. *The Hobo: The Sociology of the Homeless Man.* Chicago, IL: University of Chicago Press.

Barker, Roger G. and Herbert F. Wright. 1954. *The Midwest and Its Children: The Psychological Ecology of an American Town.* Evanston, IL: Peterson.

Baumol, William J., Sue Anne Batey Blackman, and Edward N. Wolff. 1989. *Productivity and American Leadership: The Long View.* Cambridge: MIT Press.

Bechtel, Robert B. 1997. *Environment and Behavior: An Introduction.* Thousand Oaks, CA: Sage.

Becker, Gary S. 1976. "Irrational Behavior and Economic Theory." In *The Economic Approach to Human Behavior,* edited by G. S. Becker. Chicago, IL: University of Chicago Press.

Beniger, James R. 1986. *The Control Revolution: Technological and Economic Origins of the Information Society.* Cambridge, MA: Harvard University Press.

Berlinski, David. 2000. *The Advent of the Algorithm: The Idea That Rules the World.* New York: Harcourt Brace.

Berry, Brian J. and John D. Kasarda. 1977. *Contemporary Urban Ecology.* New York: Macmillan.

Bidwell, Charles E. and John D. Kasarda. 1985. *The Organization and Its Ecosystem: A Theory of Structuring in Organizations.* Greenwich, CT: JAI Press.

Blau, Judith R. 1989. *The Shape of Culture: A Study of Contemporary Cultural Patterns in the United States.* Cambridge, England: Cambridge University Press.

Blau, Peter M. 1964. *Exchange and Power in Social Life.* New York: Wiley.

Bogue, Donald J. 1949. *The Structure of the Metropolitan Community: A Study of Dominance and Subdominance.* Ann Arbor: University of Michigan, Horace M. Rackman School of Graduate Studies.

Booth, Charles. 1902. *Life and Labour of the People in London.* London, England: Macmillan.

Boserup, Ester. 1966. *The Conditions of Agricultural Growth: The Economics of Agrarian Change under Population Pressure.* Chicago, IL: Aldine.

Burgess, Ernest W. 1925. "The Growth of the City: An Introduction to a Research Project." Pp. 47–62 in *The City,* edited by R. Park, E. W. Burgess, and R. D. McKenzie. Chicago, IL: University of Chicago Press.

Carroll, Glenn R. and Michael T. Hannan. 2000. *The Demography of Corporations and Industries.* Princeton, NJ: Princeton University Press.

Chandler, Alfred D. 1977. *The Visible Hand: The Managerial Revolution in American Business.* Cambridge, MA: Harvard University Press.

Clements, Frederic E. 1916. *Plant Succession: An Analysis of the Development of Vegetation.* Washington, DC: Carnegie Institution of Washington.

Coleman, James S. 1990. *Foundations of Social Theory.* Cambridge, MA: Harvard University Press.

Collins, Randall. 2004. *Interaction Ritual Chains.* Princeton, NJ: Princeton University Press.

Cooley, Charles H. 1930a. "Personal Competition." In *Sociological Theory and Social Research,* edited by R. C. Angell. New York: Henry Holt.

Cooley, Charles H. [1894] 1930b. "The Theory of Transportation." Pp. 75–83 in *Sociological Theory and Social Research,* edited by R. C. Angell. New York: Henry Holt.

Coser, Lewis A. 1965. *Men of Ideas: A Sociologist's View.* New York: Free Press.

Duncan, Beverly and Stanley Lieberson. 1970. *Metropolis and Region in Transition.* Beverly Hills, CA: Sage.

Duncan, Otis D. 1951. "Optimum Size of Cities." Pp. 759–72 in *Cities and Society: The Revised Reader in Urban Sociology,* edited by P. K. Hatt and A. J. Reiss. Glencoe, IL: Free Press.

Duncan, Otis D. 1959. "Human Ecology and Population Studies." Pp. 678–716 in *The Study of Population: An Inventory and Appraisal,* edited by P. M. Hauser and O. D. Duncan. Chicago, IL: University of Chicago Press.

Duncan, Otis D. 1964. "Social Organization and the Ecosystem." Pp. 37–82 in *Handbook of Modern Sociology,* edited by R. E. Faris. Chicago, IL: Rand McNally.

Duncan, Otis D. 1965. "The Trend of Occupational Mobility in the United States." *American Sociological Review* 30:491–98.

Duncan, Otis D., W. Richard Scott, Stanley Lieberson, Beverly Duncan, and Hal H. Winsborough. 1960. *Metropolis and Region.* Baltimore, MD: Johns Hopkins University Press.

Ehrenreich, Barbara. 1989. *Fear of Falling: The Inner Life of the Middle Class.* New York: Pantheon Books.

Firey, Walter I. 1947. *Land Use in Central Boston.* Cambridge, MA: Harvard University Press.

Freese, Lee. 2001. "Human Ecology." Pp. 6974–78 in *International Encyclopedia of the Social and Behavioral Sciences,* edited by N. J. Smelser and P. B. Baltes. Amsterdam, The Netherlands: Elsevier.

Frobel, Folker, Jurgen Heinrichs, and Otto Kreye. 1980. *The New International Division of Labour: Structural Unemployment in Industrialised Countries and Industrialisation in Developing Countries.* Cambridge, England: Cambridge University Press.

Galpin, Charles J. 1915. "Anatomy of an Agricultural Community." Research Bulletin 34, University of Wisconsin Agricultural Experiment Station, Madison, WI.

Geddes, Patrick. 1915. *Cities in Evolution: An Introduction to the Town Planning Movement and to the Study of Civics.* London, England: Williams & Norgate.

Gerth, Hans H. and C. Wright Mills. 1953. *Character and Social Structure: The Psychology of Social Institutions.* New York: Harcourt Brace.

Gibbs, Jack P. and Walter T. Martin. 1959. "Toward a Theoretical System of Human Ecology." *Pacific Sociological Review* 2:29–36.

Gras, Norman S. B. 1922. *An Introduction to Economic History.* New York: Harper.

Hannan, Michael T. and John Freeman. 1977. "The Population Ecology of Organizations." *American Journal of Sociology* 82:929–64.

Harvey, David. 1989. *The Condition of Postmodernity: An Enquiry into the Origins of Cultural Change.* Oxford, England: Blackwell.

Hawley, Amos H. 1944. "Ecology and Human Ecology." *Social Forces* 22:398–405.

Hawley, Amos H. 1950. *Human Ecology: A Theory of Community Structure.* New York: Ronald Press.

Hawley, Amos H. 1986. *Human Ecology: A Theoretical Essay.* Chicago, IL: University of Chicago Press.

Hochschild, Arlie R. 1989. *The Second Shift: Working Parents and the Revolution at Home.* New York: Viking.

Hollingshead, August B. 1940. "Human Ecology and Human Society." *Ecological Monographs* 10:354–66.

Homans, George C. 1949. "The Strategy of Industrial Sociology." *American Journal of Sociology* 54:330–37.

Homans, George C. 1950. *The Human Group.* New York: Harcourt Brace.

Irwin, Michael D. and John D. Kasarda. 1991. "Air Passenger Linkages and Employment Growth in U.S. Metropolitan Areas." *American Sociological Review* 56:524–37.

Jacobsen, Joyce P. 1997. "Trends in Workforce Segregation: 1980 and 1990 Census Figures." *Social Science Quarterly* 78:234–35.

Kasarda, John D. 1989. "Urban Industrial Transition and the Underclass." *Annals of the American Academy of Political and Social Science* 501:26–47.

Latour, Bruno. 1991. "Technology Is Society Made Durable." Pp. 103–31 in *A Sociology of Monsters: Essays on Power, Technology, and Domination,* edited by J. Law. London, England: Routledge.

Leccese, Michael and Kathleen McCormick. 1999. *The Charter of the New Urbanism.* New York: McGraw-Hill.

Lenski, Gerhard E. 1966. *Power and Privilege: A Theory of Social Stratification.* New York: McGraw-Hill.

Logan, John A. 1996. "Opportunity and Choice in Socially Structured Labor Markets." *American Journal of Sociology* 102:114–60.

Logan, John R. and Kyle D. Crowder. 2002. "Political Regimes and Suburban Growth, 1980–1990." *City and Community* 1:113–35.

Lynd, Robert S. and Helen Merrell Lynd. 1929. *Middletown: A Study in American Culture.* New York: Harcourt Brace.

Mann, Michael. 1986. *The Sources of Social Power.* Cambridge, England: Cambridge University Press.

Mannheim, Karl. 1936. *Ideology and Utopia: An Introduction to the Sociology of Knowledge.* London, England: Routledge & Kegan Paul.

March, James G. and Johan P. Olsen. 1976. *Ambiguity and Choice in Organizations.* Bergen, Germany: Universitetsforlaget.

Massey, Douglas S. and Nancy A. Denton. 1993. *American Apartheid: Segregation and the Making of the Underclass.* Cambridge, MA: Harvard University Press.

McKenzie, Roderick D. 1924. "The Ecological Approach to the Study of the Human Community." *American Journal of Sociology* 30:287–301.

McKenzie, Roderick D. 1927. "The Concept of Dominance and World-Organization." *American Journal of Sociology* 33:28–42.

McKenzie, Roderick D. 1933. "Industrial Expansion and the Interrelations of Peoples." In *Race and Culture Contacts,* edited by E. B. Reuter. New York: McGraw-Hill.

McKenzie, Roderick D. [1933] 1997. *The Metropolitan Community.* London, England: Routledge/Thoemmes Press.

McPherson, J. Miller. 1983. "An Ecology of Affiliation." *American Sociological Review* 48:519–32.

Mead, George H. 1934. *Mind, Self, and Society from the Standpoint of a Social Behaviorist.* Chicago, IL: University of Chicago Press.

Micklin, Michael and Dudley L. Poston. 1998. *Continuities in Sociological Human Ecology.* New York: Plenum Press.

Mills, C. Wright. [1959] 1967. *The Sociological Imagination.* New York: Oxford University Press.

Moore, Barrington. 1920. "The Scope of Ecology." *Ecology* 1:3–5.

Nadel, Siegfried F. 1957. *The Theory of Social Structure.* Glencoe, IL: Free Press.

Nielsen, Francois. 1985. "Toward a Theory of Ethnic Solidarity in Modern Societies." *American Sociological Review* 50:133–49.

Nolan, Patrick and Gerhard Lenski. 1999. *Human Societies: An Introduction to Macrosociology.* 8th ed. New York: McGraw-Hill.

Ogburn, William F. 1946. "Inventions of Local Transportation and the Patterns of Cities." *Social Forces* 24:373–79.

Ogburn, William F. 1964. *On Culture and Social Change: Selected Papers.* Chicago, IL: University of Chicago Press.

Olzak, Susan. 1986. "A Competition Model of Ethnic Collective Action in American Cities, 1877–1889." Pp. 17–46 in *Competitive Ethnic Relations,* edited by S. Olzak and J. Nagel. Orlando, FL: Academic Press.

Oxford English Dictionary. 2000. *OED Online.* Oxford, England: Oxford University Press.

Park, Robert E. 1915. "The City: Suggestions for the Investigation of Human Behavior in the City Environment." *American Journal of Sociology* 20:577–612.

Park, Robert E. 1921. "Sociology and the Social Sciences." *American Journal of Sociology* 26:401–24; 27:1–21, 169–83.

Park, Robert E. 1923. "The Natural History of the Newspaper." *American Journal of Sociology* 29:273–89.

Park, Robert E. 1936. "Human Ecology." *American Journal of Sociology* 42:1–15.

Park, Robert E. [1904] 1972. *Masse und Publikum; Eine Methodologische Und Soziologische Untersuchung.* Bern, Switzerland: Buchdruckerei Lack and Grunau. Republished as *The Crowd and the Public, and Other Essays.* Chicago, IL: University of Chicago Press.

Park, Robert E. and Ernest W. Burgess. [1921] 1969. *Introduction to the Science of Sociology.* 3d ed. Chicago, IL: University of Chicago Press.

Petersen, Trond and Laurie A. Morgan. 1995. "Separate and Unequal: Occupation–Establishment Sex Segregation and the Gender Wage Gap." *American Journal of Sociology* 101:329–65.

Piore, Michael J. and Charles F. Sabel. 1984. *The Second Industrial Divide: Possibilities for Prosperity.* New York: Basic Books.

Pred, Allan R. 1966. *The Spatial Dynamics of U.S. Urban-Industrial Growth, 1800–1914: Interpretive and Theoretical Essays.* Cambridge: MIT Press.

Quinn, James A. 1940. "Topical Summary of Current Literature: On Human Ecology." *American Journal of Sociology* 46:191–226.

Quinn, James A. 1950. *Human Ecology.* New York: Prentice Hall.

Reskin, Barbara and Naomi Cassirer. 1996. "Occupational Segregation by Gender, Race and Ethnicity." *Sociological Focus* 29:231–43.

Riesman, David. 1950. *The Lonely Crowd: A Study of the Changing American Character.* New Haven, CT: Yale University Press.

Schnore, Leo. 1958. "Social Morphology and Human Ecology." *American Journal of Sociology* 63:620–34.

Schumpeter, Joseph A. 1950. *Capitalism, Socialism, and Democracy.* New York: Harper.

Stewman, Shelby and Suresh L. Konda. 1983. "Careers and Organizational Labor Markets: Demographic Models of Organizational Behavior." *American Journal of Sociology* 88:637–85.

Suttles, Gerald D. 1990. *The Man-made City: The Land-Use Confidence Game in Chicago.* Chicago, IL: University of Chicago Press.

Thomson, J. Arthur and Patrick Geddes. 1931. *Life: Outlines of General Biology.* London, England: Williams & Norgate.

Ullman, Edward L. 1980. *Geography as Spatial Interaction.* Seattle: University of Washington Press.

Useem, Michael. 1989. *Liberal Education and the Corporation: The Hiring and Advancement of College Graduates.* New York: Aldine de Gruyter.

Vance, Rupert B. and Sara Smith. 1954. "Metropolitan Dominance and Integration." Pp. 114–34 in *The Urban South,* edited by R. B. Vance and N. J. Demerath. Chapel Hill: University of North Carolina Press.

Vernon, Raymond. 1960. *Metropolis 1985.* Cambridge, MA: Harvard University Press.

Vernon, Raymond. 1966. "International Investment and International Trade in the Product Cycle." *Quarterly Journal of Economics* 80:190–207.

Warming, Eugenius. 1909. *Oecology of Plants: An Introduction to the Study of Plant-Communities.* Oxford, England: Clarendon Press.

Weber, Adna F. 1899. *The Growth of Cities in the Nineteenth Century.* New York: Macmillan.

Weber, Marianne. 1975. *Max Weber: A Biography.* New York: Wiley.

Weber, Max. 1958. *The City.* London, England: Heinemann.

Wells, Herbert G. 1921. *The Outline of History, Being a Plain History of Life and Mankind.* New York: Macmillan.

White, Harrison C. 1992. *Identity and Control: A Structural Theory of Social Action.* Princeton, NJ: Princeton University Press.

Whitehead, Alfred N. 1933. *Adventures of Ideas.* New York: Macmillan.

Wilson, William Julius. 1978. *The Declining Significance of Race: Blacks and Changing American Institutions.* Chicago, IL: University Of Chicago Press.

Wirth, Louis. 1945. "Human Ecology." *American Journal of Sociology* 50:483–88.

Wuthnow, Robert. 1987. *Meaning and Moral Order: Explorations in Cultural Analysis.* Berkeley: University of California Press.

Zimmerman, Carle C. and Merle E. Frampton. 1935. *Family and Society: A Study of the Sociology of Reconstruction.* New York: Van Nostrand.

Zorbaugh, Harvey W. 1929. *The Gold Coast and the Slum: A Sociological Study of Chicago's Near North Side.* Chicago, IL: University of Chicago Press.

Chapter 46. The Sociology of Community

Anderson, Elijah. 1990. *Streetwise: Race, Class, and Change in an Urban Community.* Chicago, IL: University of Chicago Press.

Anderson, Elijah. 2000. *Code of the Street: Decency, Violence, and the Moral Life of the Inner City.* New York: W. W. Norton.

Bell, Colin and Howard Newby. 1971. *Community Studies: An Introduction to the Sociology of the Local Community.* Boston, MA: George Allen & Unwin.

Berry, Brian J. L. and John D. Kasarda. 1977. *Contemporary Urban Ecology*. New York: Macmillan.

Bobo, Lawrence. 2000. *Prismatic Metropolis: Inequality in Los Angeles*. New York: Russell Sage.

Bogue, Donald J. [1949] 1961. "The Structure of the Metropolitan Community." Pp. 524–38 in *Studies in Human Ecology*, edited by G. A. Theordorson. New York: Harper & Row.

Castells, Manuel. 1977. *The Urban Question: A Marxist Approach*. Cambridge: MIT Press.

Castells, Manuel. 1983. *The City and the Grassroots: A Cross-Cultural Theory of Urban Social Movements*. Berkeley: University of California Press.

Castells, Manuel. 1996. *The Rise of the Network Society*. Malden, MA: Blackwell.

Castells, Manuel. 1997. *The Power of Identity*. Malden, MA: Blackwell.

Castells, Manuel. 1998. *End of Millennium*. Malden, MA: Blackwell.

Clark, Terry Nichols. 2004. "Urban Amenities: Lakes, Opera, and Juice Bars: Do They Drive Development?" Pp. 103–40 in *Research in Urban Policy*, vol. 9, *The City as an Entertainment Machine*, edited by T. N. Clark. Oxford, England: Elsevier.

Cooley, Charles Horton. 1909. *Social Organization*. New York: Charles Scribner's Sons.

Dossani, R. and M. Kenney. 2004. "'Lift and Shift': Moving the Back Office to India." *Information Technologies and International Development* (Winter)1(2):21–37.

Dossani, R. and M. Kenney. 2003. "Went for Cost, Stayed for Quality? Moving the Back Office to India." Working Paper No. 156, Berkeley Roundtable on the International Economy.

Duncan, Cynthia M. 1999. *Worlds Apart: Why Poverty Persists in Rural America*. New Haven, CT: Yale University Press.

Duneier, Mitchell. 1999. *Sidewalk*. New York: Farrar, Straus, & Giroux.

Etzioni, Amitai. 1996. "The Responsive Community: A Communitarian Perspective." *American Sociological Review* 61:1–11.

Fischer, Claude S. 1977. "Perspectives on Community and Personal Relations." Pp. 1–16 in *Networks and Places: Social Relations in the Urban Setting*, edited by C. S. Fischer, R. M. Jackson, C. A. Stueve, K. Gerson, L. M. Jones, with M. Baldassare. New York: Free Press.

Florida, Richard. 2002. *The Rise of the Creative Class: And How It's Transforming Work, Leisure, Community and Everyday Life*. New York: Basic Books.

Florida, Richard. 2003. "Cities and the Creative Class." *City & Community* 2(1):3–19.

Florida, Richard. 2005. *Cities and the Creative Class*. New York: Routledge.

Freudenburg, William. 1986. "The Density of Acquaintanceship: An Overlooked Variable in Community Research." *American Journal of Sociology* 92:27–63.

Gans, Herbert. 1962. *The Urban Villagers*. New York: Free Press.

Geertz, Clifford. 1963. "The Integrative Revolution." Pp. 105–57 in *Old Societies and New States*, edited by C. Geertz. Glencoe, IL: Free Press.

Gereffi, Gary. 1994. "The International Economy and Economic Development." Pp. 206–33 in *The Handbook of Economic Sociology*, edited by N. J. Smelser and R. Swedberg. Princeton, NJ: Princeton University Press.

Gereffi, Gary, John Humphrey, and Timothy Sturgeon. 2005. "The Governance of Global Value Chains." *Review of International Political Economy* 12:78–104.

Giddings, Franklin H. 1922. *Studies in the Theory of Human Society*. New York: Macmillan.

Gordon, David. 1977. "Class Struggle and the States of American Urban Development." Pp. 55–82 in *The Rise of the Sunbelt Cities*, edited by D. C. Perry and A. J. Watkins. Beverly Hills, CA: Sage.

Granovetter, Mark. 1973. "The Strength of Weak Ties." *American Journal of Sociology* 78:1360–80.

Gusfield, Joseph. 1975. *Community: A Critical Response*. New York: Harper & Row.

Hampton, Keith and Barry Wellman. 2002. "The Not-So Global Village of Netville." Pp. 345–71 in *The Internet in Everyday Life*, edited by B. Wellman and C. Haythornthwaite. Oxford, England: Blackwell.

Harvey, David. 1982. *Limits to Capital*. Oxford, England: Blackwell.

Harvey, David. 1985. *The Urban Experience*. Baltimore, MA: Johns Hopkins University Press.

Harvey, David. 1990. *The Condition of Postmodernity*. Oxford, England: Blackwell.

Hawley, Amos H. 1950. *Human Ecology: A Theory of Community Structure*. New York: Ronald Press.

Hillery, George A. 1955. "Definitions of Community: Areas of Agreement." *Rural Sociology* 20:111–23.

Jonas, Andrew E. G. and David Wilson. 1999. *The Urban Growth Machine: Critical Perspectives, Two Decades Later*. Albany: State University New York Press.

Keller, Suzanne. 2003. *Community: Pursuing the Dream, Living the Reality*. Princeton, NJ: Princeton University Press.

Kumar, Krishan. 1978. *Prophecy and Progress: The Sociology of Industrial and Post-Industrial Society*. New York: Penguin Books.

Liebow, Elliot. 1967. *Tally's Corner*. Boston, MA: Little, Brown.

Lloyd, Richard and Terry Nichols Clark. 2001. "The City as Entertainment Machine." Pp. 357–78 in *Research in Urban Sociology*, vol. 6, *Critical Perspectives on Urban Redevelopment*, edited by K. F. Gotham. Oxford, England: JAI Press/Elsevier.

Logan, John R. and Kyle D. Crowder. 2002. "Political Regimes and Suburban Growth, 1980–1990." *City & Community* 1(1):113–35.

Logan, John R. and Harvey L. Molotch. 1987. *Urban Fortunes: The Political Economy of Place*. Berkeley: University of California Press.

Logan, John R. and Mark Schneider. 1984. "Racial Segregation and Racial Change in American Suburbs, 1970–1980." *American Journal of Sociology*. 89(4):874–88.

Logan, John R. and Linda B. Stearns. 1981. "Suburban Racial Segregation as a Nonecological Process." *Social Forces* 60(1):61–73.

Loomis, Charles P. and J. Allan Beegle. 1957. *Rural Sociology: The Strategy of Change*. Englewood Cliffs, NJ: Prentice Hall.

Lynd, Robert S. and Helen Merrell Lynd. 1929. *Middletown: A Study in American Culture*. New York: Harcourt, Brace.

Manis, Jerome G. and Bernard N. Meltzer. 1967. *Symbolic Interaction: A Reader in Social Psychology*. Boston, MA: Allyn & Bacon.

Massey, Douglas and Nancy Denton. 1993. *America Apartheid: Segregation and the Making of the Underclass*. Cambridge, MA: Harvard University Press.

McKenzie, Roderick D. 1933. *The Metropolitan Community.* New York: Russell & Russell.

McKenzie, Roderick D. [1925] 1967. "The Ecological Approach to the Study of the Human Community." Pp. 63–79 in *The City,* edited by R. Park and E. Burgess. Chicago, IL: University of Chicago Press.

Molotch, Harvey L. 1976. "The City as a Growth Machine." *American Journal of Sociology* 82(2):309–30.

Naples, Nancy. 1998. *Grassroots Warrior: Activists Mothering, Community Work and the War on Poverty.* New York: Routledge.

Nisbet, Robert A. 1966. *The Sociological Tradition.* New York: Basic Books.

Park, Robert. 1936. "Human Ecology." *American Journal of Sociology* 42(July):1–15.

Parsons, Talcott. 1951. *The Social System.* Glencoe, IL: Free Press.

Poplin, Dennis E. 1979. *Communities: A Survey of Theories and Methods of Research.* New York: Macmillan.

Portes, Alejandro and Alex Stepik. 1993. *City on the Edge: The Transformation of Miami.* Berkeley: University of California Press.

Salamon, Sonya. 2003. *Newcomers to Old Towns: Suburbanization of the Heartland.* Chicago, IL: University of Chicago Press.

Schwab, William A. 1982. *Urban Sociology: A Human Ecological Perspective.* Reading, MA: Addison-Wesley.

Shaw, Clifford, F. M. Zorbaugh, Henry McKay, and Leonard Cottrell. 1929. *Delinquency Areas.* Chicago, IL: University of Chicago Press.

Simmel, Georg. [1902–1903] 1950. "The Metropolis and Mental Life." Pp. 409–24 in *The Sociology of Georg Simmel,* edited by K. H. Wolff. Glencoe, IL: Free Press.

Small, Mario. 2004. *Villa Victoria: The Transformation of Social Capital in a Boston Barrio.* Chicago, IL: University of Chicago Press.

Spain, Daphne. 1992. *Gendered Spaces.* Chapel Hill: University of North Carolina Press.

Stueve, C. Ann and Kathleen Gerson. 1977. "Personal Relations across the Life Cycle." Pp. 79–98 in *Networks and Places: Social Relations in the Urban Setting,* edited by C. S. Fischer, R. M. Jackson, C. A. Stueve, K. Gerson, L. M. Jones, with M. Baldassare. New York: Free Press.

Suttles, Gerald D. 1968. *The Social Order of the Slum: Ethnicity and Territory in the Inner City.* Chicago, IL: University of Chicago Press.

Thrasher, Frederick. 1927. *The Gang.* Chicago, IL: University of Chicago Press.

Tönnies, Ferdinand. [1893] 1957. *Community and Society.* Lansing: Michigan State University Press.

Warren, Roland L. [1963] 1978. *The Community in America.* 3d ed. Chicago, IL: Rand McNally.

Weber, Max. 1978. *Economy and Society.* Berkeley: University of California Press.

Wellman, Barry. 1979. "The Community Question: The Intimate Networks of East Yorkers." *American Journal of Sociology* 84(5):1201–31.

Wellman, Barry. 2001. "Physical Place and Cyberplace: The Rise of Personalized Networking." *International Journal of Urban and Regional Research* 25(2):227–52.

Wellman, Barry and Caroline Haythornthwaite. 2002. *The Internet in Everyday Life.* Oxford, England: Blackwell.

Wellman, Barry, Janet Salaff, Dimitrina Dimitrova, Laura Garton, Milena Gulia, and Caroline Haythornthwaite. 1996. "Computer Networks as Social Networks: Collaborative Work, Telework, and Virtual Community." *Annual Review of Sociology* 22:213–38.

Wilkinson, Kenneth P. 1991. *The Community in Rural America.* New York: Greenwood Press.

Wirth, Louis. 1928. *The Ghetto.* Chicago, IL: University of Chicago Press.

Wirth, Louis. 1938. "Urbanism as a Way of Life." *American Journal of Sociology* 44:3–24.

Zorbaugh, Harvey W. [1926] 1961. "The Natural Areas of the City." Pp. 45–49 in *Studies in Human Ecology,* edited by G. A. Theodorson. New York: Harper & Row. (Reprinted from *Publications of the American Sociological Society* 20:188–97)

Zorbaugh, Harvey W. 1929. *The Gold Coast and the Slum.* Chicago, IL: University of Chicago Press.

Zukin, Sharon. 1982. *Loft Living.* Baltimore, MD: Johns Hopkins University Press.

Zukin, Sharon. 1991. *Landscapes of Power: From Detroit to Disney World.* Berkeley: University of California Press.

Zukin, Sharon. 1995. *The Cultures of Cities.* Cambridge, MA: Blackwell.

Chapter 47. Rural Sociology

Albrecht, Don E. and Steve H. Murdock. 1990. *The Sociology of U.S. Agriculture: An Ecological Perspective.* Ames: Iowa State University Press.

Allen, Patricia. 2004. *Together at the Table: Sustainability and Sustenance in the American Agrifood System.* University Park: Pennsylvania State University Press.

Anderson, Cynthia. 2000. *The Social Consequences of Economic Restructuring in the Textile Industry.* New York: Garland.

Barlett, Peggy. 1993. *American Dreams, Rural Realities: Family Farms in Crisis.* Chapel Hill: University of North Carolina Press.

Bell, Michael M. 1994. *Childerly: Nature and Morality in a Country Village.* Chicago, IL: University of Chicago Press.

Bell, Michael M. 2004. *Farming for Us All: Practical Agriculture and the Cultivation of Sustainability.* University Park: Pennsylvania State University Press.

Bertrand, Alvin. 1982. "Foreward." Pp. xi–xiii in *Rural Society in the U.S.: Issues for the 1980s,* edited by D. A. Dillman and D. J. Hobbs. Boulder, CO: Westview Press.

Billings, Dwight B. and Kathleen M. Blee. 2000. *The Road to Poverty: The Making of Wealth and Hardship in Appalachia.* Cambridge, England: Cambridge University Press.

Bonanno, Alessandro, Lawrence A. Busch, William H. Friedland, Lourdes Gouveia, and Enzo Mingione, eds. 1994. *From Columbus to CongAgra: The Globalization of Agriculture and Food.* Lawrence: University Press of Kansas.

Brown, David L. and Marlene A. Lee. 1999. "Persisting Inequality between Metropolitan and Nonmetropolitan America: Implications for Theory and Policy." Pp. 151–67 in *A Nation Divided,* edited by P. Moen, D. Dempster-McClain, and H. A. Walker. Ithaca, NY: Cornell University Press.

Brown, David L. and Louis E. Swanson, eds. 2003. *Challenges for Rural America in the Twenty-First Century*. University Park: Pennsylvania State University Press.

Bunker, Stephen G. 1985. *Underdeveloping the Amazon*. Chicago: University of Illinois Press.

Burdge, Rabel J. 1999. *A Conceptual Approach to Social Impact Assessment*. Middleton, WI: Social Ecology Press.

Busch, Lawrence, William Lacy, Jeffrey Burkhardt, and Laura Lacy. 1991. *Plants, Power, and Profit*. Oxford, England: Basil Blackwell.

Buttel, Fredrick H. 1996. "Environmental and Resource Sociology: Theoretical Issues and Opportunities for Synthesis." *Rural Sociology* 61(1):56–66.

Buttel, Fredrick H. 1997. "Rural Sociology." Pp. 631–34 in *Encyclopedia of Rural America*, edited by G. Goreham. Santa Barbara, CA: ABC-CLIO.

Buttel, Fredrick H. 2002. "Environmental Sociology and the Sociology of Natural Resources: Institutional Histories and Intellectual Legacies." *Society and Natural Resources* 15:205–11.

Buttel, Frederick H. 2003. "Continuities and Disjunctures in the Transformation of the U.S. Agro-Food System." Pp. 177–89 in *Challenges for Rural America in the Twenty-First Century*, edited by D. L. Brown and L. E. Swanson. University Park: Pennsylvania State University Press.

Buttel, Frederick and Howard Newby, eds. 1980. *The Rural Sociology of Advanced Societies*. Montclair, NJ: Allanheld Osmun.

Campbell, Hugh, Michael Mayerfield Bell, and Margaret Finney. eds. 2006. *Country Boys: Masculinity and Rural Life*. University Park: Pennsylvania State University Press.

Champion, Tony and Graeme Hugo, eds. 2004. *New Forms of Urbanization: Beyond the Urban-Rural Dichotomy*. Aldershot, England: Ashgate.

Christenson, James A. and Lorraine E. Garkovich. 1985. "Fifty Years of Rural Sociology: Status, Trends, and Impressions." *Rural Sociology* 50(4):503–22.

Cotter, David A. 2002. "Poor People in Poor Places: Local Opportunity Structure and Household Poverty." *Rural Sociology* 67(2):534–55.

Dewees, Sarah, Linda Lobao, and Louis E. Swanson. 2003. "Local Economic Development in an Age of Devolution: The Question of Rural Localities." *Rural Sociology* 68(2):182–206.

Dillman, Don A. and Daryl J. Hobbs, eds. 1982. *Rural Society in the U.S.: Issues for the 1980s*. Boulder, CO: Westview Press.

Duncan, Cynthia M. 1999. *Worlds Apart: Why Poverty Persists in Rural America*. New Haven, CT: Yale University Press.

Dunlap, Riley E., Frederick H. Buttel, Peter Dickens, and August Gijswijt, eds. 2002. *Sociology Theory and the Environment*. Lanham, MD: Rowman & Littlefield.

DuPuis, E. Melanie. 2002. *Nature's Perfect Food: How Milk Became America's Drink*. New York: New York University Press.

Elder, Glen W. and Rand D. Conger. 2000. *Children of the Land: Adversity and Success in Rural America*. Chicago, IL: University of Chicago Press.

Falk, William W. 1996. "The Assertion of Identity in Rural Sociology." *Rural Sociology* 61(1):159–74.

Falk, William W. 2004. *Rooted in Place: Family and Belonging in a Southern Black Community*. New Brunswick, NJ: Rutgers University Press.

Falk, William W., Michael D. Schulman, and Ann Tickamyer, eds. 2003. *Communities of Work: Rural Restructuring in Local and Global Contexts*. Athens: Ohio University Press.

Falk, William W. and Shanyang Zhao. 1989. "Paradigms, Theories, and Methods in Contemporary Rural Sociology: A Partial Replication and Extension." *Rural Sociology* 54(4):587–600.

Field, Donald R. and William R. Burch Jr. 1988. *Rural Sociology and the Environment*. Westport, CT: Greenwood Press.

Fine, Ben. 2004. "Debating Production-Consumption Linkages in Food Studies." *Sociologia Ruralis* 44(3): 332–42.

Fitchen, Janet M. 1991. *Endangered Spaces, Enduring Places: Change, Identity, and Survival in Rural America*. Boulder, CO: Westview Press.

Flora, Cornelia B. and James A. Christenson, eds. 1991. *Rural Policies for the 1990s*. Boulder, CO: Westview Press.

Flora, Cornelia B. and Jan L. Flora. 2003. "Social Capital." Pp. 214–27 in *Challenges for Rural America in the Twenty-First Century*, edited by D. L. Brown and L. E. Swanson. University Park: Pennsylvania State University Press.

Flora, Jan L., Jeff Sharp, Cornelia B. Flora, and Bonnie Newlon. 1997. "Entrepreneurial Social Infrastructure and Locally-Initiated Economic Development in the Nonmetropolitan United States." *Sociological Quarterly* 38(4):623–45.

Ford, Thomas. 1985. "Rural Sociology and the Passing of Scientific Chivalry." *Rural Sociology* 50(4):523–38.

Fosset, Mark and M. T. Seibert. 1997. *Long Time Coming: Racial Inequality in Southern Nonmetropolitan Areas*. Boulder, CO: Westview Press.

Freudenberg, William R. 1986. "Social Impact Assessment." *Annual Review of Sociology* 12:451–78.

Freudenberg, William R. and Robert Gramling. 1994. *Oil in Troubled Waters: Perceptions, Politics, and the Battle over Offshore Drilling*. Albany: State University of New York Press.

Friedland, William. 1982. "The End of Rural Society and the Future of Rural Sociology." *Rural Sociology* 47:589–608.

Friedland, William. 1991. "Introduction: Shaping the New Political Economy of Advanced Capitalist Agriculture." Pp. 1–34 in *Towards a New Political Economy of Agriculture*, edited by W. H. Friedland, L. Busch, F. H. Buttel, and A. P. Rudy. Boulder, CO: Westview Press.

Friedland, William. 2001. "Reprise on Commodity Systems Methodology." *International Journal of Sociology of Agriculture and Food* 9(1):82–103.

Friedland, William H., Amy Barton, and Robert J. Thomas. 1981. *Manufacturing Green Gold*. Cambridge, England: Cambridge University Press.

Friedland, William H, Lawrence Busch, Frederick H. Buttel, and Alan Rudy, eds. 1981. *Towards a New Political Economy of Agriculture*. Boulder, CO: Westview Press.

Fuguitt, Glen, David L. Brown, and Calvin L Beale. 1989. *Rural and Small Town America*. New York: Russell Sage.

Garkovich, Lorraine and Ann M. Bell. 1995. "Charting Trends in Rural Sociology: 1986–1995." *Rural Sociology* 60(4):571–84.

Gillette, John M. 1913. *Constructive Rural Sociology*. New York: Sturgis and Walton.

Goldschmidt, Walter. 1978. *As You Sow: Three Studies in the Social Consequences of Agribusiness*. Montclair, NJ: Allanheld, Osmun.

Goodman, David. 2002. "Rethinking Food Production-Consumption: Integrative Perspectives." *Sociologia Ruralis* 42(4):271–77.

Goreham, Gary A., ed. 1997. *Encyclopedia of Rural America*. Santa Barbara, CA: ABC-CLIO.

Goudy, Willis. 2005. "Notes on a 1925 Newsletter on Rural Sociology from the RSS Archives." *Rural Sociologist* 25(1):24–25.

Green, Gary. 2003. "What Role Can Community Play in Local Economic Development?" Pp. 343–52 in *Challenges for Rural America in the Twenty-First Century*, edited by D. L. Brown and L. E. Swanson. University Park: Pennsylvania State University Press.

Haney, Wava. 1997. "Rural Women." Pp. 634–38 in *Encyclopedia of Rural America*, edited by G. Goreham. Santa Barbara, CA: ABC-CLIO.

Hooks, Gregory and William Flinn. 1981. "The Country Life Commission and Early Rural Sociology." *Rural Sociologist* 1:95–100.

Jackson-Smith, D. B. 2003. "The Challenges of Land Use Change in the Twenty-First Century." Pp. 305–16 in *Challenges for Rural America in the Twenty-First Century*, edited by D. L. Brown and L. E. Swanson. University Park: Pennsylvania State University Press.

Jensen, Leif, Diane K. McLaughlin, and Tim Slack. 2003. "Rural Poverty: The Persisting Challenge." Pp. 118–31 in *Challenges for Rural America in the Twenty-First Century*, edited by D. L. Brown and L. E. Swanson. University Park: Pennsylvania State University Press.

Jischke, Martin C. 2004. "Adapting Justin Morrill's Vision to a New Century: The Imperative of Change for Land-Grant Universities." Presented at the 177th annual meeting of the National Association of State Universities and Land Grant Colleges, November 16, San Diego, CA.

Johnson, Kenneth M. and Glen Fuguitt. 2000. "Continuity and Change in Rural Migration Patterns, 1950–1995." *Rural Sociology* 65(1):27–49.

Killian, Molly S. and Charles M. Tolbert. 1993. "Mapping Social and Economic Space: The Delineation of Local Labor Markets in the United States." Pp. 69–82 in *Inequalities in Labor Market Areas*, edited by J. Singelmann and F. A. Deseran. Boulder, CO: Westview Press.

Larson, Olaf F. and Julie N. Zimmerman. 2003. *Sociology in Government: The Galpin-Taylor Years in the U.S. Department of Agriculture, 1919–1953*. University Park: Pennsylvania State University Press.

Lasley, Paul, F. Larry Leistritz, Linda M. Lobao, and Katherine Meyer. 1995. *Beyond the Amber Waves of Grain: An Examination of Social and Economic Restructuring in the Heartland*. Boulder, CO: Westview Press.

Liepens, Ruth. 2000. "New Energies for an Old Idea: Reworking Approaches to 'Community' in Contemporary Rural Studies." *Journal of Rural Studies* 16:23–25.

Lichter, Daniel and Diane McLaughlin. 1995. "Changing Economic Opportunities, Family Structure, and Poverty in Rural Areas." *Rural Sociology* 60:688–706.

Lobao, Linda. 1990. *Locality and Inequality: Farm and Industrial Structure and Socioeconomic Conditions*. Albany: State University of New York Press.

Lobao, Linda. 1996. "A Sociology of the Periphery versus a Peripheral Sociology: Rural Sociology and the Dimension of Space." *Rural Sociology* 61(1):77–102.

Lobao, Linda. 2004. "Continuity and Change in Place Stratification: Spatial Inequality and Middle-Range Territorial Units." *Rural Sociology* 69(1):1–30.

Lobao, Linda and Katherine Meyer. 1995. "Economic Decline, Gender, and Labor Flexibility in Family-Based Enterprises: The Case of Midwestern Farming." *Social Forces* 74(2):575–608.

Lobao, Linda and Katherine Meyer. 2001. "The Great Agricultural Transition: Crisis, Change, and Social Consequences of Twentieth Century U.S. Farming." *Annual Review of Sociology* 27:103–24.

Lobao, Linda and Rogelio Saenz. 2002. "Spatial Inequality and Diversity as an Emerging Research Agenda." *Rural Sociology* 67(4):497–512.

Luloff, A. E. and Jeffrey C. Bridger. 2003. "Community Agency and Local Development." Pp. 203–13 in *Challenges for Rural America in the Twenty-First Century*, edited by D. L. Brown and L. E. Swanson. University Park: Pennsylvania State University Press.

Lyson, Thomas. 2004. *Civic Agriculture: Reconnecting Farm, Food, and Community*. Medford, MA: Tufts University Press.

Lyson, Thomas and William Falk, eds. 1993. *Forgotten Places: Uneven Development in Rural America*. Lawrence: University of Kansas Press.

Mann, Susan A. 1990. *Agrarian Capitalism in Theory and Practice*. Chapel Hill: University of North Carolina Press.

Marsden, Terry. 2004. "The Quest for Ecological Modernization: Re-Spacing Rural Development and Agri-Food Studies." *Sociologia Ruralis* 44(2):129–46.

Molnar, Joseph J. and Henry Kinnucan. 1989. *Biotechnology and the New Agricultural Revolution*. Boulder, CO: Westview Press.

Murdock, Steve, Richard S. Krannich, and F. Larry Leistritz. 1999. *Hazardous Waste in Rural America: Impacts, Implications, and Options for Rural Communities*. Lanham, MD: Rowman & Littlefield.

Nelson, Lowry. 1969. *Rural Sociology: Its Origin and Growth in the United States*. Minneapolis: University of Minnesota Press.

Newby, Howard. 1983. "The Sociology of Agriculture: Toward a New Rural Sociology." *Annual Review of Sociology* 9:67–81.

Olsen, Wallace C. 1991. *Agricultural Economics and Rural Sociology: The Contemporary Core Literature*. Ithaca, NY: Cornell University Press.

Picou, J. Steven, Richard H. Wells, and Kenneth L. Nyberg. 1978. "Paradigms, Theories, and Methods in Contemporary Rural Sociology." *Rural Sociology* 43(4):559–83.

Ramirez-Ferrero, Eric. 2005. *Troubled Fields: Men, Emotions, and the Crisis in American Farming*. New York: Columbia University Press.

Rogers, Everett M., with F. Floyd Shoemaker. 1971. *Communication of Innnovations: A Cross-Cultural Approach*. New York: Free Press.

Rogers, Everett M., Rabel Burdge, Peter F. Korsching, and Joseph F. Donnermeyer. 1988. *Social Change in Rural Societies*. Englewood Cliffs, NJ: Prentice Hall.

Rural Sociological Task Force on Persistent Rural Poverty. 1993. *Persistent Poverty in Rural America*. Boulder, CO: Westview Press.

Sachs, Carolyn E. 1983. *The Invisible Farmers: Women in Agricultural Production*. Totowa, NJ: Rowman & Allenheld.

Sachs, Carolyn E. 1996. *Gendered Fields: Rural Women, Agriculture, and the Environment*. Boulder, CO: Westview Press.

Saenz, Rogelio. 1997. "Ethnic Concentration and Chicano Poverty: A Comparative Approach." *Social Science Research* 26:205–28.

Salamon, Sonya. 2003. *Newcomers to Old Towns: Suburbanization of the Heartland.* Chicago, IL: University of Chicago Press.

Sewell, William H. 1965. "Rural Sociological Research, 1936–1965." *Rural Sociology* 30:428–51.

Sharp, Jeff. 2001. "Locating the Community Field: A Study of Interorganizational Network Structure and Capacity for Community Action." *Rural Sociology* 66:403–24.

Singelmann, Joachim and Forrest A. Deseran, eds. 1993. *Inequalities in Labor Market Areas.* Boulder, CO: Westview Press.

Snipp, Mathew. 1996. "Understanding Race and Ethnicity in Rural America." *Rural Sociology* 61:125–42.

Stanton, Bernard F. 1991. "Trends and Development of Agricultural Economics and Rural Sociology in the United States." Pp. 1–21 in *Agricultural Economics and Rural Sociology: The Contemporary Core Literature,* edited by W. C. Olsen. Ithaca, NY: Cornell University Press.

Stokes, C. Shannon and Michael K. Miller. 1985. "A Methodological Review of Fifty Years of Research in Rural Sociology." *Rural Sociology* 50(4):539–60.

Swanson, Louis E., ed. 1988. *Agriculture and Community Change in the U.S.: The Congressional Research Reports.* Boulder, CO: Westview Press.

Swanson, Louis E. 2001. "Rural Policy and Direct Local Participation: Democracy, Inclusiveness, Collective Agency, and Locality-Based Policy." *Rural Sociology* 66:1–21.

Thu, Kendall M. and E. Paul Durrenberger, eds. 1998. *Pigs, Profits, and Rural Communities.* Albany: State University of New York Press.

Tickamyer, Ann R. 1996. "Sex, Lies, and Statistics: Can Rural Sociology Survive Restructuring? (or) What Is Right with Rural Sociology and How Can We Fix It?" *Rural Sociology* 61(1):5–24.

Tickamyer, Ann R. and Debra A. Henderson. 2003. "Rural Women: New Roles for a New Century." Pp. 109–17 in *Challenges for Rural America in the Twenty-First Century,* edited by D. L. Brown and L. E. Swanson. University Park: Pennsylvania State University Press.

Tickamyer, Ann, R., Debra A. Henderson, Julie A While, and Bradley L. Tadlock. 2000. "Voices of Welfare Reform: Bureaucratic Rationality versus the Perceptions of Welfare." *AFFILIA* 15(2):173–92.

Tigges, Leann M. and Deborah M. Tootle. 1990. "Labor Supply, Labor Demand, and Men's Underemployment in Rural and Urban Labor Markets." *Rural Sociology* 55:328–56.

Tolbert, Charles M., Thomas A. Lyson, and Michael D. Irwin. 1998. "Local Capitalism, Civic Engagement and Socio-economic Well-being." *Social Forces* 77:401–28.

Tolbert, Charles M., Michael D. Irwin, Thomas A. Lyson, and Alfred R. Nucci. 2002. "Civic Community in Small Town America: How Civic Welfare Is Influenced by Local Capitalism and Civic Engagement." *Rural Sociology* 67:90–113.

Voss, Paul R., David D. Long, Roger B. Hammer, and Samantha Friedman. Forthcoming. "County Child Poverty Rates in the U.S.: A Spatial Regression Approach." *Population Research and Policy Review.*

Warner, Mildred and Robert Hebdon. 2001. "Local Government Restructuring: Privatization and Its Alternatives." *Journal of Policy Analysis and Management* 20:315–36.

Weber, Bruce, Gregory J. Duncan, and Leslie A. Whitener, eds. 2002. *Rural Dimensions of Welfare Reform.* Kalamazoo, MI: W. E. Upjohn Institute.

Wilkinson, Kenneth. 1991. *The Community in Rural America.* New York: Greenwood Press.

Wimberley, Ronald C. and Libby Morris. 2002. "The Regionalization of Poverty: Assistance for the Black Belt South." *Southern Rural Sociology* 18(1):294–306.

Winson, A. 1997. "Does Class Consciousness Exist in Rural Communities? The Impact of Restructuring and Plant Shutdowns in Rural Canada." *Rural Sociology* 62(4):429–53.

Zimmerman, Julie. 2002. "Contextualizing Cash Assistance in the South." *Southern Rural Sociology* 18(1):1–20.

Chapter 48. Urban Sociology in the 21st Century

Abrahamson, Mark. 2004. *Global Cities.* New York: Oxford University Press.

Abu-Lughod, J. L. 1994. *From Urban Village to "East Village": The Battle for New York's Lower East Side.* Cambridge, England: Blackwell.

Abu-Lughod, J. L. 1999. *New York, Los Angeles, Chicago: America's Global Cities.* Minneapolis: University of Minnesota Press.

Abu-Lughod, J. L. 2000. *Sociology for the 21st Century.* Chicago, IL: University of Chicago Press.

Allen, J., D. Massey, and M. Pryke., eds. 1999. *Unsettling Cities.* New York: Routledge.

Amen, Mark M., Kevin Archer, and M. Martin Bosman, eds. 2006. *Relocating Global Cities: From the Center to the Margins.* Boulder, CO: Rowman & Littlefield.

Amin, Ash and Nigel Thrift. 2002. *Cities: Reimagining the Urban.* Cambridge: Polity.

Anderson, E. 1990. *Streetwise.* Chicago, IL: University of Chicago Press.

APCWNSP (Association for Progressive Communications Women's Networking Support Programme). 2000. "Women in Sync: Toolkit for Electronic Networking." Acting Locally, connecting Globally: Stories from the Regions. Vol. 3. Available at: http://www.apcwomen.org/netsupport/sync/sync.html.

Axel, Brian K. 2002. "The Diasporic Imaginary." *Public Culture* 14(2):411–28.

Bartlett, Anne. 2007. "The City and the Self: The Emergence of New Political Subjects in London." In *Deciphering the Global: Its Spaces, Scales and Subjects,* edited by S. Sassen. New York and London: Routledge.

Basch, Linda, Nina Glick-Schiller, and Cristina Blanc-Szanton. 1994. *Nations Unbound: Transnational Projects, Postcolonial Predicaments, and Deterritorialized Nation-States.* Langhorne, PA: Gordon and Breach.

Beck, Ulrich. 2000. *The Risk Society and Beyond: Critical Issues for Social Theory.* Thousand Oaks, CA: Sage.

Beck, Ulrich. 2006. *Cosmopolitan Vision.* Cambridge, England: Polity Press.

Bhachu, P. 1985. *Twice Immigrants.* London, England: Tavistock.

Body-Gendrot, S. 1993. *Ville et violence.* Paris, France: Presses Universitaires de France.

Body-Gendrot, S. 1999. *The Social Control of Cities.* London, England: Blackwell.

Bonacich, E., Lucie Cheng, Nora Chinchilla, Norma Hamilton, and Paul Ong, eds. 1994. *Global Production: The Apparel Industry in the Pacific Rim.* Philadelphia, PA: Temple University Press.

Bonilla, F., E. Melendez, R. Morales, and M. de los Angeles Torres, eds. 1998. Borderless Borders. Philadelphia, PA: Temple University Press.

Boyd, M. 1989. "Family and Personal Networks in International Migration: Recent Developments and New Agendas." *International Migration Review* 23(3):638–70.

Brenner, N. 1998. "Global Cities, Glocal States: Global City Formation and State Territorial Restructuring in Contemporary Europe." *Review of International Political Economy* 5(1):1–37.

Brenner, N. 2004. *New State Spaces: Urban Governance and the Rescaling of Statehood.* Oxford, England: Oxford University Press.

Brenner, N. and R. Keil. 2006. *The Global Cities Reader.* New York: Routledge.

Brenner, N. and N. Theodore, eds. 2002. *Spaces of Neoliberalism: Urban Restructuring in Western Europe and North America.* Malden, MA: Blackwell.

Bryson, J. R. and P. W. Daniels, eds. 2006. *Handbook of Producer Services.* Oxford, England: Oxford University Press.

Buechler, Simone. 2007. "Municipal Politics in a Global Context." In *Deciphering the Global: Its Spaces, Scales and Subjects*, edited by S. Sassen. New York and London: Routledge.

Burawoy, M., A. Burton, A. Ferguson, K. Fox, J. Gamson, N. Gartrell, et al. 1991. *Ethnography Unbound: Power and Resistance in the Modern Metropolis.* Berkeley: University of California Press.

Castells, M. 1972. *La Question Urbaine.* Paris, France: Maspero.

Castells, M. 1989. *The Informational City.* London, England: Blackwell.

Chase-Dunn, C. 1984. "Urbanization in the World System: New Directions for Research." Pp. 111–20 in *Cities in Transformation*, edited by M. P. Smith. Beverly Hills, CA: Sage.

Chinchilla, Norma and Norah Hamilton. 2001. *Seeking Community in the Global City: Salvadorians and Guatemalans in Los Angeles.* Philadelphia, PA: Temple University Press.

Ciccolella, P. and I. Mignaqui. 2002. "Buenos Aires: Sociospatial Impacts of the Development of Global City Functions." Pp. 309–26 in *Global Networks, Linked Cities*, edited by S. Sassen. New York: Routledge.

Clark, T. and V. Hoffman-Martinot, eds. 1998. *The New Public Culture.* Oxford, England: Westview Press.

Cohen, M., B. Ruble, J. Tulchin, and A. Garland, eds. 1996. *Preparing for the Urban Future: Global Pressures and Local Forces.* Washington, DC: Woodrow Wilson Center Press.

Cordero-Guzman, Hector, R. R. C. Smith, and R. Grosfoguel, eds. 2001. *Migration, Transnationalization, and Race in a Changing New York.* Philadelphia, PA: Temple University Press.

Daniels, Peter W. 1991. "Producer Services and the Development of the Space Economy." Pp. 135–50 in *The Changing Geography of Advanced Producer Services,* edited by P. W. Daniels and F. Moulaert. London, England: Belhaven.

Dawson, M. 1999. "Globalization, the Racial Divide, and a New Citizenship." Pp. 373–86 in *Race, Identity, and Citizenship*, edited by R. Torres, L. Miron, and J. X. Inda. Oxford, England: Blackwell.

Dean, J., J. Anderson, and G. Lovink, eds. 2006. *Formatting Networked Societies: Information Technology in and as Global Civil Society.* New York: Routledge.

Dear, Michael. 2001. "Los Angeles and the Chicago School: Invitation to a Debate." *Cities and Communities* 1(1):5–32.

Drainville, Andre. 2004. *Contesting Globalization: Space and Place in the World Economy.* London, England: Routledge.

Dogan, M. and J. D. Kasarda, eds. 1988. *A World of Giant Cities.* Newbury Park, CA: Sage.

Duncan, O. D. 1959. "Human Ecology and Population Studies." Pp. 678–716 in *The Study of Population,* edited by P. Hauser and O. D. Duncan. Chicago, IL: University of Chicago Press.

Duneier, M. 1999. *Sidewalk.* New York: Farrar, Strauss & Giroux.

Dunn, S., ed. 1994. *Managing Divided Cities.* Staffs, England: Keele University Press.

Ehrenreich, Barbara and Arlie Hochschild, eds. 2003. *Global Woman.* New York: Metropolitan Books.

El-Shakhs, Salah. 1972. "Development, Primacy and Systems of Cities." *Journal of Developing Areas* 7(October):11–36.

Ernst, Dieter. 2005. "The New Mobility of Knowledge: Digital Information Systems and Global Flagship Networks." Pp. 89–114 in *Digital Formations: IT and New Architectures in the Global Realm*, edited by R. Latham and S. Sassen. Princeton, NJ: Princeton University Press.

Espinoza, V. 1999. "Social Networks among the Poor: Inequality and Integration in a Latin American City." Pp. 147–84 in *Networks in the Global Village: Life in Contemporary Communities*, edited by B. Wellman. Boulder, CO: Westview Press.

Fainstein, Susan. 1993. *The City Builders.* Oxford, England: Blackwell.

Fainstein, Susan and Dennis Judd, eds. 1999. *Urban Tourism.* New Haven, CT: Yale University Press.

Feldbauer, P., E. Pilz, D. Runzler, and I. Stacher, eds. 1993. *Megastädte: Zur Rolle von Metropolen in der Weltgesellschaft.* Vienna, Austria: Boehlau Verlag.

Friedmann, John. 1986. "The World City Hypothesis." *Development and Change* 17:69–84.

Friedmann, J. and G. Wolff. 1982. "World City Formation: An Agenda for Research and Action." *International Journal of Urban and Regional Research* 15(1):269–83.

Gereffi, G., J. Humphrey, and T. Sturgeon. 2005. "The Governance of Global Value Chains." *Review of International Political Economy* 12(1):78–104.

Giddens, A. 1990. *The Consequences of Modernity.* Oxford, England: Polity Press.

Gilbert, Allan, ed. 1996. *Cities in Latin America.* Tokyo, Japan: United Nations University Press.

Glaeser, Andreas. 2000. *Divided in Unity: Identity, Germany and the Berlin Police.* Chicago, IL: University of Chicago Press.

Glasius, Marlies, Mary Kaldor, and Helmut Anheier, eds. 2002. *Global Civil Society Yearbook 2002.* London, England: Oxford University Press.

Gottdiener, M. 1985. *The Social Production of Urban Space.* Austin: University of Texas Press.

Graham, S. and S. Marvin. 1996. *Telecommunications and the City: Electronic Spaces, Urban Places.* London, England: Routledge.

Gugler, Joseph. 2004. *World Cities beyond the West.* Cambridge, England: Cambridge University Press.

Hagedorn, John, ed. 2006. *Gangs in the Global City: Exploring Alternatives to Traditional Criminology.* Chicago, IL: University of Illinois Press.

Hall, Peter. 1966. *The World Cities.* New York: McGraw-Hill.

Hardoy, J. E. 1975. *Urbanization in Latin America.* Garden City, NJ: Anchor.

Harvey, David. 1985. *The Urbanization of Capital.* Oxford, England: Blackwell.

Harvey, Rachel. 2007. "The Sub-National Constitution of Global Markets." In *Deciphering the Global: Its Spaces, Scales and Subjects*, edited by S. Sassen. New York and London: Routledge.

Holston, J., ed. 1996. "Cities and Citizenship." *Public Culture* (special issue)8(2).

Isin, Engin F., ed. 2000. *Democracy, Citizenship and the Global City.* London, England: Routledge.

Katznelson, I. 1992. *Marxism and the City.* Oxford, England: Clarendon Press.

Keil, Roger. 1998. *Los Angeles: Globalization, Urbanization, and Social Struggles.* Chichester, UK: John Wiley & Sons Ltd.

Kerbo, Harold R. 2005. *World Poverty: The Roots of Global Inequality and the Modern World-System.* New York: McGraw-Hill.

Kerbo, Harold R. 2006. *World Poverty: Global Inequality and the Modern World System.* Boston: McGraw-Hill.

King, A. D. 1990. *Urbanism, Colonialism, and the World Economy. Culture and Spatial Foundations of the World Urban System* (The International Library of Sociology). London, England: Routledge.

King, A. D., ed. 1996. *Representing the City. Ethnicity, Capital and Culture in the 21st Century.* London, England: Macmillan.

Klinenberg, Eric. 2003. *Heat Wave: A Social Autopsy of Disaster in Chicago.* Chicago, IL: University of Chicago Press.

Knox, P. and Taylor, P. J. eds. 1995. *World Cities in a World-System.* Cambridge, England: Cambridge University Press.

Kowarick, L., A. M. Campos, and M. C. de Mello. 1991. "Os Percursos de Desigualdade." In *São Paulo, Crise e Mudanca,* edited by R. Rolnik, L. Kowarick, and N. Somekh. Sao Paulo, Brazil: Brasiliense.

Krause, Linda and Patrice Petro, eds. 2003. *Global Cities: Cinema, Architecture, and Urbanism in a Digital Age.* New Brunswick, NJ: Rutgers University Press.

Landell-Mills, Pierre, Ramgopal Agarwala, and Stanley Please. 1989. *Sub-Saharan Africa: From Crisis to Sustainable Growth.* Washington, DC: World Bank.

Lash, Scott and John Urry. 1994. *Economies of Signs and Space.* London, England: Sage.

Lefebvre, Henri. [1974] 1991. *The Production of Space.* Oxford, England: Blackwell.

Levitt, Peggy. 2001. *The Transnational Villagers.* Berkeley: University of California Press.

Linn, Johannes F. 1983. *Cities in the Developing World: Policies for Their Equitable and Efficient Growth.* New York: Oxford University Press.

Lloyd, Richard. 2005. *NeoBohemia.* London, England: Routledge.

Logan, J. R. and H. Molotch. 1987. *Urban Fortunes: The Political Economy of Place.* Berkeley: University of California Press.

Lustiger-Thaler, H. and F. Dubet, eds. 2004. "Social Movements in a Global World." *Current Sociology* (special issue) 52(4).

Madigan, Charles, ed. 2004. *Global Chicago.* Chicago: University of Illinois Press.

Mahler, S. 1995. *American Dreaming: Immigrant Life on the Margins.* Princeton, NJ: Princeton University Press.

Marcuse, Peter and Ronald van Kempen. 2000. *Globalizing Cities: A New Spatial Order.* Oxford, England: Blackwell.

Martinotti, G. 1993. *Metropolis.* Bologna, Italy: Il Mulino.

Massey, D. and N. Denton. 1993. *American Apartheid.* Cambridge, MA: Harvard University Press.

McRoberts, Omar. 2005. *Streets of Glory: Church and Community in a Black Urban Neighborhood.* Chicago, IL: University of Chicago Press.

Mele, Christopher. 1999. "Cyberspace and Disadvantaged Communities: The Internet as a Tool for Collective Action." Pp. 264–89 in *Communities in Cyberspace,* edited by M. A. Smith and P. Kollock. London, England: Routledge.

Meyer, Carrie A. 1997. "The Political Economy of NGOs and Information Sharing." *World Development* 25:1127–40.

Miller, Daniel and Don Slater. 2000. *The Internet: An Ethnographic Approach.* Oxford, England: Berg.

Mills, Kurt. 2002. "Cybernations: Identity, Self-Determination, Democracy, and the 'Internet Effect' in the Emerging Information Order." *Global Society* 16:69–87.

Nashashibi, Rami. 2007. "Ghetto Cosmopolitanism: Making Theory at the Margins." In *Deciphering the Global: Its Spaces, Scales and Subjects*, edited by S. Sassen. New York and London: Routledge.

Noyelle, T. and A. B. Dutka. 1988. *International Trade in Business Services: Accounting, Advertising, Law and Management Consulting.* Cambridge, MA: Ballinger.

Ong, Aihwa and Donald Nonini, eds. 1997. *Underground Empires.* New York: Routledge.

Orum, Anthony and Xianming Chen. 2004. *A World of Cities.* Malden, MA: Blackwell.

Paddison, Ronan, ed. 2001. "Introduction." *Handbook of Urban Studies.* London, England: Sage.

Park, R. E., E. W. Burgess, and R. D. McKenzie, eds. 1967. *The City.* Chicago, IL: University of Chicago Press.

Parnreiter, Christof. 2002. "Mexico: The Making of a Global City." Pp. 145–82 in *Global Networks/Linked Cities,* edited by S. Sassen. New York: Routledge.

Parsa, Ali and Ramin Keivani. 2002. "The Hormuz Corridor: Building a Cross-Border Region between Iran and the United Arab Emirates." Pp. 183–208 in *Global Networks, Linked Cities,* edited by S. Sassen. New York: Routledge.

Portes, A. and M. Lungo, eds. 1992a. *Urbanización en Centroamerica.* San José, Costa Rica: Facultad Latino-americana de Ciencias Sociales.

Portes, A. and M. Lungo, eds. 1992b. *Urbanización en el Caribe.* San Jose, Costa Rica: Facultad Latinoamericana de Ciencias Sociales.

Poster, Mark. 1997. "Cyberdemocracy: Internet and the Public Sphere." Pp. 201–18 in *Internet Culture,* edited by D. Porter. London, England: Routledge.

Regional Employment Program for Latin America and the Caribbean. 1987. *Ajuste y Deuda Social: Un Enfoque Estructural.* Santiago, Chile: International Labour Office.

Riemens, Patrice and Geert Lovink. 2002. "Local Networks: Digital City Amsterdam." Pp. 327–45 in *Global Networks, Linked Cities,* edited by S. Sassen. London, England: Routledge.

Roberts, B. 1976. *Cities of Peasants.* London, England: Edward Arnold.

Roberts, B. and A. Portes. 2006. "Coping with the Free Market City: Collective Action in Six Latin American Cities at the End of the Twentieth Century." Unpublished manuscript. (On file with authors)

Rodriguez, N. P. and J. R. Feagin. 1986. "Urban Specialization in the World System." *Urban Affairs Quarterly* 22(2):187–220.

Ruggiero, V. and N. South. 1997. "The Late-Modern City as Bazaar: Drug Markets, Illegal Enterprise and the Barricades." *British Journal of Sociology* 48(1):54–71.

Rutherford, Jonathan. 2004. *A Tale of Two Global Cities: Comparing the Territorialities of Telecommunications Developments in Paris and London.* Aldershot, England: Ashgate.

Samers, Michael. 2002. "Immigration and the Global City Hypothesis: Towards and Alternative Research Agenda." *International Journal of Urban and Regional Research* 26(2):389–402.

Sandercock, Leonie. 2003. *Cosmopolis II: Mongrel Cities in the 21st Century.* New York: Continuum.

Santos, M., M. A. De Souze, and M. L. Silveira, eds. 1994. *Territorio Globalizacao e Fragmentacao.* São Paulo, Brazil: Editorial Hucitec.

Sassen, Saskia. [1991] 2001. *The Global City: New York, London and Tokyo.* Princeton, NJ: Princeton University Press.

Sassen, Saskia. 2004. "Local Actors in Global Politics." *Current Sociology* 52(4):657–74.

Sassen-Koob, Saskia. 1982. "Recomposition and Peripheralization at the Core." Pp. 88–100 in *Immigration and Change in the International Division of Labor.* San Francisco, CA: Synthesis.

Schiffer Ramos, Sueli. 2002. "Sao Paulo: Articulating a Cross-Border Regional Economy." Pp. 209–36 in *Global Networks/Linked Cities,* edited by S. Sassen. New York: Routledge.

Scott, A. J. 2001. *Global City-Regions.* Oxford, England: Oxford University Press.

Sennett, R. 1990. *The Conscience of the Eye.* New York: Knopf.

Sennett, R. 1994. *Flesh and Stone: The Body and the City in Western Civilization.* New York: Norton.

Short, John Rennie. 2006. *Urban Theory: A Critical Assessment.* New York: Palgrave Macmillan.

Short, John Rennie and Yeong-Hyun Kim. 1999. *Globalization and the City.* Essex, England: Longman.

Simmonds, Roger and Gary Hack. 2000. *Global City Regions: Their Emerging Forms.* London, England: E&FN Spon/ Taylor & Francis.

Skillington, T. 1998. "The City as Text: Constructing Dublin's Identity through Discourse on Transportation and Urban Re-development in the Press." *British Journal of Sociology* 49(3):456–74.

Smith, Carol A. 1985. "Theories and Measures of Urban Primacy: A Critique." Pp. 87–116 in *Urbanization in the World-Economy,* edited by M. Timberlake. Orlando, FL: Academic Press.

Smith, D. A. 1995. "The New Urban Sociology Meets the Old: Re-reading Some Classical Human Ecology." *Urban Affairs Review* 30(3):432–57.

Smith, D. A. and M. Timberlake. 2002. "Hierarchies of Dominance among World Cities: A Network Approach." Pp. 117–43 in *Global Networks, Linked Cities,* edited by S. Sassen. London, England: Routledge.

Smith, Michael Peter and Luis Guarnizo. 2001. *Transnationalism from Below.* Piscataway, NJ: Transaction Publishers.

Soja, Edward W. 2000. *Postmetropolis: Critical Studies of Cities and Regions.* Oxford, England: Blackwell.

Stren, R. 1996. "The Studies of Cities: Popular Perceptions, Academic Disciplines, and Emerging Agendas." Pp. 392–419 in *Preparing for the Urban Future: Global Pressures and Local Forces,* edited by M. Cohen, B. Ruble, J. Tulchin, and A. Garland. Washington, DC: Woodrow Wilson Center Press (distributed by Johns Hopkins University Press).

Stren, R. E. and R. R. White. 1989. *African Cities in Crisis: Managing Rapid Urban Growth.* Boulder, CO: Westview Press.

Suttles, G. D. 1968. *The Social Order of the Slum.* Chicago, IL: University of Chicago Press.

Taylor, Peter J. 1995. "World Cities and Territorial States: The Rise and Fall of Their Mutuality." Pp. 48–62 in *World Cities in a World-System,* edited by P. J. Taylor and P. L. Knox. Cambridge, England: Cambridge University Press.

Taylor, Peter J. 2004. *World City Network: A Global Urban Analysis.* London: Routledge.

Taylor, Peter J., D. R. F. Walker, and J. V. Beaverstock. 2002. "Firms and Their Global Service Networks." Pp. 93–116 in *Global Networks, Linked Cities,* edited by S. Sassen. New York: Routledge.

Thrift, Nigel and Ash Amin. 2002. *Cities: Reimagining the Urban.* Cambridge, England: Polity Press.

Timberlake, M., ed. 1985. *Urbanization in the World Economy.* Orlando, FL: Academic Press.

Torres, R., L. Miron, and J. X. Inda, eds. 1999. *Race, Identity, and Citizenship.* Oxford, England: Blackwell.

Valle, Victor M. and Rodolfo D. Torres. 2000. *Latino Metropolis.* Minneapolis: University of Minnesota Press.

Van de Donk, W. B. D. Loader, P. G. Nixon, and D. Rucht, eds. 2005. *Cyberprotest: New Media, Citizens, and Social Movements.* London, England: Routledge.

Veltz, P. 2005. *Mondialisation, villes et territoires: L'économie d'archipel.* Paris, France: Presses Universitaires de France.

Wacquant, L. 1997. "Inside the Zone." *Theory, Culture, and Society* 15(2):1–36.

Wajcman, Judy, ed. 2002. "Information Technologies and the Social Sciences." *Current Sociology* (special issue)50(3).

Walters, Pamela Barnhouse. 1985. "Systems of Cities and Urban Primacy: Problems of Definition and Measurement." Pp. 63–85 in *Urbanization in the World-Economy,* edited by M. Timberlake. Orlando, FL: Academic Press.

Watson, S. and G. Bridges, eds. 1999. *Spaces of Culture.* London, England: Sage.

Wellman, Barry. 1998. *Networks in the Global Village: Life in Contemporary Communities.* Boulder, CO: Westview Press.

Wellman, Barry, ed. 1999. *Networks in the Global Village: Life in Contemporary Communities.* Boulder, CO: Westview Press.

Wilson, W. J. 1997. *When Work Disappears.* New York: Alfred A. Knopf.

Wright, T. 1997. *Out of Place.* Albany: State University of New York Press.

Yang, Guobin. 2003. "Weaving a Green Web: The Internet and Environmental Activism in China." *China Environment*

Series, No. 6. Washington, DC: Woodrow Wilson International Centers for Scholars.

Yuval-Davis, N. 1999. "Ethnicity, Gender Relations and Multiculturalism." Pp. 112–25 in *Race, Identity, and Citizenship,* edited by R. Torres, L. Miron, and J. X. Inda. Oxford, England: Blackwell.

Zelinksy, Wilbur. 1991. "The Twinning of the World: Sister Cities in Geographic and Historical Perspective." *Annals of the Association of American Geographers* 81(1):1–31.

Zukin, S. 1991. *Landscapes of Power.* Berkeley: University of California Press.

Chapter 49. The Sociology of Migration

Alba, Richard. 2005. "Bright and Blurred Boundaries: Second Generation Assimilation and Exclusion in France, Germany, and the United States." *Ethnic and Racial Studies* 28:20–49.

Alba, Richard and Victor Nee. 2003. *Remaking of the American Mainstream: Assimilation and Contemporary Immigration.* Cambridge, MA: Harvard University Press.

Axinn, William and Scott Yabiku. 2001. "Social Change, the Social Organization of Families, and Fertility Limitations." *American Journal of Sociology* 106:1219–61.

Borjas, George. 1999. *Heaven's Door.* Princeton, NJ: Princeton University Press.

Brockerhoff, Martin. 2000. *An Urbanizing World.* Vol. 55(3). Washington, DC: Population Reference Bureau.

Bulmer, Martin. 1984. *The Chicago School of Sociology: Institutionalization, Diversity, and the Rise of Sociological Research.* Chicago, IL: University of Chicago Press.

Caldwell, John. 1973. *African Migration.* New York: Columbia University Press.

Collins, W. J. 1997. "When the Tide Turned: Immigration and the Delay of the Great Black Migration." *Journal of Economic History* 56:607–32.

Davis, Kinsley. 1974. "The Migrations of Human Populations." Pp. 53–65 in *The Human Population.* San Francisco, CA: W. H. Freeman.

Diamond, Jered. 1997. *The Third Chimpanzee: The Evolution and Future of the Human Animal.* New York: HarperPerennial.

Gmelch, George. 1980. "Return Migration." *Annual Review of Sociology* 9:135–59.

Goldstein, Sidney. 1976. "Facets of Redistribution: Research Challenges, Opportunities." *Demography* 13(1):423–43.

Gordon, Milton. 1964. *Assimilation in American Life.* New York: Oxford University Press.

Gurr, Ted Robert. 1969. *Why Men Rebel.* Princeton, NJ: Princeton University Press.

Hatton, Timothy J. and Jeffery G. Williamson. 1998. *The Age of Migration: Causes and Economic Impact.* New York: Oxford University Press.

Hirschman, Charles. 2005. "Population and Society: Historical Trends and Future Prospects." Pp. 381–402 in *The Sage Handbook of Sociology,* edited by C. Calhoun, C. Rojek, and B. S. Turner. London, England: Sage.

Jasso, Guillermina. 2004. "Have the Occupational Skills of New Immigrants to the United States Declined over Time? Evidence from the Immigrant Cohorts of 1977, 1982, and 1994." Pp. 261–85 in *International Migration: Prospects and Policies in a Global Market,* edited by D. S. Massey and J. E. Taylor. New York: Oxford University Press.

Jasso, Guillermina and Mark R. Rosenzweig. 1982. "Estimating the Emigration Rates of Legal Immigrants Using Administrative and Survey Data: The 1971 Cohort of Immigrants to the United States." *Demography* 19:279–90.

Landale, Nancy, R. S. Oropesa, and Bridget K. Gorman. 2000. "Migration and Infant Death: Assimilation or Selective Migration among Puerto Ricans?" *American Sociological Review* 65:888–909.

Landry, Pierre and Mingming Shen. 2005. "Reaching Migrants in Survey Research: The Use of the Global Position System to Reduce Coverage Bias in China." *Political Analysis* 13:1–22.

Lee, Everett S. 1966. "A Theory of Migration." *Demography* 3(1):47–57.

Liang, Zai. 2001. "The Age of Migration in China." *Population and Development Review* 27:499–524.

Liang, Zai and Zhongdong Ma. 2004. "China's Floating Population: New Evidence from the 2000 Census." *Population and Development Review* 30(3):467–88.

Liang, Zai and Hideki Morooka. 2005. "Migration Networks, *Hukou,* and Destination Choices." Presented at the annual meeting of the Population Association of America, March, Philadelphia, PA.

Liang, Zai and Toni Zhang. 2004. "Emigration, Housing Conditions, and Social Stratification in China." *International Migration Review* 38(1):302–24.

Lieberson, Stanley. 1980. *A Piece of the Pie: Blacks and Immigrants Since 1880.* Berkeley: University of California Press.

Lieberson, Stanley and C. Wilkinson. 1976. "A Comparison between Northern and Southern Blacks Residing in the North." *Demography* 13:199–224.

Long, Larry H. 1974. "Poverty Status and Receipt of Welfare among Migrants and Nonmigrants in Large Cities." *American Sociological Review* 39:46–56.

Ma, Laurence J. C. and Biao Xiang. 1998. "Native Place, Migration and the Emergence of Peasant Enclaves in Beijing." *China Quarterly* 155:548–81.

Massey, Douglas S. 1988. "Economic Development and International Migration in Comparative Perspective." *Population and Development Review* 14:383–413.

Massey, Douglas S., Rafael Alarcón, and Humberto González. 1987. *Return to Aztlan: The Social Process of International Migration from Western Mexico.* Berkeley: University of California Press.

Massey, Douglas S., Joaqin Arango, Graeme Hugo, Ali Kouaouci, Adela Pellegrino, and J. Edward Taylor. 1993. "Theories of International Migration: A Review and Appraisal." *Population and Development Review* 19:431–66.

Massey, Douglas S., Joaqin Arango, Graeme Hugo, Ali Kouaouci, Adela Pellegrino, and J. Edward Taylor. 1998. *World in Motion: Understanding International Migration at the End of the Millennium.* Oxford, England: Oxford University Press.

Massey, Douglas S. and Nancy A. Denton. 1993. *American Apartheid: Segregation and Making of the Underclass.* Cambridge, MA: Harvard University Press.

Massey, Douglas S., Andrew Gross, and Kumiko Shibuya. 1994. "Migration, Segregation, and the Geographic Concentration of Poverty." *American Sociological Review* 59:425–45.

McDonald, John S. and Leatrice D. McDonald. 1974. "Chain Migration, Ethnic Neighborhood Formation, and Social Networks." Pp. 226–36 in *An Urban World*, edited by C. Tilly. Boston, MA: Little, Brown.

Park, Robert Ezra and Ernest W. Burgess. 1969. *Introduction to the Science of Sociology*. Chicago, IL: University of Chicago Press.

Portes, Alejandro and Min Zhou. 1993. "The New Second Generation: Segmented Assimilation and Its Variants among Post-1965 Immigrant Youth." *Annals of the American Academy of Political and Social Science* 530(November):74–96.

Quillian, Lincoln. 1999. "Migration Patterns and the Growth of High-Poverty Neighborhoods, 1970–1990." *American Journal of Sociology* 105:1–37.

Ravenstein, E. G. 1889. "The Laws of Migration." *Journal of the Royal Statistical Society* 48:167–227.

Rogers, Andrei and Frank Willekens, eds. 1986. *Migration and Settlement: A Multiregional Comparative Study*. Dordrecht, The Netherlands: D. Reidel.

Sjaastad, Larry. 1969. "The Costs and Returns of Human Migration." *Journal of Political Economy* 70:80–93.

South, Scott and Kyle Crowder. 1997. "Escaping Distressed Neighborhoods: Individual, Community, and Metropolitan Influences." *American Journal of Sociology* 102:1040–84.

Stark, Oded. 1991. *The Migration of Labor*. Cambridge, MA: Blackwell.

Stark, Oded and J. Edward Taylor. 1988. "Relative Deprivation and International Migration." *Demography* 16:1–14.

Steinberg, Stephen. 1989. *The Ethnic Myth: Race, Ethnicity, and Class in America*. Boston, MA: Beacon Press.

Stouffer, Samuel. 1949–1950. *The American Soldier*. Princeton, NJ: Princeton University Press.

Thomas, William I. and Florian Znaniecki. 1984. *The Polish Peasants in Europe and America*, edited by E. Zaresky. 2 vols. Urbana: University of Illinois.

Tilly, Charles. 1978. *From Mobilization to Revolution*. New York: Random House.

Tilly, Charles and C. H. Brown. 1967. "On Uprooting, Kinship, and the Auspices of Migration." *International Journal of Comparative Sociology* 8:139–64.

Todaro, Michael. 1976. *Internal Migration in Developing Countries*. Geneva, Switzerland: International Labour Office.

Tolnay, Stewart. 1998. "Educational Selection in Migration of Southern Blacks, 1880–1990." *Social Forces* 77(3): 487–514.

Tolnay, Stewart E. 2003. "The African American 'Great Migration' and Beyond." *Annual Review of Sociology* 29:209–32.

Tolnay, Stewart E. and Kyle Crowder. 1999. "Regional Origin and Family Stability in Northern Cities: The Role of Context." *American Sociological Review* 64:97–112.

Tucker, Robert C. 1978. *The Marx-Engels Reader*. 2d ed. New York: W. W. Norton.

Van Tubergen, Fran, Ineke Maas, and Henk Flap. 2004. "The Economic Incorporation of Immigrants in 18 Western Countries: Origin, Destination, and Community Effects." *American Sociological Review* 69:704–27.

Walker, Robert and Michael Hannan. 1989. "Dynamic Settlement Processes: The Case of US Immigration." *Professional Geographer* 41:172–83.

Warren, Robert and Ellen P. Kraly. 1985. "The Elusive Exodus: Emigration from the United States." *Population Trends and Public Policy, No. 8*. Washington, DC: Population Reference Bureau.

Weeks, John R. 2004. "The Role of Spatial Analysis in Demographic Research." Pp. 381–99 in *Spatially Integrated Social Science: Examples in Best Practice*, edited by M. F. Goodchild and D. G. Janelle. New York: Oxford University Press.

Wilson, Thomas C. 2001. "'Explaining Black Southern Migrants' Advantage in Family Stability." *Social Forces* 80:555–71.

Wilson, William Julius. 1987. *The Truly Disadvantaged: The Inner City, the Underclass, and Public Policy*. Chicago, IL: University of Chicago Press.

World Commission on Social Dimension of Globalization (WCSDG). 2004. "On the Cross-Border Movement of People." *Population and Development Review* 30:375–80.

Yang, Xiushi. 2002. "Migration, Socioeconomic Milieu, and Migrants' HIV Risk Behavior: A Theoretical Framework." Presented at the annual meeting of the Population Association of America, May 9–11, Atlanta, GA.

Zelinsky, Wilbur. 1971. "The Hypothesis of Mobility Transition." *The Geographical Review* 61:219–49.

Zhou, Min. 1999. "Segmented Assimilation: Issues, Controversies, and Recent Research on the New Second Generation." Pp. 196–211 in *The Handbook of International Migration: The American Experience*, edited by C. Hirschman, P. Kasinitz, and J. DeWind. New York: Russell Sage.

Chapter 50. The Sociology of Development

Allen, D. L. and L. O. Laney. 1982. "The Global Dollar: Trends and Issues in Official and Private International Finance." *Annals of the American Academy of Political and Social Science* 460:29–37.

Amin, S. 1976. *Unequal Development: An Essay on the Social Formation of Peripheral Capitalism*. New York: Monthly Review Press.

Ayres, Robert L. 1983. *Banking on the Poor: The World Bank and World Poverty*. Cambridge: MIT Press.

Banerjee, Abhijit V. 2005. "Comments on 'A Half-Century of Development' by Richard N. Cooper and 'The Evolution of Development Thinking: Theory and Policy' by Gustav Ranis. Pp. 141–44 in *Lessons of Experience*, edited by F. Baourguignon and B. Pleskovic. Washington, DC: World Bank and Oxford University Press.

Barsky, Osvaldo and G. Cosse. 1981. *Technologia y Cambio Social: Las Haciendas Lecheras del Ecuador*. Quito, Ecuador: Facultad Latinoamericana de Ciencias Sociales (FLACSO).

Baumann, Pari, Marta Bruno, Dervla Cleary, Olivier Dubois, and Ximena Flores. 2004. "Applying People Centered Development Approaches Within FAO: Some Practical Lessons." Livelihood Support Program Working Paper No. 15, Food and Agriculture Organization, Rome, Italy.

Bellah, Robert N. 1957. *Tokugawa Religion*. Boston, MA: Beacon Press.

Berberoglu, Berch. 1992. *The Political Economy of Development: Development Theory and the Prospects for*

Change in the Third World. Albany: State University of New York Press.

Black, Jan Knippers. 1991. *Development in Theory and Practice: Bridging the Gap.* Boulder, CO: Westview Press.

Blomstrom, Magnum and Björn Hettne. 1984. *Development Theory in Transition: The Dependency Debate and Beyond—Third World Responses.* London, England: Zed Books.

Boserup, Esther. 1970. *Women's Role in Economic Development.* New York: St. Martin's Press.

Bromley, Daniel W. 1991. *Environment and Economy: Property Rights and Public Policy.* Oxford, England: Blackwell.

Cardoso, Fernando Henrique and Enzo Faletto. 1979. *Dependency and Development in Latin America.* Berkeley: University of California Press.

Carroll, Thomas F. 1992. *Intermediary NGOs: The Supporting Link in Grassroots Development.* West Hartford, CT: Kumarian Press.

Chambers, Robert. 1983. *Rural Development: Putting the Last First.* New York: Longman.

Charlton, Sue Ellen, Jana Everett, and Kathleen Staudt, eds. 1989. *Women, Development, and the State.* Albany: State University of New York Press.

Chilcote, Ronald. 1974. "Dependency: A Critical Synthesis of the Literature." *Latin American Perspectives* 1:4–29.

Chirot, Daniel and Thomas D. Hall. 1982. "World System Theory." *Annual Review of Sociology* 8:81–106.

Cohen, John M. and Stephen B. Peterson. 1999. *Administrative Decentralization: Strategies for Developing Countries.* West Hartford, CT: Kumarian Press.

Dos Santos, Theotônio. 1973. "The Crisis of Development Theory and the Problem of Dependence in Latin America." Pp. 57–80 in *Underdevelopment and Development,* edited by H. Berstein. Harmondsworth, England: Penguin.

Elliott, Jennifer A. 1994. *An Introduction to Sustainable Development.* London, England: Routledge.

Evans, P. 1996. "Government Action, Social Capital and Development: Reviewing the Evidence on Synergy." *World Development* 24(6):1119–32.

Fanon, Frantz. 1965. *The Wretched of the Earth.* Translated by C. Farrington. New York: Grove Press.

Flora, Cornelia Butler. 1987. "Income Generation Projects for Rural Women." Pp. 212–38 in *Rural Women and State Policy,* edited by C. Deere and M. Leon. Boulder, CO: Westview Press.

Flora, Cornelia Butler. 1990. "Rural Peoples in a Global Economy." *Rural Sociology* 55:157–77.

Flora, Cornelia Butler. 2003. "Democracy: Balancing Market, State and Civil Society." Pp. 89–100 in *Walking toward Justice: Democratization in Rural Life,* edited by M. M. Bell and F. T. Hendricks. Boston, MA: Elsevier.

Frazier, Arvonne S. and Irene Tinker, eds. 2004. *Developing Power: How Women Transformed International Development.* New York: Feminist Press.

Friedman, Milton. 1973. *Money and Economic Development.* New York: Praeger.

George, Susan. 1988. *A Fate Worse Than Debt.* New York: Grove Press.

Gereffi, Gary. 1994. "Rethinking Development Theory: Insights from East Asia and Latin America." Pp. 26–56 in *Comparative National Development: Society and Economy in the New Global Order,* edited by A. D. Kincaid and A. Portes. Chapel Hill: University of North Carolina Press.

Gunder Frank, A. 1968. *Development and Underdevelopment in Latin America.* New York: Monthly Review Press.

Gutiérrez, Gustavo. 1973. *A Theology of Liberation: History, Politics, and Salvation.* Maryknoll, NY: Orbis Books. (Published in Spanish [1972] *Teología de la Liberación: Perspectives.* Salamanca, Spain: Ediciones Sígueme)

Holdcroft, Lane E. 1978. "The Rise and Fall of Community Development in Developing Countries, 1950–1965: A Critical Analysis and an Annotated Bibliography." MSU Rural Development Paper No. 2, Department of Agricultural Economics, Michigan State University, East Lansing.

Inkeles, Alex. 1964. "Making Men Modern: On the Causes and Consequences of Individual Change in Six Developing Countries." Pp. 341–61 in *Social Change,* edited by A. Etzioni and E. Etzioni. New York: Basic Books.

Korten, David and Ruth Klaus, eds. 1984. *People Centered Development: Contributions toward Theory and Planning Frameworks.* West Hartford, CT: Kumarian Press.

Lipton, Michael. 1984. "Urban Bias Revisited." Pp. 126–58 in *Development and the Rural Urban Divide,* edited by J. Harris and M. Moore. London, England: Frank Casso.

Long, Norman. 2001. *Development Sociology: Actor Perspectives.* New York: Routledge.

Mazur, R. and S. Titilola. 1992. "Social and Economic Dimensions of Local Knowledge Systems in African Sustainable Agriculture." *Sociologia Ruralis* 32:264–86.

McClelland, D. Cartwright. 1964. "Business Drive and National Achievement." Pp. 165–78 in *Social Change,* edited by A. Etzioni and E. Etzioni. New York: Basic Books.

McMichael, Phillip. 2000. *Development and Social Change: A Global Perspective.* 2d ed. Thousand Oaks, CA: Pine Forge Press.

Memmi, Albert. 1965. *The Colonizer and the Colonized.* Translated by H. Greenfield. New York: Orion Press.

Morss, Elliott R. and Victoria A. Morss. 1982. *U.S. Foreign Aid: An Assessment of New and Traditional Development Strategies.* Boulder, CO: Westview Press.

Moser, Caroline O. N. 1993. *Gender Planning and Development: Theory, Practice and Training.* New York: Routledge.

Murdock, J. 2000. "Networks—A New Paradigm of Rural Development?" *Journal of Rural Studies* 16:407–19.

Myren, D. 1969. "The Rockefeller Program in Corn and Wheat in Mexico." Pp. 438–52 in *Subsistence Agriculture and Economic Development,* edited by C. Wharton. Chicago, IL: Aldine.

Narayan, Deepa. 1999. *Bonds and Bridges: Social Capital and Poverty.* Washington, DC: World Bank Poverty Group.

Narayan, Deepa. 2002. *Empowerment and Poverty Reduction: A Sourcebook.* Washington, DC: The World Bank.

Nicholson, N. K. 1979. "The Congressional Mandate for Aid and Rural Development Strategies." Pp. 215–41 in *The Role of U.S. Agriculture in Foreign Policy,* edited by R. Fraenke, D. Hadwiger, and W. P. Brown. New York: Praeger.

Parsons, Talcott. 1951. *The Social System.* Glencoe, IL: Free Press.

Prebisch, Raul. 1950. *Theoretical and Practical Problems of Economic Growth.* Santiago, Chile: Economic Commission on Latin America.

Ranis, G. 2005. "The Evolution of Development Thinking." Pp. 119–40 in *Lessons of Experience,* edited by F. Bourguignon and B. Pleskovic. Washington, DC: World Bank and Oxford University Press.

Rostow, Walter W. 1951. *The Stages of Economic Growth: A Non-Communist Manifesto.* London, England: Cambridge University Press.

Rostow, Walter W. 1952. *The Process of Economic Growth.* New York: Norton.

Rostow, Walter W. 1964. *The Steps of Economic Growth.* Cambridge, England: Cambridge University Press.

Sachs, Jeffrey. 2005. *The End of Poverty: Economic Possibilities for Our Time.* New York: Penguin Press.

Schultz, Theodore W. 1964. *The Transformation of Traditional Agriculture.* New Haven, CT: Yale University Press.

Schnitz, H. 1984. "Industrialization Strategies in Less Developed Countries: Some Lessons of Historical Experience." *Journal of Development Studies* 21:1–21.

Smith, T. L. 1947. "Colonization and Settlement in Colombia." *Rural Sociology* 129–140.

Snyder, M. 1972. "Women, the Neglected Human Resources for National Development." *Canadian Journal of African Studies* 6:359–70.

Snyder, M. 2004. "Walking My Own Road: How a Sabbatical Year Led to a United National Career." Pp. 37–49 in *Developing Power: How Women Transformed International Development,* edited by A. S. Frazier and I. Tinker. New York: The Feminist Press.

So, Alvin Y. 1990. *Social Change and Development: Modernization, Dependency, and World-Systems Theories.* Newbury Park, CA: Sage.

Staudt, Kathleen. 1985. *Women, Foreign Assistance, and Advocacy Administration.* New York: Praeger.

Staudt, Kathleen. 1991. *Women, International Development, and Politics: The Bureaucratic Mire.* Philadelphia, PA: Temple University Press.

Tendler, Judith. 1975. *Inside Foreign Aid.* Baltimore, MD: Johns Hopkins University Press.

Thiesenhusen, William C. 1995. *Broken Promises: Agrarian Reform and the Latin American Campesino.* Boulder, CO: Westview Press.

Tinker, Irene. 1990. *Persistent Inequalities: Women and World Development.* New York: Oxford University Press.

Tinker, Irene and Michele Bo Bramsen. 1980. *Women and World Development.* New York: Praeger.

Torres, C. 1965. *La Revolución: Imperativo Cristiano.* Bogotá, Colombia: Ediciones del Caribe.

United Nations Development Programme. 2005a. "The Global Challenge." Retrieved July 12, 2005 (www.undp.org/mdg/).

United Nations Development Programme. 2005b. "Coordinating Global and National Efforts." Retrieved July 12, 200 (www.undp.org/mdg/).

Uphoff, Norman. 1986. *Local Institutional Development: An Analytical Sourcebook with Cases.* West Hartford, CT: Kumarian Press.

U.S. Agency for International Development. 2005. "USAID History." Retrieved May 11, 2005 (www.usaid.gov/about_usaid/usaidhist.html).

Wallerstein, Immanuel Maurice. 1974. *The Modern World System: Capitalist Agriculture and the Origins of the European World-Economy in the Sixteenth Century.* New York: Academic Press.

Wallerstein, Immanuel Maurice. 1979. *The Capitalist World-Economy: Essays.* Cambridge, England: Cambridge University Press.

Wallerstein, Immanuel Maurice. 1986. "Societal Development, or Development of the World-System?" *International Sociology* 1:3–17.

Ward, Kathryn B. 1984. *Women in the World Systems: Its Impact on Status and Fertility.* New York: Praeger.

Watkins, Alfred J. 1986. *Till Debt Do Us Part.* Lanham, MD: University Press of America.

Weber, Max. 1947. *The Theory of Social and Economic Organization.* New York: Oxford University Press.

Woolcock, Michael. 1998. "Social and Economic Development: Towards a Theoretical Synthesis and Policy Framework." *Theory and Society* 27:151–208.

World Bank. 1988. *World Development Report.* New York: Oxford University Press.

World Bank Operations Evaluation Department. 2005. *Putting Social Development to Work for the Poor: An OED Review of World Bank Activities.* Washington, DC: World Bank.

PART X: THE QUANTIFICATION OF SOCIAL LIFE

Chapter 51. Demography

Abbott, Andrew. 2001. *Chaos of Disciplines.* Chicago, IL: University of Chicago Press.

Adamchak, Donald J. and Akinwumi Adebayo. 1987. "Male Fertility Attitudes: A Neglected Dimension in Nigerian Fertility Research." *Social Biology* 34:57–67.

Ahlburg, Dennis A. and Wolfgang Lutz. 1998. "Introduction: The Need to Rethink Approaches to Population Forecasts." *Population and Development Review* 24(Suppl.):1–14.

Ahlburg, Dennis A., Wolfgang Lutz, and James W. Vaupel. 1998. "Ways to Improve Population Forecasting: What Should Be Done Differently in the Future?" *Population and Development Review* 24(Suppl.):191–98.

Aitken R. J., S. Irvine, J. S. Clarkson, and D. W. Richardson. 1986. "Predictive Value of In Vitro Sperm Function Tests." Pp. 138–51 in *Male Contraception: Advances and Future Prospects,* edited by G. I. Zatuchni, A. Goldsmith, J. M. Spieler, and J. J. Sciarra. Philadelphia, PA: Harper & Row.

Badgett, M. V. Lee 1995. "The Wage Effects of Sexual Orientation Discrimination." *Industrial and Labor Relations Review* 48:726–39.

Baumle, Amanda K., D'Lane Compton, and Dudley L. Poston Jr. Forthcoming. *The Demography of Sexual Orientation.* Albany: State University of New York Press.

Black, Dan, Gary Gates, Seth Sanders, and Lowell Taylor. 2000. "Demographics of the Gay and Lesbian Population in the United States: Evidence from Available Systematic Data Sources." *Demography* 37:138–54.

Black, Dan, Gary Gates, Seth Sanders, and Lowell Taylor. 2002. "Why Do Gay Men Live in San Francisco?" *Journal of Urban Economics* 51:54–76.

Black, Dan, Hoda R. Makar, Seth Sanders, and Lowell Taylor. 2003. "The Earnings Effects of Sexual Orientation." *Industrial and Labor Relations Review* 56:449–69.

Bledsoe, Caroline, Susanna Lerner, and Jane I. Guyer, eds. 2000. *Fertility and the Male Life-Cycle in the Era of Fertility Decline.* New York: Oxford University Press.

Bogue, Donald J. 1969. *Principles of Demography.* New York: John Wiley.

Brass, William. 1996. "Demographic Data Analysis in Less Developed Countries 1946–1996." *Population Studies* 50(3):451–67.

Caldwell, John C. 1996. "Demography and Social Science." *Population Studies* 50:305–33.

Caldwell, John C. 1997. "The Global Fertility Transition: The Need for a Unifying Theory." *Population and Development Review* 23:803–12.

Casterline, John B. 1995. "Biosocial Models: Can Demographers Ignore Them?" *Population Research and Policy Review* 14:359–71.

Cleland, John. 1996. "Demographic Data Collection in Less Developed Countries 1946–1996." *Population Studies* 50(3):433–50.

Cleland, John and John Hobcroft. 1985. *Reproductive Change in Developing Countries: Insights from the World Fertility Survey.* New York: Oxford University Press.

Cleland, J. and C. Scott. 1987. *The World Fertility Survey: An Assessment.* New York: Oxford University Press.

Coale, Ansley J. and Paul Demeny. 1968. *Methods of Evaluating Basic Demographic Measures from Limited and Defective Data.* New York: United Nations.

Coale, Ansely J. and James Trussell. 1996. "The Development and Use of Demographic Models." *Population Studies* 50(3):469–84.

Coleman, David. 2000. "Male Fertility Trends in Industrial Countries: Theories in Search of Some Evidence." Pp. 29–60 in *Fertility and the Male Life-Cycle in the Era of Fertility Decline,* edited by C. Bledsoe, S. Lerner, and J. I. Guyer. New York: Oxford University Press.

Coleman, David and Roger Schofield. 1986. *The State of Population Theory: Forward from Malthus.* Oxford, England: Basil Blackwell.

Crimmins, Eileen M. 1993. "Demography: The Past 30 Years, the Present, and the Future." *Demography* 30(4):579–91.

Davis, Kingsley. 1948. *Human Society.* New York: Macmillan.

Gates, G. J. and J. Ost. 2004. *The Gay and Lesbian Atlas.* Washington, DC: Urban Institute Press.

Goodridge et al. v. Department of Public Health, 798 N.E.2d 941 (Mass. 2003).

Greene, Margaret E. and Ann E. Biddlecom. 2000. "Absent and Problematic Men: Demographic Accounts of Male Reproductive Roles." *Population and Development Review* 26:81–115.

Gryn, Thomas A. 1997. "Internet Resources for Demographers." *Population Index* 63(2):189–204.

Gutman, Robert. 1960. "In Defense of Population Theory." *American Sociological Review* 25(3):325–33.

Guyer, Jane I. 2000. "Traditions of Studying Paternity in Social Anthropology." Pp. 61–90 in *Fertility and the Male Life-Cycle in the Era of Fertility Decline,* edited by C. Bledsoe, S. Lerner, and J. I. Guyer. New York: Oxford University Press.

Hauser, Philip M. and Otis Dudley Duncan. 1959a. "The Data and Methods." Pp. 45–75 in *The Study of Population: An Inventory and Appraisal,* edited by P. M. Hauser and O. D. Duncan. Chicago, IL: University of Chicago Press.

Hauser, Philip M. and Otis Dudley Duncan. 1959b. "Demography as a Body of Knowledge." Pp. 76–105 in *The Study of Population: An Inventory and Appraisal,* edited by P. M. Hauser and O. D. Duncan. Chicago, IL: University of Chicago Press.

Hauser, Philip M. and Otis Dudley Duncan, eds. 1959c. *The Study of Population: An Inventory and Appraisal.* Chicago, IL: University of Chicago Press.

Hill, Reuben, J. Mayone Stycos, and Kurt Back. 1959. *The Family and Population Control: A Puerto Rican Experiment in Social Change.* Chapel Hill: University of North Carolina Press.

Hirschman, Charles. 1994. "Why Fertility Changes." *Annual Review of Sociology* 20:203–33.

Horton, Hayward D. 1999. "Critical Demography: The Paradigm of the Future?" *Sociological Forum* 14:363–67.

Kammeyer, Kenneth C. W. and Helen Ginn. 1986. *An Introduction to Population.* Chicago, IL: Dorsey Press.

Keyfitz, Nathan. 1975. "How Do We Know the Facts of Demography?" *Population and Development Review* 1(2):267–88.

Keyfitz, Nathan. 1977. *Applied Mathematical Demography.* New York: John Wiley.

Keyfitz, Nathan. 1981. "The Limits of Population Forecasting." *Population and Development Review* 7(4):579–93.

Kirk, Dudley. 1996. "Demographic Transition Theory." *Population Studies* 50(3):361–87.

Kiser, Clyde V. 1953. "The Indianapolis Fertility Study: An Example of Planned Observational Research." *Public Opinion Quarterly* 17(4):496–510.

Kiser, Clyde V. and Pascal K. Whelpton. 1953. "Resume of the Indianapolis Study of Social and Psychological Factors Affecting Fertility." *Population Studies* 7(2):95–110.

Klawitter, Marieka M. and Victor Flatt. 1998. "The Effects of State and Local Antidiscrimination Policies on Earnings for Gays and Lesbians." *Journal of Policy Analysis and Management* 17:658–86.

Lawrence et al. v. Texas, 123 S. Ct. 2472 (2003).

Lee, Ronald. 2003. "The Demographic Transition: Three Centuries of Fundamental Change." *Journal of Economic Perspectives* 17(4):167–90.

Merin, Yuval. 2002. *Equality for Same-Sex Couples: The Legal Recognition of Gay Partnerships in Europe and the United States.* Chicago, IL: University of Chicago Press.

Mbizvo, M. T. and Donald J. Adamchak. 1992. "Male Fertility Regulation: A Study on Acceptance among Men in Zimbabwe." *Central African Journal of Medicine* 38:52–57.

Micklin, Michael. 1969. "Traditionalism, Social Class, and Differential Fertility in Guatemala. *America Latina* 12:59–77.

Micklin, Michael. 1992. "LDC Population Policies: A Challenge for Applied Demography." *Journal of Applied Sociology* 9:45–63.

Micklin, Michael and Dudley L. Poston Jr. 2005. "Prologue: The Demographer's Ken: 50 Years of Growth and Change." Pp. 1–15 in *Handbook of Population,* edited by Dudley L. Poston Jr. and Michael Micklin. New York: Springer.

Moore, Wilbert E. 1959. "Sociology and Demography." Pp. 832–851 in *The Study of Population: An Inventory and Appraisal,* edited by P. M. Hauser and O. D. Duncan. Chicago, IL: University of Chicago Press.

Muvandi, Ityai. 1995. "Determinants of Male Fertility and Sexual Behaviour in Kenya." Centre for African Family Studies [CAFS], CAFS Research Reports, Series No. 2.

Nam, Charles B. 1979. "The Progress of Demography as a Scientific Discipline." *Demography* 16(4):485–92.

Poston, Dudley L., Jr. 2000. "Conceptual and Methodological Advances and Challenges in Demography." Pp. 273–98 in *The International Handbook of Sociology,* edited by S. R. Quah and A. Sales. Thousand Oaks, CA: Sage.

Poston, Dudley L., Jr., Amanda K. Baumle, and Michael Micklin. 2005. "Epilogue: Needed Research in Demography." Pp. 853–81 in *Handbook of Population,* edited by D. L. Poston Jr. and Michael Micklin. New York: Springer.

Poston, Dudley L., Jr. and Michael Micklin, eds. 2005. *Handbook of Population.* New York: Springer.

Preston, Samuel. H. 1993. "The Contours of Demography: Estimates and Projections." *Demography* 30:593–606.

Schofield, Roger and David A. Coleman. 1986. "Introduction: The State of Population Theory." Pp. 1–13 in *The State of Population Theory: Forward from Malthus,* edited by D. A. Coleman and R. Schofield. New York: Basil Blackwell.

Shi, Anqing. 2003. "The Impact of Population Pressure on Global Carbon Dioxide Emissions 1975–1996: Evidence from Pooled Cross-Country Data." *Ecological Economics* 44:29–42.

Siegel, Jacob S. 2002. *Applied Demography: Applications to Business, Government, Law and Public Policy.* San Diego, CA: Academic Press.

Siegel, Jacob S. and David Swanson. 2004. *The Methods and Materials of Demography.* 2d ed. Boston, MA: Academic Press.

Simmons, Tavia and Martin O'Connell. 2003. "Married Couple and Unmarried-Partner Households: 2000." *Census 2000 Special Reports. CENSR-5.* Washington, DC: U.S. Bureau of the Census.

Singh, K. and Shan S. Ratnam. 1991. "New Developments in Contraceptive Technology." *Advances in Contraception* 7:137–57.

Stycos, J. Mayone. 1955. *Family and Fertility in Puerto Rico: A Study of the Lower Income Group.* New York: Columbia University Press.

Stycos, J. Mayone. 1987. "Demography as an Interdiscipline." *Sociological Forum* 2:615–28.

Udry, J. Richard. 1988. "Biological Predispositions and Social Control in Adolescent Sexual Behavior." *American Sociological Review* 53:709–22.

Udry, J. Richard. 1994. "The Nature of Gender." *Demography* 31:561–73.

Udry, J. Richard. 1995. "Policy and Ethical Implications of Biosocial Research." *Population Research and Policy Review* 14:347–57.

Udry, J. Richard. 1996. "Biosocial Models of Low-Fertility Societies." *Population and Development Review* 22(Suppl.): 325–26.

Udry, J. Richard, Naomi M. Morris, and Judith Kovenock. 1995. "Androgen Effects on Women's Gendered Behavior." *Journal of Biosocial Science* 27:359–68.

Udry, J. Richard, L. M. Talbert, and Naomi M. Morris. 1986. "Biosocial Foundations for Adolescent Female Sexuality." *Demography* 23:217–30.

United Nations. 2001. *World Population Monitoring 2001: Population, Environment and Development.* New York: United Nations.

United Nations. 2002. *Demographic Yearbook, Natality Statistics.* CD-ROM Special Topic, DYB-CD, No. E/F.02.XII.6. New York: United Nations.

Vance, Rupert B. 1952. "Is Theory for Demographers?" *Social Forces* 31(1):9–13.

Walther, Carol S. and Dudley L. Poston Jr. 2004. "Patterns of Gay and Lesbian Partnering in the Larger Metropolitan Areas of the United States." *Journal of Sex Research* 41:201–14.

Weeks, John R. 2005. *Population: An Introduction to Concepts and Issues.* 9th ed. Belmont, CA: Wadsworth.

Weller, Bob. 1995. "Biosocial Models of Demographic Behavior: An Introduction." *Population Research and Policy Review* 14:277–82.

Westoff, Charles F., Robert Potter, and Philip Sagi. 1963. *The Third Child: A Study in the Prediction of Fertility.* Princeton, NJ: Princeton University Press.

Westoff, Charles F., Robert Potter, Philip Sagi, and Elliot G. Mishler. 1961. *Family Growth in Metropolitan America.* Princeton, NJ: Princeton University Press.

York, Richard, Eugene A. Rosa, and Thomas Dietz. 2003. "Footprints on the Earth: The Environmental Consequences of Modernity." *American Sociological Review* 68:279–300.

Chapter 52. The Sociology of Social Indicators

Ahuvia, Aaron C. and Douglas C. Friedman. 1998. "Income, Consumption, and Subjective Well-Being: Toward a Composite Macromarketing Model." *Journal of Macromarketing* 18:153–68.

Andrews, Frank M., ed. 1986. *Research on the Quality of Life.* Ann Arbor, MI: Institute for Social Research.

Andrews, Frank M. 1990. "The Evolution of a Movement." *Journal of Public Policy* 9:401–405.

Andrews, Frank M. and Stephen B. Withey. 1976. *Social Indicators of Well-Being: Americans' Perceptions of Life Quality.* New York: Plenum Press.

Bauer, Raymond A., ed. 1966. *Social Indicators.* Cambridge: MIT Press.

Biderman, Albert D. 1970. "Information, Intelligence, Enlightened Public Policy: Functions and Organization of Societal Feedback." *Policy Sciences* 1:217–30.

Bulmer, Martin. 1990. "Problems of Theory and Measurement." *Journal of Public Policy* 9:407–12.

Campbell, Angus and Philip E. Converse. 1972. *The Human Meaning of Social Change.* New York: Russell Sage.

Campbell, Angus, Philip E. Converse, and Willard L. Rodgers. 1976. *The Quality of American Life: Perceptions, Evaluations, and Satisfactions.* New York: Russell Sage.

Campbell, T. Colin, with Thomas M. Campbell II. 2005. *The China Study.* Dallas, TX: BenBella Books.

Caplow, Theodore, Howard M. Bahr, John Modell, and Bruce A. Chadwick. 1991. *Recent Social Trends in the United States, 1960–1990.* Montreal, Québec, Canada: McGill-Queens University Press.

Carley, Michael. 1981. *Social Measurement and Social Indicators: Issues of Policy and Theory.* London, England: George Allen and Unwin.

Centers for Disease Control and Prevention. 1989. "The Surgeon General's 1989 Report on Reducing the Health Consequences of Smoking: 25 Years of Progress" (Executive Summary). *Morbidity and Mortality Weekly Report* 38(Suppl. 2):1–32.

Commager, Henry Steele, 1967. *Lester Ward and the Welfare State*. Indianapolis, IN: Bobbs-Merrill.

Cummins, Robert A. 1995. "On the Trail of the Gold Standard for Subjective Well-Being." *Social Indicators Research* 35:170–200.

Cummins, Robert A. 1996. "The Domains of Life Satisfaction: An Attempt to Order Chaos." *Social Indicators Research* 38:303–28.

Cummins, Robert A. 1998. "The Second Approximation to an International Standard for Life Satisfaction." *Social Indicators Research* 43:307–34.

Cummins, Robert A., Eleonora Gullone, and Anna L. D. Lau. 2002. "A Model of Subjective Well-Being Homeostasis: The Role of Personality." Pp. 7–46 in *The Universality of Subjective Wellbeing Indicators,* edited by E. Gullone and R. A. Cummin. Boston, MA: Kluwer.

Davis, James A. 1984. "New Money, An Old Man/Lady and 'Two's Company': Subjective Welfare in the NORC General Social Survey." *Social Indicators Research* 15:319–51.

Diener, Ed. 1994. "Assessing Subjective Well-Being: Progress and Opportunities." *Social Indicators Research* 31:103–57.

Diener, Ed. 1995. "A Value Based Index for Measuring National Quality of Life." *Social Indicators Research* 36:107–27.

Diener, Ed and Robert Biswas-Diener. 2002. "Will Money Increase Subjective Well-Being? A Literature Review and Guide to Needed Research." *Social Indicators Research* 57:119–69.

Diener, Ed and E. Suh. 1997. "Measuring the Quality of Life: Economic, Social and Subjective Indicators." *Social Indicators Research* 40:189–216.

Diener, Ed, Eunkook M. Suh, Richard E. Lucas, and Heidi L. Smith. 1999. "Subjective Well-Being: Three Decades of Progress." *Psychological Bulletin* 125:276–302.

Duncan, Otis Dudley. 1969. *Toward Social Reporting: Next Steps.* New York: Russell Sage.

Easterlin, Richard. 1973. "Does Money Buy Happiness?" *The Public Interest* 30:3–10.

Estes, Richard J. 1988. *Trends in World Development.* New York: Praeger.

Estes, Richard J. 1998. "Social Development Trends in Transition Economies, 1970–95." Pp. 13–30 in *Challenges of Transformation and Transition from Centrally Planned to Market Economies,* UNCRD Research Report Series, No. 26, edited by K. R. Hope Sr. Nagoya, Japan: United Nations Centre for Regional Development.

Ferriss, Abbott L. 1979. "The U.S. Federal Effort in Developing Social Indicators." *Social Indicators Research* 6:129–49.

Ferriss, Abbott L. 1988. "The Uses of Social Indicators." *Social Forces* 66:601–17.

Ferriss, Abbott L. 1990a. "The Quality of Life in the United States." *SINET: Social Indicators Network News* 21:1–8.

Ferriss, Abbott L. 1990b. "Whatever Happened, Indeed!" *Journal of Public Policy* 9:413–17.

Ferriss, Abbott L. 1998. "Slow Progress toward Education 2000 Goals." *SINET: Social Indicators Network News* 53:11–12.

Ferriss, Abbott L. 2000. "A Brief History of Social Indicators Developments." *SINET: Social Indicators Network News* 61:8–9; 62:14–15.

Ferriss, Abbott L. 2001. "The Domains of the Quality of Life." *Bulletin de Methodologie Sociologique* 72(October):5–19.

Ferriss, Abbott L. 2002a. "Telesis: The Uses of Indicators to Set Goals and Develop Programs to Change Conditions." *Social Indicators Research* 58(1–3):229–65.

Ferriss, Abbott L. 2002b. "Reports on Data on the Quality of Life of Children in the United States." *SINET: Social Indicators Network News* 70/71(May/August):1–5.

Ferriss, Abbott L. 2004. "The Quality of Life Concept in Sociology." *American Sociologist* 35(3):37–51.

Finsterbusch, Kurt. 1980. *Understanding Social Impacts: Assessing the Effects of Public Projects.* Beverly Hills, CA: Sage.

Fox, Karl A. 1974. *Social Indicators and Social Theory: Elements of an Operational System.* New York: Wiley-Interscience.

Gore, Albert, Jr. 1990. "The Critical Trends Assessment Act: Futurizing the United States Government." *Futurist* 24:22–28.

Greenwald, Peter and Edward J. Sondik, eds. 1986. *Cancer Control Objectives for the Nation: 1985–2000.* National Cancer Institute Monographs, No. 2. Washington, DC: U.S. Government Printing Office.

Gross, Bertram M., ed. 1967. "Social Goals and Indicators for American Society: Vol. I." *Annals of the American Academy of Political and Social Sciences* 371(May).

Gross, Bertram and Michael Springer. 1967. "A New Orientation in American Government." *Annals of the American Academy of Political and Social Sciences* 371:1–19.

Inglehart, Ronald. 1990. *Culture Shift in Advanced Industrial Society.* Princeton, NJ: Princeton University Press.

Innes, Judith Eleanor. 1990. "Disappointment and Legacies of Social Indicators." *Journal of Public Policy* 9:429–32.

Johnston, Denis F. 1990. "Some Reflections on the United States." *Journal of Public Policy* 9:433–36.

Juster, F. Thomas and Kenneth C. Land, eds. 1981. *Social Accounting Systems: Essays on the State of the Art.* New York: Academic Press.

Kane, Hal. 2001. *The Triumph of the Mundane: Unseen Trends That Shape Our Lives and Environment.* Washington, DC: Island Press.

Land, Kenneth C. 1975. "Theories, Models and Indicators of Social Change." *International Social Science Journal* 27:7–37.

Land, Kenneth C. 1982. "Ex Ante and Ex Post Assessment of the Social Consequences of Public Projects and Policies." *Contemporary Sociology* 11:512–14.

Land, Kenneth C. 1983. "Social Indicators." *Annual Review of Sociology* 9:1–26.

Land, Kenneth C. 1996. "Social Indicators and the Quality-of-Life: Where Do We Stand in the Mid-1990s?" *SINET: Social Indicators Network News* 45:5–8.

Land, Kenneth C. 2000. "Social Indicators." Pp. 2682–90 in *The Encyclopedia of Sociology,* Rev. ed., edited by E. F. Borgatta and R. V. Montgomery. New York: Macmillan.

Land, Kenneth C. 2004. "An Evidence-Based Approach to the Construction of Summary Quality-of-Life Indices." Pp. 107–124 in *Challenges for Quality of Life in the Contemporary World,* edited by W. Glatzer, S. von Below, and M. Stoffregen. New York: Springer.

Land, Kenneth C. and Abbott L. Ferriss. 2002. "Conceptual Models for the Development and Use of Social Indicators." Pp. 337–52 in *Sozialer Wandel und gesellschaftliche Dauerbeobachtung,* edited by W. Glatzer, R. Habich, and K. U. Mayer. Festschrift for Wolfgang Zapf. Opladen, Germany: Leske+Budrich.

Land, Kenneth C., Vicki L. Lamb, and Sarah Kahler Mustillo. 2001. "Child and Youth Well-Being in the United States, 1975–1998: Some Findings from a New Index." *Social Indicators Research* 56(December):241–320.

Land, Kenneth C., Vicki L. Lamb, and Sarah Kahler Mustillo. 2004. "The Child Well-Being Index." *SINET: Social Indicators Network News* 77(February):1–6.

Land, Kenneth C. and Stephen H. Schneider. 1987. "Forecasting in the Social and Natural Sciences: An Overview and Statement of Isomorphisms." Pp. 7–31 in *Forecasting in the Social and Natural Sciences,* edited by K. C. Land and S. H. Schneider. Boston, MA: D. Reidel.

MacRae, Duncan, Jr. 1985. *Policy Indicators: Links between Social Science and Public Policy.* Chapel Hill: University of North Carolina Press.

Miringoff, Marc L. and Marque Luisa Miringoff. 1999. *The Social Health of the Nation: How America Is Really Doing.* New York: Oxford University Press.

National Commission on Technology, Automation and Economic Progress. 1966. *Technology and the American Economy,* vol. 1. Washington, DC: U.S. Government Printing Office.

Noll, Heinz-Herbert and Wolfgang Zapf. 1994. "Social Indicators Research: Societal Monitoring and Social Reporting." Pp. 168–206 in *Trends and Perspectives in Empirical Social Research,* edited by I. Borg and P. P. Mohler. New York: Walter de Gruyter.

Odum, Howard W. 1936. *Southern Regions of the United States.* Chapel Hill: University of North Carolina Press.

O'Hare, William P. and Vicki L. Lamb. 2004. "Comparing the 50 U.S. States Based on Improvement in Child Well-Being during the 1990's." *SINET: Social Indicators Network News* 78/79(August):1–3.

Parke, Robert and David Seidman. 1978. "Social Indicators and Social Reporting." *Annals of the American Academy of Political and Social Sciences* 435:1–22.

President's Research Committee on Social Trends. 1933. *Recent Trends in the United States.* New York: McGraw-Hill.

Redefining Progress. 1995. *The Genuine Progress Indicator: Summary of Data and Methodology.* San Francisco, CA: Redefining Progress.

Rockwell, Richard C. 1987. "Prospect for Social Reporting in the United States: A Receding Horizon." Pp. 251–62 in *The Tocqueville Review,* vol. 8, edited by J. R. Pitts and H. Mendras. Charlottesville: University Press of Virginia.

Rose, Richard, ed. 1990. "Whatever Happened to Social Indicators? A Symposium." *Journal of Public Policy* 9:399–450.

Samli, A. Coskun. 1987. *Marketing and the Quality-of-Life Interface.* Westport, CT: Quorum Books.

Schyns, Peggy. 2001. "Income and Satisfaction in Russia." *Journal of Happiness Studies* 2:173–204.

Sheldon, Eleanor B. and Wilbert E. Moore, eds. 1968. *Indicators of Social Change: Concepts and Measurements.* New York: Russell Sage.

Sheldon, Eleanor B. and Robert Parke. 1975. "Social Indicators." *Science* 188:693–99.

Sirgy, M. Joseph and A. Coskun Samli, eds. 1995. *New Dimensions in Marketing/Quality-of-Life Research.* Westport, CT: Quorum Books.

Social Science Research Council. 1983. "The Council's Program in Social Indicators." *Items* 37(4, December):74–102.

Stones, M. J., T. Hadjistavropoulos, J. Tuuko, and A. Kozma. 1995. "Happiness Has Traitlike and Statelike Properties." *Social Indicators Research* 36:129–44.

Taueber, Conrad, ed. 1978. "American in the Seventies: Some Social Indicators." *Annals of the American Academy of Political and Social Sciences* 435(January):1–355.

Taueber, Conrad, ed. 1981. "America Enters the Eighties: Some Social Indicators." *Annals of the American Academy of Political and Social Sciences* 453(January):1–253.

United Nations Development Programme. 2004. *Human Development Report 2004.* New York: Oxford University Press.

U.S. Bureau of the Census. 1981. *Social Indicators, III.* Washington, DC: U.S. Government Printing Office.

U.S. Department of Health and Human Services. 1990. *Healthy People: 2000. National Health Promotion and Disease Prevention Objectives.* Washington, DC: U.S. Government Printing Office.

U.S. Department of Health, Education, and Welfare. 1969. *Toward a Social Report.* Washington, DC: U.S. Government Printing Office.

U.S. General Accounting Office. 2003. *Forum on Key National Indicators: Assessing the Nation's Position and Progress.* Washington, DC: U.S. Government Printing Office.

U.S. Office of Management and Budget. 1974. *Social Indicators, 1973.* Washington, DC: U.S. Government Printing Office.

U.S. Office of Management and Budget. 1978. *Social Indicators, 1977.* Washington, DC: U.S. Government Printing Office.

U.S. President's Commission for a National Agenda for the Eighties, Panel on the Quality of American Life. 1980. *The Quality of American Life.* Washington, DC: U.S. Government Printing Office.

U.S. President's National Goals Research Staff. 1970. *Toward Balanced Growth: Quantity with Quality.* Washington, DC: U.S. Government Printing Office.

Veenhoven, Ruut. 1984. *Conditions of Happiness.* Boston, MA: D. Reidel.

Veenhoven, Ruut. 1994. "Is Happiness a Trait? Tests of the Theory That a Better Society Does Not Make People Any Happier." *Social Indicators Research* 33:101–60.

Veenhoven, Ruut. 1996. "Developments in Satisfaction Research." *Social Indicators Research* 37:1–46.

Veenhoven, Ruut. 1998. "Two State-Trait Discussions on Happiness: A Reply to Stones et al." *Social Indicators Research* 43:211–25.

Ward, Lester F. 1903. *Pure Sociology.* New York: Macmillan.

Ward, Lester F. 1906. *Applied Sociology.* New York: Ginn.

Webster's New Collegiate Dictionary. 1977. Springfield, MA: G. & C. Merriam.

Williams, Robin M., Jr. 1967. "Individual and Group Values." *Annals of the American Academy of Political and Social Sciences: Social Goals and Indicators for American Society* 371(May):20–37.

PART XI: COLLECTIVE BEHAVIOR AND SOCIAL MOVEMENTS

Chapter 53. The Sociology of Collective Behavior

Abramson, Leon. 1961. *The Political Context of Sociology.* Princeton, NJ: Princeton University Press.

Adamek, Raymond and Jerry M. Lewis. 1973. "Social Control Violence and Radicalization: The Kent State Case." *Social Forces* 51:342–47.

Aguirre, Benigno E. 1994. "Collective Behavior and Social Movement Theory." Pp. 257–72 in *Disasters, Collective Behavior, and Social Organization,* edited by R. R. Dynes and K. Tierney. Newark: University of Delaware Press.

Aguirre, Benigno E. 2002. "Sustainable Development as a Collective Surge." *Social Science Quarterly* 83(1):101–18.

Aguirre, Benigno E. 2005. "Emergency Evacuation, Panic, and Social Psychology." *Psychiatry* 68(2):121–29.

Aguirre, B. E., D. Wenger, and G. Vigo. 1998. "A Test of Emergent Norm Theory of Collective Behavior." *Sociological Forum* 13:301–20.

Aguirre, B. E. and E. L. Quarantelli. 1983. "Methodological, Ideological, and Conceptual-Theoretical Criticisms of the Field of Collective Behavior: A Critical Evaluation and Implications for Future Studies." *Sociological Focus* 16:195–216.

Aguirre, B. E., E. L. Quarantelli, and Jorge L. Mendoza. 1988. "The Collective Behavior of Fads: The Characteristics, Effects and Career of Streaking." *American Sociological Review* 53:569–84.

Aguirre, Benigno E. 1984. "The Conventionalization of Collective Behavior in Cuba." *American Journal of Sociology* 90:541–66.

Alexander, Jeffrey C., R. Eyerman, B. Giesen, N. J. Smelser, and P. Sztompka. 2004. *Cultural Trauma and Collective Identity.* Berkeley: University of California Press.

Allport, Floyd. 1924. *Social Psychology.* Boston, MA: Houghton Mifflin.

Anderson, L., D. Snow, and D. Cress. 1994. "Negotiating the Public Realm: Stigma Management and Collective Action among the Homeless." Pp. 121–43 in *The Community of "The Streets,"* edited by S. Cahill and L. Lofland. Greenwich, CT: JAI Press.

Ash, Timothy Garton. 1990. *We the People. The Revolution of '89 Witnessed in Warsaw, Budapest, Berlin, and Prague.* Cambridge, England: Granta Books.

Baldassarre, Gianluca, S. Nolfi, and D. Parisi. 2003. "Evolving Mobile Robots Able to Display Collective Behaviors." *Artificial Life* 9:255–67.

Benford, Robert D. and D. A. Snow. 2000. "Framing Processes and Social Movements: An Overview and Assessment." *Annual Review of Sociology* 26:11–39.

Berk, Richard A. 1974. "A Gaming Approach to Crowd Behavior." *American Sociological Review* 39:355–73.

Best, Joel. 1995. "Lost in the Ozone Again: The Postmodernist Fad and Interactionist Foibles." *Studies in Symbolic Interaction* 17:125–30.

Blumer, Herbert. 1939. "Collective Behavior." In *An Outline of the Principles of Sociology,* edited by R. E. Park. New York: Barnes & Noble.

Blumer, Herbert. 1946. "Elementary Collective Groupings." Pp. 178–96 in *New Outlines of the Principles of Sociology,* edited by A. M. Lee. New York: Barnes & Noble.

Blumer, Herbert. 1948. "Public Opinion and Public Opinion Polling." *American Sociological Review* 13:542–54.

Blumer, Herbert. 1969. "Fashion: From Class Differentiation to Collective Selection." *The Sociological Quarterly* 10:275–91.

Blumer, Herbert. 1971. "Social Problems as Collective Behavior." *Social Problems* 18:298–306.

Brass, Paul R. 1996. *Riots and Pogroms.* New York: New York University Press.

Brass, Paul R. 1997. *Theft of an Idol: Text and Context in the Representation of Collective Violence.* Princeton, NJ: Princeton University Press.

Brown, Michael and A. Goldin. 1973. *Collective Behavior.* Pacific Palisades, CA: Goodyear.

Buechler, Steven M. and F. Kurt Cylke Jr., eds. 1997. *Social Movements: Perspectives and Issues.* Mountain View, CA: Mayfield.

Cilliers, Jakkie. 1989. "Crowd Dynamics, the Value Added Approach." *South African Journal of Sociology* 20:176–86.

Cress, Daniel M. and D. A. Snow. 2000. "The Outcomes of Homeless Mobilization: The Influence of Organization, Disruption, Political Mediation, and Framing." *American Journal of Sociology* 105:1063–1104.

Davis, Phillip W. and J. Boles. 2003. "Pilgrim Apparition Work." *Journal of Contemporary Ethnography* 32:371–402.

De Biasi, Rocco. 1998. "The Policing of Hooliganism in Italy." Pp. 213–27 in *Policing Protest,* edited by D. Della Porta and H. Reiter. Minneapolis: University of Minnesota Press.

De Vreese, Stefan. 2000. "Hooliganism under the Statistical Magnifying Glass: A Belgian Case Study." *European Journal on Criminal Policy and Research* 8:201–23.

Drury, John and S. Reicher. 1999. "The Intergroup Dynamics of Collective Empowerment: Substantiating the Social Identity Model of Crowd Behavior." *Group Processes and Intergroup Relations* 2:381–402.

Durkheim, Émile. [1897] 1951. *Suicide: A Study in Sociology.* Translated by J. A. Spaulding and G. Simpson. New York: Free Press of Glencoe.

Durkheim, Émile. [1893] 1997. *The Division of Labor in Society.* New York: Free Press.

Edelman, Murray. 1988. *Constructing the Political Spectacle.* Chicago, IL: University of Chicago Press.

Elliott, Dominic and Denis Smith. 1993. "Football Stadium Disasters in the United Kingdom: Learning from Tragedy?" *Industrial and Environmental Crisis Quarterly* 7:205–29.

Eyerman, Ron and A. Jamison. 1998. *Music and Social Movements.* Cambridge, England: Cambridge University Press.

Faris, Ellsworth. 1926. "The Concept of Imitation." *American Journal of Sociology* 32:367–78.

Feinberg, William E. and Norris R. Johnson. 1988. "Outside Agitators and Crowds: Results from a Computer Simulation Model." *Social Forces* 67:398–423.

Feinberg, William E. and Norris R. Johnson. 1989. "Crowd Structure and Process: Theoretical Framework and Computer Simulation Model." *Advances in Group Processes* 6:49–86.

Feinberg, William E. and Norris R. Johnson. 1995. "Fire Escape: A Computer Simulation Model of Reaction to a Fire Alarm." *Journal of Mathematical Sociology* 20:247–69.

Feinberg, William E. and Norris R. Johnson. 1997a. "Decision Making in a Dyad: Response to a Fire Alarm: A Computer Simulation Investigation." *Advances in Group Processes* 14:59–80.

Feinberg, William E. and Norris R. Johnson. 1997b. "The Impact of Exit Instructions and Number of Exits in Fire Emergencies: A Computer Simulation Investigation." *Environmental Psychology* 17:123–33.

Feinberg, William E. and Norris R. Johnson. 1998. "Queuing, Exit Sorting, and Evacuation in Fire Emergencies: A Computer Simulation Investigation." In *Proceedings of First International Symposium on Human Behavior in Fire,* edited by J. Shields. Ulster, UK: University of Ulster, Fire Safety Engineering Research and Technology Center.

Feinberg, William E. and Norris R. Johnson. n.d. "A Computer Simulation of the Emergence of Consensus in Crowds." Unpublished manuscript.

Ferree, Myra Marx and Frederick D. Miller. 1985. "Mobilization and Meaning: Toward an Integration of Social Psychological and Resource Perspectives on Social Movements." *Sociological Inquiry* 55:38–61.

Freud, Sigmund. 1938. *The Basic Writings of Sigmund Freud.* Edited and translated by A. A. Brill. New York: Modern Library.

Freud, Sigmund. 2001. *Group Psychology and the Analysis of the Ego.* Hillsdale, NJ: Analytic Press.

Gamson, William A. 1990. *The Strategy of Social Protest.* 2d ed. Belmont, CA: Wadsworth.

Gilje, Paul A. 1999. *Rioting in America.* Bloomington: Indiana University Press.

Goffman, Erving. 1963. *Stigma: Notes on the Management of Spoiled Identity.* New York: Simon & Schuster.

Goode, Erich and Nachman Ben-Yehuda. 1994. *Moral Panics: The Social Construction of Deviance.* Cambridge, England: Oxford University Press.

Granovetter, M. 1978. "Threshold Models of Collective Behavior." *American Journal of Sociology* 83:1420–43.

Griswold, Wendy. 1987. "A Methodological Framework for the Sociology of Culture." *Sociological Methodology* 17:1–35.

Gross, Jan T., ed. 1984. *Poland's Self-Limiting Revolution: Jadwiga Staniskis.* Princeton, NJ: Princeton University Press.

Gusfield, Joseph R. 1986. *Symbolic Crusade: Status Politics and the American Temperance Movement.* Urbana: University of Illinois Press.

Johnson, Norris R. and William E. Feinberg. 1990. "Ambiguity and Crowds: Results from a Computer Simulation Model." *Research in Social Movements, Conflict and Change* 12:35–66.

Kaizoji, Taisei. 2000. "Speculative Bubbles and Crashes in Stock Markets: An Interacting-Agent Model of Speculative Activity." *Physica A* 287:493–506.

Killian, Lewis. 1980. "Theory of Collective Behavior: The Mainstream Revisited." Pp. 275–89 in *Sociological Theory and Research,* edited by H. Blalock. New York: Free Press.

Killian, Lewis. 1984. "Organization, Rationality and Spontaneity in the Civil Rights Movements." *American Sociological Review* 49:770–83.

Killian, Lewis. 1994. "Are Social Movements Irrational or Are They Collective Behavior?" Pp. 273–80 in *Disasters, Collective Behavior, and Social Organization,* edited by R. R. Dynes and K. J. Tierney. Newark: University of Delaware Press.

Klapp, Orrin. 1962. *Heroes, Villains, Fools.* Englewood Cliffs, NJ: Prentice Hall.

Klapp, Orrin. 1964. *Symbolic Leaders, Public Dramas, and Public Men.* New York: Minerva Press.

Klapp, Orrin. 1969. *Collective Search for Identity.* New York: Holt, Rinehart & Winston.

Klapp, Orrin. 1970. "Style Rebellion and Identity Crisis." Pp. 69–89 in *Human Nature and Collective Behavior: Papers in Honor of Herbert Blumer,* edited by T. Shibutani. Englewood Cliffs, NJ: Prentice Hall.

Lang, Gladys Engel. 1983. *The Battle for Public Opinion: The President, the Press, and the Polls during Watergate.* New York: Columbia University Press.

Lang, Kurt and Gladys Engel Lang. 1961. *Collective Dynamics.* New York: Thomas Y. Crowell.

LaPiere, Richard. 1938. *Collective Behavior.* New York: McGraw-Hill.

LaPiere, Richard and Paul R. Farnsworth. 1936. *Social Psychology.* New York: McGraw-Hill.

Larana, Enrique, H. Johnston, and J. R. Gusfield. 1994. *New Social Movements: From Ideology to Identity.* Philadelphia, PA: Temple University Press.

Lebeuf, Marcel-Eugene and Nicole Soulliere. 1996. *Social Order and Disorder in Canada: A Summary of the Facts.* Ottawa, Ontario, Canada: Canadian Police Institute, Canadian Police College.

Levy, Linda. 1989. "A Study of Crowd Behavior: The Case of the Great Pumpkin Incident." *Journal of Sports and Social Issues* 13:69–91.

Lewis, Jerry M. 1982. "Social Control at English Football Matches." *Sociological Focus* 15:417–23.

Lewis, Jerry M. 1986. "A Protocol for the Comparative Analysis of Sports Crowd Violence." *International Journal of Mass Emergencies and Disasters* 4:211–25.

Lewis, Jerry M. 1987. "Crisis Resolution: The Bradford Fire and English Society." *Sociological Focus* 20:155–68.

Lewis, J. M. 1989. "A Value-Added Analysis of the Heysel Stadium Soccer Riot." *Current Psychology* 8:15–29.

Locher, David A. 2002. *Collective Behavior.* Englewood Cliffs, NJ: Prentice Hall.

Lofland, John. 1966. *Doomsday Cult: A Study of Conversion, Proselytization, and Maintenance of Faith.* Englewood Cliffs, NJ: Prentice Hall.

Lofland, John. 1985. *Protest.* New Brunswick, NJ: Transaction Books.

Lofland, John. 1993a. *Polite Protesters: The American Peace Movement of the 1980's.* Syracuse, NY: Syracuse University Press.

Lofland, John. 1993b. "Theory Bashing and Answer Improving in the Study of Social Movements." *The American Sociologist* 24:37–58.

Lofland, John. 1996. "Charting Degrees of Movement Culture: Tasks of the Cultural Cartographer." Pp. 188–216 in *Social Movements and Culture,* edited by H. Johnston and B. Klandermans. Minneapolis: University of Minnesota Press.

Mann, Leon, T. Nagel, and P. Dowling. 1976. "A Study of Economic Panic: The 'Run' on the Hindmarsh Building Society." *Sociometry* 39:223–35.

Martin, Richard J. 1974. "Cultic Aspects of Sociology: Speculative Essay." *British Journal of Sociology* 25:15–31.

Marwell, G. and P. Oliver. 1993. *The Critical Mass in Collective Action.* Cambridge, England: Cambridge University Press.

Marx, Gary. 1970. "Issueless Riots." Pp. 21–33 in *Collective Violence: Annals of the American Academy of Political and Social Science,* edited by M. Wolfgang and J. F. Short. Philadelphia, PA: American Academy of Political Science.

Marx, Gary. 1974. "Thoughts on a Neglected Category of Social Movement Participants: The Agent Provocateur and the Informant." *American Journal of Sociology* 80:402–42.

Marx, Gary T. and D. McAdam. 1994. *Collective Behavior and Social Movements.* New York: Prentice Hall.

Mattern, Mark. 1998. *Acting in Concert: Music, Community, and Political Action.* New Brunswick, NJ: Rutgers University Press.

McAllister, Kevin Michael. 2002. "Analysis of Sport Crowd Behavior Adapting Smelser's Theory of Collective Behavior." Ph.D. dissertation, Department of Education, Boston University, Boston, MA.

McCarthy, John D. and Mayer N. Zald. 1977. "Resource Mobilization and Social Movements: A Partial Theory." *American Journal of Sociology* 82:1212–41.

McPhail, Clark. 1991. *The Myth of the Madding Crowd.* New York: Aldine.

McPhail, Clark and Charles W. Tucker. 2003. "From Collective Behavior to Collective Action and Beyond." In *The Handbook of Symbolic Interactionism,* edited by L. T. Reynolds and N. J. Herman. Walnut Creek, CA: AltaMira Press.

Melucci, Alberto. 1988. "Getting Involved: Identity and Mobilization in Social Movements." *International Social Movement Research* 1:329–48.

Meyer, Katherine and John Seidler. 1978. "The Structure of Gatherings." *Sociology and Social Research* 63:131–53.

Milgram, Stanley, L. Bickman, and L. Berkowitz. 1969. "Note on the Drawing Power of Crowds of Different Size." *Journal of Personality and Social Psychology* 13:79–82.

Miller, Neil and John Dollard. 1941. *Social Learning and Imitation.* New Haven, CT: Yale University Press.

Mukerji, Chandra and Michael Schudson. 1986. "Popular Culture." *Annual Review of Sociology* 12:47–66.

Neil, David M. and Brenda D. Phillips. 1988. "An Examination of Emergent Norms and Emergent Social Structures in Collective Behavior Situations." *Sociological Focus* 21:233–43.

Newton, James and Leon Mann. 1980. "Crowd Size as a Factor in the Persuasion Process: A Study of Religious Crusade Meetings." *Journal of Personality and Social Psychology* 39:874–83.

Nye, Robert A. 1975. *The Origins of Crowd Psychology: Gustave LeBon and the Crisis of Mass Democracy in the Third Republic.* Beverly Hills, CA: Sage.

Oberschall, Anthony. 1973. *Social Conflict and Social Movements.* Englewood Cliffs, NJ: Prentice Hall.

Oberschall, Anthony. 1978. "The Decline of the 1960s Social Movement." *Research in Social Movements, Conflicts and Change* 1:257–89.

Oberschall, Anthony. 1980. "Loosely Structured Collective Conflict: A Theory and an Application." *Research in Social Movements, Conflicts and Change* 3:45–68.

Oberschall, Anthony. 1989a. "Culture Change and Social Movements." Presentation at the 84th annual meeting of the ASA, August 9–13, San Francisco, CA.

Oberschall, Anthony. 1989b. "The 1960's Sit-Ins: Protest Diffusion and Movement Take-Off." *Research in Social Movements, Conflict, and Change* 11:31–53.

Oberschall, Anthony. 1993. *Social Movements: Interests, Ideologies and Identities.* New Brunswick, NJ: Transaction.

Oberschall, Anthony. 1994. "Protest Demonstrations and the End of Communist Regimes in 1989." *Research in Social Movements, Conflict and Change* 17:1–24.

Olson, Mancur. 1971. *The Logic of Collective Action: Public Goods and the Theory of Groups.* Cambridge, MA: Harvard University Press.

Pakulski, Jan. 1986. "Leaders of the Solidarity Movement: A Sociological Portrait." *Sociology* 20:64–81.

Park, Robert E. [1904] 1972. *The Crowd and the Public.* Reprint. Chicago, IL: University of Chicago Press.

Park, Robert E. and Ernest Burgess. 1921. *Introduction to the Science of Sociology.* Chicago, IL: University of Chicago Press.

Parsons, Talcott. 1971. *The System of Modern Societies.* Englewood Cliffs, NJ: Prentice Hall.

Piven, Frances Fox and Richard A. Cloward. 1979. *Poor People's Movements: Why They Succeed, How They Fail.* New York: Vintage Books.

Piven, Frances Fox and Richard A. Cloward. 1991. "Collective Protest: A Critique of Resource Mobilization Theory." *International Journal of Politics, Culture, and Society* 4:435–58.

Prechter, Robert R., Jr. 2001. "Unconscious Herding Behavior as the Psychological Basis of Financial Market Trends and Patterns." *Journal of Psychology and Financial Markets* 2:120–25.

Quarantelli, E. L. 1974. "The Structural Problem of a Sociological Specialty: Collective Behavior's Lack of a Critical Mass." *American Sociologist* 9:59–67.

Quarantelli, E. L. and J. Hundley. 1969. "A Test of Some Propositions about Crowd Formation and Behavior." Pp. 317–86 in *Readings in Collective Behavior,* edited by R. R. Evans. Chicago, IL: Rand-McNally.

Rafael, Vicente L. 2003. "The Cell Phone and the Crowd: Messianic Politics in the Contemporary Philippines." *Public Culture* 15:399–425.

Rheingold, Howard. 2002. *Smart Mobs: The Next Social Revolution.* New York: Basic Books.

Roberts, Carl W. and Kurt Lang. 1985. "Generations and Ideological Change: Some Observations." *Public Opinion Quarterly* 49:460–73.

Rule, James B. 1988. *Theories of Civil Violence.* Berkeley: University of California Press.

Rule, James B. 1989. "Rationality and Non-Rationality in Militant Collective Action." *Sociological Theory* 7:145–60.

Santos, Gabriel. 2004. "The Manufacture of Collective Behavior by the Tobacco Industry." Unpublished manuscript.

Santos, Gabriel and B. E. Aguirre. 2005. "A Critical Review of Emergency Evacuation Simulation Models." Pp. 27–52 in *Workshop on Building Occupant Movement during Fire Emergencies,* edited by R. D. Peacock and E. D. Kuligowski. Retrieved July 2, 2005 (http://fire.nist.gov/CDPUBS/NISTSP_1032/Papers/Santos_Paper.pdf).

Schuessler, Alexander A. 2000. "Expressive Voting." *Rationality and Society* 12:87–119.

Schweingruber, David. 2000. "Mob Sociology and Escalated Force: Sociology's Contributions to Repressive Police Tactics." *Sociological Quarterly* 41:371–89.

Seidler, John, K. Meyer, and L. M. Gillivray. 1976. "Collecting Data on Crowds and Rallies: A New Method of Stationary Sampling." *Social Forces* 55:507–19.

Smelser, Neil J. 1963. *Theory of Collective Behavior.* New York: Free Press.

Smelser, Neil J. 1966. "Mechanisms of Change and Adjustment to Change." Pp. 32–54 in *Industrialization and Society,* edited by B. F. Hoselitz and W. E. Moore. The Hague, The Netherlands: Mouton.

Smelser, Neil J. 1968. *Essays in Sociological Explanation.* Englewood Cliffs, NJ: Prentice Hall.

Smelser, Neil J. 1970. "Two Critics in Search of a Bias." *Annals of the American Academy of Political and Social Science* 391:46–55.

Smelser, Neil J. 1992. "External and Internal Factors in Theories of Social Change." Pp. 369–94 in *Social Change and Modernity,* edited by H. Haferkkamp and N. J. Smelser. Berkeley: University of California Press.

Smelser, Neil J. 2004. "Psychological Trauma and Cultural Trauma." Pp. 31–59 in *Cultural Trauma and Collective Identity,* edited by J. C. Alexander, R. Eyerman, B. Giesen, N. J. Smelser, and P. Sztompka. Berkeley: University of California Press.

Snow, David A. 2004. *The Blackwell Companion to Social Movements.* Malden, MA: Blackwell.

Snow, David A., E. B. Rochford, S. K. Worden, and R. D. Benford. 1986. "Frame Alignment Processes, Micromobilization, and Movement Participation," *American Sociological Review* 51:464–81.

Snow, David A., L. Zurcher, and R. Peters. 1981. "Victory Celebrations as Theater: A Dramaturgical Approach to Crowd Behavior." *Symbolic Interaction* 4:21–41.

Sornette, D. 2003. "Critical Market Crashes." *Physics Reports* 378:1–98.

Sorokin, P. and R. E. Merton. 1937. "Social Time: A Methodological and Functional Analysis." *American Journal of Sociology* 42:615–29.

Spotton Visano, Brenda. 2002. "Financial Manias and Panics: A Socioeconomic Perspective." *American Journal of Economics and Sociology* 61:801–27.

Stark, Margaret J. A., W. J. Raine, S. L. Burbeck, and K. K. Davison. 1974. "Some Empirical Patterns in a Riot Process." *American Sociological Review* 39:865–76.

Steigerwalt, Judi. 1974. "Gabriel Tarde's Theory of Collective Behavior." Unpublished manuscript.

Stott, Clifford and Steve Reicher. 1998a. "Crowd Action as Intergroup Process: Introducing the Police Perspective." *European Journal of Social Psychology* 28:509–29.

Stott, Clifford and Steve Reicher. 1998b. "How Conflict Escalates: The Inter-Group Dynamics of Collective Football Crowd Violence." *Sociology* 32:353–77.

Strauss, Anselm L. 1993. *Continual Permutations of Action.* New York: Aldine de Gruyter.

Szabo, Mate. 1996. "Repertoires of Contention in Post Communist Protest Cultures: An East Central European Comparative Survey." *Social Research* 63:1155–82.

Sztompka, Piotr. 1993. "Lessons on Post Communist Transition for Sociological Theories of Change." Pp. 131–49 in *Post Communist Poland: From Totalitarianism to Democracy,* edited by J. Coenen-Huther and B. Synak. New York: Nova Science.

Tambiah, Stanley J. 1997. "Friends, Neighbors, Enemies, Strangers: Aggressor and Victim in Civilian Ethnic Riots." *Social Science of Medicine* 45:1177–88.

Tarde, Gabriel. 1969. *On Communication and Social Influence: Selected Papers.* Chicago, IL: University of Chicago Press.

Tilly, Charles. 1978. *From Mobilization to Revolution.* Reading, MA: Addison-Wesley.

Turner, Ralph H. 1981. "Collective Behavior and Resource Mobilization as Approaches to Social Movements: Issues and Continuities." *Research in Social Movements, Conflict, and Change* 4:1–24.

Turner, Ralph H., ed. 1967. *Robert E. Park on Social Control and Collective Behavior.* Chicago, IL: University of Chicago Press.

Turner, Ralph H. and Lewis M. Killian. 1987. *Collective Behavior.* 3d ed. Englewood Cliffs, NJ: Prentice Hall.

Useem, Bert. 1985. "Disorganization and the New Mexico Prison Riot of 1980." *American Sociological Review* 50:677–88.

Useem, Bert. 1998. "Breakdown Theories of Collective Action." *Annual Review of Sociology* 24:215–38.

Useem, Bert and Peter A. Kimball. 1989. *States of Siege: U.S. Prison Riots, 1971–1986.* New York: Oxford University Press.

Van Ginneken, Jaap. 2003. *Collective Behavior and Public Opinion: Rapid Shifts in Opinion and Communication.* Mahwah, NJ: Lawrence Erlbaum.

Waddington, D. 1992. *Contemporary Issues in Public Disorder: A Comparative and Historical Approach.* London, England: Routledge.

Waddington, D., K. Jones, and C. Critcher. 1987. "Flashpoints of Public Disorder." Pp. 155–99 in *The Crowd in Contemporary Britain,* edited by G. Gaskell and R. Benewick. London, England: Sage.

Walker, Iaian and Heather J. Smith, eds. 2002. *Relative Deprivation: Specification, Development, and Integration.* Cambridge, England: Cambridge University Press.

Ward, Christopher R., F. Gobet, and G. Kendall. 2001. "Evolving Collective Behavior in an Artificial Ecology." *Artificial Life* 7:191–209.

Watts, Meredith W. 2001. "Aggressive Youth Cultures and Hate Crime: Skinheads and Xenophobic Youth in Germany." *American Behavioral Scientist* 45:600–15.

Weeber, Stan C. and Daniel G. Rodeheaver. 2003. "Militias at the Millennium: A Test of Smelser's Theory of Collective Behavior." *Sociological Quarterly* 44(2):181–204.

Weller, Jack and E. L. Quarantelli. 1973. "Neglected Characteristics of Collective Behavior." *American Journal of Sociology* 79:665–85.

Wilson, Robert A. 2001. "Group Level Cognition." *Philosophy of Science* 68(3):s262–73.

Wright, Sam. 1978. *Crowds and Riots: A Study in Social Organization.* Beverly Hills, CA: Sage.

Zald, Mayer N. and Michael A. Berger. 1971. "Social Movements in Organizations: Coup d'Etat, Insurgency, and Mass Movements." *American Journal of Sociology* 83:833–61.

Zald, Mayer N. and Bert Useem. 1987. "Movement and Countermovement Interaction: Mobilization, Tactics, and State Involvement." Pp. 247–71 in *Social Movements in an Organizational Society,* edited by M. N. Zald and J. McCarthy. New Brunswick, NJ: Transaction.

Zucker, L. G. 1977. "The Role of Institutionalization in Cultural Persistence." *American Sociological Review* 42:726–43.

Zygmunt, Joseph F. 1986. "Collective Behavior as a Phase of Societal Life: Blumer's Emergent Views and Their Implications." *Research in Social Movements, Conflicts and Change* 9:15–46.

Chapter 54. Social Movements

Almeida, Paul D. 2003. "Opportunity Organizations and Threat-Induced Contention: Protest Waves in Authoritarian Settings." *American Journal of Sociology* 109:345–400.

Amenta, Edwin. 1998. *Bold Relief: Institutional Politics and the Origins of Modern American Social Policy.* Princeton, NJ: Princeton University Press.

Banaszak, Lee Ann. 1996. *Why Movements Succeed or Fail: Opportunity, Culture, and the Struggle for Women Suffrage.* Princeton, NJ: Princeton University Press.

Boudreau, Vincent. 2004. *Resisting Dictatorship: Repression and Protest in Southeast Asia.* New York: Cambridge University Press.

Clemens, Elisabeth S. and Debra C. Minkoff. 2004. "Beyond the Iron Law: Rethinking the Place of Organization in Social Movement Research." Pp. 155–70 in *The Blackwell Companion to Social Movements,* edited by D. A. Snow, S. A. Soule, and H. Kriesi. Malden, MA: Blackwell.

Costain, Anne N. 1992. *Inviting Women's Rebellion.* Baltimore, MD: Johns Hopkins University.

Downs, Anthony. 1972. "Up and Down with Ecology: The Issue Attention Cycle." *Public Interest* 28:38–50.

Durkheim, Émile. [1933] 1979. *The Division of Labor in Society.* Translated by W. D. Halls, introduction by L. Coser. New York: Free Press.

Durkheim, Émile. [1951] 1997. *Suicide.* Translated by J. A. Spaulding and G. Simpson, edited with introduction by G. Simpson. New York: Free Press.

Edelman, Murray. 1971. *Politics as Symbolic Action.* Chicago, IL: Markham.

Einwohner, Rachel L. 2003. "Opportunity, Honor, and Action in the Warsaw Ghetto Uprising, 1943." *American Journal of Sociology* 109:650–75.

Eisinger, Peter K. 1973. "Conditions of Protest Behavior in American Cities." *American Political Science Review* 67:11–23.

Fantasia, Rick. 1988. *Cultures of Solidarity.* Berkeley: University of California Press.

Gamson, William A. 1990. *The Strategy of Social Protest.* 2d ed. Belmont, CA: Wadsworth.

Gamson, William A. 1992. "The Social Psychology of Collective Action." Pp. 53–76 in *Frontiers of Social Movement Theory,* edited by C. M. Mueller and A. D. Morris. New Haven, CT: Yale University Press.

Gamson, William A. and David S. Meyer. 1996. "Framing Political Opportunity." Pp. 185–215 in *Comparative Perspectives on Social Movements: Opportunities, Mobilizing Structures, and Cultural Framings,* edited by D. McAdam, J. D. McCarthy, and M. N. Zald. Cambridge, England: Cambridge University Press.

Goodwin, Jeff and James Jasper, eds. 2003. *Rethinking Social Movements.* Lanham, MD: Rowman & Littlefield.

Hirschman, Albert O. 1982. *Shifting Involvements: Private Interest and Public Action.* Princeton, NJ: Princeton University Press.

Hoffer, Eric. 1951. *The True Believer: Thoughts on the Nature of Mass Movements.* New York: New American Library.

Jenkins, J. Craig. 1983. "Resource Mobilization Theory and the Study of Social Movements." *Annual Review of Sociology* 9:527–53.

Katzenstein, Mary F. 1998. *Faithful and Fearless: Moving Feminist Protest Inside the Church and the Military.* Princeton, NJ: Princeton University Press.

Keck, Margaret E. and Kathryn Sikkink. 1998. *Activists beyond Borders.* Ithaca, NY: Cornell University Press.

Keniston, Kenneth. 1968. *Young Radicals.* New York: Harcourt, Brace, and World.

Kitschelt, Herbert. 1986. "Political Opportunity Structures and Political Protest: Anti-nuclear Movements in Four Democracies." *British Journal of Political Science* 16:57–85.

Kornhauser, William. 1959. *The Politics of Mass Society.* Glencoe, IL: Free Press.

Le Bon, Gustave. 1977. *The Crowd: A Study of the Popular Mind.* New York: Penguin.

Lipset, Seymour Martin and Earl Raab. 1970. *The Politics of Unreason: Right Wing Extremism in America, 1790–1970.* New York: Harper & Row.

Lipsky, Michael. 1968. "Protest as a Political Resource," *American Political Science Review* 62:1144–58.

Mansbridge, Jane. 1987. *Why We Lost the ERA.* Chicago, IL: University of Chicago Press.

McAdam, Doug. 1982. *Political Process and the Development of Black Insurgency.* Chicago, IL: University of Chicago Press.

McAdam, Doug. 1988. *Freedom Summer.* New York: Oxford University Press.

McAdam, Doug, Robert J. Sampson, Simon Weffer, and Heather MacIndoe. 2005. "'There Will Be Fighting in the Streets': The Distorting Lens of Social Movement Theory." *Mobilization* 10:1–18.

McAdam, Doug, Sidney Tarrow, and Charles Tilly. 2001. *Dynamics of Contention.* New York: Cambridge University Press.

McCarthy, John D. and Mayer N. Zald. 1977. "Resource Mobilization and Social Movements: A Partial Theory." *American Journal of Sociology* 82:1212–41.

"Meet FFL Activists." 2002. *American Feminist,* Fall, p. 7.

Meyer, David S. 1990. *A Winter of Discontent: The Nuclear Freeze and American Politics.* New York: Praeger.

Meyer, David S. 2004. "Protest and Political Opportunities." *Annual Review of Sociology* 30:125–40.

Meyer, David S. 2005. "Social Movements and Public Policy: Eggs, Chicken, and Theory." Pp. 1–26 in *Routing the Opposition: Social Movements, Public Policy, and Democracy in America,* edited by D. S. Meyer, V. Jenness, and H. Ingram. Minneapolis: University of Minnesota Press.

Meyer, David S. 2007. *The Politics of Protest: Social Movements in America.* New York: Oxford University Press.

Meyer, David S. and Catherine Corrigall-Brown. 2005. "Coalitions and Political Context: U.S. Movements against Wars in Iraq." *Mobilization* 10(3):327–44.

Meyer, David S. and Doug Imig. 1993. "Political Opportunity and the Rise and Decline of Interest Group Sectors." *Social Science Journal* 30:253–70.

Meyer, David S. and Sidney Tarrow, eds. 1998. *The Social Movement Society.* Lanham, MD: Rowman & Littlefield.

Meyer, David S. and Suzanne Staggenborg. 1996. "Movements, Countermovements, and the Structure of Political Opportunity." *American Journal of Sociology* 101:1628–60.

Meyer, David S. and Nancy Whittier. 1994. "Social Movement Spillover." *Social Problems* 41:277–98.

Minkoff, Debra C. 1995. *Organizing for Equality: The Evolution of Women's and Racial-Ethnic Organizations in America, 1955–1985.* New Brunswick, NJ: Rutgers University Press.

Nepstad, Sharon Erickson. 2004. *Convictions of the Soul: Religion, Culture, and Agency in the Central America Solidarity Movement.* New York: Oxford University Press.

Olson, Mancur. 1965. *The Logic of Collective Action.* Cambridge, MA: Harvard University Press.

Osa, Maryjane. 2003. *Solidarity and Contention: The Networks of Polish Opposition.* Minneapolis: University of Minnesota Press.

Piven, Frances Fox and Richard A. Cloward. 1971. *Regulating the Poor.* New York: Pantheon.

Piven, Frances Fox and Richard A. Cloward. 1977. *Poor People's Movements.* New York: Vintage.

Rochon, Thomas R. 1998. *Culture Shift.* Princeton, NJ: Princeton University Press.

Rochon, Thomas R. and David S. Meyer, eds. 1997. *Coalitions and Political Movements: The Lessons of the Nuclear Freeze.* Boulder, CO: Lynne-Rienner.

Rohlinger, Deana A. 2002. "Framing the Abortion Debate: Organizational Resources, Media Strategies, and Movement-Countermovement Dynamics." *Sociological Quarterly* 43:479–507.

Rupp, Leila and Verta A. Taylor. 1987. *Survival in the Doldrums: The American Women's Rights Movement, 1945 to the 1960s.* New York: Oxford University Press.

Ryan, Charlotte. 1991. *Prime Time Activism.* Boston, MA: South End Press.

Sawyers, Traci M. and David S. Meyer. 1999. "Missed Opportunities: Social Movement Abeyance and Public Policy." *Social Problems* 46:187–206.

Schattschneider, E. E. 1960. *The Semi-Sovereign People.* New York: Holt, Rinehart & Winston.

Smelser, Neil. 1962. *Theory of Collective Behavior.* New York: Free Press.

Smith, Christian. 1996. *Resisting Reagan: The U.S. Central America Peace Movement.* Chicago, IL: University of Chicago Press.

Snow, David A. 2005. "Social Movements as Challenges to Authority: Resistance to an Emerging Hegemony." Pp. 3–25 in *Authority in Contention. Research in Social Movements, Conflicts and Change,* vol. 25, edited by D. J. Myers and D. M. Cress. Greenwich, CT: JAI Press.

Snow, David A. and Robert D. Benford. 1992. "Master Frames and Cycles of Protest." Pp. 133–55 in *Frontiers of Social Movement Theory,* edited by C. M. Mueller and A. D. Morris. New Haven, CT: Yale University Press.

Staggenborg, Suzanne. 1988. "The Consequences of Professionalization and Formalization in the Pro-Choice Movement." *American Sociological Review* 53:585–605.

Tarrow, Sidney. 1989. *Democracy and Disorder.* Oxford, England: Clarendon Press.

Tarrow, Sidney. 1998. *Power in Movement.* 2d ed. Cambridge, England: Cambridge University Press.

Taylor, Verta A. and Nancy Whittier. 1992. "Collective Identity in Social Movement Communities: Lesbian Feminist Mobilization." Pp. 104–29 in *Frontiers of Social Movement Theory,* edited by C. M. Mueller and A. D. Morris. New Haven, CT: Yale University Press.

Tilly, Charles. 1978. *From Mobilization to Revolution.* Reading, MA: Addison-Wesley.

Tilly, Charles. 1993. "Contentious Repertoires in Great Britain, 1758–1834." *Social Science History* 17:253–80.

Tismaneanu, Vladimir. 1989. "Nascent Civil Society in the German Democratic Republic." *Problems of Communism* 38:43–56.

Whittier, Nancy E. 1995. *Feminist Generations: The Persistence of the Radical Women's Movement.* Philadelphia, PA: Temple University Press.

Wilson, James Q. 1995. *Political Organizations.* 2d ed. Princeton, NJ: Princeton University Press.

Chapter 55. Mass Communications

Abercrombie, Nicholas, Stuart Hill, and Bryan Turner. 1980. *The Dominant Ideology Thesis.* London, England: Allen and Unwin.

Abercrombie, Nicholas and Brian Longhurst. 1998. *Audiences: A Sociological Theory of Performance and Imagination.* London, England: Sage.

Allor, Martin. 1988. "Relocating the Site of the Audience." *Critical Studies in Mass Communication* 5(3):217–33.

Bagdikian, Ben. 2004. *The New Media Monopoly.* Boston, MA: Beacon Press.

Barnouw, Erik. 1966. *A Tower in Babel: A History of Broadcasting in the United States to 1933.* New York: Oxford University Press.

Barnouw, Erik. 1968. *The Golden Web: 1933–1953.* New York: Oxford University Press.

Boczkowski, Pablo J. 2004. *Digitizing the News.* Cambridge: MIT Press.

Butsch, Richard. 2000. *The Making of American Audiences, 1750–1990.* New York: Cambridge University Press.

Buxton, William. 1994. "The Political Economy of Communication Research: The Rockefeller Foundation, the 'Radio Wars' and the Princeton Radio Research Project." Pp. 147–75 in *Information and Communication in Economics,* edited by R. E. Babe. Boston, MA: Kluwer Academic.

Carey, James W. 1979. "Mass Communication Research and Cultural Studies: An American View." Pp. 409–25 in *Mass Communication and Society,* edited by J. Curran, M. Gurevitch, and J. Woollacott. Beverly Hills, CA: Sage.

Carey, James W. 1992. *Communication as Culture.* New York: Routledge.

Castells, Manuel. 2001. *The Internet Galaxy.* New York: Oxford University Press.

Compaine, Benjamin. 2000. *Who Owns the Media?* 3d ed. New York: Lawrence Erlbaum.

Compaine, Benjamin, ed. 2001. *The Digital Divide: Facing a Crisis or Creating a Myth?* Cambridge: MIT Press.

Davis, Susan. 1986. *Parades and Power: Street Theatre in Nineteenth-Century Philadelphia.* Philadelphia, PA: Temple University Press.

Eaman, Ross. 1994. *Channels of Influence: CBC Audience Research and the Canadian Public.* Toronto, Ontario, Canada: University of Toronto Press.

Elmer, Greg and Mike Gasher, eds. 2005. *Contracting Out Hollywood: Runaway Productions and Foreign Location Shooting.* Lanham, MD: Rowman & Littlefield.

Ewen, Stuart. 1976. *Captains of Consciousness.* New York: McGraw-Hill.

Ewen, Stuart. 1998. *PR: A Social History of Spin.* New York: Basic Books.

Featherstone, Mike. 2003. *Undoing Culture: Globalization, Postmodernism, and Identity.* London, England: Sage.

Fishman, Mark. 1990. *Manufacturing the News.* Austin: University of Texas Press.

Gans, Herbert. 2004. *Democracy and the News.* New York: Oxford University Press.

Garnham, Nicholas. 2000. *Emancipation, the Media and Modernity: Arguments about the Media and Social Theory,* New York: Oxford University Press.

Gerbner, George and Larry Gross. 1980. "The Violent Face of Television and its Lessons." Pp. 149–62 in *Children and the Faces of Television: Teaching, Violence, Selling,* edited by E. L. Palmer and A. Dorr. New York: Academic Press.

Gitlin, Todd. 1978. "Media Sociology: The Dominant Paradigm." *Theory and Society* 6:205–53.

Gitlin, Todd. 2003. *Media Unlimited.* New York: Owl Books.

Hagen, Ingunn and Janet Wasko, eds. 2000. *Consuming Audiences.* Creskill, NJ: Hampton.

Hall, Stuart. 1982. "The Rediscovery of Ideology: Return of the Repressed in Cultural Studies." Pp. 56–90 in *Culture, Society, and the Media,* edited by M. Gurevitch, T. Bennett, J. Curran, and J. Woollacott. New York: Methuen.

Herman, Edward and Noam Chomsky. 2002. *Manufacturing Consent: The Political Economy of the Mass Media.* New York: Pantheon Books.

Katz, Elihu and Paul F. Lazarsfeld. 1955. *Personal Influence.* New York: Free Press.

Klein, Naomi. 2002. *Fences and Windows: Dispatches from the Front Lines of the Anti-Globalization Movement.* New York: Picador Press.

Lazarsfeld, Paul F. and Patricia Kendall. 1948. *Radio Listening in America.* New York: Prentice Hall.

Lessig, Lawrence. 2004. *Free Culture.* New York: Penguin Books.

Long, Elizabeth. 1994. "Textual Interpretation as Collective Action." Pp. 181–211 in *Viewing, Reading, Listening: Audiences and Cultural Reception,* edited by J. Cruz and J. Lewis. Boulder, CO: Westview Press.

Lowery, Shearon A. and Melvin L. DeFleur. 1995. *Milestones of Mass Communication Research: Media Effects.* New York: Longman.

Mattelart, Armand. 1983. "Introduction: For a Class and Group Analysis of Popular and Communication Practices." Pp. 17–67 in *Communication and Class Struggle,* vol. 2, *Liberation, Socialism,* edited by A. Mattelart and S. Siegelaub. New York: International General.

McChesney, Robert W. 1994. *Telecommunications, Mass Media, and Democracy: The Battle for the Control of U.S. Broadcasting, 1928–1935.* New York: Oxford University Press.

McChesney, Robert W. 1999. *Rich Media/Poor Democracy: Communication Politics in Dubious Times.* Urbana: University of Illinois Press.

McKercher, Catherine. 2002. *Newsworkers Unite: Labor, Convergence and North American Newspapers.* Lanham, MD: Rowman & Littlefield.

McQuail, Dennis. 1983. *Mass Communication Theory: An Introduction.* London, England: Sage.

Meehan, Eileen. 1990. "Why We Don't Count: The Commodity Audience." Pp. 117–37 in *Logics of Television,* edited by P. Mellencamp. Bloomington: Indiana University Press.

Meehan, Eileen and Ellen Riordan, eds. 2002. *Sex and Money: Feminism and Political Economy in the Media.* Minneapolis: University of Minnesota Press.

Mosco, Vincent. 1996. *The Political Economy of Communication.* London, England: Sage.

Mosco, Vincent. 2004. *The Digital Sublime: Myth, Power, and Cyberspace.* Cambridge: MIT Press.

Mosco, Vincent. 2005. "Here Today, Outsourced Tomorrow: Knowledge Workers in the Global Economy." *Javnost/The Public* 12:39–56.

Mosco, Vincent and Dan Schiller, eds. 2001. *Continental Order? Integrating North America for Cybercapitalism.* Lanham, MD: Rowman & Littlefield.

Murdock, Graham. 2000. "Reconstructing the Ruined Tower: Contemporary Communications and Questions of Class." Pp. 7–26 in *Mass Media and Society,* edited by J. Curran and M. Gurevitch. 3d ed. London, England: Arnold.

Murdock, Graham and Peter Golding. 2000. "Culture, Communications and Political Economy." Pp. 70–92 in *Mass Media and Society,* edited by J. Curran and M. Gurevitch. 3d ed. London, England: Arnold.

Murdock, Graham and Peter Golding. 2004. "Dismantling the Digital Divide: Rethinking the Dynamics of Participation and Exclusion." Pp. 244–60 in *Towards a Political Economy of Culture: Capitalism and Communication in the Twenty-First Century,* edited by A. Calabrese and C. Sparks. Lanham, MD: Rowman & Littlefield.

Press, Andrea L. 1991. *Women Watching Television: Gender, Class, and Generation in the American Television Experience.* Philadelphia: University of Pennsylvania Press.

Ross, Karen and Virginia Nightingale. 2003. *Media and Audiences: New Perspectives.* Buckinghamshire, England: Open University Press/McGraw-Hill.

Schiffrin, Deborah, Deborah Tannen, and Heidie Hamilton. 2001. *Handbook of Discourse Analysis.* Oxford, England: Blackwell.

Schiller, Dan. 1981. *Objectivity and the News.* Philadelphia: University of Pennsylvania Press.

Schiller, Dan. 1999. *Digital Capitalism.* Cambridge: MIT Press.

Schiller, Herbert I. 1992. *Mass Communication and American Empire.* 2d ed. Boston, MA: Beacon Press.

Schudson, Michael. 1978. *Discovering the News.* New York: Basic Books.

Schudson, Michael. 1984. *Advertising: The Uneasy Persuasion.* New York: Basic Books.

Servon, Lisa. 2002. *Bridging the Digital Divide.* Oxford, England: Blackwell.

Shannon, Claude E. and Warren Weaver. 1949. *The Mathematical Theory of Communication.* Urbana: University of Illinois Press.

Smythe, Dallas W. 1977. "Communications: Blindspot of Western Marxism." *Canadian Journal of Political and Social Theory* 1(3):1–27.

Starr, Paul. 2004. *The Creation of the Media: Political Origins of Modern Communications.* New York: Basic Books.

Thompson, Edward P. 1963. *The Making of the English Working Class.* London, England: Victor Gollancz.

Tuchman, Gaye. 1990. *Making the News: A Study in the Construction of Social Reality.* New York: Simon & Schuster.

Tunstall, Jeremy. 1981. *Journalists at Work.* London, England: Constable.

Vaidhyanathan, Siva. 2004. *The Anarchist in the Library.* New York: Basic Books.

Wasko, Janet. 2003. *How Hollywood Works.* Thousand Oaks, CA: Sage.

Wayne, Michael. 2003. "Post-Fordism, Monopoly Capitalism, and Hollywood's Media Industrial Complex." *International Journal of Cultural Studies* 6(1):82–103.

Willis, Paul. 1977. *Learning to Labor: How Working Class Kids Get Working Class Jobs.* New York: Columbia University Press.

Zhao, Yuezhi. 2001. *Media, Market, and Democracy in China: Between the Party Line and the Bottom Line.* Urbana: University of Illinois Press.

PART XII: SOCIETY IN MOTION

Chapter 56. Social Change

Agger, Ben. 2004. *Speeding Up Fast Capitalism.* Boulder, CO: Paradigm.

Anderson, Perry. 1974a. *Passages from Antiquity to Feudalism.* London, England: New Left Books.

Anderson, Perry. 1974b. *Lineages of the Absolutist State.* London, England: New Left Books.

Beckfield, Jason. 2003. "Inequality in the World Polity: The Structure of International Organization." *American Sociological Review* 68:401–24.

Bell, Daniel. 1973. *The Coming of Post-Industrial Society.* New York: Basic Books.

Bellah, Robert N. 1957. *Tokugawa Religion.* Glencoe, IL: Free Press.

Bornschier, Volker and Christopher Chase-Dunn. 1985. *Transnational Corporations and Underdevelopment.* New York: Praeger.

Bornschier, Volker, Christopher Chase-Dunn, and Richard Rubinson. 1978. "Cross-National Evidence of the Effects of Foreign Investment and Aid on Economic Growth and Inequality: A Survey of Findings and a Reanalysis." *American Journal of Sociology* 84:651–83.

Browne, Kingsley R. 2002. *Biology at Work: Rethinking Sexual Equality.* New Brunswick, NJ: Rutgers University Press.

Browne, Kingsley R. 2005. "Women in Science: Biological Factors Should Not Be Ignored." *Cardozo Women's Law Journal* 11:509–28.

Carneiro, Robert L. 1970. "A Theory of the Origin of the State." *Science* 169:733–38.

Chase-Dunn, Christopher and Thomas D. Hall. 1997. *Rise and Demise: Comparing World-Systems.* Boulder, CO: Westview Press.

Childe, V. Gordon. 1936. *Man Makes Himself.* London, England: Watts.

Childe, V. Gordon. 1951. *Social Evolution.* London, England: Watts.

Chirot, Daniel. 1985. "The Rise of the West." *American Sociological Review* 50:181–95.

Chirot, Daniel. 1986. *Social Change in the Modern Era.* New York: Harcourt Brace Jovanovich.

Collins, Randall. 1985. *Sociology of Marriage and the Family.* Chicago, IL: Nelson-Hall.

Collins, Randall. 1986. *Weberian Sociological Theory.* New York: Cambridge University Press.

Collins, Randall. 1995. "Prediction in Macrosociology: The Case of the Soviet Collapse." *American Journal of Sociology* 100:1552–93.

Collins, Randall. 1997. "An Asian Route to Capitalism: Religious Economy and the Origins of Self-Transforming Growth in Japan." *American Sociological Review* 62:843–65.

Coontz, Stephanie. 1992. *The Way We Never Were: American Families and the Nostalgia Trap.* New York: Basic Books.

Coontz, Stephanie. 2005. *Marriage, A History: From Obedience to Intimacy, or How Love Conquered Marriage.* New York: Viking.

Davies, James C. 1962. "Toward a Theory of Revolution." *American Sociological Review* 27:5–18.

Dobb, Maurice. [1947] 1963. *Studies in the Development of Capitalism.* Rev. ed. New York: International Publishers.

Eisenstadt, S. N. 1963. *The Political Systems of Empires.* New York: Free Press.

Eisenstadt, S. N. 1964. "Social Change, Differentiation, and Evolution." *American Sociological Review* 29:375–86.

Emigh, Rebecca Jean. 2005. "The Great Debates: Transitions to Capitalisms." Pp. 355–80 in *Remaking Modernity: Politics, History, and Sociology,* edited by J. A. Adams, E. S. Clemens, and A. S. Orloff. Durham, NC: Duke University Press.

Esping-Andersen, Gosta. 1990. *The Three Worlds of Welfare Capitalism.* Princeton, NJ: Princeton University Press.

Firebaugh, Glenn. 1992. "Growth Effects of Foreign and Domestic Investment." *American Journal of Sociology* 98:105–30.

Firebaugh, Glenn. 2003. *The New Geography of Global Income Inequality.* Cambridge, MA: Harvard University Press.

Firebaugh, Glenn and Brian Goesling. 2004. "Accounting for the Recent Decline in Global Income Inequality." *American Journal of Sociology* 110:283–312.

Frank, Andre Gunder. 1998. *Reorient: Global Economy in the Asian Age.* Berkeley: University of California Press.

Frank, Andre Gunder and Barry K. Gills, eds. 1993. *The World System: Five Hundred Years or Five Thousand?* New York: Routledge.

Gamson, William A. 1990. *The Strategy of Social Protest.* 2d ed. Belmont, CA: Wadsworth.

Giddens, Anthony. 1990. *The Consequences of Modernity.* Stanford, CA: Stanford University Press.

Giddens, Anthony. 2002. *Runaway World: How Globalization Is Reshaping Our Lives.* Rev. ed. London, England: Routledge.

Goesling, Brian. 2001. "Changing Income Inequalities Within and between Nations: New Evidence." *American Sociological Review* 66:745–61.

Goldstone, Jack A. 1991. *Revolution and Rebellion in the Early Modern World.* Berkeley: University of California Press.

Goldstone, Jack A., ed. 2003. *States, Parties, and Social Movements.* New York: Cambridge University Press.

Green, Daniel M. 1999. "Liberal Moments and Democracy's Durability: Comparing Global Outbreaks of Democracy— 1918, 1945, 1989." *Studies in Comparative International Development* 34:83–120.

Gurr, Ted Robert. 1970. *Why Men Rebel.* Princeton, NJ: Princeton University Press.

Hahn, Gordon M. 2002. *Russia's Revolution from Above, 1985–2000: Reform, Transition, and Revolution in the Fall of the Soviet Communist Regime.* New Brunswick, NJ: Transaction.

Harris, Marvin. 1977. *Cannibals and Kings: The Origins of Cultures.* New York: Random House.

Harvey, David. 1989. *The Condition of Postmodernity.* Oxford, England: Blackwell.

Held, David, Anthony McGrew, David Goldblatt, and Jonathan Perraton. 1999. *Global Transformations.* Stanford, CA: Stanford University Press.

Hobson, John M. 2004. *The Eastern Origins of Western Civilisation.* Cambridge, England: Cambridge University Press.

International Organization for Migration. 2003. *World Migration Report 2003.* Geneva, Switzerland: International Organization for Migration.

Kentor, Jeffrey and Terry Boswell. 2003. "Foreign Capital Dependence and Development: A New Direction." *American Sociological Review* 68:301–13.

Korzeniewicz, Roberto P. and Timothy P. Moran. 1997. "World-Economic Trends in the Distribution of Income, 1965–1992." *American Journal of Sociology* 102:1000–39.

Kumar, Krishan. 1995. *From Post-Industrial to Post-Modern Society.* Oxford, England: Blackwell.

Kumar, Krishan. 2001. *1989: Revolutionary Ideas and Ideals.* Minneapolis: University of Minnesota Press.

Kurzman, Charles. 1998. "Waves of Democratization." *Studies in Comparative International Development* 33:42–64.

Landes, David S. 1998. *The Wealth and Poverty of Nations.* New York: Norton.

Lenski, Gerhard E. 1966. *Power and Privilege: A Theory of Social Stratification.* New York: McGraw-Hill.

Lenski, Gerhard E. 1970. *Human Societies: An Introduction to Macro-Level Sociology.* New York: McGraw-Hill.

Lenski, Gerhard E. 2005. *Ecological-Evolutionary Theory: Principles and Applications.* Boulder, CO: Paradigm.

Lomborg, Bjørn. 2001. *The Skeptical Environmentalist: Measuring the Real State of the World.* Cambridge, England: Cambridge University Press.

McAdam, Doug, John D. McCarthy, and Mayer N. Zald, eds. 1996. *Comparative Perspectives on Social Movements.* New York: Cambridge University Press.

Mahoney, James. 2003. "Long-Run Development and the Legacy of Colonialism in Spanish America." *American Journal of Sociology* 109:50–106.

Mann, Michael. 1986. *The Sources of Social Power,* vol. 1: *A History of Power from the Beginning to AD 1760.* Cambridge, England: Cambridge University Press.

Marx, Karl and Friedrich Engels. [1848] 1978. "Manifesto of the Communist Party." Pp. 469–500 in *The Marx-Engels Reader,* 2d ed., edited by R. C. Tucker. New York: Norton.

Meyer, John W., John Boli, George M. Thomas, and Francisco O. Ramirez. 1997. "World Society and the Nation-State." *American Journal of Sociology* 103:144–81.

Meyer, John W., Francisco O. Ramirez, Richard Rubinson, and John Boli-Bennett. 1977. "The World Educational Revolution, 1950–1970." *Sociology of Education* 50:242–58.

Moore, Barrington, Jr. 1966. *Social Origins of Dictatorship and Democracy.* Boston, MA: Beacon Press.

Paige, Jeffery M. 1975. *Agrarian Revolution.* New York: Free Press.

Parsons, Talcott. 1966. *Societies: Evolutionary and Comparative Perspectives.* Englewood Cliffs, NJ: Prentice Hall.

Parsons, Talcott. 1971. *The System of Modern Societies.* Englewood Cliffs, NJ: Prentice Hall.

Pomeranz, Kenneth. 2000. *The Great Divergence: China, Europe, and the Making of the Modern World Economy.* Princeton, NJ: Princeton University Press.

Rossides, Daniel. 1990. *Social Stratification: The American Class System in Comparative Perspective.* Englewood Cliffs, NJ: Prentice Hall.

Rostow, W. W. 1960. *The Stages of Economic Growth: A Non-Communist Manifesto.* New York: Cambridge University Press.

Rueschemeyer, Dietrich, Evelyne Huber Stephens, and John D. Stephens. 1992. *Capitalist Development and Democracy.* Chicago, IL: University of Chicago Press.

Sanderson, Stephen K. 1994a. "Evolutionary Materialism: A Theoretical Strategy for the Study of Social Evolution." *Sociological Perspectives* 37:47–73.

Sanderson, Stephen K. 1994b. "The Transition from Feudalism to Capitalism: The Theoretical Significance of the Japanese Case." *Review (Fernand Braudel Center)* 17:15–55.

Sanderson, Stephen K. 1995a. *Macrosociology: An Introduction to Human Societies.* 3d ed. New York: HarperCollins.

Sanderson, Stephen K. 1995b. *Social Transformations: A General Theory of Historical Development.* Oxford, England: Blackwell.

Sanderson, Stephen K. 1999a. *Macrosociology: An Introduction to Human Societies.* 4th ed. New York: Addison-Wesley-Longman.

Sanderson, Stephen K. 1999b. *Social Transformations: A General Theory of Historical Development.* Rev. ed. Boulder, CO: Rowman & Littlefield.

Sanderson, Stephen K. 2004. "World Democratization, 1850–2000: A Cross-National Test of Modernization and Power Resource Theories." Paper presented at the annual meetings of the American Sociological Association, San Francisco, CA.

Sanderson, Stephen K. 2005a. *Revolutions: A Worldwide Introduction to Political and Social Change.* Boulder, CO: Paradigm.

Sanderson, Stephen K. 2005b. "World-Systems Analysis after Thirty Years: Should It Rest in Peace?" *International Journal of Comparative Sociology* 46:179–213.

Sanderson, Stephen K. 2007. *Evolutionism and Its Critics: Deconstructing and Reconstructing an Evolutionary Interpretation of Human Society.* Boulder, CO: Paradigm.

Sanderson, Stephen K. and Arthur S. Alderson. 2005. *World Societies: The Evolution of Human Social Life.* Boston, MA: Allyn & Bacon.

Service, Elman R. 1970. *Primitive Social Organization: An Evolutionary Perspective.* 2d ed. New York: Random House.

Shofer, Evan and John W. Meyer. 2005. "The World-Wide Expansion of Higher Education in the Twentieth Century." *American Sociological Review* 70:898–920.

Singer, Peter. 2002. *One World: The Ethics of Globalization.* New Haven, CT: Yale University Press.

Skocpol, Theda. 1979. *States and Social Revolutions: A Comparative Analysis of France, Russia, and China.* New York: Cambridge University Press.

Snow, David A. and Robert D. Benford. 1992. "Master Frames and Cycles of Protest." Pp. 133–55 in *Frontiers in Social Movement Theory,* edited by A. Morris and C. M. Mueller. New Haven, CT: Yale University Press.

Steward, Julian H. 1955. *Theory of Culture Change.* Urbana: University of Illinois Press.

Stiglitz, Joseph E. 2003. *Globalization and Its Discontents.* Rev. ed. New York: Norton.

Sweezy, Paul. [1950] 1976. "A Critique." Pp. 33–56 in *The Transition from Feudalism to Capitalism,* edited by R. Hilton. London, England: New Left Books.

Szymanski, Albert. 1981. *The Logic of Imperialism*. New York: Praeger.

Tiger, Lionel. 1999. *The Decline of Males*. New York: St. Martin's Press.

Tilly, Charles. 1978. *From Mobilization to Revolution*. New York: McGraw-Hill.

Tilly, Charles. 1990. *Coercion, Capital, and European States, 990–1990*. Oxford, England: Blackwell.

Tilly, Charles. 2004. *Social Movements, 1768–2004*. Boulder, CO: Paradigm.

Turner, Jonathan H. 1995. *Macrodynamics: Toward a Theory on the Organization of Human Populations*. New Brunswick, NJ: Rutgers University Press.

Turner, Jonathan H. 2003. *Human Institutions: A Theory of Societal Evolution*. Lanham, MD: Rowman & Littlefield.

Wallerstein, Immanuel. 1974a. *The Modern World-System: Capitalist Agriculture and the Origins of the European World-Economy in the Sixteenth Century*. New York: Academic Press.

Wallerstein, Immanuel. 1974b. "The Rise and Future Demise of the World Capitalist System: Concepts for Comparative Analysis." *Comparative Studies in Society and History* 16:387–415.

Wallerstein, Immanuel. 1979. *The Capitalist World-Economy*. New York: Cambridge University Press.

Wallerstein, Immanuel. 1980. *The Modern World-System II: Mercantilism and the Consolidation of the European World-Economy, 1600–1750*. New York: Academic Press.

Wallerstein, Immanuel. 1989. *The Modern World-System III: The Second Era of Great Expansion of the Capitalist World-Economy, 1730–1840s*. San Diego, CA: Academic Press.

Warren, Bill. 1980. *Imperialism: Pioneer of Capitalism*. London, England: Verso.

Weber, Max. [1904] 1958. *The Protestant Ethic and the Spirit of Capitalism*. Translated by T. Parsons. New York: Charles Scribner's Sons.

White, Leslie A. 1943. "Energy and the Evolution of Culture." *American Anthropologist* 45:335–56.

White, Leslie A. 1959. *The Evolution of Culture*. New York: McGraw-Hill.

Wickham-Crowley, Timothy P. 1992. *Guerrillas and Revolution in Latin America*. Princeton, NJ: Princeton University Press.

Wolf, Eric R. 1969. *Peasant Wars of the Twentieth Century*. New York: Harper & Row.

World Bank. 2002. *World Development Indicators*. Washington, DC: World Bank.

Wright, Erik Olin. 1985. *Classes*. London, England: Verso.

Wright, Erik Olin. 1997. *Class Counts: Comparative Studies in Class Analysis*. New York: Cambridge University Press.

Chapter 57. Dynamic Systems Theory

Anderson, P. 1976. *Considerations on Western Marxism*. London, England: New Left Books.

Archer, M. S. 1995. *Realist Social Theory: The Morphogenetic Approach*. Cambridge, England: Cambridge University Press.

Baumgartner, T. 1978. "An Actor-Oriented Systems Model for the Analysis of Industrial Democracy Measures." Pp. 55–77 in *Sociocybernetics*, vol. 1, edited by R. F. Geyer and J. van der Zouwen. Leiden, The Netherlands: Martinus Nijhoff.

Baumgartner, T., W. Buckley, and T. R. Burns. 1975. "Relational Control: The Human Structuring of Cooperation and Conflict." *Journal of Conflict Resolution* 19:417–40.

Baumgartner, T., T. R. Burns, and P. R. DeVillé. 1975. "The Structuring of International Economic Relations." *International Studies Quarterly* 19:126–59.

Baumgartner, T., T. R. Burns, and P. R. DeVillé. 1979. "Work, Politics, and Social Structuring under Capitalism." Pp. 173–221 in *Work and Power*, edited by T. R. Burns and V. Rus. London, England: Sage.

Baumgartner, T., T. R. Burns, and P. R. DeVillé. 1986. *The Shaping of Socio-Economic Systems*. London, England: Gordon and Breach.

Bergesen, A. 1983. *Crises in the World-System*. Beverly Hills, CA: Sage.

Buckley, W. 1967. *Sociology and Modern Systems Theory*. Englewood Cliffs, NJ: Prentice Hall.

Buckley, W. 1998. *Society—A Complex Adaptive System: Essays in Social Theory*. Amsterdam, The Netherlands: Gordon and Breach.

Burawoy, M. and T. Skocpol, eds. 1982. "Marxist Inquiries: Studies of Labor, Class, and States." *American Journal of Sociology* 88(Suppl.).

Burawoy, M. and E. O. Wright. 2001. "Sociological Marxism." In *Handbook of Sociological Theory*, edited by J. Turner. New York: Kluwer/Plenum.

Burns, T. R. 1999. "The Evolution of Parliaments and Societies in Europe: Challenges and Prospects." *European Journal of Social Theory* 2(2):167–94.

Burns, T. R. Forthcoming. "System Theories." In *The Encyclopedia of Sociology*, edited by G. Ritzer. Oxford, England: Blackwell.

Burns, T. R., T. Baumgartner, and P. R. DeVillé. 1985. *Man, Decisions, and Society*. London, England: Gordon and Breach.

Burns, T. R., T. Baumgartner, T. Dietz, and Nora Machado. 2002. "The Theory of Actor-System Dynamics: Human Agency, Rule Systems and Cultural Evolution." In *Encyclopedia of Life Support Systems* (EOLSS). Oxford, England: UNESCO, EOLSS. www.eolss.net.

Burns, T. R. and M. Carson. 2002. "Actors, Paradigms, and Institutional Dynamics: The Theory of Social Rule Systems Applied to Radical Reforms." Pp. 109–145 in *Advancing Socio-Economics: An Institutionalist Perspective*, edited by R. Hollingsworth, K. H. Muller, and E. J. Hollingsworth. Oxford, England: Rowman & Littlefield.

Burns, T. R. and M. Carson. 2005. "Social Order and Disorder: Institutions, Policy Paradigms and Discourses—An Interdisciplinary Approach." Pp. 283–310 in *A New Agenda in Critical Discourse Analysis: Theory and Interdisciplinarity*, edited by P. Chilton and R. Wodak. Amsterdam, The Netherlands: John Benjamins.

Burns, T. R. and P. R. DeVillé. 2003. "The Three Faces of the Coin: A Socio-Economic Approach to the Institution of Money." *European Journal of Economic and Social Systems* 16(2):149–95.

Burns, T. R. and H. Flam. [1987] 1990. *The Shaping of Social Organization: Social Rule System Theory with Applications*. London, England: Sage.

Burns, T. R. and M. Kamali. 2003. "The Evolution of Parliaments: A Comparative, Historical Perspective on Assemblies and Political Decision-Making." Pp. 261–75 in *Handbook of Historical Sociology,* edited by G. Delanty and E. Isin. London, England: Sage.

Burns, T. R. and E. Roszkowska. Forthcoming. "Conflict and Conflict Resolution: A Societal-Institutional Approach." In *Procedural Approaches to Conflict Resolution,* edited by M. Raith. London, England: Springer Press.

Chase-Dunn, C. 1997. *Rise and Demise: Comparing World-Systems.* Boulder, CO: Westview Press.

Chase-Dunn, C. and P. Grimes. 1995. "World-Systems Analysis." *Annual Review of Sociology* 21:387–417.

Chase-Dunn, C. and T. D. Hall. 1993. "Comparing World-Systems: Concepts and Working Hypotheses." *Social Forces* 71:851–86.

Chirot, D. and T. D. Hall. 1982. "World-System Theory." *Annual Review of Sociology* 8:81–106.

Collins, R. 1988. *Theoretical Sociology.* New York: Harcourt Brace Jovanovich.

Dahrendorf, R. 1959. *Class and Class Conflict in Industrial Society.* Stanford, CA: Stanford University Press.

DeVillé, P. R. and T. R. Burns. 2004. "Contemporary Capitalism, Its Discontents and Dynamics: Institutional and Political Considerations." Presented at the 36th World Congress of the International Institute of Sociology, July, Beijing, People's Republic of China.

Fukuyama, F. 1992. *The End of History and the Last Man.* New York: Free Press.

Geyer, R. F. and J. van der Zouwen, eds.1978. *Sociocybernetics: An Actor-Oriented Social Systems Approach.* Leiden, The Netherlands: Martinus Nijhoff.

Gindoff, P. and G. Ritzer. 1994. "Agency-Structure, Micro-Macro, Individualism-Holism-Relationism: A Metatheoretical Explanation of Theoretical Convergence between the United States and Europe." Pp. 3–23 in *Agency and Structure: Reorienting Social Theory,* edited by P. Sztompka. London, England: Gordon & Breach.

Granovetter, M. 1985. "Economic Action and Social Structure: The Problem of Embeddedness." *American Journal of Sociology* 50:481–510.

Hollingsworth, J. R. and R. Boyer. 1997. *Contemporary Capitalism: The Embeddedness of Institutions.* New York: Cambridge University Press.

Hopkins, T. K. and I. Wallerstein. 1982. *World-Systems Analysis: Theory and Methodology.* Beverly Hills, CA: Sage.

Jaeger, C. C. 1994. *Taming the Dragon. Transforming Economic Institutions in the Face of Global Change.* Amsterdam, The Netherlands: Gordon and Breach.

Janowitz, M. 1977. "A Sociological Perspective on Wallerstein." *American Journal of Sociology* 82(5):1090–97.

Lockwood, D. 1964. "Social Integration and System Integration." In *Explorations in Social Change,* edited by G. K. Zollschan and H. W. Hirsch. Boston, MA: Houghton Mifflin.

Mandel, E. 1993. *Revolutionary Marxism and Social Reality in the 20th Century: Collected Essays.* Edited by S. Bloom. Atlantic Highlands, NJ: Humanities Press.

Martinelli, A. 2005. *Global Modernization: Rethinking the Project of Modernity.* London, England: Sage.

Marx, K. [1867] 1967. *Capital.* New York: International Publishers.

Marx, K. 1973a. *Grundrisse: Foundations of the Critique of Political Economy.* London, England: Penguin Books.

Marx, K. 1973b. "The Eighteenth Brumaire of Louis Bonaparte." In *Surveys from Exile.* Harmondsworth, Middlesex, England: Penguin Books.

Moore, B. 1966. *Social Origins of Dictatorship and Democracy.* Boston, MA: Beacon Press.

O'Connor, J. 1973. *The Fiscal Crisis of the State.* New York: St. Martin's Press.

Olson, M. 2000. *Power and Prosperity: Outgrowing Communist and Capitalist Dictatorship.* New York: Basic Books.

Parsons, Talcott. 1951. *The Social System.* Glencoe, IL: Free Press.

Parsons, Talcott. 1966. *Societies: Evolutionary and Comparative Perspectives.* Englewood Cliffs, NJ: Prentice Hall.

Poulantzas, N. 1978. *Classes in Contemporary Capitalism.* London, England: Verso.

Przeworski, A. 1985. *Capitalism and Social Democracy.* Cambridge, England: Cambridge University Press.

Skocpol, T. 1977. "Wallerstein's World Capitalist System: A Theoretical and Historical Critique." *American Journal of Sociology* 82(5):1075–90.

Stinchombe, A. L. 1968. *Constructing Social Theories.* New York: Harcourt, Brace, & World.

van Parijs, P. 1993. *Marxism Recycled.* Cambridge, England: Cambridge University Press.

Wallerstein, I. 1974. *The Modern World System.* New York: Academic Press.

Wallerstein, I. 2004. *World-Systems Analysis: An Introduction.* Durham, NC: Duke University Press.

Weber, M. 1951. *The Religion of China.* New York: Macmillan.

Weber, M. 1976. *The Protestant Ethic and the Spirit of Capitalism.* London, England: Allen and Unwin.

Weber, M. 1981. *General Economic History.* New Brunswick, NJ: Transaction.

Wright, E. O., A. L. Levine, and E. Sober. 1992. *Reconstructing Marxism.* New York: Verso.